Nineteenth-Century Literature Criticism

Guide to Thomson Gale Literary Criticism Series

For criticism on	Consult these Thomson Gale series
Authors now living or who died after December 31, 1999	*CONTEMPORARY LITERARY CRITICISM (CLC)*
Authors who died between 1900 and 1999	*TWENTIETH-CENTURY LITERARY CRITICISM (TCLC)*
Authors who died between 1800 and 1899	*NINETEENTH-CENTURY LITERATURE CRITICISM (NCLC)*
Authors who died between 1400 and 1799	*LITERATURE CRITICISM FROM 1400 TO 1800 (LC)* *SHAKESPEAREAN CRITICISM (SC)*
Authors who died before 1400	*CLASSICAL AND MEDIEVAL LITERATURE CRITICISM (CMLC)*
Authors of books for children and young adults	*CHILDREN'S LITERATURE REVIEW (CLR)*
Dramatists	*DRAMA CRITICISM (DC)*
Poets	*POETRY CRITICISM (PC)*
Short story writers	*SHORT STORY CRITICISM (SSC)*
Literary topics and movements	*HARLEM RENAISSANCE: A GALE CRITICAL COMPANION (HR)* *THE BEAT GENERATION: A GALE CRITICAL COMPANION (BG)* *FEMINISM IN LITERATURE: A GALE CRITICAL COMPANION (FL)* *GOTHIC LITERATURE: A GALE CRITICAL COMPANION (GL)*
Asian American writers of the last two hundred years	*ASIAN AMERICAN LITERATURE (AAL)*
Black writers of the past two hundred years	*BLACK LITERATURE CRITICISM (BLC)* *BLACK LITERATURE CRITICISM SUPPLEMENT (BLCS)*
Hispanic writers of the late nineteenth and twentieth centuries	*HISPANIC LITERATURE CRITICISM (HLC)* *HISPANIC LITERATURE CRITICISM SUPPLEMENT (HLCS)*
Native North American writers and orators of the eighteenth, nineteenth, and twentieth centuries	*NATIVE NORTH AMERICAN LITERATURE (NNAL)*
Major authors from the Renaissance to the present	*WORLD LITERATURE CRITICISM, 1500 TO THE PRESENT (WLC)* *WORLD LITERATURE CRITICISM SUPPLEMENT (WLCS)*

ISSN 0732-1864

Volume 167

Nineteenth-Century Literature Criticism

Criticism of the
Works of Novelists, Philosophers, and Other
Creative Writers Who Died between 1800
and 1899, from the First Published Critical
Appraisals to Current Evaluations

Jessica Bomarito
Russel Whitaker
Project Editors

THOMSON

GALE

Detroit • New York • San Francisco • San Diego • New Haven, Conn. • Waterville, Maine • London • Munich

Nineteenth-Century Literature Criticism, Vol. 167

Project Editors
Jessica Bomarito and Russel Whitaker

Editorial
Kathy D. Darrow, Jeffrey W. Hunter, Jelena O. Krstović, Michelle Lee, Thomas J. Schoenberg, Noah Schusterbauer, Lawrence J. Trudeau

Data Capture
Frances Monroe, Gwen Tucker

Indexing Services
Laurie Andriot

Rights and Acquisitions
Ron Montgomery, Sue Rudolph, Andrew Specht

Imaging and Multimedia
Dean Dauphinais, Robert Duncan, Leitha Etheridge-Sims, Lezlie Light, Michael Logusz, Dan Newell, Kelly A. Quin, Denay Wilding

Composition and Electronic Capture
Amy Darga

Manufacturing
Rhonda Dover

Associate Product Manager
Marc Cormier

LIBRARY OF CONGRESS CATALOG CARD NUMBER 84-643008

ISBN 0-7876-8651-4
ISSN 0732-1864

Printed in the United States of America
10 9 8 7 6 5 4 3 2 1

Contents

Preface vii

Acknowledgments xi

Literary Criticism Series Advisory Board xiii

Preface

Since its inception in 1981, *Nineteeth-Century Literature Criticism* (*NCLC*) has been a valuable resource for students and librarians seeking critical commentary on writers of this transitional period in world history. Designated an "Outstanding Reference Source" by the American Library Association with the publication of is first volume, *NCLC* has since been purchased by over 6,000 school, public, and university libraries. The series has covered more than 450 authors representing 33 nationalities and over 17,000 titles. No other reference source has surveyed the critical reaction to nineteenth-century authors and literature as thoroughly as *NCLC*.

Scope of the Series

NCLC is designed to introduce students and advanced readers to the authors of the nineteenth century and to the most significant interpretations of these authors' works. The great poets, novelists, short story writers, playwrights, and philosophers of this period are frequently studied in high school and college literature courses. By organizing and reprinting commentary written on these authors, *NCLC* helps students develop valuable insight into literary history, promotes a better understanding of the texts, and sparks ideas for papers and assignments. Each entry in *NCLC* presents a comprehensive survey of an author's career or an individual work of literature and provides the user with a multiplicity of interpretations and assessments. Such variety allows students to pursue their own interests; furthermore, it fosters an awareness that literature is dynamic and responsive to many different opinions.

Every fourth volume of *NCLC* is devoted to literary topics that cannot be covered under the author approach used in the rest of the series. Such topics include literary movements, prominent themes in nineteenth-century literature, literary reaction to political and historical events, significant eras in literary history, prominent literary anniversaries, and the literatures of cultures that are often overlooked by English-speaking readers.

NCLC continues the survey of criticism of world literature begun by Thomson Gale's *Contemporary Literary Criticism* (*CLC*) and *Twentieth-Century Literary Criticism* (*TCLC*).

Organization of the Book

An *NCLC* entry consists of the following elements:

- The **Author Heading** cites the name under which the author most commonly wrote, followed by birth and death dates. Also located here are any name variations under which an author wrote, including transliterated forms for authors whose native languages use nonroman alphabets. If the author wrote consistently under a pseudonym, the pseudonym will be listed in the author heading and the author's actual name given in parenthesis on the first line of the biographical and critical information. Uncertain birth or death dates are indicated by question marks. Single-work entries are preceded by a heading that consists of the most common form of the title in English translation (if applicable) and the original date of composition.

- The **Introduction** contains background information that introduces the reader to the author, work, or topic that is the subject of the entry.

- A **Portrait of the Author** is included when available.

- The list of **Principal Works** is ordered chronologically by date of first publication and lists the most important works by the author. The genre and publication date of each work is given. In the case of foreign authors whose works have been translated into English, the list will focus primarily on twentieth-century translations, selecting those works most commonly considered the best by critics. Unless otherwise indicated, dramas are dated by first performance, not first publication. Lists of **Representative Works** by different authors appear with topic entries.

■ Reprinted **Criticism** is arranged chronologically in each entry to provide a useful perspective on changes in critical evaluation over time. The critic's name and the date of composition or publication of the critical work are given at the beginning of each piece of criticism. Unsigned criticism is preceded by the title of the source in which it appeared. All titles by the author featured in the text are printed in boldface type. Footnotes are reprinted at the end of each essay or excerpt. In the case of excerpted criticism, only those footnotes that pertain to the excerpted texts are included. Criticism in topic entries is arranged chronologically under a variety of subheadings to facilitate the study of different aspects of the topic.

■ A complete **Bibliographical Citation** of the original essay or book precedes each piece of criticism.

■ Critical essays are prefaced by brief **Annotations** explicating each piece.

■ An annotated bibliography of **Further Reading** appears at the end of each entry and suggests resources for additional study. In some cases, significant essays for which the editors could not obtain reprint rights are included here. Boxed material following the further reading list provides references to other biographical and critical sources on the author in series published by Thomson Gale.

Indexes

Each volume of *NCLC* contains a **Cumulative Author Index** listing all authors who have appeared in a wide variety of reference sources published by Thomson Gale, including *NCLC*. A complete list of these sources is found facing the first page of the Author Index. The index also includes birth and death dates and cross references between pseudonyms and actual names.

A **Cumulative Nationality Index** lists all authors featured in *NCLC* by nationality, followed by the number of the *NCLC* volume in which their entry appears.

A **Cumulative Topic Index** lists the literary themes and topics treated in the series as well as in *Classical and Medieval Literature Criticism, Literature Criticism from 1400 to 1800, Twentieth-Century Literary Criticism,* and the *Contemporary Literary Criticism* Yearbook, which was discontinued in 1998.

An alphabetical **Title Index** accompanies each volume of *NCLC*, with the exception of the Topics volumes. Listings of titles by authors covered in the given volume are followed by the author's name and the corresponding page numbers where the titles are discussed. English translations of foreign titles and variations of titles are cross-referenced to the title under which a work was originally published. Titles of novels, dramas, nonfiction books, and poetry, short story, or essay collections are printed in italics, while individual poems, short stories, and essays are printed in roman type within quotation marks.

In response to numerous suggestions from librarians, Thomson Gale also produces an annual paperbound edition of the *NCLC* cumulative title index. This annual cumulation, which alphabetically lists all titles reviewed in the series, is available to all customers. Additional copies of this index are available upon request. Librarians and patrons will welcome this separate index; it saves shelf space, is easy to use, and is recyclable upon receipt of the next edition.

Citing *Nineteenth-Century Literature Criticism*

When citing criticism reprinted in the Literary Criticism Series, students should provide complete bibliographic information so that the cited essay can be located in the original print or electronic source. Students who quote directly from reprinted criticism may use any accepted bibliographic format, such as University of Chicago Press style or Modern Language Association style.

The examples below follow recommendations for preparing a bibliography set forth in *The Chicago Manual of Style,* 14th ed. (Chicago: The University of Chicago Press, 1993); the first example pertains to material drawn from periodicals, the second to material reprinted from books:

Guerard, Albert J. "On the Composition of Dostoevsky's *The Idiot.*" *Mosaic: A Journal for the Interdisciplinary Study of Literature* 8, no. 1 (fall 1974): 201-15. Reprinted in *Nineteenth-Century Literature Criticism.* Vol. 119, edited by Lynn M. Zott, 81-104. Detroit: Gale, 2003.

Berstein, Carol L. "Subjectivity as Critique and the Critique of Subjectivity in Keats's *Hyperion.*" In *After the Future: Postmodern Times and Places,* edited by Gary Shapiro, 41-52. Albany, N. Y.: State University of New York Press, 1990. Reprinted in *Nineteeth-Century Literature Criticism.* Vol. 121, edited by Lynn M. Zott, 155-60. Detroit: Gale, 2003.

The examples below follow recommendations for preparing a works cited list set forth in the *MLA Handbook for Writers of Research Papers,* 5th ed. (New York: The Modern Language Association of America, 1999); the first example pertains to material drawn from periodicals, the second to material reprinted from books:

Guerard, Albert J. "On the Composition of Dostoevsky's *The Idiot.*" *Mosaic: A Journal for the Interdisciplinary Study of Literature* 8. 1 (fall 1974): 201-15. Reprinted in *Nineteenth-Century Literature Criticism.* Ed. Lynn M. Zott. Vol. 119. Detroit: Gale, 2003. 81-104.

Berstein, Carol L. "Subjectivity as Critique and the Critique of Subjectivity in Keats's *Hyperion.*" *After the Future: Postmodern Times and Places.* Ed. Gary Shapiro. Albany, N. Y.: State University of New York Press, 1990. 41-52. Reprinted in *Nineteeth-Century Literature Criticism.* Ed. Lynn M. Zott. Vol. 121. Detroit: Gale, 2003. 155-60.

Suggestions are Welcome

Readers who wish to suggest new features, topics, or authors to appear in future volumes, or who have other suggestions or comments are cordially invited to call, write, or fax the Associate Product Manager:

Associate Product Manager, Literary Criticism Series
Thomson Gale
27500 Drake Road
Farmington Hills, MI 48331-3535
1-800-347-4253 (GALE)
Fax: 248-699-8054

Acknowledgments

The editors wish to thank the copyright holders of the criticism included in this volume and the permissions managers of many book and magazine publishing companies for assisting us in securing reproduction rights. Following is a list of the copyright holders who have granted us permission to reproduce material in this volume of *NCLC*. Every effort has been made to trace copyright, but if omissions have been made, please let us know.

COPYRIGHTED MATERIAL IN *NCLC*, VOLUME 167, WAS REPRODUCED FROM THE FOLLOWING PERIODICALS:

American Transcendental Quarterly, spring, 1978; v. 1, March, 1987; v. 8, December, 1994. Copyright © 1978, 1987, 1994 by The University of Rhode Island. All reproduced by permission.—*Canadian Slavonic Papers,* v. 33, September, 1981. Copyright © Canadian Slavonic Papers, Canada, 1981. Reproduced by permission of the publisher.—*Comparative Drama,* v. 12, winter, 1978-79. Copyright © 1978-79, by the Editors of Comparative Drama. Reproduced by permission.— *The Concord Saunterer,* v. 19, December, 1987. Reproduced by permission. The Concord Saunterer is published annually by the Thoreau Society. www.thoreausociety.org.—*Criticism,* v. 13, spring, 1971. Copyright © 1971 Wayne State University Press. Reproduced with permission of the Wayne State University Press.—*Dalhousie Review,* v. 54, winter, 1974-75. Reproduced by permission.—*Dostoevsky Studies,* v. 3, 1982. Copyright © 1982 by the International Dostoevsky Society. Both reproduced by permission.—*The Durham University Journal,* v. 74, December, 1981. Reproduced by permission.—*The Eighteenth Century: Theory and Interpretation,* v. 37, spring, 1996 for "'Inexhaustible Generosity': The Fictions of Eighteenth-Century British Imperialism in Richard Cumberland's *The West Indian*" by Maaja A. Stewart. Copyright © 1996 by Texas Tech University Press. Reproduced by permission of the publisher and the author.—*English Language Notes,* v. 10, September, 1972. Copyright © 1972, Regents of the University of Colorado. Reproduced by permission.—*The Hudson Review,* v. 13, summer, 1960. Copyright © 1960 by The Hudson Review, Inc. Renewed 1988. Reproduced by permission.— *Literature and Psychology,* v. 26, 1976. Copyright © Morton Kaplan 1976. Reproduced by permission of *Literature & Psychology: A Psychoanalytic and Cultural Criticism.*—*The New England Quarterly,* v. 48, September, 1975 for "The Kinetic Revolution: Transformation in the Language of the Transcendentalists" by Catherine Albanese. Copyright 1975 by The New England Quarterly. Reproduced by permission of the publisher and author.—*New Zealand Slavonic Journal,* 1980. Reproduced by permission.—*School and Society,* v. 81, February 19, 1955. Reproduced by permission.—*Slavic and East European Journal,* v. 16, spring, 1972; v. 17, summer, 1973. Copyright © 1972, 1973 by AATSEEL of the U.S., Inc. Both reproduced by permission.—*Studia Mystica,* v. 2, summer, 1979. Reproduced by permission.

COPYRIGHTED MATERIAL IN *NCLC*, VOLUME 167, WAS REPRODUCED FROM THE FOLLOWING BOOKS:

Bakhtin, Mikhail. From "Characteristics of Genre and Plot Composition in Dostoevsky's Works," in *Problems of Dostoevsky's Poetics.* Edited and translated by Caryl Emerson. University of Minnesota Press, 1984. Copyright © 1984 by the Regents of the University of Minnesota. All rights reserved. Reproduced by permission.—Bem, Alfred L. From "The Problem of Guilt," in *Twentieth-Century Interpretations of* Crime and Punishment. Edited and translated by Robert Louis Jackson. Engelwood Ciffs, N.J.: Prentice-Hall, 1974. Reproduced by permission of Robert Louis Jackson.—Bennett, Fordyce Richard. From "Bronson Alcott and Free Religion," in *Studies in the American Renaissance.* Edited by Joel Myerson. Twayne Publishers, 1981. Copyright © 1981 by G.K. Hall & Co. All rights reserved. Reproduced by permission.— Boas, Frederick S. From *An Introduction to Eighteenth-Century Drama, 1700-1780.* Oxford University Press, 1953. Reproduced by permission of Oxford University Press.—Carlson, Larry A. From "Emerson, Friendship, and the Problem of Alcott's *Psyche,*" in *Emersonian Circles: Essays in Honor of Joel Myerson.* Edited by Wesley T. Mott and Robert E. Burkholder. University of Rochester Press, 1997. Copyright © 1997 Larry A. Carlson. All rights reserved. Reproduced by permission.—Christy, Arthur. From *The Orient in American Transcendentalism: A Study of Emerson, Thoreau, and Alcott.* Columbia University Press, 1932. Copyright 1932 Columbia University. Renewed by Gertrude N. Christy 1960. Reproduced by permission.—Cox, Gary. From *Crime and Punishment: A Mind to Murder.* Twayne Publishers, 1990. Copyright 1990 by G.K. Hall & Co. All rights reserved. Reproduced by permission of Thomson Gale.—Dircks, Richard J. From *The Unpublished Plays of Richard Cumberland, Volume I.* AMS Press, 1991. Copyright © 1991 by AMS Press, Inc. All rights reserved. Reproduced by permission.—Dircks, Richard J. From *The Unpublished Plays of Richard Cumberland,*

PHOTOGRAPHS AND ILLUSTRATIONS APPEARING IN *NCLC*, VOLUME 167, WERE RECEIVED FROM THE FOLLOWING SOURCES:

Thomson Gale Literature Product Advisory Board

Amos Bronson Alcott
1799-1888

American essayist, poet, prose writer, and biographer.

The following entry presents criticism on Alcott from 1836 to 1997. For additional information on Alcott's career, see *NCLC,* Volume 1.

INTRODUCTION

Writer, educator, conversationalist, and mystic, Alcott was, in many ways, the embodiment of the American Transcendentalist movement. He lived during an era of intellectual ferment and radical social change in America, and his essays and poetry reflect the confidence and enthusiasm of his age. Antigovernment and nonconformist in his philosophy, Alcott devoted his life to exploring the potential of the human spirit as both a source of new ideas and as a repository for limitless optimism, with the aim of teaching the individual how to overcome the repressive burden of society's conventions. While Alcott possessed an indomitable will and great intellectual passion, he never succeeded, however, in reining in his powerful energies in the service of a single, coherent purpose. Throughout his life he struggled to find a practical application for his energies, and his dogged refusal to work within the framework of American capitalist society often placed his family in serious economic jeopardy. For much of his life he struggled to earn a living, generally relying on the generosity of friends for his family's survival. During his own lifetime his reputation rested primarily on his gifts as a raconteur, and contemporary accounts testify to the eloquent and engaging, albeit unstructured and improvisational, qualities of Alcott's conversational style. Modern critics and scholars generally find Alcott's writings to be labored and unoriginal, and his work attracts few readers today. In spite of his failings as an author, however, Alcott remains a representative figure of his age, and his ideas played an indisputable role in the formation of a distinctly American intellectual culture in mid-nineteenth-century New England.

BIOGRAPHICAL INTRODUCTION

Alcott was born in Wolcott, Connecticut, on November 29, 1799, the son of a poor farmer. After abandoning his education at the age of thirteen, he worked briefly in

a clock factory before becoming an itinerant peddler, an occupation that took him to the Carolinas. Alcott's first-hand observations of slavery in the South, coupled with his brief sojourn in a Quaker community, exerted a powerful impact on his intellectual and moral development and helped shape the radical social views that would form the foundation of his life's work. He struggled for several years to earn a living selling his wares, and by his early twenties Alcott found himself burdened by numerous debts. He returned to Connecticut and embarked on a career as a teacher. He taught for a few years at schools in the towns of Bristol and Cheshire and became increasingly interested in school reform, but found little support and eventually felt pressured to quit. He then taught at an infant school in Boston, where he hoped to find greater enthusiasm for progressiveness and reform. In 1830 Alcott married Abigail May; they would eventually have four daughters. Alcott spent the next few years teaching at various schools in Philadelphia before returning with his family to Boston in 1834 to found the Temple School.

Inspired by his early experiences as an educator, Alcott set out to develop a new system of instruction that cultivated the innate spiritual and imaginative potential of the child. He eschewed traditional rote instruction and forms of discipline in favor of a conversational, Socratic method of teaching, encouraging his students to seek knowledge from intuition rather than memorization. As his teaching philosophy evolved, Alcott had begun to write essays describing his pedagogical methods. In these early writings, published in the *American Journal of Education* and its successor, *American Annals of Education and Instruction,* Alcott expounded his conviction that the educational process was essentially moral and that instructors could impart a strong sense of values only by nurturing the unique spiritual development of each student. In 1834 Alcott's assistant, Elizabeth Palmer Peabody, began keeping an account of activities at the Temple School, which she published in 1835 as *Record of a School.* With the publication of Peabody's work, Alcott's educational methods quickly achieved notoriety among critics and readers, who were troubled by his liberal attitudes toward religion and sex. But also during these years Alcott became acquainted with like-minded writers and intellectuals, among them Ralph Waldo Emerson and Orestes Brownson. In 1836 Alcott helped form the Transcendental Club, a society devoted to progressive ideas of social reform, art, and spirituality. That same year Alcott also published the first volume of his *Conversations with Children on the Gospels,* with a second volume appearing in the following year. This work exacerbated the public's suspicions concerning Alcott's educational philosophy, and by 1839 Alcott found enrollment at his school in such serious decline that he was forced to close. In April 1840, disenchanted with what he perceived to be the corruption and degradation of city life, Alcott moved his family to Concord, where he managed to eke out a modest living as a farmer. While living in Concord, Alcott also played a role in creating a Transcendentalist journal entitled the *Dial,* which published his aphorisms known as the "Orphic Sayings"; fifty of them appeared in the *Dial* in 1840, another fifty in 1841, and twelve in 1842. Unfortunately the "Orphic Sayings" met with widespread ridicule among critics and readers, and more than two decades would pass before Alcott published again. In spite of the difficulties of these years, Alcott's ideas began to attract supporters abroad, and in 1842 he traveled to England to meet with a group of Transcendentalists led by Henry Wright. At this time Alcott became friends with Charles Lane, with whom, in 1843, he founded a short-lived commune, Fruitlands, in Harvard, Massachusetts.

For the next decade and a half Alcott and his family lived in various New England towns, finally settling permanently in Concord in 1857. At around this time Alcott began to secure speaking engagements, and for the next several years he engaged in numerous public "conversations" throughout the Midwest, which earned him a modest following. In 1868 Alcott finally achieved financial stability when his daughter, Louisa May, published her best-selling novel *Little Women.* Alcott himself wrote prolifically over the last two decades of his career, largely poetry and essays, but also an acclaimed biography of Emerson. As he grew older, Alcott became increasingly conservative in his views, and he even embraced organized Christianity in the face of new ideas concerning human evolution and women's suffrage, theories he found too radical. In the last years of his life Alcott gained acclaim as an elder spokesman for the Transcendentalist movement, delivering lectures and helping to found the Concord School of Philosophy in 1879. Alcott's career was cut short in 1882, however, when he suffered a massive stroke, leaving him unable to speak or write. He died six years later, on March 4, 1888.

MAJOR WORKS

While during his lifetime Alcott achieved greater renown as a conversationalist than an author, he did produce a handful of literary works of some merit and lasting significance. His first published work, "Observations on the Principals and Methods of Infant Instruction," which appeared in 1830, was based on his experiences teaching at the infant school in Boston and provides a record of American educational theories in the early nineteenth century. The two-volume *Conversations with Children on the Gospels,* which provides a valuable chronicle of the spiritual views of Alcott's students, helped promulgate new attitudes toward the importance of early education in America. Alcott generally enjoyed greater success with his later works. He published the well-respected biography *Ralph Waldo Emerson* in 1865. *Concord Days* (1872), a collection of essays and poems, represents the culmination of Alcott's mature philosophical thought. Alcott produced another collection, *Table-Talk,* in 1877 and that was followed by a volume of poetry, *New Connecticut,* in 1881. His last work, *Sonnets and Canzonets,* appeared in 1882. Although unpublished during his lifetime, Alcott's exhaustive journals, which first appeared in 1938 under the title *The Journals of Bronson Alcott,* represent the most articulate and complete expression of his ideas concerning spirituality, literature, and politics. Equally valuable as a document of Alcott's life and times is *The Letters of A. Bronson Alcott,* published in 1969.

CRITICAL RECEPTION

Alcott's writings were generally met with indifference and, at times, derision. Emerson himself, while one of Alcott's closest and most loyal friends, had little praise for Alcott's writings and even discouraged his friend from publishing his book-length documentation of his daughter Elizabeth's first years, *Psyche.* By the time of Alcott's death, however, he had begun to gain recognition as an important and highly original thinker. In 1893 Franklin Benjamin Sanborn and William T. Harris published *A. Bronson Alcott, His Life and Philosophy,* a valuable early appraisal of his life and work. A more detailed and objective account of Alcott's career, Odell Shepard's *Pedlar's Progress,* appeared in 1937. Also in the 1930s, Arthur Christy was among the first to recognize Alcott's pivotal role in introducing and popularizing Eastern philosophy in New England, and during the 1940s scholars of education such as Dorothy McCuskey produced book-length studies of Alcott's educational philosophy. Since the 1970s scholars of the American Renaissance, notably Joel Myerson, have begun to recognize Alcott's crucial contribution to the development of Transcendentalist philosophy as well as his indisputable influence on the writings of Emerson. Although Alcott has never attracted substantial critical interest as a poet or prose stylist, the diversity and versatility of his ideas and interests have struck a chord with prominent thinkers and writers outside literary circles. In recent years Alcott's teaching philosophy has attracted renewed interest, and child psychologists such as Robert Coles and Joseph Chilton Pearce have praised Alcott's *Conversations with Children on the Gospels* as a seminal work in the field of early childhood education.

PRINCIPAL WORKS

Observations on the Principals and Methods of Infant Instruction (essay) 1830

Conversations with Children on the Gospels. 2 vols. (essays) 1836-37; also published as *Record of Conversations on the Gospels, Held at Mr. Alcott's School*

Ralph Waldo Emerson (biography) 1865; also published as *Ralph Waldo Emerson: An Estimate of His Character and Genius,* 1882

Tablets (essays and poetry) 1868

Concord Days (essays and poetry) 1872

Table-Talk (essays and poetry) 1877

New Connecticut: An Autobiographical Poem (poetry and prose) 1881

Sonnets and Canzonets (poetry) 1882

The Journals of Bronson Alcott (journals) 1938; also published as *Journals,* 1966

†*Orphic Sayings* (prose) 1939

The Letters of A. Bronson Alcott (letters) 1969

†Originally published in 1840, 1841, and 1842 in the journal *Dial.*

CRITICISM

Ralph Waldo Emerson (journal date 24 June 1836)

SOURCE: Emerson, Ralph Waldo. Journal entry from *Journals of Ralph Waldo Emerson, with Annotations, 1836-1838,* edited by Edward Waldo Emerson and Waldo Emerson Forbes, p. 75. Boston: Houghton Mifflin Company, 1910.

[*In the following excerpted journal entry dated 24 June 1836, Emerson responds to Alcott's* Conversations with Children on the Gospels.]

I have read with great pleasure, sometimes with delight, No. 5 of Mr. Alcott's **Record of Conversations on the Gospels.** The internal evidence of the genuineness of the thinking on the part of the children is often very strong. Their wisdom is something the less surprising because of the simplicity of the instrument on which they play these fine airs. It is a harp of two strings, Matter and Spirit, and in whatever combination or contrast or harmony you strike them, always the effect is sublime.[1]

Note

1. This passage is followed by those about Prayer being "a true study of truth" (*Nature,* "Prospects," p. 74, Centenary Ed.[; Boston and New York: Houghton Mifflin, 1903-4]), and that about every man or boy having a trust of power, whether over a potato-field or the laws of a state. (*Lectures and Biographical Sketches* [in *The Complete Works of Ralph Waldo Emerson* (Boston: Houghton Mifflin, 1883)], "Education," p. 128.)

Orestes A. Brownson (review date October 1838)

SOURCE: Brownson, Orestes A. Review of *Conversations with Children on the Gospels,* by Amos Bronson Alcott. *Boston Quarterly Review* 1 (October 1838): 417-32.

[*In the following excerpt, Brownson praises Alcott's idealism and originality as a thinker, while critiquing the limitations of his philosophy.*]

This [**Conversations with Children on the Gospels**] is a difficult book for Reviewers. It is not easy to say what it is, or what it is not. It is hardly safe to assume it as an index to the views and opinions of its editor, or to the character and worth of the school in which these **Conversations** were held. The **Conversations** published are incomplete; they comprise only one year of what was intended to be a four years' course. The very nature of such conversations precludes the possibility of recording them with perfect accuracy, though these were recorded with great fidelity; and then, they constituted the exercise of the scholars for only a part of one half-day in a week, the rest of the time being taken up with the studies common in other schools. As it regards Mr. Alcott, these **Conversations** very imperfectly reveal him, or his system of instruction. One is in constant danger of misapprehending him, and of ascribing to him views and opinions which belong solely to the children. Even his own questions, if we are not on our guard, may mislead us; for they were frequently suggested by the remarks of the scholars, and designed merely to induce them to carry out their own thought. . . .

Still we are not at all surprised that Mr. Alcott and his publications are so little appreciated, and so greatly misapprehended. Mr. Alcott is a reformer. He does not believe that the Past has realized the highest worth man may aspire to; he does not believe that the methods of teaching usually adopted, or the systems of education contended for by our teachers and professors generally, are at all adapted to the purpose of rearing up MEN, and of making them walk as becomes moral and intellectual beings, made in the image of God and possessing a Divine Nature; he thinks that the aim of our systems of education, whether private, public, domestic, or social, is too low, and that the methods adopted are destitute of science, above all of vitality, that they are too mechanical, and make of our schools only commendable "treadmills." Now to think and say all this is to reflect no great credit on our thousands of school-teachers and learned professors and their friends, nor upon those who boast the efforts we have made and are making in the cause of Education. This is as much as to tell his disciples, that unless their righteousness, in this respect, exceed that of the Scribes and Pharisees, the Chief Priests and Elders in the teaching Art, they shall in no wise be qualified for undertaking to rear up men and women, fit to be the citizens of a free and Christian Republic. Can the Chief Priests and Elders, the Scribes and Pharisees, be made to believe this; or to regard him who utters it in any other light than that of a reviler, a blasphemer? Reformers are never understood and appreciated, till the reforms for which they contend are to a good degree realized.

Then again, Mr. Alcott is a peculiar man. He has observed more than he has read, and reflected more than he has observed. He is a man, though eminently social in his feelings and tastes, who has lived mostly in communion with himself, with children, and with Nature. His system is one which he has thought out for himself and by himself. It has therefore almost necessarily taken the hues of his own mind, and become somewhat difficult to communicate to minds not constructed like his own. The terms he has made use of in his solitary reflections to express his thoughts to himself have a special meaning, a special value in his use of them, of which those with whom he converses are ignorant, and of which it is often extremely difficult for them to conceive. In consequence of his solitary reflections, of his little intercourse with the world at large, and his limited acquaintance with books, he has framed to himself a peculiar language, which, though formed of the choicest English, is almost, if not quite wholly unintelligible to all who have not become extensively acquainted with his mode of thinking. He very easily translates the thoughts of others into his language, but it is with great difficulty that he translates his thoughts into their language. People generally in hearing him converse form no conception of his real meaning; and if they attach any meaning to what he says, it will in nine cases out of ten be a false one. This, however, though it accounts for the misapprehension of people, in regard to him, is not altogether his fault. People may misapprehend him, because they do not understand themselves. There are not many men who have thoroughly analyzed their own minds, become masters of their own ideas, and so familiar with them that they can recognise them when clothed in a new dress. We are familiar with certain words, which we suppose we use as signs of ideas, but which we use very often as substitutes for ideas. When we find these words defined, or hear them used indeed as signs of ideas, and as signs of the very ideas for which we should have used them, had we used them for any, we are at fault; we find ourselves introduced to entire strangers with whom we can hold no conversation. We know not our own ideas; and very likely are frightened at them, and run away from them as though they were the Evil One himself. . . .

Mr. Alcott is known mainly as a schoolmaster, but as a schoolmaster, as we usually think of schoolmasters, he must not be viewed. Unblessed with an abundance of this world's goods, he has often been obliged to confine himself to the drudgery of mere schoolmaster duties; but he is an original thinker, and he aspires to be an educator, not of children only, but of mankind. His system of Human Culture is designed for the human race, and is valued by him as true in itself, and as the means of raising all men to the stature of perfect men in Christ Jesus. He professes to have a whole system of Theology, Morality,—a philosophy of Man, of Nature, of God. His method of teaching is but the means by which men are to be led ideally and actually to the Absolute. His philosophy he regards as the philosophy of the Absolute. It is as the theologian, the philosopher, the moralist, and the philanthropist, rather than as a schoolmaster, that he is to be regarded. But we proceed to develop his system.

Suppose a man who has no means of knowledge but his five senses. Such a man can take cognizance, of only material objects, of sensible qualities. Color, form, extension, solidity, sound, odor, taste, comprise all the objects of knowledge he can consistently admit. In a word, external nature is all he knows. External nature is to him what it appears. It is real, not symbolical. It indicates nothing which it is not,—nothing on which it depends, and of which it may be regarded as the sign or apparition. It is what it appears, and when seen it is known, and when known that is the end of knowledge. Nothing more is to be known.

In Nature everything, as known by this man of five senses, and of five senses only, is concrete. Nothing is abstract. There are particulars but no generals. Mankind is merely a collective name, and has no meaning beyond the number of individual men and women it designates. A tree is a tree and nothing more. Truth and virtue are abstract nouns, invented for the convenience of conversation, but void of meaning. There may be true stories, true views, but not truth, conformity to which makes the individual story or view a true one. There may be virtuous men and women, but no virtue, conformity to which makes one virtuous.

But is this true? Are all things what they appear? And does all that is appear? Is the Appearance the Thing? Or is the Thing that appears always back of the Appearance? Is it the Thing that we recognise with our senses, or is it only the sign, symbol, or shadow of the Thing? In man, is it the man that is apparent to the senses? The senses perceive the body, but is the body anything more than the symbol of the man? Take all the phenomena with regard to a man, presented us by the senses, and do they constitute the man? The man is evidently a collection of forces, moral, intellectual, and physical. We observe in him moral affections; we know that he performs the act of thinking; we see that such things as growth, decay, digestion, nutrition, and the like, are constantly going on in him. Now is there not back of these Something that produces them? Is it the feet that walk, or is it the man that walks? Does the brain think, or is it the man that thinks? The stomach, does it digest, or is it the man that digests? The heart, does it love, or is it the man that loves? Back then of the sense-phenomena lies the real Man, the Thing, the Reality, of which what is apparent to the senses is the mere symbol, or sign. The appearance, the apparition is not the man, but a mere index to point us to where the man is and to what he does.

Take a plant. The senses show us a certain number of phenomena. But in that plant are there not things which the senses do not show us, of which they can take no cognizance? Back of this sense-plant is there not the spirit-plant, that is, the real plant of which the senses show us only the appearance or symbol? The real plant is the law that is manifesting itself; the force which pushes itself out in what we call growth, in the bud, the

blossom, the fruit; and which makes it precisely what it is, and not something else. It is not meant by this that the senses deceive us; it is only meant that they do not show us the Thing, but its sign; not the reality, but the phenomenon, as a word is not the idea, but its sign or symbol.

We do not give these examples as demonstrations, but merely as illustrations to make our meaning obvious. Now apply the remarks we have made of man and of the plant to all nature, and you have Mr. Alcott's doctrine of Nature, or more properly of the external world. The external world is merely the world of the senses; it is not a real but an apparent world, not substantial, but phenomenal. He does not distrust the senses as do the Idealists, but he denies their power to attain to realities. They stop short of the Thing, and merely give us its sign. They show us where the Thing is, but leave it for the spirit to see what it is.

Pursuing the path in which we have started we may go much further. The Real is always the Invisible. But the invisible world which we have found lying immediately back of the sensible or apparent world, is it the ultimate world? Is there not another world which the soul may discover back of that? All effects are included in their causes, and we have not attained to the Thing till we have attained to the ultimate cause. Absolute reality of all things can then be found only in the absolute cause of all things. A cause in order to be a cause must be free, self-sufficing, and self-acting. If absolute then it must be one, for more absolute causes than one is an absurdity which the reason rejects. The world of the senses must then be resolved into the invisible world of the reason, which may for distinction's sake be called the *intelligible* world; and the intelligible world must then be resolved into the Absolute world, the world of Unity, which, if we understand Mr. Alcott in his terminology, may be called the world of Faith. In man he recognises sense, understanding, or reason, and Faith or Instinct; each of these has a world of its own. The absolute world, that is, Absolute Reality is found only by Faith or Instinct, and is the world of Absolute Unity.

Now, Absolute Unity, in the bosom of which all things exist, is God. In the last analysis all Reality resolves itself into God. God is the sum total of all that is; the only Substance, the only absolute Being, the only absolute Reality. God is the Universe, and the Universe is God;—not the sensible universe, nor the intelligible, but the Instinctive;—not the universe seen by the eye of sense, nor that seen by the eye of reason or understanding, but that seen by the inner eye of the soul, by Faith or Instinct.

Now the universe of the senses and that of the understanding are both manifestations of God. The sensible universe is God as he appears to the senses; the intelligible universe is God as he unfolds himself to the intellect; the universe beheld by Faith or Instinct, that is, by the highest in man, is God in his absoluteness; as he is in himself, the real, not the manifested God. We take our stand now on the revelations of Instinct; that is, in God himself, and from his point of view examine and interpret all phenomenal worlds and beings. In descending from him through the intelligible world and the sensible, we perceive that all laws, all forces, all things, so far forth as they have any real being, are identical with God. God is not the plant as it exists to the understanding, or the senses; nevertheless, he is all the reality, all the absolute being there is in the plant; God is not man, and man is not God, as he exists to the senses, or to the understanding; nevertheless all the real being there is in man, all that is not phenomenal, appearance merely, is God, "in whom we live, and move, and have our *being*."

By a psychological examination of man, we find that he takes cognizance of the three worlds, or universes we have enumerated. Man must have then three orders of faculties, corresponding to these three worlds. He is not then merely endowed with five senses, as we supposed in the beginning; he has, above his five senses, reason or understanding; and above this, as that which attains to the Absolute, Faith or Instinct; which, so far as we can perceive, is very nearly identical with what M. Cousin calls Spontaneity or the Spontaneous Reason. Now in the business of education, we should have reference to these three worlds, or these three orders of faculties, and according to their relative importance. The education which has been and is most common has reference almost exclusively to the world of the senses; some few philosophers and teachers are laboring to make it conform to the world of the understanding; few or none labor to make it conform to the world of Instinct, to the absolute Truth and Reality of things. This last is Mr. Alcott's work. To call attention to this work, to show by his instructions what it is, and by his example how it may be and is to be done, is what he regards as his mission. As a partial experiment, as an intimation of what may under more favorable circumstances be accomplished, he had these **Conversations** recorded as they occurred, and has finally published them to the world.

Having thus far glanced at what may be called Mr. Alcott's metaphysical system, we may now proceed without much difficulty to seize his theory of education, and to a general comprehension of his views of Childhood and of Religion. These views have struck many minds as absurd, but the absurdity, we think we find in the views of others, is often an absurdity for which we alone are responsible. We assign to others very frequently the absurd views which originate with ourselves; and it is a good rule for us to observe, that so long as a man's views appear to us to be wholly absurd, if he be a man of but tolerable understanding, we should judge ourselves ignorant of his real meaning.

Instinct, which must be carefully distinguished from Impulse, is according to Mr. Alcott's theory the Divine in Man. It is the Incarnate God. Our instincts are all divine and holy, and being the immediate actings, or promptings of the Divinity, they constitute the criterion of Truth and Duty. They are what there is in man the most real and absolute. They are then the most Godlike, the most Divine, partake the most of God; they are then to be regarded as the highest in man, to which all else in him is to be subordinated. The instincts are to be followed as the supreme law of the soul.

The instincts, inasmuch as they are the Divine in man, the Incarnate God, contain all the truth, goodness, reality there is in man. The Divine in man, or the God Incarnate, is one with the Universal, the Absolute God. There is nothing in the sensible universe, nor in the intelligible universe, that is not in the Absolute God. All things are in God, and God is in man. In our instincts then are included, in their law, their reality, both the world of sense and the world of the understanding. To know these worlds then we must look within, not abroad. To become acquainted with God and his manifestations we must study the instincts. Knowledge, truth, goodness, all that can deserve to be called by either name, must be drawn out of the soul, not poured into it. Human culture, therefore, as the word *education,* (from *e* and *duco,*) literally implies, is merely drawing forth what exists, though enveloped, in the soul from the beginning.

As the child is born with all the instincts and with them more active and pure than they are in after life, it follows that the child is born in possession of all truth, goodness, worth, human nature can aspire to. Therefore said Jesus, "Suffer little children to come unto me, for of such is the kingdom of heaven." Childhood is therefore to be reverenced. The wise men from the East do always hail with joy the star of the new-born babe, and haste to the cradle to present their offerings and to worship. The educator must sit down with reverence and awe at the feet of the child, and listen. Till this be done, little progress can be expected in human culture.

The child is pure and holy. It obeys freely and without reserve its Divine Instincts. It smiles, loves, acts, as God commands. The true end, or one of the great ends of Human Culture must be to preserve the child in the grown up man. Most people at a very early day lose the child, and go through life bewailing their lost childhood. The whole family of man may be represented as the distracted mother, who wept with loud lamentation for her children, because they were not. The only exception to this is, that they too often lose their childhood without being conscious of their loss. Childhood is lost; the innocency, the freedom, the light of the instincts are obscured, and all but annihilated, by the false modes of life which are adopted; by the wrong state of society which prevails; by intemperance, in eating, drinking, sleeping, and the like; and by the mistaken education which men have unwisely encouraged,—an education which tends perpetually to raise sense and understanding above Divine Instinct, and to subject us to shadows and illusions, rather than to truth and reality. Hence, the necessity of strict temperance in all the habits of the body, and of early attention to the instincts, so that they may be called forth and strengthened before the senses and the understanding have established their dominion over us.

The body in its true state is to the soul what the outward universe is to God,—its veil or covering, or more properly, its symbol which marks to the senses the place where it is. What are called bodily appetites and inclinations, come from the soul, not from the body; proceeding from the soul, they should be regarded, in themselves, as of like purity and divinity, as any of the instincts of our nature. The exercise of them all, and in all cases, should be regarded as a religious exercise, and should be performed with all the feelings of awe and responsibleness, with which we accompany the most solemn act of religious worship. All the functions of the body, as we call them, but which are really functions of the soul, are holy, and should be early surrounded with holy and purifying associations. Hence the conversations in the volumes before us with the children, on the mysterious phenomena attending the production and birth of a new member to the human family, or what Mr. Alcott calls the Incarnation of Spirit,—conversations which have caused him much reproach, and done him, for the moment, we fear no little injury. His motives were pure and praiseworthy, and his theory seemed to require him to take the course he did, and he should not be censured; but for ourselves, we regard as one of the most certain instincts of our nature, that one which leads us to throw a veil over the mysterious phenomena by which the human race is preserved and its members multiplied. Mr. Alcott's theory requires him to respect all the Instincts, and why this less than others? In attempting to eradicate it, he appears to us to be inconsistent with himself, and likely to encourage more prurient fancies than he will be able to suppress. Nature in this has provided better, in our judgment, for the preservation of chastity in thought and in deed, than man can do by any system of culture he can devise.

Pursuing the rules implied in these general principles, the educator aims to call forth into full glory and activity the grace and truth with which man is endowed. He labors to train up the human being committed to his care, in obedience to the Highest, to see, and respect, and love all things in the light, not of the senses, not of the intellect even, but of Faith, of Instinct, of the Spirit of God,—the "true light, which enlighteneth every man that cometh into the world." If he succeeds in realizing his aim, the result is a perfect Man, "armed at all points, to use the Body, Nature, and Life for his growth and re-

newal, and to hold dominion over the fluctuating things of the Outward." Realize this in the case of every child born into the world, and you have reformed the world,—made earth a heaven, and men the sons of God in very deed. This is the end Mr. Alcott contemplates; this end he believes can be attained by his method of viewing and disciplining the soul, and by no other. Hence the magnitude of the work he is engaged in,—the importance of his doctrine, and his method of culture to the human race.

If now for the word *God,* we substitute the word *Spirit,* and call spirit absolute Being, and the absolute, the real universe, which lies back of the sensible universe and the intelligible, also spirit, and therefore regard all power, force, cause, reality, as spirit, and spirit everywhere as identical, we may, with the expositions we have made, attain to a proximate notion of Mr. Alcott's theory of God, Man, and Nature, as well as of Human Culture. He sees spirit everywhere, and in everything he seeks spirit. Spirit regarded as the cause and law of organization is God; spirit organized is the universe; spirit incarnated is man. An identity therefore runs through God, Man, and Nature; they are all one in the fulness of universal and everlasting spirit.

Spirit, though incarnate in the case of every human being, attains rarely to anything like a perfect manifestation. A perfect manifestation, however, is not to be expected, because there are no bounds to the growth of spirit. Many bright specimens of the worth men may attain to have been exhibited at distant intervals in the world's history; among which Moses, Socrates, and Jesus are the worthiest. Of these three Jesus stands first.

With this estimate of the character of Jesus, the Records of his life must of course be regarded as the most suitable text book for the educator. They give the children for their study the model nearest to perfection, that can as yet be found. Besides all this, the identity of spirit, and therefore of human nature in all ages and countries of the world, implies an identity between Jesus, or the Instincts of Jesus, and the Instincts of the child. The coincidence, which we may discover between the manifestations of the pure Instincts of Childhood and those recorded of Jesus, becomes therefore a proof of the accuracy of the Record. If we can reproduce in children, as yet unspoiled, the phenomena recorded of Jesus, then we have a new proof, and a strong proof, that the Record is a faithful one. These ***Conversations on the Gospels,*** therefore, so far as the answers of the children may be regarded as a reproduction of Jesus, the doctrines or precepts ascribed to Jesus, constitute a class of evidence for Christianity, which the Christian theologian will find not without value.

These are, rudely and imperfectly sketched, the chief outlines of Mr. Alcott's system, so far as we have ourselves been able to comprehend it. Of the two volumes before us we will not attempt to form an estimate. Different minds will estimate them differently. That they do in part accomplish the end for which they were designed we think no one can reasonably deny. They may be read with profit by all students of the New Testament; and to minds of some quickness of apprehension they will open up, in that often read but poorly comprehended volume, many views of rich and varied beauty on which the soul may feast with delight. Parents and Sunday School teachers will find them a valuable help in their work of instructing their children, and in conversing with children on religious subjects; and to them we conscientiously commend these volumes, not for the doctrines they may be supposed to teach, but for the suggestions they contain, and for the method of approaching the young mind they in part unfold.

As it regards Mr. Alcott's religious and metaphysical system, we have not much to offer. We have aimed to state it, not to criticise it. It strikes us as neither absurd nor alarming. We see much truth in it, and we recognise in it the marks of a mind earnestly in love with truth and willing to labor to gain it. The system, though original with Mr. Alcott, is by no means new or peculiar. As a whole we do not embrace it. We differ from him in several essential particulars. We do not admit that identity between Man and God, and God and Nature, which he does. God is in his works; but he is also separate from them. Creation does not exhaust the Creator. Without Him his works are nothing; but He nevertheless *is,* and *all* He is, without them. I am in my intention, but my intention makes up no part of me. I am in the word I utter; and yet I am the same without the word that I am with it. In uttering it I have put forth a creative energy, but I nevertheless retain, after uttering it and independently of it, all the creative energy I had before. So of God. The universe is his intention, his word, and we may find him in it; but he remains independent of it, and is no more identical with it, than my resolution is identical with the power I have of forming resolutions, or than my word is identical with the power that utters it. Mr. Alcott appears to us not to distinguish with sufficient accuracy between the Creation and the Creator. The relation of the universe to God, according to him, is the relation of a word to the idea it stands for, whereas we regard it as the relation of an effect to its cause. It would be hard for us to entertain his views, without becoming more pantheistic than we believe truth and piety warrant.

But notwithstanding this, Mr. Alcott's views of education, as he reduces them to practice, are unexceptionable. If he runs into an extreme in some cases, if he dwells too much in the Inward, and insists too much on Spontaneity, he probably goes not farther than is necessary to counteract the strong tendency in an opposite direction, which is the most striking characteristic of our schools as they are. What we regard as erroneous in his theory, can in the actual state of things amongst us have

no bad effect. We have overlooked the Inward; we have lost our faith in the Spiritual; and it is well that a man comes amongst us, who persists in directing our attention to the voice of God that speaks to us, is ever speaking to us, in the soul of man. The Instincts, as Mr. Alcott calls them, are no doubt from God; they deserve to be studied and reverenced; we must, however, be on our guard that we do not become exclusively devoted to them, for if we do we shall become Mystics.

Ralph Waldo Emerson (journal date 23 March 1842)

SOURCE: Emerson, Ralph Waldo. Journal entry from *Journals of Ralph Waldo Emerson, with Annotations, 1841-1844,* edited by Edward Waldo Emerson and Waldo Emerson Forbes, pp. 166-82. Boston: Houghton Mifflin Company, 1911.

[*In the following excerpted journal entry dated 23 March 1842, Emerson records his impressions of Alcott's character. While Emerson has high praise for Alcott's conversational skills, he shows less regard for his friend's writings, which he describes as offering "more pain than pleasure from the perusal."*]

Here prepares now the good Alcott to go to England,[1] after so long and strict acquaintance as I have had with him for seven years. I saw him for the first time in Boston in 1835.

What shall we say of him to the wise Englishman?[2]

He is a man of ideas, a man of faith. Expect contempt for all usages which are simply such. His social nature and his taste for beauty and magnificence will betray him into tolerance and indulgence, even, to men and to magnificence, but a statute or a practice he is condemned to measure by its essential wisdom or folly.

He delights in speculation, in nothing so much, and is very well endowed and weaponed for that work with a copious, accurate and elegant vocabulary; I may say poetic; so that I know no man who speaks such good English as he, and is so inventive withal. He speaks truth truly; or the expression is adequate. Yet he knows only this one language. He hardly needs an antagonist,—he needs only an intelligent ear. Where he is greeted by loving and intelligent persons, his discourse soars to a wonderful height, so regular, so lucid, so playful, so new and disdainful of all boundaries of tradition and experience, that the hearers seem no longer to have bodies or material gravity, but almost they can mount into the air at pleasure, or leap at one bound out of this poor solar system. I say this of his speech exclusively, for when he attempts to write, he loses, in my judgment, all his power, and I derive more pain than pleasure from the perusal. The *Post* expresses the feeling of most readers in its rude joke, when it said of his **"Orphic Sayings"** that they "resembled a train of fifteen railroad cars with one passenger." He has moreover the greatest possession both of mind and of temper in his discourse, so that the mastery and moderation and foresight, and yet felicity, with which he unfolds his thought, are not to be surpassed. This is of importance to such a broacher of novelties as he is, and to one baited, as he is very apt to be, by the sticklers for old books or old institutions. He takes such delight in the exercise of this faculty that he will willingly talk the whole of a day, and most part of the night, and then again to-morrow, for days successively, and if I, who am impatient of much speaking, draw him out to walk in the woods or fields, he will stop at the first fence and very soon propose either to sit down or to return. He seems to think society exists for this function, and that all literature is good or bad as it approaches colloquy, which is its perfection. Poems and histories may be good, but only as adumbrations of this; and the only true manner of writing the literature of a nation would be to convene the best heads in the community, set them talking, and then introduce stenographers to record what they say. He so swiftly and naturally plants himself on the moral sentiment in any conversation that no man will ever get any advantage of him, unless he be a saint, as Jones Very was. Every one else Alcott will put in the wrong.

It must be conceded that it is speculation which he loves, and not action. Therefore he dissatisfies everybody and disgusts many. When the conversation is ended, all is over. He lives to-morrow, as he lived to-day, for further discourse, not to begin, as he seemed pledged to do, a new celestial life. The ladies fancied that he loved cake; very likely; most people do. Yet in the last two years he has changed his way of living, which was perhaps a little easy and self-indulgent for such a Zeno, so far as to become ascetically temperate. He has no vocation to labor, and, although he strenuously preached it for a time, and made some efforts to practise it, he soon found he had no genius for it, and that it was a cruel waste of his time. It depressed his spirits even to tears.

He is very noble in his carriage to all men, of a serene and lofty aspect and deportment in the street and in the house. Of simple but graceful and majestic manners, having a great sense of his own worth, so that not willingly will he give his hand to a merchant, though he be never so rich,—yet with a strong love of men, and an insatiable curiosity concerning all who were distinguished either by their intellect or by their character. He is the most generous and hospitable of men, so that he has been as munificent in his long poverty as Mr. Perkins in his wealth, or I should say much more munificent. And for his hospitality, every thing in the form of man that entered his door as a suppliant would be made

master of all the house contained. Moreover, every man who converses with him is presently made sensible that, although this person has no faculty or patience for our trivial hodiernal labors, yet if there were a great courage, a great sacrifice, a self-immolation to be made, this and no other is the man for a crisis,—and with such grandeur, yet with such temperance in his mien.

Such a man, with no talent for household uses, none for action, and whose taste is for precisely that which is most rare and unattainable, could not be popular,—he could never be a doll, nor a beau, nor a bestower of money or presents, nor even a model of good daily life to propose to virtuous young persons. His greatness consists in his attitude merely; of course he found very few to relish or appreciate him; and very many to dispraise him. Somebody called him a "moral Sam Patch."

Another circumstance marks this extreme love of speculation. He carries all his opinions and all his condition and manner of life in his hand, and, whilst you talk with him, it is plain he has put out no roots, but is an air-plant, which can readily and without any ill consequence be transported to any place. He is quite ready at any moment to abandon his present residence and employment, his country, nay, his wife and children, on very short notice, to put any new dream into practice which has bubbled up in the effervescence of discourse. If it is so with his way of living, much more so is it with his opinions. He never remembers. He never affirms anything to-day because he has affirmed it before. You are rather astonished, having left him in the morning with one set of opinions, to find him in the evening totally escaped from all recollection of them, as confident of a new line of conduct and heedless of his old advocacy. *Sauve qui peut.*

Another effect of this speculation is that he is preternaturally acute and ingenious to the extent sometimes of a little jesuitry in his action. He contemns the facts so far that his poetic representations have the effect of a falsehood, and those who are deceived by them ascribe the falsehood to him: and sometimes he plays with actions unimportant to him in a manner not justifiable to any observers but those who are competent to do justice to his real magnanimity and conscience.

Like all virtuous persons he is destitute of the appearance of virtue, and so shocks all persons of decorum by the imprudence of his behavior and the enormity of his expressions. . . .

This man entertained in his spirit all vast and magnificent problems. None came to him so much recommended as the most universal. He delighted in the fable of Prometheus; in all the dim, gigantic pictures of the most ancient mythology; in the Indian and Egyptian traditions; in the history of magic, of palmistry, of temperaments, of astrology, of whatever showed any impatience of custom and limits, any impulse to dare the solution of the total problem of man's nature, finding in every such experiment an implied pledge and prophecy of worlds of science and power yet unknown to us. He seems often to realize the pictures of the old alchemists: for he stood brooding on the edge of discovery of the Absolute from month to month, ever and anon affirming that it was within his reach, and nowise discomfited by uniform shortcomings.

The other tendency of his mind was to realize a reform in the Life of Man. This was the steadily returning, the monotonous topic of years of conversation. This drew him to a constant intercourse with the projectors and saints of all shades, who preached or practised any part or particle of reform, and to a continual coldness, quarrel, and non-intercourse with the scholars and men of refinement who are usually found in the ranks of conservatism. Very soon the Reformers whom he had joined would disappoint him; they were pitiful persons, and, in their coarseness and ignorance, he began to pine again for literary society. In these oscillations from the Scholars to the Reformers, and back again, he spent his days.

His vice, an intellectual vice, grew out of this constitution, and was that to which almost all spiritualists have been liable,—a certain brooding on the private thought which produces monotony in the conversation, and egotism in the character. Steadily subjective himself, the variety of facts which seem necessary to the health of most minds, yielded him no variety of meaning, and he quickly quitted the play on objects, to come to *the Subject*, which was always the same, viz., *Alcott in reference to the World of To-day.*

From a stray leaf I copy this:—

Alcott sees the law of man truer and farther than any one ever did. Unhappily, his conversation never loses sight of his own personality. He never quotes; he never refers; his only illustration is his own biography. His topic yesterday is Alcott on the 17th October; to-day, Alcott on the 18th October; to-morrow, on the 19th. So will it be always. The poet, rapt into future times or into deeps of nature admired for themselves, lost in their law, cheers us with a lively charm; but this noble genius discredits genius to me. I do not want any more such persons to exist.[3]

Notes

1. Mr. Alcott's high thoughts on life and on the education of the young had reached certain Englishmen, notably James Pierrepont Greaves, a retired merchant turned scholar and philanthropist, a friend of Pestalozzi and of Strauss, and of Mr. John A. Heraud, editor of a reform magazine. Mr. Alcott's "Records of a School" so interested these and others that a school was established at Ham, Surrey, on Alcott's principles and named for him.

Letters from these friends urged Mr. Alcott to come where he would be warmly welcomed and eagerly heard. The voyage was made possible by the good offices of his friends here.

2. The subjoined letter, and not what follows in the succeeding pages of the Journal, is what Mr. Emerson did write to Carlyle of his friend, over and above some note of introduction, kindly and brief:—

CONCORD, March 21, 1842.

I write now to tell you of a piece of life. I wish you to know that there is shortly coming to you a man by the name of Bronson Alcott. If you have heard his name before, forget what you have heard. Especially if you have read anything to which his name was attached, be sure to forget that; and, inasmuch as in you lies, permit this stranger, when he arrives at your gate, to make a new and primary impression. I do not wish to bespeak any courtesies, or good or bad opinion concerning him. You may love him or hate him, or apathetically pass by him, as your genius shall dictate; only I entreat this, that you do not let him quite go out of your reach until you are sure you have seen him and know for certain the nature of the man. And so I leave contentedly my pilgrim to his fate.

3. It would seem that Mr. Emerson sat down to make a rough draft of a letter of introduction for Mr. Alcott and was led on by interest in the subject to write the above (never sent) resultant of seven years' experience of this strange Nineteenth-Century Apostle with his gifts and his gaps.

Twenty-five years later, Mr. Emerson said to his son, "It will be a thousand pities if I don't outlive Alcott and Ellery Channing, for nobody else knows them well enough to do them justice."

This long entry in the Journal is the fullest statement that Mr. Emerson left, and it was written at the time when Mr. Alcott's theories were at their highest flight, just before the tragic fall to earth in the winter of the following year when the Fruitlands community went to wreck.

Henry David Thoreau (journal date 1845-47)

SOURCE: Thoreau, Henry David. Journal entry from *The Writings of Henry David Thoreau.* Vol. 1, edited by Bradford Torrey, p. 432. Boston: Houghton Mifflin Company, 1906.

[*In the following journal entry from the years 1845-47, Thoreau offers a favorable assessment of Alcott's intellectual and spiritual qualities.*]

Alcott is a geometer, a visionary, the Laplace of ethics, more intellect, less of the affections, sight beyond talents, a substratum of practical skill and knowledge unquestionable, but overlaid and concealed by a faith in the unseen and impracticable. Seeks to realize an entire life; a catholic observer; habitually takes in the farthest star and nebula into his scheme. Will be the last man to be disappointed as the ages revolve. His attitude is one of greater faith and expectation than that of any man I know; with little to show; with undue share, for a philosopher, of the weaknesses of humanity. The most hospitable intellect, embracing high and low. For children how much that means, for the insane and vagabond, for the poet and scholar![1]

Note

1. [*Walden* (Boston: Houghton Mifflin, 1906), p. 296; Riverside edition (1893) 415, 416.]

F. B. Sanborn (essay date 1882)

SOURCE: Sanborn, F. B. "An Essay on the Sonnet." In *Sonnets and Canzonets,* by A. Bronson Alcott. 1882. Reprint, pp. 13-35. New York: AMS Press, 1969.

[*In the following excerpt, Sanborn praises Alcott's command of language in his poetry.*]

Mr. Alcott in these new sonnets [**Sonnets and Canzonets**], the ripe fruit of an aged tree, has used the freedom that nature gave him, and years allow: he has written with little uniformity in the order and number of his rhymes, but with much regard to the spirit of the sonnet as a high form of verse. I fancy that Dante (who may be called the father of the sonnet, though not the first to write it) chose this graceful and courteous verse, because it is so well suited to themes of love and friendship. When he would express sorrow or anger, or light and jesting humor, he had recourse to the canzonet, the *terza rima,* or what he called the ballad,—something quite unlike what we know by that name. Mr. Alcott has followed in the same general course; his sonnets are one thing, his canzonets another: though the difference in feeling, which prompts him to use one form rather than the other, cannot always be definitely expressed. It is felt rather than seen, and seen rather by the effect of the finished poem than by the light of any rule or formal definition.

Definiteness, in fact, must not be looked for in these poems; nor is it the characteristic of the highest poetry in any language. Verse may be powerful and suggestive, or even clear in the sense of producing a distinct impression on the mind, without being definite, and responding to all the claims of analysis. I take it that few readers will fail to see the central thought, or the vivid portraiture in each of these sonnets and canzonets; but

fewer still will be able to explain precisely, even to their own minds, what each suggestive phrase and period includes and excludes in its meaning. For this fine vagueness of utterance, the sonnet has always given poets a fair field, and our present author has not gone beyond his due privilege in this respect, though he has availed himself of it more frequently than many would have done. The mottoes and citations accompanying each sonnet may help the reader to a meaning that does not at once flash in his eyes. But he must not expect to conquer these verses at a single reading. The thought of years, the labor of months, has been given to the writing of them; and the reader ought not to complain if he take as much time to comprehend them as the author took to write them. They are worth the pains of reading many times over, and even of learning them by heart, for which their compendious form well fits them.

It may be complained that these sonnets lack variety. This is indeed a fault into which sonneteers often fall,—our best collection of American sonnets hitherto—those of Jones Very—being open to this censure. It will be found, perhaps, that the sameness of rhyme and thought is often but an appearance,—the delicate shade of meaning being expressed, in a vocabulary of no large extent, by a rare process of combining and collocating words. Certain phrases recur, too, because the thought necessarily recurs,—as when the oratory of Phillips and of Parker, as of others, is characterized by the general term, *eloquence.* In the poverty of our language, there is no other term to use, while the qualifying words and their connection sufficiently distinguish between one person and another. The critical are referred to Homer, who never fails to repeat the same word, or the same verse, when it comes in his way to do so.

Mrs. Ednah D. Cheney (lecture date summer 1888)

SOURCE: Cheney, Mrs. Ednah D. "Reminiscences of Mr. Alcott's Conversations." *Open Court* 2 (9 August 1888): 1131-33, 1142-44.

[*In the following essay, originally read at a meeting in summer 1888, Cheney offers a thorough and detailed account of Alcott's abilities as a conversationalist. Quoting from a number of Alcott's friends and acquaintances, Cheney paints a vivid portrait of the Transcendentalist philosopher's intellectual and moral powers.*]

PART I.

Gentlemen and Ladies.[1]—It is a difficult task to give any idea of Mr. Alcott's conversations to those who never had the happiness of listening to him, for he was unlike every other in the charm and fascination of his speech. He delighted in conversation, and celebrated it ever as the highest form of human expression. Lowell, in the "Fable for Critics," has hardly caricatured him in saying:

For his highest conceit of a happiest state is
Where they'd live upon acorns, and hear him talk
  gratis,
And indeed, I believe, no man ever talked better,
Each sentence hangs perfectly poised to a letter;
He seems piling words, but there's royal dust hid
In the heart of each sky-piercing pyramid.

This comparison to a pyramid is striking, because most people think of Mr. Alcott's speech as more like a free balloon, with no attachment to earth—but I find in an old letter this remark of a critic: "The company that night formed a pyramid, whose base was deep in earth, but whose summit bathed itself in the clouds."

Little justice has been done to the keen sagacity, the fine perception of character, the wit, the satire, even, I may say, audacity of Mr. Alcott's speech, which made his conversation not only elevating, but exhilarating, for these traits were always in subordination to the prevailing quality of high spirituality which left the deepest impression upon you. I find such expressions as these written at the time of hearing him:

"That atmosphere of thought was like sea air to an invalid."

"Mr. Alcott's conversation was a great deal to me, it led me into the Universal, out of myself. It had the same effect that Genius always does." "He was more genial, more humane than I expected." Again, "There is a sort of charm in his voice which, like the music of a song, diverts the attention from the words." And, "I feel like a child with him, and am quite sure that he will accept all with gentleness and forbearance."

At times he was a pure rhapsodist and carried you along by the music of his thought and speech, which it was impossible to define. Theodore Parker said: "Sometimes Mr. Alcott talks like an angel."

I think he never prepared himself by writing, or made notes of what he wished to say or even to quote, although he sometimes opened the conversation by reading, but he sought to bring his mind into the right condition for fruitful meditations. He was wont to read his favorite authors, the philosophers Pythagoras, Plato, Plotinus, etc., or his quaint old poets, Quarles or Donne, Spencer or Herbert, and then as the day began to decline he took his walk around the Common, letting the bracing air and the glow of the sunset tune his mind to harmony, and fill him with inspiration. He never cared to have any one speak to him before the meeting opened.

Yet in the strict sense of the word, Mr. Alcott was not a master of conversation, for his speech was mainly a monologue, and he was not greatly helped by contact with other minds, even by the rich company which he drew about him. He needed a listener rather than an interlocutor. He once said to me: "I wish I had some one with infinite leisure and unbounded patience to listen to my journals," and he liked the same for his speech. He wanted to hear the echo of his own thought from another mind, but he liked as well that it should be reflected back to him unchanged, as to have it remoulded by another's personality. He was little helped by opposition or criticism—it seldom struck out sparks to hammer upon him, but rather he was deafened and deadened by the concussion. He did not seek debate, but communion. He never came to a close grip with an antagonist, he always had a protecting space about him, an air cushion which neutralized the effect of the blows. Yet there was nothing overbearing in his manner, this very buoyant atmosphere made every one feel freedom as if he were floating and held by no barriers, except the impossibilities of arriving anywhere for want of assistance.

He often repeated his thought, even in precisely the same form and words, and yet it always had a certain freshness of originality, and those who really entered into his mind found him always suggestive and fresh. He said: "No book is worth reading that is not as fresh the thousandth time as the first," and his statements were so full of meaning, that after many hearings you often found yourself puzzling over them with new interest in the explanation. I was delighted to find young people of the second generation feeling the same charm in his conversation that we had done, when we sat as young girls at his feet.

Yet it was inevitable that he should sometimes find himself unable to sustain his angelic flights, and should mount a hobby which he rode over the level ground. The repetition of talk on his favorite themes of Temperament, Complexion, Diet, became wearisome to his hearers, especially to those who only perceived the outward features of the subject, and by no means recognized the wide relations which they held in Mr. Alcott's mind. There was always in the company some one to whom his treatment of these topics was new, and who, taking them in their most literal sense, combated his views with superficial arguments, so that the weariness of the discussion was due more to his opponents than to himself. The meat-eater was unwilling to be classed with beasts of prey, and the dark-haired man did not understand being called a demon, and the round of explanation had to be gone through with again and again. He was too much in earnest in his thought to turn away from the discussion of these deep topics, which were full of deep meaning to him.

My own first recollection of Mr. Alcott is of one conversation heard in his house in Beach street, which must have been between the years 1838 and 1840. I was a mere school-girl and went with an older friend who admired and valued him. I was entirely befogged and gained nothing from the conversation but a certain personal impression of dignity and power, which inclined me to hear him again when the right time came. I remember that walking home with my father, I remarked that I could not understand his denying the miracles, which seemed to me a perfectly reasonable exercise of power by a personal God.

I did not hear him again for about ten years, when I began to attend his conversations and to make abstracts of them. In opening, he said: "We must devote the first evening principally to forming acquaintance. We must grope and blunder, and in some moment the inspiring light will come to some mind, and perhaps four or five happy episodes will be all we shall get from the conversation." In the course of these remarks Mr. Alcott said: "Words, if rigidly adhered to, become tombs of thought"; whereupon some one suggested that then "dictionaries are grave-yards!" Mr. Alcott said, he hoped we should go struggling on, we might possibly get into so deep waters of thought that we should drown therein, but he hoped not, "at any rate he had rather drown in a sea of ideas than of words."

By way of commencement he read Plato's Parable of Man, as a figure with a hundred heads of bird and beast, which represented the desires; then the figure of a Lion which was Anger; and then the figure of a Man; and he who loves justice gives the rule to this man over the beasts.

This was discussed by Miss Elizabeth Peabody, Mr. Parker, and by Mr. Scherb, a very brilliant German lecturer, then in Boston.

He then gave some phrases as: instincts, which desire; understanding, which apprehends; fancy, which images; reason, which comprehends; imagination, which seizes truths; conscience, which perceives laws, inspiration or intuition.

Mr. Parker asked him to define Understanding and Reason. He declined, saying: "God only can define, Man can only confine!" Well, will you confine them then? said Mr. Parker.

When the conversation turned to language, Mr. Alcott said: "All language is fluent, a word means what we will have it to mean at the time, it needs the whole experience of life to explain it, and no definitions can make it convey the thought to one not in a condition to receive it."

He followed this theory and often put his own meaning into words which made him liable to misunderstanding from others. "Taken in a certain fine sense," was a favorite expression of his used of old words which were to express new ideas.

While Theodore Parker admired Mr. Alcott and recognized his peculiar value, he was not helpful to him in the conversation on account of their very different intellectual methods. Yet Mr. Parker would sum up the whole talk of the evening in a masterly manner, showing how each person had brought out some necessary phase of the question, and presenting such a curious contrast between his definite statement, and the floating mist which had appeared before, as moved us all to laughter. He did so this evening, closing by accepting Mr. Alcott's definition of the object of man's culture "being to free him from institutions," and asking, "what methods would help to this end?"

Instead of answering this question, Mr. Alcott spoke of conversation and said: "I wish you constantly to draw me from the centre to the surface, into the region where men buy and sell. Here sits a man whose blessing or curse it is, that he dwells in the region of the Ideal, he cannot come down to the region of the Understanding, he has no common sense. Will you not take his case kindly into consideration?"

Among those present was Wm. Henry Channing, who usually helped Mr. Alcott more than any one, unless it were John W. Brown, who always comprehended and sympathized with him. But when Mr. Alcott once appealed to him to know if he used words vaguely, Mr. Brown frankly replied: "You do, and I should not understand you if I did not already know your theories." Mr. J. F. Clark was also present at the conversations.

Among the company was a German of much learning, but skeptical and excessively critical who once apologized to Mr. Alcott for having perhaps said too much and hurt the conversation. "Oh!" said Mr. Alcott, very coolly, "do not be troubled, I don't know upon the whole, but you have helped as much as you have hindered."

But the subject which never failed to puzzle his audience and to draw out much questioning and philistinism was his favorite theory of the Temperaments and Complexions and their illustration in the Angelic and Demonic Man. It was not pleasant to those who had inherited the brunette complexion and dark hair of Southern ancestors, to hear this fair, blue-eyed, light-haired man calmly class them as demons, which word they took, not in its Socratic sense, but as our own German ancestors used it.

A dark-eyed lady once said to him after such a conversation, "I believe your theory, Mr. Alcott, but I don't like to think I belong to the Demons." "Oh! Mrs.——!" he replied, "there are many shades darker than you, there is the Negro."

When he was thus discoursing once, as I felt a sensitiveness for my friends, the Negroes, I said, "Swedenborg says, 'the Negroes are the most beloved of all the races in Heaven.'" "That is very kind in Mr. Swedenborg," was the answer which stopped all comment.

But the most remarkable passage of arms that I remember was with the late Col. Greene. Col. Greene was a master of the art of logic and almost rivaled Socrates in his skill in winding an adversary up into a complete snarl. Of course, he was quite antipathetic to Mr. Alcott. On one occasion, Mr. Alcott described the demonic man and it was point for point a portrait of Mr. Greene, then Reverend and not Colonel, who sat directly before him. "The demonic man is strong, he has dark hair and eyes, his eye is full of fire, he has great energy, strong will. He is logical, and loves disputation and argument. The demonic man smokes, etc." The company silently made the application, but Mr. Greene said, "But has not the demonic man his value?" "Oh, yes!" said Mr. Alcott, "the demonic man is good in his place, very good, he is good to build railroads, but I do not quite like to see him in pulpits, begging Mr. Greene's pardon."

Mr. Greene took the thrust very pleasantly but sharpened his weapons for a retort. On the first convenient occasion he had a string of questions arranged so artfully that while beginning very simply, they would inevitably lead to a *reductio ad absurdum,* if Mr. Alcott answered them frankly, according to his theory. Mr. Alcott replied with a simple affirmative or negative as Mr. Greene had planned, until the company began to perceive his intention, and that if the next question were answered as it must be, Mr. Alcott would be driven to the wall. The question was put, but instead of the simple answer, Mr. Alcott began to talk, and that most delightfully. He soared higher and higher, as if he had taken the wings of the morning, and brought us all the glories of heaven. I believe none of us could tell what he said, but we listened in rapture. Mr. Greene sat with one finger crossed upon another waiting for a pause to put in his question, but the time never came, his opponent was borne away in a cloud far out of sight.

I always queried whether this was intentional, or whether his good angel carried him away, but Louisa said, "O, he knew well enough what he was about."

These anecdotes may appear trivial, but they show Mr. Alcott's keenness of wit and sagacity, and his remarkable power of saying the most cutting things without wounding those to whom he talked.

PART II.

The different way in which he and Mr. Parker regarded Jesus's severe denunciations of the Scribes and Pharisees was characteristic. Mr. Alcott thought they were spoken with such divine serenity that nobody's feelings were hurt, but Mr. Parker said, "No man uttered those words without his pulse running up to a hundred and twenty, and his heart beating as if it would burst out of his bosom."

A witty lady once said Mr. Alcott was "so much of a lamb, he was a little bit of a sheep;" but he had weapons of defence, wit, sarcasm, and irony, which he could use on occasion.

A lady once saying to him, "Mr. Alcott, why have you not come to see me, as you ought to have done?" he replied, "There are many oughts, some of them quite as important as Mrs.———."

To a person who was very much troubled about the Free Love movements, saying, "I ought to do something about them. What shall I do? I wish some one would tell me what to do," he quietly replied, "Meantime, there is Providence."

It is easy to understand that it is far more possible to give such salient exceptions to the usual tenor of the conversation, than any idea of the real height and depth of his thought; you must seek for that in his writings and in the noble criticism of his philosophy we shall have from the one, I may almost say, alone able to give it to us.

While Mr. Alcott's only means of earning money at this time was from these conversations, it was very hard for him to make a pecuniary bargain for them, and he was so unskillful in money matters that one year, in making out his circular, he had put the price of single tickets so low that it was cheaper to buy them all than a ticket for the course. He was very generous in giving free tickets to those who desired them, even to those who added nothing to the pleasure of the company. I remember one woman, somewhat crazed in mind, who occasionally threw the company into convulsions of laughter by her ill-timed remarks, but whom he bore with patiently, always giving her free tickets and escorting her down to the North End after the conversation was over, because he did not think it safe for her to go alone.

With all his seeming unpracticality, Mr. Alcott was not slipshod in his arrangements. He loved thoroughness, good form, good manners. He was never unpunctual either in opening or closing the conversation. He respected his audience and treated them with justice.

The greatest advantage gained from the Town and Country Club established about this time was, that it gave Mr. Alcott a large room in which to hold conversations, and as he thus had no expense for rent, he indulged himself in inviting the company to take tickets, I am not quite sure whether without pay or not. There were to be four conversations, and it was hoped that none would be present but those who felt real interest in him, and who would not be liable to misunderstand him. It hardly proved so, however, for his abounding generosity would not allow him to refuse a ticket to any one who wished it, and as Mr. Emerson's name was joined in the invitation, many wished to attend from curiosity or a very superficial interest. The room was generally crowded. Miss Bremer was once or twice among the guests, very much delighted, but not quite agreeing with his theories. Mr. Emerson came and kept his promise to speak, although with painful effort as he shrank from extemporaneous speech. Among others was a Jewish gentleman who objected to everything other people believed in and who annoyed Mr. Alcott more than I ever saw any one else do. "That raised Lazarus," was his common expression for him. Mr. Sumner was among the guests, and Dr. Elder of Philadelphia. I think it was this winter that Mr. Lowell was occasionally present, and tried to catch Mr. Alcott in some of his theories, but his good genius usually saved him.

In 1851, Mr. Alcott managed his conversations in a novel way, which brought out his rare power of appreciating and delineating character. He proposed a series of seven conversations of Representative men, most of them living and all of our own times.

He first spoke of the true American type as not having yet appeared, and introduced Daniel Webster as not a representative American, not combining all the races which are going to form the new type. He said, "Nature meant to make a noble man, she built the forehead nobly, but the backhead is too powerful even for that, and the crown is wanting. She put in four or five Romans, two or three Saxons, but not the Hebrew. On the plane of the memory and understanding he is great, he deals wisely with affairs, with coarse material interests, but not in the imagination not in the pure reason, not in the conscience. We do not go to Webster for metaphysics. No mother would ask him how to educate her child."

Mr. Alcott drew a comparison between Webster and Cromwell and added that Webster "lacked the feminine. He was old too early, and without the feminine we can have no true manhood."

"Not until we get the feminine element in Congress, whether in a man or a woman, shall we have the right spirit there."

He spoke of him as a conservative. "There is," he said, "a true conservatism, but in the popular sense, the conservative is a man behind himself, and behind his times. He is a demonic man." Probably, Webster was the best type of what Mr. Alcott really meant by the Demonic Man. He said also "that the characteristic of the great men of the last century, from Goethe to Webster, had been this duplicity, this divided nature. We see it in Byron, in Coleridge—eminently in Carlyle. Coleridge did

not sin as Webster, but he was also guilty of that which prevented his doing the things he was capable of doing. The serene single man is yet wanting."

Mr. Garrison represented the Liberal on the second evening, and the conversation was carried on more by others than usual. Mr. Alcott spoke of the Liberator, as Mr. Garrison's diary and best exponent, and of its value as History. In my abstract I have said that I fear I have not fully presented the bread and ample justice Mr. Alcott did to Mr. Garrison. Theodore Parker was the third topic, and Mr. Alcott called him the representative of "popular rights." "He is a great Saxon, with perhaps a little of the Roman. He speaks a thing because it is so, not because he will have it so. We have said all when we have called him 'a man.' Books and libraries serve him, he serves humanity."

"If Mr. Parker is not our priest, he indicates him. He is the silence of the priest, greater than his speech. He moves us not by words alone, but by his port, manner, disposition. There is a soul alive deified in him. He is pre-eminently gifted to operate on the people's heart."

Even in re-reading my poor abstract, I am very much struck with the genial appreciation which Mr. Alcott showed of one so unlike himself. Mr. Parker did not quite suit his imagination, but his heart and conscience responded to him.

Mr. Wm. Henry Channing was the subject of the next discussion. Of him Mr. Alcott said, "He partakes more largely of the fluid element, he is liberated and freed and is an enthusiast. Mr. Channing has not a great imagination, but a lively fancy. As Mr. Parker represents Rights, he represents Love." In answer to a question as to Mr. Channing's failure, Mr. Alcott said, "That is failure when a man's idea ruins *him,* when he is dwarfed and killed by it, but when he is ever growing by it, ever true to it, and does not lose it by any partial or immediate failures—that is success whatever it seems to the world." Again, he said, "True discrimination can come only from a genuine love. It is the paint for our canvass-portrait. He only can truly paint the Devil who for the time loves him!"

I am sorry to find my abstracts of the remaining evenings quite incomplete. Of Dr. Wm. Ellery Channing he spoke as among men of sentiment. My impression of the evening is that he hardly accounted for the wide mark which Dr. Channing has made, but he summed up the conversation thus:

"It is character that does the work. We have one man here who knows how to do his work, he hits the nail on the head. It is not the hammer that hits the nail, it is the man that holds it."

Of the discussion of Mr. Emerson, I have unfortunately no record, I was absent from illness, but it was reported to me as very beautiful. Neither have I any abstract of the conversation on Margaret Fuller as the representative of woman, but in a private letter written at the time, I speak of it as a painful disappointment, so that I sat in agony until I resigned the evening as hopelessly lost. It appears to have been taken out of Mr. Alcott's hands. An old-school physician made a disagreeable attack on Harriet K. Hunt and the Medical College, at which all the company were indignant and which she very properly answered:

Those who love poetical justice may be glad to know that this same physician, very high in his profession, from a bitter opponent became a kind advocate and most helpful friend to women physicians.

Mr. Alcott, however, as well as Mr. Higginson, spoke very beautifully of Margaret Fuller, as I have also recorded his doing in private conversation. I am sorry that I have not his words, for it is a popular error to suppose that these two noble souls were not in cordial harmony of feeling, although so different in expression. Mr. Alcott summed up these conversations as a series of seven pictures.

Our first, Mr. Webster, was a colossal bronze statue.

Our second, Mr. Garrison, was a phrenological head illuminated.

Our third, Mr. Parker, was a bold crayon drawing, wanting in some richness of coloring, but still a good crayon sketch—we were pretty well satisfied with it.

Our fourth, Mr. Channing, was a profile.

Our fifth, Margaret Fuller, was only an outline with the features left out and is left on the easel, it is not yet painted.

Our sixth, Mr. Emerson, was a finely cut medallion and when it was done we fell in love with it ourselves.

Our seventh, Dr. Channing, we hoped would be a miniature. It has not been quite perfect, but we guess it is a miniature.

A new course of fifteen lectures was proposed (on what I have in a letter disrespectfully called the old fellows, by which I presume was meant the philosophers) from Hermes to Goethe.

I think this course was never given. I have no record or remembrance of it.

Beside these public courses Mr. Alcott had occasionally classes of young ladies, to whom he read from the philosophers and poets. Sometimes he required us to write,

transposing a poem into prose. Wordsworth's "Intimations of Immortality" was a favorite subject for this exercise. He frequently attended the meetings of a class who were reading Plato and gave them inspiration and help in understanding his works.

I find three hours mentioned as the length of one of these lessons and no weariness is expressed.

In 1849, Mr. Emerson gave a course of lectures in Freeman Place Chapel. Mr. Alcott invited his friends to come to his room in West Street, after the lecture, to meet Mr. Emerson. They were delightful hours of free social converse, with the lecture for a subject of discussion interesting to all. One evening I noted as present, Mr. Alcott, Mr. Emerson, Mr. Lowell, Mrs. Holland, Mrs. Payne, Mr. and Mrs. Whipple, Mr. Gould, Mr. Woodman, Mr. Fernald, Miss Sarah Dana and others. Mr. Parker was usually there, and Miss Peabody.

It is difficult to show by any figures or even any definite statement of theories or principles, the result of all this work of Mr. Alcott's. For myself, I find his influence so inwoven with all my reading and my hearing at that time, so rich in intellectual life, that I cannot refer things very decidedly to his teaching, but the stimulus to thought was very great. Every subject was treated in its highest relations. No personal or party aims crept in to bias the judgment. There was no sneer for enthusiasm, no putting down of the standard in ethics to meet temporary exigencies. For the time as was said of one of the company by a wit, we were like "disembodied intelligences" seeking for pure thought. In looking over old correspondence I find many minds responding to this influence, even those who could not receive it directly, and this I believe was the way in which Mr. Alcott's thought was spread abroad in wider and wider circles until at last many were helped who never knew from whence the first impulse came.

Yet there were those who did not then and never have accepted this teacher. He had to be content with the recognition of the few who were like-minded or receptive, and leave others to study the great problem by other methods. He had his limitations, but they were not rigid bars. He was unique in his special power, and there were enough to translate the music of his thought into the language of the world.

In speaking of his teaching and his relation to children I think these same limitations must be borne in mind. I wish very much that we could have the testimony of those who were his scholars in childhood. I find a great discrepancy in their views, and am constrained to think he had the same power of impressing a few deeply while he could not influence others at all, with children as with grown people. I know of one pupil, that, in the language of her wise aunt, "he opened her mind," and they felt she was a changed being from his instructions, while others will not confess to any benefit and have kept the same indifference through life. I think he regarded the child too abstractly as an angel, and did not always see what was working in the pupil's thought or what was merely an attempt to reflect his suggestions. He could hardly escape this illusion entirely.

How lasting and wide his influence will become, I cannot venture to predict, but unique and beneficent as it was, to those near to him, I cannot think that it will be lost, but will continue to fashion the thoughts and minds of those who find they can breathe in his atmosphere as in their native air.

If the form of conversation to which he committed his thought seem slight and perishable, we must remember that words are as lasting as temples and statues, and are all that the greatest of teachers has left to us.

Note

1. Read at the Memorial Meeting of the Concord School of Philosophy, Summer of 1888.

Arthur Christy (essay date 1932)

SOURCE: Christy, Arthur. "Alcott the Propagandist." In *The Orient in American Transcendentalism: A Study of Emerson, Thoreau, and Alcott,* pp. 235-59. New York: Columbia University Press, 1932.

[*In the following essay, Christy examines Alcott's interest in Eastern philosophy. Christy asserts that of all the Transcendentalists, Alcott proved the most instrumental in disseminating Eastern ideas in America during the mid-nineteenth century.*]

> Very desirable it were since the gates of the East are now opening wide and giving the free commerce of mind with mind, to collect and compare the Bibles of the races for general circulation and careful reading.
>
> —Alcott, *Tablets,* p. 135.

> I dine and pass the afternoon with the Adams and read 'Bhagavad Gita' to a large audience in the evening, with lively discussions, etc.
>
> —Alcott, *Manuscript Journals.*

> The ideal world I might have treated as a cloud-land, had I not known Alcott, who is a native of that country and makes it as solid as Massachusetts for me.
>
> —Emerson, *Works,* I, xxxiv.

I

The personality of Amos Bronson Alcott, as did that of Emerson and Thoreau, determined the nature of his work. Emerson, as we have seen, was the sage. An

iconoclast in things of the spirit, he nevertheless built, in the place of the dogmas he had scrapped, a new philosophy, a synthesis of all the congenial ideas he found in the thought-life of his time, with much from the Orientals. Thoreau we have studied in his own peculiar temper. It is easy enough to charge him in one sense with being an imitator of his elder friend. He was not in the large sense the pioneer; Emerson was that. Emerson, it was, who like Tennyson's Ulysses sailed beyond the utmost bound, not of human but of Occidental thought. He breathed the yeasty air of intellectual territories which none of his countrymen had explored before him. His essays are the log books of these journeys. But always he returned home to domestic conventionality and propriety. One may describe Emerson as he will—level-headed or urbane. The truth is that he never carried all his theories to their logical conclusion. He is regarded as the most important exponent of American Transcendental thought. There are many reasons for this, the chief being his eloquence and his extensive writing. Yet Thoreau surpassed his friend in many ways. Emerson's intellectual honesty was superb and his heart stout, but his was a different rôle. Without the thoughts with which Emerson returned from his explorations, Thoreau might never have gone to Walden. And Alcott's place in the Transcendental sun was that of educator and dreamer—naturally enough a dreamer. His practical contribution to the cause of the East in America was that of a teacher. His talents were used where they were the most effective. Brilliant as a teacher and conversationalist, in these rôles he sowed the Oriental seed. He also proposed a series of books which no single human being before or since his time has ever written. The plan never was realized, and Alcott, of the three Concord friends, is a man whose influence and work have never been appraised, because so little of his personality ever found its way into the printed page. For this reason his individual color and contribution must be determined from quite a different angle. The bathos[1] which in a purely literary sense is the result of the transition to his pages from those of Emerson and Thoreau, is completely displaced by the fact that in his time Alcott probably had no equal as a popularizer of Orientalism. Though his work was different from that of his friends, it was essentially no less important.

II

The unpublished *Journals* of Bronson Alcott, as they rest securely on their shelves in Concord today, consist of fifty heavy leather-backed volumes. The closely written pages have been preserved from the fate of most scattered loose leaves by the foresight of Louisa Alcott, who ordered the binding of all her father's manuscripts before her death. But slightly explored by Mrs. Morrow[2] and Sanborn, who based his *Life* largely on notes for a biography which Alcott himself had prepared,[3] these diary pages remain unpublished. That they are of value no one who has dipped into them can doubt. There is not the fluency of Emerson's and Thoreau's diaries, but Alcott's nevertheless reflect the high intellectual and spiritual life which he lived, and his personality. Within their covers are embalmed his thoughts after the failure of Fruitlands; the fortitude with which he faced the future after the dismal failures of his Philadelphia and Boston schools; the clear expression of the theories which marked him as an enlightened educator, but unfortunately a prophet whose time was not ripe for his message; the plans he had for regenerating humanity; and, of most value here, a record of his activities and schemes for educating men in the Oriental religions. In the earlier years of his life Alcott wrote at greater length. After the forties, his duties and responsibilities grew, the conversations increased in number, and the labor entailed in preparing them robbed him of time he might have used in elaborating his thought. One must read in between the lines of the entries for these years, if their complete significance is to be grasped.

What is known of the chronology of Alcott's Oriental interests is extremely slight. His earliest reading of consequence was done in the libraries of Philadelphia, while he was a school master there. It was during this period of his life, around the year 1831, that he seems from evidence outside of his *Journals*[4] to have first read about the Orientals. The unpublished journal manuscript pages themselves contain few tell-tale sentences to disclose the fact that Orientalism of any sort was getting a hold. Alcott became expansive when he wrote on the educational theories which later brought him both fame and opprobrium. On other matters he was most laconic. As late as January 25, 1849, after he had met Emerson and Thoreau and had become a lover of the Orientals, this sentence, with its unique spelling, "I read the Bagvat Geeta," was all that appeared to indicate how a Sunday had been spent. Emerson and Thoreau would not have failed to expand that simple sentence into an interesting passage of self-revelation. But not Alcott. He had less ink. He was not a born scribbler.

There can be little doubt that Alcott's active Oriental interests commenced when he, like Thoreau before him, first met Emerson. There was nothing in the man to make him immune. Had there been any reason for resistance, it would nevertheless have been difficult to remain aloof from such enthusiasm as had taken hold of Emerson and Thoreau; and rather ungracious, in view of the kindness they showed him during luckless days. There was a brotherly bond between the three men. Belonging to the confraternity of mystics, mutually sharing each other's sentiments of what was wrong with their world ecclesiastically, politically and socially, they lived as neighbors for many years. During this time Alcott reflected the influence of his friends. But instead of immersing himself in nature, as did Thoreau, or brooding on and writing about the Over-Soul, as did Emerson, he made his chief interest the universal scriptures of men.

III

One of the most interesting pages of all in Alcott's *Journals* was drawn up at a time when he was diagraming his tablets, a name which he frequently applied to the pages of his diary, and subsequently gave to one of his published books.[5] There is the following which appeared under the date of August, 1849:

Tablet   Tuesday 21.

MANKIND LIBRARY

The Sacred Scriptures, with Mythological and Biographical elucidation, first collected and edited: being the Lives, works and times of

Moses	Plato
Confucius	Christ
Zoroaster	Mahomet
Pythagoras	Behmen
Socrates	Swedenborg

Mythology

I. Hebrew and Egyptian	III. Greek and Roman
II. Oriental and Indian	IV. Christian and Cosmic

There can be little doubt as to what it was—the title page of a volume, or series, to be published under the caption of *Mankind Library*. And Alcott was to be the author and editor! Here was one of the man's great plans.[6] No dishonor falls upon him for having failed in the realization. It was a task which no man has ever accomplished, almost commensurate with the editing of *The Sacred Books of the East*, which required the cooperation of the world's best Oriental scholars and thirty-one years of assiduous labor to complete.[7] It is unnecessary to discuss at further length the significance of this dream in Alcott's life work. Nothing could demonstrate more clearly how anxious he was to propagate the Newness. The stark facts are themselves the most eloquent exposition of their own significance.

IV

But the dream persisted and Alcott read constantly in the Oriental scriptures. He had been doing this for several years. On Tuesday, June 17, 1849, the following was entered upon the pages of the diary: "I read the 'Bhagavad Gita'; also write to Louisa and Abby who are passing some weeks at Samuel May's."[8] Reading over other entries we find that two months later he was doing the same thing, re-reading a book which he could have perused at one sitting. On Wednesday, June 27, he writes: "I dine and pass the afternoon with the Adams⁹ and read 'Bhagavad Gita' to a large audience in the evening, with lively discussions etc." One is gratified that Alcott's neighbors were capable of entering into "lively discussions, etc." with him on the subject of Hindu mysticism. It may be taken as evidence that the leaven was at work in Concord.

During the month of March, 1849, even before he had drawn upon the proposed title-page for the *Mankind Library,* he planned for a series of public conversations on the teachings of the Oriental sages. One of the most interesting pages of Alcott's diary is that on which he had prepared an advance notice of the meetings, leaving the place and date blank, but probably otherwise ready to turn over to the printer. This notice was confided to the diary on Saturday, March 17:

Sunday Readings and Conversations

Mr. A. Bronson Alcott will give the first of several Readings from the Sacred Books of Mankind, with interpretations and original teachings interspersed at——Street, on Sunday morning, next, March——, commencing at 10 o'clock.

All persons disposed to give hospitable entertainment to the words of illuminated Mind of all times, are respectfully invited to attend the Readings, and express their sentiments on the text, interpretations and teachings. Admission free.

The clergymen of Concord and Boston may have frowned on such competition on the Sabbath day, and their parishioners remained loyal to the established services. Alcott's hope that he could get a following was too venturous, and two years passed before anything came of the plan.

But meanwhile he was reading and collecting material for the course. He consulted James Freeman Clarke, the author of the *Ten Great Religions,* and on March 24 recorded as follows the suggestions he had received:

Oriental Readings. List of Authors to be sought at the Athenaeum. (Given me by J. F. Clarke).

Collier's Four Books of Confucius,
History of China, (by the Jesuit)
The Kings of Confucius,
The Vedas,
The Saama Vedas,
Vishnu Parana,
Saadi,
Firdusi,
The Zendavesta,
The Koran.

This was in 1849, as already intimated. Whether he made an immediate attempt to follow Clarke's suggestions is not indicated in his diary. But that he probably continued to search widely and persistently for books is suggested by the entry of February 11, 1851:

I brought from the Athenaeum, this afternoon, for my Readings, "Marshman's Confucius," containing the Life of Confucius and translation of the "Lun Gnee" or Dialogues, being the third of the Four Classical Books of the Chinese. Also from Burnham's "The Phoenix a collection of Ancient Fragments," "The Morals of Confucius," "The Oracles of Zoroaster" etc. Emerson sent me, a day or two since, the "Hermes Trismegistus," the only copy, I suppose, there is to be had in the country, and which I brought out from England.¹⁰ "Saadi's Gulistan," I can obtain from the Cambridge Library; and of the other Books, from which I propose to give Selections, Socrates, Plato, Behmen, I possess copies; also Dante, by Dr. Carlyle, Buckley's Aeschylus; and Wellington's Swedenborg. Of Goethe I must purchase a copy. Bohn has just published an edition of Faust, Iphigeneia, Torquato Tasso and Egmont.

The fact that Alcott read critically cannot be proved by more substantial evidence than the following passage which was written two days later: "Cory's translations are so superior to Stanley's or Thomas Taylor's of the Oracles of Zoroaster, that I shall transcribe some of them to these pages from my journal of 1849."¹¹ The transcription followed, five pages of them. They show what Alcott thought the best, and give some conception of what he planned to read to his audiences. "Look not on Nature for her name is Fatal," was one; "Who knows himself knows all things in himself," was another; and still a third was this unique statement of a favorite idealistic doctrine: "Evil, according to the oracle, is more frail than non-entity." The following, which was among the transcribed texts, seems but another way of stating Emerson's favorite doctrine of Compensation: "Our voluntary sorrows germinate in us as the growth of the particular life we lead." More in Alcott's personal manner were these sentences: "The Furies are the constrainers of men," and "There is a certain Intelligible which it becomes you to understand with the flower of the mind."¹²

Alcott continues under the same date:

"The History of Ancient Philosophy" (Ritter's) is not to be had from our Athenaeum; nor have I been able to find there anything of Saadi's. Harvard College Library, and Longfellow,¹³ supplied me with the works of these Orientalists, but I have found less in Ritter for my purposes, than either Stanley or Cudworth had for me.

With all this reading and assiduous preparation for the proposed course, Alcott never lacked for time to share his findings with his friends. Since what is presented here has never been published before, I continue in his own words. It is still February, 1851.

Saturday 15.

Afternoon, came Goodwin¹⁴ to see me, and discussed profoundly on the soul of Music. Mr. G. is recently from Cincinnati; and now organist at St. Paul's in this city. He is familiar with the highest, or Transcendental Music, and himself a composer and critic. Like all minds of this fine cast, he is a receiver of Emerson, and a reader of the biblical literatures of the world. I shall send him tickets to the Select Readings and Conversations on the Poets and Philosophers.

Eight days later H. G. O. Blake, Thoreau's intimate friend and literary executor, called, and we find the following record: "Blake came, and I read some passages from my Diary, the sketch of Thoreau, whom he esteems highly; and the passages from Zoroaster. A man of delicate tastes and much sharpness of intellect is this Mr. Blake; a reader of choice things; and a come-outer in spirit."

At last satisfactory arrangements were made and the day for the first of the conversations arrived. On Monday, February 24, 1851, Alcott pasted one of the admission cards into the *Journal.* The order of the subjects is interesting evidence of the use he planned to make of some of his reading which we have followed.

ADMIT
TO
MR. ALCOTT'S CONVERSATIONS
ON THE
POETS AND PHILOSOPHERS

———

I. Hermes Trismegistus	V. Aeschylus
II. Zoroaster	VI. Pythagoras
III. Confucius	VII. Socrates
IV. Saadi	VIII. Plato

IX. JESUS CHRIST

X. Dante	XIII. Milton
XI. Behmen	XIV. Swedenborg
XII. Shakespeare	XV. Goethe

———

The readings will be held on Monday Evenings, No. 7, Montgomery Place, and will commence Feb. 24, at 7½ o'clock. *Boston, February,* 1851.

Late on the same evening, after the first meeting had passed into history, he wrote:

> Evening. Few persons to hear and discuss Hermes, in consequence of the rain. But we had a very good time of it. Mrs. Dall, Miss Parsons, Norton, etc. having something to say about our Egyptian of whom I gave them a taste, with an introduction on the Oracles, Sacred and Profane; their subjects and law. Hermes is the least popular of the names on my card, and of him we know less than of any one of these persons. He is even more fabulous than Zoroaster or Confucius and as mythological as Pythagoras. I did not expect to make much of him but to find a text or two for conversation.[15]

So ended the first of the conversations on that rainy night. If they were continued, I found no evidence of the fact as I browsed through the *Journal.* A few more meetings might have been held, but Alcott did not comment on their success or failure.

But what was Alcott's purpose in holding these conversations? I do not know that scholars have ever told or known. Assuredly any funds that might have accrued from them were negligible. A self-appointed educator and propagator of the things of illuminated Mind, to use his own phrase, Alcott found in these readings and conversations a double outlet. Since he was not a man of the cloth, the occasions afforded him an opportunity to preach his own philosophy to adult audiences, and to gratify the one passion of his life which had never left him, the love of the game of playing school. But let Alcott confess his own purpose in offering the course of 1851. He is writing in his diary on Wednesday, February 12, 1851, a week and a half before the rainy night on which the Egyptian Hermes was used as a springboard:

> A few texts, very few, will serve, and more than serve, for the Readings. Of all Mind, Zoroaster whether he were one or several, a real or mythological Personage, is the more occult and astral, of my cycle, doubled, and opening into a third in Goethe—the void-mind, mythology and history alike twisted into the web of his Genius, and himself but the spokesman of the Fate that ruled him. Hermes Trismegistus is no less oracular in the text of his "Divine Pymander" and suggestive of the intellectuals. Behmen and Swedenborg follow, precede perhaps, in comprehensiveness and depth of insight into natural things, as Pythagoras includes the wisdom of Society and of Education; and Christ of Divinity. Plato was the Scholar and Occultist; Socrates, great master of Practical morals. Saadi is a Persian Come-outer; Dante and Milton are theological poets; as Aeschylus is a mythic bard, and Shakespeare the pure poet, of humanity. *With such vast and universal cyphers as these minds afford of existence, I shall not want suggestions of the depth and height of Being, nor occasion for declaring some private experiences as they rise.*

With this commitment on the position in human history of the men with whom he planned to deal, and the confession of what he hoped to do, we may conclude this phase of Alcott's labors as a propagandist in behalf of the Orientals and turn to another, a work in which the boulders he started rolling eventually became an avalanche.

V

The marriage of Fannie Maria Adelaide Channing, the daughter of William Henry Channing, to the famous author of *The Light of Asia,* brought the American Transcendentalists into close contact with one of the most eminent popularizers of Buddhism in the Old World.[16] In a very short time interesting results appeared. Alcott's *Journal* is the evidence. The story is best presented with passages culled from its pages. On August 19, 1879, he wrote:

I have a letter from my esteemed friend Rev. William Henry Channing of London, with a book. He dates from 3 Campdon House Road, Huntington, August 4, and presents the book to

> *A. Bronson Alcott,*
> *Wm. T. Harris,*
> *F. B. Sanborn, and*
> *Their confreres in Concord Summer School of*
> *Philosophy and Literature*

The book is entitled:

> *The Light of Asia, or The Great Renunciation, Being the Life and Teachings of Gautama, Prince of India and Founder of Buddhism.* By Edwin Arnold, London, 1879.

The purpose of Channing's writing to Alcott is disclosed when the latter continues:

> Channing gives a brief account of the Author, and desired to have the book presented to the school, before its close. It came a day too late. But Harris and Sanborn may review it after perusal. It is written in flowing blank verse, and has great literary merit at best. I shall find time now to give it a closer reading.
>
> Mr. Arnold is, I understand a brother of Matthew, and son of Dr. Arnold of Rugby School. He married a daughter of Mr. Channing.

Alcott must have obtained the concluding note on Edwin's relationship to Matthew Arnold from his own imagination, certainly not from Channing. There is no evidence of any close relationship between the men. Alcott was probably hazarding a guess because of the correspondence in the names.[17] The conclusion of Channing's letter he quotes as follows:

> My friend, Edwin Arnold, gave me this volume amongst others to dispose of: and the best use of the gift, as fulfilling the poet's wish seemed to me to be,— the putting it at the disposal of your company. Will our friend, Mr. Harris, introduce it with such notice as he deems most befitting to the readers of his Journal?[18] Will Mr. Sanborn and other friends do likewise in their own appropriate way. Poem and Poet should be widely known, and be heartily welcomed by the nation that providentially serves as mediator between Europe and Asia, to unite the East and West, the Ancient and the Modern Ages, in unity.
>
> And now with hearty friendly regards for yourself, my dear "Ever Young Artist" and with all the company of generous and great compeers around you, believe me,
>
> Yours ever respectfully and hopefully,
> WILLIAM HENRY CHANNING.

Channing does not state the fact, but it seems likely that he wrote to Alcott for two reasons. First, he was the dean of the Concord Summer School of Philosophy and Literature, and secondly, Channing probably knew that it would have been difficult to find a more active agita-

tor in all America than Alcott. The suggestion that Sanborn and Harris write notices of the book and that "other friends do likewise in their own appropriate way" was ingenious. Alcott took the hint and went to work. Six days later he notes in his diary that "Sanborn gives . . . notice of Edwin Arnold's 'Light of Asia' in yesterday's *Republican,* with some account of the author taken from Channing's letter to me."[19]

The book arrived in Concord on August 19. The note regarding Sanborn's review which has just been quoted was dated August 25. Alcott was only beginning his work. He made trips forthwith to Boston and arranged for the immediate publication of the American edition. Early in September his *Journal* bears the following entry:

> Friday 5. To Boston and find Arnold's *Light of Asia* is already in Press and to be published forthwith. An appendix is to be added of Channing's account of the author, Ripley's and Sanborn's notices, and that of the London Athanaeum. Thus the book will come before our American public chiefly on its own merits. (Holmes also writes a review.)

The parenthetical comment about Holmes does not indicate whether it was at the direct solicitation of Alcott or Channing that the review was written. It might have been either, but most probably Alcott, since he was on the immediate field and Channing was in Europe. What Holmes wrote of Edwin Arnold's book will be discussed presently.

A passage under the date of September 27 from the *Journal* shows that it was from Alcott's personal copy of *The Light of Asia,* the very copy received from Channing, that the Boston printers set type for the American edition. Alcott had moved quickly. Almost immediately he negotiated for the printing, and since he probably possessed one of the very first copies to reach America, and quick action was desirable in presenting to the public so valuable a work as Edwin Arnold's, he gladly relinquished the treasure. But he was not the loser, for he writes:

> Mr. Niles[20] gives me the English copy of Arnold's *Light of Asia* in exchange for the copy sent me by Mr. Channing which the printers defaced in printing the American edition, now nearly ready for publication. Dr. Holmes' characteristic review, George Ripley's, and Channing's letter to me, are published as a supplement.
>
> The book will be read with surprise by most, and raise curious questions in the minds of Christians generally.

Alcott had done his work effectively. The nature of the comment he elicited in behalf of the book from his friends will be seen when we take note of the American reviews. The book was safely in press. The business details had all been satisfactorily attended to. Alcott gave himself to enjoyment of the volume, carrying it with him when he called on all his friends. On October 14 he is "At Emerson's. I take my copy of Arnold's *Light of Asia* for his perusal." And he continues the work of sending the good news afield:

> Sunday 19th. Also wrote to Mills[21] of Syracuse sending him Sanborn's notice of "Arnold's Light of Asia." Charles Mills has been almost the only American scholar who has cultivated Oriental studies, and written books on Buddhist literature. This poem of Arnold's must interest him, perhaps add to his knowledge of that old learning.

Alcott's excitement and feverish activity gradually subsided. When in January, 1880, *The Light of Asia* was published in Boston, he did not even comment upon the fact in his ***Journal,*** nor have I found record of his ever having corresponded with Edwin Arnold. The last entry which deals in any way with the book appears in connection with a letter from Channing:

> Tuesday 20. My esteemed friend Wm. Henry Channing writes from London dating January 1st. He informs me of his intention of visiting America next April . . . He expects to pass the summer with us, and will doubtless attend our School at the Orchard House. We shall expect good words from him then and there.[22] He forwards thanks for our interest in the reprinting of "Light of Asia."

And thus Alcott's activity in behalf of the book seems to have ended. Nothing could show better the results of the work which he started and the interest of the American public in Orientalism than the words of Edwin Arnold's biographer in the *Dictionary of National Biography:* "The poem aroused the animosity of many pulpits, but there were *sixty editions in England and eighty in America,* and translations were numerous."[23]

VI

The phenomenal success of Edwin Arnold's poem in America was of course due to its own intrinsic merit and appeal. But there can be no doubt that it was also partly due to the warm reception the book received even from the few New England writers whom Alcott mentioned as contributing to an appendix in the American edition.[24] Alcott's account seems to have indicated what was contemplated rather than what actually appeared in the appendix. Nevertheless Ripley, Channing, Sanborn and Holmes did write enthusiastic accounts. It is not outside of the interests of this study to take brief note of the verdict of Alcott's friends.

Ripley's *New York Tribune* review and the excerpt from Channing's letter to Alcott were the only notices printed in the supplement to the 1880 Boston edition of *The Light of Asia* which I have examined. The review from the pen of Oliver Wendell Holmes was the feature article in *The International Review* for October, 1879, and never, to my knowledge, appeared as a supplement in any of the books.[25] The probable reason, and a good one, was the length at which Holmes wrote. As printed in *The International Review,* the article filled twenty-six full pages. It was based on the 1879 edition of the book which appeared in London. One may well imagine the anticipation with which the American audience awaited the volume, after a man of Holmes's literary repute had prepared the way by such pronouncement as:

> For it is a work of great beauty. It tells a story of intense interest, which never flags for a moment; its descriptions are drawn by the hand of a master with the eye of a poet and the familiarity of an expert with the objects described; its tone is so lofty that there is nothing with which to compare it but the New Testament; it is full of variety, now picturesque, now pathetic; now rising into the noblest realms of thought and aspirations; it finds language penetrating, fluent, elevated, impassioned, musical always, to clothe its varied thoughts and sentiments.

The concluding sentence of Holmes's essay was:

> To lay down this poem and take up a book of popular rhymes is like stepping from the carpet of a Persian palace upon the small tradesman's Kidderminster, or exchanging the shawl of an Indian empress for the printed calico which graces the matinees of the basement.

Writing with greater detail than Ripley, Holmes practically discusses at length each of the eight books which comprised Arnold's poem. The story is told and many of the descriptive scenes repeated. The quotations which were chosen to bait American poetasters were fortunate. We may choose one to serve a double purpose as a sample of Holmes's tastes in the poem and an instance of the early experience of the young Buddha which led to his own renunciation:

> All things spoke peace and plenty, and the Prince
> Saw and rejoiced. But, looking deep, he saw
> The thorns which grow upon this stem of life;
> How the swart peasant sweated for his wage,
> Toiling for leave to live; and how he urged
> The great-eyed oxen through the flaming hours,
> Goading their velvet flanks; then marked he, too,
> How lizzard fed on ant, and snake on him,
> And kite on both; and how fish-hawk robbed
> The fish tiger of that which he had seized;
> The shrike chasing the bulbul, which did chase
> The jewelled butterflies; till everywhere
> Each slew a slayer and in turn was slain,—
> Life living upon death. So the fair show
> Veiled one vast, savage, grim conspiracy
> Of mutual murder, from the worm to man,
> Who himself kills his fellow . . .
> The Prince Siddartha sighed. "Is this," he said,
> "That happy earth they brought me forth to see?"

But the most interesting thing in Holmes's entire review is the manner in which he prepared his readers, hostile most probably to Buddhism, for what was to follow. One can read in the sentences a deliberate and tactful attempt to break down aversion:

> If one were told that many centuries ago a celestial ray shone into the body of a sleeping woman, as it seemed to her in her dream; that thereupon the advent of a wondrous child was predicted by the soothsayers; that angels appeared at this child's birth; that merchants came from afar, bearing gifts to him; that an ancient saint recognized the babe as divine and fell at his feet and worshipped him; that in his eighth year the child confounded his teachers with the amount of his knowledge, still showing them due reverence; that he grew up full of compassionate tenderness to all that lived and suffered; that to help his fellow-creatures he sacrificed every worldly prospect and enjoyment; that he went through the ordeal of a terrible temptation, in which all the powers of evil were let loose upon him, and came out a conqueror over them all; that he preached holiness and practised charity; that he gathered disciples and sent out apostles, who spread his doctrine over many lands and peoples; that this "Helper of the Worlds" could claim a more than earthly lineage and a life that dated from long before Abraham was,—of whom would he think this wonderful tale was told? Would he not say at once that this must be another version of the story of One who came upon our earth in a Syrian village, during the reign of Augustus Caesar, and died by violence during the reign of Tiberius? What would he say if he were told that the narrative was between five and six centuries older than that of the Founder of Christianity? Such is the story of this Poem. Such is the date assigned to the personage of whom it is told. The religion he taught is reckoned by many authorities as the most widely prevalent of all beliefs.

George Ripley's review in the *New York Tribune* was interpretive rather than critical, quoting long passages from the original attempts to retell the story of the Buddha, his princely birth, the palace in which the father confined him in order to shield him from knowledge of the world's evil and pain. With the retelling of the story, Ripley paraphrased Arnold's introduction, which deals with the worldwide scope of the Buddhist faith and its influence as the spiritual stay of "not less than four hundred and seventy millions of our race." A sense of Ripley's verdict on the poem may be gathered from the following passage:

> From the dim and shadowy legends of the princely founder of the great religion of the East, scanty and uncertain as they prove to be under the hand of critical research, Mr. Arnold has constructed a poem, which for affluence of imagination, splendor of diction, and virile descriptive power, will not be easily matched among the most remarkable productions in the literature of the day.

The conclusion of Ripley's review was even more laudatory. Readers of the *New York Tribune* could not have failed to be affected by such praise as, "Mr. Arnold's imaginative gifts are combined with a singularly acute historical sense, and a rare perception of the music of rhythmical harmonies and the curious significance of a felicitous phrase. . . . [The poem] is illustrated with all the charms of a fascinating narrative and the enchantments of melodious verse." Such sentences undoubtedly were instrumental in promoting the sale of the book.

But there probably were more reasons for the success of *The Light of Asia* than reviews such as those written by Sanborn, Holmes, and Ripley. In America few English authors have fared better than Edwin Arnold. William Henry Channing would have been interested in the book under all ordinary circumstances. As Arnold's father-in-law he had personal reasons for using all the influence at his command. There is scant reason for believing that his activity in behalf of the book ceased after he had secured Alcott's services in seeing the American edition through the press. Nor was his judgment at fault when he asked Alcott to negotiate with influential men for reviews. Channing knew that Alcott would do his work well, and he did. Also, the poem itself must have counted for a great deal. America was ready to receive it. The reason is best stated in a sentence from the review which W. C. Brownell wrote for *The Nation*: "It [*The Light of Asia*] not only has charm for all students and men of letters, and it is not only the gospel of 'countless millions', as Mr. Arnold says, but to certain Occidental transcendentalists has long offered a comfort and assuagement."[26]

To the end of his life Alcott continued to work as educator and promulgator of mystic lore, but gradually his labor became less personal and centered around his administrative duties as dean of the Concord Summer School of Philosophy. He was not regarded as a great writer by his contemporaries. But they knew him to be a great talker. Lowell, with marked insight, described him in the *Fable for Critics*:

> And indeed, I believe, no man ever talked better,—
> Each sentence hangs perfectly poised to a letter;
> He seems piling words, but there's royal dust hid
> In the heart of each sky-piercing pyramid.
> While he talks he is great, but goes out like a taper,
> If you shut him up closely with pen, ink, and paper;
> Yet his fingers itch for 'em from morning till night,
> And he thinks he does wrong if he don't always write;
> In this, as in all things, a lamb among men,
> He goes to sure death when he goes to his pen.

Posterity will find no reason to change this estimate. It will also add the fact that Alcott's name can never be separated from Fruitlands and the Temple School, important attempts in the social history of America to promote the good life. While it is unfair to think of these ventures as failures, Alcott nevertheless appears as something of a Don Quixote in them, an idealist in conflict with a crass world, and "lamb among men." It is pleasant to think of him as having backed a luckier horse when he took the rôle of propagandist for the new Orientalism. American interest in the Orientals, if it was to take quick hold, needed a man who would work as a house to house colporteur, with his personal enthusiasm and brilliant talk in drawing-rooms doing what the pen of Emerson and Thoreau could not do in the study and hermitage. Alcott was that man. His was a humbler, but essential and successful part.

Notes

1. A textual examination of Alcott's published works reveals that quotations from the *Bhagavadgita* which deal with the subject of food predominate. An example is the following from *Tablets,* (p. 16): "'All living things,' said the Bhagavad Gita, 'are generated from the bread they eat; bread is generated from rain, rain from divine worship, and divine worship from good works.'" The following is Alcott's commentary in the same context: "A creed dealing thus super-sensibly with the elements must have fertilizing properties, and bring the gardener to his task little tinctured by noxious notions of any kind. If he fall short of being the reverent naturalist, the devout divine, surrounded thus by shapes of skill, types of beauty, tokens of design, every hue in the chromatic, every device in the symbolic gamut, I see not what shall make him these. . . ." Another similar passage, with quotation from the *Bhagavadgita,* will be found in *Table-Talk* ([Boston: Roberts Brothers, 1877;] p. 72). The most readable use of Oriental material in Alcott's books, in this connection probably taken from a Sufi poet, is to be found in *Sonnets and Canzonets* ([Boston: Roberts Brothers, 1882;] p. 114): "One knocked at the Beloved's door, and a Voice asked from within, Who is there? And he answered, It is I. Then the Voice said, This house will not hold me and thee, and the door was not opened. Then went the lover into the desert, and fasted and prayed in solitude. And after a year he returned, and knocked again at the door. And again the Voice asked, Who is there? and he said, It is Thyself. And the door was opened to him." The closest resemblance to a Confucian influence to be found in Alcott's work is the following from *Table-Talk,* (p. 60): "Reverence for superiors is the source of filial piety and obedience. We are told that the times of remote antiquity bore so great a reverence for parents as to venture to call them gods." Such a passage may equally be ascribed to Greek influence, however. In *Concord Days* [(Boston: Roberts Brothers, 1872)], p. 117, Alcott wrote: "'He that in the morning hath heard the voice of virtue,' says Confucius, 'may die at night.' And it were virtuous to rise early during our June mornings to breakfast on strawberries with the robins. . . ." The original Confucian passage source read: "If in the morning I hear of the right way, and in the evening die, I can be happy." (*Analects,* IV. 8.) Emerson had used the quotation in his *Works* [(*Complete Works of Ralph Waldo Emerson,* Boston: Houghton Mifflin, 1883)], X, 117. The passage also appeared in the *Dial,* III, 493. Alcott, in what is probably his characteristic manner in quoting, garbled it.

2. Honoré Willsie Morrow in *The Father of Little Women,* Boston, Little Brown, 1927, has dealt mostly with Alcott's educational theories and their exemplification in the Philadelphia and Boston experiments.

3. I am indebted to Mrs. F. Alcott Pratt of Concord for the information presented here. The Alcott *Journals* are being held for publication in entirety at some future time. They are therefore not available for reference. Mrs. Pratt, however, graciously consented to my using a limited number of excerpts dealing with Alcott's Oriental interests, and to include the following unpublished paragraph, dated July 3, 1859: "Thoreau comes and stays an hour or two. Students of nature alike: our methods differ. He is an observer of Nature pure, and I discern her as exalted and mingled in Man. Her brute aspects and qualities interest him, and these he discriminates with a sagacity unsurpassed. He is less thinker than observer: a naturalist in tendency but of a mystic habit, and a genius for detecting the essence in the form, and giving forth the soul of things seen. He knows more of Nature's secrets than any man I have known, and of Man as related to Nature. He thinks and sees for himself in ways eminently original and is formidably individual and persistent."

4. See page 10.

5. *Tablets* appeared in Boston, 1868.

6. See Sanborn and Harris [*A. Bronson Alcott, His Life and Philosophy* (Boston, 1893)], *op. cit.,* I, 332.

7. Max Müller edited *The Sacred Books of the East,* which appeared 1879-1910. For statistics see Mudge, *Guide to Reference Books,* fifth edition, 1929, p. 87.

8. Abby and Louisa were Alcott's daughters. Mrs. Alcott's maiden name was May.

9. I am informed by Mrs. F. Alcott Pratt of Concord that the reference was to Alvin Adams, the founder of the Adams Express Company.

10. With Charles Lane for the Fruitlands Library.

11. Cory's translation will be found in *The Phenix* [New York, Gowan, 1835]. See Appendix for the others.

12. These quotations were taken from *The Phenix,* New York, Gowan, 1835. The following completes the list which Alcott copied into his diary as texts for conversational meetings:

> Ether "in which the things without figure are figured."
>
> "Defile not the Spirit nor deepen a superficies."
>
> "Enlarge not thy destiny."
>
> "Oh how the world has inflexible intellectual rulers."
>
> "All fountains and principles whirl round, And always remain in ceaseless revolution."
>
> "Never change barbarous names, For there are names in every nation given by God, Having unspeakable efficacy in the mysteries."
>
> "Nature persuades us that there are pure demons, Even the blossoms of evil matter are useful and good."
>
> "From the cavities Of the earth leap forth terrestrial dogs, Showing no true sign to mortal men."
>
> "Let the immortal depth of your soul lead you, But earnestly extend your eyes upward."
>
> "It is not proper to understand that Intelligible with vehemence, But with the extended flame of an extended mind measuring all things Except the Intelligible. But it is ignoble to understand this; For if you incline your mind you will understand it Not correctly, but it becomes you to bring with you a pure and inquiring eye, To extend the void mind of your Soul to the Intelligible, That you may learn the Intelligible *Because it subsists beyond mind.*"
>
> "You will not understand it, as when understanding some particular thing."
>
> "Things divine are not attainable by mortals who understand body, But only as many as are lightly armed arrive at the Summit."
>
> "Rhea, the fountain and river of the blessed Intellectuals, Having first received the power of all things in her ineffable bosom, Pours forth perpetual generation upon every thing."
>
> "But the paternal mind receives not her will Until she has gone out of oblivion and pronounces the word Assuming the memory of the pure fraternal Symbol."
>
> "The Soul of man will in a manner clasp God to herself, Having nothing mortal she is wholly For the glories in the harmony under which the mortal body exists."
>
> "For thy vessel the beasts of the earth shall inherit."
>
> "The Paternal Mind has sowed Symbols in souls."

13. In the appendix of this book will be found a list of the Oriental volumes in Henry Wadsworth Longfellow's library which Alcott might have used. It is not impossible that Emerson also drew from this source.

14. A note in Alcott's diary adds the information that William Goodwin was a Greek scholar of note and the husband of Ellen Channing. He was probably William Watson Goodwin, listed in *Appleton's Cyclopedia of American Biography* as born in Concord, Massachusetts, May 9, 1831. He graduated from Harvard in 1851, studied at Bonn, Berlin and Göttingen, and became Eliot Professor of Greek literature at Harvard in 1856. He was the first director of the American school of classical studies at Athens.

15. The identity of the persons mentioned by Alcott is probably as follows: Mrs. C. H. Dall, a later Transcendentalist and a blue-stocking. She is most interesting because of her marriage to William Healey Dall, the first foreign missionary of the Unitarian Church to India. Mr. Dall established himself in Calcutta in 1855, returning to visit his family once every five years. Emerson wrote in his *Journals*, X, 163: "In India, a Brahmin may be very poor, and perform daily menial tasks for the English, as porters or servants, but the natives still kneel to him, and show him the highest respect.—Mr. Dall testified this fact to me on his return from India." For the identity of Miss Parsons, see the preface, *Letters from Brook Farm* 1844-47, edited by Amy L. Reed, Vassar College, 1928. In this book appears a brief sketch of Anna Q. T. Parsons, who was a frequent visitor to Brook Farm, but never a member. Charles Eliot Norton needs no identification.

16. The date of the marriage is not in the account of Arnold's life given in the *Dictionary of National Biography,* Second Supplement [(New York: Macmillan Company, 1912)]. The death of Arnold's first wife occurred in the year 1864 and that of Mrs. Fannie Channing Arnold in 1889. Arnold's third wife was a Japanese, Tama Kuro Kawa, of Sendai.

17. Edwin Arnold (1832-1904) was the second son of Robert Coles Arnold of Whartons, Framfield, En-

gland. He graduated B.A. from University College, Oxford, in 1854, and M.A. in 1856. For a detailed account of his life see *Dictionary of National Biography,* Second Supplement.

18. I found no review of the book in *The Journal of Speculative Philosophy.* It is singular that the book was not even listed under the head of "books received."

19. Sanborn's notice of the book, which appeared in the *Springfield Republican* of August 24, 1879, consisted principally of excerpts from the introduction and Channing's letter, the latter being biographical. Only in the last paragraph did Sanborn write anything of a contribution: "Unable to be present with his friends at the Orchard House, Mr. Channing sent Mr. Arnold's book to Mr. Alcott, Prof. Harris and Mr. Sanborn: but it arrived too late to be even a text for one of the conversations. It will, perhaps, be reprinted in Boston and thus become better known to the American public than it well could be in the London edition. Its poetic merits are considerable, but it has a higher value as an exposition in a sympathetic spirit of the true ideal that inspires the great philanthropic religion of Asia,—the harbinger, and, for half-civilized men the complement, of Christianity."

20. Little, Brown and Company, the successors to Roberts Brothers, have written me that they are unable to supply data regarding Alcott's dealings with the publishers. They stated that Mr. Niles was the publishing manager for Roberts Brothers and came in direct contact with the authors and editors.

21. I quote from a letter by a member of the Mills family, graciously written in response to my request for information of Charles Mills's friendship with Alcott: "Charles de Berard Mills was a student of Oriental literatures and philosophies. He was also a friend both to Emerson and to Thoreau. He exchanged visits and letters with them and the bond of mutual interests and sympathies was strong. . . . As a boy he knew when Alcott was expected for a visit as his father laid in a barrel of special apples and cheese for the vegetarian philosopher. . . . Mr. Mills secured a lecture for Emerson in Syracuse. . . . Of Mr. Mills's books I can give the title of three, *The Indian Saint or Buddha and Buddhism; Pebbles, Pearls and Gems of the Orient,* and *The Tree of Mythology.*"

22. Channing gave four lectures in Concord in 1880. They were listed under the head of "Oriental and Mystical Philosophy." Specific titles were 1. "Historical Mysticism." 2. "Man's Fourfold Being." 3. "True Buddhism." 4. "Modern Pessimism." *The Journal of Speculative Philosophy,* XIV, 252-53, presents a prospectus of the lectures.

23. *Dictionary of National Biography,* Second Supplement. The italics are added.

24. See page 251.

25. O. W. Holmes, "The Light of Asia," *International Review,* VII (Oct. 1879), 345-71.

26. W. C. Brownell, "Recent Poetry," *Nation,* DCCXLIX (Nov. 6, 1879), 314.

Odell Shepard (essay date 1937)

SOURCE: Shepard, Odell. "City Schoolmaster." In *Pedlar's Progress: The Life of Bronson Alcott.* 1937. Reprint, pp. 112-218. Boston: Little, Brown and Company, 1938.

[*In the following excerpt, Shepard describes the circumstances surrounding the composition and publication of* Conversations with Children on the Gospels.]

Alcott liked best to talk about Jesus with children, thinking that they were best able to understand that essentially childlike mind. Such talks had, for him, a triple value: they were instructive to the children, they helped him to understand the nature of childhood, and they taught him about Jesus. He expected to learn from them more than he taught, and the probability is that he did so.

In this spirit of the student Alcott began, in the autumn of 1835, a series of Conversations on the Gospels with the children of his own school. It was one of the most characteristic things he ever did. His whole personality and character went into it, as one piece. The conception and the execution show the boldest reach of his mind. Some contemporaries thought that God was with him and others that the Devil was in him, but all agreed that he was like a man possessed. And so it was appropriate enough that, in its effects upon his public standing and professional career, this series of Conversations on the holiest theme should have been his most disastrous failure. Having soared highest, he fell farthest. The fall broke his life in two, and brought his work as a teacher of children to a close.

There were thirty-seven children in the Temple School while these Conversations continued, nine of whom were between ten and twelve years of age, eighteen between seven and ten, and the rest six years old or less. One of the most profound, little Josiah Quincy, who certainly spoke very like Wordsworth's "mighty philosopher," "seer blest," and "eye among the blind," was six. The children came from homes of various sectarian affiliations: Universalist, Unitarian, Baptist, Episcopalian, Methodist, Swedenborgian, and Free Enquirer. There were twenty-nine boys and eight girls—just enough to ensure that "purity" which the teacher considered so important, but enough also, alas, to make it seem particularly horrible that the teacher himself should have allowed and even promoted the discussion of themes about which "female children," at any rate, should never speak, never hear, and never even think.

These Conversations were in fact what their name implied. They were not lectures or monologues, for Alcott talked far less than the children did, and most of his contributions were questions. "I ask and ask till I get something fit and worthy," he said one day. "I am not thinking, generally, of any particular answer. Sometimes I ask because I do not think myself, and hope that you will find some word that will embody the spirit of the Conversation. Sometimes—always, indeed—I seek to assist you by my questions in finding the answer, by the free exercise of your own minds. All truth is within. My business is to lead you to find it in your own Souls."

In a language which had at last become admirably simple, using images drawn from the common fund of childhood's experience, Alcott followed along the thin clue of his pupils' thoughts, with extraordinary skill and unmistakable reverence, as far as that thread could lead him. There he stopped. For he was not trying to tell his children anything. Rather, he was hoping to be told. The whole manner of the man and all his words—set down by Miss Peabody or by her sister Sophia, soon to be Mrs. Nathaniel Hawthorne, or by Miss Margaret Fuller—suggested that as he moved onward into the penetralia of a child's mind he felt that he was approaching a shrine. And yet he had also a scientific purpose in mind. It was a psychological investigation that he had on hand, as it had been a few years before when he had gazed interrogatively down upon Anna and Louisa in their cradles. They had been less articulate philosophers than these of the Temple School, and so had obliged him to contribute more than his share to the Conversation. He was still contributing to it in that manuscript, now called *Psyche,* which Mr. Emerson was reading with mingled joy and pain. But the question in his mind, or rather the hypothesis, had not changed.

"You all appear to think," he said once, "that you have something within you godlike, spiritual, like Jesus, though not so much. And what is this?"

"Spirit, Conscience," piped a dozen young voices in chorus. And one boy added, "Conscience is God within us."

One smiles, at first, to observe how Alcottian were the answers that Alcott drew from his young friends. "If you call Jesus God, and God God," said a six-year-old boy, "then I think there would be two Gods, and that is the same as worshipping statues." When the teacher asked whether there were any idolaters in Boston, the prompt answer was "Yes; a great many of them. They worship money." When Alcott asked what person in history had "kept his babyhood," several children replied that Jesus had done so, and one lad volunteered the startling remark that "God is babyhood." At this answer, however, Alcott showed some hesitation. One can almost see him think. "I believe," said he, "that there is truth in that; and yet it is a language so liable to be misunderstood that it had better not be used."

If Alcott's cautious and skillful questioning did elicit, too frequently, no more than a reflection and an echo of himself, it was certainly against his will. Again and again he told the children that he did not wish to control their minds or even suggest their answers. More than once he declined to state his own opinion on a question which had led to disagreement among them. One of his pupils remarked to him, with the polite freedom which he always cultivated in the classroom: "I don't think it has been much of an argument on your side, for your side was only asking questions." And Alcott replied: "No; it is my object to make you argue, make you reason, by giving the terms. I have not sought in these Conversations to present my own views of truth, but to call forth yours; and by so doing to make you conscious of your own powers of finding it. It is the part of a wise instructor to tempt forth from the minds of his pupils the facts of their inmost consciousness, and make them apprehend the gifts and faculties of their own being. Education, when rightly understood, will be found to lie in the art of asking apt and fit questions, and in thus leading the mind by its own light to the perception of truth"—in which remark there was perhaps more of Socrates than of Jesus. Once more in his *Journal* for 1836 Alcott says that good instruction is always the lending of one's own mind to another, so that he may see how truth looks through that prismatic glass.

Like every other good teacher, Alcott was aware that it was his business to set his pupils free—and free, perhaps most of all, from himself; but he must also have known the extreme difficulty of this final achievement. Had Jesus succeeded in it? He had hardly even tried; and that would mean that He was not, after all, quite the perfect teacher. Had Socrates succeeded? He tried, and with some success; yet there was much of Socrates in Plato, as there was of Plato in Aristotle. The wisest and most loving father could not avoid leaving some mark of his own mind upon a son. The most cautious and careful scientist would always reach a result in his experiment strongly warped by the bias of his own mind. Alcott did all that the most thoughtful scientist, parent, or teacher could do to escape or erase his "personal equation." As much as possible he strove to be not Bronson Alcott but the smooth clear pipe for the breath of the Spirit. Of a session in which he felt that he had failed he said: "It is remarkable that this is the only instance in which I have premeditated one of these Conversations. I studied this passage beforehand, and in no instance have we succeeded so ill. It is better to give the subject up to the children and let them lead us where they will."

Yet of course it was impossible for Alcott to exclude himself entirely from the Conversations. More than once, to illustrate the soul's contrition for sin, he told a story about his three-year-old Louisa, not mentioning her by name, and her swift oscillations between passionate anger and love. And again, to show what might be the effect of nature's beauty and peace upon the soul, he recalled his own hours of vision on New Connecticut Hill: "I knew a boy once who lived in a small farmhouse under the brow of a hill covered with trees and beautiful retired coves and solitudes; and he used to rise early in the morning and go out and choose one of these beautiful places, when the dew was on the ground and the trees and the birds were singing and the sun was glittering, and there he would say his prayers; and he found it easy to be good and kind all day when he practised this. I knew this boy very intimately."

Yes, in spite of him, the Conversations were full of Bronson Alcott. There was more idiosyncrasy in his way of asking a question than in most men's emphatic statements. Little by little he drew and deepened an indelible image on those young minds that would last through their lives and go on to their children's children. He taught, or at any rate he enforced, no theological system, no sectarian doctrine, no Christology. He was content to set Jesus of Nazareth in those young minds and hearts as an unforgettable example and ideal, to bring Him near, to make Him dear, to draw Him down to Boston. And, for his own share in the profit, he felt when he was through that his children had told him many a thing he had not guessed before. Also he felt that his long-standing belief in the Platonic theory of "recollection" had been confirmed. The children had said such wonderful things! They amazed even him by their wisdom, which could never have been learned in this dark and forgetful world; and others were impressed as much as he.

Mr. Emerson came on the fifteenth of June, 1836, to hear a Conversation upon the Gospel of St. John. The next day he wrote in his Journal:—

> I felt strongly, as I watched the gradual dawn of thought upon the minds of all, that to truth is no age or season. It appears, or it does not appear; and when the child perceives it he is no more a child. Age, sex, are nothing. We are all alike before the great whole. Little Josiah Quincy, now six years six months old, is a child having something wonderful and divine in him. He is a youthful prophet.

One week later, Emerson wrote in the same Journal:—

> Mr. Alcott has been here with his Olympian dreams. He is a world-builder. Evermore he toils to solve the problem: Whence is the world? The point at which he prefers to begin is the mystery of the Birth of a Child.

Yes, ever since the advent of Anna and his long brooding beside her cradle, Alcott had preferred to begin there. The mystery of birth was to him what the "flower in the crannied wall" would soon be to Tennyson—a central and symbolic mystery which, if he could solve it, would help him to the further solution of "what God and man is." For it involved, of course, the multiform question how the soul takes on a body, why it needs one, what it does with it, what it was and did before it had one, and what it will do when it has that strange encumbrance no longer.

A good place to begin such inquiries was with the mystery of birth. When he came to the birth of Christ in his discussion of the Gospels, Alcott asked his children what they thought about the matter—supposing, perhaps, with his sometimes astonishing naïveté, that they might have more authentic opinions than adults about an event which was in their own experience so recent. He found, or thought he did, that the children were absolutely ignorant about the physiology of birth. On that subject he did not attempt to enlighten them, but merely said that it was a matter with which they were "not acquainted," and passed on. One lad, he discovered, believed that bodies came out of the ground and lay about upon it here and there, waiting for souls, which came directly from God, to inhabit them. Such a theory suited Alcott's purpose well enough, for he wished his pupils to understand that "the deliverance of the spirit is the first thing. . . . The physiological facts, sometimes referred to, are only a sign of the spiritual birth. You have seen the rose opening from the seed with the assistance of the atmosphere. This is the birth of the rose. It typifies the bringing forth of the spirit by pain and labor and patience. . . . And a mother suffers when she has a child. When she is going to have a child she gives up her body to God, and He works upon it in a mysterious way and, with her aid, brings forth the child's Spirit in a little Body of its own; and when it has come she is blissful."

These are the only recorded words in which Bronson Alcott ever called the attention of his children to the physiology of reproduction. Not only are they delicate and gentle words in themselves, but, like a cloud in the sunrise, they are caught up into a context of thoughtful beauty that suffuses and all but erases them in the splendor of Spirit. Alcott could not have avoided saying as much as this without leaving one of those fearful *lacunae* over which most parents and teachers of his time were wont to "draw a veil." What he said, moreover, though certainly slight in amount, was sufficient to place and to leave the whole matter of sex where he always thought it belonged, in the Shekinah glory of holiness. . . .

Bronson Alcott, having written his Introduction—Emerson called it "an admirable piece, full of profound anticipations"—[to the first volume of the **Record of Conversations on the Gospels, Held in Mr. Alcott's School**] and having paid as much as he could borrow of the printer's bill, sat down to await the grateful acclaims of the community. He did not expect an immediate success, and indeed he was a little anxious about the first reception of his book, yet he could modestly confide to his Journal that the work would "date a new era in the history of education, as well as a prophecy of the renovation of philosophy and of Christianity." However this might turn out to be, the whispers that Miss Peabody had heard months before in the parlors of Tremont and Beacon Street—feminine whispers only, no doubt accompanied by lowered eyes and crimsoned cheeks—were deepened soon by the rumble of masculine voices until the clamor culminated in the authoritative thunder of the Boston Press. There was going to be a storm.

* * *

Alcott's answer to the first flashes of premonitory lightning was to issue, in February, the second volume of the **Conversations**. After that he sat silent—listening, thinking, suffering, and watching his beloved school go to pieces. No mob shouted at the door of the Temple School, demanding that he give up the keys or that he retract his devilish book. That would have been a relief, but it was denied him. He made no impressive speeches to mobs or to irate parents, and neither did his five-year-old daughter Louisa. One denies these things because they have been asserted. But there was drama going on, not histrionics. There was the inward tragedy going on of a slow and silent heartbreak. The more imaginatively one enters into and shares the man's sorrow, the more one will wish to say of it only the sober truth.

The first bolt from Olympus aimed at Alcott's little book was launched by Nathan Hale,—brother-in-law of Governor Edward Everett, father of Edward Everett Hale, Bostonian Federalist, soon to be a railroad president, for forty years owner and editor of the Boston *Daily Advertiser*, and a Deacon of the Brattle Street Church. The fact that he was the nephew of another Connecticut schoolmaster who had regretted that he had but one life to give to his country did not incline him to mercy toward this one. Almost anywhere in Boston it would have been enough merely to know that Mr. Hale did not approve of the **Conversations on the Gospels**, but it was soon common knowledge that Mr. Hale disliked that book extremely. His keen nose had scented

four or five different kinds of heresy in it, but he summed up his remarks with the scathing sarcasm: "These conversations appear to be the first fruits of the new attempt to draw wisdom from babes and sucklings."

After this there followed certain voluble and abusive inanities in *The Boston Courier*, signed by "A Parent," which one would hesitate to quote even in part if they did not so clearly reveal the sort of mentality with which every man who thinks a little in advance of his generation has to contend. Accusing Alcott of "diving deep into solemn mysteries," the Parent bursts forth:—

> We cannot repress our indignation at the love of notoriety, for it can be nothing else, which will lead a man to scorn the truth & the best interests of society—& boldly defying public opinion & the sentiments of the wise & good, to pollute the moral atmosphere, throw a stumbling block in the path of improvement, & say to the travellers therein "Thus far shalt thou go, & no further!" . . . It were a venial error in Mr. Alcott had he simply published the crude remarks of his pupils, but he has gone further. He seemed to delight in his own person in directing their attention to the more improper subjects—& when they appeared with intuitive perception to shrink from contact with them, he has forced their minds to grapple with them. . . . Mr. Alcott should hide his head in shame.

Thus encouraged, the Editor of the *Courier*, Mr. Joseph T. Buckingham—probably with the intent of disinfecting the moral atmosphere and removing the stumbling-block from the path of improvement—gave it as his opinion

> . . . upon the honesty of a man, that the **Conversations on the Gospels** is a more indecent and obscene book (we say nothing of its absurdity) than any other we ever saw exposed for sale on a bookseller's counter. Mr. A. interrogates his pupils on subjects which are universally excluded from promiscuous companies of men and women. . . . We doubt, too, whether the clergymen who are so ambitious to outdo each other in the force of their puffs upon the **Conversations** would deem it wise or expedient to read in their pulpits some of those portions of the Gospels which Mr. Alcott reads to his pupils as containing topics of juvenile conversations and discussions; or if they should read such passages and offer to their congregations the remarks that would naturally be suggested thereby, we apprehend it would be among their last readings in any pulpit.

Having thus charged the Gospels themselves with obscenity,—and certainly they are quite as obscene as Alcott's **Conversations** upon them,—Mr. Buckingham rested for that day. But there were noble powers of indignation in this man. He it was who, a few years before, had poured the vials of contempt upon "two natural and experimental philosophers" who were trying to get up a project for a railroad from Boston to Albany—a project, he said, "which every one knows, who knows the simplest rule in arithmetic, to be impracticable . . . and which, if practicable, every person of common sense knows would be as useless as a railroad from Boston to the moon." Some practical jester it may have been—one rather suspects that transcendental humorist James Freeman Clarke—who inserted in the *Christian Register* a letter in which Alcott was defended and praised, citing as the letter's source the *Boston Courier.* If it was done in order to see how Mr. Joseph T. Buckingham would perform, the perpetrator was not disappointed. On this occasion the editor ended his diatribe by saying: "We are told that a clergyman living no great distance from Boston, when asked his opinion of the **Conversations on the Gospels,** said that one-third was absurd, one-third blasphemous, and one-third obscene. And such, we apprehend, will be the deliberate opinion of those who diligently read and soberly reflect."

All of these vilifications Alcott pasted very neatly and methodically in his commonplace book, making no comment of any sort upon them. Beside the remark quoted from "a clergyman living no great distance from Boston," however, he wrote in the margin, in lead pencil, the name "Rev. Andrews Norton, D.D." It was the name of transcendentalism's most redoubtable foe.

* * *

Not all the comments upon Alcott's book, by any means, were adverse. There came comforting letters from the mother of Josiah Quincy and from the famous and influential fathers of Lemuel Shaw and Emma Savage. James Freeman Clarke wrote two highly favorable notices of the book in the *Western Messenger,* that brilliant little forerunner of the *Dial.* Clarke it was, too, who made the gravely ironical suggestion to Editor Buckingham:—

> We perceive that the Boston *Courier* recommends that Mr. Alcott be presented to the Grand Jury on account of his book. We respectfully suggest, in addition, that the indictment be in the words of that formerly found against Socrates, the son of Sophroniscus. In Xenophon's *Memorabilia,* chapter 1, it runs thus: "Socrates is accused of not believing in the gods in which the city believes, but introducing other new divinities; he is also accused of corrupting the minds of the young." The two cases would then be exactly parallel.

The *Christian Register,* most influential of Unitarian journals, also defended Alcott's book with warmth and ability; but by far the most important of all the comments, favorable or adverse, was the long and brilliant article entitled "Alcott on Human Culture" which appeared in October, 1838, in the *Boston Quarterly Review,* written by the religious stormy petrel of those days, Orestes A. Brownson. The article runs to some five thousand words. It is a thoughtful and highly intelligent discussion of Alcott's educational, religious, and

philosophical theories, written from the inside by a close personal acquaintance—Alcott and Brownson believed, indeed, that they were distantly related—who knows not only his man's present opinions but how he reached them. Few men in America at that time had been so elaborately explained to their contemporaries as Alcott was in Brownson's study. This was, in fact, the first sympathetic, deeply considered, and fully informed examination ever made of an American transcendental thinker.

To Alcott himself praise was hardly more disturbing than blame. What he wanted, now as ever, was a friendly association, a sense of coöperation with "worthy" men and women toward some "worthy" end. This end or goal might be ever so vague, dim, and distant; he cared less than perhaps he should have cared about that, because what he really desired—in his teaching, his reforming, his conversing, and in all the travel of his later years up and down the land—was the warmth of human sympathy. He had of course read the broken-down translated version of Zimmermann's *Einsamkeit,* or *Solitude,* now in its twentieth American edition. What reading man of his time had not? He liked to think and speak of himself as a "solitary" because it had long been established, partly with Zimmermann's help, that every man of "genius" must be that. Yet nothing could have been farther from the truth. From the earliest years of his bashful boyhood he had been an outsider, looking in; and now what was worst about this calamity of the School and the **Conversations** was not the public hue and cry, the loss of pupils, the increase of poverty, the forced auction of his school furniture and of the busts of Socrates and Plato, the sale of his books, the threat of a mob, or even that the children pointed at him as he walked in the street and called out derisive names. The worst was that he who had been for a little while definitely inside was now thrust forth again into a world either hostile or indifferent, a world that knew him not and had no wish for his gifts or for his service.

Dorothy McCuskey (essay date 1940)

SOURCE: McCuskey, Dorothy. "Philosophical Backgrounds." In *Bronson Alcott, Teacher,* pp. 60-81. New York: Macmillan Company, 1940.

[*In the following excerpt, McCuskey examines the origins of* Conversations with Children on the Gospels.]

> Time doth but tell the story of the Spirit's doings, and the true historian is he who doth apprehend its features and will aright. Every man's life is but a phase of the *One Divine Nature* that flows through all visible things, by whose subtle breath all are fed and sustained.
>
> Alcott *Journals,* January, 1837.

In the first six years of Alcott's teaching, the school had been the center of his life. He kept discovering new things, first about his profession, and then about children. In Philadelphia, though, it was different. There his chief stimulation came from outside his school. The change came about, however, very easily and naturally. As Alcott began his teaching in Connecticut, he was at first carried away by the apparent power in the hands of the schoolmaster, and he began to experiment, gravely, prayerfully, finding better ways to use that power. His first efforts were in the direction of external changes, and, working with his Cousin William, he let in light and air, designed new furniture, and introduced slates and blackboards. These were genuine innovations, which were accepted rather rapidly, even though the cost was at first objected to. However, in the process of making physical changes, Alcott's thinking employed, more and more, terms in their psychological meanings. As his teaching with such tangible aids as slates and blocks of wood developed, he began to wonder how children did learn. He watched them more carefully. He saw that they reacted to the pleasing appearance of the schoolroom, and to the pleasant, affectionate manner of the teacher, and he thought they learned better under such circumstances. And so, for a time in Alcott's teaching, he searched for better and better ways of teaching in accordance with "the laws of thought."

He kept going deeper and deeper. The children sometimes said the most amazing things, things that had no apparent connection with observable circumstance. What were the laws of thought? As Alcott went from the common schools of Connecticut, where he taught children of all school ages, to the Boston infant school of two-to-four-year olds, he noticed a great change. These little children were more frank, more naive. They had not learned to hide their feelings in deference to the ideas of adults. Alcott saw here that children are primarily active, and so he let them play, and he watched. He saw another thing. He saw that they did more than respond to the stimuli about them; they were self-initiating. Their drives to action seemed to come from within themselves. That would take some thinking about. What were the implications for a schoolmaster?

And more, what were the implications of such observations for a psychologist, or a philosopher? For by this time, teaching five children in Germantown did not occupy much of Alcott's thought and energy. In Germantown, too, there were no Sunday School Associations, no reform meetings, and no Unitarian sermons to occupy him. Rather, Alcott had, for the first time, access to great libraries and leisure to read; he had daily association with his friend William Russell; and he had his infant daughter Anna. These might lead him to answer the questions he had begun to wonder about. In the lives of many men there may be discovered some point upon which all lines of thought seem to converge, some

event for which all others were but preparatory. So it was with Alcott. All things, but chiefly these three—his daughter Anna, his friend William Russell, and great books—combined to make Alcott a transcendental thinker. Events might well have been contrived to keep him from thinking—he might have been too busy, or he might have had no stimulation—but the fates arranged otherwise.

It was with the intent of a scientist that Alcott turned to observe his daughter Anna, who was born in Germantown, March 16, 1831. Within ten days of her birth, he had commenced "an Historical account of the Development of the Intellect and Moral Conduct of my little girl, from birth, to be continued as her mind and heart make progress." The history of a human mind, he felt, begun in infancy by the parent and carried on by the child when he was able, would be a treasure of greater value to the world than all the philosophical systems ever built up. It would be a history of human nature. Before Anna was born, Alcott had seen in *Nicholson's Journal* an article on observations of a child. The idea caught fire with him, but the conclusions of the article, he thought, were imaginative and unsound. He would try to avoid that, in his observations. And so, he set out to be a fact-finder.

To be sure, Alcott was not the sort of fact-finder who delighted in facts. He wanted to know what they meant. He observed his new-born child that he might discover the birth of Soul, and the foundations of character. He wanted to find out something about Body and Mind, how they were related, how they worked. It is breathtaking to see this untrained man set himself, a hundred years before Arnold Gesell, the specific scientific task of observing children. For help, he turned to all the scientific books he could find. He read chiefly Broussais' *Physiology,* Jackson's *Principles of Medicine* and Combe's *Phrenology.* But unfortunately, Alcott never defined with sufficient precision the object of his search. He made patient, minute, regular physiological and psychological observations, but he was not primarily interested in physical and mental development. If that had been his object, he might have succeeded in anticipating some of the discoveries of modern psychologists. In his search for the Soul he became lost:

> I sit down to make some remarks on the lives and circumstances of my children, but e'er I am aware I have left the consideration of them as individuals and have merged their separate existences into the common life of the Spirit. I have left their terrestrial life, with the varied phenomena that typify its action, and am roaming at large over the domain of the celestial world—beholding not only these, my children, in the gladsome existence there, but also the unnumberable children of the Infinite Parent Himself, the common Father.[1]

As Alcott failed to find his answer with Anna, he tried again with Louisa, who was born in Germantown on her father's birthday, November 29, 1832; and a third time, with Elizabeth, born in Boston, June 24, 1835. From the dark, dynamic Louisa, Bronson Alcott may never have expected to discover much about the Soul, for she was not a "child of light." The fiery-tempered Louisa taught her father, perhaps, more of the "Demon" than of Soul. Alcott persevered, however. The progress of his investigations is reflected in the titles of the manuscripts in which his records were kept. He began very strictly with **"Observations on An Infant."** Then came *The Breath of Childhood, Evangele,* and finally, *Psyche.* This last manuscript represents the refined gold of three observations, and the dross of many, many re-writings. But the more Alcott wrote, the more coy his subject became, and there was little hint of Psyche in the final draft.

What did Alcott mean by Psyche, or Soul? Partly, he used the word in a religious sense, to mean the spiritual, aspiring part of man's being. At other times it was meant to refer to the intellect, to the active agent in the learning process; and sometimes Alcott used the word with a hint of the physiological *élan vital* in his meaning. Perhaps the soul does manifest itself in those various ways, perhaps its chief characteristic is its illimitability. But a single man cannot do all things at once. Alcott was seeking, not whatever answer his data produced, but was attempting to discover by objective means something which did not exist in a substantive form.

At the same time that one records Alcott's failure either to make a scientific "contribution to knowledge" or to discover the elusive birth of Soul, one must applaud the reasonableness of his attempt, as well as its daring. He was seeking to understand the manifestations of spiritual law in the natural universe. The soul was in all things, yet not of them; it caused change, yet was itself changeless. It was at once the doer and the thing done. Alcott never encompassed Psyche on the bulky pages of his manuscripts, but he grew more and more sure of her presence. . . .

Alcott's excursions into general literature widened his horizons immensely. As a boy he had read good literature—Milton, Cowper, Thomson, and Bunyan, but since then he had read very little. This reading, then, marks a real literary renaissance for Alcott. He particularly enjoyed the English romantic poets, Wordsworth, Coleridge, Byron, Shelley, and Keats, who, with Milton, he considered the "first poets in the language." Wordsworth had the advantage of saying for him his own best thoughts and intuitions, for Alcott was literal in his acceptance of the ideas about children in the "Ode on Intimations of Immortality from Recollections of Early Childhood," for example. Coleridge the philosopher and religious thinker was such a shining light to Alcott that he had little to say about the man as a poet. In October, 1832, he wrote:

In Coleridge in particular there are passages of surpassing beauty and deep wisdom. He seems to have studied man more thoroughly, and to understand him better, than any previous poetic writer, unless it be Wordsworth. And his prose writings are full of splendid ideas clothed in the most awful and imposing imagery. There is in this man's soul a deep well of wisdom, and it is a wisdom not of earth. No writer ever benefited me more than he has done.[2]

The presence of the life and works of Byron on Alcott's list of important books seems odd at first glance. It was, of course, not the Byron of *Don Juan* that would appeal to Alcott (he would ignore such a poem), but Byron's humanitarian efforts in Italy and Greece; and Moore's account of his pathetic death at Missolonghi in the service of human freedom could not but touch Alcott.

"The frequent perusal of poetry seems necessary to the vigor, vivacity and freshness of the mind," wrote Alcott, but it was chiefly the philosophic message or the symbolism of poetry that he appreciated. He was much annoyed at the criticism of Shelly's personal life, probably comparing it with the reaction to his own attempts at reform. Alcott must have recognized in Shelley, too, that ethereal quality that was a kindred element in his own character. He chose "Queen Mab" as the poem upon which Shelley's fame would chiefly rest.

Since Alcott liked the sort of volume in which he could read at random, the works of William Hazlitt were eminently satisfactory. He read not only Hazlitt's *Lectures on English Poets,* and his *Select British Poets,* but the *Spirit of the Age,* and *Table Talk.* Lamb's *Elia* pleased Alcott's whimsical fancies and More's *Utopia* delighted his idealistic mind. Shakespeare Alcott now read for the first time, but in him Alcott found few "correspondencies." He was doubtless too earthy, and so Alcott read his work desultorily, "chiefly for the vocabulary."

Alcott never learned to read a foreign language, but, from the month he moved to Philadelphia (March, 1833) German literature in translation appeared on his reading lists. He was reading Carlyle's *Sartor Resartus,* and works of Victor Cousin or Coleridge might have further stimulated his interest. From the standpoint of the growth of Alcott's philosophy, perhaps no book was more important than F. A. Nitsch's *View of Professor Kant's Principles concerning Man, the World, and the Deity.* From this book Alcott copied out ninety-four of Kant's theoretical principles into his Commonplace Book for 1833. This means that Alcott had knowledge of Kant, other than through the interpretations of Coleridge and other English transcendentalists.

Other philosophical reading was important as well. Alcott used three histories of philosophy—those by Cousin, Formay, and Fennerman, though he was not at all interested in the history of ideas. He liked historical writings only when they demonstrated to him the truth of his own beliefs. In the works of Emanuel Swedenborg, especially that on "Influx, Correspondence, and Faith" Alcott would find much to his liking. He had always looked at the world in terms of allegories, hence Swedenborg's doctrine of the "correspondence" of natural phenomena and spiritual realities merely served Alcott as proof that truth is of no particular time or place.

Coleridge was the most important of the English philosophers, as Alcott now read *Aids to Reflection, The Friend, Biographia Literaria,* and *Lay Sermons.* Locke had previously been read rather completely, so that only the discussion of "innate ideas" appears on this list. It was probably reread in connection with some of the theories which attempted to discredit it. Bacon, however, was read in the *Novum Organum,* the *Advancement of Learning,* and the *Interpreter of Nature.* Alcott strongly approved of Bacon's inductive methods, and felt that Bacon relied on the spiritual principle, though there was nowhere a definite statement of it. "*He beheld all things in the concrete.*"

Alcott's classical readings began with Aristotle's *Ethics* and the volumes he used, carefully annotated, remain in his library today. Aristotle, as well as Bacon, appealed to the pedagogic Alcott, and he describes his devotion to their teachings at the same time that he tells of one of the most important events in his educational history. He says, "In 1833 I was a disciple of Experience, trying to bring my theories within the Baconian method of induction, and took the philosophy of Aristotle as the exponent of humanity while my heart was even then lingering around the theories of Plato without being conscious of it. A follower of Aristotle was I in theory, yet a true Platonist in practice."[3]

The discovery of Plato served to inaugurate a new period in Alcott's thinking. He wrote, in May, 1833, "Plato I had long wished to read, but could never before find a translation. It had long been my impression that there were in his writings great and profound ideas which the light of existing thought and science had not been bright enough to attain."[4] Alcott read the *Cratylus, Phaedo, Parmenides* and *Timaeus,* and at the time supposed these "fragments" were all of Plato that Taylor had translated. It was natural that Alcott should read Proclus and Plotinus immediately afterward, for Thomas Taylor felt that the Neo-Platonic ideas represented by these men were necessary to an understanding of Plato. It would be futile, then, to try to distinguish Platonic and Neo-Platonic ideas in Alcott's thinking, for they were presented to him as one. It would be equally impossible to try to assert that Plato contributed any particular doctrines to Bronson Alcott's thinking.

In Plato, Alcott found a world where he could live, a world he was later to make seem "as solid as Massachusetts" to Emerson. In Plato, Alcott found expressed

an intuitive theory of knowledge which agreed with his own experience, and he found spirit set forth as the unconditioned substance upon which all conditioned experience is based. In the doctrine of nature as the shadow, or copy, of the primal Idea, Alcott found a further clue to the relationship he had been trying to discover through his children. This Platonic theory explained, as the Lockean could not, man's direct relationship with the Supreme Being. Of the validity of this idea Alcott now had no doubts.

Reinforced in this belief by one of the great minds of all time, Alcott set down a bold attack on the "dead and corrupt materialism" of the contemporary Lockean philosophy. Locke had asserted that all phenomena were based on the operation of the law of cause and effect, thus making no distinction between the natural and the spiritual. To Alcott the conclusions from such a premise were necessarily false: "It [modern philosophy, or Locke] shuts God from the universe, and, carried to its legitimate issues, results in Pantheism building up on an inconceivable basis the whole fabrick of religion, which it must assume as independent of man, and nature. It makes of exterior nature a self-existent substance, and sees not in the laws and vicissitudes of things the movement of spirit."[5] With the reading of Plato, however, all these illusions of Lockean theory were swept away. Alcott saw clearly "what before was obscured by the gloss of exterior matter—spirit all in all—matter its form and shadow."

Alcott's spiritual philosophy was not completed upon the discovery of Plato, however; as he read Coleridge, there grew in his mind a conception of Jesus Christ as the physical embodiment of God or Spirit, which added to Alcott's philosophy a Christian element it had hitherto lacked. The reading of *Aids to Reflection, The Friend,* and the *Biographia Literaria* served Alcott both from the point of view of philosophical theory and of religious experience. In *The Friend,* Coleridge has set forth a method of scientific thought which he had formulated after an examination of many systems of philosophy. The most notable characteristic of this method is its reconciliation of Plato's idealism and Bacon's material view of the world. Coleridge correlates the two in this fashion:

> Thus the difference, or rather distinction between Plato and Lord Bacon is simply this: that philosophy being necessarily bipolar, Plato treats principally of the truth, as it manifests itself at the *ideal* pole, as the science of intellect (i.e. *de mundo intelligibili*); while Bacon confines himself, for the most part, to the same truth, as it is manifested at the other, or material pole, as the science of nature (i.e. *de mundo sensibili*).[6]

Coleridge thus corroborated Alcott's feeling (it was scarcely more than that) that Bacon was, in some way, related to the spiritual principle. By applying Aristotelian logic to the principles of intuitive knowledge, Coleridge gave philosophic respectability to the doctrines which formed the basis of the transcendental philosophy. Alcott particularly delighted in Coleridge's eclecticism—his inclusion of Plato, Aristotle, Jesus, Bacon, and the German philosophers in one system.

It was as a religious thinker that Coleridge most affected Alcott, however. In the latter part of his life and in the generation that followed, Coleridge was ranked by many young clergymen of liberal views as the greatest religious thinker of their time, and he did much to deepen and liberalize religious thought in England and the United States. After reading Coleridge, Alcott realized that he had been studying outward phenomena in his search for the origin of human powers, without a sense of the grounds on which phenomena were dependent for their form and existence. Coleridge lifted him out of this difficulty and turned his attention to Spirit, not as an abstract entity, but as manifested in Jesus Christ. The lights of Aristotle, Plato, Bacon were all lost in the "transparent radiance of the gospel of Christ." This enthusiasm was not a temporary one—in 1836 Alcott read *Aids to Reflection* for the fifth time with unabated interest. It was likewise this philosophy of Jesus Christ as the emblem of spirit which became embodied in the practice of the Temple School. Evidences of Alcott's high regard for Coleridge recur throughout the journals. In him, Alcott felt, were blended the poet and the philosopher; a teeming, vivid imagination, and a profound, clear understanding, each reflecting light and beauty on the other. Of Coleridge's service to his own age and to the future, Alcott wrote, January 17, 1836:

> Coleridge was not of this age but of one to come; and the aspiring of this, and coming time, will be led, by his prophetic vision, to the perception of the era, of which the present is only the herald. They must look through his *Eye* and behold that which they are seeking. In this lieth his greatness—not that he hath created aught anew, or declared aught before unknown—but that he hath erected a Telescope, and pointed it towards the Spiritual Country, so that all who will make discoveries, or view the Divine Realities of *Humanity,* or of *Divinity,* shall accept his guidance, use his instruments, with grateful and reverential hearts! . . . The English tongue is restored to its purity in his writings; and where will the thoughtful find more to enkindle and enlighten, than in the pages of '*The Friend*'—the '*Biographia*' and the '*Aids to Reflection*'!

What effect did all these varied types of reading have upon Alcott's philosophy? This was a question that Bronson Alcott asked of himself. Books, he felt, had called forth truths from the inward darkness in which his self-ignorance had wrapped them. The books he had read had encouraged him; and if they had not often supplied him with new views, they had held sympathetic communion on the way. His mind did not readily take the ideas of another, but ever sought to subordinate all facts to his own scheme of things. Yet he found it consoling to discover "that the mind, at various ages, and under all possible aspects, and circumstances, has taken similar views of truth. It shows how trifling is the influence of time and of institutions, on the vision of great minds; how these rise above all circumstances to behold the self-same truths, and, at their eras, to publish these to the world. *Truth is of no age nor nation; it is ever contemporaneous with genius and virtue.*"[7]

Notes

1. Shepard, *Pedlar's Progress,* 143.

2. Shepard, Editor, *Alcott Journals,* 32.

3. Shepard, Editor, *Alcott Journals,* 66 f.

4. *Ibid.,* 36.

5. *Ibid.,* 36.

6. Samuel Taylor Coleridge, *The Friend,* Burlington, Vermont, 1831, 431.

7. *Alcott Journals,* May, 1837.

Bibliography

Samuel Taylor Coleridge, *The Friend*: A Series of Essays, to Aid in the Formation of Fixed Principles in Politics, Morals, and Religion, with Literary Amusements Interspersed, First American, from the Second London Edition, Burlington, Vermont, Chauncey Goodrich, 1831, 510 pp.

The third part contains the famous essay on method, which was so admired by the thinkers of the early nineteenth century.

Odell Shepard, *Pedlar's Progress,* Boston, Little, Brown and Co., 1937, 137-163.

Odell Shepard, Editor, *The Journals of Bronson Alcott,* Boston, Little, Brown and Co., 1938, 27-45.

John B. Wilson (essay date 19 February 1955)

SOURCE: Wilson, John B. "Bronson Alcott, Platonist or Pestalozzian?" *School and Society* 81, no. 2053 (19 February 1955): 49-53.

[*In the following essay, Wilson examines the primary influences behind Alcott's teaching methods.*]

Father of "Little Women," friend of Emerson, and founder of the progressive Masonic Temple School in Boston, Bronson Alcott in his own lifetime earned the title "The American Pestalozzi." American scholars today have rediscovered Alcott and have re-emphasized the Pestalozzian influence.[1] But to Emerson, to other members of the "Hedge Club" of transcendentalists, and to his fellow teachers of New England Alcott was more Pythagorean than Pestalozzian in educational practice, more the follower of Plato than of Rousseau in educational theory. A reconsideration of Alcott's development as an educational philosopher will prove that his concern with the ideals and strategies of Rousseau, Pestalozzi, Basedow, Froebel, and other "progressive" teachers of his day was a passing phase, supplementing only for a short while his permanent interest in ancient Greek and early Christian experiments in "soul-culture."

Recently Dorothy S. McCuskey has disproved the "classic" statement of W. S. Monroe, that Alcott was "Pestalozzian without knowing the basis of his pedagogic creed,"[2] although she is obliged to admit that the Concord philosopher had his Pestalozzianism from secondary sources before 1830.[3]

After 1825, during his four years as master of the Centre Street District School in Cheshire, Conn., Alcott was a subscriber to William Russell's *American Journal of Education.* In nearly every issue of that periodical writers debated the relative merits of the "Lancastrian or Monitorial Plan" of teaching and the "Pestalozzian or Mutual Plan," and Alcott's diary for this period was entitled "The Cheshire Pestalozzian School." Listed among his readings for 1826 was a book by William Maclure, *Epitome of Pestalozzian Instruction.* Two years later Alcott was studying J. P. Greaves' *Exposition of Conducting Infant Instruction,* a tract on the Pestalozzian system, and in 1830 he purchased Dr. E. Biber's *Henry Pestalozzi.* Meanwhile he was corresponding with Maclure, Dr. J. M. Keagy, the Rev. William Woodbridge, and other disciples of Pestalozzi.[4] In 1828 Alcott contributed six articles to Russell's *Journal* regarding the newly organized American "Infant School Society," patterned after J. P. Greaves' British society of the same name. The following year Alcott wrote for the *Journal* two critiques directly concerning Pestalozzi's methods of instruction.

These articles and Alcott's advanced pedagogy at the Temple School in Boston won him the title of "The American Pestalozzi," bestowed by the Englishman J. P. Greaves, associate to Pestalozzi for 10 years. Even earlier a scholarly minister of New England, Samuel J. May, had noted similarities between Alcott's theories and those of the Swiss educator.[5] May had urged Alcott to submit an analysis of his own classroom experimentation to Russell's *American Journal of Education.* Later, techniques of Alcott and Pestalozzi were compared in detail by Charles Lane in an article contributed to the *Dial* for April, 1843.[6] Shortly afterwards Lane expanded this article into a book, *The Law and Method of Spirit-Culture, An Interpretation of Bronson Alcott's Idea and Practice at the Masonic Temple.*

But even Alcott's "discoverer," the ardent Pestalozzian Samuel J. May, felt impelled to modify his thesis of similarity and influence: "Alcott added a mystic, Platonic tinge to his system, which was not evident in Pestalozzi."[7]

In commenting on Alcott's school William Russell denied that it was a copy of Pestalozzi's or any other, for Alcott "had acted in the true spirit of the method of Pestalozzi, keeping the mechanical part of teaching strictly subordinate to the mental."[8]

In fact, Pestalozzi's system of object-teaching, the basis of Greaves' and Russell's "infant schools," was almost entirely neglected by Alcott. For that reason his assistant in the Temple School, Miss Elizabeth Peabody, later abandoned Alcott's method and adopted that of Froebel in her kindergartens. She maintained that the European educator had made capital of the play instincts of children as a part of the educational process, whereas Alcott had sought to subordinate everything physical to his "spiritual" tuition and had recognized play only as a necessary interruption by means of which the children worked off their surplus energies.[9]

In his two articles on Pestalozzi's methods Alcott commended the Swiss educator for adopting the mother-child relationship as the foundation for all teaching, approved his use of Socratic questioning to determine what moral and religious ideas existed in the child's mind, and praised his efforts to train head, heart, and hand by "leading out" potential elements present from birth.[10] But to Alcott, Pestalozzi's educational procedure was a dialectic rather than a dogmatic system, an exercise whereby the teacher could know the child and enable the child to know himself:

> By an attentive study of the primary operations of the infant mind in acquiring, retaining, and expressing its ideas, the distinguished philosopher [Pestalozzi] obtained a knowledge of its nature so accurate, and devised such methods for the harmonious development of all its powers, as to be able to operate upon it himself, with certainty and success. An observer of nature, by this he was taught to lead the infant mind onward in a regular and continuous progress toward truth and virtue . . . and to induce it to put forth its own volitions, and become the chief agent of its own advancement.[11]

Alcott, therefore, found nothing prescriptive in Pestalozzi's system. To him it was merely a means to the end of good instruction based on the nature, needs and interests of the child. Furthermore, he concluded his final article on Pestalozzi with the comment that this educator's techniques were greatly similar to the teaching procedures of Pythagoras and other ancients.[12]

Emerson placed Pythagoras first and Pestalozzi last in the pantheon of Bronson Alcott, not solely on the basis of chronology. "He measures ages by teachers, and reckons history by Pythagoras, Plato, Jesus, and Pestalozzi."[13] Frequently, Emerson attested the Platonic basis of Alcott's teaching: "Alcott declares that a teacher is one who can assist a child in obeying his own mind, and who can remove all unfavorable circumstances. He believes that from a circle of twenty well-selected children he could draw in their conversation everything that is in Plato, and as much better in form than it is in Plato, as the passages I read him from the *Heimskringla* are than Bancroft."[14]

Another contemporary, George P. Bradford, wrote that Wordsworth's platonic "Ode on the Intimations of Immortality" could be considered as Alcott's point of departure in dealing with children:

> His school was founded on the principle of the Platonic philosophy that all abstract truth exists in the soul of man; and its aim was not to impart knowledge from without, but to educe both truth and knowledge from the mind of the child, where it lies, unrecognized and unknown perhaps, but still existing in a purer form, or less encumbered by errors, than in later life.[15]

Elizabeth Peabody, more familiar than anyone else with Alcott's educational philosophy and teaching procedures, emphasized the influence of Pythagoras, Plato, and Jesus almost to the exclusion of that of Pestalozzi. In her *Record of Mr. Alcott's School,* a stenographic reporting of his conversations with the children of the Temple School in Boston while she was assistant teacher there, she maintained that Christ's parables and Plato's dialogues were the models for Alcott's pedagogy:

> The manner of Jesus and Plato is authority, were any needed, to show what the mind requires in order to be quickened and renewed. "Without a parable spake he not unto them." Neither should the teacher of spiritual truth nowadays. By neglecting this mode of instruction we have shorn the young mind of its beams. We have made it prosaic, literal, worldly.[16]

Miss Peabody recalled that Alcott had often quoted as the foundations of his method of spiritual culture Wordsworth's "Ode," Plato's *Symposium,* and Christ's declaration that children were of the kingdom of heaven. As early as 1826, while at Cheshire, Alcott had declared his intention "To teach with reference to Eternity, to teach as an agent of the Great Instructor, to teach as the former of character and the promoter of the collective happiness of man."[17] Always he contended that proofs of pre-existence resided in the consciousness of children and that these could be drawn out by skillful Socratic questioning. He believed that "Contemplation of spirit is the first principle of human culture, the foundation of self-education."[18]

In directing the intellectual activities of his pupils toward a "contemplation of spirit," Alcott used four techniques: contemplation of spirit in themselves by exercises in introspection; contemplation of spirit in Christ by readings from the New Testament; contemplation of spirit in language by semantic discussions regarding figurative meanings of words; contemplation of spirit in literature by consideration of moral truths contained in fables, parables, and allegories.[19]

Alcott defended his pedagogy, not by quoting the precepts and examples of latter-day progressive educators, but by relying on the ancient transcendental doctrine that spirit is the only true reality and that matter is a "temporary accident." When critics protested that his tuition did not result in the well-rounded development which Pestalozzi sought, Alcott replied: "The soul's very life consists in its actions; . . . there is not, over and above the soul's very life, conscience, intellect, affections, happiness, virtue, salvation—but . . . the soul has its substantial existence in these various modes and degrees of action, and . . . to educate the soul is to make common cause with its action. . . ."[20] This statement represented a clean break with the object-teaching and activity-learning advocated by Pestalozzi and his followers.

Alcott did not entirely disregard the external world. He promised his pupils that others would come to the school and talk with them about "outward things." "I can teach better about inward things," he assured them. An oft-recurring question in his school was this: "Is truth [or virture, or law, or justice] in the mind or out of the mind?" Invariably, the answer was "In the mind,"[21] for his students had been well indoctrinated with transcendental idealism.

So certain was Alcott of the rightness of his theories, arrived at by practice in the schools of Cheshire, Bristol, Germantown, Philadelphia, and Boston, that he became a propagandist for his own system in a series of pamphlets.

In the first of these publications, **"Observations on the Principles and Methods of Infant Instruction,"** Alcott presented as the basis for his entire program of culture the following Platonic thesis:

> . . . infant instruction when adapted to the human being, is founded on the great principle, that every infant is already in possession of the faculties and apparatus required for his instruction, and that, by a law of his constitution he uses these to a great extent himself; that the office of instruction is chiefly to facilitate this process, and to accompany the child in his progress rather than to drive or even to lead him.[22]

In his **"Doctrine and Discipline of Human Culture,"** Alcott defined education as "inspiration" and named as the greatest teacher of all times Jesus Christ, who knew that He must "inspire in order to unfold, to arouse every faculty, and to awaken the Godlike in man."[23] Christ's method of spiritual instruction was the conversation:

This preference of Jesus for Conversation, as the highest organ of utterance, is striking proof of his comprehensive Idea of Education. He saw what was in man, and the means of perfecting his being. He saw the Superiority of this exercise over others for quickening the Spirit. For, in this, all the faculties of the being are touched. It tempts forth all the powers.[24]

Through his own use of the conversation, Alcott was certain that he had perfected a technique of child culture that would revolutionize not only secular education, but also religious instruction, and in issuing his two volumes of *Conversations with Children on the Gospels* in 1836-1837, he presented the conversation in this dual function, as Miss Peabody observed in her "Recorder's Preface":

These conversations were recorded, because it was thought that they might prove a model for parents and teachers who were desirous of giving a spiritual culture to the young; and also because Mr. Alcott felt that what the children should freely say would prove to be a new order of Christian Evidences, by showing the affinity of their natures with that of Jesus Christ.[25]

A fellow transcendentalist, Orestes Brownson, defended Alcott's thesis in a review appearing in the *Boston Quarterly*. Spirit had attained an almost perfect manifestation in Socrates and Jesus, Brownson contended. Thus, the record of Christ's life became the most illustrious model for what is latent in the child. Furthermore, "if we can reproduce in children, as yet unspoiled, the phenomena recorded of Jesus, then we have a new proof, and a strong proof, that the Record is a faithful one."[26] Brownson therefore presented Alcott not only as a teacher, but also as a philosopher, a moralist, and a theologian, to the disgust of many orthodox ministers and professors of divinity, who had attacked the "Record" as another transcendental "form of infidelity."

It was in this larger sphere of "defender of the transcendental faith" that Alcott began to believe his mission lay. Even after he was forced to close his school in Boston, was refused a teaching position in Concord because of his "heresies," and lost much of his faith in the educational process through correspondence with Greaves and associations with the British Alcott House group, he still retained confidence in what had been his mainstay as a teacher—the conversation.

As early as 1835 Alcott was planning an ambitious program of adult education, nation-wide in scope, to begin with a series of "conversations with some of the thinking spirits . . . on subjects connected with the nature and destiny of man."[27] In his *Journal* for that year he referred to Socrates, Plato, and Jesus as his authorities, for they used the conversation as "the medium of instruction to the docile disciples"; they "resigned themselves to the simple promptings and intuitions of the spirit."[28]

"Garrison made the Convention, Greeley made the Newspaper, and Alcott is making the Conversation," he wrote in 1856.[29] His book *Concord Days* contains lengthy passages defending "conversation by Dialogue" as first practiced by Socrates, refined by Plato, and modernized by Alcott.

A little exasperated with his friend's constant talk fests, Emerson wrote: "He seems to think society exists for this function, and that all literature is good or bad as it approaches colloquy, which is its perfection."[30] Education had come to be synonymous with conversation to Alcott. He stated in his Superintendent's Report of the Concord Schools, 1860-1861: "Certainly the best we can do is to teach ourselves and our children how to talk. . . . So taught the masters: Plato, Plutarch, Pythagoras, Pestalozzi, so Christianity was first published from lovely lips; so everyone teaches deserving the name of teacher or interpreter."[31]

James Russell Lowell, attending one of Alcott's conversations in a little room on Boston's West Street, next to Elizabeth Peabody's bookshop, wrote:

Hear him but speak, and you will feel
    The shadow of the Portico
Over your tranquil spirit steal.[32]

Lowell felt that Alcott had successfully recreated the atmosphere, and had effectively reproduced the techniques, of Plato's Lyceum.

But also Alcott's teaching had degenerated into pure verbalism. More loyal followers of Pestalozzi—Goethe, Fellenberg, and Froebel—had adopted that educator's formula of growth through pleasurable activity.

At the time Alcott published his first Superintendent's Report, his one-time assistant, Elizabeth Peabody, did not offer her usual dissent. She had sailed for Europe to observe the new Froebelian kindergartens, or activity schools, in Germany, France, and Switzerland.

Notes

1. G. E. Haefner, *A Critical Estimate of the Educational Theories and Practices of A. Bronson Alcott* (New York: Columbia University Press, 1937); O. Shepard, *Pedlar's Progress, the Life of Bronson Alcott* (Boston: Little, Brown and Co., 1937); D. McCuskey, *Bronson Alcott, Teacher* (New York: Macmillan Co., 1940).

2. W. S. Monroe, *History of the Pestalozzian Movement in the United States* (Syracuse, N. Y.: Bardeen, 1907).

3. D. McCuskey, "Bronson Alcott, Progressive Educator" (unpublished Ph.D. dissertation, Yale University, 1936).

4. B. A. Hinsdale, *Horace Mann and the Common School Revival* (New York: Charles Scribner's Sons, 1900); McCuskey, *Bronson Alcott, Progressive Educator,* 73-77, 82-84.

5. F. Sanborn and W. T. Harris, *A. Bronson Alcott, His Life and Philosophy* (Boston: Roberts Brothers, 1893), I, 87.

6. *Dial,* 3: 417-454, April, 1843.

7. Sanborn and Harris, *op. cit.,* I, 87.

8. *American Journal of Education,* 3: 563, 1828.

9. *The Record of Mr. Alcott's School* (third ed., Boston: Roberts Brothers, 1874), 4.

10. *American Journal of Education,* 4: 54-55, Jan., 1829; *American Journal of Education,* 4: 99, March, 1829.

11. *American Journal of Education,* 4: 54-55, Jan., 1829.

12. *Ibid.,* 106.

13. *The Journals of Ralph Waldo Emerson,* edited by Edward Waldo Emerson and Waldo Emerson Forbes (Boston: Houghton Mifflin, 1909-1914), VII, 500.

14. *Ibid.,* VII, 499.

15. *Memorial History of Boston,* edited by Justin Winsor (Boston: Osgood, 1881), IV, 326.

16. *Record of Mr. Alcott's School,* 25-26.

17. Shepard, *Pedlar's Progress,* 92.

18. *Record of Mr. Alcott's School,* 245.

19. *Ibid.,* 247.

20. *Record of Mr. Alcott's School,* 237.

21. *Ibid.,* 235.

22. *Observations on the Principles and Methods of Infant Instruction* (Boston: Carter, Hendee, 1830), 27.

23. *Doctrine and Discipline of Human Culture* (Boston: Munroe, 1836), 18.

24. *Observations on the Principles and Methods of Infant Instruction,* 9-10.

25. *Conversations with Children on the Gospels* (Boston: Munroe, 1836-1837), I, i-ii.

26. *Boston Quarterly Review,* 1: 429, 1838.

27. *The Journals of Bronson Alcott,* edited by Odell Shepard (Boston: Little, Brown, 1938), 104.

28. *Ibid.,* 104.

29. *Ibid.,* 281.

30. Sanborn and Harris, *op. cit.,* II, 249.

31. Quoted by Haefner, *op. cit.,* 124.

32. Sanborn and Harris, *op. cit.,* II, 392.

Joel Myerson (essay date September 1972)

SOURCE: Myerson, Joel. "'In the Transcendental Emporium': Bronson Alcott's 'Orphic Sayings' in the *Dial*." *English Language Notes* 10, no. 1 (September 1972): 31-8.

[*In the following essay, Myerson examines the diverse critical reactions that followed the publication of the "Orphic Sayings."*]

One of the most controversial publications of the American Transcendentalists was Amos Bronson Alcott's **"Orphic Sayings"** in the July 1840 and January 1841 numbers of the *Dial*. But unlike Emerson's Divinity School Address or Theodore Parker's *Discourse on the Transient and Permanent in Christianity,* Alcott's **"Sayings"** did not constitute a call to arms signalling a visible break with the established order; rather, they became a lightning-rod which drew down upon the *Dial* and the Transcendentalists the satiric and often violent outbursts of press and public alike. Later historians of Transcendentalism were also less than kind: Octavius Brooks Frothingham called the **"Sayings"** "an amazement to the uninitiated and an amusement to the profane," and Harold Clarke Goddard flatly declared that Alcott's pieces, "more than all the other contributions to the *Dial* combined, served to bring down the ridicule of the community without discrimination on its pages."[1] An examination of the contemporary reception of the **"Sayings"** will unfortunately bear out these later comments on Alcott's writings.[2]

Alcott had been at the Transcendental Club meeting on September 18, 1839, at which it was proposed that a journal "designed as the organ of views more in accordance with the Soul" be started.[3] And Alcott even gave the magazine its title, "The Dial," named after the heading he had given a collection of his thoughts which he had been assembling from his journals over the past few years.[4] Naturally Alcott wished to contribute to the new magazine and in April he read some **"Orphic Sayings"** to Emerson. But Emerson felt they were not very good and told Margaret Fuller, who had been appointed editor of the *Dial,* that Alcott would never "write as well as he talks."[5] A few weeks later Alcott returned with new and revised **"Sayings"** which Emerson found better than he had expected, though still laden with Alcott's "inveterate faults." Nonetheless he believed they would "pass muster & even pass for just & great," and he promised to forward them to Margaret for the *Dial* soon.[6] Yet as May began, Emerson urged their printing for different reasons, for he again said he did not like them, and he predicted that neither Margaret nor George Ripley, the *Dial*'s business manager, would either. But they should be printed, he explained, even with their "cold vague generalities," and with Alcott's name over them, for "if people are properly acquainted with the prophet himself" they would make proper allowances and "the sayings will have a majestical sound."[7] Emerson did not have to repeat this plea, for when Alcott visited Margaret to discuss the **"Sayings"** in May they had a successful meeting.[8] She had read the Sayings earlier and had found them "quite grand," though 'oft-times too grandiloquent." Therefore when Alcott agreed to her "strictures" with "great sweetness," apparently promising to do more revisions, the publication of his **"Sayings"** was assured.[9]

When the first number of the *Dial* appeared in July 1840 with fifty of Alcott's **"Orphic Sayings,"** the public and private reaction to them was both disappointing and upsetting. Although Margaret had felt the **"Sayings"** "read well," and though Emerson had considered them "quite a necessary ingredient" in the *Dial*, Alcott's own statement that they had been "ridiculed by the general Press" was more to the point.[10] At least three reviewers picked this one Saying as showing the dubious heights to which Transcendental folly could climb:

Genesis

The popular genesis is historical. It is written to sense not to the soul. Two principles, diverse and alien, interchange the Godhead and sway the world by turns. God is dual. Spirit is derivative. Identity halts in diversity. Unity is actual merely. The poles of things are not integrated: creation globed and orbed. Yet in the true genesis, nature is globed in the material, souls orbed in the spiritual firmament. Love globes, wisdom orbs, all things. As magnet the steel, so spirit attracts matter, which trembles to traverse the poles of diversity, and rests in the bosom of unity. All genesis is of love. Wisdom is her form; beauty her costume.[11]

Few reviewers treated Alcott as kindly as a correspondent of the *Boston Daily Advertiser* (July 15), who wrote in asking the paper to reprint one of the **"Sayings,"** not being sure whether it would "excite or allay" curiosity about the new *Dial*. The "absurdity of the Dial ectic nonsense" in Alcott's contribution was used by the *Philadelphia Gazette* to attack its political foes in this parody: "All Locofocoism is of desperation. Deceit is her form—disorder her costume."[12] The *Boston Morning Post* (July 14) warned that the "genuine transcendentalism" of the **"Sayings"** would bring a "shower of brick-bats" down upon the *Dial*.

The *Post*'s reviewer was correct: the next month two mostly unfavorable reviews of the *Dial* centered their attacks upon Alcott's contribution. The prestigious *Knickerbocker* said the *Dial* could "scarcely edify the public, or improve American letters," and pointed to the **"Orphic Sayings"** as a prime example of the "*Literary Euphuism*" that the Transcendentalists practiced. In Philadelphia, the *National Gazette and Literary Register* (August 18) mentioned only the **"Sayings"** in its review of the *Dial*. Calling them "neither natural nor intellectual philosophy," the reviewer warned that if the *Dial* could not do better than this, the "utility of its publication was doubtful." The *New World* (August 8) of New York also dismissed Alcott, saying that his meaning was "clear as mud."

With such a negative public reaction it is little wonder that Margaret Fuller declined to publish more of Alcott's **"Sayings"** in the October *Dial*, even though he had offered them to her.[13] The more temperate and favorable reception of the next *Dial* seemed to bear her out. The *Boston Daily Advertiser* (October 16) commented favorably upon the absence of the **"Sayings."** In a generally favorable review, the *Boston Morning Post* (October 12) chided its editorial brethren for their merciless treatment of the July *Dial*, but noted that "the tomahawk and the scalping knife were used with an Indian barbarity" quite "*justly*" upon Alcott's "nonsense." The November *Knickerbocker*, while calling the new *Dial* a "decided improvement" over the last, still felt called upon to attack people who "*think* they think" and printed some "Gastric Sayings" in imitation of Alcott:

The popular cookery is dietetical. . . . Appetite is dual. Satiety is derivative. Simplicity halts in compounds. Mastication is actual merely. The poles of potatoes are integrated; eggs globed and orbed: yet in the true cookery, flour is globed in the material, wine orbed in the transparent. . . . As magnet the steel, so the palate abstracts matter, which trembles to traverse the mouths of diversity, and rest in the bowels of unity.

In November Margaret Fuller, aware that she had hurt Alcott's feelings by omitting him from the October *Dial* and believing that the furor created by the reviews had died down, asked Emerson to approach Alcott for another contribution.[14] As a result Alcott sent fifty more **"Sayings"** to the *Dial* and Margaret had them set in type almost at once.[15]

When the January 1841 *Dial* was published the reviewers had not forgotten Alcott's earlier contribution and they attacked his newest one with the same spirit. The *Boston Morning Post* (January 13) printed three **"Sayings"** in illustrating "the step from the sublime to the ridiculous." The "quintesence of folly and extravagance—affected, mystical, bombastic—and, in some instances, puerile," was the Boston *Evening Mercantile Journal*'s (January 15) description of the *Dial*; Alcott's "unintelligible" **"Sayings"** were quoted as evidence. One bright spot was the *New-Yorker* (January 23), edited by the sympathetic Horace Greeley. It printed some **"Sayings"** and announced that "they need not frighten any body." But the *Knickerbocker* (February), which thought the new *Dial* the best yet, devoted a quarter of its review to attacking Alcott, a "second-hand imitator of a second-hand model [Thomas Carlyle]," who dressed up "meagre thoughts in the 'garb of a mountebank,'" and it printed a parody of the **"Sayings"** called "Putty," beginning, "Ever the true Putty fast-sticketh." Small wonder Alcott warned his father to beware of all the "Dial slanders" which he was sure would be printed.[16]

Individual reactions to the **"Orphic Sayings"** were also unenthusiastic. The comment of Rhoda Newcomb, an aspiring young Providence blue-stocking, that the **"Sayings"** were "full of the highest wisdom" was definitely a minority view.[17] The Reverend William Ellery Channing told Elizabeth Peabody that Alcott's "flights" in the *Dial* "amuse rather than edify me,"[18] and the young Transcendental minister James Freeman Clarke caustically noted that the **"Sayings"** were so typical of Alcott that his name "needed not to have been appended."[19] Lydia Maria Child laughingly described her own inability to "talk common sense" at times as her own "Orphic Sayings."[20] In Buffalo G. W. Hosmer, in whose family house at Concord Alcott now lived, wrote that the ghost of his great-aunt, who was "a spiritualist in her way," might like the **"Sayings,"** but that the spirit of his more conservative great-uncle would call Alcott a "condemned soul."[21] A friend of Caroline Dall, a member of Margaret Fuller's circle, made up some more "Gastric Sayings" which parodied Alcott's "Love globes, wisdom orbs, all things," with: "The frying-pan globes, the griddle orbs all things."[22] George William Curtis said that he practiced the "Orphic, which says: 'Baptize thyself in pure water every morning when thou leavest thy couch,'" but which Curtis more concisely rendered as "Wash betimes."[23]

Even after the initial laughter had died down the memory of Alcott's **"Sayings"** was kept alive. On January 1, 1842, a letter to the *Boston Post* complained that the "Orphic bombast" had rattled down upon the American public like "a train of fifteen railroad cars with one passenger."[24] The *Knickerbocker* made a running joke of the **"Sayings"** for the next four years, especially when it found similar examples of Alcott's "style" like this one in March 1841:

> They all went down the garden to cut cabbages to make an apple-pie. A great she-bear ran through the village. What, no soap? So he died! And she very imprudently married the barber. There were present the Jammaninnies; the Pica-ninnies, the Dooboobies, and the Great Ram Jam Nam himself. With a little round button at the top. They all set to playing catch who can, till the gunpowder ran out of the heels of their boots!

When a Boston silhouette maker's circular contained such phrases as "The Front Face, in the Looking Glass; is not accurately perceivable," the *Knickerbocker* called it "'Orphic' style of advertising . . . in the Transcendental Emporium" (October 1842). In quoting from a French cookbook, the reviewer subjoined "a few 'Orphic Sayings' of the kitchen" (July 1844). The most cruel parody took place when the *Knickerbocker* compared Alcott's work to the composition of an eighth-grader at the New York Asylum for Deaf Mutes, which contained such passages as

> I stood near the water. I undressed my feet. . . . I looked at large water came. . . . The large water floated fast. I afraid. . . . I seen at the hog ate grass. The hog seen at me. I went on the ground. I ran. . . . The hog ran under the fence and got his head under the fence and want to ran out the fence! I caught ears its hog. . . . I rided on the hog ran and jumped fast. The hog ran fell on near the water. I rided off a hog.
>
> (June 1844)

Other magazines joined in the fun. One "Moonshine Milky-water" of "SUNDIAL AVENUE" supposedly wrote this letter—in unacknowledged but obvious imitation of Alcott—to the committee planning a dinner for the visiting Charles Dickens in 1842 and *Brother Jonathan* published it on March 26:

> *Gentlemen of the Committee:*
>
> The wonder-sign of Great Goslington's furibundity is world-absorbing. Quozdom yawns abysmal. Lionized humanity, ephemeral though, floats upon the time-stream of newspapers, and peradventure may avoid fuliginous obliviscity. . . . Penny-trumpetism is orbed:—small-talkism is cubed:—in the abyss of Quozdom ingulfed are both—re-nascent nevertheless. A dinner is, and it is not.
>
> Savory, committee-gentlemen, is the order of fried smelts, pork-fat in potatoism pan-borne, harmoniously liquidating. But wherefore fried? Are not gridirons extant in perenniel parallelism?

In a review of "Carlyle's Miscellanies" in February 1843 the *Magnolia* asked: "what mortal man (except the compositor) ever read the **'Orphic Sayings'** of Alcott." In that same month the *Boston Post,* wishing to fill up space with a series of apothegms, prefaced them with "Sayings not Orphic by people not Transcendentalists" (February 14). As late as April 1844 the *North American Review* complained, in a review of James Russell Lowell's *Poems,* of the **"Orphic Sayings,"** those "most unmeaning and witless effusions—we cannot say of the brain, for the smallest modicum of brains would have rendered their appearance an impossibility,—but of mere intellectual inanity." To Alcott, who genuinely believed his **"Sayings"** to be wise and farsighted, this reception was a great blow, even though he continued to produce and believe in similar works.[25]

In the late 1850's, when Alcott made out "an inventory of his spiritual real estate," one of its five items was the twelfth **"Orphic Saying"** from the July *Dial*.[26] This **"Saying,"** "Greater is he, who is above temptation, than he, who, being tempted, overcomes," was also on the masthead of the first number of the English reform journal, the *Healthian* (January 1842). Three years later Alcott received an "elaborately bound volume" from a "famous German Philosopher"; on the cover was imprinted a bust of Alcott and, "in letters of gold," one of the **"Sayings."**[27] Another favorable reaction to the **"Sayings"** was registered by William T. Harris, later editor of the *Journal of Speculative Philosophy* and influential in the Concord School of Philosophy, who felt that the **"Orphic Sayings"** had "aroused that there was in me of the speculative power."[28] Later audiences, though, were not always as appreciative. In 1866 Alcott read more **"Sayings"** to the St. Louis Philosophical Society and at least one onlooker felt that even Alcott suspected "his oracles were made to contradict themselves by some Hegelian process which he did not understand." When pressed for more concrete explanations, Alcott replied: "It requires a Christ to interpret a Christ." The meeting was then adjourned, "among little tidbits of tee-hees," by the pronouncement that Alcott's "hidden meaning" was that "only an Alcott can rightly interpret an Alcott."[29] The net result of all this was the placing of Alcott and his **"Orphic Sayings"** in a permanent place among the more ludicrous aspects of American Transcendentalism. Thus, when Henry A. Beers visited Concord in 1905 and asked an innkeeper about Alcott, he received this answer: "Oh, Alcott! The best thing he ever did was his daughters."[30]

Notes

1. *Transcendentalism in New England* (New York, 1876), p. 133; *Studies in New England Transcendentalism* (New York, 1908), p. 115.

2. A more complete account of Alcott's relations with the *Dial* will be found in George Willis Cooke, *An Historical and Biographical Introduction to Accompany THE DIAL* (Cleveland, 1902) and the present author's "A History of the *Dial* (1840-1844)," Ph.D. dissertation, Northwestern University, 1971.

3. September 18, Alcott, "Diary July-December 1839," p. 249, Houghton Library, Harvard University; this and other manuscripts at the Houghton Library are used by permission of the Harvard College Library.

4. February, Alcott, "Scripture for 1840," p. 47, Houghton Library, Harvard University.

5. April 8, 1840, *The Letters of Ralph Waldo Emerson,* ed. Ralph L. Rusk (New York, 1939), II, 276; hereafter cited as *EmL.*

6. April 24, 1840, *EmL,* II, 291-292.

7. Letter to Margaret Fuller, May 8, 1840, *EmL,* II, 294.

8. May, Alcott, "Scripture for 1840," p. 80.

9. Margaret Fuller to Emerson, May 31, 1840, *EmL,* II, 297n.

10. Letter to Emerson, July 5, 1840, Thomas Wentworth Higginson, *Margaret Fuller Ossoli* (Boston, 1884), p. 155; letter to Margaret Fuller, July 2, 1840, *EmL,* II, 311; Alcott, "Autobiographical Index," Houghton Library, Harvard University.

11. Alcott's cause was not helped any by the *Dial*'s omission of the bracketed word in the following sentence: "The poles of things are not integrated: creation [not] globed and orbed" (Alcott's correction, "Scripture for 1840," p. 109).

12. N.d., pasted in Alcott, "Scripture for 1840," p. 110.

13. By the end of July Alcott was preparing about fifty of his Sayings for the *Dial* and in August he transcribed them for submission. Apparently when he saw Margaret Fuller in the middle of the month she rejected his offer of help. Upset, Alcott lamented that there was "no place for him" in the *Dial* and he unsuccessfully tried to get the English *Monthly Magazine* to publish his Sayings (Emerson to Margaret Fuller, July 21, 1840, *EmL,* II, 316; August, Alcott, "Scripture for 1840," p. 132; Emerson to Margaret Fuller, August 16, 1840, *EmL,* II, 324; September 23, 1840, Theodore Parker, "Journal," I, 467, Unitarian Universalist Association, Boston).

14. November 7, 1840, *EmL,* II, 354n.

15. November, Alcott, "Scripture for 1840," p. 200; Margaret Fuller to Emerson, December 6, 1840, *EmL,* II, 362n.

16. In a supreme show of egotism Alcott described his critics so: "A fool may laugh at a sage, but takes nothing from his stature in wisdom, but adds much to his own weight of folly" (January 27, 1841, Houghton Library, Harvard University).

17. Letter to C. K. Newcomb, July 6, 1840, Brown University; used with permission of the Brown University Library.

18. He did not "care much for Orpheus in the 'Dial' . . . but Orpheus at the plough" was after his own heart. Miss Peabody showed the letter to Alcott, who copied it into his journal without comment (September 1840, *Reminiscences of Rev. Wm. Ellergy Channing* [Boston, 1880], p. 414; Alcott, "Scripture for 1840," pp. 141-142).

19. Letter to Sarah Clarke, July 8, 1840, Houghton Library, Harvard University.

20. Letter to Augusta King, October 21, 1840, *Letters of Lydia Maria Child,* ed. Harriet Winslow Sewall (Boston, 1883), p. 38.

21. September 2, 1840, *Memorial of George Washington Hosmer,* ed. J. K. Hosmer (n.p., 1882), pp. 85-86.

22. Dall, *Transcendentalism in New England* (Boston, 1897), p. 30.

23. May 10, 1844, *Early Letters of George Wm. Curtis to John S. Dwight: Brook Farm and Concord,* ed. George Willis Cooke (New York, 1898), p. 185.

24. Emerson felt that though this was a "rude joke" it unhappily expressed "the feeling of most readers" (March 1842, *The Journals and Miscellaneous Notebooks of Ralph Waldo Emerson,* ed. William H. Gilman *et al.* [Cambridge, Mass., 1960-], VIII, 211).

25. During these same years Alcott produced "Orphic" or "Pythagorean" Sayings for the Providence *Plain Speaker* (May, December 1841), the *Boston Quarterly Review* (October 1841), the *Healthian* (September 1842), and the *Present* (December 15, 1843; January 15, 1844).

26. F. B. Sanborn and William T. Harris, *A. Bronson Alcott: His Life and Philosophy* (Boston, 1893), II, 553.

27. Frederick L. H. Willis, *Alcott Memoirs* (Boston, 1915), p. 51.

28. Sanborn and Harris, *Alcott,* II, 551.

29. Denton J. Snider, *A Writer of Books* (St. Louis, [1910]), pp. 335-337.

30. Beers, *Four Americans: Roosevelt, Hawthorne, Emerson, Whitman* (New Haven, Conn., 1920), p. 75.

Lewis Perry (essay date 1973)

SOURCE: Perry, Lewis. "Nonresistant Anarchism and Antislavery." In *Radical Abolitionism: Anarchy and the Government of God in Antislavery Thought,* pp. 55-91. Ithaca, N.Y.: Cornell University Press, 1973.

[*In the following excerpt, Perry examines Alcott's role in the abolitionist movement of the 1830s and 1840s. Perry traces the evolution of Alcott's attitude toward the antislavery cause, from his early collaboration with William Lloyd Garrison to his eventual break with the* movement. *According to Perry, Alcott became particularly critical of the bellicose nature of Garrison's methods, as well as of his single-minded concern with political rather than spiritual or moral issues.*]

IV

One of the clearest-thinking nonresistants was Bronson Alcott, who is usually thought of in other connections, such as in his role as a controversial educational reformer or as a transcendentalist consociate of Emerson and Thoreau.[1] Alcott was an active Garrisonian reformer, having been one of his earliest converts to abolitionism. In November 1830 he and Garrison, with four others, formed what he later called the "preliminary Anti-Slavery Society."[2] His acquaintance with greater writers did not diminish even the literary dimensions of his respect for Garrison; thus he once wrote his brother-in-law, Samuel Joseph May, that he had been moved to weeping while reading five of Garrison's sonnets.[3] As a reformer Alcott was especially inspired by the nonresistance movement, and he participated vigorously in virtually every convention. Close examination of Alcott's point of view clarifies further the origins and the theoretical problems of nonresistance.

In the first place, Alcott was a transcendentalist. In tracing the origins of the New England Non-Resistance Society, we have discussed developments in the benevolence societies and in evangelical Protestantism. It might be asked whether transcendentalism has been overlooked. In fact Alcott was the only well-known transcendentalist to join the new movement. Nonresistance flourished in Boston and elsewhere in New England, but not in Concord. Although Emerson took note of the Garrisonians in lectures and essays, neither he nor Thoreau was prompted by theory or temperament to join a reform association. Not even antislavery gained much of Emerson's attention; the idea of the government of God was associated with a fatalistic attitude in Emersonism as surely as with militancy in Garrisonism. Emerson confessed in his journal that sometimes he berated himself for not giving greater support to abolitionism: "But then, in hours of sanity, I recover myself, and say, 'God must govern his own world, and knows his way out of this pit, without my desertion of my post, which has none to guard it but me. I have quite other slaves to free than those negroes, to wit, imprisoned spirits, imprisoned thoughts, far back in the brain of man.'" Nor do the nonresistants appear to have been influenced by Emerson. Nonresistance was not justified, as it might have been, in terms of such Emersonian notions as the sacredness of the private man or the permanency of laws reflected in human consciousness. Nonresistance stayed close to the sovereignty of God, and to Emerson the Garrisonians were simply "the continuation of Puritanism."[4]

Alcott, though a transcendentalist, was an important figure in the Non-Resistance Society and helped in such tasks as the revision of the Declaration of Sentiments and the planning of conventions.[5] His excitement concerning the new movement was virtually unrestrained. "I regard Non-Resistance as the germ of the New Church," he wrote in his diary. "This doctrine is destined to work deeper than any other now proposed to the consideration of the people." On one hand, nonresistance reasserted "the primitive doctrine of the Cross"; on the other, it heralded new types of organization, both secular and religious, which would not trample on the human soul. "It is an Assertion of the right of Selfgovernment, and of private judgement, in which both Church and State take root."[6] His enthusiasm was most clearly revealed in a letter written to his brother after attending the 1841 nonresistance convention. He prophesied that "all things are doomed." The world of sin and error was about to be cleansed, and reformers were gathering who would "restore the worship of the True and loving God in the Hearts of men." He chose to join in the work.[7]

In Alcott's case, transcendentalist beliefs were not irrelevant to nonresistance. When other nonresistants spoke of the inconsistency between divine and human government, they tended to depict God as a distant, supernatural sovereign. Alcott identified the operation of divine government more nearly with unwritten laws of conscience knowable to the private man. From this point of view he called the democratic theory of government diabolical because it valued the decisions of masses of men over the will of God which may be discovered in "the seclusion of a single soul." "Beelzebub rules the masses," he wrote, "God individuals. The Kingdom of Truth is within, not out there in Church or State."[8]

Alcott had mastered the paradoxes of nonresistance in which divine government, self-government, and self-control became interchangeable. If he revealed a distinctive, transcendentalist understanding of the natural conscience, he also obeyed his heavenly sovereign. At one time, for example, he grew impatient with the nonresistants' discussion of whether force was sinful in circumstances of great danger. "Whoever, says Christ, is not ready to give up father and mother, wife and children, brothers and sisters, *yea, even his own life,* cannot be my disciple. Yet we make it a question!" This concern to be uncompromisingly submissive to the Almighty, however, implied an antinomian freedom on earth. Alcott went on: "I look upon the Non-Resistance Society as an assertion of the right of self-government. Why should I employ a church to write my creed or a state to govern me? Why not write my own creed? Why not govern myself?" Then follows the paradox: the nonresistant who should enjoy such freedom is the man "who has overcome himself."[9]

One of the most enthusiastic and talkative participants in the new movement, Alcott was also very critical of his fellow nonresistants. To some extent his criticisms

were derived from his transcendentalist emphasis on the private man; nevertheless, they may help to clarify the ambiguities in the movement. In brief, he found the nonresistants too combative, too political, and too narrow in their conception of their goals.

As early as September 1839, Alcott began to show misgivings about the combativeness of the movement. He recorded in his diary doubts that the people at the nonresistance meetings could be the source of better institutions because they lacked "faith in meekness: they assume a warlike manner."[10] At the 1841 meetings he warned nonresistants against "vocabulary . . . taken from the camp." How seriously others took this warning may be guessed from the fact that, a few minutes later, Garrison was saying: "I believe in 'fighting the good fight of faith'; and I like the expression well." Alcott was arguing for a philosophy of reform in which the general behavior of reformers was their most important means of converting others, while Garrison spoke simply to the point that "the philosophy of all reform is commotion—agitation."[11] In time Alcott arrived at a perceptive, though rather bitter, analysis of Garrison's fighting spirit:

> It is much to have a platform as free as the minds of the freest of the time; and this service Garrison has done for us moderns. But Garrison himself, I now discern, is far from catholicism and the comprehension of the whole truth. He does not see it. The most intolerant of men, as trenchant as an Ajax, he has not yet won those self-victories which lead to the discovery of the unconquered territory of the enemy, and so of the superior powers of t hose who have won themselves and are the willing subjects of self-rule.

> He snuffs the prey like a vulture, nor will he rest till his beak and talons are fast in the eagle's breast and the lion has seen him torn in pieces. He has perfect skill in the use of his own weapons, nor has he ever lost a battle. He cannot give quarter even, and is as unrelenting to friends as enemies. Mercy is no attribute of his justice. He knows all the manners of the snake, and, were he self-freed, might crush his head; but, as it is, will only scotch the hydra and play with his tail.[12]

Besides finding nonresistance too combative, Alcott criticized its concern with politics. He told the first anniversary convention that he wished "governments occupied less of our thoughts." Something was amiss, he felt, in the constant debates about the evils of governments. They would be ended "whether we make it an object or not," and did not deserve much attention: "Our only reliance is in the Theocracy in the human soul. We take too much notice of states and masses, if we think them more mighty than individuals." Even the manner of the nonresistants betrayed touches of politics, that is, they declaimed at one another rather than conversing freely and spontaneously.[13]

Nonresistance appeared too political in the way in which it thought of "*influence.*" In Alcott's view, the movement did not need to be concerned with the number of its adherents or their position in society. Men are most deeply impressed, he said, not by those with power, prestige, or followers, but instead by those who, like Jesus, "speak and act most simply and heartily." Reform ought to be conducted as the revival of true, simple ideas: "I believe we might get statements so clear and true, that there would no argument be needed about them." Reform, in other words, was a matter of appealing properly to the conscience, of reawakening moral sentiments. It was not a matter of mass action or political power. "Speak to the feelings and instincts," he said, "and that will be sufficient."[14] He thus urged the simplification of their methods.

Alcott's third general criticism was that their goals were too narrowly conceived. For one thing, the society's name, with its stress on nonviolence, limited its scope. There was a broad movement in the land against the authority of church and state, and it should have been allowed time to clarify itself before being confined by a name. What was sought was not nonviolence, but "an entire revision of Society."[15] Moreover, the concerns of nonresistance should have extended beyond church and state; a principal concern should have been the family. "The family is the church—the family is the state—is the school." Nonresistants should attempt to govern all of their own domestic relationships with love and meekness and then try to extend the same spirit throughout society.[16] To put it another way, he thought the society should be directed toward sentimental rather than political reform.

Alcott was best known as an educational reformer. While he felt nonresistance was too narrowly conceived, an interest in education was actually a repeated theme among nonresistants.[17] Furthermore, Alcott's belief in vicarious punishment, in which the teacher insisted that he be punished for a pupil's misbehavior, bore some resemblance to nonresistance, or the refusal to inflict punishment.[18]

Behind all of Alcott's criticisms was his desire for comprehensive, universal reform. Garrisonian nonresistance was a secular reform to be fought for with military zeal and with tactics that might be termed political. The Garrisonians often spoke of nonresistance as the fundamental principal of all reform, but they kept it as a separate reform and usually advocated a piecemeal approach to the renovation of social relations. None of this satisfied Alcott. If Alcott was clearer and more consistent than some other nonresistants and if his criticisms were frequently on target, it was in part because his interest in secular reforms, such as the abolition of slavery, took second place to his aspiration for a complete overhaul of society. His search for a broader approach to reform led him to believe that opposition to property was more important than either antislavery or nonresistance and that Garrison's cause would for a time be "lost" behind that of the transcendentalist labor

reformer, Orestes Brownson (who soon became a leading convert to Roman Catholicism).[19] Alcott's search took him briefly in 1843 to a utopian attempt to found the community known as Fruitlands. He moved away from the Garrisonians, though there is no reason to believe he was ever anything but a nonresistant. As such, he was capable of clear gestures. In 1843 he refused to pay taxes to the government and finally went to jail. One of his associates explained to the *Liberator* that, while everyone agreed it was wrong to establish a religion by force, no one previously had dared to act on the principle that it was wrong to compel support of a government. The communication was aptly captioned, "State Slavery."[20] Henry David Thoreau, who was not a nonresistant, was nonetheless familiar with this precedent when he spent his celebrated night in jail.[21]

Notes

1. There is no fully adequate study of Alcott. Odell Shepard's *Pedlar's Progress: The Life of Bronson Alcott* (Boston, 1937) was meant to be supplemented with Shepard, ed., *Journals* [(Boston, 1938)]. Also helpful is F. B. Sanborn and William T. Harris, *A Bronson Alcott: His Life and Philosophy,* 2 vols. (New York, 1965; 1st pub. 1893).

2. Shepard, ed., *Journals,* p. 26.

3. Garrisons, *Garrison* [Wendell Phillip and Francis Jackson Garrison, *William Lloyd Garrison: The Story of His Life, Told by His Children,* 4 vols. (New York: The Century Company, 1885)], II, 99.

4. Quoted in Stephen E. Whicher, ed., *Selections from Ralph Waldo Emerson* (Boston, 1957), pp. 355, 186. On Emerson and reform, see Whicher, *Freedom and Fate: An Inner Life of Ralph Waldo Emerson* (New York, 1961); and Maurice Gonnaud, *Individu et société dans l'oeuvre de Ralph Waldo Emerson. Essai de biographie spirituelle* (Paris, 1964).

5. See Garrison to Samuel Joseph May, Sept. 24, 1838, Garrison Papers, Boston Public Library; Edmund Quincy to Alcott, Jan. 4, 1842, Alcott Papers, Harvard College Library.

6. Alcott, Diary, XIII, 180, Aug. 28, 1839, Alcott Papers, Harvard College Library.

7. Richard L. Herrnstadt, ed., *The Letters of A. Bronson Alcott* (Ames, Ia., 1969), p. 57.

8. Shepard, ed., *Journals,* p. 136.

9. *Non-Resistant,* Oct. 19, 1839, p. 4.

10. Alcott, Diary, XIII, 262, Sept. 27, 1839, Alcott Papers, Harvard College Library.

11. *Non-Resistant,* Nov. 19, 1841, p. 4.

12. Shepard, ed., *Journals,* p. 191, by permission of Little, Brown and Co. Copyright 1938, by Odell

Shepard. Copyright renewed © 1966 by Odell Shepard. The entry is for Feb. 1847.

13. *Non-Resistant,* Nov. 19, 1841, p. 4.

14. *Ibid.,* Nov. 16, 1839, p. 3.

15. Alcott, Diary, XIII, 263, Sept. 27, 1839, Alcott Papers, Harvard College Library.

16. *Liberator,* Nov. 19, 1841, p. 4.

17. A Michigan delegate to the 1841 convention described a school of sixty or seventy pupils in a newly settled area run on nonresistance principles (*Liberator,* Nov. 19, 1841, p. 4). Rowland Robinson, a prominent nonresistant whose son later achieved fame as a Vermont writer, began a similar venture. Oliver Johnson described Robinson's school after Alcott had explained that children's instincts are less perverted than those of adults (*Non-Resistant,* Nov. 16, 1839, p. 3). Maria Weston Chapman illustrated the truth of nonresistance from her long experience as a teacher: "The school that is managed by coercion—by force—is, in the most important respects, ungoverned" (*ibid.,* Sept. 21, 1839, p. 3). The founding convention (*ibid.,* Jan. 1839, p. 3) criticized the warlike toys and books given to children as "among the most effectual means of laying the foundation of slavery, anarchy, bloodshed and ruin." No nonresistant was more interested in education than Henry Wright, who called his two years of service as a children's minister the happiest and most useful in his lifetime (see Mary Howitt, "Memoir of Henry Clarke Wright," *Howitt's Journal,* II [1847], 133).

18. Edmund Quincy distinguished nonresistance from armed resistance: both fight evil, but "the one believes that the evil which is in the world, is to be overcome by the infliction of suffering or death upon the evil-doer; the other, by the voluntary endurance of suffering or death themselves in his stead" (*Non-Resistant,* Nov. 16, 1839, p. 3).

19. Herrnstadt, ed., *Letters,* p. 53.

20. *Liberator,* Jan. 27, 1843, p. 4.

21. See John C. Broderick, "Thoreau, Alcott, and the Poll Tax," *Studies in Philology,* LIII (1956), 612-626.

Catherine Albanese (essay date September 1975)

SOURCE: Albanese, Catherine. "The Kinetic Revolution: Transformation in the Language of the Transcendentalists." *New England Quarterly* 48, no. 3 (September 1975): 319-40.

[In the following excerpt, Albanese discusses Alcott's interest in using birth and creation as metaphors and analyzes how these images helped shape his philosophy.]

Bronson Alcott, in his turn, was a man in love with the symbolism of birth. There was the intriguing passage in his *Journal*:

> Fluids form solids. Mettle [sperm] is the Godhead proceeding into the matrix of nature to organize Man. Behold the creative jet! And hear the morning stars sing for joy at the sacred generation of the Gods![1]

And there was his custom of sending birthday letters to his daughters as well as Christmas letters to remind them of the birth of Jesus. In *Conversations on the Gospels,* birth emerged as an important theme. Like the rose seed, Alcott told his young students, "so the seed of a human being is placed in the midst of matter which nourishes it, and it grows and becomes perfected." "Where is the Life that causes a seed to spring out and seek the light?" he asked. The answer lay with the spirit which "makes the body just as the rose throws out the rose leaves."[2]

For Alcott, a contemplation of birth should lead to a disclosure of the nature of spirit; and, based on this perception, it would be the task of education to lead forth the spirit implicit in the child and existing still in much of its original state of innocence. Education thus was an active and moving endeavor, a far cry from the humdrum of the recitation system of the Boston Latin School and Harvard University. Alcott explained his notion of education in **"The Doctrine and Discipline of Human Culture"** (1836). Significantly, the title page bore the quotation of Jesus: "The wind bloweth where it listeth, and ye hear the sound thereof; but ye cannot tell whence it cometh nor whither it goeth; so is everyone that is born of the Spirit."[3]

But the symbol of birth was only one example of Alcott's concern for movement and life in the realm of education. Another favorite was spiritual culture, and in Alcott's mind this abstraction was decidedly kinetic. For Alcott, spiritual culture "lifts the body from the drowsy couch; opens the eyes upon the rising sun; tempts it forth to breathe the invigorating air; plunges it into the purifying bath, and thus whets all its functions for the duties of the coming day."[4] The movement corresponded to the activity of all creation, since "not only the whole universe is in motion, but every thing is in a state of change within it."[5]

Alcott interwove traditional gospel symbols with natural symbols of flux and flow in a view of the world which shared Emerson's basic perceptions. Matter was "like a great sea" moved by the living spirit which pervaded it.[6] "Do you think God flowed through all the forefathers of Jesus down to Joseph," Alcott asked his pupils. "Do you think his spirit flowed on through your ancestors and down to you?"[7] He told of a man in Boston whose spirit could "be made to flow out through his fingers, and make the sick person well."[8] Another time, he recalled for them the effect the sight of the ocean had produced in him when he first saw it at the age of twelve,[9] and again he painted the joy of country life where there were "living springs" from which water sprang up and was never dry. Water meant "Spirit pure and unspoiled," he told them, and asked, "Have you a living Spring?" "The waters become impure by standing still—by your not trying."[10]

Another part of the changing universe which Alcott often noted was light. Religious light was moving light, and in *The Dial* he wrote that the "prophet, whose eye is coincident with the celestial ray, receives this into his breast, and intensifying there, it kindles on his brow a serene and perpetual day."[11] In another offering he pictured inspiration which "darts like lightning, straight to its quarry, and rends all formulas of the schools as it illuminates the firmament of the mind."[12] Again, the soul was a Prometheus who received the divine fires and fashioned them into a man who was image of God and model for all other natural forms.[13] The child was gentle (and sacred) because "there, for a little while, fed by divine fires, the serene flame glows."[14]

Notes

1. [Amos Bronson] Alcott, *Journals* (March 31, 1839), [quoted in Odell Shepard, *Pedlar's Progress: The Life of Bronson Alcott* (Boston, 1937),] 121.

2. Amos Bronson Alcott, *Conversations with Children on the Gospels* (Boston, 1836-1837), I, 132; II, 15; I, 233.

3. John 3:8, as quoted on the title page of Amos Bronson Alcott, *The Doctrine and Discipline of Human Culture* (Boston, 1836).

4. Alcott, *The Doctrine and Discipline of Human Culture,* 22.

5. Alcott, *Conversations with Children on the Gospels,* I, 135.

6. Alcott, *Conversations . . . ,* II, 27.

7. Alcott, *Conversations . . . ,* I, 137.

8. Alcott, *Conversations . . . ,* II, 176.

9. Alcott, *Conversations . . . ,* I, 229.

10. Alcott, *Conversations . . . ,* II, 72-77.

11. Amos Bronson Alcott, "Orphic Sayings," *The Dial,* I, 357 (Jan., 1841).

12. Amos Bronson Alcott, "Days from a Diary," *The Dial,* II, 416 (April, 1842).

13. Alcott, "Orphic Sayings," *The Dial,* I, 97 (July, 1840).

14. Alcott, "Orphic Sayings," *The Dial,* I, 359.

Fordyce Richard Bennett (essay date spring 1978)

SOURCE: Bennett, Fordyce Richard. "A Note on Alcott and Analogy." *American Transcendental Quarterly,* no. 38 (spring 1978): 151-52.

[*In the following essay, Bennett examines Alcott's earliest written expressions of Transcendental ideas.*]

Bronson Alcott's essay, **"On the Nature and Means of Early Intellectual Education, as Deduced from Experience"** (1833), lying between the earlier **"Observations of the Principles and Methods of Infant Instruction"** (1830) and the later **"Doctrine and Discipline of Human Culture"** (1836) and forming a transition between Alcott's earlier Pestalozzian and Lockean tendencies and his later Transcendentalism, reveals, according to the traditional interpretation, "Alcott's impressive intellectual growth between his departure from Boston in 1830 and his return in 1834" and the "shedding of some Lockean preconceptions during the early 1830's."[1] Nevertheless, it has never been shown how the 1833 essay indicates Alcott's growth toward Transcendentalism.

"Interested this month," Alcott wrote in his diaries for January, 1832,

> in reading and reflecting on the nature of man. The special topic of thought was *Analogy* as the prototype—the object of all psychological operations—the renovating power of humanity, . . . There is an instructive and intuitive depth which the light of general intellect as reflected from faith, has not as yet pierced. It is the "Spirit Land" of the soul. . . . Analogy is the key which unlocks the inward gates and reveals the mystic field of life and light.[2]

The diary distinguishes the mystic light associated with analogy from "the light of general intellect" and the 1833 essay suggests separation between the dim light surrounding the shadowy, material forms of sense and the spiritual light permeating the realm of ideality. The effects of analogy are at once moral and intellectual: its operation purifies the soul in addition to guaranteeing intuitive and certain knowledge. For those who, in Alcott's words from the 1833 essay,

> have preserved their beings, in mature life, a faithful mirror of outward analogy. Their minds are pure and undefiled. Truth flows through them as from a sweet and lucid fountain.[3]

Such passages indicate the individual's direct relation to what Emerson would later term the Oversoul.

To supplement his use of analogy, Alcott introduces his metaphor of the soul as mirror and he repeats it in the last installment of his **"Principles and Methods of Intellectual Instruction Exhibited in the Exercises of**

Young Children." Alcott rejects the *tabula rasa* metaphor of Locke, in the May 1833 section of the latter essay, substituting his own of the soul as mirror, as a receptacle of ideas and a source for intuitions of correspondences and analogies:

> Education, rightly regarded, is not only an influence by which ideas are imparted, but an agency which calls them forth, in clear and palpable forms, from the sentient mind. It is a process of *expression* as well of *impression*. Its office consists, not in shedding light upon an opaque substance, but on the transparent mirror of the soul, whose surface reflects the images cast upon it, in their true proportions.[4]

Alcott handily compresses two central Transcendental tenets into the 1833 essay by his use of the analogy concept and the mirror metaphor—microcosm and correspondence—thereby anticipating the concept of reason as defined by Carlyle and Coleridge, a concept later embraced by Emerson, and "shedding some Lockean preconceptions."

Notes

1. John C. Broderick, "Emerson, Alcott, and the American Institution of Instruction," *Emerson Society Quarterly,* No. 13 (1958), 27.

2. Bronson Alcott, *Journal for 1832-3,* VI, 1-2. Material from the unpublished diaries is used by permission of the Houghton Library, Harvard University.

3. Bronson Alcott, "On the Nature and Means of Early Intellectual Education, as Deduced from Experience" in *The Transcendentalists and Minerva. Cultural Backgrounds of the American Renaissance with Fresh Discoveries in the Intellectual Climate of Emerson, Alcott, and Thoreau,* ed. Kenneth Walter Cameron (Hartford: Transcendental Books, 1958), II, 443.

4. Bronson Alcott, "Principles and Methods of Intellectual Instruction Exhibited in the Exercises of Young Children," *Annals of Education,* III (May, 1833), 219.

Robert D. Richardson, Jr. (essay date 1978)

SOURCE: Richardson, Robert D., Jr. "Parker and Alcott: The Affirmation of Myth: Bronson Alcott and the Orphic Mode." In *Myth and Literature in the American Renaissance,* pp. 48-64. Bloomington: Indiana University Press, 1978.

[*In the following essay, Richardson examines Alcott's efforts to invent a modern myth of the spirit, both in his conversations and in his writings. According to Richardson, Alcott's wholehearted espousal of the mythic form represents the purest "American affirmation of myth" of the Transcendental era.*]

Modern acceptance of myth as an authentic form of imaginative truth arose as part of the reaction against the Enlightenment's skeptical rejection of myth as superstition. Indeed, the affirmation of myth is a hallmark of romanticism; the revaluation of myth is just one result of the romantic emphasis on the integrity of what the imagination seizes upon as true. In another way, the resurgence during the early nineteenth century of a new, broader and more philosophical Christianity created a climate favorable to the reassessment of myth as the religious expression of other peoples and times. Though the impulse to accept myth as somehow true is present, at least fitfully in America in a Barlow or a Freneau, it remained for the Transcendentalists to work out a thoroughgoing acceptance of myth and to carry that acceptance over importantly into their writing. Though its roots reach back well into the eighteenth century, it is only from about 1820 on that the various elements making up the characteristic American affirmation of myth begin clearly to emerge and it is only from about 1835 on that these elements creatively coalesce into literary achievement.

Sometime between 1819 and 1824 Emerson read both Lowth and Blackwell, two of the eighteenth-century writers from whom so much of the nineteenth-century revaluation of myth—both skeptical and affirmative—seems to spring. In 1825 appeared a French translation of Friedrich Creuzer's *Symbolik und Mythologie der alten Völker* (1810), an epoch-making work of German classical scholarship which impressively argues that myths were an essentially symbolic—*not* allegorical—mode in which ancient Eastern wisdom had expressed itself.[1] Creuzer's views spread widely in England and America after the French edition (incredibly there never has been an English translation) and may be traced to Emerson through several channels. Edward Everett's lectures, which began in 1820 and which Emerson heard, were laced with references to Creuzer; Degerando's *Histoire comparée des systèmes de philosophie* (2d ed., Paris, 1822-23), which Emerson studied carefully beginning in 1830, is full of Creuzer; and Creuzer's ideas also appear in G. Oegger's *The True Messiah* (published 1842), which had been partially translated earlier (by Elizabeth Peabody), and used in manuscript by Emerson around 1835.[2] Creuzer's views were taken up also by Francis Lieber, and the articles on mythology in the *Encyclopedia Americana* (1829-33) are openly Creuzerian. Finally, Charles Anthon inserted Creuzer's interpretations into the various editions of Lempriere's *Classical Dictionary,* which he (Anthon) began editing in 1825 and finally put his own name to in 1841.

K. O. Müller's *Introduction to a Scientific System of Mythology* also appeared in German in 1825 (English translation, 1844). From this book and from the same author's study of *The Dorians* (translated into English in 1830) came another view of myth, opposed in part to Creuzer but also essentially affirmative to myth itself. Müller, the most eminent classicist of his time, agreed that myths were essentially symbolic representations, but he insisted that Greek myths revealed not transplanted Asian wisdom but the earliest era of Greek history.[3] Müller's ideas strongly marked the writings and conversations of Elizabeth Peabody. Her textbooks on Greek history from 1833 on treat myth seriously as the earliest record of the Greek mind. One of her conversation "classes" went so deeply into the problem that one of the ladies did a translation of another of Müller's books for the occasion. Elizabeth Peabody's own later essay "The Dorian Measure" (1849) links Greek myth to Greek religion and education.[4] For Emerson, who first read Müller's *The Dorians* in 1831, or indeed for anyone in the 1830s, Müller was the preeminent authority on early Greek history. Müller held Greek myths to be imaginative accounts of that history; he considered the myths to be the key to the Greek mind, and rigorous philological analysis the key to myth. From about 1825 on, then, Creuzer's work lent new weight to the effort to understand myth as symbolic form, while Müller's work gave myth research pride of place in investigations into early Greek history.

By 1826 Emerson was reading Thomas Taylor's translation of Plato, with its startling reinterpretation of Greek mythological thought as a symbolic representation of the "perennial philosophy" (which Taylor said originated with Orpheus) that assumes the primacy of mind and sees nature as a system of appearances or images in which a metaphysical order is reflected. In 1829 Coleridge's *Aids to Reflection* was published in New England by James Marsh. The book quickly became important to Emerson and others because of its opposition to Locke and its persuasive call for a philosophy that would be religious and a religion that would be philosophical. Also in 1829, at Andover Theological Seminary, Calvin Stowe reannotated the translation of Lowth's *Lectures on the Sacred Poetry of the Hebrews*. By 1833 Alcott was discovering Taylor's Plato, James Marsh was bringing out his English translation of Herder's *Spirit of Hebrew Poetry* in Vermont, Margaret Fuller was reading and translating some of Goethe's modern poetic reinterpretations of such Greek myths as that of Prometheus, and Elizabeth Peabody was writing textbooks that treat Greek myth sympathetically as Greek religion. It is a far cry from the old charge of "heathen idolatry" and shows how far the new affirmative spirit had penetrated when Miss Peabody could say, in a book intended for children, "The Religion of the Greeks is strikingly different from any other which has been seen on earth. The principle of fear seems hardly recognizable in any of its earlier expressions, whether we consider the festivals and other religious rites, or the earliest records of it in the Homeric poems, which are the most joyous strains that the human mind has ever sent forth toward the Superior Powers."[5]

By the mid thirties, then, the materials for a new view of myth were at hand in New England. The ideas of Lowth, Blackwell, Herder, Taylor, Creuzer, Müller, and Goethe were in the air. Emerson's reading in Oriental myth, going back to Edward Everett's Creuzerian insistence that everything comes from the mysterious East, and becoming especially strong after 1837, together with the impact from 1841 on of Carlyle's brilliant interpretation of Nordic myth, added other important bodies of myth to the ferment of mythic ideas. These began to yield literary results as early as 1835, when Alcott began work on his *Psyche,* a modern myth of the Soul, and 1836, when Emerson's lectures on the philosophy of history began to urge that myth is the truest history. It is a great irony that during this same year, 1836, Theodore Parker was beginning work on his translation of De Wette, whose purpose, diametrically opposite to Emerson's, was to dissolve myth by turning the light of history on it. It is one of Emerson's strengths that he saw both sides of the argument. But in order to see clearly the American affirmation of myth at its wholehearted, unalloyed, one-sided fullest, one must turn not to Emerson, but to Alcott.

Amos Bronson Alcott (1799-1888), the gentle mystic who had once been a peddler and who taught school with the passion of a reformer, was known as the American Pestalozzi. He was also known as an impractical dreamer who founded the short-lived model community Fruitlands, an enthusiastic admirer of Thomas Taylor the Platonist, a spreader of Neoplatonism in midwest America, and the "dean" of the Concord School of Philosophy in the 1880s. Alcott was considered by Emerson to have been a great man. Others found him incomprehensible, and part of the problem, no doubt, was Alcott's fondness for the then rather novel terminology of myth. In an essay called **"The Garden,"** which argues that nature is best reflected in the civilized activity of gardening, Alcott presses his argument by claiming "Our human history neither opens in forests nor in cities, but in gardens and orchards whose mythologies are woven into the faith of our race."[6] The mythologies he means are those both of Eden and of Arcadia. Alcott never uses words such as "myth" or "mythology" in pejorative or negative ways. Myth for him is always something fine and creative. Myth is not just the past, either; it is something to which we still have access in these latter days. He points out that "we associate gardens and orchards with the perfect condition of mankind," and he adds, "Gardeners ourselves by birthright, we also mythologize and plant our Edens in the East of us, like our ancestors; the sacredness of earth and heaven still clinging to the tiller of the ground.'"[7] Even more direct is his praise of Thoreau, whom he calls a modern mythmaker, an assessment Thoreau himself would have been pleased with:

> Like Homer, Hesiod, and the earliest poets, Thoreau saw and treated Nature as a symbolism of the mind, as a physiological theology. His mysticism is alike solid and organic, animal and ideal. He is the mythologist of these last days—reminds more of the ancients in his mode of seeing and saying than any recent naturalist and poet.[8]

Alcott is at home with the terminology of myth, he sees great significance in it, and while he talks about it often in connection with the Greeks or the Bible, he seems usually to be concerned more with the present than with the past. Alcott is always making the case for *modern* myth. Myth is, for Alcott, entitled to serious consideration because it seems to provide a way to reconcile classical and Christian ideas with modern philosophical thought. As the following passage suggests, classical ideas and Christianity can both be dealt with in terms of myth if one thinks of myth as something positive, noble, and compelling—in short, as a high ideal, held with genuine religious conviction.

> The Greek gods had the infirmities of men, and hence stood nearer to men than if they had been conceived as perfect. So the Christian view aids the weakness of man's conception by the humanities of the second person in the Trinity.
>
> The Greek gods were men ennobled by the attributes of poetry, exalted by art and religion, never monstrous, as were the Eastern, but shaped in accordance with the ideal of the human figure.
>
> Our gods are partly pagan—composites of Greek, Roman, British; and the process of humanizing them, modifying their forms and attributes from the Puritans, is fast going forward. Ours are not our own. Hebrew largely. Not in accordance with western genius.[9]

At least one reason for Alcott's interest in myth, then, is his sense that new gods, new religions, and new beliefs were in the very process of being formed as he was writing. Indeed, one of the most attractive aspects of New England Transcendentalism is its sense of excitement, adventure, and discovery, its enthusiastic prizing of the momentous present. Myth played an important part in the Transcendental movement, for some of the various thinkers and writers who can be gathered together under that vague label shared a belief that myth was not solely something in the distant past of mankind but was a live force in their modern world.

This is not the place to discuss the Transcendental movement as a whole, but even a treatment of the part played by ideas of myth in the movement necessitates mention of a few general points. As Harold Goddard has put it, Transcendentalism was "the mingling of an old world and a new world element, the blending of an idealistic, Platonistic metaphysics and the Puritan spirit, the fusion—at a high revolutionary temperature—of a philosophy and a character."[10] Leaving aside the complex problems of greater and lesser influence, which differed almost from person to person among the Transcendentalists, it is clear that the movement has an English strain from Coleridge, Carlyle, and Thomas Taylor the Platonist, German strains partly through the above, partly directly through the translated works of Herder, Goethe, and the philosophers of German idealism, Kant, Fichte, and Jacobi, French strains from Constant and Jouffroy and Cousin, and a strong native American strain. The point to be stressed here is the rich profusion, the variety which was scooped up and more or less assimilated by the excited group of New Englanders. Of course the mingling and the fusion were done differently by an Alcott and by a Thoreau, but taken all together, the impressive inpouring of new ideas and the transformations in thought and literature wrought with the new ideas were underlain by a drive to revitalize the religious spirit in the America of the time. As a movement, Transcendentalism was simultaneously religious, philosophical, and literary in emphasis; in its religious aspect it was sufficiently radical to lead a modern scholar to say "Transcendentalism was the French Revolution of American Religion."[11] The description is apt, if we take it to suggest not the destruction but the democratizing and radical transformation of religious ideas. Transcendentalism revitalized Christianity by applying idealist thought to inherited Christian concepts. As spirit manifested itself in matter (or as form evolved through the concrete), so God manifested himself in man. The parallel with the Christian idea of incarnation and with Christ is apparent. Pushed one more step and taken out of history into the present, spirit must manifest itself in all men at all times. All men participate in spirit or—as it could still be called then—divinity. The Christian parallel here is in the implication that all men, not just Christ, are in the incarnated condition of Christ. The second way in which Transcendentalism revitalized the religious spirit of the times follows from and is really only an extension of the above; it was an effort to reconcile classical paganism and Christianity in a modern way which would then enjoy the best aspects of each outlook.

It is with this idea that Bronson Alcott was concerned; his **"Orphic Sayings"** try to reconcile German philosophy and Christian teachings through Greek forms modified for nineteenth-century America. Myth is the catalyst, the common denominator, and at times the form of Alcott's Orphism. Fifty of his often ridiculed **"Orphic Sayings"** were printed in *The Dial* in July 1840, and another fifty the following January. They are not only deliberately mythic, but quite complex and not to be understood apart from Transcendentalism in general and the work of Thomas Taylor the Platonist in particular.

Taylor's five-volume *Works of Plato,* published in England in 1804, was a major though not always recognized force behind the American Transcendentalist movement. As George Mills Harper says, "In any discussion of the influence of Plato on English and American literature for the next half century or so [after 1804], we should be mindful of two facts about Taylor's *Plato*; it was the only complete English translation, and it was a book with a mission." That mission, "to convey the idealistic convictions about the nature of man and the universe which he had acquired from a lifetime of reading in the Neoplatonists," was exactly what interested Alcott and Emerson in Taylor.[12] Taylor's numerous books included translations from Proclus, Plotinus, Iamblichus, Porphyry, and it is never forgotten, even in the briefest discussions of Taylor, that he was much more a Neoplatonist of the Alexandrian school than what is now understood as a student of Plato. Alcott and Emerson both read Taylor over and over; they collected his works, inquired after him in England (where he was, it seems, all but forgotten), and spread Taylor's Platonism as far as the middle western states of America, where Plato clubs sprang up in such places as Jacksonville and Quincy, Illinois.[13]

It was Taylor's version of Orphism that had such great mythological significance in Alcott's eyes and which led Alcott to his own attempt to compose Orphic Hymns for his own times. Alcott's own Orphism is not a bizarre aberration or even an unexpected outcropping, but only an extreme expression of the philosophical idealism common at the time, an expression couched in deliberately "mythic" terms.

According to Taylor, the Orphic theology—that is, the idea that can be drawn from the Orphic Hymns—asserts the primacy of mind and regards physical nature as a system of appearances. Taylor's "A Dissertation on the life and theology of Orpheus" contains a characteristic account:

> . . . the deity is an immense and perpetually exuberant fountain whose streams originally filled and continually replenish the world with life. Hence the universe contains in its ample bosom all general natures, divinities visible and invisible, the illustrious race of daemons, the noble army of exalted souls, and men rendered happy by wisdom and virtue. According to this theology, the power of universal soul does not alone diffuse itself to the sea, and become bounded by its circumfluent waters, while the wide expanse of air and aether is destitute of life and soul; but the celestial spaces are filled with souls, supplying life to the stars, and directing their revolutions in everlasting order. So that the celestial orbs in imitation of intellect, which seeks after nothing external, are wisely agitated in perpetual circuit round the central sun. While some things participate of being alone, others of life, and others are endued with sentient powers; some possess the still higher faculty of reason; and lastly others are all life and intelligence.[14]

This is abstruse stuff; high, noble, rarified, and with very little dirt clinging to its roots. Taylor's prose is no doubt a major source of the characteristic vices of the Transcendental style, but if one can look on the above as an effort not only to present the idea of pantheism but to urge us to see it, and to describe the world as the pantheist sees it, not heaving and throbbing with animal life or Dionysian urge but shining and awake with a life of mind or spirit, then one may glimpse the attractiveness of this rather elusive view of the world. Like Plato, Taylor concludes "that there is another certain nature exempt from the passivity and imperfection of bodies, existing not only in the heavens, but in the ever-changing elements, from which the motion of bodies is primarily derived. And this nature is no other than soul, from which animals derive their life and motive power, and which even affords an image of self-motion to the unstable order of bodies."[15]

Here, too, the difficulty of the passage may be forgiven when it is seen that Taylor is questioning the material assumption, common since Hobbes and reasserted by Holbach, that the universe is only matter and motion, both of which have always existed. When he is summarizing, Taylor can be quite straightforward. "Hence we may with reason conclude, that not only the universe, but each of its eternal parts is animated, and endued with intellect, and is, in its capacity similar to the universe."[16] Taylor's argument presents a conception of mind as deity which seems to fit both a pagan and a Christian outlook. The "grand arcanum of the Orphic theology" is finally "that God is all things; which is likewise an Egyptian doctrine, from whence it was derived through Orpheus into Greece; and this sublime truth Plotinus himself proves with his usual sagacity and depth. But here it is necessary to observe, that Orpheus and the Platonists do not conceive the Deity to be all things, as if he were a divisible, corporeal nature, but that he is all things, because present everywhere, and to every being totally, though more or less intimately present, according to the various gradations and approximations of being."[17] What all this leads to is the perception that the best of pagan philosophy and its mythological expression and the best of Christian theology come to the same point, that God is all things.

Alcott's **"Orphic Sayings"** do not set out to demonstrate the above: they take it for granted and proceed from there. Alcott is not a chronicler of divinity; he takes the idea of pantheism seriously and thus sets out to record the appearances of deity in his own life and his own times. He bears witness, and the form in which the witness is expressed is half that of Orphic Hymns and half that of biblical Scripture. His **"Orphic Sayings"** are clearly intended as new scripture, resulting from new revelation. They are filled with a sense of the divine, but it is made quite clear that the divine is a quite common appearance. Alcott deals in the deific, but it is a daily, all-purpose concept, the modern equivalent of which might be expressed as "the sense of the sacred" as opposed to the profane. The third saying shows Alcott's workaday idea of deification as well as his undeniable sincerity.

> Hope deifies man; it is the apotheosis of the soul; the prophecy and fulfillment of her destinies. The nobler her aspirations, the sublimer her conceptions of the Godhead. As the man, so his God; God is his idea of excellence; the complement of his own being.[18]

What looks like merely a standard Unitarian and Humanist earnestness becomes here a fresh way of saying man creates god in his own image. This is not meant satirically of course; the power of creating or becoming godlike is the source of Alcott's sense of the divine. This is strongly expressed in the tenth saying, on **"Apotheosis"**:

> Every soul feels at times her own possibility of becoming a God; she cannot rest in the human, she aspires after the Godlike. This instinctive tendency is an authentic augury of its own fulfillment. Men shall become Gods. Every act of admiration, prayer, praise, worship, desire, hope, implies and predicts the future apotheosis of the soul.

Saying number thirty-nine, called **"Embryon,"** is put more simply, and with an effort at eloquent pithiness. "Man is a rudiment and embryon of God: eternity shall develop in him the divine image."

Like some other Transcendentalists, Alcott found it difficult to express or explain adequately some of his ideas. What he struggled for, often without success, was a way to demonstrate and prove his intuitive convictions about the primacy of mind or spirit. In saying number thirty-one, on **"Calculus,"** he puts his idea of deity or deific energy and at the same time snows his awareness of the need for a better means of expressing the difficult, easily mocked doctrines of his Yankee Platonism.

> We need, what Genius is unconsciously seeking, and, by some daring generalization of the universe, shall assuredly discover, a spiritual calculus, a novum organon, whereby nature shall be divined in the soul, the soul in God, matter in spirit, polarity resolved into unity; and that power which pulsates in all life, animates and builds all organizations, shall manifest itself as one universal deific energy, present alike at the outskirts and center of the universe, whose center and circumference are one. . . .

What Alcott does not quite say, though it is hinted at when he admiringly calls Thoreau or Elizabeth Peabody a mythologist, is that myth is the "spiritual calculus" of "universal deific energy."

Though it is not put so bluntly, this is the idea that animates the last three of the first group of **"Orphic Sayings."** Number forty-eight, on **"Beauty,"** begins with

what the modern reader quickly recognizes as Alcott's standard attempt to fuse Neoplatonism and Christian ideas; here the Christian idea is that of fall or lapse:

> All departures from perfect beauty are degradations of the divine image. God is the one type, which the soul strives to incarnate in all organizations. Varieties are historical. The one form embosoms all form; all having a common likeness at the base of difference. Human heads are images, more or less perfect, of the soul's or God's head. But the divine features do not fix in flesh; in the coarse and brittle clay. Beauty is fluent, art of highest order represents her always in flux, giving fluency and motion to bodies solid and immovable to sense. The line of beauty symbolizes motion.

Something quite remarkable grows out of this seemingly routine fusion of Platonic and Christian versions of lapse. It is as though Alcott had rediscovered the whole idea of metamorphosis. Alcott's language stresses change; "flux," "fluency," "incarnate," and "embosom" all work to create the idea of some essential breath or spirit passing from one form to another. What Alcott would call "Deific energy" is not fixed; it is always becoming, transforming, changing, evolving, or devolving.

The argument of saying forty-eight is carried on in the next. In fact, the last three sayings are a unit, forming a short essay on modern metamorphosis. Forty-nine is called **"Transfiguration"** and concerns itself directly and explicitly with the process of transformation:

> Never have we beheld a purely human face; as yet, the beast, demon, rather than the man or God, predominate in its expression. The face of the soul is not extant in flesh. Yet she has a face, and virtue and genius shall one day reveal her celestial lineaments: a beauty, a majesty shall then radiate from her that shall transcend the rapt ideal of love and hope. So have I seen glimpses of this spiritual glory, when, inspired by some thought or sentiment, she was transfigured from the image of the earthly to that of the heavenly, the ignoble melting out of her features, lost in the supersensual life.

Alcott's apprehension of change, transformation, or metamorphosis is clearer here, though still put in completely abstract terms. The center of Alcott's conception of metamorphosis, the reason for dwelling on it and using it to conclude the first group of sayings, is the need to search out and distinguish what is divine, what human, and what bestial. Rather than argue that the human contains in it both the divine and the bestial—a rather static conception—Alcott approaches the problem as one of transformation from one state or form to another. And, interestingly, in the final saying Alcott changes his mode and expresses his conception of metamorphosis in mythical and imaginative terms. For once he rescued an idea from the barrenness of neo-Alexandrian abstraction:

> Know, O man, that your soul is the Prometheus who, receiving the divine fire, builds up this majestic statue of clay and moulds it in the deific image, the pride of

gods, the model and analogon of all forms. He chiselled that godlike brow, arched those mystic temples from whose fanes she herself looks forth, formed that miraculous globe above, and planted that sylvan grove below; graved those massive blades yoked in armed powers; carved that heaven-containing bosom, wreathed those puissant thighs, and hewed those stable columns, diffusing over all the grandeur, the grace of his own divine lineaments, and delighting in this cunning work of his hand. Mar not its beauty, spoil not its symmetry, by the deforming lines of lust and sin; dethroning the divinity incarnated therein, and transforming yourself into the Satyr and the beast.

There is a compelling quality to this baroque, romantic language which is redolent of Victor Hugo.[19] Alcott here combined the mythologist and the reformer; the passage starts with a remarkable vision of metamorphosis—physically imagined—of man into god. Despite the moralistic ending, however, the passage as a whole suggests that Alcott really did rediscover the live idea behind the classical, Ovidian concept of metamorphosis. It would be Hawthorne who would give it a satisfactory modern literary form, but it was Alcott who showed the way, who suggested how the modern reformer or moralist could use the classical myths of transformation to illuminate modern problems of internal, perhaps psychological, metamorphoses. Alcott's weakness is not a lack of ideas, but rather a deficiency of concretizing imagination and a pallid style of writing. He prefers to discuss the idea of metamorphosis in philosophical terms most of the time, rather than try to imagine a story through which the idea could work itself out in concrete human terms. He preferred abstract reasoning to literature, not knowing apparently that the "mythology" he so admired in Thoreau was not possible except when literary expression succeeded in embodying those philosophical ideas. Like his beloved Neoplatonists, he was usually content to write *about* myth, leaving the actual creation of myth to others.

Yet Alcott did try on occasion to do something that looks very much like the deliberate creation of myth. In the manuscript versions of a book that began as observations on the birth and development of his first daughter, Anna, and that grew into the odd narrative called *Psyche,* Alcott blended his reading and his experience in a book about the origins and growth of the soul. It is beyond question that certain books were important to him. He himself laid great stress on the importance of his having read Coleridge's *Aids to Reflections* in 1832 and Thomas Taylor's translations of Plato's *Cratylus, Phaedo, Timaeus,* and *Parmenides* in 1833. He continued to read and reread Coleridge and Taylor's Plato for the rest of his life, but, as Odell Shepard notes, Alcott read mainly to find extension and corroboration of his own ideas. "As a reader, Bronson Alcott had neither talent nor training, so that he was obliged to get on as best he could with a thin streak of genius."[20] This thin streak stamped all his writing and thinking, it fused his read-

ing with his daily life, and it may be observed at work in the successive books or versions of one book which he began to produce in 1831, when Anna was born. The first manuscript was called **"A Record of Observations on the Phenomena of Life as Developed in the History of an Infant During the First Year of its Existence,"** and it is full of detailed comment, much of which bears out a more or less Lockean view of mind, then generally accepted, that the child is an empty vessel, a blank slate on which experience begins to record impressions taken in through the senses.[21] This manuscript was reworked into one called *Psyche or the Breath of Childhood,* which Alcott wrote from June 24, 1835 to June 24, 1836. In this work, childhood has become an emblem of the spiritual. "The infant is to all an emblem of goodness," Alcott wrote, in language that seeks to modify, but does not openly contradict Locke.[22] Later, in the same manuscript, the child has progressed from being an emblem of revelation to being the Revelation itself. As the following passage shows, Alcott was clearly and consciously aware that he was engaged in penning scripture, or as we might call it, in mythopoesis.

> Of the various media of Revelation, the child is, perhaps, the most significant of all. The *history of a child,* including its inner as well as outer movements, with its relations both spiritual and material and the varying phenomena of the sensual and the supersensual—this would be a Revelation indeed—an Incarnate Word to humanity. We have the history of an adult in the life of Jesus. In the Gospels both his inner and outer experience is given. The supremacy of the spiritual comes forth to our senses. The Word is incarnated, and man looketh on the face of his brother in the flesh, seeing it in the image of the Divine Life that he inheriteth. Yet the revelation of childhood hath not yet been promulgated. The "eyes have not seen nor the hands yet handled the Word of God" as presented in infancy. To the penning of this gospel let me apply myself.[23]

The central point here is that the child is more than a mere emblem of the spiritual, the child is in fact the vehicle of the spiritual, the form through which Spirit manifests itself. Alcott's final version, called *Psyche an Evangele,* finished in 1838, is a narrative working-out of this idea. It is no less than a new myth of the soul. Not content to follow Apuleius' version of the story of Psyche, Alcott took ideas from Coleridge and from Taylor's Plato, and, with his own daughter's growth and development before his eyes, he tried to write a modern myth of Psyche as an inspiration—a scripture—for his own times.

There is no model or parallel for this extraordinary piece of writing that I know of in American literature of this era. But Alcott's fable, when set beside certain productions of German romanticism, such as Klingsohr's Fairy Tale in Novalis's *Henry of Ofterdingen* (1802; tr. by J. Owen and published at Cambridge, Mass. in

1842), would seem to be a perfectly explicable work of romantic idealism. Alcott's ***Psyche an Evangele*** has never been published. (The opening chapter is printed in an appendix to this volume.) The trouble, as Alcott himself knew, was that he, like Emerson, distrusted the adequacy of language itself. In a letter to Sophia Peabody, Alcott wrote, with his own ***Psyche*** in mind, that his words "have a significance borrowed from their inmost being; and are to be interpreted, not by ordinary and popular acceptation, but by the genius of the individual that utters them. These [especially gifted minds] have a significance of their own. They commune not with words but in spite of them. Ordinary minds mistake them. For they cannot be revealed through the illusory medium of words."[24] ***Psyche*** has a sort of late eighteenth-century quality in its diction, its capitalization, and its vague resemblance to William Blake's prophetic works. It is written in an unusual style to be sure, but we can indeed perceive its main lines through his incantatory and unliterate language. No longer is the child a mere emblem of spirit; the child is now the important thing. To give an adequate account of the manifestation of spirit as child requires nothing less than a new myth, a narrative fable of Psyche in Concord, a modern scripture, a gospel of childhood.

It is not quite fair to leave Alcott without emphasizing that myth touched him as it touched a few others of his time, such as Emerson or Margaret Fuller, not just in their ideas and writings, but in their lives. As Alcott understood the story, Orpheus was a bringer of civilization, one who could charm beasts and draw the very rivers out of their courses by the sweetness of his song. As a teacher of the young, as the reformer who founded "Fruitlands," as "dean" of the Concord School of Philosophy, and even or perhaps especially as a gardener, Alcott lived the life of a religious teacher and philosopher. Emerson thought him a sage and a prophet, recognizing in him a man bringing a gospel. Judged by what he tried to be rather than by what he actually wrote or accomplished—and Emerson's judgment here must be respected—Alcott was a kind of minor modern Orpheus. But he was an Orpheus of intention, for he lacked the instrumental imagination. Alcott could say, grandly, that "the world is but the symbol of mind, and speech a mythology woven of both."[25] He himself never published his major effort. Final judgment will have to wait, however, until his ***Psyche*** has had its critics. That he, along with other Transcendentalists, was trying to make myths is undeniable. Even the enemies of the "movement" saw that much. Noah Porter noted in 1842 that "Transcendentalism was rather unbelief than belief. Subtle, refining, symbolizing all living truths and real facts into inert and powerless mythi."[26] The description fits Alcott and other minor Transcendentalists, and with a few exceptions it characterizes the literary side of Transcendentalism up to 1842. But the main work of Emerson and that of Thoreau and Whitman, not to mention the counter-Transcendental writing of Hawthorne and Melville, cannot be so dismissed as "inert and powerless" myths. Avoiding Parker's one-sided rejection of myth and Alcott's too-easy acceptance of it, these writers pursued various middle courses, exploring the problem of myth both skeptically and affirmatively at the same time. The result was a powerful, vital literature which deliberately and extensively used myth as subject, as form, and as process.

Notes

1. Creuzer's great work is his *Symbolik und Mythologie der alten Völker, besonders der Griechen,* 4 vols. (Leipzig/Darmstadt, 1810-12). The French translation is J. D. Guignaut, *Religions de l'antiquité considerées principalement dans leurs formes symboliques et mythologiques,* 4 vols. (Paris, 1825-51). For Creuzer's impact on modern myth study, see Feldman and Richardson, *The Rise of Modern Mythology* [*1680-1860* (Bloomington: Indiana University Press, 1972)], and Jan de Vries, *The Study of Religion,* tr. Kees W. Bolle (New York; Harcourt Brace Jovanovich, 1967).

2. Emerson discusses Everett in "Life and Letters in New England," [*The Complete Works of Ralph Waldo Emerson,* ed. Edward Waldo Emerson (12 vols.; Boston: Riverside Press, 1903-04)], vol. 10, p. 312. Everett's use of Creuzer may be seen in Edward Everett's *Synopsis of a course of Lectures on the History of Greek Literature* (n.d.) in the Harvard College Library. Emerson's use of Joseph Marie de Gérando's *Histoire Comparée* is discussed by F. I. Carpenter in *Emerson's Asia* (Cambridge: Harvard University Press, 1930), pp. 10-11. J. G. E. Oegger's *The True Messiah,* tr. and pub. by E. P. Peabody (Boston, 1842), is discussed in K. W. Cameron, *Emerson the Essayist* (Raleigh, N.C., 1945), vol. 1, and reprinted in vol. 2.

3. Karl Otfried Müller's *Prolegomena zu einer wissenschaftlichen Mythologie . . .* (Göttingen, 1825) was not translated into English until 1844, but his two-volume work on *The Dorians* was available in English from 1830, and his influence in Europe and America was very great by the time his *History of the Literature of Ancient Greece* appeared in English in 1840. For a general estimate of Müller, see Feldman and Richardson, *The Rise of Modern Mythology,* and G. P. Gooch, *History and Historians in the Nineteenth Century* (London: Longmans & Co., 1913).

4. The influence of K. O. Müller on Elizabeth Peabody may be traced from her *Key to History, Part III, the Greeks* (Boston: Marsh, Capen & Lyon, 1833) through her conversations as discussed by G. W. Cooke, *Historical and Biographical Introduction to Accompany The Dial* (1855; repr. New

York: Russell & Russell, 1961), to her essay on "The Dorian Measure," in *Aesthetic Papers* (Boston, 1849; repr. Gainesville, Fla.: Scholar's Facsimiles & Reprints, 1957), and her "Introduction to Bem's History," in her *Universal History* (1859; rev. ed., 1875).

5. E. Peabody, *Key to History, Part III, The Greeks,* p. 8. By 1859, in her *Universal History,* this remarkable and too little studied woman could confidently say, ". . . the time is past for supposing mythology to be the *fictions* of vanity or superstition. It was an inevitable expression of truth whose keys we have lost, and which only can be restored by the imagination, cultivated by research into facts" (p. xxvi).

6. A. B. Alcott, *Tablets* (Boston: Roberts Brothers, 1868), p. 7.

7. Ibid., p. 10.

8. *The Journals of Bronson Alcott,* sel. and ed. Odell Shepard (Boston: Little, Brown and Company, 1938), p. 350.

9. *Journals of Bronson Alcott,* pp. 350-351.

10. Harold C. Goddard, *Studies in New England Transcendentalism* (New York: Hillary House, 1960), p. 189.

11. Ibid., p. 186.

12. George Mills Harper, "Thomas Taylor in America," in *Thomas Taylor, the Platonist,* ed. K. Raine and G. M. Harper (Princeton: Princeton University Press, 1969), p. 51. This volume has an excellent and extensive bibliography.

13. See also G. M. Harper, "Towards the Holy Land, Platonism in the Middle West," *South Atlantic Bulletin,* 32 (1967), pp. 1-6.

14. Thomas Taylor, "A Dissertation on the life and theology of Orpheus," in *Thomas Taylor, the Platonist,* p. 171. See also Kathleen Raine's excellent account, "Thomas Taylor in England," in the same volume.

15. *Thomas Taylor, the Platonist,* p. 173.

16. Ibid., p. 175.

17. Ibid., p. 179.

18. This and subsequent quotations from Alcott's "Orphic Sayings" are taken from *The Dial.* Numbers one through fifty appeared in the issue for July 1840, numbers fifty-one through one hundred in that for January 1841.

19. See, for example, the section "Satyr" in Hugo's *La Légende des Siècles* [(1859)].

20. Odell Shepard, *Pedlar's Progress* (Boston: Little, Brown and Company, 1937), p. 155.

21. See *Pedlar's Progress,* pp. 139-145.

22. K. W. Cameron, *Emerson the Essayist* (Raleigh, N.C.: The Thistle Press, 1945), vol. II, p. 108. Cameron has printed, from *Psyche or the Breath of Childhood,* "chiefly those passages which Emerson said were worthy of being saved." It is well known that Emerson read, edited, and advised against the publication of *Psyche.*

23. *Emerson the Essayist,* vol. II, p. 120.

24. Richard L. Herrnstadt, *The Letters of A. Bronson Alcott* (Ames: Iowa State University Press, 1969), p. 28.

25. A. B. Alcott, *Tablets,* p. 176.

26. Noah Porter, "Transcendentalism," in the *American Biblical Repository,* 2d series, VIII, 1842, p. 198.

Barbara Harrell Carson (essay date summer 1979)

SOURCE: Carson, Barbara Harrell. "Bronson Alcott and the New England Mysteries." *Studia Mystica* 2, no. 2 (summer 1979): 56-69.

[*In the following essay, Carson examines the philosophical and literary antecedents that inspired Alcott's ideas. Carson argues that it was the manner in which Alcott mythologized his own life, rather than his actual writings, that exerted the most powerful influence on the development of Transcendentalism.*]

The man who today is remembered mainly as the father of the "Little Women" achieved in his own time a marked, if not always flattering, renown. It has even been suggested that, in 1837, it was Bronson Alcott, and not Emerson, who was considered the leader of that group designated the "Transcendentalists" by their more practical fellow New Englanders.[1] In his later years his influence spread far beyond New England. His repeated tours of the "West," where he lectured on his favorite mystical themes, made it possible for him to claim a "Bishoprick" (as he and Mrs. Alcott called it) that embraced "a dozen states, extending from Western N[ew] York to the Missouri and South to St. Louis."[2] There had been an earlier diocese stretching over to England, where the Alcott House, founded by his admirers in that country, had provided a meeting place for Englishmen interested in the Pythagorean life. From both East and West had come proof of his reputation, the one sending followers to establish with him the tiny commune at Fruitlands, the other contributing Hegelian and Neoplatonic philosophers to help him set up the Concord School of Philosophy.

This widespread admiration was not the product of Alcott's writings. His works are repetitious, sometimes bombastic, and often trivial.[3] He deserves the attention of students of literature and the humanities today, however, since the ideas he held and the influences that touched him help to point out intellectual forces at work in the Transcendental era. The influences that many of his contemporaries transmitted in their writings, Alcott translated into his life. Even in his own day, his fame derived from the mysticism that directed his actions, rather than from the theories he wrote of. His eighty-nine years were filled with daring and original—and often quixotic—attempts to restore the ascendency of man's spiritual nature. Alcott himself seems to have recognized his failure as a writer, and as if in justification of it, he once declared: "It is life, not scripture; character, not biography, that renovates mankind. The letter of life vitiates its spirit. Virtue and genius refuse to be written."[4] Indeed, Alcott's life itself might be considered his most successful artistic creation.

The symbolism which most dominated his vision—the mythology which he was most concerned to revise for the modern world and present through his life—was that associated with Orphism and Pythagoreanism, which he had begun to study in 1833. Orpheus is today remembered best for the power of his music to tame wild beasts and for his descent to Hades to free his wife Eurydice. But for Alcott there was a more significant side to the story of the mythical hero: Orpheus was credited by ancient writers with establishing the Mystery cults of ancient Greece.[5] The rites which he instituted were said to have been passed on to Pythagoras, and, indeed the Pythagorean colony at Croton was judged to be essentially an Orphic community. So similar were the Orphic and Pythagorean teachings, particularly concerning the history of the soul and the way to a life of purity, that the two became practically indistinguishable.[6] Very often, Pythagoreanism was thought of as the philosophical side and Orphism as the religious side of the same mystical system. After Pythagoras the cloak of Orphic succession was thought to have fallen to Plato. Next in the lineage of Orphic mysticism were the philosophers largely responsible for emphasizing Plato's association with Orphism: the Neoplatonists (Plotinus, Porphyry, Jamblichus, Proclus), whose goal was a mystical return to the realm of the absolutely Good—as Plotinus described it, "the flight of the alone to the alone."

Word of this congenial philosophy came to Alcott and his New England contemporaries primarily through the writings and translations of Thomas Taylor. Born in England in 1758, Taylor had by his death in 1835, published more than forty separate titles, at least two-thirds of which concerned Platonism, Neoplatonism, mysticism, and the occult.[7] Enormous as his achievement was, however, censure rather than praise was his lot.

The extent of Taylor's command of Greek is conjectural; he seems to have turned frequently to Latin translations; and the English of his versions is often awkward. In addition, he emended freely in the direction of his bias, making no distinction between the ideas of Pythagoras, Plato, and the Neoplatonists. His notes collate not only these, but draw upon the Orphic literature, as well as the Chaldean Oracles and Zoroastrian and Hermetic writings, to explain Platonic concepts and to reveal the "hidden" meanings of various myths.

But neither his imperfect Greek nor his poor style—nor even his penchant for unscholarly annotation—can account for the vindictiveness of the contemporary denunciation of his works. It now seems clear that the ridicule he suffered was occasioned not so much by his critical lapses as by his personal beliefs. He was a man with a message—he defended Neoplatonic idealism against the materialism of his day—and it was this message that threatened his fellows and stirred up their animosity.[8] His enthusiasm for paganism and the occult and his apparently serious acceptance of Orphic and Pythagorean beliefs (including vegetarianism) led to his being depicted in Disraeli's *Curiosities of Literature* as "a Modern Pletho," who, like his fifteenth-century counterpart, was trying to revive polytheism.[9] To Horace Walpole he was "this half-witted Taylor" who preferred those unintelligible ancient Platonists to Bacon and Locke, the apostles of common sense.[10] In the early nineteenth century Thomas Love Peacock joined the derision in *Melincourt* by having Mr. Forester (Shelley) describe how Taylor, the "learned mythologist," would greet Sir Oran Haut-ton (an orang-outan from Angola) with part of an Orphic invocation to Pan.[11] And Peacock's granddaughter colored further the later nineteenth-century view of Taylor by spreading apocryphal tales of his sacrificing lambs and pouring out libations to the gods in his apartment.[12]

Nevertheless, there were others whose admiration equalled this derision. Coleridge intented praise when he referred to Taylor as "the English pagan," and when, in 1788, Godefroi Yzarn, a young French nobleman who had converted to vegetarianism, came to London, he was directed to "'Mr. Thomas Taylor, of Walmouth, [who] was generally considered as the principal Pythagorean in England.'"[13] Moreover, it is becoming increasingly evident that what Taylor failed to achieve as a first-rate translator and historian of philosophy, he made up for in his value to literary authors of the early nineteenth century. And it was precisely his eclecticism, his unscholarly enthusiasm, his occult symbolizing, and what one critic has called his "contagious ardor for the divine"[14] that led Emerson to call him "a better feeder to a poet than any man between Milton and Wordsworth."[15]

In America, among those most affected by Taylor's "contagious ardor" were Alcott and his fellow Transcendentalists. Alcott judged his own discovery in 1833 of Taylor's translation of *The Cratylus, Phaedo, Parmenides, and Timaeus* so significant that years later when recording the event he wrote in red ink, a distinction otherwise reserved for signalizing his marriage, the births of his daughters, the beginning of the Civil War, and the assassination of Lincoln.[16] An even greater influence on Alcott's life was the book that became his favorite: Jamblichus' *Life of Pythagoras* in Taylor's translation.[17] Further indication of Taylor's importance to Alcott may be seen in the library he brought back from England in 1842. To the books bequeathed him by the English Pythagorean, James Pierrepont Greaves, Alcott had himself added, during his English tour, "many works of a like character." In the selected bibliography printed in the Transcendental magazine, *The Dial,* Alcott declared his library "a richer collection of mystical writers than any other library in this country"; and he heralded the arrival in America of "this cabinet of mystic and theosophic lore" as "a remarkable fact in our literary history." Among the one-thousand volumes (which included an *Orpheus* in Greek and Latin [1689]) were at least twenty-three by Taylor, whose works represented the greatest number by any single author or translator. The most significant of these were Porphyry's *Select Works,* containing *On Abstinence from Animal Food*; Jamblichus' *On the Mysteries of the Egyptians, Chaldeans, and Assyrians* and his *Life of Pythagoras*; and the five volumes of Plato's *Works.*[18]

In these works—particularly in their presentation of Orphic and Pythagorean mysticism—Alcott found a philosophical *raison d'etre* and an historical precedent for the life he had already chosen. Pythagoras of Samos became the master of the sage of Concord. Some measure of the extent of Alcott's adulation can be seen in his judgment that Pythagoras stood at the head of all the great men of the past. His claims concerning Pythagoras' influence were enormous. "Any one conversant with the history of thought," he wrote,

> must perceive that the Germs of all modern philosophy are properly speaking Pythagorean, and that speculative theology is deeply tinged with its essence. One shall find the best of our 'New Testament' intimated, if not expressed, in these Pythagorean and Platonic Books. . . .
>
> Perhaps we might claim for our modern Transcendentalism . . . little more more than a following forth into the manifold relations of life and nature, the central truths and ideas of the Samian sage. I consider him the *only Educator* the world has known. We are yet far from treating the human being with any thing like the skill which history shows was his, and wait for the first . . . hint of an institution for training youth into the principles and victories of a divinely human life.[19]

To say that Pythagoras became his ideal, that he tried to follow Pythagoras' example in his life, does not adequately describe Alcott's response to the Greek phi-

losopher and mystic. It would actually be closer to the truth to say that Alcott came to see himself as a nineteenth-century Pythagoras—or Pythagoras as an ancient Alcott. In almost every major undertaking, in almost all his ideals, he could find evidence of his similarity to Pythagoras. It was in this way that his life became the medium of his mythology, the source of his influence on other Transcendentalists. Living, better than writing, could show mankind the way to a new spiritual existence through the Pythagorean way.

Even his early years—before he had studied the life of Pythagoras—seemed to offer evidence of his Pythagorean nature, when he looked back on them. Odell Shepard, Alcott's biographer, has detected an example of such an identification after-the-fact in Alcott's accounts of his peddling trips south. As an old man, he often wondered why the dogs guarding the gates of the southern plantations had never bothered him, but had instead, as he wrote in his autobiographical poem *New Connecticut,* escorted him kindly to their masters' doors.[20] The answer to the mystery, Shepard theorizes, came to him from the pages of Jamblichus' *Life of Pythagoras.* By his old age, Alcott had read many times Jamblichus' account of Pythagoras' taming a bear, talking to an ox, and stroking an eagle he had called down from its flight over Olympus. All these, Jamblichus had written, were acts which "demonstrated that [Pythagoras] possessed the same dominion as Orpheus, over savage animals, and that he allured and detained them by the power of voice proceeding from the mouth."[21] It was surely this legend that had led Alcott, in a typical movement toward mythologizing his own life, to decide that "those fierce and formidable beasts recognized in him not so much a pedlar as the spirit of Pythagoras come back to earth. At any rate, he addressed himself to the gentleman whom he believed to be imprisoned in each of those shaggy breasts. . . ."[22]

In the teaching career that followed his years as a peddler, Alcott also felt that he had measured up to his predecessor. Again and again he emphasized that Pythagoras was the greatest teacher history had known. One such declaration appears in the letter quoted above, where Alcott also traced his Transcendental philosophy to Pythagoras.[23] At another time, he described Pythagoras as "the father of the method of Conversation."[24] It should not be surprising that Alcott himself was considered by his contemporaries to be the originator and master of the "Conversation." He had introduced the term to describe that peculiar combination of monologue and discussion by which he presented to culture-hungry New Englanders his own occult theories as well as his version of the doctrines of the Neoplatonists. In linking this technique to Pythagoras, Alcott was obviously projecting back into the admired figure one of his own salient achievements, quite willing for the sake of the mythology he was creating to adjust the stories concerning Pythagoras so as better to present himself as Pythagoras' modern incarnation.

Perhaps the most dramatic evidence for this claim was his attempt in 1843 to establish a commune at Fruitlands Farm in Harvard, Massachusetts. It seems indisputable that from the beginning of the venture, Alcott was striving to model Fruitlands after Pythagoras' Croton. It was while he was in England from May through October, 1842, that the plans for the commune began to take shape. During that time he was in close association with a number of Englishmen who considered themselves Pythagoreans, among them the men who returned to Massachusetts with him to set up Fruitlands. That his thoughts were very much on the Pythagorean life in those months abroad can also be seen in his contributing, at this time, a brief article on the subject to the *Healthian* magazine.[25] In 1848, he was still thinking of the Harvard farm as a nineteenth-century counterpart of Pythagoras' community. That year he wrote in his journal:

> Thoreau came in while I was reading Thir[l]wall's account of Pythagoras and of his aims, philosophy, and endeavors, and we discussed a little the possibility of reaching the people by means of a similar character in our day.

> I was reminded by the perusal of the views and purposes of this illustrious teacher of our enterprise at Fruitlands, and of the many points which it had in common, both in idea and form, with the institution at Croton.[26]

Those common points included almost all the precepts that were to guide his community. In fact, when he outlined in one of his books the disciplines established by Pythagoras, he might just as well have been listing the rules set up at Fruitlands (rules which he himself followed most of his life, even after the fall of the commune). Pythagoras, Alcott wrote, had taught silence and solitude, abstinence from animal foods and temperance in the use of other foods, the employment of baths and music for the health of body and soul, and the practice of wearing garments of pure white linen.[27] In other of his writings, Alcott expanded on the significance of these methods to the pursuit of spiritual perfection—both in his own life and in the lives of the Pythagoreans.

One idea that strikes the reader of Alcott's discussions of these practices is his insistence on their links to Pythagoras, even when more immediate sources were obvious. The importance of meditative silence, for example, Alcott had probably learned from the Quakers of Germantown and Philadelphia, where he had taught school from 1830-34. Nevertheless, it was to Pythagoras that he traced this precept, writing at some length on the significance to the Pythagoreans of "that most difficult of all victories—the victory over the tongue."[28]

Alcott knew that the silence of the Pythagoreans (like that of the Quakers) was not an end in itself. The Mysteries taught that only in quietness of the spirit can one perceive the voiceless messages of the gods. Among those who had discussed this silent communication was Plutarch, himself supposedly an initiate in the Mysteries, as Alcott was aware.[29] Alcott could have found Plutarch's comments on the subject in the notes to Jamblichus' *On the Mysteries*. There Taylor had quoted Plutarch's explanation that the "divine reason is unindigent of voice, . . . proceeding through a silent path. . . ."[30] Alcott's emphasis was much the same in one of his own **"Orphic Sayings"**:

> Silence is the initiative to wisdom. Wit is silent, and justifies her children by their reverence of the voiceless oracles of the breast. Inspiration is dumb, a listener to the oracles during her nonage; suddenly she speaks, to mock the emptiness of all speech. Silence is the dialect of heaven; the utterance of Gods.[31]

It was this same recognition of the inspiration derived from silence that, at another time, brought Orpheus to his mind and led him to decide that although they spoke different languages, he was united with Orpheus in the wisdom coming to the silent spirit:

> The tongues are oftener hindrances than helps to the Mind. . . . I thought today, as I inscribed my thought by the woodside on a fly-leaf, of Orpheus, whose dialect I spake not nor could read—that to all divinities the babblements of men were nought, since the Spirit spake one tongue, nor could the faintest of its voices fall meaningless on their ears, in what track of place or time soever.[32]

Like meditative silence, the Pythagorean practice of ritual bathing also became part of Alcott's preparation for inspiration, especially during the Fruitlands period.[33] It even led to his hearing a sort of music of the spheres, a perceptive power traditionally thought to belong only to Pythagoras—further evidence to Alcott of the validity of his personal mythology.[34] It is hard to keep from smiling at the seriousness with which he transformed the routine of a bath into a ritual in which the effects wrought by the shock of freezing water were viewed as an encounter with the divine, resulting in his own elevation into a resplendent spiritual state. Alcott was, however, quite serious when he described the winter at Fruitlands, where he bathed "twice a day, at morning and again at sunset":

> I bathed in cold water, ducking head and shoulders for several times successively to the bottom of the capacious tub in which I stood, and poured water by pailsful over the whole body, rubbing down briskly afterwards with crash towels, and practiced friction with the flesh brush. In the coldest mornings there was a cracking and lambent flash following the passage of my hand over the pile of the skin, and I shook flames from my finger ends, which seemed erect and blazing with

phosphoric light. The eyes, too, were lustrous, and shot sparkles whenever I closed them. On raising my head from the flood there was heard a melody in the ear, as of the sound of many waters; and rubbing the eyes gave out an iris of the primitive colors, beautiful to behold, but as evanescent as a twinkling. It was not easy to write prose while thus exalted and transfigured. I tasted mannas, and all the aromas of field and orchard scented the fountains, and the brain was haunted by the rhythm of many voiced melodies.[35]

The most obviously Pythagorean part of Alcott's life was, of course, his diet. As in the case of his practice of meditative silence, there were other more immediate influences leading to his vegetarianism. One was his cousin William, who preceded Alcott in this path and in 1835—the year Alcott became a vegetarian—founded the monthly magazine *Moral Reformer,* which proclaimed the virtues of the meatless diet. Another influential voice calling for dietary reform was that of Dr. Sylvester Graham, who, in 1836, spoke at Alcott's school in Boston.[36] But Alcott's vegetarianism also began within two years of his first readings of Taylor's translations, and it was to Orpheus and Pythagoras, rather than to contemporary sources, that Alcott linked his abstinence from meat. Particularly important to him was the discussion of vegetarianism in his favorite book, Jamblicus' *Life of Pythagoras.* He found an even stronger denunciation of meat-eating in Taylor's translation of Porphyry's *On Abstinence from Animal Food,* which he also owned. In excerpts from his journal printed in *The Dial,* Alcott identified both Pythagoras and Porphyry as his predecessors in the dietary regimen that he described as follows:

> I brought from our village a bag of wheaten flour for our board. Pythagorean is our diet, we yet make small demands on foreign products; but harvest our dust mostly from this hired acre. I would abstain from the fruits of oppression and blood, and am seeking means of entire independence. . . . One miracle we have wrought, nevertheless, and shall soon work all of them, our wine is water,—flesh, bread,—drugs, fruits, and we defy, meekly, the satyrs all, and Esculapius.[37]

Like Pythagoras, Alcott based his vegetarianism on the theory that animals are kin to man (since the One Spirit, though in different degrees, flows through both)[38] and on the belief that eating animal flesh would excite man's bestial nature and detract from his spiritual side.

For specific suggestions concerning the diet most favorable to the man who desires the greatest possible influx of Spirit, Alcott seems to have turned to the Orphic and Neoplatonic symbolism of the sun as the highest Good. Characteristically transporting mythological imagery into life and treating metaphor literally, Alcott advised that *"whatever grows above ground, and tempered in the solar ray, is most friendly to the strength, genius and beauty proper to man."*[39] Fruits he considered the

best of all foods, since they are so much closer to the sun than dirt-bound vegetables. Their effects are also of a higher sort. "Like Orpheus," he wrote, "[fruits] tame the human passions to consonance and harmony by their lyric influence."[40]

In yet another way the program at Fruitlands became a part of Alcott's living symbolism: his use of only linen for clothing also had an analogue in Pythagorean practice and in Orphic mythology. His refusal to wear wool was based, at least partially, on his belief that in using it man deprived and enslaved the sheep; cotton was, of course, proscribed because it was derived from Negro slavery.[41] But there was also a positive reason for the choice of linen. Alcott may have recalled that a linen garment was the dress required of an initiate in the Mysteries.[42] He was, at any rate, clearly aware that wearing it was an important part of Pythagorean practice,[43] so it must have pleased him—at the time of his Fruitlands venture or in retrospect—that his use of linen was one more instance in which he brought to life the symbolic role he had chosen.

Possibly, there was also another reason for his linen clothing. It is quite likely that Alcott knew the reason behind the choice of linen by the Pythagoreans and the initiates in the Mysteries. Their rules concerning clothing materials could be traced to the Orphic prohibition of wool. As Taylor reported in his dissertation on *The Eleusinian and Bacchic Mysteries* (a work that Alcott seems to have known),[44] a fleece of wool was included in the Orphic ceremonies as a symbol of the "laceration or distribution of intellect, or Dionysus, into matter."[45] According to Orphic theogony, Dionysus, the god at the center of Orphic worship, had been born to Zeus and his daughter Kore-Persephone. To Dionysus, Zeus had given rule over the other gods. However, Zeus' rivals, the Titans—children of Gaia, the Earth—had become jealous of the young god, so they distracted him with a number of trinkets, including a fleece of wool, killed him, and tore his body to pieces. The Titans had then tasted the flesh of Dionysus, so infuriating Zeus that he destroyed them with a thunderbolt. From the smoldering remains of the Titans, the Orphic Mysteries taught, arose the race of man, a being of twofold nature, born from the Titans, the impious offspring of the Earth, but retaining—since they had partially consumed Dionysus—a small part of the god. The Orphic desire was to be freed from the dominion of the Titanic heritage through the exaltation of the Dionysus within. If Alcott did have this Orphic myth in the back of his mind as he donned his linen clothes, he would have seen in his renunciation of wool yet another emblem of his desire to escape, as much as possible, from the material life to which man is subjected.

Although in the mythologizing of his life Alcott more often compared himself to Pythagoras than to Orpheus, the latter analogy did occur to him. We have seen it already in the ties to silence which he felt united him with Orpheus, in the abstinence from meat which he regarded as the heart of "the Orphic life," and in the diet of fruit which also linked him with Orpheus, at least in metaphor. He discerned another similarity between himself and Orpheus in his desire, as he expressed it, to "take the beast out and put in the man—to tame the beast, rather, and develope [sic] the man in the man, disqualifying him for howling longer with the wolves or glutting himself with the swine. . . ."[46] He summed up this goal in his journal in what he called a "little Orphic fancy" about "the Gentle Tamer" who "dwelt on the skirts of the forest, and whose chambers were roughly invaded from day to day by the beasts from the woods, but who tamed them into gentleness by his soft manners and kind disciplines and behaviors. . . ."[47] It is hard not to see in such a picture both the archetypal Orpheus and Alcott himself, who tried to tame the beast in men by showing them, in his own life, the Orphic way.

Alcott may have failed in many of his ventures, but he did succeed in living his chosen symbolism—a success attested by the number of his contemporaries who acquiesced in Alcott's claim (spoken and implied) of being a modern Pythagoras or Orpheus. Robert Carter (at one time an editor of the magazine *The Pioneer*) wrote of Alcott's role in the revival of Pythagorean asceticism.[48] George William Curtis (essayist, editor, and a member of Brook Farm) spoke of "the Orphic Alcott" who designed and built for Emerson that strange and symbolic summer house of curved wood.[49] To William Emerson, he was "the Orphic philosopher," into whose sieve William warned his brother not to throw even his cheapest acres.[50] To Dr. Channing, however, (who seems to have recognized something of the power of Alcott's living symbolism) he was "Orpheus at the plow," teaching a greater lesson through his life "than most of us teach by the pen."[51] And even before he wrote his **"Orphic Sayings,"** it was widely assumed that he was the "Orphic poet" in Emerson's *Nature*—indeed, he made such an identification himself.[52] In recognizing the success of Alcott's spiritual venture, Thoreau's tribute in *Walden* was perhaps the most perceptive of all:

> . . . Connecticut gave him to the world,—he peddled first her wares, afterwards, as he declares, his brains. These he peddles still, prompting God and disgracing man, bearing for fruit his brain only, like the nut its kernel. I think that he must be the man of the most faith of any alive. His words and attitude always suppose a better state of things than other men are acquainted with. . . . He has no venture in the present. . . . I think that he should keep a caravansary on the world's highway, where philosophers of all nations might put up, and on his sign should be printed, 'Entertainment for man, but not for his beast. . . .' A blue-robed man, whose fittest roof is the overarching sky which reflects his serenity. I do not see how he can ever die; Nature cannot spare him.[53]

Notes

1. Octavius Brooks Frothingham, *Transcendentalism in New England: A History* (New York: Harper, 1959; 1st edition, 1876), p. 257.

2. *The Letters of A. Bronson Alcott,* ed. Richard L. Herrnstadt (Ames, Iowa: Iowa State University Press, 1969), p. 643.

3. In addition to his journal contributions, Alcott published ten books. Four were on his theories of education. The others were *Concord Days* (1872), *Table-Talk* (1877), *Tablets* (1879), two volumes of poetry—*New Connecticut* (1881) and *Sonnets and Canzonets* (1879)—, and *Ralph Waldo Emerson: An Estimate of His Character and Genius* (1888).

4. "Orphic Sayings," *The Dial,* I (January 1841), 355.

5. Modern studies of Orphic religion include W. K. C. Guthrie, *Orpheus and Greek Religion,* rev. ed. (New York: Norton Library, 1966); Jane Harrison, *Prolegomena to the Study of Greek Religion,* rev. ed. (New York: Meridian Books, 1960); Ivan M. Linforth, *The Arts of Orpheus* (Berkeley: University of California Press, 1941); Vittorio D. Macchioro, *From Orpheus to Paul: A History of Orphism* (New York: Holt, 1930); Erwin Rodhe, *Psyche: The Cult of Souls and Belief in Immortality among the Greeks,* trans. W. B. Hillis (London, 1925); J. R. Watmough, *Orphism* (Cambridge: The University Press, 1934).

6. We see Alcott's equation of the terms "Orphic" and "Pythagorean" in his explanation that "anciently, there existed what is called the Orphic Life, men keeping fast to all things without life, and abstaining wholly from those that had [life]," for the purpose of preparing themselves to receive the "deepest wisdom." This, Alcott continued, was the way of life that Pythagoras had followed. *Tablets,* pp. 37, 115-118. This directly echoes Plato's description of the Orphic life in *Laws* 6.782c.

7. Among these was *The Works of Plato* in five volumes, issued in 1804, the first English publication of the whole of Plato.

8. Perhaps the best summary of Taylor's contemporary reputation and publishing history is Frank B. Evans II, "Thomas Taylor, Platonist of the Romantic Period," *PMLA,* LV (1940), 1060-79. For other evaluations of Taylor's translations, see Kathleen Raine and George Mills Harper, eds. *Thomas Taylor the Platonist: Selected Writings,* Bollingen Series no. 88 (Princeton: Princeton University Press, 1969), pp. 19-25, and the introduction to R. Catesby Taliaferro's edition of Taylor's translation of *The Timaeus and the Critias,* Bollingen Series no. 3 (n.p., 1944), pp. 9-34.

9. [Isaac Disraeli], *Curiosities of Literature* (5th ed.; London, 1807), I, 370.

10. *Letters of Horace Walpole,* ed. P. Toynbee (Oxford, 1903-5), XIV, 238.

11. *Melincourt; or, Sir Oran Haut-ton* (London, 1896; first ed., 1818), pp. 51-52.

12. William E. A. Axon, "Thomas Taylor, the Platonist: A Biographical and Bibliographical Sketch," reprinted from *The Library* (July and August, 1890) in *Pamphlets on Biography* (London, 1890), IX, 9.

13. Evans, "Thomas Taylor, Platonist of the Romantic Period," *PMLA,* 1074, 1077.

14. J. A. Notopoulos, "Shelley and Thomas Taylor," *PMLA,* LI (1936), 502.

15. *The Complete Works of Ralph Waldo Emerson,* ed. Edward Waldo Emerson (12 vols.; Boston: Riverside Press, 1903-04), VIII, 50.

16. Odell Shepard, *Pedlar's Progress: The Life of Bronson Alcott* (Boston: Little, Brown, 1937), p. 160.

17. F. B. Sanborn and William T. Harris, *A. Bronson Alcott: His Life and Philosophy* (2 vols.; Boston: Roberts Brothers, 1893), II, 641.

18. "Catalogue of Books," *The Dial,* III (April 1843), 545-48.

19. *The Letters of A. Bronson Alcott,* p. 403.

20. *New Connecticut,* p. 62.

21. Jamblichus, *Life of Pythagoras,* trans. Thomas Taylor (London, 1818), p. 41.

22. Shepard, *Pedlar's Progress,* p. 51.

23. See also *Concord Days,* p. 88.

24. *The Letters of A. Bronson Alcott,* p. 444.

25. Shepard, *Pedlar's Progress,* p. 336.

26. *The Journals of Bronson Alcott,* ed. Odell Shepard (Boston: Little, Brown, 1938), p. 200. The discussion of Pythagoras Alcott refers to is in Connop Thirlwall, *History of Greece* (New York, 1848-51), I, 214-219.

27. *Concord Days,* pp. 88-92, 186.

28. *Tablets,* pp. 113-114. Alcott's discussion is actually a very close, unacknowledged paraphrase of Jamblichus' *Life of Pythagoras,* trans. Thomas Taylor (London, 1818), p. 51. Jamblichus ends his passage on silence by saying that its importance was "unfolded to us [by those] who instituted the Mysteries."

29. *Concord Days,* pp. 111-112.

30. Jamblichus, *On the Mysteries of the Egyptians, Chaldeans, and Assyrians,* trans. Thomas Taylor (London, 1821), p. 237n.

31. "Orphic Sayings," *The Dial,* I (January 1841), 361.

32. *The Journals of Bronson Alcott,* p. 187.

33. *Concord Days,* p. 92; *Tablets,* p. 115; *cf.* Jamblichus, *Life of Pythagoras,* p. 72.

34. Jamblichus, *Life of Pythagoras,* p. 44.

35. *The Journals of Bronson Alcott,* pp. 240-241.

36. Shepard, *Pedlar's Progress,* p. 437; Sanborn and Harris, *A. Bronson Alcott,* I, 270.

37. "Days from a Diary," *The Dial,* II (April 1842), 427.

38. In fact, Alcott even elaborated on the Pythagorean concept of man's relation to animals, deciding that animals are incarnations of man's lower self, having "lapsed" from man in the same way man had emanated from the Divine. *The Journals of Bronson Alcott,* p. 379.

39. *Tablets,* p. 36. *cf.* his poem, "The Seer's Rations," in which part of the prescribed diet is sunbeams (*Tablets,* p. 39).

40. *Tablets,* p. 35. The identification of the sun as Good probably contributed also to Alcott's theory of complexions. As he explained in his Conversations, blonds partake more of the angelic or solar temperament and brunettes more of the demonic or lunar. (It would have taken a compassionate listener—or an unobservant one—to fail to note that Alcott, himself a blond, was by his own theory "a child of light," while his dark wife was relegated to the status of a demonic "descendent of night.") *The Journals of Bronson Alcott,* p. 453.

41. Shepard, *Pedlar's Progress,* p. 368.

42. *The Metamorphosis, or Golden Ass, and Philosophical Works of Apuleius,* trans. Thomas Taylor (London, 1822), p. 208.

43. *Concord Days,* p. 92; *cf.* Jamblichus, *Life of Pythagoras,* p. 108.

44. *The Letters of A. Bronson Alcott,* p. 657.

45. Thomas Taylor, *Eleusinian and Bacchic Mysteries, A Dissertation* (London, 1875), p. 156.

46. *The Journals of Bronson Alcott,* pp. 267-268.

47. *The Journals of Bronson Alcott,* p. 170.

48. Cited in Clara Endicott Sears, comp., *Bronson Alcott's Fruitlands* (Boston: Houghton, Mifflin,

1915), p. 38; Sanborn and Harris, *A Bronson Alcott,* II, 379-380.

49. Sanborn and Harris, *A. Bronson Alcott,* II, 432.

50. *The Letters of Ralph Waldo Emerson,* ed. Ralph L. Rush (6 vols.; New York: Columbia University Press, 1939), III, 263n.

51. Frothingham, *Transcendentalism in New England,* p. 259.

52. *The Journals of Bronson Alcott,* p. 78.

53. *The Writings of Henry David Thoreau* (20 vols.; Boston: Houghton, Mifflin, 1906), II, pp. 296-297.

Fordyce Richard Bennett (essay date 1981)

SOURCE: Bennett, Fordyce Richard. "Bronson Alcott and Free Religion." In *Studies in the American Renaissance,* edited by Joel Myerson, pp. 403-21. Boston: Twayne Publishers, 1981.

[*In the following essay, Bennett examines Alcott's involvement with "free religion," a Unitarian movement of the 1860s and 1870s that embraced an inclusive attitude toward all religious creeds. Bennett argues that Alcott's eventual criticism of the movement was rooted in his increasing conservatism and in his desire to embrace orthodox religion in his later years.*]

"A curious jumble of fools and philosophers," wrote Louisa May Alcott of the Radical Club, a place "where the philosophers mount their hobbies and prance away into time and space, while we gaze after them and try to look wise."[1] And in the same vein, she wrote in a letter of 1872 to her mother: "Had a very transcendental day yesterday, and at night my head was 'swelling visibly' with the ideas cast into it. The club was a funny mixture of rabbis and weedy old ladies, the 'oversoul' and oysters. Papa and [Cyrus A.] B[artol]. flew clean out of sight like a pair of Platonic balloons, and we tried to follow, but couldn't."[2] A serious account of the Radical Club, an adjunct of the Free Religious Association, is Mrs. Sargent's *Sketches and Reminiscences.* Yet, neither Mrs. Sargent nor Alcott's biographer, Odell Shepard, nor the historian of Free Religion, Stow Persons, gives more than passing reference to Alcott's place in Free Religion,[3] even though Alcott's activities, as recorded in his diaries, indicate his involvement in this reaffirmation of a Transcendental theme: rebellion against conservative Unitarianism.

On Sunday, 1 January 1865, Alcott, always eager to exploit his genius for conversation, pondered the "avenues open": drawing room, platform, pulpit, and schoolhouse.[4] Eleven days later he wrote: "Thursday 12. To

Boston. See the Fraternity people about giving a series of Sunday Evening Lectures on Religious Themes."[5] He discussed his purpose with Daniel Ricketson in a 12 February 1865 letter: "Lately it has seemed as if the call had come for me to speak, not <from> in parlours alone and privately, but from public platforms and pulpits: as if our ripest thinkers and best men's utterances needed to be followed out into clearness, to be complemented in Ass[ocia]tions of a *Personal God,* a *vital theology,* answering to the claims of our revolutionary times."[6]

A course of Sunday evening lectures on religious themes in the Fraternity Rooms at 554 Washington Street, lectures for the Twenty-Eighth Congregational Society at the Melodeon on 5 February ("American Religion") and 5 March ("Religious Veins and Issues of Our Time"), and preaching for Charles G. Ames at Albany, Charles T. Brooks at Newport, Sidney H. Morse (editor of the *Radical*) at Haverhill, and Charles C. Burleigh at Florence, comprised Alcott's activities in a year in which his reading of Strauss and Renan made him increasingly dissatisfied with even the likes of James Freeman Clarke, whose preaching was "far too Hebrew," of the "ancient type," not of the party of the present, "of faith and of today."[7] Alcott spoke of Frederic Henry Hedge, another target of his dissatisfaction, on 24 January 1865: "Hedge is learned, thoughtful, discreet and while speculatively free, plants himself practically on the old traditions in Church and State. He declines giving a lecture in our series on Sunday evenings."[8] Instead of Hedge and Clarke, Alcott invited Samuel Johnson as speaker for the Sunday Evening lectures, and he drew the lines explicitly in a February 1865 list entitled "Names of Our Men"—a list including, among others, Ralph Waldo Emerson, David A. Wasson, John Weiss, Samuel Longfellow, Johnson, Octavius Brooks Frothingham, Robert Collyer, William J. Potter, Brooks, Joseph B. Marvin, and Thomas Wentworth Higginson.[9]

Alcott's critiquing, listing, and line drawing seem innocent enough unless placed in context and then they appear ominous, for spring promised the first National Unitarian Convention.[10] "I am to go to Florence," Alcott wrote on 11 March 1865, "to New York City, probably attend the Convention there, and hope to meet Brooks of Newport, J. W. Chadwick of Brooklyn, Frothingham, and others of the liberal faith."[11] In his 3 April letter to Mrs. Stearns, he added: "Tomorrow, I am off for New York, expecting to join Wasson at Worcester, and we go on together to the Convention. The Free Congregational Society at Florence, where I passed Sunday last, send me as their delegate. If not admitted, we shall question the *Liberal* name the Convention has taken, and may rightly plead for Christendom's enlargement."[12]

On Sunday, 2 April 1865, Alcott, considering himself a delegate from Florence, readied himself for the trip to

New York City and, as he recorded in his diary, "the representative of that growing part of our population which abstains mostly from supporting the existing Churches in New England, finding little or nothing in the weekly services to further their piety."[13] Leaving with Wasson and other delegates, Alcott traveled to New York, arriving Tuesday, briefly visiting Samuel Johnson in Brooklyn and then taking his spot at the Convention (his credentials brought by Burleigh of Florence) on Wednesday, 5 April.[14] Alcott was pleased with Clarke's pacification sermon at All-Souls of the preceding evening, terming it "Catholic in spirit, recommending sympathy and union on the broadest grounds" in his letter to his wife Abba of 8 April, and remarking as follows in his diary: "But for claims urged for the Unitarian name and notions, his discourse was catholic and urged the broadest grounds for union."[15] At the two o'clock session on Wednesday afternoon, Alcott recommended the lyceum as a model for refurbishing the Unitarian pulpits and the addition of lay speakers.[16] All was not placid on these two early spring days, for when Clarke suggested the Convention amend the constitution to read "Unitarian and Independent churches," Bellows squelched the amendment and Edward C. Towne objected.[17] Wasson, disturbed by the stress on the lordship of Christ in the Preamble and First Article, said he "could not accept a Lord according to the interpretation of the Orthodox churches . . . that Jesus never intended that he should be considered a Lord who had come to dominate over men. . . . A form has been thrust between us and God, and an authority placed over the soul."[18] "I am present," Alcott wrote of the 5-6 April events, "at the sittings Wednesday and Thursday. Here see W. H. Channing, Towne of Medford, Ames of Albany, O. B. Frothingham, [Lucy] Stone, Morse, Marvin, Longfellow, and find myself in sympathy with them. Wasson makes a good speech. . . . Towne also speaks to the point. Bellows and Co disinclined to open the doors for debate of opinions: jealous of their good orthodox name and fame as a denomination. . . . Frothingham feels agrieved by their ignoring his place and claims."[19]

The following day Alcott left for home and noted in his diary: "Friday 7. Take the train for New Haven. Towne comes on with me. I propose a meeting of our friends sometime soon for consultation on measures of teaching and influence and give him the names."[20] Earnest plans for such a meeting would only begin after the failure to achieve unanimity at the Syracuse Conference of October 1866, but until then Alcott consoled himself with talks on the "New Church" and "New Divinity" with F. B. Sanborn, Emerson, Ames, Brooks, Wasson, and Morse, and with publication of the *Radical,* edited by Morse, termed by Alcott "a live Journal—an indication of an American theology planted in the everlasting laws of man's being."[21] Alcott hoped the *Radical* would join the radicals of the East with the St. Louis Hege-

lians of the West: "Sunday 15. I read Morse several papers, and we discuss the times at length. His journal is finding unexpected favor, and bids fair to become the leading organ of free thought for New England and the West. We consider the propriety of holding a Conference of thoughtful persons in Boston during Anniversary Week. I advise it, and wish him to speak with Emerson about the movement, also with Johnson and Weiss. If they approve, write our friends in the May number of the *Radical*."[22]

In the third week of May 1866, Alcott wrote Wasson and Morse about the meeting but Morse cancelled the plans a few days later.[23] On Sunday, 6 May 1866, Alcott had spoken at the Melodeon on "The Radical Church and Movement," calling for an itinerant priesthood, a parlorlike temple (reminiscent of the Temple School), and eclecticism with regard to sacred books.[24] Yet Alcott was not content, as his diary for Sunday, 29 July, indicates: "It would please me to speak often on Sundays, but for this service I have few invitations and must consent to wait. The New Divinity is fashioning itself almost unconsciously in the faith of the fervent of my time."[25] Alcott outlined this "New Divinity" in his publication in the *Radical*. Admitting the historic basis of faiths, Alcott argued for the permanent in religion: "It is pure theism, the sense of the spirit's presence, and pulsating in every breast, revealing itself as Law, Idea, Person, the source of life, the spring of thought, sense of duty. This immanent deity, once admitted as the postulate of existence, solves all questions the mind asks, the heart proposes, and plants man's being on imperishable foundations."[26] The "inner sense" implied revelation accessible to all through intuition, a direct critique of the senses as avenues to spiritual truths, a catholicity of response to the scriptures of other religions and a concomitant antisectarianism.[27] "We require," Alcott wrote in demanding a comparative divinity, "the modern divine to be familiar with the thought of all times; with Plato's texts as with St. Paul's, with Zoroaster as with Jesus, Hermes as Moses, Herbert as David; himself drinking not less at the fountains."[28]

Circumstances auspicious for a "New Divinity" arose later in 1866. In his diary for 8-13 October, Alcott wrote:

> The Unitarian National Conference has met at Syracuse and discussed denominational topics chiefly. Dr. Hedge's discourse, like every public utterance of his, tells for institutions holding fast to historic grounds. . . . Abbot of Dover, N.H. introduced very liberal grounds for union, which the Conference withdrew, greatly to its discredit. I see nothing to prevent the denomination from hardening into a refined Episcopal Hierarchy, as formidable as the English establishment, and with all its professions, illiberal and Sectarian like that. The friends of free thought and of a free Church, may now take steps independent of this orga-

nization and plant theology in ideas becoming the advanced civilization of our time. The Radical should speak openly for that large and increasing class of thoughtful men and women who find themselves outside of existing sects, and desirous of uniting on the broadest grounds, as a Church befitting humanity. 'Tis plain the Unitarian body designs casting them out as heretical and foes to its organization.[29]

Francis Ellingwood Abbot, soon to be a central figure in Free Religion, displayed, so Alcott thought, "depth of thinking and liberality of Spirit."[30]

Within two months of the Syracuse Convention, Alcott was contemplating reviving the Sunday lectures and holding a convention for the radicals: "I am willing to revive the Sunday Evening Course of Lectures. And must consult Weiss, Johnson, Towne about the same. Also about holding a Convention of liberal minds wishing for a more efficient religious ministry. We might invite Johnson, Weiss, Emerson, Frothingham, Wasson, Towne, Chadwick, Higginson, Morse, Marvin, Potter, Abbot, [John T.] Sargent, Burleigh, Sanborn, perhaps some others, to meet somewhere in Boston, and discuss ideas and measures at length, and this very soon."[31] The Sunday "Radical Lectures on Religion" were organized by Morse to be given at the Parker Fraternity Hall and Alcott (who seems to have replaced Abbot) delivered the fourth lecture on 17 February 1867. Discussing "Modern Religion," Alcott spoke on "instrumentalities" (newspapers, theatre, lectures, and conversation), church architecture, and religion's essence: "Religion—true religion—is man's life. It exists in his soul. It has a divine life and a human life. Religion flows down into our humanity, and its function is to make us divine."[32] Under the dates 13-21 January, Alcott mentioned receipt of an announcement: "Towne sends me a circular note for a meeting at Bartol's on Tuesday, February 5."[33] The circular note, bearing the names of O. B. Frothingham, Weiss, Towne, Abbot, and Potter, and inviting Alcott to 17 Chestnut Street, Bartol's residence, for an eleven o'clock meeting, read as follows:

> Since all prevailing denominational religious organizations set limits, more or less strict, to religious inquiry and fellowship, and since the recent attempts to organize even the most liberal denomination of Christians, as shown in the National Conference of Unitarian Churches, have fallen into the same error, and so have failed to satisfy the demands of Liberal Faith, it is believed that the time has come to form a new association, in spiritual bonds, on the basis of Free Thought, for the purpose of bringing like-minded men together, of gathering to a head powers that are working too aimlessly in the same general direction, and of diffusing rational truths by rational methods. The desire is to make a fellowship, not a party; to promote the scientific study of religious truth, not to defend the legacy of theological tradition; to keep open the lines of spiritual freedom, not to close the lines of speculative belief.[34]

Though suffering from rheumatism during January, Alcott attended the momentous early February meeting which led to plans for the first Free Religious Association convention in late May. On 5 February he went to Boston to

> meet the Conference at Bartols. A large attendance—mostly preachers: many young men. Dr. Bartol made Chairman, Towne Secretary. Potter submits a paper for a Fellowship of Persons to promote the interests of pure religion, to encourage the scientific study of theology, and to increase fellowship in the spirit, all persons cordially invited to become members. Membership in the association shall leave each individual responsible for his own opinion alone, and affect in no degree his relation to other associations.
>
> The paper is discussed freely by Frothingham, Potter, Weiss, Longfellow, [Charles Eliot] Norton, [Charles K.] Whipple, and others. I take an earnest part in the proceedings. Tis agreed to submit the paper to a Committee, who shall call a conference of the people sometime during the spring and present the doings of this meeting for further consideration. The spirit of the speakers is hopeful, catholic, and intellectual. . . . This concert of thoughtful persons, bids fair and commends itself to my feelings, and I return with satisfaction to my thoughts and studies.[35]

Alcott wrote to his St. Louis comrade, William Torrey Harris, that the "Association purposes building a Hall for Pure Theological Teaching, and promises to do good work in the way of Conversation and Lecture."[36] Near the beginning of the fourth week in May 1867, Alcott received an announcement of a public meeting to consider the "wants and prospects" of Free Religion, at Horticultural Hall on the morning of 30 May. Under that date, Alcott recorded in his diary: "Come into the city and attend 'The Free Religion Convention' setting in Horticultural Hall. The Hall is crowded. The speeches free and effective, only [Robert Dale] Owen's is too long. Weiss's, Abbot's, Higginson's and Emerson's were excellent. Had the meeting been open for discussions during the afternoon and evening, it would have been far more satisfying to many. What action shall follow the organization remains to be seen."[37]

Alcott's ideas of action are apparent from a diary entry made only a few days later:

> Tuesday 4. To Watertown and pass the day with Weiss. Find him feeling with me concerning the new Radical Religious Association hoping it may serve the practical needs of the time. . . . Nothing were better than Conventions held in various places, inviting the people to come and discuss, at least hear discussed the great questions about which our people are more or less interested. I am purposing to venture upon some held alike on Sundays and week-days, and I shall be strengthened in my purpose by the sympathy and cooperation of others. Had more time been allowed for speaking of *instrumentalities* I should have dealt more at length, at the late Convention [first Free Religious Association meeting], on *Conversations, Conventions* and *Lectures* as measures for awake[n]ing and informing the minds of the community concerning the needs and duties of our time.[38]

And before the Free Religious Club at No. 13 Chestnut Street on 17 June 1867, he addressed the problem of "the Religious wants of the time and ways of meeting them."[39] In addition to use of teachers, conversations, conventions, club rooms, and journals, Alcott wished to "send missionaries into the cities and towns to speak wherever pulpits are open on Sundays, and on week days in Conversations, or lecture, as opportunity may open."[40] Alcott spread the radical gospel in the years following the Free Religious Association's formation in churches at Dover (Abbot), Medford (Towne), Haverhill (Morse), Newport (Brooks), Albany (Ames), Florence (Burleigh), and elsewhere, the letters and diaries of 1867-68 expressing uncritical enthusiasm for the *Radical,* Free Religious Association, and Free Religious Club, and criticism of such men as Judge Ebenezer Rockwood Hoar, who felt that Alcott's desire to open the Unitarian Church to "free thought" would "come to nothing but dissensions," and Samuel J. May, who, Alcott concluded, "still clings to the Christian traditions and fails to comprehend the spiritual condition of the people. His sympathies are with the Conservative Unitarian body, its men and measures."[41] Alcott considered a "school for the New Divinity" to be held at his residence with Emerson, Johnson, Wasson, Weiss, and Harris as professors.[42] Alcott revealed his enthusiasm for Free Religion while drawing significant parallels in this diary comment: "I consider the [Free Religious] Club as offering opportunity for the widest discussion of all questions affecting human welfare. We have had nothing like it since the times of the Transcendental Aurora: nothing so free, fresh inspiring. Perhaps it were true to call this the ripe fruit of that sapling there planted, and since grown to something of majesty and maturity."[43] And again upon receipt of a copy of the 1867 proceedings of the Free Religious Association, he commented: "This pamphlet of 54 pages has just come to hand. I regard the meeting, addresses, association here reported as a most significant fact in the religious movements of our time, perhaps forming an era in the Christian Church to which reference will be made hereafter. Whether a new religious order is to spring from the views and purposes of those who promoted this meeting, and who are bent on pursuing discussions in this connexion of thought and endeavor, remains to be seen."[44]

The "school for the New Divinity" did not materialize but a more workable plan was proposed by Towne in the fall of 1867, a plan indicating that Alcott's conversations in various churches, clubs, and semi-official gatherings were part of Free Religious Association propaganda: "Towne comes up with me in the 11 o'clock train. We discuss religious reform at length. He thinks the Committee appointed at the meeting of the Free Religious Association last May will take measures for opening a course of instruction for the benefit of the

Cambridge Students, and that Emerson, Weiss, Bartol, Wasson, Johnson (if he will) give courses of Lectures in Cambridge during the coming autumn and winter. I am also to have my Conversations as part of the plan."[45] Perhaps one of Alcott's most significant practical efforts for Free Religion was organizing the Sunday Evening Horticultural Hall Lectures in 1868-69 and 1869-70, lectures thereafter conducted directly by the Free Religious Association. Alcott established the lecture course initially in collaboration with Morse of Haverhill and J. J. Locke of Greenwood but later with Edwin Morton, a Boston attorney. On 10 October 1868, Alcott recorded:

> A desirable Hall in the Horticultural Building is offered us for three months, with the privilege of holding morning and evening meetings at $30 the Sunday. This last will suit us. And Locke engages to solicit subscriptions to defray expenses.
>
> I think Emerson, Wasson, Abbot, Potter, and perhaps Weiss, may assist me in the speaking. It may be a rash adventure not worth the trial. The sectarians are active on Sundays. I think some of us who would speak for freedom from the yoke of sect, may becomingly try our wits also.
>
> Shall I own that I deem myself a Priest of the Free Faith, and entitled alike by thought and experience, if not by Gifts, to be heard by any who may find profit in my words.[46]

The first speaker in the course was Weiss, who lectured on the "Real Relation of Man to God" on 17 January 1869, drawing this response from Alcott: "A good audiance assemble at Horticultural Hall to hear Weiss. His discourse was firmly conceived, delivered with a graceful impassioned eloquence and gave much satisfaction to his thoughtful auditors. We think our course opens with prospects of brilliant success."[47] Other speakers included Abbot, Weiss, Higginson, and Frothingham, the concluding lecture given by Wendell Phillips, "Christianity a Battle, not a Dream," on 11 April 1869. Emerson, who declined speaking the following year, chose "Natural Religion" as his subject for the series' twelfth lecture on 4 April 1869, reasserting themes of the "primal sentiments," the unity in creation, correspondence, "beneficent necessity," and natural above creedal/ historical religion. Emphasizing the grandeur of the moral laws within man, Emerson echoed sentiments of three decades before: "Now can anything be so great as that inward Copernican system, whose equilibrium is perfect as the other, whose periodicities are as compensatory; which never tilts, and never decays; to which nothing can be added, from which nothing subtracted; which was before the other, and will be after it; and to which that is only a shadow and a type;—which builds and unbuilds the men and kingdoms of earth, and is the Source and Law of all existence? Space, eternity, godhead, are of the mind: wherever there is wrong the response is pain. We do not live by times, but by qualities. We pass for what we are. The evils we suffer are the measure of those we have done."[48]

In addition to the Horticultural Hall Free Religious Course, Alcott added one further substantial contribution—missionary proselytizing at the West. During the winters of 1869-70 and 1870-71, for example, Alcott toured Connecticut, New York, Illinois, Ohio, Missouri, Iowa, and Michigan speaking often on "The Ideal Church," "The Coming Church," or "Worship." The content varied little, the emphases being on belief in a personal God, church architecture (semi-circular pews, statuary, painting, slightly elevated pulpit), an oratory less rhetorical and more extemporaneous, greater variety of speakers including women, children's choir, prayer (silent but extemporaneous when spoken), sermons consisting of scriptures and poetry from various nations to be read while seated, primacy of ideas, fluidity of the religious forms and instrumentalities for each age, the church universal (inclusive not exclusive), the intuitive method as a means to religious truth, belief in immortality of the soul, reform of church music by reducing the number of hymns, home as the "initial Church," worship as primarily planting oneself in spirit, services conducted in Saxon speech (a plain, not bookish, language), and the need for sacraments and symbols.

* * *

Though one of the founders and prime movers behind the early workings of Free Religion and a self-styled "Priest of the Free Faith," Alcott eventually became its critic, his views moving from uncritical praise toward a criticism qualified by limited appreciation. In January 1869, Alcott praised his own brainchild, the Horticultural Hall Radical Lectures: "I shall be disappointed if it is not found to serve the religious needs of our time, and become an organic institution here and elsewhere."[49] But by 6 May 1870, he wrote: "I am dissatisfied with the Sunday lectures as falling short of the highest aims of religious teaching, and wish to see a Church fairly planted in Absolute ideas."[50] And on 7 January 1872, Alcott characterized the Sunday Lectures, as he would Free Religion as a whole: "They mark the transition from our older to newer forms of instruction and worship."[51] Alcott, involved in the first meetings of the Radical Club in 1867 and its early enthusiastic supporter, criticized the Club as early as 1869 for its divisiveness and materialism.[52] And ten years later, when the Radical Club had become the Chestnut Street Club, Alcott noted: "I have seldom attended these meetings since the drift of thought and discussion has become less spiritual and philosophical than at first; and find myself less and less in sympathy with the members. Its scientific pretensions appear to me mostly of the doubtful kind and tending to merely negative results at best."[53]

"I find," he wrote after a meeting of the Club on 13 November 1876, "my idealism wholly mistimed and inopportune in this setting of individualists and extreme radicals."[54] Its stress on scientific method (especially on Darwinian thought), on the historical and concrete rather than the abstract and ideal, and its disputatious "extreme Individualism," placed the Club with the Free Religious Association in Alcott's estimation.[55]

Alcott, hopeful that Free Religion would fulfill dreams frustrated in the 1830s and 1840s, became disillusioned with the organization and its hostility to Christianity, as expressed by its agnosticism and scientific leanings.[56] A group of individuals not a Church, he called it on 7 January 1872, and two years later termed the members "agitators rather than builders."[57] After an early honeymoon, Alcott settled into an uneasy marriage with the Free Religious Association: "I cannot feel in perfect sympathy with the views of the leading minds in it [Free Religious Association], but as an organ for diffusing a freer spirit, consider it among the most effective of any, and shall belong to it in this way.—It stands apparently in like relations to the Church that the Antislavery Societies stood to the State as an instrumentality for reforming the Church, but has little of a positive nature in itself. It is Transcendental Idealism, not this negative Positivism that is to build a Church for these times."[58] Negative, destructive, narrow, transitional—these were the labels Alcott later gave the Free Religious Association, an organization to clear away superstition, idols of the tribe, preparing the way for the Universal Church.[59]

Alcott's changing attitudes toward Abbot, the Free Religious Association's leading figure, reflect in microcosm his attitudes toward Free Religion as a whole. In an early diary entry, dated 23 December 1866, Alcott placed Abbot with Harris as the two youths upon whom to build the future: "Among the young ministers he [Abbot] chiefly interests me by his depth of thinking and liberality of Spirit. His metaphysical ability has already gained him notice, and his attitude as regards the religious movements of the time leads me to hope much of him. With him and Harris, both still very young men and strong, I shall feel there is a foundation for the new ideas, and the possibility of planting an American Culture."[60] Again, on 16 August 1868, Alcott noted of Abbot: "Abbot is here. He is disposed to hold fast and sure his independence of sects and schools, thinking freely and acting from his own convictions as opportunities open to him. I think he has a useful future before him. On the whole, he seems one of the more spiritual thinkers of the time."[61] And, after Abbot had been prosecuted and driven from his pulpit, Alcott remarked: "I regard Abbot as one of the priests of the New Faith, the Universal religion, and likely to promote this in ways not yet clear to any of us. A man of faith, insight, thought, learning, and method, he must make his mark, like Harris, on the philosophy of our time."[62] Alcott, however, revised his opinion in August 1879, when he wrote beneath the passage that this estimate was an "overstatement as to theology."[63] But a decade before Alcott had said of Abbot that "his is a logical rather than an ideal mind."[64] And the following day, 13 December 1869, he added these strictures: "I find Abbot inclining to Rationalism as distinguished from Idealism, and more of a scholar than a thinker apparently. His reading, I judge, has been confined mostly to the later British and French writers on metaphysical subjects, the German and Greek writers having interested him less. But no man is master who is not familiar with the types of thought which the great masters of those countries represent and I shall look to Harris and St. Louis rather for the freshest and deepest things."[65] Abbot, in his 28 February 1870 Horticultural Hall lecture, "Jesus and Socrates in the History of Religion," insisted that Free Religion could have no "ideal men" as Christianity had in Jesus, that the Socratic virtue of knowledge must supplement the Christian one of love, and that Socrates, in this sense superior to Jesus, had harbored no secrets in religion, avoiding mysteries "too sacred for the uninitiated."[66] Alcott found the treatment of Jesus "impious and audacious" and claimed that Jesus stood "permanent and alone, an exceptional being above classifying or being comprehended—to be worshiped by Christendom at large."[67] The preceding month Alcott had concluded that the doctrine of Abbot's *Index* could not "find acceptance with many," stating bluntly: "A Godman is essential to the mass of mankind, and may answer to all needs of heart and head."[68] Alcott's perspective had changed from that 18 February 1865, when he had praised Renan's "good service in disabusing Christendom of many superstitions about Christ."[69] Abbot's logical, rational mind and his humanism that placed Christ in a secondary role irked Alcott, who attacked the *Index* as "representative of the Evolution theories" and "destitute of a positive faith, scientific or religious."[70] Abbot, his *Index,* and disciples, received all the labels Alcott used to characterize Free Religion—negative, destructive, disputatious, divisive, rationalistic, and individualistic. Abbot and Free Religion symbolized a transitional period of negative, though necessary, criticism preparatory to a constructive phase embodying the "Ideal Church" (as outlined by Alcott). No consideration of Alcott and Abbot should overlook Abbot's 5 February 1871 Horticultural Hall Radical Lecture on "Intuitionism Versus Science, or the Civil War in Free Religion." Here Abbott, taking the intuitionists to task for their dogmatic adherence to notions of direct revelations of truths such as God's existence and the immortality of the soul, termed them a "spiritual aristocracy" to be compared with the scientific rationalists, humbly accepting nothing till established by

proof, "evidence" not "assertion."[71] Of course, Alcott combined his idealism with the intuitive method and so fell on the side of the opponents of Abbot and the *Index* in this "Civil War" among Free Religionists.[72]

* * *

On 1 June 1877, William Henry Channing spoke before the Free Religious Association on the "men eminent as promoters of freedom in religion."[73] The "four representative men" included Jonathan Edwards and Theodore Parker and the remaining two Channing introduced as follows: "But who is the man,—or rather who make the *pair* of men, from whom sprang this grand, transcendental movement in New England, which Francis Ellingwood Abbot now questions? They are both here this morning. There sits one,—this blessed, white-haired patriarch (A. Bronson Alcott), who is younger today than I ever saw him before. And the other sits here also, looking on, unseen by you, whose name I have already mentioned,—Ralph Waldo Emerson. I tell you those are the men out of whose thought and from whose heart Theodore Parker himself drew in his inspiration; and from them Free Religion came."[74] Nine years before, at the first annual meeting of the Free Religious Association (May 1868), Alcott termed Emerson the father of "the thought that brought us here" and continued: "This meeting is transcendentalism. This is the fruit of forty years of earnest, private, self-respecting modest thought."[75] The articles defined the Free Religious Association's intent as "being to promote the interests of pure religion, to encourage the scientific study of theology" and left "each individual responsible for his own opinions alone."[76] The stress on individualism and the loose organizational structure indeed suggested Transcendentalism.

Emerson's unrehearsed remarks at the Free Religious Association's first public meeting at Horticultural Hall, Thursday, 30 May 1867, were unmistakably Transcendental, finding churches and creeds "outgrown": "The church is not large enough for the man, it cannot inspire the enthusiasm which is the parent of everything good in history, which makes the romance of history . . . in churches, every healthy and thoughtful mind finds itself in something less; it is checked, cribbed, confined. . . . The church should always be new and extemporized, because it is eternal, and springs from the sentiment of men, or it does not exist."[77] Emerson, finding the personages and sacraments of historical religion "mortifying puerilities," affirmed that "as soon as every man is apprised of the Divine presence within his own mind,—is apprised that the perfect law of duty corresponds with the laws of chemistry, of vegetation, of astronomy, as face to face in a glass; that the basis of duty, the order of society, the power of character, the wealth of culture, the perfection of taste, all draw their essence from this moral sentiment, then we have a religion that exalts; that commands all the social and all the private action."[78] At the second annual meeting of the Free Religious Association on 28 May 1869, Emerson criticized the notion of the "miraculous dispensation" as coming "the wrong way, from without, not from within. This positive, historical authoritative scheme is not coincident with our experience or our expectations."[79] Emerson's main points were two: first, do not "elevate [Jesus] out of humanity" and, second, radical individualism based upon the self's reliance on conscience or the moral sentiment.[80] The result of self-reliance, Emerson concluded, was that "every believer holds a different Christianity, i.e. All the Churches are churches of one member."[81] And in his two Horticultural Hall Radical Lectures given for the Free Religious Association, "Natural Religion" (number twelve in the series, given 4 April 1869) and "The Rule of Life" (number fourteen in the series, given 12 March 1871), Emerson retained the purity of the early essays' Transcendentalism.[82] Therefore, because of Emerson's position as a vice-president of the Free Religious Association and his activities as a Horticultural Hall lecturer, and because of Bronson Alcott's concern with the "instrumentalities" of Free Religion, it seems safe to conclude that Transcendentalism had more than an inspirational role in Free Religion.

However, this is not to ignore the dominant stream of scientific rationalism in Free Religion nor to overlook the fact of the shifting bases for Alcott's estimates of Free Religion, for if his early enthusiasms for Free Religion were inspired by Transcendentalism, his later criticisms were increasingly the result of his attempts to domesticate Transcendentalism, admitting it to the parlors of orthodoxy. His personal theism, with its emphasis on the personality of the Creator and Jesus as an incarnate deity, flirted with orthodox Trinitarian conceptions and, though he maintained to the end a commitment to intuitive method, he rejected Emerson's "churches of one member" by his emphasis upon an "Ideal Church," which in practical terms represented modifications in present churches according to his instructions regarding architecture, poetry, music, sermonizing, and scriptures. The church should be planted in the ideal, the trans-individual, and Alcott placed strictures on Free Religion for making a religion of Emersonian radical individualism. The prototype of this extreme individualism was Roger Williams, as Alcott pointed out in an address to the Providence Free Religious Society on 30 May 1875.[83] Abbot and Frothingham exemplified this extreme antinomianism, perhaps most succinctly summarized in Alcott's critique of the *Radical*'s editor, S. H. Morse, "who," Alcott noted, "wishes political rule abolished altogether, and everyone['s] life untouched by Church and State. Subject polity to his own individual sense of right. Once, I

might have accepted fully his doctrine of Individual Sovereignty, ignoring all interference from institutions, convention, and creeds of all kinds, as during the Fruitlands' and non-taxpaying periods of my life. It was putting the logic to its ultimate consequences. . . ."[84] So much so had he retreated from his earlier radicalism that in his diary for February 1880, Alcott could write: "I believe it is agreed that I am sufficiently orthodox to be claimed no longer by Unitarians, either of the conservative or radical type, but Emerson's faith appears to remain a debatable question still."[85] An additional indication of Alcott's "failure of nerve" came in the final volume of his diary: "Sunday 14. Neither Calvinism nor Unitarianism, if one would claim the medium and moderate creed, appear as reasonable avoiding the extremes of both as Episcopacy wherein is room for the private judgment without breaking the thread of tradition, and all that good men in the past have found in its ritual and doctrines. I suspect that I am a better Churchman than I have known hitherto; and, if not within the scope of the articles literally, am spiritually and by Spirit descent."[86]

Following the lead of the conservative Joseph Cook, Alcott categorized Free Religionists as the leftists of Transcendentalism, while the impersonal and personal theists represented the center and right respectively.[87] In April 1877, Alcott used Cook as an example of an orthodoxy "approaching a Transcendental standpoint."[88] "The fair-minded," Alcott then insisted, "are perceiving that Christianity in its essential purity is Transcendental—Jesus the Transcendentalist of his race."[89] Obviously, for Alcott, Transcendentalism no longer claimed kinship with the ideas of forty years before—the ideas surrounding the Temple School and Fruitlands. It is fair to ask if this later "ism" was Transcendentalism and whether Alcott should not have applied Emerson's warning about nature to Transcendentalism, that she "will no longer be kinged, or churched, or colleged, or drawing-roomed"?[90]

Notes

1. *Louisa May Alcott: Her Life, Letters, and Journals,* ed. Ednah D. Cheney (Boston: Roberts, 1890), pp. 197-98, 261. A National Endowment for the Humanities Fellowship supported the research for this paper.

2. *Louisa May Alcott,* ed. Cheney, p. 268.

3. *Sketches and Reminiscences of the Radical Club,* ed. Mrs. John T. Sargent (Boston: James R. Osgood, 1880), Odell Shepard, *Pedlar's Progress: The Life of Bronson Alcott* (Boston: Little, Brown, 1937), and Stow Persons, *Free Religion: An American Faith* (New Haven: Yale University Press, 1947). An excellent discussion of the place

of Free Religion in Alcott's intellectual development may be found in Frederick C. Dahlstrand, "Amos Bronson Alcott: An Intellectual Biography" (Ph.D. diss., University of Kansas, 1977), pp. 423-68.

4. Alcott, "Diary for 1865," p. 4, MH [Harvard University manuscript]. Material from the Alcott-Pratt Collection is used by permission of the Houghton Library of Harvard University. All manuscripts are transcribed literally.

5. Alcott, "Diary for 1865," p. 14.

6. *The Letters of A. Bronson Alcott,* ed. Richard L. Herrnstadt (Ames: Iowa State University Press, 1969), p. 363. Angle brackets (<>) indicate cancelled material in the manuscript.

7. Alcott, "Diary for 1865," pp. 95-96.

8. Alcott, "Diary for 1865," p. 24.

9. Alcott, "Diary for 1865," p. 87.

10. See the account of the first National Unitarian Convention in Conrad Wright, *The Liberal Christians: Essays in American Unitarian History* (Boston: Beacon, 1970), pp. 81-109.

11. Alcott, "Diary for 1865," p. 109.

12. Alcott, *Letters,* p. 366.

13. Alcott, "Diary for 1865," p. 128.

14. Alcott, "Diary for 1865," pp. 129-30.

15. Alcott, *Letters,* p. 367; Alcott, "Diary for 1865," p. 130.

16. Alcott, "Autobiographical Collections, 1856-1867," p. 222[, MH].

17. Alcott, "Diary for 1865," pp. 135-36.

18. Alcott, "Autobiographical Collections, 1856-1867," p. 222.

19. Alcott, "Diary for 1865," p. 141. Conrad Wright, in his *The Liberal Christians,* implies that Bellows was an ogre to the Transcendentalists and their later sympathetic interpreters. If anything, Alcott was predisposed in Bellows' favor since during his residence in Walpole, New Hampshire (beginning June 1855), Alcott often heard Bellows preach, and, when the latter left for New York City, he invited Alcott (in October 1856) to hold conversations at All-Souls Church (a visit allowing Alcott to contact Walt Whitman). "Perhaps I shall give him," Alcott noted of Bellows, "the first place as the preacher of the nobler divinity of our Time, and its best representative in pulpits" (10 August, "Diary for 1856," p. 666). And the next day Alcott wrote of his "sympathy and agreement"

with Bellows (p. 668). The preceding month he had listed Bellows with such men as Horace Bushnell, Henry Ward Beecher, Theodore Parker, and Emerson as leading "Americans" and "New Englanders" (13 July 1856, p. 599). Further, on 16 November 1855, Alcott had categorized Clarke, Hedge, and Bellows as true "Transcendentalists" while future Free Religionists, Johnson and Frothingham, were labelled "Natural" ("Diary for 1855," p. 472).

20. Alcott, "Diary for 1855," p. 142.

21. Alcott, "Diary for 1866," p. 8.

22. Alcott, "Diary for 1866," p. 106.

23. Alcott, "Diary for 1866," pp. 132, 157.

24. Alcott, "Diary for 1866," p. 139.

25. Alcott, "Diary for 1866," p. 201.

26. Alcott, "Tablets," *Radical,* 2 (November 1866): 179.

27. Alcott, "Tablets," *Radical,* 1 (May 1866): 328-29; "Tablets" (November 1866), 177-79.

28. Alcott, "Tablets" (November 1866), 178.

29. Alcott, "Diary for 1866," pp. 260-61.

30. Alcott, "Diary for 1866," p. 323.

31. Alcott, "Diary for 1867," pp. 9-10.

32. Alcott, "Autobiographical Collections, 1856-1867," p. 254.

33. Alcott, "Diary for 1867," p. 26. Hedge had just written in the *Christian Examiner* on the old Transcendental Club and Alcott's comments on that old club in relation to present prospects are revealing: "As to the new Church discussed in the Club, we fancy there are signs in the air intimating its speedy planting" ("Diary for 1867," p. 23).

34. Alcott, "Diary for 1867," p. 41. In a 19 January 1867 cover letter for the circular, Towne wrote to Alcott: "I send you enclosed a call issued in the interest of organization of the radical movement. If you can give it your attention, it will be of service to our cause. It is hoped that we may be able to form a Religious Science Association, to provide for a May meeting, and to secure a Conference biennially of a whole free character" (Alcott, "Letter Books, 1867").

35. Alcott, "Diary for 1867," pp. 43-44.

36. Alcott, *Letters,* p. 428.

37. Alcott, "Diary for 1867," p. 210.

38. Alcott, "Diary for 1867," pp. 218-19.

39. Alcott, "Diary for 1867," p. 229.

40. Alcott, "Diary for 1867," p. 230.

41. Alcott, "Diary for 1867," pp. 252, 268.

42. Alcott, "Diary for 1867," pp. 276-77.

43. 16 September, Alcott, "Diary for 1867," pp. 339-40.

44. 13 October, Alcott, "Diary for 1867," pp. 387-88. After reading a copy of the 1867 proceedings for Harris, Alcott wrote in his diary for 23 October 1867: "I mail to Harris a copy of The Report of Addresses at the Free Religious Association meeting last May. It is proper that he should learn the spirit and aims of the speakers on that occasion, representative as these are, of the advanced religious thought of New England. Had views and purposes which have long been cherished by myself been favored with expression at the meeting, I should regard the Report as a fuller statement of the ideas now rising into importance and soon to embody themselves in an institution, perhaps conceived by none" (p. 407).

45. 15 October, Alcott, "Diary for 1867," p. 396.

46. Alcott, "Diary for 1868," pp. 305-306. See also the letters to Locke and Chandler in *Letters,* pp. 450, 456, and the following: "Diary for 1868," pp. 304-305, 400, 445-46, 459-60, 477; "Diary for 1869," pp. 12-13, 31-32, 35, 69, 97-98, 118, 568-69, 595, 632, 780.

47. Alcott, "Diary for 1869," p. 35.

48. Emerson, "Sovereignty of Ethics," p. 41, MH (Am 1280.211 [15]). This and other manuscript material from the Emerson Collection is used by permission of the Houghton Library of Harvard University.

49. 17 January, Alcott, "Diary for 1869," p. 35.

50. Alcott, "Diary for 1870," p. 260.

51. Alcott, "Diary for 1872," p. 31. Alcott thought enough of the Radical Lectures to consider possible topics for a speech, though early in January 1874 he did not consider himself "in full sympathy and spiritual accord with the speakers." He continued: "I judge their present phase of thought and action traditional and is to be overborne by more enlightened and devout views of life and destiny. Every step in human progress has its critical period, but these men are critics rather than reformers; agitators rather than builders" ("Diary for 1874," pp. 19-20). Nevertheless, two weeks later Alcott pondered giving an address to the radicals: "Had I the opportunity of speaking in this course, or in a separate lecture, I would take for my sub-ject, 'The Modern Reformatory Ideas and Methods,' illustrating these metaphysically and historically. My travelling experiences would serve to show how widely the spirit of reform is stirring in the community East and West, and in what methods it is working out its issues. Conversations, Clubs, lectures, in pulpits and schools, in families, all intimate the undertide of thought and sentiment now active in our time" (18 January, "Diary for 1874," p. 70). On 15 February 1874, Alcott lectured for the Free Religious Association at Horticultural Hall on "Modern Reformatory Ideas and Methods," emphasizing "the need of missionary enterprize for diffusing philosophy and religion" and giving an account "of the interest felt at the West in ideas and new instrumentalities already in existence in numerous cities for discussing questions in the most natural and exhaustive manner, by Clubs, associations, held together by the simplest ties" ("Diary for 1874," p. 194). The content of the lecture included oft-repeated themes of the influence of Idealism in contemporary thought, the validity of the intuitive method, the reconciling, unifying power of radical truth, the primacy of ideas in nature ("forms in which all things in nature are cast"), the example of Jesus as the perfect idealist, the equivalence of the kingdoms of heaven and ideas, and the need for a universal scripture ("Autobiographical Collections, 1872-1877," p. 161[, MH]).

52. 20 May, 18 October, 15 November, Alcott, "Diary for 1869," pp. 431, 734, 782.

53. 17 February, Alcott, "Diary for 1879," p. 99.

54. Alcott, "Diary for 1876," p. 610.

55. 15 April, Alcott, "Diary for 1870," p. 205; 12 February, Alcott, "Diary for 1872," p. 93; 19 January, 8 February, Alcott, "Diary for 1874," pp. 71-72, 170.

56. Alcott, "Diary for 1882," p. 164; Alcott, "Diary for 1880-1881," p. 492; Alcott, "Diary for 1874," p. 224.

57. Alcott, "Diary for 1872," pp. 31-33; Alcott, "Diary for 1874," pp. 19-20.

58. 30 May, Alcott, "Diary for 1872," p. 324.

59. Alcott's disenchantment spread to his relationship with the Florence Free Congregational Society, the organization he had represented at the first National Unitarian Convention in April 1865. By March 1874, Alcott, after attending the evening dedication of the Florence Society's Cosmian Hall, found the Free Congregationalists there "not a little tinctured with the shallow scientific notions so current" and guilty of a certain "bigotry of dis-

sent" (25 March, "Diary for 1874," p. 343). Alcott's final diary entry on this Cosmian Society, on 9 February 1879, was severe: "Free thinking is here cultivated to the verge of atheism and nihilism even. Excellent people, but for the most part, without spiritual culture or literary attainments. Their former teacher, Charles Burleigh, was a devout and able leader—a rationalist rather than idealist. Since his death, the Society appears to have lapsed largely into the Free Religious School of thinking, and, what with their individualism and atheistic teachings, have become distracted and adrift" ("Diary for 1879," pp. 78-79).

60. Alcott, "Diary for 1866," p. 323.

61. Alcott, "Diary for 1868," p. 181.

62. 14 February, Alcott, "Diary for 1869," p. 123.

63. 14 February, Alcott, "Diary for 1869," p. 123.

64. 12 December, Alcott, "Diary for 1869," p. 839.

65. 12 December, Alcott, "Diary for 1869," p. 842.

66. Alcott, "Diary for 1870," p. 125.

67. 28 February, Alcott, "Diary for 1870," p. 122.

68. 25 January, Alcott, "Diary for 1870," p. 42.

69. Alcott, "Diary for 1865," p. 67.

70. Alcott, "Diary for 1877," p. 364; Alcott, "Diary for 1878," p. 287.

71. Alcott, "Diary for 1871," p. 122.

72. For example, at a 17 March 1873 meeting of the Radical Club, Alcott spoke out on this matter: "I assert the intuition as the ground of authority in all matters of religious faith" ("Diary for 1873," p. 147).

73. Channing, "Address," *Proceedings of the Tenth Annual Meeting of the Free Religious Association* (Boston: Free Religious Association, 1877), p. 44.

74. Channing, "Address," p. 47.

75. Alcott, "Remarks," *Proceedings at the First Annual Meeting of the Free Religious Association* (Boston: Adams, 1868), p. 78.

76. "Articles of Association," *Free Religion. Report of Addresses at a Meeting Held in Boston, May 30, 1867, to Consider the Conditions, Wants, and Prospects of Free Religion in America* (Boston: Adams, 1867), p. 54.

77. "Remarks of Ralph Waldo Emerson," *Free Religion,* pp. 52-53.

78. "Remarks of Ralph Waldo Emerson," *Free Religion,* p. 53.

79. Emerson, "Speech at the Second Annual Meeting of the Free Religious Association, 28 May 1869," p. 1, MH (Am 1280.211 [18]).

80. Emerson, "Speech at the Second Annual Meeting," pp. 3-4; "Address of Ralph Waldo Emerson," *Proceedings of the Second Annual Meeting of the Free Religious Association* (Boston: Roberts, 1869), pp. 43-44.

81. Emerson, "Speech at the Second Annual Meeting," p. 5.

82. Emerson, "Sovereignty of Ethics," delivered for the Free Religious Association under the title "Natural Religion"; Emerson, "The Rule of Life," MH (Am 1280.210 [2]).

83. Alcott, "Diary for 1875," p. 127.

84. Alcott, "Diary for 1873," pp. 1019-20

85. Alcott, "Diary for 1880," pp. 51-52.

86. 14 May, Alcott, "Diary for 1882," p. 131. A further indication of Alcott's shift from moralism back to piety was registered in his changed attitude toward his essay "The Doctrine and Discipline of Human Culture" and the two-volume *Conversations with Children on the Gospels* it introduced (an essay highly praised by Emerson and giving a summary of Alcott's early Transcendentalism). On 21 March 1879, Alcott wrote: "I certainly entertain at present views more in harmony with if not identical with, *Evangelical orthodoxy,* than I did at the time these Conversations were conducted and should modify, if not suppress, some portions of the text, were I to venture to alter this in the least to suit my present views" ("Diary for 1879," p. 166). Another indication was Alcott's revealing reinterpretation of the Reverend William Ellery Channing, who had freed him from his Episcopalian orthodoxy in the late 1820s. On 16 December 1878, Alcott spoke in Joseph Cook's parlors on Channing, an address placing Channing upon the Procrustean bed of Trinitarianism and precipitating the vehement dissent of Higginson and Bartol. Alcott made the following entry in his diary that evening: "His [Channing's] *Arianism* is deemed by me the loftier doctrine of his theological belief, and Unitarianism has lapsed into Rationalism, Humanitarianism, Naturalism, since his departure. I consider the Free Religious Movement a legitimate outcome of this lapse from Channing's Personal Faith, and he may be claimed as having been more in sympathy, if not in doctrine, with the Orthodox Trinitarian, than with the current Unitarianism of this time" ("Diary for 1878," pp. 683-84).

87. Alcott, "Diary for 1877," p. 31.

88. Alcott, "Diary for 1877," p. 240.

89. Alcott, "Diary for 1877," p. 240.

90. Emerson, "Sovereignty of Ethics," p. 3.

Harry De Puy (essay date March 1987)

SOURCE: De Puy, Harry. "Amos Bronson Alcott: Natural Resource, or 'Consecrated Crank'?" *American Transcendental Quarterly* n.s. 1, no. 1 (March 1987): 49-68.

[*In the following essay, De Puy offers a reassessment of Alcott's lasting influence.*]

The sparkling blue eyes of Amos Bronson Alcott first opened to the blue American skies on November 29, 1799. Eighty-nine years later, on March 4, 1888, he died—just two days before Louisa May, the most famous of his four "Little Women." In the interim, Alcott followed a somewhat checkered career as pedlar, teacher, day-laborer, philosopher, reformer, omnivorous reader and talker, committee-man, traveler, gardener, club founder, writer, fond (if improvident) husband and father, friend and associate of the great, and collaborator in "crackpot" schemes.

Thanks to the obscene jibes to which he was subjected in boyhood by his playmates, he changed the family name from Alcock to Alcox, and then to Alcott. In later years Alcott became interested in genealogy, tracing his lineage directly from Catholic Bishop John Alcocke, who served Henry VII as Lord High Chancellor of England. Though Barclay's "Eclogues" noted that "this Cock trode never hen," Alcott's faith in his ancestry lay undisturbed.

A phrenologist for whom Alcott sat in 1838 found that the volume of his brain was "full, with great activity," and that his temperament was "nervo-sanguineous." Concerning Alcott's "organs," those classified as "very large" were Philoprogenitiveness, Adhesiveness, Approbativeness, Veneration and Ardor; considered "usually large" were Amativeness, Inhabitiveness, Circumspection, Firmness and Self-Esteem.

In *The Journals of Bronson Alcott,* Odell Shepard cites this Journal entry for December 12, 1856:

> Walt Whitman comes, and we dine at Taylor's Saloon, discussing America, its men and institutions. Walt thinks that the best thing it has done is the growing of Emerson, the only man there is in it—unless it be himself. Alcott, he fancies, may be somebody, perhaps, to be named by way of courtesy in a country so crude and so pregnant with coming great men and women. . . . If a broader and finer intercourse with men serves to cure something of [Whitman's] arrogance and take out his egotism, good may come, and great things, of him.
>
> (293-294)

With his remark, Whitman may unwittingly have set the tone for future commentary on Bronson Alcott. Although a bit rudely, he has placed the man in his precise rank in American literary history: a forerunner at a time when America was not quite ready for serious literary activity (struggling young countries seldom are). What Whitman didn't see, of course, was that no one of Alcott's "type" can ever be ignored. His active life encompassed years of great ferment and excitement, and he knew nearly all the famous people of his time. He was a splendid buffer for some of them, generously absorbing numerous thwacks that might otherwise have been directed toward more sensitive and more productive minds than his own. Perhaps what Whitman failed to perceive was the goodness and altruism native to Alcott, virtues that were not lost on milder acquaintances. Whitman was altogether too abrupt and uncharitable toward a man whose humanitarian instincts were demonstrably superior to his own.

While some effort is required to take him seriously, it is not too difficult to treat him sympathetically for—to paraphrase Étienne Gilson—there is more than one excuse for being an Alcott, though there is no excuse for being his disciple. In a sense, Alcott's was the tragedy of the self-made man: only too often, self-made is haphazardly made. Partly by what he did and partly by what he did not do, he left his contemporaries with the impression of a man "ineffectually good, mild, vague, and somewhat absurd" (*Journals* xvi).

To treat him as a failure, though, is to judge him hastily or from a biased point of view. In his own eyes he was not a failure. Alcott tells us in **"Orphic Saying XXVI,"** "Experience is both law and method of all tuition, all influence. This holds alike of physical as of spiritual truths; the demonstration must be *epical*; the method living, not empirical." He is implying what every teacher knows, that true immortality lies in passing on to others the larger view of life, which is accomplished as much by example as by precept: the teacher must live what he teaches. If, in the eyes of the world, Alcott was a failure, he was a splendid one who might have adorned the lines of an E. A. Robinson poem at a later date.

His personal faults were legion. More than one of his contemporaries—Hecker and Trowbridge, for example—recorded the opinion that "he loved to sit on platforms" and "delighted in the sound of his own voice." This was probably true but, as Shepard remarks in *Pedlar's Progress,* "the reason for it was something other, or at any rate something more, than simple vanity" (281). In his *Alcott Memoirs,* Doctor Willis remarks,

> As much as I reverenced and admired Mr. Alcott—(he had a peculiar charm for the young)—I remember feeling a burning sense of indignation at his seeming indif-

ference to the domestic burden that was resting upon his devoted wife and the actual poverty that enshrouded the little family.

(22)

His indifference to the practical affairs of life and the heroic struggle of his wife were no indication of lack of affection for her or for their children. No man loved his family more, and although at times he sorely tried them, their affection and reverence for him never wavered. "Mrs. Alcott struck the keynote of his character," continues Dr. Willis (27), "when I heard her say, 'He carries his head in the clouds.'" Let it be noted that his wife was not the "compleat" martyr: "Give me one day of practical philosophy," she once exclaimed, "it is worth a century of speculation and discussion."

Alcott lived and talked and wrote as if he thought the world owed him a living, and his friend Emerson thought he was in the right of it. Odell Shepard (*Pedlar* 428) accurately observes that "few or none of Alcott's contemporaries whose opinions are worth recording ever seriously entertained the notion that he was either lazy or a 'dead beat.'" Seemingly always in "hot water," yet (declares Shepard in *Pedlar* 441), "In Alcott's own life the uses of adversity were almost always sweet. He reminds one of a sentence written by his wife in one of her darkest hours: 'There are some plants that must be bruised to give forth their sweetest odors.'"

Even his Pythagorean practices he carried to embarrassing lengths. At the monthly meetings of the Saturday Club in Boston he was known as the "after-dinner member" because he usually came in "for the best of the feast—the nuts and the apples, the wit and philosophy abounding—after the abominations were removed." He took no great pleasure in the dinners Emerson often gave for persons of distinction who visited Concord. On one such occasion the host is said to have dilated at considerable length (while carving a roast) upon the horrors of cannibalism. "Bronson Alcott's face was working with amusement and barely suppressed glee until he suddenly burst forth with 'But Mr. Emerson, if we are to eat meat at all why should we *not* eat the best?'" (*Pedlar* 428).

One very grave weakness contributed most to the differences between his being remembered as one of the literary greats of his time and as merely the father of Louisa May: he couldn't "communicate" via the written page. Consider the facts: Bronson Alcott wrote more, by millions of words, than almost anyone else of his time. His *Journals* alone run to over fifty volumes. In mature years he was the friend and neighbor of three men who were writing English prose as well as anyone then alive. "Moreover, he had abundant leisure, wide reading, great themes, an intelligent public, and more practice with the pen than almost any of his associates,"

asserts Shepard (*Journals* xvii). Sadly it must be said that Alcott misused a finer set of literary opportunities than most writers are ever granted. He never let a day pass without writing something, and the heart of his teaching method—discounting the "Conversation"—was the keeping of journals by all of his pupils. We might here have a clue to his failure: journals are a repository for ideas, but literature is not merely a collection of ideas. Alcott did not regard his *Journals* in the way of Emerson and Thoreau: as a quarry from which future lectures and essays might be carved. Keeping a journal is a fine habit, but a writer dare not neglect another wholesome habit that was, for the French classicists, the keystone: "Polish, polish and repolish." Louisa May learned this, at least. She also learned to publish, publish and republish: criticism helped supply the polish. Her father neither polished nor published beyond a few trifles. Also, journal entries tend to be aphoristic, and often they never expand into literature, because aphorisms have a way of dazzling their creator. Ultimately, however, they must be served up in a palatable form; jaded appetites refuse to be tempted by bare, unadorned aphorisms. It is all very well for a prophet to preach and practice heroically, but he shouldn't be surprised that his revelations court oblivion if he fails to brighten them for a discerning posterity.

His *Journals* are on a par with his published works which—in the judgment of Shepard (*Pedlar* 505)—are "flat, dull, and lifeless." As with Margaret Fuller and Wendell Phillips, Alcott's natural mode of expression was that of speech, in which he was more or less gifted. Nevertheless, the *Journals* gradually took on the easy and simple conversational style for which he was famous in speech, and by "conversing" with himself he did a large amount of good (though never distinguished) writing. *Tablets* (1868), *Concord Days* (1872), *Table Talk* (1877), *Sonnets and Canzonets* (1882) and *New Connecticut* (1877) proved that his fundamental error with regard to style was natural enough to a self-made man. He thought of style as "something remote, difficult, involving constant strain, rather than as a free and fearless expression of one's own idiom," Shepard says (*Journals* xix). His long essay, *Ralph Waldo Emerson,* privately printed in 1865 and published in 1882, is considered the best extended piece of prose he ever produced—and that is no masterpiece. The best of his poems is **"Ion,"** a "monody" for Emerson.

Both Alcott and Emerson represented Protestantism at its most "protestant" extreme. Obviously, Alcott was aware that Americans of his time were a religious people, though in no haste to organize their religion. Said he,

> The doctrines of the last thirty years (1833-1863) have gone against efforts of that kind. We have been Protestants—protesting against what was; have taken sides

with the iconoclast, and been rather demolishing idols than planting new institutions.

(Ghodes 25)

The time was coming, he thought, when new institutions would spring up, but not just yet. The iconoclasts were in pursuit of a church, yet the tendency of their teaching was rather to favor individualism—to conform the inquirer toward what was peculiar to himself more than to blend into a "personality which all share in common." Clarence Ghodes quotes Alcott:

> We are so very individual that we *meet* with difficulty; nor till parties become partakers of that personality which relates them to one another, that which is common to all, is it possible to plant a Church. We belong now to a Church with one member only—very largely so all over the country, and it is with difficulty that we can find any brother with whom we can commune. And, indeed, the doctrine of reformers has been, for the last thirty years—and how natural it was that it should be so—to protest against all organizations. Well, very good, if we can at last get free of our individuality, and become persons indeed—partake that which unites and relates us to one another.
>
> (25)

Just such a Church was almost founded in September 1836 when George Ripley brought together five persons at his Boston home "to see how far it would be possible for earnest minds to meet." Invitations were issued and a club was formed. According to Alcott's account (in Ghodes 17),

> This club was called the 'Transcendental Club' because its members imagined the senses did not contain the mind. Contrary to Locke and all the modern philosophers, they ventured to believe that Plato and the Alexandrians—the ancients—had a metaphysics which corresponded to the wants of the human mind, and was adequate to its expression. They were called 'Transcendentalists' from the philosopher Kant, as parties present well know; but 'symposium' seemed to be the better name for a Club or company of earnest persons enjoying their conversation. . . . I believe there was seldom an inclination on the part of any to be silent.

The "Transcendentalists" wasted no time in pushing Protestantism to its logical extreme and beyond: they were not at all loath to advance the cause of their own divinity. Each member entertained the belief that he might be a prophet—at the very least. There was much talk of a Man, a modern Messiah, who could be expected; Alcott was by no means the only one to entertain a strong suspicion that he himself would be chosen.

Transcendentalism was in essence both a philosophy and a religion of reform, no mean combination, especially when we consider that none of its exponents had ever been subjected to any rigorous scientific, logical or mathematical training. In their consequent lack of intellectual patience and caution, they did not display the mental qualities which later generations learned to respect. They showed—wryly observes Shepard (*Pedlar* 257)—a careless ease in their speculations, "a noble disregard of evidence, which somehow recalls the mood of the pioneer." They were loud, too, but perhaps they had to shout in order to be heard in a country bustling with industry and exploitation of its vast potentialities. What the nation thought of them apparently didn't bother them a whit—Alcott always held that "the Pegasus of the multitude is a mule" and could therefore be disregarded. He made many wonderful discoveries through his conversations and readings, and hastened to deposit his newly-minted ideas in order to get them into currency before something else filled the vacuum left by the seeming abdication of the established churches.

The intoxicating language of the Transcendentalists failed to win more than a handful of converts; most were people who can be found, in any age, only too willing to slough off restrictions, exhibit themselves, and shock the "squares." The facile mumbo-jumbo of the Transcendentalists is only slightly less unintelligible—not to say humorous—than that of the "Beatniks" of a few decades ago. Two converts—William Chace and Christopher Greene—are described by Odell Shepard (*Pedlar* 299) as "so intensely religious that they were constantly trying to shock the 'unco' guid' by the most outrageous blasphemies against 'the Nazarene.'" Christ's presumption to divinity was apparently more than their "intensely religious" souls could bear. "What a pity," Emerson was writing, "that we cannot curse and swear in good society." Chace and Greene did not share Emerson's reticence.

Transcendentalism was eager to sponsor reform. No reformer was too wild to be embraced. Thoreau gave impassioned speeches on behalf of a rash activist named John Brown. Alcott was a staunch backer of the fiery abolitionist, William Lloyd Garrison, who once wrote of him (Shepard, *Pedlar* 304):

> Mr. Alcott is a . . . warm-hearted philanthropist, a resolute and uncompromising foe of priestcraft, bigotry, and sectarianism under every guise, a Reformer who is for laying the axe at the root of the tree and not for pruning its branches. . . . May his visit be greatly blessed to the promotion of 'peace on earth, good will to men,' and to the demolition of all those national and geographical distinctions and prejudices which alienate and curse our race.

Reform movements were not overly-popular in those turbulent days, nor was Transcendentalism. Lacking both appeal to and support of the masses, which it all but ignored, Transcendentalism was doomed to failure.

It failed as a religion because it pruned too drastically, leaving little or no opportunity for grafting or future growth: the baby, so to speak, was flung out with the bath water. It failed as social reform because it rejected the unwashed, while dealing violently with those whom it condescended to notice. As a philosophy it failed because it was absurdly inadequate: it was less a philosophy than an intuition, which patently cannot readily be communicated—if at all. Expecting someone to accept another's intuition is merely another way of asking someone to accept the other's authority—and isn't it just that which began the whole affair? Men were being asked to give over the world of matter and Mammon in order to live in a world of spirit: exactly what Christ had preached. Yet Alcott denied Christ's divinity with one breath, while affirming his own in the next. One can hardly blame cross materialists for ignoring Alcott's message along with Christ's. Perhaps Americans who hesitated to replace a cast-off, logical Calvinism with the illogical, intuitive Transcendentalism of Alcott were trying to say (long before James Joyce), "We've lost our faith, not our senses."

As for Alcott's attempt to "Christianize Plato," that had been tried many times before, hence it wasn't to be marveled that hardly anyone was struck dumb with wonder. Since he steadfastly refused to learn from the mistakes of others, he spent a good portion of his life recovering from the effects of errors that many had committed before him: now and then the blow nearly finished him. If one wished to be uncharitable, one might quote Ben Franklin (another "household Plato") at him: "Experience is a hard school, and only a fool will learn in no other."

The "house organ" of the Transcendental Club was launched officially in September of 1839, but the first issue of the *Dial* (so christened by Bronson Alcott) did not appear until the following year. In this issue were fifty **"Orphic Sayings"** authored by Alcott. In the amused opinion of the Boston newspapers, the **"Sayings"** were like a "train of fifty coaches going by, with only one passenger." Try as he might, Alcott failed to appreciate the analogy. Says Shepard in *Pedlar* (293), "The best answer to the public ridicule of **'Orphic Sayings'** seemed to be the composition of more **'Orphic Sayings.'**" Whereupon, he wrote fifty more. The laughter continued to ripple through the Boston newspapers and the drawingrooms of Beacon Hill. The **"Sayings"** were thought to furnish a fitting *reductio ad absurdum* of Transcendental pretentions, both substance and form striking the uninitiated as novel, extravagant and esoteric. Alcott's hope that the **"Sayings"** would comprise a "complete series of sentences, which would carry the appreciative reader through the descent from spirit to matter, and upward again to the first origin, [was] scantily realized" (Warren 11).

In substance, the **"Sayings"** combined the familiar doctrines of Transcendental individualism as found in Emerson's early *Essays* with an added strain peculiar to

Alcott among the Transcendentalists, his neo-Platonism. Emerson was, of course, sympathetic to some aspects of the Plotinian teaching. He, however, was an evolutionist. Alcott was an emanationist, holding his theory of creation by lapse from the One:

> The first Principle, or God, is a Person—self-determining or creative, self-directing or self-dissecting.
>
> He creates that which is most like Himself, hence self-determined or creative beings. They differ from the Absolute Person only in degree; they are pure souls.
>
> These pure souls may lapse or may not. They have the possibility of lapse, since they are free.
>
> Those that lapse create thereby bodies for themselves; and lapsing still further, generate the lower animals, and these continuing the lapse, beget the plant world—and thence results the inorganic world.
>
> The limit to the lapse is the atom (i.e., complete self-externality, or space, or chaos).

This is not pure Plotinus or Proclus, but is close enough to be considered one and the same theory.

With Emerson, Alcott deplored dependence upon majorities, institutions and Mammon (though "sore annoyed" was Alcott without it); with Emerson he invoked self-reliance, religion of the spirit, plain living and high thinking. Warren says of him,

> No doubt there were subsidiary elements of the fantastic in the mind of Bronson Alcott, but in the main that mind grasped with clarity and maintained with persistence a world view which has ever retained the respect of the philosophically minded.
>
> (13)

Alcott enjoyed the double-profession of sage and educationist. In 1835 he began to teach the doctrine of the preexistence and subsequent lapse of the soul. It was Coleridge, he said later, who introduced him to metaphysical idealism. Chapter XII of the *Biographia Literaria,* with its citations from Plotinus, Warren suggests, "may well have introduced Alcott to that historic school of thought with which he was in temperamental harmony" (6).

The **"Orphic Sayings"** are not as ridiculous as Alcott's detractors like to let on, though the archaic (even then) mode of expression does appear to invite sarcastic comment. Also, they are often pugnacious and melodramatic, but there is a consistent undertone of serious conviction that cannot be denied. Patient, attentive reading reveals the line of thought that orders his ideals. Had he been a creative writer like Melville or Whitman, there is no doubt that he would have gone many leagues farther toward successfully promulgating his ideas, mad as they may appear on bare exposition.

Using a slight twist on the age-old argument for the soul's immortality, Alcott presents his doctrine of **"Apotheosis"** (**"Saying X"**):

Every soul feels at times her own possibility of becoming a God; she cannot rest in the human, she aspires after the Godlike. This instinctive tendency is an authentic augury of its own fulfillment. Men shall become Gods. Every act of admiration, prayer, praise, worship, desire, hope, implies future apotheosis of the soul.

In **"Saying XIV"** he re-works the theological doctrine of original sin and its philosophical complement of man's loss of the state of natural (intuitive) wisdom along with Eden: "Reason is the left hand of instinct; it is tardy, awkward, but the right is ready and dextrous. By reasoning the soul strives to recover her lost intuitions, . . . sinners must needs reason; saints behold." He eulogizes speech in **"Saying XVIII"**: "Great, indeed, is the delight of speech; sweet the sound of one's bosom thought, as it returns laden with the fragrance of a brother's approval." He appears to be sniping gently at Emerson in **"Saying XIX"** when he writes, "Great thoughts exalt and deify the thinker; still more ennobling is the effect of great deeds on the actor." **"Saying XXI"** on **"Originality"** makes one pause to wonder where Alcott fits into his own scheme of things: "Only the noble and heroic," he writes, "outlive in time their exit from it." At least one Saying (**"XLVII"**) on the **"Actual and Ideal"** displays latent poetic appeal: "The actual and ideal are twins of one mother, Reality, who failing to incarnate her conceptions in time, meanwhile contents herself with admiring in each the complement of the other, herself integrant of both. Always are the divine Gemini intertwined, Pan and Psyche, man and woman, the soul and nature."

Emerson began to sense that Alcott was limited in his themes of discourse, somewhat the same feeling that Melville evoked in Hawthorne. For Alcott, life found interpretation through two or three persistent doctrines, and Emerson wearied of him from time to time: "He is, to be sure, monotonous. You may say, one gets tired of the uniformity,—he will not be amused, he never cares for the pleasant side of things, but always truth and their origin he seeketh after." Unfortunately for Emerson, Alcott saved his ideas for the Essayist's abused ears: "There were others in plenty to whom one could talk of cabbages and kings, neighbors whose minds ran on politics and agriculture," quotes Austin Warren (6).

Inhospitality to his extreme views and practices Alcott expected of nonbelievers, so his meeting with Thomas Carlyle shook him a little. The Connecticut prophet and Scottish historian had much in common—friends, social origins, intellectual ancestry—yet each thought the other a little mad. According to Shepard (*Pedlar* 318) there is a story that the two men went walking in Mayfair, and that the one peasant's son said to the other, proudly pointing out the expensive magnificence of the houses: "Do you see this, mon? This has stood for a thousand years, and will stand when you and your dom'd Potato Gospel have gone to the dogs." Nevertheless, Carlyle was to write to Emerson of "the good Alcott, with his long lean face and figure, with his gray worn temples and mild radiant eyes; all bent on saving the world by a return to acorns and the golden age; he comes before one like a venerable Don Quixote, whom nobody can laugh at without loving."

Their "bickering" elicited widespread hilarity among those who appreciated the adamantine natures of the belligerants. Twenty years after, the elder Henry James was saying in Boston that Carlyle had been vexed at Alcott's refusal to eat what was set before him at breakfast. He had sent out for some strawberries for the American vegetarian's special benefit (undoubtedly a painful financial sacrifice for the frugal Scot). When these were put on the table, reads Shepard's *Pedlar* (317), "Alcott was said to have taken them on the same plate with his potatoes, so that 'the two juices ran together and fraternized.' Carlyle was made almost ill, apparently, by this revolting spectacle, so that he could eat nothing himself, but stormed up and down the room instead."

That Transcendentalism "failed" is no great wonder, even ignoring theological and philosophical weaknesses. Its only true "Apostle" was Alcott. Only he believed implicitly in the basic neo-Platonism that formed its matrix: the One, creation by lapse (emanation) from the One, preexistence of the soul (reminiscence), personalism ("togetherness") and apotheosis (co-divinity). Only Alcott, with near-monomaniacal zeal, went among the barbarians to spread the gospel. Only Alcott exposed himself, in person, to the laughter—both good-natured and spiteful—of the philistines. Only Alcott sacrificed his personal and family life to the dissemination of the Word. His was action in a sea of passion. He was the prophet of Transcendentalism, whereas Emerson was the scribe; he saved Emerson the trouble of practicing what he preached.

Since Emerson and Alcott are so often mentioned in the same breath—often irreverently, sometimes otherwise—it would be pointless to deny that there was a great common bond between them. Despite bridgeless differences in background, education and temperament, they complemented one another so well that it is difficult to picture the life of one without the influence of the other. Each considered himself a genius, while politely conceding equal status to the other. Emerson had the modesty to affect a slight concealment, though he was quite certain of both his genius and his prophetic role. Bronson Alcott could not be bothered with subterfuge: a simple, direct man, he refused to let modesty stand in his way. Each, however, was somewhat annoyed by the course that genius took in the other. Alcott couldn't countenance Emerson's "inactive," scholarly ways, nor could Emerson quite accustom himself to his friend's "boorish" zest and garrulity. Theirs, still, was a fruitful symbiotic relationship: Alcott supplied enthusiasm, idealism, thoughts cut free of deadwood, conversation and a practiced ear; Emerson contributed beauty, balance, money, sympathy and protection, along with his own ideas and criticism. Indeed, Shepard remarks, "Had it not been for the broad aegis that Emerson held over him, the reputation of Alcott would have entirely succumbed, long since, to an environment either hostile or indifferent" (*Journals* xvi).

Alcott removed to Concord to be near the man who may almost be called his other self, for Emerson and he were "carved out of the same cloud." It is one main value of Alcott's journals that they help us see how much was given and how much was gained by each partner of the intellectual friendship. Alcott could listen as well as expound, and Emerson required a creative auditor who could evoke, by his understanding and sympathy, the lofty and immortal in the Essayist's nature. He found in Alcott's spirit hospitality to all conceivable ideas and ideals.

Alcott could never quite evolve a settled opinion of his friend. After only five pages of his essay, *Ralph Waldo Emerson—His Character and Genius,* he did a complete about-face. On page fifteen he writes, "Now were Emerson less individual, according to our distinction; that is, more personal and national,—as American as America,—then were his influence so much the more diffusive, and he the Priest of the Faith earnest hearts are seeking." On page twenty, he generously shifts his stance:

> His [writing] I consider original and American; the earliest, purest our country has produced,—best answering the needs of the American mind. Consider how largely our letters have been enriched by his contributions. Consider, too, the change his views have wrought in our methods of thinking. . . .

One learns early to expect sudden reappraisal from Alcott.

Emerson was quite as reversible in his evaluations in return. No sooner had he written in exasperation of his friend's shortcomings than he entered in his *Journal* (1857) this paean: "Yesterday Alcott left me after three days spent here. . . . I could see plainly that I conversed with the most extraordinary man and highest genius of the time. He is a man. He is erect; he sees. . . ." He shared with Carlyle the view that Alcott was a sort of contemporary Don Quixote, with his audience playing Sancho Panza. But he found the knight-errant venerable rather than absurd, reports Austin Warren: "he had wandered in from another world, a little dazed and inarticulate, but none the less luminous" (7). "Our Alcott," Emerson wrote, "has only just missed being a

seraph. A little English finish and articulation to his potentialities, and he would have compared with the greatest." As usual, Emerson wrote volumes in a sentence.

Alcott prized the poetic spirit in Emerson, though he was less certain of his poetic form. He declared in **"Emerson"** that anyone was fortunate who could be admitted of a morning to his high discourse, or be permitted to join the poet in his afternoon walks to Walden, the Cliffs, or elsewhere—"hours to be remembered, as unlike any others in [one's] calendar of experiences" (43). Emerson and Thoreau he recognized as "forcible protestants against the materialism of their own, as of preceding times, these masterly Idealists [discerning] beyond all question their right to the empires they swayed—the rich estates of an original genius" (**"Emerson"** 56).

Emerson's death came as a terrible blow to Alcott. He expressed his grief at the loss of his friend in a monody entitled **"Ion,"** read before the Concord School of Philosophy in July 1882.

> Now wave and shore and wood are mute and chill,
> Ion, melodious bard, hath dropped her quill,
> His harp is silent, and his voice is still.

So tragic an event, however, lay in the future, as yet un-intuited by "Our Alcott."

In his **"Conversation"** on the Transcendental Club and the *Dial,* Alcott mentions, tongue-in-cheek, two articles that appeared in the magazine:

> Here, too, is a curious article entitled 'Fruitlands.' Then came 'English Reformers.' Not finding any Americans who could help to plant Paradise, it was imagined there might be some in Old England, and a sample or two came over, who, not content to remain long, returned soon to die, and Paradise remains still to be planted.

There is just a hint of "I shall be telling this with a sigh" in his remarks. Fruitlands was Alcott's great dream, and when it expired before his eyes, he very nearly died with it. There were several obvious reasons, almost too patent for mention, why Fruitlands could scarcely have been expected to succeed. Ghodes declares that "From the commonsense point of view it was a crack-brained scheme, attracting only such brains as were themselves a little flawed" (27).

Fruitlands was about three miles from the town of Harvard, and nearly a mile from Still River Village. Its distance from Boston was about thirty miles. When Alcott and Lane bought it for the purpose of creating utopia, it was an unnamed, land-worn farm of ninety acres. The persons actually becoming members of the Community were Lane and his son, William; Alcott, his wife, and four daughters; one other woman, Anna Page; along with Isaac Hecker, Christopher Greene, Joseph Palmer, Abraham Everett, Samuel Larned, Charles Bowers and H. C. Wright (an Englishman who remained but a few weeks). The experiment lasted less than a year. Clara Sears writes:

> This matter of getting the right kind of persons to join the Community required a keen insight into human nature, and on this point Mr. Alcott was not very strong. His own sincerity and depth of purpose were so great that he looked for these same attributes in every one who approached him, and often failed to detect the superficial qualities that lurked underneath the surface enthusiasm of some of his followers.
>
> (19)

At this time, Transcendentalism (superficially, at least) "was rife through the land." Some called it "the Newness," and the expression "Apostles of the Newness" was popular. The apostles could be recognized by their long hair, Byron collars, flowing ties, and eccentric habits and manners. Nothing seemed too excessive to prove their emancipation from the shackles of convention. It is said that one day three young men of this stamp turned up at Emerson's in Concord and entered into an animated conversation with him on his front porch. With them, freedom of thought and allegiance to "the Newness" took the form of preceding every remark, however trivial, with resounding oaths. This so startled passersby, and Emerson as well, that he hastily invited them "to move round to the back of the house where the vibrations of their sulphurous ejaculations might roll harmlessly across the meadow instead of exploding in through the windows of the houses near by" (Sears 19).

One Fruitlander, Everett, was a cooper by trade, profoundly serious, and a man, says Lane, "of rather deep experience, having been imprisoned in a mad-house by his relations because he has a little property." Even with this "advantage," however, he was not, in Lane's opinion, "a spiritual being—at least not consciously and wishfully so" (Shepard, *Pedlar* 34).

Fruitlands also possessed—even flaunted—the most famous beard in America. With the beard went gnarled, muscular, cantankerous Joseph Palmer to protect it. He had been through many sufferings and persecutions in its defense. As a general rule, Palmer agreed with no one, but he liked Bronson Alcott, and Alcott liked him.

Questioned about Fruitlands many years later, Father Hecker gave the following interview:

> Alcott was a man of great intellectual gifts or acquirements. His knowledge came chiefly from experience and instinct. He had an insinuating and persuasive way with him.
>
> (*Question:*) *What if he had been a Catholic, and thoroughly sanctified?*

He could have been nothing but a hermit like those of the fourth century—he was naturally and constitutionally so odd. Emerson, Alcott, and Thoreau were three consecrated cranks.

> (*Question:*) *What did Mr. Alcott say when you left?*

He went to Lane and said, 'Well, Hecker has flunked out. He hadn't the courage to persevere. He's a coward.' But Lane said, 'No; you're mistaken. Hecker is right. He wanted more than we had to give him.'

> (Quoted in Sears 84-85)

Hecker added, "[Alcott] was unquestionably one of those who liked to sit upon a platform, and he may have liked to feel that his venerable aspect had the effect of a benediction. But with this mild criticism, censure of him is well-night exhausted."

The farmers of the surrounding neighborhood were uproarious over the practice of their craft as pursued at Fruitlands, particularly because Alcott would not permit the worn acres to be enriched, upon the theory that it would be an offense against Nature to scatter fertilizer upon her bosom, and that the forcing of her processes was wholly unjustifiable. Much sarcastic comment was occasioned, too, over the fact that there was neither horse, nor cow, nor pig, nor even poultry on the place. Alcott's explanations convulsed the resident tillers of the soil. He contended that animals had equal rights to life, liberty and happiness with mankind. The cow should not be robbed of the milk which belonged to her calf. Chickens' lives were as sacred as those of human babies. He even went to the extreme of directing that the canker worms infesting the ancient apple trees at Fruitlands should in no wise be disturbed, maintaining that they were equal claimants to the fruit with anyone else. All of these things were commented upon in the town of Harvard, the farmers saying, "They have a lot of crazy fools out there."

The widespread belief that Alcott and Lane were "unbalanced" was examined in a book by an English alienist, Doctor Tuke, who visited the United States in 1885. His assessment, as found in Willis, *Alcott Memoirs*:

> Was Alcott insane? That such a man could induce others to imitate him and found such a community as at the farm of Fruitlands in Massachusetts would astonish were it an isolated case. But other persons passed through very similar phases about the same period in America. In an exhaustive study of Mr. Alcott, who interested me very much, I find no evidence whatsoever of mental disease, and I regard his Fruitlands idea as but an illustration of that peculiar psychological condition which under abnormal religious thought, will develop eccentric courses. A cold winter was sufficient to convert Mr. Alcott to common sense notions.
>
> (37)

One of Lane's curious ideas was his partition of man into three states: the disconscious, the conscious, and the unconscious. The disconscious was the state of swine, the conscious a baptism by water, the unconscious a baptism by fire. He advanced his notion in a "conversation" with Alcott and W. H. Channing in the presence of some few others. One of the listeners attempted to explain it later to Dr. Willis, who remembers: "I laughed and said, 'I cannot get that clear in my mind.' 'Well,' he replied, 'after I heard them talk for a few minutes I did not think I had any mind at all!'" (Willis 86).

Of all those who endeavored to analyze the Fruitlands experiment, either to explain it or explain it away, none has done so well as Louisa May Alcott in her essay-play, "Transcendental Wild Oats." By far the most prominent of Alcott's triumphs, Louisa was precisely the one of his four children from whom he had expected the least. Neither fully understood the other; Louisa's moods, language and conduct often seemed to her father strangely uneven and abrupt. Yet, while Anna Alcott was summing up the other children's attitude toward the Fruitlands community with a single sentence in her journal—"It is a pleasant place to live in, I think"—Louisa was storing her observations in the manner of Dickens, whose works she so greatly admired. The characters in "Wild Oats" are equally Dickensian and allegorical: Charles Lane is called "Timon Lion," Alcott is "Abel Lamb," Mrs. Alcott is "Sister Hope," and so on, their names providing a clue to their personalities. Her reaction to the experiment, while never completely censorious (she loved her father too much for that), still reflected the disturbance she felt over Alcott's subjecting his family to hardships, poverty and the world's sneers. Particularly did she resent the strain placed upon her mother. Dr. Willis says in his *Memoirs*:

> Mrs Alcott, who had to bear the full burden of housework for a family of sixteen people, told me a great deal about it in after years, saying she marveled she came out of it alive. She could not afford help. . . . 'I worked like a galley slave, Llewellyn,' she said, 'but mercifully the crash came in a few months or I should have died.' In after years, Louisa, being asked in my presence if there had been any beasts of burden at Fruitlands, replied, 'There was but one and she a woman.'
>
> (80-81)

Lane ("Timon Lion") was Louisa's villain of the piece. He had resided in the Alcott household for some time before the Fruitlands project, having come from "Alcott House" in England to realize with Alcott their dream of the "consociate family." Louisa and Mrs. Alcott had come to dislike him for his dictatorial ways, sustaining his conduct later at Fruitlands. He was so busy telling everyone else what to do that, not surprisingly, he neglected to find work for himself. Following are some excerpts from Louisa's play, as quoted in Sears' *Alcott's Fruitlands*:

> 'Each member is to perform the work for which experience, strength, and taste best fit him,' continued Dic-

tator Lion. 'Thus drudgery and disorder will be avoided and harmony prevail.'

> 'What part of the work do you incline to yourself?' asked Sister Hope, with a humorous glimmer in her keen eyes.

> 'I shall wait till it is made clear to me. *Being* in preference to *doing* is the great aim, and this comes to us rather by a resigned willingness than a wilful activity, which is a check to all divine growth,' responded Brother Timon.

> 'I thought so.' And Mrs. Lamb sighed audibly, for during the year he had spent in her family Brother Timon had so faithfully carried out his idea of 'being, not doing,' that she had found his 'divine growth' both an expensive and unsatisfactory process.
>
> (154-155)

Unlike his partner, Alcott did not consider labor a check to spiritual growth:

> Abel Lamb simply revelled in the Newness, firmly believing that his dream was to be beautifully realized and in time not only little Fruitlands, but the whole earth, be turned into a Happy Valley. He worked with every muscle of his body, for *he* was in deadly earnest. He taught with his whole heart and head; planned and sacrificed, preached and prophesied, with a soul full of the purest aspirations, most unselfish purposes and desires for a life devoted to God and man, too high and tender to bear the rough usage of this world.
>
> (161-162)

Other than chafing at their impracticality, Louisa did not indict the other adult members. Often she found them amusing. Samuel Bower ("Brother Pease") expected to be saved by eating uncooked food and going without clothes. He was required, however, to curtail his nudist propensities, being allowed to wear his primeval costume only while out of sight of the other members. Normally he wore an airy cotton poncho, but in midsummer he frolicked among the unprejudiced woodchucks and huckleberry bushes. "A sunstroke unfortunately spoilt his plan, and he returned to semicivilization a sadder and wiser man" (161).

Apparently Christopher Greene was the "youth" who, believing that language was of little consequence if the spirit were only right, startled newcomers by blandly greeting them with "Good morning, damn you," and other remarks "of an equally mixed order" (154).

Another irrepressible being held that all the emotions of the soul should be freely expressed. Illustrating this theory "by antics that would have sent him to a lunatic asylum, if, as an unregenerate wag said, he had not already been in one" (159). When his spirit soared, he climbed trees and shouted; when doubt assailed him, he lay on the floor and groaned. "At joyful periods, he raced, leaped, and sang; when sad, he wept aloud; and when a great thought burst upon him in the watches of the night, he crowed like a jocund cockerel, to the great delight of the children and the great annoyance of the elders" (159).

Anna Page ("Miss Jane Gage")—fat, amiable, lazy, sentimental—couldn't abide the spartan diet. She cladestinely filled herself with forbidden tidbits and was observed one day eating fish at a neighbor's house. For this she was publicly reprimanded by "Brother Timon." The lady protested that she had taken only a little bit of the tail. "Yes," answered Timon, "but the whole fish had to be tortured and slain that you might tempt your carnal appetite with that one taste of the tail. Know ye not, consumers of flesh meat, that ye are nourishing the wolf and tiger in your bosoms?" (163).

Salt and spice were forbidden as vain luxuries by Lane and Alcott. "Sister Hope" was supported through many trying scenes by her sense of the ludicrous—she's had ten years' experience of her husband's vegetarian vagaries as training for this new freak.

Writes Louisa, "No teapot profaned that sacred stove, no gory steak cried aloud for vengeance from her chaste gridiron; and only a brave woman's taste, time, and temper were sacrificed on that domestic altar" (157).

Palmer ("Brother Moses") brought a yoke of oxen from his farm when finally the philosophers had had enough of blistered hands and aching backs. At least they thought it was a yoke of oxen, until someone discovered that one of the animals was a cow. Not wishing to break the cow's heart, they decided to keep her in ignorance for a while longer. The garden was planted with a generous supply of useful roots and herbs, but "as manure was not allowed to profane the virgin soil, few of these vegetable treasures ever came up" (159). The sowing, too, was peculiar. Owing to some unfortunate error, the three brethren who devoted themselves to this graceful task found—when nearly halfway through— that each had been sowing a different sort of grain in the same field. The mistake could not be remedied.

The rule was to do what the spirit urged; on more than one occasion, work was abandoned by the brethren in favor of attendance at reform conventions. At about the time the grain was ready to be stored, "some call of the Oversoul wafted the men away" (166). A rainstorm was approaching and the grain was sure to be ruined. Since there was no help to be had from the men "who said many wise things and did many foolish ones," "Sister Hope" and the children were obliged to save the harvest as best they could.

With the first frosts, "the butterflies, who had sunned themselves in the new light through the summer, took flight, leaving the bees to see what honey they had

stored for winter use" (167). Beyond the satisfaction of a few months of exemplary living, very little remained, and they were faced with the prospect of severe dearth. Lane, disgusted with the scheme's failure, retired to the Shakers, who appeared to have the only successful community in operation.

> Desolation and despair fell upon Abel. . . . Silently he lay down upon his bed, turned his face to the wall, and waited with pathetic patience for death to cut the knot which he could not untie. Days and nights went by, and neither food nor water passed his lips. Soul and body were dumbly struggling together, and no word of complaint betrayed what either suffered.
>
> (170)

He rallied his spirits, however, and the Alcotts left the farm in Palmer's hands. "'Poor Fruitlands! The name was as great a failure as the rest!' [said] Abel, with a sigh, as a frostbitten apple fell from a leafless bough at his feet" (173).

Louisa was to go on to fame as a writer of children's stories. Dr. Willis, her former playmate, said of her in his *Memoirs,* "[She] left to the young people of her own and coming generations the legacy of her clean, sweet, and pure books. One might look in vain for any great art in them, but her ethics cannot be questioned nor the brilliancy and sparkling quality of her style" (39). One must assume that Louisa's friend intended his remarks as a compliment; there was more of the earthy artist in her, but there was also her father. She was seldom able to write for anything but money: her father's debts were pressing, as were the comforts of life for the rest of the family. In *Pedlar,* Shepard asserts:

> Her fame, when she could be made to understand it or to think of it at all, seemed to her an impertinence, a wholly unwarranted intrusion. What mattered to her far more than fame or the art of letters was that Henry Ward Beecher should offer her three thousand dollars for one story and that her publishers could send her thirty-three thousand dollars as the royalties of one quadrennium. One sets down these facts not to her discredit but to the honor of a brave and gallant woman. She was a mercenary soldier, but she fought with body and mind and soul in the holy cause of Family.
>
> (504)

It was her "misfortune" to have a philosopher as a father. Dr. Willis gives us her definition of a philosopher: "A man up in a balloon with his family at the strings trying to pull him down" (41).

Had she read Herman Melville's *Pierre,* Louisa May would have taken some cold comfort from the following passage—partially in reference to Fruitlands— though she might have objected to its tone. Of the "new-light Apostles," Melville writes:

Among all the innate, hyena-like repellants to the reception of any set form of a spiritually-minded and pure archetypical faith, there is nothing so potent as its skeptical tendencies, so that inevitable perverse ridiculousness, which so often bestreaks some of the essentially finest and noblest aspirations of those men, who disgusted with the common conventional quackeries, strive in their clogged terrestrial humanities, after some imperfectly discerned, but heavenly ideals: ideals, not only imperfectly discerned in themselves, but the path to them so little traceable that no two minds will entirely agree upon it. . . . Know this: that while many a consumptive dietarian has but produced the merest literary flatulencies to the world, convivial authors have alike given utterance to the sublimest wisdom, and created the least gross and most ethereal forms.

(332)

Nevertheless, Alcott's name and fame have been attested in other directions, notably in the field of primary education. For a number of years he actually taught in the classrooms—sometimes "public," sometimes those of his own formation. His methods were both a marvel and scandal in years when "education" of the young was either a private affair or a travesty on the word. Alcott loved children, and it was his especial delight to watch their minds develop. Combining an uncommon amount of educational common sense with the methods of a European innovator, Pestalozzi, he admonished New England that the schoolroom need not be a torture chamber for whipping the Devil out of children. For perhaps the first time in America, learning became a joy for children rather than a painful, mechanical process. Alcott was much too successful and novel for the times, so the public schools disowned him. Using his own methods he should have been a success in private ventures, notably at his Temple School in Boston. An unfortunate combination of circumstances destroyed the undertaking: a national economic panic, his indebtedness, and his insistence on teaching his version of Christianity to his pupils. He also slipped into an error that our modern "educators" have adopted: placing too great an emphasis on method.

Not surprisingly, one of the more important elements of his teaching method was the "Conversation." Teacher and class discussed freely any aspect of learning that happened to be under investigation at the time. In his enthusiasm, Alcott ignored his own injunction against the teacher's forcing ideas on his pupils. In all fairness, though, it must be said that he probably wasn't aware of what he was doing. Yet, his *Conversations on the Gospels,* which so outraged Boston, were in reality thinly disguised regurgitations of Alcott's own reflections on Christianity. They were obviously not intuitive truths (as he would have us believe) issuing from the mouths of sucklings, and bobbing to the surface of baby souls via Platonic reminiscence. Yet more than thirty years later he was still convinced that they were. Ghodes quotes him:

You will excuse me if I venture to mention a book of *Conversations on the Gospels,* also printed this year [1836], and which I value for this, among other reasons—it intimated what children might say on subjects about which senior divines were no better informed than they; and I confess I have since thought, had the divines themselves, many of them, been pupils of the young divinity students, they, too, might have graduated with advantage.

(16)

No profound insight was required to observe that his "Conversations" were actually rambling, long-winded lectures. Very little was contributed by anyone other than Alcott. If he chanced to have a "hostile" audience—one that asked searching questions and demanded facts instead of fancies—he refused to talk until the interruptions ceased. These, then, were no more "conversations" than Plato's works were "dialogues."

Despite his faults, he made lasting contributions. Even today, his reports, made when he was Concord superintendent of schools, are highly praised. His methods are in general acceptance everywhere. It is perhaps a shame that he gave up teaching so quickly. His name, rather than some that we see daily, might now be engraved in concrete over the entries of our public schools.

His "Conversations" for adults had a certain impact, too. What other reason could cause Thoreau, in the original manuscript of *Walden* (quoted in Shepard, *Pedlar* 504), to say of him, "A thought floats as serenely and as much at home in his mind as a duck pluming herself on a far inland lake. He is perhaps the sanest man, and has the fewest crotchets, of any I chance to know—the same yesterday and tomorrow." He wasn't as successful with Ellery Channing or with Hawthorne—the "boned pirate," as Channing called him—who always looked in an assembly of men like a criminal at a convention of detectives. (Both were present, nonetheless.) To quote again Emerson's *Journal* of 1857:

Life [Alcott] would have and enact, and not nestle into any cast-off shell or form of the old time, and now proposes to preach to the people, or to take his staff and walk through the country, conversing with the schoolteachers, and holding conversations in the villages. And so he ought to go, publishing through the land his gospel like them of old time.

In his last decades, Bronson Alcott gradually let fall one long-cherished heresy after another, "until it was hard to distinguish him from almost any orthodox person" (Shepard, *Pedlar* 472). Had he mellowed with age, or was it Louisa's prosperity and his own that forced on him a fine old house in a fine old town with its demand for a harmonizing set of social, political and theological opinions? Perhaps the family had finally pulled hard enough on the strings and the philosopher in the balloon had been brought out of the clouds, down to the everyday earth. Or perhaps the balloon inevitably lost some of its hot air.

Whatever the reason, let it not be said that one has attempted to bury Alcott in derision. If one has made free with him it is in the same spirit with which Melville has done the same, for in *Pierre* he says of such thinkers as Alcott:

> Yet let me here offer three locks of my hair, to the memory of all such glorious paupers who have lived and died in this world. Surely, and truly I honor them—noble men often at bottom—and for that very reason I make bold to be gamesome about them; for where fundamental nobleness is, and fundamental honor is due, merriment is never accounted irreverent.

(297-98)

Works Cited

Alcott, A. Bronson. *Ralph Waldo Emerson: His Character and Genius.* Boston: A. Williams, 1882.

Ghodes, Clarence. "Alcott's 'Conversation' on the Transcendental Club and the Dial." *American Literature* March 1931: 14-27.

Melville, Herman. *Pierre: or the Ambiguities.* New York: Harper, 1852.

Sears, Clara Endicott. *Bronson Alcott's Fruitlands.* Boston: Little, Brown, 1938.

Shepard, Odell. *The Journals of Bronson Alcott.* Boston: Little, Brown, 1938.

———. *Pedlar's Progress.* Boston: Little, Brown, 1937.

Warren, Austin. "The Orphic Sage: Bronson Alcott." *American Literature* March 1931: 3-13.

Willis, Frederick L. H. *Alcott Memoirs.* Boston: Richard G. Badger, 1915.

Michael Thurston (essay date December 1987)

SOURCE: Thurston, Michael. "Alcott's Doctrine of Human Culture." *Concord Saunterer* 19, no. 2 (December 1987): 47-54.

[*In the following essay, Thurston examines Alcott's efforts to reconcile religion and rationality in his philosophical writings.*]

We know Bronson Alcott the teacher, the innovator of classroom teaching techniques. In his work we see the educational system his daughter Louisa May Alcott presented in *Little Men.* We also know Alcott the mystic, "the magnificent dreamer, brooding as ever, on the renewal or reedification of the social fabric after ideal

law."[1] The image often presented is reminiscent of the opinion shared by Emerson and Carlyle, that Alcott seemed to have "wandered in from another world, a little dazed and inarticulate, but none the less luminous."[2] There is, though, some good solid philosophy beneath the perceptions we have of Alcott, some 150 year after his *Conversations with Children on the Gospels* appeared. Alcott was driven since his youth by the seemingly insoluble conflict between the deep religious faith he learned from his family and the ideas of human worth and perfectability that came out of the Enlightenment. Through his wide reading and his personal experience, he arrived at a theory which seemed to solve the problem of reconciling rational faith in man and faith in (and emotional reliance upon) an eternal deity.

In 1835 Alcott discovered the path to a reconciliation of religion and reason. In July of that year he met Ralph Waldo Emerson and became, by degrees, a part of the informal collection of thinkers known as Transcendentalists. The Transcendentalists, like Alcott, "sought to combine the mystical, emotional element of the old Puritan faith with Enlightenment rationalism's celebration of human worth and dignity."[3] Their basic premise was best defined perhaps by Emerson in his lecture, "The Transcendentalist":

> It is well known to most of my audience that the Idealism of the present day acquired the name Transcendental from the use of the term by Immanuel Kant, of Königsberg, who replied to the skeptical philosophy of Locke . . . by showing that there was a very important class of ideas or imperative forms, which did not come by experience, but through which experience was acquired, that these were intuitions of the mind itself; and he denominated them *Transcendental* forms.[4]

Dissatisfied with "the thin porridge or cold tea of Unitarianism," Emerson and the others desired a more authentic religious experience. With their own religious beliefs as a starting point, the Transcendentalists absorbed Kant's ideas, through Coleridge's *Aids to Reflection,* and Plato's ideas, and developed a philosophy which emphasized a quest for truth, in the shape of Kant's Transcendental forms, based on individual intuition and interaction with the omnipresent divinity.[5] Once Alcott met and spoke with these people, it did not take long for him to realize that he had, unknowingly, been a Transcendentalist for some time. Alcott was familiar with Coleridge's influential *Aids to Reflection* and the Platonism of Thomas Taylor and others. In the Transcendentalists he found confirmation of the validity of his interpretations of those philosophies and his incorporation of key ideas into his own theories. His interactions with this group also provided intellectual stimulation and a receptive and interested sounding board for his ideas.

The ex-ministers in the group knew the work of such mystics as Swedenborg, Fichte, and Schelling. They introduced Alcott to these ideas and these principles became an integral part of his thought. Mysticism came to be, finally, Alcott's defining quality:

> Instead of seeking wisdom by intellectual processes . . . he appeals at once to the testimony of the Consciousness, claims immediate insight, and . . . announces a truth he has seen.[6]

The sympathy of the Transcendentalists for his ideas buoyed Alcott's own confidence in them. There were, of course, some disagreements. Alcott was the leading challenger of church doctrine among the group.[7] While they often agreed with his statements to a point, most of the Transcendentalists saw something "of the impractical, even the ridiculous" in Alcott.[8] As the extreme, he caused them to more closely examine their own ideas so as not to follow him "to positions both dangerous and indefensible."[9] The cohesion of this group which had formed to expound the "newness" in theology and philosophy, in spite of the great diversity among them, convinced Alcott that the ideas they shared were the basis of a unified movement. Transcendentalism he felt, "was imminently going to change the world."[10] It would be a mainspring of reform. Alcott's desire to translate the "newness" into practical reform and his desire to draw attention to the Temple School in Boston, the forum in which he was implementing his pedagogical innovations, prompted him to attempt to spread his ideas more widely. Late in 1836 he published the first volume of *Conversations with Children on the Gospels,* intended as a demonstration of the "special insight of children into the workings of the spirit," as well as of the new methods of teaching that were employed at the Temple School.[11] For our purposes, the real importance of the volume lies in the fact that it included as a preface an essay which Alcott had published earlier that year in pamphlet form. **"Doctrine and Discipline of Human Culture"** is a manifesto of Alcott's philosophy as of 1836. It received little attention except from Emerson, who said it was "full of profound anticipations,"[12] and Thoreau, who recommended it as an introduction to Transcendentalism.[13] The essay is well worth analyzing because it contains the seminal ideas of Alcott's philosophy of Human Culture.

"Doctrine and Discipline of Human Culture" is one of several works in which Alcott tried to provide a distilled, powerful statement of his brand of Transcendentalism. **"Orphic Sayings,"** another such attempt, was called "meaningless, even absurd," by many readers because it lacked the unity necessary to tie together ideas in a system and contained what Emerson called inveterate faults, "airiness, verbosity, and lack of concreteness."[14] Unfortunately, the earlier essay suffers from these faults as well. The organization of the piece is esoteric. The essay is divided under subheadings between which there is no transition and it is often diffi-

cult to perceive the flow of Alcott's logic. The language of the essay is laden with religious terminology and passionate exhortation. One is quite justified in calling the piece a sermon. Alcott thought of himself as a prophet, the harbinger of a new age to be ushered in by Transcendentalism.[15] This essay is an articulation of the philosophical and spiritual content of that new age.

Given the rather muddled organization of the essay, it is convenient to use the terms of the title as a starting place for the analysis of the work. Alcott's choice of the word "doctrine" is important. Because of his sense of mission and his peculiar image of himself as a prophet, Alcott is not proposing a "theory" or "approach." By "doctrine" he means a religious tenet or dogma: "It is the mission of this age to revive this idea, give it currency, and reinstate it in the faith of men."[16] Alcott adds force to this exposition of doctrine by criticizing the society to which it is addressed. The idea of Human Culture, "so clearly announced, and so fully demonstrated in the being and life of Jesus, has made but little evidence in the minds of men." "We have," Alcott writes, "neither great men nor good institutions." Children come out of the poor education system "destitute of that high principle, and those simple aims, that alone ennoble human nature." He criticizes the existing epistemology and theology on the grounds that neither has realized the true importance of Jesus and the principle of Human Culture that he epitomized. "It has not become," he writes, "the ground and law of human consciousness. They have not married their nature to it by a living faith." He adds, "Disowning him in their minds, unable to grasp his Idea, they have deified him in their hearts. They have worshipped the Holiness which they could not define." Since the cause of these problems is the misapprehension of the idea of Human Culture, the solution lies in the revival of that idea. This is the doctrine that Alcott advocates in the essay.

The word "discipline" is meant here in two senses: the mental discipline of the mystic and the vocation of fostering and nurturing the development of Genius. Alcott calls the first of these "Faith," the second, "Human Culture." Institutions of learning, Alcott writes, have built their discipline on "shallow principles." Teaching is uninspired and too much emphasis is placed on coercion of mind and body to conform to socially prescribed standards. The discipline that must be developed in children instead is "the will of an Idea": "To work worthily, man must aspire worthily." It is the intellectual strength required for such aspirations that must be developed, for "without this faith, an Idea works no good." This faith "is the possession of all who apprehend Ideas," especially the most important idea, Genius. Alcott's solution to the lack of such faith that he sees in society is his concept of Human Culture.

The meanings of the two terms, Genius and Human Culture, form the crux of the essay. The term "Genius" is borrowed from Coleridge and is related to the Romantic concept of childhood associated with William Blake. Alcott calls Genius "the free and harmonious play of all the faculties of a human being, . . . human nature rising superior to things . . . and transfiguring them into the image of its own spiritual idea." Genius is the residue of each individual's primordial experience of the infinite, "an original, indestructable element of every spirit." It is "the Divine Idea of a Man." This Genius, however, is "encumbered by the gluts of the appetites, sunk in the corporeal senses," in much the same way as Plotinus's "Soul" is bound up in the inferior body. Genius must be tempted forth, drawn out of the worldly concerns that cloud it. So long as man is unconscious of the divinity that resides in each person, he is incomplete, incapable of realizing his position as "rightful Sovereign of the Earth, fitted to subdue all things to himself and to know of no superior save God." The process by which man can be made to recognize the divinity within is Human Culture:

> Human Culture is the art of revealing to a man the true Idea of his Being—his endowments—his possessions—and of fitting him to use these for the growth, and perfection of the Spirit . . . it seeks to realize in the Soul the Image of its Creator.

It is this concept that Alcott offers as the solution to the problems he has pointed out. Human Culture, the unfolding of the hidden divinity, the Genius, within each person is the "divine Art, including all others, or subordinating them to its Idea," and it is best seen in the life and teachings of Jesus:

> His achievements are a glimpse of the Apotheosis of Humanity. They are a glorious unfolding of the God like in man. They disclose the Idea of Spirit.

It has been demonstrated that Alcott admired Jesus; so much so, in fact, that he used the Gospels as textbooks. He writes of them here as "those Records wherein his [Jesus's] career is delineated with so much fidelity, simplicity, and truth." They are valuable not only as a "fit Text-Book for the study of Spirit," but, even more important, "they are a specimen also of the true method of instruction." Teachers should teach, Alcott writes, as Jesus taught: "From facts and objects the most familiar, he slid easily and simply into the highest and holiest themes. . . . Conversation was the form of utterance he sought." Jesus exercised a comprehensive idea of education which woke the Genius of the soul. Alcott's Human Culture is simply that idea of education. The method of instruction described and explained in *Record of a School* could easily be the one described above and attributed to Jesus. Teachers, Alcott wrote,

> alone can pierce the customs and conventions that hide the Soul from itself . . . They revive in Humanity the lost idea of its destiny and reveal its fearful endowments. They indicate the divinity of man's nature.

The mystery, the question of how to realize the great potential in man, is solved: "This is but the unfolding of human nature in its fullness; working free of every encumbrance, by possessing itself."

Alcott resolved in the idea of Human Culture the conflict that had concerned him since youth. This synthesis of Christian ethics, Neo-Platonic metaphysics, and practical observation yielded an acceptable answer to the problem of reconciling religious faith and rationalism. That answer was the concept of self-knowledge and self-possession that depended upon a combination of individual intuition of the underlying divinity and rational observation of observable phenomena. The idea of Human Culture is the centerpiece of Alcott's philosophy. By the time of the publication of the essay on Human Culture, he had "appropriated the main elements of his philosophy," among them the doctrine of Human Culture.[17] The reconciliation Alcott strove for is found in the idea of a transcendental process through which the divinity within each person is unfolded. The God that Alcott so desperately needed could exist within this concept, and the potential for human perfectibility could as well.

The transcendental character of this philosophy is seen in its fundamental emphasis: Self-reliance, the idea of a search for truth through individual intuition, the function of the material world, or Nature, all characteristics of Transcendentalism, are found in the doctrine of Human Culture. The pantheistic idea of divinity in all things appears in the mainstream of Transcendentalism as well as in Alcott's essay. The central difference between that mainstream, perhaps best articulated by Emerson, and Alcott's brand of Transcendentalism lies in divergent attitudes toward Nature. Emerson saw Nature as the locus of a "transcendental Spirit," and thought man must strive to know Nature as a tool to be used by man in his search for self-knowledge. The locus of divinity was within himself:

> With Emerson, Alcott deplores reliance upon majorities, reliance upon institutions, reliance upon Mammon; with Emerson, Alcott invokes self-reliance, invokes religion of the spirit, invokes plain living and high thinking. But for his ethics Alcott presupposes the metaphysics not of Kant or Schelling, but of Plotinus and Procrus.[18]

Rather than the transcendental Spirit written of by Emerson, Parker and others, Alcott emphasized a transcendental process, education, in the guise of Human Culture. This philosophical conclusion was manifested in pedagogical innovations like the use of conversations, teaching through stories, the use of Nature, and the idea of a holistic educational experience involving home life as well as classroom training. While it is for these practical innovations that Alcott is best known, the philosophical base on which they were built is also important. Alcott, less educated than most of the Transcendentalists, saw, through practical experience, the value of education. With the concept of Human Culture, he built a philosophy around that value and informed American education with his philosophical conclusions.

Notes

1. Joel Porte, ed., *Emerson in His Journals* (Cambridge, 1982), p. 7.

2. Joseph Slater, ed., *The Correspondence of Emerson and Carlyle* (New York, 1964), p. 163.

3. Frederick C. Dahlstrand, *Amos Bronson Alcott: An Intellectual Biography* (Toronto, 1982), pp. 130, 131.

4. Ralph Waldo Emerson, *Nature, Addresses, and Lectures* (Boston, 1903), pp. 339-340.

5. Harold Clarke Goddard, *Studies in New England Transcendentalism* (New York, 1960), p. 4.

6. Octavius Brooks Frothingham, *Transcendentalism in New England* (Boston, 1876), pp. 249, 251.

7. Dahlstrand, *Alcott*, p. 132.

8. Dahlstrand, *Alcott*, p. 132.

9. Dahlstrand, *Alcott*, p. 132.

10. Dahlstrand, *Alcott*, p. 137.

11. Dahlstrand, *Alcott*, pp. 139-140.

12. Dahlstrand, *Alcott*, p. 140.

13. Robert D. Richardson, *Henry Thoreau: A Life of the Mind* (Los Angeles, 1986), p. 110.

14. Dahlstrand, *Alcott*, p. 182.

15. E. B. Schlesinger, "The Philosopher's Wife and the Wolf at the Door," *American Heritage* (August 1957), pp. 32-37.

16. Amos B. Alcott, *Conversations with Children on the Gospels* (New York, 1972), p. 29. Quotations which follow are from this text unless otherwise indicated.

17. Goddard, *Studies in Transcendentalism*, p. 57.

18. John C. Broderick, "Alcott and the American Institute of Education," *Emerson Society Quarterly* (March 1958), pp. 27-29.

Arthur Versluis (essay date 1993)

SOURCE: Versluis, Arthur. "Bronson Alcott and Jacob Böhme." In *Studies in the American Renaissance,* edited by Joel Myerson, pp. 153-59. Charlottesville: University Press of Virginia, 1993.

[*In the following essay, Versluis explores the influence of German mystic Jacob Böhme on Alcott's Transcendental philosophy.*]

None of the American transcendentalists were so ridiculed as Amos Bronson Alcott. Throughout his life, Alcott was a thoroughgoing religious radical whose pronouncements often were too much even for Transcendentalists like Emerson, although they themselves had abandoned Unitarian liberalism as too conservative. Yet while many critics have noted and lampooned Alcott's eccentric modes of "prophetic" expression from his **"Orphic Sayings"** in the *Dial* onward—some considering him deluded and even insane—Alcott's work becomes more comprehensible when one considers a central hidden source of his inspiration: German mysticism exemplified in the work of the seventeenth-century Protestant mystic Jacob Böhme.

This is not to defend Alcott completely from the charge of unfortunate expression, of course. It is no accident that Alcott, with his often incoherent **"Orphic Sayings,"** inspired more derision of the early Transcendentalist periodical the *Dial* than anyone else. Even Alcott's friend Emerson criticized the **"Sayings,"** published in the first issue of the *Dial* in 1840, as containing Alcott's "inveterate faults": verbosity, imprecise expression, extreme abstractness, and incoherence. Emerson suspected that his friend would never write so well as he talked, but he still encouraged Margaret Fuller—who shared his assessment of Alcott—to publish **"Orphic Sayings,"** since they would distinguish the *Dial* from other publications.[1]

Distinguish it they did. Newspaper writers ridiculed the *Dial* as "the ravings of Alcott and his fellow zanies," even though Alcott's was the only genuinely eccentric writing in the new magazine. The *Knickerbocker,* in its issue of November 1840, parodied Alcott's contribution to the *Dial* with its "Gastric Sayings," and such pronouncements as "The popular cookery is dietetical. . . . Appetite is dual. Satiety is derivative. Simplicity halts in compounds. Mastication is actual merely." One sees how close Alcott's writing was to this mockery in this genuine **"Orphic Saying"**:

> The popular genesis is historical. It is written to sense not to the soul. Two principles, diverse and alien, interchange the Godhead and sway the world by turns. God is dual. Spirit is derivative. Identity halts in diversity. Unity is actual merely. The poles of things are not integrated: creation [not] globed and orbed. Yet in the true genesis, nature is globed in the actual, souls orbed in the spiritual firmament. Love globes, wisdom orbs, all things. As magnet the steel, so spirit attracts matter, which trembles to traverse the poles of diversity, and rests in the bosom of unity. All genesis is of love. Wisdom is her form: beauty her costume.

Another newspaper wag said Alcott's prose was like "a train of fifteen cars going by with only one passenger."[2] Margaret Fuller's assessment was apt: "The break of your spirit in the crag of the actual makes surf and foam but leaves no gem behind. Yet it is a great wave Mr. Alcott."[3]

What on earth was Alcott trying to say in such a passage? Without reference to German mysticism, it makes no sense whatever. But consider this excerpt in light of medieval and Protestant German mysticism. The classical medieval mysticism of Tauler and Eckhart emphasizes the imageless transcendent divine unity, toward which the contemplative ascends. The Protestant mysticism of Böhme likewise emphasizes this divine unity, but also includes a cosmological dualism seen in the antinomy of divine love and wrath, both of which derive from transcendent divine unity. And the English Böhmean mystic John Pordage (whose work Alcott had read, as we shall see) speaks of the contemplative ascent to the divine unity using the visionary image of a globe. For Alcott to write that "Nature is globed" or that souls are "orbed" is for him to rephrase Pordage, and to reiterate the traditional mystical understanding of correspondences between man as microcosm and nature as macrocosm, both of which have their origin in the divine, the perfection of which is symbolized by the orb or globe.

No question that Alcott's phrasing here is cryptic, to say the least. Indeed, without a thorough knowledge of such writers as Böhme and Pordage, one can only regard Alcott's writings as a complete cipher. But the key to this cipher is definitely found in the Protestant mystics, especially in Böhme. For Alcott is contrasting historical Christianity with spiritual or mystical Christianity in this passage, contrasting the dualistic, materialistic understanding of God, man, and nature seen in historical, literalist religion with the transcendent unity of God, man, and nature when seen in a mystical light as found in the writings of Böhme. Alcott's passage is implicitly urging us to "traverse the poles of diversity, and rest in the bosom of unity."

Unfortunately, as is more often the case than not, Alcott's phrasing is grotesque and virtually incomprehensible even for those who are familiar with his sources. Why say that "two principles, diverse and alien, interchange the Godhead?" The verb is not only unfamiliar but imprecise as well—and worst of all, unnecessary. Later, what he writes is "The poles are not integrated: creation [not] globed and orbed." What he apparently means is: "In fallen nature, polarities are not integrated in a greater harmony, nor is creation seen in the light of its transcendent unity." But with the utterly unnecessary use of the colon, he makes the sentence incoherent and grammatically wrong. This kind of imprecise expression—and the incompetent attempts at grandiloquence or oracular utterance it represents—meant that Alcott was to meet with little success even among Böhmenist mystics, much less among the general public.

Böhmenist mysticism appears overtly in virtually all of Alcott's books, especially in *Tablets* (1868), *Concord Days* (1872), and *Table-Talk* (1877). In *Tablets,* Alcott writes on what was to become his own central attack on Darwinist evolutionism, emanationist mysticism based in Genesis and in Böhme: "Boehme, the subtilest thinker on Genesis since Moses, conceives that nature fell from its original oneness by fault of Lucifer before man rose physically from its ruins." But Alcott corrects Böhme as well: "We think it needs no Lucifer other than mankind collectively conspiring, to account for nature's mishaps, or man's."[4] Regardless of Alcott's anthropocentrism, however, his Christian emanationism opposed to Darwinian evolutionism drew much on Böhme's *Mysterium Magnum,* his enormous commentary on the first book of the Old Testament.

In *Concord Days* Böhme again reappears, here in a section on him written by Alcott, along with a lengthy letter from the British Böhmenist Christopher Walton praising Böhme to the skies and explaining his own never completed project of publishing many works of Böhme and his disciples. Alcott's comments on Böhme here say volumes about his indebtedness:

> Mysticism is the sacred spark that has lighted the piety and illuminated the philosophy of all places and times. It has kindled especially and kept alive the profoundest thinking of Germany and of the continent since Böhme's first work, "The Aurora," appeared. Some of the deepest thinkers since then have openly acknowledged their debt to Böhme, or secretly borrowed without acknowledging their best illustrations from his writings. It is conceded that his was one of the most original and subtlest of minds, and that he has exercised a deeper influence on the progress of thought than anyone since Plotinus.[5]

Implied here, but not said outright, is that American Transcendentalism also is indebted to Böhme.

Perhaps most illustrative of how Alcott saw himself as an American Böhmean—as a deep thinker who at times acknowledged his debt to Böhme, and at times did not—appears in *Table-Talk.* Here, as in **"Orphic Sayings,"** Alcott is at his most oracular: "Instinct, intuition, volition, embosom and express whatsoever the Spirit vaticinates and verifies in experience."[6] Why use a word like vaticinate? What does this sentence mean? It is unclear, to say the least. However, in the same book, we find an illustration entitled "Orbis Pictus" that very much echoes similar illustrations Alcott had seen adorning Böhmean books in England (see illustration below [in *Studies in the American Renaissance*]).

While in England more than thirty years before, Alcott had read the works of Böhmenists John Pordage and Dionysius Andreas Freher, and had seen the numerous alchemically based diagrams and illustrations that accompany not only these English works, but many German Böhmenist works as well. Not surprisingly Alcott, who saw himself as a kind of fresh American Böhme, included in *Table-Talk* this quasi-Böhmenist illustration "Orbis Pictus," along with the following, which strongly reminds us of **"Orphic Sayings"** and its "orbed thoughts":

> To the senses, things appear linear, orbed to thought. The lines of genesis, like flames, show spirally and aspirant. The spiral includes all known figures.
> "Principles, like fountains, flow round ceaselessly, Whirling in eddying evolutions of wavelets."[7]

This is, I would argue, Alcott's brand of American Böhmenism; admittedly incoherent, by and large, but definitely finding its inspiration in Böhmean thought, especially of the English variety. The references here to "figures" and "orbed," to "fountains" and "flames" reflect quite precisely the visionary nature of Böhmean thought, which works like alchemy in images, not in logical succession of thought.

That Alcott was intensely drawn to Böhmenist mysticism we can see not only in his search for books by such authors as Law and Pordage while in England in 1842, and by references in his books to Böhme, but also in his later attempts to forge connections between the American Transcendentalist movement and British Böhmenist disciples Christopher Walton and Edward Burton Penny. However, despite their common love for Böhme's works, Alcott and the British mystics only made a sporadic alliance. In 1867, Alcott wrote Walton—editor of a proposed massive series of theosophical writings called the *Cyclopaedia of Pure Christian Theology and Theosophic Science, or Law's Memorial*—warmly proposing that Walton contribute to the New England Transcendentalist publications and organizations like the Free Religious Association: "My studies for many years have lain in the direction of the Mystic authors, Jacob Behmen being a favorite, and, as I judge, the master mind of these last centuries. I was fortunate, when in England in 1842, to find not only his works in Law's edition, but most of the works of his disciples; Taylor, Pordage, Frances Lee, Law, and others."[8] Walton replied with an extensive letter, but it was a year before Alcott responded.

However, Alcott's belated reply revealed how much he was interested in Böhme and in the publications Walton and Penny were bringing out in England. Alcott had been able to read copies of the English Böhmenists's translations and other works through the Harvard library, and through his friend W. M. Fernald; he had, he writes Walton, read them all.[9] This intensive reading of the letters of Louis Claude de Saint-Martin, an ardent French Böhmenist, and other works "deepened" Alcott's "conviction" of "the exceeding importance of giving to the world full accounts of the lives of Behmen's illustrious desciples."[10] "I hope nothing will defeat your purpose of doing this," Alcott wrote, for "it is a kind of thought with which our advanced thinkers should be familiar in order to justify any claims to a real knowledge of spiritual things. . . . I wish I could add that any considerable number of our advanced thinkers had penetrated the core of the Mystery."[11]

Alcott did what he could to cement connections between W. T. Harris' *Journal of Speculative Philosophy,* a chiefly Hegelian organ of St. Louis Transcendentalism with which Alcott was affiliated, and the British Böhmenists, coaxing Penny or Walton to write articles on Böhme for it: "You will see by his table of contents how comprehensive his [Harris'] range is, and yet that without Boehme it is not inclusive." But by 1873, Alcott was still writing Walton, trying to coax him to write an article on Böhme for Harris' journal. And although Alcott took the liberty of having Harris publish a letter from Walton as a sort of advertisement for him—and even sent Walton copies of the journal, as well as of Alcott's latest book, the bonds between American Transcendentalism and British mysticism never really materialized, save in Alcott himself.

When in 1878, Thomas Johnson—a young Platonist from Osceola, Missouri—wrote Alcott about establishing a "Journal of Mysticism and Idealism," Alcott wrote back enthusiastically, hoping that in Johnson's publication he would find a vehicle for American publication of Böhmenist and other mystical writers. Revealingly, Alcott wrote that

> I think much of republications of authors now little known, but whose thoughts must find acceptance with our religious and thinking public once brought to their notice. The religious element has always attached the liveliest significance to the mystic and Ideal in life and thought, and we have no Journal, or newspaper even, doing any justice to its force and power.
>
> And biographical sketches of the great founders of these schools would form a most attractive feature of your magazine.[12]

Johnson's proposed journal became the *Platonist,* published from 1881 to 1888, continuing Alcott's love for Platonism, but not becoming a vehicle for Böhmenist mysticism.

During Alcott's last years—when his dream, the Concord School of Philosophy, became a reality—there was considerable public confusion about whether he had reverted or converted to "Christian orthodoxy" more amenable to the Unitarian and other Protestant clergy of his day, and here again Böhme provides an explanation. Especially as a result of his association with popular Congregationalist minister Joseph Cook, Alcott found himself answering letters and questions from many people who wondered what his precise sectarian or doctrinal position was. In his lectures at the Concord School and elsewhere, Alcott propounded a "Christian theism" that fiercely opposed Darwinist materialism, and he even underwent several doctrinal examinations by various Protestant clergy, who concluded that Alcott was more or less doctrinally sound. All of this drove the *Index*, a radical Transcendentalist publication, to condemn Alcott as having become "orthodox."[13]

But in fact, Alcott had been deeply drawn to universalist Protestant Böhmean mysticism more than forty years before, and he had not undergone a great change in attitude. In the 1870s and 1880s, as he did much earlier, Alcott sought to propagate a non-sectarian Christianity rooted in Protestant mysticism, especially that of his "Arch-mystic," Böhme. But circumstances had changed. Where in the 1840s Alcott's mysticism was perceived as part of Transcendentalist radicalism, and hence as a threat to more conservative Protestantism, by the 1880s, his views were opposed to Darwinist evolutionism and materialism—and hence his mysticism was allied with more conservative Protestants who also opposed the Darwinist evolutionism that had permeated postbellum Transcendentalist religious radicalism.

Nearly all of the "second cycle" Transcendentalists who embraced "Free Religion" radicalism also fervently embraced Darwinist science, their most fanatic apostle being John Fiske. But Alcott adamantly opposed Darwinism in all its social and other applications, recognizing in it, and in the dogma of "progress," an anti-spiritual sentiment that was effectively countered by Böhmenist mysticism.[14] In fact, Alcott was able to exclude proponents of Darwinism from the Concord School of Philosophy, and never failed to rail against Darwinism from his "Christian theist" position, which he drew from such authors as St. John, Plotinus, Tauler, Eckhart, and Böhme.[15]

In sum, then, we may say that the theosophy of Jacob Böhme was extremely important for Bronson Alcott from the beginning to the end of his career. Indeed, like Böhme himself, Alcott has often been mocked for his incomprehensibility. Yet his attraction to Böhmean mysticism has been little explored, either as a key to his often otherwise inexplicable oracular writings, or as a reason for his later attacks on evolutionism and his association with more conservative Protestant clergy. What is more, this "hidden" association between Alcott and Protestant Böhmean mysticism suggests a deeper affiliation between Emersonian Transcendentalism and earlier Protestant non-sectarian theosophy—including affiliations between Alcott's Fruitlands experiment and earlier American Böhmean communities like Ephrata, in the eighteenth century—that certainly could bear further exploration.

Notes

1. See Frederick C. Dahlstrand, *Amos Bronson Alcott: An Intellectual Biography* (Rutherford, N.J.: Fairleigh Dickinson University Press, 1982), pp. 182-83.

2. See Joel Myerson, "'In the Transcendental Emporium': Bronson Alcott's 'Orphic Sayings' in the *Dial*," *English Language Notes,* 10 (September 1972): 31-38, and Harry De Puy, "Amos Bronson Alcott: Natural Resource, or Consecrated Crank?" *American Transcendental Quarterly,* n.s. 1 (March 1987): 55. Myerson points out that the *Dial* omitted the bracketed word in the following sentence: "The poles of things are not integrated: creation [not] globed and orbed" (33*n*).

3. Dahlstrand, *Alcott,* p. 183.

4. "Genesis," *Tablets* (Boston: Roberts Brothers, 1868), p. 181.

5. *Concord Days* (Boston: Roberts Brothers, 1872), p. 237.

6. *Table-Talk* (Boston: Roberts Brothers, 1877), p. 133.

7. *Table-Talk,* p. 132.

8. *The Letters of A. Bronson Alcott,* ed. Richard L. Herrnstadt (Ames: Iowa State University Press, 1969), p. 417.

9. *Letters,* p. 469.

10. *Letters,* p. 470.

11. *Letters,* p. 470.

12. *Letters,* p. 736.

13. See Dahlstrand, *Alcott,* pp. 343ff.

14. One might well say that Alcott was one hundred years ahead of his time—since in his book *Science, Meaning, and Evolution: The Cosmology of Jacob Boehme* (New York: Parabola, 1991), French physicist Basarab Nicolescu argues that Böhme provides an alternative paradigm suitable for understanding modern physics in the context of post-Darwinian science. Böhmean mysticism can indeed provide a non-materialist cosmology for science, as Böhmean writers like Franz von Baader have pointed out.

15. See Dahlstrand, *Alcott,* p. 353.

Bernard Schmidt (essay date December 1994)

SOURCE: Schmidt, Bernard. "Bronson Alcott's Developing Personalism and the Argument with Emerson." *American Transcendental Quarterly* n.s. 8, no. 4 (December 1994): 311-27.

[*In the following essay, Schmidt discusses the influence of Walt Whitman's 1868 essay "Personalism" on the development of Alcott's later thought. Alcott's subse-*

quent espousal of "Personal Theism," according to Schmidt, represented a distinct challenge to Emerson's abstract notions of divinity and created an intellectual divide between the two friends.]

In "The Divinity School Address" (1838), Emerson publicly declared that God was too important to be diminished by the mundane concept of personality. Both Perry Miller in *The Transcendentalists* (1950) and David Van Leer in *Emerson's Epistemology* (1986) thoroughly emphasize the fact that by renouncing the concept of a personal deity Emerson separated himself from both traditional and Unitarian Christianity in an uproarious embroilment in which his enemies, such as the editors of the Unitarian organ *The Christian Examiner,* accused him of preaching theology that was not only "distasteful" and "repugnant" but "neither good divinity nor good sense" (qtd. in Miller 197). Whether the reader studies the plea in sermon form of Henry Ware Jr. for "The Personality of the Deity" or the diatribes of the conservative Unitarian spokesman Andrews Norton against what he perceives to be an atheistic attack on the structure of Christianity, one of the key points of Emerson's break with the traditional Christian church was his stand on the need for an impersonal deity, and Bronson Alcott, the pioneer Personalist, argued with Emerson for the desirability of a personal deity throughout the course of their friendship. As David P. Edgell, William Ellery Channing's biographer has noted, Emerson accused traditional Christianity of a "noxious" emphasis on the "person of Jesus." To many Christians of the older denominations, certainly including Unitarianism, Emerson's rejection of the personal deity who can make miracles and reveal Biblical dogma was the work of a corrupt atheist. Alcott did not join the attacks on his friend, but their argument helps to characterize their different forms of theism.

Writing in 1934, Harvey Gates Townsend described the Transcendental state of mind as originating "in the universal desire to find a satisfactory set of personal beliefs by which a man can live and call his soul his own" (Townsend 133). Whitman and Alcott were Transcendentalists, who not only conducted a thorough search for workable, livable "personal beliefs," but who came to consider the initiator of this search, the individual self, to be the prime mover and receiver of the vital perceptual and conceptual messages in the universe. Whether acting or acted upon, the personal self was the focal point of perception. If the actor in a given situation were God, then the scene would be centered on a super-human self. If the actor were human, then the self would not be supernatural, but would still be the manufacturer of knowledge. So the rather prosaic assumption that the center of the universe is the individual—not nature, the Oversoul, or even God—eventually grew into American Personalistic Idealism, a system of philosophy that took form in the time of the Transcendental ferment, but had its own course to follow.

In a little-known article called "Personalism," published in the fifth volume of the *Galaxy* in 1868, Walt Whitman set down some of the key ideas of this Personalistic philosophy which were to be further developed by later more systematic thinkers; the *Galaxy* manifesto marks Whitman as the ostensible father of this movement within Transcendentalism. In "Personalism," Whitman wrote that the tendency to consider the members of a democracy as masses must be balanced by a contrary impulse to see them as individual selves. The center of the universe is "me," and "even for the treatment of the universal, in politics, metaphysics, or anything, sooner or later we come down to one single, solitary Soul" (Whitman 541). Artificial conventions and barriers to the wholesome development of character fall away as men consider their own personal selves the primary source of insight. Then, a perfect democratic society begins to evolve as "our model, a clear-blooded, strong-fibered" man, "under control," attends to the promptings of "Personality" (Whitman 543).

This article is concerned with a Personalistic thinker, who is, however, much more closely associated with Emersonian Transcendentalism than Whitman: Amos Bronson Alcott, who has never been given proper credit for the new direction he helped to give American thought. The object of this study is to show that Alcott was much more than a piper who played a foolish tune; he was a pioneer in the impulse that became American Personalism. Also, Alcott's Personalism was a foil to Emerson's abstract idealism, and the two Transcendentalists argued about the personality of the deity until the end of their active lives. The argument alone makes Alcott a significant part of American Transcendentalism. As Helen R. Deese reminds us, "historians of transcendentalism have noted the difficulty of chronicling a movement which expressed itself to a great extent in oral forms," and which included "lectures, sermons," and "Bronson Alcott's conversations" (17). In dialogue and informal writings, Alcott preserved the conflict between his Personalism and Emerson's absolute idealism, a conflict that is important to American intellectual history.

That Alcott and Whitman communicated about their common interest in the universe as a product of personality is a matter of record. In April of 1868, Whitman wrote to his mother that he had sent Alcott his article, "Personalism," and that his older friend "compliments me highly" (Whitman, *Complete Writings* 233). How highly Alcott complimented Whitman and his Personalistic article was recorded in the journal of April 23, 1868:

> Letter from Whitman, with his paper on Personalism in the *Galaxy.* Is pleased with my letter of January 19,

last. This Personalism is in the same grand vein of democracy, and he promises a third on literature.

Say what men say, this man is a power in thought, and likely to make his mark on times and institutions. American Gallery: Emerson, Thoreau, and Walt. If there be an ideal personalism, so is there an actual individualism, of which Thoreau and Whitman are prodigious impersonations—Walt for institutions, Thoreau for things.

Write to Whitman and send him my Emerson.

Read "Personalism" again after day's work. Verily, great grand doctrine, and great grand Walt, grown since I saw him in his Brooklyn garret in 1850—. Greater and grown more open-eyed, as perhaps oneself, since then.

(Shepard, *Journals* 391)

Alcott's tone of approval here is unmistakable, as it is in a letter sent to Whitman on the same day of the journal entry, April 28, 1868. The "noble paper" on "Personalism" shows "the route to Personal Power for the nation as for the individual," says Alcott (Herrnstadt 435). The idea that truly free individuals have a personal power that must create and maintain a free, democratic state is Personalistic. Although Alcott had his own desire to see American institutions influenced by Personalistic Idealism, his support of Whitman's manifesto, the first real codification of Personalistic view in the United States, is one clear way in which Alcott placed himself in the formal history of the movement.

Alcott, the conversationalist, the enthusiastic speaker with the mission of the preacher, made a significant contribution to American Personalistic Idealism by maintaining a little-known series of arguments with his closest friend and strongest supporter, Ralph Waldo Emerson. By the time Alcott's philosophical thoughts were committed to books, namely *Tablets* (1868), *Concord Days* (1872), and *Table Talk* (1877), the two leaders of Transcendentalism had gone their separate philosophical ways, parting on friendly but irreconcilable terms. By refusing to succumb to the persuasions of his prestigious friend, Alcott developed his own personalized brand of Transcendentalism and gave the Personalistic movement a rigor that could not be derived from the abstract, often sterile appeal of the Emersonian cosmos and its Oversoul.

Although the argument was primarily documented in Alcott's journals and letters in the mid-nineteenth century, there is evidence that Alcott's Personalistic impulses were stirring within his mind as early as 1837, and that by then his formulation and discussions of Personalism had begun. Hubert H. Hoeltje marks Alcott's first visit to Concord in the fall of 1835 as the beginning of the conflict between Emerson's abstract idealism and Alcott's Personalism. Alcott was overwhelmed

with Emerson's blend of humane sensitivity and deep scholarship, but there was a tension between the two men that later blossomed into an ideological conflict:

Beneath these first impressions, had he been able to see deeply enough, or clearly enough, Alcott might have read much that the future had in store for his friendship with Emerson. He might have read his growing awareness of his friend's apparently meticulous care for form, a flaw which Emerson himself, many years later, was to call one of the chief defects of Plato, a man revered by him almost above all. Alcott might have observed too, had his own convictions been plain to him, that some time long hence in the declining days of their lives, they should approach disagreement in what he now chose to regard as a mere difference of association rather than of thought. But Alcott was still to formulate his conception of Personality, and now he was content to quiet his doubts with the obvious kinship of thought with his friend.

(Hoeltje 25-26)

Hoeltje's summary of the situation is reasonable, but he does not mention that during the early meetings of the Transcendental Club Alcott's Personalistic theories were subject of discussion.

Although Alcott missed the first meeting of the Transcendental Club, held on September 8, 1836, he was among the new members in the group gathered for the second meeting held on September 19, 1836 (Myerson 27-28). From nineteenth-century newspaper accounts, Clarence Gohdes has reconstructed Alcott's "'Conversations' on the Transcendental Club and the *Dial*," and notes that Alcott's Personalistic doctrines were often set upon by proponents of "Impersonality," an abstract, impersonal idealism of the coldest Platonic sort. In an effort to find through continuing and lively discussion a set of religious views free from the superstitions of Calvinism and the lifelessness of Unitarianism, the parties involved took "individuality" to be the center of thought (qtd. in Gohdes 17). Conversation centered on this concept, as well as "impersonality—Law, Right, Justice, Truth—," but to the intense philosopher from Spindle Hill, some element seemed to be missing (qtd. in Gohdes 17). In his search for the dynamic element that would bind together and give vitality to the dead abstractions passed from mind to mind in the arguments of the Transcendental Club, Alcott slowly forged his doctrine of Personalism. A superpersonality, a pulsing, dynamic consciousness with an omnipotent and omnipresent intelligence was the answer, and Alcott's search concluded in a manner that definitively separated his Personalism from Emerson's Transcendentalism.

For Alcott, abstractions lost their impact on the mind without the binding element of personality, and this fact forced him to ask questions which did not occur to other members of the group:

But where the power was in which they inhered, how they were related to one another, what was to give them vitality—these questions were quite neglected, and left out of sight. Hence we read in the books and journals published about that time, of Law, Justice, Right, and the rest. That view pervades *Nature,* also the lectures of Mr. Emerson, and, indeed almost all the writing of his school. . . . I think that was the deficiency of the transcendental school; is its deficiency still; is the reason why it has not incorporated itself into a church, and been found equal to compete with orthodoxy, and the old Puritanism, which, whatsoever may have been its blunders—whatsoever superstitions may have been mingled with its doctrines—did believe in a Person, and did not allow itself to discriminate personality away into laws and ideas.

(qtd. in Gohdes 17-18)

As Alcott thought through his doctrine of personalism with increasing assurance, he did not allow any creed, religion, or philosophy "to discriminate personality away into laws and ideas." His God had a definite, vital personality. However, Emerson preferred to consider the Deity "a universal soul within or behind his individual life," a "universal soul" which he eventually called the Oversoul, and consequently, the vitality of a real personality in his world of abstractions was unacceptable (Atkinson 15). This contrast illustrates the difference between the characters of the social, people-minded Alcott and the retiring, somewhat aloof Emerson. With their basic differences in disposition crystallizing in their individual philosophies, the two friends could not put aside their conflict concerning the theory of "Personality." Emerson made rare references to the Personality of God, but these are of little significance compared to his much more fully developed descriptions of the One or Oversoul as an entity with no personality.

By 1858, statements of the dispute were increasingly evident in the journals and letters of Alcott. For instance, the journal note for February 12, 1858, mentioned that, after tea, Emerson and his friend talked "late on intellect and individualism discriminating the latter from personality" (Shepard, *Journals* 306). In much of Alcott's later work, an "individualism" took on a distinctly pejorative, anti-social note, often representing a deviation from love of fellow-man, rather than the individualized Transcendental search for higher truths. Again, in a journal entry for April 16, 1863, Alcott criticized Emerson's notion of Deity. In the discussion for that evening, Alcott found his friend's reaction to his Personalistic theories "deficient, his Individuality overpowering, and he only saved by his liberating imagination from Fate," which here means fatalism (Shepard, *Journals* 356). That the friends disputed the issue of Personalism, but agreed on the need to combat fatalism is shown by Emerson's reaction in his journal to this discussion:

Alcott defended his thesis of personality last night, but it is not a quite satisfactory use of words. We speak daily of a government of power used to personal ends, and I see profound needs of distinguishing the first cause as super personal. It deluges us with power, we are filled with it, but there are skies of immensity between us and it. But Alcott's true strength is in the emphasis he gives to partnership of power against the doctrine of Fate. There is no passive reception. The receiver to receive, must play the God also.

(Emerson and Forbes 503)[1]

Odell Shepard sees Emerson's insistence on an impersonal "first cause" as a product of "lingering Calvinism" or a rationalization for "his reluctance toward all intimate association" (Shepard, *Pedlar's Progress* 465). David Williams has shown that Emerson's aunt, Mary Moody Emerson, was a clear and strong connection between Emerson and his Calvinist heritage (3). Integral to Personalism, however, is the social tendency, which was as much a part of Alcott's character and philosophy, as a certain aloofness was natural to Emerson. Alcott's social proclivity, his feeling for the importance of the community of selves, was anticipated in Leibniz's *Monadology.* Leibniz, a founder of Personalistic thought, took great care to describe the integrity and autonomy of the self. What is commonly overlooked in his explication of a monadic universe is that individual selves are inextricably linked together. In the limited sphere or universe in which human beings function, each body responds to, and is affected by, whatever happens to the others with which they are in contact: "by means of these beings the body responds to those bodies adjoining them, and their intercommunication reaches to any distance whatsoever" (Von Leibniz 465). The "knowledge of eternal and necessary truth," provided by a God who gives definite moral laws, creates a social structure in which man can live in peace and harmony (Von Leibniz 459). This feeling for social intercourse became a pillar to the Personalist tradition. Whitman's *Galaxy* article stresses the importance of self as the center of society, and the democratic framework as the perfect structure for the self. Democracy, "a great word whose history remains unwritten, because that history has yet to be enacted," describes the political environment within which the superior American self will fulfill its potential (Whitman 541). Whitman's marriage of two concepts, the concern of the individual for society and the belief that such a concern can best flourish in a democracy, was never to be relinquished by Personalistic thinkers.[2] In the Personalistic view, social interaction and political freedom were inextricably linked together. Emmanuel Mounier, the foremost thinker in the French School of Personalism, was adamant in his statement that no man is truly "isolated," and that society has a certain holistic personality that must be trained to be morally alert and ethically sensitive (Mounier 84). Alcott, as well as most other Personalists, would have agreed with Mounier:

The effort to achieve truth and justice is a collective effort. Not that a million consciences necessarily produce a higher consciousness than does a single strict conscience. Numbers, before they are organized, may only produce mediocrity, confusion, weariness, or passion. And at the first attempt, organization often does not more than harden the mass emotions thus brought together. It is only through their personalization that numbers achieve human significance, insure free cooperation and exchange of gifts, and bring under control the follies and mystifications into which individuals are led through separation.

(Mounier 84)

The process of "Personalization" to which Mounier refers offsets the damaging effects of the individual selfishness or "separation" that approximates Alcott's idea of "individuality." In his lecture at the Concord School of Philosophy, given on July 19, 1882, Dean Alcott defined "Personality" as the soul-like quality or spiritual essence "which is universal and common to men—all that is central and absolute in each one" (Bridgman 31). The Personalist Edgar Sheffield Brightman would later explain that a self is merely a unit of consciousness that may only function by instinct, but a person has a personality and is able to reason and develop a value system (341). "Individuality," in Alcott's pejorative, disruptive sense, is "that which is particular and special, which distinguishes one person from another," which prevents men from achieving a universal oneness of mind and a unification with God, because of their temperamental weaknesses and petty concerns (Bridgman 31). In a later lecture at the school entitled "Individualism," Alcott further defined this key concept as a "separation from a oneness with God—a becoming divided from Him and willfully pursuing the path that leads away from Him" (Bridgman 129). Not only does individuality lead to social deviation and unfriendly behavior, but the egotism of the man given to individuality ultimately sets him against the building of the institutions valuable to mankind. Theologically, the individualist is a fallen man; his willfulness and selfishness give him kinship with Adam and even Satan, the classical rebels of Christian mythology. Not only does the failure to maintain harmony with God and mankind lead to "separateness from good and truth and beauty," it also leads man to become the adversary to goodness, a satanic character" who isolates himself with a hell of denial and evil, of oppositeness to the highest" (Bridgman 130). The family, schools, church, and state must survive the individualist's pursuit of his own way.

To Alcott, the ordinary distinction between individuals, that is, individuality in the modern, positive sense, is a separate phenomenon which he refers to as "Differentiation" (Bridgman 130). Nicholas Berdyaev, the modern Russian Personalistic theologian and historian, takes a position similar to that of Alcott and most other American Transcendentalists: as part of a biological ge-

nus, the single man must consciously control his relation to society. The individual must fight an existential battle to develop his rights to territory, personal sovereignty, and a general independence from the impositions of hostile wills. The Russian philosopher goes on to describe individualism as a problem that must be solved to create a Personalistic universe. Although his thought is couched in the language of the laboratory, it is linked with Alcott's, and his similar, comparable ideas shed light on those of the American:

The individual in his biological self-assertion and self-centeredness may sever himself from the life of the genus, but this alone never leads to the affirmation of personality, its growth and expansion. Hence Christian ethics is personalistic, but not individualistic. The narrow isolation of personality in modern individualism is the destruction and not the triumph of personality. Hardened self-hood—the result of original sin—is not personality. It is only when the hardened self-hood melts away and is transcended that personality manifests itself.

(Berdyaev 58)

In Alcott's view, as in Berdyaev's, "hardened self-hood" is the result of original sin and is a grave threat to human well-being and progress. In the Personalistic tradition, and in the mind of Bronson Alcott, individualism is a crime against God and society.

This pejorative view of individualism helps to reveal the depth and seriousness of Alcott's dispute with Emerson. Writing in 1872 to Thomas Davidson, the Orphic Sage criticized Emerson for "Individualism idealized" and a hesitation to commit himself to "the ground of Personality in the exercise of free choice" (Herrnstadt 548). In this letter Alcott included Emerson in a list of men who had fatalistic tendencies. If his criticism of his friend seemed farfetched, for Emerson was hardly a pure fatalist or hard determinist, and obscure, for "Individualism idealized" in Alcott's terms would seem to be anti-fatalistic, the tone of censure is clear and unmistakable. As early as January of 1846, Alcott had criticized Emerson in words that accused him of hiding in his idealistic retreat to avoid emotional interaction with his peers and his God; Emerson's path seemed to lead to atheism:

Emerson is Constitutionally a pantheistic sophist. The idealism of his mind, defacing the primitive ascendancy of the moral sentiment, leaves him without basis for upholding the verity of Being. He is unable to escape wholly his taint of unbelief, in which he was bred, and his fine powers carry this mark into all his designs.

(Shepard, *Journals* 72)

According to Paul F. Boller, Jr., Emerson often spoke and wrote like a pantheist, once he no longer saw pantheism as a road to atheism. An idealist rather than a theist, Emerson usually "emphasized immanence rather than transcendence and his inclinations were toward pantheism" (Boller 81). The predecessor to Gay Wilson Allen as Emerson's biographer, Ralph L. Rusk, says that his subject "approved mysticism, pantheism, idealism in varying degrees, by turns" (241). Alcott, on the other hand, avoided pantheism by his creation of the omnipotent personality, through which each person or soul had a reality of its own beyond its role as a component of all-encompassing nature. Alcott saw Emerson not only as a pantheist as opposed to a theist, but also as a "sophist" tainted by "unbelief."

In numerous utterances Alcott designated Emerson a pantheist, and this term makes their theological disagreement international rather than just purely local. The larger conflict of atheism versus theism subsumes the more limited dispute over the personal versus impersonal nature of God. The threat of atheism was a significant source of torment to the western European and, to some extent, the American nineteenth-century intellect and would have made most American Unitarians and Transcendentalists quickly forget their disputes over miracles, revelation, the nature of the deity, and the function of human reason to band together against a common foe. Historically, the name of the debate over the brand of atheism called pantheism is the *Pantheismusstreit* or pantheism controversy. Friedrich Heinrich Jacobi brought it to the public in 1785 when he published his discussion with Moses Mendelssohn of Lessing's acceptance of Spinoza's controversial pantheistic doctrines (Weinberg 36). Mendelssohn planned to write a book about Lessing, and he was not about to associate his famous friend with the Spinozist acceptance of God as an impersonal "absolute substance" without definite proof (Weinberg 37). By taking God out of a supernatural realm and making Him part of nature or material reality, the thinker begins with pantheism but might finish with an atheism in which no supernatural events or deities exist, a threatening evolution indeed for the person with religious inclinations. Of course, divesting God of his dominating, paternal, supra-natural personality is inherent to this process. Conventional systems of Christianity will not work if a person's fate is predetermined; the older forms emphasized rewards and punishments which were a product of the individual's will or choice. Perry Miller has shown that even Calvinism was forced to soften its stand on election by the device of covenant theology. The Covenant of Grace allowed sinners to claim salvation by imitating the purified behavior of the saved. Spinoza takes choice away from mankind by making his God a subsuming nature, which moves a person like a "stone," which is "thinking and knowing," but is actually rolled along by an impersonal force (qtd. in Lamont 39).

Mendelssohn's role in the controversy was to clear Lessing of adherence to "Spinozism," but when Jacobi inconsiderately published his correspondence with Less-

ing's protector, the private nature of the discussion was destroyed. The controversy exploded so that thinkers as famous and diverse as Kant, Herder, Goethe, and later Schleiermacher, Schelling, and Hegel participated in its often vituperative polemics (Weinberg 36-37). For his role as its pious, perhaps sanctimonious master of ceremonies, Jacobi earned the epithet of "gossiping old woman" in Heinrich Heine's retrospective assessment written in 1834 (79). Nonetheless, Jacobi had declared that "Spinozism is atheism" making sure that the title of pantheist was not comfortable and that the *Pantheismusstreit* would become an interesting segment of Western theological history (Weinberg 36). Alcott had used a rather mystical utterance of Jacobi for his epigraph to the section of his book *Table Talk* called "Person." When Isaiah Berlin says of Jacobi and his mentor, Johann Georg Hamann, pietistic proponents of the *Pantheismusstreit*, that "the God they worshipped was personal—they looked on pantheism as a species of atheism—" he could well have been describing Alcott's rationale in his argument with Emerson (186).

Although Emerson scholars do not emphasize his interest in Spinoza, it did exist. Two of his journal entries in 1838 place Spinoza in a list of the world's profound thinkers. Joining Socrates and Jesus, Spinoza is in the elite group of "trismegisti," "that lofty and sequestered class" of "prophets and oracles, the high priesthood of the pure reason . . ." (Plunstead, *Journals* 37). To Emerson, great thinkers help a person find his or her own thoughts, so there is no reason to fear any thinker or philosophical system. Dogma was mankind's true intellectual nemesis. Therefore, Spinoza could be a "hobgoblin" in Emerson's youth and a "saint" in his maturity (Bosco, *Journals* 99). If Spinoza or Emerson had conferred with other religious philosophers in any era in history, they would have found that they were of one mind, and to have heard any of their words or read any of their books could have been nothing other than delightful (Bosco, *Journals* 91, 329). Emerson refused to be threatened by the gentle lens grinder who had been reviled by both Jewish and Christian theologians. In fact, Emerson often approached the concept of religious dispute with blatant nonchalance. In the mundane philosophical environment of the United States, a *Pantheismusstreit*, a pantheism controversy, was for Andrews Norton. To most citizens it would be "clatter" (Orth, *Journals* 109). To Emerson, the down-to-earth proudly anti-intellectual American thought "the pinelog was God, and that God was in the jakes" (Orth, *Journals* 103-104). Therefore, Emerson asked in his *Journals*, even with his theory of reality as "but one substance," "what can Spinoza tell" such a person to threaten his or her equanimity (Orth, *Journals* 104)? Spinoza was deep and wise, but he was very much the European idealist; Emerson, the American idealist, knew that American practicality and xenophobia precluded lasting attention to European theological disputes. Besides, according to

Rusk, Emerson's friend and sometimes mentor, Elliot Cabot, tried to instill in Emerson his own combative enthusiasm for Spinoza, but he failed (309).

Theological disputes were futile and "childish" (Porte, *Journals* 548). The philosopher gives you what is yours; "if Spinoza cannot, perhaps Kant will: If Kant cannot, then perhaps Alcott" (Sealts Jr., *Journals* 390). In "The Latest Form of Infidelity," the vituperative, humorless Unitarian divine, Andrews Norton, named Emerson a priest of "the celebrated atheist Spinoza" (qtd. in Allen 321). Norton fought Emerson, but the gentle transcendentalist fought not at all. He argued with Alcott and rejected his personal God and in the process inadvertently became a participant in an American version of the *Pantheismusstreit*.

Alcott wanted to see "humanity and nature alike in a complete genius," not a disembodied intellect so idealistic, so impersonal, that it seemed to be part of a being who dwelled in "some fancied realm, some Atlantides of this Columbia, very clearly discernible to him [self] but not by us" (Shepard, *Journals* 194-195). Ironically, however, Emerson at times described Alcott as a "tedious archangel," a man whose entire being was high in the clouds (Linscott 190). For Emerson, the Orphic Sage was a man who would "never finish a sentence" without revolving "in spirals until he is lost in air," and, with all his kindness, wisdom, and admirable idealistic tendencies and beliefs, Alcott sometimes seemed to Emerson to have the perspective of a madman. Emerson's violent disapproval of the Fruitlands experiment provoked him to describe Alcott and his English friend Lane as needing "feet": "They are always feeling of their shoulders to find if their wings are sprouting" (Linscott 270).

Nevertheless, the substance of Alcott's complaint with Emerson would give birth to a doctrine that became traditional in American Personalism. A part of the greater idea of individualism is the lesser idea of impersonalism. To Alcott, Emerson's impersonalism began with his refusal to associate the individual personality in a warm and intimate way with those of the people in society. The younger man was doomed to a nearly misanthropic isolation. The brilliant Emerson

> assumed the first of our poets, was forbidden pure companionship with Nature. He dwelt rather in an intellectual grove, and looked at society from this his retreat through the glass of imagination, coming rarely into positive contact and sympathy with it through the heart and understanding and set never a firm foot on the Yankee-land in which he nominally dwelt. He was a citizen of the crystal palace, but of no country because of all.
>
> (Shepard, *Journals* 253-254)

The man with no "country," hiding in his sacred "grove," was not truly individualistic in the manner of the reformers; his conceptual thrashing about did not

threaten to dismember society through the destruction of its institutions. Yet, Alcott continued to refer to Emerson as an individualist, a term which Odell Shepard says Alcott associated with "all human ignorance, strife, misunderstanding," and even fairly respectable controversy (*Pedlar's Progress* 494).

In the published work of both Alcott and Borden Parker Bowne, leader of the Boston school of Personalism, there is no evidence that they exchanged ideas. The only direct link between the two men was forged in 1880: Bowne was a member of the committee in charge, when Alcott was invited to suggest speakers for the Boston Monday Lectureship (Herrnstadt 818). However, Alcott did think through many of the same concepts as Bowne, and the two men were pioneers in the development of American Personalism.

Alcott's references to impersonalism were never systematized; later, Bowne molded his own concept of impersonalism into a clear, conceptual foil to personalistic theism. Whether or not Alcott discussed Personalism with Bowne, the Orphic Sage could never have sustained the logical concentration and attention to theme that Bowne displayed in "The Failure of Impersonalism," the critical chapter in *Personalism* (1908). According to Bowne, impersonalism arises from two general sources: either a deification of the world of sense, which leads to the belief that all beings, laws, and occurrences are part of a mechanistic process called nature, or a compulsion to go beyond the personal god to an impersonal or absolute first cause in the search for a prime mover. The first source of impersonalism is Naturalism; with its materialistic and sensual tendencies, it had little attraction to the Transcendentalists. The second is much more treacherous in its appeal to those who seek deity in abstraction, but for a Personalist, the human self, the perceiver of God, is not an abstraction. Ideas actually belong to a particular person, and the reality of the individual is the beginning point in the assumption that a supreme Person exists. Thus, Bowne argued, "we must really say that complete personality can be found only in the Infinite and Absolute Being, as only in him can we find that complete and perfect selfhood and self-possession which are necessary to the fullness of personality" (Bowne, *Personalism* 284). Alcott would have rejoiced in Bowne's formulation of these thoughts, and he would have agreed with Bowne that a strictly abstract idealism or even materialism "is a pure fiction," because "All actual ideas are owned, or belong to someone, and mean nothing as floating free" (Bowne, *Personalism* 284).[3]

The argument between the two leaders of American Transcendentalism continued until the end of their active lives. On February 13, 1865, Alcott complained:

> E. thinks his lecture on "Character" should content people. I tell him it will not satisfy the religious mind, and needs the compliment of Personality to stand good

for the Universal Faith. He claims "Nature" as the best word on the whole, for the All, and is not disturbed by any scandal of his pantheistic notions or idealism.

(Shepard, *Journals* 370)

And on May 30, of that year:

> After tea, he reads me his lecture on "Character," as revised, to which I give generally my hearty assent. Perhaps something more of warmth of coloring, a Godhead more personal, would have pleased me better; but 'tis his, and as the deification of his intelligence, admirable.

(Shepard, *Journals* 372)

In Alcott's opinion, Emerson looked for God and found the reflection of his own dry intellectualism. Emerson's thought was akin to the "Old Light" anti-revival impulse born in conservative Congregationalism and bred in Unitarianism.

Alcott insisted on a Personal Theism and on the "instrumental action for planting it" (Shepard, *Journals* 390). Ultimately, both men argued for action and, thus, were progenitors of the Pragmatists; when Alcott said that his Personalistic doctrines needed "instrumental" action, or gained validity through implementation, he was using a term common to his vocabulary and one which John Dewey would use to describe his early Pragmatism. Alcott's Personalistic position was almost a challenge to Emerson, but by 1877 his criticisms of Emerson's thought were less severe, even though similar, to those of the previous decades:

> My friend's persistent Individualism appears to mellow with years and some apparent infirmities, as should be the rule with poets and idealists. Perhaps I should find still deeper sympathy with him in thought and social intercourse were his drift of temperament less dominant and determined—But then Emerson were not Emerson, and the fine forces of his genius had not the emphasis that tells so truly the man he is. An evening with him is a rare privilege—too rare to be sought too often, for the profit of Individualism or Personalism alike.

(Shepard, *Journals* 475)

As this late journal entry shows, the argument was never settled. Although "Transcendental method, as Emerson conceived it and used it, was wholly and entirely intuitive" and was "an individual, immediate raid on universal truth," his God was the impersonal Oversoul (Blau 122). Although the "Reason was primarily a power of the mind to feel moral and religious truth," and Emerson's individual person was allowed intuitive, affective, and emotional perceptions of universal knowledge, his God was purely an abstraction (White 99). On March 22, 1878, in the latter days of their friendship and active lives, Alcott summarized his dispute with Emerson over Personalism:

The old topic of Personal Immortality comes into our discussion, and I find my friend as persistent as formerly in his individualism. His faith is purely ethical, and demands the certainty of facts experienced individually. His idealism hesitates and pauses, appalled at the dread facts of the Personality. True to his convictions, he modestly rests in his Individualism, and is silent concerning what lies beyond. Perhaps he may be classed as an ideal theist, with that film of pantheistic haze that hovers always about that school of thinkers. This latent pantheism has from the first characterized the New England school of Transcendentalists, and has not yet cleared itself from the clouds, most of its disciples being still touched with its indefiniteness, unable to find the certainty they seek. While it has modified favorably the materialistic tendencies of New England thinking, it has failed of planting itself upon the intuition of the Personal and Immortal.

(Shepard, *Journals* 485)

Emerson had taken the mechanical concept of human reason and, in the tradition of Coleridge and the Scottish Common Sense philosopher Duglad Stuart, molded it into the function that "intuitively and not by a syllogistic or logical process" allows man to see "absolute and universal right and truth" (Davis 210). Thus, he could free himself from Locke, but not from Plato. Through the influence of Emerson, absolute idealism became integral to American Transcendentalism; for Alcott, the absolutist impulse needed to be limited by personality. Robert M. Greenberg makes the point that for Emerson human consciousness is a process, which constantly composes an ever-changing reality out of an influx of perceptions (214). For the Personalist Alcott, Emerson hobbled that consciousness by delivering its sovereignty to the absolute One. There is no real individual integrity or self-reliance when personality is devalued to the status of a character defect.

In his introduction to *The Transcendentalists,* Perry Miller attempted to describe the motivating force that united Emerson, Alcott, and their Transcendental comrades in New England:

> The Transcendental movement is most accurately to be defined as a religious demonstration. The real drive in the souls of the participants was a hunger of the spirit for values which Unitarianism had concluded were no longer estimable. It had, to all appearances irrevocably, codified into manageable and safe formularies appetites that hitherto in America had been glutted with the terrors of hell and the ecstasies of grace. Unless this literature be read as fundamentally an expression of a religious radicalism in revolt against a rational conservatism, it will not be understood; if it is so interpreted, then the deeper undertone can be heard. Once it is heard, the literature becomes, even in its more fatuous reaches, a protest of the human spirit against emotional starvation.

(Miller 8)

Miller's vision of the sterility of Unitarianism has a parallel in Morton White's vision of the weakness in Emerson's Oversoul and its idealistic successor, Josiah

Royce's Absolute, both constructs that deprive religion of its vitality by extracting its emotional content (White 113). Alcott knew that his friend's abstract deity was a deficiency, which could cause American Transcendentalism to lose its impetus. In Emerson's absolute idealism, "emotional starvation" was perpetuated, and the dryness of Unitarianism lived on. Transcendentalism, with its emphasis on individuality, finally lost touch with man as a single unit, a personality, and never became the new religion that some of its proponents had hoped it would. In the early twentieth century, William James echoed Alcott's complaint with Emersonian idealism, and in so doing, wrote the obituary of Transcendentalism as a religious force:

> An entire world is the smallest unit with which the Absolute can work, whereas to our finite minds work for the better ought to be done within this world, setting in at single points. Our difficulties and our ideals are all piecemeal affairs, but the Absolute can do no piecework for us; so that all the interests which our poor souls compass raise their heads too late. We should have spoken earlier, prayed for another world absolutely, before this world was born. It is strange, I have heard a friend say, to see this blind corner into which Christian thought has worked itself at last, with its god who can raise no particular weight whatsoever, who can help us with no private burden.
>
> (James 404)

James saw what Alcott deeply felt, and by incorporating Personalistic concerns into some of his books, James showed his respect for the legacy of Alcott and Whitman.

Notes

1. For the sake of clarity, I list all Emerson journal entries by editor in the internal notes and Works Cited. I list Alcott's lectures, journals, and letters by editor in the internal notes.

2. In a 1940 article on Personalism, Ralph T. Flewelling continued the emphasis on the need for a democratic society for the healthiest growth of the mind and the character of the individual:

> The development of the person can be achieved only under the highest possible conditions of freedom. But freedom is discovered as possessing limits in an orderly society. The person can be free only to the extent of not impinging on the reasonable rights and opportunities of others. It is obvious then that freedom must be practiced with self-control on the part of each citizen. . . . The person can realize his own highest gifts and happiness only in the service of all.
>
> (340-341)

3. See Bowne, *Personalism* 284. Bowne argued that scientists continually mistake their abstractions and classification processes for reality and called this simple error the "fallacy of the universal" (Bowne, *Theory of Thought* 244). Because it causes people to replace religious faith with a fanatic belief in science as a source of truth, it is a dangerous and "perennial source of atheistic and evolutionary speculation" (Bowne, *Theory of Thought* 246). Bowne felt that this fallacy was behind Spinoza's pantheism in which the living person is confused with the category of humanity, and all the categories are subsumed by an amorphous, impersonal one (*Theory of Thought* 247). Bowne's "fallacy of the universal" is a detailed outgrowth of the impulse, which led Alcott to fear the scientist who "methodizes life and spirit all away" (Shepard, *Journals* 71).

Works Cited

Alcott, A. Bronson. *Concord Lectures on Philosophy*. Ed. Raymond L. Bridgman. Cambridge, 1883; rpt. Philadelphia: Albert Saifer, 1969.

———. *The Journals of Bronson Alcott*. Ed. Odell Shepard. Boston: Little, Brown, 1938.

———. *The Letters of A. Bronson Alcott*. Ed. Richard L. Herrnstadt. Ames: Iowa State University Press, 1969.

———. *Table Talk*. Boston: Roberts Brothers, 1877.

Allen, Gay Wilson. *Waldo Emerson*. New York: Viking, 1981.

Atkinson, Brooks, ed. *The Complete Essays and Other Writings of Ralph Waldo Emerson*. New York: Random House, 1940.

Berdyaev, Nicholas. *The Destiny of Man*. New York: Harper & Row, 1960.

Berlin, Isaiah. *Against the Current*. Ed. Henry Hardy. Intro. Roger Hausheer. Middlesex, England: Penguin, 1982.

Blau, Joseph L. *Men and Movements in American Philosophy*. Englewood Cliffs: Prentice Hall, 1952.

Boller, Paul F., Jr. *American Transcendentalism, 1830-1860*. New York: Putnam & Sons, 1974.

Bosco, Ronald A. and Glen M. Johnson, eds. *The Journals and Miscellaneous Notebooks of Ralph Waldo Emerson*. 16 vols. Cambridge: Harvard University Press, 1960-1982.

Bowne, Borden Parker. "The Failure of Impersonalism." In *The Development of American Philosophy*. Eds. Muelder, Sears, and Schlabach. Boston: Houghton Mifflin, 1960.

————. *Theory of Thought and Knowledge.* New York: American Book, 1987.

Brightman, Edgar Sheffield. "Personalism." *A History of Philosophical Systems.* Ed. Vergilius Ferm. New York: Philosophical Library, 1950. 340-352.

Davis, Merrill R. "Emerson's 'Reason' and the Scottish Philosophers." *The New England Quarterly* 17 (1944): 209-228.

Deese, Helen R. "Alcott's Conversations on the Transcendentalists: The Record of Carolina Dall." *American Literature* 6 (1988): 17-25.

Edgell, David P. *William Ellery Channing.* Boston: Beacon Press, 1955.

Emerson, Edward Waldo and Waldo Emerson Forbes, eds. *The Journals of Ralph Waldo Emerson.* Vol. IX. Boston and New York: Houghton Mifflin, 1913.

Flewelling, Ralph T. "Personalism." In *Twentieth Century Philosophy.* Ed. Dagobert D. Runes. New York: Philosophical Library, 1943.

Gohdes, Clarence. "Alcott's 'Conversation' on the Transcendental Club and *The Dial.*" *American Literature* 3 (1931): 14-27.

Greenberg, Robert M. "Shooting the Gulf: Emerson's Sense of Experience." *ESQ* 31 (1985): 211-229.

Heine, Heinrich. *Religion and Philosophy in Germany.* 1882. Introd. Ludwig Marcuse. Trans. John Snodgrass. Boston: Beacon, 1959.

Hoeltje, Hubert H. *Sheltering Tree.* Port Washington, New York: Kennikat Press, 1943.

James, William. *The Varieties of Religious Experience.* New York: Macmillan, 1961.

Lamont, Corliss. *Freedom of Choice Affirmed.* New York: Continuum, 1990.

Linscott, Robert N., ed. *The Journals of Ralph Waldo Emerson.* New York: Random House, 1960.

Miller, Perry, ed. *The Transcendentalists.* Cambridge: Harvard University Press, 1950.

Mounier, Emmanuel. *Personalism.* London: University of Notre Dame, 1952.

Myerson, Joel. "A History of the Transcendental Club." *Emerson Society Quarterly* 23 (1977): 27-35.

Orth, Ralph H. and Alfred R. Ferguson, eds. *The Journals and Miscellaneous Notebooks of Ralph Waldo Emerson.* 16 vols. Cambridge: Harvard University Press, 1960-1982.

Plumstead, A. W. and Harrison Hayford, eds. *The Journals and Miscellaneous Notebooks of Ralph Waldo Emerson.* 16 vols. Cambridge: Harvard University Press, 1960-1982.

Porte, Joel, ed. *Emerson in His Journals.* Cambridge: Harvard University Press, 1982.

Rusk, Ralph L. *The Life of Ralph Waldo Emerson.* New York: Columbia University Press, 1949.

Saelts, Merton M., Jr., ed. *The Journals and Miscellaneous Notebooks of Ralph Waldo Emerson.* 16 vols. Cambridge: Harvard University Press, 1960-1982.

Shepard, Odell. *Pedlar's Progress.* London: Williams and Norgate, 1938.

Townsend, Harvey Gates. *Philosophical Ideas in the United States.* New York: American Book, 1934.

Van Leer, David. *Emerson's Epistemology.* New York: Cambridge, 1986.

Von Leibniz, Gottfried Wilhelm Freiherr. "The Monodology." In *The Rationalists.* Trans. John Veitch. Garden City, New York: Dolphin Books, 1960. 455-471.

Weinberg, Kurt. "Pantheismusstreit." *The Encyclopedia of Philosophy.* Ed. Paul Edwards. Trans. Albert Weinberg. New York: Macmillan, 1972.

White, Morton. *Science and Sentiment in America.* London: Oxford University Press, 1972.

Whitman, Walt. "Personalism." *The Galaxy 5,* No. 5 (1868): 540-547.

————. *The Complete Writings of Walt Whitman,* Vol. 8. Ed. R. M. Bucke, et al. New York and London: Putnam, 1902.

Williams, David R. "The Wilderness Rapture of Mary Moody Emerson." *Studies in the American Renaissance.* Ed. Joel Myerson. Charlottesville: University Press of Virginia, 1986. 1-16.

Larry A. Carlson (essay date 1997)

SOURCE: Carlson, Larry A. "Emerson, Friendship, and the Problem of Alcott's *Psyche.*" In *Emersonian Circles: Essays in Honor of Joel Myerson,* edited by Wesley T. Mott and Robert E. Burkholder, pp. 115-25. Rochester, N.Y.: University of Rochester Press, 1997.

[*In the following essay, Carlson examines the circumstances surrounding the composition of Alcott's* Psyche. *Carlson asserts that Emerson's unflinchingly honest appraisal of the manuscript, which he considered unworthy of publication, ultimately strengthened the friendship between the two men.*]

In late spring of 1838 Emerson found himself in a painfully uncomfortable position as critic and friend of Bronson Alcott, who had asked for a reading of a book he hoped to publish. The problem for Emerson was explaining to Alcott that his voluminous manuscript on the divinity of childhood was unfit for publication because of its lack of focus, its stylistic mannerisms, its verboseness, and its abstractness. Its principal problem, Emerson thought, was "a want of unity of design." He told Alcott that "If the book were mine, I would on no account print it; and the book being yours, I do not know but it behoves you to print it in defiance of all the critics" (L [*Letters of Ralph Waldo Emerson*; 1939-] 2:139, 138). "Judg[ing] the counsel wise," Alcott accepted Emerson's opinion of the manuscript, entitled *Psyche,* and abandoned the project altogether, focusing his efforts instead on rethinking his career in the face of the closing of his Temple School caused by the publication of his controversial *Conversations with Children on the Gospels.*[1]

The surface of this story does not seem even to hint at much of a problem at all. Emerson was simply doing a favor for a friend, acting as a perceptive critic for someone whose writing skills turned out to have serious shortcomings. What this brief summary fails to reveal, however, is the extent to which Emerson was involved with the manuscript, which he had repeatedly volunteered to publish at his own risk, and with the life of the person who at that point had arguably become his closest friend. Emerson had looked at the manuscript several times over the course of nearly two and a half years, during which time his confidence and fame had risen as writer and lecturer with the publication of *Nature,* his lecture series on *The Philosophy of History, Human Culture,* and *Human Life,* as well as his Phi Beta Kappa Address on the American Scholar; in contrast, over the same period Alcott had fallen from being heralded as a new prophet of education to being pilloried and nearly mobbed as a corrupter of children. When Emerson composed the letter on *Psyche* at the end of June 1838, much indeed had changed in both their lives since he first saw the manuscript in early February 1836. That the letter and accompanying notes on specific flaws in *Psyche* came to eighteen pages is but one measure of how troubling a task this proved for Emerson. While many studies of Emerson and Alcott record the outward facts of the former's role in evaluating *Psyche* and in considering the ways it may have influenced the composition of *Nature,* none have fully explored the inner drama of this story as it helps us to understand Emerson's concept of friendship. Even the two newest biographies of Emerson, superb studies both, Robert Richardson's *Emerson: The Mind on Fire* and Carlos Baker's posthumous and aptly titled *Emerson Among the Eccentrics,* do not analyze this episode from the perspective of what it says about one of the central concerns in Emerson's life and thought, which received its fullest expression in 1841 in his essay on the topic in *Essays: First Series.*[2] Emerson's involvement with Alcott and with *Psyche* illustrates the complexities and tensions inherent in Emerson's concept of friendship, especially his two essential necessities—truth and tenderness—which make ideal friendship virtually impossible to achieve and any attempt at doing so mined with emotional risks and frustrations.

Before they first met in the summer of 1835 Emerson and Alcott were each in varying degrees aware of the other's existence. Alcott had heard Emerson preach in 1828 at Chauncy Place Sunday School in Boston; Emerson's sermon on "the Universality of the Notion of the Deity" Alcott deemed "a very respectable effort."[3] So too did he like Emerson's January 1830 sermon on "*Conscience* as a fundamental principle in morals and human nature" (*JBA* [*The Journals of Bronson Alcott*] 22). In January 1835 Alcott noted in his journal his range of acquaintances and friends, including among others the Reverend William Ellery Channing, Elizabeth Palmer Peabody (then assisting Alcott at the Temple School), and Washington Allston. He concluded the entry by writing, "I wish to know Mr. R. Emerson and Mr. Hedge" (*JBA* 56). A week later he heard Emerson lecture on "The Character of Michaelangelo" and wrote, "Few men among us take nobler views of the mission, powers, and destinies of man than Mr. E[merson]. I hope the people of this city will go and learn of him the conditions of virtue and vision . . ." (*JBA* 56). Alcott clearly saw in Emerson a like-minded soul who could share his hopes for the possibilities of self-culture and a more harmonious world.

Emerson's introduction to Alcott first came in early July 1835 when he heard their mutual friend George Partridge Bradford describe the master of the Temple School as "a consistent spiritualist" (*JMN* [*The Journals and Miscellaneous Notebooks of Ralph Waldo Emerson*; 1960-] 5:57). A few days later, as fate would have it, they actually met, at an evening gathering in Boston. Among those present were Waldo's brilliant younger brother Charles and his fiancée, Elizabeth Hoar; Aunt Mary Moody Emerson; Elizabeth and Mary Peabody; and Lydia Maria Child (*JBA* 57-58). So in what appeared to be a crowd of sorts began the meeting that would lead to a friendship that lasted the better part of five decades. By the end of the month Emerson had read "with great delight" Elizabeth Peabody's *Record of a School,* which attempted to capture the actual day-to-day innovative practices at Bronson's Temple School (*JMN* 5:63).[4] So enamored was he with Alcott's genius that he immediately recommended the book to his brother William, whose wife had recently given birth to their first child: "To the parents of the little Willy I cannot doubt it will be engaging" (*L* 1:448).

In October, accompanied by Bradford, Alcott made the first of what became regular visits to Concord. After spending an exhilarating weekend with Emerson, Lidian, his bride of a month, and Charles discussing "various interesting topics of an intellectual and spiritual character," Alcott thought the newly married couple to be representative of "a new idea of life." He enjoyed too his conversation with Charles, who struck him as having "much of his brother's spirit"; in both brothers the "man" was "not lost in the scholar." It was surely an important moment in the history of the relationship between Alcott and Emerson. "To have a few such friends is the joy and content of life," Alcott recorded in his journal. "In communion with such the spirit finds itself, and for the brief time of their presence forgets its independent life, being lost in the common being of humanity" (*JBA* 69). For his part Emerson characterized the self-taught Alcott, four years his senior, as "A wise man, simple, superior to display . . . [who] drops the best things as quietly as the least." He also included in his journal entry Charles's remark on "the nimbleness & buoyancy which the conversation of a spiritualist awakens; the world begins to dislimn" (*JMN* 5:98-99).

Their relationship matured quickly and steadily over the next year, this at precisely the period when Emerson was meditating on friendship, several journal entries about which later ended up in his essay on the subject. Alcott continued to admire Emerson's "eloquent and passionous views of the Spiritual Philosophy,"[5] attended his lectures on English literature, and lent him his journals. In turn Emerson eagerly sought Alcott's company, visited the Temple School, copied passages from Alcott's journals into his own, and considered his friend "a great genius" (*L* 2:27), "a world-builder" with "Olympian dreams" (*JMN* 5:178). Over the summer, wanting to give Alcott a wider field of action, Emerson made arrangements for his friend to join the Transcendental Club, then being formed by Frederic Henry Hedge, who envisioned a forum only for ministers. "You must admit Mr Alcott over the professional limits," Emerson urged Hedge, "for he is a god-made priest. That man grows on me every time I see him" (*L* 2:29).

Of special note during this period are several events that helped intensify and shape the relationship between the two men into something more than an uncomplicated mutual admiration society. Out of chronological order, they include the death of Charles in May, which devastated Waldo and no doubt deepened the bond between him and Bronson. Indeed, Merton Sealts is right in observing that "Perhaps Bronson Alcott came closest to filling the particular void left in Emerson's life after the death of Charles" (*JMN* 5:xi). Second was Alcott's decision to publish the record of his Wednesday morning Socratic conversations with his young pupils, female as well as male, on the New Testament. These frank, innocent, wide-ranging discussions were designed, like *Record of a School,* to take Alcott's message about educational reform outside his school, to show society that children were not "young vipers" but were instead incarnations of holiness with the capacity to deal with subjects ordinarily assumed to be the sole

and proper province of adults. Among other subjects Alcott covered were money-worshipping, idolatry, the nature and meaning of birth, and the pain of Christ's Circumcision, these with children ranging in age from six to thirteen. Emerson read the introduction, praised it, and persuaded Alcott to publish it separately. Volume one of *Conversations with Children on the Gospels* was published in late December for the Christmas trade, volume two in February 1837.[6] Neither Emerson nor Alcott was prepared for the unrelenting, vitriolic attacks that eventually destroyed the Temple School and that prompted Emerson to public defense of and private consolation to Alcott.

The third crucial event of 1836 was Emerson's initial involvement with *Psyche.* Upon concluding a visit with Alcott in Boston in early February, Emerson left with the manuscript of several hundred pages, his curiosity apparently piqued by his friend's description of it as a revelation of childhood. Alcott was delighted and looked forward to "the opinion of one so well qualified to judge of the merits of English composition." Alcott added that "His opinion—frankly given—will be of great service to me. There is not among us, a scholar of a riper judgment or purer taste" (**"J 36"** [**"Bronson Alcott's 'Journal for 1836'"**]:29). An opinion "frankly given" proved from the beginning to be problematical for Emerson. At the end of the month, having read over half of the tome, he returned the manuscript along with a lengthy, tactfully written letter. He called it "original and vital in all its parts; manifestly, the production of a man in earnest, & written to convince"; some passages, he felt, even "possess[ed] . . . the rare power to awaken the highest faculties, to awaken the apprehension of the Absolute" (*L* 2:4). He liked several passages well enough in fact to copy into his journal (*JMN* 5:122-23).

Emerson then gently summarized its many "defects," significantly attributing them to the "subtlety and extent of the subject" rather than to Alcott's demonstrable failings as a wordsmith. In contrast to Alcott's Journal for 1835, which he would read in June and which he found filled with "perfectly simple and elegant utterance," *Psyche* was full of the "inflation" and "cramp" that was happily and mercifully absent in Alcott's diary (*JMN* 5:170). Recognizing Alcott's intention to have it published, Emerson urged massive cutting and appended a six-page list of what he charitably labeled as "verbal inaccuracies"—that just for the first hundred pages that he found time to run over in line-by-line fashion. He apparently hoped Alcott would get the point and himself clean up the other gaffes, as well, of course, as condensing the whole manuscript (*L* 2:4-6). Alcott, always cognizant of the severe limitations of his formal education, found the criticisms "valuable" and was pleased that for the first time in his life he had someone who could be "the voice of advice or encouragement." He acknowledged the "errors" and vowed "ultimately [to] master them" (**"J 36"**:39).

But master them he could not. In some ways, perhaps, what Emerson first looked over in February was as good as *Psyche* would be or ever could be given the temperament and training of its author. Weighing in at 503 pages—one understands why Emerson urged "compression"—and subtitled *The Breath of Childhood,* the manuscript was inspired by the birth of his third daughter, Elizabeth, in 1835, and grew out of the record-keeping he had done for his first two children, Anna, born in 1831, and Louisa May, in 1832. These journals, variously entitled "observations" and totalling nearly 1,400 pages, attempt to capture the psychological, moral, and spiritual development of his children.[7] Besides recording Anna's and Louisa May's reactions to their new sister and his own on Elizabeth's growth in her early months, Alcott's latest effort incorporated long passages couched in what he believed were effective poetic style and biblical tones on the mysteries and beauty of childhood. Here is a brief sample:

> Spirit doth ever send an herald before to announce her own coming. She commissioneth matter to this end, and maketh this her docile errand boy to await her own bidding. . . . Nought happeneth within her own Primeval Realm, that she doth not ordain. Nought addresseth to the *Outward Sense* that she doth not herself substantiate and shape forth in matter,—her vassal and servant. She fortelleth and remembereth all.
>
> (1-2)

Even with this short excerpt one can see what Emerson was up against when he tackled the manuscript—these were clearly ideas that spoke to his soul and his transcendental vision of life, but they were just as clearly cast in stilted, affected language, for page after page after page. Still, though, Emerson continued to be sanguine that it could be revised into something worthy of publication. He took the manuscript again in early August (**"J 36"**:141), when he was nail-biting over the final draft of *Nature,* and kept *Psyche* for several months. When in early September *Nature* was published, Alcott called it a "gem" and—doubtless thinking of his own *Conversations with Children on the Gospels,* soon to go to press, and of *Psyche*—declared that "it is the harbinger of an order of works, given to the elucidation and establishment of the Spiritual." And he added, with what must have been great pleasure, that "Mr E[merson] adverts, indirectly, to my '*Psyche*' (now in his hands) in the work" (**"J 36"**:72). Emerson returned *Psyche* in mid-December, a week before volume one of Alcott's *Conversations* was released. Alcott noted in his journal that both Emerson and Elizabeth Hoar, who had read it, "urge its publication." Ever the optimist at this point in his life, Alcott planned to publish it between what he expected would be the third and fourth volumes of the *Conversations* (**"J 36"**:88).[8]

What happened during the next year and a half sorely tested Emerson's friendship. Alcott was plunged into hopeless despair when the *Conversations* was blasted from every quarter. Andrews Norton, for instance, Unitarian "Pope" at Harvard and one of Emerson's former professors, thought it a mixture of obscenity, blasphemy, and absurdity.[9] When the editors of the two leading Boston dailies, the *Advertiser* and the *Courier,* began their attacks on Alcott, Emerson insisted that he be given an opportunity to defend his friend. Successful at the latter, he proclaimed that the book is "pervaded with original thought and sincere piety" and urged of the public, "Let it be read."[10] In a private letter of consolation, Emerson told Alcott, who he believed was "deeply grounded in God," to forget "the little barking dogs" and, come what may of the school, "pray let not the pen halt, for that must be your last & longest lever to lift the world withal" (*L* 2:61-62).[11] By the end of summer the number of Alcott's pupils had dwindled from a one-time high of forty to but a handful, with little prospect that the situation would improve. And he was five thousand dollars in debt, the start-up costs of the school still not having been recouped. The situation obviously demanded of Emerson sympathy and encouragement.

In subsequent notes and visits Emerson again expressed concern that Alcott not abandon his writing. There is much irony in this advice given the final disposition of *Psyche* and the general consensus of Alcott's other peers. Even Alcott himself seemed puzzled. After meeting with Emerson at the end of April and hearing the same suggestion, Alcott wrote in his journal that "He values my professional labours somewhat lower than most of my friends. Herein, I think he errs; while, as a writer, he overestimates my ability." Alcott acknowledged his deep respect for Emerson's opinion and added, with considerable insight, that Emerson's

> friendship springs from worthier qualities of my nature. . . . There mingles less of reward for personal rights and abilities, than happens in the intercourse of similar minds, acting in similar pursuits. His manner and bearing toward me are noble and manly.[12]

Little did Emerson understand how powerful his advice was or what consequences it ultimately proved to have for Alcott. Throughout the humiliating financial and personal events that followed—the threat of mob action, a steady visit of duns, the auction of his prized library and statuary from the school, moving the school to a much less attractive but less costly room, and moving his family to a less costly house—Alcott threw himself into revising *Psyche.* With all the revisions he intended to make, it would be a great book; it would be his claim on the age; it would be his place in the sun. After all, Emerson had expressed faith in his abilities. Alcott's journal entries for this period dramatize the intensity of the shift of his emotional and intellectual energies away from his school to *Psyche*.[13] As she later would worry upon the demise of Fruitlands, Alcott's wife, Abba, worried about how the spectre of failure affected her husband's health, especially with the family "as poor as rats": "in producing the life of Psyche," she confided to her brother Samuel J. May in the fall of 1837, "he will also produce the death of his body."[14]

Over the course of the ensuing months, as they met on various occasions, Alcott surely must have given Emerson progress reports of one kind or another to which Emerson must have responded with encouragement. In early November, in a major expression of generosity to the ego-battered Alcott, Emerson offered to publish *Psyche* at his own risk after bringing out an edition of Carlyle's *French Revolution* ("**J 37, 2**" ["**Bronson Alcott's 'Journal for 1837' (Part Two)**"]:115). The offer was repeated in February 1838 when the Carlyle volume was selling well. Recalling their meeting in the Boston Athenaeum, when the offer was again made, and reflecting on Emerson's kind assistance to Carlyle, Alcott wrote in his journal: "(it was published at his risk, in friendship for the author) [and its success gives] him leave to publish, in like manner, my MS. volume."[15]

As a writer Alcott was no Carlyle to be sure, and when Emerson looked at the manuscript of *Psyche* for the final time, in early June 1838, he despaired over the changes Alcott had made and his failure to correct many of the problems he had pointed out nearly two and a half years earlier. Now subtitled *An Evangele,* it had been trimmed to a mere 346 pages. At the same time, though, many of the stylistic glitches and affectations were still there. Worse, Alcott struck a prophetic tone in various places. The new Jeremiah, bitter and angry over society and institutions, railed against the unbelieving, materialistic age even as he extolled the spirituality of childhood. The city, for instance, was an "offense": "It is feculent. It hath seventy plagues. Behold its markets, kitchens, distillers, sewers. . . ." (43).

What was Emerson to make of all this? What was he to do? Was this still a time in Alcott's life, and everything suggested it was, to show tenderness and generosity? Or was this a time for frankness and truth? Emerson prized the blessed solitude of self, which might have led to a minimal kind of reaction, leaving himself disentangled as much as possible, but he also understood that the claims of friendship required a thoughtful, elaborate response. That assessing the revised version pained him deeply is evidenced not only in the tone and substance of the letter Alcott received but also in the draft of the letter, replete with hesitations and searches for the right word.[16] If the first version of *Psyche* suffered from want of condensation, this one he viewed as lacking focus. Is it, he queried his friend, a "gospel"? Or "a book of thought addressed to literary men"? Most of the letter, pointing out its many flaws, is obviously

the work of a person who believed that honesty was called for. Yet at the very end of the letter—after first having informed him that if it were his he would not publish it, and then after having delivered nearly ten pages of what he admitted was his "critical bludgeon"— Emerson entertained the possibility that in "inducing" Alcott to "with hold the volume," he might be doing his friend "a great harm." If Alcott wanted it published, Emerson would make the appropriate arrangements with Metcalf and Company as promised (*L* 2:138-41).[17]

Though Alcott would quietly accept the honest appraisal of the work, which at Harvard University remains unpublished, Emerson fretted over the letter.[18] On the very day he sent it, 28 June, he vented his dissatisfaction and frustration in a letter to Margaret Fuller, which he was happy to write, he said, after finishing "a very irksome piece of work, namely a faithful criticism of *Psyche.* . . ." In sentiments that later found their way into his essay on friendship, Emerson elaborated:

> I had few smooth things to say but I hope he will feel the truth as better, as I should my brother's strictures. . . . Of so many fine people it is true that being so much, they ought to be a little more, & missing that, are naught. The omnipresent tragedy of More & Less never moves us to such sadness as in these unperfect favorites, the missing windows in Aladdins palace.
>
> (*L* 2:142)

As David Robinson has so succinctly and ably put it: "Emerson was burdened by what he felt to be an awkward capacity in personal relations, but nevertheless longed for passionate attachments. In a way that typified his entire circle, however, he regarded friendships with an air of holiness that often crippled them with impossible expectations."[19] In an often remarked sentence from his essay on friendship that speaks to his intense relationship with Alcott as pointedly as it does to Fuller or any other of his soul-mates, Emerson said that a friend should be "forever a sort of beautiful enemy, untamable, devoutly revered, and not a trivial conveniency to be soon outgrown and cast aside" (*CW* [*Collected Works of Ralph Waldo Emerson*; 1971-] 2:124). That Emerson continued to support Alcott for decades to come, in emotional, intellectual, and even material ways, despite the sour experience with *Psyche,* is enduring and eloquent testimony to the passion with which he pursued the ideal of friendship.

Notes

1. Larry A. Carlson, "Bronson Alcott's 'Journal for 1838' (Part Two)," *SAR* [*Studies in the American Renaissance*] 1994: 128. *Psyche* exists in two versions, both at the Houghton Library at Harvard University. The earlier of the two manuscripts, which Emerson first looked over in February 1836, is subtitled "The Breath of Childhood" (59M-306

[8]). The later version, to which Emerson is here responding, is subtitled "An Evangele" (59M-306 [9]).

2. Robert D. Richardson, Jr., *Emerson: The Mind on Fire* (Berkeley: University of California Press, 1995); Carlos Baker, *Emerson Among the Eccentrics: A Group Portrait* (New York: Viking, 1996). Even Hubert H. Hoeltje's book-length study of the two friends, *Sheltering Tree: A Story of the Friendship of Ralph Waldo Emerson and Amos Bronson Alcott* (Durham, N.C.: Duke University Press, 1943), does not explore the episode in terms of Emerson's theory of friendship.

3. *The Journals of Bronson Alcott,* ed. Odell Shepard (Boston: Little, Brown, 1938), p. 12; hereafter cited parenthetically as *JBA.*

4. Elizabeth Peabody, *Record of a School* (Boston: James Munroe and Company, 1835); a second edition was published in 1836 (Boston: Russell, Shattuck).

5. Joel Myerson, "Bronson Alcott's 'Journal for 1836,'" *SAR* 1978: 25; hereafter cited parenthetically as *J* 36.

6. A. Bronson Alcott, *Conversations with Children on the Gospels,* 2 vols. (Boston: James Munroe and Company, 1836-37). The introduction was published separately as *The Doctrine and Discipline of Human Culture* (Boston: James Munroe and Company, 1836).

7. These manuscripts, which have never been published, are at the Houghton Library at Harvard University (59M-306 [1], [2], [3], [6]).

8. This journal entry also indicates that Orestes Brownson and his wife were now reading *Psyche* and that Alcott hoped to have their approval for publication as well; what if anything the Brownsons thought of the manuscript is not known.

9. *Boston Courier,* 9 May 1837, p. 2. The comments are anonymous in the paper: Alcott later identified Norton as the author in his "Autobiographical Collection, 1834-1839," p. 134 (Houghton Library, Harvard University, 59M-307 [3]).

10. *Boston Courier,* 4 April 1837, p. 2.

11. At the end of this letter, dated 24 March 1837, Emerson wrote that when he visited Boston in the next few days he would return Alcott's "*astonishing* MSS." Ralph L. Rusk's note following the letter speculates that the "MSS" was "presumably *Psyche*"; however, Alcott was working on several projects at this point and there is no conclusive evidence in either person's letters or journals that the one referred to by Emerson was *Psyche.*

12. Larry A. Carlson, "Bronson Alcott's 'Journal for 1837' (Part One)," *SAR* 1981: 112.

13. Larry A. Carlson, "Bronson Alcott's 'Journal for 1837' (Part Two)," *SAR* 1982: 82-85, 89, 93-96, 99-103, 125; hereafter cited parenthetically as "J 37, 2."

14. 3 October 1837. A. Bronson Alcott, "Family Letters, 1828-1861" (Houghton Library, Harvard University, 59M-305 [25]).

15. Larry A. Carlson, "Bronson Alcott's 'Journal for 1838' (Part One)," *SAR* 1993: 210.

16. The draft of Emerson's letter to Alcott, dated 27 June 1838, is at the Houghton Library at Harvard University (bMS AM 1280.226 [1404]).

17. Subsequently Emerson believed that Alcott's genius was expressed better in conversation than in writing. In a letter to an English correspondent in the spring of 1842, shortly before Alcott set sail for England, Emerson said that "we shall send you a large piece of spiritual New England in the Shape of A. Bronson Alcott . . . whom you must not fail to see, if you can compass it. A man who cannot write but whose conversation is unrivalled in its way; such insight, such discernment of spirits, such revolutionary impulses of thought; whilst he speaks he has no peer. . . . Since Plato and Plotinus, we have not had his like" (1 April 1842, to Rev. John Sterling [*L* 7:496]).

18. Only very small portions of *Psyche* have been printed. In *Emerson the Essayist,* Vol. II (Raleigh, N.C.: Thistle Press, 1945), pp. 101-25, Kenneth Walter Cameron incorporates some passages from the first version that Emerson thought worth saving. Robert D. Richardson, Jr., includes a brief section of Book One of the later version in *Myth and Literature in the American Renaissance* (Bloomington: Indiana University Press, 1978), pp. 234-35.

19. David M. Robinson, *Emerson and the Conduct of Life: Pragmatism and Ethical Purpose in the Later Work* (Cambridge: Cambridge University Press, 1993), p. 36.

FURTHER READING

Biographies

Dahlstrand, Frederick C. *Amos Bronson Alcott: An Intellectual Biography.* East Brunswick, N.J.: Associated University Presses, 1982, 397 p.

Overview of Alcott's life and work.

Sanborn, F. B., and William T. Harris. *A. Bronson Alcott: His Life and Philosophy.* 2 vols. Boston: Roberts Brothers, 1893, 679 p.

    Studies Alcott's life and career against the backdrop of American education in the nineteenth century.

Criticism

Beer, Thomas. "Irritating Archangel." *Bookman* 66 (December 1927): 357-66.

    Critique of Alcott's life and career.

Bennett, Fordyce Richard. "Alcott's Earliest Writings on Education." *American Transcendental Quarterly,* no. 31 (summer 1976): 25-6.

    Analysis of Alcott's pedagogical theories.

Berry, Edmund G. "Bronson Alcott: Educational Reformer." *Queen's Quarterly* 52 (spring 1945): 44-52.

    Examines Alcott's philosophy of education.

Blankenship, Russell. "Amos Bronson Alcott (1799-1888)." In *American Literature as an Expression of the National Mind,* pp. 312-15. New York: Henry Holt and Company, 1931.

    Assesses Alcott's role in the Transcendentalist movement.

Carlson, Larry A. "'Those Pure Pages of Yours': Bronson Alcott's *Conversations with Children on the Gospels.*" *American Literature* 60, no. 3 (October 1988): 451-60.

    Investigates the controversy surrounding the original publication of *Conversations with Children on the Gospels.*

Caruthers, J. Wade. "The Transcendentalist as Mystic: Amos Bronson Alcott." *Connecticut Review* 9, no. 2 (May 1976): 90-9.

    Examines the various literary, theological, and social influences underlying Alcott's philosophy.

Francis, Richard. "Circumstances and Salvation: The Ideology of the Fruitlands Utopia." *American Quarterly* 25, no. 2 (May 1973): 202-34.

    Examines Alcott's short-lived Utopian community.

Gay, Carol. "The Philosopher and His Daughter: Amos Bronson Alcott and Louisa." *Essays in Literature* 2, no. 2 (fall 1975): 181-91.

    Explores the relationship between Alcott and his daughter, the novelist Louisa May Alcott.

Haefner, George E. *A Critical Estimate of the Educational Theories and Practices of A. Bronson Alcott.* 1937. Reprint. Westport, Conn.: Greenwood Press, 1970, 130 p.

    Analyzes Alcott's educational philosophy, and evaluates his various schools.

Hoeltje, Hubert H. *Sheltering Tree: A Story of the Friendship of Ralph Waldo Emerson and Amos Bronson Alcott.* Durham, N.C.: Duke University Press, 1943, 209 p.

    Examines the close friendship between the two philosophers.

Pannill, H. Burnell. "Bronson Alcott: Emerson's 'Tedious Archangel.'" In *A Miscellany of American Christianity: Essays in Honor of H. Shelton Smith,* edited by Stuart C. Henry, pp. 225-47. Durham, N.C.: Duke University Press, 1963.

    Examines the evolution of Alcott's Transcendental ideals between the years 1835 and 1845.

Pietras, Thomas P. "Amos Bronson Alcott: A Transcendental Philosophy of Education." *Educational Theory* 21 (winter 1971): 105-11.

    Studies the irreconcilable contradictions between Transcendentalism and Alcott's pedagogical theories.

Stiem, Marjorie. "Beginnings of Modern Education: Bronson Alcott." *Peabody Journal of Education* 38, no. 1 (July 1960): 7-9.

    Evaluates the progressive elements in Alcott's approach to education.

Ward, Rev. J. H. "Bronson Alcott's Career." *Outlook* (8 July 1893): 69-71.

    Assesses Alcott's life and work.

Warren, Austin. "The Orphic Sage: Bronson Alcott." *American Literature* 3, no. 1 (March 1931): 3-13.

    Examines Alcott's significance as a thinker.

Additional coverage of Alcott's life and career is contained in the following sources published by Thomson Gale: *Dictionary of Literary Biography,* **Vols. 1, 223;** *Literature Resource Center;* **and** *Nineteenth-Century Literature Criticism,* **Vol. 1.**

Richard Cumberland
1732-1811

English playwright, essayist, novelist, and poet.

INTRODUCTION

Cumberland was one of the most prolific comic playwrights of the Restoration era. He was a dramatist whose talent for humorous characterizations, combined with a steadfast faith in human goodness, contributed to the rise of sentimental stage drama in the late eighteenth and early nineteenth centuries. Over the course of his long career he wrote more than fifty plays, in addition to three novels, hundreds of essays, poetry, and a memoir, all marked by skillful, elegant prose and a strong sense of moral purpose. Cumberland drew his principal inspiration from the classics, in particular the Greek dramatists Aristophanes and Euripides, and was also influenced by the works of Shakespeare. More than anything, Cumberland possessed a great passion for the theater, and he regarded the stage as an ideal venue for exploring questions of right and wrong. In such comedies as *The West Indian* (1771) and *The Jew* (1794), Cumberland addressed issues of prejudice toward minorities in the British Empire, lending qualities of humanity and complexity to exhausted stereotypes. Although Cumberland enjoyed popular and critical success at the height of his career, he was also notorious in literary circles for his vanity, and he was ridiculed mercilessly by his contemporaries. While most modern scholars consider Cumberland a minor playwright, a few of his best-known plays, in particular *The West Indian, The Fashionable Lover* (1772), and *The Choleric Man* (1774), have endured. Cumberland also remains noteworthy for founding the short-lived *London Review,* the first major literary journal to require critics to sign their names to their reviews.

BIOGRAPHICAL INFORMATION

Cumberland was born in Cambridge on February 19, 1732, the son of an Anglican minister. His great-grandfather, Richard Cumberland, was the bishop of Peterborough, while his maternal grandfather, Richard Bentley, was a renowned Cambridge scholar. Under the tutelage of Bentley, Cumberland quickly proved himself an exceptional student, mastering the classics at a young age, first at public schools in Bury and Westminster and later at Trinity College, Cambridge. After completing

his education, he received an invitation to become personal secretary to the Earl of Halifax, and in 1760 he became the lord lieutenant of Ireland. Cumberland remained in government service for more than two decades, working in such far-flung outposts as North Carolina, Nova Scotia, and Spain. His experiences on the edges of the British Empire helped shape his attitude toward people living in the colonies, and his rejection of political oppression and social prejudice would inspire several of his most important stage writings. Cumberland began writing for the stage in his late twenties. In 1761 he published his first dramatic work, the historical tragedy *The Banishment of Cicero*. The play's complicated plot and explicit violence proved too daunting for theater producers of the age, however, and the work never appeared on the stage in Cumberland's lifetime. His next effort, the operetta *The Summer's Tale,* did manage to reach the stage in 1765, appearing at the Covent Garden Theatre for nine performances, although the work was not well received. In 1769 he saw the debut of his first successful comedy, *The Brothers,* at the Covent Garden Theatre. The work proved popular with theatergoers and attracted the attention of the renowned producer David Garrick, with whom Cumberland soon developed a close friendship. Cumberland wrote steadily over the next decade, producing such popular works as *The West Indian* and *The Choleric Man,* while also continuing to perform his government duties. As his popularity grew, so did Cumberland's ego, and he quickly became the most tireless and vocal promoter of his own work. Cumberland's self-serving attitude and extreme vulnerability to criticism, coupled with recurring accusations that he had plagiarized much of his work, rankled his contemporaries, among them the acclaimed comedic playwrights Oliver Goldsmith and Richard Brinsley Sheridan. At the same time Cumberland's sentimentality and overly optimistic view of human nature was becoming tiresome to many theatergoers, prompting a backlash against his plays. Amid mounting criticism of his work, Cumberland authored the essay "Dedication to Detraction," first published as the preface to *The Choleric Man,* in which he defended his approach to stage comedy. Sheridan captured Cumberland's self-absorption and sensitivity most astutely in his portrayal of Sir Fretful Plagiary, the vain, pompous dramatist at the center of Sheridan's 1779 play *The Critic.* Cumberland's career as a bureaucrat ended abruptly in 1780, when a misguided attempt to broker a secret peace with Spain resulted in the loss of his commission. Out of work and in serious debt, Cumberland retired to Tunbridge Wells, where he devoted himself full-time to writing. Over the next decade a number of his plays, including *The Mysterious Husband* (1783), *The Natural Son* (1784), *The Imposters* (1789), and *The School for Widows* (1789), enjoyed decent runs on the London stage, and in 1789 he published his first novel, *Arundel.* Cumberland produced some of his best dramatic works in the 1790s, among them *The Jew* and *The Wheel of Fortune* (1795). In his last years he devoted himself to his memoirs, wrote numerous essays on classic drama, and founded the *London Review,* a journal intended to compete with such periodicals as the *Edinburgh Review* and the *Quarterly.* Cumberland died on May 11, 1811, in London.

MAJOR WORKS

Only a handful of Cumberland's plays are of interest to modern scholars. In *The West Indian,* widely regarded as his most important work, Cumberland mingles comedy with pathos as he tackles questions of race and intolerance in the British colonies. The play's protagonist, the wealthy West Indian planter Belcour, is one of Cumberland's most complex and sympathetic characters. Combining shrewd business acumen with an impulsive, idiosyncratic personality, Belcour alienates and confuses many members of London high society through his naive, yet always well-intentioned, efforts to assimilate. Although the play's other main character, Major

O'Flaherty, embodies many of the characteristics of the stereotypical Irishman as a belligerent hard drinker, he also serves, like Belcour, as a model of sincerity and virtue. In the end the essential goodness of Belcour and O'Flaherty conquers the hypocrisy and ostentation of elite British society, and the play's final message is one of optimism and goodwill. Most of Cumberland's other well-known dramatic works focus on similar moral themes. *The Note of Hand* (1774) is a cautionary tale condemning the perils of gambling, while *The Choleric Man* extols the importance of education in cultivating strong moral principles. Like *The West Indian, The Jew* questions society's preconceptions about race and social background. *The Wheel of Fortune,* arguably the most successful play of Cumberland's later career, revolves around the character of Penruddock, who flees society after his best friend, Woodville, seduces the love of his life. Twenty years later Penruddock emerges from his forest isolation a wiser, more temperate man; although he is tempted to enact revenge on Woodville, whose gambling problem has resulted in the loss of his fortune, in the end Penruddock acts with restraint and uses his own newfound fortune to help restore honor and integrity to Woodville's son, Henry.

In addition to his abundant output as a dramatist, Cumberland also authored three novels of interest. In the autobiographical *Arundel,* he portrayed an aspiring author who embarks on a career in government service, while *Henry* (1795) tells the story of Ezekiel Daw, a Methodist preacher. Both works demonstrate the influence of Henry Fielding and Laurence Sterne, particularly in their ironic tone and sentimental character portrayals. Cumberland's last novel, *John de Lancaster* (1809), appeared two years before his death. At the height of his career Cumberland also produced a six-volume series titled *The Observer* (1786-90, 1798), approximately two-thirds of which consists of original writings by Cumberland, and the rest of which Cumberland compiled or translated. His autobiography, *Memoirs of Richard Cumberland* (1806), recounts the major events of his life and career. The work offers a strikingly candid portrayal of the author's professional jealousies and insecurities, as well as valuable anecdotes concerning other well-known theater personalities of the age.

CRITICAL RECEPTION

Cumberland enjoyed modest success as a playwright during his lifetime, and his best plays ran for extended periods at some of London's most popular theaters. At the same time Cumberland was a sensitive and vain man who quarreled openly with many of his contemporaries. These public feuds prompted attacks on his personality and his work, most memorably in Sheridan's parody of Cumberland in *The Critic.* Few reviewers or dramatists considered Cumberland a leading playwright of the period, and at the time of its publication his final novel, *John de Lancaster,* received a negative review from Sir Walter Scott. In 1824 Scott published an extensive overview of Cumberland's career, in which he offered critical evaluations of his major works. Although no other major critical studies appeared at that time, Cumberland's work remained a topic of interest for journalists and critics, and reviews of his works appeared with some regularity throughout the nineteenth century. The bulk of these articles, however, dismissed Cumberland's work as derivative and insubstantial. The turn of the century saw renewed scholarly interest in Cumberland's career. In his essay "The English Terence," which appeared in the *Fortnightly Review* in January 1900, G. Barnett Smith offered one of the earliest modern assessments of Cumberland's body of work, as well as a survey of contemporary critical reactions to his plays. George Paston's *Little Memoirs of the Eighteenth Century,* which appeared in 1901, included a lengthy appreciation of the playwright's career and also helped spark renewed academic interest in Cumberland's work. In 1917 Stanley T. Williams published *Richard Cumberland,* the first significant book-length study of Cumberland's career. By the 1970s and 1980s scholars had begun to pay closer attention to the social and political relevance of Cumberland's works, particularly in his depictions of minorities and colonial power in such plays as *The West Indian* and *The Jew.* The early 1990s saw the appearance of two volumes of his uncollected dramatic works, *The Unpublished Plays of Richard Cumberland* (1991-92), edited by Richard J. Dircks.

PRINCIPAL WORKS

*The Banishment of Cicero (play) 1761

The Summer's Tale (play) 1765; revised as *Amelia,* 1768

The Brothers (play) 1769

Timon of Athens [adaptor; from the play by William Shakespeare] (play) 1771

The West Indian (play) 1771

The Fashionable Lover (play) 1772

The Choleric Man (play) 1774

The Election (play) 1774

The Note of Hand (play) 1774

The Princess of Parma (play) 1774

Odes (poetry) 1776

The Battle of Hastings (play) 1778

Miscellaneous Poems Consisting of Elegies, Odes, Pastorals, &c. together with Calypso, a Masque (poetry and play) 1778

The Bondman [adaptor; from the play by Philip Massinger] (play) 1779

Calypso (play) 1779

The Critic (play) 1779

The Duke of Milan [adaptor; from the play by Philip Massinger, and *Mariamne,* by Elijah Fenton] (play) 1779

The Widow of Delphi (play) 1780

Anecdotes of Eminent Painters in Spain, during the Sixteenth and Seventeenth Centuries, with Cursory Remarks upon the Present State of Arts in That Kingdom. 2 vols. (essays) 1782

The Walloons (play) 1782

The Mysterious Husband (play) 1783

The Carmelite (play) 1784

The Natural Son (play) 1784

†*The Arab* (play) 1785

The Country Attorney (play) 1787

Arundel. 2 vols. (novel) 1789

The Impostors [adaptor; from *The Beaux Stratagem,* by George Farquhar] (play) 1789

‡*The School for Widows* (play) 1789

Calvary: or the Death of Christ. A Poem, in Eight Books (poem) 1792

Prelude for the Opening of the Theatre Royal Covent Garden (play) 1792

#*Richard the Second* (play) 1792

#*The Armorer* (play) 1793

The Box-Lobby Challenge (play) 1794

The Jew (play) 1794

The Dependent (play) 1795

First Love (play) 1795

Henry. 4 vols. (novel) 1795

The Wheel of Fortune (play) 1795

Days of Yore (play) 1796

Don Pedro (play) 1796

The Last of the Family (play) 1797

The Village Fete (play) 1797

The Observer. 6 vols. (criticism and essays) 1786-90, 1798

‖*A Word for Nature* (play) 1798

Joanna of Montfaucon [adaptor; from *Johanna von Montfaucon,* by August von Kotzebue] (play) 1800

Lovers' Resolutions (play) 1802

The Sailor's Daughter (play) 1804

A Melo-Dramatic Piece: Being an Occasional Attempt to Commemorate the Death and Victory of Lord Viscount Nelson (play) 1805

A Hint to Husbands (play) 1806

Memoirs of Richard Cumberland, Written by Himself; containing an Account of his Life and Writings Interspersed with Anecdotes and Characters of Several of the Most Distinguished Persons of his Time, with whom he has had intercourse and Connection (memoirs) 1806; enlarged edition, 1807

The Exodiad [with Sir James Bland Burgess] (poem) 1807

The Jew of Mogadore (play) 1808

John de Lancaster. 3 vols. (novel) 1809

The Widow's Only Son (play) 1810

Retrospection, A Poem in Familiar Verse (poem) 1811

The Posthumous Dramatick Works of the Late Richard Cumberland, Esq. 2 vols. (plays) 1813
The Plays of Richard Cumberland. 6 vols. (plays) 1982
The Unpublished Plays of Richard Cumberland. 2 vols. (plays) 1991-92

*The Banishment of Cicero has not been staged; it was published in 1761.

†Critics believe Cumberland derived *The Arab* from his never staged and now lost play *Salome. The Arab* was later revised, but never staged, as *Alcanor.*

‡Largely a revision of *The Country Attorney.*

#Cumberland attempted to stage *Richard the Second* in 1792, but was denied a license to do so, due to the play's sensitive political content. He subsequently revised and then staged the play in 1793 as *The Armorer.*

‖*A Word for Nature* was published in *The Posthumous Dramatick Works of Richard Cumberland* as *The Passive Husband.*

CRITICISM

Edinburgh Review (review date April 1806)

SOURCE: Review of *Memoirs of Richard Cumberland,* by Richard Cumberland. *Edinburgh Review* 8, no. 15 (April 1806): 107-28.

[*In the following excerpt, the anonymous critic discusses important aspects of Cumberland's upbringing and education, as well as highlights from his literary career. The critic clearly admires Cumberland as a playwright, but finds numerous faults with his memoirs, criticizing in particular the work's disjointed structure and tedious prose style.*]

We certainly have no wish for the death of Mr Cumberland; on the contrary, we hope he will live long enough to make a large supplement to these memoirs [***Memoirs of Richard Cumberland***]: but he has embarrassed us a little by publishing this volume in his lifetime. We are extremely unwilling to say any thing that may hurt the feelings of a man of distinguished talents, who is drawing to the end of his career, and imagines that he has hitherto been ill used by the world: but he has shown in this publication, such an appetite for praise, and such a jealousy of censure, that we are afraid we cannot do our duty conscientiously, without giving him offence. The truth is, that the book has rather disappointed us. We expected it to be extremely amusing; and it is not. There is too much of the first part of the title in it, and too little of the last. Of the life and writings of Richard Cumberland, we hear more than enough; but of the distinguished persons with whom he lived, we have many fewer characters and anecdotes than we could have wished. We are the more inclined to regret this, both

because the general style of Mr Cumberland's compositions has convinced us that no one could have exhibited characters and anecdotes in a more engaging manner, and because, from what he has put into this book, we actually see that he had excellent opportunities for collecting, and still better talents for relating them. The anecdotes and characters which we have, are given in a very pleasing and animated manner, and form the chief merit of the publication; but they do not occupy one tenth part of it; and the rest is filled with details that do not often interest, and observations that do not always amuse.

Authors, we think, should not be encouraged to write their own lives. The genius of Rousseau, his enthusiasm, and the novelty of his plan, have rendered the *Confessions,* in some respects, the most interesting of books. But a writer, who is in full possession of his senses, who has lived in the world like the men and women who compose it, and whose vanity aims only at the praise of great talents and accomplishments, must not hope to write a book like the *Confessions*; and is scarcely to be trusted with the delineation of his own character, or the narrative of his own adventures. We have no objection, however, to let authors tell their own story, as an apology for telling that of all their acquaintances; and can easily forgive them for grouping and assorting their anecdotes of their contemporaries, according to the chronology and incidents of their own lives. This is but indulging the painter of a great gallery of worthies with a panel for his own portrait; and though it will probably be the least like of the whole collection, it would be hard to grudge him this little gratification.

Life has often been compared to a journey; and the simile seems to hold better in nothing than in the identity of the rules by which those who write their travels, and those who write their lives, should be governed. When a man returns from visiting any celebrated region, we expect to hear much more of the things and persons he has seen, than of his own personal transactions; and are naturally disappointed if, after saying that he lived much with illustrious statesmen or heroes, he chooses rather to tell us of his own travelling equipage, or of his cookery and servants, than to give us any account of the character and conversation of those distinguished persons. In the same manner, when, at the close of a long life, spent in circles of literary and political celebrity, an author sits down to give the world an account of his retrospections, it is reasonable to stipulate that he shall talk less of himself than of his associates, and natural to complain, if he tells long stories of his schoolmasters and grandmothers, while he passes over some of the most illustrious of his companions, with a bare mention of their names.

Mr Cumberland has offended a little in this way. He has also composed these memoirs, we think, in too diffuse, rambling, and careless a style. There is evidently no se-

lection or method in his narrative; and unweighed remarks, and fatiguing apologies and protestations are tediously interwoven with it in the genuine style of good-
natured but irrepressible loquacity. The whole
composition, indeed, has not only too much the air of
conversation; it has sometimes an unfortunate resemblance to the conversation of a professed talker; and we
meet with many passages in which the author appears
to work himself up to an artificial vivacity, and to give
a certain air of smartness to his expression, by the introduction of cant phrases, odd metaphors, and a sort of
practised and theatrical originality. The work, however,
is well worth going over, and contains many more
amusing passages than we can afford to extract on the
present occasion.

Mr Cumberland was born in 1732; and he has a very
natural pride in relating, that his paternal great grandfather was the learned and most exemplary Bishop Cumberland, author of the treatise *De Legibus Naturæ*; and
that his maternal grandfather was the celebrated Dr Richard Bentley. Of the last of these distinguished persons
he has given, from the distinct recollection of his childhood, a much more amiable and engaging representation than has hitherto been made public. Instead of the
haughty and morose critic and controversialist, we learn,
with pleasure, that he was as remarkable for mildness
and kind affections in private life, as for profound erudition and sagacity as an author. . . .

The most valuable part of his early education was that
for which he was indebted to the taste and intelligence
of his mother. We insert with pleasure the following
amiable paragraph.

> It was in these intervals from school that my mother
> began to form both my taste and my ear for poetry, by
> employing me every evening to read to her, of which
> art she was a very able mistress. Our readings were,
> with very few exceptions, confined to the chosen plays
> of Shakespear, whom she both admired and understood
> in the true spirit and sense of the author. Under her in-
> struction I became passionately fond of these our
> evening entertainments; in the mean time, she was at-
> tentive to model my recitation, and correct my manner
> with exact precision. Her comments and illustrations
> were such aids and instructions to a pupil in poetry, as
> few could have given. What I could not else have un-
> derstood, she could aptly explain; and what I ought to
> admire and feel, nobody could more happily select and
> recommend. I well remember the care she took to mark
> out for my observation, the peculiar excellence of that
> unrivalled poet, in the consistency and preservation of
> his characters; and wherever instances occurred
> amongst the starts and sallies of his unfettered fancy, of
> the extravagant and false sublime, her discernment of-
> tentimes prevented me from being so dazzled by the
> glitter of the period as to misapply my admiration, and
> betray my want of taste. With all her father's critical
> *acumen,* she could trace, and teach me to unravel, all
> the meanders of his metaphor, and point out where it

illuminated, or where it only loaded and obscured the
meaning. These were happy hours and interesting lectures to me, whilst my beloved father, ever placid and
complacent, sate beside us, and took part in our amusement: his voice was never heard but in the tone of approbation; his countenance never marked but with the
natural traces of his indelible and hereditary benevolence.

> pp. 39, 40

The effect of these readings was, that the young author,
at twelve years of age, produced a sort of drama, called
Shakespeare in the Shades, composed almost entirely
of passages from that great writer, strung together and
assorted with no despicable ingenuity. He has inserted
rather a long extract from this juvenile compilation.
There is next an animated and minute account of his
studies at Westminster, with flattering characters of the
head masters, from Nichols to Vincent. Throughout the
work, indeed, he is too full of eulogies, and seems resolved to deserve every body's good word, by the most
profuse and indulgent commendation. . . .

In his fourteenth year he was entered of Trinity College, Cambridge, where he seems to have lived a very
regular, studious, and innocent life; and acquired great
reputation by *keeping an act,* at the age of seventeen,
against 'a finished mathematician, and black-bearded
philosopher from the North country.' He took his bachelor's degree with equal honour; and obtained a high
place among *the wranglers* of his year. Upon this occasion he makes a considerable digression in praise of
mathematical learning, and contends, with much zeal,
that it is to the neglect of these studies that we should
impute all the bad argument we hear in common conversation. We do not think this proposition made out by
demonstrative evidence; but it leads the author to make
some lively observations, which we shall subjoin as a
fair specimen of the general disquisitions which he has
occasionally introduced into these memoirs.

> Hear the crude opinions that are let loose upon society
> in our table conversations; mark the wild and wander-
> ing arguments that are launched at random, without
> ever hitting the mark they should be levelled at: what
> does all this noise and nonsense prove, but that the
> talker has indeed acquired the fluency of words, but
> never known the exercise of thought, or attended to the
> development of a single proposition? . . .

> These gentlemen are very entertaining, as long as nov-
> elties with no meaning can entertain you; they have a
> great variety of opinions, which, if you oppose, they do
> not defend, and if you agree with, they desert. Their
> talk is like the wild notes of birds, amongst which you
> shall distinguish some of pleasant tone, but out of
> which you compose no tune or harmony of song. These
> men would have set down Archimedes for a fool, when
> he danced for joy at the solution of a proposition, and
> mistaken Newton for a madman, when, in the surplice
> which he put on for chapel over night, he was found

the next morning, in the same place and posture, fixed in profound meditation on his theory of the prismatic colours. So great is their distaste for demonstration, they think no truth is worth the waiting for: the mountain must come to them: they are not by half so complaisant as Mahomet. They are not easily reconciled to truisms, but have no particular objection to impossibilities. For argument they have no ear; it does not touch them; it fetters fancy, and dulls the edge of repartee . . .

pp. 81-84

This is certainly very brisk and lively; but it does not correspond at all with our notions of good writing. It is the style of a smart talker, spoiled by the habit of writing comedies; every thing is broken into points, and varnished into brilliancy; there is a constant exaggeration, which offends against candour and sober judgment; and an unremitting and visible effort, which is painful and oppressive to the imagination. His characters of individuals have something of the same faults; he seems always to study effect, much more than truth of delineation; and exaggerates the characteristic, till the natural can no longer be recognized. On the stage this is necessary, like rouge and false eyebrows; but it defeats the very end of delineating real characters; and begets a distrust, that stands equally in the way of our pleasure and our information. . . .

He left London for a short time, to stand candidate for his fellowship, which he obtained with great honour, though not without considerable struggle and opposition; and, on his return to town, ventured for the first time to the press with a churchyard elegy, in imitation of Gray. Soon after, he projected an epic poem on the discovery of India, of which a considerable part was executed. He has inserted six or seven pages, as a specimen, in this work; but we hope the public is to see no more of it: it is cumbrous, prosaic, and utterly uninteresting. . . .

In the end of the Lieutenancy of Lord Halifax, Mr Cumberland's father was promoted to the see of Clonfert in Ireland; and upon that noble Lord's nomination to the high office of Secretary of State, our author suffered the mortification of being superseded in his situation of secretary, and seems to have thought himself but indifferently compensated by the appointment of clerk to the Board of Trade. In this situation, he wrote an opera, and the Comedy of **The Brothers,** which was acted with considerable applause. There is some good dramatic criticism in this and in other parts of the book; but we are more edified by his characteristic anecdotes of Irish manners and characters, which he had an opportunity of collecting when upon a visit to his father in his residence of Clonfert. They are all a little overcharged, we suspect; but are very amusing. Our readers may take the following picture of a native Irish baron.

> On this visit to Mr Talbot, I was accompanied by Lord Eyre of Eyre Court, a near neighbour and friend of my

father. This noble Lord, though pretty far advanced in years, was so correctly indigenous, as never to have been out of Ireland in his life, and not often so far from Eyre Court as in this tour to Mr Talbot's. Proprietor of a vast extent of soil, not very productive, and inhabiting a spacious mansion, not in the best repair, he lived, according to the style of the country, with more hospitality than elegance: whilst his table groaned with abundance, the order and good taste of its arrangement were little thought of: the slaughtered ox was hung up whole, and the hungry servitor supplied himself with his dole of flesh, sliced from off the carcase. His Lordship's day was so apportioned, as to give the afternoon by much the largest share of it, during which, from an early dinner, to the hour of rest, he never left his chair, nor did the claret ever quit the table. This did not produce inebriety; for it was sipping rather than drinking, that filled up the time: and this mechanical process of gradually moistening the human clay, was carried on with very little aid from conversation; for his Lordship's companions were not very communicative, and fortunately he was not very curious. He lived in an enviable independence as to reading, and of course he had no books. Not one of the windows of his castle was made to open, but luckily he had no liking for fresh air; and the consequence may be better conceived than described.

pp. 206-7

The following traits are from the opposite extreme in the scale of society.

> Amongst the labourers in my father's garden, there were three brothers of the name of O'Rourke, regularly descended from the kings of Connaught, if they were exactly to be credited for the correctness of their genealogy. There was also an elder brother of these, Thomas O'Rourke, who filled the superior station of hind, or headman; it was his wife that burnt the bewitched turkies, whilst Tom burnt his wig for joy of my victory at the cock-match, and threw a proper parcel of oatmeal into the air, as a votive offering for my glorious success. One of the younger brothers was upon crutches in consequence of a contusion on his hip, which he literally acquired as follows—When my father came down to Clonfert from Dublin, it was announced to him that the bishop was arrived: the poor fellow was then in the act of lopping a tree in the garden: transported at the tidings, he exclaimed—'Is my lord come? Then I'll throw myself out of this same tree for joy.'—He exactly fulfilled his word; and laid himself up for some months . . .

pp. 212-13

. . . . .

On his return from Ireland, Mr Cumberland brought out his excellent play of the West Indian, which was received with unbounded applause, and seems to have decided him in favour of this species of composition. He also wrote a pamphlet vindicating the memory of his grandfather Dr Bentley from what appeared to him an illiberal attack of Bishop Lowth.

At this period of his story he introduces several sketches and characters of his literary friends, which are executed, for the most part, with great force and vivacity. Of Garrick he says—

> Nature had done so much for him, that he could not help being an actor; she gave him a frame of so manageable a proportion, and, from its flexibility, so perfectly under command, that, by its aptitude and elasticity, he could draw it out to fit any sizes of character that tragedy could offer to him, and contract it to any scale of ridiculous diminution that his Abel Drugger, Scrub or Fribble, could require of him to sink it to. His eye, in the mean time, was so penetrating, so speaking; his brow so moveable; and all his features so plastic, and so accommodating, that wherever his mind impelled them, they would go; and, before his tongue could give the text, his countenance would express the spirit and the passion of the part he was encharged with.
>
> pp. 245-46

. . . Foote is frequently introduced. The following story we think very ludicrous.

> I remember well, when Garrick and I made him a visit, poor Foote had something worse than a dull man to struggle with, and matter of fact brought home to him in a way that, for a time, entirely overthrew his spirits, and most completely *frighted him from his propriety.* We had taken him by surprise, and of course were with him some hours before dinner, to make sure of our own if we had missed of his. He seemed overjoyed to see us, engaged us to stay, walked with us in his garden, and read to us some scenes roughly sketched for his Maid of Bath. His dinner was quite good enough, and his wine superlative. Sir Robert Fletcher, who had served in the East Indies, dropt in before dinner, and made the fourth of our party. When we had passed about two hours in perfect harmony and hilarity, Garrick called for his tea, and Sir Robert rose to depart. There was an unlucky screen in the room that hid the door, and behind which Sir Robert hid himself for some purpose, whether natural or artificial I know not; but Foote, supposing him gone, instantly began to play off his ridicule at the expense of his departed guest. I must confess it was (in the cant phrase) *a way that he had,* and just now a very unlucky way; for Sir Robert, bolting from behind the screen, cried out—'I am not gone, Foote; spare me till I am out of hearing; and now, with your leave, I will stay till these gentlemen depart, and then you shall amuse me at their cost, as you have amused them at mine.'
>
> pp. 250-51

Of Goldsmith he says,—

> That he was fantastically and whimsically vain, all the world knows; but there was no settled and inherent malice in his heart. He was tenacious to a ridiculous extreme of certain pretensions that did not, and by nature could not, belong to him; and at the same time inexcusably careless of the fame which he had powers to command. His table-talk was, as Garrick aptly compared it, like that of a parrot; whilst he wrote like Apollo. He had gleams of eloquence, and at times a

majesty of thought; but, in general, his tongue and his pen had two very different styles of talking. What foibles he had, he took no pains to conceal: the good qualities of his heart were too frequently obscured by the carelessness of his conduct, and the frivolity of his manners. Sir Joshua Reynolds was very good to him, and would have drilled him into better trim and order for society, if he would have been amenable; for Reynolds was a perfect gentleman, had good sense, great propriety, with all the social attributes, and all the graces of hospitality, equal to any man.

> Distress drove Goldsmith upon undertakings neither congenial with his studies nor worthy of his talents. I remember him, when in his chamber in the Temple, he showed me the beginning of his *Animated Nature*; it was with a sigh, such as genius draws, when hard necessity diverts it from its bent to drudge for bread, and talk of birds and beasts and creeping things, which Pidcock's show-man would have done as well. Poor fellow, he hardly knew an ass from a mule, nor a turkey from a goose, but when he saw it on the table.
>
> pp. 257-9

In pursuing the same speculation, he introduces another still more celebrated character.

> Who will say that Johnson himself would have been such a champion in literature, such a front-rank soldier in the fields of fame, if he had not been pressed into the service, and driven on to glory with the bayonet of sharp necessity pointed at his back? If fortune had turned him into a field of clover, he would have laid down and rolled in it. The mere manual labour of writing would not have allowed his lassitude and love of ease to have taken the pen out of the inkhorn, unless the cravings of hunger had reminded him that he must fill the sheet before he saw the tablecloth. He might, indeed, have knocked down Osbourne for a blockhead, but he would not have knocked him down with a folio of his own writing. He would perhaps have been the dictator of a club; and wherever he sate down to conversation, there must have been that splash of strong, bold thought about him, that we might still have had a collectanea after his death; but of prose, I guess, not much; of works of labour, none; of fancy perhaps something more, especially of poetry, which, under favour, I conceive was not his tower of strength.
>
> pp. 259-60

> Anecdotes of times past, scenes of his own life, and characters of humourists, enthusiasts, crack-brained projectors, and a variety of strange beings, that he had chanced upon, when detailed by him at length, and garnished with those episodical remarks, sometimes comic, sometimes grave, which he would throw in with infinite fertility of fancy, were a treat, which, though not always to be purchased by five and twenty cups of tea, I have often had the happiness to enjoy for less than half the number. He was easily led into topics; it was not easy to turn him from them; but who would wish it? If a man wanted to show himself off by getting up and riding upon him, he was sure to run restive, and kick him off: you might as safely have backed Bucephalus, before Alexander had lunged him. Neither did he

always like to be over-fondled:—when a certain gentle-man outacted his part in this way, he is said to have de-manded of him—'What provokes your risibility, Sir? Have I said any thing that you understand?—Then I ask pardon of the rest of the company—' But this is Henderson's anecdote of him, and I won't swear he did not make it himself.

pp. 263-4

I have heard Dr Johnson relate with infinite humour the circumstance of his rescuing Goldsmith from a ridicu-lous dilemma, by the purchase-money of his *Vicar of Wakefield,* which he sold on his behalf of Dodsley, and, as I think, for the sum of ten pounds only. He had run up a debt with his landlady, for board and lodging, of some few pounds, and was at his wit's-end how to wipe off the score, and keep a roof over his head, ex-cept by closing with a very staggering proposal on her part, and taking his creditor to wife, whose charms were very far from alluring, whilst her demands were extremely urgent. In this crisis of his fate he was found by Johnson, in the act of meditating on the melancholy alternative before him. He showed Johnson his manu-script of the *Vicar of Wakefield,* but seemed to be with-out any plan, or even hope, of raising money upon the disposal of it: when Johnson cast his eye upon it, he discovered something that gave him hope, and immedi-ately took it to Dodsley, who paid down the price above mentioned in ready money, and added an eventual con-dition upon its future sale. Johnson described the pre-cautions he took in concealing the amount of the sum he had in hand, which he prudently administered to him by a guinea at a time. In the event, he paid off the landlady's score, and redeemed the person of his friend from her embraces.

p. 273

These are almost all the literary characters of whom Mr Cumberland has made any particular mention; and though we are little more than half through the volume, we believe we are not very far from the conclusion of our extracts. The remainder of it is occupied, chiefly, with the personal transactions and family arrangements of the author, in which, it is not reasonable to suppose that the public should take any great interest. His father was translated to the see of Kilmore, and died soon af-ter. Our author himself wrote a variety of plays, and some odes and other poems, which had respectively their merited success, and was appointed Secretary to the Colonial Department, through the friendly interest of Lord George Germain, then at the head of that Board. He was ever afterwards the zealous friend and defender of his patron; and spent much of his time in his society. The following anecdote struck us as curious and impor-tant.

It happened to me to be present, and sitting next to Ad-miral Rodney at table, when the thought seemed first to occur to him of breaking the French line, by passing through it in the heat of the action. It was at Lord George Germain's house at Stoneland, after dinner, when, having asked a number of questions about the

manoeuvring of columns, and the effect of charging with them on a line of infantry, he proceeded to ar-range a parcel of cherry-stones, which he had collected from the table, and forming them as two fleets drawn up in line, and opposed to each other, he at once ar-rested our attention, which had not been very generally engaged by his preparatory inquiries, by declaring he was determined so to pierce the enemy's line of battle (arranging his manoeuvre at the same time on the table), if ever it was his fortune to bring them into action.

p. 298

This statement, at first sight, appears to be inconsistent with the claim of our ingenious countryman Mr Clerk of Eldin to the brilliant and important discovery to which it alludes; and to say the truth, we cannot help entertaining some doubts of Mr Cumberland's accuracy in the detail of a conversation which took place five and twenty years before he committed it to writing; but upon attending to the circumstances of the case, it does not appear to us that the anecdote, even if recorded with perfect correctness, affords the slightest ground for calling in question the originality or importance of Mr Clerk's admitted discovery. Even if Admiral Rodney had really conceived this brilliant idea at the very mo-ment commemorated by Mr Cumberland, it is apparent that Mr Clerk had been beforehand with him in the conception; and we should only have the extraordinary, though not unprecedented, case of the same discovery having been made successively by two separate indi-viduals. The conversation recorded by Mr Cumberland appears to have taken place recently before the Admi-ral's departure for the West Indies in January 1780; but Mr Clerk had brought his plan to maturity, and commu-nicated the particulars of it to several persons, immedi-ately after Keppel's action off Ushant, nearly two years before, and while Admiral Rodney was resident abroad. But this is not all. Mr Clerk has himself stated, in his preface, that having gone to London in the end of the year 1779, he had a meeting, by appointment, with Mr R. Atkinson, Admiral Rodney's particular friend, and another with Sir Charles Douglas his Captain, at which he detailed, and fully explained to these gentlemen, ev-ery part of his system, for the express purpose of hav-ing it communicated to the Admiral before his depar-ture with the fleet which he had been appointed to command. Mr Clerk adds, that he understood that such a communication was accordingly made, and that he has it from the best authority, that the Admiral expressed his zealous approbation of the scheme before he left London, and, after his return, made no scruple to ac-knowledge that it was Mr Clerk who had suggested the manoeuvres by which he had obtained the victory of the 12th April 1782. These facts, we have no doubt, may still be established; and it is pleasing to observe, that they rather serve to explain, than to contradict, the par-ticulars related by Mr Cumberland. It is not very likely that a scheme of such magnitude should suggest itself, for the first time, in the gaiety of a conversation at table; but if it had been recently communicated to the noble Admiral, it is abundantly natural that the accidental mention of breaking lines of infantry in land battles, should lead him to speak of it; and if he did not happen to mention with whom the suggestion had originated, it was equally natural for Mr Cumberland to suppose that it had that moment presented itself.

Soon after this, Mr Cumberland was induced to undertake a private mission to the Court of Spain, of which he has introduced a very long and languishing account; and for the trouble and expenses of which, he complains very vehemently that he has received no compensation on the part of the British Government. Our tribunal is not competent to the determination of such causes. Nor would any tribunal, we suppose, think it expedient to hazard an opinion upon the statement of one of the parties. There are some little pieces of good description interspersed in the dull diplomacy of the hundred quarto pages to which the Spanish biography is extended; and a curious account of a wonderful gypsey actress at Madrid, which we regret not being able to extract.

Upon his return, Mr Cumberland had soon to witness the demolition of the Board of Trade, in consequence of Mr Burke's Reform Bill; and was deprived of his secretaryship, on a compensation scarcely amounting to a moiety of what was taken away. Upon this diminished income he retired with his family to Tunbridge Wells, where he has continued ever since to reside, and to amuse himself by writing essays, comedies, novels, and these memoirs.

There is little in the subsequent part of the book that seems to require any detail. The author criticizes his own works with considerable candour and acuteness, and with little more than a natural partiality. He assures us, that the Israelites never made him any acknowledgment for the exertions he made in their favour; and this strain of ingratitude seems to have gone far to ruin them in his good opinion. He gives a long account of the retirement and death of Lord Sackville; and runs into a very silly and splenetic rhapsody on the fame of the Young Roscius, whose gains and popularity have evidently afflicted him more than was necessary. He praises the poetical labours of Sir James Bland Burges and Mr Hayley; and informs us, that Junius is savage; Sterne, frivolous and pathetic; and Edmund Burke, graceful in his anger, and musical even in his madness. The volume closes with a tribute to the filial piety of his youngest daughter.

We will pronounce no general judgment on the literary merits of Mr Cumberland; but our opinion of them certainly has not been raised by the perusal of these memoirs. There is no depth of thought, nor dignity of sentiment about him;—he is too frisky for an old man, and

too gossiping for an historian. His style is too negligent even for the most familiar composition; and though he has proved himself, upon other occasions, to be a great master of good English, he has admitted a number of phrases into this work, which, we are inclined to think, would scarcely pass comment even in conversation. 'I declare to truth'—'with the greatest pleasure in life'— 'She would lead off in her best manner,' & c.—are expressions which we should not expect to hear in the society to which Mr Cumberland belongs;—'laid,' for lay, is still more insufferable from the antagonist of Lowth, and the descendant of Bentley;—'querulential' strikes our ear as exotic;—'locate, location, and locality,' for situation simply, seem also to be bad; and 'intuition,' for observation, sounds very pedantic, to say the least of it. Upon the whole, however, this volume is not the work of an ordinary writer; and we should probably have been more indulgent to its faults, if the excellence of some of the author's former productions had not sent us to its perusal with expectations perhaps somewhat extravagant.

Quarterly Review (review date May 1809)

SOURCE: Review of *John de Lancaster,* by Richard Cumberland. *Quarterly Review* 1, no. 2 (May 1809): 337-48.

[*In the following review, the anonymous critic compares Cumberland's prose style unfavorably to his dramatic writing.*]

Mr. Cumberland has now borne arms in the fields of literature for more than half a century: the nature of his service has been as various as its date has been protracted; nor has his warfare been without its success and its honours. If he has never been found in the very van and front of battle, he has seldom lagged in the rear: and although we cannot find that he has on any occasion brought home the *spolia opima,* or qualified himself for the grand triumph, it must be allowed that he has often merited and obtained the humbler meed of an ovation. His dramatic pieces are those on which his fame will hereafter most probably rest. But the 'Terence of England, the mender of hearts', unsatisfied with having made more than one successful effort in modern comedy, perhaps the most difficult of all compositions, seemed determined to shew us that his vein though fertile was not inexhaustible, and that the friend of Garrick, of Goldsmith, and of Johnson, could write plays fit only to be prefatory to the more important matter of Mother Goose. These must be forgotten ere the author of **The West Indian, The Brothers, The Jew,** and **The Wheel of Fortune,** can enjoy his full honours; but we can comfort him with the assurance that the date of their memory is already nearly expired. As a periodical writer, Mr. Cumberland's classical learning and accurate taste, his beautiful and flowing stile, and the pleasing subjects on which he usually loves to employ himself, compensate in some degree for want of depth of thought, or novelty of conception. It is hardly possible to speak too highly of his translations from Aristophanes and the ancient Greek fragments, they are not only equal, but superior, to any thing of the kind in our language; and so great is our respect for the author of these exquisite versions, that we will not say a single word of his original poetry.

But it is as a novelist that we are at present to examine Mr. Cumberland's literary powers. We cannot place **Arundel** and **Henry** on the same shelf with the works of Fielding or Smollet, and we are the less inclined to do so as the latter novel, being a close imitation of Tom Jones, serves particularly to shew the wide difference between the authors. Yet Mr. Cumberland's novels rank far above the usual stock in trade of the circulating library, are written in easy and elegant language, and evince considerable powers of observing generic, though not individual, characters. Excepting Smollett alone, whose sailors are, moreover, of a more ancient and rugged school, none has better delineated the characteristic and professional traits of the British navy, than Mr. Cumberland. The mission to Spain filled his portfolio with interesting sketches of that people, and of the persecuted Jews, who yet reside amongst them, which we often trace in his novels, tales and dramatic labours. The works of former authors he has laid liberally under contribution, and sometimes new-dressed their characters so well, as to give them an air of originality. Thus Ephraim Daw, in **Henry,** is a methodistical parson Adams, having the same simplicity of character, the same goodness of heart, and the same disposition to use the carnal arm in a good cause, qualified by the enthusiastic tenets and language of the sect from which the author derives him. It is therefore, we repeat, rather in delineating a species than an individual that the art of Mr. Cumberland consists, so far as it is original, the distinguishing personal features which he introduces being usually borrowed from others. Indeed we know but two remarkable peculiarities of taste in manners and incident which are completely his own, and run through all his works. The first is an odd and rather unnatural transfer of the task of courtship from the hero to the heroine of the piece. Mr. Cumberland seems to have found an inexpressible charm in exchanging the attributes of the sexes, so that the weaker may turn the chase upon the stronger, and the pigeon become the pursuer of the hawk. The frank and exacting manners of Charlotte Rusport, and his other ladies, (which, should they ever become fashionable, would be no slight inconvenience to our modish gentlemen,) were carried to their height in the novel of Henry, in which the virtues of continence and chastity, which, ever since the days of Heliodorus, the first novelist on record,

have been esteemed the indispensable and inalienable property of the heroine of the tale, were, *vi et armis,* transferred to the hero, leaving the unfortunate damsel to whom they rightfully belonged as bare of both as the birch tree of leaves upon Christmas eve. This singular taste seemed so deeply ingrafted in Mr. Cumberland's system of writing, that when we understood that he had selected a scriptural subject for his last poem, we never doubted for an instant that he had given the preference to the history of Joseph and Potiphar's wife. And though then mistaken, we find the present novel exhibiting symptoms too peculiar to be over-looked in a general view of Mr. Cumberland's literary character. The second predilection to which we alluded, is the peculiar pleasure which this author finds in a duel with all its previous pomp and circumstance of gentlemanlike defiance, retort, and reproof valiant. A single combat, either commenced or completed, makes a part of almost all his narratives, and Doctor Caranza himself cannot be estimated a more perfect judge of points of honour concerning the distance, the arms, and all the punctilio of the duello. Of this there is enough, and to spare, in the following pages.

The story of **John de Lancaster** is neither long nor complicated. The principal character and real hero of the novel is Robert de Lancaster, an ancient Welch Esquire, whose character is derived from that of Mr. Shandy, senior, chequered with the hundred attributes of Cornelius Scriblerus, father of the renowned Martinus. He is a great reader of all such learned works as convey neither instruction nor information, and in perusing the ancient historians, whether of the classical or Gothic periods, 'holds each stranger tale devoutly true.' This humour is pushed into the regions of utter and raving extravagance, especially as, saving in points of learning or science, we are required to believe that the old gentleman is not only of a sane mind, but endowed with uncommon good sense and talents, as well as with an admirable temper and most benevolent disposition, the cast whereof we think he derived from a certain 'Squire Allworthy, of Allworthy Hall in Somersetshire, who may not be utterly unknown to some of our readers. The credulity of this worthy person being seconded by no small quantity of family pride, he places implicit reliance on a pedigree which deduces his family in a direct line, not from Brutus or Hewel Dha, but from Samothes, son of Japhet the third son of Noah; and believes that his ancestors acquired the family-estate sixty-six years after the taking of Troy, and eleven hundred thirty and two years before the Christian era. He credits another tradition, which affirms that his ancestor taught King Bladud to fly; and another concerning an island in Ireland where the natives are immortal. As if this burden were not sufficient for his faith, he believes with Mr. Shandy in the effect of Christian-names upon their owners, with Cornelius Scriblerus in the influence of the harp in appeasing insurrections, and contends that 'soft airs well executed on the flute, were found to be a never-failing cure for the sciatica or hipgout.'—p. 289, Vol. I.

When the tale opens, Robert de Lancaster is residing quietly in his hereditary castle with his daughter Cecilia an amiable old maid, his son Philip a sort of cousin germain to the author's excellent Ned Drowsy, and his daughter-in-law wife of the said Philip, who is then just about to add an heir to Kray-Castle, and a link to the lineage of Samothes ap Japheth ap Noah. This desirable event is hastened in a very undesirable manner by an awkward Welsh Baronet named Sir Owen ap Owen, who, in a fit of tumultuous gallantry, overturns the tea-equipage into the lap of Mrs. De Lancaster. While she receives the necessary attendance in her premature accouchement, the group below are left in circumstances which again fatally remind us of the *Life and Opinions of Tristram Shandy*. The elder De Lancaster on this occasion harangues his friend Colonel Wilson, a maimed officer on half-pay, the Uncle Toby of the tale, whose blunt, soldier-like simplicity is meant to contrast the absurd ingenuity of his patron.

> So many things are assumed without being examined, and so many disbelieved without being disproved, that I am not hasty to assent, or dissent in compliment to the multitude; and on this account perhaps I am considered as a man affecting singularity: I hope I am not to be found guilty of that idle affectation, only because I would not be a dealer in opinions, which I have not weighed before I deliver them out. Above all things I would not traffic in conjectures, but carefully avoid imposing upon others or myself by confident anticipation, when nothing can be affirmed with certainty in this mortal state of chance and change, that is not grounded on conviction; for instance, in the case of the lady above stairs, whose situation keeps our hopes and fears upon the balance, our presumption is, that Mrs. De Lancaster shall be delivered of a child, either male or female, and in all respects like other children—
>
> I confess, said Wilson, that is my presumption, and I should be most outrageously astonished, should it happen otherwise.
>
> I don't think it likely, murmured Philip.
>
> No, no, no, replied De Lancaster; but we need not be reminded how many præternatural and prodigious births have occurred and been recorded in the annals of mankind. Whether the natives of the town of Stroud near Rochester are to this day under the ban of Thomas à Becket I am not informed; but when, in contempt of that holy person, they wantonly cut off the tail of his mule as he rode through their street, you have it from authority that every child thenceforward born to an inhabitant of Stroud was punished by the appendage of an incommodious and enormous tail, exactly corresponding with that, which had been amputated from the archbishop's mule.
>
> Here a whistle from the colonel (to the tune of Lilibulero, we presume) struck the auditory nerves of Philip, who, gently laying his hand upon his stump, gravely reminded him that Becket was a saint—

> De Lancaster proceeded—What then shall we say of the famous Martin Luther, who being ordained to act so conspicuous a part in opposition to the papal power, came into the world fully equipped for controversy; his mother being delivered of her infant, (wonderful to relate) habited in all points as a theologian, and (which I conceive must have sensibly incommoded her) wearing a square cap on his head, according to academic costuma. This, Colonel Wilson, may perhaps appear to you, as no doubt it did to the midwife, and all present at his birth, as a very extraordinary and præternatural circumstance.
>
> It does indeed appear so, said the Colonel. I know you don't invent the fable; I should like to know your authority for it.
>
> My authority, replied De Lancaster, in this case is the same as in that of Becket's mule; Martinus Delrius is my authority for both; and when we find this gravely set forth by a writer of such high dignity and credit, himself a doctor of theology, and public professor of the Holy Scriptures in the university of Salamanca, who is bold enough to question it?
>
> I am not bold enough to believe it, said Wilson.
>
> p. 25-29

During this learned discussion, which we produce as a specimen of the dialogue and manners, Mrs. Philip de Lancaster is disencumbered of a boy, who after such absurd ceremony as suited an old humourist, that half expected his grandson's arrival with a tail at one extremity, and a doctor's cap at the other, is christened by the name of John de Lancaster. We are next treated with a long account of a visit actually achieved by the ancient De Lancaster to another old gentleman called Ap Morgan, the father of Mrs. Philip de Lancaster, and maternal grandfather to the infantine hero. Ap Morgan, it seems, had discovered (something of the latest) that when through paternal influence his daughter was induced to bestow her hand upon the descendant of King Samothes, she had sacrificed to filial duty a tender predilection in favour of a certain gallant young officer, by name Captain Jones. This circumstance he communicates to old De Lancaster, acquainting him at the same time, in very civil terms, that he was grieved to death at having conferred his daughter on so stupid a fellow as his son Philip, when she had made so much better choice for herself. To repay this confidence, De Lancaster proves to Morgan, without the assistance of Delrius, that he was not responsible for the consequences of her obstinate silence, that their son and daughter were admirably matched, the lady being a religious hypochondriac, and the gentleman a mere cypher; and that their parental tenderness ought to overlook both as a blank in their lineage, fixing their only hopes upon the grandson, whom, under Providence, they had been the means of producing to the De Lancasters and Ap Morgans.—All which is admitted by old Morgan as 'a cure of the mournfuls'; his taste in consolation being at least as peculiar as that of his friend in history and philosophy.—Meanwhile, Penruth Abbey, the seat of Sir Owen ap Owen, receives two important inmates. These are a Spanish lady, or rather a Spanish Jewess, widow to a brother of the baronet who had settled in Spain, and her son, the heir of the title and estate.

The descendants of Israel were heretofore favourites with Mr. Cumberland. The characters of Abraham Abrahams in *The Observer,* of Sheva in *The Jew,* even of Nicolas Pedrosa in the lively tale which bears his name, are honourable and able testimonies of his efforts to stem popular prejudice in favour of a people degraded because they are oppressed, and ridiculed because they are degraded. Apparently, however, he hath repented him of his inclination towards the Jews, for not only do this same Mrs. Ap Owen and her son exhibit characters the most base, malicious, and detestable, but their descent from the stock of Abraham is thrown at their heads by all who speak of them, and is obviously held out as one source at least of their enormities. There is a singular passage in Mr. Cumberland's *Memoirs,* from which it would seem that the guilt of negligence at least, if not of ingratitude, worse than witchcraft, has, in his opinion, attached to the synagogue.[1] Perhaps this may be one cause why he now spits upon their Jewish gaberdine.

In tracing the crimes of the Ap Owens, Mr. Cumberland follows the maxim 'Nemo repente turpissimus.' The mother sets out by entrapping the leisure, if not the heart, of Mr. Philip de Lancaster, whose hypochondriac spouse is now expected to bid the world good night, under the influence of a slow decline. The character of David Ap Owen also opens gradually on the reader. He first pinches the tail of a lap-dog: secondly, he gallops past young John de Lancaster, in hunting, and maliciously bespatters him with mud and gravel, to the great damage of his clothes, and danger of his precious eyesight: thirdly, this 'Jew-born miscreant,' as De Lancaster terms him, insults the youthful heir of Kray Castle at a festive meeting of the family harpers. But a darker scene is soon to open,—Sir Owen Ap Owen worried out of his life by his sister-in-law and nephew, dies about the period when John De Lancaster, from an amiable and promising boy, has become a gallant youth. The baronet had bequeathed to Cecilia de Lancaster, a valuable diamond ring,—to young John, a favourite hunter. The ring is stolen by Mrs. Ap Owen, the horse ham-strung by her son, now Sir David. Their villainy and cruelty are detected. The gentlemen of the country, attached to the interest of the house of Owen, and members of a hunt over which the heir of that family presided, proceed to hold, what, for want of a better word, we shall call *a grand palaver,* upon this important occasion; and, after a solemn investigation of these delinquencies, transfer, in all form, their friendship and allegiance to the rival house of De Lancaster. Sir David and his mother are hooted from Wales, and obliged to retreat to Portugal. This dark picture is mingled with

softer shades: John de Lancaster falls in love with a beautiful girl, the daughter of that same Captain Jones to whom his mother had been early attached. Mrs. Philip de Lancaster had placed all her earthly hopes on planning a match between her son and the daughter of her lover. Yet this seemed an untoward project, for at their very first interview, John, as he is usually and concisely termed, being so much struck with the young lady's beauty as to substitute an ardent embrace for the more formal salutation of a bow, alarms the discreet *gouvernante,* who, ignorant of Mrs. De Lancaster's views, secludes the young lady from so unceremonious a visitor. This occasions some slight misunderstandings and embarrassments, which we have not time to trace or disentangle, as we hasten to the conclusion of the novel.

While Mrs. Philip de Lancaster was quietly dying at Kray Castle, her husband was suddenly seized with the fancy of setting out to take lodgings for her at Montpellier. Most people would have thought his company on the road more necessary to the invalid than his exertions as an avant courier. But this worthy *poco curante* was exactly in the situation of the Jolly Miller, who cared for nobody and nobody for him, so he was permitted to execute his plan of travelling without remonstrance or interference. His evil destiny guided him to Lisbon, where he received news of his lady's decease, and immediately after fell into the society, and of course into the toils, of the Ap Owens. These Jewish-Spanish-Welch reprobates, by the assistance of a Portugueze bravo with long whiskers, compelled poor Philip to sign a bond, obliging himself, under a high penalty, to marry Mrs. Ap Owen before the expiration of three months. No sooner had he submitted to this degrading engagement, than he became anxious to evade the completion, and wrote a most dismal penitentiary letter to his son John, imploring him to hasten to Lisbon and rescue him from the matrimonial shackles about to be forcibly imposed on him. This epistle was delivered at Kray Castle by a Mr. Devereux, who had sailed for England to learn something of the character of Sir David ap Owen, ere he countenanced his addresses to his sister. He is soon convinced of the infamy of the baronet, and returns to Portugal with young Lancaster, who loses not a moment in flying to his father's assistance. He came, however, too late. Philip was doomed to lose his life through the only exertion of courage which its course exhibited. Sir David had urged the fulfilment of the bond, and, in a rencontre which followed, basely availed himself of the assistance of his bravo, to murder his intended father-in-law. When John arrived, he found his father mortally wounded, and his enemy in the hands of justice. The former dies—the latter commits suicide, and Mrs. Ap Owen throws herself into a convent or a synagogue, we forget which. The fair hand of Miss Devereux is conferred upon the son of Colonel Wilson, a gallant young officer, who had accompanied John on his Portuguese crusade. Her hand indeed he had proudly refused to solicit, and almost to accept; for we are told that her father's coffers overflowed with the gold of Brazil, and that his daughter was a rock of diamonds, while her lover was in all respects a soldier of fortune. But this difficulty is overcome as is usual in Mr. Cumberland's plots, by the express solicitations of the fair lady. The return of the whole party to England is followed by the nuptials of Amelia and John de Lancaster. His grandfather, for their guidance, was pleased to compose a code of rules for domestic happiness in the married state, which are thus described:

> They consisted chiefly of truisms, which he was at the pains of proving; and of errors so obvious, that examination could not make them clearer. He pointed out so many ways, by which man and wife must render each other miserable, that he seemed to have forgot that the purport of his rules was to make them happy. So little was this learned work adapted to the object held out in the title, that, if it had been pasted up for general use on the door of a church, it may be doubted if any, who had read it, would have entered there to be married.

In *John de Lancaster,* although we cannot attach the importance to it which is claimed by the author, we find a good deal to praise. The language is uniformly elegant and well-turned, some of the repartees are neatly introduced, and the occasional observations of the author are in general pointed and sensible. Some scenes of pathetic interest arise from the death of a young woman, robbed of her virtue by the nefarious Sir David Owen. A Welch harper and poet is repeatedly introduced, and many of his lyrical effusions are not inferior to those of Mr. Dibdin. The following verses might be sung to advantage at a charity dinner when the subscription books were opened, provided a few bumper toasts had previously circulated.

> Let thy cash buy the blessing and pray'r of the poor,
> And let them intercede when death comes to thy door;
> They perhaps may appease that importunate power,
> When thy coffers can't buy the reprieve of an hour.
> Foolish man, don't you know every grain of your gold,
> May give food to the hungry and warmth to the cold,
> A purchase in this world shall soon pass away,
> But a treasure in Heaven will never decay.—& c. & c.

Of the skill exhibited in conducting the incidents, we cannot speak with much applause. The black and flagitious villainy of Owen is without any adequate motive, and is therefore inartificial and revolting. Besides, John and he squabble and affront and threaten each other through the whole book, without coming to any personal issue. They are constantly levelling their pistols, and alarming our nerves with the apprehension that they will go off at half-cock. We have, however, in this, as in all Mr. Cumberland's novels, the pleasing feeling that virtue goes on from triumph to triumph, and that vice is baffled in its schemes, even by their own baseness and atrocity. There is, we think, no attempt at peculiarity of character, unless in the outline of the grandfather, whose extravagance is neither original nor

consistent. Mr. Cumberland assures us that he has turned over many volumes to supply Robert de Lancaster with the absurd hobby-horsical erudition diffused through his conversation. No one will dispute Mr. Cumberland's learning, but the allusions to the classics might have been taken from any ordinary work on antiquities; and to black letter lore, he makes no pretence, almost all his hero's references being to imaginary authors, and the quotations devised for the nonce by Mr. Cumberland himself. This is the more unpardonable, as a display of ancient Welch manners, and appropriate allusions to the history, legends and traditions of Gyneth, Prestatyn, and Deheubarth, would have given his hero's character the air, if not the substance, of originality. The insertion of vague gibberish is a wretched substitute. Had Ritson been alive he might have rued his rash intrusion on this sacred ground. The invention (even in jest) of supposititious authorities and quotations, would certainly have brought down castigation under some quaint and newly furbished title, which had already served to introduce the satire of Nash, Harvey, or Martin Marprelate, such as '*Pap with a Hatchet, or a Fig for my Grannum*'; or '*A very merrie and pithie Comedie, intituled, The longer thou livest the more Fool thou art.*'

Mr. Cumberland has made an affecting apology for the imperfections of his novel, by calling upon us to consider his long services and advanced age. It is perhaps a harsh answer, that every work must be judged of by its internal merit, whether composed like that of Lipsius upon the day in which he was born, or like the last tragedy of Sophocles, upon the very verge of human existence. We should, therefore, have listened more favourably to this personal plea, had we not been provoked by a strain of querulous discontent, neither worthy of the author's years, of his philosophy, nor of his real goodness of heart. We have, for example, the following doleful lamentation over the praise and the pudding, which, he alleges, have been gobbled up by his contemporaries.

> If in the long course of my literary labours I had been less studious to adhere to nature and simplicity, I am perfectly convinced I should have stood higher in estimation with the purchasers of copy rights, and probably been read and patronized by my contemporaries in the proportion of ten to one. To acquire a popularity of name, which might set the speculating publishers upon out-bidding one another for an embryo work (perhaps in meditation only) seems to be as proud and enviable a pre-eminence as human genius can arrive at: but if that pre-eminence has been acquired by a fashion of writing, that luckily falls in with the prevailing taste for the romantic and unnatural, that writer, whosoever he may be, has only made his advantage of the present hour, and forfeited his claim upon the time to come: having paid this tribute to popularity, he certainly may enjoy the profits of deception, and take his chance for being marked out by posterity (whenever a true taste for nature shall revive) as the misleader and impostor of the age he lived in.

The circulation of a work is propagated by the cry of the many; its perpetuity is established by the fiat of the few. If we have no concern for our good name after we have left this world, how do we greatly differ from the robber and assassin?—But this is nothing but an old man's prattle. Nobody regards it—We will return to our history.

Vol. ii. p. 176

By our troth, Mr. Cumberland, these be very bitter words. We are no defenders of ghost-seeing and diablerie.—That mode of exciting interest ought to be despised as too obvious and too much in vulgar use; but, when the appeal is made to nature, we must recollect that there are incredibilities in the moral, as well as physical, world. Whole nations have believed in dæmons and witches; but who can believe that such a caricature as Robert de Lancaster ever existed out of the precincts of Bedlam!—There is no one that has not, at some period of his life, felt interested in a ghost-story; but it is impossible to sympathize with a character who pins his faith to figments as gross as if in his respect for green cheese he had conceived the moon to be composed of that savoury edible. Mr. Cumberland's assumed contempt of public applause we cannot but consider as an unworthy affectation. In fact, few men have shewn more eagerness to engross the public favour, of which he now grudges his contemporaries their slight and transitory share. His papers have come flying abroad on the wings of the hawkers. He has written comedies at which we have cried, and tragedies at which we have laughed: he has composed indecent novels and religious epics. He has pandered to the public lust for personal anecdote, by writing his own life and the private history of his acquaintances.

> At length he took his muse and dipt her
> Full in the middle of the Scripture:
> What wonders there the man grown old did!
> Sternhold himself he out-Sternholded.

Popularity we own to be a frail nymph, and far too free of her favours; but we cannot see her lashed by an author, who has strained every nerve to gain a share of them, without recollecting the exclamation of Lear:—

> Thou rascal beadle, hold thy bloody hand!
> Why dost though lash that whore?—Strip thine own
>   back,
> Thou hotly lust'st to use her in that kind
> For which thou whip'st her—

Neither can we offer Mr. Cumberland much consolation on the other topic of his complaint. He seems to think of this predilection of the public as Trinculo did of losing his bottle in the pool, and grows doubly indignant at the pipe and tabor of the deluding Dæmonologist—'There is not only dishonour in it, but an infinite loss—yet this is your innocent goblin!' The gentlemen of Paternoster-row we are afraid, notwithstanding Mr. Cumberland's diatribe, will continue obstinately to prefer discounting drafts on the present generation, payable at sight, to long-dated bills on posterity, which cannot be accepted till both the drawer and holder have become immortal in every sense of the word.

Upon the whole we rejoice that an old and valued friend has, at the advanced age of seventy-six, strength and spirits to amuse himself and the public with his compositions; and we think it will conduce greatly to both, if he will cease to fret himself because of the success of ballad-singers, ghost-seers, and the young Roscius. If they flourish at present, let him console himself with the transitory quality of their prosperity. We dare not soothe him too much by assenting to the counter-part of his prophesy: for, although the hopes of future glory have been the consolation of every bard under immediate neglect, yet experience compels us to confess that they are usually fallacious. Contemporary applause does not once, perhaps, in an hundred times, ensure that of posterity: few names are handed down to immortality, which have not been distinguished in their own generation; and least of all do we anticipate any splendid accession to the posthumous fame of an author, whose talents do not in the present day rank him above a dignified and respectable mediocrity.

Note

1. 'The public prints gave the Jews credit for their sensibility in acknowledging my well-intended services; my friends gave me joy of honorary presents, and some even accused me of ingratitude for not making public my thanks for their munificence, I will speak plainly on this point; I do most heartily wish they had flattered me with some token, however small, of which I might have said *this is a tribute to my philanthropy,* and delivered it down to my children, as my beloved father did to me his badge of favour from the citizens of Dublin: but not a word from the lips, not a line did I ever receive from the pen of any Jew, though I have found myself in company with many of their nation; and in this perhaps the gentlemen are quite right, whilst I had formed expectations, that were quite wrong; for if I have said for them only what they deserve, why should I be thanked for it? But if I have said more, much more, than they deserve, can they do a wiser thing than hold their tongues?'

Sir Walter Scott (essay date 1824)

SOURCE: Scott, Sir Walter. "Richard Cumberland." In *Lives of Eminent Novelists and Dramatists,* pp. 468-87. London: Frederick Warne and Co., 1887.

[*In the following essay, originally published in 1824, Scott offers an overview of Cumberland's literary career. In addition to critiquing Cumberland's major works, Scott examines the often tempestuous relationships that developed between Cumberland and other prominent authors and theater personalities of his era.*]

This author, distinguished in the eighteenth century, survived till the present was considerably advanced, interesting to the public, as well as to private society, not only on account of his own claims to distinction, but as the last of that constellation of genius which the predominating spirit of Johnson had assembled about him, and in which he presided a stern Aristarchus. Cumberland's character and writings are associated with those of Goldsmith, of Burke, of Percy, of Reynolds, names which sound in our ears as those of English classics. He was his own biographer; and from his *Memoirs* we are enabled to trace a brief sketch of his life and labours, as also of his temper and character; on which latter subject we have the evidence of contemporaries, and perhaps some recollections of our own.

Richard Cumberland boasted himself, with honest pride, the descendant of parents respectable for their station, eminent in learning, and no less for worth and piety. The celebrated Richard Bentley was his maternal grandfather, a name dreaded as well as respected in literature, and which his descendant, on several occasions, protected with filial respect against those who continued over his grave the insults which he had received from the wits of Queen Anne's reign. This eminent scholar had one son, the well-known author of *The Wishes*, and two daughters. The second, Joanna, the Phœbe of Byron's pastoral, married Dennis Cumberland, son of an archdeacon, and grandson of Richard Cumberland, Bishop of Peterborough.[1] Though possessed of some independence, he became rector of Stanwick, at the instance of his father-in-law, Dr. Bentley, and, in course of time, Bishop of Clonfert, and was afterwards translated to the see of Kilmore.

Richard Cumberland, the subject of this memoir, was the second child of this marriage, the eldest being Joanna, a daughter. He was born on the 19th of February, 1732: and, as he naturally delights to record with precision, in an apartment called the Judge's Chamber, of the Master's Lodge of Trinity College, then occupied by his celebrated maternal grandfather—*inter sylvas Academi.* With equal minuteness the grandson of the learned Bentley goes through the course of his earlier studies, and registers his progress under Kinsman of St. Edmondsbury, afterwards at Westminster, and finally at Cambridge; in all which seminaries of classical erudition, he highly distinguished himself. At college he endangered his health by the severity with which he followed his studies, obtained his Bachelor's degree with honour, and passed with triumph a peculiarly difficult examination; the result of which was his being elected to a Fellowship.

Amid his classical pursuits, the cultivation of English letters was not neglected, and Cumberland became the author of many poems of considerable merit. It may be observed, however, that he seldom seems to have struck out an original path for himself, but rather wrote because others had written successfully, and in the manner of which they had set an example, than from the strong impulse of that inward fire, which makes or forces a way for its own coruscations, without respect to the course of others. Thus Cumberland wrote an Elegy in a Churchyard on St. Mark's Eve [**"An Elegy Written on St. Mark's Eve"**], because Gray had, with general applause, published an Elegy in a Country Churchyard. He composed a drama on the subject of Elfrida, and with a chorus, in imitation of Mason; he imitated Hammond, and he imitated Spenser, and seems to display a mind full of information and activity, abounding with the natural desire of distinction, but which had not yet attained sufficient confidence in its own resources, to attempt a road to eminence of his own discovery; and this is a defeat from which none of his compositions are entirely free.

Mr. Cumberland's original destiny was to have walked the respectable and retired path by which his ancestors had ascended to church dignity; and there is every reason to believe, that, as he was their equal in worth and learning, his success in life might have been the same as theirs. But a temptation, difficult to be resisted, turned him from the study of divinity to that of politics.

The Rev. Mr. Cumberland, father of the poet, had it in his power to render some important political services to the Marquis of Halifax, then distinguished as a public character; and in recompense or acknowledgement of this, young Richard was withdrawn from the groves of Cam, and the tranquil pursuit of a learned profession, to attend the noble lord in the advantageous and confidential situation of private secretary. Amidst much circumlocution and moral reflection, which Cumberland bestows on this promotion and change of pursuit, the reader may fairly infer, that though he discharged with regularity the ostensible duties of his office, it was not suited to him: nor did he give the full satisfaction which perhaps he might have done, had a raw academician, his head full, as he says, of Greek and Latin, and little acquainted with the affairs of the existing world, been in the first place introduced for a time to busy life as a spectator, ere called to take an active part in it as a duty. His situation, however, led him into the best society, and insured liberal favour and patronage (so far as praise and recommendation went) to the efforts of his muse. In particular, his connexion with Lord Halifax introduced our author to Bubb Doddington, afterwards Lord Melcombe, of *Diary* memory, who affected the character of Mæcenas, and was in reality an accomplished man.

It was under the joint auspices of Lords Halifax and Melcombe, that Cumberland executed what he has entitled his first legitimate drama, ***The Banishment of Cicero***—an unhappy subject, the deficiencies of which are not redeemed by much powerful writing. This tragedy was recommended to Garrick by the two noble patrons of Cumberland; but, in despite of his deference for great names and high authorities, the manager would not venture on so unpromising a subject of representation. *The Banishment of Cicero* was published by the author, who frankly admits, that in doing so he printed Garrick's vindication.

About this time, as an earnest of future favours, Cumberland obtained, through the influence of Lord Halifax, the office of crown-agent for the province of Nova Scotia, and conceived his fortune sufficiently advanced in the world, to settle himself by marriage. In 1759, therefore, he united himself to Elizabeth, only daughter of George Ridge, of Kilmerton, by Miss Brooke, a niece of Cumberland's grandfather, Bentley. Mrs. Cumberland was accomplished and beautiful, and the path of promotion appeared to brighten before the happy bridegroom.

Lord Bute's star was now rising fast in the political horizon, and both the Marquis of Halifax and the versatile Bubb Doddington had determined to worship the influence of this short-lived luminary. The latter obtained a British peerage, a barren honour, which only entitled him to walk in the procession at the coronation, and the former had the Lieutenancy of Ireland. The celebrated Single-Speech Hamilton held the post of Chief Secretary to the Lord-Lieutenant, while Cumberland, not to his perfect content, was obliged to confine himself to the secondary department of Ulster Secretary. There was wisdom, perhaps, in the selection, though it would have been unreasonable to expect the disappointed private secretary to concur in that opinion. No one ever doubted the acute political and practical talents of William Gerard Hamilton, while Cumberland possessed, perhaps, too much of the poetical temperament to rival him as a man of business. A vivid imagination, eager on its own schemes, and unapt to be stirred by matter of duller import; a sanguine temper, to which hopes too often seem as certainties, joined to a certain portion both of self-opinion and self-will, although they are delightful, considered as the attributes of an intimate friend, are inconvenient ingredients in the character of a dependent, whose duty lies in the paths of ordinary business. Besides, Mr. D'Israeli has produced the following curious evidence, to show that Cumberland's habits were not those which fit a man for ordinary affairs: "A friend who was in office with the late Mr. Cumberland, assures me that he was so intractable to the forms of business, and so easily induced to do more or to do less than he ought, that he was compelled to perform the official business of this literary man, to free himself from his annoyance; and yet Cumberland could not be reproached with any deficiency in a knowledge of the human character, which he was always touching with a caustic pleasantry."[2]

Cumberland, however, rendered his principal some effectual service, even in the most worldly application of the phrase—he discovered a number of lapsed patents, the renewal of which the Lord-Lieutenant found a convenient fund of influence; but the Ulster Secretary had no other reward than the empty offer of a baronetcy, which he wisely declined. He was gratified, however, though less directly, by the promotion of his father to the see of Clonfert in Ireland. The new prelate shifted his residence to that kingdom, where, during his subsequent life, his son, with pious duty, spent some considerable part of every year in attendance on his declining age.

Lord Halifax, on his return to England, obtained the seals of Secretary of State, and Cumberland, a candidate for the office of Under Secretary, received the cold answer from his patron, that "he was not fit for every situation"; a reason scarce rendered more palatable by the special addition, that he did not possess the necessary fluency in the French tongue. Sedgwick, the successful competitor, vacated a situation at the Board of Trade, called Clerk of Reports, and Cumberland became desirous to hold it in his room. As this was in the gift of Lord Hillsborough, the proposal to apply for it was in a manner withdrawing from the patronage of Lord Halifax, who seems to have considered it as such, and there ensued some coldness betwixt the minister and his late private secretary. On looking at these events, we can see that Cumberland was probably no good man of business, as it is called, certainly no good courtier; for, holding such a confidential situation with Lord Halifax, he must otherwise have rendered himself either too useful, or too agreeable, to be easily parted with.

An attempt of Cumberland's to fill up the poetical part of an English opera, incurred the jealousy of Bickerstaff, the author of *Love in a Village,* then in possession of that department of dramatic composition. The piece, called the *Summer's Tale,* succeeded in such a degree, as induced the rival writer to vent his indignation in every species of abuse against the author and the drama. In a much better spirit, Cumberland ascribed Bickerstaff's hostility to an anxious apprehension for his interest, and generously intimated his intention to interfere no further with him as a writer of operas. The dispute led to important consequences; for Smith, well known by the deserved appellation of Gentleman Smith, then of Covent-Garden, turned the author's dramatic genius into a better channel, by strongly recommending to him to attempt the legitimate drama. By this encouragement, Mr. Cumberland was induced to commence his dramatic career, which he often pursued with success, and almost always with such indefatigable industry, as has no parallel in our theatrical history.

The Brothers was the first fruit of this ample harvest. It was received with applause, and is still on the stock-list of acting plays. The sudden assumption of spirit by Sir Benjamin Dove, like Luke's change from servility to insolence, is one of those incidents which always tell well upon the spectator. The author acknowledges his obligations to Fletcher's *Little French Lawyer*; but the comedy is brought to bear on a point so different, that little is in this instance detracted from its merit.

But the *West Indian,* which succeeded in the following year, raised its author much higher in the class of dramatic writers of the period, and—had Sheridan not been—must have placed Cumberland decidedly at the head of the list. It is a classical comedy; the dialogue spirited and elegant; the characters well conceived, and presenting bold features, though still within the line of probability; and the plot regularly conducted, and happily extricated. The character of Major O'Flaherty, those who have seen it represented by Jack Johnstone[3] will always consider as one of the most efficient in the British drama. It could only have been drawn by one who, like Cumberland, had enjoyed repeated opportunities of forming a true estimate of the Irish gentleman; and the Austrian cockade in his hat, might serve to remind the British administration, that they had sacrificed the services of this noble and martial race to unjust restrictions and political prejudices. The character of Major O'Flaherty may have had the additional merit of suggesting that of Sir Lucius O'Trigger; but the latter is a companion, not a copy, of Cumberland's portrait.

Garrick, reconciled with the author by a happy touch of praise in the prologue to *The Brothers,* contributed an epilogue, and Tom King supported the character of Belcour with that elastic energy which gave reality to all the freaks of a child of the sun, whose benevolence seems as instinctive as his passion.

The *Fashionable Lover,* which followed the *West Indian,* was an addition to Cumberland's reputation. There was the same elegance of dialogue, but much less of the *vis comica.* The scenes hang heavy on the stage, and the character of Colin M'Leod, the honest Scotch servant, not being drawn from nature, has little, excepting tameness, to distinguish it from the Gibbies and Sawnies which had hitherto possession of the stage as the popular representatives of the Scottish nation. The author himself is, doubtless, of a different opinion, and labours hard to place his *Fashionable Lovers* by the side of the *West Indian,* in point of merit; but the critic cannot avoid assenting to the judgment of the audience. The *Choleric Man* was next acted, and was well received, though now forgotten: and other dramatic sketches, of minor importance, were given by Cumberland to the public, before the production of his *Battle of Hastings,* a tragedy, in which the language, often uncommonly striking, has more merit than the characters or the plot. The latter has the inconvenient fault of being inconsistent with history, which at once affords a

hold to every critic of the most ordinary degree of information. It was successful, however, Henderson performing the principal character. Bickerstaff being off the stage, our author also wrote *Calypso,* and another opera, with the view of serving a meritorious young composer, named Butler.

Neither did these dramatic labours entirely occupy Cumberland's time. He found leisure to defend the memory of his grandfather, Bentley, in a controversy with Lowth, and to plead the cause of the unhappy Daniel Perreau, over whose fate hangs a veil so mysterious. Cumberland drew up his address to the jury, an elegant and affecting piece of composition, which had much effect on the audience in general, though it failed in moving those who had the fate of the accused in their hands.

The satisfaction which the author must have derived from the success of his various dramatic labours, seems to have been embittered by the criticisms to which, whether just or invidious, all authors, but especially those who write for the theatre, are exposed. He acknowledges that he gave too much attention to the calumnies and abuse of the public press, and tells us, that Garrick used to call him the man without a skin. Unquestionably, toughness of hide is necessary on such occasions; but, on the whole, it will be found that they who give but slight attention to such poisoned arrows, experience least pain from their venom.

There was, indeed, in Cumberland's situation, enough to console him for greater mortifications than malevolent criticism ought to have had power to inflict. He was happy in his family, consisting of four sons and two daughters. All the former entered the king's service; the first and third as soldiers, the second and fourth in the navy. Besides these domestic blessings, Cumberland stood in the first ranks of literature, and, as a matter of course, in the first rank in society, to which, in England, successful literature is a ready passport. His habits and manners qualified him for enjoying this distinguished situation, and his fortune, including the profits of his office, and his literary revenues, seems not to have been inadequate to his maintaining his ground in society. It was shortly after improved by Lord George Germain, afterwards Lord Sackville, who promoted him in the handsomest manner to the situation of Secretary to the Board of Trade, at which he had hitherto held a subordinate situation.

A distant relation also, Decimus Reynolds, constituted Mr. Cumberland heir to a considerable property, and placed his will in the hands of his intended successor, in order that he might not be tempted to alter it at a future period. Cumberland was too honourably minded to accept of it, otherwise than as a deposit to be called back at the testator's pleasure. After the course of several years, Mr. Reynolds resumed it accordingly. Another remarkable disappointment had in the meanwhile befallen, which, while it closed his further progress in political life, gave a blow to his private fortune which it never seems to have recovered, and, in the author's own words, "very strongly contrasted and changed the complexion of his latter days from that of the preceding ones."

In the year 1780, hopes were entertained of detaching Spain from the hostile confederacy by which Britain was all but overwhelmed. That kingdom could not but dread the example held out by the North Americans to their own colonies. It was supposed possible to open a negotiation with the minister, Florida Blanca, and Richard Cumberland was the agent privately entrusted with conducting this political intrigue. He was to proceed in a frigate to Lisbon, under pretence of a voyage for health or pleasure; and either to go on to Madrid, or to return to Britain, as he should be advised, after communicating with the Abbé Hussey, chaplain to his Catholic Majesty, the secret agent in this important affair. Mrs. Cumberland and her daughters accompanied him on this expedition. On the voyage, the envoy had an opportunity, precious to an author and dramatist, of seeing British courage displayed on its own proper element, by an action betwixt the "Milford" and a French frigate, in which the latter was captured. He celebrated this action in a very spirited sea-song, which we remember popular some years afterwards.

There was one point of the utmost consequence in the proposed treaty, a point which always has been so in negotiations with Spain, and which will again become so whenever she shall regain her place in the European republic. This point respects Gibraltar. There is little doubt that the temptation of recovering this important fortress was the bait which drew the Spanish nation into the American war; and could this fortress have been ceded to its natural possessor, mere regard to the Family Compact would not have opposed any insurmountable obstacle to a separate peace with England. But the hearts of the English people were as unalterably fixed on retaining this badge of conquest, as those of the Spaniards upon regaining it; and in truth its surrender must have been generally regarded at home and abroad as a dereliction of national honour, and a confession of national weakness. Mr. Cumberland was, therefore instructed not to proceed to Madrid until he should learn from the Abbé Hussey whether the cession of this important fortress was, or was not, to be made, on the part of Spain, the basis of the proposed negotiation. In the former event, the secret envoy of England was not to advance to Madrid; but, on the contrary, to return to Britain. It was to ascertain this point that Hussey went to Madrid; but unhappily his letters to Cumberland, who remained at Lisbon, while they encouraged him to try the event of a negotiation, being desirous perhaps, on his own account, that the negotiations should not be

broken off, gave him no assurances whatever upon the point by which his motions were to be regulated. Walpole, the British Minister at Lisbon, seems to have seen through the Abbé's duplicity, and advised Cumberland to conform implicitly to his instructions, and either return home, or at least not leave Lisbon without fresh orders from England. Unluckily, Mr. Cumberland had adopted the idea that delay would be fatal to the success of the treaty, and, sanguine respecting the peaceful dispositions of the Spanish ministry, and confident in the integrity of Hussey, he resolved to proceed to Madrid upon his own responsibility—a temerity against which the event ought to warn all political agents.

The following paragraph of a letter to Lord Hillsborough, shows Mr. Cumberland's sense of the risk which he thought it his duty to incur:—

> I am sensible I have taken a step which exposes me to censure upon failure of success, unless the reasons on which I have acted be weighed with candour, and even with indulgence. In the decision I have taken for entering Spain, I have had no other object but to keep alive a treaty to which any backwardness or evasion on my part would, I am persuaded, be immediate extinction. I know where my danger lies; but as my endeavours for the public service, and the honour of your administration, are sincere, I have no doubt that I shall obtain your protection.

From this quotation, to which others might be added, it is evident that, even in Cumberland's own eyes, nothing but his success could entirely vindicate him from the charge of officious temerity; and the events which were in the meantime occurring in London, removed this chance to an incalculable distance. When he arrived at Madrid, he found Florida Blanca in full possession of the whole history of the mob termed Lord George Gordon's, and, like foreigners on all such occasions, bent to perceive in the explosion of a popular tumult the downfall of the British monarch and ministry. A negotiation, of a delicate nature at any rate, and opened under such auspices, could hardly be expected to prosper, although Mr. Cumberland did his best to keep it alive. Under a reluctant permission of the British ministry, rather extorted than granted, the envoy resided about twelve months in Madrid, trying earnestly to knit the bonds of amity between ministers, who seem to have had little serious hope or intention of pacification, until at length Cumberland's return was commanded in express terms, on the 18th January, 1781. The point upon which his negotiation finally shipwrecked, was that very article to which his instructions from the beginning had especially directed him, the cession of Gibraltar. According to Cumberland, the Spaniards only wanted to talk on this subject; and if he had been permitted to have given accommodation in a matter of mere punctilio, the object of a separate treaty might have been accomplished. To this sanguine statement we can give no credit. Spain was at the very moment employed in actively combining the whole strength of her kingdom for the recovery of this fortress, with which she naturally esteemed her national honour peculiarly connected. She was bribed by the promise of the most active and powerful assistance from France; and it is very improbable that her ministry would have sacrificed the high hopes which they entertained of carrying this important place by force of arms, in exchange for anything short of its specific surrender.

Still, however, as Mr. Cumberland acted with the most perfect good faith, and with a zeal, the fault of which was only its excess, the reader can scarce be prepared, by our account of his errors, for the unworthy treatment to which he was subjected. Our author affirms, and we must presume with perfect accuracy, that when he set out upon this mission, besides receiving a thousand pounds in hand, he had assurance from the Secretary of the Treasury, that all bills drawn by Mr. Cumberland on his own bank, should be instantly replaced from the treasury; and he states, that, notwithstanding this positive pledge, accompanied by the naming a very large sum as placed at his discretion, no one penny was ever so replaced by government; and that he was obliged to repay from his private fortune, to a ruinous extent. the bankers who had advanced money on his private credit; for which, by no species of appeal, or application, was he ever able to obtain reimbursement.

Whatever may be thought of Mr. Cumberland's political prudence in venturing beyond his commission, or of his sanguine disposition, which too long continued to hope a favourable issue to a desperate negotiation, there can be no doubt that he was suffered to remain at Madrid, in the character of a British agent, recognised as such by the ministry, in constant correspondence with the Secretary of State, and receiving from him directions respecting his residence at, or departure from, Madrid. There seems, therefore, to have been neither humanity nor justice in refusing the payment of his drafts, and subjecting him to such wants and difficulties, that, after having declined the liberal offer of the Spanish monarch to defray his expenses, the British agent was only extricated from the situation of a penniless bankrupt, by the compassion of a private friend, who advanced him a seasonable loan of five hundred pounds. The state of the balance due to him was indeed considerable, being no less than four thousand five hundred pounds; and it may be thought, that, as Mr. Cumberland's situation was ostensibly that of a private gentleman, travelling for health, much expense could not—at least ought not—to have attended his establishment. But his wife and daughters were in family with him; and we must allow for domestic comfort, and even some sort of splendour, in an individual, who was to hold communication with the principal servants of the Spanish crown. Besides, he had been promised an ample

allowance for secret-service money, out of a sum placed at his own discretion. The truth seems to be, that Lord North's administration thought a thousand pounds was enough to have lost on an unsuccessful negotiation; and as Cumberland had certainly made himself in some degree responsible for the event, the same ministers, who, doubtless, would have had no objection to avow the issue of his intrigues had they been successful, chose, in the contrary event, to disown them.

To encounter the unexpected losses to which he was thus subjected, Mr. Cumberland was under the necessity of parting with his paternal property at an unfavourable season, and when its value could not be obtained. Shortly after followed the dissolution of the Board of Trade; and the situation of Secretary fell under Burke's economical pruning-knife—a compensation amounting only to one-half the value being appointed to the holder. Thus unpleasingly relieved from official and political duties, Mr. Cumberland adopted the prudent resolution of relinquishing his town residence, and settling himself and his family at Tunbridge, where he continued to live in retirement, yet not without the exercise of an elegant hospitality, till the final close of his long life.

The *Anecdotes of Eminent Painters in Spain,* in two volumes, together with a Catalogue of the Pictures which adorn the Escurial, suffered to be made by the King of Spain's express permission, were the principal fruits of our author's visit to the continent. Yet we ought to except the very pretty story of Nicolas Pedrosa, an excellent imitation of Le Sage, which appeared in the *Observer,* a periodical paper, which Cumberland edited with considerable success. This was one of the literary enterprises in which the author, from his acquaintance with men and manners, as well as his taste and learning, was well qualified to excel, and the work continues to afford amusement both to the general reader and the scholar. The latter is deeply interested in the curious and classical account which the *Observer* contains of the early Greek drama. In this department, Cumberland has acknowledged his debts to the celebrated Bentley, his grandfather, and to his less known, but scarce less ingenious relation, Richard Bentley, son of the celebrated scholar, and author of the comedy or farce termed *The Wishes.* The aid of the former was derived from the notes which Cumberland possessed, but that of Richard Bentley was more direct.

This learned and ingenious, but rather eccentric person, was the friend of Horace Walpole, who, as his nephew Cumberland complains with some justice, exercised the rights of patronage rather unmercifully. He had been unsuccessful as a dramatic author. His comic piece entitled *The Wishes,* was written with a view of ridiculing the ancient drama of Greece, particularly in their pedantic adherence to the unities. This was a purpose which could scarcely be understood by a vulgar audience, for much of it turned on the absurd structure of the stage of Athens, and the peculiar stoicism with which the Chorus, supposed to be spectators of the scene, deduce moral lessons of the justice of the gods from the atrocities which the action exhibits, but without stirring a finger to interfere or to prevent them. In ridicule of this absurdity, the Chorus in *The Wishes* are informed that a madman has just broken his way into the cellars, with a torch in his hand, to set fire to a magazine of gunpowder; on which, instead of using any means of prevention or escape, they began, in strophe and antistrophe, to lament their own condition, and exclaim against the thrice-unhappy madman, or rather the thrice-unhappy friends of the madman, who had not taken measures of securing him—or rather upon the six-times unhappy fate of themselves, thus exposed to the madman's fury. All this is a good jest to those who remember the stoicism with which the Choruses of Æschylus and Euripides view and comment upon the horrors which they witness on the stage, but it might have been esteemed caviare to the British audience in general; yet the entertainment was well received until the extravagant incident of hanging Harlequin on the stage. The author was so sensible of the absurdity of this exhibition, that he whispered to his nephew, Cumberland, during the representation—"If they do not damn this, they deserve to be d—d themselves;" and, as he spoke, the condemnation of the piece was complete. It is much to be wished that this singular performance were given to the public in print.—The notice of Richard Bentley has led us something from our purpose, which only called on us to remark, that he furnished Cumberland with those splendid translations from the Greek dramatists which adorn the *Observer.* The author, however, claims for himself the praise due to a version of the *Clouds* of Aristophanes, afterwards incorporated with this periodical work.

The modern characters introduced by Cumberland in his *Observer,* were his own; and that of the benevolent Israelite, Abraham Abrahams, was, he informs us, written upon principle, in behalf of a persecuted race. He followed up this generous intention in a popular comedy, entitled *The Jew.* The dramatic character of Sheva, combining the extremes of habitual parsimony and native philanthropy, was written in the same spirit of benevolence as that of Abrahams, and was excellently performed by Jack Bannister. The public prints gave the Jews credit for acknowledging their gratitude in a very substantial form. The author, in his *Memoirs,* does not disguise his wish, that they had flattered him with some token of the debt which he conceives them to have owed. We think, however, that a prior token of regard should have been bestowed on the author of Joshua, in the tale of *Count Fathom*: and, moreover, we cannot be surprised that the people in question felt a portrait in which they were rendered ludicrous as well as interesting, to be something between an affront and a compliment. Few of the better class of the Jewish persuasion would, we believe, be disposed to admit either Abrahams or Sheva as fitting representatives of their tribe.

In his retreat at Tunbridge, labouring in the bosom of his family, and making their common sitting-room his place of study, Cumberland continued to compose a number of dramatic pieces, of which he himself seems almost to have forgotten the names, and of which a modern reader can trace very few. We have subjoined, however, a list of them, with his other works, taken from the Index of his *Memoirs.* Several were successful; several unfortunate; many never performed at all; but the spirit of the author continued unwearied and undismayed. *The Arab, The Walloons,* and many other plays, are forgotten; but the character of Penruddock, in the *Wheel of Fortune,* well conceived in itself, and admirably supported by Kemble, and since by Charles Young, continues to command attention and applause. *The Carmelite,* a tragedy, on the regular tragic plan, attracted much attention, as the inimitable Siddons played the part of the Lady of Saint Valois, and Kemble that of Montgomeri. The plot, however, had that fault which, after all, clings to many of Cumberland's pieces—there was a want of originality. The spectator, or reader, was by the story irresistibly reminded of *Douglas,* and there was more taste than genius in the dialogue. The language was better than the sentiments; but the grace of the one could not always disguise that the other wanted novelty. *The Brothers, The West Indian,* and *The Wheel of Fortune,* stand high in the list of acting plays, and we are assured, by a very competent judge, that *First Love,* which we have not ourselves lately seen, is an excellent comedy, and maintains possession of the stage. The drama must have been Cumberland's favourite style of composition, for he went on, shooting shaft after shaft at the mark which he did not always hit, and often effacing by failures the memory of triumphant successes. His plays at last amounted to upwards of fifty, and intercession and flattery were sometimes necessary to force their way to the stage. On these occasions, the Green-room traditions avow that the veteran bard did not hesitate to bestow the most copious praises on the company who were to bring forward a new piece, at the expense of their rivals of the other house, who had his tribute of commendation in their turn, when their acceptance of a play put them in his good graces. It was also said, that when many of the dramatic authors united in a complaint to the Lord Chancellor against the late Mr. Sheridan, then manager of Drury Lane, he prevented Cumberland from joining the confederacy, by offering to bring out any manuscript play which he should select for performance. But selection was not an easy task to an author, to whom all the offspring of his genius was equally dear. After much nervous hesitation, he trusted the chance to fortune; and out of a dozen of manuscript plays which lay by him, is said to have reached the manager the first which came to hand, without reading the title. Yet if Cumberland had the fondness of an author for his own productions, it must be owned he had also the fortitude to submit without murmuring, to the decision of the public. "I have had my full share of success, and I trust I have paid my tax for it," he says, good-humouredly, "always without mutiny, and very generally without murmuring. I have never irritated the town by making a sturdy stand against their opposition, when they have been pleased to point it against any one of my productions. I never failed to withdraw myself on the very first intimation that I was unwelcome; and the only offence that I have been guilty of, is, that I have not always thought the worse of a composition, only because the public did not think well of it."

The Sacred Muse shared with her dramatic sisters in Cumberland's worship. In his poem of **Calvary,** he treated of a subject which, notwithstanding Klopstock's success, may be termed too lofty and too awful to be the subject of verse. He also wrote, in a literary partnership with Sir James Bland Burgess (well known as the author of *Richard Cœur de Lion,* and other compositions), **The Exodiad,** an epic poem, founded on sacred history. By **Calvary** the author sustained the inconvenient loss of an hundred pounds, and **The Exodiad** did not prove generally successful.

The author also undertook the task of compiling his own **Memoirs**; and the well-known Mr. Richard Sharpe, equally beloved for his virtues, and admired for the extent of his information, and the grace with which he communicates it, by encouraging Mr. Cumberland to become his own biographer, has performed a most acceptable service to the public. It is indeed one of the author's most pleasing works, and conveys a very accurate idea of his talents, feelings, and character, with many powerful sketches of the age which has passed away. It is impossible to read, without deep interest, Cumberland's account of the theatre in Goodman's Fields, where Garrick, in the flower of his youth, and all the energy of genius, bounded on the stage as Lothario, and pointed out to ridicule the wittol husband and the heavy-paced Horatio; while in the last character, Mr. Quin, contrasting the old with the modern dramatic manner, surly and solemn, in a dark-green coat profusely embroidered, an enormous periwig, rolled stockings, and high-heeled, square-toed shoes, mouthed out his heroics in a deep, full, unvaried tone of declamation, accompanied by a kind of sawing action, which had more of the senate than the stage. Several characters of distinguished individuals were also drawn in the **Memoirs** with much force; particularly those of Doddington, Lord Halifax, Lord Sackville, George Selwyn, and others of the past age. There are some traits of satire and ridicule which are perhaps a little overcharged. This work was to have remained in manuscript until the author's death, when certainly such a publication appears with a better grace than while the autobiographer still treads the stage. But Mr. Cumberland, notwithstanding his indefatigable labours, had never been in easy circumstances since his unlucky negotiation in Spain; and in the work itself, he makes the affecting confession, that circumstances, paramount to prudence and propriety, urged him to anticipate the date of publication. The **Memoirs** were bought by Lackington's house for 500*l.,* and passed speedily from a quarto to an octavo shape.

We have yet to mention another undertaking of this unwearied author, at a period of life advanced beyond the ordinary date of humanity. The *Edinburgh Review* was now in possession of a full tide of popularity, and the *Quarterly Review* was just commenced, or about to commence, under powerful auspices, when Mr. Cumberland undertook the conduct of a critical work, which he entitled *The London Review* on an entirely new plan, inasmuch as each article was to be published with the author's name annexed. He was supported by assistants of very considerable talents; but, after two or three numbers, the scheme became abortive. In fact, though the plan contained an appearance of more boldness and fairness than the ordinary scheme of anonymous criticism, yet it involved certain inconveniences which its author did not foresee. It is true, no one seriously believes that, because the imposing personal plural *We* is adopted in a critical article, the reader is from that circumstance to infer that the various pieces in a periodical review are subjected to the revisal of a board of literary judges, and that each criticism is sanctioned by their general suffrage, and bears the stamp of their joint wisdom. Still, however, the use of the first person plural is so far legitimate, that in every well-governed publication of the kind, the articles, by whomsoever written, are at least revised by the competent person selected as editor, which affords a better warrant to the public for candour and caution, than if each were to rest on the separate responsibility of the individual writer. It is even more important to remark, that the anonymous character of periodical criticism has a tendency to give freedom to literary discussion, and at the same time, to soften the animosities to which it might otherwise give rise; and, in that respect, the peculiar language which members of the senate hold towards each other, and which is for that reason called parliamentary, resembles the ordinary style of critical discussion. An author who is severely criticised in a review, can hardly be entitled, in the ordinary case, to take notice of it otherwise than as a literary question; whereas a direct and immediate collision with a particular individual, seems to tend either, on the one hand, to limit the freedom of criticism, by placing it under the regulation of a timid complaisance, or, on the other, to render it (which is, to say the least, needless) of a fiercer and more personal cast, and thereby endanger the decorum, and perhaps the peace of society. Besides this, there will always be a greater authority ascribed by the generality of readers to the oracular opinion issued from the cloudy sanctuary of an invisible body, than to the mere dictum of a man with a Christian name and surname, which may not sound much better than those of the author over whom he predominates. In the far-famed Secret Tribunal of Germany, it was the invisibility of the judges which gave them all their awful jurisdiction.

So numerous were Cumberland's publications, that, having hurried through the greater part of them, we have yet to mention his novels, though it is as a writer of fictitious history he is here introduced. They were three in number, *Arundel, Henry,* and *John de Lancaster.* The two first were deservedly well received by the public; the last was a labour of old age, and was less fortunate. It would be altogether unfair to dwell upon it, as forming a part of those productions on which the author's literary reputation must permanently rest.

Arundel, the first of these novels, was hastily written during the residence of a few weeks at Brighthelmstone, and sent to the press by detached parcels. It showed at the first glance what is seldom to be found in novels, the certainty that the author had been well acquainted with schools, with courts, and with fashionable life, and knew the topics on which he was employing his pen. The style, also, was easy and clear, and the characters boldly and firmly sketched. Cumberland, in describing Arundel's feelings at exchanging his college society, and the pursuits of learning, to become secretary to the Earl of G., unquestionably remembered the alteration of his own destination in early life. But there is no reason to think that in the darker shades of the Earl of G. he had any intention to satirize his patron, the Earl of Halifax, whom he paints in his *Memoirs* in much more agreeable colours.

The success which this work obtained, without labour, induced the author to write *Henry,* on which he bestowed his utmost attention. He formed it upon Fielding's model, and employed two years in polishing and correcting the style. Perhaps it does not, after all, claim such great precedence over *Arundel* as the labour of the author induced him to expect. Yet it would be unjust to deny to *Henry* the praise of an excellent novel. There is much beauty of description, and considerable display of acquaintance with English life in the lower ranks; indeed, Cumberland's clowns, sketched from his favourite men of Kent, amongst whom he spent his life, may be placed by the side of similar portraits by the first masters.

Above all, the character of Ezekiel Daw, though the outline must have been suggested by that of Abraham Adams, is so well distinguished by original and spirited conception, that it may pass for an excellent original. The Methodists, as they abhor the lighter arts of literature, and perhaps contemn those which are more serious, have, as might have been expected, met much rough usage at the hands of novelists and dramatic authors, who generally represent them either as idiots or hypocrites. A very different feeling is due to many, perhaps to most, of this enthusiastic sect; nor is it rashly to be inferred, that he who makes religion the general object of his life, is for that sole reason to be held either a fool or an impostor. The professions of strict piety are inconsistent with open vice, and therefore must, in the general case, lead men to avoid the secret practice of what, openly known, must be attended with loss of character; and thus the Methodists, and other rigid sectaries, oppose to temptation the strong barriers of interest and habitual restraint, in addition to those restrictions which religion and morality impose on all men. The touch of enthusiasm connected with Methodism renders it a species of devotion, warmly affecting the feelings, and therefore peculiarly calculated to operate upon the millions of ignorant poor, whose understandings the most learned divines would in vain address by mere force of argument; and doubtless many such simple enthusiasts as Ezekiel Daw, by their well-meant and indefatigable exertions amongst the stubborn and ignorant, have been the instruments of Providence to call such men from a state of degrading and brutal profligacy, to a life more worthy of rational beings, and of the name of Christians. Thus thinking, we are of opinion that the character of Ezekiel Daw, which shows the Methodist preacher in his strength and in his weakness, bold and fervent when in discharge of his mission, simple, well-meaning, and even absurd, in the ordinary affairs of life, is not only an exquisite, but a just portrait.

Cumberland seems to have been less happy in some of the incidents of low life which he has introduced. He forced, as we have some reason to suspect, his own elegance of ideas, into an imitation of Fielding's scenes of this nature; and, as bashful men sometimes turn impudent in labouring to be easy, our ingenious author has occasionally, in his descriptions of Zachary Cawdle and his spouse, become disgusting, when he meant to be humorous.

The author of *Henry* piqued himself particularly on the conduct of the story, but we confess ourselves unable to discover much sufficient reason. His skein is neither more artfully perplexed, nor more happily disentangled, than in many tales of the same kind; there is the usual, perhaps we should call it the necessary, degree of improbability, for which the reader must make the usual and necessary allowance, and little can be said in this respect, either to praise or censure the author. But there is one series of incidents, connected with a train of sentiment rather peculiar to Cumberland, which may be traced through several of his dramas, which appears in *Arundel,* and which makes a principal part of the interest in *Henry.* He had a peculiar taste in love affairs, which induced him to reverse the usual and natural practice of courtship, and to throw upon the softer sex the task of wooing, which is more gracefully, as well as naturally, the province of the man. In *Henry,* he has carried this farther, and endowed his hero with all the self-denial of the Hebrew patriarch, when he has placed him within the influence of a seductive being, much more fascinating in her address, than the frail Egyptian matron. In this point, Cumberland either did not copy his master, Fielding, at all, or, what cannot be conceived of an author so acute, he mistook for serious that author's ironical account of the continence of Joseph Andrews. We do not desire to bestow many words on this topic; but we are afraid, such is the universal inaccuracy of moral feeling in this age, that a more judicious author would not have striven against the stream, by holding up his hero as an example of what is likely to create more ridicule than imitation.

It might be also justly urged against the author, that the situations in which Henry is placed with Susan May, exceed the decent licence permitted to modern writers; and certainly they do so. But Cumberland himself entertained a different opinion, and concludes with this apology:—"If, in my zeal to exhibit virtue triumphant over the most tempting allurements, I have painted those allurements in too vivid colours, I am sorry, and ask pardon of all those who think the moral did not heal the mischief."

Another peculiarity of our author's plot is, that an affair of honour, a duel either designed or actually fought, forms an ordinary part of them. This may be expected in fictitious history, as a frequent incident, since the remains of the Gothic customs survive in that particular only, and since the indulgence which it yields to the angry passions gives an opportunity, valuable to the novelist, of stepping beyond the limits prescribed by the ordinary rules of society, and introducing scenes of violence, without incurring the charge of improbability. But Cumberland himself had something of a chivalrous disposition. His mind was nurtured in sentiments of honour, and in the necessity of maintaining reputation with the hazard of life; in which he resembled another dramatic poet, the celebrated author of *Douglas,* who was also an enthusiast on the point of honour. In private life, Cumberland has proved his courage; and in his *Memoirs* he mentions, with some complacency, his having extorted from a "rough and boisterous captain of the sea" an apology for some expressions reflecting on his friend and patron, Lord Sackville. In his *Memoirs,* he dwells with pleasure on the attachment shown to him by two companies of Volunteers, raised in the town of Tunbridge, and attaches considerable importance to the commission of Commandant, with which their

choice had invested him. They presented their commander with a sword, and, when their pay was withdrawn, offered to continue their service, gratuitously, under him.

The long and active literary life of this amiable man and ingenious author, was concluded on the 7th May, 1811, in his eightieth year, at the house of Mr. Henry Fry, in Bedford Place, Russell Square, and he was interred in Poet's Corner, Westminster Abbey.

His literary executors were Mr. Richard Sharpe, already mentioned, Mr. Rogers, the distinguished author of *The Pleasures of Memory,* and Sir James Bland Burgess; but we have seen none of his posthumous works, except *Retrospection,* a poem in blank verse, which appeared in 1812, and which appears to have been wrought up out of the ideas which had suggested themselves, while he was engaged in writing his *Memoirs.*

Mr. Cumberland had the misfortune to outlive his lady and several of his family. His surviving offspring were Charles, who, we believe, held high rank in the army, and William, a post-captain in the navy. His eldest daughter, Elizabeth, married Lord Edward Bentinck, son of the Duke of Portland; his second, Sophia, was less happily wedded to William Badcock, Esq., who died in the prime of life, and left a family of four grandchildren, whom Chancery awarded to the care of Mr. Cumberland. His third surviving daughter was Frances Marianne, born during his unlucky embassy to Spain. To her the author affectionately inscribed his *Memoirs,* "as having found, in her filial affection, all the comforts that the best of friends could give, and derived, from her talents and understanding, all the enjoyments that the most pleasing of companions could communicate."

In youth, Mr. Cumberland must have been handsome; in age, he possessed a pleasing external appearance, and the polite ease of a gentleman accustomed to the best company. In society he was eloquent, well-informed, and full of anecdote; a willing dealer in the commerce of praise, or—for he took no great pains to ascertain its sincerity—we should rather say, of flattery. His conversation often showed the author in his strong and in his weak points. The foibles are well known which Sheridan embodied on the stage, in the character of Sir Fretful Plagiary. But it is not from a caricature that a just picture can be drawn, and in the little pettish sub-acidity of temper which Cumberland sometimes exhibited, there was more of humorous sadness than of ill-will, either to his critics or his contemporaries. He certainly, like most poets, was little disposed to yield to the assaults of the former, and often, like a gallant commander, drew all his forces together to defend the point which was least tenable. He was a veteran also, the last living representative of the literature of his own age, and conceived himself the surviving depository of their fame, obliged to lay lance in rest against all which was inconsistent with the rules which they had laid down or observed. In these characters it cannot be denied, that while he was stoutly combating for the cause of legitimate comedy and the regular novel, Cumberland manifested something of personal feeling in his zeal against those contemporaries who had found new roads, or by-paths, as he thought them, to fame and popularity, and forestalled such as were scrupulously treading the beaten highway, without turning to the right or to the left. These imperfections, arising, perhaps, from natural temper, from a sense of unmerited neglect, and the pressure of disadvantageous circumstances of fortune, or from the keen spirit of rivalry proper to men of an ardent disposition, rendered irritable by the eagerness of a contest for public applause, are the foibles rather of the profession than the individual; and though the man of letters might have been more happy had he been able entirely to subdue them, they detract nothing from the character of the man of worth, the scholar, and the gentleman.

We believe Cumberland's character to have been justly, as well as affectionately, summed up in the sermon preached on occasion of his funeral, by his venerable friend, Dr. Vincent, then Dean of Westminster. "The person you now see deposited, is Richard Cumberland, an author of no small merit; his writings were chiefly for the stage, but of strict moral tendency—they were not without their faults, but these were not of a gross description. He wrote as much as any, and few wrote better; and his works will be held in the highest estimation, so long as the English language is understood. He considered the theatre as a school for moral improvement, and his remains are truly worthy of mingling with the illustrious dead which surround us. In his subjects on Divinity, you find the true Christian spirit; and may God, in His mercy, assign him the true Christian reward!"

Notes

1. The following amiable picture of Richard Cumberland occurs in the very interesting *Memoirs* of Samuel Pepys:—

   "18*th March,* 1667.—Comes my old friend Mr. Richard Cumberland to see me, being newly come to town, whom I have not seen almost, if not quite, these seven years. In a plain country parson's dress. I could not spend much time with him, but prayed him to come with his brother, who was with him, to dine with me to-day; which he did do: and I had a great deal of his good company; and a most excellent person he is as any I know, and one that I am sorry should be lost and buried in a little country-town, and would be glad to remove him thence; and the truth is, if he would accept of my sister's fortune, I should give 100*l.*

   more with him than to a man able to settle her four times as much as I fear he is able to do."

   It is impossible to suppress a smile at the manner in which the candid journalist describes the brother-in-law whom he finally adopted, not without a glance of regret towards Cumberland;—

   "*February* 7*th,* 1667-8.—Met my cosen Roger again, and Mr. Jackson, who is a plain young man, handsome enough for her, one of no education nor discourse, but of few words, and one altogether that, I think, will please me well enough. My cosen had got me to give the odd sixth 100*l.* presently, which I intended to keep to the birth of the first child: and let it go—I shall be eased of the care. So there parted, my mind pretty well satisfied with this plain fellow for my sister; though I shall, I see, have no pleasure nor content in him, as if he had been a man of reading and parts, like Cumberland."—Pepys' *Diary,* vol. ii. pp. 29 and 189.

2. [Isaac D'Israeli,] *The Literary Character Illustrated* [(London, John Murray, 1818)].

3. Commonly called Irish Johnstone. The judgment displayed by this excellent actor, in his by-play, as it is called, was peculiarly exquisite. When he intercepted the cordial designed for Lady Rusport, and which her attendant asserted was only good for ladies' complaints, the quiet and sly expression of surprise, admirably subdued by good breeding, and by the respect of a man of gallantry even to the foibles of the fair sex, and the dry mode in which he pronounced that the potion was very "good for some gentlemen's complaints, too," intimated at once the quality of her ladyship's composing draught, but in a manner accurately consistent with the perfect politeness of the discoverer, enjoying the jest himself, yet anxious to avoid the most distant appearance of insulting or ridiculing the lady's frailty. Go thy ways, old Jack! we shall hardly see thy like in thy range of character.

United States Democratic Review (review date May 1856)

SOURCE: Review of *Memoirs of Richard Cumberland,* by Richard Cumberland. *United States Democratic Review* n.s. 6, no. 2 (May 1856): 389-97.

[*In the following review, the anonymous critic offers a biting critique of Cumberland's memoirs, regarding the work as little more than the product of Cumberland's excessive vanity.*]

The present American edition of Cumberland's Autobiography [*Memoirs of Richard Cumberland*] is generally a reprint from the London edition of 1806. What was the ruling motive in the mind of the "Professor of his own history," as Jean Paul calls himself, in the production of the work, we are by no means certain that we know. He says: "The copyright of these memoirs produced to me the sum of five hundred pounds." That perhaps was the leading inducement to their preparation, since at the time they were undertaken, the failure of his Spanish embassy, and the refusal or neglect of the English government to refund the advances its prosecution had forced upon him, left him in a very straitened pecuniary position. But the motive and the inducement are two things. We have said that we are not certain of the motive. We wish we were quite certain that it *was not* what it seems to us to have been. Nothing goes more against the grain of our thinking, than an ill opinion of any one who has done the world service in any department of art. We never yield to its influence until we have exhausted every word of testimony against it. In the present instance, unfortunately, we can discover nothing upon which to build up a more charitable hypothesis than that which at first suggests itself. The motive of Cumberland in his autobiography appears to be the same which mainly characterized his efforts through life—vanity. Nor is his vanity of a common and ordinary kind. It is not the pleasant surface-vanity which revels in its own good opinion, and wears its satisfaction as a cloak, beneath which the owner is shielded from the biting wind of criticism, or the foggy breath of envy. Garrick described him as "a man without a skin"; and if, in fact, he was fitted by nature with the ordinary cuticle and epidermis of humanity, both were so amazingly thin that a child's arrow, headed with a bent pin, and shot from a bow of lath, would always find his heart and poison his moments of greatest happiness. His vanity was, in fact, morbid and intense. This, then, is the motive of the memoir, and has given it its peculiar shape and character. He professes to use no embellishment, and asserts that he will say no more of himself than honor and conscience demand. Living as he did, therefore, among the wits and great ones of his time, we naturally expect that his memoirs will be a kind of table-talk, where the best things of the best men shall be found spicily embalmed. That, however, would be the very opposite of what he intends, since it would give that prominence to others, which his pretended modesty seeks to secure for his own figure. It is, indeed, Mr. Cumberland he desires to keep before us perpetually, with my Lord this, and the Duke of that surrounding him, for the mere purpose of reflecting an added brilliancy upon him. Great men, artists, every body are merely the setting: Mr. Cumberland is the Kooh-i-noor, the precious jewel in the heads of all the toads who are made to hop about him. Vanity of vanities—all is vanity.

Richard Cumberland was born February 19th, 1732. He was the grandson of Dr. Richard Bentley, and great-grandson of Richard Cumberland, Bishop of Peterborough. His father was a minister of the Established Church, and afterwards Bishop of Clonfert, from which See he was translated to that of Kilmore. He studied at the public schools of Bury, and Westminster, and entered Trinity College, Cambridge, when very young. His intention was to follow the profession of which many of his family had been distinguished members; but he was diverted from it by the Earl of Halifax, who appointed him his private secretary, and afterwards took him with him when, in 1760, he was appointed Lord-Lieutenant of Ireland. On the accession of Lord George Germaine to the Cabinet he was appointed Secretary of the Board of Trade, and continued to hold that office until 1782. In 1780 he was dispatched upon a secret mission to the Court of Spain. This mission proved ultimately very unfortunate for him. He appears to have been led by his vanity into a false position, and to have exceeded the powers granted him. He was recalled. His expenses, beyond his outfit, were nearly five thousand pounds. Government never refunded him a penny of it, although he long besieged Lord North with petitions and remonstrances. His wife very nobly surrendered her jointure, and he applied whatever property he possessed to the liquidation of his debts. The family removed from London to Tunbridge, and lived in a much smaller way than they had been in the habit of doing. Prior to the unfortunate Spanish mission he had written frequently, but after it he devoted himself entirely to literature, and produced the greater part of the numerous dramatic pieces by which he is commonly known as an author. He wrote some poems also, but none above mediocrity, and his novels have long been forgotten.

His best comedies are *The West Indian* and the *Wheel of Fortune.* Both of these keep the stage, and are likely to do so.

Whilst still a school-boy he gets a little liberty, and is treated with the sight of Garrick in the character of Lothario. And "when," he says,

> after long and eager expectation, I first beheld little Garrick, then young and light, and alive in every muscle and in every feature, come bounding on the stage, and pointing at the wittol Altamont and heavy-paced Horatio—heavens, what a transition!—it seemed as if a whole century had been stepped over in the transition of a single scene; old things were done away, and a new order at once brought forward, bright and luminous, and clearly destined to dispel the barbarisms and bigotry of a tasteless age, too long attached to the prejudices of custom, and superstitiously devoted to the illusions of imposing declamation. This heaven-born actor was then struggling to emancipate his audience from the slavery they were resigned to, and though at times he succeeded in throwing in some gleams of new-born light upon them, yet in general they seemed to love darkness better than light, and in the dialogue of altercation between Horatio and Lothario, bestowed far the greater show of hands upon the master of the old school

than upon the founder of the new. I thank my stars, my feelings in those moments led me right; they were those of nature, and therefore could not err.

Apropos to several things, Cumberland gives some exceedingly good advice in the following. How much he took of it himself, and whether he took any part of it, our general knowledge of his character renders doubtful. We can well believe that he never liked his own productions less because the public failed to agree with him as to their merits; but for the rest—it is good advice, that's all.

> I am not to learn that dramatic authors are to arm themselves with fortitude before they take a post so open to attack; they, who are to act in the public eye, and speak in the public ear, have no right to expect a very smooth and peaceful career. I have had my full share of success, and I trust I have paid my tax for it always without mutiny, and very generally without murmuring. I have never irritated the town by making a sturdy stand against their opposition, when they have been pleased to point it against any one of my productions; I never failed to withdraw myself on the very first intimation that I was unwelcome, and the only offense I have been guilty of is, that I have not always thought the worse of a composition only because the public did not think well of it.
>
> It is a truth not sufficiently enforced, and when enforced, not always admitted, though one of the most useful and important for the government of our conduct, and this it is—that every man, however great in station or in fortune, is mutually dependent upon those who are dependent upon him. In a social state, no man can be truly said to be safe who is not under the protection of his fellow-creatures; no man can be called happy, who is not possessed of their good-will and good opinion; for God never yet endowed a human creature with sensibility to feel an insult, but that he gave him also powers to express his feelings, and propensity to revenge it.
>
> The meanest and most feeble insect, that is provided with a sting, may pierce the eye of the elephant, on whose very ordure it subsists and feeds.
>
> Every human being has a sting; why then does an overgrown piece of mortal clay arrogantly attempt to bestride the narrow world, and launch his artificial thunder from a bridge of brass upon us poor underlings in creation? And when we venture to lift up our heads in the crowd, and cry out to the folks about us—"This is mere mock thunder; this is no true Jupiter; we'll not truckle to his tyranny"—why will some good-natured friend be ever ready to pluck us by the sleeve, and whisper in our ear, "What are you about? Recollect yourself! he is a giant, a man-mountain; you are a grub, a worm, a beetle; he'll crush you under his foot; he'll tread you into atoms," not considering, or rather not caring,
>
>> "That the poor beetle, which he trode upon,
>> In mental suff'rance felt a pang as great
>> As what a monarch feels."
>
> Let no man who belongs to a community presume to say that he is independent; there is no such condition in

society. Thank God, our virtues are our best defense: conciliation, mildness, charity, benevolence. *Hæ tibi erunt artes.*

Every body, probably, has heard the anecdote illustrative of "vaulting ambition which o'erleaped its selle," in the case of the young man who played "Yankee Doodle" to perfection on a penny whistle, but not content with that, attempted the variations, and blew his brains out. Our author gives another anecdote of the passion, which carries the moral as strongly with it.

> I recollect the fate of a young artist in Northamptonshire, who was famous for his adroitness in pointing and repairing the spires of church-steeples; he formed his scaffolds with consummate ingenuity, and mounted his ladders with incredible success. The spire of the church of Raunds was of prodigious height; it overpeered all its neighbors, as Shakspeare does all his rivals; the young adventurer was employed to fix the weather-cock; he mounted to the topmost stone, in which the spindle was bedded; universal plaudits hailed him in his ascent; he found himself at the very acme of his fame, but glorious ambition tempted him to quit his ladder, and occupy the place of the weather-cock, standing upon one leg, while he sung a song to amaze the rustic multitude below: what the song was, and how many stanzas he lived to get through, I do not know; he sung it in too large a theatre, and was somewhat out of hearing; but it is in my memory to know that he came to his cadence before his song did, and falling from his height, left the world to draw its moral from his melancholy fate.

In the following we are treated to some good sketches of men, and some very bad criticism. The sketches of individual character are worth reading; the criticism scarcely worth criticising, as the world has set all that right long ago:

> At this time I did not know Oliver Goldsmith even by person; I think our first meeting chanced to be at the British Coffee-House; when we came together we very speedily coälesced, and I believe he forgave me for all the little fame I had got by the success of my **"West Indian,"** which had put him to some trouble, for it was not his nature to be unkind, and I had soon an opportunity of convincing him how incapable I was of harboring resentment, and how zealously I took my share in what concerned his interest and reputation. That he was fantastically and whimsically vain all the world knows, but there was no settled and inherent malice in his heart. He was tenacious to a ridiculous extreme of certain pretensions, that did not, and by nature could not, belong to him, and at the same time inexcusably careless of the fame which he had powers to command. His table-talk was, as Garrick aptly compared it, like that of a parrot, whilst he wrote like Apollo; he had gleams of eloquence, and at times a majesty of thought, but in general his tongue and his pen had two very different styles of talking. What foibles he had he took no pains to conceal; the good qualities of his heart were too frequently obscured by the carelessness of his conduct, and the frivolity of his manners. Sir Joshua Reynolds

was very good to him, and would have drilled him into better trim and order for society, if he would have been amenable, for Reynolds was a perfect gentleman, had good sense, great propriety, with all the social attributes, and all the graces of hospitality, equal to any man. He well knew how to appreciate men of talents, and how near a kin the muse of poetry was to that art of which he was so eminent a master. From Goldsmith he caught the subject of his famous Ugolino; what aids he got from others, if he got any, were worthily bestowed and happily applied.

There is something in Goldsmith's prose, that to my ear is uncommonly sweet and harmonious; it is clear, simple, easy to be understood; we never want to read his period twice over, except for the pleasure it bestows; obscurity never calls us back to a repetition of it. That he was a poet there is no doubt, but the paucity of his verses does not allow us to rank him in that high station, where his genius might have carried him. There must be bulk, variety and grandeur of design to constitute a first-rate poet. The "Deserted Village," "Traveller," and "Hermit" are all specimens beautiful as such, but they are only birds' eggs on a string, and eggs of small birds too. One great magnificent *whole* must be accomplished before we can pronounce upon the *maker* to be the ὁ ποιήτης. Pope himself never earned this title by a work of any magnitude but his Homer, and that being a translation, only constitutes him an accomplished versifier. Distress drove Goldsmith upon undertakings neither congenial with his studies nor worthy of his talents. I remember him, when in his chamber in the Temple, he showed me the beginning of his "Animated Nature"; it was with a sigh, such as genius draws, when hard necessity diverts it from its bent to drudge for bread, and talk of birds, and beasts, and creeping things, which Pidcock's show-man would have done as well. Poor fellow, he hardly knew an ass from a mule, nor a turkey from a goose but when he saw it on the table. But publishers hate poetry, and Paternoster Row is not Parnassus. Even the mighty Doctor Hill, who was not a very delicate feeder, could not make a dinner out of the press till by a happy transformation into Hannah Glass, he turned himself into a cook, and sold receipts for made dishes to all the savory readers in the kingdom. Then indeed the press acknowledged him second in fame only to John Bunyan; his feasts kept pace in sale with Nelson's fasts, and when his own name was fairly written out of credit, he wrote himself into immortality under an alias. Now, though necessity, or I should rather say, the desire of finding money for a masquerade, drove Oliver Goldsmith upon abridging histories and turning Buffon into English, yet I much doubt, if without that spur he would ever have put his Pegasus into action: no, if he had been rich, the world would have been poorer than it is by the loss of all the treasures of his genius and the contributions of his pen.

Who will say that Johnson himself would have been such a champion in literature, such a front-rank soldier in the fields of fame, if he had not been pressed into the service, and driven on to glory with the bayonet of sharp necessity pointed at his back? If fortune had turned him into a field of clover, he would have lain down and rolled in it. The mere manual labor of writing would not have allowed his lassitude and love of

ease to have taken the pen out of the inkhorn, unless the cravings of hunger had reminded him that he must fill the sheet before he saw the table-cloth. He might indeed have knocked down Osbourne for a blockhead, but he would not have knocked him down with a folio of his own writing. He would, perhaps, have been the dictator of a club, and wherever he sat down to conversation, there must have been that splash of strong, bold thought about him, that we might still have had a collectanea after his death; but of prose I guess not much, of works of labor none, of fancy perhaps something more, especially of poetry, which, under favor, I conceive was not his tower of strength. I think we should have had his Rasselas at all events, for he was likely enough to have written at Voltaire, and brought the question to the test, if infidelity is any aid to wit.

A characteristic anecdote of Johnson follows on the next page:

> I remember when Sir Joshua Reynolds, at my house, reminded him that he had drank eleven cups, he replied: "Sir, I did not count your glasses of wine, why should you number up my cups of tea?" And then laughing, in perfect good humor he added: "Sir, I should have released the lady from any further trouble, if it had not been for your remark; but you have reminded me that I want one of the dozen, and I must request Mrs. Cumberland to round up my number." When he saw the readiness and complacency with which my wife obeyed his call, he turned a kind and cheerful look upon her, and said: "Madam, I must tell you for your comfort, you have escaped much better than a certain lady did awhile ago, upon whose patience I intruded greatly more than I have done on yours; but the lady asked me for no other purpose but to make a Zany of me, and set me gabbling to a parcel of people I knew nothing of; so, madam, I had my revenge of her; for I swallowed five-and-twenty cups of her tea, and did not treat her with as many words."

In the following there is sound sense and good morality. The principle inculcated can not be too often urged upon those who cater to the public taste. It is claimed that the drama is the school of virtue. That it should be so, the common consent of all good and wise men has long since decreed. That it is at the present day to such an extent as to claim the benefit of the rule in its favor, we distinctly deny. When the "Dame aux Camelias" of *Dumas-fils* nightly crowds the boxes of one metropolitan theatre, and a troupe of Model Artists, representing the crucifixion of our Saviour, crowds the benches of another, we are compelled, reluctantly, to say that the Theatre has thrown away every claim to the support or countenance of virtuous or God-fearing men and women, and prostituted itself below the reach even of their censure. Let managers, as well as playwrights, ponder the following:

> As the writer for the stage is a writer to the passions, I hold it matter of conscience and duty in the dramatic poet to reserve his brightest coloring for the best characters, to give no false attractions to vice and immoral-

ity, but to endeavor, as far as is consistent with that contrast, which is the very essence of his art, to turn the fairer side of human nature to the public, and, as much as in him lies, to contrive so as to put men into good humor with one another. Let him, therefore, in the first place, strive to make worthy characters amiable, but take great care not to make them insipid; if he does not put life and spirit into his man or woman of virtue, and render them entertaining as well as good, their morality is not a whit more attractive than the morality of a Greek chorus. He had better have let them alone altogether.

Congreve, Farquhar, and some others have made vice and villainy so playful and amusing, that either they could not find in their hearts to punish them, or not caring how wicked they were, so long as they were witty, paid no attention to what became of them: Shadwell's comedy is little better than a brothel. Poetical justice, which has armed the tragic poet with the weapons of death, and commissioned him to wash out the offense in the blood of the offender, has not left the comic writer without his instruments of vengeance; for, surely, if he knows how to employ the authority that is in him, the scourge of ridicule alone is sharp enough for the chastisement of any crimes which can fall within his province to exhibit.

If the following be a true fairy story, we shall be of the faction of the "small grey men," of whom Burton, in his Anatomy, saith, "they do walk about in little coats not two foot high," for the rest of our lives. The anecdote of the good bishop, his father, has more true Christianity in it than many a barrel of sermons:

> The fairies were extremely prevalent at Clonfert. Visions of burials, attended by long processions of mourners, were seen to circle the churchyard by night; and there was no lack of oaths and attestations to enforce the truth of it. My mother suffered a loss by them of a large brood of fine turkeys, who were every one burnt to ashes, bones and feathers, and their dust scattered in the air by their provident nurse and feeder, to appease those mischievous little beings, and prevent worse consequences. The good dame credited herself very highly for this act of atonement; but my mother did not see it quite in so meritorious a light.

> A few days after, as my father and I were riding in the grounds, we crossed upon the Catholic priest of the parish. My father began a conversation with him, and expressed a wish that he would caution his flock against this idle superstition of the fairies; the good man assured the bishop, that in the first place he could not do it if he would, and in the next place confessed that he himself was far from being an unbeliever in their existence. My father thereupon turned the subject, and observed to him with concern that his steed was a very sorry one, and in very wretched condition. "Truly, my good lord," he replied, "the beast himself is but an ugly garron, and, whereby I have no provender to spare him, mightily out of heart, as I may truly say; but your lordship must think a poor priest like me has a mighty deal of work, and very little pay." "Why, then, brother," said my good father, whilst benevolence beamed in his countenance, "'tis fit that I, who have the advantage of

you in both respects, should mount you on a better horse, and furnish you with provender to maintain him." This parley with the priest passed in the very hayfield where the bishop's people were at work. Orders were instantly given for a stack of hay to be made at the priest's cabin; and in a few days after a steady horse was purchased and presented to him. Surely, they could not be true-born Irish fairies that would spite my father, or even his turkeys, after this.

We think not; for, if Irish fairies are not capable of appreciating a good deed or reciprocating a kindness, they are mighty little like Irishmen. God bless the good bishop; if six more like him had ever sprouted on the leaves of the Established Church in Ireland, heaven and earth would have both been a deal richer by this time.

Our space, and not our will, consents to abandon the subject at this point. Cumberland died in London, May 7th, 1811, being then in the 79th year of his age. "The evening of his day was clouded by pecuniary embarrassments, from which he endeavored, in vain, to relieve himself by his literary labors." The summary of his qualities as a man and an author, given by the Encyclopædist, is so just and happy, that we feel it unnecessary to "sum up" in other words.

> Of the personal character of Cumberland, a pretty accurate judgment may be formed from his memoirs. His self-esteem was great, and his vanity overweening, but, although extremely sensitive to criticism, and intolerant of censure, he had not real malignity in his composition, and, like most excitable persons, seems to have been as placable as he was irritable. His temperament was of a kind which, if easily disturbed, as quickly recovered its balance; and there is every reason to believe, that the predominant tone of his feelings was alike generous and liberal. On the only occasion of his life when his moral principles were put to the test, they appeared to the very greatest advantage. His conduct respecting the bequest of Mr. Reynolds, who had devised to Mr. Cumberland his estate, to the exclusion of the natural heir, evinced the greatest disinterestedness, and the highest sense of honor and probity. It was his misfortune to have been bred a courtier, and never to have taken his degrees in that school. He evidently wanted the suppleness and versatility necessary to insure success in such a career. In a subordinate station, which merely required attention to formal and technical duties, he acquitted himself indifferently well; but in venturing to act as minister, he found himself wofully deficient in those qualities, without the possession of which genius and talents are of little avail. . . . In society, his chief aim was to please; and, by the admission of his contemporaries, few men appeared to more advantage in conversation, or evinced a more perfect mastery, when he chose to exercise it, of the art of pleasing. The great faults of his character were a tendency to lavish hollow compliments on those who were present, and a propensity, without provocation or necessity, to indulge in bitter sarcasms against individuals after they had taken their departure. . . . As a writer, he is more remarkable for the number than for the excellence of his works; but many of them, it should be

remembered, were hastily produced, in order to better his income, and some of them are marked by no ordinary degree of intellectual power. In every variety of fortune the drama was his favorite pursuit; and if he has produced much that is perishable or forgotten, he has also evolved orations which have been inregistered as among the finest efforts of genius. The character of Penruddock in **"The Wheel of Fortune,"** for example, is a masterpiece, which received a double consecration from the histrionic talents of John Kemble, by whom it was so often, so nobly personated. As a poet he can not by any means rank high; for, while he had a play of imagination, which unfitted him for the concerns of actual life and business, his warmest admirers can only claim for him the praise of correct versification and elegant sentiment, which, however, has secured for some of his poetical works a considerable share of popularity.

His *Memoirs* are already a favorite work. The present edition is not only handsomely got up, well printed, etc., but presented in a form which must make it generally popular.

J. F. H. (essay date July 1865)

SOURCE: H., J. F. "Richard Cumberland." *Temple Bar* 14 (July 1865): 580-99.

[*In the following excerpt, the critic evaluates Cumberland's significance as a dramatist more than 50 years after his death.*]

Amongst the numerous ghosts of the men of past times evoked by the genius of the author of the *Roundabout Papers,* it is rather a remarkable fact that the once famous author of **The West Indian,** and innumerable other plays, all more or less successful in their time, should never once make his appearance. And yet Richard Cumberland was conspicuous enough in his own day. A learned and successful author; a playwright whose works, though they do not now keep the stage, were nevertheless important in their time; a friend of Johnson, Reynolds, Goldsmith, and Garrick; a poet, politician, essayist, and critic of no mean attainments,—he was in every sense a man of mark in his own day; so much so, indeed, as to make it somewhat extraordinary that he should be so entirely forgotten in ours. One reason possibly may be found in the jealousy with which the world is apt to regard a man of too varied accomplishments. He "who in the course of one revolving moon" essays the various *rôles* of "poet, statesman, fiddler, and buffoon," stands a great chance of being remembered by posterity as neither one nor the other, unless he be possessed of consummate genius. A Michael Angelo may, it is true, devote himself with impunity—nay, even with success—to half-a-dozen different arts and sciences; but it is not given to every man "to wear the armour of

Achilles." Those things which a man of great genius may do successfully, will prove sources of ruin and destruction to those men of more moderate abilities who may be unwise enough to attempt them. Thus it not unfrequently happens that he who, by devoting his entire attention to one single object, might have attained, if not fame, at least a fair and enduring reputation, may, by frittering away his talents on half-a-dozen different objects, wholly lose the applause that might have attached to him through steadfast devotion to one, and may become, as has been the case with Cumberland, the mere shadow of a name.

To nine readers out of every ten of the present day it is probable that the name which stands at the head of this paper is almost wholly unknown, while in the minds of at least half the remainder it will simply arouse vague and cloudy visions of a figure in a bag wig and sword, mixed up in some half-intelligible way with Johnson and the men of his era. Yet it is hardly fifty years ago since the announcement of his name threw James Smith ("Mr. Smith the poet") into a flutter of delight only equalled by that with which the young Victor Hugo received the visit of the veteran poet of his youth, Chateaubriand. Richard Cumberland forms, indeed, one of the great connecting links between the last and the present centuries; and those who know him, though only at second-hand, can (like Mr. Thackeray with the old friend whom he mentions at the beginning of his lecture on the reign of George I.) "travel back for seven score years of time; have glimpses of Brummell, Selwyn, Chesterfield, and the men of pleasure; of Walpole and Conway; of Johnson, Reynolds, Goldsmith; of North, Chatham, Newcastle; of the fair maids of honour of George II.'s court; and of the German retainers of George I."—nay, they may even go back farther still, and, by dwelling on the founder of the family, obtain glimpses of the latter half of the seventeenth century, in the person of that Dr. Cumberland who was made Bishop of Peterborough in 1691; or be admitted to the literary quarrels of Pope, Swift, and their clique in that maternal grandfather of our playwright, who was that Dr. Bentley whom Swift hitched into the *Battle of the Books,* and whom Pope impaled for all posterity as "slashing Bentley," side by side with the less known, though equally ill-used, commentator "piddling Tibbald." . . .

The first attempt of Cumberland in the dramatic art was the production of a tragedy on a subject taken from Middleton's *Life of Cicero,* then just published. **The Banishment of Cicero,** in five acts, was presented by Lord Halifax to Garrick; but the little manager, though by no means given to what Cibber used to call the "choking of singing birds," was too wise to risk his reputation by the production of a tragedy such as this. He was certainly under considerable obligations to Halifax, and would without doubt have been glad to oblige a powerful nobleman such as he, had it been possible; but it is evident, in spite of Cumberland's attempts to disguise the fact, that the play was really too bad for representation. In the first place, his choice of subject was most unhappy. Cicero is not a character for whom the play-going public are at any time likely to care, and his banishment is an exceedingly trivial matter to form the catastrophe of a long five-act tragedy. However, the author was proud of his bantling, and liked not the idea of the world losing so much instruction and amusement as he thought his tragedy likely to offer. It was published, therefore, but, greatly to his credit, with no preface in explanation of the circumstances under which Garrick had refused it. Copies were sent to the Primate and to Warburton, the latter of whom returned a courteous note of thanks, in which he assures Cumberland that his "very fine dramatic poem is (like Mr. Mason's) much too good for a prostitute stage." What Warburton meant by his phrases of flattery probably he himself best knew, but there is an odd "sour-grapes" flavour about his consolation, which could not have been very pleasant to Cumberland, in spite of the pride with which he publishes the letter. The play is not very easy to get at, but those who do attempt to read it are more likely to "sleep o'er Cato's drowsy theme" than to agree with the author in his opinion that though "inaccuracies may be discovered here and there as a dramatic poem, for the closet it will bear examination." His fault, indeed, is never a want of appreciation of his own merits. Whatever blame may attach to him on other grounds, none can on this; and in order to prove his case he does not hesitate to assume the most difficult position that can be devised—that of censor and critic of his own works. He has executed his task with as much impartiality as could be expected, with the usual, and indeed necessary result, that of disgusting his readers with his vanity and of irritating them by his incompetency. . . .

Comic opera was the order of the day on the stage, and Bickerstaff was at the head of this school of composition. His two works, *Love in a Village* and *The Maid of the Mill,* having been very successful, Cumberland was stimulated to attempt something of the same kind, and produced accordingly what he very appropriately styles "a thing in three acts," which he named *The Summer's Tale.* It was miserably dull and tedious; but being merely the vehicle for music, and not greatly regarded, it was moderately successful. Abel supplied the overture; Bach, Dr. Arne, and Dr. Arnold the music to the songs; and Beard, Shuter, and Miss Brent—all then in high favour—filled the principal characters.

His friends were not particularly struck by this, his first success. On leaving the theatre one day he met an old acquaintance, with whom he entered into conversation, and who told him frankly that he could never achieve a reputation by compiling the nonsense which usually goes to the formation of an opera. He wound up his ar-

guments by suggesting that he should devote himself to writing comedies, by which both fame and money might be gained; and on this hint Cumberland had the good sense to act. In the following summer, as soon as he was released from his duties at the Board of Trade, he set out on a visit to his father, whom he found comfortably settled at Clonfert, and with whom he stayed for some little time, returning to England in the autumn. His time had not been wasted in this long recess; for in the course of the winter he produced his first comedy, *The Brothers,* at Covent Garden. It was very fairly received, and appears to have fixed the destiny of its author, inasmuch as from this time we have more of the gestation and production of new comedies than of any thing else. This play of Cumberland's can hardly be called his first, seeing he had already produced a tragedy for the benefit of the trunk-makers, and an opera which had lived nine nights; but it was assuredly his first attempt in the style in which he was to gain his greatest successes, and in which he was to reign unquestioned king for many years to come. Those who have the courage to disinter it from the thousand-and-one works of the same class—successful and unsuccessful—which supplied the stage a century ago, will find little to praise in it more than is to be found in hundreds of other comedies which have long been forgotten. The characters are all old and conventional, the humour is of the stage, stagey, and the dialogue inexpressibly tedious. Mrs. Inchbald, it is but fair to say, however, is not of this opinion, though she carefully enshrines her opinions in the decisions of other people. "*The Brothers,*" she says, "is acknowledged by all critics to be a very good play."

If this play did nothing else, it had one very good effect—it produced a reconciliation between Cumberland and Garrick, who had not been upon the best of terms since the rejection of the *Banishment of Cicero.* This was brought about by means of a simple and graceful allusion in the epilogue. The play over, Mr. Yates stepped forward to deliver it, in accordance with the kindly but disused practice of the time, and began:

> Who but hath seen the celebrated strife,
> Where Reynolds calls the canvas into life;
> And 'twixt the Tragic and the Comic Muse,
> Courted of both, and dubious where to choose,
> Th' immortal actor stands——

"The immortal actor" was taken somewhat by surprise; but Garrick, with all his good qualities—and they were not few—was of all men one of the most open to flattery. In this instance it was so delicately applied, and so palpably sincere—for Cumberland could not know, though he might guess, that he would be present—that it could not fail of its desired effect. Mr. Fitzherbert, whose intimacy with Garrick has preserved his name, was with him in the box, and came round straightway "to assure Mr. Cumberland of the gratification he had afforded to Mr. Garrick." An intimacy, broken only by death, thus commenced. The actor visited the dramatist in Queen Anne Street, and the latter returned his attentions both at his house at Hampton and in Southampton Street.

Somewhere about this time he came into collision with Sheridan. With an inexplicable want of taste, he could never be brought to see, or at all events to acknowledge, the genius of his immortal rival, Sheridan. He is said even to have sat through a representation of *The School for Scandal* without a smile, and to have inquired what his friends could see to laugh at in it. He had not long before produced a tragedy, **The Battle of Hastings,** which has long been consigned to the limbo of forgotten works, and Sheridan did not forget this tragedy when Cumberland's behaviour at his comedy was reported to him. "Not laugh at my comedy!" said he; "somewhat ungracious, to say the least, for I laughed at his tragedy the other night from beginning to end." The retort was severe, but a more terrible revenge was in store. The immortal *Critic* came out in 1779, and the world there saw Cumberland at full length in the character of Sir Fretful Plagiary. The resemblance was perfect; one of his sons was the first to recognise it, and it soon became the talk of the town. It is only fair to add, however, that there is another account which states that the provocation was not a personal, but a political one, and this, for Sheridan's sake, one would rather accept. In Cumberland's farce, **The Note of Hand, or a Trip to Newmarket,** there is a certain amount of satire levelled at the Duke of Devonshire, Charles Fox, and other heads of that political party to which Sheridan was attached, and the tradition says that Sir Fretful was designed as a retaliation. Whichever be the true version of the story, it is certain that the satire was aimed at Cumberland, and equally certain that it was most bitterly felt. The injury rankled in his mind, and in spite of the attempts to disguise it, it was a sore point even a quarter of a century after.

The work by which Cumberland is best known was next set upon the stocks. The usual annual visit to his father at Clonfert was occupied by the composition of **The West Indian,** which, with a minuteness that would be amusing were it not tedious, he has told the world, was planned and written in a little closet at the back of the palace, which had no other prospect than that of a turf stack with which it was almost in contact. On his return to England, he submitted the manuscript of **The West Indian** to the friendly criticism of Garrick, who gave him a number of exceedingly valuable hints as to the conduct of his plot, the arrangement of his scenes, and the like, and who bestowed a great deal of attention on the arrangements for the rehearsal and cast of the play. The author's expectations were not high—indeed, he says that he offered to resign the profits of his work to Garrick, if he would give him a certain picture which

hung over his chimney-piece in Southampton Street—a copy of a Holy Family, by Andrea del Sarto—and the bargain would have been completed had not the picture been a gift from Lord Baltimore to the manager. Public curiosity had been aroused, and a good deal of hostility excited by the title of the new piece. The West Indians of London came down to the theatre on the first night in great force, disposed to resent any attack of the author on their class in an exceedingly summary manner. Their temper manifested itself the moment the prologue commenced, and the first four lines were spoken in the midst of such a tremendous uproar that not a word could be heard. Garrick grew painfully agitated; but the cry came for the speaker to recommence. He did so amidst a sulky kind of attention, and the audience, calmed a little by the promise that the hero should discover "some emanations of a noble mind," waited for the evolution of the plot and the development of the character with more patience than had at first been anticipated. The galleryful of Irish servants was conciliated by the promise of an Irishman in the piece who should differ in some respects from the conventional stage Irishman, who had hitherto "been treated," to use Cumberland's words, only "with kicks and cuffs," and prepared itself for lusty applause. The play opened amidst mingled silence of one party and cheering of another; but when the curtain dropped, the enthusiasm was unanimous, and the success of the piece was determined. To the reader of the present day it seems tame enough; not so was it esteemed at the time of its production. It ran for eight-and-twenty nights without the help of an afterpiece; the author's night produced a great sum, and he sold the copyright besides for 150*l.* The bookseller who bought it made no bad bargain; he was accustomed to boast in later days that he had sold no less than 12,000 copies—a number which would leave him a tolerable margin of profit.

The critics abused the piece in but few instances. Chiefly through Garrick's influence, they were very merciful as a rule; but the little manager's sense of humour prepared a wholesome antidote to the author's vanity. Calling upon him one morning, he found Garrick busy reading the St. James's evening paper. "Here, here," he cried, immediately on seeing Cumberland, "if your skin is less thick than a rhinoceros's hide, egad, here is that will cut you to the bone. This is a terrible fellow; I wonder who it can be!" He began apparently reading from the paper a violent attack upon the play, no one feature of which was spared, character, diction, and plot being alike assailed. The miserable author wriggled in his chair under the torment, which was not lessened when Garrick laid down the paper and condoled for a while with him on the cruelty of the journalists. When he had sufficiently enjoyed his joke, he resumed his reading, cheering up the distressed dramatist as the criticism began to soften, until he closed his amusement with a really genuine panegyric, of which he was himself the writer, and which was contained in the paper from which he had apparently been reading. One hardly knows which to admire most—the wit of Garrick or the delicacy of his flattery and of his warnings. It was one of those things that only he could have done, and is one of the pleasantest proofs of the genuine amiability of his character. . . .

The author of **The West Indian** had now become a somewhat distinguished member of London society, and was accustomed to entertain a large and brilliant circle of friends at his house in Queen Anne Street; Johnson, Burke, Reynolds, Garrick, Soame Jenyns, and a host of others, were constant visitors, and all appear to have entertained a very high respect for their host. Johnson was particularly attached to "Cumbey," and his friendship was not diminished by the very high estimation in which he held his friend's wife. In a note of Boswell's he quotes from Johnson's letters to Mrs. Thrale the opinion expressed by "the great lexicographer" of "that learned, ingenious, and accomplished gentleman:" "the want of company," says Johnson, "is an inconvenience; but Mr. Cumberland is a million." Besides Johnson, Cumberland also made acquaintance about this time with Foote, through Garrick's introduction; and also came to know Goldsmith, of whom he has related a number of anecdotes of no great importance. Those that really deserve attention have been incorporated by Mr. Forster in his charming life of Goldsmith; and as that book is probably in every reader's hand, it is unnecessary to repeat them here. His opinion of Goldsmith is, perhaps, of less importance than even his stories about him. The simple exterior and general quietude of the little poet led him to think less of his powers than they deserved; but as he looks from the heights of an imaginary superiority upon the less conspicuous though more enduring genius of his friend, his criticisms become sometimes rather amusing. . . .

Shortly after his return from Spain he commenced that course of literary labour which was to fill the remainder of his life, by the publication of two small octavo volumes of anecdotes of eminent painters in Spain. This was succeeded by those essays under the title of **The Observer,** on which chiefly rest his claims to a reputation for scholarship. Though they are now nearly forgotten, they had considerable reputation in their day, and Cumberland himself thought very highly of them. In one place, indeed, he congratulates himself that they had been incorporated in a collection of the British Essayists, and "may therefore be regarded as fairly enrolled among the standard classics of our native language." They did not appear singly, as was the case with those of the founders of the art of English essay-writing, but when sufficient were accumulated to form a volume it was brought out. The quantity of space covered by these 152 essays is rather greater than that occupied by the *Rambler,* which consists of 208; but while

Johnson received help from friends but rarely (only six pages of the whole being by other hands), and from books not at all, more than a third of **The Observer** is compiled or translated from the works of other writers. It is hardly fair, however, to institute comparisons between these two writers; while Cumberland was simply a man of ordinary capacity and considerable power of application, Johnson was a man of really unusual genius, and possessed of a wonderful power of execution. Some of the **Observers** will, notwithstanding the general air of heaviness which pervades them, always be valuable to the scholar and the critic. His inquiries into the history of the Greek writers, especially into that of the comic poets, are perhaps his happiest efforts, and his translations from Aristophanes are not destitute of value. He was probably greatly indebted, though he has not acknowledged the fact, to the annotated copies of the authors whom he criticised, which said copies had formerly been the property of his grandfather Dr. Bentley, and had come into the possession of Cumberland through his uncle. They are always likely to be commended rather than read; neither style nor subject is sufficiently attractive for this bustling nineteenth century. He has been rather scurvily treated of late years, his works being used as a quarry from which some "popular" authors have dug a great deal of good material without the smallest acknowledgment. An amusing instance of this "conveyance" occurred a short time ago. In one of the numbers of *Household Words,* shortly before that paper changed its name, appeared an article which has since been republished, in which the writer occupies himself by imagining the sort of treatment which would be dealt out to Shakespeare did his works appear now for the first time. The topic is treated pleasantly enough, but one of the numbers of **The Observer** contains the development of the same idea, not less skilfully worked out.

From his retirement at Tunbridge Wells, Cumberland sent forth his tragedy of **The Carmelite,** which being a little less dull than **The Battle of Hastings,** and having the inestimable advantage of the support of Kemble and Mrs. Siddons, was performed with moderate success. Controversy, too, presented her attractions, and these our author could never resist. The Bishop of Llandaff, "one of the ablest scholars and finest writers in the kingdom," by Cumberland's own account, published a proposal for equalising the revenues of the Church. Cumberland opposed the proposition in a pamphlet, to which the bishop deigned no reply. His opponent thereupon assumed that he "had the best of the argument," though possibly others may take a rather different view of the transaction. In the same way he addressed a pamphlet to Dr. Parr, with the somewhat boastful title of **"Curtius rescued from the Gulf."** To this also he obtained no reply, and probably had the same idea of the wisdom of the learned doctor as he had of that of the Bishop of Llandaff, who, he considers, "did a wiser thing in declining the controversy than in throwing out the occasion."

Cumberland produced one more comedy, *The Impostors,* with indifferent success; and then, finding that the stage would none of him, he thought that he might find greater acceptance amongst the publishers. In the course of two or three years he produced a series of novels—*Arundel, Henry,* and *John de Lancaster.* The first is a story in the Richardsonian manner, told in a series of letters; the second is modelled upon Fielding, from whom he borrowed his plan and the externals of his work; and the last, which appeared in 1809, was in the manner of the new school of romantic fiction. The three novels are all equally dull and unreal; their tediousness can only be imagined by those who have attempted to read them. They give, indeed, painful evidence of failing powers, and of the numbing influence of advancing age. The review of his declining years is no pleasant task. He had set out with high hopes and noble ambitions; he sank ere his death into a drivelling egotist. By and by he began to fancy himself an epic poet, and produced a new version of the great tragedy of the Christian faith—a poem with the title of *Calvary.* Afterwards, in conjunction with his friend Sir James Bland Burges, he brought forth another epic, the subject taken from the Old Testament, and the title *The Exodiad.* It is very smooth, very fluent, and excessively tedious. From beginning to end there seems no trace of the genuine poetic fire; an observation which will apply with equal force to the former poem, *Calvary.* They are both exemplifications of the most monotonous mediocrity, and prove, were any proof needed, the truth of the saying,

> Mediocribus esse poetis
> Non dii, non homines, non concessere columnæ.

Not much more time was, however, left to the veteran dramatist for labour of any sort. Driven by stern necessity, he published his autobiography, by which, in spite of its faults, he will best be remembered; and a few days before his death issued his poem of *Retrospection,* the only one of his works which appears, to those who have no interest in him beyond a literary one, worthy in any degree of his fame. He was in London on business, and was staying in the house of a friend, when his mortal disease attacked him. A few days of suffering, and he had done with the world and its struggles, its joys and its griefs. He died peacefully and calmly on the 7th of May 1811, and was buried on the 14th in Westminster Abbey, close to the spot where rests the body of his old and generous friend Garrick. The funeral-service was read over him by the Dean of Westminster, Dr. Vincent, with whom he had been a schoolfellow, and who had not forgotten their ancient friendship. The Dean delivered a panegyrical oration at the conclusion of the service, in which the poet received an ample measure of praise for his conduct in both public and private capacities. Unhappily, however, the speaker selected for his eulogium those very points in Cumberland's character to which exception may most readily be taken; such, for instance, as the freedom of his plays from profane oaths, and the purity of his novels both in moral and incidents. The only excuse which can be offered for this reckless misrepresentation is, that in all probability the venerable Dean had no personal acquaintance with the works of his friend, and that he had therefore been compelled to rely upon some not overscrupulous intermediary, who had described the dead man not as he was, but as he desired to be thought.

It has been necessary in the preceding pages to rely to a considerable extent upon the autobiography which Cumberland himself drew up. In that work his merits and defects are alike conspicuous. There is a great air of frankness and sincerity about his tone; but it is impossible to avoid an occasional suspicion that the writer has been tempted to gloss over and over-colour some events and some actions which, seen in the full light of truth, might have a rather different effect. With La Fontaine we may say:

> Je soupçonne fort une histoire
> Quand l'héros en est l'auteur;
> L'amour propre et la vaine gloire
> Rendent souvent l'homme vanteur:
> On fait toujours si bien son compte
> Qu'on tire de l'honneur de tout ce qu'on raconte.

That his name will be remembered for any other reason than on account of his connection with greater men, it would be folly to assert; yet, on the other hand, it cannot be denied that as a servant of the State he was eminently faithful, and exceedingly ill-rewarded; while his services to literature, though not, perhaps, enduring, were good and valuable in their time, and contained but little that even their author would wish to see destroyed.

Temple Bar (essay date May-August 1879)

SOURCE: "Richard Cumberland." *Temple Bar* 56 (May-August 1879): 171-87.

[*In the following essay, the anonymous critic offers a survey of Cumberland's literary career. The critic concedes that Cumberland's plays enjoyed great success during the playwright's lifetime, but asserts that they are ultimately derivative and unoriginal and questions whether they have any enduring value.*]

Cumberland was born on the 19th of February 1732, in the master's lodge of Trinity College—"*inter silvas Academi,*" he says—under the roof of his maternal grandfather, Richard Bentley, the famous scholar. His great-grandfather was Richard Cumberland, Bishop of

Peterborough; his father was a clergyman, the rector of Stanwick, in Northamptonshire, and was some years afterwards made Bishop of Clonfert, in Ireland. After receiving the rudiments of his education at Bury St. Edmunds, Richard was removed to Westminster. He seems to have been principally indebted to his mother for the cultivation of his literary tastes; during the vacations she accustomed him to read aloud to her every evening. These readings, with few exceptions, were confined to the plays of Shakespeare, and she supplemented them by critical remarks. In his twelfth year he wrote a drama entitled *Shakespeare in the Shades,* into which he introduced Hamlet and Ophelia, Romeo and Juliet, Lear and Cordelia, Ariel and the great poet himself. Some specimens of this juvenile effort are preserved in his *Memoirs,* and the imitations and paraphrases are rather clever for so youthful a hand, although not to be ranked with the juvenilia of such precocious prodigies as Cowley and Pope.

At fourteen he was sufficiently advanced in his studies to be admitted to the University, and at seventeen he was pursuing a course of study that allowed him only six hours sleep. He held a disputation with a "north-country, black-bearded philosopher," and beat him, this being but the first of four such contests during the year, all of which were maintained by him with honour. He also planned a Universal History, and, inspired by Mason's *Elfrida,* wrote a drama on the Greek model, upon the subject of Caractacus, which, strange to say, Mason some time after took as his theme for another so-called classic tragedy.

At a much earlier age than that honour is usually bestowed he received his B.A. degree, and immediately afterwards received the offer of a private secretaryship from the Earl of Halifax, then President of the Board of Trade. It was considered by all his friends too advantageous an opening to be declined; but all his desires pointed to a scholarship and a life devoted to learning, so with disappointed hopes and a head stuffed full of Greek and Latin he felt himself at Whitehall completely out of his element. His duties, however, which consisted only in copying a few private letters to governors and civil officers abroad, were very light, and in his private lodging in Mount Street, Grosvenor Square, he was able to continue his studies; well stocked with books, he sought no other society, and lived a hermit's life. Not, however, without scribbling poetry, which came into the world still-born, and a ponderous tragedy, entitled *The Banishment of Cicero,* inspired by Middleton's Life of the great orator. This he read to Lord Halifax, who was so delighted with it that he proposed they should at once walk over from Bushey, where they were staying at the time, to Hampton and offer it to Garrick. Such ponderosities were thrust upon the Drury Lane manager every day, and our young author had penetration enough to perceive that, although the little great

man was all bows and politeness to his noble visitor, the chances of the tragedy were desperate. And a few days afterwards the manuscript was returned as not being adapted for representation. Nevertheless the play was published, probably at Lord Halifax's desire, my lord being extremely angry with Garrick for not accepting it.

Cumberland obtained a scholarship, but soon had to relinquish it, for in 1759 he married the daughter of Mr. George Ridge, a gentleman of Hants; and the lady brought him some fortune.

In the meantime he made but little progress in the career his friends had selected for him. When the Earl of Halifax was appointed Lord Lieutenant of Ireland, he had to content himself with the secondary post of Ulster Secretary, while "Single Speech" Hamilton was appointed to the first position; and although he added considerably to the earl's powers of patronage by the discovery of certain lapsed patents, his only reward was the offer of an empty baronetcy, which he prudently declined. Lord Halifax, upon his return to England, received the seals of Secretary of State, and Cumberland then solicited the office of Under Secretary, but was refused, with the answer that he was not fit for every situation, and the excuse that he could not speak French with sufficient fluency. Upon which Cumberland, withdrawing from the Earl's service, obtained through Lord Hillsborough the somewhat derogatory appointment of assistant secretary to the Board of Trade. The fact is he seems to have been a bad business man, capricious and intractable, and, as Sir Walter Scott observes, not a good courtier; otherwise, holding, as he did, so confidential a situation near Lord Halifax's person, he must have rendered himself either too useful or too agreeable to have been easily parted with.

It was probably these failures and disappointments which first caused him to turn his attention seriously to literature.

The success which had attended Bickerstaff's operettas induced him to try his hand upon that species of composition, and in 1765 he wrote a three-act musical drama, entitled *The Summer's Tale.* Abel composed the overture, Bach, Arne, and Arnold supplied some original music; Beard, Miss Brent, Mr. and Mrs. Mattocks, and Shuter filled the principal parts. It was performed nine or ten nights with but very indifferent success, and afterwards, cut down to two acts, figured in his list of plays as *Amelia.* It brought down upon him the abuse of that disreputable personage, Isaac Bickerstaff, who considered he ought to have the monopoly of the musical drama; and as the experiment was not a successful one, Cumberland next employed his pen upon a more ambitious effort, a comedy, which he entitled *The Brothers.* It was brought out at Covent Garden, and admirably cast, the principal parts being performed by Woodward, Yates, Quick, Smith, Mrs. Green, and Mrs. Yates. Although it was successful and kept the stage for some years, it is but poor stuff; the abrupt and disjointed scenes betray the hand of a novice, neither plot nor dialogue ever rises above the tamest commonplace, while the characters are conventional and drawn with little power. Indeed the only one worthy of notice is Sir Benjamin Dove, the hen-pecked husband who, having been goaded by his wife to some display of courage, suddenly turns the tables upon her and becomes her tyrant. So doubtful were the Covent Garden powers of this play, that Harris had to take the responsibility of its production entirely upon his own shoulders. An artful compliment introduced into the epilogue, in which Garrick was styled the immortal actor, brought about reconciliation and friendship with Garrick, between Cumberland and whom there had been a coolness since the rejection of *The Banishment of Cicero.*

During a visit to his father at Clonfert, "in a little closet at the back of the palace, as it was called, unfurnished and out of use, with no other prospect from my single window but that of a turf stack, with which it was almost in contact, I seated myself by choice, and began to plan and compose *The West Indian.*" This work, written with much care, was an immense advance upon the previous one. It was offered to and accepted by Garrick, who wrote a capital epilogue for it. Cumberland gives us, in his *Memoirs,* an illustration of the care and the judgment which Garrick bestowed upon the production of a new play. Barry, according to our author, was very desirous of playing Major O'Flaherty, but Garrick, after a long deliberation, determined to entrust it to Moody, who was at the time an actor little known, and receiving only a low salary. He did not see Barry in the whole part, there were certain points in the humour where he thought he might fail, "and in that case his failure, like his name, would be more conspicuous than Moody's. In short, Moody would take pains; it might make him, it might mar the other; so Moody had it, and succeeded to our utmost wishes." King was the hero, Belcour, and Mrs. Abington played Charlotte Rusport, as a favour.

The production of a new play was an event in those days, and all the boxes were taken for several nights in succession. But a rumour having got abroad that the comedy was intended as a satire upon West Indians and Creoles in general, a strong body of partisans assembled in the theatre on the first night to do battle, if need be, for the maligned. The opening lines of the prologue, which ran—

> Critics, hark forward! noble game and new;
> A fine West Indian started full in view:
> Hot as the soil, the clime which gave him birth,
> You'll run him on a burning scent to earth,

seemingly countenanced the report, and raised such a tumult, that it became doubtful whether another word would be heard. Garrick was very uneasy, and was heard to say that he had never before seen the pit so hostile. At length, however, silence being restored, the prologue was recommenced, and suffered to proceed amidst sullen silence, only once broken at the lines—

> Laugh, but despise him not, for on his lip
> His errors lie; his heart can never trip,

which refer to Major O'Flaherty, and which raised a hearty round of applause from the Irish in the gallery. The crisis was past, and the comedy proceeded smoothly and successfully to the end. It was played twenty-eight nights, without an after-piece, and proved very profitable to the author, for he tells us how the treasurer of Drury Lane came to his house in Queen-Ann Street in a hackney coach, with a huge bag of money, and spread it all in gold upon his table, saying he had never paid an author so much before. Cumberland also received £150 for the copyright from Griffin, the publisher, who afterwards boasted that he sold 12,000 copies of this play. Such a sale, however, was not so extraordinary an occurrence as it would appear in the present day, for it must be remembered that the dramatic was *the* light literature of that age, in which novels were few and little read.

Cumberland was now fairly launched as a dramatist, and his success drew around him many of the most famous people of the day. Some of his sketches of contemporary celebrities are excellent. Here is one of the eccentric Soame Jenyns, the author of *The Origin of Evil,* which Johnson reviewed. "He was the man who bore his part in all societies with the most even temper and undisturbed hilarity of all the good companions whom I ever knew. He came into your house at the very moment you had put upon your card; he dressed himself to do your party honour in all the colours of the jay; his lace, indeed, had long since lost its lustre, but his coat had faithfully retained its cut since the days when gentlemen wore embroidered figured velvets with short sleeves, boot cuffs, and buckram shirts; as nature had cast him in the exact mould of an ill-made pair of stiff stays, he followed her so close in the fashion of his coat, that it was doubted if he did not wear them; because he had a protuberant wen just under his pole, he wore a wig, that did not cover above half his head. His eyes were protruded like the eyes of the lobster, who wears them at the end of his feelers, and yet there was room between these and his nose for another wen, that added nothing to his beauty; yet I heard this good man remark, when Gibbon published his history, that he wondered anybody so ugly could write a book." Yet Cumberland goes on to say that he was the charm of every circle, and gave a zest to every company he came into. He told no long stories, did not engross much of your attention, and was not angry with those who did. Although his thoughts were original, he was inclined to paradox. He wrote verses upon dancing, and prose upon metaphysics, without knowing much of either. Mrs. Jenyns had a great respect for her husband's good sayings, but "so imperfect a recollection of them, that though she always prefaced her recitals with 'as Mr. Jenyns says,' it was not always what Mr. Jenyns said, and never, I am apt to think, as Mr. Jenyns said; but she was an excellent old lady, and twirled her fan with as much mechanical address as her ingenious husband twirled his snuff-box."

His sketches of Garrick are also very good. After paying a high tribute to his talents and goodness of heart, and relating how he would charm a circle of children by imitating turkey-cocks, peacocks, and water-wagtails, he tells a capital story of that restless vanity which never slumbered for a moment. "The brilliant vivacity of Garrick was subject to be clouded, little flying stories had too much of his attention, and more of his credit than they should have had; and certainly there were too many babblers, who had access to his ear. There was some precaution necessary as to the company you associated him with at your table; Fitzherbert understood that in general admirably well, yet he told me of a certain day when Garrick, who had, perhaps, been put a little out of his way, and was missing from the company, was found in the back yard acting a turkey-cock to a black boy, who was capering for joy and continually crying out, 'Massa Garrick do so make me laugh: I shall die with laughing.'" There is another good story, in connection with Foote, which illustrates "little David's" readiness and good-nature. He and Cumberland dining with Foote one day, a certain Sir Robert Fletcher dropped in and made a fourth at table. Presently Sir Robert rose to depart; but instead of quitting the room he loitered behind a screen, which stood before and entirely concealed the door, long enough to hear his host commence ridiculing him. "I am not gone, Foote," he said, suddenly reappearing; "spare me till I am out of hearing; and now with your leave I'll stay till these gentlemen depart, and then you shall amuse me at their cost, as you have amused them at mine." Even Foote's impudence was not proof against such a shock as this; but what threatened to be a very disagreeable *contretemps* was averted by Garrick's genius and good-nature. "I never saw him," says the narrator, "in a more amiable light; the infinite address and ingenuity that he exhibited, in softening the enraged guest, and reconciling him to pass over an affront, as gross as could well be put upon a man, were at once the most comic and the most complete I ever witnessed."

Of Johnson too he tells an anecdote which will bear repeating. Sir Joshua Reynolds having remarked that Johnson had drunk eleven cups of tea, he requested Mrs. Cumberland to "round up his numbers" by making the dozen. "Madam," he said, as he took the cup, "I must tell you for your comfort you have escaped much better than a certain lady did a while ago, upon whose patience I intruded greatly more than I have done on yours; but the lady asked me for no other purpose than to make a zany of me, and set me gabbling to a parcel of people I knew nothing of; so, madam, I had my revenge of her; for I swallowed five-and-twenty cups of her tea, and did not treat her with as many words."

Cumberland was a frequenter of the British Coffee House, which was a great resort of North Britons, as well as of some of the most famous men of the time, Foote, Garrick, Goldsmith, Reynolds. Here it was one day suggested that he should write a comedy with a Scotchman in it, as a companion to his Irish Major. He objected that he had never been in Scotland, and knew very little of the dialect. "Give your Scotchman a character," remarked one of the company, "and take your chance for dialect. If you bring a Roman upon the stage, you don't make him speak Latin." "No, no," cried Foote, "and if you don't make him wear breeches, Garrick will be much obliged to you. When I was in Stranraer I went to the kirk, where the Mess-John was declaiming most furiously against luxury, and, as heaven shall judge me, there was not a pair of shoes in the whole congregation." From this conversation originated the character of Colin Macleod, in his next comedy, **The Fashionable Lover,** produced in 1772; it was a success, and became his favourite work.

The Choleric Man, a comedy to which Garrick wrote the epilogue, was brought out in 1775. His next production was an alteration of *Timon of Athens.* Shadwell, in his alteration of this play, had given Timon a mistress who remained steadfast to him in all his troubles. Cumberland gave him a sister whose wealth he had squandered with his own, thereby degrading the character of the noble Greek. He also rewrote a large portion of the dialogue. What havoc his cold turgid pen made with Shakespeare's tragedy may be imagined. For the credit of the audience, be it said the abortion was still-born, and never appeared in print.

A bombastic tragedy, entitled **The Battle of Hastings,** was produced at Drury Lane, under Sheridan's management, in 1778. Henderson, who had just been transferred thither from the Haymarket, played Edgar Atheling. During a residence in Bath, Cumberland had seen this actor play Shylock, and was so struck by his powers that he highly recommended him to Garrick, who empowered him to treat for his services. But while the negotiation was pending, David having received an unfavourable report of Henderson's talents from his brother George, who was in a bad state of health at the time, grew cool upon the business, and the engagement fell through. The next season Henderson opened at the Haymarket, and made an immediate success. Garrick, however, could not or would not recognise his talent, and after seeing him play Shylock had no word of praise except for the Tubal. Yet he was an actor of genius, the best Falstaff since Quin, and excellent in several tragic parts: John Kemble considered his Shylock the finest tragic effort he had ever witnessed. Still he was not what his admirers dubbed him—a second Garrick. His flow of spirits, boundless fund of wit, humour, and of all other social qualities, rendered him a universal favourite in private life. As a reader he was inimitable. He was once concerned with the elder Sheridan in a course of public readings: among the selections was Cowper's John Gilpin, which, although three years had elapsed since its publication, was little known; but he gave it with such verse and drollery that it at once became the rage. "He broke the people's heart with the story of 'Le Fèvre,'" writes Tom Dibdin, "and then nearly killed them over again with laughing at Johnny Gilpin." His career was a short one; he died in 1785, and lies in the Abbey, close to Garrick, who had been his model in life.

But to return to Cumberland. The appointment of principal secretary to the Board of Trade made a considerable addition to his private means. Not so fortunate, however, proved another appointment, which promised great things. In the year 1780 the Government despatched him upon a secret mission to the Court of Spain, the object of which would seem to have been the conclusion of a separate peace with that power. Unfortunately, while he was negotiating, the Gordon riots against the Catholics broke out, and to this he ascribes his failure. But whatever might have been his merits as a playwright, Richard Cumberland's diplomatic talents were not brilliant; he was recalled, and the administration, then under Lord North, meanly and dishonestly refused to reimburse him one farthing of his expenses, although these had been guaranteed by Robinson, the Secretary of the Treasury. Such had been the cost of this expedition, in which his wife and all his family accompanied him, that it brought him almost to ruin. "I wearied the door of Lord North," he said, "until his very servants drove me from it. I withstood the offer of a benevolent monarch whose munificence would have rescued me, and I embraced ruin in my own country to preserve my honour as a subject of it; selling every acre of my hereditary estate, jointured on my wife by marriage settlement, who generously concurred in the sacrifice which my improvident reliance upon the faith of Government compelled me to make."

During his stay at Madrid he witnessed a performance of the great Spanish and gipsy actress, Tiranna, about whom he tells some amusing anecdotes. Upon hearing that a famous English play-writer desired to see her act, she sent word that he was not to come to the theatre until she desired him, as it was only when she liked the part and was in the humour that she could play well.

After waiting several days he at length received the expected summons. But he had not been many minutes in his box when she sent word that as she felt no inclination for acting that night, she would not be able to do justice to her talents or to his expectations, and that he was to go home again. He obeyed the capricious creature, and another week elapsed before he received permission to attend the theatre again. "I had not then," he says, "enough of the language to understand much more than the incidents and action of the play, which was of the deepest cast of tragedy, for in the course of the plot she murdered her infant children, and exhibited them dead on the stage lying on each side of her, whilst she, sitting on the bare floor between them (her attitude, action and features, defying all description) presented such a high-wrought picture of hysteric frenzy, laughing wild amidst severest woe, as placed her in my judgment at the very summit of her art." So tremendous was the effect of this acting upon the audience, who rose in a kind of tumultuous frenzy, that the play was not suffered to terminate, and the curtain was abruptly dropped. Presently a gentleman brought her round to Cumberland's box. "The artificial paleness of her cheeks, her eyes, which she had dyed of a bright vermilion round the edges of the lids, her fine arms bare to the shoulders, the wild magnificence of her attire, and the profusion of her dishevelled locks, glossy black as the plumage of the raven, gave her the appearance of something so more than human, such a Sybil, such an imaginary being, so awful, so impressive, that my blood chilled as she approached me, not to ask but to claim my applause, demanding of me if I had ever seen any actress that could be compared with her in my own or any other country. 'I was determined,' she said, 'to exert myself for you this night; and if the sensibility of the audience would have suffered me to have concluded the scene, I should have convinced you that I do not boast of my own performances without reason.'" The Duke of Osuna, the commander of the Spanish guards, considered it indispensable to his honour to be the admirer of the finest woman in Spain, and he had paid her large sums of money, but had never once visited or seen her. One day, by the persuasion of a friend, he sent an intimation that he should come and take chocolate with her. But on his way to her house he fell fast asleep in the carriage, and upon arriving there no one had the temerity to awaken him. So after halting for a considerable time, and finding the duke still slumbered, the coachman wheeled round and took him home again.

Soon after Cumberland's return to England a new misfortune befell him. Under Burke's bill the Board of Trade, of which he was secretary, was dismissed, and for the loss of his office he received only a moderate compensation. Compelled to retrench his expenditure, he gave up his house in Portland Place and retired to Tunbridge Wells. He resided there more than twenty years, "inhabiting the same house, and cultivating a plot of ground embowered with trees and amply sufficient for a profusion of flowers, which my old servant, Thomas Cairns, nursed and took delight in."

His eldest daughter had married Lord Edward Bentick, the Duke of Portland's brother, an alliance he did not forget to parade, for he dearly loved a lord. There is an amusing story told of him and another, whose son or daughter had also entered a noble family, meeting at a dinner-party, and mutually entertaining one another with inquiries about my lord and my lady and anecdotes of the same, until the patience of everybody was exhausted. He now devoted himself to literary pursuits in earnest. Some experiences of his Spanish trip were given to the world in his *Anecdotes of Eminent Painters in Spain*; he also commenced the *Observer,* a series of essays, in the style of the *Spectator,* which ran to five volumes, the entire work being composed without assistance from any other hand. It is included among the British Essayists. *The Walloons,* a comedy, brought out at Covent Garden in 1782, and *The Mysterious Husband,* 1783, were written for his favourite, Henderson, as was also a play called *The Arab,* 1785, performed only one night, for that actor's benefit, and never published. Henderson's great failing was an unconquerable avarice. "I have now in my mind's eye," writes Cumberland, "the look he gave me, so comically conscious of taking what his judgment told him he ought to refuse, when I put into his hand my tributary guineas for the few places I had taken in his theatre. 'If I were not the most covetous dog in creation,' he cried, 'I should not take your money, but I cannot help it.' I gave up my tragedy to his use for one night only, and have never put it to any use since. His death soon followed, and he was hurried to the grave in the vigour of his talents and the meridian of his fame." The tragedy of *The Carmelite,* 1784, was written for the theatrical star, Mrs. Siddons. *The Natural Son,* 1785, was composed to display the talents of Miss Farren in the part of Lady Paragon. His dramatic labours were now varied by the composition of two novels, *Arundel* and *Henry. Arundel,* he tells us, was hastily put together while he was passing a few idle weeks at Brighthelmstone, and sent to the press in parcels. It seems to have contained something of his own early life, and Sir Walter Scott says the style is easy and clear, and the characters boldly and firmly sketched. The same good authority characterises *Henry* as an excellent novel. "There is much beauty of description, and considerable display of acquaintance with English life in the lower ranks; indeed Cumberland's colours, sketched from his favourite men of Kent, amongst whom he spent his life, may be placed by the side of similar portraits by the first masters . . . The character of Ezekiel Daw, which shows the Methodist preacher in his strength and in his weakness, bold and fervent when in discharge of his mission, simple, well-meaning, and even absurd, in the ordinary affairs of life, is not only an exquisite, but a just, portrait." The

books are now probably *introuvables,* at least I have never come across a copy of either. A third novel, *John de Lancaster,* written years afterwards, was not so successful as its predecessors. A sacred poem, called *Calvary,* modelled upon *Paradise Lost,* and a second, an epic entitled *The Exodiad,* written in conjunction with Sir James Bland Burgess, were also among his miscellaneous works. Dr. Drake compared *Calvary* with the compositions of Shakespeare and Milton, but both have long since sunk into the oblivion of unread and unreadable books. Indeed in the author's lifetime they met with no success. *Calvary* had so languid a sale that he says he lost "at least a hundred pounds by it," at which he "feels a proud indignant consciousness that it deserved better treatment," but consoles himself with the hope there would be a tribunal, meaning posterity, that would deal out justice to him when he could not be a gainer by it, and speak favourably of his performance when he could not hear their praises. Alas, his hopes have proved fallacious.

He continued to pour forth dramatic works, good, bad, and indifferent, with a wonderful fecundity. Among them was *The Jew,* in which Bannister played so admirably as Sheva. This was followed by the finest of all his plays, *The Wheel of Fortune,* 1795. Penruddock, of which John Kemble gave so splendid a rendering, remained a favourite part with all actors of tragic character from that time to the days of Samuel Phelps. In the same year was produced another successful comedy, *First Love*; yet, notwithstanding these incessant labours, when the fears of French invasion brought about a general arming, he found time to head a volunteer movement among the inhabitants of Tunbridge Wells, and every evening until ten o'clock was incessantly at drill, and sometimes after that turned out for a march by moonlight or torchlight. The news of the battle of Trafalgar inspired him with the idea of a piece entitled *The Victory and Death of Lord Nelson.* The music was composed and the drama was in rehearsal, when an interdiction came from the Lord Chamberlain and stopped the performance.

Cumberland survived his wife several years, and his youngest daughter became the comfort of his old age; fortunately for him she was of a studious turn, with a passion for books that dated from her earliest infancy. Among his last literary labours were his *Memoirs,* which were published during his lifetime. His dramatic works, including twelve plays published after his death, were fifty-four in number. He died in Bedford Place, Russell Square, on the 7th of May 1811, in his eightieth year, and is buried, as every one knows, in Poets' Corner.

Cumberland may at least be accredited with having brought a style of dramatic composition into vogue which held the stage until within the memory of the present generation, and some of the features of which still linger in the productions of the minor theatres. He, however, was no more the originator of sentimental comedy than was another author, Hugh Kelly, to whom that doubtful honour has been assigned; it belongs to a name far more illustrious than either. *The Conscious Lovers, The Tender Husband, The Lying Lover,* are the earliest specimens of the *comédie larmoyante*; they were suggested by Jeremy Collier's celebrated book against the stage, and were an attempt to supersede the licentiousness and immorality of the Wycherley and Congreve School by purer pictures of men and manners. But the wit that was so charming in the pages of *The Tatler* and *The Spectator* was not adapted for the stage, and the high-flown sentimentality of such characters as Bevil and Indiana is tedious and artificial in the extreme. A more moderate reformer of comedy, Colley Cibber, succeeded better. He rejected the gross indecency of the Restoration and Queen Anne writers, and yet retained something of their wit, and Steele's tearful Thalia remained unwooed until Richard Cumberland brought her into fashion again.

One year previous to the production of **The Brothers,** that is to say, in 1768, Hugh Kelly brought out his comedy *False Delicacy.* Kelly, according to John Taylor, was in his youth a potboy in a Dublin tavern much frequented by actors, and to this circumstance he was indebted for his first taste for the stage. Very early in life he wrote dramatic critiques for the newspapers. He was afterwards apprenticed to a staymaker. But such a mechanical employment could not content his soaring ambition, and in the year 1760, being then twenty-one years old, he added another to the number of Irish adventurers who swarmed in London at that period. At first he worked at his trade and did some copying for an attorney, whose acquaintance he had made in a Covent Garden tavern. But in 1762, he abandoned all other callings for authorship by profession; obtained employment upon several periodicals, then became editor of *The Public Ledger,* wrote for the Government, and was rewarded with a pension of £200 a year. In 1767 he published a satire entitled *Thespis,* a poor imitation of Churchill's *Rosciad,* in which all the principal actors of the day were reviewed with bitter malignity. This production, however, procured him the notice of Garrick, whose policy was always to convert enemies into friends, and in the next year he accepted and produced Kelly's first dramatic work. A kind of celebrity is still attached to this comedy as the supposed original of the sentimental school. Although destitute of originality, since it follows the old lines of fashionable comedy laid down by his predecessors, in which all the characters are fine ladies and gentlemen; and although in the dialogue there is very little wit, in the conduct of the plot very little invention, it is not deserving of the unmitigated contempt which the biographers of Goldsmith—for between Kelly and Goldy there was a rivalry—have

cast upon it. Cecil, the slovenly old bachelor, who at fifty makes overtures to a young lady, but finding that he does not prove acceptable, abandons all such hopes for the future, and gives friendly aid to his successful rival, is the best character, and the elder Farren once thought of reviving the comedy for the sake of acting it. Mrs. Harley is a sprightly widow, but is only a more decent descendant of many a lady who figured in the old scenes of Congreve and his contemporaries; the loves of Lord Winworth and Lady Betty, of Sidney and Miss Marchmont, are insipid enough; but the object of the author is to laugh at the false delicacies of such courtships, and not to set them up for admiration, as his critics insinuate he does. The writing is much too fine at times, but that was a vice of the age, in which every writer indulged with the exception of Goldsmith; but there is nothing *larmoyante* about the sentimentality, and it is never seriously meant by the author, who by the mouth of Mrs. Harley is always ready to cast ridicule upon it. When we come to the consideration of Cumberland's comedies we shall find very different conditions.

False Delicacy was very successful: it ran eight successive nights, and might have run longer had not Garrick pledged himself a little before this time that no new piece should be played nine nights in succession. It was, however, performed twenty times afterwards in the same season. Three thousand copies were sold by two o'clock upon the day after its publication, and ten thousand during the year. It was translated into French and Portuguese, and its author became quite the rage. After this he studied for and practised at the bar, wrote five more plays, and died at the early age of thirty-eight. There is much in such a fight with fortune and with the accidents of birth, as is witnessed in poor Hugh Kelly's career, to excite our admiration, more especially after reading Davies's epitaph upon him (*Life of Garrick*): "No man ever profited more by a sudden change of fortune in his favour; prosperity caused an immediate and remarkable alteration in his whole conduct: from a low, petulant, absurd, and ill-bred censurer, he was transformed to the humane, affable, good-natured, well-bred man." *The School for Wives,* the only other of his works I am acquainted with, is still further removed from the sentimental style than *False Delicacy,* to which it is a much superior production. There is one situation in it really admirable, where the rake who, under the character of a theatrical manager, has seduced a stage-struck girl from her home, being at her lodgings is introduced to two ladies, who are very anxious to hear her rehearse Juliet, and finds himself confronted by his wife and her aunt. For the rest, the work is far more like an imitation of one of Colley Cibber's comedies than a *comédie larmoyante.*

But it is time to leave Kelly, the supposed originator of the sentimental comedy, and turn to, after Steele, the real Simon Pure, Cumberland. There is not much to be said for the genius of a man who wrote fifty-four plays and yet did not add one original or permanent character to the stage. Penruddock, in *The Wheel of Fortune,* is the most powerful of all his *dramatis personæ,* but it is only Kotzebue's *Stranger* anglicised and brought down to commonplace. Sheva was a celebrated part with several famous actors, but a Jew miser who denies himself the commonest necessaries of life to lavish hundreds and thousands upon virtuous poverty is a monstrosity. There is a terrible sameness in all Cumberland's comedies. There is one group, of which he was the creator, which has excited the tears of lack-a-daisical women and bored sterner-hearted playgoers for many generations. Holcroft, Mrs. Inchbald, Morton, the younger Colman, and after them the writers of domestic drama until the present day, have posed these dreadful people with slight variations in nearly all their serious plays. A widowed mother who has known better days, but who is now reduced to poverty, a son who is an ensign, or a clerk to some stony-hearted merchant, and a lovely daughter, was Cumberland's favourite arrangement of the group. He sometimes brought in a father. Mrs. Inchbald and Holcroft usually made the interesting personages a young married couple with a child; the wife is a Lady Somebody who has married a poor officer, and has been in consequence discarded by a flinty-hearted parent; being reduced to a state of starvation, the husband becomes gloomy, desperate, and attempts suicide or robbery. Of course everything comes right in the end, the flinty heart is suddenly transformed into tender flesh, or some generous friend interposes and the pair live happy ever afterwards. This is still a stock group upon the stage of the minor theatres. But Cumberland was too moral and genteel to drive his characters to an improper state of despair; it was all very well for such red republicans as Holcroft and Mrs. Inchbald, but it would not have been becoming in the father-in-law of one of the house of Portland; with him the mother is the meekest and most suffering of angels, the daughter is equally angelic, the son is another angel in top-boots; there is always an heiress desperately in love with him, but although she intimates her preference in the most unequivocal terms, he is too modest to understand her, too nobly proud to marry her, although he may break her heart by his backwardness. It has been objected that Cumberland has reversed the ordinary relations of the sexes, and that in his plays it is usually the lady who makes love; such things, however, do happen even in real life, and we should not blame him for one of the few glimpses of real human nature that he has vouchsafed us in such spirited girls as Emily Tempest and Charlotte Rusport. All his good people are as full of sentiment as Joseph Surface, whom Sheridan probably intended as a satire upon such characters. There is very little vivacity about his rakes, with the exception of Belcour (*The West Indian*), who, notwithstanding exaggerations, is probably the best character he ever drew; his comic personages are most ponderous in their mirth, and have always a sentiment upon their lip.

> A flattering painter, who made it his care,
> To draw men as they ought to be, not as they are.
> His gallants are all faultless, his women divine,
> And comedy wonders at being so fine!
> Like a tragedy queen he has dizen'd her out,
> Or rather like Tragedy giving a rout.
> His fools have their follies so lost in a crowd
> Of virtues and feelings, that Folly grows proud;
> And coxcombs, alike in their failings alone,
> Adopting his portraits, are pleased with their own.

Like Molière, he took his property wherever he found it, but, unlike the great Frenchman, he had not the art of concealing his thefts or of so assimilating another's substance with his own that it derived a new charm for the combination. Plagiaries are often glaringly apparent in his comedies, but his tragedies are little else. The plot of *The Carmelite* is little more than a reproduction of that of Douglass, but the work is very inferior. From this mass of frigid bombast I cull a few specimens of Cumberland's blank verse. Matilda, the Lady Randolph of the play, is describing the murder of her husband to his dying assassin.

> Mercy! thou man of blood, thou hast destroy'd it.
> It came from heaven to save St. Valori:
> You saw the cherub messenger alight
> From its descent; with outspread wings it sate,
> Covering his breast; you drew your cursed steel,
> And through the pleading angel pierced his heart.
> Then, then the moon, by whose pale light you struck,
> Turn'd fiery red, and from her angry orb
> Darted contagious sickness on the earth;
> The planets in their courses shriek'd for horror;
> Heaven dropt maternal tears.

When the husband, who is alive all the time, is, in the disguise of a monk, describing to her the manner of his death, she exclaims:

> Oh, follow him no further,
> For see, the accursed Pyreneans rise,
> Streaming with blood; there hellish murder howls;
> There madness rages, and with haggard eyes
> Glares in the craggy pass! she'll spring upon me
> If I advance. Oh, shield me from the sight!

And when at last he discloses himself to his frantic widow, she bursts forth again in the Pistol vein:

> This transport is too quick, it melts my brain,
> The sky runs round; the earth is all in motion:
> Nay, now it whirls too fast.

And upon such trash as this the splendid genius of Siddons was wasted.

If he laid Home under contribution in *The Carmelite,* he flew at far higher game in *The Battle of Hastings,* in which he attempted an imitation of some of the famous passages of Shakespeare. Here are a couple of specimens of his manipulation.

> The poet, by the magic of his song,
> Can chain the listening moon around the spheres,
> End in his airy and extravagant flight,
> Belt wide creation round.

> You did ride
> As you'd o'ertake the couriers of the sky,
> Hors'd on the sightless winds.

The originals of these passages are too well known to need a reference. Another specimen of bathos from the same play is decidedly original:

> Power supreme!
> Whose words can bid the gathering clouds disperse,
> And chain the stubborn and contentious winds,
> *When they unseat the everlasting rocks,*
> *And cast them to the sky!*

To blow a horn, clothed in the language of this modern euphuist, becomes "Provoke the bugle," while a simple command to open a door is phrased:

> The wooden guardian of our privacy
> Quick on its axle turn.

No burlesque could surpass this, and yet this man presumed in *Timon of Athens* to place his nonsense beside the sublime diction of Shakespeare. Some choice passages might be culled from a tragedy in prose entitled *The Mysterious Husband,* which contains a monstrosity of character, Lord Davenant, that a transpontine stage would nowadays be ashamed of, but sufficient have been quoted to give the reader an idea of our author's tragic powers.

Never even did the wit of Sheridan conceive a happier appellative for Richard Cumberland than that of Sir Fretful Plagiary; while professing the most philosophical indifference to hostile criticism he so smarted beneath the least attack that Garrick called him a man without a skin, and in his prefaces and prologues he was perpetually descanting upon his injuries. Of his jealousy of contemporary dramatists some amusing anecdotes are told. Being present with his family at one of the performances of *The School for Scandal,* the children screamed with delight when the screen fell. Cumberland looked black as thunder; and, pinching the one nearest to him, he asked, "What are you laughing at, my dear little folks? There's nothing to laugh at"; then in an under-tone, "Keep still, you little dunces." "That was most ungrateful of Cumberland," remarked Sheridan, upon the story being reported to him; "for when I saw his tragedy I laughed from beginning to end." It is *The Battle of Hastings* that Sheridan is supposed to have burlesqued in *The Critic,* partly as a punishment

for his ill-natured remark, and partly because in a farce called *The Note of Hand* Cumberland had satirised Sheridan's associates, Charles Fox, the Duke of Devonshire, and the Whig party. But Cumberland and his bombast were such admirable themes for Sheridan to exercise his wicked wit upon, that the mere pleasure of the thing would be quite sufficient cause, without seeking for any other. How humorously under the character of Sir Fretful he has hit off his fellow-dramatist's failings! While smarting under Dangle's remarks, he exclaims in the spirit of his prototype's prefaces, "For my part I am never so well pleased as when a judicious critic points out any defect," Sir Fretful bursts into invectives against the newspapers, although he never looks into them, considers their abuse the best panegyric, and likes it of all things. But he is very anxious to know what the paper of Thursday has said about him. Dangle's report is in Sheridan's most malicious vein.

"Why, he roundly asserts that you have not the slightest invention or original genius whatsoever; though you are the greatest traducer of all other authors living. That as to comedy you have not one idea of your own, he believes, even in your commonplace book, where stray jokes and pilfered witticisms are kept with as much method as the ledger of the lost and stolen office. Nay, that you are so unlucky as not even to start with taste; but that you glean from the refuse of obscure volumes, where more judicious plagiarists have been before you; so that the body of your work is a composition of dregs and sediments, like a bad tavern's worst wine. In your more serious efforts, he says, your bombast would be less intolerable, if the thoughts were ever suited to the expression; but the homeliness of the sentiment stares through the fantastic incumbrance of its fine language, like a clown in one of the new uniforms. That your occasional tropes and flowers suit the general coarseness of your style, as tambour sprigs would a linsey-wolsey; while your imitations of Shakespeare resemble the mimicry of Falstaff's page, and are about as near the standard of the original. In fine, that even the finest passages you steal are of no service to you, for the poverty of your own language prevents them assimilating; so that they lie on the surface like lumps of marl on a barren moor, encumbering what is not in their power to fertilise."

In these witty strictures much allowance must be made for the licence of wit, but in their bearing they are terribly true.

G. Barnett Smith (essay date 1 January 1900)

SOURCE: Smith, G. Barnett. "The English Terence." *Fortnightly Review* n.s. 67, no. 397 (1 January 1900): 243-57.

[In the following essay, Smith offers a general assessment of Cumberland's literary career, while examining

contemporary critical reactions to the playwright's major dramatic works. Responding to Oliver Goldsmith's assertion that Cumberland was "the Terence of England," Smith argues that Cumberland lacked the talent or originality to merit the comparison. Smith concludes that, while he was an admirable man, Cumberland was decidedly a minor writer.]

The caustic wit of the brilliant Sheridan made havoc for a time, in certain circles, with the reputation of Richard Cumberland, the novelist and dramatist. Wit is an iconoclastic power, and especially so in the hands of a man like Sheridan; but it is not always just. Truth generally lies midway between extremes; and so, while the author of *The School for Scandal* unmercifully flayed the author of **The Wheel of Fortune,** it must not be forgotten that another illustrious contemporary, Oliver Goldsmith, described Cumberland, in his charming poem "Retaliation," as "The Terence of England, the mender of hearts."

There was a good deal of jealousy between Sheridan and Cumberland. While the former was much the more original in genius, the latter was the more successful in the outset. In fact his dramatic productions were all the vogue for some years, and were instrumental in introducing him to all the literary and distinguished society of his day. Although Cumberland praised the judicious introduction of the screen scene in *The School for Scandal,* he was charged with being the irritable opponent of all merit but his own. The story goes that he was present with his young family at an early performance of the famous comedy just named, *The School for Scandal.* They were seated in the stage box, and the children screamed with delight; but the less easily pleased fretful author pinched them, exclaiming, "What are you laughing at, my dear little folks? You should not laugh, my angels, there is nothing to laugh at!" And he added in an undertone, "Keep still, you little dunces." When Sheridan was told of this, he said, "It was ungrateful of Cumberland to have been displeased with his children for laughing at my comedy, for when I went to see his tragedy I laughed from beginning to end." But there must have been something beyond this to account for Sheridan's animosity towards Cumberland, whom he ultimately pilloried as the irritable and conceited dramatist, Sir Fretful Plagiary, in *The Critic.* Those who knew them both account for it thus. Sheridan, being most anxious to collect the opinions of the acknowledged judges of dramatic merit on *The School for Scandal,* asked what Mr. Cumberland had said on the first night of the performance. "Not a syllable," was the answer. "But did he seem amused?" "Why, faith," was the reply, "he might have been hung up beside Uncle Oliver's picture. He had the villanous disinheriting countenance; like the ladies and gentlemen on the walls, he never moved a muscle."

"Devilish ungrateful that," remarked Sheridan, "for I sat out his tragedy last week, and laughed from beginning to end." The tragedy in question was the **The Carmelites,** which the authors of *The Rolliad* mauled and stamped upon with great glee. It is only fair to Cumberland to state that he strenuously denied being present when *The School for Scandal* was first performed. There seems to be no doubt, however, that Sheridan was determined to hold up his fellow-dramatist to public ridicule, and the whole affair might well have formed an additional chapter in Isaac D'Israeli's *Quarrels of Authors.*

Cumberland was somewhat notably descended on both sides. His great-grandfather was Dr. Richard Cumberland, an able Protestant divine, who was consecrated Bishop of Peterborough in 1691. He is said to have doubled up that wicked philosopher, Hobbes of Malmesbury, in a learned work entitled *De Legibus Naturæ;* but, as life is short, I must leave it to others to find out how he accomplished his task. What is certainly to his credit—and at the same time extraordinary conduct on the part of a Bishop—is the fact that he gave away his income to the poor while living, and only left £25 at his death to bury himself with. Such instances of mental aberration among prelates are extremely rare. Cumberland's maternal grandfather was Dr. Richard Bentley, the erudite scholar and critic, whom Swift describes as "a writer of infinite wit and humour;" Pope, as "slashing Bentley." Macaulay affirmed that he was "the greatest scholar that had appeared in Europe since the revival of letters." Joanna, the younger of Dr. Bentley's daughters, and the mother of the dramatist, was the Phœbe of Byron's fine pastoral, "My time, O ye Muses, was happily spent." Cumberland's paternal grandfather was an Archdeacon; and his father also, Denison Cumberland, was in the church, and became Bishop of Clonfert and afterwards of Kilmore.

The dramatist was born in 1732. He was educated at Bury St. Edmund's, then at Westminster School, and when only in his fourteenth year was admitted at Trinity College, Cambridge, being one of the youngest undergraduates ever seen there. He seems to have been a model youth, for he says in his **Memoirs,** "I did not wantonly misuse my time, or yield to any even of the slightest excesses that youth is prone to: I never frequented any tavern, neither gave nor received entertainments; nor partook in any parties of pleasure, except now and then in a ride to the hills, so that I thank God I have not to reproach myself with any instances of misconduct towards a generous father, who at this tender age committed me to my own discretion and confided in me." In fact, as Disraeli said of his illustrious political rival, Cumberland does not seem to have been possessed of "a single redeeming vice." The classics were Cumberland's strong point; but he must have been good at mathematics too, for he occupied a high position among the Wranglers of Lis year and took his Bachelor's Degree with honours.

He left the University while still quite young, and was destined, like so many of his family, for the Church. But in return for some services rendered by his father he was appointed private secretary to the Whig Earl of Halifax, whom he accompanied to Ireland. Cumberland's family thought this appointment excellent, but he took a different view, and would have much preferred quiet employment in connection with his University studies. Dependence was repugnant to him, and moreover he was a student of books, not of men. Lord and Lady Halifax were courteous and considerate to a degree, and many young men about town, seeking an opening in political life, envied the young secretary, but he felt like a fish out of water. In his intervals of leisure he made his first small offering to the press, following the steps of Gray with another churchyard elegy, written on St. Mark's Eve, when, according to rural tradition, the ghosts of those who are to die within the year ensuing are seen to walk at midnight across the churchyard. Financially, the quotation for ghosts seems to have been very low at that time, for Dodsley, the publisher, reaped as little pecuniary profit from the poet's plaintive ditty as the general public took literary interest in it.

At Horton, the country seat of Lord Halifax, Cumberland was thrown into the society of many gifted men, and he greatly pleased the brilliant Charles Townshend by unearthing for him a recondite quotation from the *Troades* of Seneca. At the house of Bubb Dodington, in Dorsetshire, Cumberland met Alderman Beckford, "Leonidas" Glover, and many others, with whom occurred various literary passages of arms and wit contests. "Beckford, loud, voluble, self-sufficient, and galled by hits which he could not parry and probably did not expect, laid himself more and more open in the vehemence of his argument; Dodington, lolling in his chair in perfect apathy and self-command, dozing, and even snoring at intervals in his lethargic way, broke out every now and then into such gleams and flashes of wit and irony, as by the contrast of his phlegm with the other's impetuosity, made his humour irresistible, and set the table in a roar." Yet Dodington had his graver hours of solemnity of thought and language, which Cumberland highly appreciated.

In 1767 Cumberland wrote his first legitimate drama in five acts, *The Banishment of Cicero.* Bishop Warburton declared it to be too good for a degraded stage, and Halifax was so delighted with it that he took it to Garrick. The Jupiter of the stage, however, returned it, stating that he despaired of accommodating a play on such a subject to the purposes of the stage. The language of this drama is hard and stilted, though fine lines now and again occur; and it is somewhat extraordinary in that it

has no subordinate characters—they are all principals. As an example of Cumberland's style, we may give the closing lines of the first act of this play, in which the dramatist looks forward to the birth of some scientific genius of the calibre of Sir Isaac Newton:—

> When flaming comets vex our frighted sphere,
> Though now the nations melt with awful fear,
> From the dread omen fatal ills presage,
> Dire plague and famine, and war's wasting rage;
> In time some brighter genius may arise,
> And banish signs and omens from the skies,
> Expound the comet's nature and its cause,
> Assign its periods, and prescribe its laws;
> Whilst man grown wise, with his discoveries fraught,
> Shall wonder how he needed to be taught.

Cumberland married, in 1759, the only daughter of Mr. George Ridge, of Kilmiston, Hampshire, and he looked forward to a prosperous future under the auspices of Lord Halifax. But William Gerrard Hamilton, who was Chief Secretary of Ireland—Lord Halifax being Lord Lieutenant—stood in the way. Hamilton was known in England as "Single-Speech Hamilton," from his one brilliant speech at Westminster, but in the Irish House of Commons he spoke well and frequently. Halifax offered Cumberland a Baronetcy, but the honour was declined as one utterly unsuited to his tastes and inclinations. Just before Halifax went out of office, however, he promoted the dramatist's father to the See of Clonfert, which he seems to have adorned by his benevolence, equity, and integrity.

For some reason or other Halifax did not treat Cumberland with the consideration he deserved, considering the assiduous attention which the latter had always paid to the Statesman's public and private affairs. But Cumberland did not pursue him with bitter animosity in consequence; on the contrary, he behaved with dignity and magnanimity. One of the best and most discriminating passages in Cumberland's prose is this, in which he describes the character of his patron Halifax: "I am persuaded he was formed to be a good man, he might also have been a great one: his mind was large, his spirit active, his ambition honourable: he had a carriage noble and imposing; his first approach attracted notice, his consequent address ensured respect: if his talents were not quite so solid as some, nor altogether so deep as others, yet they were brilliant, popular, and made to glitter in the eyes of men: splendour was his passion; his good fortune threw opportunities in his way to have supported it; his ill fortune blasted all those energies which should have been reserved for the crisis of his public fame; the first offices of State, the highest honours which his Sovereign could bestow, were showered upon him, when the spring of his mind was broken, and his genius, like a vessel overloaded with treasure, but far gone in decay, was only precipitated to ruin by the very freight that, in its better days, would have crowned it with prosperity and riches."

A little piece by Cumberland, named *The Summer's Tale,* led to a quarrel between the writer and Isaac Bickerstaff. The latter had just enjoyed great success with his operas of *Love in a Village* and *The Maid of the Mill,* and he resented as an intrusion into his own domain Cumberland's excursion in the same field. *The Summer's Tale* was powerfully supported by its music, Abel furnishing the overture, and Sebastian Bach and Doctors Arne and Arnold supplying some original compositions. It ran successfully for a time, but Bickerstaff was furious, and set all the engines of abuse to work against his rival. Cumberland carried himself well under the infliction, and wrote such a letter that it drew forth warm commendation from Garrick, and induced Bickerstaff himself to confess that he had acted unjustly. It was the quiet answer again turning away wrath. In 1769 Cumberland wrote his first comedy, *The Brothers,* which was brought out at Covent Garden. The author acknowledged his obligations in the construction of this piece to Fletcher's *Little French Lawyer.* It was well received, and held the stage until Sir Walter Scott's time, being prominent in the stock list of acting plays. The sudden assumption of spirit on the part of one of the characters, Sir Benjamin Dove, with the rapid change of another from servility to insolence is one of those incidents which will always bring down the house. A compliment to Garrick in the epilogue brought about a friendship between the actor and the dramatist; but by some observations in the prologue Cumberland incurred the hostility of a host of newspaper writers. However, what was of far more importance was the fact that the comedy kept possession of the stage, and that those famous actors, Woodward and Yates, lost no credit by appearing in it.

During two visits paid to his father at Clonfert, Cumberland planned and partially wrote his play of *The West Indian.* This comedy still remains one of the best of English stage-plays. Its incidents, plot, and characters—including the first representation of an Irish gentleman which the theatre had witnessed—are all well sustained. The West Indian is a man of generous spirit and strict honour, but with a vivacious and giddy disposition; the Irishman, who takes service under Austria, is courageous and honourable, with none of that vulgarity and those gross absurdities which generally disfigure his delineation upon the stage. While visiting his father in Ireland Cumberland made the acquaintance of the eccentric Lord Eyre, of Eyre Court, a nobleman who had never been out of Ireland in his life, and very seldom more than a few miles from Eyre Court. With him he made excursions on the Shannon, where he met with an irascible Irishman, who furnished the sketch for one of his best characters, Major O'Flaherty. Lord Eyre lived in a spacious mansion, and his table groaned with abundance; but there was no order in the place, and the slaughtered ox was hung up whole, while the hungry servitor sliced his own food off the carcase. Lord Eyre

dined early in the day, and then never left his chair till bed-time. He sat sipping his claret the whole time, passing the hours without reading or conversation. He had no liking for fresh air, and not one of the windows of the castle was made to open. But he could indoctrinate his visitor into the mysteries of cock-fighting.

On the occasion of accompanying his father to Dublin—where the Bishop was presented with the freedom of the city in a gold box—Cumberland was made an honorary LL.D. of the University.

Garrick accepted *The West Indian,* and agreed to play the principal character, but he objected to the abrupt way in which he first appeared. "Never," said he, "let me see a hero step upon the stage without his trumpeters of some sort or other." So at the actor's instigation he wrote a preparatory scene. Although all the best parts of the house were booked for several nights in succession, Cumberland offered to give his whole rights to Garrick for a picture that hung over his chimney-piece in Southampton Street. It was only a copy from a Holy Family of Andrea del Sarto, and Garrick would have closed with the offer had not the picture been a present to him from Lord Baltimore. Such was the fortune of *The West Indian* that it ran for twenty-eight successive nights without the buttress of an afterpiece—a most unusual circumstance. Garrick himself passed a panegyric upon the piece in the St. James's evening paper, and the author made a large sum of money by it. He also sold the copyright for £150 to Griffin, who averred that in a few months he sold 12,000 copies of the work.

Cumberland now entered the lists of controversy, and vindicated the insulted character of his grandfather, Dr. Richard Bentley. In a pamphlet, which went through two large editions, he successfully repelled the charges of Bishop Lowth; and when Hayley, the biographer of Cowper, made merciless and uncivil sport with Dr. Bentley's character, he neatly turned the tables upon him by publishing a copy of verses by Hayley of a most laudatory character. Cumberland gives us several graphic pictures of celebrated men *en deshabille.* For example, there was Soame Jenyns, who wrote verses upon dancing, and prose upon the origin of evil; yet he was a very indifferent metaphysician, and a worse dancer. He was ill-favoured in appearance, for his eyes protruded like lobsters, and between them and his nose there was room for a large wen; yet this was the man who said when Gibbon published his immortal history, that he wondered anybody so ugly could write a book. But Jenyns had a brevity of expression, that was sometime very pointed, as when speaking of the difference between laying out money upon land or purchasing into the funds, he remarked, "One was principal without interest, and the other interest without principal." Then we have a picture of Garrick on one occasion, found by his friends in a back yard, acting a turkey-cock to a black boy, who was capering for joy, and continually crying out, "Massa Garrick do so make me laugh: I shall die with laughing." Once Cumberland and Garrick had gone to dine with Foote, the dramatist, who was never very particular in flaying his friends with ridicule. A certain Sir Robert Fletcher made a fourth at the merry party, and after he had left, as Foote thought—though he was only hiding behind a screen—Foote began to make merry at his expense. But it appeared to be a case of the biter bit. Appearing from behind the screen, Sir Robert said: "I am not gone, Foote; spare me till I am out of hearing; and now, with your leave, I will stay till these gentlemen depart, and then you shall amuse me at their cost, as you have amused them at mine."

The next dramatic venture of Cumberland was **The Fashionable Lover,** a drama which he regarded as of a moral, grave, and tender cast, inasmuch as he discovered in it sentiments laudably directed against national prejudice, breach of trust, seduction, gaming, and the generally dissipated tendencies of the age. But it did not please the critics, and Cumberland, sensitive and irritable, replied to them so copiously that Garrick called him "the man without a skin." At this period Cumberland met for the first time Oliver Goldsmith, of whom he draws a just portrait with his foibles and his genius. Speaking of him as a poet, he says, "There must be bulk, variety, and grandeur of design to constitute a first-rate poet. 'The Deserted Village,' 'Traveller,' and 'Hermit' are all specimens beautiful as such, but they are only birds' eggs on a string, and eggs of small birds too. One great magnificent *whole* must be accomplished before we can pronounce the maker to be a king among poets." Goldsmith was earning money from the publishers by writing on natural history, when he hardly knew an ass from a mule, or a turkey from a goose. Cumberland admired Dr. Johnson, though he believed necessity and not inclination was the spur to most of his literary labours. "He would have put up prayers for early rising, and lain in bed all day, and with the most active resolutions possible, been the most indolent mortal living. He was a good man by nature, a great man by genius." Over the tea-table he was unrivalled in the brilliancy of his wit, the flow of his humour, and the energy of his language." Cumberland's lines upon Johnson are happy in defining the great lexicographer's characteristics:—

> Herculean strength and a stentorian voice,
> Of wit a fund, of words a countless choice;
> In learning rather various than profound,
> In truth intrepid, in religion sound;
> A trembling form and a distorted sight,
> But firm in judgment and in genius bright;
> In controversy seldom known to spare,
> But humble as the Publican in prayer;
> To more than merited his kindness, kind,
> And, though in manners harsh, of friendly mind;
> Deep tinged with melancholy's blackest shade,

> And, though prepar'd to die, of death afraid:
> Such Johnson was; of him with justice vain,
> When will this nation see his like again?

The idea of Goldsmith's poem of *Retaliation* arose out of a previous meeting at St. James's coffee house, where a number of distinguished men assembled, after dining at Cumberland's and Sir Joshua Reynolds's. Edmund Burke suggested that extempore epitaphs should be written, and Garrick at once dashed off a valedictory poem to poor Goldsmith, little imagining that he would be the first in reality, as in jest, to be committed to the grave. Garrick's was not a kindly effort, and, by way of counteracting it, Cumberland wrote one of a more serious and, at the same time, complimentary character, which closed with the line, "All mourn the poet, I lament the man." Goldsmith was much touched by this, and kept repeating the line over to himself; and at the next meeting he produced the famous poem in which he paid his fine tribute to Cumberland. Death soon made havoc in the dramatist's family, as well as amongst his friends, for he lost within a very short space both his father and his mother. Being ill himself at the time at Bath, he was unable to watch over their last hours with the deep filial affection he felt for them. Some time before his death, Bishop Cumberland had been translated to the see of Kilmore.

The Choleric Man, Cumberland's fourth comedy, was brought out by Garrick, and among those who performed in it were Mrs. Abington, then in the height of her fame, and Messrs. King, Aikin, and Weston. The chief point in the comedy, which was formed on the plan of Terence's *Adelphi,* was the striking contrast between two brothers—one a courtly gentleman, the other a rustic booby. There was a good deal of humour in the piece, but the last three Acts dragged heavily. As is often the case, being inferior work, the author had a manifest partiality for it, and rated it amongst his best pieces. Cumberland next had the temerity to produce a new version of Shakespeare's *Timon of Athens.* He observes respecting this: "Barry played the part of Timon, and Mrs. Barry that of Evanthe, which was engrafted in the original for the purpose of writing up the character of Alcibiades. As the entire part of Evanthe and, with very few exceptions, that of Alcibiades are new, the author of this alteration has much to answer for." The public apparently thought so too, for the play was not popular, and it has perished in the waters of Lethe. Let us not fish it out from thence to vex the spirit of the dramatist.

To satisfy Moody, a noted performer of Irish characters, Cumberland wrote **The Note of Hand, or A Trip to Newmarket,** which was the last piece of his produced by Garrick before the latter disposed of his property in Drury Lane Theatre, and withdrew from stage management. Shortly afterwards our author produced his tragedy of **The Battle of Hastings,** with Henderson in the part of Edgar Atheling. The drama was ill adapted to the stage, and it may be relegated to a deserved obscurity. Meanwhile Cumberland was not neglecting business. He was still a subaltern in the Board of Trade, but when Lord George Germain took the seals of the Colonial Department, he interested himself in procuring the post of Secretary for Cumberland, who thus unexpectedly found himself comfortably provided for. On various occasions during the conflict with America, the new Secretary manifested a zeal which was not unprofitable for his friend and patron. At this time Cumberland took a house at Tetworth, in order to be near his friend Lady Frances Burgoyne, sister of his old patron, Lord Halifax, who had just passed away. Here, to introduce the compositions of a promising young musician named Butler, he wrote *Calypso* and *The Widow of Delphi*; but the public failed to respond with enthusiasm to his efforts.

In the year 1780, Cumberland went on a secret mission to Spain. He had discovered certain machinations by French and Spanish agents against England, and went out to counteract them. He was accompanied by his wife and daughters, and sailed with Sir William Bunbury in the *Milford* frigate. The vessel was nearly destroyed on two occasions; first by a storm, secondly by an engagement with the enemy. Mrs. Cumberland seems to have behaved with great fortitude, and when the dangers of the seas were over, the dramatist composed a song upon the victory won by the British frigate. The vessel, however, was thrown out of its course, and after landing at Belem Castle, Cumberland and his family visited Buenos Ayres for a time, and eventually sailed for Spain. He reached the Spanish capital at a time most unfavourable for negotiations, for the Lord George Gordon riots were exciting great alarm in London. After a series of interesting adventures in Spain, Cumberland was obliged to return to England without having accomplished his mission, being also about £5,000 out of pocket. He memorialised Lord North for redress, but could obtain no adequate compensation.

Shortly afterwards, the Board of Trade, as then constituted, was abolished under a Bill brought in by Edmund Burke. Cumberland was now set adrift upon a compensation which, though much nearer to an equivalent than what he had received upon his Spanish claims, was yet hardly a moiety of the salary of which he had been deprived. His means being thus straitened, he reduced his establishment, and went to live at Tunbridge Wells, then a very fashionable resort. Considering the rapid means of communication existing at this day, it is amusing to read these observations by our author upon Tunbridge Wells, a town distant only thirty-four miles from London: "Its vicinity to the capital brings quick intelligence of all that passes there; the morning papers reach us before the hour of dinner, and the evening ones before breakfast the next day; whilst between the arrival of the general post and its departure, there is an interval of twelve hours; an accommodation in point of correspondence that even London cannot boast of." Nor would wish to boast of, London might add. The new denizen of Tunbridge found the place very healthful and beautiful, and was never tired of singing its praises, and of eulogising the Men of Kent for their physical attractions, their courage, and their moral sentiments.

In 1782 Cumberland published his ***Anecdotes of Eminent Spanish Painters,*** a work which was interesting and curious enough for the general mass of readers, as up to this period there had been no such regular history of the Spanish school in the English language. Moreover, when the author added to it an authentic catalogue of the paintings in the royal palace at Madrid, he gave the world what it had not seen before, as that catalogue was the first that had been made, and one undertaken by special permission of the King of Spain. The author's comedy of *The Walloons* was brought out at Covent Garden Theatre, with Henderson in the chief part. Henderson seems to have been a man of great parts away from the stage. He was widely read, had a brilliant wit, and no mean power of versification. On the stage he was greatly admired, his Falstaff, Shylock, Sir Giles Overreach, & c., being striking impersonations. When Cumberland proposed to write something for him, he asked that the character should be after the cast of Congreve's *Double Dealer*. "Make me a fine, bold-faced villain," he said, "the direst and the deepest in nature I care not, so you do but give me motives, strong enough to bear me out, and such a prominency of natural character, as shall secure me from the contempt of my audience; whatever other passions I can inspire them with will never sink me in their esteem." The dramatist fulfilled his request, and also conceived for him the character of Lord Davenant in *The Mysterious Husband,* in which he achieved a conspicuous success. On the last night of this play, King George III. and his Queen were present, and Henderson's agonies were such in the concluding scene, where he died upon the stage, that realistic spectacles of this kind were for some time afterwards banished from the boards.

The Observer, a collection of moral, literary, and familiar essays by Cumberland, appeared in 1785. These essays contain by far his best efforts in prose. In comparisons like this, for example, he shows discrimination and judgment as a critic:—

> I believe there is no ancient poet that bears so close a resemblance in point of genius to any of the moderns, as Æschylus bears to Shakespeare: the comparison might afford a pleasing subject to a man of learning and leisure; if I was farther to compare the relation in which Æschylus stands to Sophocles and Euripides, with that of Shakespeare to any of our later dramatists, I should be inclined to put Sophocles in the line with Rowe, and Euripides with Lillo.

The following is a really eloquent passage upon the Athenian stage:—

> The spirit of a free people will discover itself in the productions of their stage; the comic drama, being a professed representation of living manners, will paint these likenesses in stronger or in fainter colours, according to the degree of licence or restraint which may prevail in different places, or in the same place at different periods. We are now upon the particular era in the Athenian constitution, when it began to feel such a degree of control under the rising power of the Macedonian princes, as put a stop to the personal licentiousness of the comic poets. If we are to consider Athens only as the capital seat of genius, we must bewail this declension from her former state of freedom, which had produced so brilliant a period in the annals of her literature; but speak of her in a political sense, and it must be acknowledged that, whatever restraints were put upon her liberty, and however humbling the disgraces were which she incurred, they could not well be more than she merited by her notorious abuse of public prosperity, and more ungrateful treatment of her best and most deserving citizens. When the thunder of oratory was silenced, the flashes of wit were no longer displayed. Death stopped the impetuous tongue of Demosthenes, and the hand of power controlled the acrimonious muse of Aristophanes.

One more play by Cumberland, **The Arab,** Henderson took part in, and shortly afterwards he died, in the full vigour of his talents, and the meridian of his fame. "Garrick died also, and was followed to the Abbey by a long-extended train of friends, illustrious for their rank and genius, who truly mourned a man, so perfect in his art, that Nature hath not yet produced an actor worthy to be called his second." Continuing his reminiscences, Cumberland says: "I saw old Samuel Johnson standing beside his grave, at the foot of Shakespeare's monument, and bathed in tears: a few succeeding years laid him in earth, and though the marble shall preserve for ages the exact resemblance of his form and features, his own strong pen has pictured out a transcript of his mind, that shall outlive that, and the very language which he laboured to perpetuate." Eight years after the loss of Johnson, Sir Joshua Reynolds died. "When he was lost to the world, his death was the dispersion of a bright and luminous circle of ingenious friends, whom the elegance of his manners, the equability of his temper, and the attraction of his talents, had caused to assemble round him as the centre of their society. In all the most engaging graces of his art; in disposition, attitude, employment, character of his figures, and above all, in giving mind and meaning to his portraits, if I were to say Sir Joshua never was excelled, I am inclined to believe so many better opinions would be with me, that I should not be found to have said too much."

Romney went some years after Reynolds. It would be impossible to say which was the nobler portrait painter, but Reynolds finished his course happy and respected, Romney his in a sad and truly pathetic manner. Cumberland knew Romney well, and when he first saw him he was painting three-quarter portraits for eight guineas. The dramatist was the first person to sit to him at the voluntarily higher charge of ten guineas. In considerably less than a century after his death one of his works fetched £3,045 in London. Romney was of a shy and studious nature, with a touch of hypochondria. He was both the rival and the antithesis of Reynolds. "He was at once so eager to begin, and so slow in finishing his portraits, that he was for ever disappointed of receiving payment for them by the casualties and revolutions in the families they were designed for—so many of his sitters were *killed off,* so many favourite ladies were dismissed, so many fond wives divorced, before he would bestow half an hour's pain upon their petticoats, that his unsaleable stock was immense, whilst with a little more regularity and decision he would more than have doubled his fortune, and escaped an infinitude of petty troubles that disturbed his temper. At length, exhausted rather by the languor than the labour of his mind, this admirable artist retired to his native county in the north of England, and there, after hovering between life and death, neither wholly deprived of the one nor completely rescued by the other, he continued to decline, till at last he sank into a distant and inglorious grave." His fame, however, is now as assured as that of the great Sir Joshua himself.

Cumberland produced at Drury Lane his tragedy of **The Carmelite,** with Mrs. Siddons in the part of the Lady of Saint Valori, and the great Kemble, who was then at the commencement of his career, in the character of the youthful Montgomeri. But, good as was the acting, and by no means indifferent the play, the theatrical world was greatly agitated at this time by the appearance of Master Betty, the Infant Roscius. Cumberland is very severe upon this child of fortune, and the way in which he was foisted upon the public. Our author now began to write less and less for the stage, and he was greatly distressed by its apparent symptoms of degradation. But the drama has its ups and downs in every age, and will continue to do so until the end of time. Sometimes it is a slave to buffoonery, sometimes to the shapely forms of the burlesque, and the latter invariably means a negation of the intellect. But it manages after these visitations to pull itself together again, and take a new lease of life. For that reason, it did not sink into eclipse after Cumberland gave up writing for it, neither will it expire because of the present rage for frivolity.

The comedy of **The Natural Son,** brought out with Miss Farren in the principal character, was assailed by Cumberland's critics with a bitterness which it did not deserve. The performers themselves felt this, and manfully supported its interests. It certainly has many witty passages which, if penned by a Sheridan, would have elicited hearty applause. One only of many may be cited. One society lady, expostulating with another as to reading being destructive to the complexion, remarks: "Dr. Calomel says that a lady, to preserve her beauty, should not even think; he has wrote a book purposely to dissuade people from reading." *"Every book he writes will do that,"* exclaims the other. Another comedy, ***The Impostors,*** followed ***The Natural Son,*** the principal characters in the former being sustained by Baddeley, Palmer, and Mrs. Jordan.

We now find Cumberland essaying a new vein, and publishing in 1789 his first novel, ***Arundel.*** It was very rapidly composed; but as the scene was laid partly in college and partly at court, and treated of incidents and characters in high life, the author was able to draw upon his recollections, and paint vigorously what he had felt and witnessed. The ladies of the story were sometimes placed in critical situations, but he brought them safely through their trials, and married them respectively to the men of their choice. This novel was followed in a few years by another entitled ***Henry,*** founded upon Fielding's model. But although the author laboured at it carefully, he was not successful. The fact is, he was unable to describe low life truthfully, which is a more difficult feat than the delineation of individuals in a more refined sphere. Yet Scott praised the character of Ezekiel Dow, a Methodist preacher, as not only an exquisite but a just portrait. But while it may be faithful enough, it cannot compare with Fielding's *Parson Adams,* a worthy of most natural simplicity of mind and heart, learned and human. Alluding to another peculiarity of Cumberland as a novelist, Scott says: "He had a peculiar taste in love affairs, which induced him to reverse the natural and usual practice of courtship, and to throw upon the softer sex the task of wooing, which is more gracefully, as well as naturally, the province of the man." There was also a want of delicacy and propriety in these wooing scenes. A third novel, ***John de Lancaster,*** written by Cumberland in his declining years, was far inferior to its predecessors, and has rightfully sunk into oblivion. Two plays still remain to be mentioned, which will do more for his permanent fame than his novels, and these are ***The Wheel of Fortune*** and ***The Jew.*** These and ***The West Indian*** are by far the ablest of his dramatic productions.

One more field Cumberland strayed into, that of epic poetry, but without success. He lacked the genius for compositions of this high type, which require something more than a mere flow of turgid eloquence, or even a display of taste and erudition. His first epic, ***Calvary,*** was a poem in eight books, published in 1792. Dr. Nathan Drake, who had some pretensions as a literary critic, described it as "a work imbued with the genuine spirit of Milton, and destined, therefore, most probably to immortality." But, alas! Drake was mistaken; and so was Cumberland too, in imagining that Drake's eulogy had obtained for the poem a place amongst the great British classics. ***The Exodiad,*** the dramatist's second venture in epic poetry, was written in conjunction with Sir James Bland Burgess. We may agree with the joint authors that the leading of the Israelites out of Egypt to the death of Moses upon Mount Horeb, contains all that is necessary for the production of a grand and sacred epic poem; but that is a very different thing from saying that Cumberland and Bland Burgess produced it. On the contrary, they do not pilot metaphorically the Jews out of Egypt with that efficiency and Miltonic grandeur which alone are sufficient to justify them in the eyes of posterity.

Cumberland was still living when Pitt was stricken down by the hand of death, and Fox speedily followed him. He paid a warm tribute to the extraordinary qualities of those celebrated men, but wisely deprecated the idea that the sun of England was bound to set in consequence. Napoleon was still disturbing Great Britain and Europe; but it seems to me that the following is an admirable passage, where Cumberland points out the true nature of our national powers of resistance:—

> We should recollect that it is upon the general spirit of our countrymen that we rest our confidence; when Nelson breathed his last, be breathed out nothing but his own brave soul; our fleets are not become less terrible to our enemies because he no longer lives to command them: if it were so, it were time indeed to withdraw from the contest, for there is one at no great distance from us, who is fearfully and anxiously alert to watch our waverings, and engraft his own advantages upon them; but as the courage of our soldiers has recently chastised his arrogance, so I trust that the harmony of our councils will disappoint his artifice, and enable our nation to maintain that attitude, which alone is worthy of its character, and consistent with its security.

Thus it has ever been with England, and thus we trust it ever will be, that with the time of crisis comes the master-spirit to guide her through her dangers and her perplexities.

Having outlived all his early friends, Cumberland died on the 7th of May, 1811, in his eightieth year. He had survived Goldsmith by nearly forty years, Johnson by twenty-seven years, Soame Jenyns by twenty-four years, Garrick by thirty-two years, Reynolds by nineteen years, and Bubb Dodington (Lord Melcombe) by nearly fifty years. He was thrown into contact with most of the distinguished men of his time, which was partly owing to his official, and partly to his dramatic and social connections.

As a writer, Cumberland was not great; he was not even of the second rank, if we count men like Goldsmith and Sheridan in that degree; but he frequently wrote with effect, and invariably as a scholar and a gentleman. Like too many people, he tried to succeed in too many things, and has in consequence just missed high distinction, alike as a poet, a novelist, and a dramatist. Goldsmith's comparison of him with Terence might pass muster as a compliment, but certainly could not be defended on the score of accuracy. No doubt the later dramatist's methods were framed on those of Terence, but in all the latter's great literary qualities Cumberland was but a shadow of him. Where is that pure and perfect style which have caused some eminent critics to class Terence with Cicero, Cæsar, and Lucretius? Where the fine individualisation of character, the cosmopolitanism, the metrical skill, the coruscating wit, the exquisite pathos?

Cumberland's *Memoirs* are garrulous, but interesting, though some of his stories and recollections require taking with a considerable grain of salt. But he is so overshadowed by his contemporaries, that something less than justice has been done to his literary powers. In private life he was all that was excellent and sincere; he had varied stores of information, which he was never backward in imparting; and he was ever moved by a genuine consideration for the claims and feelings of others.

George M. Baker (essay date June 1911)

SOURCE: Baker, George M. "An Echo of Schiller's *Räuber* in England." *Modern Language Notes* 26, no. 6 (June 1911): 171-72.

[*In the following essay, Baker examines similarities between Friedrich Schiller's 1782 play* Die Räuber *and Cumberland's* Don Pedro.]

Recent investigation has shown that Schiller's *Räuber* called forth very few imitations in England. In spite of four translations between 1790-1800, one of which passed through four editions, there appeared very few native tragedies which, either in plot or diction, followed directly in its track. Thomas Rea[1] mentions only two plays which owe their origin to Schiller's drama, Holman's *Red Cross Knights,* 1799, and Gandy's "Lorenzo," 1823. The reason for this poverty of imitation is not far to seek. The striking characteristics of the *Robbers,* revolutionary sentiment and extravagant diction rendered it popular with liberal readers, but at the same time subjected it to the veto of the dramatic censor. It could reach the English stage only in a mutilated form. This is what happened to it at the hands of Holman, who diluted the sentiments and substituted a melodramatic for a tragic catastrophe.

To these plays mentioned by Rea may be added a third, Richard Cumberland's *Don Pedro,* which, though not a professed imitation, bears a resemblance close enough to stamp it as an offspring of the *Robbers.* An outline of the plot will show that Cumberland seized upon certain external characteristics of Schiller's play, which appealed to him because of their dramatic effectiveness, and upon these as a framework constructed a romantic drama which preserves little of the vigor and strength of the original.

Don Pedro, called El Diablo, the son of a Spanish nobleman, has been discarded by his family on account of his liberal principles and savage character. He joins a band of robbers, and by his superior vices is raised to the dignity of being their leader. Henrique, his brother, is the very antithesis of Don Pedro and the embodiment of all that is good and amiable. He falls by chance into the hands of the robbers, is stabbed, and left for dead by his brother. Pedro now disguises himself in Henrique's clothes and gains admission to the house of his uncle, who, believing him to be Henrique, is about to bestow upon him the hand of his daughter Celestina; but Celestina has a dream in which she is apprised of the villainy of Pedro and his supposed murder of Henrique. But the father will not be convinced by any such flimsy evidence. An inquiry concerning the supposed murder of Henrique is instigated by the inquisitor. Nicholas, a messenger to whom Henrique had given a letter recommending that his brother should take flight before his infamy should be revealed, is condemned. The evidence is supplied by Pedro, who represents that he, as Henrique, had written the letter and that Nicholas had robbed him. But the real Henrique has followed after his messenger, and relates to the inquisitor the true state of affairs. Nicholas is set free, Henrique is joined to Celestina and Don Pedro, crowded to the wall, commits suicide.

Cumberland is indebted to Schiller not so much for the details of the plot, as for the idea of the banditti, the hostility between the two brothers and, above all, for the general characteristics of Don Pedro, bearer of the title rôle. In his person the author combined the worst characteristics of both Karl and Franz Moor, resulting in an enormity so unnatural and grotesque that the human element is scarcely recognizable. He is, like Karl Moor, a free, unrestrained spirit, has Karl's disregard for established custom and social order and finally falls a prey of his own pernicious appetites and desires. There is, however, in his character, no suggestion of the human and pathetic side of Karl's nature, his intense love for Emilia and his father, his ultimate regret for the waywardness of his life and his fatalistic conviction that he was the victim of inevitable circumstances. For these redeeming qualities are substituted Franz's cunning and cruelty, unscrupulousness, and atheism. The fusion of the two brothers Karl and Franz into one character made it necessary to create a new figure, Henrique, who is the virtuous and injured lover of the conventional type. Schiller's style is reflected in Cumberland's diction by the employment of extravagant language calculated to express violent emotion. It is, however, a feeble echo of his model and has the effect of bombast and inflation. We are conscious that behind the words there is no convincing personality, and behind the personality no burning experience in the author's life.

Don Pedro was produced for the first time at the Haymarket Theatre July 26, 1796, and met with little success. It was announced for a second representation with a "mixture of applause and approval." After four performances it was taken off and never revived. That Cumberland himself was not very well satisfied with his effort may be inferred from the fact that he scarcely mentions it in his ***Memoirs.***

Note

1. Schiller's *Dramas and Poems in England*, 1906.

Ernest Bernbaum (essay date 1915)

SOURCE: Bernbaum, Ernest. "Kelly, Goldsmith, Mrs. Griffith, and Cumberland: 1768-1772." In *The Drama of Sensibility: A Sketch of the History of English Sentimental Comedy and Domestic Tragedy, 1696-1780*, pp. 224-46. Boston: Ginn and Company, 1915.

[*In the following excerpt, Bernbaum offers a critical analysis of Cumberland's* The West Indian. *Bernbaum argues that the play marks a watershed moment in Cumberland's career, while also representing a significant step forward in the development of sentimental dramatic comedy.*]

Extraordinary enthusiasm greeted Cumberland's ***The West Indian*** (19 January, 1771), which was performed twenty-eight nights in its first season, and survived longer than any other sentimental comedy of this period. Its author, conscious that it would always be considered his masterpiece, recorded in his ***Memoirs***[1] the place and the circumstances of its composition with a particularity and seriousness resembling Gibbon's on an incomparably worthier occasion. Making some allowance for Cumberland's vanity, one may grant that he had reason to be proud of his achievement. He surpassed the merits of his previous play, and repeated its faults only in a lesser degree. Again he constructed, by borrowing and ingeniously rearranging old themes, a plot that was thronged with action. He conducted familiar figures,—an heiress courted by a poor young man; a father in disguise watching the career of his son, the issue of a clandestine marriage; the son reformed through love for a virtuous girl,—through varying scenes that were never inactive and that seemed new. As in ***The Brothers,*** he had not leisure to express the emotions of his characters in detail. He managed, however, more frequently and forcefully than heretofore, to find opportunity to voice those emotions in well-worded, though somewhat platitudinous, sentiments. To the serious characters he added some that were by turns comic and villainous, including a female Puritan, who, it is interesting to observe, was despised because "her heart is flint." He combined anew those elements which recent history had shown to be popular, and was careful not to repeat any of the unappreciated experiments made by his rivals.

Though a sedulous observer of conventions in vogue, Cumberland was not destitute of originality and enterprise. He perceived that the sentimental dramatists had not carried their idealization of life far enough. He thought that the goodness of human nature should henceforth be illustrated, not only by those types of character which had been repeatedly exalted, but also by those which had been disregarded or treated in comic and disdainful fashion. This programme, an intelligent and sincere one, he described in his ***Memoirs*** as follows:

> I fancied there was an opening for some originality, and an opportunity for showing at least my good will to mankind, if I introduced the characters of persons who had been usually exhibited on the stage as the butts for ridicule and abuse, and endeavored to present them in such lights as might tend to reconcile the world to them, and them to the world. I thereupon looked into society for the purpose of discovering such as were the victims of its national, professional, or religious prejudices, in short, for those suffering characters which stood in need of an advocate; and out of these I meditated to select and form heroes for my future dramas, of which I would study to make such favorable and reconciliatory delineations as might incline the spectators to look upon them with pity and receive them into their good opinion and esteem.[2]

The purpose thus undertaken resulted in an important forward step in sentimental comedy, and gave Cumberland his securest claim to remembrance.[3] First carried out in ***The West Indian,*** it guided his subsequent work, and appeared in some of his plays which, like ***The Jew*** (1794), lie beyond the chronological limits of this book.

"I took," he says, "the characters of an Irishman and a West Indian for the heroes of my plot." The public had not associated the heroic with those types. The Irish had, with inconsiderable exceptions, been portrayed on the stage as utterly ridiculous;[4] but Cumberland's Major O'Flaherty in ***The West Indian*** was, though humorous, never unattractive. Concerning him, Cumberland wrote:

> The art, as I conceive it, of finding language for the Irish character on the stage, consists not in making him foolish, vulgar, or absurd; but on the contrary, whilst you furnish him with expressions that excite laughter, you must graft upon him sentiments that deserve applause.[5]

O'Flaherty's bravery; his patriotism, voiced in such sentences as, "I am an Irishman; mine is not the country of dishonor"; his ready sympathy, which led him to "share the little modicum that thirty years' hard service had left him" with the destitute; and his fiery scorn of meanness,—these were traits as engaging as they were novel.[6]

The colonials from the West Indies were looked upon in London as ill-bred, violent, and grossly ostentatious. As such they had been lampooned in Foote's Sir Peter Pepperpot in *The Patron* (1764). When Cumberland's play was announced, it was assumed that he too would cast ridicule upon them; and some West Indians went to the theatre "to chastise the author."[7] They found, however, in Cumberland's Belcour a young gentleman who did honor to their land, whose passionate temperament was excused on the ground of the tropical climate, and of whom it was said that "his very failings set him off." He was a sentimental prodigal, with all the instinctive goodness of heart proper to such a character, and the additional charm of delightful vivacity. It was not, as Arthur Murphy complained, an accurate delineation of the manners of a West Indian planter; but it was a variation of the sentimental hero that took the town by storm.[8]

The national prejudice which Cumberland tried to overcome in his next sentimental comedy, **The Fashionable Lover** (20 January, 1772), was that against the Scotch. For the benefit of those Englishmen who still nursed a grudge against the nation that had risen against them in 1745, Cumberland had his Colin Macleod utter this appeal:

> When you have shad the blude of the offenders, it is na' generous to revive the offense. As for mine awn particular, Heaven be my judge, the realms of England does na' haud a heart more loyal than the one I strike my hond upon![9]

The last words of the play, spoken by its Sir Friendly Moral, protested against those whose charity "never circulated beyond the Tweed," and declared: "I'd rather weed out one such unmanly prejudice from the hearts of my countrymen than add another Indies to their empire." Colin Macleod stood in marked contrast to the contemptible Scotch characters that had predominated on the stage.[10] In him the niggardliness imputed to the North Briton was shown as unselfish economy. Colin faithfully guards against extravagance in his master's household, and bestows the greater part of his wages upon poor relations. He helps to rescue the heroine of the play from a precarious situation; and he is favorably contrasted with his master, Lord Abberville, who "in a distinguished rank openly assaults innocence" while Colin "in his humble post secretly supports it."[11]

The frame into which this kindly portrait of the Scotch steward is inserted is pieced together from parts of earlier sentimental comedies like *The Foundling, The Clandestine Marriage,* and *The School for Rakes.* The heroine, Miss Aubrey, a dependant in a rich merchant's family, is beloved by the poor but deserving Tyrrel and pursued by the fashionable libertine, Lord Abberville. In the end the rake reforms; and the heroine, discovered to be an heiress, is married to her worthy lover. Most of the scenes,—like that in which Miss Aubrey, at a moment when Abberville is forcing his unwelcome attentions upon her, is surprised by his fiancée and accused of giving him encouragement,—are theatrically effective. So frequent are the turns in the plot, however, and so unusually numerous the characters with important parts, that only the greatest care for unity of action could have kept the play from disorganization. That care Cumberland did in this instance not exercise, and consequently the work leaves a confused impression.[12] His public, however, though not admiring **The Fashionable Lover** as much as **The West Indian,** overlooked its looseness of structure on account of its many vigorous scenes and appealing characters.

Notes

1. Ed. 1806, p. 114.

2. Pp. 115-116.

3. This is usually ignored, emphasis being laid upon Cumberland's moralizing,—a tendency which he shares with his rivals.

4. For example, Foigard in Farquhar's *The Beaux' Stratagem,* the Irish apprentice in Murphy's *The Apprentice,* Captain O'Cutter in Colman's *The Jealous Wife,* Patrick O'Connell in Reed's *The Register Office,* and the Irish sharpers in Colman's *The Oxonian in Town.* Exceptions are the comparatively amiable Irishmen in Thomas Sheridan's *The Brave Irishman* and Macklin's *Love à la Mode.*

5. *Memoirs,* p. 116.

6. There was difficulty about finding a suitable actor for this rôle. Cf. *Memoirs,* p. 123, and [John] Genest, [*Some Account of the English Stage from the Restoration in 1660 to 1830* (New York: B. Franklin, 1832)] V, 297-298.

7. *Memoirs,* p. 122.

8. It may be noted in passing that in this year (1771) Charles Jenner published *The Man of Family,* an adaptation of Diderot's *Le Père de Famille,* with a rather interesting preface explaining why the work seemed unsuited to the British stage.

9. Act III, scene iii.

10. For example, Macruthen in Foote's *The Englishman Returned from Paris,* Donald Macgregor in his *The Orators,* Johnny Macpherson in his *The*

Devil upon Two Sticks, the Scotch apprentice in Murphy's *The Apprentice,* and Maclaymore in Smollett's *The Reprisal.* Later than Cumberland's Colin Macleod appeared Foote's ridiculous Lady Catherine Coldstream in *The Maid of Bath*; and the absurd, though not unamiable, Rhodolpha Macsycophant in Macklin's *The Man of the World* (performed in Dublin in 1760, in London not until 1781). Macklin's play, however, preaches against provincialism.

11. Act II, scene i; Act III, scenes i, ii, v; Act V, scene ii.

12. It was probably against criticisms of this nature that he was replying in his preface when he said that the British drama, with its traditions of freedom, should not imitate the French.

Stanley T. Williams (essay date March 1921)

SOURCE: Williams, Stanley T. "The Early Sentimental Dramas of Richard Cumberland." *Modern Language Notes* 36, no. 3 (March 1921): 160-65.

[*In the following essay, Williams provides an overview of Cumberland's early plays.*]

Richard Cumberland, the dramatist, speaks in his *Memoirs* of his plays as "a long list of dramas, such as I presume no English author has yet equalled *in point of number.*" This is a statement disingenuous enough, unless we suppose Cumberland ignorant of the prolific Elizabethans, Marston, Decker, and Heywood. The dramatist is equally pompous, but more truthful when he says, later: "When I attempt to look into the mass of my productions, I can keep no order in the enumeration of them; I have not patience to arrange them according to their dates: I believe I have written at least fifty dramas published and unpublished."

Cumberland's carelessness in losing sight of his dramas has rendered a complete collection of them difficult. He himself in the *Memoirs* indexes thirty-eight dramatic pieces; Genest assigns him forty-three; *Biographia Dramatica* credits him with fifty-four; and a student more patient than the author himself may record others. Neither of the two dramatic dictionaries makes mention of a play called *The Confession,* printed in a collection of plays called *The Posthumous Dramatic Works of Richard Cumberland.* Three other plays may be attributed to Cumberland upon more or less reputable authority.[1]

The Banishment of Cicero, written about 1761, and concerned with the conspiracy of Clodius, Piso, and Gabinius against Tully, never found an audience, save

David Garrick, whose friendship for Cumberland began at this time. *Biographia Dramatica* finds the unpleasant scenes "too vicious and shocking to come within the decent clothing of tragic muse."[2]

In 1765 Cumberland ventured into a dramatic field for which he was totally unfitted. On December 6, an operetta, *The Summer's Tale,* with music by Abel, Bach, and Arne was produced at Covent Garden Theatre. The piece had a run of nine nights.[3] The play was judged a failure by the critics, but Cumberland brought it forward three years later under another name; it was altered, and acted as *Amelia* at Covent Garden on April 12, 1768. The piece was again acted, with alterations, on December 14, 1771, at Drury Lane Theatre. Mudford, in his *Life of Cumberland,* asserts that *Amelia* is a convincing proof of the dramatist's unwillingness to admit any play of his to be a failure.

On December 2, 1769, at Covent Garden Theatre, was acted *The Brothers.* "It was written," Cumberland affirms, "after my desultory manner, at such short periods of time and leisure as I could snatch from business or the society of my family . . . Neither was it any interruption, if my children were playing about me in the room."[4] The comedy was probably finished early in 1768, for a letter of March 21 of this year to Garrick can hardly refer to another play: "I have," says Cumberland, "a comedy in my possession which has never been in any hands but my own, and is, both in plot and execution, entirely new and original."[5] The offer was apparently refused, but the comedy was subsequently accepted by Covent Garden Theatre. Cumberland's happiest inspiration in the writing of *The Brothers* was a passage in the epilogue which won for him the friendship of Garrick. The play was acted about twenty-two times, and enjoyed many revivals. The popularity of *The Brothers*[6] secured for Cumberland the patronage and protection of Garrick, and definitely established him as a writer of "legitimate comedy." Its success gave him courage to begin *The West Indian. The West Indian,* acted on January 19, 1771, has been discussed in an earlier issue of this periodical.

The same year which brought forth *The West Indian* offered the first of Cumberland's adaptations of Shakespeare. *Timon of Athens* was acted at Drury Lane on December 4, 1771. This play was followed on January 20, 1772, at the same playhouse, by *The Fashionable Lover.* This production, a comedy of manners with a Scotch hero, found favor second only to that of *The West Indian. The Fashionable Lover* was acted, at its first appearance, about fifteen times. There were two revivals of the play at Covent Garden, on May 9, 1786, and April 9, 1808. A performance followed on December 8, 1808, at Bath, and a revival occurred at Drury Lane in 1818, seven years after the author's death. Cumberland was partial to *The Fashionable Lover,* and openly prefers it in the Prologue to either *The Brothers* or *The West Indian,* saying to the audience:

> Two you have reared; but between you and me,
> This youngest is the fav'rite of the three.

"I confess," Cumberland says in the **Memoirs,** "I flattered myself that I had outgone *The West Indian* in point of composition."

The Note of Hand,[7] a farce, was acted at Drury Lane on February 9, 1774, and later on October 19, at the same theatre, *The Election,* "the production of a hasty hour."[8] "Considered as a literary composition," says *Lloyd's Evening Post* of October 21, "this interlude is the most execrable we ever met with," but declares that it is timely: "As all Election matter depends upon being well timed than well written, we doubt not it will be a favorite with the audience when it is more perfect in the Performance, as it really has a very good stage effect." *The Election* manifests Cumberland's usual idealistic tendency: "The author flatters himself it breathes throughout that freedom and independency which is ever so grateful to us all tempered with that loyalty and harmony which is so necessary to promote the general happiness."[9]

The Choleric Man, produced at Drury Lane on December 19, 1774, was another venture of the same year. A character named Old Nightshade bore the brunt of the critics' assaults, and seemed to violate all the decorum of sentimental comedy. Davies denounced him as "a wretch without the least tincture of humanity," and one who was "fit for no place but Bedlam,"[10] and *The St. James Chronicle,* after praising his analogues in the *Adelphi, L'École des Maris,* and *The Squire of Alsatia,* almost shouts that he is "a despicable Character, made up of Noise, Nonsense, Outrage, and Madness."[11] "We can scarcely recognize," says the dramatic critic of *Lloyd's Evening Post* of December 19, "the nature and humour exhibited in the paternal severity of Terence's Demea in the grim distortions and wild ravings of Old Nightshade." "Nightshade," says Arthur Murphy, ". . . is in one continued rage from beginning to end. The author should have considered that no man lives in a perpetual whirlwind of passion. . . . If Mr. Cumberland," concludes Murphy, "had copied nature, the audience would have had the pleasure resulting from variety; and the fits and starts of his angry boy might have helped to retard, and, at times, to forward the main business of the plot."[12]

Young Nightshade, who reminds the reader of Tony Lumpkin, was thought "too knowing and too shrewd," at least for a "Country Put;" Gregory fell below the standard set in *The Squire of Alsatia;* and—alas! for Cumberland's learning!—Young Manlove was reckoned "but a faint copy of the ingenious Æschines."[13]

The Battle of Hastings was finally accepted by Sheridan, it is supposed, only by the grace of Garrick's influence. The hand of the universal mender of plays is apparent upon every page of the tragedy, and, as usual, Cumberland is amusingly busy, revising, and rewriting. We have, at first, Cumberland's sour thanks for Garrick's candid opinion of an epilogue, with the enclosure of another, fortified by a host of apologies, and a conclusion saying that he "wrote it post-haste directly upon reading Garrick's letter." Of the amendments Cumberland writes: "The whole which you recommend is done: Edwina's simile of the Tower (act the first) is made very impassioned; the conclusion of the fourth act was before your criticism came to hand entirely reformed, and I owed the correction to Miss Young's protest against the simile of the lightning;[14] your observation tallying with what I had done was particularly pleasing."[15] The anticipated criticism is characteristic. The letters reflect Sheridan's and Cumberland's uneasiness. "We have as yet had no rehearsal," he writes Garrick, "nor can I tell when we shall. . . . Without some prudence and patience I should never have got the ladies cordially into their business, nor should I not only have avoided a jar with Mr. Smith,[16] but so far have impressed him in my favor as to draw an offer from him (though too late) of taking the part of Edwin."[17] Cumberland wrote Henderson, the actor, concerning the role. On October 25, 1777, Henderson replies to Cumberland: "I am much obliged and honoured by your intelligence respect the Battle of Hastings. . . . As soon as I have gone through the Roman Father, which I now have in rehearsals, I shall dedicate my studies to the Battle."[18] Early in January Henderson is well established as Edgar, for Cumberland tells Garrick that "Henderson returns Saturday next, and we shall have three practices this week."[19] The success of Henderson in Edgar was dubious, and Cumberland chose to blame his friend rather than the heavy and unnatural character he himself had created. "He did not possess," says the dramatist, "the graces of person or deportment, and that character demanded both; an actor might have been found who with inferior abilities would have been a fitter representative for it."[20] "I am not surprised," writes J. H. Pye, in regard to the failure of this actor in *The Battle of Hastings,* "at the fate of Henderson."[21] The first performance of *The Battle of Hastings* was on January 24, 1778. It was acted twelve times.[22]

During the same year in which *The Battle of Hastings* was acted, Cumberland produced *The Princess of Parma,* a tragedy. This play was acted privately, on October 20 and October 21, 1778, in Mr. Hanbury's theatre at Kelmarsh, Northamptonshire. Cumberland himself was one of the *dramatis personæ.*

Notes

1. *The Elders,* a farce acted at Kelmarsh, Northamptonshire; *The Days of Geri,* in a list compiled by

Sir Walter Scott; *Palamon and Arcite,* in manuscript form in the British Museum.

2. *Biographia Dramatica* [(London: Longman, et. al., 1812)], III, 47.

3. Further comment upon *The Summer's Tale* may be found in *The Gentleman's Magazine* for December, 1765, *The Universal Magazine* for December, 1765, *The Universal Museum* for December, 1765, *The London Magazine* for December, 1765, and *The Royal Magazine* for December, 1765. All these periodicals contain specimens of the lyrics of the musical comedy.

4. *Memoirs* [(London, 1806)], I, 264. Cumberland has a tendency to emphasize his casual method of composition. See Mudford, *Life of Cumberland* [(London: Sherwood, Neely and Jones, 1812)], p. 188.

5. *Private Correspondence of David Garrick* [(London, 1831)], I, 293. Cumberland to Garrick, March 21, 1768.

6. A version of *The Brothers* in prose may be found in Miss Macauley's *Tales of the Drama* [(Chiswick: Sherwood, Neely and Jones, 1877)], p. 239. *The Brothers* was not at first definitely known to be Cumberland's.

The Whitehall Evening Post of December 4, 1769, says: "Notwithstanding some reports to the contrary, we can assure our readers that the new Comedy called *The Brothers,* is written by——Cumberland; who possesses a considerable post in the Treasury, and is the author of a tragedy called, *The Banishment of Cicero,* and a musical Comedy, entitled *The Summer's Tale.*"

Further comment upon *The Brothers* may be found in *The Weekly Magazine* of December 14, and December 21, 1769, *Scot's Magazine* for December, 1769, Boaden, *Life of Mrs. Jordan* [(London: Bull, 1831)], II, 106, Mrs. Inchbald, *The British Theatre* [(London: Longman et. al., 1808)], p. 18.

For American productions of *The Brothers,* see Seilhamer [Philadelphia, 1888)], *History of the American Theatre,* 1749-1774, I, 330 (sometimes named *The Shipwreck*).

7. *The London Magazine,* February, 1774. See also *The Oxford Magazine,* February, 1774. Further comment upon *The Note of Hand* may be found in *The Sentimental Magazine* for February, 1774, *The Westminster Magazine* for February, 1774, *The London Chronicle* of February 10, 1774, *Memoirs,* I, 388, Mudford, *Life of Cumberland,* p. 318, and *Private Correspondence of David Garrick,* I, 621, Doctor Hoadly to Garrick, April 10, 1774.

8. *The Town and Country Magazine,* October, 1774.

9. *The Town and Country Magazine,* October, 1774.

Biographia Dramatica says that *The Election* was never printed, but *The Gentleman's Magazine* for January, 1775, contains the following item: "A new musical interlude, called the election, as it is performed at the theatre royal in Drury Lane, 8vo. 6d. Griffin."

Further comment upon *The Election* may be found in *The Universal Magazine* for October, 1774, and *The London Magazine* for October, 1774.

10. *Memoirs of the Life of David Garrick,* II, 273-4.

11. *The St. James Chronicle,* December 22, 1774.

12. *Life of David Garrick,* II, 108.

13. *The St. James Evening Chronicle,* December 22, 1774.

14. *The Town and Country Magazine* for January, 1778, complains that Cumberland, "a volunteer in the service of his favourite muse Thalia," "aims too much at the sublime, and the gods themselves often were incapable of understanding him."

15. *Private Correspondence of David Garrick,* II, 283, Cumberland to Garrick, January 4, 1778.

16. Cumberland writes Garrick: "Mr. Smith has made good my apprehensions, and refused taking any part in my tragedy but that of Edgar."

17. *Private Correspondence of David Garrick,* II, 283.

18. *Letters and Poems by the late Mr. John Henderson,* p. 293, Henderson to Cumberland, October 25, 1777.

19. *Private Correspondence of David Garrick,* II, 285, Cumberland to Garrick, Monday evening (probably February 5, 1778).

20. *Memoirs,* I, 391.

21. *Private Correspondence of David Garrick,* II, 291, J. H. Pye to Garrick, February 21, 1778.

22. [John] Genest [*Some account of the English stage from the Restoration in 1660 to 1830* (New York: B. Franklin, 1832)], VI, 6-8. See *Ibid.,* VI, 6, for a comparison of *The Battle of Hastings* with Boyce's *Harold.* Further comment upon this play may be found in *Lloyd's Evening Post* of January 26, 1778, *The London Chronicle* of January 25, 1778, *Biographia Dramatica,* III, 51, and Mudford, *Life of Cumberland,* p. 320.

Stanley T. Williams (essay date November 1921)

SOURCE: Williams, Stanley T. "The Dramas of Richard Cumberland, 1779-1785." *Modern Language Notes* 36, no. 7 (November 1921): 403-8.

[*In the following essay, Williams examines Cumberland's experiments with various dramatic styles during the early 1780s.*]

Richard Cumberland's sentimental masque, *Calypso,* was acted March 20, 1779, at Covent Garden Theatre. This play tells a moral tale of the struggle of Telemachus to resist Calypso. On a "rocky shore, wild and desart," (I, i) Calypso mourns Ulysses, and even Proteus can give no news of the wanderer. Telemachus is wrecked upon the island, and, despite the protests of Mentor, yields to Calypso. He is moved to repentance by discovering the real wickedness of Calypso, and, with the moral awakening of Telemachus, the palace of Calypso vanishes. "The plot," as *Biographia Dramatica* (III, 77) says, "is well known to every school boy and girl who has read Telemachus," and "the adventures of Telemachus, in different shapes, have already surfeited the world. Opera, masque, and Tragedy have all maintained this hero in a languishing kind of existence." *Calypso* was, however, effective as eighteenth-century stage-craft. "It has," says *The London Review* for March, "something in it picturesque and poetical, we wish we could say equally dramatic and theatrical; but in these points it is somewhat defective, altho' we think it by no means so deficient as our play-house and newspaper criticks pretend." The prophecy of *The London Magazine* for April that *Calypso* was "not likely to outlive the nine nights that include three benefits" was true, since the masque was acted but three times. *Calypso* must be set down as one more unfortunate experiment by Cumberland in a field for which he was totally unfitted.[1]

The Bondman, an adaptation of Massinger's play, was acted on October 13, 1779. It is probable that the play was offered to the world anonymously. *The Public Advertiser* of October 14 reviews it, "altered, as 'tis said, by Mr. Hall." *The Bondman* was "acted only about six nights."[2]

The failure of *The Duke of Milan,* acted November 10, 1779, at Covent Garden, marked Cumberland's third unsuccessful attempt within two years to adapt Elizabethan tragedies. Revision of the plays of Shakespeare, of Massinger, or even of Fenton, could never result with any degree of credit to Cumberland, since he was in no sense a writer of good tragedies, nor even a capable adapter of them. Exactly what he professes in his Advertisement to *Timon of Athens* he never achieves, namely, the bringing of plays "upon the stage with less violence to their authors, and not so much responsibility on his part."[3]

Cumberland now turned again to musical comedy. On February 1, 1780, Covent Garden Theatre advertised *The Widow of Delphi, or The Descent of the Deities.* The author's powers in this species of drama had not improved. *The Widow of Delphi* was performed six times.[4]

The Walloons, written during Cumberland's sojourn in Spain as ambassador, was acted April 20, 1782, at Cov-

ent Garden. On January 28, 1783, there appeared at the same theatre *The Mysterious Husband,* a good example of eighteenth-century domestic tragedy. Lord Davenant, the villain, was played by Henderson. "Well, Mr. Cumberland," Mrs. Henderson is reported to have said, "I hope at last you will allow Mr. Henderson to be good for something on the stage." "Madam," replied the poet, "I can't afford it—a villain he must be."[5] This was Henderson's third appearance as Cumberland's leading character in a tragedy. Certain lines in the prologue of *The Mysterious Husband* have interest as a possible allusion to *The Critic*:

> Now parody has ventured all its spite
> Let Tragedy resume her ancient right.[6]

The Carmelite, a so-called Gothic tragedy, was acted with some measure of success at Drury Lane on December 2, 1784. Mrs. Siddons won fame as Matilda. On the twenty-second of the same month appeared a sentimental comedy of Cumberland's, *The Natural Son.* The story of this piece follows: Blushenly, without name or fortune, but with all the other graces of a sentimental comedy hero, escapes the meshes of Phoebe, an elderly spinster, and wins, in spite of his diffidence, the hand of Lady Paragon. Rueful, moved to remorse by the virtues of his natural son, Blushenly, acknowledges him, and repents publicly of his wrong-doing. *The Natural Son* is sadly deficient in incident for a five-act play, and the December *Westminster Magazine* points out that "it must require a considerable husbandry to draw out so slight a fable into five acts." This fault, and Cumberland's ancient weakness of firing all his artillery in the first two acts, destroyed a promising comedy. "It has of late," says *The Universal Magazine* for the same month, "been remarkably the lot of the theatres to produce plays which began well, and sink both in interest and effect as they proceed. *The Natural Son* is a piece which comes within this description. The first and second acts are good ones, and though there are many happy incidents, excellent sentiments, and pointed witticisms and remarks in the third, fourth and fifth, yet considered as acts, they are by no means equal to those that precede them. It were to be wished that Mr. Cumberland had compressed his plot, and written the comedy in three acts only; all would then have been alive and interesting."

Cumberland, with undying belief that any "unequal production"[7] of his, if properly cared for, would ultimately succeed, reduced the five acts of *The Natural Son* to four, and the play in this form was acted at Drury Lane on June 10, 1794. "The omissions," says *The European Magazine,* "were chiefly the exclusion of a character called Rueful, which certainly added nothing to the merit of the play. In its present state it is much improved."[8] The worth of *The Natural Son*—and it has worth—lies partly in "well delineated character."[9] Cumberland was bold enough to use old wine. Major O'Flaherty re-appears, and is effective, although he lacks the wit of earlier days. "Upon the whole well contrived," is one judgment, though the same writer laments that "Major O'Flaherty throws sad disgrace on young Dudley,"[10] for the votaries of the early play knew the promise that "Dudley made . . . at the conclusion of *The West Indian*,"[11] and now the Major is "totally unprovided for."[12] In the production of a decade later the Major's name "was changed to Captain O'Carol."[13] *Biographia Dramatica* praises the characters of Rueful and Dumps, and *The Westminster Magazine* discerns in "Jack Husting's first interview with Sir Jeoffrey, and his address to Miss Phoebe . . . abundant humour."

The Arab, or *Alcanor,* acted March 8, 1785, at Covent Garden Theatre, has the familiar Cumberland plot: Mariamne, the former queen, having been imprisoned, the royal Augusta exults over the faded charms of her rival. Herodian, the son of Mariamne, has returned only to find his mother dethroned, while Alcanor, lost for years past in the desert, arrives as the heir-presumptive, magnificent in his simplicity, his naïveté, his fierce and generous passions. When he is made aware of the just claims of Herodian to the throne, in spite of the imprecations of Augusta, he yields the kingdom to his rival. Shortly afterwards, he learns that Glaphyra loves and is loved by Herodian. Since Alcanor has earlier saved the maiden's life, and loves her, this crisis is the supreme test of his generous nature. He wavers, sending Barzilla, who proves to be his own father, to kill Herodian, but virtue conquers, and Alcanor's suicide liberates Herodian and Glaphyra. In all likelihood, *Salome,* a lost tragedy by Cumberland, *The Arab,* as acted at Covent Garden, and *Alcanor,* as found in *The Posthumous Dramatick Works,* are successive versions of the same drama. In letters to Garrick in 1770 Cumberland describes *Salome,* and says he has made her life "twice attempted by Mariamne."[14] "If yet," he writes two months later, "the catastrophe is too shocking, by the danger in which Glaphyra is kept, I have a plan for softening that, though I am humbly of the opinion it has a very great effect as it is."[15] What became of the unfortunate *Salome* it is impossible to tell, but the mention of the characters of Mariamne, Glaphyra, and Bethanor links the lost play with both *The Arab* and *Alcanor.* Mariamne appears in *Alcanor,* Bethanor in *The Arab,* and Glaphyra in both. The relationship of *The Arab* to *Alcanor* is clear. *Biographia Dramatica* does not realize that these are essentially the same play.[16] Listed as separate plays, *The Arab* is said to have been never published, and *Alcanor* never performed. *Alcanor* is, in fact, a later evolution of *The Arab.* Of *The Arab*'s *dramatis personæ* of five characters, two, Herodian and Glaphyra, reappear in *Alcanor.* Contemporary references to incidents of *The Arab* prove that the plots were substantially alike. "There can hardly be a doubt," says Genest of *The Arab,* "that this is the T. published

in Cumberland's posthumous works as *Alcanor.*"[17] *The Arab* was acted but once. In the cast were Henderson, Lewis, Wroughton, Mrs. Bates,[18] and Miss Young. "This tragedy," says *The London Magazine* for March, 1785, "abounds in business; some of the incidents are effected by great contrivance and ingenuity. Several of the situations are as full of force as any we have observed in tragedies of a late period. Glaphira's avowal of Herodian being her lover; the confession Bathanor[19] [*sic*] makes, of his being the father of Abidah;[20] the interview between Herodian and Glaphira; and the death of Bathanor, deserve particular attention. The language is full of imagery, some of which possesses novelty. The tragedy was well got up, and the performers played with infinite spirit." At his last benefit Henderson[21] acted the part of Alcanor with success. A friend, E. T., wrote to him: "I saw in one paper, Bensley preferred to you in Horatius. I have not seen your Horatius, but I have your Alcanor, and I am sure your Horatius must be good."[22]

From this time on Cumberland's pen was never idle. During the Summer Season at the Haymarket Theatre was produced *The Country Attorney.* It was withdrawn after the fourth performance. Genest (VI, 452) gives the number of performances of *The Country Attorney* as four, but The Theatrical Register of *The Gentleman's Magazine* records six. The play was never printed, and Cumberland hardly mentions it in the *Memoirs* (II, 278). *The European Magazine* justly calls *The Country Attorney* "one of those hasty productions by which Mr. Cumberland has been gradually writing down his reputation, ever since the appearance of *The West Indian.*"[23]

Notes

1. Cumberland says that *Calypso* was written to bring Butler forward, *Memoirs* [(London, 1806)], I, 800. See *The Widow of Delphi.* Further comment upon *Calypso* may be found in the *St. James Chronicle* of March 23, 1779; *The London Chronicle* of March 22, 1779, and Genest, VI, 95.

2. *Biographia Dramatica,* [(London, Longman et al., 1812)] III, 64. Further comment upon *The Bondman* may be found in *The London Chronicle* of October 15, 1779; *Lloyd's Evening Post* of October 13, 1779, and in Boaden, *Life of Mrs. Siddons* [(London: Henry Colburn, 1827)], p. 117.

3. *Memoirs,* I, 384. The prologue of *The Duke of Milan* was said to be written *en revanche* for the attack on Cumberland in *The Critic.* Further comment upon *The Duke of Milan* may be found in *Lloyd's Evening Post* of November 15, 1779.

4. Further comment upon *The Widow of Delphi* may be found in *The Westminster Magazine* for February, 1780; *The Town and Country Magazine* for February, 1780; *The Universal Magazine* for February, 1780; *The London Chronicle* of February 2,

1780; *The Public Advertiser* of February 1, and February 2, 1780; *Biographia Dramatica*, IV, 405, Mudford, *Life of Cumberland* [(London: Sherwood, Neely and Jones, 1812)], p. 341; and [John] Genest [*Some account of the English stage from the Restoration in 1660 to 1830* (New York: B. Franklin, 1832)], VI, 146.

5. *Life of Mrs. Siddons,* p. 229.

6. Further comment upon *The Mysterious Husband* may be found in *The Lady's Magazine* for February, 1783; *The Critical Review* for February, 1783; *Aickin's Review* for 1783; Genest, VI, 268; Mudford, p. 413; Oulton, *History of the Theatres of London* [(1796)], II, 2; and Dunlap, *Life of George Frederick Cooke* [(1813)], I, 338, 341, 343.

7. *The London Chronicle,* December 25, 1784.

8. *The European Magazine,* June, 1794.

9. *Biographica Dramatica,* IV, 74.

10. *The Westminster Magazine,* December, 1784.

11. *Idem.*

12. *Idem.*

13. Genest, VI, 152.

14. *Private Correspondence of David Garrick* [(London: H. Colburn and R. Bentley, 1831-32)], I, 380, Cumberland to Garrick, January 25, 1770.

15. *Idem.,* March 17, 1770.

16. *Biographia Dramatica: The Arab,* III, 35, *Alcanor,* III, 12.

17. Genest, VI 360.

18. Mrs. Bates acted regularly at Drury Lane.

19. Bethanor = Barzilla in the play of *Alcanor.*

20. Abidah = Alcanor in the play of *Alcanor.*

21. In the *Memoirs,* II, 207, Cumberland says: "I have now in my mind's eye that look he (Henderson) gave me, so comically conscious of taking what his judgment told him he ought to refuse, when I put into his hand my tributary guineas for the few places I had taken in his theatre: 'If I were not the most covetous dog in creation,' he cried, 'I should not take your money; but I cannot help it.'"

22. *The European Magazine,* July, 1787. Further comment upon *The Country Attorney* may be found in *The Town and Country Magazine* for July, 1787; *The London Chronicle* of July 9, 1787; Adolphus, *Life of John Bannister,* I, 160; *Memoirs of Mrs. Crouch,* II, 24, 56; and Mudford, p. 547.

23. *Letters and Poems by the late Mr. John Henderson,* p. 213, E. T. to Henderson, November 13,

1777. Further comment upon *The Arab* may be found in the *Memoirs of Mrs. Crouch,* I, 238.

M. J. Landa (essay date October 1925)

SOURCE: Landa, M. J. "The Grandfather of Melodrama." *Cornhill Magazine* n.s. 59 (October 1925): 476-84.

[*In the following excerpt, Landa examines the impact of Cumberland's plays on the emergence of melodrama in England.*]

One of the persistent delusions is that melodrama is a French importation. Holcroft's *A Tale of Mystery,* produced at Covent Garden, November 13, 1802, is regularly cited as the first play of this kind staged in England. It was an adaptation of *Cœlina,* by Guilbert de Pixerécourt (1773-1844), who, according to the learned, was the inventor of this type of drama. Pixerécourt's own life might be responsible for the legend of his fatherhood. He was the son of a nobleman, was in danger of his life in the French Revolution, afterwards lived in a garret where he painted fans for two francs a day, subsequently made a fortune with some fifty-nine plays and lost it in litigation.

But six years before Holcroft's adaptation, on September 10, 1796, a play by S. J. Arnold, entitled *Shipwreck,* was produced at Drury Lane with great success, and was actually condemned by the critics as 'abounding in claptraps,' quite a modern denunciation of melodrama. Some eighteen months earlier than *A Tale of Mystery,* on February 28, 1801, J. Fawcett's *Pérouse, or Desolate Island,* based on Kotzebue's *Pérouse,* contained a good deal of dumb action with descriptive music—the principal feature of the first melodramas—and also the character of a chimpanzee! This would give Germany a claim over France. Kotzebue, too, had a melodramatic career. A diplomatist as well as a dramatist, he entered the Russian service, and was assassinated in Mannheim in 1819 for his Russian sympathies. The speed and thoroughness of the march of melodrama in England was such that, on December 5, 1803, there was produced at Drury Lane *The Caravan, or The Driver and His Dog,* in which a dog saved an infant from drowning in real water, drawing from Sheridan the witty comment that it also saved the theatre. But even if actually melodrama in its definite form came across the sea, the ground was prepared by Englishmen whose literary work influenced foreign writers, certainly Pixerécourt. Walpole's *Castle of Otranto* was written in 1765, a year after the birth of Mrs. Radcliffe, of whose wild romances *The Mysteries of Udolpho,* 1794, is the most sensational and celebrated. The greatest of these writers, 'Monk' Lewis, was born in 1775 (two years later than Pixerécourt), and his *Castle Spectre* was staged at Drury Lane in 1797.

Apart from these literary forerunners, more definite stage precursors of melodrama were the plays of Richard Cumberland (1732-1811), who was a successful dramatist before Pixerécourt saw the light. Cumberland, who lies buried in Westminster Abbey, is invariably remembered, when remembered at all, as the original of Sir Fretful Plagiary, in which character Sheridan mercilessly pilloried and immortalised him in *The Critic*. There was some measure of justification, and Garrick termed Cumberland 'the man without a skin,' owing to his sensitiveness. Nevertheless, Richard Cumberland has claims to a place in literary and dramatic history. The son of one Bishop and the grandson of another, he took a serious and even a fastidious view of his profession as playwright. He deemed the stage a pulpit for the ventilation of grievances, the denunciation of evils, and appeals on behalf of the unfavoured and unfortunate. He endeavoured to break down the prejudices against the Irishman in *The West Indian*, 1771, against the Scot in *The Fashionable Lover*, 1772, and made a still bolder plea on behalf of the Jews in *The Jew* in 1794.

He was the first to introduce purpose into drama in an age of artificiality. This undoubtedly redeems him from the charge of plagiarism levelled freely at him; his work widened the horizon of the stage and registers him as one of the pioneers of the problem play. By superimposing extraneous things on sentimental comedy, of which he regarded himself the High Priest, he laid the unmistakable foundations of melodrama. It seems only natural now that this form of play should be evolved from the sentimental comedy of the eighteenth century; for, after all, melodrama is sentimentality, crudely and vigorously expressed. Sentimental comedy, born of Colley Cibber, found in Cumberland its last and most frank exponent. As developed by him, there were divagations on the lines subsequently styled the formula of Pixerécourt. If the latter is to be termed the Father of Melodrama then is Cumberland distinctly the Grandfather. The definite form of the play in England owes more to Cumberland than to the French parent. It was Cumberland who invented the turgid dialogue, which, quite as much as the incident, gives English melodrama its special character.

Pixerécourt is credited with establishing the principle that four leading characters are essential—the hero, the villain, the persecuted heroine, and the simpleton (such as the village idiot, or stupid servant) for comic relief. These four characters, of course, are to be found long before. Shakespeare's *Othello* with Othello, Iago, Desdemona, and Roderigo at once occurs to mind. Pixerécourt, however, may have standardised them as a framework for incidents—or rather, his critics and admirers afterwards thus analysed his work. The subdivision of dramatic effort is none the less to be found in Cumberland before Pixerécourt was born. It is less conscious perhaps, but it is there, most definitely in *The Fashion-able Lover,* produced at Drury Lane, January 1772, a year before the birth of Pixerécourt. The latter divided a piece into three acts devoted to love, persecution or misfortune, and triumph. Cumberland followed the fashion of five acts, but the content of *The Fashionable Lover* conforms to the three divisions of the French writer, which are nothing novel and as inexorable in well-made drama as are exordium, argument, and peroration in a well-made speech. More important is it that in *The Fashionable Lover,* which was Cumberland's third play, deemed by the author, according to his prologue, his best, and proudly proclaimed as original, without indebtedness to any French source, the English dramatist created the much-harried heroine of melodrama and endowed her with language which may be declared to be still in use to-day. The persecuted lachrymose heroine, luxuriating in her sufferings, is completely embodied in Augusta Aubrey and enshrined in gems of perfervid threnody:

> How I am watched in this house you well know; therefore you must not stay. What you have suffered for my sake I can never forget. May your life never again be exposed on my account.

> 'Tis vain to urge my innocence to you; heaven and my own heart acquit me; I must endure the censure of the world. . . . The last surviving orphan of a noble house, I'll not disgrace it.

> Wretched, unfriended creature that I am, what shall I do?

> I have no home, no father, friend, or refuge in the world; nor do I, at this moment, fainting as I am with affliction and fatigue, know where to find a hospitable door.

> Put me, I beseech you, in some present shelter, till the labour of my hands can keep me; and hold me up but for a breathing space, till I can rally my exhausted spirits, and learn to struggle with the world.

> You have mischief in your minds, but I beseech you, leave me to my misfortunes, nor cast away a thought on a wretch like me.

> I accuse no one; I submit with patience; I am content to be the only sufferer in this business, and earnestly entreat you to desist from any altercation on my account.

> No, my lord, you've made me wretched—guilty you shall never make me.

> Why should I urge my innocence? I am unfortunate, I am poor.

> The prayer and intercession of an orphan draw heaven's righteous benediction upon you!

> I have a father, then, at last! Pardon my tears; I'm little used to happiness.

> Upon my knees I do beseech you mitigate your severity; it is my first petition; he's detected; let his conscience add the rest.

There are other melodramatic characters in this same play, equipped with similar convulsions. The villain is Bridgemore, Augusta's guardian, who robs his ward of her money. There is the long-lost father with 'The overflowings of a father's heart bless and reward you!' and his gallery-appealing denunciation of the villain, 'Raised by the bounty of my family, is this your gratitude? When, in the bitterness of my distress, I put an infant daughter in your hands, the last weak scion of a noble stock, was it to rob me you received her?—to plunder and defraud a helpless orphan, as you thought her. . . . Villain, I have the proofs!' There is the blundering, good-natured servant, a Scot, who befriends the heroine and—like the perfect comic-relief—dares to admonish his master, 'Pay your poor tradesmen; those are debts of honour,' and other comic 'foreigners,' indispensable to melodrama, in a French servant, a Welsh tutor, and a Jew. There is also a villainess, Lucy Bridgemore, who tries to ruin the reputation of the heroine; and the impulsive hero, 'I drew my sword in the defence of innocence; every man of honour would have done the same. . . . As for my poverty, in that I glory.' The entrance of the hero, or other person to put matters right at the crucial moment, is in this play, too, and virtue rewarded is the supreme tenet of Cumberland's dramaturgy.

The Fashionable Lover, if staged to-day, would seem by melodrama lovers to be a perfectly modern play.

In Cumberland's best play, *The West Indian,* produced a year earlier than Augusta's tearful Odyssey, there is a scene in which a titled lady and a lawyer plot the destruction of a will, with one of the earliest stage Irishmen overhearing and subsequently emerging from his hiding-place to snatch the document—an episode that has been the model for hundreds such in melodrama. In this play there are no fewer than three high-souled, high falutin heroes—Cumberland was young (in playwriting) and prodigal—the Irishman aforesaid, and two soldiers, father and son; whilst in the author's first play, *The Brothers,* December 1769, the hero is a sailor, with patriotic speeches of the type that made the Adelphi ring a century later:

> You now breathe the air of England—a rough reception it has given you; but be not, therefore, discouraged; our hearts are more accessible than our shores; nor can you find inhospitality in Britain, save only in our climate. . . . This I will say for my countrymen, that where you can point out one rascal with a heart to wrong you, I will produce fifty honest fellows ready and resolute to redress you. . . . One villain, however base, can no more involve a whole nation in his crimes, than one example, however dignified, can inspire it with his virtues.

This play ends with an interrupted marriage, the bridegroom-villain (the wicked squire) being confronted by his discarded wife!

There is the discarded wife again in *First Love* (Drury Lane, 1795), who, in the person of the famous Mrs. Jordan, had to utter the heartrending words, 'I am a miserable, solitary relict.' Cumberland bundled all his *clichés* into this, his poorest play, and his effeminate, quixotic hero, played by Mr. Palmer, the creator of Joseph Surface, must have revelled in such phrases as: 'May you find your happiness where mine was lost! Oh, Lady Ruby, pardon a distracted mind. . . . What she has to reveal to you, I know not: if misfortunes, you will pity them; if mistakes, you will pardon them—wronged she may be, guilty she cannot be. . . . I consider money but as dust to dust.' These sentiments are of the litany of the conventional hero of melodrama.

Poor Cumberland suffered much because of his sensitiveness to criticism; but in common fairness it must be admitted as strange that a Frenchman, not yet born when the Englishman's melodramatic bombast was being applauded in London, has been credited with something that, whatever its worth, should be attributed to an author, forgotten, although he sleeps in our national Valhalla. Study of the plays of the facile hacks of the first half of the nineteenth century, craftsmen of startling speed and precocity, leads to the irresistible conclusion that they must have written with the plays of Cumberland in front of them. They found him a well-stocked Army and Navy and Civilian Stores for stagewrights.

Frederick S. Boas (essay date 1953)

SOURCE: Boas, Frederick S. "Richard Cumberland." In *An Introduction to Eighteenth-Century Drama, 1700-1780,* pp. 301-9. Oxford: Oxford University Press, 1953.

[*In the following excerpt, Boas offers an overview of Cumberland's major dramatic works, giving a particularly close reading of the plays* The West Indian *and* The Choleric Man.]

Another dramatist who, like Kelly, made a resounding success with an early play which he never repeated was Richard Cumberland. Son of a Northamptonshire rector who later became an Irish bishop, he was born on 19 February 1732 in the house of his maternal grandfather, Richard Bentley, Master of Trinity College, Cambridge. Educated at Westminster and Trinity, he became secretary to the Earl of Halifax, whom, when Lord Lieutenant, he accompanied to Ireland in 1761. Turning later from an official to a literary and theatrical career he began with a tragedy and two comic operas, followed by a comedy, *The Brothers,* produced at Covent Garden, 2 December 1769, which showed greater promise. This was amply fulfilled in *The West Indian,* produced at Drury Lane on 19 January 1771. The title was taken from the central figure of the play, Belcour, just arrived in London as inheritor of large estates in Jamaica. He is the unacknowledged son of the prosperous merchant Stockwell, who in the opening scene confides the secret of his birth to his clerk Stukely. This is a departure from the usual convention where, as in *A Word to the Wise,* such a disclosure is not made to the audience till the end. Stockwell conceals their relationship from Belcour because he will discover much more of his real character as his merchant than as his father. In their first interview Belcour gives him an insight into its opposite aspects by his frank confession.

> I am the offspring of distress, and every child of sorrow is my brother. While I have hands to hold, therefore, I will hold them open to mankind. But, sir, my passions are my masters; they take me where they will; and oftentimes they leave to reason and to virtue nothing but my wishes and my sighs.

It is not long before he gives proofs of this self-accusation. He becomes infatuated with the beauty of a girl whom he sees by chance in the crowded London streets, and follows her home. She is Louisa Dudley, daughter of a half-pay Captain, and sister to Charles, an ensign. The mother had been the eldest daughter of Sir Oliver Roundhead who, indignant at her marrying an impecunious soldier, had cut the family out of his will. The veteran Captain, to improve his fortunes, is now seeking an exchange into a commission with full pay 'in the fatal heats of Senegambia', but needs a sum of money to equip him for the expedition. Charles appeals for this to his hard-hearted puritan aunt, Lady Rusport, to whom Sir Oliver Roundhead had left his whole estate. But his plea is in vain, though supported by her stepdaughter Charlotte who is in love with the ensign.

The Dudleys are lodging with a Mr. and Mrs. Fulmer, who are in even worse plight than themselves. Fulmer has tried different trades and failed in all. Now he has set up as a bookseller, with the result, as he complains, that 'men left off reading; and if I was to turn butcher, I believe, o' my conscience, they'd leave off eating'. Now Mrs. Fulmer is planning a more disreputable way of earning their livelihood. Meanwhile Belcour arrives in pursuit of Louisa, and, on hearing of the Captain's plight, shows that it was no boast when he called every child of sorrow his brother. He hands the astonished Captain a sealed paper containing his necessary expenses of travel in two hundred-pound notes. Thus when another veteran soldier, the Irish Major O'Flaherty, who is paying court to Lady Rusport, comes with a letter from her ordering Dudley to leave London at once, he is able to give a promise to that effect. Nor is Belcour his only would-be benefactor. In a stolen interview with Charles Charlotte entrusts him with a box containing her jewels, to be deposited with Stockwell for the accommodation of £200. The merchant agrees to send her the money but hands the jewels to Belcour to be returned to her.

During their dialogue the West Indian is transported by receiving a letter from Mrs. Fulmer telling him that she can arrange an interview with his charmer at her house. On hearing that she is the daughter of his beneficiary, the Captain, he declares that this is the end of the matter. Finding that he is 'one of your conscientious sinners', Mrs. Fulmer plays her trump card. She tells Belcour that 'sister' to Charles Dudley is merely cover for 'mistress', and it is in that sense that she is daughter to the Captain. Belcour eagerly swallows the bait, and lets Mrs. Fulmer wheedle him out of Charlotte's jewels which she is to hold in trust for Louisa. The girl begins to thank him for his civilities, but he cuts her short by an impassioned declaration of love and an assurance that 'this good lady, Mrs. Fulmer, has something to offer in my behalf'. Louisa demands a better proof of the sincerity of his abrupt professions than 'a little superfluous dross', which Mrs. Fulmer interprets to him as meaning jewels instead of coin.

He tries to atone to his conscience by bringing Charlotte a more valuable case of diamonds than her own, and when she refuses them, he makes a clean confession.

> I cannot invent a lie for my life; and, if it was to save it, I couldn't tell one. I am an idle, dissipated, unthinking fellow, not worth your notice; in short, I am a West Indian; and you must try me according to the charter of my colony, not by a jury of English spinsters. Truth is, I have given away your jewels.

His sincerity disarms Charlotte into forgiveness, and when a letter comes from Charles revealing that Belcour is his father's rescuer, she is prompted by his generous action to disclose to him her love for the son, and her readiness, as soon as she is of age, to share her fortune with him. Belcour is struck silent by the sudden entrance of Louisa, to whom Charlotte shows the diamonds in the belief that her own are now with her cousin, who protests that such things are infinitely above her reach. They have been retained by Mrs. Fulmer, who is preparing to make them the means of escape from their creditors.

Still believing the slander about Louisa, Belcour begs from the girl 'love, free, disencumbered, anti-matrimonial love', and takes hold of her. She throws him off, calling for rescue from Charles, who salutes Belcour as 'villain' and bids him defend himself. They begin a fight till, at a cry from Louisa, Major O'Flaherty knocks up their swords, and, finding Charles to be the son of an old companion-in-arms, warns him, 'Never, while you live, draw your sword before a woman.' The Major, outraged by Lady Rusport's callous treatment of her kinsfolk, has forsaken her house. She is now to receive a shattering blow. A lawyer, Varland, informs her that Sir Oliver Roundhead left in his last illness a second will by which his grandson, Charles Dudley, inherited his whole estate. Lady Rusport offers him a bribe of £5,000 to let her destroy the will, and with sundry twinges of conscience he accepts it. But the bargain is overheard by O'Flaherty who threatens Varland with a beating unless he surrenders the will. The lawyer bids him give it to Charles Dudley, if he is an honest man, to which the Major indignantly retorts, 'An honest man! Look at me, friend. I am a soldier. This is not the livery of a knave. I am an Irishman, honey; mine is not the country of dishonour.' Thus Dudley becomes a man of fortune at the very moment when Charlotte, overcoming false delicacy, offers herself in marriage to him, thinking that he is still poor, and that she will have enough for both.

In somewhat too-protracted fashion the various complications are resolved. O'Flaherty bears a formal challenge from Charles to Belcour, for whom Stockwell acts as second, in order that, when they meet on the duelling-ground, he may produce the Fulmers in custody as witnesses to their slander of Miss Dudley, and as guilty of trying to sell Charlotte's diamonds. Charles thus withdraws his epithet of 'villain', and Louisa accepts Belcour's now honourably proffered hand. Charlotte and Charles can be united without eloping to Scotland. Lady Rusport flounces out in a rage, bidding the pair marry and be wretched. O'Flaherty looks forward to a retreat in his native country, where he has not set foot for thirty years, but which he thinks worth all the rest of the world put together. Finally, Stockwell reveals to Belcour that in him he has found a father 'who observes, who knows, who loves you'.

The West Indian has been called 'the extreme example of English sentimental comedy', and it took the town by storm. It had an initial run of thirty nights and was revived from time to time. It has therefore called for a somewhat detailed analysis of its elaborate plot. But today it has lost much of its attraction. For a mid-eighteenth-century audience a stranger coming from Jamaica to London had something of the glamour of the unknown. And he could be credited with blunders in getting to know the ways of the unfamiliar capital city. But it passes reasonable belief that even a novice should be so easily taken in by a Mrs. Fulmer and should persist so obstinately in the conviction that Miss Dudley is a professional wanton. Belcour is one of the least persuasive of the favourite eighteenth-century type, the good-hearted rake. The other characters are on more or less conventional lines except Major O'Flaherty, who brings a refreshingly piquant note into the usually high-flown dialogue. But, whatever may be posterity's verdict, *The West Indian* can claim to have proved 'good theatre'.

Towards the end of the same year, in December 1771, Cumberland ventured into a different field with an adaptation of *Timon of Athens*, but returned in January 1772 to sentimental comedy with *The Fashionable Lover* which, however, failed to repeat the success of *The West Indian.*

Nor, in spite of his indefatigable labours for the stage, did Cumberland ever again repeat his early triumph. Amongst his pieces of various types in the same decade *The Choleric Man,* produced at Drury Lane on 19 December 1774, presents some features of interest, especially in its printed form. It went through three London editions in 1775, as well as one in Dublin. It contained an ironical dedication by Cumberland to 'the high and mighty Sir, Detraction'.

> When any play, like this now submitted to the public, meets a favourable reception on its first appearance, the very next morning by break of day out comes your manifesto. . . . They who have been pleas'd, being told they ought not to have been pleas'd, go no more and avoid an error in judgement; they who would have gone stay at home and save their money.

Here is a clue to Sheridan's caricature of Cumberland as Sir Fretful Plagiary in *The Critic.*

The titular figure of *The Choleric Man* is Nightshade, who comes up to London from the country to consult his brother, the lawyer Manlove, about a case against a neighbouring parson concerning a pigeon-house, and gets involved by his temper in serious difficulties. But the main interest is in two contrasted sons, Jack, whom Nightshade keeps with him under severe discipline, and Charles, brought up by his uncle Manlove, whose name he has adopted, with the social advantages of a public school and university education. What distinguishes Charles from most of the gallants in eighteenth-century comedy is that he is also an artist, having studied chiefly in Rome as the grand repository of the antique, and having acquired a collection of paintings. Manlove suggests that this will be a link between him and Miss Laetitia Fairfax, an heiress who is also a painter and has been two years in Italy. He chooses to meet her incognito, and presents himself under the guise of an artistic young man, a friend of Charles Manlove whose pictures he invites her to visit with Mrs. Stapleton, her guardian's wife.

There the ladies have a surprise. Jack Nightshade has taken advantage of his father's absence to follow him secretly to London. Here, to let him pose as a man of quality, Charles lends him a fashionable suit and gives him a handsome sum to spend. Then, for a freak, Jack poses as Charles and receives the ladies in the picture-gallery. In what is apparently a unique scene in the comedies of the period, and one which shows Cumberland's interest in the fine arts, Laetitia comments to Mrs. Stapleton on the paintings as a connoisseur, while Jack takes them aback by his Philistine retorts.

LAET.

> Look, dear madam, here is grace and dignity, Guido's Lucretia, the dagger in her breast, and in the act of heroic self-destruction. What resolution! what a spirit has the great artist thrown into those eyes!

JACK.

> Yes, she had a devil of a spirit. She stabb'd herself in a pique upon being cross'd in love.

. . . . .

LAET.

> Do you observe that picture, madam? 'Tis a melancholy story, very finely told by Poussin. It is a view of Marseilles at the time of the plague, with a capital figure of the good bishop in the midst of the group.

JACK.

> Bishop, madam! That person which you look upon is a physician, and the people round about him are his patients; they are in a desperate way it must be confest.

The ladies can stand no more when Jack gives an immodest explanation of a picture of Actaeon being turned into a stag, in which Laetitia sees the colouring of the Venetian school, probably by 'Tintoret'. Sadly disillusioned, Laetitia will have nothing more to do with this vulgarian. Jack on his part is pleased because, while posing as Charles Manlove, he has been tricked into making love to Laetitia's maid, Lucy, pretending to be her mistress. Lucy has been pressed into this by her brother, Dibble, and under interrogation by Laetitia reveals the secret of the various impersonations. Knowing the truth Laetitia, seen as a painter in her own studio, makes play with Charles by asking his judgement and help about a portrait of Mr. Stapleton till he is forced to confess that he is pleading for himself. It is appropriate that it is in this studio that the final all-round explanations take place. Nightshade is aghast at the idea of his son marrying a chambermaid. When reminded that he cannot disinherit him, he shouts, 'I'll live for ever on purpose to plague him; I'll starve the whelp; he shall have nothing to live upon but rainwater and pignuts.' But when Manlove offers to keep him Nightshade retorts, 'I'll forgive him and keep him to myself', and they go off together. With his 'rival' gone Charles and Laetitia are free to fall into each other's arms and thus end a comedy with some unusual features.

Undeterred by 'Detraction' and by Sheridan's satire, Cumberland continued to write plays, novels, translations, and an epic till towards the close of his long life on 7 May 1811.

Oliver W. Ferguson (essay date 1974)

SOURCE: Ferguson, Oliver W. "Sir Fretful Plagiary and Goldsmith's 'An Essay on the Theatre': The Background of Richard Cumberland's 'Dedication to Detraction.'" In *Quick Springs of Sense: Studies in the Eighteenth Century,* edited by Larry S. Champion, pp. 113-20. Athens: University of Georgia Press, 1974.

[*In the following essay, Ferguson examines the controversy surrounding "Dedication to Detraction," Cumberland's preface to* The Choleric Man.]

SIR FRETFUL.

> The newspapers! Sir, they are the most villainous—licentious—abominable—infernal.—Not that I ever read them—no—I make it a rule never to look into a newspaper.

(R. B. Sheridan, *The Critic*, I, i)

At the end of his biography of Richard Cumberland, Stanley Williams exclaims, "What the talent and industry of Cumberland could not effect in fifty years of effort, the careless genius of Sheridan won for him in a few hours. Sir Fretful Plagiary!"[1] Allowing for the exaggeration that is burlesque's due, Sheridan's portrayal of Cumberland as Sir Fretful Plagiary in *The Critic* (1779) is accurate. Cumberland's borrowings—usually underscored by his sturdy assertions of originality—were notorious.[2] Equally so were the traits of personality that inform Sheridan's caricature: Cumberland's insatiable vanity and his contentious responses to adverse criticism. Williams termed him, of all the playwrights of his day "the most thievish, the most sensitive, the most proud, and the most pilloried."[3]

In the course of a full career Cumberland had and took advantage of numerous opportunities to reveal this side of his personality to his contemporaries, but nowhere did he do so more clearly and at greater length than in the essay entitled **"Dedication to Detraction,"** which he wrote on the occasion of the publication in 1775 of his comedy **The Choleric Man.** The play had opened at Drury Lane on 19 December 1774. It was a moderate success, but its reception did not answer Cumberland's high expectations. And though the reviewers were by no means uniformly hostile, they were unfavorable. In particular, there was widespread agreement that the playwright had failed to live up to the excellence of his acknowledged model, Terence's *Adelphi,* and that he had failed to acknowledge an even more helpful predecessor, Shadwell's *Squire of Alsatia.*[4] When Cumberland arranged for the publication of **The Choleric Man,** he replied to these objections, personifying the reviewers collectively as "Detraction," to whom he "dedicated" the published version of his play.

The mock dedication embarrasses as much by its heavy and obvious sarcasm as by the various tones—aggrieved patience, indifference, righteous anger, self-pity—in which Cumberland addresses his adversary:

High and Mighty Sir,

The attention, with which you have been pleased to distinguish this inconsiderable production, makes it a duty with me to lay it at your feet. The applauses of the Theatre gave me assurance of its success, but it was your testimony alone, which could inspire me with any opinion of its merit: Nor is it on this occasion only I am to thank you; in whatever proportion I have been happy enough to attract the regards of the public, in the same degree I have never failed being honoured with your's.

How I have merited these marks of your partiality I am not able to guess: I can take my conscience to witness, I have paid you no sacrifice, devoted no time or study to your service, nor am a man in any respect qualified to repay your favours: Give me credit, therefore, when I tell you, that your liberality oppresses me. Was I apt to rate my pretensions highly, and presume upon the indulgence of the public, I might have some claim to your favor; but 'till you hear me complain that my reward is not equal to my merit, I pray you let me enjoy my content and my obscurity.[5]

The Monthly Review for January 1775 remarked on the unintentional appropriateness of Cumberland's diatribe as a preface to a play called **The Choleric Man**: "In a long dedication worthy the pen of *Scriblerus*, the Author of this comedy has, in his own person, given a very lively image of **The Choleric Man.** This prince of the *genus irritabile* will allow no man's dog to bark in his presence; although he courts applause, he will not consider himself as liable to censure; and he proscribes the whole generation of *annotators, remarkers, observers,* & c. from the minor critic of a newspaper, to the grave *Aristarchus* of a Review." This last remark—which refers to Cumberland's assertion that Londoners owe to Detraction "the great encrease of *news-papers* (not to mention *magazines, reviews,* & c)"—is suggestive. Cumberland does indeed "proscribe the whole generation" of reviewers. As one reads the **"Dedication,"** he realizes that the personified dedicatee is more than a rhetorical flourish: "Detraction" is for the playwright the composite of every unfavorable review he has ever received, the sum of all the anonymous critics who have persecuted him from the outset of his career to the present.

The extreme bitterness—and the imprudence—of the **"Dedication to Detraction"** can only be understood in terms of this wider context. The reception accorded his latest play was the immediate occasion for Cumberland's essay. But from the cumulative injuries which he fancied had been done him, Cumberland chose to cite one specifically and to elaborate on it in remarkable detail. Halfway through the **"Dedication,"** he says to "Detraction," "But there remains a word to be said on some learned animadversions of your's, entitled *An Essay on the Theatre,* in which you profess to draw a *Comparison between Laughing* and *Sentimental Comedy*; and in which you are pleased evidently to point some observations at my comedy of the **Fashionable Lover**" (p. ix). Cumberland's comedy had been produced in January 1772; the "animadversions" are, of course, Oliver Goldsmith's. "An Essay on the Theatre," which appeared in the *Westminster Magazine* for January, 1773, is the *locus classicus* for his objections to sentimental comedy.

It has commonly been assumed that Goldsmith's authorship of "An Essay on the Theatre" was recognized during his lifetime. The editors of *Boswell for the Defence,* for example, say that Boswell sought to flatter Goldsmith in his letter of congratulation on the successful opening of *She Stoops to Conquer* by playing "variations on the theme" of "An Essay on the Theatre," despite the fact that Boswell was in Edinburgh at the time and had been there when the essay was published; and a recent study of Goldsmith observes that "many of Goldsmith's contemporaries were unable to accept his antisentimental attitudes . . . even though there was unmistakable evidence elsewhere ('An Essay on the Theatre')."[6] Because of this assumption scholars have failed to comprehend how Cumberland could have been unaware that the attack which he singled out for rebuttal in the **"Dedication of Detraction"** was Goldsmith's. In his study of sentimental comedy Ernest Bernbaum expressed amazement at Cumberland's ignorance. More recently Ricardo Quintana has marveled that Cumberland nowhere indicated "that he had the remotest idea that the 'Essay' in question was Goldsmith's," a fact which in his opinion adds to "the difficulty of determining the precise relationship" between the two men.[7] Cumberland's ignorance, however, appears surprising only from our vantage point. We have no doubt that Goldsmith wrote "An Essay on the Theatre," but we should remember that he never acknowledged the essay and that it was first attributed to him in 1798, when it was printed in *Essays and Criticisms, by Dr. Goldsmith,* on the authority of Thomas Wright, the printer of the *Westminster Magazine*.[8] Wright is a qualified witness, and the case for Goldsmith's authorship is supported by internal evidence, but these points should not obscure the fact that the "Essay on the Theatre" appeared as an unsigned essay in the first number of a new periodical. Not only is there no evidence that any of Goldsmith's friends knew of his authorship of the piece (or, indeed, that any of them even knew of its existence at the time of its publication); there is explicit and firsthand testimony—testimony that has not heretofore been recognized—that a member of Goldsmith's circle who might be supposed to have been better informed ascribed it to someone else.

On 12 January 1775, the day the **"Dedication to Detraction"** was published, George Steevens inquired of David Garrick, "To what Essay on the Theatre does Mr. C. refer at the top of p. 9 of his dedication?" The following day Garrick answered Steevens: "*[T]he Cho-*

leric Man came in just as I had receiv'd yr letter—the *Essay on ye Theatre,* was anonymous, & printed in the Morning Chron^e against Sentimental Comedy & written (as he has been told) by our Lincoln's Inn friend—It was a Stroke at y^e *[F]ashionable Lover.*"[9] "Our Lincoln's Inn friend" is the lawyer-playwright, Arthur Murphy; and Cumberland's error is altogether understandable: Murphy's opposition to sentimental comedy was as well known as Goldsmith's, and he and Cumberland openly disliked each other.[10] Cumberland's mistaken attribution, then, is not remarkable. Nor is the fact that he had forgotten, two years after the event, where "An Essay on the Theatre" had been published.[11] His lapse of memory emphasizes the obvious fact that the essay appeared in a notoriously ephemeral medium. And his ignorance of the essay's authorship—an ignorance shared by such knowledgeable men of the theater as Steevens and Garrick—serves to remind us that had it not been for Thomas Wright, the best-known contemporary criticism of sentimental comedy in eighteenth-century England could very well have remained out of the Goldsmith canon.

If Cumberland's misapprehensions about the authorship of "An Essay on the Theatre" are not surprising, his reading of the piece is. "An Essay on the Theatre" neither refers to *The Fashionable Lover* by name nor alludes to any episodes or characters that could be associated exclusively with Cumberland's comedy. The only possible echo is in Goldsmith's remark that as the hero of a typical sentimental comedy is "but a tradesman, it is indifferent to me whether he be turned out of his Counting-house on Fish-street Hill, since he will still have enough left to open shop in St. Giles's" (*Works,* III, 213). Bridgemore, the unscrupulous merchant in *The Fashionable Lover,* lives on Fish-street Hill, and the name occurs several times throughout the play; but he is not turned out of his shop, and his role in the play is anything but heroic. That Cumberland should have built on so tenuous a base is extraordinary (and that Garrick should have tacitly accepted his reading suggests that he was not familiar with Goldsmith's essay). Even had he known that Goldsmith was the author of "An Essay on the Theatre," he would have had no grounds to regard his comedy as the particular object of Goldsmith's scorn. The essay, after all, was written a full year after the production of *The Fashionable Lover*; and it objected to the ubiquity of the type rather than to a specific sentimental comedy—indeed, one of its chief criticisms is that all sentimental comedies were alike!

The explanation for Cumberland's error must lie in Cumberland's vanity—a vanity that almost defies successful caricature. To read the playwright's *Memoirs* is to appreciate fully Sheridan's art: Sir Fretful is funny; there is little mirth to be got from Cumberland's evaluation of his dramatic career. Interestingly, he is most nearly modest (or he affects to be) about the best of his comedies, *The West Indian*: "Such was the good fortune of an author, who happened to strike upon a popular and taking plan." Of *The Brothers,* a thoroughly meretricious piece, he boasts, "I believe I may say that it brought some advantage to the theatre as well as some reputation to its author." *The Fashionable Lover* was in his judgment superior to his previous comedies: "I verily believe if *The Fashionable Lover* was not my composition, and I were called upon to give my opinion of it . . . I could not deny it a preference to *[T]he West-Indian* in a moral light, and perhaps, if I were in very good humour with its author, I might be tempted to say that in point of diction it approached very nearly to what I conceived to be the true style of comedy." And to bring our survey up to the time of *The Choleric Man,* of that play Cumberland declares, "If ever there shall be found an editor of my dramatic works as an entire collection, this comedy will stand forward as one of the most prominent among them."[12] When one reads such passages as these, Cumberland's misapplication of "An Essay on the Theatre" to *The Fashionable Lover* is somewhat more understandable: the essay derided sentimental comedy, and Cumberland was the most popular author of sentimental comedies; therefore, *The Fashionable Lover,* his most recent contribution to the genre (and the play that in his considered opinion "approached very nearly to . . . the true style of comedy"), had to be the example the anonymous critic had in mind.

"An Essay on the Theatre" had appeared in 1773; the **"Dedication to Detraction"** followed in 1775. For two years Cumberland had brooded over what he construed as an attack on *The Fashionable Lover*; and when his next comedy provoked adverse criticism, he not only responded to this but also reverted to his earlier grievance, devoting approximately half of the **"Dedication to Detraction"** to a querulous and pedantic vindication of sentimental comedy. It is easy to see why Sheridan emphasized Sir Fretful's morbid sensitivity: "He is the sorest man alive, and shrinks like scorched parchment from the fiery ordeal of true criticism."

Cumberland remained convinced that "An Essay on the Theatre" had singled out *The Fashionable Lover* for attack. In his *Memoirs* (begun in 1804 and published in 1807) he reiterated the charge and now asserted that "the chief object" of the **"Dedication to Detraction"** had been to refute the essay (I, 379-380). He also remained ignorant of the identity of his supposed assailant. In fact, in his *Memoirs* he had nothing but kind words (delivered in the most condescending of tones) for Goldsmith. He was especially proud of the lines with which he is portrayed in "Retaliation," the poem of mock epitaphs which Goldsmith had written shortly before his death and which was published in April of 1774. Here is the portrait that excited Cumberland's gratitude:

Here Cumberland lies having acted his parts,
The Terence of England, the mender of hearts;
A flattering painter, who made it his care
To draw men as they ought to be, not as they are.
His gallants are all faultless, his women divine,
And comedy wonders at being so fine;
Like a tragedy queen he has dizen'd her out,
Or rather like tragedy giving a rout.
His fools have their follies so lost in a croud
Of virtues and feelings, that folly grows proud,
And coxcombs alike in their failings alone,
Adopting his portraits are pleas'd with their own.
Say, where has our poet this malady caught,
Or wherefore his characters thus without fault?
Say was it that vainly directing his view,
To find out mens virtues and finding them few,
Quite sick of pursuing each troublesome elf,
He grew lazy at last and drew from himself?

(lines 61-78, *Works,* IV, 355-356)

Cumberland's self-esteem not only led him to miss altogether the delicate ambiguity of Goldsmith's portrait; it also blinded him to strictures on sentimental comedy that had enraged him when he had read them in the "Essay on the Theatre." The description of his comic muse as "dizen'd out" with the trappings of tragedy parallels the essay's assertion that classical comic playwrights never exalted their characters into "buskined pomp" or created "a Tradesman's Tragedy" (*Works,* III, 211). The account of Cumberland's perfect characters and the moral laxity of his comedy that allows folly to escape punishment under cover of "virtues and feelings" is a compressed version of a similar criticism in the essay: "In these Plays almost all the Characters are good. . . . If they happen to have Faults or Foibles, the Spectator is taught not only to pardon, but to applaud them, in consideration of the goodness of their hearts; so that Folly, instead of being ridiculed, is commended" (p. 212). Even the sobriquet "Terence" which Goldsmith bestows on Cumberland echoes the essay, in which that playwright is cited as the ancient who went furthest in mixing comedy and tragedy (p. 211).

Had Cumberland read these lines with his usual hypersensitivity, he would surely have been aware of the subtle irony of Goldsmith's portrait. He might even have recognized the parallels between the portrait and the anonymous essay that had so angered him the previous year, and he might then have taken the next step and guessed at Goldsmith's authorship of the essay. But Goldsmith's solemn observation that Cumberland himself was the model for all his perfect characters was irresistible, and for once Sir Fretful's paranoia was lulled. Vanity does not always leave its subject vulnerable. Sometimes it can protect him.

Notes

1. *Richard Cumberland* (New Haven, 1917), p. 301.

2. Williams's book is the most convenient source for examples of Cumberland's plagiarisms. See especially his comments on Cumberland's first four comedies, *The Brothers, The West Indian, The Fashionable Lover,* and *The Choleric Man,* and on his tragedy, *The Battle of Hastings.* This last appeared in 1778, the year before Sheridan's creation of Sir Fretful Plagiary.

3. "The English Sentimental Drama from Steele to Cumberland," *Sewanee Review,* XXXIII (1925), 422.

4. Williams, pp. 111-113.

5. *The Choleric Man,* 3rd ed. (1775), p. iii.

6. William K. Wimsatt, Jr., and Frederick A. Pottle, eds., *Boswell for the Defence* (New York, 1959), p. 151; Robert H. Hopkins, *The True Genius of Oliver Goldsmith* (Baltimore, 1969), p. 11.

7. Ernest Bernbaum, *The Drama of Sensibility* (1915; rpt. Gloucester, Mass., 1958), p. 251 n 1; Ricardo Quintana, "Oliver Goldsmith as a Critic of the Drama," *SEL,* V (1965), 452-453.

8. Arthur Friedman, ed., *Collected Works of Oliver Goldsmith* (Oxford, 1966), III, 205. Hereafter cited as *Works.*

9. *The Letters of David Garrick,* ed. David M. Little and George M. Kahrl (Cambridge, Mass., 1963), III, 985 and n. 3.

10. Howard H. Dunbar, *The Dramatic Career of Arthur Murphy* (New York, 1946), p. 225.

11. In his *Memoirs* (1807), Cumberland described the essay as "a tract then in some degree of circulation" (1, 379).

12. Ibid., 1, 296-297, 264-265, 346-347, 381.

Eugene M. Waith (essay date winter 1978-79)

SOURCE: Waith, Eugene M. "Richard Cumberland, Comic Force, and Misanthropy." *Comparative Drama* 12, no. 4 (winter 1978-79): 283-99.

[*In the following essay, Waith examines Cumberland's unique approach to dramatic comedy.*]

I

In 1775 Richard Cumberland published an ill-natured dedication with his comedy *The Choleric Man,* prompting Arthur Murphy to say, at the end of a severely unfavorable criticism of the principal character, that the true idea of a choleric man was to be found in the dedication.[1] That this dedication should be a sample of Cumberland at his thorniest is especially ironic, since his chief concern was a theory of comedy to support his own benevolent comedies. He was replying to the charge that his comedy was (without acknowledgement) based on Shadwell's *Squire of Alsatia,* and above all, to what he saw as an attack on him in "An Essay on the Theatre, or a Comparison between Laughing and Sentimental Comedy," published in the *Westminster Magazine,* 1 January 1773. Both the tone of the dedication and Cumberland's unconvincing denial that he had borrowed from Shadwell provided Sheridan with material for his devastating portrait of Cumberland as Sir Fretful Plagiary in *The Critic.* The reply to "An Essay on the Theatre," however, was much more than a demonstration of spleen and wounded vanity. It was a serious attempt to challenge certain widely accepted ideas about the development and the nature of comedy.

The **"Dedication to Detraction"** addressed in this one personified abstraction all those who had attacked Cumberland—the newspaper drama critics and the author of the "Essay on the Theatre," who was not then known to be Oliver Goldsmith.[2] Cumberland assumed that his comedy *The Fashionable Lover* (1772) was the specific butt of this attack on sentimental comedy, though there is little in the "Essay" to suggest that such was the case. What no one could miss was the attempt to show that sentimental comedy, by soliciting tears, ignored the function of comedy, which "should excite our laughter by ridiculously exhibiting the follies of the Lower part of Mankind." The "one Argument in favour of Sentimental Comedy" was said to be that it was "of all others, the most easily written."[3] This sneer obviously hurt ("You insinuate that every blockhead can write *Sentimental or pathetic Comedy*"),[4] but not so much as the implication that the writers of this kind of comedy were unaware of the traditional generic distinctions. Goldsmith had cited Aristotle and Boileau as examples of the "Great Masters in the Dramatic Art," all of whom had agreed that pity was the province of tragedy, as laughter and ridicule were of comedy. He admitted that Terence sometimes approached, yet always stopped short of, "the downright pathetic," and pointed out that even he was "reproached by Caesar for wanting the *vis comica.* All the other comic writers of antiquity aim only at rendering folly or vice ridiculous. . . ."[5]

To be lectured to like a schoolboy, and, of all things, on the subject of classical tradition, was intolerable to Richard Bentley's grandson, who had received an excellent education in the classics. He set out to demolish his unknown assailant with a truly formidable display of learning, accompanied by numerous footnotes in both Latin and English:

> By this specimen of your acquaintance with the *comic writers of antiquity, most learned Sir,* I suspect that from the great attention you have bestowed upon the moderns, you have had little to spare to their predeces-

sors; for if it is your opinion that *Terence* of all the ancient comic poets made the *nearest approaches* to the *pathetic,* I fear you will have an host of authorities to combat?

(p. ix)

The most remarkable feature of the ensuing polemic is that under the guise of expounding the tradition to an ignoramus who has got it all wrong, Cumberland actually presents a little-known, eccentric interpretation of Caesar's words and a minority view of Terence.[6] For Goldsmith was with the majority of commentators then as now in understanding Caesar to mean that Terence provided less laughter than other comic writers. While some eighteenth-century critics admired Terence for his departures from Aristophanic and Plautine comedy,[7] and others, like Goldsmith, praised him for not going too far, there was a general consensus that he was exceptional in his "approaches to the pathetic." Now Cumberland cites Varro, whom Quintilian called "the most learned of Romans," to show that three other "comic poets of the Roman stage" were thought to excel Terence in *pathos,* or the portrayal of emotion, while he was supreme in *ethos,* or the depiction of character. As to Caesar's poem on Terence (which Cumberland quotes in full), the seventeenth-century classicist Tanneguy Le Fèvre, who took the Latin name Tanaquillus Faber, believed that Caesar was lamenting an insufficiency of pathos. Cumberland translates:

> *Caesar thought* (says the commentator) *that Terence, in moving the passions, was inferior to some others, which indeed is the case; and Caesar's opinion is confirmed by the decree of Varro, the most learned of the Romans.*

(p. x)[8]

Although Le Fèvre's interpretation was not widely accepted, and not even by his learned daughter, Anne Dacier,[9] it precisely suited Cumberland's argument, allowing him to recapitulate: "the *pathetic* is the very essence of the *vis comica,* or in other words, *requires force and energy, especially* in *the comic province* [Le Fèvre's words again]; the very opposite doctrine to what you, *most learned Sir,* have maintained" (p. xi).

Cumberland then seizes upon Goldsmith's rash claim that "All the other comic writers of antiquity aim only at rendering folly or vice ridiculous." Not so, says the translator of the *Comicorum Graecorum Fragmenta.* If Old and Middle Comedy in Greece aimed mainly at satire and ridicule, New Comedy, as seen in the surviving fragments, consisted of "moral sententious passages, elegant in their phrase, but grave, and many of them, especially those of *Diphilus,* of a religious cast . . ." (p. xii). He mentions the belief of the second-century Christian apologist Clement of Alexandria that "many *passages* in *Menander* are copied from the Hebrew prophets. . . . It will appear therefore that *sentiment* or the *pathetic* in comedy was not neglected by the ancients . . ." (pp. xii-xiii). He concludes by assuring the anonymous author that he bears him no ill-will.

Some years later, publishing his translations of the extant fragments of the Greek comic writers in his series of papers called *The Observer,* Cumberland comments on "the tender and religious sentiments" to be found in a fragment of Moschion preserved by Clement of Alexandria.[10] In the same number he says of a fragment by Sotades that it "seems to prove, amongst many other instances, how much the grave and sentimental comedy now began to be in fashion with the Athenians" (p. 186). The passage concerns the lamentable deaths of such "benefactors to mankind" as Socrates, Diogenes, Aeschylus, Euripides, and Homer. Cumberland comments: "There is a melancholy grandeur in these sentiments, with a simplicity of expression, which prove to us that these authors occasionally digressed from the gay spirit of comedy into passages not only of the most serious, but sublimest cast" (p. 187). Again we hear of a fragment of Menander "which breathes the spirit, and nearly the very words of the Hebrew prophets" (No. 149, p. 195), and Cumberland observes that in most of the surviving fragments of this author we find, not "those facetious and sprightly sallies to be expected from a comic writer," but "a melancholy display of the miseries, the enormities, the repinings of mankind" (No. 150, p. 201). Indeed, so great is the "general disgust against mankind" that it "can hardly be considered as falling within the province of comedy in any case" (p. 202). Of the fragments of Philemon, Menander's contemporary, Cumberland says that they are "in general of a sentimental, tender cast, and though they enforce sound and strict morality, yet no one instance occurs of that gloomy misanthropy, that harsh and dogmatizing spirit, which too often marks the maxims of his more illustrious rival" (No. 151, p. 212). Happily, Menander is not always misanthropic: "Amongst the smaller fragments there are several good apothegms, some brief moral maxims well expressed, and though not many of those witty points, which are so frequent in Aristophanes, yet there are some specimens of the *vis comica,* which have a very ingenious turn of words in their own tongue" (No. 150, p. 207). Some of the best comedy is both serious and touching, but it must also be entertaining.

In this last quotation the Le Fèvre interpretation of *vis comica* seems to be abandoned in favor of the more usual association with what is amusing, and when, at the very end of his life, Cumberland writes of "the many striking proofs of the true *vis comica*"[11] in *The Beaux' Strategem* he appears to mean all that conduces to "delight and entertainment." Although he uses this key term in more than one sense, he clearly sets great store by "comic force," and his opinion of Aristophanes gives a further idea of what it means to him. In another number of *The Observer* he defends Aristophanes against Plutarch, who preferred Menander. If there is obscenity in the older comic writer there are also "the loftiest flights of poetry." Like Juvenal, he "chastises vice by an open exposure of its turpitude, offending the ear, whilst he aims to mend the heart" (No. 138, pp. 122-23). Cumberland accepts the highly improbable story first printed by Aldo Manuzio in the *editio princeps* of Aristophanes (Venice, 1498) that the Greek playwright was "the pillow companion" of St. John Chrysostom (p. 123), presumably because of his moral force. "The even suavity of Menander's style" is contrasted with "the irregular sublimity of Aristophanes's" (No. 139, p. 127).

Admiration for Aristophanes by the defender of sentimental comedy (he eventually included a complete translation of *The Clouds* in *The Observer*) may at first be startling, but "the loftiest flights of poetry," the aim of mending the heart, the morality which might recommend itself to a Christian saint, and the "irregular sublimity" explain the attraction. Cumberland did not believe that the ridicule of vice or folly should be or ever had been the sole aim of comedy, but he was by no means opposed to it. In his *Memoirs,* written in 1806-07, he reproves Congreve, Farquhar, and others for not using "the scourge of ridicule" to punish some of their vicious wits (p. 141). Properly used, it can contribute to the forceful effect which Cumberland admires.[12]

He relates comic force to characterization in the same passage of the *Memoirs* when he speaks of the playwright as a "writer to the passions," who should strive to make worthy characters amiable but not insipid. To make them entertaining he must put "life and spirit" into them. He recalls how, at the beginning of his career, seeking to write "something that might be lasting," and believing that in his time "great eccentricity of character was pretty nearly gone by," he determined to show "at least [his] good-will to mankind" by portraying in a favorable light "persons who had been usually exhibited on the stage, as the butts for ridicule and abuse" (pp. 141-42). Hence his "West Indian" and the Irishman in the same play. No stage-Irishman was to serve as a model for the latter, since the usual "gross absurdities and unnatural contrarieties have not a shade of character in them" (p. 142). He concludes:

> and the art, as I conceive it, of finding language for the Irish character on the stage consists not in making him foolish, vulgar, or absurd, but, on the contrary, whilst you furnish him with expressions that excite laughter, you must graft them upon sentiments that deserve applause.
>
> (p. 143)

In this account of his aims Cumberland characteristically invites an approving look, a pat on the back. But both his emphasis on showing the good side of persons usually ridiculed on the stage and his directions for the presentation of an Irishman correspond so closely to his practice that they may be taken as genuine indicators of certain of his ideas of comedy. Here once more is the hope of improving the spectators, in this case by making them feel more kindly toward some whom they might normally scorn. Such characters are not to be caricatured, but rather, based on nature, like the characters of all good drama, but especially comedy. They may excite laughter, but finally must move the audience to sympathy and approval. The Advertisement prefixed to his successful comedy *The Fashionable Lover* states that it is "design'd as an attempt upon [the reader's] heart."[13]

The conspicuously affective cast of the theory of comedy which emerges from all of Cumberland's remarks is not unusual in this period of classically educated writers, but Cumberland came by it more naturally than most. For not only had his grandfather, Richard Bentley, seen to his training in classical rhetoric, but the writings of his great-grandfather, Richard Cumberland, Bishop of Peterborough, had familiarized him with Christian apologetics. No wonder he was attracted by the story of a saint who slept on the comedies of Aristophanes. No wonder he thought that the best comedy should mend the heart.

Two scenes which Cumberland especially admired come close to embodying his comic ideal, and show what becomes in his plays a characteristic form of comic force. One is the famous "steinkirk" scene in Cibber's *The Careless Husband,* a comedy which he considered inferior to none. In the critique prefixed to Cooke's edition of this play, he asks the reader to note that Cibber "with great art" describes Sir Charles Easy as:

> perfectly secure that he had raised no suspicion in Lady Easy, and therefore it is in nature, that the discovery, coming upon him by surprise, is an incident of sufficient weight to alarm his conscience, and awaken his remorse; this is a circumstance that should by no means be overlooked, though perhaps it has never yet been pointed out, for upon this the whole probability and reasonableness of his reformation turns, as it would have been quite out of nature, to have made him feel the force of a candour which he had frequently imposed upon, or to have described him on a sudden penitent for an offence in which long impunity had hardened him.[14]

The repentance of Sir Charles is matched by that of Lady Townly in another Cibber play, *The Provoked Husband,* based on an unfinished comedy by Vanbrugh. Cumberland comments:

> We . . . know to a certainty, that it is to the author of *The Careless Husband* we are indebted for that beautiful and affecting scene, in which Lady Townly, awaking to a consciousness of her misconduct, . . . [makes]

her last appeal . . . she then proceeds to relate what she rightly terms "the story of her heart," and a story it is, which never failed to reach the hearts of the hearers, when representation did it justice.[15]

Both scenes present an unexpected goodness. One is praised for being natural, the other for reaching "the hearts of the hearers," and I think it is apparent that in Cumberland's eyes each scene also has the virtue for which the other is praised. The best comedy, then, is Terentian in the faithful delineation of character, but goes beyond Terence in forcefulness of effect, adding *pathos* to *ethos.*

II

The Choleric Man, to which the **"Dedication to Detraction"** was prefixed, was admittedly based on the *Adelphi,* Terence's play about the two brothers, one strict and one tolerant, and their contrasting ways of bringing up boys. In Cumberland's play the choleric Nightshade has been very strict with his son Jack, whom he has kept in the country, while his son Charles has been brought up in town by the tolerant brother, Manlove. Cumberland later comments:

> The chief effect in this play is produced by the strong contrast of character between Manlove and the Choleric Man, and again, with more comic force, between Charles, the courtly gentleman, and Jack, the rustic booby. . . .

> *(Memoirs,* p. 194)

"Comic force" here seems to be the result of striking contrasts between pairs of characters—contrasts based on the Terentian model, though heightened and altered in several ways. One conspicuous alteration is the introduction of an episode, having nothing to do with systems of education, in which Nightshade puts himself clearly in the wrong by beating a newspaper-vendor in the street. (Knowing how Cumberland felt about newspaper reviewers, one is tempted to see Nightshade's misdeed as a wish-fulfillment fantasy.) After being urged by Manlove's friends to give up this kind of behavior, Nightshade finally succumbs in the last act to his brother's arguments. Throwing down his cane, he promises: "I'll never take another stick in hand, till I'm obliged to go upon crutches" (V.ii; p. 80).

This is the first of two moments into which Cumberland has split the climax of the contrast between Manlove and Nightshade. The second of these moments focuses attention on the showing up of Nightshade's son Jack, and hence on the outcome of the rival systems of education. Here Jack, who has disguised himself as his brother, is shown to have offered marriage to a disguised chambermaid. Usually an engaging oaf, he has inherited enough of his father's temperament to fly into a rage when he discovers his mistake, but quickly subsides when the girl, the daughter of a footman, points out that "the footman bred his daughter as a gentleman shou'd, and the gentleman gave his son the education of a footman." "Father, that last wipe was at you," he says (V.iii; p. 89). It is Nightshade's turn to explode, and he orders his son to go back to the country to "till the soil, and be a beast of burden; 'tis what nature meant you for." Manlove admonishes Nightshade, almost in Raphael's words to Adam: "Nay, brother, blame not nature, she has done her part: 'Tis you that shou'd have till'd the soil" (p. 90). The "choleric man" is made to admit that his system has failed but also to forgive Jack. He is still "an incorrigible humorist," as Manlove calls him, but has been reduced to harmless—and amusing—bluster.

As the most recent editor of the play, Olaf Olsen, correctly points out, Cumberland avoids a sentimental scene here by not having Jack repent like his prototype in *The Squire of Alsatia*.[16] Shadwell's country boy falls on his knees, and his father weeps. Yet in Cumberland's play the triumph of good nature is far more decisive than in Terence, where the last laugh is at the expense of the tolerant brother. The contrasts between both pairs of brothers, constituting "the chief effect of the play," are closely tied to the taming of a choleric disposition. Though not as a whole a sentimental play, this version of Terence appeals to our faith in benevolence, adding an emotional component to the comic force of the contrasted characters.

In many of Cumberland's best known plays an unexpected display of goodness makes the desired emotional appeal. Where the goodness consists not simply in giving up a bad habit, such as beating people in the street, but in doing good for others, the appeal is even stronger. Thus in the play for which Cumberland is remembered today (if at all), a West Indian and an Irishman, two of the characters he seeks to rescue from the ridicule and abuse usually heaped on them, are conspicuously large-hearted. Belcour, the impulsive, passionate, irresponsible West Indian, cannot resist "rescuing a fellow creature from distress,"[17] prompting one of the heroines to say, "O blessed be the torrid zone for ever whose rapid vegetation quickens nature into such benignity!" (III.vii; p. 58). O'Flaherty, a "humorous" Irishman, many of whose expressions "excite laughter," as they were intended to do, endears himself to the audience by saying to the villainous Lady Rusport, "You preach, and you pray, and you turn up your eyes, and all the while you're as hard-hearted as a hyena—A hyena, truly! By my soul there isn't in the whole creation so savage an animal as a human creature without pity" (II.xi; p. 40).

The Scotsman, Colin Macleod, in *The Fashionable Lover,* is cut from the same cloth. Cumberland admittedly depended on earlier plays for the dialect, and was criticized for getting it wrong; but while taking a short-

cut to this comic effect, he took pains to model the character on a Highland servant whose "scrupulous integrity" had made him a trusted manager of his master's household and "a great favorite of everybody who resorted there" (*Memoirs,* p. 174). It is Colin, trusted servant to a bad master, who takes pity on the forlorn heroine and brings about the happy ending. As Stanley Williams says, "He is at once the buffoon and the mainspring of the action."[18] Cumberland later wrote of this play that "it was a drama of a moral, grave, and tender cast" (*Memoirs,* p. 175)—a comment that recalls some of his statements about both Middle and New Comedy: "tender and religious sentiments," "grave and sentimental comedy," "moral . . . grave . . . religious."[19] He evidently thought he had captured some of the qualities he most admired in Greek comedy and found lacking in Terence.

Of all the characters who transcend the comic stereotype to reveal unsuspected virtues, Sheva in *The Jew,* a relatively late play (1794), is the most striking. When Cumberland is busy rehabilitating Scotsmen in *The Fashionable Lover* he is content to portray "little Napthali of St. Mary Axe" as a scheming Shylock, who is in league with the villain, but betrays him when it becomes expedient to do so. The stereotype is untouched. To extract the greatest possible theatrical effect from the revelation of Sheva's exemplary generosity, Cumberland has one of the young heroes of the later play describe the Jew in terms even more opprobrious than those applied to Napthali: "Here comes . . . old Sheva, the rich Jew, the meerest muck-worm in the city of London: How the old Hebrew casts about for prodigals to snap at."[20] The other young hero has a more charitable view of Sheva, whom he once rescued from a mob of tormentors, but even he does not realize that Sheva is in every way the antithesis of the cruel and materialistic merchant, Sir Stephen Bertram, who is about to make both heroes miserable. He dismisses Charles from his counting-house and orders him to leave town with his family, so as to end the involvement of Sir Stephen's son Frederic with Charles's sister Eliza. Sir Stephen's objection is to Eliza's unsuitable poverty. It is Sheva who changes everything by generous loans and the gift of a dowry. Hence in the fifth act Charles can introduce him to the assembled company as "My benefactor; your's, Eliza; Frederic's; your's, dear mother; all mankind's: The widow's friend, the orphan's father, the poor man's protector, the universal philanthropist" (p. 73). As the benefactions are poured out at the end of a Cumberland comedy, the impulse is to cry with Dryden's Dorax, "O stop this headlong Torrent of your goodness: / It comes too fast upon a feeble Soul. . . ."[21] And indeed the emotional effect for which Cumberland strives is closely related to that of the quarrel-and-reconciliation scene which Dryden knew to be sure-fire, exploiting it in *All for Love* and *Troilus and Cressida* before he came to *Don Sebastian.* In both kinds of scene triumphant good nature brings harmony out of chaos. In tragedy, where most early examples of the quarrel-and-reconciliation scene are found, the harmony cannot last, but the display of good nature adds a dimension to the hero's stature. At the end of a comedy, where the establishment of harmony is the expectation set up by the genre, the display of good nature offers a comparable enhancement of character. The admiration thus aroused fits perfectly into Cumberland's program for comedy.

If a performer of unexpected benefactions is wanted, it is hard to beat a reformed misanthropist, and the emotional appeal of one of Cumberland's most successful late comedies, *The Wheel of Fortune,* performed in 1795, one year after *The Jew,* derives in large part from the reformation of the misanthropic Penruddock. Boaden considered John Philip Kemble's interpretation of this role "one of the most perfect impersonations that had ever excited human sympathy."[22] But the figure of the misanthrope seems to have fascinated Cumberland much earlier. In 1768, before he had had a major dramatic success, he wrote an alteration of Shakespeare's *Timon of Athens.* In this version Timon has a daughter, Evanthe, with whom Alcibiades is in love. When he comes with his army to crush Athens, it is she, even more than the senators, who persuades him to give up his revenge. Having accomplished this part of her design, she says, "I've sav'd a city; grant me now, kind Gods, / To save a father."[23] Cumberland makes the death of Timon the final scene, for which the setting establishes the emotional context:

> *The prospect of a rude wild country, to a considerable extent, with the ruins of a temple to* Faunus, Timon *is discovered at the extremity of the stage led in by* Flavius: *At the same time* Evanthe *enters at the front, surveys him some time, and while he slowly advances, speaks.*

> (p. 57)

Evanthe tries to persuade Timon to return to the now friendly Athens, but he refuses. When Alcibiades arrives to add his plea, Timon still refuses, but he immediately agrees to give his daughter to the victorious hero. Although he is still a misanthrope ("Shun mankind," he tells them), he is affectionate to his daughter and quick to reward his old friend. In Shakespeare's play Timon's epitaph is read in the penultimate moment:

> Seek not my name. A plague consume you, wicked caitiffs left!

> Here lie I, Timon, who, alive, all living men did hate.

> Pass by and curse thy fill, but pass and stay not here thy gait.[24]

Alcibiades then calls him "noble Timon," but it is a terrible nobility we hear in that voice from the grave. Cumberland manages to drain much of the bitterness

out of the death of his misanthrope by having Timon, just before he dies, invoke heaven's blessing on Alcibiades and Evanthe. Visually there is a balance of opposing impressions: the scene is bleak, but Timon dies on the steps of the ruined temple, surrounded by his daughter, his friend, and his faithful steward Flavius.

In Nos. 17 and 18 of the first edition of *The Observer* Cumberland tells the story of a misanthrope to illustrate the false opinions a man may have of good or bad fortune, "overreacting," as we should say, to either one, only to find later that it was not so good or so bad as it seemed: "An extraordinary example occurs to me of this criminal excess of sensibility in the person of a Frenchman named Chaubert, who happily lived long enough to repent the extravagance of his misanthropy."[25] As to the causes of this "excess of sensibility," "the principal disgust, which turned him furious against mankind, seems to have arisen from the treachery of a friend, who ran away with his mistress, just when Chaubert was on the point of marrying her. . . ." (An identical treachery is later made the cause of Penruddock's misanthropy.) Chaubert, "whose passions were always in extremes, had given a thousand instances of romantic generosity to this unworthy friend, and . . . had even saved him from drowning one day . . ." (p. 156).

These details are revealing. Within each misanthrope, it seems (Timon is the classic example), is a disillusioned benefactor. Chaubert, after years of wandering, meets the master of an English ship who has been ruined by the man who stole Chaubert's wife-to-be. Yet this Englishman has forgiven his enemy and has adopted the man's maltreated son. Chaubert begins to admire the mariner and pity the boy until finally "The long-repressed emotions of humanity now burst so violently upon me, that they choaked my speech, and I could only clasp the galant boy in my arms and shower my tears upon his neck" (p. 168). When, by an amazing coincidence, Chaubert discovers that his former friend and mistress once attempted to poison him, he sees that the loss of this woman was a blessing. The moral of the story is "resignation to Providence," which serves as a title in the table of contents, and the second instalment ends with a long fragment of a comedy by Menander's contemporary, Philemon, where a servant advises his master not to complain of misfortune: "You may send yourself out of the world with sorrow," he says, "but I think it better to stay my time in it and be happy" (p. 174). It will be remembered that in another *Observer* Cumberland praises Philemon for avoiding the misanthropy into which Menander sometimes sinks. The best kind of comedy is the obvious analogue to a story of discarded misanthropy.

Penruddock's life, like Chaubert's, is dominated by unexpected turns of "the wheel of fortune," his problems are essentially similar, and like Chaubert, he turns from hatred to benevolence. While the final gesture of the *Observer* story is resignation, however, the final gesture of the play—one that has a far greater dramatic impact—is forgiveness.[26]

The opening scene presents the hero at the nadir of his fortunes, living in a cottage in a remote part of the country. The forest setting and the opening dialogue immediately convey the impression of Penruddock's isolation, and his first words display his "surly humor." By a nicely contrived irony a stroke of unexpected good fortune brings out the worst in him. He finds that he has inherited a fortune and the means to ruin Woodville, the treacherous friend who stole his fiancée, Arabella, gambled away both his money and hers, and then, overcome by remorse, left her. Like the villain of melodrama, Penruddock gloats: "Woodville at my mercy! If there's a man on earth, that can inspire me with revenge, it is that treacherous, base, deceitful rival."[27] The remainder of the play shows why Penruddock does not take that revenge.

First, in a London street, he compares the noise and crowds to the solitude he has left: "How rich was I in my contented poverty! how poor has Fortune made me by these soul-tormenting riches!" (II; p. 31). Later, in "a magnificent Ball Room" of the house he has inherited, he exclaims, "'Sdeath! can a man that has look'd Nature in the face, gaze on these fripperies?" (III; p. 44). With these Stoic sentiments, worthy of a Senecan chorus, the opposition of simple Nature to corrupt society is neatly superimposed on the opposition of misanthropic retreat to living with one's fellow man. Each locale, the forest and the ball room, has a double significance.

In the ball room, during the third act, Penruddock receives two visits which move him and, for the audience, deepen the contradictions in his relationship to society. The first is from Henry, the son of Woodville and Arabella. At an earlier encounter Henry described Penruddock as a "gloomy misanthrope, . . . harden'd into savage insensibility, . . . [issuing] like a hungry lion from his den, to ravage and devour" (II; pp. 34-35), unaware that he was addressing the lion. Now Penruddock tells him the story of Woodville's treachery in order to justify this lion-like behavior.

After Henry's departure Sydenham, a plain-speaking acquaintance of Penruddock, arrives to reproach him for not forgiving Woodville, ". . . when you might have conquer'd him by generosity" (p. 49). He goes on to say that Henry's poverty is likely to prevent his marriage to an admirable but indigent young lady. Unless Penruddock relents, these two will also be the victims of his revenge. Penruddock does not alter his grim bearing during the interview (Sydenham later compares him to "a gloomy nightpiece in a gilded frame") but he gives hints of inner alteration in his closing soliloquy:

Here's a bold spirit! These are the loud-tongu'd moralists, who make benevolence a bully, and mouth us into mercy by the dint of noise and impudence—but I shall lower his tone.—Who waits?—[JENKINS *appears*]—Tell my Attorney I wou'd speak with him.

[*Exit.*]

END OF ACT III

(p. 51)

Here some of those "ingenious turns of words" which Cumberland sometimes recognized as components of the *vis comica* provide amusement as they support a facade which is beginning to crumble. As the curtain drops we do not know how Penruddock will lower Sydenham's tone or what he wants to discuss with his attorney, but our suspicions are shrewdly aroused.

In fact, as the next act makes clear, Penruddock has already changed his plans. As Chaubert began to admire the mariner, he has seen that "Sydenham has a heart" (p. 57), and, like Chaubert, he has been touched by the son of his former love. The consequences are also similar: "the long-repressed emotions of humanity" burst upon him, and he arranges with his lawyer to settle money on both Arabella and Henry. His benefactions are finally made known in the highly emotional scenes of Act V, in which Arabella, Henry, Sydenham, and Woodville, come to thank him. Having made possible Henry's wedding and the reuniting of Arabella and Woodville, Penruddock now plans to return to his cottage, not as a misanthrope but as one who has learned "that the true use of riches is to share them with the worthy; and the sole remedy for injuries, to forgive them" (p. 79).

These are the concluding words of the play. In this climactic position Cumberland placed the sort of "tender and religious sentiments" which he admired in the fragments of Moschion. It is a reasonable guess that for him they contributed to the moral and emotional uplift which he thought to be an important part of comic force. The ending of the play has much in common with melodrama,[28] but it also accords perfectly with the pattern that Northrop Frye derives from Greek New Comedy, and designates as the distinctive "mythos" of comedy.[29] What makes *The Wheel of Fortune* pure Cumberland does not invalidate his claim to be a traditionalist.

III

From the eighteenth century to the twentieth, people have marvelled how Cumberland could have failed (as he apparently did) to detect the irony in Goldsmith's mock epitaph of him in *Retaliation*. Some of the key lines are:

Here Cumberland lies having acted his parts,
The Terence of England, the mender of hearts;

A flattering painter, who made it his care
To draw men as they ought to be not as they are.
His gallants are all faultless, his women divine,
And comedy wonders at being so fine; . . .

* * *

Say, where has our poet this malady caught,
Or wherefore his characters thus without fault?
Say, was it that vainly directing his view,
To find out mens virtues and finding them few,
Quite sick of pursuing each troublesome elf,
He grew lazy at last and drew from himself?[30]

The answer may be that he dismissed some of it as
friendly rallying (for example, the accusation of flattery,
which he would have resented if he had taken it
seriously), and wanted to believe that he was the English Terence—still better, "the mender of hearts."
Above all, this choleric man may have fancied the picture of himself as a somewhat disillusioned seeker after
virtue, who, like Penruddock, looks at last for the benevolence beneath his own rough exterior. To the reader
of the *Memoirs* it is clear that the part Cumberland always wanted to play was the benefactor in one of his
own comedies.

Notes

1. *The Life of Garrick* (London, 1801), II, 109.

2. See Oliver W. Ferguson, "Sir Fretful Plagiary and
Goldsmith's 'An Essay on the Theatre': The Background of Richard Cumberland's 'Dedication to
Detraction,'" *Quick Springs of Sense,* ed. Larry S.
Champion (Athens: Univ. of Georgia Press, 1974),
pp. 113-20; and Richard Cumberland, *The Choleric Man,* ed. Olaf S. Olsen, Diss. NYU 1968, p.
13. Although Goldsmith's authorship of the essay
was revealed in 1798, Cumberland's flattering portrait of him and account of the "Dedication to Detraction" in his *Memoirs of Richard Cumberland*
(1806; ed. Henry Flanders [Philadelphia, 1856],
pp. 176-79, 185-90, 193-94) suggest that, surprisingly, he had remained in the dark. For a differing
opinion on these matters see John Loftis, *Sheridan
and the Drama of Georgian England* (Oxford:
Blackwell, 1976), pp. 15-17.

3. *Collected Works of Oliver Goldsmith,* ed. Arthur
Friedman (Oxford: Clarendon Press, 1966), III,
210, 213.

4. *The Choleric Man* (London, 1775), p. ix. Quotations from Cumberland's plays are taken from the
first editions. Several of them are also to be found
in the volumes of *Bell's British Theatre,* Mrs.
Inchbald's *British Theatre,* and *Cumberland's
British Theatre.*

5. *Collected Works,* III, 210-11. These comments
were apparently borrowed from Voltaire (see p.

211, n. 4), but were in any case characteristic of
what had been standard opinion for hundreds of
years.

6. A number of different interpretations have been
offered in this century. See, for example, L. A.
Post, "The Art of Terence," *Classical Weekly,* 23
(1929-30), 121-28; Roy C. Flickinger, "Terence
and Menander," *Classical Journal,* 26 (1930-31),
676-94; Alfred et Maurice Croiset, *Histoire de la
littérature grecque,* III, 3d. ed. (Paris: Fontemo-
ing, 1913), 653; *The Choleric Man,* ed. Olsen, p.
16.

7. See my "Aristophanes, Plautus, Terence, and the
Refinement of English Comedy," *Studies in the
Literary Imagination,* 10 (1977), 91-108.

8. See the edition of Terence by Le Fèvre (Saumur,
1571), where he quotes and comments on the opinions of the "ancients" in his prefatory address "Ad
Lectorem."

9. See her very polite dissent from her father's opinion in *Les Comédies de Térence* (Amsterdam and
Leipzig, 1747), pp. lviii-lix. The first edition of
her translation appeared in 1688.

10. *Observer* No. 147 in Alexander Chalmers, *British
Essayists* (London, 1802-03), XLIV, 183. *The Observer* first appeared in 1785 with forty papers.
Many more were added in volumes published in
the next five years; Chalmers then included them
in his series, where they are most readily available. The translations (without the comments in
The Observer) were later reprinted in Robert Walpole's *Comicorum Graecorum Fragmenta* (1805)
and in James Bailey's work of the same title
(1840).

11. P. vi of the critique prefixed to C. Cooke's edition
of the play, which was first published separately
(no date), then in Vol. IV of Cooke's *British
Drama* (London, 1817).

12. Bishop Hurd, in criticizing Fontenelle's theory of
comedy, speaks of "the passion of ridicule,"
though he does not think other kinds of pleasantry
can be said to "move" the spectator. See Horace,
*Epistolae ad Pisones . . . To which are added
Critical Dissertations by the Reverend Mr. Hurd,*
5th ed., II (Dublin, 1768), 55.

13. (London, 1772), p. vi.

14. Critique, p. viii, in Cooke's *British Drama,* XIV.

15. Critique, p. xxi, in Cooke's *British Drama,* XIV.

16. *The Choleric Man,* Introduction, p. xliii.

17. *The West Indian* (London, 1771), II.vi; p. 27.

18. *Richard Cumberland: His Life and Dramatic
Works* (New Haven: Yale Univ. Press, 1917), p.

99. Joseph Keenan, in his unpublished dissertation, "The Poetics of High Georgian Comedy" (U. Wisconsin, 1969), prefers to call "serious comedies" such as *The Fashionable Lover, The Jew,* and *The Wheel of Fortune* melodramas (pp. 222-41), but although melodramatic elements are clearly present, it seems to me a mistake to distinguish so sharply between these plays and others written according to the same principles. Cumberland called them all comedies.

19. Quoted more fully above from *Observer,* No. 147 and the "Dedication to Detraction."

20. *The Jew* (London, 1794), Li; p. 4.

21. *Don Sebastian,* IV.iii.628-29 in California Dryden, XV (Berkeley: Univ. of California Press, 1976), 190.

22. James Boaden, *Memoirs of the Life of John Philip Kemble, Esq.* (London, 1825), II, 140.

23. *Timon of Athens* (London, 1771), V; p. 50.

24. *Timon of Athens,* ed. H. J. Oliver (London: Methuen, 1959), V.iv.71-73.

25. (London, 1785), p. 156; in Chalmers' *British Essayists,* XLI, the story appears in a slightly altered form in Nos. 15 and 16.

26. Mrs. Inchbald and others assumed that Cumberland took the idea for his play from Kotzebue's *The Stranger* (see her introduction to *The Wheel of Fortune* in *The British Theatre,* XVIII [London, 1808]); but although misanthropy and repentance are also the subject of that play (whose German title is *Menschenhass und Reue*), the plot is totally different.

27. *The Wheel of Fortune* (London, 1795), I; p. 11.

28. See M. J. Landa, "The Grandfather of Melodrama," *Cornhill Magazine,* n.s. 59 (1925), 476-84; and Keenan, "Poetics," pp. 222-41.

29. *Anatomy of Criticism* (Princeton, N. J.: Princeton Univ. Press, 1957), p. 163.

30. *Collected Works,* IV, 355-56; see also *Memoirs,* pp. 188-89; Williams, *Richard Cumberland* [(1917)], pp. 126-31.

Elizabeth M. Yearling (essay date December 1981)

SOURCE: Yearling, Elizabeth M. "Victims of Society in Three Plays by Cumberland." *Durham University Journal* 74, no. 1 (December 1981): 23-30.

[*In the following essay, Yearling analyzes Cumberland's attitudes toward social prejudice in the plays* The West Indian, The Fashionable Lover, *and* The Jew.]

An avowed aim of sentimental drama was to encourage moral behaviour. Often this remained a generalized ideal, as in Steele's desire to help the proprietors of the established theatre 'to make their Representations as beneficial, and instructive, as they are delightful to the People'.[1] Sometimes the intention was more specific. In 1771, Richard Cumberland set about his task of instruction with **The West Indian** which contained, he hoped, a new moral message. He believed 'there was an opening for some originality, and an opportunity for shewing at least my good will to mankind, if I introduced the characters of persons, who had been usually exhibited on the stage, as the butts for ridicule and abuse, and endeavoured to present them in such lights, as might tend to reconcile the world to them, and them to the world'.[2] The victims of national, professional, or religious biases were to be his heroes, and the major results of this policy were **The West Indian, The Fashionable Lover** (1772), and **The Jew** (1794). There are problems in such a programme of reform. When eighteenth-century writers discussed other nations, and particularly those they considered to be of another race, they frequently cast doubts on the foreigners' intelligence.[3] Sentimental drama is not properly equipped to defend anyone against charges of mental inferiority, because its tendency is to reject the intellect and exalt the emotions. The philosophy which lies behind the drama was prepared to give a role to reason, and to be realistic about human nature: early in the eighteenth century, Shaftesbury emphasized the need for everyone to 'reason concerning his own Happiness: "What his *Good* his, and what his *Ill*"'[4] and Lord Kames, arguing that benevolence which damages oneself is undesirable, asserted that 'the true moral balance depends on a subordination of self-love to duty, and of arbitrary benevolence to self-love'.[5] But Cumberland, with a sentimental dramatist's soft-centred approach to the current benevolent philosophy, leaves little room in his characters' good natures for the rational element which more seasoned thinkers saw was necessary. How successful then can the dramatist be in his difficult task of countering charges of mental—and moral—inferiority with evidence of good-heartedness?

In **The West Indian,** Cumberland stands up for a creole planter and an Irishman. The latter, a standard comic figure in English drama, represents victims of religious and national prejudice. David Hume, for example, in his essay 'Of National Characters' comments disparagingly on the honesty of the Irish.[6] Cumberland highlights the drawbacks of Irish birth by enlisting Major O'Flaherty in the service of Austria to show the 'melancholy and impolitic alternative' that religion condemned him to (**Memoirs,** p. 204), and also presents him as positively likeable: 'whilst you furnish him with expressions, that excite laughter, you must graft them upon sentiments, that deserve applause' (**Memoirs,** p. 205). The creole planter is less familiar but had become a type much resented in London and criticized in the literature of the late eighteenth century.[7] Cumberland had himself seen Samuel Foote's *The Patron* (1764) with its caricatured West Indian, Sir Peter Pepperpot, who describes a woman in sugar-planter's imagery: 'sweet as a sugar-cane, strait as a bamboo'.[8] The breed was particularly associated with sexual immorality.

Cumberland's planter, Belcour, is a sentimental hero who with all his faults is good-hearted and generous: 'as I could not keep consistency of character without a mixture of failings, when I gave him charity, I gave him that, which can cover a multitude' (*Memoirs,* p. 204). His failings consist mainly in a hot-headed pursuit of Louisa Dudley, a girl of respectable birth but low fortune. She appears fair game to Belcour since her wicked landlady pretends to him that Louisa is the mistress, not the sister, of Charles Dudley. Belcour's charity emerges in his financial aid to Charles's father, whose impossible sister-in-law. Lady Rusport, has refused help. In the end Belcour learns the truth about Louisa, is forgiven by everyone because of his generosity, and acknowledged by his host, Stockwell, as his own son.

The critics were not happy with the play, and although the modern reader may find odd their stress on moral issues, instead of any detailed discussion of the play's effectiveness as a blow against prejudice, their comments indicate very well where the dramatist's propaganda goes astray. Cumberland himself admits that 'the moral of the West Indian is not quite unexceptionable' (*Memoirs,* p. 219), and the *Monthly Review* found several weaknesses. The reviewer begins with praise: 'the sentiment is at once elevated and tender. It excites a curiosity strongly interested, and has so blended the pathetic and ridiculous, that if the spectator or reader has sensibility and discernment, he will be kept almost continually laughing with tears in his eyes.'[9] The objections follow: Lady Rusport's step-daughter Charlotte is wrong to defend Dudley Senior's marriage since over-hasty marriages of penniless young men to penniless young women are one of life's sources of misery. The reviewer had supposed that a marriage which made being dead 'eligible to the wife', threatened the husband with finding employment in Senegambia, and left the son and daughter poor, 'would be pointed out as a warning to the young and thoughtless against such engagements' (p. 143). Cumberland irresponsibly supports Charlotte's attitude, although he does not adventure far in doing so. He dodges moral and practical problems by revealing in the end that the Dudley family has been robbed of its inheritance only by Lady Rusport's amateurish machinations. Stockwell is variously criticized. He is tactless in entrusting a financial deal with Charlotte Rusport to Belcour, who is a stranger to her: indeed Stockwell sends Belcour off on this delicate mission with an active encouragement to indulge in 'gallantry'. He is accused of giving 'a bad lesson both to children and to parents' (p. 147) in his admission that he has no right to stop Belcour's libertine course. His desire to correct his son is checked by his inability at this stage to divulge his own relationship to the young man. If his reticence is, as Cumberland's reviewer suggests, misguided, it is passed off by the dramatist as humanity. 'O Nature, what it is to be a father! Just such a thoughtless headlong thing was I when I beguiled his mother into love' (III. i: p. 371). This further moral flaw is unaccountably overlooked by the reviewer. Stockwell himself was guilty as a young man of embarking on a secret marriage: 'the inferiority of my condition made it hopeless to expect her father's consent' (I. i: p. 346). No doubt the Monthly reviewer could have traced Stockwell's shaky morality back to this inauspicious beginning. Within the play it provides some explanation of the merchant's extraordinary complaisance over his son's bad behaviour and it indicates that Cumberland was not worrying much about the morality or immorality of inappropriate matches. Not surprisingly, the reviewer finds him as culpable as his characters. He 'makes high spirits, strong feelings, and warm passions, a kind of dispensation for debauchery' (p. 144); 'to represent the irregularities of a young fellow like this as *necessary,* is absolving him from every tie, which it should be the labour of the moralist to strengthen' (p. 145).

These criticisms may be rather priggish but the reviewer is, I think, right in his attack on Cumberland's presentation of Belcour. Within the play's moral context his pardon and repentance come too easily. Even if we consider his irregularities fairly harmless, the characters Cumberland manipulates all believe very strongly that Belcour's behaviour over Louisa has been reprehensible and for them to forgive him so easily because he is good-hearted betrays softening of the brain and of the moral fibre. Although Cumberland's biographer, Stanley Williams, pauses to comment that eighteenth-century dramatic 'critiques were impressionistic, unscholarly, and often absurd,'[10] they sometimes include objections we are inclined to accept, and they are helpful through being more in touch with the moral attitudes of their own period than we can hope to be. Contemporary attitudes to Major O'Flaherty also illustrate this. The casual moral comments of Cumberland's acquaintances have much in common with published criticism. Lord Clare (*Memoirs,* p. 226) and the Monthly reviewer (p. 148) were both disturbed by a passing reference to O'Flaherty's five wives. The actor Moody was left to solve this problem and added the phrase '*en militaire*' to O'Flaherty's mention of his wives (*Memoirs,* p. 226). I find it difficult to imagine that his contribution did much to smooth moral hackles. The *Monthly Review* found the Major inconsistent since a fortune-hunter cannot also be an honourable man (p. 148). And his eavesdropping, although it discovers Lady Rusport's deception, was considered by Lord Lyttelton 'unbecoming of him as a man of honour' (*Memoirs,* p. 223).

Cumberland, ever-anxious to please but not making too good a job of it added 'a few words of palliation into the Major's part, by making him say upon resorting to his hiding place—*I'll step behind this screen and listen; a good soldier must sometimes fight in ambush as well as in the open field*' (**Memoirs**, p. 223).

From all these comments we learn that however much good nature Cumberland lavishes on these representatives of minority groups, he still leaves them open to charges of immoral and dishonourable behaviour. And with Belcour he does little to dispel current notions about West Indian planters. He underlines the origins of his good-hearted hero. Stockwell prepares us for Belcour's behaviour by expecting him to be 'wild, perhaps, as the manner of his country is' (I. iv: p. 348), and before his first entrance Belcour provokes a riot by treating all the wharf-side hangers-on as if they were slaves (I. v: p. 349). The climate of his birth is either blamed for his wildness or acclaimed as a cause of good nature. He laments his 'cursed tropical constitution' which results in 'inflammatory passions' (IV. x: p. 392); he is not yet, claims Stockwell, 'assimilated to this climate' (V. iii: p. 399). But for Charles Dudley he has 'a warmth of heart peculiar to his climate' (III. vii: p. 379), and Charlotte is impelled to bless 'the torrid zone for ever, whose rapid vegetation quickens nature into such benignity!' (III. vii: p. 380).

Here Cumberland falls in with one contemporary explanation of national differences, that the climate of the different parts of the world has a strong effect on the inhabitants. According to Buffon, 'Climate, food, manners and customs produce not only a difference in sentiment, but even in the external form of different people.'[11] Lord Kames opposed this view with the argument that the differences between peoples were not *caused* by different climates but that men were actually of different races which were suited to different climates. This gets rid of Buffon's causality but still associates varieties of appearance and behaviour with varieties of climate.[12] David Hume, while arguing against the influence of climate, admitted his suspicion that all those living beyond the poles or between the tropics were 'inferior to the rest of the species' and advanced, very tentatively, an explanation for southerners' liking of women: 'the genial heat of the sun, in the countries exposed to his beams, inflames the blood, and exalts the passion between the sexes.'[13] Belcour is a white West Indian, not an indigenous native, but the characters' comments indicate that Cumberland is applying the climate theory to his hero. Belcour is also given some imagery fitting his homeland: 'I declare I know no more than if I was in the Blue Mountains'; 'I shall be wasted to the size of a sugar-cane' (II. v: p. 358). And Mrs Fulmer, the wicked landlady, alludes to plantation conditions in her jibe that 'girls of her sort are not to be kept waiting like negro slaves in your sugar plantations' (III. iii: p. 372). All this scarcely amounts to precise and unprejudiced characterization. Cumberland's approach is kindlier than Foote's in *The Patron*, but Belcour shares traits and imagery (the 'sugar-cane' reference) with Sir Peter Pepperpot, and one of the few extra details, Mrs Fulmer's joke, is derogatory. The accusation is ignored by Belcour. Not only does the play not answer this fairly standard belief about West Indian planters but the action almost corroborates it, since Belcour repents of his ill-intentioned pursuit of Louisa only when he discovers she is a lady. Part of Cumberland's trouble was perhaps that the charge was often true,[14] but this is no complete excuse for creating a character whose nationality though sketchily portrayed conforms to the image Cumberland is supposed to be changing. He has united a series of clichés about West Indians with the stereotype of the benevolent man.

Cumberland reveals his sanguine attitude to the problems of re-educating the public when he describes Belcour: 'To the West Indian I devoted a generous spirit, and a vivacious giddy dissipation; I resolved he should love pleasure much, but honour more' (**Memoirs**, p. 204). The character is founded on an idea, not on any observation.

The treatment of O'Flaherty has similar flaws. Cumberland wrote the play while visiting his father in Ireland, but he did not make full use of his experience there. He was entertained by the Irish: 'I . . . was withal uncommonly delighted with their wild eccentric humours, mixing with all ranks and descriptions of men, to my infinite amusement' (**Memoirs**, p. 192). The reaction is honest enough but the 'wild eccentric humours' have been pared down in O'Flaherty to a verbal trait—'expressions, that excite laughter' (**Memoirs**, p. 205). This seems a move away from the Irishmen Cumberland had met to the stage Irishman who is laughed at because of the odd way he talks. Indeed whatever his personal observation, Cumberland admitted to having used a glossary for O'Flaherty's phraseology. Also he mentally blue-pencilled some of his first-hand knowledge. He wrote of the Irish character, 'Though I strove to present it in its fairest and best light upon the stage, truth obliges me to confess there was another side of the picture, which could not have been contemplated without affright and horror! Atrocities and violences, which set all law and justice at defiance, were occasionally committed in this savage and licentious quarter, and suffered to pass over with impunity' (**Memoirs**, p. 193). Since Cumberland was engaged in a defence of the Irish, the purging of these disturbing traits is understandable, but his inability to make full use of what he learned in Ireland results in a flattening of the Irishman who is reduced, like Belcour, to a compound of stage type and generous nature. The treatment of these characters clarifies what is wrong with **The West Indian**: Cumberland wrote it partly to change attitudes to national types who were traditionally mocked, but he fell back on accepted ideas about these types and added little from his own experience. As a result Belcour and O'Flaherty remain unconvincing figures, unlikely to win general approval for their real-life compatriots.

The same is true of Cumberland's next attempt at corrective dramaturgy. An acquaintance suggested that he should do for the Scots what he had done for the Irishman and the West Indian. In *The Fashionable Lover* he took up the idea. 'I began to frame the character of Colin Macleod upon the model of a Highland servant, who with scrupulous integrity, and a great deal of nationality about him, managed all the domestic affairs of Sir Thomas Mills's household . . . With no other guide for the dialect of my Macleod than what the Scotch characters of the stage supplied me with, I endowed him with a good heart, and sent him to seek his fortune' (*Memoirs,* p. 254). This sounds more promising. Colin Macleod is at least founded on a real person. But why do Cumberland's observations go only half-way? Why take his dialect from stage Scotsmen? It looks as if Cumberland may again resort to clichéd national peculiarities combined with good-heartedness. It is not encouraging that the play's first line is 'Hoot! fellows, haud your honds.'[15]

The Fashionable Lover has the complicated plot involving long-lost relations that gives sentimental comedy an opportunity for joyful tears. Lord Abberville, a fashionable spendthrift, is to marry Miss Bridgemore but is fascinated with Augusta Aubrey, the orphan who is Cinderella to the Bridgemore family. He forces an entry into her bedroom where he is found by Miss Bridgemore, herself no stricken betrothed but a rival for Augusta's wooer, Tyrrel. The ensuing disturbance causes Augusta to flee, but she is intercepted in the street by Colin Macleod, Lord Abberville's Scots servant and lodged safely with a Mrs. Macintosh whom Colin does not know but whose house stands nearby. He assumes that a Scots name on the door guarantees honesty; her name, alas, conceals a thoroughly English whoremonger, Nan Rawlins. Tyrrel learns Augusta's whereabouts and visits her, encountering Lord Abberville who has been enticed there by news of fresh blood: the former leaves scornfully, persuaded of her guilt, and Lord Abberville tries to rape Augusta but is interrupted by Colin and Tyrrel's uncle, Mortimer. Augusta becomes the latter's ward and eventually the arrival of her lost father tidies up the mess. Bridgemore, trusted with Aubrey's daughter and his money, has swindled him and has also ruined Lord Abberville. Everyone is tricked into visiting Mortimer's home where Bridgemore is exposed but pardoned at Augusta's request, and Tyrrel and Augusta betrothed. Lord Abberville repents.

The play mounts a general attack on vice. Cumberland speaks in his *Memoirs* of its including 'sentiments, laudably directed against national prejudice, breach of trust, seduction, gaming, and the general dissipation of the time then present. I could not deny it a preference to *[T]he West-Indian* in a moral light' (p. 255). The *Monthly Review* agreed with him: the later play was 'more correct, more chaste, and, consequently, on the whole, a more moral performance' but also less spirited.[16] It is unquestionably an inferior play. The rehabilitation of the Scots is carried out in a manner that rouses neither enthusiasm nor belief: no other people on the globe, we learn, 'have more love and charity for one another' (III. i: p. 45). Also Colin lacks the vitality of Belcour and O'Flaherty and much of his good-heartedness is demonstrated by unconvincing remarks such as, 'in England he that wants money wants every thing; in Scotland now, few have it, but every one can do without it' (II. i: p. 33). His attempts to help those in distress are only partially successful. And it rather tells against the Scots that they are deceived by 'Mrs Macintosh' who has adopted her pseudonym because it brings all the Scots to buy in her shop. To leave Augusta with a stranger on the assumption that anyone with the surname Macintosh must be honest and kindly betrays another, ill-founded kind of racial prejudice. Augusta, temporarily astringent—a welcome change—accuses Colin of 'a partiality to your country rather than to virtue' (III. v: p. 63). His behaviour confirms the lack of thought that seems the natural partner of benevolence in Cumberland's racial protégés. No nation is likely to be grateful to Cumberland for being presented as lovable but stupid. In giving this impression he confirms ideas of mental inferiority.

Cumberland's attitude to Macleod reveals more than he guesses. In his Advertisement he discusses the sources of comedy available to him. 'The level manners of a polished country like this, do not supply much matter for the comic muse, which delights in variety and extravagance; wherever, therefore, I have made any attempt at novelty, I have found myself obliged either to dive into the lower class of men, or betake myself to the outskirts of the empire: the centre is too equal and refined for such purposes' (p. iv). His words should warn us that Colin will be Cumberland's good-natured man with a Scots accent. Sir Walter Scott, who liked O'Flaherty, sniffed at Macleod: 'the character of Colin Macleod, the honest Scotch servant, not being drawn from nature, has little, excepting tameness, to distinguish it from the Gibbies and Sawnies which had hitherto possession of the stage, as the popular representatives of the Scottish nation'.[17] Cumberland has his eyes wide open for comic eccentrics since the stage Scotsman of *The Fashionable Lover* is briefly joined by a stage Frenchman, La Jeunesse, and a stage Welshman, Dr. Druid, a relatively sympathetic character, but an obsessive variously labelled as 'that old piece of pedantry' and 'that buffoon' (I. i: p. 13) and addicted to alliterative word pairs and triplets. It is also slightly disturbing to find the author of *The Jew* including in this earlier play the stock assumptions about Jews: a Jewish usurer, Napthali, helps Bridgemore to appropriate Aubrey's money and to ruin Abberville. Louis Zangwill comments, in a paper read to the Jewish Historical Society, that 'unless specially alive to injustice, Cumberland would as a matter of course avail himself of the usual stock figures that were at the disposal of dramatists. Whilst drawing Napthali he was so engrossed with Colin that he did not stop to reflect.'[18] And a similar oversight troubled Sir Walter Scott who commented on Cumberland's prejudiced description of Jewish characters in his novel, *John de Lancaster.*[19]

Further weakening any claim by Cumberland of rescuing the Scots from prejudice is his own generosity in handing round benevolence. As a philanthropist Colin is matched by Mortimer, a man of 'marble outside' (II. i: p. 27) but secret generosity, who is more efficient at doing good than is Abberville's highland retainer. Mortimer's faithful servant, Jarvis, is good-hearted; Tyrrel is credited with generosity and virtue. Aubrey loves his fellow men: 'he has made the human heart his study; he loves his own species' (v. ii: p. 88). Some of the wrong-doers develop consciences. A maid who has compromised Augusta is anxious to confess, and Lord Abberville eventually repents—'I have been lost in error' (v. ii: p. 97). This is one of Cumberland's irritating weaknesses. He is so free with generosity and humanity that particular cases lose their force. It comes as no surprise that Colin is warm-hearted since practically everyone else is, and his Scottishness becomes quite incidental. Cumberland claims in the Advertisement that 'the Comedy now submitted to the reader, is designed as an attempt upon his heart, and as such, proceeds with little deviation from mine' (p. iii). The reader, his heart distended, begins to long for an attempt on his head.

The demonstration is finally taken to self-defeating extremes in *The Jew.* Frederic Bertram secretly marries Eliza Ratcliffe who has no money, and is cut off by his father. The marriage horrifies Eliza's brother, Charles, and a quarrel with Frederic leads to a challenge. Perhaps the memory of attacks on *The West Indian* led to Cumberland's giving Charles an attitude which resembles that of the *Monthly Review*: 'The woman without fortune, that consents to a clandestine marriage with a man, whose whole dependence is upon an unforgiving father, never can be justified.'[20] But Sheva the Jew promises to help Charles, lends Frederic three hundred pounds and settles ten thousand pounds on Eliza. Only after these generous actions is the lucky chance revealed that Ratcliffe Senior had helped Sheva to escape from Spain. The play ends in the home of Mrs. Goodison, one of Sheva's beneficiaries, who also just happens to be Frederic and Eliza's landlady. There Eliza's charm wins over her father-in-law, the two young men return safely after a token duel, and Sheva's generosity is fully recognized and commended—'The widow's

friend, the orphan's father, the poor man's protector, the universal philanthropist' (v: p. 73). He has made Charles Ratcliffe his heir.

The play blurs its issues in the same way as does *The Fashionable Lover.* Charles has been kind and helpful to Sheva; Charles's father had saved Sheva's life; Frederic, inspired by love, is eloquent about 'the luxury of relieving honor, innocence and beauty from distress' (I: p. 10); even Frederic's harsh father, Sir Stephen, is won over by Eliza who then speaks of his 'generosity' (v: p. 69). Everyone in the play is ultimately soft-hearted, which emasculates Cumberland's defence of the Jew, particularly since Sheva's character is padded out with traits of the stage Jew. He has an appearance of avarice which puzzles Charles Ratcliffe: 'You give away your money, it should seem, with the generosity of a prince, and I hear you lament over it in the language of a miser.' Sheva explains that 'I love my monies, I do love them dearly; but I love my fellow-creatures a little better' (II: p. 21). He lives like a miser, starving himself and his servants, but only in order to give his money to others. Cumberland has it both ways by including the stock notion of a Jew—'I shall be ruin'd, starv'd, wasted to a watch-light'—but also suggesting that the usual assumptions are inaccurate—'thou dost stint thine appetites to pamper thine affections' (I: p. 10). There are even reminders of Shylock and Launcelot Gobbo in the relationship of Sheva and his underfed servant Jabal who has to share an egg for dinner. Once again Cumberland achieves some of his comic effect by exploiting the very character he is supposed to be showing in an unprejudiced light: Jews, Scotsmen, Irishmen, West Indians may not in his plays have all the expected faults, but they are still odd enough for that social norm, the Englishman, to find them amusing.

Sheva is part of a programme of moral improvement which has lost its initial freshness. Also he is Cumberland's second attempt at defending the Jews. The dramatist first took up the cause of 'these poor people' who 'seem the butt at which all sects and persuasions level their contempt' in his periodical, *The Observer.*[21] There he concocts a letter from 'Abraham Abrahams' who complains of the treatment of the Jews in Britain, particularly on the stage, and requests in a postscript: 'if you could persuade one of the gentlemen or ladies who write plays . . . to give us poor Jews a kind lift in a new comedy, I am bold to promise we should not prove ungrateful on a third night' (I, 248-49). Cumberland records in his *Memoirs*: 'I wrote it upon principle, thinking it high time that something should be done for a persecuted race: I seconded my appeal to the charity of mankind by the character of Sheva, which I copied from this of Abrahams' (*Memoirs,* p. 457). Sheva is drawn from Cumberland's own earlier fictional invention, not from a living example, and like Abraham Abrahams, he is self-consciously aware of his ill-treatment as a literary figure. He has been called 'a blood-sucker, an extortioner, a Shylock' (I: p. 6); 'if your playwriters want a butt or a buffoon, or a knave to make sport of, out comes a Jew to be baited and buffeted' (I: p. 7). This echoes Abrahams's complaint about dramatists: 'if ever they are in search of a rogue, a usurer, or a buffoon, they are sure to make a Jew serve the turn' (*The Observer*, I, 248). Sheva's alliterative word pairs have more rhetorical flair but the similar construction of the sentences and the repetition of "buffoon" shows that Cumberland was not trying very hard to create any individual utterance for Sheva. He falls back on a paler version of the character in Nadab, the Jew in his later musical play, *The Jew of Mogadore.* Nadab, who 'is a hard hand at a bargain' but has 'a soft place in his heart' rejoices that 'thou hast monies, Nadab, and that makes my heart so merry',[22] but he passes his days buying slaves in order to redeem them. He is surrounded by other equally generous people, who encompass several nationalities—a blanket coverage of prejudice. Sheva, Abrahams, Nadab, all are Cumberland's spokesmen: 'The benevolence of the audience assisted me in rescuing a forlorn and persecuted character, which till then had only been brought upon the stage for the unmanly purpose of being made a spectacle of contempt, and a butt for ridicule' (*Memoirs,* p. 514).

The attempt to unite in Sheva a morally impressive Jew with the expected comic characteristics satisfied the *British Critic* only in outline. The incidents of the play, the reviewer claims:

> tend to place in an honourable light a description of people too generally stigmatized as base and corrupt. The design is, therefore, deserving of every encomium . . . As a drama, however the production before us cannot claim any distinguished merit. . . . That a Jew should possess the feelings of a man and the virtues of a Christian; that such a Jew, if opulent and wealthy, should be secretly charitable, and make an indigent Christian his heir, are surely probable things, in defiance of vulgar prejudice; but that with qualities like these should be connected avarice abroad and parsimony at home, usury in his contracts and cruelty to his domestics; that his good deeds should take so perfectly the resemblance of bad ones; and that his humanity, alive to strangers, should be dead to those of his own household, are circumstances which appear to pass the line of probable events. Admitting them credible, they would offer such an unnatural alliance of the best, with the worst qualities, as would effectually violate the properties of comedy; whose office it is to reflect the features of human life in its more usual and general forms.[23]

Stanley Williams in his biography of Cumberland (p. 232) quotes several critiques which praise the play's philanthropy and its ability to draw tears, but one of these, from the *Analytical Review,* again betrays the way Cumberland is still working with racial clichés. In Sheva are united 'with the peculiarities of his sect eminent virtues'; 'an uncommon, but perhaps not an unnatural compound of extreme frugality and noble generosity, mixed with a dash of oddity, which throws a comic cast of delicate humour over the whole'.[24] It is this last ingredient which M. J. Landa objects to, pointing out that where Cumberland could have made Sheva's loneliness impressive, he merely shows it as comic.[25] It is in connection with their sabbath observance that Kames asserts 'We laugh at the Jews, and we have reason'[26] but Cumberland makes little attempt to protect them from the patronizing laughter of their host nation.

The closest he comes to making a serious point is when he gives Sheva the following words: 'We have no abiding place on earth—no country, no home. Everybody rails at us, everybody flouts us, everybody points us out for their maygame and their mockery . . . How can you expect us to show kindness, when we receive none?' (I: p. 7). Here he touches on an argument advanced by Hume: 'A small sect or society amidst a greater are commonly most regular in their morals; because they are more remarked, and the faults of individuals draw dishonour on the whole. The only exception to this rule is, when the superstition and prejudices of the large society are so strong as to throw an infamy on the smaller society, independent of their morals. For in that case, having no character either to save or gain, they become careless of their behaviour, except among themselves.'[27] In fact it is more likely that Cumberland is following Shylock than introducing philosophical argument. For his rescuing of a traditional victim is once again not really complete. Zangwill argues that Cumberland wins the audience's attention and acceptance by portraying the standard Jew and then surprises them with the truth (p. 169), but such a revelation in a Cumberland play can no longer have been much of a surprise. The portrayal of Sheva is more likely to derive from the dramatist's desire for comic effects and his falling back on the stage Jew.

The Prologue to *The Jew* speaks of Cumberland's desire to destroy prejudice in Britain:

> 'Tis but one species in the wide extent
> Of Prejudice, at which our shaft is sent,
> 'Tis but this simple lesson of the heart—
> Judge not the Man by his exterior part:
> Virtue's strong root in every soil will grow,
> Rich ores lie buried under piles of snow.

It is clear that he likes to show good nature under an unlikely exterior wherever it occurs. The victims of specific national or religious prejudices are not very different from characters such as Mortimer in *The Fashionable Lover* who hides his heart of gold beneath a harsh surface, the elder Bertram in *The Jew* whose heart melts at the sight of Eliza, or Ruefull in *The Natural Son.* Characteristics are carried across from play to play. Ruefull, like Sheva, is apparently a miser who lives in a poor home and starves himself and his servant, but 'he does good to people out of spite'[28] and hates the thought of admitting to benevolent actions. Mortimer sees mankind as being without the merit to entitle him to happiness; Ruefull does not believe in human goodness. Vocabulary also is carried over. Mortimer's is 'a soft heart in a rough case' (II. i. p. 27); Ruefull is a 'rough shell, but there's virtue at the heart of him' (III. i: p. 43), a sentiment repeated later in the play—'a rough humour, but a most benevolent nature' (IV. i: p. 65). Cumberland's effects derive in each case from the contrast of a misanthropic exterior and a tender heart. And so comments such as that in the Advertisement to *The Fashionable Lover* about portraying the 'outskirts' of the empire mean that the recognizable victim figures were useful to Cumberland in providing him with comic national peculiarities which allowed him to individualize and which he did not therefore try to prove untrue. These central figures are Scots, Irish, and so on, partly because this provides Cumberland with unusual characters; they are benevolent because he liked to show all men as benevolent. But by spreading benevolence around he dilutes its flavour and devalues the major virtue of his heroes.

Although he claims to be dispelling prejudices, Cumberland is in danger of reinforcing them. His only defence of his central characters is their benevolence, and in underlining good-heartedness he risks suggesting mental inferiority. Occasionally he not only fails to answer criticism but confirms it: as was expected of creole planters, Belcour is a woman-chaser, besides being easy to dupe. And a result of the stress on heart rather than head is the impression Cumberland gives of patronizing his heroes: at times they are close to being lovable pets, and this emphasizes the racial difference which he was trying to play down. He also avoids the most difficult case of racial prejudice of the time—the negro. Scots and Irish could hardly be described as a different race; the Jew was acknowledged intelligent. Negroes were by some believed to be of a different species, and their intelligence was doubted. Hume could say little for them, though their defence was later taken up by the Abbé Grégoire.[29] Cumberland does not explore such awkward territory, despite venturing into warmer climates with Belcour and with *The Jew of Mogadore*'s Selim, Prince of Morocco. Cumberland was not really combatting national prejudice. He has an advantage on his own good-natured ground but it is an advantage tempered by his desire to illustrate virtually universal benevolence; and he would have to cede victory on his opponents' ground since his victim figures tend to conform to national stereotypes and to establish the mental inferiority and oddity of anyone who is not English. But it is interesting that *The West Indian, The Fashionable Lover,* and *The Jew* were among Cumberland's most successful plays: in these he was able to in-

dividualize the hero by uniting his own type figure of the unlikely good fellow with the stage clichés expected of his protégés. Ultimately Cumberland was benefited as much by his chosen victims of society as they benefit from him.

Notes

1. *Richard Steele's The Theatre 1720,* ed. John Loftis (Oxford, 1962), p. 8.

2. *Memoirs of Richard Cumberland* (London, 1806), pp. 203-204.

3. For details of racial theories see Richard H. Popkin, 'The Philosophical Basis of Eighteenth-Century Racism', *Studies in Eighteenth Century Culture,* III (1973), 245-262.

4. *Characteristicks of Men, Manners, Opinions, Times,* 3rd ed., 3 vols. (London, 1723), II, 442.

5. *Sketches of the History of Man,* 2 vols. (Edinburgh, 1774), II, 286. The 1778 edition, interestingly, substitutes 'discretionary' for 'arbitrary'.

6. *The Philosophical Works of David Hume,* ed. T. H. Green and T. H. Grose, 4 vols. (London, 1874-5), III, 244.

7. Wylie Sypher, 'The West-Indian as a "character" in the eighteenth century', *Studies in Philology,* XXXVI (1939), 503-520.

8. *The Dramatic Works of Samuel Foote,* 2 vols. (London, 1809), I, 16. Cumberland comments on the play in his *Memoirs,* p. 162.

9. XLIV (1771), 142.

10. *Richard Cumberland* (New Haven, 1917), p. 49.

11. *Buffon's Natural History,* abridged (London, 1791), p. 54.

12. 'Diversity of men and of languages', *Sketches of the History of Man,* I, 1-43.

13. *Philosophical Works,* III, 252 and 256.

14. Peter Abrahams, *Jamaica* (London, 1957), p. 50. Plantation owners were frequently absent, leaving behind them overseers and book-keepers who often kept slave mistresses.

15. *The Fashionable Lover* (London, 1793), p. 9.

16. XLVI (1772), 167.

17. *The Miscellaneous Prose Works of Sir Walter Scott,* 28 vols. (Edinburgh, 1834-6), III, 201.

18. 'Richard Cumberland Centenary Memorial Paper', *Transactions of the Jewish Historical Society of England,* VII (1911-14), 147-79 (p. 162).

19. *On Novelists and Fiction,* ed. Ioan Williams (London, 1968), p. 218.

20. *The Jew* (London, 1794), p. 54.

21. 3 vols. (London, 1822), no. 38, i, 244. Cumberland tells the story of Abraham Abrahams in nos. 40-46, i, 259-313. Abrahams, in the prose tale, rescues the widow of a Captain Goodison and her daughter: the name shared with Mrs Goodison of *The Jew* suggests some laziness of imagination.

22. *The Jew of Mogadore* (London, 1808), pp. 8 and 13.

23. vi (1795), 11.

24. xx (1794), 437.

25. *The Jew in Drama* (1926; rpt. Port Washington, N.Y., 1968), p. 136.

26. *Sketches of the History of Man,* ii, 449.

27. *Philosophical Works,* iii, 250, footnote.

28. *The Natural Son* (London, 1792), p. 74.

29. Eighteenth-century attitudes to the negro are summed up in Popkin, 'The Philosophical Basis of Eighteenth-Century Racism.' See also Hume, *Philosophical Works,* iii, 252, footnote, and Kames, *Sketches of the History of Man,* i, 32, where there is a suggestion that 'inferiority in their understanding' is not innate but caused by environment.

Oskar Wellens (essay date July 1985)

SOURCE: Wellens, Oskar. "The *London Review* (1809)." *Neophilologus* 69, no. 3 (July 1985): 452-63.

[*In the following excerpt, Wellens examines the circumstances surrounding the formation of the* London Review, *Cumberland's short-lived literary journal.*]

Whereas in the latter half of the eighteenth century a mere handful of journals allowed the English reader to keep himself informed about the latest publications, the opening decades of the nineteenth century witnessed an explosion in the number and variety of reviewing periodicals. As is well known, the journal that gave the strongest impulse to a new reviewing style and was to remain the prototype for all nineteenth-century literary periodicals was the *Edinburgh Review.* Launched in October 1802 with an impression of only 800 copies, it soon emerged as the leading literary journal, reaching its peak circulation of 14,000 copies in 1814. As a quarterly paper the *Edinburgh* chose to be selective in its material for review. Compared with its predecessors, the *Edinburgh* gave more prominence to opinion and comment; and at times it departed completely from eighteenth-century reviewing traditions by publishing what were virtually original essays. It is not surprising that its immediate triumphs generated imitators, the best-known of these being the *Quarterly Review,* which made its first appearance at the end of February 1809. However, in late 1808, while attempts were being made to get the *Quarterly* under way, the advent of a similar quarterly journal, the *London Review,* was advertised, the first number of which reached the bookshops a few weeks before the *Quarterly* did. Although short-lived and less capably written than the *Edinburgh* and *Quarterly,* the *London* however takes for several reasons a special position among Romantic journals and therefore deserves more attention than it has so far received.[1] It is the object of the present article to throw some light on the *London's* background as well as to assess its performance.

In nearly all of London's leading newspapers, including the *Morning Chronicle,* the *British Press, The Times,* the *Morning Herald,* and the *Morning Post,* there appeared on either 20 or 22 October 1808 the following "Prospectus of a New Review":

> Shortly will be published, by Samuel Tipper of Leadenhall-street, the First Number of a new and original work, in which the recent Productions of our contemporary Writers will be reviewed by a Society of Literary Friends, who, in the true and manly spirit of fair and candid Criticism, have agreed that each Contributor shall, with his Contributions, give his Name to be undersigned, so that the candidate for literary fame may distinctly know to whom he is idebted, either for the commendation that encourages, or the admonition that enlightens him.—Till the time shall come when the parties associated in this liberal and well-intentioned undertaking publish themselves to the world, it is thought proper to premise, that there is not one amongst them, that holds correspondence, interest, or connection, with any Review, Satire, or Magazine whatever; and as it must be obvious that a compilation of this miscellaneous nature must require the inspection and arrangement of some one person, by practice and experience qualified for that charge, the Publisher flatters himself it will not be unacceptable to the patrons of his Work to know that this charge, at once so indispensable, and yet so delicate, will by general desire, be undertaken by *Richard Cumberland, Esq.* who is anxious, if life and health be granted him, to add this last conclusive proof of his unwearied zeal for the fame, the feelings, and the rightful claims of his contemporaries.

Contemporary reactions to this notice were not long in coming. The secret planners of the *Quarterly* in particular were understandably somewhat alarmed at the news that the emergence of their journal would coincide with that of a rival, but they felt confident that the latter's proposed rejection of anonymity would soon cause its downfall. John Murray, pressing forward his plans for the *Quarterly,* wrote to Scott: "You have probably seen the advertisement of the *New Review, . . . ,* each critique to be signed by its author, and the whole phalanx to be headed by the notorious veteran Richard Cumberland, Esq. The miserable existence of such a Review cannot possibly linger beyond the third number; but it assists in showing practically how much a good Review is wanted in London by every class".[2] Scott himself felt "surprised at the inexhaustible activity of Mr. Cumberland's spirit. His proposed *Review* cannot be very long-lived"[3], and writing to Sharpe about the *Quarterly* project, he added: "Observe carefully, this plan is altogether distinct from one which has been proposed by the veteran Cumberland to which is annexed the extraordinary proposal that each Contributor shall place his name before the article, a stipulation which must prove fatal to the undertaking".[4] Jeffrey, too, writing to Horner, referred to Cumberland's forthcoming periodical.[5] That Cumberland should appear as the editor caused many eyebrows to be raised. Aged seventy-six when about to launch the *London,* Cumberland could look back upon an exceedingly rich, if chequered, career in practically every branch of literature. What motive animated this literary veteran, considered by many as slightly *passé,* to burden himself with the hazards of producing a literary journal, and, still more astonishingly, filling it with signed articles, a phenomenon quite unprecedented in English reviewing[6], but of course much in advance of his own time? There can be little doubt that this late literary initiative of Cumberland's was largely provoked by mortification at the *Edinburgh*'s treatment of his own writings. Until the turn of the century the leading journals had generally given his works a flattering reception, which had been deeply satisfying to one hypersensitive to criticism. Looking back in his *Memoirs* (1806) upon the consideration granted him by periodical critics, he acknowledged that they had "universally treated me with the greatest liberality, and in several instances bestowed upon my labours those encomiums which (. . .) I am duly sensible are above my deservings; but it is charitable in them to praise the efforts of a worn-out veteran, and fan the sparks of an expiring flame".[7] However, the brilliant though perverse set of young *Edinburgh* men was not prepared to swell the chorus of praise. Unlike other reviewers, they began by ignoring his newly published belletristic works, Jeffrey instead focussing his attention on the first edition of Cumberland's *Memoirs.* Despite a show of deference for Cumberland's years, Jeffrey found much to criticize in these *Memoirs,* too much, evidently, for Cumberland's sensibility. Concluding his review, Jeffrey aptly remarked that "There is no depth of thought, nor dignity of sentiment about him;—he is too frisky for an old man, and too gossiping for an historian." He also found that Cumberland had composed his memoirs "in too diffuse, rambling, and careless a style. There is evidently no selection or method in his narrative; and unweighed remarks, and fatiguing apologies and protestations are tediously interwoven with it in the genuine style of good-natured but irrepressible loquacity."[8] Such harsh criticisms had apparently a shattering effect on Cumberland, who, as his *Memoirs* abundantly illustrate, was beginning to view himself as the contemporary literary celebrity *par excellence.* A demonstrative character, he did not stifle his bitterness, declaiming loudly against the *Edinburgh* reviewers. A. G. Hunter, describing a banquet at the D'Israelis where a number of literati had assembled, recorded that Cumberland's "whole conversation is sadly disgusting, from irony and detraction, conveyed in a cunning sort of way, and directed constantly against the *Edinburgh Review,* Walter Scott (who is a poor ignorant boy, and *no poet,* and never wrote a five-feet line in his life) and such other d . . . d stuff".[9] In the second enlarged edition of his *Memoirs* (1807) Cumberland could not refrain from inserting in his typical "irrepressible loquacity" the following thrust at the *Edinburgh* men: "There is a northern junto of periodical critics, who have rendered themselves extremely formidable to us, poor authors, and to whom such of us, as have viands at command, offer them up, as Indians do their oblations to the devil; whilst they, who know we do not incense them out of love but fear, receive our knee-worship with indifference and despise us for our meanness. I have not the honour of being personally acquainted with any of these gentlemen, but I perceive that my sheets amongst others have been taken into their laundry, and have gone through the usual process of *mangling.* I am truly and sincerely obliged to them for the great consideration they have had for the feeble fabric of my manufacture, on which they have bestowed so very gentle a squeezing as not to break a thread, that was not rotten before they handled it, nor make one hole but what a housewife's hand may darn. In short, though it is so much my wish to be well with them, I cannot compliment them on their sagacity, forasmuch as they have not hit upon a single fault in my imperfact work that was not much too obvious for any common marksman to have missed . . . I understand that these acrimonious North-Britons are young men; I rejoice to hear it, not only for the honour of old age, but in the hope that they will live long enough to discover the error of their ambition, the misapplication of their talents and that the combination they have formed to mortify their contemporaries is, in fact a conspiracy to undo themselves."[10] As Cumberland well knew, his was not the only voice to be raised against the "northern junto." Infuriated at the *Edinburgh*'s anonymous severity, numerous authors thinking that a conspiracy of Scottish critics harboured designs upon them dashed to their pens to retaliate. However, the spate of public letters, tracts, pamphlets, and the like, in which they poured forth their grievances, did not in the least check the *Edinburgh*'s arrogance and destructiveness. The best way to give this journal a heavy blow was, Cumberland reasoned, to start a close equivalent, which he significantly called the *London Review*.[11] Evidently this rival was meant to undermine the *Edinburgh*'s circulation, and more constructively to offer the London-based reading public a first-rate quarterly journal, which, as the above extract from Murray's letter suggests, the originators of the *Quarterly* had likewise found missing in the capital.

As to Cumberland's revolutionary principle of discarding anonymity in British reviewing, ever since the emergence of professional periodical criticism in about the middle of the eighteenth century, writers had lamented this anonymity, because it sheltered adverse critics from direct retaliation and even from having to show their credentials. The *Edinburgh* had maintained the practice of anonymity, and this was all the more galling because of the frequent insolence of its criticism. In the **"Introductory Address"** accompanying the *London*'s first issue Cumberland eloquently justified his adopted principle of signature. "The man, who in the genuine spirit of criticism impartially distributes praise or blame to the works he reviews", he wrote, "has no more need to hide his name than the tradesman has, who records himself over his shop-door; for whom has he to fear, or what to be ashamed"? Cumberland not unjustly pointed at "a dangerous temptation, an unmanly security, an unfair advantage in anonymous criticism", and clearly having the *Edinburgh* reviewers in mind, he wondered "why some men take such pains to underrate the talents of their contemporaries", reproaching such critics for "a marvellous great bathos in their ambition." Interestingly enough, while an overwhelming majority of periodical critics did not cease to lament the alleged degenerate state of contemporary literature, Cumberland was firmly convinced that "there is no sympton of decay", prophesying that his final days were witnessing an era which "no past period will eclipse." After then putting in a strong plea for criticism free from political animus, Cumberland promised, though he had "one foot in the grave", to "do my duty and maintain my post to the last."

As we have seen, the contemporary reaction to Cumberland's initiative was extremely sceptical, unanimously predicting that it would soon kill the whole *London* project. Cumberland was well aware that he took risks with his introduction of signed articles. Many persons, he confessed in a short public notice, appended to the *London*'s Number one, "had given to understand that this plan would not succeed", but if not successful in the immediate present he regarded himself as a precursor to future generations of reviewers. He wrote that he saw himself as "a public-spirited citizen, who, being seized in his latter days with the romantic idea of doing something, for which he may be remembered by posterity, lays the foundation-stone of a school or college, and endows it for the benefit of those, who may come after him; and rise to fame, when his remains are mingled with the dust. A few more experiments, like the present, will decide for or against the permanency of my plan."

How far the *London*'s premature collapse must be attributed to its open policy remains debatable. What had probably more weight in bringing about its early failure was, according to well-qualified contemporaries, the poor quality of its criticism. After having glanced through the *London*'s first number, Scott wrote to Murray: "It is universally agreed here that Cumberland is five hundred degrees beneath contempt."[12] Referring to the same issue, William Taylor of Norwich, himself an extremely prolific reviewer, told Southey that it was "poor stuff."[13] Sidney Smith likewise found the *London* "miserable"[14], and Josiah Conder, in a survey of contemporary journals, condemned Cumberland's Review as "a vile and contemptible production".[15] To Thomas Moore the *London*'s demise was due to "the original disease of dulness."[16] A further adverse factor was no doubt the precarious financial situation of the *London*'s notorious publisher Samuel Tipper. In the course of 1809 Tipper found himself involved in a lawsuit started against him by Peter Finnerty on account of libel in the *Satirist,* a chiefly political monthly magazine, then owned and edited by George Manners, but brought out by Tipper.[17] Apparently this trial, combined with the *London*'s ill-starred inception, caused Tipper's official bankruptcy at the end of 1809. The *Satirist* found another publisher in W. N. Jones; the *London* was abandoned altogether.

Before turning to the men mustered by Cumberland for his literary venture, let us first briefly consider his own performance as a *London* reviewer. Though he wrote only six reviews, three of them appeared in the first issue, where their eccentricities must have alienated many readers. Cumberland's writing was egotistical and prolix. Instead of giving full scope to the works under review, Cumberland constantly turned the spotlight of attention on himself, interspersing his remarks with copious, often irrelevant, digressions and references to his own authorship and old age, and making shameless use of an obtrusive first person, which was at the time regarded as bad manners in a reviewer. Perhaps a few specimens of this selfcentred style are worth quoting here. In the *London*'s opening article, i.e. on C. J. Fox's *History of the Early Part of the Reign of James II* (1808), Cumberland confides that he writes "upon an empty table without authorities to aid me; but I dictate what I write from honest motives to befriend the living and not wrong the dead. How to execute that purpose I need no instruction: I have that within me, which requires no teacher" (I, 8-9). Further he refers to his "humble capacity as a writer" of which, he adds, "in spite of its humility, I must confess I have made no sparing use" (I, 13). Witness also the following idiosyncratic passage, which is, in addition, entirely unconnected with the work under consideration:" I could wish, . . . , that all authors, who commit their *weak parts* to my investigation, would comfort themselves with the reflection, that I have my *weak parts* also, and am very likely not to spy out theirs. And what is there, after all, even in a whole host of critics of which to be afraid? When drawn up in array, their manoeuvres to appearance may be rather alarming; but when the word is given to *present* and *fire,* if it shall turn out that these terrific warriors are not flinted, and have only *wooden* snappers in their pieces etc." (I, 194). It is not surprising that contemporary readers turned away from such diffuse and rambling observations which scarcely touched upon the merits of the works discussed. Furthermore, in commenting at great length on George Townsend's *Armageddon,* an ambitious epic still in manuscript, and in quoting extracts from it, Cumberland introduced in the first issue of the *London* a novelty which, though interesting and no longer unusual in a modern journal, was ill-executed in his hands. This essay (I, 73-82) was not only marred throughout by Cumberland's characteristically discursive and self-indulgent pose, but what was worse, it left no room for doubt that Cumberland's chief purpose was to advertise his friend's genius.[18]

Cumberland's unpropitious presence in the *London*'s first issue could apparently not be counterbalanced by the articles of his collaborators, few of whom had any claims to eminence, though several were gradually to rise into some note.

Notes

1. Brief accounts of the *London* are found in Walter Graham, *English Literary Periodicals* (New York, 1930), p. 258 ff., and in John O. Hayden, *The Romantic Reviewers 1802-1824* (London, 1969), pp. 50-51.

2. Samuel Smiles, *A Publisher and His Friends—Memoir and Correspondence of John Murray* (London, 1891), Vol. I, p. 98 (Letter dated 26 October 1808).

3. *The Letters of Sir Walter Scott,* ed. H. J. C. Grierson (London, 1932-37), Vol. II (1808-1815), p. 123 (Letter dated 2 November 1808).

4. *Letters from and to Charles Kirkpatrick Sharpe,* ed. A. Allardyce (London, 1888), Vol. I, p. 351 (Letter dated 30 December 1808).

5. See *Letters of Scott,* II, 138n.

6. In a "Prospectus" (1788) announcing the *Analytical*'s advent, and also in a letter to John Nichols (*Literary Anecdotes of the Eighteenth Century* (London, 1812-1815), Vol. IX, pp. 384-385n), Thomas Christie had given hints to the effect that his new journal would be conducted on the prin-

ciple of signature, attacking reviewers who "without a name, from the shade of obscurity in which they were concealed, have ventured to abuse at random the first literary characters". But his plans never got beyond their inception, for the *Analytical* stuck to anonymous or vaguely initialled criticism.

7. *Memoirs* (London, 2nd edition, 1807), "Supplement", p. 17.

8. *Edinburgh Review,* Vol. VIII (April, 1806), p. 108 and 128. Jeffrey's review is reprinted in *Contributions to the Edinburgh Review* (London, 1844), Vol. IV, pp. 402-413.

9. Thomas Constable, *Archibald Constable and His Literary Correspondents* (Edinburgh, 1873), p. 127. Scott, until his connection with the *Quarterly,* was known as an *Edinburgh* reviewer.

10. *Memoirs,* "Supplement", pp. 48-50.

11. Originally the planners of the *Quarterly* intended to name their periodical the "London Review". Gifford had told S. Rogers that Murray's venture would be so called (*Memoirs, Journal, and Correspondence of Thomas Moore,* ed. John Russell (London, 1856), Vol. VIII, p. 70), and Murray's Prospectus in the papers for December 20, 1808 announced the forthcoming publication of a "London Quarterly Review". By being slightly in advance of Murray's men, Cumberland forced them to drop at the last minute the "London" from the original title of their venture. Indeed, Scott had warned Murray on January 4, 1809 that their journal was "publicly talked of here, though by some confounded with Cumberland's attempt" (Smiles, *A Publisher and His Friends,* I, 140).

12. *Letters of Scott,* II, 70 (Letter dated 25 February 1809).

13. J. W. Robberds, *A Memoir of the Life and Writings of the Late William Taylor of Norwich* (London, 1843), Vol. II, p. 274.

14. *The Letters of Sydney Smith,* ed. N. C. Smith (Oxford, 1953), Vol. I, p. 157 (Letter to Lady Holland, dated March 7th, 1809). N. C. Smith is clearly mistaken when, in a note, he takes Sydney Smith's statement "Cumberland's review miserable" to refer to Scott's review of Cumberland's novel *John of Lancaster* (1809) for the *Quarterly,* for this article appeared in the *Quarterly*'s issue for May 1809.

15. *Reviewers Reviewed* (Oxford, 1811), p. 67.

16. *The Works of Lord Byron,* ed. T. Moore (London, 1832), Vol. IX, p. 62n.

17. For an account of the trial see *Finnerty v. Tipper* (London, 1809).

18. Cumberland's immoderate praises caused Townsend some embarrassment, for as they had raised the public's expectations, the poet found himself forced to publish, after several delays, in 1815 eight out of the twelve books of which *Armegeddon* was to consist. In the "Dedication" he confessed that he would not have brought out this epic "had I not considered myself bound to subdue every anxious feeling for its success, and make every effort to gratify in some degree the curiosity excited by my late revered friend Mr. Cumberland."

Byron must have read Cumberland's article on Townsend with keen interest. In his *Hints from Horace* he alluded to it (*Works,* ed. Moore, IX, 62-63 and note), and in a letter to R. C. Dallas he still remembered "a sucking Epic Poet . . . a Mr. Townsend protegee of the late Cumberland" (*Byron's Letters and Journals,* ed. L. A. Marchand (London, 1973), Vol. 11, p. 82.)

Richard J. Dircks (essay date 1991)

SOURCE: Dircks, Richard J. Introduction to *The Unpublished Plays of Richard Cumberland.* Vol. 1, pp. vii-xl. New York: AMS Press, 1991.

[*In the following excerpt, Dircks discusses the stage history of Cumberland's early unpublished plays.*]

I

When Richard Cumberland died on May 7, 1811, at the age of seventy-nine, he was a recognized member of the world of letters leaving behind him more than forty plays, three novels, five volumes of essays, two volumes of odes and miscellaneous poetry, two epic poems, a translation of the psalms, a two-volume discussion of Spanish painting, several pamphlets on religious and philosophical questions, two volumes of memoirs, and a number of less significant shorter pieces.

A minor functionary in government and an important member of the intellectual and artistic society of the time, his interests embraced most of the knowledge of his time and was fashioned by the observation of three-quarters of a century of important political and social changes. As absentee Provost Marshall of South Carolina, he was involved with American affairs just prior to the American revolution and, as an undercover agent, attempted to bring about peace between England and Spain in 1780. Acutely aware of the impact of the French revolution on English interests, he headed, during the later years of his life, a corps of civilian volunteers, formed as part of the nation's defense against Napoleon's threat to England in the early part of the nineteenth century.

Part of a diversified social scene, he frequently mixed with members of the nobility, most significantly Lord Halifax, whom he served as a clerk in the Board of Trade, and George Germain, later Lord Sackville, who elevated him to the position of Secretary. Despite earlier disagreements with Lord North over compensation for his Spanish mission, he became the statesman's close friend when both lived at Tunbridge Wells after North's retirement from public life. Always conscious of the value of upper society in the eighteenth century, Cumberland was proud of the marriage of his daughter, Elizabeth, to Lord Edward Bentinck. During the latter part of his life, he collaborated with his close friend, Sir James Bland Burgess, on a number of literary ventures.

After the production of his great play, *The West Indian,* the dramatist moved freely through the literary and cultural world of his time. An intimate of Samuel Johnson and his circle, he came to know, not only other significant literary personalities, such as Oliver Goldsmith, but also the portrait painter, Sir Joshua Reynolds, the politician, Edmund Burke, the manager of the Drury Lane Theatre, David Garrick, and many additional representatives of the art, political, and theatrical world. Cumberland had his detractors, however, and Horace Walpole seems to have detested him, losing no opportunity to belittle his *Odes.* On the other hand, Johnson, who understood the value of his company, describes his personality in a letter to Hester Lynch Thrale: "The want of company is an inconvenience, but Mr. Cumberland is a million, make the most of what you have" (*Letters of [Samuel] Johnson,* ed. [R.W.] Chapman, II, 311).

The dramatist saw himself as a significant classical scholar and looked back with pride to his birth in the Master's lodge of Trinity College, Cambridge, where his grandfather, Richard Bentley, one of the great classicists England has produced and one of the most controversial heads of the college, resided. Sensitive to a fault about attacks on Bentley, he attempts, in his *Memoirs,* to defend his relative against what he feels to be the unfair attacks by Jonathan Swift, Alexander Pope and less significant detractors.

Despite the obvious interest that social and political historians might have in Cumberland, students of the theatre will find a study of his work most valuable. While still in the employ of Lord Halifax, Cumberland wrote three plays, each significantly different from the others, and produced them with varying success.

Cumberland's first contact with David Garrick, the manager of the Drury Lane theatre, was through his efforts to stage *The Banishment of Cicero* in 1761. Choosing a classical subject, the attempts of Claudius and Gabinus to effect the downfall of Cicero, he tried to combine a complicated love plot with political intrigue, a formula that succeeded for Joseph Addison in *Cato,* but Cumberland's drama fails to integrate the two. The play did, however, offer promise of future success, and John Genest notes that much of the tragedy is "well written." Unfortunately, even a letter of support by Bishop Warburton and the influence of Lord Halifax failed to bring it to the stage.

Four years later, in 1765, Cumberland tried again, this time with a musical play, and met with more success. Buttressing his work with music, he turned to comedy, a genre that was much more congenial to his abilities. *The Summer's Tale* is a slight play that had only moderate acceptance by the public, but the score was a fortunate combination of old and new work by distinguished musicians, Karl Friedrich Abel, who composed the overture, Thomas Augustine Arne, Samuel Arnold, and Johann Christian Bach. The central story concerning the familiar conflict between parental authority and youthful desire for independence in selecting a mate is supported by a subplot concerning the romantic problems of lovers from different social strata. The tale gives ample opportunity for the expression of sentiment and in its subplot points towards Cumberland's later mastery of sentimental themes. The country locale of the comedy, moreover, provides opportunities for entertaining song and dance.

Undaunted by the failure of *The Banishment of Cicero,* Cumberland tried tragedy again with an adaptation of *Timon of Athens,* one of Shakespeare's most puzzling and least successful plays. Built around Timon's mistaken generosity and later misanthropy, the drama touches one of the important satiric themes of the eighteenth-century, human ingratitude. Fielding focussed on this vice, by making it the primary reason for Allworthy's expelling Tom Jones from the squire's estate in his great novel. The play also treats a subject that fascinated Cumberland throughout his life and became a major motif in many of his plays, the misuse of inherited wealth. When Timon, in his apparent madness, discovers a fortune in the woods, he feeds his desire for vengeance by distributing it, in Cumberland's adaptation, to those whom he feels will do the most harm to society, most notably the banished Alcibiades, while neglecting the needs of his own daughter. The two previous adaptations of the story by Thomas Shadwell and James Love had added romantic entanglements to Shakespeare's plot, recognizing that such complications provided a formula that was almost uniformly employed in successful dramas of the period. Cumberland's approach is different from either, emphasizing through the presence of a new character, Evanthe, Timon's daughter, the moral relevance of Timon's defrauding his child of her rightful inheritance. She is also important for through her return of the affections of Alcibiades, she influences him to soften his punishment of Athens. The final act, almost entirely the work of Cumberland, effects the return of Timon, cured of his misanthropic views through his daughter's influence, thus heightening the tragic irony of his death.

Although the three dramas brought little public recognition to Cumberland, they did provide a training ground that would lead to future success. Through them he mastered the language of the stage, modified his veneration of the classics so that their influence was enriched by the effect of his experience in the pragmatic world of the theatre, and, finally, heightened his perception of the sentimental and its potential for dramatic presentation.

Timon of Athens was not produced until 1771 after Cumberland had firmly established himself as one of the leading writers for the stage through the production of *The Brothers* and *The West Indian.* In the quiet Irish city of Clonfert, where Cumberland and his family visited his father during the summer of 1767, the dramatist found inspiration for his first important comedy, catching, in *The Brothers,* the spirit of sentiment that contributed to the success of Hugh Kelly's *The False Delicacy* in 1768. Cumberland contrasts the lives of two brothers, the older, Andrew Belfield, who is corrupted by the ruthless power his inheritance of the family fortune gives him, and his younger brother, who finds himself socially vulnerable. Andrew deserts his wife, Violetta, and drives his brother away to facilitate his pursuit of Sophia. Not content with one amour, Andrew pursues Lucy at the expense of the ruin of his tenant, Goodwin.

Such crimes are familiar vices among fictitious elder brothers who, according to British custom, generally inherited the entire family fortune in order to preserve its integrity, while often neglecting the remaining children of the family. Despite the range of Andrew's vicious and selfish cruelty, however, reform is possible on the sentimental stage, and, with the help of an improbable shipwreck off Cornwall that brings all parties together on the Belfield estate, Violetta returns to Andrew, Sophia is reunited with Belfield Jr. and the brothers are reconciled. Cumberland also discovered that the presence of an important comic character was often an essential ingredient in creating successful sentimental plays. In this case he creates Captain Ironsides whose his salty dialogue and rugged individualism resembles the great sea characters of Smollett. Comedy in the play is further developed through Sir Benjamin Dove's being beset by a shrewish wife.

Encouraged by the success of *The Brothers,* Cumberland returned to Clonfert and its peaceful environs to structure another comedy, this time with the assistance of the great theatrical manager and play-doctor, David Garrick, who made valuable suggestions to Cumberland about structuring his drama, particularly concerning the proper preparation for the appearance on stage of Belcour, the West Indian. The dramatist took advantage of his opportunity to observe the Irish personality to fashion one of his most successful comic characters, Major O'Flaherty.

In *The West Indian,* a natural benevolence of spirit is found in the central character, Belcour, but his naturally effusive sexual attitudes are not balanced by prudence and virtue. Such a character had been well established by Fielding in the title character in *Tom Jones,* and Cumberland borrows much of the spirit of Tom for his West Indian whose philosophy of life dominates the thematic structure of the play. Just as Tom Jones matures in Christian virtue, so Belcour's sexual misconduct is ultimately overcome by the overriding force of natural goodness. The presence of the Dudley family complicates the return of Belcour who is unaware that he is the son of the merchant, Stockwell, who withholds this fact in order better to observe the true nature of his son. Belcour offensively pursues Louisa Dudley, mistakenly thinking she is fair game as a prostitute, but, on the other hand, displays admirable charity in unhesitatingly offering to rescue her family from financial ruin. The wealthy Lady Rusport, in her refusal to assist the Dudley family despite the romantic interest of her stepdaughter, Charlotte, in Charles Dudley, provides the superb comic Irishman, Major O'Flaherty with some of his finest moments in condemning her lack of charity and social justice. Bits of stage wizardry, such as Dudley's misuse of Charlotte's jewelry and O'Flaherty's forgetting that he has in his possession a newly discovered will that can provide financial stability for the Dudley's, are handled expertly by Cumberland, so that the improbability inherent in much of the action seems perfectly natural on stage.

Cumberland quickly followed this success with his second great comedy, *The Fashionable Lover,* produced during the 1771-72 season. The fourth of the dramatist's plays to appear that season, the comedy arrived at a time that Cumberland's popularity was high. *The Brothers* was being acted at Covent Garden, while *The West Indian* was performed at Drury Lane, along with *Timon of Athens,* the tragedy Garrick had rejected some years before.

Eagerly awaited, *The Fashionable Lover* met with immediate popular success. Although its appearance was marred by accusations of plagiarism like those of Charles Dibdin, who accused Cumberland of borrowing from the work of Richard Steele, Hugh Kelly, Samuel Foote, and the novelist, Samuel Richardson, the comedy was received with almost universal enthusiasm. Most sentimental plays and novels have elements in common, and the resemblance of the comedy to other works does not detract from its original contribution to the theatre. In the same spirit in which he portrayed the

Irish character favorably in the role of Major O'Flaherty in *The West Indian,* the dramatist raised his voice once again against national prejudice in presenting a highly original treatment of the Scottish personality. The comedy also develops two dominant themes much cherished by Cumberland, benevolence as a desirable characteristic of human actions, and the problem of inheritance.

Lord Abberville is a profligate who has foolishly dissipated his entire inherited fortune. The usual instances of conflicting romantic interests among an interesting array of characters is strengthened by the portrayal of a poor and defenceless orphan in Augusta Aubrey. Although she will ultimately inherit a substantial fortune, she is drawn to Tyrrel, a penniless but highly attractive young man. The story, expertly handled by Cumberland, is only one ingredient in this fine sentimental comedy. The characterization of Colin McLeod, the Scottish servant of the Abberville family, is brilliantly done. Also notable is the unusual treatment of the merchant, Bridgemore, who dishonestly sells cargo entrusted to him in order to finance the loans the Jew, Napthali, makes to Abberville. One of the dominant characteristics of sentimental drama is its glorification of merchants as a class, and rarely are they portrayed in the unfavorable way Bridgemore is here. Although the treatment of Napthali is not far removed from the intolerant portrait of the Jew on the English stage of the time, it is somewhat softened by placing the onus for his actions on the Christian, Bridgemore, and anticipates Cumberland's favorable portrayal of the Jewish moneylender in *The Jew,* produced almost a quarter of a century later. Mortimer, whose rough exterior belies his generous heart, prudently dispenses charity, a characteristic of many of Cumberlands sentimental personalities.

Before producing his next full-length comedy, *The Choleric Man,* Cumberland wrote a highly entertaining afterpiece that met with favorable reception by the public. *The Note of Hand,* a slight but humorous play produced in 1774, further explores the use and misuse of inherited wealth. Employing the traditional comic devices of disguise and appearance incognito, the play touches the frequent eighteenth-century practice of gambling to excess, by having Rivers lose his fortune to his uncle, who is disguised as Sunderland. Cumberland also created a fine comic role for the actor, John Moody, in O'Connor MacCormuck, who manages to outwit an assortment of sharpers seeking to defraud the inexperienced.

The Choleric Man brought Cumberland's record of spectacular success to an end, the comedy receiving only moderate acceptance by the public. The dramatist's sensitivity to criticism, ultimately satirized by Richard Brinsley Sheridan in *The Critic* through the character of Sir Fretful Plagiary, emerged in his reaction to Oliver Goldsmith's discussion of comedy in an essay in *The Westminister Magazine* (December 1772), "A Comparison between Laughing and Sentimental Comedy." Always intolerant of adverse reactions of the press, Cumberland responded to this and to charges of plagiarism in his preface to **The Choleric Man.** Cumberland's defense against plagiarism is unnecessary, for except for the central idea of comparing the effects of passive as opposed to strict education on two brothers, the comedy bears little resemblance to *The Adelphi* of Terence or to the adaptation of that classical comedy by Thomas Shadwell in *The Squire of Alsatia.*

While the two brothers pursue romances involving mistaken identity, Cumberland creates their irascible father, Andrew Nightshade, who overcomes his unbridled temper only after he injures a newspaper hawker in a fit of passion and comes to realize the possible consequences of his actions. His acid character, not mollified until near the end of the comedy, dominates much of the play. Despite many positive values, the drama is seriously flawed by a failure to achieve a satisfactory integration of the two plots, the reform of Nightshade and the effect of different types of education on his sons. The tepid response of the public reflects this failure.

Although Cumberland was consistently more successful in comedy than tragedy, he achieved moderate to good audience response to three tragedies, **The Battle of Hastings** (1778), **The Mysterious Husband** (1783), and **The Carmelite** (1784).

The first of these plays transposes late eighteenth-century notions of sentiment to the eleventh century and the battle in which William of Normandy defeated Harold II of England in 1066. The story borrows familiar elements of romance in having the legitimate heir to the throne, Edgar, disguised as Edmund to prevent his discovery by the usurper, Harold II, fall in love with Edwina, the daughter of the man who has secretly reared him. Mistaken identity and chance force the action to a climax in which the usurper's daughter, Matilda, who also loves Edgar, kills herself to preserve her beloved's happiness with her rival.

Such is the material of which sentimental plays are built, and although Edgar assumes his country's leadership after Harold is slain in battle and calls all his countrymen to action, throughout the tragedy he finds nothing more important than love, and the relationship between his commitment to love and his patriotism is not adequately developed. When the drama ends, the force of tragedy is blunted by having the usurper and his daughter die, while the sentimental lovers, Edgar and Edwina, survive.

The production of an operatic masque, **Calypso** (1779), a musical drama, **The Widow of Delphi** (1780), and a comedy, **The Walloons** (1780), followed by a political mission to Spain, preceded his next effort at tragedy. **The Mysterious Husband,** a play in the sentimental tradition was in many ways more suited to Cumberland's muse than **The Battle of Hastings.** In this play, the dramatist shares with Edward Moore's *Gamester* (1753) the theme of the disastrous effects of gambling on private life. Lord Davenant marries his wife because, as a gamester, he is in need of money, and she, deceived by her uncle into believing that Captain Dormer no longer loves her, seeks solace in a loveless marriage. Although she acts the part of a model spouse despite the absence of romantic love in her marriage, her husband does not, and finds an outlet for his passion with Marianne, the sister of Captain Dormer, without either being aware of the Captain's involvement with Lady Davenant. Finding two marriages too much, Lord Davenant provides convincing evidence that he is dead. The plot moves inevitably to a revelation of the truth which he is unable to face. In his distress, he takes poison and then stabs himself, praying for his wife as he dies.

Cumberland in this tragedy treats seriously a theme often the subject of comic plots, the effects of arranged marriages on those who enter them. Davenant's wife, although willing to live up to the obligations of a wife, is a knowing participant in a loveless marriage because she feels deserted by her true love. Davenant is not deceived, for his sole motivation is the acquisition of wealth in order to support his gambling. Although not truly villainous or unnatural, his crimes are substantial. His deceit in promoting his marriage to Lady Davenant, and his subsequent irresponsible marriage to and desertion of Marianne Dormer, may not cry out for vengeance, but they reveal the extreme selfishness of his willingness to exploit women. In sentimental fashion, however, when he does come to recognize the extent of his moral degradation, it is too late and only suicide remains a viable choice to his distorted mind. In this first attempt at genuine sentimental tragedy, Cumberland is not faithful to the tradition of setting the drama among middle-class merchants, choosing the lesser nobility as more suited to his treatment of marital deception and gambling.

Although Cumberland had created successful sentimental women in his comedies, such as Louisa Dudley and Charlotte Rusport in **The West Indian** and Augusta Aubrey in **The Fashionable Lover,** creating Lady Davenant is significantly different, since the dramatist must present a woman whose unsentimental action in marrying without love is offset by her remarkable virtue and fidelity in the most trying of marital circumstances. To do this in a believable fashion, he had to avoid creating either an excessively passive individual with no vitality, or one whose moral convictions are so scrupulously moral that they prevent the expression of the feeling and emotion needed to make her recognizably human.

Such models existed in previous eighteenth-century literature in both the theatre and the novel. Richardson's heroine, Pamela, is forced to accept with grace not only the domination of her husband, Mr. B—, but also, after their marriage, the discovery that he was the father of a child by another servant before their marriage, and to sustain the impact of his abortive post-marital romance with a wealthy countess. Beverley's wife, in *The Gamester,* although she is not faced with her husband's infidelity, must maintain a spirit of affection for a husband with horrendous shortcomings as a gambler. Amelia, in Fielding's last novel, is still more to the point, for she must endure Captain Booth, who despite his underlying love for her, finds himself, while in prison, sharing room and bed with a former woman acquaintance. Amelia must learn through sentimental virtue to recognize not only the lack of viciousness in his flaccid view of life, but to see in his ultimate reform a predictable reversal of his conduct. These models undoubtedly helped Cumberland to fashion his sentimental heroine, but she is an original success. The firmness of her convictions about her marital obligations is not achieved at the expense of prideful criticism of the conduct of others, and the charm and dignity that sustains her makes her portrayal on stage believable. Although **The Mysterious Husband** did not meet with the success of Cumberland's great early comedies, it foreshadows his ability to deal with complicated social situations in **The Jew** and **The Wheel of Fortune,** plays that restored him to dominance in the theatre in the 1790s.

In a similar way, his next tragedy, **The Carmelite,** taught him how to use the dark shadows of the Gothic mood. Setting **The Carmelite** in the melancholy shadows of a castle overlooking the sea, he successfully modulates the mood to heighten the effects of his tragic tale.

Cumberland was a good student of popular taste, not only recognizing the demand for sentiment but anticipating the development of a love of the melodramatic that had begun with the plays of Lillo, particularly in *The London Merchant,* with its emphasis on heightened passion expressed in scenes such as that in which Barnwell murders his uncle, and those that depend on the effect of passionate love on the life of the inexperienced Barnwell. This preoccupation with excessive displays of passion eventually came to be associated with the preromantic interest in medieval surroundings and gothic mystery. The mystery of Lady Matilda's seeming madness and presence in the castle terrifies the countryside, providing a somber note that is intensified by the proximity of the action to the sea. Matilda, a role fashioned to display the talents of the great actress, Sarah Siddons, made good use of the inherent terror of the setting, combining it with the story of attempted murder, usurped land, disguise, mistaken identity, shipwreck and other familiar appurtenances of Romance. The heroic stature of Hildebrand, whose guilt makes inevitable

his eventual demise, is balanced by the seemingly ineffectual actions of St. Valori, whose indecisive actions can only be explained by a Christian sensibility and idealized love that is willing to risk his own unhappiness for what he perceives to be the happiness of Matilda, who, he is convinced, has married Montgomeri in his absence. The play, which received considerable success, is significant in tracing the artistic development of Cumberland and in explaining his resurgence as a major dramatic figure in the 1790s. Cumberland's two remaining tragedies, **The Arab** (1785), performed only once as a benefit for the actor, John Henderson, and **Don Pedro** (1796), presented only four times at the Haymarket theatre, add little to his reputation as a tragedian.

Cumberland's production of the sentimental masque, **Calypso** (1779), is marred by a lack of judgment in the way the moral theme of the play is presented. The battle between evil sensuality (Calypso) and virtue (Telemachus) is presented with heavy-handed moralizing and never achieves dramatic vitality, even in the less demanding structure of the masque form.

The use of music on stage was increasing in popularity, not only in afterpieces, but also in major plays. **The Widow of Delphi** (1780) sought to take advantage of the desire of the public for what Cumberland felt was a lesser form of theatre. The use of a comic and frivolous treatment of the classical gods had been popular on the stage since Kane O'Hara presented his popular burlettas, *Midas* (1764) and the *Golden Pippin* (1773). There is some good fun and pleasant music in **Calypso,** but the play is marred by excessive length that dilutes a good idea, the pursuit of Lucretia by Mercury, into an Olympian comedy of sentiment.

Cumberland was a prolific worker, and, following his return from Spain, he sought to reestablish his reputation as a comic dramatist of importance. Like a boxer trying to work his way to a championship he had lost, he produced a rapid succession of plays, most of which were disappointing. Characteristically, he capitalized on his recent travels to present in **The Walloons** (1782) a drama that takes advantage of his experiences in Spain. Cumberland denied that the character of Father Sullivan was based on that of Abbé Hussey, the Irish clergyman and chaplain to the Spanish embassy in London, with whom he had dealt frequently on his mission, but there can be little doubt that his choice of a priest as the villain of the play evolved from his Spanish experiences. His presence during a sea-battle on his journey to Spain probably shaped that part of the story that recounts the defense, by Dangle's son, Davy, of his ship against the charge of cowardice in striking its colors.

Father Sullivan's malevolence in plotting against the British is explained by bitterness over the injury done him for his religious beliefs, and his morbid seeking of revenge points to the motivation of Penruddock in *The Wheel of Fortune.* The effect of the dramatist's proximity to the conflict with Spain on the action of the play is evident. The part of Father Sullivan was well acted by John Henderson, but the drama met with only limited success. Revenge, Father Sullivan's motivation for treason, is one of three aspects of betrayal examined in the play. Montgomery is determined to fight for Spain for his personal beliefs and because of the religion of his family, but he ultimately rejects the betrayal of his own country when conflict breaks out. Similarly, Daggerly, the accomplice of Father Sullivan, is overcome by remorse before he is seized as a traitor.

Cumberland's next three efforts were even less successful. In *The Natural Son* (1784), he attempted to capitalize on the character of Major O'Flaherty from *The West Indian,* but with little success. In the same way, the study of rights of inheritance in *The Country Attorney* (1787) and *The School for Widows* (1789), two plays on one theme in somewhat different dramatic styles, added little to his reputation. *The Impostors* (1789) also failed, the dramatist unable to find an original approach to the overworked idea of two young men seeking through fraud to meet wealthy wives, an idea that had been treated brilliantly by George Farquhar in *The Beaux Stratagem* (1707).

Improbable as it might seem, the dramatist ran into trouble with the licensing act in attempting to stage a comic musical drama, *Richard II,* in 1792. Despite Cumberland's known patriotism, so sensitive was the nation to the threat of rebellion in the aftermath of the French Revolution that even the mention of Wat Tyler's medieval insurgence was enough to deny the play a license. When it was later produced in 1793 as *The Armorer,* most of the comedy was diluted and the main background of rebellion set aside and replaced by a weak attack on Rosamund by a local tyrant.

Cumberland was, however, working his way back into public favor. In *The Box Lobby Challenge* (1794), the dramatist avoids the excessive moralizing that marked some of his recent unsuccessful work, and turns, instead, to comedy that exploits themes dealing with lower-class characters, whose relationship to the landed family that largely controls their lives is pursued in a relaxed and spirited mood. The challenge which Captain Waterland presents to Jack Crotchet in the box-lobby of the theatre over an insult to Diana Grampus's niece, Laetitia, might have had more disastrous consequence had not Jack, wishing to avoid a duel, presented to Waterland the card of Fulsome whose suit he had borrowed with the identification still in the pocket. Jack's father, a printer who sees little value in education, prefers to train his son as an apprentice, but Jack himself prefers to loaf and, when he learns that Diana Grampus is seeking a companion for her nephew when

he takes his grand tour of the continent, he passes himself off as a Cambridge scholar.

The play's situations are ripe for comedy, and Cumberland exploits them in highspirits. Cumberland is comfortable in his handling of the story, allowing the interaction of social classes to work toward their natural comic potential. Significantly, he shows a tolerance for people of the lower classes and is able to use the current broadening of social sympathies for them to emerge. His sense of human worth has expanded, and he has learned how to exploit it in the theatre. Decades before he had become a champion of those who had been the butt of theatrical comedy, the stage Irishman enobled in the character of Major O'Flaherty, and that of the Scottish servant Colin McLeod. Cumberland was ready to defend an even more difficult target of prejudice, the Jewish money lender.

The Jew (1794) links a sentimental drama with melodramatic overtones to an unusual portrait of a Jew who acts with charity toward the Christians who persecute him. Sir Stephen Bertram, a true villain in the sentimental tradition, callously dismisses Charles Ratcliffe, his clerk, and drives from home his own son, Frederick, whose romantic interest in Ratcliffe's sister, Eliza, interferes with his father's amorous designs. When Charles is slightly wounded by Frederick in a duel, the basis is laid for their reconciliation and the eventual marriage of Charles to Eliza. This potentially interesting story of sentiment is greatly buttressed by the appearance of the Jew, Sheva.

Although Cumberland was willing to use the traditional stage Jew when it suited him, as in the character of Napthali in *The Fashionable Lover,* and to have characters occasionally refer to Jews in derogatory terms, his essays in *The Observer* (1786-90) provide clear evidence of a tolerance that was unusual at the time. For example, Abraham Abrahams complains of the stage treatment of the Jew, and persuasively details his ill-treatment when he attends the theatre (III, 30-31). In Cumberland's creation of Sheva, he gives his Jewish character sufficient balance and rational control to enable him to permit Christians to hold the mistaken notion of him as a usurious money lender, because he knows that it is a false picture, but one that it would be impossible to alter. He, himself, lives simply and does not hoard up the riches he accumulates, but, rather, dispenses them in charitable ways. His attitude is not wildly altruistic, but born of gratitude and a desire to repay the Christian world for kindnesses it had shown him in the past.

Part of the genius of Cumberland's portrait is that Sheva does not act as a Jew in his altruism but as a human being whose actions do not depend upon any necessary relationship to his religion or social position. Sheva understands charity in a way that few Christians portrayed in dramatic literature do. In many ways it is fitting and significant that Sheva's altruism is exercised by one who is a social outcast, allowing his perception by the public to enable him to achieve anonymity in his charity. The great popularity of the play, not only in England but on the continent, attests to the significance of its message and the skill with which it was presented. Imitated in Paris, and on three occasions translated into German, as well as into both Hebrew and Yiddish, *The Jew* was performed as late as June 15, 1919, at a synagogue in New York.

Cumberland's success with *The Jew* was soon followed by a similar triumph in *The Wheel of Fortune* (1795). Taking a hint from a play by the German dramatist, August von Kotzebue, that had appeared in England as *The Stranger,* Cumberland brilliantly grafted familiar sentimental themes, the unfortunate effects of gambling and the harbored resentment of lost love, to a penetrating study of conscience.

The character of Roderick Penruddock is one of Cumberland's finest creations and was performed skillfully by John Kemble. Having suppressed his resentment against Harry Woodville, the close friend who had snatched Arabelle from his affections some years before, and having adjusted his life to make peace with the world, Penruddock, through an act of fate is given the power to exact terrible revenge on his rival. Woodville's son, Henry, has in the intervening years reached a point in his life where he desires to marry Emily Tempest, but this is made difficult because his father has lost not only his own fortune, but also that of his wife, at the gaming table. The sentimental story of the ruined gambler, Woodville, is not unlike that of Beverly in Moore's *The Gamester.* Cumberland, however, moves the interest in the story away from Woodville to the potential villain, Penruddock, who could pursue devastating revenge against his former rival.

The psychological struggle that tortures Penruddock, when Weazle points out to him that, because he has inherited the estate of the wealthy George Penruddock who had purchased the debts of Woodville, he is capable of destroying his former rival, is brilliantly depicted. Penruddock, still in love with Arabelle, discovers that within the peace that he has achieved lurks the insidious serpent of revenge, and he becomes a pathetic figure as his mental equilibrium is shattered. In the end, he listens to the pleas of Arabelle and her son and abandons the thoughts of revenge to emerge as a morally heroic figure at the end of the drama.

In *The Wheel of Fortune,* Cumberland read accurately the movement of public interest toward melodrama, but Penruddock is a much more subtle and penetrating creation than most protagonists of that genre. Using much of the thrust of sentimental tragedy, Cumberland effects a seemingly happy ending, but it is at the great personal cost of the happiness of his hero. Unlike Beverly, who is driven to suicide in Moore's *Gamester,* Woodville is saved from that fate by the generosity of Penruddock, who in the end cannot persuade himself to destroy his former rival or Arabelle, but assures their happiness at the sacrifice of his own, achieving peace of mind only after a turbulent trial of conscience.

Cumberland followed *The Wheel of Fortune* with a fourth successful drama in the space of two years, producing *First Love* on May 12, 1795. Lacking the dramatic bite of its precessor, the play is a romantic comedy built around the sentimental theme that love rather than economic interests should prevail in the choice of a marriage partner. Rejecting parental interference in their choices, Frederick returns to Lady Ruby, and Lord Sensitive and Sabina discover that their true happiness lies with the objects of their first passion. Cumberland, following this success, produced plays in such rapid succession that they lacked the care and time for composition that marked his most brilliant efforts. The result was a series of works that survived few performances. *The Dependent* (1795) was acted only once, and its successors, *The Days of Yore* and *Don Pedro,* were received indifferently.

Finally, in 1797, *The Last of the Family* was greeted with enthusiasm. Returning to his familiar theme of the ethics of inherited wealth, Cumberland develops a story with sufficient complication to maintain interest. Lady Cypress, a poor judge of people, misuses her fortune when, deceived by her lawyer, Early, she disinherits her nephew, Algernon, in favor of Emily, a young woman staying with her. As the result of a complicated plot involving deception, assault, and assorted villainy, Algernon and Emily finally are united in romantic bliss. Sir Oliver Montrath's balanced judgment establishes a standard for prudent action.

Cumberland continued to produce about a play a year until his death in 1811, only a few of which were successful or are of notable interest. The most significant of these plays is the adaptation of a drama by August von Kotzebue, *Joanna of Montfaucon.* Cumberland credits the German dramatist with providing him with the plot, but with little more. Genest calls it the best of the irregular dramas produced in the early nineteenth century in which music and spectacle were an important part of the presentation (VI, 476). Cumberland, in the "Introduction" to the play, bemoaned the fact that legitimate comedy and tragedy had to be reinforced by artificial, nondramatic elements such as spectacle, and he often suggests that only financial exigency persuaded him to write such dramas (xiv).

Despite his reservations, the play is a fine dramatic vehicle to which the addition of music is appropriate. A story of melodramatic passion, involving the usurping of Thurm castle by Lord Albert, his marriage to Joanna, and their eventual decision to make amends by restoring the castle to its rightful owner. Lazarra, the rejected suitor of Joanna, storms the castle, defeating Albert, but when a hermit is revealed as the true heir and allows Albert to possess it for life, a conclusion is reached that justifies a happy ending that is punctuated by a joyful chorus. Most of the many changes that Cumberland made in the original story of Kotzebue catered to English sensibilities, demonstrating that, even during the final years of his life, Cumberland had the ability to read the public taste and to fashion it into effective theatre.

Among Cumberland's last works for the theatre was *The Jew of Mogadore,* a comic opera in which he transposed the benevolent Jew from his great success of the 1790s into a Middle-Eastern character, Nadab, in a tale, built around slavery and piracy, that offers much opportunity for the use of music, pomp, and ceremony. His last work for the stage was another musical *The Privateer,* an adaptation of *The Brothers,* his successful comedy of years before.

Throughout his life, Cumberland devoted much energy to literary work other than the theatre. In his twilight years, he completed his third novel, *John de Lancaster* (1809), his epic poem, *Calvary, The Exodiad* in collaboration with Sir James Bland Burgess, and two volumes of *Memoirs.* Energetic to the end of his long life, he left behind a rich legacy of published works that establish him, not only as a dramatist, but as a significant man of letters.

Richard J. Dircks (essay date 1992)

SOURCE: Dircks, Richard J. Introduction to *The Unpublished Plays of Richard Cumberland.* Vol. 2, pp. vii-xl. New York: AMS Press, 1992.

[*In the following excerpt, Dircks evaluates Cumberland's later dramatic works.*]

II

Students of the theatre have generally assumed that Cumberland's comedy, *A Word For Nature,* produced at Drury Lane on 5 December 1798, is the same play as *The Passive Husband* that appears in the dramatist's *Posthumous Dramatic Works.* A comparison of the manuscript approved by the Lord Chamberlain with the published text reveals significant differences between them, that suggest a major revision of a play that had only moderate success in its original London production. When this revision took place cannot be determined, but it was not unusual for Cumberland to revise

an unsuccessful play, changing its dramatic emphasis to give it a fresh look, as he had done earlier in altering *The Country Attorney* to *The School for Widows.*

The change of title indicates the basic difference between the two plays. The first, *A Word for Nature,* places the emphasis on the natural goodness of Leonard and the operations of his heart despite his lack of social and educational advantages. Leonard sees the world from the point of view of natural goodness rather than worldly success, a vision that differs from that of his mother. From his vantage point, her actions, taken to promote his worldly success by marrying him to Matilda, are shameful since they disregard affection and love. His concern that Matilda must love him and not merely agree to marry him out of duty prompts him to trick his mother out of the bond of marriage and change the name to Clifton once he is convinced that Matilda loves his friend. *The Passive Husband,* on the other hand, shifts the emphasis of the drama to Sir Toby Truckle's inability to deal with his domineering and deceitful wife. Much is done to restructure the play, alter characterizations, and introduce stage business that is designed to achieve the different effect.

The names of the servants in the manuscript are changed in the printed play from John and Ruth to Patrick Malooney and Mrs. Lofty, using comic elements suitable to the Irish stage character and giving a heightened imperiousness to the character of Mrs. Lofty. Since the change of names seems to have taken place for the first production according to the cast of characters given in *The London Stage,* based on *The Monthly Visitor* for December 1798, it is possible that at least the changes appropriate to them had been made hastily between the submission of the manuscript to the Lord Chamberlain on 27 October 1798 and its London production in December.

Both versions concern the efforts of the widow, Lady Truckle, to provide for her son by arranging his marriage to the daughter of the widower, Sir Toby Truckle, whom she has recently married and domineers to such an extent that it disrupts the household domestic staff. Part of her strategy has been to insist on the education of her son, Leonard, under the tutelage of the good-hearted but pedantic Runic, while extracting from Sir Toby a legal contract for the marriage of the young man to his daughter, Matilda, when he comes of legal age. Matilda is reluctantly willing to live up to the contract for the sake of her father. This part of the story is retained in both versions, although with some variations.

The arrival of Lord Glendary and his nephew set the action of the play in motion and serves to define the different emphases in the two versions. Clifton and his uncle are on the way to war when they stop at the estate of Glendary's old friend, Sir Toby. In *A Word for Nature* there is little doubt that the marriage between Matilda and Leonard has been arranged, although Toby makes it clear that, if had it not been for pressure from his wife, he would have favored Matilda for Clifton, something Glendary had proposed. The closeness of the two families is stressed through the revelation that Lord Glendary is Matilda's godfather.

The character of Starling is a key factor in both versions, but it is significantly different in each play. In *A Word for Nature,* Starling is a hanger-on in the Truckle household, a friend of Lady Truckle who is able to abuse Toby's hospitality because of his wife's tyranny. The first view we have of Starling in *A Word for Nature* is his taking Toby's favorite horse without permission, arrogantly relying on the dominance of Lady Truckle to support him. Toby tries to have Starling leave, but the latter professes friendship and will not quarrel. Clearly he lives by his wits and, although he irritates Toby, there is little evidence of deep-seated antagonism or jealousy. A conversation between Lord Glendary and Uncle Toby is interrupted by Starling who forces his introduction to Glendary, but this action is fortuitous since both Toby and Glendary see Starling as a possible intermediary between Toby and his wife and suggest to him that he might be helpful. He does, in fact, become such an intermediary, seeing an opportunity of advancing both Toby's cause and his own.

When, in *A Word for Nature,* Starling meets with Lady Truckle, he counters her characterization of Glendary as a Scottish trickster by asserting that he is an honorable man, while, at the same time, persuading Lady Truckle that her actions toward Toby are not in her own best interests or in those of her son: "You are imprudent above measure to irritate a Husband whose good will, once gain'd, might give you all you desire (112). She subsequently moderates her assault on Toby and a marked change takes place among the servants. This alteration of her behavior is matched by that of Leonard, who, desiring to obtain the marriage contract, becomes sufficiently friendly and loving toward his mother that he persuades her to let him have it to study. On this occasion, Starling's supporting of the notion of natural virtue separates him substantially from the almost villainous character he is in *The Passive Husband.* When the pedantic Runic speaks of Leonard's "full Maturity of Manliness and Generosity," Starling counters in *A Word for Nature*: "I am sure you did not see it in your Books; at least not in your Ovid, learned Sir; there's no such thing in his whole Art of Love. So throw them all away—Let Nature teach—She's wiser than the Ancients" (131).

Starling's support of natural goodness is a far cry from the pragmatism that defines his character in *The Passive Husband,* where he carries on an unculminated romantic intrigue with Lady Truckle. A sinister figure, he becomes an avowed rival of Runic, often engaging in arguments about Runic's pedantry or his own reputation and skill as an author. Early in the play Lady Truckle reacts jealously to Starling's involvement with Matilda's confidant and is dissatisfied with his explanation that he made love to her only to find out if Matilda had another attachment.

As in *A Word for Nature,* Lord Glendary tries to enlist Starling's support for Toby, but, when Starling meets with Lady Truckle on Toby's behalf, he appears as a suitor who loves her "more than all the world," arguing that he has had no intrigue with Matilda's confidant. When he fails to convince her that she is acting imprudently, she adamantly defends her actions. Only because he has come to her as an intermediary from Toby does she deceitfully lend credibility to his role by embracing new measures, milder in appearance only, but no less efficacious in pursuing her designs. She urges him to avoid Glendary and vows that she herself will go into seclusion until Clifton and Glendary leave. She agrees, however, to admit him secretly to her rooms with the help of Lofty.

The planned assignation between Starling and Lady Truckle serves in the long run to discredit both of them when her letter to Starling planning it falls into the hands of Glendary. At Lord Glendary's request, Starling arranges an interview with Lady Truckle ostensibly to make peace between them, but Starling is chagrined to find that Glendary has the letter. Throwing himself on Glendary's mercy, Starling admits the projected meeting with Lady Truckle, but maintains that he and Lady Truckle are innocent of adultery and agrees to break any connection he has with her. She is revealed, in turn, to have prepared to leave Toby once the terms of the contract had been completed. Leonard, of course, frustrates her wishes by delivering the bond to Clifton. Starling's role is crucial to altering the play from primarily a study of the power and goodness of natural instincts in Leonard, to a portrayal of the danger of the passivity of Toby that almost destroys the happiness of his daughter. This emphasis is accentuated by Matilda's revelation of a letter from Lord Glenandry to her "passive father" offering Clifton to be her husband.

On another level, the two plays focus on the responsibilities of children to parents, and parents to children. In *The Passive Husband* Matilda is portrayed as agreeing to marry Leonard in order to save her father from the tyranny of Lady Truckle, but unlike in *A Word for Nature* it is far from definitively arranged. Although Toby has signed the contract, yielding to the tyranny of his new wife, it would not have happened, nor could the agreement be enforced without Matilda's consent. Her making the promise to marry is not merely consenting to a father's demand, but a generous decision to help her father at the expense of her own happiness. "Penetrated by the sufferings of my father," she declares to Clifton, "and by his importunity beseig'd, I did—but wherefore should I boast myself? What did I more than many others would, and all should do? I sacrificed myself to save a father" (271). Not seeing it as primarily a legal question, Matilda considers it a matter of honor not to break her word. Unlike in *A Word for Nature,* where the legal force of the contract is more strongly relied on in structuring the action, here moral force is as significant as legal force. In *A Word for Nature,* for example, in explaining to Lord Glendary why he could not consent to Clifton's marriage to Matilda, Sir Toby notes: "I am bound hand and foot as fast as law can fetter me. What will a man not do to purchase his domestic peace." The matter has been decided, and Matilda is legally bound to the agreement.

The tone is very different in *The Passive Husband.* Lady Truckle still feels it appropriate to try to persuade Toby that he should cooperate in having his daughter marry Leonard, and she discusses the same matter with Starling in an effort to enlist his assistance in bringing it about. Matilda does not love Leonard. Although she recognizes all his virtues, she knows she could never fail to see his deceitful mother in him and will always see her "father's tyrant reflected in his image (271)." But, she avers, she will not break her promise.

The relationship between Leonard and Clifton is much more measured and rational in *The Passive Husband,* than in *A Word for Nature,* where their rivalry breaks into apparent enmity, with Clifton declaring, "We are at open war—and now I tell you—I love Matilda. Love her to distraction" (116). In contrast, in *The Passive Husband,* Clifton discusses his situation with Matilda, fully recognizing friendship as a major factor: "I have, like you, betroth'd myself to Leonard: he has a heart for friendship; but the man exists not that can behold such beauty and resign it" (282).

While Matilda's love for her father causes her accept the loss of her happiness in *A Word for Nature,* and willingly to sacrifice it in *The Passive Husband,* no such motivation exists for Leonard. His mother's concerns mean little to him. Matilda's actions are largely dictated by the consequences of her father's passively accepting the dictates of his shrewish wife. Leonard's, on the other hand, react to his mother's pragmatic ambition, which his natural goodness sees as essentially evil. Unlike Matilda he finds no spring of loyalty toward a parent. His main interest is in determining whether or not Matilda loves him.

The extent to which Lady Truckle acts in her own interests rather than in those of her son is never truly clarified. She clearly wishes to take care of Leonard and, with that, achieve her own preservation. She tolerates

and apparently loves her abusive son, and, in his interests, is ruthless and unfeeling, willing to sacrifice Sir Toby in their pursuit, and unmindful of the happiness of his daughter. The romantic side of love yields to the materialistic values she espouses. But her callous actions remain sexually decent in *A Word for Nature.* In *The Passive Husband,* however, her actions take on much darker suggestions. She plans to rid herself of Toby and has begun an intrigue with Starling. More than a shrewish wife and domineering tyrant, she is prepared to dissolve her marriage as soon as she has legally provided for her son.

Sir Toby's attitude toward his child is very different from that of Lady Truckle toward hers, and the reactions of their children can only be understood in sentimental terms. The unscrupulous Lady Truckle works energetically to promote her son's interest and earns thereby his dislike and condemnation, while Sir Toby, clearly a sympathetic character, accepts in one play and engineers in the other the sacrifice of his daughter's happiness for his peace of mind. For his action he receives the sympathetic love of his daughter and her willingness to set aside her interests to help him.

The characters of the three young people show little difference in the two versions, although some differences in emphasis are apparent. As has been shown, Matilda willingly participates in the sacrifice of her happiness in *The Passive Husband,* where altruism and honor rather than legal force prevail. She adamantly will not break her promise, although her ability to abrogate the agreement is implied in Lady Truckle's urging her husband to cooperate in having his daughter marry Leonard.

A Word for Nature places great emphasis on Leonard's natural virtues that have been formed in the innocent atmosphere of the country. After an attempted education in worldly matters, he decides to reject formal education in favor of the instruction of nature. When Lady Truckle tells her son that "learning is not to be gain'd without labor," he responds: "For that very reason I gave up the attempt, and turn'd my thoughts to what I cou'd acquire without any labour at all—downright honesty, and common sense—In short I look'd well to my heart, and let my wits shift for themselves" (82). This sort of assurance sustains Leonard as he recognizes the mutual affection between Clifton and Matilda, the first hint of which he finds in his abortive attempt to write a sonnet for her. When Clifton reads it for him, changing it for the better artistically, but also using it as a vehicle to express his own affection for Matilda, the suspicion that she has entered the marriage agreement for reasons other than affection begins to develop. Leonard's desire to bring his suspicions to certainty dominates much of the sentimental action of the play. Once he is certain, there is little doubt that he will withdraw from the contest, but his pursuit, far from creating merely a dark comedy, provides opportunity for the revelation of a character that hates sponging on Sir Toby, and rejects the role of forcing Matilda to marry him against her romantic desires, despite his own deep affection for her. When he begins to suspect that she does not love him, the conflict between his friendship for Clifton and his affection for Matilda are brought into focus. In *A Word for Nature,* Clifton reveals much harsher feelings toward his friend than appear in *The Passive Husband.* Despair, born of a conviction that Leonard could not relinquish his claim to Matilda regardless of her lack of affection for him, leads to evasive scenes with Leonard and ultimately to an open break. Not understanding Leonard's romantic nature, Clifton fails to recognize the desperate urgency of his friend's inquiry into the state of the relationship between him and Matilda.

In *The Passive Husband,* more comic than sentimental effects are sought as Leonard tells Clifton of his affection for Matilda directly and suggests that a true friend would not rival him for her hand. The friendship of Leonard and Clifton sustains itself less effectively in *A Word for Nature,* as Leonard's efforts to discover the true direction of Matilda's love almost destroys it. Leonard suspects, incorrectly, that she dislikes him because he is unpolished and uneducated, something she is aware of but sees as a reflection of the goodness of his nature, and it does not affect her feelings for him. Despite her admiration for his character, she does not love him.

Matilda's consent to the marriage creates a problem for Leonard in *The Passive Husband,* where it is clear that he initially has reason to believe that she returns his strong feelings for her. Cumberland is not entirely successful in clarifying Leonard's unpolished nature. The three manifestations of his character that emerge, his condemnation of his mother's ruthless pragmatism, his relationship to Matilda, and his friendship for Clifton, do not seem to produce a unified result. The depth of his dislike of his mother is not explained by natural virtue. Had he merely objected to an arranged marriage, or to being pledged to a young woman without her specific declaration of love, or to his mother's domination over Sir Toby, his character would be understandable in terms of natural morality. But his reaction is excessive. He verbally abuses his mother, fails to grasp the extent of her efforts on his behalf, does not respond to efforts at education, and treats Clifton with offensive irony. Returning from an extended absence with Runic, he judges everything to be wrong and acts without any grasp of the effects of what he does on others. Sir Toby unpersuasively excuses his excesses on the grounds of his unpolished nature: "His Tongue may err, but his heart is right. He only spoke as Nature prompted him" (92). His relationship with Clifton is also marred by a lack of candor and excessive sensitivity about his friend's affection for Matilda. Wanting to demonstrate his natural generosity so much, he strains their friendship to the limit. Only in the broad outlines of his view of life, an effort to be rigorously just, not to poach on Sir Toby, not to accept a marriage that goes against the romantic interests of his friend, and to reasonably accept Matilda's explanation for rejecting him can a sense of what "nature" means in the context of the play be understood.

In *The Passive Husband,* Leonard's relationship to his mother remains the same, but his affection for Clifton and understanding of Matilda are more easily understood. Leonard welcomes Clifton's arrival and warns him about falling in love with Matilda. Seemingly confident of his position, he is open in discussing with his friend their mutual affection for Matilda. Although he lets Clifton know of his love for Matilda, he still urges him to see more of her. He is able to discuss freely with his friend the question of marital choice, and it is clear that once Leonard is certain about the direction of Matilda's affections, he will step aside.

In some ways the demands of sentiment are more fully met in *The Passive Husband* despite the shift in emphasis away from the theme of natural goodness. The more harmonious relationship among the three young people allows greater latitude for the portrayal of the effects of passivity on Sir Toby and those around him. Not simply a henpecked husband, his failure to take charge of his estate has impacted on his entire household. The servants are in virtual revolt, his daughter's life is threatened with destruction, the expectations of Lord Glenandry for his nephew are jeopardized, and he himself has found no peace and happiness. In shifting the interest of the drama to Sir Toby, many opportunities for comedy are exploited.

Cumberland creates a traditional and sympathetic character in Patrick Malooney, who, in *The Passive Husband,* substitutes for most of the part of John in *A Word for Nature.* Changing the servant to an Irishman enables the dramatist to introduce a note of comedy that is a welcome change from the dourful and complaining John. The initial scene of dialogue between John and Ruth, that introduces the audience to the household confusion that has been the rule since Sir Toby remarried, is replaced by Patrick's soliloquy that begins *The Passive Husband.* In the hands of a good comedian, it could be more effective than the combined efforts of John and Ruth. Rather than Lady Truckle's meeting Toby, as in *A Word for Nature,* Toby and Patrick engage in conversation. The incident in which Starling takes Toby's horse, thus setting into motion immediate antagonism between Toby and his hanger-on, is altered so that it is Lady Truckle who has gone riding. Toby's reaction reveals his affection for his wife when he interprets her intemperate behavior as due to an attack of nerves. "I'm glad of it," he observes, "'tis a fine morning, and a little airing will do her good: poor love, her nerves are all to pieces" (1).

In the third act, Patrick arrives covered with blood and manifests stock Irish characteristics by being emotionally intemperate, superstitious, brave, and proud of his readiness to fight. Lord Glendary bids him speak "if fear will let" him and he responds emotionally: "Fear! No, the devil of a fear have I; or, if I had, I'd sooner keep it to myself than bring it into your lordship's company, noble general, where fear was never yet, nor ever will be." Glenandry recognizes his mistake: "I have accus'd you falsely, I perceive: for you're an Irishman, and of course are not afraid of seeing your own blood" (260). There are deeper ties between the two men than wrought by their casual meeting. Glenandry recognizes their past association when Patrick tells of their having fought together: "The holy Saint Patrick give a thousand years to my lord general, for the gracious things he has said of my own dear country! Whereby I had hop'd to have been bless'd with your noble honour's remembrance, having serv'd in your regiment in America, and fitt by your side at the battle of Bunker's Hill" (160). The change of the servant from John to Patrick is a considerable improvement that adds comic touches while further developing the character of Lord Glenandry.

The substitution of Mrs. Lofty for Ruth is similarly successful, not so much in adding comedy but in providing Lady Truckle with an ally and quazi confidant who, in the end, betrays her. In the scene following Patrick's meeting with Lord Glendary, Mrs. Lofty argues briefly in favor of Patrick when Lady Truckle is prepared to dismiss him, but she quickly alters her approach and is tactfully prepared to agree with her in everything. Their conversation gives Lady Truckle an occasion to roundly condemn Lord Glenandry whom she recognizes as a threat not only to her supremacy but to her plans for Clifton: "This Lord Glendary—this old Highlander—Can't you see what it is that brings him hither? The carcase lures the eagle. All a plot to foist his nephew in upon Sir Toby, and snap the heiress: a piece of Scottish cunning, to patch up the tatters of his rebel confiscations with a good English rent-roll: that's his project, and my blind booby Leonard does not spy the trap that's set to catch him." Lofty loyally responds: "Oh the wretches! If such are their designs, they don't deserve to be let sleep beneath this roof one night" (264).

Mrs. Lofty's friendship for Runic leads to her desertion of her mistress. At the beginning of the fourth act, Mrs. Lofty chides Runic: "So, Mr. Runic, if you were as chang'd in countenance as in kindness, I should not know you. Time was you would look in upon us now and then, and take a jelly or a cup of tea, and conde-

scend to chat with us poor folks; but now you pass us by, and look so proud." His reason is not pride but a reaction to her close alliance with Lady Truckle against Sir Toby, and he terrifies her when he warns her that it will inevitably lead to her destruction. This important scene prepares for her desertion of her Lady's cause by delivering Lady Truckle's letter to Runic rather than to Starling for whom it was intended. Runic, in turn, triumphantly shows it to Lord Glendary. It not only threatens the dismissal of Runic but urges Lady Truckle's assignation with Starling in no uncertain terms: "Runic, it seems, suspects us—Runic shall be discharg'd. You say our assignation for this evening must not take place: I say it must, it shall. Guarded by faithful Lofty, and secur'd by locks and bolts, we may defy discovery. Come therefore, and fear nothing. Come, I say, or tremble at the vengeance I will take. The marriage is in train; when that is over, all points are gain'd, and I am yours for ever" (290). Mrs. Lofty and a determined Runic are far more involved in the plot than the innocuous Ruth and unaggressive Runic are in *A Word for Nature.*

Structurally, the most important alteration of the play is in the fourth act. The act begins in *A Word for Nature* with Runic meeting Lady Truckle to discuss the progress of Leonard in his education, followed by a quarrel between Leonard and His mother. Soon Ruth enters complaining to her mistress of the turmoil in the household. She counters Lady Truckle's demand that John be discharged, by observing that no one is capable of doing so. Starling's arrival reveals his friendship for Lady Truckle and he persuades her to moderate her behavior.

In *The Passive Husband,* on the other hand, the scene focusses on the conversation between Runic and Mrs. Lofty that eventually leads to her betrayal of her mistress. Starling's arrival reveals the extent of the tension between him and Runic. The sharpness of their antagonism has grown to be much more than professional disagreement or a contest for a preferred position in the household, but is rooted in Runic's belief that Starling has been having secret meetings with Lady Truckle. Starling turns this accusation temporarily against Runic by accusing Runic, in the presence of Toby, of fabricating charges against him. Starling emerges at this point as Toby's apparent friend.

Most of the manuscript submitted to the Lord Chamberlain remains intact in the version published in Cumberland's *Posthumous Dramatic Works,* but the printed text does represent a major revision. A comparison of the two reveals many small changes and a significant number of greater ones. The result is a substantial alteration of the emphasis of the play, making it less sentimental and more comic. Leonard's character retains much of its basic sentimentalism, but he is more open in his discussion of love with Clifton and Matilda, and the trick he plays on his mother to gain possession of the marriage contract is never necessary but serves to reinforces his altruistic attitude on love. The most significant change is in the sense the audience has of Sir Toby. The full ramifications of his accepting his daughter's willingness to marry Leonard are more obvious because of her participation in forming the agreement. Toby's passivity is emphasized in his closer relationship to Glenandry. The question of marital obligation to children is heightened, and Toby's failure as a parent and as an individual are more fully explored.

A comparison of the two versions of the story is instructive in tracing Cumberland's tendency to creatively change material to adjust to public reaction. The time of the revision is impossible to determine. The alteration of the names of the servants reflects the substantial changes in what they do in the drama. Since it is apparent that the names of the characters were altered before the actual production of the play, the changes in the action and dialogue also may have taken place during the month between its licensing and its production. That amount of time would have been enough for a man of Cumberland's experience and ability to revise quickly to make them. But a determination that this is what actually happened is not possible. What we do have is a drama in two substantially different versions that provide considerable room for studying the dramatist's writing methods.

III

The failure of *The Widow's Only Son,* which was acted only once on 7 June 1810, was one of a series of dramatic failures Cumberland experienced during the first decade of the nineteenth century that seem to demonstrate that his old appeal to sentiment no longer captured the interest of his audience. The most successful of his last four comedies, *The Sailor's Daughter,* was acted only six times in 1804. Both *Lovers' Resolutions* (1802) and *A Hint for Husbands* (1806), like *The Widow's Only Son,* did not survive their opening night. All four comedies had, in common, an unfortunate lack of intrigue and sentimental themes that were substantially out of date. In many ways they are idea plays, and a theatrical era that, following the enlargement of both Drury Lane and Covent Garden, found great audience response to music and spectacle, could only with great difficulty engage the same audience in the pursuit of ideals concerning social customs, honor, and natural virtue through traditional comedy. Cumberland reluctantly had turned his hand to musical plays with some success with *Joanna* and the *Jew of Mogadore,* the first an original treatment of a Kotzebue drama, and the second an effort to convert to a musical format music the story of the chief character of his great success of the previous decade, *The Jew.*

Both the central themes and the sources of comic laughter seem decidedly anachronistic in *The Widow's Only Son.* The audience seemed no longer interested in the fate of the dependent, the financial plight of the widow, the officious Lord, the niceties of honor, arranged marriages, the solidification of estates, artificial improvement of the land, or the morality of duelling. The mistaken intention device, centered in Hartley's visit to Marmaduke Montalbert in the second act, worked well in the eighteenth century, but the trick was growing thin and Cumberland's handling of it in this play produces little comic effect. Moreover, having Frederic's life saved when the ball from Lord Spangle's pistol is deflected by an amulet containing his father's picture, sentimentally worn about his neck, does not ring true even in the artificial world of sensibility the dramatist has created.

Cumberland combines his familiar themes of the plight of the widow and the expected difficulties of a dependent son with a serious treatment of duelling. Frederic Montalbert interrupts his studies at Cambridge when his mother is unexpectedly widowed by the slaying of her husband in a duel. On his return, he expresses the extent of his devotion. "The one great ruling passion of my soul," he tells his mother, "is love and undivided veneration for you, who now, unfortunately hold single possession of my filial heart" (143). Hartley has arranged with Lord Fungus to take Frederic into his household, but tension between them seems inevitable for Lord Fungus is "stately," and Frederic is "not suple." What gives hope of having the arrangement work is Lord Fungus's expectation that, since he is not being taken seriously as an uneducated nobleman, Frederic will be able to introduce into his household some of the cultivation that he lacks. Fungus is back in the world of the eighteenth century in his desire to improve his property, while tastelessly destroying nature in the process. Unaware of his lack of taste in this, as in his condemning Frederic's letter because it lacks pompous elaboration, he is a source of ridicule to many.

The duelling theme is pursued in both a comic and a serious way. When Lord Fungus rejects Sir Marmaduke's suggestion that Frederic might be a suitable wife for Caroline, the play takes a potentially serious but ultimately comic turn. When Hartley visits Marmaduke to plead Frederic's case, he is mistaken for Lord Fungus's second and directed to deliver a sealed answer, containing a response to a challenge that has not been made. Although there is little expectation that this duel will ever occur, Lord Spangle's challenge to Frederic is more serious, possesses no element of comedy, and almost leads to disaster when the duel actually takes place.

There is some originality in the treatment of the duelling sequence, since Frederic's father has been killed in a duel, and there is the suggestion, perhaps ahead of its time, that heredity is involved. Moreover, the conflict between honor and a more reasoned view of duelling centers ultimately on Frederic's unwillingness to disgrace himself in the eyes of Caroline. Significantly, he admits that his action is morally wrong, as he prepares to take Marmaduke's pistols: "perhaps the Angel that protects my Caroline will aid me also," he muses, "but I dare not ask it, for my cause is evil." He resolves, ultimately, to do what he knows is wrong, because he can find no way to avoid it. He meditates his action at the beginning of the fifth act, "I never knew that moment in my life, when I was less prepared to risk an Act I cannot justify, yet must perform.—Surely the same perverse entangling spirit, that laid my hapless father in his grave, rules in my bosom, else I might have turned this insult from me by a thousand ways without the smallest slur upon my honour" (181).

Frederic does not, therefore, emerge as a totally virtuous man, although there is much to admire in him, particularly in terms of sentiment. In rejecting the demands of wealth, position, and power he captures the admiration of Caroline. His dilemma over the duel is understandable, but his lying to his mother about the pistols when she meets him in the fourth act is a level of contrivance that surprises the reader. His determination to engage in the duel brings out an unexpected rashness. Knowingly doing what he believes is wrong because of his love for Caroline is different from Marmaduke's amoral willingness to fight. Milton's perception of Adam's committing "the mortal sin original" in *Paradise Lost* because of his love for Eve, is a prototype of Frederic's pursuing a knowingly evil course rather than risk Caroline's disapproval. "I would have suffered tortures for your sake;" he tells her, "rather than sink in your esteem, I rush'd on death."

Marmaduke's projected duel never seriously engages the audience's emotions. Neither party wants it, and Lord Fungus is terrified. All will clearly be revealed in time and the catastrophe averted. On the other hand, the quality of the act is well defined in the fourth act. This is not the first duel that Marmaduke has engaged in, the previous one resulting in the death of his opponent, Fitzmaurice. Ringworm warns him: "You'll come short home at last. I wonder what your conscience can be made of. D'ye think it no sin to fight a duel?" (173). But Marmaduke is adamant for the sake of honor. When Ringworm finally learns the enemy is Lord Fungus, he ridicules the idea of fighting and reveals to Marmaduke that Hartley, far from bringing a challenge for Lord Fungus, was there on behalf of Frederic.

The strongest the attack on the abuse of wealth and position is through the character of Sparkle, not so much in the foolishness of his appearance and actions, but in Caroline's description of his social behaviour: ". . . perhaps Lord Spangle might be said to engross the largest portion of those negatives, that make a total nothing, when summed up, and yet compound that specious nothing, a man of fashion." In response to her mother's objection she continues: "How else can I describe him? Only mark! He never deigns to dance, let who will sit by without a partner. Never stirs a foot to ring a bell, or set a chair, or hand a helpless female to her Coach. He admires nothing, looks at nothing, listens to nothing, smiles at nothing, and if he utters, utters a mere nothing" (160-61). Far removed from the comic figure of the beau often found in eighteenth-century literature, typified by Fielding's Beau Didapper, this man is a languid boor but one who is not totally without sensibility. When, following the duel, he withdraws angrily from competition for Caroline, accusing Lord Fungus of betraying him, he curiously has a good word to say about Frederic: "I will do Montalbert justice, He is a lad of spirit, and when I offer'd him to take my ground, and receive his fire, he declined it" (188). Significantly he reveals his own bravery, while praising Frederic.

The Widow's Only Son is, as almost all of Cumberland's plays are, well written and can provide considerable pleasure "in the closet," but, as a vehicle for the stage, it fell short of expectations. Ideas that had run their course form the center of the drama. There are no exceptional comic characters, and the sentimental motif lacks interesting intrigue. The two characters that might have offered substantial comic possibilities, Ringworm and Lord Spangle, are treated much too seriously, with neither Ringworm's preaching nor Spangle's pride exploited effectively. The play tells us much about Cumberland in his later years, and, when combined with a consideration of his other nineteenth-century plays, points to a remarkably active mind, still energetically working, but with an inability to adjust artistically to a world that has greatly changed. . . .

VII

When Cumberland's masque, *Calypso,* was produced at Covent Garden on March 20, 1779, it met with little success and was acted only three times. Stanley Williams condemns the dramatist's shift from his forte, comedy, and views it as a disaster. There were many elements that contributed to the critical onslaught that greeted the presentation, not the least of which may have been his dedication of the work to the Duchess of Manchester. The play was a vehicle for displaying the musical compositions of Thomas Hamley Butler who composed the overture and the score. Unlike the critics, Cumberland was impressed with Butler's music and regrets the young man's not having published the musical portions of the play observing: "I believe I may venture to say that more beautiful and original compositions were never presented to the English stage by a native master," and blaming its failure on the lack of strength of the singers. Cumberland tended from time to time to favor young artists, and he may well have overestimated the skill of Butler who set the work in the style of serious opera.

Cumberland sought to buttress *Calypso* with a new Prelude and Prologue. The Prelude, a brief comedy, *The Critic,* satirically treats members of the printing trade in a manner that was unlikely to enlist the critical support for the Prelude and the musical play that it accompanied. The new Prologue in declaring that the playwright's "Scenes a Caution, not a Charge, convey," does little to soften the attack.

The Critic, consisting of one act with three scenes, offers little that is new, from the comedy regarding the arrival of the Sheffield stage at an inn, which serves to introduce Eustace, a gentleman turned author, who is seeking a critic to examine his work, to the portrayal of Type, a disreputable editor who pragmatically pursues his craft seeking to fill his paper with sensational material without regard to the truth of what he prints. Greenwood, his employee, turns out to be the father of Eustace, and when Type asks him to casually evaluate the tragedy of the young man, he condemns Type as a "Wretch! Slanderer, betrayer of the Public trust." He continues his assault, emphasizing the potential for good that is lost by Type's corrupt violation of the ethics of his profession: "The fountain that supplies a City's thirst, is in your keeping, if you wou'd conduct the waters thro' a cleanly channel, to the Public lips, your Occupation wou'd be noble; but you invert its uses, and, by poisoning the Spring, send a contaminated Spring throughout the Kingdom, to vitiate the blood and humours of the best hearted Nation upon Earth" (353).

The comic elements of *The Critic* work well enough for a Prelude, but failed to contribute substantially to the success of the mainpiece, *Calypso.* Despite elaborate sets and spectacular stage business, the masque of a new composer and a playwright, whose genius lay in sentimental comedy, did not succeed, being acted with *The Critic* only three times, and provoking a storm of critical condemnation.

VIII

The projected size and elegance of the new Drury Lane theatre, which was under construction in the fall of 1793, although not used for performances until 12 March 1794, put competitive pressure on Covent Garden to expand its facilities. Its huge seating capacity made it the largest theatre, exclusive of opera houses, to be built in London until the twentieth century. Thomas Harris, the proprietor of Covent Garden, responded with an expensive renovation of the interior of the theatre that was completed in September 1792. The newly designed theatre did not match the size of the new Drury Lane, which seated 3611 viewers, but its capacity was considerable, with 632 seated in the pit, 1200 in three circles of boxes, 820 in the first gallery and 361 in the upper gallery, for a total of 3,013. The size of both theatres made acting less intimate and promoted the popular musical plays that were lamented by Cumberland and other devotees of pure tragedy and comedy. Although it was evident that such changes would result in some increase in prices, the elimination of the one-shilling gallery, a time-honored tradition in the London theatre, prompted loud and unruly elements in the audience to virtually stop the performance. Cumberland's *Prelude* could not be heard, any more than the plays that followed it. Harris finally restored the penny gallery, while retaining the increase in prices elsewhere. When Drury Lane opened under John Philip Kemble in 1794, the seats in the upper gallery cost the traditional one shilling.

Cumberland's *Prelude* is largely an appeal for understanding the need to increase the price of admission. The manager and a stranger appear disputing the presence on stage of the stranger, a sailor just returned from a voyage and prepared to appreciate the "rosy cheeks and sky-blue lovely eyes" of the ladies in the audience (259). The sailor cannot restrain his enthusiasm for England and bursts into song, at the end of which the manager complains that he is out of order and interrupting the performance. There is some comic discussion of the manager's lack of facility with words, but he and the stranger make it clear that the renovations have made for a trim and comfortable theatre. The sailor compares his service to his country to that of the theatrical manager, who responds, "I hope I shall never want spirit to stand by my Colours: I fight under a Chief, who is not of the sort to enrich himself by the Public, and only hopes they will not suffer him to sink under his endeavours" (362), arguing further that the proprietor "wou'd scorn to raise contributions, from a generous Public which he did not render back to them in liberal entertainment" (363). The justification for the increase in admission lies, the audience is told, in a desire to serve the public by presenting the Muse in the most favorable light: "It is to give energy to the current of her humour that we have cleansed the Channel; It is to reflect her image with the greater truth and lustre that we have polished our Mirror . . . Let her advance with wit in her discourse, modesty in her demeanour and good humour at her heart . . ." (364).

Whether or not this appeal would have proved acceptable had not the penny gallery been eliminated is impossible to judge, for the issue was obscured by the disruptions at the opening of the theatre. The *Prelude* was presented, however, without interference two days later, after Harris gave his word that the traditionally inexpensive seats would be restored.

The *Prelude* as presented to the Lord Chamberlain on 11 September 1792 seems to have been hastily put together and greatly revised, with many deletions and transfers of speeches from one part of the manuscript to another. Extensive deletions are indicated in square brackets, while shorter ones are provided in the textual notes.

IX

The Village Fete is an insubstantial one-act musical interlude written and performed in honor of the marriage of Princess Augusta of Great Britain to Frederick William, Prince of Wurttemberg on 18 May 1797. An occasional piece, it has no reason for existence except to take public notice of the wedding, and, as might be expected, has little literary value. William Shield set the play to music, although not all of it new, and it was designed to end with an "Illumination, Transparency, and a Royal Procession" (*London Stage*, V, 1695), which comprise the entire third scene.

The action of the first scene is set in the early morning before the mansion of Sir Martin Marygold who complains that the serenading of the peasants has awakened both him and his lady. When the reason for the festivities is explained, Sir Martin decides to join the celebration, accompanied by his two domestics, Kate and Nicholas. They invite Blacky to join them, and in a very brief appearance, he gives Cumberland an opportunity to imitate the language of the black servant: "Aha! here come Massa and Missis cross as a hell. Whuh! and old Kate and old Nick. Now you will pay for all your baboon tricks" (370). All take part in the celebration, led largely by the energetic Nicholas, who advises Sir Martin that there are days "when beer must flow and beef must quit the hooks" (371).

The arrival of Peter the Preacher almost destroys the celebration, but Sir Martin remembers to ask him to drink first and preach later, and, after a number of drafts, he sets aside his primary mission and joins the celebration.

The second scene prepares for the dancing in the third. A young rustic and an old woman are followed by an old man and two girls on their way to a pageant. The old man explains that a group of girls on one side and a company of boys on the other will meet on the Village Green and engage in lively dancing. The men are appropriately to be led by Farmer Fairlove and the girls by Peggy Pansey who are to be married that day. Thus the local festivities reinforce the sense of the national celebration. All ends with a dance that concludes the piece.

The Village Fete is a competent piece of fluff, happy in its conception and pleasant in its execution, its success almost entirely dependent on the energy of the dancers and the vitality of the music to flesh out its routine comedy and obvious incidents.

X

Cumberland's *An Occasional Attempt* was an effort to join in the patriotic fervor of Englishmen over the great victory of Admiral Lord Viscount Nelson at the naval battle of Trafalgar, and to take notice of his heroic death. One of three efforts by Cumberland to commemorate this event, it was the most successful. The first, a brief impromptu of eleven lines, was spoken at Covent Garden by Richard Wroughton on the day news reached London. The second, a two act play intended for performance on the evening after Nelson's funeral, was denied a license, but the *Occasional Attempt* was staged with some success and earned the dramatist a gold snuffbox.

The historical importance of Nelson's victory raised the level of public adulation far above that normally awarded a national hero. There was a real threat of an invasion of the British Isles by the French as Napoleon moved relentlessly forward in his conquest of Europe. Such an invasion, whatever the quality of English resistance might have been, could not take place without mastery of the seas. The French had attempted to lure the British fleet away from the continent to the West Indies, but failed in the attempt, and when Napoleon's fleet sought refuge in the Mediterranean, they were intercepted and decisively defeated by the English off Cape Trafalgar on 21 October 1805, thus not only ending the threat of invasion but assuring Britain's supremacy at sea.

Cumberland's tribute takes the form of the arrival of a ship that lands a Post Captain and his crew. Against the background of music of different moods, he praises England, while bringing news of the fallen hero. A solo piece, a trio, and a chorus punctuate the brief spectacle. The patriotic sense and gratitude of the country is evident in what is merely a slight vehicle designed to provide a framework for the expression of the national mood.

XI

The range of Cumberland's short pieces and fragments reveals the extent of his social concerns. **"The Impromptu after the Play of *Hamlet*"** emphasizes his interest in Garrick's affairs and adds additional data to what is known of their controversial friendship. Cumberland's sensitivity and Garrick's exasperation with the dramatist led to periods of conflict during their many years of association. This theatrical compliment to Garrick on the occasion of his important alteration of Shakespeare's play is an interesting footnote to their relationship.

The Princess of Parma and *The Election* take the reader into the world of the provinces and the presentation of dramas at private theatres such as that of William Hanbury at Kelmarsh. The tragedy and the comic afterpiece are both serious efforts undertaken with a high degree of professionalism. The historical range of the tragedy indicates an extent of interest in history that the age possessed and that provided a knowledgeable audience for historical drama. In *The Election,* the accepted sense of the corruption of politics and election bribery forms the basis for relatively urbane comedy, thus indicating how the populace in general viewed that phenomenon.

Two Preludes remind us that the mainpiece and afterpiece were not the only ingredients of the theatrical evening, but that along with music, dancing, recitations and similar presentations between the acts, short plays were used to introduce the entertainment on special occasions, and sometimes to attempt to buttress a main offering. *The Critic* is used to strengthen the presentation of the masque, *Calypso,* a vehicle in which Cumberland introduced a relatively unknown composer. The Prelude designed for the opening of Covent Garden's new theatre in September 1792 might perhaps have softened audience reaction to the rise in prices had it not been for the disturbances caused largely by the abolition of the penny gallery. The Interlude, *The Village Fete,* is a brief play, too short to be an afterpiece, but suitable for presentation between two other dramas, and is an example of occasional dramatic pieces used to celebrate important occasions, in this case, the marriage of Princess Augustus to Prince Frederic William. Finally, the short "melodramatic attempt" in honor of Lord Viscount Nelson further illustrates the occasional pieces often found on the stage of the eighteenth century. All of these theatrical efforts point to the versatility of the entertainment and the range of audience interest during the period.

Maaja A. Stewart (essay date spring 1996)

SOURCE: Stewart, Maaja A. "Inexhaustible Generosity: The Fictions of Eighteenth-Century British Imperialism in Richard Cumberland's *The West Indian.*" *Eighteenth Century* 37, no. 1 (spring 1996): 42-55.

[*In the following essay, Stewart offers a close reading of Cumberland's* The West Indian. *Stewart's analysis reveals numerous ways in which Cumberland's apparent sympathy for victims of oppression is undermined by his simultaneous endorsement of British imperialist policy.*]

In the fourth act of Richard Cumberland's *The West Indian* (1771), Major O'Flaherty stops a duel between an ensign in the British army and Belcour, the Jamaican son of a London merchant on his first visit to the home country. To justify his interference, the major invokes

the separation between the sphere of man's actions, where violence is acceptable, and the domestic sphere, where it is not: "if you've had wrong done you, young man, you need look no further for a second; Dennis O'Flaherty's your man for that; but never draw your sword before a woman, Dudley; damn it, never while you live draw your sword before a woman" (4.5).[1] The threat of violence in the London drawing room, with phallic swords unsheathed in the presence of ladies, brings the hostilities of the imperial sphere in the distant reaches of the empire dangerously into the metropolitan heart of the British culture. Brute force is part of the daily work of soldiers, colonials, and international merchants in imperial competitions with European rivals as well as with indigenous peoples; this institutionalized violence contradicts the civility required in London interactions. British eighteenth-century imperialism requires an ethical separation between the English mainland and the territories of its international activities. John Brewer, among other historians, points to "the stark contrast between the view from the metropolis and from its periphery. Englishmen may have prided themselves on their liberties and the rule of law, and praised the growth of commerce as a civilizing process, but authority was exercised very differently—often brutally and barbarously—in those distant lands and over those subject peoples which occupied the frontiers of commercial development."[2] Robert Hughes gives a specific example of this stark contrast: "A bill of 1752 introducing public chain-gang labor as punishment for criminals was rejected by the Lords partly because security was too great a problem but mainly because the sight of chain gangs in public places was felt to be degrading. How could onlookers distinguish such a punishment from outright slavery? In the New World, there would be no such problem."[3]

In the fifth act of Cumberland's play law replaces swords, just as civility replaces the ethos of personal honor and violence. Cumberland thus constructs an idealized narrative of mercantilism. Stockwell, the London Merchant, transforms the locus of the duel into that of the law court. The metropolitan counting-house civilizes and legalizes the activities of the frontiers, as the merchant with his patriarchal authority controls the wild colonials and the violently honorable army officers, those involved in exercising British authority in the "distant lands and over subject peoples" on the frontiers of commerce. The image of swords drawn in the presence of ladies remains the only explicit representation of imperial violence within the metropolitan center. The fact that this violence is so quickly contained reinforces the fiction that the metropolitan center remains immune to the effects of empire, that it can transform extraterritorial spaces without itself being transformed. This denial and the cultural work required to maintain the denial are the subjects of my essay. Specifically, my reading renders visible the discursive displacements and erasures that cluster around the intersection of imperialism and domesticity. My particular focus is on the ways in which categories of gender and class are realigned in response to imperial violence. This realignment displaces some of the major fears and desires of imperial activities onto metropolitan women, the underclass, and the aristocracy in order to reinforce the idealized narrative of trade as a "cordializing" system (as Thomas Paine called it) in spite of the violence that remains endemic to it.[4]

I offer Richard Cumberland's **The West Indian** as a particularly accessible text of such displacements. Cumberland, named "Sir Fretful Plagiary" by Richard Sheridan in *The Critic,* is the kind of derivative and conventional writer whose work registers clearly the discursive displacements that support the power structures of the dominant culture.[5] Cumberland's positioning of gender and class formations in the space created by the West Indian's effects on the London society offers a vantage point to British literature of empire needed to correct the readings that maintain separate spheres. Recent studies of British literature and imperialism have reinforced a discursive separation between domestic and imperial experiences in generic terms by positing an opposition between adventure romances and courtship novels. These generic terms remain necessarily gendered ones because they project different narratives for men, whose adventure novels traditionally marginalize women, and for women, whose courtship narratives traditionally marginalize male imperial activities of trade and war, the subjects of adventure.[6] In **The West Indian** we witness both the attempt and also the repeated failures of the attempt to keep imperial activities separate from courtship narratives. The presence of the Jamaican planter and the various army officers in London invokes the imperial narratives that will not be completely subsumed in the dominant courtship plot. Furthermore, even as the dominant textual ideology of **The West Indian** insists on a separation of imperial activities from domestic ones, narrative analogies and metaphorical echoes just as insistently connect the two spheres. The connections reveal just how centrally the distant imperial activities function to intensity metropolitan categories of difference. These categories of difference, in turn, sustain the mercantile economy and power structure.

Officially, the morality in **The West Indian** is in the keeping of the London merchant Stockwell who initiates the action by disguising his paternity from his Jamaican son, Belcour, until the last act in order "to make some experiment of my son's disposition" (1.1). The subsequent dramatic action derives from Belcour's inability to read the metropolitan women and the metropolitan underclass correctly: he mistakes the virtuous Louisa for a sexually available woman and he negotiates with the lower-class entrepreneurs, the Fulmers, for

access to her, an access that they pretend to possess. The action erupts into violence when Belcour's predatory sexual negotiations with women cannot be kept separate from his sentimental negotiations with men. Exchange of women functions centrally to reinforce male bonds. When Belcour approaches Louisa directly, he threatens the bonds he is beginning to create with her male relatives. By treating Louisa as a free woman who can negotiate for herself, Belcour insults the honor of her father, Captain Dudley, and her brother, Charles Dudley. Cumberland averts the threat of violence with the disclosure of the merchant Stockwell's paternity and authority over the West Indian. Belcour's initial identity as a Caribbean foundling yields to his new identity as a son of a London merchant. Marriage to Louisa further domesticates Belcour out of his predatory sexuality. The honor that figures centrally in the imperial sphere thus transforms into metropolitan virtue. This virtue derives from and in turn legitimizes the bourgeois family.

The same sequence that incorporates the West Indian into the metropolitan culture intensifies the identity of the metropolitan proper lady by distinguishing her from the transgressive others: the London prostitutes and the Caribbean slave women. The threat of violence in front of the ladies at the end of the play results directly from the West Indian's inability to make these distinctions in a sequence that insistently conflates the London prostitute with the Caribbean slave woman. "Accustomed to the land of slaves," Belcour approaches the virtuous Louisa as a natural sexual prey. His actions instantly restrict the proper lady's movements. Because of Belcour's harassment, her father forbids her the street that was the place of the first encounter: "You must walk no more in the streets, child, without me or your brother" (2.4). Furthermore, Belcour's attempt to buy Louisa creates the need to distinguish metropolitan sexualities from slave sexualities. His negotiations with Mrs. Fulmer for Louisa's favors is a clear financial transaction that Mrs. Fulmer herself associates with the Caribbean economy: "Girls of her sort are not to be kept waiting like negro slaves in your sugar plantations" (3.3). The distinction between Louisa and a slave girl in Mrs. Fulmer's rhetoric simply emphasizes that Louisa is more expensive "to lease" than a slave is to buy. This association with slave women's sexuality remains in Belcour's mind until the threat of violence makes clear that Louisa's honor is protected by a sword.

This threat of on-stage violence recalls the off-stage violence at the beginning of the play that marks the colonial's interaction with the "mob" when he enters the metropolitan space. "Accustomed to a land of slaves," he loses patience with "the whole tribe" of workers on the docks, who surround him "worse than a swarm of mosquitoes" (1.5). His reading of the London underclass through the Caribbean discourse of tribal, "swarming," and thus individually indistinguishable workers is abruptly corrected as the English "sturdy rogues . . . rebel" against his assumption of authority. Belcour quickly understands that common people express their freedom through "riot" in which they act as "rebels" (1.5). The ever-available fiction of "free-born Englishman" distinguishes the metropolitan workers from the colonial slaves. Cultural capital signified by the idea of freedom can stand in place of subsistence wages.

In the scene of the threatened duel and the scene of the threatened mob action, the violence constitutes a rejection of West Indian sexual and labor arrangements by the metropolitan culture. This rejection assures the discursive purity of the metropolitan women and the discursive freedom of the metropolitan underclass. Belcour's "incorrect" responses reinforce the disciplinary procedures by which metropolitan sectors are contained within the capitalist patriarchy. These disciplinary procedures are particularly visible in the construction of the proper lady. Both Louisa's father and Stockwell emphasize that the metropolitan women have to be distinguished from the women in colonial spaces where they function as a natural sexual or financial prey. Meanwhile, the amusement generated by Major O'Flaherty's multiple marriages makes startlingly clear the imperial rise of women: "I've married five wives *en militaire,* Captain . . . and, for what I know, they're all alive and merry at this very hour" (2.8). Charles Dudley's response to this bigamy, which projects his aunt, Lady Rusport, into the sixth "wife," ignores the criminality and focuses on the major's generous, if comic, offer to share the lady's wealth: "Well, sir, go on and prosper; if you can inspire Lady Rusport with half of your charity, I shall think you deserve all her fortune" (2.8). Major O'Flaherty remains one of the "good" characters because his primary loyalty is to his fellow officers at the expense of women. O'Flaherty's multiple marriages create a comic reflection of the notorious sexual license of white men in the Caribbean that all contemporary commentators noted. As Janet Schaw observed in the "crouds of Mullatoes" on the streets of Antigua in 1774, white man's sexual indulgence constitutes "a crime that seems to have gained sanction from custom."[7] In 1794 John Stedman described the "Surinam marriage" that institutionalized a white man's temporary cohabitation with a mulatto woman.[8] Such extra-legal sexual arrangements on the islands threatened the ideal of domesticity not only among the slaves but also among the Englishmen who settled there. Belcour's initial status as a foundling belongs with other images that represent the breakdown of the nuclear family: images of adultery, bigamy, incest, and illegitimacy appear compulsively in the eighteenth-century narratives about the West Indies. Placed in this context, the sentimental domestic family, which becomes the staple image of desire and resolution of conflict in metropolitan narratives, functions as a compensatory space for imperial violence and imperial sexuality.

The replacement of violence by domestic law and family further serves to construct the identity of the merchant class by its opposition to as well as its appropriation of residual aristocratic values. As V. G. Kiernan points out, the threat of personal violence was a mark of aristocratic status because

> duelling provided a warrant of aristocratic breeding, increasingly threatened with submergence. It preserved to the entire class a military character, a certificate of legitimate, descent from the nobility of the sword of feudal times, and of its title to officer the new mass armies. Duelling was in itself an assertion of superior right, a claim to immunity from the law such as a ruling class is always likely to seek. . . . For the man of noble birth it was all the more natural to put himself above the law because he, as seigneur, had been in command of justice in his own domain.[9]

A single discursive gesture allows the merchant class to reject the residual aristocratic honor in the metropolitan culture while appropriating the same honor for the colonies. Bourgeois morality waged a vigorous pamphlet war against claims to an autocratic immunity from law. Merchant capitalism appropriated such autocratic immunity, however, in the peripheries of the empire and in the rigidly hierarchical institutions like the army that served the peripheries.[10] The concept of "honor" ritualized the "consciousness of self-importance" that the contemporary West Indian historian, Bryan Edwards, attributed to the white West Indian because of the hot "climate" that fostered him.[11] It also idealized the violence that peculiarly characterizes modern slavery with its constant need "to repeat the original, violent act of transforming free man into slave."[12] Historical attempts to control the autocratic sword, or the colonial violence disguised as honor, appear a decade after *The West Indian* in the movement to abolish the slave trade and in the parliamentary trial of Warren Hastings, the former governor general of Bengal. The first step in controlling the sword was to render it discursively visible and unacceptable. Thomas Clarkson deconstructed all arguments that invoked the honor of British trade with Africa by collecting data that highlighted the horrifying death rate on the slave ships. Edmund Burke questioned the honor of British imperial activities in India by listing the various violent methods by which a private trade company subjected the indigenous population to its rule. In the decades that followed, hidden disciplinary procedures would increasingly replace open imperial force whenever possible.[13]

Elaborate idealizations support such hidden disciplinary procedures. Effacement of material conditions from mercantile narratives makes these idealizations possible.

Remarkably varied methods of erasures and denials of the activities of the market society concentrate especially around the representation of colonial wealth in ***The West Indian.*** Cumberland is exemplary in ignoring the ways this wealth is produced, while emphasizing instead Belcour's generosity in spending it in London. Thus, a kind of residual aristocratic liberality appears centrally in the mercantile narratives that are situated in the metropolitan culture, at the same time that the aristocratic sword of honor has to be excluded from the mainland. An illusion of an active gift-exchange, signified by generosity, thus detaches the West Indian wealth from its production and suggests that Belcour's wealth in fact contrasts with the exchanges in the dominant market economy, exchanges determined not by the giving of gifts that ask nothing in return, but by a compulsion to gain in competition with others who have to lose.[14] Generosity has a simple and powerful narrative function in this discourse: it transforms "excess" or luxury, attributed to colonial wealth as early as Sir Thomas More's *Utopia,* into "abundance."

Cumberland's text stresses the importance of this transformation when at Belcour's initial appearance Stockwell subjects the West Indian to metropolitan authority by sternly substituting images of abundance for the latter's images of excess: when Belcour celebrates his "happy stars" for his "good estate," which he can spend in England, "the fountain head of pleasure," Stockwell corrects his enthusiasm: "To use, not to waste it, I should hope; to treat it, Mr. Belcour, not as a vassal, over whom you have a wanton and despotic power, but as a subject, which you are bound to govern with a temperate and restrained authority" (1.5). Stockwell's speech erases the slave economy that produced the wealth—the potentially "wanton and despotic power" of the master over the workers—and focuses on a "free" economy in which the wealth itself replaces the slaves as Belcour's subjects. The substitution of money for slaves brings us to the center of the capitalist economy in which the circulation of money does the "work." Indeed, as Fernand Braudel points out, plantations "were capitalist creations *par excellence*: money, credit, trade and exchange tied them to the east side of the Atlantic."[15] European trade created Caribbean plantations, because everything except the land that went into the plantation economy—masters, slaves, and materials—was imported to the islands. However, many plantation owners conveniently forgot their economic basis and "expected to live the serene life of country nobles, aloof from the cares of the speculative, capitalistic environment which gave them their wealth."[16]

Stockwell's admonitions thus simultaneously recognize and deny the importance of capital exchanges. With his substitution of money for slaves he stresses the centrality of capital formation and circulation. With his insistence that Belcour govern his wealth according to the limits established by the English ideology of liberty, he evokes the residual aristocratic ideal of liberality as a way to legitimize ownership and to escape from the tendency of the market economy to subsume social relations under the uncontrollable forces of capital flow.[17]

This displacement supports others that associate the wealth gained from colonial endeavors, in reality notoriously bourgeois and mercantile, with the ethos surrounding wealth in an earlier fixed-status and aristocratic society, as this is imagined by the bourgeoisie.[18] "This man's generosity is as inexhaustible as his riches," cries the title character in Frances Sheridan's *Miss Sidney Bidulph* (1761) when she is saved from poverty by the sudden appearance of her cousin Warner after his five and twenty year absence in the West Indies.[19] Numerous other fictional Creoles and Nabobs with such god-like plenitude return to England to pour wealth on their deserving metropolitan relations in eighteenth-century fictions. Uncle Oliver in Richard Sheridan's *The School for Scandal* (1777) is characteristic in bringing moral clarity as well as financial rescue to the nephew who has exhausted his paternal inheritance and dismantled the aristocratic portrait gallery, retaining only the generosity and gratitude that mark a noble disposition. Against the bankruptcy of the old landed gentry, the returning imperialists activate a kind of aristocratic liberality. The phrase "I grow rich by giving" expresses their abundant generosity as it did for Dryden's last noble Roman, Antony, "bounteous as nature; next to nature's God" in his analogous imperial adventures.[20] Such focus on the use of wealth, informed with images of plenitude and liberality, remains central in British imperial ideology because this focus draws attention away from its accumulation. Susan Staves argues that such a fictional emphasis on generosity is "part of the schizophrenia of bourgeois culture"; it represses "the importance of the very market achievements that gave the bourgeois its wealth and power, to insist on nonmonetary motives for actions and nonmonetary sources of values, and to cry up the worth of psychic achievements."[21] One of the most economical ways of erasing the material conditions of life from the text is to posit images from a residual feudal system at the center of the emergent mercantile moral experiences.

In imperial ideology, this kind of aristocratic, ahistorical, and essentialized generosity is also an attribute of the virtuous woman. The patriarchy defines her virtue by her separation from the competition and gain of the market society. She must not enter into capital formation or exchanges, but must assure the flow of capital by freely giving of herself and her possessions. In her initial appearance, Cumberland's heiress, Charlotte Rusport, spells out clearly the obligation to generosity motivating her actions. When Lady Rusport rejects her relationship to Captain Dudley and his destitute family—"Not a shilling of mine shall ever cross the hands of any of them; because my sister chose to marry a beggar; am I bound to support him and his posterity?"—Charlotte counters unequivocally: "I think you are" (1.6). Her own actions throughout the play are directed—somewhat unsuccessfully—toward sharing her wealth with the same deserving poor relations of her step-mother, a sharing determined by her love for Charles Dudley. Love thus makes possible the non-violent transmitting of wealth from a woman to a man. Eroticized male bonding within the imperial economy functions analogously as the "natural" dispersal of Belcour's wealth when the planter helps the army officers. A liberality expressed in Major O'Flaherty's offer to share his anticipated wealth with Charles Dudley characterizes the soldiers' relationships to each other.

The appearance of actual aristocracy in the action of the play reinforces the associations to a residual aristocratic morality. The impoverished Dudleys, who become the concentrated focus of the bounty of the West Indian, the heiress, and the Irish mercenary, bear an insistently aristocratic name that descends from Queen Elizabeth's Leicester. The Dudleys in Cumberland's play are the transmitters of an "innate" nobility of the upper classes that poverty cannot disguise. They become the litmus test for the right use of riches in the play and they function to create melodramatic narratives. They themselves become typical figures of melodrama: the virtuous daughter under threat of seduction, the dignified father unrewarded in spite of years of service, and the deserving son desperately asserting his gentility by preserving his honor. Their impoverishment conveniently cancels the libertinism that bourgeois narratives traditionally attributed to the aristocrats. Their consequent "virtue" denies them an ability to act, and thus further empowers the bourgeoisie who determine their lives. The other characters in the play perform either as their victimizers or as their rescuers. The final harmonizing negotiations at the end of the play enrich the Dudleys in three different ways: they inherit Oliver Roundhead's puritan wealth, Charles marries the wealth of the former Lord Mayor of London, and Louisa marries West Indian wealth. The essentialized and ahistorical aristocratic ideal is thus confirmed not only in the generosities practiced by the West Indian and the virtuous woman, but also by the flow of commercial wealth toward old noble blood. This ennobling of fortunes gained by trade reinforces the fantasy of tradesmen that they themselves will in time become ennobled while maintaining their economic power.

When the Dudleys are dissociated from their function in the sentimental economy of generosity, their distress suggests a darker vision of the actual imperial economy. The comic flow of generosity and wealth toward the Dudley males, now "in service" to the king as army officers, only thinly disguises how much the security of the West Indian wealth depended upon the presence of British warships and soldiers in the Caribbean. Greatly outnumbered by their black slaves, the white colonists faced a constant threat of a slave revolt of the kind that destroyed the French rule in St. Domingue in 1791. Furthermore, as Bryan Edwards argued in his 1798 *History of the West Indies,* the Caribbean became the "arena" or "theatre" on which European hostilities always concentrated.[22] Most of all, like the Creole, the soldiers make visible British imperialism and its potential violence in the heart of London in a structure aptly characterized by Pollard and Crossley: "Wars were as indispensable to the development of commercial capitalism in the eighteenth century as slavery was to the development of the sugar plantation."[23] Of the three major aspects of Britain's changing international status dramatized in the play—the global expansion of commerce as represented by Stockwell, colonialization of alien lands as represented by Belcour, and the military support necessary for such global expansion and colonialization as represented by the Dudleys and Major O'Flaherty—the only part that remains both morally as well as financially intact is the merchant himself. That the metropolitan culture cannot support such soldiers, without whose support neither the extensive international trade nor the slave plantations would have been possible, points to the asymmetrical distribution of power in the play.

In particular, the desperate presence of these impoverished soldiers who populate the play makes the unequal distribution of wealth hard to ignore. It is notable that a work that sentimentalizes excessive wealth into generosity also dramatizes in so many different ways the difficulty of surviving in the metropolitan economy. The curtain rises to Stockwell's enterprises spanning the known globe, with his "many ventures of great account at sea," and to the young West Indian heir to "old Belcour's great estates in Jamaica" (1.1). The action, however, quickly focuses in turn on the poverty of the Dudleys, the Fulmers, and Major O'Flaherty. The initial association of mercantile wealth with the plural and the abundant emphasizes that the fortunes of the London merchant and his Creole son derived from God's plenitude poured upon the deserving among humans. An insistent dismissal of the "value" of money further spiritualizes the characters possessing this wealth: Stockwell, Belcour, and Charlotte all deny power to the material basis of society by compulsively designating wealth as "baubles," "a trifle," or "mere dross" that must not affect relations between individuals. This idealized vision contrasts uneasily with the pauperized desperation of those who are willing to sell their bodies to army posts in deadly climates or to colonial libertines preying on London streets.

In Cumberland's plotting, however, the cause of this poverty is not merchant capitalism. Instead, it is wealth inherited and hoarded by a woman—Lady Rusport—

that threatens to bring chaos to the social hierarchies and patriarchal transmissions of power. By hoarding, she takes wealth out of circulation. By denying family ties, she creates the poverty so epidemic in the play. Her policy of hoarding and refusal to share the wealth with her sister's son—"I renounce him as my nephew; Sir Oliver renounced him as his grandson" (1.6)—renders visible the formation of separate social classes out of one family within one generation. In making Lady Rusport responsible for the poverty, Cumberland ignores the analogy between Lady Rusport's hoarding and the concentration of wealth and power in Stockwell's hands. He focuses instead on discoveries that can redress the wrongs she has done to the Dudleys, discoveries that celebrate patriarchal generosity.

What the text represents as patriarchal generosity could, however, be read as self-interest. Sentimental aid to the deserving poor confirms Belcour's economic position as completely as Lady Rusport's denial of kinship confirms hers. Cumberland's text registers this analogy while the explicit narrative emphasizes an opposition between the actions of the man and the woman. Belcour spends on Captain Dudley the £200 he had meant to use to seduce Louisa. This choice establishes his good nature. Belcour and later Stockwell celebrate this generosity by sharply contrasting the two actions: "I've lost the girl it seems . . . but the case of this poor officer touches me; and, after all, there may be as much true delight in rescuing a fellow creature from distress, as there would be in plunging one into it" (2.6). Cumberland ignores the uncanny similarity between the actions of ruining the girl and paying for the father to serve in Africa. The money allows the captain to reassume active duty in Senegambia, a site of the slave trade that was essential to the West Indian economy because the death rate among slaves was higher than the birth rate.[24] Furthermore, numerous comments in the play emphasize that Africa's "deadly climate" would mean Captain Dudley's death as surely as sexual ruin in the sentimental narrative means death to a girl like Louisa. The actions that Cumberland opposes as seduction and generosity are thus similar in serving Belcour's self-interest at the expense of another's life.

The dominant textual ideology effaces the similarity that would conflate generosity with self-interest, a conflation perhaps more acceptable to writers in the early part of the century before the brutality of self-interest had been brought to the surface by such public forums as the movement to abolish the slave trade or the trial of Warren Hastings.[25] The attempts in sentimental fictions to establish action that escapes from the interest-based market economy efface material conditions to eroticize capitalistic negotiations between men into a liberality by which the wealthy remunerate the workers (in this case the army officers) out of generosity rather than as payment for services. Cumberland's idealized vision of the pre-market society becomes especially striking when measured against the excess of poverty created either directly or indirectly by the market society itself: except for the long distant merchant and the heirs or heiresses to estates, everyone else—the soldiers, decayed gentry, small shop-keepers, and people on the make—finds it hard to pick up a livelihood in London. As represented in the play, these impoverished people are not lifted out of their poverty by their own labor or by contractual agreements, but by the will and generosity of the wealthy. The economic morality of the old status society with its fixed social classes is, in short, imbricated with the capitalist finances in the play.

Whereas Cumberland's text rejects as well as appropriates residual aristocratic values, it criminalizes the underclass in the persons of the Fulmers. This criminalization, a direct effect of their interactions with the West Indian, serves to absolve Belcour from guilt for his own potentially criminal activities. Cumberland needs the Fulmers in order to maintain his West Indian as a positive character, one who is both a comically blundering "foreign gentleman" and also the "son" who will carry on the tradition of his father. Belcour's misreadings of his London interactions are based on serious moral issues: the slave-owner's assumptions about labor and sexual relations that Belcour attempts to impose on the underclass and on women must be rejected by the metropolitan culture. In Cumberland's plotting, however, Belcour's misreadings do not bring lasting harm. On the contrary, in spite of their serious potential to disrupt London relations, these misreadings serve a positive end in Cumberland's plot: they help to identify and consequently to dispel criminal activity from the community. The Fulmers' similar misreading of the metropolitan culture leads to their imprisonment. In their disrespect for official categories, they dismantle the discursive separation between the metropolis and the fringes of the empire: they read the London mercantile reality as if it were itself a colonial resource available to plunder, approaching the empire's capital city as a "second Eldorado, [with] rivers of gold and rocks of diamonds" (2.1). This misreading is severely punished by law at the end of the play. Significantly, the imprisonment of the Fulmers functions to resolve the tensions between the army officers and the creole. The establishment of harmony in the end requires an elaborate displacement of guilt from the West Indian for his "wild," potentially criminal, appropriation of jewels that belong to another and his attempts to prostitute a proper lady. When the Fulmers are convicted of both of these crimes, the West Indian is forgiven.

All the discursive moves I have discussed in this essay—the purification of the metropolitan women, the complex relation with residual aristocratic values, and the criminalization of the underclass—are attempts to fill the gap opened by what Fredric Jameson has called the distortion of the "structural coordinates" in bourgeois reality in its imperial pleases:

> The phenomenological experience of the individual subject—traditionally, the supreme raw materials of the work of art—becomes limited to a tiny corner of the social world, a fixed-camera view of a certain section of London or the countryside or whatever. But the truth of that experience no longer coincides with the place in which it takes place. The truth of that limited daily experience of London lies, rather, in India or Jamaica or Hong Kong; it is bound up with the whole colonial system of the British Empire that determines the very quality of the individual's subjective life. Yet these structural coordinates are no longer accessible to immediate lived experience.[26]

The discursive separation between the English mainland and the territories of its international activities assures that such structural coordinates remain out of focus and inaccessible. However, any concrete trace of the colonial system in a text does give access to the incoherences created by such attempts to contain metropolitan subjectivities and daily experiences in a "fixed-camera view of a certain section of London." Thus Cumberland's celebration of trade as a cordializing system that can embrace the differences between the London merchant and his West Indian son also, unintentionally, reveals the brutal reinforcement of other categories of difference within the metropolitan culture.

Notes

1. All references given in the text, are to Richard Cumberland, *The West Indian,* in *British Dramatists from Dryden to Sheridan,* ed. George H. Nettleton and Arthur E. Case, rev. George Winchester Stone, Jr. (Carbondale, Ill., 1969), 711-47.

2. John Brewer, *The Sinews of Power: War, Money and the English State, 1790-1930* (London, 1989), xv.

3. Robert Hughes, *The Fatal Shore: The Epic of Australia's Founding* (New York, 1988), 40.

4. *The Rights of Man, Being an Answer to Mr. Burke's Attack on the French Revolution* (London, 1930), 106.

5. Cumberland's experience with colonial material involved his profession as well as his personal life. While he served as the private secretary to Lord Halifax, the first Lord of Trade and Plantations, he found plots for tragedies in early voyages and discoveries; in contrast, information about the contemporary colonial situation remained "most discouragingly meager, and most oppressively tedious in communicating nothing" (*Memoirs of Richard Cumberland* [Philadelphia, 1856], 74). His conception of *The West Indian* did, however, grow out of his direct engagement

with present colonial material during his stay in Dublin, where he found "a state of society very different from what I observed in London," because it offered a "profuse assembly of politicians, lawyers, soldiers, and divines," together with "profuse luxury and hospitality" (*Memoirs,* 140) that centrally characterizes the colonial rulers greatly outnumbered by the colonized who surround them in a "foreign" land. Cumberland's comments on *The West Indian* stress the "novelty" of the material and the approach that can open up the closed economy of the theatrical world with new material from the outside. At the same time he shows discomfort with exotic materials unless they are thoroughly domesticated. Increasingly, in late eighteenth-century literature, such domestication was effected by comic and sentimental conventions that effaced historical and contextualized particularities. For the identification of Cumberland with Sheridan's character, see the editorial footnote to Richard Cumberland, *Memoirs,* 140.

6. See, for instance, Chris Bongie, *Exotic Memories: Literature, Colonialism, and the Fin de Siecle* (Stanford, 1991); Patrick Brantlinger, *Rule of Darkness: British Literature and Imperialism, 1830-1914* (Ithaca, 1988); and Joseph Bristow, *Empire Boys: Adventures in a Man's World* (London, 1991). For a useful analysis of how this separation functions, see Frederic Jameson, "Romance and Reification: Plot Construction and Ideological Closure in Joseph Conrad," in *The Political Unconscious: Narrative as a Socially Symbolic Act* (Ithaca, 1981), 206-80. For recent studies that are beginning to dismantle such divisions, see Edward W. Said, *Culture and Imperialism* (New York, 1993), and Laura Brown, *Ends of Empire: Women and Ideology in Early Eighteenth-Century English Literature* (Ithaca, 1993). See also my *Domestic Realities and Imperial Fictions: Jane Austen's Novels in 18th-Century Contexts* (Athens, Ga., 1993).

7. Janet Schaw, *Journal of a Lady of Quality; Being the Narrative of a Journey from Scotland to the West Indies, North Carolina, and Portugal, in the Years 1774 to 1776,* ed. Evangelina Walker Andrews (New Haven, 1934), 112.

8. John Stedman, *Narrative of a Five Years' Expedition, against the Revolted Negroes of Surinam* (London, 1796).

9. V. G. Kiernan, *The Duel in European History: Honour and the Reign of Aristocracy* (Oxford, 1988), 53.

10. See Kiernan. See also Donna T. Andrews, "Code of Honor and its Critics: Opposition to Dueling, 1700-1850," *Social History* 5 (1980):409-35.

11. *History of the West Indies,* 5 vols. (London, 1819), II, 9.

12. Orlando Patterson, *Slavery and Social Death: A Comparative Study* (Cambridge, Mass., 1982), 3.

13. See Michel Foucault, *Discipline and Punish: The Birth of the Prison,* trans. Alan Sheridan (New York, 1979).

14. For the distinction between the market society and earlier social arrangements, see Karl Polanyi, *The Great Transformation* (New York, 1944), and Jean-Christophe Agnew, *Worlds Apart: The Market and the Theater in Anglo-American Thought, 1550-1750* (Cambridge, 1986).

15. Fernand Braudel, *The Wheels of Commerce,* trans. Sian Reynolds (New York, 1986), 272-73.

16. David Brian Davis, *Problems of Slavery in Western Culture* (New York), 157. Davis goes even farther to suggest that "the sugar plantation was first of all the way to wealth for the self-made man). In a sense, the planter was the prototype for future speculators and industrialists" (157).

17. For the self-regulating market, see Karl Polanyi, *The Great Transformation,* 68-72.

18. Francis Barker in *The Tremulous Private Body: Essays on Subjection* (London, 1984) suggestively argues that the bourgeois effaced history or rewrote it to reinforce their own reality. The links between capitalism, slavery, and humanitarianism have been discussed by many modern scholars. See especially, David Brian Davis, *The Problem of Slavery*; Howard Temperley, "Capitalism, Slavery, and Ideology," *Past and Present: A Journal of Historical Studies* 75 (1977):94-118; and Thomas L. Haskell, "Capitalism and the Origins of the Humanitarian Sensibility, Part I," *The American Historical Review* 90 (1985):339-61.

19. Frances Sheridan, *Memoirs of Miss Sidney Bidulph* (London, 1987), 351.

20. John Dryden, *All for Love; or The World Well Lost,* in *British Dramatists from Dryden to Sheridan,* 1.1.182. Besides Sheridan's play, see, for example, Sarah Scott, *George Ellison,* and Jane Austen, *Sense and Sensibility.*

21. Susan Staves, *Married Women's Separate Property in England, 1660-1833* (Cambridge, Mass., 1990), 223.

22. Bryan Edwards, *History of the West Indies* IV, 586. See also Ronald Kent Richardson, *Moral Imperium: Afro-Caribbean and the Transformation of British Rule 1776-1838* (New York, 1987), and Elsa V. Goveia, *Slave Society in British Leeward Islands at the End of the Eighteenth Century* (New Haven, 1965).

23. Sidney Pollard and David W. Crossley. *The Wealth of Britain* (London, 1968), 169.

24. On the questions of slave reproduction, see Marietta Morrissey, *Slave Women in the New World: Gender Stratification in the Caribbean* (Lawrence, 1989).

25. For the early part of the century, see Laura Brown, *Alexander Pope* (Oxford, 1985).

26. "Cognitive Mapping," in *Marxism and the Interpretation of Culture,* ed. Cary Nelson and Lawrence Grossberg (Urbana, 1988), 349.

FURTHER READING

Biographies

Mudford, William. *The Life of Richard Cumberland, Esq. Embracing a Critical Examination of His Various Writings.* 2 vols. London: Sherwood, Neely & Jones, 1812, 621 p.

> Provides an early, and exhaustive, examination of Cumberland's literary career.

Paston, George [Emily Symonds]. "Richard Cumberland." In *Little Memoirs of the Eighteenth Century,* pp. 57-116. New York: Dutton, 1901.

> Surveys Cumberland's literary career, recounting numerous details and anecdotes from the author's life.

Criticism

Campbell, Thomas Joseph. *Richard Cumberland's* The Wheel of Fortune*: A Critical Edition.* New York: Garland Publishing, 1987, 289 p.

> Includes a critical analysis of the play's plot and major themes.

Detisch, Robert J. "The Synthesis of Laughing and Sentimental Comedy in *The West Indian.*" *Educational Theatre Journal* 22 (1970): 291-300.

> Argues that Cumberland's comic instincts and sharp wit help counterbalance the play's excessive sentimentality.

Dircks, Richard J. "Cumberland, Richardson, and Fielding: Changing Patterns in the Eighteenth-Century Novel." *Research Studies* 38 (December 1970): 291-99.

> Explores the novelistic techniques of the three authors.

————. *Richard Cumberland.* Boston: Twayne Publishers, 1976, 166 p.

Analyzes Cumberland's life and work.

Donohue, Joseph W. *Dramatic Character in the English Romantic Age.* Princeton: Princeton University Press, 1970, 402 p.

Examines comic elements in Cumberland's *The West Indian.*

Newman, Louis I. *Richard Cumberland, Critic and Friend of the Jews.* New York: Bloch, 1919, 124 p.

Analyzes Cumberland's treatment of Jewish characters in his writings, particularly emphasizing his play *The Jew.*

Williams, Stanley T. *Richard Cumberland: His Life and Dramatic Works.* New Haven: Yale University Press, 1917, 365 p.

Provides an overview of Cumberland's major works.

————. "Richard Cumberland's *West Indian.*" *Modern Language Notes* 35 (November 1920): 413-17.

Documents the various circumstances surrounding the play's original production, and includes contemporary critical responses.

————. "The English Sentimental Drama from Steele to Cumberland." *Sewanee Review* 33 (October 1925): 405-26.

Examines the sentimental comedies of Cumberland within the framework of eighteenth-century British drama.

Yearling, Elizabeth M. "The Good-Natured Heroes of Cumberland, Goldsmith, Sheridan." *Modern Language Review* 67, no. 3 (1972): 490-500.

Discusses the treatment of moral issues in the plays of Cumberland, Goldsmith, and Sheridan.

————. "Cumberland, Foote, and the Stage Creole." *Notes and Queries* 25, no. 1 (1978): 59-60.

Considers Cumberland's motivations for creating the character of the West Indian.

Additional coverage of Cumberland's life and career is contained in the following sources published by Thomson Gale: *Dictionary of Literary Biography,* **Vol. 89;** *Literature Resource Center***; and** *Reference Guide to English Literature,* **Ed. 2.**

Crime and Punishment

Fyodor Dostoevsky

Russian novelist, short story writer, and essayist.

The following entry provides criticism of Dostoevsky's novel *Prestuplenie i nakazanie* (1866; *Crime and Punishment*). For additional discussion of *Crime and Punishment,* see *NCLC,* Volume 7. For discussion of Dostoevsky's complete career, see *NCLC,* Volume 2. For discussion of the novel *Besy* (1871-72; *The Possessed*), see *NCLC,* Volume 21; for discussion of the novel *Zapiski iz podpol'ia* (1864; *Notes from Underground*), see *NCLC,* Volume 33; for discussion of the novel *Brat'ia Karamazovy* (1879-80; *The Brothers Karamazov*), see *NCLC,* Volume 43; and for discussion of the novel *Idiot* (1868; *The Idiot*), see *NCLC,* Volume 119.

INTRODUCTION

Dostoevsky's *Crime and Punishment* is one of the landmark novels of modern literature. A probing investigation of the ambiguous, often illusory nature of human existence, the novel examines the effects of guilt on the conscience of the individual through the story of a man whose dubious philosophical ideas compel him to commit a crime. In the character of Rodion Romanovich Raskolnikov, Dostoevsky created a representative figure of the turbulent political climate of nineteenth-century Russia. At once deeply sensitive and coldly rational, Raskolnikov struggles to comprehend his place in the world. He strives to become extraordinary—a "superman" unencumbered by the customary laws of society, as he writes in an essay—and yet he is continually moved, almost against his will, by the sufferings of the drunkards, prostitutes, widows, and other social outcasts that surround him. Believing that actions considered evil are justifiable if they lead to unselfish positive ends, he plots and carries out murder, miscalculating the impact of his actions on his own conscience. In the end his guilt drives him to the brink of despair, leaving him no recourse but to supplicate himself before the law. On one level the novel concerns the inherent contradictions of rational materialism, as the reader watches Raskolnikov's flawed assumptions reach their logical, and tragic, conclusion. In a more profound sense, however, through an examination of the ways that irrational forces control thought and behavior, the work delivers a powerful statement concerning the nature of human in-

dividuality. By treating the complex, ambivalent, and ultimately mysterious workings of the human mind as essential aspects of modern life, *Crime and Punishment* challenges conventional notions of progress and technology. Dostoevsky's ideas on these subjects find echoes in the writings of the philosopher Friedrich Nietzsche, as well as in the later existentialist novels of Jean-Paul Sartre and Albert Camus. At the same time the work's thematic complexity, coupled with its use of multiple points of view, was unprecedented in the nineteenth-century novel, and this helped usher in a new era of fiction writing. Although principally a work of realism, *Crime and Punishment* in many ways anticipates the experimental fictions of the early twentieth-century modernists.

PLOT AND MAJOR CHARACTERS

Crime and Punishment revolves around the character of Raskolnikov, a young man living in St. Petersburg. He belongs to a class of young intellectuals who believe that the oppressive monarchical government of Russia can be undone only through radical and, if necessary, violent political action. An avowed nihilist in his views, Raskolnikov spends most of his time contemplating the vital intellectual and political issues of his age. At the same time, however, he is troubled by more pedestrian concerns; he owes a number of debts, lives in a cramped, filthy apartment, and is under constant pressure from his mother to seek respectable employment. Plagued by these oppressive conditions, Raskolnikov determines to murder and rob a miserly old pawnbroker in order to pay his rent. After weeks of careful planning, he finally kills the woman, convincing himself that he is performing a public good by eliminating a selfish individual from society. His plan encounters its first obstacle, however, when the pawnbroker's simple-minded sister surprises Raskolnikov in the apartment, and he is forced to kill her as well. After narrowly eluding the notice of some visitors to the woman's apartment, Raskolnikov returns home, where he promptly falls asleep.

Shortly after he commits the murders, Raskolnikov's personality begins to undergo a powerful transformation. As he ponders the magnitude of his actions, his arrogance and egotism are supplanted by feelings of confusion and self-doubt. Dostoevsky depicts this gradual change primarily through the protagonist's diverse interactions with other characters. In one scene Raskolnikov verbally abuses Luzhin, the wealthy, hypocritical suitor of Raskolnikov's sister Dounia, threatening him with physical violence. After the death of Marmeladov, a drunkard whose daughter, Sonia, has been forced into a life of prostitution by her family's poverty, Raskolnikov impulsively gives his widow twenty rubles, a gesture that temporarily revitalizes his spirits. One of the most poignant scenes in the novel finds Raskolnikov confessing his crime to Sonia moments after she has read him the story of Lazarus from the New Testament. Razhumikin, a former classmate of Raskolnikov's who plays the role of the stable, loyal friend, provides much of the novel's moral ballast. Each of these encounters offers a fresh glimpse into Raskolnikov's evolving psyche as he moves out of his isolation into a state of exposure and vulnerability. In this respect the novel's secondary characters play important roles in elucidating Dostoevsky's major themes.

As the novel unfolds, new, more complicated motivations for the murder begin to reveal themselves. Raskolnikov justifies his actions by openly declaring his superiority to his victims on both moral and intellectual grounds. In the scenes with the police magistrate, Porfiry Petrovich, the reader learns of Raskolnikov's essay on the "superman" and how his radical notions of personal accountability and moral relativism are related to his own life. As his guilt begins to haunt him more persistently, Raskolnikov becomes increasingly reckless in his interactions with the authorities. At one point he openly admits to the crime, although the nonchalance and abruptness of his confession only make it seem unbelievable, and Raskolnikov once again eludes suspicion. In the latter half of the novel Raskolnikov also begins to interact more frequently with Svidrigailov, a wealthy intellectual whose cold amorality makes him more akin to a "superman" than any of the other characters. It is through Svidrigailov's arbitrary acts of kindness—as when he provides assistance to Marmeladov's children—that Dostoevsky heightens the sense of inscrutability surrounding the real nature of grace and redemption.

It is this overarching presence of grace, usually originating in the most unlikely places, that simultaneously fuels and ameliorates Raskolnikov's sense of guilt. The narrative continues to alternate between Raskolnikov's intense introspection and scenes of lurid intensity, as when Luzhin is exposed as a bully and a liar or when Svidrigailov commits suicide after attempting to seduce Dounia. Throughout, Raskolnikov's feelings of guilt mount with every chapter, until the weight of his secret becomes unbearable. In the book's final scene Raskolnikov finds himself at the police station in a state of near delirium, and he confesses his crime. The novel concludes with an epilogue, in which the reader sees Raskolnikov and Sonia living in Siberia, where Raskolnikov is serving his sentence. In these final pages Raskolnikov experiences for the first time feelings of love, sorrow, and hope, emotions that give him the power to endure his punishment. Most importantly, exile brings an end to Raskolnikov's arrogance; humbled by his failure to determine his own fate, he rejoins the society of other human sufferers.

MAJOR THEMES

The notion of crime as a transgression—or, taken in the Russian sense of the word, a "stepping over"—represents the central theme of *Crime and Punishment*. At the beginning of the novel Raskolnikov interprets the act of crossing the threshold of the law as the prerogative of remarkable individuals, a prerequisite for great achievements. In this sense Raskolnikov's crime becomes a measure of his own worth. Ironically his repeated, mercurial, and ultimately conflicting efforts to justify his crime, none of which prove satisfactory even to himself, come to represent Raskolnikov's failure to become an exceptional man. Within this context the attempt to conceptualize, and subsequently enact, a system of life based solely on reason becomes self-contradictory and absurd. This contradiction embodies the essence of Dostoevsky's critique of the political radicalism popular during the era. Raskolnikov becomes the representative of all nihilists, losing his individuality, or "extraordinary" aspects, in the process.

Another important question underlying the novel concerns the mutable, often absurd, nature of existence. On its most rudimentary level the sense of unreality that pervades the work arises out of Raskolnikov's intense preoccupation with his crime. Because the knowledge of his act hounds him constantly, the conversations and facial expressions of the people around him—the police inspectors, his landlady, even Razhumikin—become distorted, almost terrifying. As the narrative unfolds, it becomes clear that Raskolnikov's state of semiderangement is intended to reflect a larger, more haunting vision of the world. The novel abounds with dreamlike, often fantastical, imagery, both in its incidents of sudden, shocking violence and in the descriptions of St. Petersburg itself, which appears as a brutal and impoverished place, blighted and nightmarish. As Raskolnikov's mind becomes overwhelmed with the horror of the life around him, chaos dominates not only the physical landscape of the novel but also its imaginative landscape. Both realms become a form of hell for Raskolnikov, as he approaches the conclusion that his rationality is meaningless in the face of such widespread unpredictability and suffering. One of the most powerful scenes in the book occurs in Sonia's apartment, after a weary Raskolnikov has retreated from his family. Imploring Sonia to read the story of Lazarus aloud, Raskolnikov finally confesses his crime, and for once he experiences a moment of peace. This contrast between Raskolnikov's conception of the superior man and the humble, Christ-like redemption of Lazarus lies at the heart of the novel's power.

CRITICAL RECEPTION

Contemporary responses to the novel were almost universally enthusiastic. The noted Russian critic N. N. Strakhov was among the first to identify the conflicting themes of spirituality and social rationalism that underlie the novel. Robert Louis Stevenson, one of the earliest commentators on the novel in English, lauded the extreme inwardness and subjectivity of Dostoevsky's approach, claiming that the intensity of reading the book was akin to suffering from an "illness." Some readers viewed the work as a supreme achievement of Russian realism, an apt expression of the political climate of Russia in the 1860s. In the early twentieth century commentators such as Francis Hackett began to identify the book's weighty psychological themes, a critical approach that would come to dominate mainstream interpretations of the novel for several decades. The Russian literary theorist Mikhail Bakhtin, in his 1929 study *Problems of Dostoevsky's Art,* examined qualities of "polyphony," or multiple points of view, in the novel, asserting that these disparate, yet equally significant, narrative voices operate independently of Dostoevsky's intentions. A number of original modern perspectives on the novel began to emerge in the decades after World War II, when writers such as George Gibian and W. D. Snodgrass composed long meditations on the work's symbolic and poetic power. In the 1960s and

1970s a number of scholars, notably Richard Peace and Michael Holquist, began addressing such issues as the question of the narrator's authority in the work, the significance of Raskolnikov's dreams as manifestations of his feelings of guilt, and the role of landscape in Dostoevsky's portrayal of human consciousness. In recent years commentators have provided specialized interpretations offering feminist, sociological, and theological readings of the work. The critic Harold Bloom has edited two valuable anthologies of criticism devoted to the novel: *Fyodor Dostoevsky's Crime and Punishment,* published in 1988, and *Raskolnikov and Svidrigailov,* in 2004.

PRINCIPAL WORKS

*Bednye liudi [Poor Folk] (novel) 1846

Dvoinik [The Double: A Poem of St. Petersburg] (novella) 1846; published in journal *Otechestvennye zapiski*

Unizhennye i oskorblennye. Iz zapisok neudavshegosia literatora [Injury and Insult] (novel) 1861; published in journal *Vremia*

Zapiski iz mertvogo doma [The House of the Dead] (novel) 1860-62; published in journals *Russkii mir* and *Vremia*

Zimnie zametki o letnikh vpechatleniiakh [Winter Notes on Summer Impressions] (novel) 1863; published in journal *Vremia*

Zapiski iz podpol'ia [Notes from Underground] (novel) 1864; published in journal *Epokha*

Igrok [The Gambler] (novel) 1866

Prestuplenie i nakazanie [Crime and Punishment] (novel) 1866; published in journal *Russkii Vestnik*

Idiot [The Idiot] (novel) 1868; published in journal *Russkii Vestnik*

Vechnyi muzh [The Eternal Husband] (novel) 1870; published in journal *Zaria*

Besy [The Possessed] (novel) 1871-72; published in journal *Russkii Vestnik*

Podrostok [A Raw Youth] (novel) 1875; published in journal *Otechestvennye zapiski*

†Dnevnik pisatelia [The Diary of a Writer] (essays and short stories) 1876-77, 1880, 1881

Brat'ia Karamazovy [The Brothers Karamazov] (novel) 1879-80; published in journal *Russkii Vestnik*

Polnoe sobranie sochinenii. 14 vols. (novels, essays, and short stories) 1882-83

Pis'ma v chetyrekh tomakh. 4 vols. (letters) 1928

Sobranie Sochinenii. 10 vols. (novels, essays, and short stories) 1956-58

*Bednye liudi was published within the anthology Peterburgskii sbornik.

†*Dnevnik pisatelia was a periodical authored by Dostoevsky, and was the continuation of a column he had written while editor of another journal, the Citizen.*

CRITICISM

Leo Tolstoy (essay date 1888)

SOURCE: Tolstoy, Leo. "Tobacco and Alcohol in *Crime and Punishment*." In *Readings on Fyodor Dostoyevsky*, edited by Tamara Johnson, translated by Aylmer Maude, pp. 63-66. San Diego: Greenhaven Press, 1998.

[*In the following essay, originally published in 1888, Tolstoy suggests that Raskolnikov's "altered consciousness," a result of his use of alcohol and tobacco, is what ultimately drives him to commit murder.*]

But can such a small—such a trifling—alteration as the slight intoxication produced by the moderate use of wine or tobacco produce important consequences? "If a man smokes opium or hashish, or intoxicates himself with wine till he falls down and loses his senses, of course the consequences may be very serious; but it surely cannot have any serious consequences if a man merely comes slightly under the influence of hops or tobacco," is what is usually said. It seems to people that a slight stupefaction, a little darkening of the judgement, cannot have any important influence. But to think so is like supposing that it may harm a watch to be struck against a stone, but that a little dirt introduced into it cannot be harmful.

Remember, however, that the chief work actuating man's whole life is not done by his hands, his feet, or his back, but by his consciousness. Before a man can do anything with his feet or hands, a certain alteration has first to take place in his consciousness. And this alteration defines all the subsequent movements of the man. Yet these alterations are always minute and almost imperceptible.

[The celebrated Russian painter, K. P.] Bryullóv one day corrected a pupil's study. The pupil glanced at the altered drawing, exclaimed: "Why, you only touched it a tiny bit, but it is quite another thing." Bryullóv replied: "Art begins where the tiny bit begins."

That saying is strikingly true not only of art but of all life. One may say that true life begins where the tiny bit begins—where what seem to us minute and infinitely small alterations take place. True life is not lived where great external changes take place—where people move about, clash, fight, and slay one another—it is lived only where these tiny, tiny, infinitesimally small changes occur.

RASKÓLNIKOV'S ALTERED CONSCIOUSNESS

[*In Crime and Punishment,*] Raskólnikov did not live his true life when he murdered the old woman or her sister. When murdering the old woman herself, and still more when murdering her sister, he did not live his true life, but acted like a machine, doing what he could not help doing—discharging the cartridge with which he had long been loaded. One old woman was killed, another stood before him, the axe was in his hand.

Raskólnikov lived his true life not when he met the old woman's sister, but at the time when he had not yet killed any old woman, nor entered a stranger's lodging with intent to kill, nor held the axe in his hand, nor had the loop in his overcoat by which the axe hung. He lived his true life when he was lying on the sofa in his room, deliberating not at all about the old woman, nor even as to whether it is or is not permissible at the will of one man to wipe from the face of the earth another, unnecessary and harmful, man, but whether he ought to live in Petersburg or not, whether he ought to accept money from his mother or not, and on other questions not at all relating to the old woman. And then—in that region quite independent of animal activities—the question whether he would or would not kill the old woman was decided. That question was decided—not when, having killed one old woman, he stood before another, axe in hand—but when he was doing nothing and was only thinking, when only his consciousness was active: and in that consciousness tiny, tiny alterations were taking place. It is at such times that one needs the greatest clearness to decide correctly the questions that have arisen, and it is just then that one glass of beer, or one cigarette, may prevent the solution of the question, may postpone the decision, stifle the voice of conscience and prompt a decision of the question in favour of the lower, animal nature—as was the case with Raskólnikov.

Tiny, tiny alterations—but on them depend the most immense and terrible consequences. Many material changes may result from what happens when a man has taken a decision and begun to act: houses, riches, and people's bodies may perish, but nothing more important can happen than what was hidden in the man's consciousness. The limits of what can happen are set by consciousness.

And boundless results of unimaginable importance may follow from most minute alterations occurring in the domain of consciousness.

A WARNING FOR READERS

Do not let it be supposed that what I am saying has anything to do with the question of free will or determinism. Discussion on that question is superfluous for my purpose, or for any other for that matter. Without deciding the question whether a man can, or cannot, act as he wishes (a question in my opinion not correctly stated), I am merely saying that since human activity is conditioned by infinitesimal alterations in consciousness, it follows (no matter whether we admit the existence of free will or not) that we must pay particular attention to the condition in which these minute alterations take place, just as one must be specially attentive to the condition of scales on which other things are to be weighed. We must, as far as it depends on us, try to put ourselves and others in conditions which will not disturb the clearness and delicacy of thought necessary for the correct working of conscience, and must not act in the contrary manner—trying to hinder and confuse the work of conscience by the use of stupefying substances.

For man is a spiritual as well as an animal being. He may be moved by things that influence his spiritual nature, or by things that influence his animal nature, as a clock may be moved by its hands or by its main wheel. And just as it is best to regulate the movement of a clock by means of its inner mechanism, so a man—oneself or another—is best regulated by means of his consciousness. And as with a clock one has to take special care of that part by means of which one can best move the inner mechanism, so with a man one must take special care of the cleanness and clearness of consciousness which is the thing that best moves the whole man. To doubt this is impossible; everyone knows it. But a need to deceive oneself arises. People are not as anxious that consciousness should work correctly as they are that it should seem to them that what they are doing is right, and they deliberately make use of substances that disturb the proper working of their consciousness.

Alfred L. Bem (essay date 1938)

SOURCE: Bem, Alfred L. "Guilt in *Crime and Punishment.*" In *Readings on Fyodor Dostoyevsky,* edited by Tamara Johnson, translated by Robert Louis Jackson, pp. 58-62. San Diego: Greenhaven Press, 1998.

[*In the following essay, originally published in 1938, Bem examines Dostoevsky's portrayal of guilt in* Crime and Punishment, *particularly focusing on the psychology behind Mikolka Dementiev's puzzling self-blame for Raskolnikov's crime. Bem asserts that guilt in Dostoevsky's writings correlates with characters' "feeling of original sin" much more than with external rules of right and wrong.*]

It is often said that Dostoevsky's "novel-tragedy" gravitates toward a single major "catastrophic" event, one usually connected with a crime; what has not been sufficiently stressed is that Dostoevsky's focus is not crime at all, but its corollary—guilt. . . . We shall not be concerned here with any objective norms of guilt and crime, but only with those psychological substrata on which these norms rest. . . . Crime will be understood only as the *awareness by the subject himself of some*

moral norm which he has violated, quite apart from whether this violation has been recognized externally, morally, as a real crime. Without such a limitation [in the definition of crime] the correlation between guilt and crime, which plays such a crucial role in Dostoevsky, would be incomprehensible. Quite often, particularly in Dostoevsky's earlier works, the feeling of guilt becomes extremely and even tragically intense when only an extremely vague sense of a concrete crime lends support to this feeling. In other words, the objective crime which awakens a feeling of guilt may turn out to be so insignificant as to provide no explanation for the intense feeling of guilt. In this case the tragedy of guilt can be understood and disclosed only by presupposing that the *concrete crime serves as a surrogate for some crime not openly manifested yet present in the psyche,* like a trauma or pressure of conscience.

To understand Dostoevsky's thought one must allow for the presence in the human psyche of a feeling of sinfulness as such, independent of the existence of any concrete crime—what we might call *the feeling of original sin.* . . . We can assume, then, that the feeling of sin, of guilt can be present in the psyche unaccompanied by any consciousness of crime. Indeed, the guilt-ridden consciousness often seeks a crime, as though it wished to free itself from an overwhelming sense of fatality and enter the world of ordinary human criminality, apparently more tolerable to human consciousness than the intense pressure of metaphysical sinfulness. It is only here that we can find an explanation for Dostoevsky's idea that "each of us is guilty for all," and for his characteristic notion of the "desire to suffer." With the latter in mind we can turn to the episode in *Crime and Punishment* with the house painter Mikolka, the workman who takes on himself Raskolnikov's crime. The episode is a minor one, but of central importance for our theme.

MIKOLKA'S CONFESSION

No one first meeting the painter Mikolka Dementiev suspected in him a spiritual complexity which would lead to his puzzling assumption of guilt for the murder of the old lady. We find an ingenuous, life-loving lad, with a taste for the bottle. Porfiry Petrovich, a man not without insight, characterizes him this way:

> First he's immature, still a child; and not that he's a coward, but sensitive, a kind of artist type. Yes, really. You mustn't laugh at me for explaining him like that. He is innocent and completely impressionable. He has feelings; he is a fantast. He can sing and dance, and they say he can tell stories so people gather from all around to listen. And he'll go to school and he'll laugh himself silly because somebody somehow crooked a finger at him; and he'll drink himself senseless, not because he's a drunkard, but just every now and then, when people buy him drinks; he's like a child still.

This characterization tallies completely with our first impression of the house painters on the day of the murder. The witnesses unanimously testified that there was nothing suspicious in their conduct. Both painters, Nikolai and Dmitri, ran out of the courtyard and began to pummel each other in fun. . . . How is it possible that this apparently simple person could come to take on himself somebody else's crime? This psychological enigma must be solved, and Dostoevsky does so; but as usual when a psychological explanation is to be found in the unconscious, Dostoevsky provides an explanation on a conscious level: in this case, introducing the motif of "fear" that he, Mikolka, would be convicted. This fear overcomes Mikolka when he learns about the murder of the old lady and feels guilty because he had picked up the earrings dropped by the murderer; his fear of being accused became unbearable and he wants to hang himself. Dostoevsky tries to give the reader a convincing explanation of Mikolka's behavior by making us aware of Mikolka's internal distress; but he does not yet make it clear to us why Mikolka decided to assume somebody else's guilt. Porfiry Petrovich hints at the reason for this strange behavior; he suggests that the explanation must be sought elsewhere in Mikolka's moral experiences. The house painter turns out not to be so spiritually uncomplicated as we had imagined; he has his own enigmatic past. Porfiry Petrovich observes:

> But did you know that he was a Raskolnik? Well, not a Raskolnik, exactly, but a member of one of those religious sects. There were members of his family who were Runners; they'd run away from worldly involvement. He himself actually spent two years, not long ago, under the spiritual tutelage of some holy elder in some village. . . . He himself was moved to run off into the wilderness! He had the spirit, would pray to God at night, read the old "true" books and reread them, for hours on end. . . . Well, now, in jail it seems he remembered the honorable elder, and the Bible turned up again, too. Do you know what they mean, Rodion Romanych, when they talk of "taking suffering upon themselves?" They don't mean suffering for anybody in particular, just "one has to suffer." That means, *accept* suffering; and if it's from the authorities, so much the better. . . . You mean you won't admit that our people produce fantastic characters of this sort? Yes, many. Now the elder is beginning to have some effect again, especially after that business with the noose.

The way was clearly prepared for Mikolka's "fantastic" behavior. The news of the murder which had so disconcerted him and led him to attempt suicide was only the most immediate cause which brought to the surface those feelings of guilt that were hidden in the depths of his unconscious.

Precisely the problem of guilt lay at the root of Mikolka's act, not a superficial "fear" of conviction; indeed, Dostoevsky originally had no intention at all of introducing the latter motive. Twice in the notebooks to the

novel he stresses the basic "religious" motive in Mikolka's behavior. Thus, in one part of the manuscript we read: "A workman testifies against himself (he had got caught up with religion), wanted to suffer (but gets muddled). They start pressuring him. And an old man sits there: one has to suffer, he says." A brief note appears in another place. "News at the gathering that a man (a workman) was taken by religion."

We can see from these notes that the root of Mikolka's behavior lay in a "religious" feeling linked with his moral experiences. The fact that Dostoevsky associates these elements in Mikolka's consciousness with the influence of some old religious sectarian serving a prison term with him testifies to Dostoevsky's artistic awareness. Such views on the primordial sinfulness of man were widespread in Russian sectarian religious thought.

One might suspect Dostoevsky of using the whole Mikolka episode only as an artful manoeuvre in the development of a detective story, a way of mixing the cards and holding back the denouement. But his supreme artistry is revealed in another way: concerned with narrative technique, he nevertheless introduces instead of a shallow plot device an incident which is closely connected with the central idea of the novel— the problem of guilt. The house painter, in contradistinction to Raskolnikov who strives to evade responsibility before his conscience for his sin, assumes responsibility for a crime that he did not commit. The interplay between these two responses to the problem of guilt will become even clearer after we examine Raskolnikov's crime.

Mikolka, according to Dostoevsky, "got caught up with religion" under the influence of an old religious sectarian; but in order to get caught up on religion he must have had some spiritual motivation. We must therefore assume a feeling of general sinfulness, of primordial guilt in the depths of Mikolka's consciousness, or, more accurately, in his unconscious—a feeling which sought expression in taking suffering upon himself. The "desire to suffer" cannot be explained without the supposition that there is a primordial feeling of guilt, the experience of primordial sinfulness, at the basis of the human soul. The incident involving Mikolka in *Crime and Punishment* is only an artistic expression of this phenomenon observed by Dostoevsky in the depths of his own being. . . .

AN INTELLECTUAL JUSTIFICATION FOR CRIME

Raskolnikov, a prisoner of his *idée fixe* [obsession], kills an old money lender. The whole novel is built around the unique process of disintegration in the hero's soul: his intellectual life is split off from the life of feeling. I do not know how I can express my thought more precisely here. A state of spiritual unity and harmony gives way to a "disintegration" in which one aspect of a person's being becomes overextended and eclipses the rest. But though driven into the unconscious these other aspects of self can remain active there and affect conduct in a special way. It is still possible then, paradoxically, for a criminal in his acts to preserve some inner nobility: just this inner split in Raskolnikov is the content of *Crime and Punishment.*

Crime is presented here as an unquestioned fact, not only in the formal but also the moral sense. But this fact does not penetrate Raskolnikov's consciousness; it takes the form in his unconscious of a potential power of conscience. To the very end, mind remains unrepentant. Even in prison, after his conviction, Raskolnikov still holds inflexibly to the idea that the murder is justifiable. And yet his whole being, his entire moral nature is shaken precisely by the moral aspect of the murder. Like a shadow, Sonia continually follows him and directs him onto the path of repentance. Dostoevsky portrays this symbolic role of Sonia with amazing power. When Raskolnikov wavers in his decision to confess, Sonia at that very moment is with him as his embodied conscience. As he leaves the police station he sees her:

> There, not far from the gate, stood Sonia, numb and deathly pale; and she looked at him with a wild look. He stopped before her. There was something painful and tortured in her face, something desperate. She threw up her hands. A ghastly, lost smile forced its way to his lips. He stood there and grinned. Then he turned back upstairs to the station.

His fate is decided: he confesses to killing the old woman.

Here, then, is an extraordinary situation: in the absence of any conscious guilt feeling, guilt is not only subconsciously present but even determines the final outcome of the spiritual drama. Thus, Dostoevsky is right when he envisages the possibility, too, of Raskolnikov's spiritual resurrection, that is, the restoration of his spiritual unity.

Richard M. Eastman (essay date December 1955)

SOURCE: Eastman, Richard M. "Idea and Method in a Scene by Dostoevsky." *College English* 17, no. 3 (December 1955): 143-50.

[*In the following essay, Eastman examines Raskolnikov's first encounter with the drunkard Marmeladov in the second chapter of* Crime and Punishment. *Eastman asserts that this scene offers the reader a "window" into Dostoevsky's distinctive literary style, while elucidating the themes of sin and redemption that dominate his fiction.*]

Custom tends to select a particular passage from the works of every great writer through which most readers will see, for the first time, the unique world of that author's imagination. For Dostoevsky, so commonly represented in popular editions and in fiction courses by *Crime and Punishment,* the second chapter of that novel has come to serve as such a "window." A careful study of what it reveals can do much to prepare one for Dostoevsky's fiction as a whole.

The chapter goes as follows. The student Raskolnikov has stopped at a tavern, nervously exhausted after "rehearsing" his projected murder of a socially useless old pawnbroker-woman. He is accosted by a drunkard named Marmeladov, a stranger. For a dozen pages he listens to Marmeladov's gratuitous confession of sin. Then he escorts Marmeladov home, where he finds the drunkard's family living in abject misery. Raskolnikov leaves a few coins for them and comes away.

On the surface, the Marmeladov episode liberally violates whatever notions of narrative efficiency the reader may have brought from such Anglo-Saxon classics as *Great Expectations, Henry Esmond,* or *The Scarlet Letter.* Marmeladov is a subordinate character. He has little to do, directly, with the main story of Raskolnikov's crime and expiation. Yet Dostoevsky has no sooner opened his novel than he gives his minor actor a monologue of fantastic length: prolix, morbid, and unrealistic on several counts. One who loses Dostoevsky at this point will certainly not regain him in the many other episodes which share, in one way or another, the same qualities: Katerina Ivanovna's funeral dinner, the massive interrogations of Raskolnikov by the district attorney Porfiry, the "Grand Inquisitor" sequence of *The Brothers Karamazov,* and so on. Since his greatest puzzle will be to distinguish a structural principle in such extended passages, an analysis ought first of all to consider internal arrangement.

Marmeladov opens his conversation with Raskolnikov by a rambling overture which recapitulates more or less realistically the jumble of impulses and memories under which he suffers at the end of a five-day drunk. The overture gives way to an autobiography, the distinct divisions of which are numbered below.

(1) Marmeladov portrays the integrative forces of his second marriage. Compassion led him to marry a gentlewoman in straits (Katerina Ivanovna). Humanity induced him to make as good a husband for her as he could.

(2) Abruptly he comes to his descent into drink. Now, with equal intensity, Marmeladov paints the depths to which he sank. He lost his position. His family has come to live in squalor. The children go hungry for days on end. A painful irony darkens the account as

Marmeladov stops to pay tribute to the generosity and sufferings of those whom he has betrayed for drink. Then he arrives at the prostitution of his daughter Sonia. Before his eyes the alternatives had been debated, the desperate stepmother had urged the affirmative, Sonia had returned with her thirty roubles and lain next the wall. "And then I saw," Marmeladov tells Raskolnikov, "young man, I saw Katerina Ivanovna, in the same silence go up to Sonia's little bed; she was on her knees all the evening kissing Sonia's feet, and would not get up, and then they both fell asleep in each other's arms . . . together, together . . . yes . . . and I . . . lay drunk."

The reversal of direction between parts 1 and 2 is characteristic; the principle determines the arrangement of the remainder of the confession as well. Marmeladov, for instance, has just been seen at his presumable, irrevocable lowest. Precisely at such a moment, when the reader is persuaded that he has received the ultimate impression of a scene, Dostoevsky will shatter the impression with a sentence, to begin in a new direction.

(3) Marmeladov tells how his life miraculously mended. "Then I got up in the morning, put on my rags, lifted up my hands to heaven and set off." He got back his position. Katerina Ivanovna began to fuss over him, a new outfit was bought, the children were hushed when he rested, special dishes were cooked for him, he was bragged about to the landlady, he was called ludicrous pet names.

(4) This idyll is blotted out by Marmeladov's account of his awful relapse. He has stolen the remainder of his earnings, he has drunk for five days, the job is gone, the new clothing is bartered away. As a last device, he has gone to cadge drinking-money from his prostitute daughter, an act over which he has the sublime temerity to attempt laughing.

(5) The reader who feels that he has now seen into the depths of Marmeladov's soul has in fact seen only the inner abasement. At once, in response to the scornful question, "What are you to be pitied for?" Marmeladov rises to a vision of salvation for drunkards:

> "You too come forth," He will say. "Come forth, ye drunkards, come forth, ye weak ones, come forth, ye children of shame!" And we shall all come forth, without shame and shall stand before Him. And He will say unto us: "Ye are swine, made in the Image of the Beast and with his mark; but come ye also!" And the wise ones and those of understanding will say: "Oh Lord, why dost Thou receive these men?" And He will say: "This is why I receive them, oh ye wise, this is why I receive them, oh ye of understanding, that not one of them believed himself to be worthy of this." And He will hold out His hands to us and we shall fall down before Him . . . and we shall weep . . . and we shall understand all things!

(6) Although the episode has now attained its maximum intensity, the note of joy quickly dissipates. Raskolnikov takes Marmeladov home for a scene of external abasement bordering on slapstick, as the frightened wretch is manhandled by an hysterical wife before an amused audience of lodgers. At this point the emphasis shifts to Raskolnikov, whose reactions will be examined separately.

The characteristic dramatic structure, then, is created by the reversing of direction, by the alternating of positive and negative impressions. Its effect upon the reader is interesting. He is led to a conclusion, persuaded of it, then jerked about. A newer impression is formed, much stronger. That, too, gives way. The continued cracking up of expectations tends to loosen the reader's hold on his normal reactions. He grows uncertain; his power of orientation exhausts itself. He finds himself thrust, now morbidly receptive, into strange and often abysmal reaches of experience. The extravagance of the method, which leads Dostoevsky into massive scenes, is paid for by their overwhelming nervous momentum.

The method belongs naturally to a writer of Dostoevsky's complex outlook. Marmeladov's many-sidedness demands a series of intense, discrete revelations. The man is endlessly degraded, endlessly pure; and these two aspects of Marmeladov are integrally related; for his burning realization of the nature of infinite redemption (in his vision of the Lord's forgiveness) rises from his knowledge of infinite debasement. Dostoevsky keeps the paradox before the reader during the whole scene. One cannot take only the degradation, only the redemption; he is led by Dostoevsky's presentation to disbelieve either one, and finally to accept both as a single truth.

In almost all of Dostoevsky's extended scenes the same pattern of alternating directions appears, with the same kinds of value. It is found in Raskolnikov's three interviews with Porfiry, where the district attorney shows a blend of sympathy and calculation and the murderer shows a blend of confidence and panic. The technique is found also in Raskolnikov's baiting of the police official Zametov with reckless hints of his own guilt (Part II, Chapter VI), in Svidrigailov's attempt to seduce Dounia (Part VI, Chapter V), and elsewhere.

So much for the interior organization of the Marmeladov confession. Granting the incidental force of this episode, how does it fit Dostoevsky's total design in ***Crime and Punishment***? The rough tendency of the seven chapters of Part I is certainly to present Raskolnikov's attitudes toward a projected murder and his execution of the murder itself. At first sight Marmeladov's confession has little or no bearing upon this event; hence its context needs a close look.

In Chapter I Raskolnikov has pawned a watch with Alyona Ivanovna, the nasty old woman he means to kill. His views of the projected murder are anything but clear. On the one hand he thinks of the murder as a courageous exploit (he likens himself to Jack the Giant-killer). On the other he regards the plan as "disgusting, loathsome, loathsome." The whole preliminary visit to Alyona Ivanovna has filled him with such revulsion that he enters the tavern for relief. Miraculously, food and drink supply it. "There is nothing in it all to worry about!" he tells himself. "It's simply physical derangement. Just a glass of beer, a piece of dry bread—and in one moment the brain is stronger, the mind is clearer and the will is firm!"

The key to the Marmeladov scene is found in this remark. Raskolnikov's beer-and-bread explanation of his own state of spirit strikes the theme of materialism which Marmeladov is to develop. Now, in Chapter II, the would-be materialist, toying with the idea of murder as a kind of act of faith, confronts a drunkard who makes no sense in any materialistic terms—Marmeladov is merely a scrap of social refuse, a zero; but he impresses upon Raskolnikov the suspicion that the human soul resists quantitative reduction. Raskolnikov's reaction is by no means simple. At first his humanity is touched: he leaves part of his remaining cash in the Marmeladovs' window and departs. At once this humanity is swept aside by cynicism: "What a stupid thing I've done . . . they have Sonia and I want it myself. . . . Man grows used to everything, the scoundrel!" (Here is the pattern of alternating impressions again, now being used to expose Raskolnikov's duality.) Then the cynicism itself is displaced: "And what if I'm wrong? . . . What if man is not really a scoundrel, man in general, I mean, the whole race of mankind. . . ." This is the doubt which is to agitate Raskolnikov throughout the novel.

It is worth pointing out early that Dostoevsky's plots satisfy only partially the naive concept of plot as a network of causation. Marmeladov's confession produces, as noted earlier, no revision of Raskolnikov's murder plans. It provides him at the most with information of Sonia, the woman to whom he will turn one day; but a dozen-page monologue to lay bare the heart of a minor character is hardly an efficient device for that purpose. Of course plot does involve causation, but it also involves definition. Wishing to elaborate a human problem, a novelist with philosophic sensitivity will employ characters, episodes, sub-plots which may or may not advance the action causally but which do serve directly to clarify the central question.

In Marmeladov's confession Dostoevsky is showing Raskolnikov face to face in living terms with the alternatives of a critical question concerning the nature and value of individual personality. The drunkard's own value, as noted earlier, is ambiguous: he demonstrates the vileness and the purity of human nature; but the ambiguity intensifies Raskolnikov's adventure rather than obscures it. In a similar way, each of the opening incidents of *Crime and Punishment* defines and dramatizes the conflicting scales of value in Raskolnikov's personality.

In Chapters III and IV Raskolnikov reacts to a letter from his mother. His sister Dounia, he learns, has engaged herself to the prosperous but mean-minded lawyer Luzhin. Mother and daughter are poverty-pinched; by means of the engagement they hope to help Raskolnikov to a brilliant career. So the betrothal amounts to a contract for prostitution, as Raskolnikov sees: "Sonia, Sonia Marmeladov, the eternal victim so long as the world lasts. Have you taken the measure of your sacrifice, both of you? Is it right? Can you bear it? Is it any use? Is there sense in it? And let me tell you, Dounia, Sonia's life is no worse than life with Mr. Luzhin."

The case of the sodden Marmeladov has suddenly become the case of the proud student Raskolnikov. The idea of "Sonia the eternal victim" takes hold of Raskolnikov as he wanders along the street, expanding a sense of compassion which is in danger of shriveling. A drunken girl staggers ahead of him, being trailed by a lecherous dandy. In rags though Raskolnikov is, he calls a policeman and produces twenty kopecks so that the girl may be driven home out of harm's way. Here is another definitive incident which, like Marmeladov's confession, illuminates the acute tensions within the protagonist. Raskolnikov reacts against his own charity: "He has carried off my twenty kopecks," he murmurs of the policeman. "Well, let him take as much from the other fellow to allow him to have the girl and so let it end. . . . Let them devour each other alive—what is it to me?" Compassion returns (once more the reversal-pattern); Raskolnikov imagines the future which awaits the drunken girl and all like her. Abruptly he tries to discount the misery:

> But what does it matter? That's as it should be, they tell us. A certain percentage, they tell us, must every year go . . . that way . . . to the devil, I suppose, so that the rest may remain chaste, and not be interfered with. . . . Once you've said "percentage" there's nothing more to worry about. If we had any other word . . . maybe we might feel more uneasy . . . But what if Dounia were one of the percentage? Of another one if not that one?

The language of materialistic rationalism—so significant throughout *Crime and Punishment*—here loses force at the entrance of a personal name; and the incident closes.

The worst of Raskolnikov's developing dilemma is not that he must choose between materialism and love but that he must apparently use one to satisfy the other. He must "do something" about his mother's news, "do it at once, and do it quickly": i.e., he must regard the pawn-broker as a mere statistic to be erased so that he can use her funds to rescue the mother and sister he loves. This conflict is transversed, as one sees later, by savage pride: Raskolnikov disdains the meanness of men in the mass; he determines to rise above them, to break the law of the herd and prove his individuality. Thus his murder project is coming to represent a morbid tangle of compassionate and misanthropic impulses, so that the murder itself instead of solving anything will only precipitate an acute crisis.

The remainder of Part I continues to clarify these impulses. After Raskolnikov has rescued the drunken girl and then partially relapsed into cynicism, he dreams the purgative nightmare of the peasant clubbing his mare to death (Chapter V). Here in the most terrifying concreteness he sees what bloodshed must mean to him personally, regardless of theories. He wakes and renounces the murder. Unfortunately he has not yet extricated himself morally. Before the necessary process of definition can be completed, an overheard conversation persuades Raskolnikov that a unique chance for the murder has arrived. He is not strong enough to resist; and he drifts into the crime (Chapters VI and VII). Thus Part I closes.

The other five parts of *Crime and Punishment* and the epilogue show how the criminal is "caught"; but the network of causation, so important to the detective story, will remain subordinate. Dostoevsky's main effort will be to define, to show the full impact of a central conflict involving the worth of human life—a conflict so desperate that Raskolnikov will seem to his friends to be "alternating between two characters" (Part III, Ch. II). The kind of relevance suggested here for the Marmeladov scene can be looked for again in the episodes stressing the sensualist Svidrigailov, the muddled radical Lebeziatnikov, Luzhin the exponent of a voracious middle class, Pulcheria the selfless mother, Razumihin the naive giant who becomes Raskolikov's brother-in-law. Granting that these characters do occasionally motivate the central drama, their chief service is to outline the moral world in which Raskolnikov is trying to find his way.

But perhaps the reader of the second chapter of *Crime and Punishment* will be hardest struck, not by the structural problems discussed up to this point, but by Dostoevsky's apparently inconsistent use of realism. The tavern setting shows, on the one hand, that its author can produce a vivid selection of external detail whenever he chooses:

> [The proprietor] wore a full coat and a horribly greasy black satin waistcoat, with no cravat, and his whole face seemed smeared with oil like an iron lock. At the counter stood a boy of about fourteen, and there was another boy somewhat younger who handed whatever

was wanted. On the counter lay some sliced cucumber, some pieces of dried black bread, and some fish, chopped up small, all smelling very bad. It was insufferably close, and so heavy with the fumes of spirits that five minutes in such an atmosphere might well make a man drunk.

But realism is boldly violated in the same scene. Marmeladov begins to speak, as one might expect, with the incoherent loquacity of the alcoholic. Within a few paragraphs, however, he has shaken off the stultifying effects of a five-day drunk and attained, in common with most Dostoevsky characters, the articulate powers of a poet at white heat. Marmeladov makes—unrealistically—a fine selection of realistic detail, to put forth the shame of lying drunk while his daughter brought in the proceeds of prostitution. He goes on and on, rising at last to prophetic eloquence in his vision of the Lord's forgiveness; for a Dostoevsky character has always the gift of tongues, and in a strong Dostoevsky scene everyone has plenty of time to listen. Elsewhere the reader will find (in Raskolnikov's nightmares for instance) that Dostoevsky's characters dream with the same dramatic continuity and exquisite concreteness that mark their conversation.

This apparent incongruity of manner is partially explained by the familiar principle that realistic detail can reinforce a highly selective vision. Realism is a great convincer, in other words. Dostoevsky uses it, partly no doubt to bolster the more theatrical element in his work, but mainly as running support for what might be called psychological poetry: the extraordinarily dramatic and consecutive rendering of the inner life. Thus Marmeladov is made to display an abnormal mastery of realistic detail in his own confession: like Dostoevsky's other characters he is given the power to endorse his experience with all the physical detail necessary.

More important, whenever an author treats the objective world—the world of the senses, the world of material fact—he reveals the kind and degree of value which he attaches to that world. Dostoevsky creates an external world of great solidity; but he frequently suspends that world in order to let his characters feel and express without limitation—and from this one infers that Dostoevsky sees a serious incompatibility between the world of material fact and the world of feeling. Certainly the particular kind of external reality which Dostoevsky presents is sordid, almost never physically beautiful. Marmeladov is found in a dive; his person is bedraggled, his face greenish; his home is "littered up with rags of all sorts." Raskolnikov, though "exceptionally handsome," appears in rags and fever, starving in a garret where the yellow paper is peeling off the walls. Beauty in Dostoevsky is beauty of feeling, especially beauty of compassion, forgiveness, generosity which transcend the behavior ordinarily permitted by such external conditions. Marmeladov's vision of forgiveness for drunkards illustrates such beauty: the man has no real hope of escaping his sin, of making good the evil he has done, of regaining self-respect; but his ardor for purity bursts through for one moment of realization in the middle of a fume-ridden tavern.

As a further instance of this marked antithesis between the inner life and the world of objective fact, economic power rarely increases the store of human happiness in Dostoevsky's fiction. Exalted moments occur chiefly in the lives of those least fortified by material security: e.g., the prostitute Sonia, Razumihin the threadbare scholar, the disgraced Captain Snegiryov of *The Brothers Karamazov,* the monk Zossima, Kolya Krassotkin and his playmates. Some of Dostoevsky's deepest pathos arises from the clumsiness of gentle souls compelled to grub for a living in an irrelevant economic system. Marmeladov cannot cope with breadwinning; his consumptive wife ends her life in a fantastic bid to raise money by street-dancing; Raskolnikov's mother "knits her eyes out" in an ineffective effort to eke out her pension. Even the damned—whose materialism takes the forms of sensuality or political opportunism—are strangely indifferent to ownership as a medium of self-realization: Raskolnikov neglects to count the spoils of murder; Dmitri Karamazov handles his financial interests like a drunken sailor. It is only in humanity at its meanest that the acquisitive drive seriously governs action. Dounia's suitor, Luzhin, lives by acquisition; so do Alyona Ivanovna, the pawnbroker, and Ratikin, the venomous divinity student of *The Brothers Karamazov.* These are beings beneath damnation, so to speak.

The deeper one goes into the Marmeladov episode, the more he is likely to find that most of its distinctive features express, in one way or another, a basic opposition which will later emerge wherever he reads in Dostoevsky. The question of mood may be taken as a final illustration. Marmeladov's confession gives many readers their first experience of that quality in Dostoevsky's work which may aptly be called demonic, rising from the sordid surroundings, the poverty and feverish behavior of the actors, the agonies of humiliation, guilt, and suffering far beyond any middle-class concept of normality and made all the more poignant by broken visions of nobility. Scene after scene may open into hell—the dreams of Raskolnikov, the death of Katerina Ivanovna, the last night of Svidrigailov, the symposium at Fyodor Karamazov's, Dmitri Karamazov's orgy at Mokroe on the night of the murder, Ivan Karamazov's fantasy of the Grand Inquisitor and Ivan's hallucinated dialogue with his alter ego the devil. All in all, Dostoevsky's inferno is tremendous, but it must be related to an opposite force in him, his power of laughter.

Though Marmeladov is a lost soul, he is also a clown. With grandiloquent politeness he inquires whether Raskolnikov, a perfect stranger, has ever spent the night on a hay barge on the Neva (Marmeladov himself has, and carries bits of hay on his clothing to prove it). The chaotic disappearance of the family possessions, all bargained for drink, injects a humorous disorder into Marmeladov's efforts to give a coherent account of himself. "Sonia, as you may well fancy, has had no education. I did make an effort four years ago to give her a course of geography and universal history, but as I was not very well up in these subjects myself and we had no suitable books, and what books we had . . . hm, anyway, we have not even those now, so all our instruction came to an end. We stopped at Cyprus of Persia." Again, when Raskolnikov brings him home, Marmeladov helpfully lifts both arms so that his furious wife may search his empty pockets. She drags him into the room by the hair; he assists her by crawling along on his knees. With his head banging against the floor, he stammers out to Raskolnikov: "This . . . is a positive con-so-la-tion, ho-nou-red, sir." The sentiment is so preposterous and yet so true of both the man's probity and his downfall that one may easily laugh, without in the last losing compassion for the victim. Broad comedy like this may appear in flashes at the moments of greatest horror in Dostoevsky's fiction—for instance, when the bureaucratic soldier tries to prohibit Svidrigailov's suicide, or when the devil of Ivan Karamazov's hallucination begins to chaff his creator. Its effect is twofold. Through its incongruity the comedy enlarges one's sense of the ugly; but its lightness attests the sanity of the imagination which produced the whole and thus lends sublimity to scenes which otherwise might seem savagely morbid.

The inferno of Marmeladov's drunkenness cannot illustrate, except by contrast, that far extreme in Dostoevsky's mood: those episodes in *Crime and Punishment* and elsewhere which radiate good humor and which can be called his paradise. In particular Razumihin, the fellow-student of the murderer, brings with him an open-hearted exuberance. As he crashes drunkenly into love with Dounia, writhes in gigantic remorse the next morning, takes up steadily the burdens of "son and brother" to Raskolnikov's family—in every appearance his childlike eagerness conquers embarrassments, dispels the miasmic air in which the novel began. In Dostoevsky's later masterpieces this sunny quality goes beyond humor and becomes something tranquil and benign, both naive and wise, as in the personalities of Prince Myshkin of *The Idiot* and Alyosha of *The Brothers Karamazov.* (A better illustration of Dostoevsky's paradise would be harder to find than Book X, Chapter VI, of *The Brothers Karamazov,* in which Alyosha wins the devotion of that patronizing thirteen-year-old cynic, Kolya Krassotkin.)

What lies behind all these dualities of treatment? A dialogue, I think—a religious question and a religious answer, neither complete alone, both together containing

Dostoevsky's truth. This novelist questions the moral relativism which has rushed in wherever religious faith has crumbled. In particular, he has traced out the spiritual implications of "scientific" materialism as it encourages men to interpret their happiness in a quantitative framework. Raskolnikov and Ivan Karamazov are in part the New Man. Raskolnikov has become infatuated with the incubus of the Superman, the hero who finds law and certainty in his own individuality and who proves it by imposing it upon the world. Ivan's hypothesis is the same, that for the man without God "egoism, even to crime, must become, not only lawful but even recognised as the inevitable, the most rational, even honourable outcome of his position" (Bk. II, Ch. VI). Where George Eliot, pioneer in sociology that she was, remained persuaded that society changes conservatively, her Russian contemporary foresaw the leap into the bloody era of "reptile devouring reptile" which men would make once personality had lost its absolute worth. Raskolnikov's final nightmare (Ch. II of the Epilogue) could be taken as a premonition of the twentieth century; and so could the madness of Ivan.

Marmeladov stands as a kind of prologue to the reader's experience of Dostoevsky. In the midst of the netherworld he foreshadows so well, where victor and victim share the same depravity and torment, the truths of human worth and solidarity will prove themselves inextinguishable. Marmeladov sees salvation at his basest moment. The loveliness of Sonia "the eternal victim" will brighten as the darkness deepens. The Grand Inquisitor of *The Brothers Karamazov,* at the end of his calculated blasphemy, will receive the kiss of Christ. Dostoevsky has been accused of making abysmal sin a prerequisite for redemption. It would be fairer to say that abysmal sin is implicit in modern man and that Dostoevsky has provided an art which takes account of it and transforms it. His ambiguity arises from his conviction that faith and despair are a single truth, that redemption perpetually draws its full force from the terrible fact of damnation. Thus a double vision penetrates his great novels: the infernal mood alternates with the celestial; sordid material detail alternates with poetry of feeling; the personality of his protagonists splits between angel and demon; given scenes oscillate from positive to negative. Such a distinctive fusion of outlook and technique gives to Dostoevsky's fiction that fateful tenseness and harmonious fullness which in one way or another belong to great narrative literature.

W. D. Snodgrass (essay date summer 1960)

SOURCE: Snodgrass, W. D. "Crime for Punishment: The Tenor of Part One." *Hudson Review* 13, no. 2 (summer 1960): 202-53.

[*In the following essay, Snodgrass examines Raskolnikov's motives in* Crime and Punishment. *Through a close reading of Part One of the novel, Snodgrass ar-* gues that Raskolnikov's actions leading up to the murder, rather than his subsequent attempts to rationalize his crime, contain the real clues that explain his behavior.]

> It's a bad novel. You spend hours on the crime, hours on the punishment and nobody cares about either one.
>
> —*Cornell professor to a committee*

> A hurtful act is the transference to others of the degradation which we bear in ourselves. That is why we are inclined to commit such acts as a way of deliverance.
>
> —*Simone Weil*

Late in the novel [*Crime and Punishment*], when Raskolnikov can live no longer without confessing, he goes to Sonia and tells her that it was he who killed the old woman money-lender and her sister. For seconds Sonia is silent with shock and horror. Then, throwing herself to her knees before him, she cries, "Oh, what have you done to yourself?"[1]

There can be few moments of more dazzling illumination. Yet, it takes Raskolnikov only a few seconds to cloud the issue completely, to tangle both Sonia and himself in a huge web of pseudo-motives: he wanted to prove himself a superman, beyond authority; he wanted the old woman's money for a grandiose humanitarian scheme; he wanted to be independent of his impoverished mother; he merely wanted to prove that he had "the courage to dare." Though each of these has its truth, each reveals something of Raskolnikov, none is finally convincing either to the characters or to the author. Unfortunately, Raskolnikov's rationalizations have confused most of his critics almost as completely as himself.[2] Raskolnikov never discovers his basic motive; none of the other characters suspect it, excepting only Porfiry, the chief inspector. Porfiry, recognizing Raskolnikov's desire for punishment, first preaches to him the need for confession, then makes that confession possible by setting an example—by dropping his tone of accusation and, himself, confessing first to Raskolnikov:

> "I frankly confess—for if I am to confess I may as well confess everything—that it was I who was the first to suspect you. . . . I'm afraid I've caused you a lot of suffering. . . . I consider you in any case . . . a most honorable man. . . . I want . . . to show you that I am a man who possesses feelings as well as a conscience. I mean it."[3]

This change to a tone of dignified sympathy and respect for Raskolnikov is crucial; in making it, Porfiry advances from the role of chief inspector into the roles of the priest and father who can help Raskolnikov regain self-respect through, first, confession and, next, punishment or "suffering." I take it, then, that Raskolnikov's original motive in murder was to achieve punishment.

"Never tell the reader the real motive," said Dostoievsky; how admirably he follows his own precept!

He was thoroughly aware that such a motive might exist. In a letter to his publisher, Katkov, he suggested this motive for Raskolnikov:

> . . . I find it difficult to explain my idea. My novel, besides, contains the hint that the punishment laid down by the law frightens the criminal much less than our legislators think, partly because he himself feels the desire to be punished.[4]

Further, in the novel itself, Dostoievsky offers this motive for the crimes and confessions of lesser characters. Nikolay the painter (who resembles Raskolnikov in coming from the province of Ryazan and who is, moreover, a "Raskolnik" or "Old Believer") confesses to Raskolnikov's crime because of a religious compulsion to "accept suffering." Again, an unnamed prisoner, whom Porfiry implicitly compares to Raskolnikov, read his Bible so well that he threw a brick at the governor in order to get more punishment, yet "deliberately missed . . . to make sure he did him no injury."[5]

Yet, if Dostoievsky is conscious of such motives, why *not* tell the reader? First, Dostoievsky usually reveals the greatest truths when he works by hints and indirections. Second, he would be even more reticent than usual about stating abstractly and conspicuously an idea which most readers would then have thought merely absurd. Finally, this novel has a very large autobiographical element; he must have felt not only a literary, but a personal reticence.

In the Autumn of 1866, when he began work on *Crime and Punishment*, Dostoievsky's circumstances were remarkably like those of his hero. Having unnecessarily assumed great debts, he went to Wiesbaden to gamble. There, he had lost all he had and all he could borrow. He had pawned his wardrobe and valuables, then had been cheated on an object he especially loved by a woman pawnbroker. When he could not keep up room rent, he was abused by the hotel manager and the waiters who (like the landlady and the maid in the novel) would not deliver any food except tea, "because he didn't deserve it." The servant who watched him at night reported that he had "murder on the mind." Thus, his own Wiesbaden situation, though translated into the terms of his earlier life in St. Petersburg,[6] is carried directly into the novel as the situation of the student, Raskolnikov. There, it is offered as one of the factors leading *him* to murder. Yet, it is not misfortune or poverty which are decisive; they occur to most of us with no such drastic result. The crux lies in the protagonist's reaction to those difficulties.

It is hardly surprising, then, that Dostoievsky hesitates to offer, abstractly, a motive which might be so damaging to his readers' (or his own) opinion of himself. Yet, with steady insistence and with overwhelming insight, he does demonstrate and dramatize throughout the novel

just such a belief. And, after all, it is the special business of a novel to recreate the texture of living, not necessarily to explain it.

The special business of the first Part of *Crime and Punishment* is to recreate the circumstances in which a man will commit murder. If, as most critics suppose, this novel aimed only to show remorse *after* crime, then Part I (events before and during the crime) would be extraneous. Yet the removal of Part I, or even of that portion which precedes the murder, would terribly damage the book. This is true simply because the action of Part I accounts for the murder, which is its climax, far better than any of the rationalizations later offered either by the murderer or by the novelist.

Establishing the motive, however, does more than merely account for the murder; in large part, it accounts for the whole structure of the novel. First, nearly all Raskolnikov's later actions depend upon his first great decision—to kill Alyona Ivanovna. Second, only if we understand Raskolnikov do such secondary characters as Marmeladov, Luzhin and Svidrigaylov fall into proper perspective. Their torments are not incidental displays of horror, but sidelong analyses of Raskolnikov himself. Third, this motive (the desire to achieve a punishment which will reinstate him as a worthy member of a moral universe)—this motive complements and clarifies the doctrine of suffering put forward by Sonia and Porfiry. Finally, it accounts for Raskolnikov's second great decision, the climax toward which the book so carefully builds. It explains why Raskolnikov cannot commit a perfect crime, why he must blunder, must flirt with capture and, finally, confess. To escape would defeat the very purpose of the murder.

To trace the workings of this motive, I will investigate here the action of Part I. I will follow the strict narrative sequence of the book, interrupting that sequence only when its events can be more clearly understood in the light of later events, or of events from Dostoievsky's life. I do hope, however, that these comparisons may throw some light upon the meaning and structure of the book as a whole.

The opening scene—Raskolnikov sneaking past the kitchen of his landlady, Pashenka—is more important than one at first suspects. His discomfort—he owes rent for a shabby little fifth floor room—is of a kind we usually think amusing or trivial. Besides, Raskolnikov himself wants to believe that these actions and feelings are not significant. He tries to tell himself that he is terrified to meet Pashenka merely because he does not want to "listen to all that dreary nonsense which [does] not concern him at all," that he has "lost all interest in matters that [require] his most immediate attention," and, finally, in a kind of comic paranoia, that he is "not in the least afraid of his landlady, whatever plots she might be hatching against him." Though at first reading, such a view of Pashenka may seem reasonable, by the time one reaches Part III, it should be clear that this is palpable nonsense. As Razumikhin will demonstrate, Pashenka is pleasant enough—shy, pliable, even generous, when well-handled. Raskolnikov has chosen not to face her, explain his position and ask decent treatment. Instead, he hides from her, aggravates his debt, lets her injure him and pockets the injury in silence. It is, after all, a sort of comfort to be plotted against.

Nonetheless, Raskolnikov cannot convince himself that this "dreary nonsense . . . does not at all concern him." He is obsessed by it. The words "shame" and "fear" recur to him again and again. He has a "sickening sensation of terror which [makes] him feel ashamed. . . . His fear . . . surpris[es] even himself." We must not let him convince us—as he tries constantly to convince himself—that he is indifferent or callous, that he lacks conscience. He has, if anything, too much. At any rate, his conscience drives him the wrong way—away from people, away from any solution. He has withdrawn not only from Pashenka, but from everyone, been almost totally "absorbed in himself . . . lying about all day long in that beastly hole and thinking . . . talking to himself . . . amusing himself by indulging in fantastic dreams." This is partly because he *is* aware of guilt and debt. This debt and his response to it—the first of a long series of similar situations in the book—is a sort of trap into which he is slipping further and further. At this point, we needn't decide how much Raskolnikov himself has devised his trap; he is caught and is furious.

The scene which follows on the streets of St. Petersburg develops further these conflicting feelings of shame and rage, withdrawal and violence. We notice, first, Raskolnikov's intense isolation as he passes through the crowded streets "in a kind of coma," self-absorbed and talking to himself. In any *literal* sense, he is almost entirely cut off from the life around him. Yet, symbolically, he is very much at one with it. "The proximity of the Hay Market, the great number of disorderly houses, and most of all, the working-class population which crammed into these streets and alleyways . . . the unendurable stench from the pubs," the drunkards and prostitutes—all suggest Raskolnikov's sense of internal corruption. The crowds of people, the "summer stench," the heat and the dusty, stifling air, all suggest Raskolnikov's own constriction and compression, the rage and filth he has shut up inside himself. This sense of stifling constriction will continue unrelieved almost to the end of the novel—until the rain breaks during that night when Svidrigaylov is on the brink of suicide, and Raskolnikov on the brink of confession. It is Raskolnikov's sense of disgrace which, now, hangs over the whole scene. The squalor he sees is mainly an objectification of the degradation he feels; the disgust he expresses for those around him, mainly an expression of

self-disgust. To resolve this ambivalence in Raskolnikov's view of the street, and his corresponding preference for just such scenes of degradation, would lead us farther afield than we can go at this time.

There is another ambiguity which is more obvious and more pressing. We have never been quite sure why Raskolnikov acts so stealthily—because of shame that he cannot pay his rent and is shabbily dressed, or because he is doing something disgusting or criminal? This ambiguity becomes specially noticeable when Raskolnikov sees a drunkard, being carried in a "huge empty cart drawn by an enormous dray-horse," who suddenly points at him and shouts, "'Hey, you there, German hatter!' . . . The young man at once stopped in his tracks and clutched nervously at his hat." We suppose that Raskolnikov, sensitive and refined, is embarrassed by ridicule. Dostoievsky at once corrects us:

> But it was not shame, it was quite another feeling, a feeling that was more like fear, that had overtaken him.
>
> "I knew it!" he muttered in confusion . . . "it is just such an idiotic thing, such a trivial detail, that could ruin the whole plan! Yes, I'm afraid my hat is too noticeable . . . people might remember it, and there's your clue."

For the first time, we know that this "rehearsal" of the "plan" does involve something actively criminal. This ambiguity is important, for the criminal violence of the murder rises directly from the other side of the ambiguity—from Raskolnikov's sense of shame and personal disgrace. So also, this chapter's movement from the stealth of shame to the stealth of violence is highly significant for the same reason.

Having slipped past Pashenka and gone like a sleepwalker through the crowded streets, Raskolnikov arrives at the house of the usurer, Alyona Ivanovna. Here, he repeats the pattern of the first scene—but with very significant differences. Once again we see him slipping past the caretakers; this time he sneaks *up* the stairs, not *down* them. Earlier, we have seen him in debt to his landlady; now we see him setting up another debt to another woman, Alyona Ivanovna. But this debt will trap *her,* not him. We must never forget his real purpose in this visit. As he must remind himself, he is not pawning his watch for money, he is putting himself in debt in order to rehearse the murder. No causal relation is stated between the scene at the landlady's and the scene at the pawnbroker's; one is easily felt: Raskolnikov will kill his pawnbroker *partly* in revenge against his landlady; the rage withheld from Pashenka will gather interest and destroy Alyona Ivanovna. Incidentally, this relationship between the landlady and the pawnbroker also partly explains why, later in the novel, immediately after he has killed the pawnbroker, Raskolnikov has a nightmare in which the Assistant Superintendent of Police beats Pashenka. As Nastasya, the maid, tells him:

"That was your blood making a noise inside you. It always does that when it can't come out and it starts getting clotted up in your liver. That's when you start seeing things."

In part, this nightmare is one interpretation of motive for the murder just preceding it: the murder was one way of beating Pashenka. This linkage between the two women will need development later; now we need only note that Raskolnikov is indebted to both and has fantasies of violence against both.

I have remarked that Pashenka is a fairly reasonable and generous woman; whatever may be said of Alyona Ivanovna, she is certainly neither of *those* things. She is, in fact, all the vicious things Raskolnikov would like to think of Pashenka. That may be why he chose her. He knew her bad qualities from the beginning and detested her from the first moment he saw her,[7] yet he decided to do business with her. No one can say whether he could have found a better pawnbroker. But this much is certain: it is essential that his victim *be* a pawnbroker, a money-lender, a collector of debts; that she be old, ugly, vicious; that she mistreat her sister, Lisaveta. These qualities "justify" the crime he has so long been planning. Now, in the present scene, she cheats him; gives him an unfair price for a pledge of great sentimental and symbolic value—his only memento of his father, a silver watch with the globe engraved on its back. He can hardly be surprised that she cheats him; he would surely have been surprised—and, perhaps, disappointed—if she had not.

If Chapter 1, then, is a rehearsal and prediction of the violence Raskolnikov will commit, Chapter 2 is a premonition of the passivity he embodies. Having rehearsed the murder, having turned at least one of his fantasies into something approaching a reality, his rage is momentarily eased; he feels hungry for company, for humanity. Stepping into a tavern, he sees Marmeladov, and is drawn to him "from the very first moment . . . before a word had been spoken . . . he even explained it as a kind of presentiment." Marmeladov, too, finds Raskolnikov a kindred soul. He launches at once upon a flood of self-hatred and self-pity: his wife is ill, the children hungry; he has lost job after job by drinking, filching the money from his family; the neighbors beat his wife and he dare not interfere; his wife beats him and has driven his daughter, Sonia, to prostitution; Sonia has been forced out of their lodgings. On and on: an astounding self-display of mismanagement, abasement, bathos.

However much we want to weep for Marmeladov, still something in us wants to join with the tavern loungers and jeer. He has so deliberately chosen all of his miseries, and chosen them to flaunt before us. Again and again, he has been offered work and its rewards; he

does not want them, deliberately throws them away. Why, then, take a position at all? Why not lie around the house all day; why not beg or steal; why not wander away? Such reasonable approaches would save him most of his troubles. This is exactly what's wrong with them. Imagine the loss: if he stopped "trying" to hold a position, no wife would make sacrifices to help him, grow excited and hopeful when he seemed to reform, be happy and affectionate when he brought home his check, then, when he threw away the job and the better life he had dangled under her nose, tear her hair and beat him. Next, if he had not lost the job and his wife's affection, strangers could no longer sympathize with him about his strange compulsion, about his cruel wife. The strangest thing about this compulsion is that even he knows its source:

"That's why I drink, for it is in drink that I'm trying to find sympathy and compassion. It is not happiness but sorrow that I seek. I drink, sir, that I may suffer, that I may suffer more and more."

He has been most appallingly successful at that.

No doubt his marriage *is* painful. One must agree with Raskolnikov, when he meets Katerina Ivanovna later in the chapter, that she is "certainly . . . not the right sort of wife for Marmeladov." She does not want a husband; she wants someone to blame life on. Her every motion is an accusation against her husband, her neighbors, against the whole world for mistreating her. Later in the book, this will culminate in the grotesque display of herself and her children begging under the windows of the supposedly callous officials who (she will convince herself) have injured and starved her family. But it appears most concisely and far-reachingly in this very chapter, where she delivers her curse: "Damn, damn, damn this life." *She* has been all too successful at that.

She is at least as subtle a technician as Marmeladov, and her methods are destroying her almost as quickly. She has become ill; her consumption (like Anna Petrovna's, in Chekhov's *Ivanov*) may be seen as another accusation of her husband. Whether or not she originally so intended it, her illness certainly has *become* an accusation—both for her, and for Marmeladov:

"It's her eyes I'm afraid of—her eyes. And also the red spots on her cheeks and—her breathing. Have you ever noticed how people with her illness breathe when—when they are excited?"

It is worth noting, incidentally, that this is a literary portrait of Dostoievsky's first wife, who had died of consumption in 1864 after a long illness involving much neglect and blame, and to whom he felt very guilty indeed. It is also worth noting that throughout his life, Dostoievsky often bungled his affairs to punish himself and those around him for a variety of guilts.

The worst sort of wife—for anyone. Yet Marmeladov chose her; and with adequate warning. Her first husband had died, leaving her in the provinces with no way to support her children. Marmeladov, thinking he pitied her, offered to marry her. Instead of being relieved and grateful, she went to the altar "weeping and sobbing and wringing her hands." Surely that would have scared off any man concerned for his own preservation, any man who did not want to crucify himself in a marital contest of injury collecting. I have suggested that Raskolnikov wanted a bad pawnbroker; Marmeladov certainly wants a bad wife.

He is now very skillfully making her worse—shrewish, parasitic and violent. He knows that his own deepest need is for understanding:

> "And He will stretch forth His arm to us, and we shall fall down before Him and we shall weep. And we shall understand all . . . and all will understand, and my wife, too, my wife, will understand. Lord, thy kingdom come!"

Yet he does not ask for understanding, but rather pity:

> "Oh, if only she'd take pity on me! For surely, surely, my dear sir, every man ought to have at least one place where people take pity on him!"

That demand for pity amounts to an accusation. The accusation, in turn, makes her less able to understand. Besides, consider Marmeladov's claims for pity: first, that he has thrown away job after job to torment her; second, that she is a monster. How should she sympathize with *those* complaints? Besides, she must always have been completely absorbed in self-pity, even before those injuries which he actually has heaped upon her. What hope of pity from her? Or of understanding? It is more practical to seek disapproval and punishment; they are her chief stock in trade and, further, his habitual demand:

> "I like her to pull me by the hair . . . I'm not afraid of blows. Lord no. For you must know, sir, that far from hurting me, such blows are a real pleasure to me. I can't do without them. It's better like that. Let her beat me."

It takes much abuse to replace even a little affection. And, if she beats him, he can at least feel punished for his "chronic destitution," for starving his family, cruelly tricking his wife, punished for her flushed cheeks and labored breathing.

Yet, at the very same time, when she beats him he collects a new injustice from her—one which he can display in the taverns and streets to anyone who will listen and perhaps supply a pity to match and confirm his own flagrant self-pity. Yet even this does not exhaust the possibilities for manipulating the balance sheet.

This new injury and abuse (even though he, quite as much as she, has sought and caused it) may, after enough self-pity has been brought to bear upon it, become an excuse for his next "failure." And so the cycle is perpetuated.

We must never miss the ambivalences of Marmeladov's story. Though couched in the language of a confession, whose aim is understanding, it is really an accusation meant to condemn his wife, justify himself, and so gain pity. He openly abases himself at every moment and has only praise and respect for his wife. Yet, how deftly he paints her as trivial, greedy and vicious; himself as victimized. His own faults seem mild by comparison, especially since he both "confesses" so readily and tries so hard to "excuse" *all* her faults:

> "She can't help herself, I'm afraid. It's her character, you see."

No man in his right mind could consider that a mitigation! He has, in short, heaped coals of forgiveness upon her.

Marmeladov's techniques center around an almost invincible parody of Christian humility. If his techniques of telling his story should fail, if he should be jeered by his hearer in the tavern, that too can be turned to his advantage—that can serve as another punishment and another martyrdom to display to his next audience. For he *will* die a martyr. If Raskolnikov will not supply the requisite pity, he will find it—of all places—in Heaven:

> "It's not on earth but up there that they grieve over people and weep, but they never blame them, they never blame them! And that hurts more . . . And He who takes pity on all men will also take pity on me, and He who understands all men and things, He alone, He too, is the judge."

His final self-aggrandizement is an attempt to identify his own self-induced and rancorous martyrdom with that of Christ:

> "Behold the man! . . . I don't deserve any pity. I ought to be crucified—crucified, and not pitied. But crucify him, O judge, crucify him, and having crucified him, have pity on him! Then I, too, will come to you to be crucified; for it's not joy I thirst for, but sorrow and tears!"

They do not seem hard to find. For a year, the marriage had gone well enough. But at the first appearance of trouble, when Marmeladov lost his job because of personnel changes in his office, all the destructive possibilities of the marriage took control. Moving from place to place, their agonies have grown steadily sharper. When we first see them, (in the present chapter), they have lived in St. Petersburg for sixteen months and have brought themselves to a horrifying pitch of degradation. Within the course of the novel—not more than a few weeks—both will die. First, Marmeladov will step in front of a cart to find the death which even his wife will recognize as "what he asked for." Then she will complete her own destruction by conspicuous suffering and disease. Their deaths are the natural culmination of their techniques; final acts of blame against their world and each other.

Though at first Raskolnikov and Marmeladov seem completely opposite—Raskolnikov, self-aggrandizing, aggressive, murderous; Marmeladov, self-abasing, passive, suicidal—they are ultimately similar. We have already moved far into the Raskolnikovian element of Marmeladov's character. And Raskolnikov will come, finally, to see in Marmeladov a large part of his own soul, and to be deeply affected by that recognition. But for the moment it is Marmeladov's family which moves him—moves him to pity. As he goes, he leaves them all the change he has in his pocket.

This is the first of Raskolnikov's several attempts to save his self-respect, to prove himself good, through charity. This time, however, any self-approval he might have gained is soured immediately by the recollection that he has no money, that this gift to the Marmeladovs helps to impoverish his own mother and sister. Ironically, his act of charity has only thrown him deeper into the guilt he was trying to escape. He smiles sardonically at the Marmeladovs' victimization of Sonia:

> What a girl! What a gold mine they have found! And they are making jolly good use of it! Took it for granted. Wept bitter tears and got used to it! Man gets used to everything—the beast!

We recall that Marmeladov had frequently called himself a beast. We do not recognize until the next chapter that Raskolnikov is calling himself a beast for victimizing his own mother and sister. His judgement upon Marmeladov, his judgement upon Man, is only a reflection of his opinion of himself.

Chapter 3 has several crucial functions. Not the least of these is the inter-relating of Chapters 1 and 2, and of their heroes. I have noted that, at first, Raskolnikov and Marmeladov, as character types, seem diametrically opposed. The same may be said of the two chapters which present them: Raskolnikov's rehearsal of the murder seems to have nothing to do with Marmeladov's recital of his self-destruction. In the novel as a whole, these two thematic problems, murder and suicide, are ultimately related and joined by the psychological and religious doctrine that Raskolnikov's hatred of others is only a reflection of his self-hatred, that the murder he commits is actually a blow struck against himself, and so a form of suicide. But now, immediately, these two chapters are related and resolved by Chapter 3, which

reveals and explores the basic similarities of Raskolnikov and Marmeladov and suggests that underlying (and causal to) Raskolnikov's apparent viciousness lies a deeper passivity and self-destructiveness.

In the tavern the day before, Raskolnikov had heard the bartender shout at Marmeladov:

> "And why ain't you working? . . . why ain't you got a job seeing as how you're a civil servant?"

Next morning, at the beginning of Chapter 3, the maid Nastasya brings Raskolnikov some tea and asks him:

> "Why are you asleep? It's almost ten o'clock . . . why does a clever man like you lie about like a sack of coals, of no use to himself or anybody else? You used to give lessons to children before, didn't you? Well, why is it you do nothing now?"

When he answers that he is "doing something . . . working . . . thinking," she only laughs convulsively, just as the drunkards had laughed at Marmeladov. Raskolnikov, however, compares her not only to the drunkards, but to something much more intimate. She says nothing but what has constantly been in his own mind. We have already heard him scolding himself:

> I talk too much because I do nothing . . . Lying about all day long in that beastly hole and thinking . . .

Now he answers Nastasya "reluctantly and sternly . . . as though in answer to his own thoughts," for she has lined up with his conscience against him.

Raskolnikov has just failed, at the end of Chapter 2, in one attempt to save himself from his conscience; his gift to the Marmeladovs backfired. Now, Nastasya's answers are driving him back further, step by step, into a corner:

> "You shouldn't bite the hand that feeds you, sir . . . You don't want to get rich all at once, do you?"

He answers truthfully that he *does* want to get rich all at once; he does not admit the whole truth—that he wants terribly to bite the hand that feeds him and that if he can't get rich all at once, he'd rather starve. It's hard to say those things to one's conscience. Nastasya, at any rate, has made the normal blunder: Raskolnikov, because he felt guilty, hopeless and helpless, has created a bad situation; now she makes him feel more guilty, hopeless and helpless *because* of the situation. He will spend the next several chapters trying to answer the charge she has given voice to, trying to prove that he is of some use to someone and to himself. Yet anything Nastasya could say is trivial compared with the weight of guilt she carries into Raskolnikov's room in a letter from his mother.

This letter has one function already suggested—revealing the similarities between Raskolnikov and Marmeladov. At the same time, it has several more obvious functions. First, it gives the reader much essential information about past events, about the context of forces which have brought Raskolnikov to the tormented and murderous state of mind we have seen. Again, it introduces characters of greatest importance for the later development of the novel—Dunia, Luzhin, Svidrigaylov. Aside from this, however, the letter has a vital dramatic function in its effect upon Raskolnikov: it not only explains his past torments, but cruelly tightens those torments in upon him, and so impels him, very much more drastically, on toward the murder.

Raskolnikov has waited two months for this letter; he must anticipate at least some of its bad news. He should know his mother well enough to expect some of her self-sacrificing tone, some of the implications of his unworthiness, some of the hidden accusations. Yet he must also have hoped to be spared at least some of the disgrace which the letter heaps upon him. Compared to these coals of forgiveness, the techniques of the Marmeladovs seem childish and heavy-handed. Like Marmeladov's wife, Raskolnikov's mother accuses everything around her; like Marmeladov, she knows how to impart a tone of deepest blame and disapproval while using terms of approval and open praise. At every moment she appears to be praising her son. She has learned the tender motherly art of introducing each item of accusation as if it were a matter of praise for her son or blame for herself. Thus she is able to insinuate as much blame as she likes without once relinquishing a convincing tone of saintly unselfishness and concern for others.

The letter begins with what looks like praise of her son, but is actually a demand that he take immediate action, a reminder that everything depends upon him:

> you are our only hope of a better and brighter future.

Then, under pretence of accusing herself, she confronts him with his own past failures:

> You can't imagine what I felt when I learned that you had left the university some months ago because you hadn't the means to keep yourself and that you had lost your lessons and had no other resources.

Next, under color of excusing her failure to help him (while actually drawing attention to *his* failure to help *her*), she makes a long list of all the past debts which she and Dunya have incurred on his account: she, by borrowing against her widow's pension; Dunya, by taking an advance against her wages as governess to the Svidrigaylovs. As a result, the mother has had to live in great hardship, while Dunya was forced to remain at a post where she was subjected first to the brutalities,

then to the lustful advances of Svidrigaylov, and finally to his wife's campaign of character assassination. Both debts have been traps, and both were contracted for Raskolnikov's sake.

Having reminded Raskolnikov of these past sacrifices made for him, his mother turns to reveal the new plans she and Dunya have made: Dunya is to marry Peter Luzhin, a civil counsellor. The duplicity which I have been noting in the mother's tone is especially useful to her here. Thus, beneath her open defense of Luzhin, she is able to convey a feeling of great distaste:

> It is true he is forty-five years old, but . . . I daresay women might still find him attractive. He is altogether a highly respectable and dignified man, though perhaps a little morose and overbearing. But quite possibly that is only the first impression he makes on people . . . He said a lot more, for he seems a little vain and he likes people to listen to him, but this is hardly a vice.

If she really wanted to reassure her son, she would scarcely think out loud so often and so very pointedly; neither would she make it so plain to him that she expects him to object to Luzhin and the proposed marriage:

> And, please, Roddy dear, I must ask you not to judge him too hastily and too heatedly when you meet him . . . as I'm afraid you're all too likely to do . . . I'm saying this, dear, just in case, for I'm quite sure that he will make a good impression on you. And besides to get to know any man properly one must do it gradually . . .

One can't imagine a more effective way of setting two men against each other. Again, she is able to convey to Raskolnikov a complete lack of hope for happiness in the marriage:

> There is of course no special love either on her side or on his, but Dunya is a clever girl and as nobleminded as an angel, and she will consider it her duty to make her husband happy, and he too will probably do his best to make her happy, at least we have no good reason to doubt it, though I must say the whole thing has happened rather in a hurry.

Raskolnikov's mother has, of course, very good "reason to doubt it," as she immediately goes on to demonstrate. She knows perfectly well Luzhin's motive in the marriage and that this cannot possibly work toward Dunya's happiness:

> even before meeting Dunya he had made up his mind to marry some honest girl who had no dowry . . . for, as he explained, a husband should never be under any obligation to his wife for anything, . . . it seemed just to have slipped out in the course of the conversation, so that later he even tried to correct himself and make it sound much nicer.

She is aware, then,—and makes Raskolnikov aware—that Dunya is being sold into a hopeless slavery where she will be controlled by debt to Luzhin. Not only does the mother expect Dunya to be miserable; she expects nothing better for herself[8]:

> it would perhaps be much better if I lived on my own after their wedding . . . I am quite sure he will be so nice and considerate as to ask me himself to live with them so as not to be separated from my daughter and that, if he has said nothing about it so far, it is simply because no other arrangement has even occurred to him.

This amounts to a proclamation that both she and Dunya are to be sacrificed once more. And she leaves no ground for mistake about who is to bear the blame for the sacrifice:

> He has been practising law for many years and . . . he may, therefore, . . . be very useful to you, too, in lots of ways; in fact, Dunya and I have already decided that even now you could start on your career . . . We have even ventured to drop a few words about it to Mr. Luzhin . . . We, of course, were very careful not to say anything about . . . our great hopes that he would help us to advance you some money for your university studies . . . or about your becoming his partner.

This is, in itself, quite bad enough, quite enough of a threat to Raskolnikov's conscience. His sense of indebtedness is already almost unbearable. This new plan threatens to hurl him far deeper still. But what is worse, there is no faintest hope that this scheme could work. Even his mother knows that; and she lets him know it:

> he did immediately express some doubts as to whether your university studies would leave you much time for work at his office . . . in spite of Mr. Luzhin's present quite understandably evasive attitude . . . Dunya is firmly convinced that she will be able to arrange everything.

Even the briefest reflection, or the first glimpse of Luzhin, would convince anyone of the patent folly of this plan. Small wonder that (in the next chapter) Raskolnikov will cry out "Are they blind, both of them, or don't they notice anything on purpose? And how pleased they are!" Raskolnikov seems to suspect that this plan was deliberately chosen just because it *was* such a bad plan, and so could bring more guilt and dependency down upon his head. Whether true or not, Raskolnikov must *suspect* some such motive; whether intended or not, that will be the plan's effect. He surely feels that he has previously been trapped into debt to his mother and sister. Now they, and he with them, are to be indebted to Luzhin. And Luzhin is clearly all the things he could suspect (correctly or not) about his family—an underhanded tyrant who manipulates people through the debts he can collect against them.

The marriage arrangements completed, Luzhin has sent for Dunya and Mrs. Raskolnikov to come to St. Petersburg, though he has given only the barest minimum of help with their trip, so as to humiliate them. (He later recognizes this as his greatest tactical blunder; if he had given them money, he could have controlled their consciences.[9]) The imminent arrival of his mother and sister is perhaps the worst news of all for Raskolnikov: he will have to face directly these two women who have made themselves his victims, whom he has injured, and who seem intent upon suffering more for him, upon deepening that guilt that he is already frantic to escape. A mere letter from them has brought him all the blame he can bear, not only of the sorts I have outlined, but a whole battery of unconscious and disguised reproaches, besides:

> not only do I hate the idea of being in any way a burden to anyone, but I myself want to be entirely independent so long as I still have something to live on, and such children as you and Dunya.

The mother closes her letter, then, with an intimation of how fearful is the sacrifice Dunya is to make, and (as at the beginning of her letter) a reminder that everything depends upon Raskolnikov, a demand that he take some sort of immediate action:

> Love Dunya, Roddy. Love your sister. Love her as she loves you, and remember she loves you very much, much more than herself. She is an angel, and you, Roddy, are all we have in the world, our only hope of a better and brighter future. If only you are happy, we shall be happy.

Small wonder that Raskolnikov hates them both; that he is more miserably unhappy than ever, that he rushes out into the streets "muttering and even talking aloud to himself, to the astonishment of the passers-by, many of whom thought he was drunk."

The parallel to Marmeladov is clear, even to the suggestion of drunkenness. Raskolnikov too, is being destroyed by accumulated guilt and debt to his dependents, again an older and a younger woman, though in his case a mother and sister, not a wife and daughter. And the parallel is extensive. Just as Marmeladov has sold his sick wife's shawl and stockings for drink, Raskolnikov has accepted an advance on the pension of his aging and sick mother. The comparison of Dunya to Sonia is even stronger. Sonia became a prostitute to support the Marmeladov family, so filling the gap of Marmeladov's failure; thereupon Marmeladov, refusing to be helped, took her earnings for drink. Similarly, Dunya has just escaped what was very like prostitution (governess to the Svidrigaylovs), only to be sold into something much nearer prostitution (marriage to Luzhin); Raskolnikov, refusing to be helped, has left the university and given up his pupils. Both men have refused any intermediate position; if they cannot support their family, they will hang helplessly upon them, until they drag them to the ground. At least one of these men has deliberately set the standard of success impossibly high, so as to retain his failure and the position of the dependent child.

So far, I have compared Raskolnikov's mother to Marmeladov's wife; Marmeladov's wife makes openly the accusations which Raskolnikov's mother only implies. (This does not make the accusation less threatening; when only implied, it is much harder to answer.) Seeing Marmeladov beaten by his wife, Raskolnikov must have imagined himself—and to some extent wished himself—beaten by his mother. Yet this letter from the mother makes plain a stronger and even more frightening resemblance of the mother, Pulcheria Alexandrovna, to the landlady, Pashenka, and so finally to the pawnbroker, Alyona Ivanovna. For if Raskolnikov has intentionally picked Alyona Ivanovna to stand in the image of Pashenka, he has picked both to stand in the image of his mother. They form a triumvirate of older women, each accompanied by a younger woman, each a widow. From each Raskolnikov has asked and received something; to each he is indebted. They hold his spirit as a pledge. They seem to him tormentors, since it is on their account that he torments himself. When Raskolnikov strikes down the pawnbroker with an axe, he will strike at Pashenka; but he will also strike behind her at the image of his greatest creditor, his mother. Good reason then that, later in the book, when he is ready to face the police and confess to murdering the pawnbroker, meeting instead his mother, still alive and ready to accuse him not only for his past failures, but for this new stroke against her as well, he will fall in a dead faint. Good reason, too, that when he recovers and she offers to sit up beside him that night, he cries, "Don't torture me!"

Thus, his mother's letter brings Raskolnikov to a very low point—very near the murder. Yet, several torments remain before he will be ready for that. Those torments are provided in Chapter 4. All of Raskolnikov's actions in this chapter seem quite trivial in themselves, but by now very small things can tip the scale. By the end of this chapter he will be ready to turn his back on sanity and kindliness.

The first of his added torments, as he wanders through the streets talking to himself, are self-torments. True, he does seem to feel, as I have already noted, that the proposed marriage is a sort of plot against him. He is in a surprising rage against his mother:

> Oh, the cunning woman . . . Is it possible that her conscience is secretly pricking her for agreeing to sacrifice her daughter to her son? Are they blind both of them, or don't they notice anything on purpose? . . . Well, of course mother can't help being the person she is, but Dunya . . .

Again, he has already made a comment on Dunya—

No, dear Dunya . . . the ascent to Golgotha is certainly not so easy. No.

which tacitly compares her with Marmeladov and his ludicrous desire to be crucified. No doubt he is enraged by the accusations buried in the letter, yet his anger must rise also from a suspicion that they have intentionally planned a bad match so that he will be responsible for it, or else (as I think more probably) so as to prove to him conclusively what wretchedness he has forced upon them, thus forcing him to save them. If correct, this would indicate a certain familial resemblance between the techniques of the mother and those of the son.

Yet, even if I am right in thinking Raskolnikov has such suspicions, they are surely not conscious. His principal conscious feelings are quite opposite: rage against himself and, as I have noted, self-torment which is, if anything, only aggravated by his rage against his mother:

> he kept torturing himself, tormenting himself with these questions, and he seemed even to derive some pleasure from it. Still, all these questions were not new, nor did they . . . occur to him just at that moment; they were old, old questions, questions that had long worried him.

In exactly the same way that being beaten by his wife had two opposed purposes for Marmeladov, Raskolnikov's worrying has two opposed purposes. First, it is a self-punishment for the debts he has already collected by inaction. At the same time, it further prevents him from taking any action; it is as much a technique of "stalling" as is his day-dreaming. Clearly, it is collecting new guilt even faster than it can pay off the old; he must give it over:

> It was clear that he ought not now to brood or to suffer passively, to waste his time in idle thoughts about how impossible it was to solve those questions, but that he had to do something at once and quickly, too. He had to make up his mind at all costs, do something, anything, or—"Or renounce life altogether!"

"To suffer passively"—that is the crucial accusation.[10] He must no longer withdraw to his room to lie about day-dreaming of riches on one hand, or of revenge on the other. He must no longer rationalize, no longer worry. The background material which the letter has filled in, the implied comparison to the passive masochist Marmeladov, the accusations of Nastasya, the whole tenor of his mother's letter, her coming visit to St. Petersburg, the impending marriage,—all lay upon Raskolnikov a demand for some immediate action.

He has reached, already, one crucial decision:

> While I'm alive this marriage will not take place, and to hell with Mr. Luzhin . . . I don't want your sacrifice Dunya! . . . mother! It shall not be, as long as I live.

He will not permit them to aggravate his debt to them. But this only leads him to a greater dilemma:

> He suddenly recollected himself and stopped. . . . It shall not be? And what can you do to prevent it? Will you forbid it? What right have you to do that? What can you promise them in return, to lay claim to such a right? To devote all your future, all your life to them *after* you have finished your course at the university and got yourself a job? We've heard that before, old chap! Those are only words. But what now? You simply have to do something now, do you understand that? And what are you doing now? You're robbing them. . . . How are you going to protect them from the Svidrigaylovs or from Vakrushin, you future millionaire . . .

Once again, he feels unable. It seems absurd to give lessons to children, work at odd jobs, or do translations as does Razumikhin;[11] that would not begin to cover the debt he feels. But if he rejects these ordinary accomplishments, then the demand for decisive action, and for extraordinary achievement, is only the greater. He must "get rich all at once." Besides, his refusal to work at some such ordinary job makes his actual need for money (as opposed to his feeling of need for action) more severe. He dare not sit out the game any longer; yet he dare not play, either, for he has made the stakes too high to dare any loss.

He has, moreover, lost confidence in himself. Because of his past failures, he now feels not only unable to solve his personal problems, but unworthy to perform any good act. "What right have you to do that?" he asks himself. The same phrase, and paraphrases of it, will turn up repeatedly. It holds his deepest sense of degradation. All "good" acts are being removed from him; he has no "right" to perform one. Yet if he cannot find one, he must

> "renounce life altogether!" he suddenly cried . . .

Immediately upon the heels of that thought comes the recollection of the man who *has* renounced life altogether, who seeks his own destruction:

> "Do you realize, . . . sir, what it means when you have nowhere to go to?" he suddenly recalled the question Marmeladov had asked him the night before.

This comparison of himself to Marmeladov is so anguishing that his mind must blot it out, must replace it with something at least less painful. That less painful thought is the murder:

> Suddenly he gave a start; a thought flashed through his mind, a thought that had also occurred to him the day before . . . he knew, he *felt* that it would most certainly cross his mind and was already waiting for it . . . it was only a dream, but in a sort of new, terrifying and completely unfamiliar guise, and he himself suddenly realized it. The blood rushed to his head and everything went black before his eyes.

Raskolnikov replaces the image of himself as Marmeladov, then, with the image of himself as murderer; and finds a relief in that; if he cannot see himself as good, then he must either see himself as nothing ("renounce life altogether") or else see himself as evil. The latter, of course, is less agonizing. He nearly faints trying to escape the mere thought of the murder; yet, the more horrible that thought, the better; for his mind must use this violence both to discharge his accumulated rage and to refute its own cruellest accusation of Marmeladov-like passivity and nothingness.

Yet he has one chance to rescue himself. He is on the Horse Guards' Boulevard, giddy with horror; as he tries to clear his vision and stagger toward a seat, he becomes involved in an episode with a drunken teen-aged girl. This episode—which at first seems out of place as well as puzzling in itself—is of very highest importance. It is Raskolnikov's last opportunity to save his self-respect. When it fails, he will feel that he has no choice but to seek an active evil. First, his refusal to help this girl has a passive destructiveness which does much to explain his past actions, and explain them in a way which is anything but flattering to him; second, it is a step in the direction of an active destructiveness. For the first time, his feelings of helplessness, self-hatred, his urge to punish himself will turn toward an open and avowed viciousness directed outward.

This scene on the boulevard is one of a closely related series running through the novel, which involve either Raskolnikov or Svidrigaylov (in many ways, Raskolnikov's *alter ego*) with younger girls, especially girls who have some air of sexual degradation. These scenes are specially significant as indexes to Raskolnikov's or Svidrigaylov's current view of the world and especially in presenting and investigating that ambiguous attitude to degradation which I have already noted. Many of these scenes will spring into the reader's mind with ease: Raskolnikov with Sonia; Svidrigaylov with Katya, with his fiancee, with Dunya. There are two scenes, however, so closely related to this one, that I would like to interrupt the natural flow of the narrative sequence for a moment to discuss them before returning to the scene on the boulevard.

I want first to draw the reader's attention to that scene near the end of the book when Svidrigaylov, having finally given up Dunya, is sleeping drunkenly in a little attic room, very much like Raskolnikov's attic. There, he suffers three evil and tormented dreams, each more terrifying and archetypal than the one before. The first is a disgusting dream of a mouse which runs about over his body beneath his clothes and which he cannot catch. The second is of the coffined body of a young girl whom he must have sexually assaulted in earlier life, so causing her to commit suicide. The third dream (after he *thinks* he has wakened) is a scene markedly analogous to Raskolnikov's discovery of the girl on the boulevard—Svidrigaylov finds a five year old girl who has been beaten and has fallen asleep on the stairs. Picking her up, he takes her to his room and tenderly puts her to bed. Seeing the feverish flush of her face, he thinks she is drunk, but suddenly decides instead, "It was lust, it was the face of a whore, the shameless face of a French whore." We had not imagined that the old roue, Svidrigaylov, so detested lust, that his libertinism (as revealed in the second dream) rises so directly from his Puritanism, his accusation of the world as evil (as revealed in the final dream). The order of his dreams strongly suggests that Svidrigaylov's own evil is produced directly by his vision of the world as evil. (Similarly, Raskolnikov will kill when he decides the world is too evil to be coped with except by evil.) As he tries to strike the little girl, Svidrigaylov *does* wake, horror-stricken, then goes out at once and shoots himself.

Against this series of nightmares, I want to contrast that scene, much earlier in the novel, where Raskolnikov, after the murder and his subsequent illness, goes into the streets looking for company. There he makes his first steps toward redemption. First, he gives some money to a fifteen year old street-singer. This is the first of his two "successful" attempts to be charitable; the second happens only when he is on the way to the police station to confess at the end of the novel. (Throughout Part I, Raskolnikov is unable to perform a "successful" charity; he must first have reached some sort of peace with himself and so with the people around him.) Having given the money to the street-singer, he tries to start conversations with passersby, then goes to a tavern, looks at a young prostitute named Duklida and says, "What a pretty face." When he gives her some money, he hears her shamed for begging by an older prostitute with a "bruised face and swollen upper lip." He moves at once to his first affirmation: "Live under any circumstances—only to live!"

Let me return, then, to the scene on the Horse Guards' Boulevard. Svidrigaylov is specially pertinent here, since at this very moment Raskolnikov is reacting to his first knowledge of him: in her letter, his mother had mentioned him as Dunya's persecutor. He has already asked himself, "How are you going to protect them from the Svidrigaylovs . . . you future millionaire. . . ." Now he introduces the name, himself, into the scene: when he first sees the fat dandy approaching the drunken teenager, who has apparently been raped already and then turned loose on the streets, Raskolnikov rushes at him calling, "Hey you! Svidrigaylov! What do you want here?" He obviously identifies the girl, whom he wants to help, with Dunya. Moreover, he *is* able to help her, at least with the aid of the elderly policeman who shortly arrives. Raskolnikov gives the policeman twenty copecks, telling him to get a cab and

take the girl home. Suddenly, however, as the policeman is about to do this, Raskolnikov makes a shocking about-face:

> in an instant he became quite a different man. "I say! Hey, there!" he shouted after the policeman . . . "Leave them alone! It's not your business! Let them be! Let him . . . have his fun!"

Once again, he feels:

> Who am I to help her? Have I any right to help anyone? Let them devour each other alive for all I care. What business is it of mine? And what right had I to give away the twenty copecks? They weren't mine, were they?

On the verge of absurdity, he complains that the policeman "walked off with my twenty copecks." From this, he goes on to try to justify his about-face on the "modernistic" grounds that

> It's essential . . . that such a percentage should every year go—that way—to the devil—It's essential so that the others should be kept fresh and healthy and not be interfered with.

Once again he has failed to help; he believes (at least consciously) that this is because he has no money of his own, is dependent. Yet we must not too readily accept his evaluation of the situation. Something is very odd here; after all, Raskolnikov *was* able to help this girl; may even have helped against his will.

The problem of the twenty copecks is a distraction from the real problem. After all, if Raskolnikov had wanted to help this girl, he could have done so just as well (or nearly as well) without any money at all. Besides, money is hardly the only kind of help, for this girl or anyone else. Raskolnikov himself gets his greatest help from Razumikhin, Porfiry and Sonia; not one of them offers him a cent. Those characters in the novel who give money to others, often injure them with it, and sometimes intentionally: Raskolnikov feels he has been injured by advances of money from his mother, his landlady, the pawnbroker; Svidrigaylov offers money to nearly everyone he meets, but no one dares accept it for fear of being in debt to him; worse, Luzhin again and again "helps" people with money by which he quite consciously intends to trap them—as I have previously noted, he openly defines this as his best strategy. The most extreme example of this sort of thing, of course, is the gift Luzhin makes to Sonia for no other purpose than to call her a thief.

The problem for Raskolnikov, though, is that a gift of money may not only fail to help the receiver, it may equally fail to help the giver. One can almost sum up this novel as a structure of financial and emotional debts which the debtors try to pay off with charities, on one hand, or self-punishments on the other. Though the charities of Raskolnikov and Svidrigaylov may not be so malevolent as those of Luzhin, yet their motives are badly mixed, and their charities show little real concern for the person supposedly helped. Has Raskolnikov, really, any care for the needs of the girl on the Boulevard? Any more than Svidrigaylov has for Dunya's? Not really. All Svidrigaylov wants of Dunya is her virtue—if she loves him, or will submit to him, or even only accept his money, that may prove once and for all that he is not evil—or so he hopes. Similarly, Raskolnikov has no interest in this teen-aged girl as an individual personality (which might be paraphrased "as a soul"); he is using her to answer the accusations of Nastasya and his mother, to raise his own self-appraisal.

This selfishness, however, is not in itself so terribly damaging. The real problem lies in a crucial displacement which prevents these charitable acts from having even the designed effect of raising the giver's view of himself. Both Raskolnikov and Svidrigaylov try to use their money in one area to solve a problem which lies in another. Svidrigaylov wants to buy off his conscience; yet even if Dunya should accept his money, his love, his bed, that could not cancel the debt he feels to his wife, to his servant John, to the young girl he must have assaulted. Similarly, Raskolnikov must know that he is demanding an unreasonable return from whatever investment he might make in this teen-aged girl. Since she is only symbolically related to Dunya and his mother, he can do nothing for her which will *drastically* alter his self-evaluation. Yet he needs something drastic, wants "to get rich (emotionally) all at once." So he must realize that this charity is doomed to failure and abandons it and the girl together.

Yet this does not fully account for his turning against the girl; surely not for the viciousness with which he does so. I have suggested so far that Raskolnikov has failed because of a feeling of shame and guilt, of helplessness and dependency, because of a lack of self-confidence. These are all true, yet there may also be reasons less flattering. He may have encouraged himself to fail. He identifies this drunken girl with Dunya; he wants to help both. He does not help either and claims that this is because he is not able, does not have the right. Yet in this case, that is clearly a rationalization; he has both the right and the ability. This strongly suggests that his past statements have also been rationalizations; that he could have helped Dunya or his mother if he had really wanted to. He knows that by dismissing his students and dropping out of the university, he has injured his family. I suggest that is the reason he did so; like Marmeladov, he found a way not only of "passive suffering," but of "passively injuring" his family when he has a grudge against them. (The full nature of that grudge is far from clear, although I will later hazard a guess about a part of it.) By such a method of revenge,

he could not only hurt his family, but in the very same act punish himself for so doing, while gaining the secondary benefits of self-pity. This would account, also, for his terrible isolation: those energies which should have been directed outward into ordered action have been withheld and withdrawn, but then have turned against him as self-violence in punishment for his passivity.

To have helped this girl, then, would not have helped his view of himself, but worsened it. Again, his conscience has driven him the wrong way: he feels so very guilty that he must continue acting badly or else admit that he *has* been wrong. He has not the basic sense of worth which would let him admit to any particular wrong act. Not being able to admit the wrong of having injured himself and his family, he cannot now turn to help this teen-aged girl. It seems less painful to carry on the tendencies, the self-definition, already started. So he tells the policeman, "It's not your business . . ." just as he has already told himself "It's not your business" whether you pay your landlady, whether you help your family out of their troubles. Yet, in one sense, this episode differs from anything earlier. This is not mere passive destructiveness, as was giving up his lessons. This is not only a refusal to help, but has an element of active viciousness. Raskolnikov, trying to escape the figure of Marmeladov, driven to "do something, anything," has made a first step in the direction of that very man he detests and wishes to attack—Svidrigaylov.

He has refused, then, an act whose performance was of greatest importance to his view of himself and of his world. Svidrigaylov would give such a refusal the inverted Puritanical rationale that the girl was evil anyway, hence a proper victim; Raskolnikov gives it the "modernistic" rationale that a certain percentage must "go . . . to the devil anyway." This is only a disguised statement of his own (self-encouraged) weakness: i.e., I am helpless to prevent suffering, therefore I may as well join the persecutors, so as to have at least *some* active role, some escape from passivity, from being nothing. Later, he will expand this rationale of "scientific percentage" into the "modernist" and "scientific" justification of the murder of Alyona Ivanovna. He now claims that he has not "any right to help anyone . . . to give away twenty copecks," that he is powerless to act in the direction of good; he will shortly commit a hideous murder in a desperate hope of proving that he *has* "the right to possess power;" a power which, he thinks, can only act in the direction of evil. (He is powerless to act in the direction of good, only because to do so now would point to the evil of his past actions.) Further, just as he did with the pawnbroker, Raskolnikov has tricked the girl on the boulevard into a position where he can claim that *she* has injured *him* by taking his money. This, in some absurd way, seems to excuse his attempt to injure her. What we have, then, in the Boulevard scene, is really a second, and much more dangerous, rehearsal of the murder.

Yet this moment on the very brink of despair is relieved by a single, momentary ray of light and sanity. Raskolnikov suddenly asks himself a singularly pertinent question:

> "And where am I going to?" he thought suddenly. "Curious! I came out for something. Came out as soon as I had read the letter. Oh, yes, I was going to Vasilyevsky Island to call on Razumikhin. That's it."

If he had planned to visit Razumikhin, we had not known it; perhaps he had not known it, himself. Yet, after reading his mother's letter, he clearly *should* go to Razumikhin. Razumikhin can help him to repair and replace his clothing, get some lessons or translations to do; can, in general, help him to a practical approach to his difficulties.

Razumikhin's function as a contrast to (and relief from) Raskolnikov is obvious. Razumikhin has all the external problems of Raskolnikov; none of the internal ones. Like Raskolnikov, he is a student who has had to leave the University for lack of money. He, however, has responded directly to this hardship by taking whatever work he could find, then doing it happily and well until he could resume his studies. Both strong and intelligent, he has "managed to keep himself without any outside assistance whatever," so owes no one and has not complicated his problems. He never takes "any of his failures to heart" for he has never demanded more of the world than it gives and so has no desire to see himself as a martyr. Again, not demanding much from the world, he does not hear it demanding so much in return; his conscience remains free and untroubled. Simple, frank and outgoing: when angry, he knocks someone down; when chagrined, he bangs his fist into the stove; when spreeing, he is liable to fell policemen. Unlike Raskolnikov, he is "extraordinarily cheerful and communicative" and even Raskolnikov finds it "hardly possible to be on any but friendly terms with Razumikhin." Above all, he knows who he is, what he wants, what he stands for, and preserves in himself that "sense of dignity" which Raskolnikov so desperately needs.

Though Dostoievsky does not insist on this, the names of the two characters tend to define them: the name Raskolnikov refers to that which is divided, suggested both the schismatic in religion (the heretic or "Old Believer"), and also the schizoid in personality; the name Razumikhin stands for reason, reasonability, efficiency and practicality, the very qualities he both preaches and exhibits as a character. There is also some significance in the fact that Razumikhin lives on Vasilyevsky Island and that Raskolnikov finds himself headed

in that direction at this moment. Vasilyevsky Island is the home of the University, the Academy of Arts and the Academy of Sciences[12]; it must have stood in the minds of most Russians as the very center of enlightenment, culture and reason. It is precisely the place, as Razumikhin is the man, to which Raskolnikov should turn in these difficulties.

As Chapter 5 opens, however, we discover that Razumikhin has been introduced only to suggest what Raskolnikov is turning against. Even the thought of visiting him suggests to Raskolnikov's bitter and tormented brain, "some ominous meaning." It would mean to give up being bitter and tormented, to reverse his strategy and, to some degree, overhaul his personality. It must seem to Raskolnikov, just as it often seemed to Dostoievsky, that the very bases of his personality lay in the unreasonable and cranky; to give up those qualities might, he fears, also threaten to make him nothing. It would surely deprive him of the great triumph which he has imagined would prove once and for all his transcendent worth and repay his conscience:

> Suppose (Razumikhin) does get me some lessons, suppose he even shares his last penny with me, . . . so that I could buy myself a pair of boots and mend my clothes to be able to give lessons, what then? What shall I do with my few coppers afterwards? Is that what I want? . . . did I really think of putting everything right . . . a solution of all my difficulties in Razumikhin?

Nothing small or partial will do—Raskolnikov is nothing if not proud. He has put off his visit too long; to go now to Razumikhin would mean admitting he has been wrong, must accept other men's way out of his dilemma. He knows that eventually he *must* go to reason and to Razumikhin ("I shall call on Razumikhin, of course") . . . Yet, to save his pride, he must first "solve" his own problem his own way:

> I shall call on him . . . on the day after I've *done* it, after *that* [the murder] has been settled, and when everything is different.

This, in its way, is true enough—he *will* go to Razumikhin after the murder; further, Razumikhin (and reason) will then visit *him*. Again, after the murder everything will be different, yet Raskolnikov must suspect even now that in a more crucial sense everything will be just the same. Nonetheless, he has made his decision. He jumps up, crying, "Will it really happen?" His answer comes, very fittingly, as a nightmare.

Thus far, in the book's first four chapters, Dostoievsky has investigated his hero through a few highly significant bits of action and by means of comparisons and contrasts. At the same time, as I have already noted, he has laid the ground-work for all the remaining structure of the novel[13] by introducing all the important secondary characters, excepting only Porfiry Petrovich, the chief inspector, who obviously cannot enter the story until after the murder. We have met first, Marmeladov, the key secondary figure of Part I: he has shown to Raskolnikov his own passive masochism, a revelation which, as I have said, is crucial in driving Raskolnikov toward violence. We have also met, though at second hand, Razumikhin, who will step in after the murder and dominate Part II, bringing Raskolnikov to the very verge of confession and redemption. In the letter, we have met Raskolnikov's mother and sister, who will appear just when he is ready to confess (at the end of Part II); they, together with other "accusers"—Porfiry Petrovich and that unnamed workman who calls Raskolnikov "Murderer!"—will hurl Raskolnikov back into the terrible depths of Parts III and IV. We have been told about the book's one true saint, Sonia, and its one true villain, Luzhin—the two characters who will struggle and exert such strong and opposite attractions upon Raskolnikov through Parts IV and V. Finally, we have met Svidrigaylov, who will oppose Porfiry Petrovich as a father-figure in the struggle for Raskolnikov's soul in Part VI. Oddly enough, Svidrigaylov's influence will ultimately be for the good, showing as he so graphically does, the evil, the agony, the self-destruction which must fall on the man who tries to explain away his guilt, who will not confess. It is no accident that at the end of the novel proper, the police will hear of Svidrigaylov's death and of Raskolnikov's confession almost at the same moment.

Dostoievsky has planted the seeds, then, from which most of the novel must grow. He has made a preliminary exploration of Raskolnikov and of his torments. Now, after one brief respite, one glimpse of Razumikhin and rationality, he is ready to plunge into the depths of Raskolnikov's agonized mind, into his nightmare of himself. Turning his back on Vasilyevsky Island and on Razumikhin, Raskolnikov has fallen, characteristically, into a deep but troubled sleep. If we have had one momentary ray of light and sanity, the darkness which follows will only be the darker for that.

Raskolnikov's dream may be briefly summed up (with none of its overwhelming horror): Raskolnikov, a boy of seven, is walking with his father to the little church and cemetery where his grandmother and younger brother are buried. On the way they must pass a tavern which has an ominous atmosphere. Out of it, a group of artisans and their women swarm, climbing into a cart which belongs to one of them named Mikolka. Attached to this cart is a weak little old mare which they jeer, curse and whip, trying to force her into a gallop. When the mare can scarcely pull them, they become wild with rage, dancing about and beating her with whips and sticks. At last Mikolka, furious, kills her with an iron bar. Meantime, the young Raskolnikov runs about trying to stop them, then finally "put[s] his arms round her

dead, blood-stained muzzle and kisse[s] . . . her . . . eyes . . ." Then he suddenly "rushe[s] in a rage at Mikolka with his little fists," but is caught and restrained by his father. When he tries to cry out, he wakens.

Like any other dream, this one has day remnants which offer some hints about its significance; further, these same motifs will carry on past the dream into the later development of the novel. Carts for instance, like trunks and taverns, have a considerable textural importance throughout the book. Later, for example, Raskolnikov will pass through the gates of his victim's house hiding behind one; after the murder, he will very nearly walk under the wheels of a carriage, then will be beaten by its driver who will believe (correctly, I think) that he did it on purpose; later, Marmeladov *will* fall under the carriage and find there his own death.

At the moment, however, I am much more concerned with the carts Raskolnikov has already encountered during the day—the carts from which this dream-cart must in part derive. While reading in his mother's letter that she and Dunya would be driven to the railway station in a peasant's cart, he had recalled that he himself used to drive just such a cart. Again, we have already mentioned the scene in Chapter 1 when Raskolnikov was on the way to rehearse the murder and a man had shouted at him from a huge empty cart, "Hey, you there, German hatter!" Raskolnikov had "at once stopped in his tracks and clutched nervously at his hat."

That episode first introduced the element of ridicule which was to be pointed so strongly at Marmeladov and Raskolnikov in later scenes. The tavern loungers and the neighbors who had jeered at Marmeladov, the wife who beats him, the drunkard who shouted at Raskolnikov, Nastasya with her convulsive laughter—all are transformed in the dream into the mob who swarm, jeering, from the tavern and who drive and beat the poor old horse. From this viewpoint, then, the horse represents both Raskolnikov and Marmeladov, being jeered, beaten and finally killed because they cannot pull the load of their families.

Raskolnikov's dream has reminded him how he, as a little boy

> always liked watching those huge dray-horses with their long manes and thick legs, walking leisurely, with measured steps, and drawing a whole mountain behind them, but without the slightest strain, as though they found it so much easier going with carts than without carts. But now, curiously enough, some peasant's small, lean, greyish-brown mare was harnessed to one of these huge carts, the sort of poor old nag which—he had seen it so often—found it very hard to draw quite an ordinary cart with wood or hay piled on top of it, especially when the cart was stuck in the mud or in a rut,

and every time that happened, the peasant flogged her so brutally, sometimes even across the eyes and muzzle, and he felt so sorry, so sorry for the poor old horse that he almost burst into tears, and his mother always used to take him away from the window.

I take this to be a description, first, of the ever-capable Razumikhin (who was introduced only a short time before the dream); then, a description of Raskolnikov, the thin, little feeble mare who "doesn't earn his keep" and is most surely "stuck in the mud." In part, then, the nightmare shows Raskolnikov to himself as a man who simply cannot (or thinks he cannot) pull the vast, vulgar, sweating load laid on him and is being derided, jeered and beaten because of it. All he can do is to kick with impotent rage at his tormentors. Good reason, then, that when Raskolnikov wakes from his dream, "Every bone in his body seem[s] to ache" and "his eyes [are] burning." He wakes with the physical sensations of having actually undergone the beating he has dreamed of, and which he has been undergoing, emotionally, for many months.

Yet, the dream is not only an interpretation of the past where Raskolnikov sees himself as helpless and injured; it is also another prediction and rehearsal of the future, where he hopes to see himself filled with great and injurious power. If he recalled that he himself used to drive a peasant's cart, like the one his mother and sister will take to the station, that may suggest that he is not the horse in the dream, but the driver, Mikolka. There is much evidence to bear this out. While the peasants are beating the little mare, someone shouts to Mikolka, "Why don't you strike her with an axe? Despatch her at once!" Like the pawnbroker woman, the old mare is sickly, feeble and in some essential way inferior. Though outwardly respectable, she is actually parasitic and certainly "doesn't earn her keep"—in the next chapter, the young student will tell his officer friend that Alyona Ivanovna is "of no use to anyone." When he wakes from his dream, Raskolnikov himself immediately assumes that it *was* a vision of himself killing her:

> Good God! . . . is it possible that I will really take a hatchet, hit her on the head with it, crack her skull, slither about in warm, sticky blood, break the lock, steal and shake with fear, hide myself all covered in blood and with the hatchet—Good God! Is it possible?

He decides that it is not possible. Yet no one can miss the tone of delight with which he describes these horrors which he asserts that he will not commit.

We may also note here, incidentally, that the painter who falsely confesses to this murder is also named "Mikolka," though most translators, apparently wishing to avoid confusion, give his name as "Nikolay." I suggest that Dostoievsky created this complication intentionally as one hint to the meaning of the dream and its

relation to the murder. In the dream, Raskolnikov, disguised as a workman named Mikolka, kills a horse symbolic of a pawnbroker woman; later a painter, also named Mikolka, (I have already pointed out that he comes from Ryazan and is a Raskolnik) confesses to Raskolnikov's actual murder of that same woman.

Yet, if Mikolka is identified with Raskolnikov, and the old horse with the pawnbroker, we must not forget that the pawnbroker is always symbolically related, for Raskolnikov, to his landlady and his mother. Thus, in the dream, Raskolnikov may be seen to be beating Pashenka, and, more important, his mother. It is she who still pulls the family load, though too old and feeble to do so. It is she who is "just breaking his heart." And it is Raskolnikov who drives her on. We should notice the great emphasis upon beating the horse across the eyes; Raskolnikov feels particularly guilty about his mother's knitting shawls and cuffs at night; he fears she may go blind before he can help her. Thus, since conscience must accuse him of driving his mother and sister, in this aspect the dream presents him to himself as fearfully and essentially evil, in the past. And this self-definition must help lead him on to become evil in the future.

Still, if we are to understand this dream, we must turn it once again and see it in yet a different light. Though in one sense Raskolnikov is the horse killed in his dream, and is in another sense the brute who kills it, he is present in a much more obvious guise—as himself when seven years old. This line of interpretation is strengthened by several phrases in the dream which echo phrases in the previous episode (the scene on the Horse Guard's Boulevard). When, in the earlier scene, he had seen the dandy approaching the teen-aged girl,

> Raskolnikov rushed at him with his fists, without stopping to consider that the thick-set gentleman was a match for two men like himself.

Similarly, in the dream, the young Raskolnikov

> rushed in a rage at Mikolka with his little fists.

In the dream, the vision of himself as dependent and helpless is even more exaggerated than in the Boulevard scene: he has now become a church-going little boy who must deal with hulking, vicious workmen. Once again, as on the Boulevard, the fact that he owns nothing is offered as proof of his helplessness: Mikolka rages, as he beats the mare, "My property . . . Mine . . . My property!" In his dream, Raskolnikov again has "no right to help." Yet this may be as much a hope and an excuse as it is a fear; having no rights, one has no responsibilities. Thus Raskolnikov need not help the mare—or the girl on the Boulevard, or Dunya, or his mother. And though in his dream he credits himself with having made an heroic attempt, he has been forcibly restrained—on the Boulevard, by the policeman; in the dream, by his father who tells him:

> "Come along . . . they're drunk. Having fun, the fools. Come along and don't look. . . . Playing the fool. It's not our business."

This is a startling echo; on the Boulevard, Raskolnikov had turned to the policeman and, at the very moment of his shocking change-of-heart, shouted almost the same words:

> "Leave them alone! It's not your business! Let them be! Let him . . . have his fun! What do you care?"

This echo, when one first recognizes it, can be very misleading. Clearly, the horse has some relation to the girl on the boulevard; one is liable to think that Raskolnikov's words about her have been echoed in the dream to show why he turned against her. One is led into speculations about whether or not Raskolnikov may, in his childhood, have witnessed a scene like that in the dream, and have heard his father make such a comment. This is, of course, beyond the scope of the novel; no one will ever know. Besides, it is of no importance, since even if such an event *had* occurred, that would neither excuse nor explain Raskolnikov's actions on the Boulevard. To put his own words from that earlier scene into his father's mouth in the dream is, at best, only a rationalization, an attempt to give his father's authority to the idea that he had "no right" to help, or else an attempt to blame his own viciousness upon a supposed callousness in his father.

The deeper purpose of this echo is less simple and less flattering. Twice—once on the Boulevard, once in the dream—Raskolnikov has refused help to someone and claimed it was not his business. Both claims are, themselves, echoes of his earlier statement about his own intimate affairs, his "business"—his rent, his debts, his clothing. He has claimed that they, too—those "matters that required his most immediate attention, . . . did not concern him at all." And here again, as in the dream or on the Boulevard, the reason "he did not want to bother" about his own business, is that this is the best way he can refuse help to others. Thus, these echoes lead us back, once again, to Raskolnikov's relation with his family. This explains why Raskolnikov is restrained from going to the aid of the horse in the dream—it partly represents his mother and sister, and he wishes them to be injured. This is the same factor which restrains the horse, insofar as it represents Raskolnikov himself, and makes him too weak and feeble to pull his cart—and then makes him so furious with himself for having injured others and himself, that he feels like thrashing himself to death.

It is very suggestive that Raskolnikov picks this particular phrase—that his affairs are none of his business—to explain his method of revenge. It makes possible a guess about the nature of the grudge he wants to pay off against his mother—or, since that grudge must be very old and complicated and must involve much blame on both sides, a guess at the particular events which have triggered this particular set of weapons in Raskolnikov and this particular excuse for their use.

The only hint we have of any specific grudge, lies in the matter of the landlady's invalid daughter, Natalya Zarnitsyn, now dead, with whom Raskolnikov had been in love and whom he had contracted to marry. We do not learn about this affair until after the murder when Raskolnikov is called in to the police station because of his debt to Pashenka.[14] Later on, we learn that Raskolnikov's mother had apparently raised strong objections, and from her self-pitying account of the affair to Razumikhin, we may judge what tack she took with Raskolnikov:

> "I could never rely on his character, not even when he was a boy of fifteen. . . . Why, to take something that happened only recently. I wonder if you know that only a year and a half ago he took it into his head to marry that girl—what was her name?—the daughter of Mrs. Zarnitsyn, his landlady—oh, it was an awful shock to me! . . . Do you think . . . my tears, my appeals, my illness or perhaps even my death from grief, or our poverty would have stopped him? He would have calmly stepped over all the obstacles. But surely, surely, he does care for us a little, doesn't he?"[15]

The marriage did not take place, apparently because of Natalya's death, and it is not possible to tell how much the mother's interference may have complicated matters. She plainly has acted very possessive and blameful and now feels anything but charitable:

> "May God forgive me . . . but I couldn't help being glad when I heard of her death, though I don't know which of them would have ruined which . . ."

Raskolnikov feels the loss of Natalya more strongly than he likes to admit. It would not be surprising if he blamed his mother for her death—perhaps quite unreasonably. He certainly does blame her for the loss of the love affair, does resent her possessive interference, and the kind of technique she has used against him. Watching the first awakenings of love between Dunya and Razumikhin, he suddenly breaks in, full of nostalgia and, though he tries to deny it, resentment:

> ". . . do you remember, mother, that I was in love and wanted to get married. . . . I really don't know why I was so attached to her at the time. Because she was always ill, I suppose. If she'd been lame or a hunchback I believe I'd have loved her better still." He smiled wistfully. "Yes,—a sort of spring madness."
>
> "No, it wasn't only spring madness," Dunya said, warmly.
>
> . . . Then, completely absorbed in his thoughts, he got up, went up to his mother, kissed her, went back to his seat and sat down.

"You're still in love with her," said Mrs. Raskolnikov, touched.

"Her? Now? Oh, I see, you mean her? No. It's as if it never happened in this world at all. . . . And everything here seems to be happening quite in another world. . . . You, too, seem to be miles away."[16]

I am certainly not suggesting that Raskolnikov would have been happy with Natalya; there is every reason to think their marriage would have been just about like the Marmeladovs'. I am only pointing out that he must feel deprived of the management of his most intimate affairs, feel that his mother has made his life into her business, not his own. He, in revenge, has learned to frustrate her plans by refusing to "concern himself" with his own affairs. This also would account for the childish possessiveness of Mikolka in the dream. Raskolnikov has permitted the control of his life to pass out of his hands; recalling the incident of Natalya, he even gets up like a dutiful little boy, walks over and kisses his mother, then returns and sits down as if in a trance. Yet, however withdrawn he becomes, some part of his mind must be frantic with rage, must want to club someone or something to death, must want to shout that his affairs are:

My property . . . Mine . . . My Property!

Thus, in the dream, he beats his mother to death, mocking her all the while with her own possessiveness.

Further, Raskolnikov seems to have taken a similarly ironical method of revenge in using his mother's accusations: resenting her blamefulness, he sees to it that her worst reproaches come true. He has picked up her phrase that "he would have calmly stepped over all the obstacles" and has apparently decided to "show her;" his theory for the murder is built upon a claim that the superior man (himself) is permitted everything, has a right to "step over certain obstacles," is even entitled "to step over a corpse or wade through blood, . . . to eliminate all obstacles"[17] if his conscience leads him to do so. Again, thinking back upon the murder, Raskolnikov reflects that "I was in a great hurry to step over . . . but I did not step over—I remained on this side."[18] We should also recall that Raskolnikov always acts worse under the influence of those who accuse him— his mother and sister, the workman who calls him "Murderer," the Porfiry who torments him, Svidrigaylov who insists on seeing a likeness between them. He can only confess to, and be saved by, those who respect him regardless of whatever evil he may have committed— Sonia, Polya Marmeladov, the changed Porfiry. Not the least profound insight in this novel lies in the way its hero always tends to *become* what people tell him that he already *is*.

But I have gone far from the dream; let me return to it. I am faced, now, with the problem of resolving these seemingly disparate readings of the dream. First of all,

where is Raskolnikov in his dream? Is he the horse, the little boy, the father, or the brute Mikolka? The answer must be Yes. All of the characters of the dream are the dreamer. The problem is not to decide who is who, but rather to understand the tenor of the dreamer's apprehension of the world, that is, of his mind.

That is not so difficult as it might seem. The dream shows Raskolnikov to himself as a man too feeble in drawing his burdens, yet entirely too strong in punishing himself for that failure. Thus he is stuck on a treadmill of guilt and rage where he is beating himself to death for being stuck. At the same time, the dream shows him a world which has the same characteristics: all good characters are weak or victimized. (The dream contains but disguises the fact that these characters have chosen to be either weak or victimized.) Meantime, "the worst are full of passionate intensity." The only active role in the dream belongs to such destroyers as Mikolka. Raskolnikov's dream tells him that he must choose either murder or suicide; either kill or be killed.

For the horse, also, I have given what must seem disparate interpretations. Does the horse represent the teenaged girl, Dunya and Sonia, Or does it represent the pawnbroker, the landlady and the mother, Or Marmeladov and Raskolnikov? Once again, the answer to all the questions is Yes. To miss the identity of all these characters as symbolized by the horse is to miss an essential texture of Raskolnikov's mind. In particular, we must recognize the identity of Raskolnikov with the pawnbroker he kills. I have already pointed out that he has picked Alyona Ivanovna as exemplifying the worst qualities of his mother—debt collecting and tyranny. Again, I have shown that Raskolnikov shares many of those worst qualities (no doubt his mother was an effective teacher)—especially the technique of intentional mismanagement so as to blame others and collect debts against them. These are the very qualities he wants to punish in himself and so to annihilate. Thus, he has chosen Alyona Ivanovna to stand not only as a scapegoat for his mother, but much more important, for himself. Though outwardly respectable because she earns a living, she is at least as much a parasite as he is. In Chapter 3, Nastasya had said that he was "of no use to himself or anyone else." In Chapter 5 which follows, the young student will tell his officer friend that the pawnbroker is "no use to anyone," and Raskolnikov will recognize this as a reflection of his own thoughts. In a world, then, where he sees no alternatives but murder or suicide, Raskolnikov has carefully picked out Alyona Ivanovna to take the punishment he feels he should level at himself. I return to my initial quotation from *Gravity and Grace* by Simone Weil:

A hurtful act is the transference to others of the degradation which we bear in ourselves. That is why we are inclined to commit such acts as a way of deliverance.

The fact that Raskolnikov wakes with the assumption that the dream meant murder:

> Good God! . . . is it possible that I will really take a hatchet, hit her on the head. . . .

instead of the only other alternative, suicide, indicates what choice he has made.

In the bases of his mind, then, he has reached the first of his two great decisions—that he will kill Alyona Ivanovna. Though he believes that he has decided otherwise, he is wrong. He is, in fact, unable to reach *any* decision with his conscious mind, for the unconscious areas have taken over in a desperate, though obviously foolish, attempt to prove himself worthy of life. From this point, he is less and less able to control his actions, less and less able to understand them. He cannot imagine why he goes home so indirectly, by way of a detour through the Hay Market where he encounters Lisaveta, or why

> such a decisive, and, at the same time, such an entirely accidental meeting in the Hay Market (where he had no business to be at all) occurred just at that hour and even at that minute of his life. . . . It was as though it had happened on purpose, as though the meeting had been specially arranged for him!

It was. The meeting may be "entirely accidental" so far as Lisaveta's part in it is concerned. He, however, has deliberately placed himself where he could run into her. It is luck that he happens to find her today; but if not today, then sooner or later.

Having "accidentally" encountered Lisaveta, and "accidentally" found out that she will be away—and her sister home alone—the next evening at seven, Raskolnikov returned to his house and "entered his room like a man sentenced to death." For good reason; we have already seen how closely he identifies with his chosen victim.

> He thought of nothing, and indeed he was quite incapable of thinking; but he suddenly felt with all his being that he no longer possessed any freedom of reasoning or of will, and that everything was suddenly and irrevocably settled.

From this point on, he acts under compulsion, like a man being led or pushed, for his conscious mind is no longer in control; it has yielded to unconscious forces it does not recognize. Thus we reach a great irony; in the murder, the very act meant to prove conclusively to himself that he is an active person, he feels entirely passive, entirely as if compelled by forces outside himself. The only act which, at this point, could have felt "active" should be some practical and direct action aimed at taking command of his problems. The murder itself is, in the long run, an act of the deepest passivity.

Even though the unconscious mind has gained control, the conscious mind must still be reckoned with, must be convinced that the murder is a proper act. Chapter 6, which is concerned with preparations for the murder, demonstrates the workings of this most important of preparations. At the same time, however, the nature of Raskolnikov's preparations permits Dostoievsky to investigate the motive which still underlies those motives we have so far discussed. Here, by revealing Raskolnikov's desire to make his preparations badly and get caught, his determination to blunder, Dostoievsky can lay the groundwork for Raskolnikov's second great decision—the decision to confess.

If the conscious mind is to be assuaged, that can only be done by bringing the murder under some noble-sounding rationalization. The outlines of this rationalization are sketched in by a very cleverly contrived flashback to a scene where Raskolnikov had heard "a student he knew called Pokorev" telling an Army officer that one might kill Alyona Ivanovna as an humanitarian project. He argues that he could:

> "gladly murder that damned old woman and rob her of all she has . . . kill her, take her money, and with its help devote (himself) to the service of humanity and the good of all. Well, don't you think that one little crime could be expiated and wiped out by thousands of good deeds? . . . One death in exchange for a hundred lives—why it's a simple sum in arithmetic!"

When reminded that this is a matter of "human nature," not of arithmetic, he replies:

> "even human nature can be improved and set on the right path, for otherwise we should all drown in a sea of prejudices. Otherwise there wouldn't have been a single great man."

Raskolnikov, too, is a student, and recognizes in Pokorev his own thoughts. We meet this rationalization in its fuller form much later in the book, when Porfiry produces Raskolnikov's essay, "On Crime." This essay recounts Pokorev's ideas of the humanitarian criminal, but greatly expands the idea, only suggested by Pokorev, of the superman. Raskolnikov argues in his article that men fall into two types: the great stupid, sluggish mass of mankind who must obey and be led; second, the "great" men, the leaders who try to improve mankind's lot, or at least do *something* with it. They, the supermen, show themselves by their ability to step across any lines of already existing authority. They are feared and mistrusted by the masses and are often considered criminals and may be killed because if it. The superman must expect this and must yet dare, for if successful, he will become an object of veneration, himself.

Though on first reading the novel, one is surprised by this essay which seems to introduce a completely new motive for the murder, one should quickly recognize that it is really only the old motive obviously inverted. Raskolnikov suspects that he is a sub-man, unworthy of the notice of anyone, so invents a theory to prove himself superior to all, above all authority; he suspects himself of being completely incapable of action, so invents a theory to prove himself capable of the grandest and most far-reaching actions; he suspects himself of being a parasite upon his mother and sister, so invents a theory to prove himself a benefactor to all mankind.

Thus, if I may for a moment jump ahead to the end of this chapter where Raskolnikov will have completed his preparations, we will see there the grotesque spectacle—by no means so uncommon as one could wish—of a man walking through the public streets on his way to commit a savage and hideous murder, but speculating, as he goes, about what improvements he might make in the public gardens when he comes into power:

> Walking past Yussupov Park, he became entirely absorbed in the question of improving its amenities by high-playing fountains, and he could not help thinking that they would improve the air in all the squares marvellously. Gradually he came to the conclusion that if the Summer Gardens were extended to Mars Square and even joined on the Mikhailovsky Palace Gardens, it would be a most wonderful improvement for the town.

I cannot imagine that most political revolutionaries felt much differently when young. Neither am I sure that Raskolnikov would be so much worse than most governors and statesmen; he might very well make just such improvements as he envisages, and seems more likely to dedicate himself to the welfare of humanity than most politicians one can recall—revolutionary or conservative. His only serious miscalculation about men who overstep authority is his failure to recognize his own motive in so doing. Yet, he continually hovers about it. First, he recognizes that people, in general, may prefer less pleasant parts of the city:

> Why was it, he wondered, that in all the large cities people seemed inclined to congregate, not by any means out of sheer necessity, just in those parts where there were neither gardens nor fountains, but dirt, bad smells, and every kind of abomination?

Next, he asks why he himself prefers degradation:

> He then remembered his own walks in the Hay Market, and for a moment he seemed to wake up. "What silly nonsense!" he thought. "No, much better not to think of anything at all."

Better not indeed; he might recognize his own urge which is carrying him at this moment, not toward power and aggrandisement, but toward degradation and abasement.

This problem opens the motive that yet underlies those we have already discussed; it forces me to return to the body of the chapter and to investigate the other preparations Raskolnikov has made for the murder. For, once his unconscious has convinced his conscious mind that murder is permissible, even noble, the conscious mind must then set about making the necessary physical preparations. Yet, even as it does, it realizes that its chief problem will be to protect itself against the deeper motives of the unconscious mind—its desire that Raskolnikov should be caught:

> he had been greatly interested in the question why almost every crime was so easily solved . . . the main reason for it lay not so much in the physical impossibility of concealing a crime as in the criminal himself; the criminal himself, at least almost every criminal, is subject at the moment of the crime to a kind of breakdown of his reasoning faculties and of his will-power, which are replaced by an amazingly childish carelessness just at the moment when he is most in need of caution and reason.

This pushes our analysis of motive an important step onward. Raskolnikov knows, even before he commits the crime, that his greatest enemy will be his own mind, that once again he will defeat himself. He knows, then, at some level of his mind, that he will be trying to get caught, that there is a purpose to his "childish carelessness." The only plausible purpose is a desire for punishment. Thus, before he ever commits the crime, he knows that he belongs, and wishes to belong, not to the class of "great men" who may overstep, but to the class of "ordinary" people who, should they ever mistake themselves for advanced people or "destroyers" and get out of hand,

> "you won't even have to employ anyone to thrash them—for, being extremely law-abiding by nature, they will thrash themselves: some of them will perform this service for one another, while others will administer the thrashing to themselves with their own hands. In addition, they impose all sorts of public penances upon themselves, and the result is both beautiful and edifying. In short, you needn't worry. It's a law of nature."[19]

It may well be asked what Raskolnikov hopes to gain from so severe a punishment as that he seeks. The answer, I think, may be divided into four parts. First, he needs to feel adequately punished for his past wrongs, cleared of the deep sense of shame which has dogged him throughout Part I. This sense of shame is so severe that, as René Fuelop-Miller rightly observes, Raskolnikov has a nightmare in the Epilogue where he sees his own degradation as a great plague that spreads over and infects the whole European continent. He must somehow cleanse his view of himself and of his world. He later admits that he already knew that the sacrifice of Alyona Ivanovna, which was supposed to accomplish this, would fail:

finally, I am a louse, . . . because I myself am perhaps worse and nastier than the louse I killed, and I knew *beforehand* that I would say that to myself *after* killing her![20]

Yet, knowing this, he went on with the murder, for it was not really the murder, but its consequences which held out hope to him.

Second, he must want punishment as a proof that he is not negligible. In this sense, Raskolnikov is like a child who would rather be whipped than ignored. He needs proof that he *is* a person, and is capable of some act vicious enough to compel some kind of attention from those in authority. In *The Need for Roots,* Simone Weil has written:

Just as the only way of showing respect for somebody suffering from hunger is to give him something to eat, so the only way of showing respect for somebody who has placed himself outside the law is to reinstate him inside the law by subjecting him to the punishment ordained by the law.

And, in *The House of the Dead,* Dostoievsky himself has written of the convicts in the prison at Omsk:

This general tone was apparent externally in a certain peculiar personal dignity of which almost every inmate of the prison was acutely conscious. It was as though the status of a convict, of a condemned prisoner, was a sort of rank, and an honourable one, too.

Punishment may be one form of respect, then; at best, it may show the criminal that those in authority still hold some hope for him, believe he may yet be corrected; at worst, it shows the criminal that he is enough of a person to have some effect, if only in angering those in authority.

Third, and as an extension of this, Raskolnikov must want a punishment which will force him to act hereafter in line with his own conscience. In a sense, his problem is to accept his mother's morality, while giving up her conflicting technique. His conscience's accusations, unsupported by an external force, are driving him to act always worse and worse. Thus, he must find an authority so overwhelming, even vicious, that he will have to knuckle under to it and stop, once and for all, his painful rebellion. Simone Weil, again, has written in *Gravity and Grace*:

The powerful, if they carry oppression beyond a certain point, necessarily end by making themselves *adored* by their slaves. For the thought of being under absolute compulsion, the plaything of another, is unendurable for a human being. Hence, if every way of escape from this constraint is taken from him, there is nothing left for him to do but to persuade himself that he does the things he is forced to do willingly, that is to say, to substitute *devotion* for *obedience.*

It is just such a devotion, such an obedience, that he desires; none other will assure him to being as good as he demands of himself. Thus, no leniency on the part of the state is tolerable to him. When, during his last interview with Porfiry Petrovich, Porfiry offers him a lighter sentence if he will confess, Raskolnikov at once admits that he does not want any reduction of sentence; Porfiry admits that he had suspected as much all along.[21]

Finally, and most important, Raskolnikov wants not only to be forced into being a worthy citizen, but most especially he wants to be defined as a loved and worthy child in a God-centered, family-style universe. That universe must be founded upon moral law, and that moral law enforced by the fatherly punishing arm of the state. Raskolnikov is exactly like the child who deliberately disobeys to find out if the rules really exist, if behavior has limits, if his family lives inside solid walls. It is no use to ignore such disobedience, the child will only force attention, make his defiance conspicuous. And he will not be happy until he has received the punishment, the assurance, that he wants. This explains Porfiry's emphasis, in the later chapters, on the idea of definition:

"You see, if, for instance, I were to put my suspect under lock and key a little too soon, I may, as it were, lend him some moral support. . . . I'd give him, as it were, a definite status, I'd, as it were, satisfy him psychologically and set his mind at rest, so that he'd slip through my fingers and retire into his shell."[22]

Raskolnikov is like the ex-convict Kuzma, in Chekhov's story "An Encounter" who, if not punished and reviled for his misdeeds, is faced by the awful prospect of an empty universe where "anything is possible" and where no god-father enforces justice or order upon mankind. So it is that Dostoievsky, in *The Diary of a Writer,* warns the new jurors about their leniency:

by prison and penal servitude, perhaps, you would have saved half of them. You would have assuaged, and not burdened, them. Self-purification through suffering is easier, I tell you. . . . You are merely planting cynicism in their souls. . . . You infuse into their souls incredulity in the popular truth, in the truth of God; you are leaving them confused. . . .

It may seem strange that Dostoievsky, who had himself been a convict, should urge jurors to send more people to prison. This will not seem so strange if one recalls the paradoxical development of Dostoievsky's political and religious thought. Much of the analysis of this novel bears at least a tangential applicability to its author's life. It is well known that nearly all his adult life he was given to compulsive gambling and mismanagement of his affairs and this has often been interpreted as a form of onanism and self-punishment. It is well known, too, that much of the guilt he felt emanated from the time that his tyrannical father was killed by rebelling serfs—a time which coincided with the period that Dostoievsky was, himself, feeling most rebellious.[23] Finally, nearly everyone knows how Dostoievsky was later arrested among a group of liberal thinkers and somewhat revolutionary literati, sentenced to death, led to the scaffold with a group of other "condemned" men—all of whom had already been pardoned—then, at the last minute, "saved" and his sentence commuted to four years hard labour in Siberia and four more years as a common soldier. Anyone would expect that the exaggerated severity of this sentence and the deliberate cruelty of the mock execution (one of the prisoners never fully regained sanity)—that all this would set Dostoievsky once and for all against the established Czarist regime. Quite the opposite happened. From the moment of his imprisonment, Dostoievsky began moving, year by year, toward an ever more conservative political position, an ever more servile attitude toward the Little Father, the Czar. At the same time, he became more and more an orthodox Christian and more convinced of the mission of the Czarist state as the bearer of true Christianity to the world. He himself claimed in a letter to Dr. Yanovsky that his period in Siberia had cured him of a mental derangement. I would recommend to the reader, once again, that passage just quoted from Simone Weil, which began, "The powerful, if they carry oppression beyond a certain point, necessarily end by making themselves *adored*. . . ." Or one might compare that superb scene in *Great Expectations* where the vicious and tyrannical Mrs. Joe, after long suspense, finally confronts old Orlick who had struck her down and half killed her with his blacksmith's hammer. She politely requests him to sit down and take tea with her.

Thus it is that, to Dostoievsky, those characters who are sick or handicapped—the invalid Natalya, the near-idiot Lisaveta, the crippled and stuttering Kapernaumovs—seem to be specially godly and blessed. The crushing hand of god has already been laid upon them; they have received His attention, "accepted suffering" (which is synonymous, here, with punishment) in advance, and so are blessed.

This also explains how Dostoievsky can feel that the criminal may be the most earnest God-seeker; the naughty child may be the most earnest parent-seeker. Notice that in Raskolnikov's awful nightmare, the murder symbolized there is only an interruption of his journey toward the church. In another sense, it is another way of making a part of that journey. Several times in the novel, Raskolnikov vigorously asserts that he does believe in God; his crime is one way of provoking God to declare himself. Again, notice that Raskolnikov is a law student. He has chosen a very dear school—the experience of punishment and law. Though there *are* many other schools of universal moral law, none are too convincing. What Raskolnikov most anxiously wants to learn is that "you can't get away with it"—whatever it

is. He gets the answer he wants; it does seem a shame, however, that he has to do so much of the work involved in seeing that the answer comes out right.

And how very hard he *does* work, trying to get caught. He begins by taking his usual method of sabotaging his own plans—daydreaming; he lies half-asleep in his room fantasying about oases in the desert and sands of gold, until it is well past six o'clock, so that he is rushed in his preparations and late in arriving. This late arrival, and the resulting late departure, leads directly to the murder of Lisaveta. Then again, he has made no *real* preparations for the murder at all. He has counted the number of steps to Alyona Ivanovna's house, has invented a sling to carry the axe under his coat, has prepared a needle and thread; yet he has taken no care to see that he could find an axe, nor, what is worse, that he could return it after the murder without being seen. Neither has he made any plans for getting out of his own house, or into Alyona Ivanovna's, without being seen. Hardly conducive to the "perfect crime." Then again, as he walks through the street, glancing at no one and trying to

> make himself as inconspicuous as possible . . . he remembered his hat. "Good God! and I had the money the day before yesterday and I didn't think of getting a cap!" He swore loudly.

We should not forget (even if he does) that he *did* think of getting a cap; it was the first thing he thought of as soon as the drunkard in the cart called him a "German hatter."

It is true that Raskolnikov has found an axe, that he does get into Alyona Ivanovna's house unnoticed, screened by a passing cart, he does get up the stairs without meeting anyone, but this is all a matter of chance. Unfortunately for him, his good luck holds.

As Chapter 7 opens, Raskolnikov continues making blunder after blunder, while "luck" carries him through the murder and his escape. Though the murder scene itself is uncanny and hideous, it is at the same time, terribly ludicrous. No one has ever bungled so completely and so successfully.

After Alyona Ivanovna has been kind enough to look aside long enough for Raskolnikov to extricate his axe from the sling in which he has carried it, and to murder her, we watch him rushing about the apartment, gradually losing control, acting less reasonable with each moment that passes. First he tries the chest of drawers, then rushes back to be sure the old woman is dead—this time getting blood all over his hands and the axe. Then he returns to the chest,

> but he kept making mistakes; for instance, he would see that a key did not fit, but he kept trying it.

Then, having wasted this much time, when he should be making his escape, he forgets the decisions he had already reached:

> Suddenly he remembered the big key with the notches in the bit which was hanging there with the other small keys, and he realized that it could not possibly belong to the chest of drawers (the same idea had occurred to him the last time) but to some trunk or box . . .

Having got the trunk from under the bed and opened it, he begins to wipe the blood from his hands on the red trimmings of clothes, explaining this with the most insane logic:

> "It's red, and blood doesn't show so much on red," he thought to himself, but suddenly he came to his senses with a start. "Good Lord, am I going off my head?" he thought in a panic.

At this point, he is interrupted by the entrance of Lisaveta. Having killed her, he very nearly loses all control:

> Raskolnikov almost lost his head. He picked up her bundle, threw it down again, and rushed out into the passage.

Then he comes back, but not to prepare his escape. As if he had not lost enough time already, he now falls

> into a kind of brown study or even reverie; there were moments when he seemed to forget everything, or . . . to start worrying about something that did not matter.

He does finally rouse himself enough to try to wash his hands and the hatchet, both of which are covered with Lisaveta's blood. Yet even while he knows that he is doing a poor job of this, he cannot make himself do it well:

> He realized . . . that his examination was too perfunctory, and that there might be something that would attract attention which had escaped his notice.

At this point, he has the very sensible reflection that he is possibly not in control of himself, that he was "not able to do anything to protect himself, and that, generally, he most probably should not be doing what he was doing now. . . ." Yet an even more shocking recognition awaits him:

> He stood there unable to believe his own eyes: the door, the front door, leading from the passage to the stairs, the same door before which he had so recently stood ringing the bell and through which he had come in, stood open, at least five inches open! Neither locked nor even latched all that time!

He has committed the "perfect crime" with the front door standing open; everyone in the apartment house could have been watching him.

Yet the only person who did come through that open door was Lisaveta. Why? In a narrative sense, this second murder may seem accidental and arbitrary. Yet no one can deny that the second murder "feels right" in the novel. In the first place, it is symbolically "right" in the Christian morality of the story. It shows how wrong Raskolnikov was in taking murder as a "mathematical problem"—in thinking he could overstep the moral law in one single instance, thereafter devoting himself to the welfare of mankind. Evil leads to evil; by committing the murder of a woman he hates, he has placed himself in a position where he must murder another woman whom he admires and pities.

There is, however, a symbology far under this, which is related to Sonia's beautiful question: "What have you done to yourself?" As I have pointed out, when he killed the pawnbroker woman, Raskolnikov was, at the deepest level of his thought, striking against himself, against that part of himself which is most like Alyona Ivanovna, like his mother, like Pashenka—that part of himself which is idle, passive, debt-collecting, "not worth its keep." His irrational hatred of Alyona Ivanovna is clearly a reflection of his self-hatred; his viciousness against her, a refusal to confess to the qualities he has shared with her.

Yet he can never escape those qualities except by confessing them. In killing Alyona Ivanovna, he has not obliterated the worst part of his personality, but (as the narrator in Dostoievsky's story, **"White Nights,"** says) in committing a crime, the criminal "has destroyed what is best in him. . . ."[24] Thus it is that the simple, gentle Lisaveta (symbolically tied to Dunya, Sonia, and all the best qualities of Raskolnikov) must wander in to fall under the axe. Once dead, she does not rise again. The pawnbroker is another matter; by killing her, Raskolnikov has merely perpetuated her and everything usurious, cruel and tyrannical in his own personality. Refusing to stay dead, she will rise up and live in Raskolnikov's mind; we meet her there all too soon again in that nightmare where Raskolnikov will strike her again and again with the axe, yet she will not die. He bends down to discover that she has been laughing at him the whole time. The murder has made him more like her, not less; "What have you done to yourself," indeed!

This, too, suggests something about the sexual symbology of the murder itself, and helps account for some part of its uncanny phosphorescent glow. The murder itself has the appearance of an act of sexual aggression against the pawnbroker as a mother-figure. Raskolnikov's opening of the trunks, his theft of the purse "full to bursting," his fumbling with the keys:

> the moment he began fitting the keys into the drawers, the moment he heard their jingling, a sort of spasm passed over him. . . . He . . . picked up the keys and

again began trying them. But for some reason . . . the keys would not fit in any of the locks . . . he kept making mistakes; . . . he would see a key did not fit, but he kept trying it. Suddenly he remembered the big key with the notches in the bit which was hanging there with the other small keys . . .

all these details seem strongly sexual. Yet, because of Raskolnikov's deep identification with Alyona Ivanovna, the murder must finally be seen not as an act of sexual violence directed against another; but rather as an act of self-destruction and "self-abuse." If sex is seen as an aggressive and harmful act, then this form of aggression, too, may be turned against the self. Thus, a desire to commit some sexual violence against the mother, or some substitute figure, might be turned into sexual self-assault, into a blameful rape upon the self. For Raskolnikov, the loss of Natalya Zarnitsyn must be very important: even though one cannot imagine any great sexuality in either Natalya or Raskolnikov, to lose her might still *symbolize* an important sexual privation and so might generate new aggressive sexuality which might, then, be turned back against the self. This onanistic pattern underlying the crime must partly account for the way Raskolnikov throws away the stolen money and articles, or hides them beneath a stone beside a urinal.[25] This, too, helps explain that little scene after the murder when Raskolnikov re-enacts the murder but puts himself more obviously in the victim's role: first he wanders "accidentally" under a passing carriage, then is whipped by the driver (who may be compared with Mikolka of the nightmare); a passing woman and her daughter take pity on him and charitably give him 20 copecks. He throws the money into the river.[26]

Thus, however much the murder appears an act directed toward the outside world, Raskolnikov sees his victim—like everything else in the world—only in terms of himself. And within minutes of murdering her, he will assume the same positions and attitudes which she had taken before. As soon as he realizes that the door is open,

He rushe[s] to the door and bolt[s] it.

"But what am I doing? I must get out of here! I must get out!"

There is no out except through confession. No sooner does he step into the hall than he hears footsteps—all the way from the ground floor—and knows at once that they are coming "to the old woman." Raskolnikov darts back into the room just in time, latches the door, again, and stands breathless, clutching his hatchet.

They were now opposite each other, with only the door between them, just as he and the old woman had been a short while ago when only the door separated them and he was listening intently.

Outside the door stands Koch, "a big fat man . . . a man of authority" who is joined at once by a younger man, "a future public prosecutor." "The whole thing

was like a nightmare" to Raskolnikov, simply because he experiences these men as figures of his own creation and conscience. That is why, as he stands listening to them approaching on the steps:

he felt as though he were turned to stone, as though it were all happening in a dream, where you are chased by a murderer who is getting nearer and nearer, but you are unable to stir, you seem to be rooted to the ground, unable even to lift your arm.

He is pursued by a murderer—by the only one he knows. And he would like, terribly, to surrender to those who can save him from himself:

the thought occurred to him suddenly a few times to put an end to it all by shouting to them from behind the door. And, at times, he felt like starting cursing and taunting them, while they were still unable to open the door. "Oh, if only one could get it over quickly!" it flashed through his mind.

"Get it over quickly!" For he knows all along what he will have, eventually, to do. Yet he was never one to cut short his own suffering.

By the most fantastic set of coincidences and accidents, he will manage to escape and get back to his landlady's house, will manage to return the axe and get into his room. But only to prolong his agony. As soon as he can get on his feet again, he will be back, ringing the bell, looking around the room, asking about the blood, torturing himself in the most horrible ways. Then, too, he will be flirting with the police, hinting to them, dropping clues all over St. Petersburg. He will be in a perfect agony every time their suspicion seems to turn from him. And when, finally, Sonia and Porfiry have brought him to see what he has done to himself and Svidrigaylov has shown him the logical next step, suicide, then at last he will stop, turn, go to the police who would not come to him, and confess.

Notes

1. Part V, Ch. 2. All quotations are from the translation by David Magarshack.

2. From this remark I should exclude Avrahm Yarmolinsky, whose analysis in *Dostoievsky: His Life and Art* [(New York: Criterion Books, 1957)] hints strongly at the interpretation here offered.

3. Part VI, Ch. 2.

4. Quoted by Magarshack in his Introduction to the novel.

5. Here Dostoievsky strengthens and openly asserts an interpretation for this incident which he had previously only suggested when handling the same incident for *The House of the Dead*.

6. Cf. Alberto Moravia, "The Marx-Dostoievsky Duel," *Encounter,* November, 1956.

7. Cf. Chapter 6.

8. This is the only detail which I have displaced from its original place in the letter's sequence of ideas and details.

9. Part V, Ch. 1.

10. The ensuing interpretation owes much to discussions with Robert Hellman of C.C.N.Y. and to certain essays of Edmund Bergler. Throughout the essay I am indebted to George P. Elliott of Barnard College.

11. This becomes explicit only at the beginning of the next chapter, Chapter 5.

12. Cf. Jessie Coulson's Introduction to her own translation of *Crime and Punishment,* Oxford University Press, 1953.

13. A stimulating study by Edward Wasiolek, "On the Structure of *Crime and Punishment,*" appeared in the March 1959 issue of *PMLA.*

14. Part II, Ch. 1.

15. Part III, Ch. 2.

16. Part III, Ch. 3.

17. Part III, Ch. 5.

18. Part III, Ch. 6.

19. Part III, Ch. 5.

20. Part III, Ch. 6.

21. Part IV, Ch. 5.

22. Ibid.

23. Cf. e.g., Freud, "Dostoevsky and Parricide."

24. A cancelled passage quoted in the Introduction to David Magarshack's translation of *Crime and Punishment.*

25. Dostoievsky's second wife, Anna, reported that after they had been married a week, he took her to see the actual stone.

26. Part II, Ch. 2.

Mikhail Bakhtin (essay date 1963)

SOURCE: Bakhtin, Mikhail. "Characteristics of Genre and Plot Composition in Dostoevsky's Works." In *Problems of Dostoevsky's Poetics,* edited and translated by Caryl Emerson, pp. 101-80. Minneapolis: University of Minnesota Press, 1984.

[In the following excerpt, originally published in 1963, Bakhtin examines aspects of "carnivalization" in Crime and Punishment.*]*

The problem of *carnival* (in the sense of the sum total of all diverse festivities, rituals and forms of a carnival type)—its essence, its deep roots in the primordial order and the primordial thinking of man, its development under conditions of class society, its extraordinary life force and its undying fascination—is one of the most complex and most interesting problems in the history of culture. We cannot, of course, do justice to it here. What interests us here is essentially only the problem of carnivalization, that is, the determining influence of carnival on literature and more precisely on literary genre.

Carnival itself (we repeat: in the sense of a sum total of all diverse festivities of the carnival type) is not, of course, a literary phenomenon. It is *syncretic pageantry* of a ritualistic sort. As a form it is very complex and varied, giving rise, on a general carnivalistic base, to diverse variants and nuances depending upon the epoch, the people, the individual festivity. Carnival has worked out an entire language of symbolic concretely sensuous forms—from large and complex mass actions to individual carnivalistic gestures. This language, in a differentiated and even (as in any language) articulate way, gave expression to a unified (but complex) carnival sense of the world, permeating all its forms. This language cannot be translated in any full or adequate way into a verbal language, and much less into a language of abstract concepts, but it is amenable to a certain transposition into a language of artistic images that has something in common with its concretely sensuous nature; that is, it can be transposed into the language of literature. We are calling this transposition of carnival into the language of literature the carnivalization of literature. . . .

In all of Dostoevsky's novels, beginning with **Crime and Punishment,** there is a consistent *carnivalization* of dialogue.

We find other instances of carnivalization in **Crime and Punishment.** Everything in this novel—the fates of people, their experiences and ideas—is pushed to its boundaries, everything is prepared, as it were, to pass over into its opposite (but not, of course, in the abstractly dialectical sense), everything is taken to the extreme, to its outermost limit. There is nothing in the novel that could become stabilized, nothing that could justifiably relax within itself, enter the ordinary flow of biographical time and develop in it (the possibility of such a development for Razumikhin and Dounia is only indicated by Dostoevsky at the end of the novel, but of course he does not show it: such life lies outside his artistic world). Everything requires change and rebirth. Everything is shown in a moment of unfinalized transition.

It is characteristic that the very setting for the action of the novel—*Petersburg* (its role in the novel is enormous)—is on the borderline between existence and nonexistence, reality and phantasmagoria, always on the verge of dissipating like the fog and vanishing. Petersburg too is devoid, as it were, of any internal grounds for justifiable stabilization; it too is on the threshold.[1]

The sources of carnivalization for **Crime and Punishment** are no longer provided by Gogol. We feel here in part a Balzacian type of carnivalization, and in part elements of the social-adventure novel (Soulié and Sue). But perhaps the most vital and profound source of carnivalization for this novel was Pushkin's "Queen of Spades."

We shall pause for analysis on only one small episode of the novel, which will permit us to investigate several important characteristics of carnivalization in Dostoevsky, and at the same time clarify our claim concerning Pushkin's influence.

After the first meeting with Porfiry and the appearance of the mysterious artisan with his one word, "Murderer!", Raskolnikov has a *dream* in which he *again* commits the murder of the old woman. We quote the end of this dream:

> He stood over her. "She is afraid," he thought. He stealthily took the axe from the noose and struck her one blow, then another on the skull. But strange to say she did not stir, as though she were made of wood. He was frightened, bent down nearer and tried to look at her; but she, too, bent her head lower. He bent right down to the ground and peeped up into her face from below, he peeped and turned cold with horror; the old woman was sitting and *laughing, shaking with noiseless laughter,* doing her utmost that he should not hear it. Suddenly he fancied that the door from the bedroom was opened a little and that there was *laughter* and whispering within. He was overcome with frenzy and he began hitting the old woman on the head with all his force, but at every blow of the axe and the *laughter* and whispering from the bedroom *grew louder* and the old woman was simply shaking with mirth. He was rushing away, but the *passage was full of people, the doors* of the flats stood open and *on the landing, on the stairs* and everywhere below there were people, rows of heads, *all looking,* but huddled together in silence and expectation. Something gripped his heart, his legs were rooted to the spot, they would not move. . . . He tried to scream and woke up.

> [*SS* [(*Sobranie Sochinenii,* 10 vols.; Moscow: Goslitizdat, 1956-58)] V, 288; *Crime and Punishment* [(trans. Constance Garnett; New York: Bantam Books, 1958)], Part III, ch. 6]

Several points are of interest here.

1. The first point is already familiar to us: the fantastic logic of dreams employed here by Dostoevsky. We recall his words: ". . . you *leap over* space and time, *over all laws of life and reason,* and only pause where your *heart's desire* bids you pause" (**"Dream of a Ridiculous Man"**). This same dream logic made it possible to create here the image of a *laughing murdered old woman, to combine laughter with death and murder.* But this is also made possible by the ambivalent logic of carnival. Before us is a typical carnival combination.

The image of the laughing old woman in Dostoevsky echoes Pushkin's image of the old Countess winking from the coffin, and the winking Queen of Spades on the card (the Queen of Spades is, incidentally, a *carnival double* of the old Countess). We have here a *fundamental* resonance between two images and not a chance external similarity, for it occurs against the background of a general resonance between these two works ("The Queen of Spades" and **Crime and Punishment**). This is a resonance both in the atmosphere of images and in the basic content of ideas: "Napoleonism" on the specific terrain of early Russian capitalism. In both works this concretely historical phenomenon receives a second *carnivalistic plane,* one which recedes into infinite semantic space. The motivation for these two echoing images (the laughing dead woman) is also similar: in Pushkin it is *insanity,* in Dostoevsky, the *delirious dream.*

2. In Raskolnikov's dream it is not only the murdered woman who laughs (in the dream, to be sure, it proves impossible to murder her). Other people are also laughing, elsewhere in the apartment, in the bedroom, and they laugh louder and louder. Then a crowd appears, a multitude of people on the *stairway* and *down below* as well, and in relation to this crowd passing *below,* Raskolnikov is located at the *top of the stairs.* Before us is the image of communal ridicule on the public square decrowning a carnival king-pretender. The public square is a symbol of the communal performance, and at the end of the novel, Raskolnikov, before going to give himself up at the police station, comes out on the square and bows low to the earth before the whole people. This communal decrowning, which "came to Raskolnikov's heart" in a dream, has no *direct* echo in the "The Queen of Spades," but a distant echo is nevertheless there: Hermann's fainting spell in the presence of the people at the Countess' grave. A fuller echo of Raskolnikov's dream can be found in another of Pushkin's works, *Boris Godunov.* We have in mind the thrice-recurring prophetic *dream* of the Pretender (the scene in the cell of Chudovo Monastery):

> I dreamed I climbed a *crooked stair* that led
> Up to a tower, and there upon that *height*
> I stood, where Moscow like an ant hill lay
> *Under* my feet, and in the *marketplace*
> The *people* stared and pointed at me *laughing*;
> *I felt ashamed, a trembling overcame me,*
> I fell headfirst, and in that fall I woke.[2]

Here is the same carnival logic of self-appointed *elevation,* the communal act of comic *decrowning on the public square,* and a falling *downward.*

3. In Raskolnikov's dream, *space* assumes additional significance in the overall symbol-system of carnival. *Up, down,* the *stairway,* the *threshold,* the *foyer,* the *landing* take on the meaning of a "point" where *crisis,* radical change, an unexpected turn of fate takes place, where decisions are made, where the forbidden line is overstepped, where one is renewed or perishes.

Action in Dostoevsky's works occurs primarily at these "points." The interior spaces of a house or of rooms, spaces distant from the boundaries, that is from the threshold, are almost never used by Dostoevsky, except of course for scenes of scandals and decrownings, when interior space (the drawing room or the hall) becomes a substitute for the public square. Dostoevsky "leaps over" all that is comfortably habitable, well-arranged and stable, all that is far from the threshold, because the life that he portrays does not take place in that sort of space. Dostoevsky was least of all an estate-home-room-apartment-family writer. In comfortably habitable interior space, far from the threshold, people live a biographical life in biographical time: they are born, they pass through childhood and youth, they marry, give birth to children, die. This biographical time Dostoevsky also "leaps over." On the threshold and on the square the only time possible is *crisis time,* in which a *moment* is equal to years, decades, even to a "billion years" (as in **"The Dream of a Ridiculous Man"**).

If we now turn from Raskolnikov's *dream* to what happens in the waking life of the novel, we will be persuaded that the threshold and its substitutes are the fundamental "points" of action in the novel.

First of all, Raskolnikov lives, in essence, on a threshold: his narrow room, a "coffin" (a carnival symbol here) opens directly onto the *landing of the staircase,* and he never locks his door, even when he goes out (that is, his room is unenclosed interior space). In this "coffin" it is impossible to live a biographical life—here one can experience only crisis, make ultimate decisions, die or be reborn (as in the coffins of "Bobok" or the coffin of the Ridiculous Man). Marmeladov's family lives on the threshold as well, in a walk-through room leading directly onto a staircase (here, on the threshold, while bringing home the drunken Marmeladov, Raskolnikov meets the members of the family for the first time). Raskolnikov experiences terrible moments at the threshold of the murdered pawnbroker's when, on the other side of the door, on the stairway landing, her visitors stand and tug at the bell. It is to this place that he returns and himself rings the bell, in order to relive those moments. The scene of his half-confession to Razumikhin takes place on the threshold in the corridor by a lamp, without words, only in glances. On the threshold, near the doors leading to a neighboring apartment, his conversations with Sonya occur (with Svidrigailov eavesdropping on the other side of the door). There is certainly no need to enumerate further all the "acts" that take place on the threshold, near the threshold, or that are permeated with the living sensation of threshold in this novel.

The threshold, the foyer, the corridor, the landing, the stairway, its steps, doors opening onto the stairway, gates to front and back yards, and beyond these, the city: squares, streets, façades, taverns, dens, bridges, gutters. This is the space of the novel. And in fact absolutely nothing here ever loses touch with the threshold, there is no interior of drawing rooms, dining rooms, halls, studios, bedrooms where biographical life unfolds and where events take place in the novels of writers such as Turgenev, Tolstoy, and Goncharov. Of course, we can uncover just such an organization of space in Dostoevsky's other works as well.

Notes

1. A carnivalized sense of Petersburg first appears in Dostoevsky in his novella *A Faint Heart* (1847), and was later powerfully developed, in ways applicable to all of Dostoevsky's early works, in "Petersburg Visions in Verse and Prose."

2. Translation by Paul Schmidt in his *Meyerhold at Work* (Austin: U. of Texas Press, 1980), p. 85.

Pierre R. Hart (essay date spring 1971)

SOURCE: Hart, Pierre R. "Looking over Raskol'nikov's Shoulder: The Narrator in *Crime and Punishment.*" *Criticism* 13, no. 2 (spring 1971): 166-79.

[*In the following essay, Hart argues that Dostoevsky's narrative point of view in* Crime and Punishment *exerts a subtle influence on the reader's interpretation of Raskolnikov's motives.*]

Dostoevskij's continued experimentation with the mode of his narration suggests a concern for form which is frequently ignored. Ranging from the epistolary form of **Poor Folk** to the multi-levelled narrative structure in **The Brothers Karamazov,**[1] his works employ many of the variants of first and third person narration. Because of this diversity, attempts to arrive at a general definition of the narrator's function have not been totally successful.[2] Differences in the distance separating teller and tale would appear to make a consideration of function within the confines of a single work more instructive. In the present essay, I shall attempt to demonstrate the consequences of Dostoevskij's choice of narrative stances in **Crime and Punishment.** Although unobtrusive, the narrator of this novel makes his presence felt through a variety of devices and ultimately has a pronounced effect on our perception of Raskol'nikov and his crime.

On first examination, the overwhelming sense of Raskol'nikov's presence almost totally obscures the existence of an independent narrative voice. For the greater part of the novel, events are viewed from a physical vantage point which coincides with that occupied by the hero. Furthermore, the narrator frequently serves as a neutral transmitter of Raskol'nikov's experiences. Yet the fact that there is an intermediary between fictional character and reader introduces the possibility for independent commentary. Even in those scenes where the focus is firmly fixed on Raskol'nikov, there are occasions when parenthetic remarks, subtle contradictions of the hero's impressions, or unrelated digressions signal the presence of another, active consciousness. Technically, the position enjoyed by the narrator might best be defined as that of "editorial omniscience."[3] From this vantage point, he is able to exert a relatively high degree of control over the narration without detracting from the central importance of Raskol'nikov's personality.

In the process of planning his novel, Dostoevskij expressed particular concern over the point of view to be employed. His choice was conditioned by his explicit desire to present as his hero ". . . an educated man, a man of the new generation."[4] From the notebooks for the novel, it is evident that several approaches were considered before the final selection. Dostoevskij's original intention was to employ the hero as a first person narrator who would relate the story in the form of a confession. Subsequently, he abandoned this plan, stating that ". . . the plot's structure is such, the story must be narrated by the author and not by the hero."[5] In the absence of any thorough explanation for this change, we are obliged to speculate as to its motivation. At several points in his notes on the problem, Dostoevskij stressed the need for "complete frankness," even "naïveté." He may have recognized the difficulty of satisfying this demand with Raskol'nikov cast in the role of narrator.[6] Indeed, it might be argued that the very existence of fictional tension throughout the novel depends upon Raskol'nikov's inability or refusal to analyze his position with complete objectivity, thus disqualifying him as a possible narrator.

The basic model for the narration as it emerged in the completed novel is contained in the immediately following entry: "Narration from the point of view of the author, [a] sort of invisible but omniscient being, who doesn't leave his hero for a moment."[7] In practice, the narrator did not fully comply with this prescription, for the novel's structure required that he part from Raskol'nikov at several points. But even in such instances, his relation to other figures and events is consistent with that established in the sections dealing with the main character.

Despite the shift in the point of view, the work retains a sense of the first person narrative, an effect due to the particular combination of omniscient description and "narrated monologue"[8] employed by the narrator. Within those scenes where Raskol'nikov's impressions are primary, there is a tendency to move from the mere report of the protagonist's observations to a more dramatic form which incorporates some of the features of colloquial speech. As the narration shifts between these modes, the identities of the narrator and Raskol'nikov tend to merge, producing a category of statements that might ultimately be attributed to either of them.[9] In defining the narrator's function, then, we must take into account both the source of a remark and the possible modifications it has undergone in the process of transmission.

One of the narrator's primary functions is to provide information about Raskol'nikov which the hero is either unable or unwilling to admit to himself. As he makes the final arguments for and against his plan to murder, the reader is provided with an independent commentary on the hero's mental condition. Throughout the novel, Raskol'nikov will return to the question of whether he is in full possession of his senses. Seen from the narrator's standpoint, the issue is resolved from the outset: "It would have been difficult to sink to a lower ebb of disorder . . ." and further "This is what happens to *some monomaniacs* [emphasis mine] who are excessively concentrated on one thing."[10] Within the context of this basic analysis, various aspects of Raskol'nikov's behavior can be more readily explained. Transitions between the waking state and dreams, for example, tend to be indistinct and reflect upon the fusion of fact and fantasy in Raskol'nikov's isolated world. In introducing the first of his hero's nightmares, the mare beating scene, the narrator calls attention to the importance of these experiences: "Under the unhealthy conditions, dreams frequently are distinguished by an unusual vividness and an exceptional resemblance to reality . . . Such dreams, sick dreams, are always remembered for a long time and produce a strong impression on the distraught and excited human organism." (59-60) Here it is not simply the abnormal state which is stressed but also, the intensity and persistence of a particular subconscious experience which has important implications for Raskol'nikov's subsequent development.[11]

While stressing Raskol'nikov's psychological malfunctioning, the narrator also implies that his hero merits compassion. Although he obviously cannot condone the experiment in self-cognition that Raskol'nikov undertakes, it may be interpreted as a particularly violent consequence of temporary derangement, a crime committed by a man who otherwise demonstrates his potential for good.

It is through the narrator's commentary on specific overt actions that we most clearly perceive the almost paternalistic concern for Raskol'nikov's welfare. As an omniscient being, observing from beyond the confines of the action, he is effectively restrained from directly influencing his hero's decisions and hence, must address himself to the reader in what would appear to be a mood of frustration and anguish. Immediately following the starkly realistic description of the murders, for example, he momentarily diverts our attention from Raskol'nikov's frantic efforts to escape in order to stress the futility of it all:

> If, at that moment, he had been capable of seeing and judging more correctly; if only he could have envisioned all the difficulties of his position, all the desperation, ugliness, and absurdity of it, if he could have understood how much difficulty and perhaps, even crime, still remained for him to surmount and commit before he could tear himself from this place and make his way home, he might very well have abandoned everything and gone to give himself up, not from fear but simply because of his horror and revulsion at what he had done.
>
> (86-87)

Contrary to all expectation, the murders, as Raskol'nikov must ultimately realize, have not confirmed his theory but rather, produced the very human response of "horror and revulsion." And although he does momentarily experience revulsion, the feeling is quickly lost. It thus remains for the narrator to stress the inescapable reaction and moral judgment of this crime, to assert his function as a normative agent who is responsible for placing the acts in a proper social perspective. Raskol'nikov cannot be allowed to assume the initiative and present his view exclusively for to permit this would be to obscure the sense of transgression.

At moments of greater lucidity, Raskol'nikov may actually attempt to delude himself as to the success of his experiment and it then becomes the narrator's obligation to make the futility of such attempts clear. When pride and self-confidence rather than humility are offered as the means for achieving salvation, the narrator effectively destroys the illusion by the manner in which he reports Raskol'nikov's thoughts: "It suddenly seemed to him, as to a man clutching for a straw that 'he too could live, that there was still life, that his life had not ended with that of the old woman.' Perhaps his conclusion was too hasty but he did not think of that." (198) The hesitant manner in which the narrator concludes his report does less to alter the sense of Raskol'nikov's original thought than does the parenthetic remark "as to a man clutching for a straw." This figure of speech reinforces the impression of a desperate but still unrepentant man, who continues to seek comfort in the very qualities that led to his tragic mistake.

Since salvation can only be attained through personal acknowledgement of error, the narrator must endure the agonizingly slow progress which his hero makes, with-out hope of changing its tempo or direction. Obviously unproductive repetitions in Raskol'nikov's thought and behavior elicit expressions of somewhat impatient concern. Everything which might be offered as a justification for the crime must be evaluated against the store of previous experience. As Raskol'nikov makes one of his first attempts to understand the true motivation for his crime, he is struck by the curious fact that he failed to take the money from the pawnbroker's purse. His immediate reaction is to dismiss this as an oversight due to illness. The narrator's intrusion at this point serves to remind us that the question cannot be so readily resolved: "Yes, that's so, that's all so: But he had known that before and it was not at all a new question for him." (116) To recognize that this is an old question is to place the validity of economic motivation in doubt, something which Raskol'nikov is not yet fully prepared to do. Thus, the narrator can counter Raskol'nikov's arguments rhetorically, but it still remains for the latter to work through the welter of apparent motivations independently.

With regard to external events and objects, the narrator assumes a somewhat different function, providing supplementary detail which is quite compatible with that offered by Raskol'nikov directly. In fact, the initial portrayal of Lužin depends largely upon the narrator's commentary and it is only subsequently that Raskol'nikov makes his own scorn for this figure completely evident. The narrator picks up the epithet "fiancé" (*ženix*), uttered with such vehemence by Raskol'nikov, and uses it as the basis for an elaborate physical description which is thoroughly laced with sarcasm. Petr Petrovič's concern for his attire is, according to the narrator, "completely innocent and permissible" yet the effect is "excessively evident." (152) The word "excessively" (*sliškom*) qualifies every descriptive detail. Furthermore, by the very act of denying certain ludicrous similarities, the narrator implants suggestions of unfavorable comparisons in the reader's consciousness: "Even his hair . . . combed and curled at the barber's, did not produce a ridiculous impression or give him a stupid appearance, as is generally the case with curled hair, which gives the face an inescapable resemblance to that of a German awaiting his wedding." (153)

Additional encounters with Lužin as the novel progresses provide the narrator with the opportunity to probe more deeply into the man's character, exposing his basest qualities and preparing us for the final scandal which will completely discredit both the man and his philosophy. During the decisive meeting attended by Dunja, Raskol'nikov and Lužin, the narrator establishes an independent vantage point by describing a seating arrangement which suggests that he is no longer situated immediately behind his hero. The greater physical distance separating the narrator from Raskol'nikov makes it plausible to attribute the judgment of Lužin to the narrator alone: "In general, Petr Petrovič belonged to that class of people which is superficially very polite in society and which particularly pretends to amiability but which, at the slightest provocation, loses all composure and becomes more like sacks of flour than lively and nonchalant men of society." (307) During the ensuing argument, Lužin proves the accuracy of this observation by his behavior. Were Lužin's vanity merely an innocuous idiosyncrasy, it might be dismissed without further consideration but there is much in his doctrine of enlightened self-interest which smacks of Raskol'nikov's own ideas.[12] The narrator thus continues his attack, albeit more directly, in the scene concerning Sonja's alleged theft of money from Lužin. At the scene's beginning, the reader has no clue as to Lužin's planting of the note on her. Only the narrator and Lebezjatnikov know the whole truth of the matter and, for the moment, the general impression of Sonja's guilt is allowed to persist. Lužin's response to the bewildered girl's predicament is singled out in the narrator's description: "Petr Petrovič at any rate was at once moved to *compassion*." (narrator's emphasis) By deliberately stressing the sympathy professed by Lužin, the terrible hypocrisy of his gesture becomes the more evident when we finally learn of his implication in the affair.

Equally harsh initial judgment is passed on Lebezjatnikov although he is at least partially redeemed by his exposure of Lužin. Lebezjatnikov is subjected to merciless attack as the epitome of the unthinking "joiner" of liberal causes. Without really understanding the issues in question, he is inclined to express himself through stock slogans and behavior:

> Despite all these qualities, [the narrator is here referring to his good points] Andrej Semenovič really was stupid. He had become attached to progress and to "our younger generation" passionately. He was one of that numerous and varied legion of vulgarians (*pošljaki*), of half-animate miscarriages (*nedonoski*), of petty, half-educated tyrants (*samodury*), who immediately subscribe to the most fashionable current idea, only to vulgarize it and to instantly caricature everything that they serve in the most sincere fashion.
>
> (378)

In terms of the total structure, this obtrusive criticism scarcely seems justified. Through it, the narrator attracts attention to his own notions without appreciably contributing to the sub-plot which involves Lebezjatnikov. And because the characterization depends almost totally upon the narrator's description, Lebezjatnikov stands apart from the remaining characters who are assessed jointly by the narrator and Raskol'nikov.

At several points throughout the novel similar instances occur in which narrative commentary, at least partially out of context, suggests preoccupation with problems lying beyond the scope of the finished novel.

Raskol'nikov's first encounter with Marmeladov in the tavern provides one example for which an explanation is apparent. There is a clear distinction in this scene between Raskol'nikov's reaction to Marmeladov's grandiloquent confession and that of the narrator. Somewhat overwhelmed initially, Raskol'nikov quickly assumes that ". . . usual unpleasant and irritated feeling of aversion for any stranger who approached or even wanted to approach him." (15) But the narrator, rather than dismissing Marmeladov's loquaciousness, remarks on it specifically and attempts to provide a social-psychological explanation for the man's behavior: "This habit becomes a necessity for some drinkers, and especially for those who are treated strictly and ordered about at home. Thus, in the company of other drinkers, they always seem to try to justify themselves and, if possible, to even gain respect." (17) To a certain degree, this analysis provides us with some insight into the relationship existing between Marmeladov and Katerina Ivanovna. But it is questionable whether domestic conditions have done more than aggravate qualities inherent in Marmeladov. From the stress placed upon alcoholism, it would seem that the narrator's remarks were left-overs from the novel as Dostoevskij had originally conceived it: "My work is to be called **The Drunkards** and will be tied in with the current issue of drunkenness. Not only is the problem of drunkenness analyzed but all its conditions, etc. etc."[13] By contrast, there is no attempt to speculate on prostitution as a social problem although there is a suggestion of the narrator's attitude toward it. Sonja's first appearance is accompanied by a description which contains only one allusion to the propriety of her position: "She was also in rags; her attire was cheap, but adorned, street fashion, according to the taste and rules of her own particular world, for an obvious and shameful (*pozorno*) purpose." (192) Throughout the remainder of the description, what might be construed as moral disapprobation is really an attempt to stress the incongruity of the girl's appearance at her father's deathbed, e. g. the "impropriety" of her light dress with its ridiculous train, the parasol which serves no purpose at night, and the "absurd" straw hat. Raskol'nikov does not catch sight of Sonja until a little later and hence, these impressions can only be attributed to the narrator.

A final example of the narrator's independent judgment of social phenomena is provided by the occasion of the funeral dinner at the Marmeladov's. Raskol'nikov never indicates any regret for having given the last of his money to Katerina Ivanovna for the funeral but the narrator makes his own criticism quite explicit, terming the dinner a "senseless" one, upon which ten rubles have been "wasted." (393) These observations provide the starting point for the narrator's exposition of the psychology of the poor: "These paroxysms of pride and vanity are sometimes inflicted upon the poorest and most crushed persons and may become an irritating, irresistable necessity." (393-94) Yet the generalization does not totally apply to Katerina Ivanova for, in the very next sentence, we learn that "she, above all, is not one of the crushed." (394) Economic circumstances, plus the intense mental strain seem to account for her behavior.

Although the narrator may criticize particular actions, he does demonstrate considerable sympathy for the poor, especially when comparisons with the wealthy are involved. The coachman and policemen at the scene of Marmeladov's accident are treated with a touch of dry sarcasm. From their point of view, it would appear that the accident is not so much of a human tragedy as it is an inconvenience: "The coachman, however, was not very distressed and frightened. It was evident that the carriage belonged to some rich and important person who was awaiting its arrival somewhere; the police, of course, were somewhat concerned with disposing of this incident." (184) The narrator's "of course" (*konečno*) indicates ironic appreciation of the policeman's primary concern for factors other than Marmeladov's injuries. The hero of the moment is Raskol'nikov and the narrator accords him due recognition for his efficient supervision of the injured man's treatment. He even hastens to justify the money which Raskol'nikov gives to one of the police, apparently anxious that this gesture not be misconstrued as a common bribe. "He even managed to slip something unnoticed into the policeman's hand. It was, however, straightforward and legitimate, and, in any case, help was closer here." (185)

At times, the narrator even singles out those features among his impoverished characters which impart a sort of elegance to them. Together with Razumixin,[14] he comments upon the ability of Dunja and her mother to make a virtue out of necessity: "Her gloves were not only worn but had holes in them, as Razumixin noticed, but nevertheless, this obvious poverty of dress lent a particular air of dignity, which is always the case with those who know how to wear poor clothes." (223)

As several of the foregoing examples would suggest, the narrator does not restrict himself to mere repetition or elaboration upon Raskol'nikov's observations. His independence of judgment functions both to complement and to temper his hero's more impulsive impressions. Reflecting upon the substance of his final conversation with Svidrigailov, Raskol'nikov is disgusted that Svidrigailov had contaminated his ideologically pure crime by suggesting that it might be deserving of the same end as his own amoral crimes i.e., the perpetrator might "run off to America." He rejects Svidrigailov as a "coarse villain, a voluptuous debaucher and a scoundrel." (508) Raskol'nikov's aversion is quite probably dictated by his growing sense of self-preservation; the proposition of suicide prompts him to dismiss Svid-

rigailov as totally corrupt. It remains for the narrator to provide the more objective evaluation, to remind the reader of Svidrigailov's own duality and of the fascination which derives from it: "Actually, Raskol'nikov had made his judgment too hastily and thoughtlessly. There was something about Svidrigailov that gave him a certain originality, or even mystery." (508)

Similarly, the narrator has formulated his own opinion about Sonja. It is he rather than Raskol'nikov who notes the expression of "*insatiable* compassion" (narrator's emphases) on Sonja's face during the first meeting. At this point, the narrator wishes to make explicit the fact that Raskol'nikov is unable to understand the impulses that motivate Sonja's behavior. To him, she is simply a "holy fool." The conclusions that he draws as to her ultimate fate, namely, suicide, the madhouse, or complete depravity, are those appropriate to his own particular mental state: ". . . but he was already a sceptic, he was young and given to abstraction and therefore cruel. For that reason, he could not help believing that the last alternative, depravity, was the most likely." (336) This conjecture is almost immediately replaced by the notion of her madness, but what is significant is that he continues to consider only the desperate alternatives which have haunted him personally.

At times, the details introduced by the narrator are of a factual nature, specifically intended to correct erroneous impressions created through a character's immediate perception. Superficially, this might appear to be "factography" of the sort to which Grossman refers. But the fact itself may be of no importance to the story but rather, introduced for the purpose of substantiating observations previously made about the person whose view is being challenged. Katerina Ivanovna, for example, is prone to distort the social and economic status of those she meets: ". . . sometimes it even became embarrassing, for she invented various circumstances to his [i.e., a new acquaintance's] credit that simply did not exist, believing in their reality herself with all sincerity . . ." (394) When the list of lodgers who have been invited to the dinner in memory of her husband is reviewed, it is discovered that the "fat lieutenant colonel" is absent. This bit of miscellaneous information might be allowed to pass unchallenged. But the narrator inserts parenthetically the fact that he is a retired officer of considerably lower rank (*štabs-kapitan*). This revelation accentuates the self-deception that Katerina Ivanova has practiced without disrupting the illusion in her own mind.

A second instance in which such "corrective detail" is provided by the narrator occurs during Raskol'nikov's second visit to Porfirij Petrovič. The latter remarks on his suspect's "justifiably witty" observation that interrogations may be more confusing for the interrogator than for the interrogated. The narrator hastens to disavow

Porfirij's statement: "(Raskol'nikov had made no such observation.)" (350) Through his intervention, the narrator draws attention to the technique that Porfirij employs in his investigation: the continual bombardment of his suspect with a stream of remarks which may or may not be relevant, but which probe Raskol'nikov's defenses. Both here and at other points in the interview, the narrator's observations underscore Raskol'nikov's indignation and impatience with such tactics. But at the same time, the narrator conveys his suspicions of an ulterior motive concealed by these seemingly maladroit remarks. This is evident at the outset of the conversation when Porfirij's repeated references to his government quarters as "a capital thing" (*slavnaja vešč'*) prompt the narrator to observe: "This stupid repetition . . . contradicted, in its banality, the serious, thoughtful, and enigmatic gaze that he directed at his guest." (347)

The two examples of "corrective detail" cited above share a feature common to both characters and narrator throughout the work—that of the parenthetic remark. When used by the latter, it serves a variety of purposes and places the narrator in different relationships to his characters and reader. In the scene involving Katerina Ivanovna, the general tonality makes it apparent that the passage is to be construed as a rough transcription of her thoughts and impressions for there are sarcastic asides on some of the lodgers. Viewed in this context, the disclosure of the lieutenant colonel's real rank must be considered as one purposely directed from the plane of action at the reader. In the case of Raskol'nikov's conversation with Porfirij Petrovič, the parenthetic remark is again in an alien context, being inserted into the investigator's speech. The comment is not only distinguished mechanically by parentheses; it is separated stylistically by its directness from the circumlocutions which characterize Porfirij Petrovič's speech. Whether the narrator of Raskol'nikov should be designated as the source is difficult to determine. Certainly the latter would be capable of reacting in such fashion for he was constantly to guard against being trapped into confession and a mental note of this kind would indicate the effort he is making to stay alert. But regardless of the possible confusion of consciousnesses in attributing this thought, it differs from the first example in direction. While there can be no question that the inserted remark on Katerina Ivanovna is intended solely for the reader, the second is an unvoiced rebuttal to Porfirij Petrovič's statement and hence, more closely integrated in the action. One can imagine Raskol'nikov crying out, "I never said such a thing." It would be impossible, on the other hand, to imagine anyone denying Katerina Ivanovna the reality of her lieutenant colonel.

The parenthetic remark may also be used to establish one of several moods in the course of a conversation. During Raskol'nikov's second visit to Sonja, he at-

tempts to rationalize the motivation for his crime. Before he can complete his explanation, the narrator interjects: "(He spoke as though he had learned it in advance.)" (434) The immediate implication is that Raskol'nikov no longer has faith in his ideas nor does he really expect Sonja to believe him. The speech becomes a sort of involuntary purge rather than a sincere confession and, in a second parenthetic remark, the narrator offers a possible explanation for this unexpected garrulousness: "(Really, he had been too long without talking with anyone!)" (436)

Finally, the parenthetic remark may serve as a variant of the stressed phrase that is, the narrator may give added emphasis to a word or phrase by repeating it as an aside, within parentheses. On his first visit to the police station, Raskol'nikov excuses his eccentric behavior with the explanation that: "I am a poor student, sick and depressed (that's what he said, 'depressed') by poverty." (107) The narrator's added emphasis calls attention to the fact that Raskol'nikov, through the use of such emotionally loaded terms, is attempting to arouse his listeners' sympathy. That the narrator does not approve of this tactic is evident from his subsequent observation: "If he had cared to think a little, he would, of course, have been amazed that he had been able to speak with them like that in such manner a moment ago and had even forced his feelings upon them." (109) Raskol'nikov's conscious recognition of this lapse follows almost immediately.

The foregoing analysis offers evidence to refute the contention that: "In *Crime and Punishment,* the author is so little in evidence that the ordinary reader is not conscious of his presence."[15] Some of the difficulty in distinguishing his contribution may derive from confusion of voices which occurs as thoughts are transmitted in various manners. It is also true that the narrator does not emerge as a distinctive personality with a unique style that will identify him, except by default, from the characters. Nonetheless, he makes his impact felt through the numerous functions he performs.

He is the inventory keeper for Raskol'nikov's experience and calls attention to the errors, repetitions, and ill-advised judgments that he makes. Through his active role as commentator, he provides a point of reference external to Raskol'nikov, with which his hero's perception of the world can be compared. While Raskol'nikov's story is unquestionably the focal point of the novel, his perception of the story is not. By maintaining his perceptual initiative, the narrator prevents the novel from becoming a clinical study in psychology.

The narrator is also essential as the sole bridge between certain events and characters. It is through him alone that Lebezjatnikov's character and significance in the novel are understood. And he is the only witness to the greater part of Svidrigailov's final, fantastic night.

The means for achieving these purposes are frequently quite unspectacular. Parenthetic remarks may interrupt a stream of thought or dialogue to introduce a necessary "correction factor." Individual words may be emphasized, either to strengthen the character's case or to suggest other interpretations on the narrator's part. Thus the narrator adds his own dimension to the novel and contributes significantly to the portrayal of "a member of the new generation."

Notes

1. For an account of the latter, see Robert Belknap, *The Structure of "The Brothers Karamazov"* (The Hague, 1967), pp. 77-105.

2. Previous attempts to reach a general definition of the narrator's function in Dostoevskij's fiction have yielded conflicting results. Among Soviet literary critics, the analyses of Leonid Grossman and Mixail Baxtin might be cited as examples of the diversity of opinion. Grossman, in his article "Dostoevskij-xudožnik" in *Tvorčestvo Dostoevskogo* (Moscow, 1959), pp. 330-416, emphasizes the journalistic practice that the author utilized to establish a basis in everyday reality for the more fantastic elements of his narration. The narrator thus remains independent of the characters and events portrayed. "In his system of composition, there was a principle of objective information for the reader, of reportage or authorial direction, that is, of short inserted factographic elucidations of the tangled web of life's relationships." (p. 354)

Baxtin, on the other hand, disputes the notion of authorial omniscience, reserving for the characters the opportunity to make discoveries about their own lives. The author-narrator is conceived on the same plane as his heroes. Thus, in his *Problemy poetiki Dostoevskogo* (Moscow, 1963), he maintains that had Dostoevskij written Tolstoj's *Three Deaths,* he would have, as narrator, participated on an equal footing with his characters: "The entire work would have been constructed like a great dialogue and the author would have entered as the organizer and participant in this dialogue and would not have left the final word for himself, that is, he would have expressed in his work the 'dialogical' nature of human life and human thought." (p. 98) An interesting compromise, specifically relating to the narrator's role in *Crime and Punishment,* is developed by Ja. O. Zundelovič in *Romany Dostoevskogo* (Taškent, 1963). He perceives the author-narrator as a guiding force in the novel, determined to control Raskol'nikov's freedom of development: "Thus, Dostoevskij also infuses the 'objective' narration with subjective pathos in his attempts to stay right with his hero, whom he leads from crime to self-punishment with the passionate desire to assert the correctness of his own views." (p. 17) (It should be noted that none of the critics cited above distinguishes between the narrative voice and the author *per se.*)

3. The definition of "editorial omniscience" as one position in a symmetrical structure of possible points of view may be found in Norman Friedman, "Point of View in Fiction: The Development of a Critical Concept," *PMLA,* LXX (Dec. 1955), 1171.

4. *The Notebooks for* Crime and Punishment *by Fyodor Dostoevsky,* ed. and trans. Edward Wasiolek (Chicago, 1967), p. 173.

5. *The Notebooks,* p. 54.

6. In his introduction to *The Notebooks,* Wasiolek makes some of the same points with respect to the possible reasons for Dostoevskij's rejection of the first person narrator for *Crime and Punishment.* (p. 9) There was the danger that the author's desired sense of immediacy would be lost in disjointed introspection at the hands of the hero as Dostoevskij conceived him.

7. *The Notebooks,* p. 53.

8. Dorrit Cohn, "Narrated Monologue: Definition of a Fictional Style," *Comparative Literature,* XVIII (1966), 98, defines this concept in the following manner: "The rendering of a character's thoughts in his own idiom, while maintaining the third person form of narration." Several critics have remarked upon this feature in Dostoevskij's works without extensively studying it. Zundelovič, p. 13, terms it "partially direct speech" (*nesobstvenno prjamaja reč'*) with exclamation points, repetition and colloquial phrases producing a sense of the character's impressions in passages which cannot be categorized as being either direct or indirect speech. V. I. Etov, "Priemy psixologičeskogo analiza v romane *Prestuplenie i nakazanie,*" *Vestnik moskovskogo universiteta,* serija X, filologija (1967), No. 3, 7, describes Dostoevskij's technique as a "mixed form," with the hero's story being "veiled" by the author's narration.

9. Zundelovič, p. 14, goes so far as to state: "It's as though the author were transformed into his hero and they were speaking in unison."

10. F. M. Dostoevskij, *Sobranie sočinenij* (Moscow, 1957), V, 32. All subsequent quotations from *Crime and Punishment* are taken from this edition. Numbers in parentheses following quotations indicate the appropriate pages.

11. See W. D. Snodgrass, "Crime for Punishment: the Mare-Beating Episode," Crime and Punishment

and the Critics, ed. Edward Wasiolek (Belmont, California, 1961), pp. 90-98.

12. Ironically, Raskol'nikov is quite able to predict the ultimate consequence of Lužin's theory and anticipates the objection which Porfirij Petrovič will raise to his own notion of the "great man." Of Lužin's theory he remarks: "It follows that people's throats may be slit." (159) Porfirij Petrovič is to ask him: "Do they [the great men] begin executing people?" (271)

13. Letter written by Dostoevskij to A. A. Krajevskij, June 8, 1865, included in "Dostoevskij—Selections from the Letters," Crime and Punishment *and the Critics,* p. 3.

14. Here we are provided with a particularly good example of how the modes of narration can overlap and obscure the identity of the source. The first portion of the sentence is clearly a case of indirect speech, where the second, beginning with the words "but nevertheless . . ." might either be construed as narrated monologue or independent narrator observation, while the final portion, beginning with the words "which is always . . ." is a generalization which can be attributed readily to the narrator.

15. Joseph Warren Beach, *The Twentieth Century Novel* (New York, 1932), p. 155.

Marina Turkevich Naumann (essay date spring 1972)

SOURCE: Naumann, Marina Turkevich. "Raskol'nikov's Shadow: Porfirij Petrovič." *Slavic and East European Journal* 16, no. 1 (spring 1972): 42-54.

[*In the following essay, Naumann demonstrates how Dostoevsky employs the character of the magistrate, Porfirij Petrovič, to reveal Raskolnikov's motives for committing murder, as well as his complex feelings of guilt and remorse.*]

Porfirij Petrovič, the examining magistrate in *Crime and Punishment* is a crucial figure.[1] Although his part in the novel comes late (Part 3) and is comparatively brief (sixty pages), it is central. With boundless energy he ubiquitously shadows Raskol'nikov.[2] His ceaseless attention to detail and shrewd interrogations reveal the hero's intellect, psyche, and faith. Porfirij solves the mystery of Raskol'nikov's crime and, most important, helps the criminal through his torment of guilt and confession toward his new life with Christ.

Dostoevskij depicts Porfirij in great detail. In only four sentences he draws the following portrait:

He was a man of about thirty-five, of not quite medium height, corpulent and even paunchy, clean-shaven, with no mustache or sideburns, with closely cropped hair on a large round head which bulged out rather peculiarly at the back. He had a chubby, round, and somewhat snub-nosed face of a sickly dark yellow color but rather hearty and even mocking. It would have been even good-natured but for the expression of his eyes, which had a sort of watery glint in them and were covered with almost white, blinking eyelashes, which seemed to be winking at someone. The expression of those eyes was strangely out of keeping with his whole figure, which even had something of an old peasant woman about it and invested it with something much more serious than one would have expected at first sight.

(p. 259)[3]

Like Oblomov, Porfirij is introduced to the reader clad in a dressing gown (*xalat*) and a pair of comfortable old slippers. However, it is not a question of *xalatnost'* here. Porfirij is hardly a man of negligent inaction.

Porfirij is a hypochondriac. Throughout the novel he complains about his aches and pains. He grumbles about a hangover from Razumixin's party and says that he "somehow became unstrung" (p. 265). Yet he boasts that he does not drink. In fact Porfirij is one of the few figures in the novel who is not a drinker.[4] In another scene Porfirij frets about his "confounded laughter" (p. 349), which causes him to shake for half an hour at a time. This, he says, is very bad for a man of his nervous disposition. He fears that he might have a stroke. Then he continues about his haemorrhoids: "But you see, walking is simply indispensable for me. I'm always sitting down, and I'm glad to walk about for five minutes or so. Haemorrhoids, you know. I keep planning to take up gymnastics as a cure."[5] Later, Porfirij laments his cigarette smoking.

Now take these cigarettes. . . . Harm, pure harm, and yet I can't give them up. I'm always coughing, there's a rasping feeling in my throat, I'm short of breath. I'm a coward, you know. I went the other day to Botkin—he spends a half hour minimum examining each patient. He just laughed when he looked at me. He sounded me and listened to my chest. "Incidentally," he says to me, "tobacco is no good for you; your lungs are affected." But how can I give it up? What's there to take its place? I don't drink. That's the whole trouble, ha, ha, ha: I don't drink. Everything is relative after all, Rodion Romanyě; everything is relative.

(467-68)

Even Porfirij's doctor seems not to take Porfirij's ailments very seriously.

Porfirij's eyes are his most expressive feature. Although they are out of harmony with his figure, they are in keeping with the examining magistrate's vocation and profession. During Porfirij's meetings with Raskol'nikov, these strange liquid eyes seem to play with those of the suspect. They disturb Raskol'nikov. They screw up, glance down, squint, and roll; they also are capable of ignoring, discerning, and perceiving. They even wink at Raskol'nikov. Significantly, when the two men part for the last time Porfirij's eyes appear to avoid Raskol'nikov (p. 482).

The examining magistrate is a relative of Razumixin, but he is the only major character in *Crime and Punishment* without a family name. The notebooks suggest that Dostoevskij had difficulty choosing a patronymic for him.[6] In the early parts of the completed novel (e.g., pp. 157, 220) he is simply Porfirij; only later in the work does he become Porfirij Petrovič. Dostoevskij's choice of names for his characters is more than chance, and Porfirij Petrovič's name is no exception. Porfirij's given name is derived from the Greek word meaning purple and is thus descriptive of someone magisterial. *Porfir* 'porphyry' is a rather common hard mineral. Since *Petr-* also suggests rock, the tautology may be taken to be an allusion to the rock covering the incriminating clues uncovered by Porfirij Petrovič. More tenuously, I might suggest that Porfirij's role as the cornerstone of justice is also being symbolized. The absence of a family name lends weight to this allegorical interpretation.[7]

Dostoevskij once wrote that in *Crime and Punishment* he wanted to "rummage through all the contemporary issues."[8] Many of these timely issues are reflected in the portrayal of Porfirij. The prime current issue was crime, which had long been of interest to Dostoevskij. Vjačeslav Ivanov has even suggested that crime is at the bottom of all of Dostoevskij's novels.[9] In the criminal events reported in the newspapers of his day, Dostoevskij found justification for the subject of his novel.[10] Ernest J. Simmons notes that Dostoevskij was particularly fascinated with criminal psychology and studied criminal and legal procedure. In the portrayal of Porfirij and his successful handling of Raskol'nikov's case Dostoevskij's expertise is patent: at no point does Porfirij make the wrong move either legally or otherwise. According to Simmons, the notebooks show that Dostoevskij carefully checked the details of Porfirij's moves. For instance, Dostoevskij annotated the direction "They place him [Raskol'nikov] under surveillance" with a reminder to check the legality of this action: "Is it possible to do this?"[11]

A related contemporary event reflected in the depiction of Porfirij is the Russian judicial reform of 20 November 1864, which established in the Ministry of Justice the tenured position of examining magistrate.[12] Porfirij's relation to the Reform is clear in Dostoevskij's notebooks (p. 167): "It's true that Porfirij is proud, but he has talent, and he'll make an (excellent) inspector. Now with the Reform we need practical people like him." In the novel Porfirij mentions the Reform to Raskol'nikov:

"There's the Reform, and we will be renamed at least in our title, ha, ha ha!" (p. 350).

The Reform also provided for a new concept of justice, wherein the punishment was concerned not only with civil and social order but with the ethical and moral position of the criminal.[13] The Reform considered the personality of the criminal, his character, ethics, psychology, and the circumstances which caused him to commit the crime. The magistrate's task was to uncover this extenuating evidence. His interrogation could establish that a man technically responsible for the incriminating facts might not be completely responsible for the crime. The old theory that the punishment was to match the crime was replaced. The Reform now decreed that punishment by pain and deprivation would not rehabilitate the man.[14] The criminal had to be treated as a broken human who needed help and hope. Thus it is natural that Porfirij is not only occupied with solving Raskol'nikov's crime, but is interested in giving Raskol'nikov a chance to recover as a complete man. It is in this context that Porfirij may be considered as Dostoevskij's embodiment of the new justice.

Criminology was not an infrequent theme of belles lettres in Dostoevskij's day. When Victor Hugo's novel *Les Misérables* appeared in 1862, Dostoevskij read it and praised it highly.[15] This *roman policier* preceded Dostoevskij's novel by only four years. In Hugo's novel, as in E. T. A. Hoffmann's tale *Das Fraulein von Scudéry* (1819) and Balzac's *Le Père Goriot* (1834), the inspector plays a significant role. And Dostoevskij, an admirer of these masters,[16] was influenced by the colorful figures of Javert, La Reynie, and Vautrin.[17]

La Reynie is a Satanic figure. He performs his state duties with ferocity. He was

> betrayed by his blind zeal into acts of cruelty and terrorism. The tribunal acquired the character of an Inquisition; the most trifling suspicion was sufficient cause for strict incarceration; and it was left to chance to establish the innocence of a person accused of a capital crime. Moreover, La Reynie was hideous in appearance, and malicious by temperament, so that he aroused the hatred, alike of those whose avenger or protector he was appointed to be. The Duchesse de Bouillon being asked by him during her trial if she had seen the Devil, replied, "It seems to me, I see him this very moment."[18]

Monsieur Vautrin is more akin to Porfirij Petrovič. He is an eloquent type endowed with the curious mixture of dandyism, buffoonery, premature age, and omniscience that Porfirij displays. Balzac's description recalls Porfirij:

> He was the kind of man generally known as a "jolly fellow." He had broad shoulders, a well-developed chest, and thick square hands strongly marked on the fingers with tufts of bright red hair. His face was lined

with premature wrinkles, and showed signs of hardness, contradicted with his soft insinuating manners. His low pitched voice, in harmony with his noisy mirth, was not disagreeable. He was cheerful and obliging. . . . He seemed to be familiar with everything; with vessels, the sea, France and foreign countries, with men, business events, laws, hotels and prisons. . . . Like a stern judge, his eye seemed to probe all questions, thoughts and consciences.[19]

But Hugo's Inspector Javert seems to be Porfirij's most direct literary ancestor. Hugo's realistic description of Javert in part anticipates Dostoevskij's image of snub-nosed Porfirij:

> His human face consisted of a stub-nose, with two enormous nostrils, toward which enormous whiskers mounted on his cheeks. You felt uncomfortable the first time that you saw these two forests and these two caverns. When Javert laughed, which was rare and terrible, his thin lips parted, and displayed, not only his teeth, but his gums, and a savage flat curl formed around his nose, such as is seen on the muzzle of a wild beast. Javert when serious was a bull-dog; when he laughed he was a tiger. To sum up, he had but little skull and plenty of jaw; his hair hid his forehead and fell over his brows; he had between his eyes a central and permanent frown, like a star of anger, an obscure glance, a pinched-up and formidable mouth, and an air of ferocious command.[20]

There are other striking similarities. Most important is that, like Javert, Porfirij is first and foremost a state official who is intent on apprehending a criminal. In their final scenes the parallel between them is striking. Both characters in the deep mercy which they feel toward their criminals reveal for the first time their true humanity. Their inner voices speak out and they free their felons from the pursuit. By this act, however, they bring their missions to an end. Suddenly both Javert and Porfirij become drooped and bent over. Both die, Javert literally and Porfirij figuratively.

Porfirij Petrovič thus bears the unmistakable imprint of other nineteenth-century sleuths.[21] However, he is a more positive figure. He is not Satanic and ugly like La Reynie, nor is he sinister like the ex-convict Vautrin. He is a kinder and more developed Inspector Javert. Porfirij is better able to meld his duty to society with his duty to the individual.

Mention must be made of still another contemporary topic which influenced the depiction of Porfirij Petrovič. In 1865 Louis Napoleon of France published his *Histoire de Jules César*. In the introduction the author theorized on the role and the rights of extraordinary people.[22] The treatise was translated into Russian and had considerable impact in Russian literary circles.[23] Dostoevskij's interest in the Napoleonic idea is suggested in the "calligraphic exercise" found in the notebooks for *Crime and Punishment*: "Napoleon, Julius

Caesar and Rachel."[24] There are echoes of Louis Napoleon's thesis in Raskol'nikov's conversations with Porfirij,[25] and Porfirij's criticism of Raskol'nikov's theory (271-72), as Polonskaja notes (p. 583), appears to be based in part on an article published in *Sovremennik* in early 1865 which was sharply critical of Louis Napoleon's treatise.

The role of Porfirij did not emerge spontaneously for Dostoevskij. Originally Dostoevskij had planned to write a novel on the prevalent social question of drunkenness (*Pis'ma*, I, 408). However, as he wrote, the problems of Raskol'nikov's crime and punishment began to attract him more. In 1865 he wrote to his editor Katkov:

> Although crimes like this are terribly difficult to carry out . . . Raskol'nikov by pure accident manages to carry out his undertaking both quickly and successfully. . . . No suspicion falls or can fall on him. It is at this point that the whole psychological development of the crime unfolds. Insoluble problems confront the murderer; unsuspected and unlooked-for emotions torment his heart. Heavenly truth and earthly law claim their rights, and he ends by being *compelled* to denounce himself. Compelled so that, even at the cost of rotting in prison, he may be reunited with mankind; the feeling he experienced of being cut off and isolated from mankind as soon as the crime was committed has been torture to him. The criminal decides that he must accept suffering in order to atone for his deed. But I find it difficult to explain my idea fully.
>
> (*Pis'ma*, I, 417-18)

Dostoevskij's intention to depict Raskol'nikov's transgression and moral punishment is clear. However, the letter indicates that Dostoevskij was having difficulty. The confession form was too confining for this story, and he needed a device, a character, which would help to "explain [his] idea fully." In February 1866 Dostoevskij wrote: "A new shape, a new plan attracted me and I made a fresh start" (*Pis'ma*, I, 430). The new plan was the narrative form, while the new shape, I wish to propose, was Porfirij Petrovič. Interestingly, Porfirij is practically absent in the first drafts of *Crime and Punishment* when the story is told in the first person. He is briefly mentioned in the second notebook, while the third notebook shows Dostoevskij struggling with the characterization. In these early notebooks Porfirij is not as confident an examiner as he later emerges. In the final version of the novel Porfirij possesses the omniscient and ubiquitous traits which are properly only those of an author. Although Porfirij tells Raskol'nikov that he has learned everything from him, this is not always the case. Porfirij often knows more than what legal or human channels will afford. For example, Porfirij has an enigmatic explanation for how he searched Raskol'nikov's quarters: "What do you think: that I wasn't at your place searching? I was, I was, ha, ha, ha, I was, when you were lying sick right here in your little bed. Not officially and not in my own person, but I was. Your room was examined to the last hair. . . ." (p. 472.) Further, Porfirij is "by chance" (p. 268) familiar with Raskol'nikov's initialed article "On Crime," and inexplicably knows about the pawnbroker's clients, about Raskol'nikov's fever, and about Raskol'nikov's part in the Marmeladov tragedy.

As a central figure, or, as Blackmur suggests, an agency of the plot, Porfirij sets the wheels of the action of the novel in motion.[26] In a series of tense dialogues Porfirij compels Raskol'nikov to express his ideas, his psychology, and his glimmerings of faith. He questions and guides the student's thoughts to the point where the hero can understand the gravity of his crime, can voluntarily confess to it, and accept suffering. The magistrate and criminal meet three times.[27] Twice Raskol'nikov goes to Porfirij, once to his apartment and once to his office. The third meeting is Porfirij's surprise call on Raskol'nikov in the garret. Their conversations take place on three levels: the ideological, the psychological, and the religious.[28]

On the ideological plane Porifirij knows more about Raskol'nikov's theories than Raskol'nikov himself. He is aware that Raskol'nikov's initialed article "On Crime" has already been published. He is interested in it and forces Raskol'nikov to restate his theory and to elaborate on it. Fully aware of the flaws in Raskol'nikov's superman thesis, Porfirij checks Raskol'nikov's logic and pursues the implications of the thesis. He raises some cogent questions, proceeding from the general to the particular. His choice questions are: "How are we to distinguish these extraordinary people from the ordinary?" (p. 271); "Are there many such people—these 'extraordinary' ones—who have the right to kill other people?" (p. 272); "When you were writing this article of yours, it just, hee, hee, couldn't be that you didn't consider yourself also just a wee bit of an 'extraordinary' man, with a some *new word* to say. . . . Isn't that so?" (p. 275); "Might not you yourself have decided . . . to step over an obstacle? I mean, for example, to commit murder and robbery?" (p. 275); and lastly: ". . . that's the whole point: walking down the stairs that time—just let me ask: you were there shortly after seven, weren't you?" (p. 277). At no point does Raskol'nikov technically fall into Porfirij's trap and admit that he is the criminal. On the other hand, he knows that Porfirij has matched his intellectual powers and has all of the facts in hand.

Porfirij has not only forced Raskol'nikov to elaborate on his theory. He has made him consider the question of moral punishment. Raskol'nikov has to admit that the extraordinary, as well as the ordinary, will have a punishment of pain and suffering on top of penal servitude. He admits that essentially there can be no perfect transgression and therefore no superman.

Raskol'nikov's theory, as Baxtin notes,[29] loses its completeness. Porfirij has demonstrated to Raskol'nikov that his theory has a contradictory complexity, and he is satisfied. He knows that he has his criminal and that he has brought him to the threshold of admitting his guilt. At the succeeding encounters Porfirij continues to anatomize Raskol'nikov's theory and his crime. He takes him through the painful admission that his theory is unoriginal and intellectually worthless, and he concludes that Raskol'nikov himself does not believe it any more (p. 481).

According to Porfirij, psychology also has its place in juridical examinations. At their first meeting Porfirij analyzes Raskol'nikov's theory on "the psychology of the criminal during the whole course of the crime" (p. 268). In so doing he demonstrates that he is perhaps a better psychologist than the young author, and this Raskol'nikov readily admits (to Razumixin, p. 279). At the second rencontre, which follows the first by merely a day, Porfirij is no longer interested in Raskol'nikov's ideas on psychology: he is interested in Raskol'nikov himself. He toys with Raskol'nikov's nerves, taunting him and luring him. He tugs at the hero psychologically until he drives him into dangerous agitation, causing him to talk too much. Raskol'nikov's awareness of this makes the situation all the more painful. He realizes that this is not the cat-and-mouse game of their first meeting, but that it is a moth-and-candle situation. Raskol'nikov has committed the perfect crime and is proud of it. Porfirij knows that Raskol'nikov wants to take credit for his achievement, partly out of pride, partly from an aching conscience. The irony is that in revealing his feat Raskol'nikov renders his achievement imperfect. Further, Porfirij is cognizant of the fact that Raskol'nikov cannot live with this guilty conscience, as he had predicted in his article "On Crime." Thus Porfirij jumps again from the irrelevant to the relevant, from the general to the particular, from the theoretical to the practical, echoing all of Raskol'nikov's theories. Raskol'nikov is driven into a frenzy. He begs Porfirij to stop psychologizing and to let him know if he is free from suspicion. If he is suspect, he implores Porfirij to cross-examine him properly or arrest him. But Porfirij wants Raskol'nikov to comprehend fully the gravity of his transgression. For this reason he will not give Raskol'nikov's conscience the consolation of certainty.

Unlike the first meeting, the jocular atmosphere of the second meeting is set by Porfirij, not by Raskol'nikov. Porfirij's psychologizing is accompanied by his distracting and nerve-wracking physical motion. Porfirij's perpetual laughter, his chortling, his winking and blinking, and the rolling to and fro of his rotund figure bring the agitated student to the point of hysteria. Raskol'nikov is driven to a nervous attack and needs air (357-58). The unexpected visit of Mikolka and his surprising confession to Raskol'nikov's crime bring only momentary relief. Porfirij continues to play his game of torture. He notes that he will still have to examine the student and enigmatically bids him farewell: "If God brings us together then we will see each other very, very much. And once and for all we will get to know each other (*Esli Bog privedet, tak i očen' i očen' uvidimsja-s. I okončatel'no poznaem drug druga*)." (p. 368)

At their final meeting Porfirij maintains his psychological pitch even more artfully. He begins by telling Raskol'nikov that he regrets the torture of their previous encounters. The implication is that he considers Raskol'nikov innocent. This tactic is the most refined form of torment. It agonizes Raskol'nikov, who knows better.[30] In addition to his physical activity, the magistrate now interjects key words into his banter such as "axes," "open doors," "hag's skulls," "Napoleon," and "bells."[31] The repetition of these incriminating words push the hero even closer to madness, for he knows that Porfirij has the essential details of the crime. Finally by toying with the word *stone* (p. 472) Porfirij reveals that he has the incriminating clues to arrest Raskol'nikov. Porfirij continues with a play on words: "And do you know that he [Mikolka] is an Old Believer (*iz raskol'nikov*), and not an Old Believer (*iz raskol'nikov*) even, but a member of some sect" (p. 474). Understandably, Raskol'nikov shudders at hearing the presumed murderer referred to with a word which is homophonous with his last name. This anticipates by two pages the direct accusation: "Why you are the murderer, Rodion Romanyč" (p. 476). But Porfirij will not give Raskol'nikov the consolation of being arrested. He will let him remain free until he confesses on his own.

Having led his young friend through an intellectual and psychological transformation, Porfirij now tries to help Raskol'nikov find God and Christ. Porfirij appears as quietly as a mouse at the lodgings of the now mentally distraught Raskol'nikov for their third and final encounter. They are completely alone, like confessor and confessant. Porfirij appears to be humane, gentle, and compassionate. Here it is necessary to recall Porfirij's first conversation with Raskol'nikov, when he casually questioned Raskol'nikov on his faith in God:

> "So you do believe in the New Jerusalem?"
>
> "I do," Raskol'nikov replied firmly; as he said this and all through his long tirade he kept his eyes lowered, fixed on one spot on the carpet.
>
> "And do you believe in God? I'm sorry to be so curious."
>
> "I do," Raskol'nikov repeated, raising his eyes to Porfirij.
>
> "And do you believe in the resurrection of Lazarus?"
>
> "I do. Why do you need to know all this?"
>
> "Literally?"
>
> "Literally."
>
> (p. 271)

In this important exchange Porfirij learns that Raskol'nikov is not an empty spiritual shell, not a lost soul like Lužin or Svidrigajlov. Raskol'nikov is aware of the Christian resurrection. Porfirij now knows that there is hope for this sinner; he has the potential of being saved and of being reunited with the world from which he has become estranged. Significantly, Raskol'nikov reacts immediately to Porfirij's probing. He immediately goes to Sonja and asks her to find the passage about Lazarus and read it to him (337-38). Porfirij-Justice thus joins Sof'ja-Divine Wisdom (the Church) in rescuing the transgressor, Raskol'nikov.

At their second and third meetings Porfirij appeals more and more to Raskol'nikov's latent Christian beliefs in an effort to rehabilitate him. Despite Raskol'nikov's deep hatred for the magistrate, the latter reminds Raskol'nikov that he "truly loves [him] and sincerely wishes him well" (p. 361). Midway through their final meeting while discussing Mikolka Porfirij shows the importance of suffering and of repentance (474-75). He forces Raskol'nikov to apply his own theories of suffering to himself. Porfirij, like Sonja, has faith in the young criminal and believes that in the end he will accept suffering. At the point where Porfirij speaks of Raskol'nikov's need to repent, suffer, and start life anew, the image of air is introduced: Porfirij claims that all Raskol'nikov needs is air.[32] Complaining repeatedly about the stuffiness, he opens windows to refresh the hero. When Porfirij parts with Raskol'nikov he says: "Going for a walk? Looks like a fine evening, just as long as there is no storm. But then it would be better, if it would freshen things." (p. 481) The magistrate is speaking of Raskol'nikov's catharsis and of his resurrection. Here the storm symbolizes his purification through suffering and repentance.

Porfirij leaves Raskol'nikov "stooping somehow and as if avoiding looking at Raskol'nikov" (p. 482). Why is he stooped and why does he avoid looking at his young friend?[33] Perhaps the father confessor is himself weighed down by a burden. The burden is the question: Has he been successful in saving Raskol'nikov? and will he choose the right path, the path of suffering and repentance? For Porfirij is fully aware of still another path, Svidrigajlov's path: suicide.[34] Profirij therefore cautions: "If by chance—I'm saying this just in case—you should want in the next forty or fifty hours to put an end to the matter differently, in some fantastic way, to lay hands on yourself (the idea is nonsense but then you will forgive me for it), leave me a brief but detailed note. . . . Well, good-bye. Kind thoughts and blessed undertakings!" (481-82). Raskol'nikov in the end accepts Porfirij's parting words. Porfirij has indeed helped to save the young criminal from himself. With his guidance and Sonja's love, Raskol'nikov confesses and accepts suffering. He seeks the fresh air of Siberia and is carried right out onto the shore, just as Porfirij had predicted (p. 479).

And what becomes of Porfirij? At the end the once vibrant magistrate appears to have aged. His hypochrondria and resemblance to the old peasant woman are only a surface reflection of a possibly greater change. At their last meeting Porfirij says to Raskol'nikov: "Who am I? I'm a finished (*pokončennyj*) man, nothing more. A man who perhaps feels and sympathizes, who perhaps even knows a thing or two, but who is absolutely finished." (p. 480) Porfirij says earlier: "I'm a single man, you know, not a man of the world, an obscure man, and in addition a finished (*zakončennyj*) man, a stiff man, I've gone to seed" (p. 349). He has used all of his faculties and has transferred all of his zest for life to the more needy and promising youth. He has helped Raskol'nikov through the trauma of transgression and has shown him the way to "heavenly truth and earthly law" (*Pis'ma*, I, 417-18). Porfirij is the seed that once dead[35] produces much new fruit, a new man. This anticipates the epigraph of **The Brothers Karamazov**: "Verily, verily, I say unto you, except a corn of wheat fall into the ground and die, it abideth alone: but if it die it bringeth forth much fruit."

To summarize: Porfirij Petrovič's role in **Crime and Punishment** is central. Despite his many idiosyncrasies, he carries the authority of examining magistrate in the mid-nineteenth-century Russian judicial system. Porfirij shadows Raskol'nikov through a stifling and cramping (p. 465) St. Petersburg. He penetrates into the recesses of Raskol'nikov's intellect, psyche, and heart. He exposes both external and spiritual facets of the hero and is thus the mirror, or perhaps better, the shadow (*sledovatel'*) of Raskol'nikov himself. Finally, having led the young Raskol'nikov out of the darkness of St. Petersburg into the fresh sunlit air of Siberia, Porfirij Petrovič, as Raskol'nikov's shadow, grows shorter and finally disappears.

Notes

1. I wish to thank the Reverend Professor Georges Florovsky of Princeton University for originally suggesting this study to me and for his many helpful ideas.

2. The English translation of *sudebnyj sledovatel'* is examining magistrate or inspector. Unfortunately the translation does not convey the sense of the word *sledovatel'* which also suggests the action of following (*sledovat'*) or shadowing. This nuance is particularly relevant to this study; Porfirij does indeed shadow Raskol'nikov.

3. F. M. Dostoevskij, *Sobranie sočinenij* (10 vols.; M.: GIXL, 1956-58), V. Volume and page references in the text are to this edition. The translations are based in part on F. M. Dostoevsky, *Crime and Punishment*, trans. by D. Magarshack (Harmondsworth, England: Penguin Books, 1951).

4. Porfirij was not a character in Dostoevskij's drafts for *P'janen'kie*. His "attribute" echoes the earlier drinking theme, however.

5. Page 350. At the time that Dostoevskij was writing *Crime and Punishment* he was suffering from epileptic fits and, like Porfirij, from haemorrhoids. He wrote on 19 February 1866 that he had been suffering from haemorrhoids for a month. F. M. Dostoevskij, *Pis'ma*, 4 vols., ed. A. S. Dolinin (M., L. 1928-59), I, 431; Jessie Coulson, *Dostoevsky: A Self Portrait* (New York: Oxford Univ. Press, 1962), 144.

6. In *The Notebooks* he is called either simply Porfirij or Porfirij Ivanovič (p. 96), Porfirij Filipič (p. 167), Porfirij Stepanyč (p. 164), Inspector Semënov (p. 169), Porfirij Semënyč (202), Porfirij Petrovič (202). *The Notebooks for Crime and Punishment*, ed. and trans. E. Wasiolek (Chicago: Univ. of Chicago Press, 1967); *Iz arxiva F. M. Dostoevskogo, Prestuplenie i nakazanie: Neizdannye materialy*, ed. I. I. Glivenko, (M., L.) 1931).

7. Neljudov, a surname which suggests "not of people" is the examining magistrate in *The Brothers Karamazov*. See note 27 for a short analysis of this character.

8. "Primečanija," V, 578.

9. Vjačeslav Ivanov, *Freedom and The Tragic Life* (New York: Noonday Press, 1959), 7-22. Dostoevskij's novelistic and publicistic works are proof of this interest.

10. In 1865 Dostoevskij wrote: "Our papers are full of stories which show the general feeling of instability which leads young men to commit terrible crimes . . . (there is the case of the theological student who killed a girl he had met in a shed by appointment and who was arrested at breakfast an hour later, and so on). In short, I am quite sure that the subject of my novel is justified, to some extent at any rate, by the events that are happening in life today." *Pis'ma*, I, 418.

11. Ernest J. Simmons, *Dostoevsky: The Making of a Novelist* (New York: Vintage Books, 1940), 168.

12. *Enciklopedičeskij slovar'*, XXX, ed. K. K. Arsen'ev (SPb.: Brokgauz-Èfron, 1900), 456.

13. I am indebted for this interpretation to Georges Florovsky.

14. Father Zosima in *The Brothers Karamazov* elaborates on this problem when he states the Church's view that the criminal must be regenerated, reformed, and saved (IX, 82-83). Dmitrij Karamazov's lawyer also stresses this point when he tells the jury: "It is not for an insignificant person like me to remind you that Russian justice is not merely punishment but also the salvation of the lost one! Let other nations have punishment and the letter of the law. We will have the spirit and

the meaning, the salvation and the rebirth of the lost." (X, 305.)

15. Donald Fanger, *Dostoevsky and Romantic Realism* (Chicago: Univ. of Chicago Press, 1967), 190. In April 1877 Dostoevskij wrote: "I myself like *Les Misérables* very much. It appeared at the time that my own *Crime and Punishment* appeared. . . . The late F. I. Tjutčev, our great poet, and many others at the time thought that *Crime and Punishment* was incomparably higher than *Les Misérables*. But I argued and proved to everyone that *Les Misérables* was higher than my poem, and I argued sincerely, from my whole heart. I am sure of this even now in spite of the general opinion of all of our experts." *Pis'ma*, III, 264. Quoted by V. Šklovskij, *Za i protiv: Zametki o Dostoevskom* (M.: Sovetskij pisatel', 1957), 181.

16. The influence of Hoffmann, Balzac, and Hugo upon Dostoevskij is indisputable. See G. I. Čulkov, *Kak rabotal Dostoevskij* (M.: Sovetskij pisatel', 1939), 144-45. A letter written by Dostoevskij on 9 October 1838 points to his early interest in these authors (Coulson, 10-11). Dostoevskij's library contained the complete works of Balzac and Hugo, the French translation of Hoffmann's *Tales,* Voltaire's *Zadig* and Eugene Sue's *Les Mystères de Paris*; Leonid Grossman, *Seminarij po Dostoevskomu* (M.: Gosizdat, 1922), 43. The great influence of *Les Misérables* on Dostoevskij is considered by Grossman in *Poètika Dostoevskogo* (M.: Gos. Akad. xudožestvennyx nauk, 1925), 47.

17. In his analysis of *Das Fraulein von Scudéry* Charles Passage notes: "Both of these representatives of the law [La Reynie, the President of the special Court of Justice, and Lieutenant Desgrais] are kept more or less in the background of the story . . . yet here are ready-at-hand models for Porfirij Petrovič and the explosive Lieutenant Zamjotov in *Crime and Punishment*. Porfiry Petrovich is, of course, far more important a character than La Renyie and much more carefully delineated." *Dostoevsky the Adapter: A Study in Dostoevsky's Use of the Tales of Hoffmann* (Chapel Hill: Univ. of North Carolina Press, 1954), 145.

18. E. T. A. Hoffmann, *Tales of Hoffmann*, ed. Charles Lazare (New York: A. A. Wyn, 1946), 46.

19. Honoré de Balzac, *Le Père Goriot,* trans. Jane Sedgwick (New York: Rinehart and Co., 1950), 16.

20. Victor Hugo, *Les Misérables,* trans. Lascelles Wraxall (New York: Heritage Press, 1938), 168.

21. Other possible spiritual ancestors of Porfirij are no doubt Voltaire's *Zadig,* and Edgar Allen Poe's C. Auguste Du Pin, the detective in "The Mystery of Marie Roget" and "The Murders in the Rue Morgue." Fanger (p. 190) mentions Dickens' Inspector Becket as a possible forebear. Probably Sue's *Les Mystères* and Ponson Du Terrail's series *Rocambole* were an influence as well. I could find no substantial evidence that Porfirij influenced the depiction of Sherlock Holmes.

22. Napoleon III, *History of Julius Caesar,* 2 vols. (New York: Harper and Bros., 1866), I, ix-xv.

23. Fanger, 188-89; F. I. Evnin, "Roman Prestuplenie i nakazanie," *Tvorčestvo F. M. Dostoevskogo,* (M.: AN SSSR, 1959), 153-57.

24. Fanger, 188. Rachel is Elizabeth Rachel Félix (1821-58), a noted French tragedian, who was the mistress of Louis Napoleon. Bernard Falk, *Rachel the Immortal* (London: Hutchinson & Co., 1935), 179-204.

25. V. V. Danilov in "K voprosu o kompozicionnyx priemax v Prestuplenii i nakazanii Dostoevskogo," *Izvestija AN SSSR, Otd. obščestvennyx nauk,* 1933, No. 3, discusses the effect of Louis Napoleon on Raskol'nikov's theories. The "world-historical personage" concept developed by Hegel in *The Philosophy of History* is an important influence. Balzac's *Le Père Goriot* also contributed to Raskol'nikov's thesis.

26. R. P. Blackmur, *Eleven Essays in the European Novel* (New York: Harcourt, Brace & World, 1964), 128.

27. In *The Brothers Karamazov* (Part 3, Book IX) Dostoevskij's other examining magistrate, Nikolaj Parfenovič Neljudov takes Dmitrij Karamazov also through three ordeals. Dostoevskij has subdivided the first chapters of the "Preliminary Investigation" into chapters with a definite religious connotation: "Xoždenie duši po mytarstvam: mytarstvo pervoe," "Mytarstvo vtoroe," and "Tret'e mytarstvo." Although Neljudov is neither a central character nor a fully delineated magistrate in *The Brothers Karamazov,* he does echo Porfirij. His peculiar laugh, his warm, almost sympathetic manner, his incisive interrogating, his adroitness in catching his "criminal" on trifles, and lastly his participation in his hero's religious trials are but a few of the qualities which recall Porfirij.

28. Note the following analyses of Porfirij's conversations with Raskol'nikov: M. Baring, *Landmarks in Russian Literature* (London: Methuen and Co., 1960), 122; Leonid Grossman, *Tvorčestvo Dostoevskogo* (Sobr. soč., 2; M.: Sovremennye problemy, 1928), 7-8; Julius Meier-Graefe, *Dostoevsky: The Man and His Work* (New York: Harcourt, Brace & Co., 1928), 120-25; K. Mochulsky, *Dos-*

toevsky: His Life and Work, trans. M. Minihan (Princeton, N.J.: Princeton Univ. Press, 1967), 303-11.

29. M. M. Baxtin, *Problemy poètiki Dostoevskogo* (M.: Sovetskij pisatel', 1963), 118.

30. This incident directly echoes a scene in *Les Misérables,* I, 200-07. Inspector Javert informs Monsieur Madeleine (Jean Valjean) that a lowly man has confessed to the crime that Javert knows that Madeleine has committed. He thus implies that Madeleine is free from his pursuit. However, it is clear that Madeleine is trapped by Javert. He will be unable to endure this false freedom.

31. In the passage in question, there are many occurrences of words suggesting "bell": *Mikolka* (6 ×), *kolokol'čik* (4 ×), *kolokol'ni,* and *Raskol'nikov* (3 ×).

32. Neljudov likewise keeps offering Dmitrij Karamazov water (IX, 568).

33. This passage echoes the following final description of Inspector Javert in *Les Misérables:* "Javert retired slowly from the Rue de l'Homme Armé. He walked with drooping head for the first time in his life, and, equally for the first time in his life, with his hands behind his back. Up to that day Javert had only assumed, of Napoleon's two attitudes, the one which expresses resolution, the arms folded on the chest; the one indicating uncertainty, the arms behind the back was unknown to him. Now a change had taken place, and his whole person, slow and somber, was stamped with anxiety. He buried himself in the silent streets, but followed a certain direction; he went by the shortest road to the Seine. . . .

"Javert leaned his elbows on the parapet, his chin on his hand, and while his hands mechanically closed on his thick whiskers, he reflected. A novelty, a revolution, a catastrophe had just taken place within him, and he must examine into it. Javert was suffering horribly, and for some hours past Javert had ceased to be simple. He was troubled; this brain, so limpid in its blindness, had lost its transparency, and there was a cloud in his crystal. Javert felt in his conscience that duty was doubled, and he could not hide the fact from himself. When he met Jean Valjean so unexpectedly on the Seine bank, he had something within him of the wolf that recaptures his prey and the dog that finds its master again. . . .

"One thing had astonished him—that Jean Valjean had shown him mercy: and one thing had petrified him—that he, Javert, had shown mercy to Jean Valjean." (Vol. V, Book 5, 147-48.)

34. In one draft of the novel Raskol'nikov shoots himself. *The Notebooks,* 243.

35. Porfirij dies only figuratively. He does not appear again in the action of the novel. In the epilogue, the reader is told that Porfirij attended Razumixin's marriage to Dunja. Perhaps here too Porfirij represents "the heavenly truth and earthly law" mentioned in Dostoevskij's letter to Katkov.

J. Thomas Shaw (lecture date December 1972)

SOURCE: Shaw, J. Thomas. "Raskol'nikov's Dreams." *Slavic and East European Journal* 17, no. 2 (summer 1973): 131-45.

[*In the following essay, originally delivered as a lecture in 1972, Shaw analyzes Dostoevsky's use of dreams as a means of elucidating the central themes of* Crime and Punishment.]

It is often suggested that in the novel, and indeed in imaginative literature, nothing is "real" except what is experienced by the reader.[1] Raskol'nikov's dreams are central to the development of theme and action in **Crime and Punishment,** and they are as sharp, clear, vivid, and sensuously "present" as anything else in the novel. The novel presents five of Raskol'nikov's experiential dreams.[2] Two of them precede the murder; two follow it and precede his confession to the police, which terminates the novel proper; and one occurs in the Epilogue. Each of these dreams has its own particular quality. At the same time they fall into definite groups: the two preceding the murder are different in important ways from the two after it, and all four dreams in the novel proper are quite different from the dream in the Epilogue. This paper will examine all these dreams, which seem never to have been examined in juxtaposition with each other, particularly with regard to the vividness of the mode of presentation. It will conclude by considering the function of these dreams in the development of theme and in the structure of the novel. The function of the epilogue in fiction will also be treated.

In the novel, words for "dream" are used in two basically different senses. One is what I referred to above as the experiential dream, which is experienced, when one is asleep or half-awake, as a sequence of sensuously perceived actions and impressions. The usual word in Russian for this type of dream is *son,* which may also mean "sleep." Raskol'nikov's dreams called by the term *son* are described as sick, morbid (*boleznennyj*), or horrible (*strašnyj*), basically identifying them with the other word mainly used in the novel for experiential dreams, *greza* (plural *grezy*), a word which can mean "daydreams" or "feverish dreams," whether or not the word "feverish" is used in a particular instance. The word *son* tends to be used for a dream dreamed once. However, this word in the plural and also the usual word for "daydreams," *grezy,* are both used for Raskol'nikov's final dream in the Epilogue, and both are equated with *bred* 'delirium.'[3] A third noun for "dream" is also used in the novel, with a different application. It is *mečta,* which can be used as a general word for an experiential dream; it may also be used in the figurative sense for wish or desire, as in Martin Luther King's "I have a dream . . . ," whether or not sensory details or sequence is given. In *Crime and Punishment* the word *mečta* is used only in the figurative sense: with regard to Raskol'nikov's "dream" that he may embody his own theory of the extraordinary man to whom all is permitted. We may anticipate by saying that "dreams" in one sense are used as a measure of "dream" in another: each instance of *son* or *greza* marks a failure as regards his *mečta.*

Before looking at Raskol'nikov's dreams I should perhaps say a few words about Dostoevskij as fictional craftsman and about some of the particularities of Russian grammar relevant to vivid narrative. Twentieth-century studies of Dostoevskij are showing more and more how conscious a craftsman he was, how intensively and how successfully he worked at the art of his novels. His notebooks to *Crime and Punishment* show how much he was concerned with the problems of narrative technique, of the narrator and narrating in this novel. He had done considerable work on the novel before he decided on the omniscient narrator technique which makes Raskol'nikov's consciousness available to us through the prism of the narrator's.[4] At the same time, flashes of Raskol'nikov's consciousness can be presented to us through the device of *erlebte Rede*—primarily, indirect speech—and with special vividness in Russian, in that indirect speech (and indirect consciousness, which uses the same grammar) is presented in the tense of direct speech.[5] The third-person, past-tense narration in *Crime and Punishment* is the product of an omniscient narrator who is aware, not only of the conscious but of the subconscious, and not only of events presented within the novel itself but of those before and after it, whether or not they are ever portrayed within the bounds of the work. Thus the gradual resurrection or regeneration of Raskol'nikov, of which we are told in the Epilogue, is in the past tense of the narration as given by the narrator, is known by him before the novel begins, and is as much a "given" in the novel as anything else in it.[6]

It should be noted with regard to the past-tense narration of the novel that the historical present is available in Russian and indeed is much more prevalent in Russian usage than it is in English. However, in *Crime and Punishment* I have found no example of the historical present. The only narrator's passages in the present tense are those giving generalized observations of one kind or another. One such passage is the novel's concluding paragraph concerning Raskol'nikov *after* the

novel and the Epilogue: "But that is the beginning of a new story—the story of the gradual renewal of a man, the story of his gradual regeneration, of his passing from one world into another and learning a new, heretofore unknown reality. That might be the subject of a new story, but our present story is at an end." (472; V, 574)

The two instances in the entire novel of narration in the present tense occur in the first two dreams. In each case the narrator tells us it is a dream, and then the narrative shifts to the present tense of reported speech. In context we know the dream is a dream, and we know, in that it is embedded in past-tense narration, that events after this event are known to the narrator, though not as yet to the reader. However, the effect of the present-tense presentation in these two dreams is that they are the most vivid passages in the entire novel. The second of these dreams is short enough that it can be quoted here in its entirety. In the passage I have preserved the tenses of the Russian.

> He kept having daydreams (*emu vsë grezilos'*), and the daydreams (*grezy*) were so strange: in the most frequent one, he saw himself in Africa, in Egypt, in some sort of oasis. The caravan is resting, the camels are peacefully lying down; the palms are growing all around in a complete circle; everyone is having dinner. But he keeps drinking water, right out of a stream which is right next to him, flowing and gurgling. And it is so cool, and the wonderful, wonderful blue water, which is cold, runs over the varicolored stones and such clean glittering sand . . .

The passage has a sensuous immediacy which in the Russian is augmented in a completely natural manner by the use of the present tense. This recurring dream represents Raskol'nikov's vivid quasi-consciousness just before he goes out to commit the murder. Dreaming this dream almost prevents him from carrying out the crime by causing him to arrive at the scene late; he almost overdreamed the occasion. And the use here of the vivid present tense gives the impression, albeit temporarily, that the action of the novel has become somehow a present-tense action, that what has already happened, according to the narrator's past tense of narration, may not happen at all. This is perhaps the high point of suspense in a novel in which there is much, and continuing, use of suspense.

Raskol'nikov's second dream, as presented, occupies only some dozen lines or 100 words and may be considered as, in a sense, paralleled by many other instances of indirect speech or *erlebte Rede* utilizing the present tense and hence adding briefly its vividness to that of a briefly dramatized second consciousness. The most vivid sustained passage in the entire novel from the point of view of narrative technique is found in Raskol'nikov's first experiential dream, which ends only some half-dozen pages before the second dream. Again, the vividness comes from—or at least is augmented by—the sustained use of the present tense. The entire passage is relatively long, five and a half pages or about 2,200 words. It begins with the narrator's generalizations on dreams, which as generalizations are of course in the present tense:

> In a morbid condition of the mind, dreams often have a singular actuality, vividness, and an extraordinary semblance of reality. At times the picture which takes shape is monstrous, but the setting and the entire representation as it develops are at the same time so plausible, filled with details so fine, so unexpected, but so artistically consistent with the whole picture that the dreamer himself could never have invented them in the waking state, even if he were a Puškin or a Turgenev. Such dreams, sick dreams, always remain long in the memory and make a powerful impression on a human organism which is disturbed and already excited.

The dream begins in the narrator's words and in his past tense, with an interesting ambiguity as to whether his consciousness of Raskol'nikov at the time of dreaming is not simultaneously also Raskol'nikov's.

> Raskol'nikov had a fearful dream. He dreamt he was back in his childhood in their little town. He is about seven years old and is taking a walk in the country on a holiday toward evening. It is getting gray, the day is sultry, the countryside is exactly as he remembered it; in fact his memory of it is much more blurred than the image of it in his dream.

It is unclear whether Raskol'nikov is aware that his dream is more vivid than memory; indeed it is never made clear whether this dream is of an actual or imaginary event in the past.[7] Continuing, the passage describes the tavern "which had always aroused in him a most unpleasant impression," where there was "always" a crowd, and past which he and his father always had to go in order to visit the graves of his grandmother and his dead brother. The narrator next utilizes the technique of indirect speech for reported consciousness, shifting to the present tense for narration.

> And now he dreams: he is going with his father down the road to the graveyard and they pass the tavern; he is holding his father's hand and looking with fear at the tavern. . . . Near the tavern entrance stands a cart, but it's a strange cart. It is one of those big carts to which they hitch big draft horses, and they haul commodities and wine casks in them. He has always liked to look at these enormous draft horses. . . . But now—how strange—such a big cart and they have hitched up a thin little peasant's sorrel plug horse, one of the ones—he has often seen it—which sometimes strain with a high load of firewood or hay, especially when the cart gets stuck in the mud or in a rut, and then get painfully, oh so painfully beaten with knouts, sometimes right on the muzzle and eyes, and he feels so sorry, so very sorry looking at this that he almost cries, and mama has always led him away from the window.

So far, it will be seen that the situation dreamed of is presented in the context of similar experiences. Indeed, the specific event of the dream is anticipated in the generalized statement of the way peasants painfully beat their horses "right on the muzzle and eyes." After this much initial generalizing, the remainder of the dream is presented in one-time vivid present-tense narration of the killing of the horse by the peasant Mikolka and of the child Raskol'nikov's reactions. The vividness of the dream in its detailed sequential occurrences and in the experiences anticipates the murder itself.

> "Fetch an axe to her! Finish her off," shouts a third.
>
> "I'll show you! Stand off," Mikolka screams frantically; he throws down the shaft, reaches into the cart again and pulls out an iron crowbar. "Look out," he shouts and with all his might he stuns his poor little horse. The blow has fallen; the little mare has staggered, has sunk back, has tried to pull, but the crowbar comes down hard on her back again, and she falls on the ground. . . .
>
> But the poor boy is beside himself. He makes his way screaming through the crowd to the sorrel plug horse, puts his arms around its bleeding dead muzzle and kisses it, kisses the eyes, the lips . . . Then suddenly he jumps up and in a frenzy throws himself with his little fists at Mikolka. . . . He tries to draw a breath, to cry out, and he wakes up.
>
> He woke up all in a sweat, with hair wet with sweat, panting, and he sat up in horror.

Here we see that, though the form of the dream is that of something remembered—in which case the result would have been known—in presentation it is of a dynamic present tense in which the outcome is as it were unknown to the participant, and indeed to the narrator, until we have in double form "he wakes up" and "he woke up." (In contrast, the scene of the actual murder is presented in the "epic calm" of the third person of the narrator:

> There was not another moment to lose. He took the axe out all the way, swung it with both hands, scarcely conscious of himself, and almost without effort, almost mechanically, brought it down on her head blunt side first. It was as though there was no strength of his in this. But as soon as he had once brought the axe down, his strength returned to him. . . . The blow fell on the very top of her head, which was possible because of her short stature. She cried out, but very faintly, and suddenly collapsed to the floor, although she still managed to raise both hands to her head.
>
> [68-69; V, 83]

The details—there are many, many more—are quite vivid, but the narrator's use of the past tense assumes that both the completion of the event and the consequences are known.)

We hardly need go further into detail about the sensuous vividness of Raskol'nikov's first dream. Visual particulars are given in what Tolstoj was later to call "superfluous detail." We, as well as Raskol'nikov, hear the peasants speak and call to each other and Raskol'nikov speak to his father. We hear the thud of the cart shaft and crowbar on the head of the animal. We share the tactile impression of the blows rained on the mare and of Raskol'nikov's kissing the eyes and lips of the animal.[8] Raskol'nikov reacts to the dream as definitely as to any other experience in the novel:

> His whole body was as though broken. . . .
>
> "Good God," he cried, "can it be, can it be that I will really take an axe, start hitting her on the head, bash her skull in . . . that I will slip in the sticky warm blood, break the lock, steal, and tremble; hide, all spattered with blood . . . with the axe . . ."

He concludes for the moment that he could not bear it (*ne vyterplju*), could not bring himself to do it (*ne rešus'*), and he specifically relates this experiential dream (*son*) to his figurative dream (*mečta*): "'Lord,' he prayed, 'show me my path, and I renounce this accursed . . . dream (*mečta*) of mine!'"

Raskol'nikov's third and fourth dreams, both subsequent to the murder, are each so presented that neither the reader nor Raskol'nikov is conscious that it is a dream until it is over—although the reader and Raskol'nikov both may experience uncertainty concerning the actual moment the dream concludes, i.e., when it finally becomes clear that a dream has occurred. The third dream takes up about a page, some 400 words. I shall give a part of it. It is in the narrator's past tense.

> It was already toward evening when he came home, so that he must have walked a total of about six hours. What route he took on the way back he did not remember at all. Undressed and quivering all over like an over-driven horse, he lay down on the sofa, pulled his overcoat over him, and immediately dropped off . . .
>
> At dusk he was awakened by a terrible scream. Good God, what a scream! Such unnatural sounds, such howling, wailing, gnashing, tears, beating, and cursing he had never yet heard or seen. He could not imagine such brutality, such frenzy. In terror he sat up in his bed, almost fainting with agony all the while. But the fighting, wailing, and cursing grew louder and louder. And then to his great amazement he caught the voice of his landlady. She was howling, shrieking, and wailing, rapidly, hurriedly emitting words which could not be made out, pleading for something—no doubt, not to be beaten, for she was being mercilessly beaten up on the stairs. The voice of her assailant had become so horrible from spite and rage that it was no more than a hoarse croak, but nevertheless he was also saying something, and it was also quickly and indistinctly, hurrying and sputtering. All at once Raskol'nikov trembled like a leaf; he recognized that voice; it was the voice of Il'ja Petrovič. . . . "But why, why . . . and how can this be?" he repeated, seriously thinking that he had gone mad. But no, he hears it too distinctly! . . . Indeed, they will come to him next, if that's it, "because . . . surely it's all on account of . . . of yesterday's . . . Lord!"

This third dream, in its sensations, stands out from the others in that it consists almost entirely of sounds: shouting, beating, exclaiming, disputing, whispering. The reality of the experience of the dream for both Raskol'nikov and the reader is on the same plane as that of the "real events" of the novel. Indeed, there is no clear indication of the moment when he wakes up: "Raskol'nikov fell worn out on the sofa, but he was not able to close his eyes. He lay for half an hour with such suffering, such an intolerable sensation of infinite terror as he had never experienced before. Suddenly a bright light lit up his room." The servant Nastasja comes in. She is finally able to convince Raskol'nikov that "nobody has been beating the landlady," and she has her peasant diagnosis of his illusion: "No one has been here. That's your blood crying out. When it has no outlet and begins to clot up inside, you start imagining things" (the verb is *mereščit'sja*, familiar for "fancying, dreaming"). Raskol'nikov imagines in this dream that the police are beating up his landlady, while he trembles in fear that they are on the way to get him. The narrator's image, immediately before the dream, of Raskol'nikov's "quivering all over like an over-driven horse" connects the dream with the first dream of the novel and also suggests that the recipients of punishment of the first and third dreams are both in some sense himself. (In the early draft of this scene, written while Dostoevskij was casting the novel in the form of a first-person narrative, Raskol'nikov speaks of an "overdriven horse which I saw in childhood.")

Raskol'nikov's fourth and last dream within the novel proper is placed in a climactic position, at the very end of Part 3, where it balances the presentation of the murder itself at the end of Part 1. He has already revisited the scene of the crime and on the way back has been accosted by a man who calls him a murderer (*ubivec*, substandard for *ubijca*); he has also reached the conclusion that he has "killed a principle, not the old woman," and that he would "kill her again if she came back to life." This fourth dream is of an attempt to "kill her again."

> He lost consciousness; it seemed strange to him that he did not remember how he managed to get (*mog očutit'sja*) to the street. It was late evening. It was getting dark and the full moon was shining brighter and brighter, but the air was somehow especially sultry. The streets were crowded with people; workmen and businessmen were making their way home; other people were out walking; there was the smell of mortar, dust, and stagnant water.

Like the third dream, the fourth is presented as narrative on the same plane of reality as the "real events" of the novel. This one, however, concentrates on sight rather than sound; as in the preceding passage, it can include other impressions, even smell. Even more than the third dream, the presentation of the fourth moves in and out of *erlebte Rede,* so that Raskol'nikov's momentary reactions are given from his perspective, though the whole event is narrated in the third person.[9] He dreams he is following the man who had earlier called him a murderer.

> There's the window on the second floor; mournfully and mysteriously the moonlight passed through the panes; and there's the third floor. Hey! This is the apartment where the workmen were painting . . . How was it he hadn't recognized it at once? The steps of the man walking ahead became silent. "He must have stopped or hidden himself somewhere." Here's the fourth floor; should he go farther? And what silence there—it's even frightening . . . But he went on.

This passage is an excellent example of the combination of consciousnesses—Raskol'nikov's and the narrator's—which the technique allows, a paradoxical combination of immediacy and artistic distance. Stillness and moonlight characterize this dream, in contrast to the total focus on sound in Raskol'nikov's third dream.

> The huge, round, bronze moon was looking straight in the window. "This silence is on account of the moon," thought Raskol'nikov; "no doubt it is posing a riddle now." He stood and waited, waited a long time, and the quieter the moon, the louder beat his heart; it even started hurting. And still silence. Suddenly there was a short dry cracking noise, like someone breaking a piece of kindling wood, and all was still again. A startled fly suddenly flew up and struck the window pane and made a plaintive buzz.

The dream of the attempted re-enactment of the murder is like the presentation of the actual murder in the concreteness of detailed presentation.

> At that very moment, in the corner between the small cupboard and the window, he made out something like a cloak hanging on the wall. "Why the cloak?" he thought; "it wasn't here before . . ." He quietly drew nearer and sensed that behind the cloak someone seemed to be hiding. Cautiously he drew back the cloak with his hand and saw that there was a chair there, and on the chair in the corner there sat a little old woman, all doubled up with her head down so that he could not make out the face; but it was she. He stood over her. "She is afraid," he thought; he quietly freed the axe from the loop and hit the old woman on the top of the head, once and then again. But it was strange: she did not even stir, as though she were made of wood. He got scared, bent down nearer, and started to examine her; but she too bent her head lower. Then he bent right down to the floor and looked up into her face, looked and turned cold with horror: the old woman was sitting and laughing—she was shaking with quiet, inaudible laughter, trying very hard to keep him from hearing her. . . . He tried to scream—and woke up.

It is not clear to the reader until the final verb "woke up" that the entire experience has been a dream. Even so, *prosnulsja* (woke up) is anticipated by *esli b očnu-*

las' (if she came back to life) immediately before the start of the dream, which is echoed by *očutit'sja* in the beginning of the dream, when in dream consciousness Raskol'nikov has the impression of being awake.

> He drew a deep breath—but how strange: his dream seemed to continue; his door was wide open and there was a complete stranger standing in the doorway and he was watching him intently. . . . "Is it still a dream (*Son èto prodolžaetsja ili net*)," he wondered. . . .

> Ten minutes passed. It was still light but getting on toward evening. In the room there was complete stillness. Even from the stairs no sound could be heard. There was only the buzzing of a big fly which kept hitting against the windowpane. Finally it became unbearable. Raskol'nikov suddenly sat up on the sofa.

As eerie as the dream is Svidrigajlov's melting out of it, so that Raskol'nikov, aware now that he was dreaming, wonders whether the appearance of this, the last important character to be introduced, is a continuation of the dream. Svidrigajlov is Raskol'nikov's nightmare, and he appears as though out of a nightmare.

To summarize Raskol'nikov's four dreams in the novel proper, each of them is experiential, and three of them are one-time. Raskol'nikov participates directly in each. The first two are given frame presentation, so that the reader is always aware that they are dreams; the third and fourth are presented in the narrator's third person past tense and in the same basic style and detail as the events of the novel proper. Only one of these four dreams—that of the oasis—is said to have been repeated in Raskol'nikov's consciousness; but the nature of the one-time presentation of that dream in the novel is such that it too is experiential for the reader as well as for Raskol'nikov.

Raskol'nikov's final dream in the Epilogue, set in Siberia after he has confessed to the civil authorities that he has committed murder, is quite different. It consists of about 400 words. I shall quote only part of it.

> When he was better he remembered the dreams he had (*svoi sny*) while he was feverish and delirious. He dreamt in his illness that the whole world was condemned to a terrible new strange plague (*morovoj jazve*) that had come to Europe from the depths of Asia. All were to be destroyed except a very few elect ones. There appeared some new sorts of trichinae, microscopic creatures, which were infesting the bodies of men. But these creatures were spirits endowed with intelligence and will. Men attacked by them immediately started raving and went insane. But never, never did men consider themselves so intelligent and so unwavering in the truth as did the infected ones. Never did they consider their decisions, their scientific deductions, their moral convictions and beliefs so unshakable. Whole villages, whole towns and peoples were infected and went insane. . . . Each thought that he alone had the truth. . . . They could not agree on what

to consider evil and what good. . . . Men killed each other in a sort of senseless malice. . . . They began to accuse one another, they fought and killed one another. There were conflagrations and famine. All men and all things were perishing. The plague spread and moved further and further. Only a few men were able to be saved in the whole world. They were the pure, elect people, destined to found a new race and a new life, to renew and purify the earth, but no one had seen these people, no one had heard their words and voices.

Raskol'nikov was tormented (*mučilo*) that this senseless delirium haunted his memory so miserably and so tormentingly, that the impression of these feverish dreams (*gorjačešnyx grez*) persisted so long.

The Epilogue dream is certainly vivid enough in its themes. The dream is Apocalyptic in the strict sense: it is a vision of the general destruction of evil, to be followed by an age in which only the good remain alive. Dostoevskij was fond of the Book of Revelation, and the marginal markings in his copy of the Bible show that he interpreted apocalyptic prophecies of destruction as applying to his own day. Indeed, the image of trichina was of topical currency at the time of writing; the organism had been discovered in 1835, and the clinical characteristics of the acute disease caused by it, in 1860, five years before Dostoevskij began the novel. There was discussion of trichina in the Russian press while **Crime and Punishment** was being written.[10] Sporadic outbreaks of trichinosis were still occurring at the time, suggesting the danger of a "plague from Asia" such as the Asiatic cholera had proved to be when it first appeared in Russia, Europe, and the United States some thirty years before the novel was written.[11] For the modern day, Dostoevskij substitutes "microscopic" trichinae for such a plague of the Book of Revelation as the plague of locusts with "faces like human faces" (Revelation 9: 3-11; cf. the entire passage).[12]

A dream of almost universal destruction with only a few of the elect to survive seems vivid enough. Curiously, however, it is experientially much less vivid than any other of Raskol'nikov's dreams. Its presentation lacks their sensuous immediacy. The explanation obviously is that Raskol'nikov is not a participant in this dream as he is in the others. The reader receives the details of the dream in summary form rather than experiencing them through Raskol'nikov's consciousness, which is to say that this dream is presented thematically. With the exception of the oasis dream Raskol'nikov's other dreams are presented as one-time, consecutive, vital experiences in which he himself takes part, and they are directly apprehended by the senses: things are heard, seen, touched, tasted, smelled. And the oasis dream is sensuously "present" to touch, taste, and sight. Instead of being specific this last dream is general; instead of happening to Raskol'nikov the events, or rather process, dreamed of affects others. (Perhaps we should note that, like several of the other dreams in

the novel, this one is anticipated: Razumixin, one of Raskol'nikov's alter egos, had earlier asked him, "Caught the plague or something?" [*Očumel ty, čto li*—a folkish expression meaning something like "Are you off your nut?"]; 99; V, 118.)

Like epilogues in general, the Epilogue in **Crime and Punishment** consists mainly (its first chapter—three-fifths of it) of generalized summary of what "has happened" since the end of the novel proper. However, this one is untypical in presenting a vital experiential moment—after the dream. Raskol'nikov is looking across the river from the prison: "In the boundless steppe, bathed in sunlight, the nomads' tents appeared as distant specks. Over there was freedom, there other men were living, utterly unlike those here; there time itself seemed to stand still as though the age of Abraham and his flocks had not passed. Raskol'nikov sat, he gazed motionless, without interruption. His thoughts passed into daydreams (*grezy*), into contemplation." (470; V, 572) Immediately afterward Raskol'nikov, in spite of himself and irrespective of his will, falls at Sonja's feet and embraces her knees. The passage is directly experiential; the juxtaposition with the dream suggests a causal connection.

How it happened he did not know, but all at once something seemed to seize him and fling him at her feet. He was crying and embracing her knees. For the first instant she was terribly frightened and her face turned pale. She jumped up and looked at him trembling. But immediately, at the same instant, she understood all. A light of infinite happiness came into her eyes. . . . In place of dialectics, life had begun.

(471-72; V, 573)

Now let us consider Raskol'nikov's dreams in relation to the development of the novel's themes as they are reflected in its title. The novel proper extends from the rehearsal of the murder, through its commission and aftermath, to Raskol'nikov's confession. If the "punishment" of the title were imprisonment in Siberia, then we would have the extreme oddity that the novel proper—some 550 pages—is involved with the crime and its detection (the first half of the title) and the Epilogue—some 25 pages—with the punishment (the second half of the title). The subject is of course much more complex than that. The title **Crime and Punishment**, as many have noted, implies the question of the nature and specificity of crime and of punishment. In Russian the title is far more suggestive than in English; within the novel there is wordplay based upon the nouns in the title, making clear it possesses more than one level of meaning. Since the Russian language has no definite or indefinite article, the two nouns in the title refer simultaneously to conceptual categories and to specific crime and specific punishment. Furthermore, both nouns of the title are, in Russian, verbal nouns, so that they can be at the same time (1) concept words, (2) words referring to a particular deed, and (3) words referring to the doing of a particular deed: punishment, *a* punishment, *the* punishment, punishing, *a* punishing, *the* punishing; crime, *a* crime, *the* crime, committing a crime, *a* committing of a crime, *the* committing of a crime. In addition, the word translated thus far as "crime" (*prestuplenie*) has still further suggestiveness in that it may mean "crime" in the juridical sense, "transgressing, transgression" in the religious sense, or a figurative "stepping over or across" any boundary or obstacle or expectation established by custom, mores, or accepted norms. The novel continually asks, directly and implicitly, "What is (a, the) crime? What is (a, the) punishment?"

Perhaps no work of literature presents so graphically a man testing and *living,* psychologically and even physiologically, a theory. Raskol'nikov's theory, it will be remembered, is that crime is accompanied by sickness, by a loss of willpower and self-control, unless it is committed for sufficient reason by an "extraordinary man," in which case it is "no crime." From this point of view the story of the novel is Raskol'nikov's testing of his own capacity to commit without sickness a "crime that is no crime," thus to prove himself to be an "extraordinary man." According to his theory, the height of the sickness, manifested by loss of will and self-control, will "immediately" precede and follow the commission of the deed, and then it will pass off "like any other illness." (63-64, 225; V, 77, 268) The morning after the murder Raskol'nikov asks himself in a moment of conscious awareness of illness, "Can it be that the punishment is coming on? It is!" (81; V, 96) The word is *kazn',* which means God's punishment or punishment from the nature of things—the most definite form of *nakazanie.* Just before the fourth dream (of trying to recommit the murder) Raskol'nikov plays on the word meaning to commit a crime, to transgress, to step across: "I wanted to hurry up and step across . . . . I did not kill a human being, I killed a principle! It was the principle I killed, but as for stepping across, I did not step across but remained on this side . . . ." (238-39; V, 285.) According to Raskol'nikov's theory, sickness for the nonextraordinary man, the criminal, should simply pass off, but during the course of the novel this does not happen. For one moment, after he has helped with money for Marmeladov's funeral, he feels so well, so strong and defiant, that he thinks he may be his own "extraordinary man" after all,[13] but during the course of the novel his sickness instead of simply passing off grows worse. In terms of the logic of the novel, his choices are to commit suicide like Svidrigajlov or to confess and go to Siberia, so that he can "live."[14] But he does not begin to "live" again, as we have seen, until he can embrace Sonja and what she stands for. And he cannot embrace Sonja until he has had his dream in the Epilogue.

Now we are ready to speak of the way the dreams fit into the total pattern of the crime and punishment in the novel. In accordance with Raskol'nikov's theories, his dreams in the novel proper, both before and after committing the murder, are symptoms of a nonextraordinary man's sickness before and after a premeditated crime. The novel suggests that the intense "sickness immediately before the crime" really started six weeks or so before the novel begins, from the moment a specific crime was conceived, the moment Raskol'nikov decided to apply his theory to one particular victim as a test of himself.[15] The novel begins with the further intensification of this sickness from the rehearsal through the murder itself. Thus, in accordance with Raskol'nikov's theory, his sickness is the punishment of the nonextraordinary man who imagines himself extraordinary. Intense punishment for the crime comes from the moment it is specifically conceived, and the punishment is then heightened immediately before and after the murder is actually committed. From this point of view, the most vivid scene of the entire novel—the dream of the killing of the horse—is intense punishment for his own premeditated crime before it is actually enacted. After the murder Raskol'nikov's sickness leads, among other things, to intense punishment inflicted by the dreams of the beating of the landlady and his futile attempt to recommit the murder. The dreams of the novel proper, like the other events there, prove to Raskol'nikov that he is no extraordinary man as measured by his own theory, and they are part of the punishment that leads him to confess. Nevertheless, this confession at the end of the novel proper results not from a feeling of guilt but from weakness, the inability to endure further the punishment he had been experiencing; he still has the defiant conviction that his theory has not been refuted, though it has been shown that he himself does not embody it. Neither Raskol'nikov's conscious mind nor his conscious conscience, if I may so express it, acknowledges wrongdoing, but merely an error of judgment in self-evaluation (467; V, 567-68).

The function of the dream in the Epilogue is quite different: to provide an answer, not to any specific application, but to the general theory itself. Raskol'nikov's dream, as we have seen, is Apocalyptic; it describes what would happen in a world where almost everybody applies to himself the theory of the extraordinary man; the resulting carnage would allow only a few uninfected people to survive. The novel does not tell us there is a cause-and-effect relationship between Raskol'nikov's dreaming of this dream, his seeing a modern counterpart of Abraham's flock, and the Easter season during which he becomes capable of embracing Sonja. But the relationship of the events is clear: Raskol'nikov's theory, not merely its application, had to be refuted in his own subconscious before he could embrace a human being and "live" again. The examining magistrate Porfirij Petrovič had asked the question explicitly during the novel proper: "Who of us in Russia does not consider himself a Napoleon now?" (231; V, 276) Raskol'nikov's final dream presents and answers the question and its implications in pestilential terms. Raskol'nikov's being tortured by his final dream, the punishing but curative dream of the novel, marks the point at which his subconscious caring for others can move into the conscious. Only when his whole theory is recognized by him as evil can regeneration come.

In its nature an epilogue should be a projection of the story proper; it should not be structurally necessary, though it may make conclusions explicit which were only implicit in the story proper. There has been much discussion of Raskol'nikov's resurrection, whether it is as credible as the crime and the experiences he undergoes before confessing to the police.[16] Of course not, if only because the focus of the 550 pages of the novel proper is on experiences immediately antecedent to the murder and up to the confession. But these experiences include themes which project directly into the themes of the Epilogue: the implications of Svidrigajlov's dictum that Raskol'nikov is confronted with a choice between suicide or Siberia (confession) but that he loves life too much to commit suicide; Sonja's reading to Raskol'nikov the biblical account of the resurrection of Lazarus; Raskol'nikov's and Sonja's mutual attraction which can blossom into love when he becomes capable of fully accepting another as an individual instead of as a manifestation of statistical percentages; Raskol'nikov's overcoming the plague of the mind and coming back to a proper kind of reason, as his relationship to Razumixin and the play on the name of Razumixin suggest;[17] his acceptance of a justice represented by Porfirij Petrovič which is different from that of his own theories. Just as the dreams of the novel have the right intensity for the experiences of the novel proper, when Raskol'nikov is testing himself against his theory, in similar way the ideological dream in the Epilogue combines a generalized impression with an ideological function in a manner quite appropriate for an epilogue. **Crime and Punishment** as a novel has its primary focus on the theoretical and actual crime and on the punishment that the criminal undergoes until he not only accepts his punishment but accepts it as being just. The story of the gradual regeneration of the criminal, including his working out of a new, satisfactory way of *thinking* about life, would indeed have required another, and different, novel.

Notes

1. This paper was delivered as the banquet address at the annual meeting of AATSEEL in New York City, December 1972.

2. For convenience, the location of all the dreams in the novel will be given here. My translations are essentially those of Constance Garnett in Fedor Dostoevsky, *Crime and Punishment* (New York: Bantam, 1958, and later printings), revised as appropriate on the basis of the Russian text in volume 5 of F. M. Dostoevskij, *Sobranie sočinenij* (10 vols.; M.: GIXL, 1956-58). Unless otherwise indicated, references in the paper are first to page numbers in the Bantam edition, then to volume and page numbers in the Russian edition.

   Dream I: Part 1, chapter 5 (48-54; V, 59-65)

   Dream II: Part 1, chapter 6 (60-61; V, 73-74)

   Dream III: Part 2, chapter 2 (102-04; V, 121-23)

   Dream IV: Part 3, chapter 6 (240-42; V, 286-89)

   Dream V: Epilogue, chapter 2 (469-70; V, 570-71)

3. In the first printed edition of the novel, after the last dream it is called *ètogo sna*. In later editions this was emended to "these feverish dreams" (*ètix gorjačešnyx grez*). See F. M. Dostoevskij, *Polnoe sobranie xudožestvennyx proizvedenij*, ed. B. Tomaševskij and K. Xalabaev (13 vols.; M.: GIZ, 1926-30), V, 492.

4. For the notebooks see I. I. Glivenko, ed., *Iz arxiva F. M. Dostoevskogo*: "*Prestuplenie i nakazanie*" (M.: GIXL, 1931); Fyodor Dostoevsky, *The Notebooks for Crime and Punishment*, ed. and tr. Edward Wasiolek (Chicago: Univ. of Chicago Press, 1967); and "Rukopisnye teksty," in F. M. Dostoevskij, *Prestuplenie i nakazanie*, ed. L. D. Opul'skaja and G. F. Kogan (M.: Nauka, 1970), 427-678. The question of the difference in artistic effect produced by the third-person version rather than the planned first-person form is studied in detail by Gary Rosenshield, "The Narrator in *Crime and Punishment*" (Diss. Univ. of Wisconsin 1971).

5. The techniques of indirect speech and indirect consciousness in the novel in general are discussed, with appended bibliography, in Ronald James Lethcoe, "Narrated Speech and Narrated Consciousness" (Diss. Univ. of Wisconsin 1969); and, with specific reference to *Crime and Punishment*, in Rosenshield, "Narrator."

6. This point is emphasized by Rosenshield ("Narrator," 332) as essential not only as regards the artistry of the Epilogue but the entire novel.

7. In the early, first-person version, the scene of the horse killing is presented as direct memory. See the Opul'skaja and Kogan edition for the text (p. 458) and for a note commenting on the possible autobiographical connection for Dostoevskij himself (p. 740).

8. That Dostoevskij himself felt this to be the most vivid passage in the entire novel is shown by his

choosing it for public reading, which we are told was remarkably successful. See A. G. Dostoevskaja, *Vospominanija,* ed. L. P. Grossman (M., L.: Gosizdat, 1925), 254.

9. The unclearness of the demarcation between dream and reality in this dream is noted by Temira Pachmuss, "The Technique of Dream-Logic in the Works of Dostoevskij," *SEEJ,* 4 (1960), 231-32.

10. See the Opul'skaja and Kogan edition, p. 773.

11. For detailed description of the first cholera epidemic to reach the two Russian capitals see Roderick E. McGrew, *Russia and the Cholera, 1823-1832* (Madison: Univ. of Wisconsin Press, 1965).

12. For a summary of the information on Dostoevskij's interest in the Apochrypha and his utilization of it, see the Opul'skaja and Kogan edition, p. 773.

13. This is the scene of Raskol'nikov's reaction to Polen'ka's thanks, after Marmeladov's death (at which Raskol'nikov provided the money for his funeral from the money he had just received from his mother); see 165-66; V, 197.

14. Svidrigajlov expresses it in terms of "two roads," either a "bullet in the forehead" (i.e., suicide) or the Vladimirka road (to Siberia), presumably after confession; see 430; V, 523.

15. The scene is presented in flashback fashion in Part 1, chapter 6. Raskol'nikov overhears two students arguing that it would be no crime to kill the old pawnbroker whom Raskol'nikov had just visited. He is struck by the way they echo his own ideas in their formation. See 57-59; V, 69-72.

16. Among scholars and critics who have expressed the view that the Epilogue is unbelievable or insufficiently motivated, one may mention Zental Maurina, *A Prophet of the Soul: Fyodor Dostoevsky,* tr. C. P. Finlagson (London: Clark, 1940), 131-32; E. J. Simmons, *Dostoevski: The Making of a Novelist* (1940; rpt. London: Lehmann, 1950), 152-53; F. I. Èvnin, "Roman *Prestuplenie i nakazanie,*" in N. L. Stepanov, ed., *Tvorčestvo Dostoevskogo* (M.: AN SSSR, 1959), 165; Ja. O. Zundelovič, *Romany Dostoevskogo* (Taškent: Srednjaja i vysšaja škola, 1963), 49-50; V. I. Ètov, *Dostoevskij* (M.: Prosveščenie, 1969), 239.

17. Many have noted the emphasis in the novel on the connection of Razumixin's name with "reason." This occurs three times. Lužin emphasizes the meaning of the name by misremembering it as Rassudkin (something like "ratiocination" rather than "reason"; 262; V, 313). Svidrigajlov tells Raskol'nikov that Razumixin's name suggests him as being "sensible" (*rassuditel'nyj*; 409; V, 496).

Razumixin himself suggests his role vis-à-vis Raskol'nikov when he jokingly introduces himself, not as Razumixin but Vrazumixin (one who may bring another to his senses, to his reason; 262; V, 313).

Gennaro Santangelo (essay date winter 1974-75)

SOURCE: Santangelo, Gennaro. "The Five Motives of Raskolnikov." *Dalhousie Review* 54, no. 4 (winter 1974-75): 710-19.

[*In the following essay, Santangelo analyzes the various motives behind Raskolnikov's crime. Santangelo concludes that Raskolnikov's actions are the result of unconscious forces rather than of a single, clear rationale.*]

As an esthetic experience *Crime and Punishment* is whole and complete.[1] As a critical experience, however, the complexity of motivation causes confusion and a slight feeling of despair. The critic must untangle layers of motivation, cause, and feeling, observing at all times the depth levels on which the action is moving. The problem of the novel is why Raskolnikov killed the wretched old lady and allied to this difficulty, why he confessed, and why he was punished. The notebooks reveal that Dostoevsky, himself, tortured over the problem. He never clearly explained as he himself said, things this way or that way. The author says in the notebooks in another context, "The murder takes place almost by chance. (I myself did not expect that)."[2] This confusion in Dostoevsky's creative process does not disintegrate the novel esthetically, for its total effect is one of artistic wholeness and unity, his best constructed work. In the novel his conception of the hero's character would not permit him to explain clearly the motive for the crime because too many motives are operative. There is no clear rational key. Dostoevsky presents the character as an artistic entity and achieves the total integration of the emotional, unconscious, and rational basis of his hero. The novel then does present a mystery, a crime without a clear motivation represented in a character who is very self-aware, but knows very little about himself.

Raskolnikov in the confessional scene with Sonia says he doesn't know why he killed the old woman. But he does give five motives for the crime. First, he says he killed the old lady because he was poor and needed money. This motive is the social justification from poverty. Then he argues that he wished to benefit society, that the old woman was useless and would have let her money rot. This motive is utilitarian. These first two are coupled because they exist on the level of the consciousness. The third motivation is psychological. He says to Sonia, "And do you realize, Sonia, that low ceilings and small poky little rooms warp mind and soul." He killed the old lady out of some subconscious compulsion. Later he claims as the fourth motive that he had a right to step over the bounds of ordinary human laws, that his will was above good and evil, as well as law and order. Rather than utilitarian, this problem is moral, a question of the autonomous will and the expanded ego. Lastly, Raskolnikov unconsciously poses the problem of man's relation to God. He says to Sonia, "Was it the old hag I killed? No, I killed myself, and not the old hag. I did away with myself at one blow and for good. It was the devil who killed the old hag, not I." Raskolnikov killed because he could not place himself in the mystic structure of man's internal relationships and some entity outside self—hence his personality was split. Raskolnikov rejects almost all these motives himself during the same confession scene, but they represent different facets of his personality which are integral to his experience and cannot be disregarded. The minor characters also represent different phases of the student's personality and mirror to him his own problems, although they must stand on their own as full artistic creations.

After Raskolnikov had confessed to Sonia, he claims poverty as his first motive. The stinking city of St. Petersburg is a passive catalytic agent in the instigation to the crime. Raskolnikov, walking the city streets in a daze, passively records the squalid conditions: a young girl eager to throw herself into the canal; a sixteen-year-old girl debauched and a prey of seducers; and starving children.

The tragedy of the Marmeladov family crystallizes this theme of the insulted and the injured. Raskolnikov sees mirrored in the misery of the family his own wretchedness. They live in squalor with little to eat and to wear: a woman wasted by consumption, a young daughter driven to prostitution, and a beaten man driven to drink. Through them the reader sees the origin of Raskolnikov's protest. Mrs. Marmeladov spits up her blood on the streets of St. Petersburg in the search for a justice that does not exist on this earth.

Old Marmeladov is the first of Raskolnikov's doubles. In the drunkard, the student recognizes his own poverty and that of his family as including them among the insulted and injured. Destitute, Raskolnikov paces his hole like a starving trapped wolf. Marmeladov, the double for these insults in the soul of Raskolnikov, objectifies the conditions which Raskolnikov cannot verbalize, but feels deeply.

The motivation of the student revolutionary is quite evident. Raskolnikov killed an old lady in ineffectual fury, to protest the condition of the insulted and the injured. He killed the old woman to protest the wretched condi-

tions of the Marmeladovs, his own wretched condition, and the condition of man who from poverty of soul and body strikes in frustration at the symbol of the wretchedness which chains him. Motivated thus by social consciousness, Raskolnikov emerges as a scapegoat figure, carrying on his back to the martyrdom of Siberia the accumulated guilt, shame, and injustice of the social order.

But Raskolnikov rejects this motive. He says to Sonia, "No, Sonia, . . . I wasn't as hungry as that and I wanted to help my mother all right, but that wasn't the reason either." He knows that he did not kill the old lady merely to steal her money.

The student confesses both the social and personal basis of the utilitarian motivation by analogy to the career of Napoleon who if he had to kill an old hag to advance his career would have done so without reservation. Raskolnikov also killed to help himself and his mother. The motive from poverty is a protest: the utilitarian leads to logical action. Early in the novel Raskolnikov says, "Now begins the reign of reason and light and of will and strength. . . . And to think that I practically made up my mind to live in a square yard of space!"

Such a utilitarian rationalistic theory leads also to a tyrannical socialism. When individual liberty is denied and good and evil looked upon as prejudices in the way of achieving the greatest good of the greatest number, then the logical conclusion is tyranny. This is basically a rationalistic ethic which denies the personal and social foundations of human character. It looks merely to the "good" of man seen as a material animal. When Raskolnikov thinks of himself as a benefactor of mankind with the right to obliterate anything in his path, he is thinking rationally and not humanly. One critic observed that Raskolnikov would make a good commissar of the Soviet Republic.[3]

This idea is brought back to the student in another double who carries the utilitarian, rationalistic ethic to a grotesque extreme, Luzhin the suitor of Dunya, Raskolnikov's sister. He is an opportunistic, hypocritical liberal, the type of the *nouveau-riche* bourgeois who justifies any theory on the basis of utility.

Raskolnikov hates Luzhin passionately because in him he sees reflected in a glass darkly the image of himself as intellectual justifier of his crime. Luzhin is a parody of the greatest good of the greatest number, that in a new dispensation all will be permitted, and that the sanctity of the individual is a prejudice carried over into the present age. In the notebooks Dostoevsky says, "The fiance [Luzhin]—he unfolds completely for him [Raskolnikov] a theory by which one is justified in killing."[4] Just as the sinners in Dante's Inferno see in their punishments the true reflection of their crimes, so also Raskolnikov sees in Luzhin the true reflection of his utilitarianism and hates his double passionately.

But Raskolnikov also rejects this motive verbally in his confession, "I know—I know it! The old Lady wasn't a louse," he replied, looking strangely at her. Later he says, "I did not commit this murder to become the benefactor of humanity by gaining wealth and power—that, too, is nonsense. I just did it; I did it for myself alone, and at that moment I did not care a damn whether I would become the benefactor of someone, or would spend the rest of my life like a spider catching them all in my web and sucking the living juices out of them." Dostoevsky has Raskolnikov reject the ravages of the dangerous intellect within himself by rejecting Luzhin and all he stands for. These two motives are rational theories which Raskolnikov first mentions in his confession to Sonia because they exist on the conscious level. After discussing the utilitarian motive for some time, he says to Sonia, "There are quite, quite other motives here. I haven't spoken to anyone for ages Sonia. I have an awful headache now." He is breaking through the level of the consciousness, finding it difficult to unlock repressed unconscious motives. The headache is a reaction to the pain of revealing what he has attempted to keep hidden. Instead of the psychoanalytic couch with an administering psychiatrist, Raskolnikov reveals himself to Sonia whose gentle prodding, total unselfish commitment, and love, help to unlock the murderer's unconscious. After complaining of the headache, Raskolnikov speaks vaguely of feelings and dreams because he cannot verbalize his subconscious motivations either through a failure to understand them or admit them to himself. This third motivation is the unrevealed motive of the unconsciousness, the unresolved psychic conflicts, especially sexual, that motivated the crime.

Raskolnikov is obviously a neurotic. Many of the characters at one time or other think him mad. The basis of this neurosis could easily be incestuous. Early in the novel he had said, "Mother, sister—how I loved them! Why do I hate them now? Yes, I hate them. I hate them physically. I can't bear them to be near me." Dunya is his primary incestuous fixation. He opposes Luzhin violently not only as a pseudoliberal, but also as a rival for Dunya's affections. He has his sister and mother sit with Sonia, an attempt to lower them to the prostitute's level so that he can be free to possess them. This unresolved incestuous tendency explains his attachment to sickly, sexless girls like his landlord's daughter and Sonia.[5]

These neurotic tendencies lead to guilt feelings that cannot be eradicated and explain Raskolnikov's desire for punishment even before he commits the crime. He does everything to reveal himself because he wishes to suffer in order to alleviate the feelings of guilt. This guilt and subsequent desire for punishment become so strong that he commits the murder.

In killing the old woman and her sister, he is actually killing his mother and sister. His insistence on using only a sharp-edged weapon, such as a knife or axe, symbolizes his desire to cut away those objects that have inhibited his psychic development. This attack is aimed at Lizaveta who represents his sister. He kills the old woman with the blunt end of the axe, but splits the sister's head open; some of the phallic implications of this act should be obvious. But the murder has solved nothing because Raskolnikov's mother and sister appear on the scene almost immediately, again arousing the vicious cycle of incestuous desire and guilt. He then seeks punishment in Siberia for his unlawful desires.

Possibly as a result of this unresolved sexual problem, Raskolnikov's personality has been split. His name in Russian means either dissent or schism. This split is revealed in the dichotomies that exist in his reason and his emotions. Unable to resolve the problem, he kills the old woman to find in her death the proof of his superiority. The murder resolves nothing and is a meaningless act. Raskolnikov recognizes that he would be a louse after and knew it before he committed the crime. He cannot integrate his character as he vacillates between self abasement and self assertion. The only answer to such a split is suicide. Dostoevsky had thought of ending the novel with Raskolnikov's suicide.[6]

If the novel is a psychoanalytic casebook, then the ending has to be considered inconclusive because Raskolnikov's mental structure would not appear to change. Raskolnikov cannot reject the neurosis himself because he is not totally aware of it. This approach can be useful. Certainly it makes some sense of Lizaveta's murder. And Raskolnikov's erratic behaviour must be considered the product of an unbalanced personality. This critical approach, however, which looks upon the novel as a case book, a story of a personality disturbance, can swallow up all the others, relegating them to minor internalization of deep-seated neurosis.

Another irrational motive, the fourth, is the will to power, what I prefer to call the theory of the autonomous will. During the confession, Raskolnikov says to Sonia, after rejecting the theory about the thoughts aroused in his lonely room leading him to the crime, that the lawmaker is above good and evil. While the utilitarian motive is completely rational (I committed the crime to gain such and such an end), this desire becomes an irrational necessity, a dare, a megalomanic compulsion. Napoleon considering his career is utilitarian: Napoleon above human laws wading through blood as an exercise for his own grand personality is irrational, a megalomaniac. The human agent is above all moral considerations and steps over the boundaries of good and evil because these categories do not exist for his own autonomous will. Like the Byronic hero, he attempts to assert absolute freedom.

The moral freedom of choice is a fundamental in Dostoevsky's moral dialectics, but this freedom is not only the freedom to do good. Such a concept leads to tyrannical socialism, constrained predestination, and the ideas of the inquisition. For freedom to be exercised, evil must exist to be chosen. Such a freedom entails the possibility of great wrong, which leads to the tragedy of freedom in Dostoevsky's novels. Raskolnikov drives towards freedom, but never frees himself completely and has been perverted. This type of freedom becomes anarchy if it is not connected with some object outside itself freely chosen. If a leap of faith based on intuition is not made, the subject is lost in the dark path of his own autonomous will. This terrible freedom lays possibilities for tragic action in man's way. Svidrigaylov represents Raskolnikov's double in terms of the free autonomous will. From him, Raskolnikov has mirrored many of his own theories. Svidrigaylov believes strongly in the right to trespass all bounds. He has no particular feeling of guilt about all this and sees life as a total amusement.

He is a nihilist, a complete cynic without a sense of shame who, because he has no shame, has completely freed his will from all prejudices. Seeking suicide, he doesn't care whether Dunya shoots him or not. He releases her because he is completely free. Having no prejudices, certainly a stronger character than Luzhin, he has passed the boundaries of ordinary human values only to reach a boundary he cannot pass, some realization of the meaning of human experience. But this freedom is an illusion because it means nothing to him without a reference outside of himself. Turned back on himself, he cannot envision anything outside his will. He thinks that eternity is not a grand thing at all, but merely a bath house very small, with some loathsome spiders. His suicide follows. He could go nowhere else. Raskolnikov hates Luzhin, but fears and is fascinated by Svidrigaylov. He hunts him in the symbolic winding streets of St. Petersburg. Raskolnikov with horror recognizes in this dark looking glass, the perversion of the theory that he who dares can try anything. He is fascinated by Svidrigaylov because he recognizes there the part of his soul that dared kill the old lady. But how hideous the vision appears in this debauched middle-aged man. When Svidrigaylov kills himself, this other ego of Raskolnikov, the student, is then free to turn himself in, for that exterior symbol of what was truly dead in him has been cut away.

Raskolnikov turned down the wrong side path in seeking that road to freedom. If he had remained a utilitarian, he would have been lost like Luzhin. If he had refused to take responsibility for his behaviour, he would have been a lost, trapped psychotic. He had gone up the road toward freedom of choice and was led astray. If he had been committed completely to the nihilism of his will, he would have committed suicide like Svidrigaylov. He rejected this idea of the dare very forcefully to Sonia.

The critic must consider God or something like him when discussing the ontological motivation for the crime, Raskolnikov's fifth motive. The autonomous will represented a moral, ethical consideration. The ontological or mythic, religious problem involves a religious dimension. Sonia exclaimed, deeply shocked, that God had handed the student over to Satan and Raskolnikov replied that he imagined Satan tempted him. And later he says, "Was it the old hag I killed? No, I killed myself and not the old hag."

In saying that he killed himself, Raskolnikov recognizes that he had split himself and hoped to resolve the problem by eliminating it. This psychological and moral split, looked at from the point of view of Dostoevsky's deep-seated attachment to Russian orthodox religion, is disbelief. Raskolnikov is sick and has turned his hand against himself because he didn't have any self. Lost within himself, he struck out to find the truth. The desire for freedom is the mystic way to faith, but the sick Raskolnikov did not see it. He struck in hatred against himself so that he might avoid the self confrontation of a man without belief. But this burden of terrible freedom which he took upon himself had no adequate object to which it could attach itself, nothing really to choose. Looking outside himself, Raskolnikov found nothing and looking inside he found chaos and anarchy. He rejected humanity and God, subconsciously realizing the nature of his sin, and finally killed the old woman to prove that he was lost. The ambivalence of this murder then becomes apparent, for it represents the rejection of humanity, but Raskolnikov in his desire to be punished for the crime (a critical truism which most critics accept) mysteriously sought also salvation, because through suffering he might redeem himself.

This theme of the loss of identity without God finds its symbolic double in Sonia. Instead of distorting the image to the hideous as the other doubles had done, she purifies the image of Raskolnikov as he might become.

She had been Lizaveta's friend. In their humility, simplicity, and goodness they had much in common. More interesting is their promiscuity. Yet they both have a pietistic connection with life as symbolized by their religion. As a pledge of their mutual faith they exchange crosses. When Raskolnikov kills Lizaveta, he also kills that which Sonia represents in his psyche.

Raskolnikov kills two principles when he kills the old woman and her sister. He is obliterating his connection with God because the burden of freedom has been too much for him. He is attempting to prove that his will is autonomous, that his ego can reconstruct the universe as it wishes. He is also chopping off his connection with humanity and the earth. Lizaveta and her older sister are symbolic chthonian deities.[7] The old lady hoards her treasure and represents a terrible force. The younger sister is fertility (remember her constant pregnancy), the good earth goddess who fructifies the world and blesses it with mercy. Sonia recognizes what Raskolnikov has done and tells him to kiss that earth which he has defiled.

Raskolnikov deep in his nature has never been able to cut himself off from these life sources as he thought he could. Mr. George Gibian in an interesting article demonstrates the basis of Russian religion and folklore in *Crime and Punishment.*[8] In evidence too intricate and long to discuss here, he demonstrates that Raskolnikov never really rejected the living symbols of Russian life such as water, air, vegetation and the concept of the New Jerusalem based on the Lazarus theme.

But Raskolnikov must pay a price for his crime and his humanity. Porfiry tells him that he must suffer, that suffering is his only way. Dostoevsky believed in a mystique of suffering, that man's moral responsibility encompasses the totality of human evil, and that all men must take up their cross. Raskolnikov seeks and avoids his cross simultaneously. The motive of punishment which is part of this mythic-religious motivation persists through the novel. (The psychoanalytic critic sees clearly that Raskolnikov actually seeks detection and punishment). In this unconscious drive for punishment lies his salvation because it is through suffering that he will wipe away his crime and find peace in human identification. The psychoanalytic critic looks upon suffering as sickness; the mythic-religious, as healing.

Raskolnikov thinks he is a rebel against any entity outside himself. Unable to determine what he is because he has no outside referent, he loses a sense of his own personality and is split. To establish his identity he strikes and hopes to kill in himself his fixed place in the dialectics of eternity. In so striking he seeks the punishment that will identify him with humanity. Although he kills Lizaveta, she is resurrected in Sonia. He takes his cross and goes to the new Jerusalem of Siberia, reintegrating with God and Mother Earth. The vital interest of the novel rests in the interaction of these diverse motivations. The abstractions must not replace, however, the artistic integrity of the work. Raskolnikov is not a philosopher making abstract reflections on life. Capable of inflicting great wrong, he is also capable of great compassion. Strong and self-willed, he is also insecure and humble. Dostoevsky delves into the character to trace the diverse branches of behaviour to one common trunk, the core of Raskolnikov's character. He is not many persons, but one person. Also the other characters are not isolated from the centre of the action. They represent human beings, not as complex as Raskolnikov, who are struggling with moral problems that the student himself cannot solve. The novel is artistically integrated, a realistic portrayal of misery viewed on the social, psychological, and religious levels.

Why did Raskolnikov kill the old lady? Is there one motive that explains the action? They are all compelling because rarely is a man the product of one force. All actions are intertwined with depth levels of motive that rest in the unconscious. Dostoevsky had the courage to present a man in the totality of his personality. Raskolnikov's crime was a personal, social, moral and religious act.

Notes

1. I assume here that the ending is an integral part of the novel as demonstrated in much of modern criticism, see especially, Edward Wasiolek, "On the Structure of *Crime and Punishment*," *PMLA* (December, 1955) 979-996.

2. Edward Wasiolek, ed., *Crime and Punishment and the Critics,* (San Francisco, 1961), 11. The translation is the editor's from I. I. Glivenko's edition of the notebooks.

3. Alberto Moravia, "The Marx-Dostoevsky Duel," *Encounter,* November, 1956, 3-5.

4. Wasiolek, 9.

5. For much of this information on the sexual motivation of Raskolnikov, I am indebted to Edna C. Florence, "The Neurosis of Raskolnikov: A study in Incest and Murder," *Archives of Criminal Psychodynamics,* I (Winter, 1955), 344-396. This article presents a professional psychoanalytical discussion to which I have not been able to add very much except my disapproval.

6. In the notebooks, Wasiolek, 16.

7. For a fuller explication of this mythic interpretation see Vyacheslav Ivanov, "The Revolt Against Mother Earth," in *Freedom and the Tragic Life* (New York, 1952).

8. George Gibian, "Traditional Symbolism in *Crime and Punishment*," *PMLA* (December, 1955), 979-996.

Raymond J. Wilson, III (essay date 1976)

SOURCE: Wilson, Raymond J., III. "Raskolnikov's Dream in *Crime and Punishment*." *Literature and Psychology* 26, no. 4 (1976): 159-66.

[*In the following essay, Wilson examines the ways in which Raskolnikov's horse-beating dream serves as an expression of his character.*]

In trying to understand Raskolnikov's apparently erratic behavior in *Crime and Punishment,* readers have often resorted to the idea that Raskolnikov has a "split personality" even before they find out his name comes from the Russian root *raskol* meaning schism or split. However, the simple notion of a two-way Jekyll-Hyde or emotional-intellectual split in Raskolnikov never proved completely workable in analyzing Raskolnikov's personality. Raskolnikov cannot be forced into so limited a mold. The implications of Raskolnikov's horse-beating dream provide more flexibility for analysis. Aspects of the dream reflect facets of Raskolnikov's complex personality. This very flexibility, however, causes problems in interpreting the dream, as W. D. Snodgrass demonstrates in his analysis:

> First of all, where is Raskolnikov in his dream? Is he the horse, the little boy, the father, or the brute Mikolka? The answer must be Yes. All of the characters of the dream are the dreamer. The problem is not to decide who is who, but rather to understand the tenor of the dreamer's apprehension of the world, that is, of his mind. . . . For the horse, also, I have given what must seem disparate interpretations. Does the horse represent the teen-aged girl, Dunya and Sonia, Or does it represent the pawnbroker, the landlady and the mother, Or Marmeladov and Raskolnikov? Once again, the answer to all the questions is Yes. To miss the identity of all these characters as symbolized by the horse is to miss an essential texture of Raskolnikov's mind.[1]

Obviously needed is a way to select, from this wealth of material, the aspects of the dream which best help us explain Raskolnikov's actual behavior, without oversimplifying the character by denying that other aspects exist. Confusion in the novel over the painter Mikolka's name helps us do this.

At the moment Raskolnikov is about to confess his murder to a police examiner named Porfiry Petrovich, a painter bursts into Porfiry's office claiming the crime as "mine alone." The painter's name creates confusion. In Dostoevsky's own words, not attributed to any character, the painter is "Nikolay," the name used by both the police examiner (338)[2] and the master worker who reported Raskolnikov's return to the scene of the crime (344). Raskolnikov's friend Razumikhin calls the painter "Mikolay" (132) and "Nikolka." (427) In the painter's confession scene with Porfiry, Raskolnikov alone calls the confessing painter "Mikolka." (340) If we assume an error by the author, this confusion would be surprising. However, as Raskolnikov's mistake, the error provides a clue to our use of the dream material.[3]

The name "Mikolka" links the painter to the Mikolka of Raskolnikov's horse-beating dream (Part I, Chapter 5). Raskolnikov dreams himself as a little boy feeling guilt and horror at his inability to prevent a drunken peasant named Mikolka from beating the animal to death. Like the painter, the dream Mikolka claims full responsibility for the crime, screaming, "You keep out of this! She's mine, isn't she? I can do what I like with my own." (54) Raskolnikov had been about to reveal his murderer personality, prompted—like the dream's Mikolka—by anger and hatred. When the painter confesses, Raskolnikov listens instead to an inner voice urging him to act as if the crime were none of his business. This detached attitude is expressed in the dream by the little boy's father, an onlooker, who tells the little boy that the crime belongs to Mikolka and is none of the boy's business.

Each of the three main actors in Raskolnikov's dream—Mikolka, little boy, and onlooker—reflect ways of reacting that Raskolnikov consistently demonstrates in the novel. First the peasant Mikolka, who kills the horse, projects the Raskolnikov capable of a physically brutal axe-murder and of cruelly insulting those who love him. Second the little boy Raskolnikov, who cries agonized tears, represents the generous Raskolnikov aiding the Marmeladov family and the one who impulsively prevents a well-dressed man from pursuing a confused young girl. Finally there is the little boy's father in the dream who urges him to continue their walk to the graveyard saying, "It is none of our business. Let us go." The father has the voice of the uninvolved onlooker Raskolnikov who says, "What business is it of yours?" to the policeman he has just asked to aid the young girl (47). The same onlooker operates when Raskolnikov tells himself how "stupid" he is to give his money to the Marmeladov family (24).

We see these three personalities in Raskolnikov's three interviews with the police inspector. In the first interview, Porfiry mainly deals with Raskolnikov's onlooker personality. Raskolnikov maintains a "none-of-my-business" attitude and deals successfully with a trick question about the painters, one of whom Raskolnikov later calls by the dream nickname. Raskolnikov evades this trick. But later we discover that his hostile tone of laughter at the beginning had enabled the magistrate to guess "everything then." (434) Obviously Porfiry's trained ear detected the murderer's voice.

The murderer personality becomes even more important in the second interrogation, at the end of which Raskolnikov actually calls the painter by the dream nickname. On the way to Porfiry's office for this second examination, Raskolnikov "felt infinite, boundless hatred for him, and he even feared that his hatred would make him betray himself." (319) Whenever Raskolnikov is in one aspect of his personality and has to shift suddenly to another, it shocks his emotional system. Porfiry intentionally evokes Raskolnikov's murderer personality, the result being that "At moments" Raskolnikov "longed to throw himself on Porfiry and strangle him then and there." (327)

Porfiry's tactics make it difficult for Raskolnikov to keep from reacting like a murderer. At one point he "fell suddenly into a real frenzy . . . a perfect paroxysm of fury." (335) Alternately, Porfiry shocks Raskolnikov by reminding him that the crime is supposedly none of Raskolnikov's business, by saying variations of: "Good Lord! What are you talking about? What is there for me to question you about?" (322) Such reminders progressively upset Raskolnikov:

> As he had before, he suddenly dropped his voice to a whisper, instantly recognizing with anguish and hatred that he felt obliged to submit to the command, and driven to greater fury by the knowledge.
>
> (335)

Finally Raskolnikov "rushed at Porfiry" (336), who is quite delighted at this open display of murderous qualities telling Raskolnikov that he has already betrayed himself. But, before Porfiry can confront Raskolnikov with the implications of his actions, the painter bursts in to confess. The timing is pure coincidence. But Raskolnikov calls the painter "Mikolka" and this is not coincidence. For Dostoevsky employs the supposed error again.

In the third interview, Porfiry no longer tries to provoke the murderer in Raskolnikov. Instead, he speaks in a mild paternal tone evoking the little boy personality, urging Raskolnikov to drop his onlooker pretense. Notably, here for the first time, Porfiry calls the painter by the dream character's nickname: "No, Rodion Romanovich, my dear chap, Mikolka isn't in this at all!" (437) Raskolnikov responds "like a frightened small child caught redhanded in some misdeed." (438) He smiles "meek and sad" and speaks "as if he no longer could conceal anything at all from Porfiry." (440)

In the sense we have been using, everyone has many parts to his personality. But in Raskolnikov's case important parts are alienated from each other. The onlooker cannot see how the old woman's death can possibly concern him. The murderer has sneering contempt for the little boy's acts of impulsive generosity. The little boy is totally horrified by the murderer's acts of brutality. This alienation gives meaning to the word "split" in the term "split personality." These are not postulated interior forces or images but overt ways of acting which the other characters recognize. The real test of the dream characters' explanatory value is whether they contribute to the reader's understanding of Dostoevsky's depiction of Raskolnikov. Eight important episodes demonstrate that they do.

(1) RASKOLNIKOV'S REUNION WITH HIS SISTER.

On seeing his sister for the first time in three years, Raskolnikov brusquely denounces her marriage plans. Those present make allowances for the insult because of his "condition," which we can see as the temporary dominance of the Mikolka personality. Dr. Zosimov later recalls this in terms that could apply to Mikolka: a "monomaniac, who had been goaded almost to raving madness by the smallest word . . ." (213)

But the next morning, Raskolnikov arises talking to himself the way the dream's onlooker talked of those who tortured the animal. In the dream the onlooker implies: What business is it of ours? He says, "They are drunk, they are playing the fool." (56) And awake, Raskolnikov thinks:

> His most horrifying recollection was of how 'ignobly and disgustingly' he had behaved, not only in being drunk, but in taking advantage of a young girl's situation to abuse her fiancé in front of her, out of stupid and hastily conceived jealousy, when he knew nothing either of their mutual relationship and obligations or, properly speaking, of the man himself. And what right had he to condemn him so hastily and rashly? Who had appointed him the judge?
>
> (201)

The onlooker in the dream said: "It's none of our business. Let us go." Like him, Raskolnikov now says . . .

> of course, I can't gloss over or efface all this nastiness, now or ever . . . and so I must not even think of it, but appear before them in silence . . . and not ask forgiveness, but say nothing . . .
>
> (202)

Yet, on seeing his mother and sister again, Raskolnikov makes all right again with the charm of a little boy—astounding the others present. Their mother's face "shone with pride and happiness" as she notes "how simply and delicately" Raskolnikov achieved the reconciliation. And his friend Razumikhin thinks: "Now that's what I absolutely love him for!" (215)

(2) THE MURDER ITSELF.

Before the crime, the onlooker in Raskolnikov's personality tells him that he cannot possibly be serious in his plans—but not from any sense of moral outrage; rather, being split from the murderer, the onlooker feels no identity with the Raskolnikov who can be brutal. However, when the time comes, Raskolnikov, like Mikolka, strikes Alyona repeatedly with the blunt side of the axe. Raskolnikov then reacts in horror at his own crime just as the little boy of the dream reacts to Mikolka's cruelty. Lizaveta's arrival turns little-boy horror into terror; and as Raskolnikov flings himself forward with the axe "her lips writhed pitifully, like those of a young child when it is just beginning to be frightened . . ." (76) Lizaveta, like the old mare, responds minimally and ineffectively. And, as a voice in the dream had urged (55), Raskolnikov mercifully finishes her off with one blow from the sharp edge of the axe. Again Raskolnikov first reacts, like the little boy, with horror and repulsion for what he had done, rather than with "fear for himself."

In the dream the onlooker treats the crime as trivial: "'Come away,' said his father, '. . . Come away; don't look!'" (54) And "It is none of our business. Let us go." (56) After the crime, Raskolnikov turns more and more to this attitude:

> But a growing distraction, that almost amounted to absentmindedness, had taken possession of him; at times he seemed to forget what he was doing, or rather to forget the important things and cling to trivialities.
>
> (77)

Raskolnikov calmly washes his hands and cleans the axe, treating the bodies in the other room and the money in the bedroom as if they were none of his business. Near-discovery shakes him out of this mode. But as he escapes, we listen to an interior debate. One voice urges him to run, to hide in the doorway, to take a cab. The other, parallel to the dream's onlooker calms him and urges him to act as if nothing has happened.

(3) RASKOLNIKOV'S MEETING WITH ZAMETOV.

When he meets Zametov, the police clerk, at a bar called the "Crystal Palace," Raskolnikov tries to talk of the axe murder like an onlooker who can have only passing interest. But "in a flash he remembered, with an extraordinary intensity of feeling," the scene in the murder room. And he "was suddenly filled with a desire to shriek out, to exchange oaths with them, stick out his tongue at them, mock at them, and laugh, laugh, laugh." (155) Raskolnikov's Mikolka personality makes Zametov shiver and recoil suddenly from Raskolnikov. Dostoevsky describes the result of the struggle between the Mikolka personality and onlooker in Raskolnikov's appearance:

> The latter's eyes were glittering, he had grown shockingly pale, and his upper lip trembled and twitched. He leaned as near as possible to Zametov and began moving his lips, but no sound came from them; they remained like this for half a minute. He knew what he was doing, but he could not restrain himself.
>
> (159)

Zametov's obvious recognition of the murderer brings Raskolnikov "to his senses." The onlooker emerges again, and Raskolnikov successfully acts as if the murder is none of his business.

(4) RASKOLNIKOV'S RETURN TO THE SCENE OF THE CRIME.

When Raskolnikov leaves Zametov, the switches continue. Meeting Razumikhin at the door of the bar, Raskolnikov viciously insults him. Then he stands by, watching an attempted suicide as if it were none of his business, never even wondering if he should try to help. He goes to the murder scene where he must pretend that the crime is no business of his. Suddenly switching to the horrified little boy, he asks to be taken to the police. People hesitate and the commotion of Marmeladov's accident distracts him. He tries to help the man and impulsively gives all his money to the widow for the funeral. This little-boy generosity stirs Raskolnikov to great joy, but then his onlooker takes control and misinterprets, reinforcing the theme that Raskolnikov can go on living as if the crime were none of his business: ". . . it had come to him suddenly, as to a man clutching at a straw, that even for him it was 'possible to live, that life was still there, that his life had not died with that old woman.'" (182)

(5) THE CONFESSION TO SONYA.

In the dream the onlooker had urged the little boy on toward the cemetery, a dubious course. And another insight by the onlooker demonstrates the limited life open to Raskolnikov if he continues clutching at the straw that the onlooker offered him at the Marmeladov's:

> 'Where was it,' Raskolnikov thought, as he walked on, 'where was it that I read of how a condemned man, just before he died, said, or thought, that if he had to live on some high crag, on a ledge so small that there was no more than room for his two feet, with all about him the abyss, the ocean, eternal night, eternal solitude, eternal storm, and there he must remain, on a hand's-breadth of ground, all his life, a thousand years, through all eternity—it would be better to live so, than die within the hour? Only to live, to live! No matter how—only to live!'
>
> (152)

In effect, the onlooker urges Raskolnikov to stay up on the cliff face, a disastrous choice. But Sonya urges him to try to climb down to the solid ground, as dangerous as that effort might be.

The little boy in Raskolnikov takes the first step down when he confesses to Sonya. Raskolnikov must overcome the onlooker's urging him not to confess. But when Sonya begins to guess his secret, Raskolnikov "looked at her and suddenly in her face he seemed to see Lizaveta." (393) The expression is that of a small child and Raskolnikov's little boy personality at last emerges. Dostoevsky supplies the italics to make this point more emphatic:

> Her fear suddenly communicated itself to him: the same terror showed in his face and he gazed at her with the same fixity and almost with the same *childish* smile.
>
> (394, Dostoevsky's emphasis)

Sonya's tender reaction brings tears to Raskolnikov's eyes and, "Long unfamiliar feelings poured like a flood into his heart and melted it in an instant." (395) But on her vow to follow him to prison, Raskolnikov "felt a sudden shock" of the change of personality modes and "the old hostile, almost mocking smile played on his lips." (395) In declining the offer, Raskolnikov no longer speaks as a little boy: "In his changed tone she now suddenly heard the voice of the murderer." (395)

(6) Raskolnikov's impulse to murder Svidrigaylov and to commit suicide.

As more characters learn of Raskolnikov's murder—first Sonya, then Svidrigaylov, then Dunya—Raskolnikov finds the onlooker's indifferent position more difficult to maintain. The position erodes, leaving more and more the choice between murderer and little boy. At one point, the murderer seems dominant as Raskolnikov resolves "with cold despair" to murder Svidrigaylov (445). This proves unnecessary, but the murderer's most vulnerable victim may be Raskolnikov himself. The Mikolka part of him takes malicious pleasure in repeatedly striking a victim aspect of himself, just as the dream's peasant enjoys striking repeated blows. Raskolnikov even numbers his repeated psychological blows:

> '. . . Oh, aesthetically speaking, I am a louse, nothing more,' he added, suddenly beginning to laugh like a madman. 'Yes, I really am a louse,' he went on, clinging to the idea with malicious pleasure, burrowing into it, playing with it for his own amusement, 'if only because, first . . . secondly . . . thirdly . . . Finally, I am a louse because, . . . Oh, platitudes! What baseness!'
>
> (264)

The dream Mikolka killed the mare. There is a danger that Raskolnikov will kill himself. As Svidrigaylov puts it, "Rodion Romanovich has two ways open to him: a bullet through the brain, or Siberia." (480) Raskolnikov contemplates suicide on the canal at the very moment that Svidrigaylov actually kills *himself.*

(7) Raskolnikov's last interview with his mother.

Turning sharply away from suicide at the canal, Raskolnikov proceeds immediately to his mother where his "heart was all at once softened" just as at his confession to Sonya. Then Sonya had knelt at Raskolnikov's feet; now with his mother, Raskolnikov "fell down before her and kissed her feet, and they wept, with their arms about one another." (495) Her reaction makes clear that the little boy possesses his personality then:

> 'Rodya, my dear, my first-born,' she said, sobbing 'now you are just like the little boy you used to be; you would come to me just like this, and put your arms round me and kiss me.'
>
> (495)

Raskolnikov repeats this gesture a year later falling at Sonya's feet and accepting "resurrection into a new life" (526) at the feet of the woman whom the other prisoners called, "Little mother." (523) Like a little boy he is free to start a new life. That evening Raskolnikov for the first time combines the objectivity of the onlooker with the warm emotion of the child:

> Everything, even his crime, even his sentence and his exile, seemed to him now, in the *first rush of emotion,* to be something external and strange, as if it had not happened to him at all.
>
> (526-527, my emphasis)

The onlooker has never before been described as having strong emotions. This is a more whole, more complete feeling and indicates a process of reintegrating the split-off parts.

(8) Raskolnikov's final confession to the police, and the eventual reintegration of his personality.

The three parts of Raskolnikov's dream also explain Raskolnikov's confusing final confession scene, resolving it into the interplay of specific personality fragments. Raskolnikov has decided that he cannot act as if the crime were none of his business. First, too many people know about his guilt; and second, he cannot live like a man on a ledge of a cliff—he must confess to start a new life. But he has not repented. Saying goodby to his sister Dunya early in the very day of his confession, Raskolnikov repudiates her suggestion that he is "half atoning for your crime" by "advancing to meet your punishment." Raskolnikov's contempt for his victim still resembles the dream Mikolka's contempt for the old mare.

> 'Crime? What crime?' he cried, in a sudden access of rage. 'Killing a foul, noxious louse, that old money lender . . . was that a crime? That is not what I am thinking of, and I do not think of atoning for it.'
>
> (498)

Raskolnikov feels sorry only for the stupidity of his failure. Thus even as he prepares to confess, Raskolnikov claims he still feels as if he had committed no crime. His sister's response indicates her frustration at his inability to grasp the implications of his own action. "'Brother, brother, why are you saying this? You really did spill blood!' cried Dunya, in despair." (498)

Raskolnikov then visits Sonya to bid farewell. He goes to her, as he realizes moments later, out of Mikolka-like cruelty. "I wanted to see her terror, and watch her heart being torn and tormented!" (504) But as Raskolnikov leaves Sonya's apartment, a desperate renewal of the onlooker wonders, "Is it really impossible to stop now and revise all my intentions again . . . and not go?" (503)

Suddenly remembering Sonya's advice to "say aloud to all the world, 'I am a murderer!'" Raskolnikov has a shuddering change "like a clap of thunder" and "tears gushed out." To admit the murder as his crime, while not in the murderer aspect of his personality, would be a step towards unifying the split-off parts. Raskolnikov "almost flung himself on the possibility of this new, complete, integral sensation." (505) Desire for completeness, for this integral sensation, brings the split parts close enough to allow Raskolnikov to fall on his knees in the Haymarket. But comments by bystanders, that he is a drunk or a pilgrim to Jerusalem, encourage the onlooker by acting "as a check on Raskolnikov" stilling "the words 'I am a murderer,' which had perhaps been on the tip of his tongue." (505)

Raskolnikov's need for a "complete, integral sensation," to be obtained by claiming the murder, suggests the importance of confession for Raskolnikov. It is not the act of confessing that is important but the consequences. By confessing Raskolnikov would publicly and irrevocably claim the murderer as part of himself. In addition to any good feelings the confession might give him, claiming the murderer would make it part of his public identity. His position as prisoner would give him the sustained public identity of "the axe murderer," making the shift to onlooker difficult. For a whole year after confessing, Raskolnikov will resent this identity. But the prison situation relentlessly forces Raskolnikov to accept the reality that he did murder the old lady, this being prison's main therapeutic quality. Only when Raskolnikov finally accepts this reality can the little boy's triumph pave the way for the slow emergence of a coherent personality.

But there is danger that Raskolnikov will not confess. For personality switches continue even after the Haymarket insight. When Raskolnikov enters the office of Ilya Petrovich, this police clerk chatters on treating Raskolnikov with such complete implicit assumption of innocence that the onlooker powerfully revives in Raskolnikov. The police officer does not even exactly remember Raskolnikov's name, creating a temptation to try again to act as if the murder were "none of his business." Svidrigaylov posed the greatest threat to reveal Raskolnikov's secret. News of his death removes another obstacle to the onlooker's position, further tempting Raskolnikov to turn back. Raskolnikov staggers out of the office, but the sight of Sonya renews the little boy personality that had sent Raskolnikov into the office. He returns and confesses.

Dreams can only be interpreted in the light of other elements of personality. With a literary character, we have only those elements which the author chooses to give us. In *Crime and Punishment,* Dostoevsky consistently describes Raskolnikov in terms of Mikolka, onlooker, and little boy, even providing the italics to indicate how we are to interpret his words; he gives us the discrepancy over the name of the painter Nikolay; and he indicates that Raskolnikov's salvation must take the

form of a reintegration. Clearly, in Mikolka, the onlooker, and the little boy we have found the route by which Raskolnikov's dream carries us to a better understanding of his dilemma.

Notes

1. W. D. Snodgrass, "Crime for Punishment: The Tenor of Part One," *The Hudson Review,* XII, No. 2, Summer 1960, p. 239.

2. Feodor Dostoevsky, *Crime and Punishment,* tr. Jessie Coulson, ed. George Gibian (New York: Norton, 1964), p. 338. All references in parentheses are to this edition.

3. I am indebted to Lee T. Lemon of The University of Nebraska-Lincoln for checking Coulson's rendering of the painter's name against the original Russian text. I also want to thank Professor Lemon for the generous time he spent reading this paper and offering suggestions.

Malcolm V. Jones (essay date 1976)

SOURCE: Jones, Malcolm V. "*Crime and Punishment*: Transgression and Transcendence." In *Dostoyevsky: The Novel of Discord,* pp. 67-89. New York: Barnes & Noble Books, 1976.

[*In the following essay, Jones examines the role chance plays in determining Raskolnikov's fate.*]

> *The gloomy, oppressive atmosphere in which the opening episodes of* **Crime and Punishment** *unfold arouses an unaccountable depression in the hero. But within a page we find that his mood is in actual fact due to agonizing reflection on the infinite complexity of life.*
>
> B. Kuznetsov, *Einstein and Dostoyevsky* [(1972)]

> *'Enough!' he said solemnly and resolutely. 'No more delusions, no more imaginary terrors, no more phantom visions! There is such a thing as life! . . . My life hasn't come to an end with the death of the old woman. . . . Now begins the reign of reason and light—and of will and strength—and we'll see now! We'll try our strength now!' he added arrogantly, as though addressing some dark power and challenging it.*
>
> Raskolnikov in *Crime and Punishment*

I

Apart from *The Gambler,* which Dostoyevsky wrote at great speed between writing the fifth and sixth parts of *Crime and Punishment* in order to fulfil a contractual obligation to his publisher Stellovsky,[1] the novel which some regard as Dostoyevsky's masterpiece was to follow directly after *Notes from Underground.* There is no doubt that it is a great novel—a psychological, social and philosophical *tour de force,* a representation of amazing complexity and assurance of the experience of a young 'ideological murderer'. Yet the novel relates the psychological aspect of the crime to the social and ideological problems of the period and also to perennial philosophical questions.

The Underground Man was obsessed with progressive, 'rational', determinist doctrines, which seemed to him to constitute a scientific confirmation of his sense of impotence. But he had flung in the faces of the progressives his own intuition of the complexity and irreducible disorder of life. He had trumpeted self-will, even when used in the service of perversity. He had vaunted suffering as the origin of consciousness. A cult of perversity and emotional intensity had become a substitute for emotional balance and intellectual clear-sightedness, denied him by a combination of personal circumstance and intellectual fashion. But ultimately all he could be sure of was that life is a great deal more complicated than modern man tends to think—Hamlet had thought this too[2]—and the laws of life much more elusive and 'illogical' than the current wisdom supposed.

All these themes are taken up again in *Crime and Punishment,* though by no means in the same way. Writers on Dostoyevsky frequently remind us that the Russian word for 'crime' (*prestupleniye*) means 'transgression' or 'stepping over',[3] and that it is a 'stepping over' of the bounds of common morality into a region where there is no distinction between good and evil that is the basic motivating force in the novel. However, Raskolnikov 'transgresses' in more than one way. He not only makes a breach in the moral law or even the criminal law. He steps over the bounds of aesthetic seemliness; he offends also Dostoyevsky wished the reader to understand, against divine law.[4] Most important of all, for it is the realm in which all these 'laws' find their focus, he breaks the psychological law of his own personality and, as Dostoyevsky puts it, 'kills himself'.[5]

The Underground Man was unable to step over. He felt hemmed in on every side, and turned to hurling philosophical abuse and finding pleasure in perverse experiences. But even fantasy and vice afforded him only temporary release and literary hysterics only a temporary consolation. Raskolnikov, however, does step over. His tragedy is that in destroying the structures of 'ordinary life', he too fails to find others adequate to take their place, until, at least, the rebirth foreshadowed in the epilogue. The ethics of Napoleonism prove catastrophically inadequate.

In Wiesbaden in the first part of September 1865, Dostoyevsky drafted a letter to M. N. Katkov, the editor of the journal *Russkiy vestnik,* in which he said he hoped that his new novel would be published. This draft letter (the version he sent has been lost) is often quoted because it sums up the main idea of the novel. It also draws attention to a number of other features of the work which require comment, and it is therefore worth reproducing an extract here.

> It is the psychological account of a crime. The action is contemporary and takes place in the present year. A young man, expelled from the university, of lower middle class origins, living in utter poverty because of an inability to concentrate on day-to-day problems [*legkomysliye*] and a lack of intellectual stability, who has fallen prisoner to some of the strange 'incomplete' ideas which float about in the air, has decided to break out of his loathsome situation at one stroke. He has resolved to kill an old woman, the widow of a titular councillor who lends money on interest. The old woman is stupid, deaf, sick, greedy, charges exorbitant rates of interest, is malicious, makes other people's lives hell and torments her younger sister, whom she keeps at home and treats like a servant. 'She is no good for anything,' 'Why does she live?' 'Is she any use to anyone?' and so on. These questions thoroughly unhinge the young man. He decides to kill her, to rob her of everything, so as to bring happiness to his mother, who lives in the provinces, to rescue his sister—who lives with the family of a landowner as a paid companion—from the lascivious advances of the head of the family—advances which threaten her with ruin—to finish his university course, to go abroad and then for the rest of his life to be honest, resolute and steadfast in the performance of his 'humane duty to mankind', by means of which he will, of course, 'expiate his crime', if in fact such an act (against a deaf, stupid, malicious and sick old woman, who herself does not know why she lives on this earth and who would possibly die a natural death in a month's time) can be called a crime.

> In spite of the fact that crimes of this kind are extremely difficult to execute—i.e. it almost always happens that evidence is left around and loose ends stick out all over the place, and an enormous amount is left to chance, which almost always gives the criminal away—*he succeeds, completely by chance, in successfully and speedily committing his crime.*

> He passes almost a month between the crime and the final catastrophe. There are no suspicions against him and there can be none. It is then that the whole psychological process of the crime unwinds itself. *Insoluble questions confront the murderer, unsuspected and unforeseen feelings torment his heart.* Divine justice and truth, earthly law, claim their own, and he is ultimately *compelled* to give himself up. He is compelled, even if it means perishing in penal servitude, so that he can be reunited with other people. He has been tortured by a feeling of being separated and cut off from humanity, which came over him at the moment he committed the crime. The laws of justice and human nature have claimed their own, have killed [his] convictions, without resistance. The criminal himself decides to accept torment in order to atone for his deed. Actually, I find it difficult to explain my idea fully.

> In my story, apart from this, there is a hint of the idea that the judicial punishment meted out for a crime frightens the criminal rather less than the lawgivers suppose, partly because *he himself demands it morally.*[6]

Certainly not everything in this letter corresponds exactly to the final version of the novel, and the reader should beware of supposing that it does, yet there are a number of important clues here to the meaning of the work and to the problems it contains. Two points in particular will be selected here for special comment. The first relates to the psychology of the hero and the second to the world in which he lives.

Dostoyevsky's letter hints that apart from the fateful act itself, Raskolnikov is by no means a resolute character. As a matter of fact this irresoluteness is stressed throughout the novel. Indeed the very first sentence of the novel reads (my italics): 'Early one morning, during an exceptional heat wave at the beginning of July, a young man went out into the street from the boxroom which he rented from tenants in S. Lane, and slowly, *as though unable to make up his mind,* he set off in the direction of K. bridge.'[7] The fact of the murder, Raskolnikov's firmness in dealing with Luzhin, his resourcefulness in confronting Porfiry and his own theory of exceptional people occasionally lead readers to think of Raskolnikov as a consistently decisive person. Of course, he is capable of decisive action, when his thoughts and emotions are momentarily concentrated on one object, but such occurrences are not wholly typical of him during a period when his thoughts and emotions are disorganised by the shadow of his crime. More often than not he simply cannot make up his mind. A feature of Raskolnikov's mental confusion is the frequent irrelevance of his thoughts to the matter in hand. When he is actually on his way to commit the murder,

> . . . his mind was preoccupied with all sorts of irrelevant thoughts, though not for long. Walking past Yusupov Gardens, he was momentarily caught up in thoughts about the question of constructing high-playing fountains and how much fresher the air would be on the squares. Gradually he came to the conclusion that if the Summer Garden were extended to Mars Field and even joined on to the Mikhaylovsky Palace Gardens, then it would be a fine and useful amenity for the town.[8]

But it is not just when Raskolnikov is on his way to commit his crime that the irrelevant takes a hand. He is constantly sidetracked by thoughts and events that divert him from his intention. His mind wanders; he catches himself doing inexplicable things. First of all there is his encounter with Marmeladov and the strange attraction he has for him. Then he is distracted by his mother's letter; then by the girl who has been seduced whom he finds staggering in the street watched by a suspicious-looking gentleman; then he finds himself—though he cannot understand why—on his way to Razumikhin's house. Finally, and most important of all:

> Later, when he recalled this time and everything that had happened to him during this period, minute by minute, point by point, feature by feature, one circumstance always amazed him, and awakened superstition in him, although it was actually not all that unusual. But it later continually seemed to him to predetermine his fate.
>
> In fact he could never exactly understand or explain to himself why, tired, exhausted as he was, instead of doing the most sensible thing and taking the shortest and most direct way home, he returned home via the Haymarket, which was quite unnecessary. The detour was not a long one, but obviously took him out of his way and was quite superfluous. Of course he had returned home dozens of times without remembering which streets he had taken. But why, he always asked himself, why did such an important, and decisive, yet in the highest degree accidental meeting, take place in the Haymarket (where he had no reason to be going), exactly then, at that precise hour, and that exact moment of his life when he was in just the frame of mind and when circumstances were exactly right for that meeting to have the most decisive and conclusive influence on his whole destiny? It was as if it had been waiting for him intentionally.[9]

The element of chance in Raskolnikov's fate takes us ahead to another point to which we shall return. Here we should notice one thing: it is through being sidetracked that he happens to overhear the conversation about Alyona Ivanovna. Here a quite unnecessary and inexplicable act turns out to be fateful. The irrelevant does not always turn out to be so decisive; but in *Crime and Punishment* it is often unexpectedly so.

It is evident from the outset that Raskolnikov is not wholly in control of his thoughts and his actions. Not only does he swing from one extreme to another, from compassion to cynicism, from love to hate, but he also experiences horrific dreams, fever, fantasies, the loss of his sense of time, the blurring of subjective and objective, of dream and reality, of thought and word, morbid suspiciousness and aggressiveness, and varying degrees of confusion and clarity of thought. He is lost and trying to find a new life and a new self. His decision to break out of his situation, to do something now or never, is associated with his supposed discovery of a new historical law, with implications for morality, the life of society and the individual. This law, he is willing to admit, is not yet known, but it will be known, and it will confirm his intuitive conviction that people can be divided into two major categories. This general law does not involve the absolute division of mankind; there must be many doubtful cases. But it nevertheless holds good in general, with large samples. In principle some extraordinary people are above the criminal and the moral laws, and they may permit their consciences to step over obstacles, if this is necessary for the fulfilment of an idea on which the welfare of mankind may possibly depend. Such people are masters of the future and they all transgress the law and are destroyers.[10]

Some of the objections to this theory are expressed in the novel itself, but Raskolnikov takes a lot of convincing that he is wrong, even after his confession, trial and imprisonment. All he is willing to admit is that he made a bad job of it. This is no more than an admission that he is not a Napoleon himself, and does not imply that his understanding of socio-historical laws is mistaken. But his admission of failure is of great importance within the framework of the fiction, and particularly for Raskolnikov himself. An idea which should have focused his energies, his thoughts and emotions has had exactly the opposite effect. It is only when he is diverted from it that his personality sometimes expresses itself harmoniously.

Raskolnikov had anticipated that when it came to actually committing the murder he would be in a state of mental and emotional confusion, and so it turns out. The fact that he arrives at the scene of the murder at all, unnoticed and complete with his hatchet, is, as Dostoyevsky suggests, due to an almost incredible series of coincidences, and hardly at all to calculation. After his second, unpremeditated murder, Raskolnikov stops short: 'A tormenting, sombre thought was stirring within him—the thought that he was behaving like a madman and that at that moment he was unable to think clearly, to defend himself, that in general he should not have been doing what he was now doing. . . .'[11] The next day comes the conviction that everything, even his memory, even plain commonsense, is deserting him.[12] When he later comes to rethink what he has done, he asks himself: 'If you did all this consciously and not like an idiot, if you really had a definite and firm intention, then why haven't you all this time looked into the purse . . . ?'[13]

Almost immediately after the crime Raskolnikov begins to feel urges to give himself up. They begin before he meets Sonya. The very next day he thinks his punishment is already starting, wants to confess on his knees, and, when in the police-station, feels an urge to confess which is so strong that he even gets up to carry it out.[14] He is prevented from doing so by another coincidence.

Even if Raskolnikov's theory is correct, and the novel neither confirms nor refutes it, it offers little comfort to 'ordinary' people, nor does it offer any solution to the fundamental problems of the age. In fact, Raskolnikov's Napoleon theory, and, even more, his resolution to put it into effect by committing murder, stir up emotions within him which his theory fails to harness and control. He is made painfully aware of them by his dream of the old horse being heartlessly flogged to death by a drunken peasant. Critics, often with psychological qualifications or interests, have vied with each other in attempts to relate various characters in the dream (Raskolnikov himself as a little boy, his father, the drunken peasant, the old horse itself, the crowd) to characters and events in the novel. But the main point must not be clouded by excessive ingenuity: all the attitudes and emotions experienced by the characters in the dream are operative within Raskolnikov himself and too often, as in the dream, they come into direct conflict with each other. They underlie, moreover, his complex and fluctuating relations with other characters in the novel and explain in large measure the emotional basis for the fascination these characters exercise over him.

The other point to be extracted here from Dostoyevsky's letter to Katkov concerns the environment in which Raskolnikov operates: it is the emphasis which Dostoyevsky places on the element of chance in the novel.[15] As Philip Rahv has stressed, the hyperbole involved here should not be taken purely as a fictional device. It is true that the writers of the *romans d'aventures* traded in coincidence for its effect. As usual, Dostoyevsky learned from them, but he made their fictional devices constitutive elements in his fictional world—not artificial contrivances, but an intrinsic part of reality.

There are a number of striking situational coincidences in the novel: the fact that Porfiry is related to Razumikhin[16]; that Svidrigaylov comes to St Petersburg and takes a room next to Sonya's[17]; that Luzhin lives in the same house as the Marmeladovs, together with his former ward Lebezyatnikov,[18] and is distantly related to Svidrigaylov's wife.[19] Even allowing for the small part of the capital in which most of the action takes place, the coincidences are still striking. So too is the coincidence by which Svidrigaylov commits suicide at a spot on the other side of the Neva,[20] apparently not far from the place where Raskolnikov had his dream about the old horse.[21] As important as these situational coincidences—more important even than the singular chance which kills off Svidrigaylov's wife in time for him to pursue Dunya to St Petersburg, eventually to commit suicide and enable Sonya to follow Raskolnikov to Siberia—are the coincidences which advance the main plot. It is in the final analysis coincidence which both enables and impels Raskolnikov to commit the murder and to escape successfully, at a time when he had ceased to believe that he would really do it.[22] It is by chance that Porfiry learns that Raskolnikov is the author of the article on crime, when even Raskolnikov himself did not know it had been published.[23] It was chance which led the unfortunate Lizaveta to return home at the crucial moment to the scene of the crime.[24] It is by chance that Raskolnikov meets Marmeladov (on more than one occasion) and learns of Sonya's existence.[25] And so on. In the process leading to Raskolnikov's confession, chance also plays an important part.

Coincidence, when repeated, may have the appearance of the hand of Providence guiding events, as it does for Raskolnikov in the period immediately preceding the crime. Such a feeling is born of the conjunction of inner compulsion and outer events. On the other hand, it may prompt the reflection that events are in reality beyond man's control, and their logic—if such there be—beyond man's comprehension. It may lead to the conclusion that events sometimes seem quite arbitrarily to advance man's plans and sometimes to divert his attention, to present obstacles, and to defy his attempts to control things. It may suggest determinism and a preordained order of things or it may suggest anarchy and a world in which man is merely the flotsam and jetsam on the sea of life. In such ways Dostoyevsky creates the context in which the great philosophical questions about freedom and necessity, freewill and determinism, may naturally arise. What chance and coincidence on a large scale do not support is a view of life in which the individual can take control of events.

This is the basis for the 'indeterminacy' of which Rahv writes.[26] It infects, naturally enough, psychological processes as well as the sequence of outer events. There is no need perhaps to do more than draw the reader's attention to the complex web of motives, urges and events, both physical and spiritual, which bring about the main occurrences of the novel. That is too self-evident, and has been the subject of many analyses in critical and scholarly literature. But though it has often been noted that Raskolnikov's acts are 'overdetermined', and that they are extremely complex and not reducible to *one* 'real' motive (which, incidentally, he is slow to realise), it is perhaps not so evident that some of his acts and changes of mood are, so to speak, 'underdetermined'. That is to say, although the context is such that Raskolnikov's abrupt changes of mood are psychologically plausible, the proximate reason for the change is often not provided. If one seeks out a reason, it often turns out to be a circumstance which could equally well have had the opposite effect.[27]

All this goes to increase the atmosphere of indeterminacy, to break down common notions of cause-and-effect relationships and facilitate efforts to seek and discover alternative structures, patterns and explanations. They find their focus—inevitably in a novel of this type—in the hero's explorations into his own psyche. But these explorations turn out to be something more profound and disconcerting than talk of 'a criminal in search of his own motive' might seem to imply. For Dostoyevsky tells us that this criminal, who sets so much store by reason and will, falls prey to a quite different sensation at the moment his fate is decided: 'He went into his room, like a man condemned to death. He was reasoning about nothing and was completely incapable of reasoning; but with his whole being he suddenly felt that he no longer had any rational freedom or freedom of the will, and that everything had been irrevocably and suddenly decided.'[28]

If chance plays a major role in the novel, so too do unintended and unforeseen consequences. It would not be correct to suggest that Raskolnikov did not in any way

foresee the outcome of the murder. Even before he commits it he has doubts about his capacity to bring it off and decides that he will turn afterwards to Sonya. But the consequences of the murder are certainly unintended and the intensity of his emotional reaction unforeseen. In that sense almost the whole novel is about unintended and unforeseen consequences, and this is true not only of Raskolnikov's deed, but of the plans and deeds of other characters as well: Luzhin, Porfiry, Svidrigaylov, as well as Dunya and Sonya.[29]

Nothing in Dostoyevsky's novel invalidates a cause-and-effect explanation of events. But its very structure demonstrates the inadequacy of mechanical notions to an understanding of everyday experience. The impression given is of a world in which acts of individual freewill may sometimes determine events, but are just as often irrelevant and even contrary to the outcome.

II

Although the novel takes the hero through successive scenes of disorder, from which he only occasionally finds release, the plot itself is, by Dostoyevskian standards, a relatively orderly one. It is built around the main character and his fateful act; in the early conception of the novel this character had been the narrator and, to a significant degree, the novel retains structural features which originated in this conception. A careful study of the modes of narration would reveal considerable subtlety and variation in the way that Dostoyevsky retains much of the advantage of first-person narration while ostensibly using a third-person, omniscient narrator.[30] The use of the third-person narrator makes it possible to establish a social and personal context for Raskolnikov's subjective view of events. It also enables the focus of attention occasionally to move away from him. The most notable instances involve Luzhin and Sonya[31] on the one hand and Svidrigaylov and Dunya[32] on the other. Indeed, the working out of Svidrigaylov's fate temporarily overshadows that of Raskolnikov.

Nevertheless, the Ideas, or organising principles, of the hero, the main plot and the novel as a whole are virtually identical, and find their dramatic focus in Raskolnikov's act of murder. Such digressions as there are in the novel are thematically and psychologically closely linked with the main plot, and their outcome is of great moment to the hero, sufficient, indeed, to distract him from his preoccupation with his own predicament. Each of the digressions, moreover, is linked to the others and contributes to Raskolnikov's understanding of his own problems. Ultimately they bring him to a re-evaluation of his position. It should not be forgotten that between periods of confusion and fever, not only does Raskolnikov confront Porfiry but he also dissuades Dunya from her engagement to Luzhin,[33] organises things when Marmeladov is run over,[34] and publicly defends Sonya at Marmeladov's funeral.[35] He appears as a leading participant in all these episodes. Even Dunya and Svidrigaylov, in the scene in which Dunya shoots at Svidrigaylov, may be said to be acting out symbolically an aspect of Raskolnikov's own inner conflict; he has shown himself already to be deeply emotionally involved in the situation.

It is only in Dostoyevsky's next novel, *The Idiot,* that the digressive character of reality comes to occupy a dominant position in the structure of the work. In *Crime and Punishment* this conception is not absent but it is subordinated to the consciousness of the hero.

III

The consciousness of the hero, the way in which he formulates his problems and the solutions he seeks are themselves related to prevailing social and cultural circumstances. Many students of Dostoyevsky have pointed out the 'physiological' accuracy of his depiction of St Petersburg and his interest in contemporary social problems. Although he uses only initials to designate streets, alleyways and squares, there is no problem about identifying them on a map of St Petersburg. The modern visitor to Leningrad may have more difficulty of course, since many of the street names have been changed since the Revolution. But he may still visit 'Raskolnikov's house' on the corner of Grazhdanskaya (formerly Meshchanskaya) Street and Przheval'skaya Street (formerly Stolyarnyy Lane). Similarly he may call at 'Sonya Marmeladova's house' where Kaznacheyskaya Street meets the Griboyedov Canal. Other landmarks in the novel (and for that matter *The Idiot*) have been traced and can as easily be found.[36] The social environment is equally authentic. The newspapers of the 1860s testify to the rapid rise in money-lending in St Petersburg at different rates and for different securities. As one newspaper commented, this phenomenon bore witness equally to the poverty of the lower classes and the existence of a class of entrepreneur ready to profit from it.[37] Likewise, the rate of crime was increasing steeply: the yearly average of arrests for theft and swindling reached 40,000, an eighth of the total population of the capital.[38] One case of murder (committed by a certain Gerasim Chistov), which was reported in the papers and took place in January 1865, bore a striking resemblance to the details of Raskolnikov's crime.[39] The growth of drunkenness and prostitution was also a constant subject of comment in the papers, and it is interesting to note that current descriptions of the capital in the *feuilletons* then being published in the St Petersburg newspapers have much in common with the physical detail (the heat, the smells, the clouds of dust from the streets, the constant bustle, the closeness of the atmosphere) described in Dostoyevsky's novel.[40] Even Raskolnikov's day-dreaming about high-playing fountains echoes a scheme lately canvassed in the press.[41]

Such parallels have been traced in detail in Soviet writing on Dostoyevsky. So too have ideological parallels reflecting Dostoyevsky's polemic with the progressives of the day.

Many attempts have been made to trace Raskolnikov's ideological antecedents and to show their roots in current European and particularly Russian polemics. In an article in *Encounter* in 1966,[42] Joseph Frank describes how Raskolnikov's preoccupations reflect Russian culture in the early and mid-1860s. He points to the recent shift among the intelligentsia from utopian socialism to an 'embittered elitism' which stressed the right of a superior individual to act independently for the welfare of humanity. He also draws parallels between the views of Pisarev and his group—their use of the utilitarian calculus and social Darwinism—and Raskolnikov's ideological position. He traces the 'Nietzschean' elements in Raskolnikov to Zaytsev.[43]

But if Raskolnikov is influenced by the progressive, utilitarian creeds of the younger generation, he also falls in with Romantic traditions, notably with the Romantic tradition of Napoleon worship, and in particular its expression in a then recent book by Napoleon III.[44] B. G. Reizov traces the ideological and literary antecedents of Raskolnikov back more than half a century. He finds analogues of Raskolnikov's belief that crime may be justified in the interests of mankind as a whole, or of a needy or suffering member of it, in Schiller's Karl Moor, Balzac's Rastignac, Bulwer-Lytton's Eugene Aram, Victor Hugo's Claude Gueux and Jean Valjean and many others. In a similar way he traces the cult of the great man, the hero-figure, in the decades preceding Raskolnikov.[45] Raskolnikov's conscious ideals derive in part from this tradition, as did those of real-life progressives. There is a distinction to be made between those of his humanitarian views and feelings which are associated with his Napoleon theory and those which are associated with his intuitive sympathy for his suffering neighbour. It is the difference, in Dostoyevsky's words, between the ideals of the man-god and the God-man, between a proud, generalised sympathy for an abstract humanity, in whose interests many lives may be taken, and a humble compassion for one's neighbour, however lowly and insignificant. It is interesting to find a recent Soviet writer commending Dostoyevsky for his support of the second ethic and his opposition to the first.[46]

IV

Various forms of 'spiritual' disorder and complexity in *Crime and Punishment* have received their due in commentaries on the novel, and some of them have been mentioned in an earlier chapter of this book. Psychological, moral, aesthetic and religious disorder in a variety of forms, both social and personal, pervade the novel and are not only to be found in Raskolnikov. The workman Nikolay, who is a schismatic, believes in suffering for its own sake, and actually confesses to the murder, is a prime example of religious disorder as such.[47] Psychological disorder in a broad sense is, of course, everywhere in evidence. Both Katerina Ivanovna Marmeladova and Raskolnikov's mother eventually suffer from delusions and go out of their minds. Svidrigaylov has terrifyingly grotesque dreams which testify to the disorder of his personality, only partially hidden by his normally calm, cynical exterior; he also sees ghosts. Though he does not admit that ghosts do not exist, he concedes that it may be that they appear only to sick minds. Finally he commits suicide. There is also the confusion of mind attendant upon drunkenness, particularly important in the case of Marmeladov, whom it drives to degradation and the grave—an early example of the link between alcohol consumption and street accidents.

In an earlier chapter it was argued that though Raskolnikov may be described as a monomaniac, critics more usually dwell on his dualism, or what is often somewhat loosely termed his character as a 'double'. It turns out that the split in his personality is neither complete nor irrevocable. Neither part of his personality attains complete mastery over the other. Indeed there is one notable occasion when the two sides seem to act in concert. It is the scene where he manages to defend the meek, vulnerable and falsely accused Sonya and at the same time to attack the cynical, philistine Luzhin. Significantly, Raskolnikov '. . . spoke trenchantly, calmly, precisely, clearly and firmly. His piercing voice, his tone of conviction, and his stern countenance created a profound impression on everyone.'[48] Richard Peace has written:

> *Crime and Punishment,* in as much as it is built exclusively round one character, has all the appearance of a monolith. This is deceptive; for the fabric itself of the monolith is ordered according to a dualistic structure which informs the whole work. Dualism is both Dostoyevsky's artistic method and his polemical theme.[49]

Professor Peace goes on to write of the opposing impulses of aggression and submission in Raskolnikov, which correspond roughly to two groups of characters in the first part of the book. 'In the category of the self-assertive we have Alyona, Luzhin, Svidrigaylov; in the category of the self-effacing—Lizaveta, Marmeladov, Sonya, Dunya.'[50]

It is not just that the first group is self-assertive, or even aggressive. Its members are also malicious; they engage in some form of 'cannibalism' in Dostoyevsky's sense, contributing to the wilful destruction and desecration of life. It is not just that members of the second group are self-effacing. Indeed Dunya, in particular, is not always self-effacing. In their various ways they are also compassionate and they admit the claims of other people on them. Though this is the most obvious way of classifying the two groups, it runs the risk of oversimplification. Few readers are likely to confuse Luzhin and Svidrigaylov or Sonya and Dunya. Yet Raskolnikov enters into relations with all of these people and in varying degrees (with the partial exception of Alyona and Lizaveta) they bring out different complexes of ideas and feelings in him. They do not merely distract him; they involve his emotions, and this interaction is itself deeply disturbing and confusing. It intensifies his identity problem and complicates it. It is sometimes said (normally in relation to Sonya and Svidrigaylov) that other characters *externalise* aspects of Raskolnikov's personality. It could equally well be said that he *internalises* aspects of their personalities. At any rate a relationship is established which is not wholly reducible to the kind of positive and negative principles of which Richard Peace writes. Such relationships abound in Dostoyevsky's novels and, as it will not be possible to examine this aspect of his fictional world in relation to each of his major works, it may be useful to turn to it now.

V

That Svidrigaylov has a close psychological relationship with Raskolnikov is generally agreed by readers. Raskolnikov's emphatic denial of it is evidence enough in itself:[51] he protests too much. Svidrigaylov recognises in Raskolnikov a fellow-spirit. He shares the Underground Man's sense of boredom (ennui), his seeking of moments of intensity, his amoralism and sadistic tendencies. Although the stories in circulation about his responsibility for the deaths of his wife, manservant and a young girl are nowhere confirmed—the strongest accusations come via Luzhin who is an adept at exaggeration and false accusation[52]—he admits to striking his wife twice with a riding whip.[53] Nor can the self-indulgent and sadistic aspects of his relations with women and even Raskolnikov be overlooked. He has an aesthetic awareness—he says he loves Schiller and can write about the Raphael Madonna[54]—but this aesthetic sensibility fails to have any moral effect on him. On the contrary, he seems to enjoy defacing and destroying beauty and purity. He represents the decadent strain in late Romanticism.[55]

Svidrigaylov confronts Raskolnikov with a possible outcome of his own impulse towards amoralism. Of course, he is very far from Raskolnikov's Napoleonic ideal, which focuses on the heroic strain in the Romantic tradition. He is no more a real Napoleon than is Raskolnikov. He is doomed to an impotent suicide. Nor does his predilection for sordid sexual adventures have anything in common with Raskolnikov's ambitions. The view of some critics that Svidrigaylov is a warning to Raskolnikov of what he could become is a little far-fetched. What Svidrigaylov demonstrates to Raskolnikov is that if he opens the gates to amoralism, loses a sense of the holy, turns his back on the distinction between good and evil, then he opens the gate to such as Svidrigaylov too. A subsequent turning to philanthropy is no protection against the moral and psychological consequences. It is just such as Svidrigaylov (and Luzhin) that Raskolnikov cannot tolerate, particularly where his own sister is involved. Svidrigaylov and Raskolnikov do have some things in common, which makes Raskolnikov's dilemma worse: a cynical amoralism is but one of them. They share sadistic (cannibalistic) tendencies, the sense of being both victim and monster, a fear of death, a respect for Dunya. But there is a tremendous difference. Raskolnikov, despite his efforts to suppress it, still retains a powerful moral sense.

It must be admitted that there has been some disagreement among critics about Svidrigaylov's moral sense. It appears that he has lost all spontaneous feeling for the distinction between good and evil, as far as his conscious, waking life is concerned. One may argue, as Edward Wasiolek has done, that Svidrigaylov is 'someone beyond good and evil' and that 'those who have attempted to see some redemptive traits in Svidrigaylov . . . simply have not understood the logic of Dostoyevsky's morality.'[56] Or one may argue, as Richard Peace does, that Svidrigaylov's philanthropy after his scene with Dunya reveals him to be a changed man.[57] The text does not give us adequate grounds for certainty. Yet what is clear is that his turning to philanthropy does not save him from the consequences of his previous style of life. It is virtually irrelevant to his decline—like putting on the brakes and finding they do not work. The symbolic meaning of his final dream is also unmistakable. A five-year-old girl whom he has rescued and put to bed suddenly becomes a shameless French whore before his eyes, and he is horror-struck.[58] This surely is what finally destroys the meaning in life for Svidrigaylov. It is symbolic of the fact that even the most innocent and pure seems irresistibly to take on the appearance of corruption and to invite him to defile it. It symbolises the fact that even the sincerity of his love for Dunya is infected by the same virus. (The opposite is true for Raskolnikov. His prostitute—Sonya—turns out to be an innocent child.) There is more to Svidrigaylov's relationship with Dunya than mere animal passion. He is not merely the monster seeking another victim. He really seems to have hoped that Dunya might have saved him.[59] She is not like the others. She has a power over him which others do not have. She refuses to bend to his whim. He had come to Petersburg still entertaining hopes of supplanting Luzhin as her fiancé.[60] Now he is not only bored with life: his last hopes of regeneration have been dashed, and not only from without (Dunya) but also from within (his dream). As he says to Raskolnikov, he is left with the choice of going on a journey or marrying a young girl.[61] His horrible dream rules out the second alternative. He goes to 'America'—his euphemism for suicide.

If Svidrigaylov reflects Raskolnikov's cynicism, albeit in a distorting mirror, so, in a different fashion, does Luzhin. Both are, so to speak, petty Napoleons, in that they consider themselves justified in abandoning traditional morality. Whereas Svidrigaylov attempts to make amends by last-minute acts of generosity (if this be his motive), Luzhin builds philanthropy into his philosophy of life, like Raskolnikov. He represents capitalism with a veneer of socialist verbiage. On his first encounter with Raskolnikov he tries to impress the young people with the progressive ideas he has taken the trouble to learn:

> 'If up to now, for example, I have been told "Love thy neighbour," and I did, what came of it?' continued Pyotr Petrovich, perhaps with unnecessary haste. 'The result was that I tore my coat in half, shared it with my neighbour, and we both remained half naked. As the Russian proverb has it: If you try to catch two hares at once, you won't catch either of them. But science tells us "Love yourself most of all, because everything in this world is based on personal interest. Love yourself alone, and you'll do your business properly and your coat will remain in one piece." Economics adds that the more private business is carried on in society, and the more whole coats there are, so to speak, the firmer society's foundations will be and the more the common good will be served.'

The continuation of Luzhin's speech leads Raskolnikov to exclaim: '"Well, if the principles you've just been advocating are pushed to their logical conclusion, you'll soon be justifying murder."'[62]

For the common good, let it be noted. Luzhin's subsequent behaviour, the way in which malice and a desire for petty revenge override any other considerations, demonstrates how little the common good features in his calculations. Raskolnikov cannot ally himself with such as Luzhin, but Luzhin too holds up a distorting mirror to Raskolnikov's philosophy, and he reacts vehemently against the reflection.

If Dunya declines to save Svidrigaylov, Sonya has no such reservations about Raskolnikov. She performs the gradual and near-miraculous task of bringing him to repentance and rebirth. In the early stages she is not without motley allies: Raskolnikov himself, who is tormented by the need to straighten out his situation; Svidrigaylov, who goads him into recognition of aspects of himself and his philosophy which he is reluctant to acknowledge; Porfiry, who torments and tantalises him until he can stand it no more; and Dunya who stands before him as a moral reproach and example. But Sonya is unique in that she not only points the way but gives herself to him without reserve, follows him to Siberia, and draws out those qualities in him, those ideas and emotions, which provide the foundation for spiritual rebirth. Whereas the others can only disturb and reveal, Sonya lays the basis for a permanent change.

Like Svidrigaylov, Sonya is a character in her own right. It would be quite easy (though the point of view from which the novel is written does not encourage it) to imagine the action as seen by Sonya. Her experiences during the few days of the action cannot have been much inferior in horror and despair to those of Raskolnikov. She witnesses the deaths of her parents, one on the streets and the other after a street accident. She is at her wit's end to know what to do about her brothers and sisters. She is visited by an apparently demented young student who has appeared out of the blue to give alms to her family, and who subsequently confesses to the murder of her close friend and her friend's half-sister. She is falsely accused of theft by someone who, she had thought, was going to help her family. She is told by the unfortunate student that she ought to throw herself in the canal.[63] At the end of the novel she is in Siberia with the convicts, but looking forward to happiness with a reformed Raskolnikov. Told in such a way, the whole would be worthy of Eugène Sue, a contemporary version of the story of Fleur-de-Marie.[64]

Some readers have found Sonya incredible. But even if Sonya is not Dostoyevsky's most successful creation, she is not psychologically incredible. She declines to take up arms against God's world; she meekly accepts what she conceives to be God's will. Her humility is allied to a deep compassion for the suffering of others and a tremendous capacity for self-sacrifice. Moreover she declines to judge others. These may not be the values of the majority, either then or now, but they are not incredible. Moreover, she is not presented by Dostoyevsky as a calm contented creature, accepting her lot with unruffled equanimity. She is timid, frightened, often embarrassed and confused, with an acute sense of her own worthlessness. She shakes with fear on the occasion when she visits Raskolnikov and finds his mother and sister there.[65] She is by no means unmoved by her terrible afflictions. She dare not look the future in the face, and her blind faith in God's protection is shaken by Raskolnikov's predictions and the fate of her poor mother.[66] After Raskolnikov's first long interview with her she spends the whole night in fever and delirium.[67] After Luzhin's attempt to ensnare her, her sense of helplessness bites into her heart and she becomes hysterical.[68] Sonya too is incapable of coping with life. Her simple faith only just carries her through, but it sustains her and affects Raskolnikov, at first only fitfully, but later decisively. Sonya too stands in need of a spiritual resurrection, and Siberia not only sets the scene for Raskolnikov's spiritual rebirth, but for Sonya's too. Dostoyevsky writes: 'They were both pale and thin, but in those sick and pale faces there already shone the dawn of a renewed future, of complete resurrection to a new life. Love resurrected them. The heart of one contained infinite springs of life for the heart of the other.'[69]

In brief, the encounters with Svidrigaylov, Luzhin and Sonya bring out various aspects of Raskolnikov's personality. But the reverse is also true. Raskolnikov has a decisive influence on the fates of Svidrigaylov, Luzhin and Sonya. If Svidrigaylov and Sonya both fascinate him, he likewise exercises a fascination over them. The same is true of the relationship between Raskolnikov and Dunya. Whereas she has a crucial influence upon him, it is in large measure Raskolnikov who brings about her refusal to compromise with Luzhin or Svidrigaylov and promotes her relationship with Razumikhin.

VI

Raskolnikov exhibits many signs of being a disillusioned idealist. But in conflict with an unaccommodating reality his idealism is suppressed in favour of what he supposes to be realism. It is possible to see this process re-enacted on numerous occasions, notably when he checks himself after an act of spontaneous and what seems to him inappropriate generosity.[70]

Dostoyevsky wrote in the notebooks for *A Raw Youth*: 'nihilism is . . . the last stage of idealism.'[71] If there is a part of Raskolnikov which responds to Sonya's primitive Christianity, there is also a part which responds to the high moral principles and virtue of Dunya.

Svidrigaylov perceives Raskolnikov's latent idealism very clearly and taunts him with 'Schillerism'. He also perceives the link between Raskolnikov the idealist and Raskolnikov the nihilist:

> 'So you lay claim to strength? Ha, ha, ha! You quite surprised me, Rodion Romanich, although I knew in advance that it would turn out like that. *You* talk to me about vice and aesthetics! You are a *Schiller*! You are an *idealist*! That is just as it should be of course, and it would have been surprising if it were otherwise, but it's somehow strange when you come across it in real life. What a pity I have so little time, for you're a most interesting individual! By the way, do you like Schiller? I like him tremendously.'[72]

When Raskolnikov loses his patience and a little later exclaims: '"I've had enough of your horrible and disgusting anecdotes, you low, depraved sensualist!"' Svidrigaylov again takes up the refrain: '"Listen to the Schiller! A real Schiller! Just listen to him! *Où va-t-elle la vertu se nicher?* Do you know, I think I shall go on telling you these stories just for the pleasure of hearing your frantic protests."'[73]

Of course, Svidrigaylov touches Raskolnikov on a raw nerve. For it is not Raskolnikov's compassion for Dunya which is principally aroused. He is disgusted: it is his sense of what is honourable and dishonourable, what is virtuous and what is vile in Svidrigaylov's behaviour which is stirred. There are numerous other incidents which confirm the importance of these 'Schillerian' idealistic attitudes in Raskolnikov.[74] It is significant that he feels not only intellectually but also morally superior to both Luzhin and Svidrigaylov. If this attitude sits oddly with his claim to be above morality, there is a similar discord with regard to his aesthetic sense. He experiences an aesthetic disgust with himself for stooping to murder such an 'old louse' as the woman money-lender, when Napoleon left whole armies to perish. He tries desperately to persuade himself that Napoleon would have approved: '"Would he have felt disgusted to do it because it was far from monumental and—and wicked too? . . . he wouldn't have felt disgusted at all and . . . indeed it would never have occurred to him that it was not monumental."'[75]

But Raskolnikov has already consoled himself with the thought that Porfiry would not suspect him, precisely because he could never imagine that a person who considers himself a Napoleon would commit the two murders: '"His aesthetic sense won't allow him. 'A Napoleon crawl under an old woman's bed?' Oh, rubbish!"'[76] Shortly afterwards Raskolnikov rebukes himself with the words: '"Oh, I'm an aesthetic louse, and nothing more."'[77] Such aesthetic and moral idealism plays an important role in Raskolnikov's attitudes and behaviour, in spite of his nihilism. The Romantic idealism exhibited here is brought out even more forcibly in his last interview with Dunya where it is associated with the humanitarian motives which underlie Raskolnikov's crime. He exclaims that he is going to give himself up out of cowardice:

> 'Brother, brother, what are you saying! You shed blood, didn't you?' cried Dunya in despair.
>
> 'Which all men shed,' he answered almost in a frenzy, 'which is being shed and has always been shed on earth in torrents, which pours out like champagne, and for which people are crowned with laurels in the Capitol and called benefactors of mankind. If you look more closely, you'll see. I too wanted to do good to people, and I should have done hundreds and thousands of good deeds, to make up for one piece of stupidity. Actually, it wasn't stupid, but just clumsy; the idea itself wasn't nearly as stupid as it seems now that it has failed. . . . (Failure makes everything look stupid.) By this piece of stupidity I simply wanted to put myself in a position of independence, to take the first step, to get hold of the necessary funds, and then everything would have been put right by the immeasurable good, relatively speaking. . . . But I couldn't keep it up, because I'm rotten! That's all there is to it. All the same, I'm not going to adopt your attitude: if I'd succeeded, I should have been hailed as a benefactor to mankind, but now it's off to gaol with me!'
>
> 'But that's all wrong, Rodion, you've got it all wrong. You don't know what you're saying!'

'Ah! the wrong *form,* not the right aesthetic form! Well, I simply don't understand why blowing people up with bombs or slaughtering them in a siege according to the rules is a more acceptable form. The fear of aesthetics is the first sign of impotence! I have never, never understood that more clearly than I do now, and I understand my "crime" less than ever. I have never felt stronger and more convinced than at this moment! . . .'[78]

It is of some significance that the humanitarian motives for Raskolnikov's crime are unusually prominent in his conversation with Dunya. For Raskolnikov's Romantic idealism (Schillerism) turns out in some measure to be a family characteristic.[79] Dunya and her brother have much in common, in temperament as well as in facial features. Their mother affirms this, noting in her son the presence of those qualities of impulsiveness in defence of virtue and indignation in the face of vice[80] which Svidrigaylov also discerns. The point is made obliquely in other ways. For example, Porfiry remarks that Raskolnikov is, in his opinion, one of those men who, even if he were disembowelled, would stand and look at his torturers with a smile, provided he had found God or something to believe in.[81] Similarly, Svidrigaylov says of Dunya that, had she lived in bygone days, she would undoubtedly have suffered martyrdom, and she would most certainly have smiled when her breast was burnt with red-hot pincers.[82] The essential difference here is that, like the Man from Underground, Raskolnikov has not yet found 'something to believe in', whereas his sister apparently has. She is proud, fiery, capable of self-sacrifice for a loved one, courageous, self-confident, generous, strong-minded, sometimes patient and sensible, sometimes over-impetuous, on the look out for someone to save. She is also dazzlingly beautiful.[83]

Though it is Dunya who brings about Svidrigaylov's defeat, it is not she who brings about Raskolnikov's renewal. This is effected not by contact with Dunya's sort of Romantic idealism (which Dostoyevsky saw as the first stage of nihilism) but with the virtues of humility, compassion and insight, the voluntary acceptance of purification through suffering, and the refusal to judge others which Dostoyevsky associates with Christianity. It is the 'pure prostitute' who saves Raskolnikov, not the girl who is 'almost morbidly chaste'.[84]

If the demonic and the humanitarian are often related in Raskolnikov, as they are in his Napoleonism, it is not surprising that the primitive Christian response and the response of the Romantic idealist are also often indistinguishable. Are his acts of charity and courage described at his trial primarily beautiful Schillerian deeds or acts of spontaneous self-sacrifice and compassion? Are they acts, to use Professor Peace's distinction, of self-effacement or self-assertion? What about the episode when he defends Sonya against the false charges laid against her by Luzhin? What about the future which

Dostoyevsky projects for him? It surely cannot be imagined that Raskolnikov will become a sort of male Sonya! It is perhaps easier to imagine, as Mochulsky does, that he is not really resurrected spiritually at all, and that the last lines of the novel are a 'pious lie', a sop to the readers of Katkov's journal.[85] But it is not impossible to imagine a Raskolnikov resurrected through a synthesis of his latent idealism, his intelligence and vigour, and the experience of suffering seen through the eyes of Sonya. It is noteworthy that, from their various standpoints, Porfiry, Dunya and Sonya all foresee Raskolnikov's renewal by means of suffering.[86] It is appropriate that towards the end of the novel Sonya and Dunya come to have a deep mutual respect,[87] that Dunya marries Razumikhin and that Porfiry is among the invited guests at the wedding.[88]

In their various ways Luzhin, Svidrigaylov, Dunya and Sonya help to bring out in Raskolnikov a rejection of the crime he has perpetrated and an affirmation of moral values, values of justice, and respect and compassion for the individual. The fact that he has killed not only Alyona but also Lizaveta must also have played its part. The eternal values have not been snuffed out and they are incompatible with the wilful destruction of life. The structures of life cannot be rearranged in the way Raskolnikov has supposed without disastrous consequences.

The long interviews with Porfiry also play an important part in the process of Raskolnikov's self-illumination. They understand each other very well. Both know that Raskolnikov is the murderer. Both are playing psychological games, which they know to be two-ended instruments. Both seem to subscribe to Raskolnikov's theory that the criminal gives himself away by a breakdown of willpower at the crucial moment.[89] Each tries to put the other off his guard by play-acting and psychological tricks. Raskolnikov tries to counter Porfiry by anticipating his traps and forestalling them—for example, by entering the room laughing loudly.[90] Porfiry's principal technique is to put his victim off his guard by a confused and seemingly endless account of all manner of irrelevant things and suddenly lunge in with a question of crucial importance.[91] Although he is a representative of authority, he is something of a buffoon: he is said to be cynical, mistrustful, sceptical and to play practical jokes. Towards the end of the novel he also appears to be convinced of the possibility of Raskolnikov's spiritual rebirth.[92]

His object, it should be noted, is not to obtain material proof of Raskolnikov's guilt, but to make him confess, and he tries to do so by breaking down Raskolnikov's psychological defences. Eventually he arrives at the belief that Raskolnikov can be spiritually reborn, and even tells him so. His ultimate goal is to get Raskolnikov to abandon his theory and, as he puts it, to 'abandon himself to life'[93] without sophistry. Life will set him on his feet if he will do this.

Porfiry points to Raskolnikov's future. The dénouement of the novel, and indeed the greater part of the epilogue, depict Raskolnikov's discovery that he has failed. It is only later that he comes to abandon his theory as such, to abandon himself to life, and to find a new way of thinking and living. This the narrator does not describe.

VII

Porfiry tells Raskolnikov that what he now needs is air, and later he will accept himself again. God has prepared a life for him.[94] If the other characters in the novel pull and push Raskolnikov psychologically in directions which threaten his convictions and dominant feelings, Porfiry's role is to create a disturbance in Raskolnikov's mind, to loosen and put into a state of flux the ideas and emotions which hold him prisoner, permitting them eventually to settle into new configurations. In this perspective there is nothing improbable about his rebirth in Siberia. What William James wrote many years later about religious conversion illustrates very well the psychological processes involved:

> What brings such changes about is the way in which emotional excitement alters. Things hot and vital to us today are cold tomorrow. It is as if seen from the hot parts of the field that the other parts appear to us, and from these hot parts personal desire and volition make their sallies. They are in short the centers of our dynamic energy, whereas the cold parts leave us indifferent and passive in proportion to their coldness. . . .
>
> Now there may be great oscillation in the emotional interest, and the hot places may shift before one almost as rapidly as the sparks that run through burnt-up paper. Then we have the wavering and divided self. . . . Or the focus of excitement and heat, the point of view from which the aim is taken, may come to lie permanently within a certain system; and then, if the change be a religious one, we call it a *conversion*, especially if it be by crisis, or sudden.
>
> . . . To say that a man is 'converted' means [. . .] that religious ideas, previously peripheral in his consciousness, now take a central place, and that religious aims form the habitual center of his energy.[95]

Raskolnikov's conversion, although his preparation for it is lengthy, does indeed happen suddenly. This passage, by a psychologist who certainly did not have Dostoyevsky in mind, elucidates Raskolnikov's situation very well.

It has often been said that his ultimate motive for committing the murder is to decide once and for all the issue of whether he is a Napoleon or a louse. Undoubtedly this is a strong argument. Raskolnikov is inwardly divided, and this is how reality confronts him. But the act of murder also ultimately achieves a different and more far-reaching aim. Before the murder, after his dream of Mikolka and the old nag:

> 'O Lord,' he prayed, 'show me my way, and I renounce that damned dream of mine!'

> As he crossed the bridge he quietly and calmly looked at the Neva, and the bright glow of the bright red sunset. In spite of his weakness, he felt no tiredness at all. It was as though an abscess on his heart, which had been coming to a head for a whole month, had suddenly burst. Freedom, freedom! Now he was free from the witchcraft, magic spells, fascination and delusions.[96]

It is immediately thereafter that chance plays a fateful hand and radically alters the situation. But Raskolnikov is surely not praying for or welcoming a life of self-effacement to replace his Napoleonic delusions. He is praying for an altogether new illumination, one that transcends his dualism and frees him from all manner of spells and delusions. It is surely this that is prefigured in the epilogue and to which Porfiry Petrovich points. However, Dostoyevsky does not let the reader in on the secret. That, he tantalisingly tells us, might be the subject of another story. In fact it would appear that Dostoyevsky had a lot more problems to solve in his fiction before he would feel confident enough to address himself directly to the depiction of a character who had been 'reborn'.

In the meantime Dostoyevsky's first great novel was concluded. But the downfall of his hero is not depicted merely by juxtaposing his evil ways to the saintly ways of Sonya, nor even by showing the awakening of a conscience within him. He does something altogether more complex and more subtle than this: he maps out the shifting sands of experience on which Raskolnikov treads, the interplay of the unforeseen, the irrelevant, the fateful conjunction of multiple chance occurrences, the at times dramatic, at times scarcely perceptible effect of other consciousnesses upon his own, and of events upon his state of mind. Raskolnikov galvanises all his energies in an effort to defend himself against Porfiry's subtle (and not so subtle) psychological attacks, against the threat to his cynical Napoleonism of Dunya, Sonya and Svidrigaylov, and even Razumikhin. In Dostoyevsky's letter to Katkov he had written: 'Insoluble questions confront the murderer, unsuspected and unforeseen feelings torment his heart.' They absorb so much of his mental and physical energies that he has none left to profit from his crime. This is why he eventually has to give himself up. It was surely this which Dostoyevsky found it so difficult to explain fully to Katkov.

Notes

1. For an account of the events surrounding the publication of these two novels see, for example, K. Mochulsky, *Dostoevsky, his Life and Work,* translated by Michael A. Minihan (Princeton, 1967), pp. 270 ff. and 314 ff.

2. *Hamlet,* Act I, sc. v: 'There are more things in heaven and earth, Horatio, / than are dreamt of in your philosophy.'

3. See, for example, Vadim V. Kozhinov, '*Prestupleniye i nakazaniye* F. M. Dostoyevskogo', in *Tri shedevra russkoy klassiki* (Moscow, 1971) (pp. 107-186), part of which is translated as 'The First Sentence in *Crime and Punishment,* the Word "Crime", and Other Matters' in *Twentieth Century Interpretations of Crime and Punishment,* edited by R. L. Jackson (Englewood Cliffs, 1974) (pp. 17-25).

4. See Dostoyevsky's letter to M. N. Katkov (below), note 6.

5. *Crime and Punishment,* Part 5, ch. iv.

6. *Pis'ma,* [edited by A. S. Dolin in, 4 vols. (Moscow-Leningrad, 1928-59),] I, pp. 418-419; draft letter to M. N. Katkov from Wiesbaden, first half of September 1865.

7. *Crime and Punishment,* Part 1, ch. i. [In my references to Dostoyevsky's works I have contented myself with the chapter (and where appropriate part and book) number. There are so many editions of Dostoyevsky's works available that it seemed invidious and not very helpful to choose between them.]

8. *Ibid.,* Part 1, ch. vi.

9. *Ibid.,* Part 1, ch. v.

10. *Ibid.,* Part 3, ch. v.

11. *Ibid.,* Part 1, ch. vii.

12. *Ibid.,* Part 2, ch. i.

13. *Ibid.,* Part 2, ch. ii.

14. *Ibid.,* Part 2, ch. i.

15. It should be noted that Dostoyevsky himself intimates that an *unusual* degree of coincidence facilitates the events surrounding the murder. Their conjunction has an overwhelming effect on Raskolnikov's consciousness. Other coincidences of course do not, because they come singly or for other contingent reasons.

16. *Crime and Punishment,* Part 3, ch. iv.

17. *Ibid.,* Part 3, ch. iv.

18. *Ibid.,* Part 2, ch. v.

19. *Ibid.,* Part 1, ch. iii.

20. *Ibid.,* Part 6, ch. vi.

21. *Ibid.,* Part 1, ch. v.

22. *Ibid.,* Part 1, ch. v.

23. *Ibid.,* Part 3, ch. v.

24. *Ibid.,* Part 1, ch. vii.

25. *Ibid.,* Part 1, ch. ii.

26. Philip Rahv, 'Dostoevsky in *Crime and Punishment'*, in *Dostoevsky, a collection of critical essays,* edited by René Wellek (Englewood Cliffs, 1962) (pp. 16-38), p. 20.

27. This quality, among others, makes it essential to think in terms of unconscious elements in the psychology of Dostoyevsky's characters. Compare, for example, Raskolnikov's instinctive compassion in his reaction to the young woman staggering in a drunken fashion in the street (Part 1, ch. iv) when he mentally identifies her pursuer with Svidrigaylov, and his indifference and apathy when he witnesses the attempted suicide of a young woman at the Voznesensky Bridge (Part 2, ch. vi). It is possible to explain either reaction (i.e. they are plausible within the context); but if the reactions were reversed, with suitable modifications, they would be no less plausible. Dostoyevsky often introduces such emotions: 'For some reason. . . .'

28. *Crime and Punishment,* Part 1, ch. v. The same is true of his state of mind when he finally feels he must confess to Sonya:

    'Must I tell her who killed Lizaveta?' The question was strange because he suddenly, at the same moment, felt that he not only had to tell her, but that to put it off, even for a moment, was quite impossible. He still didn't know why it was impossible. He simply *felt* it, and this agonising consciousness of his impotence before the inevitable almost crushed him.

    (Part 5, ch. iv)

29. It is not difficult to multiply examples of this phenomenon; one notable occurrence which has unintended and fateful consequences is the receipt by Raskolnikov of his mother's letter.

30. The transition from first to third person narration is noted in the third version of his drafts for the novel: 'Narrative from the point of view of the author, an as it were invisible but omniscient being, but who doesn't leave him for a minute . . .' (*Complete Works* [(Polnoye sobraniye sochineniy v tridtsati tomakh; Leningrad, 1972-)], VII, p. 146. See chapter 2, note 15).

31. *Crime and Punishment,* Part 5, ch. i.

32. *Ibid.,* Part 6, v and vi.

33. *Ibid.,* Part 4, ch. ii.

34. *Ibid.,* Part 2, ch. vii.

35. *Ibid.,* Part 5, ch. iii.

36. See E. Sarukhanyan, *Dostoyevsky v Peterburge* (Leningrad, 1972).

37. I am indebted for the following details to the commentary to *Crime and Punishment* in *Complete Works,* VII (pp. 308-363). The writers draw attention to a single number of *Vedomosti S.-Peterburgskoy politsii* (*The St Petersburg Police Gazette*) in which no fewer than eleven advertisements for loans at different rates of interest were placed (No. 141 for 1865), and to a comment in *Golos,* No. 38, 7 February, 1865, on the social implications of this state of affairs (pp. 331-332).

38. *Ibid.,* p. 332, quoting E. Karnovich, *Sankt-Peterburg v statisticheskom otnoshenii* (St Petersburg, 1860), pp. 114-122.

39. *Ibid.,* p. 332; cf. *Golos,* Nos. 247-253, 7-13 September 1865.

40. E.g. *Crime and Punishment,* Part 1, ch. i; *Complete Works,* VII, pp. 332-333; *Golos,* No. 196, 18 July 1865.

41. *Complete Works,* VII, p. 333; *Peterburgskiy listok,* no. 106, 18 July 1865; *Crime and Punishment,* Part 1, ch. vi.

42. Joseph Frank, 'The World of Raskolnikov', *Encounter,* XXVI, June 1966 (pp. 30-35).

43. *Ibid.,* p. 33.

44. Napoleon III's *Vie de Jules César* appeared in March 1865; the first instalment of *Crime and Punishment* appeared in *Russkiy vestnik* no. 1, 1866.

45. B. G. Reizov, '*Prestupleniye i nakazaniye* i problemy yevropeyskoy deystvitel'nosti', *Izvestiya Akademii Nauk SSSR,* seriya literatury i yazyka, XXX, 5, 1971 (pp. 388-399). Cf. *Crime and Punishment,* Part 2, ch. vi, where Razumikhin calls Raskolnikov a 'translation from a foreign language'.

46. B. Kuznetsov, *Einstein and Dostoyevsky* (London, 1972), p. 103. Kuznetsov adds: 'Nowadays no one would dare to plan a general harmony which disregarded individual fates.' It is interesting to speculate on what the Underground Man would have made of this.

47. Cf. Richard Peace, *Dostoyevsky* (Cambridge, 1971), p. 45.

48. *Crime and Punishment*, Part 5, ch. iii.

49. Richard Peace, *op. cit.*, p. 34.

50. *Ibid.*, p. 37.

51. *Crime and Punishment*, Part 4, ch. 1.

52. *Ibid.*, Part 4, ch. ii. Perhaps Dunya's accusations are better founded (Part 6, ch. v.).

53. *Ibid.*, Part 4, ch. i.

54. *Ibid.*, Part 6, ch. iii; Part 4, ch. i.

55. A particularly 'decadent' touch in the characterisation of Svidrigaylov is his dream of Trinity Day in Part 6, ch. vi.

56. E. Wasiolek in *The Notebooks for Crime and Punishment*, edited and translated by Edward Wasiolek (Chicago and London, 1967), p. 8.

57. Richard Peace, *op. cit.*, p. 50.

58. *Crime and Punishment*, Part 6, ch. vi.

59. *Ibid.*, Part 6, ch. vi.

60. *Ibid.*, Part 4, ch. i.

61. *Ibid.*, Part 4. ch. i.

62. *Ibid.*, Part 2, ch. v.

63. *Ibid.*, Part 4, ch. iv.

64. Eugène Sue, *Les Mystères de Paris*, first published in serial form in the *Journal des Débats* in 1842. Dostoyevsky had a copy of the 1843 edition in his personal library. Cf. L. P. Grossman, *Seminariy po Dostoyevskomu* (Moscow and Petrograd, 192 2), p. 33.

65. *Crime and Punishment*, Part 3, ch. iv.

66. *Ibid.*, Part 4, ch. iv.

67. *Ibid.*, Part 4, ch. iv.

68. *Ibid.*, Part 5, ch. iii.

69. *Ibid.*, Epilogue, ch. ii.

70. Beginning with his gift to the Marmeladov family (*ibid.*, Part 1, ch. ii).

71. *F. M. Dostoyevsky v rabote nad romanom 'Podrostok'*, edited by I. S. Zil'bershteyn and L. M. Rozenblyum, *Literaturnoye nasledstvo*, LXXVII (Moscow, 1965), p. 128; for an English translation see *The Notebooks for a Raw Youth*, edited with an introduction by E. Wasiolek, translated by V. Terras (Chicago and London, 1969), p. 119.

72. *Crime and Punishment*, Part 6, ch. iii.

73. *Ibid.*, Part 6, ch. iv.

74. I have engaged in a more detailed discussion of these attitudes in an article entitled 'Raskol'nikov's humanitarianism', *Canadian-American Slavic Studies*, VIII, Fall 1974 (pp. 370-380).

75. *Crime and Punishment*, Part 5, ch. iv.

76. *Ibid.*, Part 3, ch. vi.

77. *Ibid.*, Part 3, ch. vi.

78. *Ibid.*, Part 6, ch. vii.

79. Raskolnikov accuses his mother and sister of 'Schillerism' (*ibid.*, Part 1, ch. iv).

80. *Ibid.*, Part 1, ch. iii.

81. *Ibid.*, Part 6, ch. ii.

82. *Ibid.*, Part 6, ch. iv.

83. *Ibid.*, Part 3, ch. i.

84. *Ibid.*, Part 3, ch. iv.

85. K. Mochulsky, *Dostoevsky, His Life and Work*, translated by Michael A. Minihan (Princeton, 1967), p. 312.

86. *Crime and Punishment*, Part 6, ch. ii; Part 6, ch. vii; Part 5, ch. iv.

87. *Ibid.*, Part 6, ch. viii.

88. Razumikhin, of course, becomes a symbol of life, normality (but not conventionality) and good sense. *Ibid.*, Epilogue, ch. i.

89. *Ibid.*, Part 1, ch. vi.

90. *Ibid.*, Part 3, ch. v.

91. Porfiry's first attempt occurs at this interview (*ibid.*, Part 3, ch. vi) but it is Porfiry's usual technique, which he uses still on the occasion when he tells Raskolnikov he knows he is guilty (Part 6, ch. ii).

92. *Ibid.*, Part 6, ch. ii.

93. *Ibid.*, Part 6, ch. ii.

94. *Ibid.*, Part 6, ch. ii.

95. William James, *The Varieties of Religious Experience* (London, 1960), pp. 200-201.

96. *Crime and Punishment*, Part 1, ch. v.

Temira Pachmuss (essay date 1980)

SOURCE: Pachmuss, Temira. "Dostoyevsky's Porfiry Petrovich: A New Socrates." *New Zealand Slavonic Journal*, no. 1 (1980): 17-24.

[*In the following essay, Pachmuss examines the similarities between the character Porfiry Petrovich from* Crime and Punishment *and Socrates.*]

The figure of Socrates appears to have fascinated Dostoyevsky. He was very pleased to hear from Dr S. D. Yanovsky, his friend in St Petersburg, that he had a phrenology similar to the Greek philosopher,[1] and avowed that he himself was aware of this similarity. There are also a few references to Socrates in Dostoevsky's texts. For example, in Notebook IV (1864-1865), which contained much of the material that went into *Prestupleniye i nakazaniye* (*Crime and Punishment*), we find the mention of Socrates in several passages. Speaking about Ivan Matveich, the hero of an early allegorical story **'Krokodil' ('The Crocodile'**, 1865), Dostoyevsky enters in his notes: "He wants to believe that he's Socrates."[2] A victim of his own sterile theories, Ivan Matveich resembles "Socrates and a fool."[3] Raising the question: "What is a philosopher?" Dostoyevsky answers: "'Philosopher' to us in Russia is an abusive word and signifies: fool."[4] His "philosopher—fool," Dostoyevsky reiterates, "wants to show that he's Socrates."[5] The present article examines a character in *Crime and Punishment* who is a philosopher but not a fool, and who strikingly resembles Socrates, on several levels.

"As a central figure . . . Porfiry sets the wheels of action of the novel [*Crime and Punishment*] in motion," Marina Turkevich Naumann observes in her well-researched article 'Raskol'nikov's Shadow: Porfiry Petrovič.'[6] "In a series of tense dialogues Porfirij compels Raskol'nikov to express his ideas, his psychology, and his glimmerings of faith. He questions and guides the student's thoughts to the point where the hero can understand the gravity of his crime, can voluntarily confess, and accept suffering."[7] Indeed, Porfiry is a crucial figure in *Crime and Punishment,* who raises several compelling questions, leads Raskolnikov through an intellectual and psychological transfiguration, and appeals to his dormant Christian beliefs in an effort to rehabilitate him.

Since Porfiry is a central character, a 'shadow' of Raskolnikov, several scholars have searched for his literary ancestors. Some have linked him to la Regnie in E. T. A. Hoffmann's tale *Das Fräulein von Scuderi* (1819),[8] whereas others claim that Dostoyevsky was influenced by the colourful figures of Inspector Javert in Victor Hugo's *Les Misérables* (1862), Vautrin in Balzac's *Le Père Goriot* (1834), Voltaire's 'Zadig; ou, La destinée. Histoire orientale' (1747), and Edgar Allan Poe's Chevalier C. Auguste Dupin, the detective in 'The Mystery of Marie Rogêt' (1842-43) and 'The Murders in the Rue Morgue' (1841). Donald Fanger mentions Dickens' Inspector Bucket as a possible forebear.[9] Eugène Sue's *Les Mystères de Paris* (1842-3) and *Les Mystères du peuple* (1849-56), and Ponson du Terrail's *Les Exploits de Rocambole* (1859), with its ensuing series, might have exercised some influence as well.

However, Porfiry is not merely a detective. As stated earlier, he is a primary motive force in the plot of the novel; he is Raskolnikov's counsellor and spiritual deliverer. Therefore, one should not limit Porfiry's ancestry to the ranks of belletristic sleuths. *Crime and Punishment* is, in the first place, a story of a spiritual pilgrimage towards enlightenment and transfiguration, and it is Porfiry (and, for that matter, Sonya Marmeladova) who helps Raskolnikov find God and Christ. When Porfiry advises Raskolnikov to accept suffering, because a man who is brought to justice suffers what is good, Raskolnikov becomes somewhat suspicious: "What sort of prophet are you? From what heights of lofty calm do you utter these all-wise exhortations?"[10] Raskolnikov is obviously aware that Porfiry aspires to be not only a clever detective, but a man of great insight and moral wisdom.

As a teacher of moral goodness and truth, Porfiry Petrovich appears to be closely modelled on the greatest champion of principles of right and wrong in behaviour that the Western world has yet produced, Socrates. This interpretation seems to agree not only with the general nature of the novel—but also with the principal moral themes presented in *Crime and Punishment.* In several of his famous dialogues, Plato presents Socrates' teachings concerning justice, injustice, punishment, the interest of the stronger who rules at the cost of the subject who obeys, and other moral issues.[11] For example, in the second half of one of the dialogues, the *Gorgias,* Callicles offers the following argument to his mentor, Socrates: "That is, in fact, how justice is determined: the stronger shall rule and have the advantage over his inferior . . . If a man appears of capacity sufficient to shake off and break through and escape from all these conventions, he will trample under foot our ordinances, . . . all this mass of unnatural legislation."[12] And elsewhere: "Nature herself reveals it to be only just and proper that the better man should lord it over his inferior: it will be the stronger over the weaker."[13] Callicles' contention that the extraordinary man has the right to trample with impunity on the laws of society in order to accomplish his ends closely resembles Raskolnikov's 'theory' concerning two categories of men: the superior who write the laws and remain exempt from the penalty of their misdeeds, and the inferior who are willing to be ruled and remain subordinate to their ruler.[14] Moreover, Socrates' argument that punishment is beneficial because it cures the transgressor's sick soul and reunites him with his fellow men by imposing suffering upon him is reminiscent of Porfiry's position that the criminal's soul is improved if he is justly punished. A man who is brought to justice is rid of the vice in his soul.[15] When facing Raskolnikov, who applied the theory of the extraordinary man and thus has transgressed "our ordinances and charms and spells, all this mass of unnatural legislation,"[16] to use the words of the sage of Athens in the *Gorgias,* Porfiry urges

Raskolnikov to accept pain and anguish to cure his sick soul. Sonya reiterates Porfiry Petrovich's views that Raskolnikov, who committed the crime, should voluntarily go to where he will get the speediest justice. "He must hurry to the judge, as though to a physician,"[17] Socrates insists.

Both Dostoyevsky and Socrates, when elaborating their positive views and possible solutions to various ethical dilemmas, avail themselves of poetic and religious myths. In *Crime and Punishment,* the myth of the regenerated sinner, the raising of Lazarus, and other Biblical allegories reveal its author's innermost convictions. Similarly, in *The Republic* in the allegory of the cave,[18] Socrates illustrates the progress of the mind from the lowest state of enlightenment to knowledge of the Good through the parable comparing the world of appearances to an underground cave. Several other dialogues (*Gorgias, Phaedo, Phaedrus*) describe the fate of the soul before birth and after death in the poetical imagery of myth—because no certain knowledge is attainable—for the Greek philosopher believed that the indestructible soul must reap the consequences of its deeds, good or bad. In the *Gorgias,* after rebuking Callicles' assertion that power is its own justification, Socrates advances the surprising proposition that incurring unjust punishment is better by far than escaping deserved penalty. Making reference to the myth about the Islands of the Blessed and the prisonhouse called Tartarus, Socrates claims that criminals who understood their own best interests would actively seek punishment, for "only in this way can they be rid of their own wrongdoings."[19] Socrates elaborates: "Those who are benefited by their punishment at the hands of men and gods are they that have committed only curable sins; none the less their improvement must come through the pangs of suffering both here and in Hades."[20]

The rejection of these ideas, then—that the stronger can plunder the property of the weaker, that the better should rule the worse, that the superior man should take the advantage over the inferior—as well as the emphatic avowal that the soul of the criminal is improved if he is justly punished, form the ethical and philosophical focus of the *Gorgias* and *Crime and Punishment* and were equally important for both Socrates and Dostoyevsky in their concern for human society and for the role of the individual within it. The main difference between Socrates and Porfiry Petrovich is that the latter deals with a more intricate compound of the human personality than Socrates had envisaged in the *Gorgias.* Aware of the complexities of human consciousness, with all its hidden layers and entanglements, Porfiry anticipates that the criminal's subconscious desire for punishment will propel him to justice, even though he consciously endeavours to escape it.

In *Crime and Punishment,* we have the essence of Socrates' argument, as developed in the *Gorgias,* played out in a gripping dramatic form: in place of theoretical discourses on the status of the extraordinary man and the hypotheses of punishment and justice, we have the actual crime and punishment—on the legal, moral and religious levels—of a man who claimed to be a 'select' one. As in the *Gorgias,* however, the argument is a disputation in conformity with the laws of logic between the young theoretician and the older teacher, during which the latter's provocative manner and penetrating questions demolish the young and inexperienced man's insolvent ideas.

Was Dostoyevsky aware that the theory propounded by Raskolnikov that the extraordinary man has the right to tread underfoot the 'unnatural laws'—if this theory is necessary to achieve his goal, which in the final analysis is nothing less than the acquisition of power—was 2300 years old? There is no direct evidence, but it is significant that Porfiry Petrovich discloses to Raskolnikov: "You invented a theory, and you were ashamed because it went wrong and because it turned out to be not even original." (p. 479) Just as Socrates refutes Callicles, a young man of Athens who, like Raskolnikov, believes himself to be a 'better' man, Porfiry tugs at his interlocutor psychologically, befuddles, and argues with him until he drives him into an admission of guilt, and a rejection of his own thesis. This was Socrates' famous method of dealing with his opponents. And as if recognizing it, Razumikhin, Raskolnikov's close friend, instructs him when the latter is on the point of leaving to see Porfiry: "He is an intelligent fellow, very intelligent, he's nobody's fool, only he has a sort of special way of looking at things, . . . he is distrustful, a skeptic, and a cynic. He likes to mislead people, or rather to baffle them . . . Well, it is an old and well-tried method." (pp. 254-5) This portrait could easily be used to describe Socrates as we know him from various sources. There is a striking pattern of resemblances between the philosopher of Athens and the police detective of St Petersburg who refute the variants of the same theory, as presented by Callicles and Raskolnikov, with compelling power. One of the salient features of Socrates' style in conducting the dialectical debate is his constant use of irony to taunt his interlocutor, to lure him until he drives him into dangerous agitation. He was famous for dealing with his opponents in this manner. In the *Symposium,* Alcibiades, recounting one of Socrates' debates, says: "With these words he replied in the ironical manner, which is so characteristic of him."[21] As Razumikhin says, Porfiry Petrovich, too, likes to mislead people by using irony—he knows that if he irritates his subject sufficiently, he may perhaps cause a fatal slip of the tongue. He also seems to enjoy the game of teasing, attracting and finally deceiving him. Fully aware of this approach, which is itself an illustration of his typical ironic self-disparagement, Porfiry avows: "I agree, I agree, I have a nasty sarcastic nature, but just look at what people have made of that!"

(p. 356) His irony, or sarcasm, was just as powerful a tool in his interrogation as it was in Socrates' discussions.

Porfiry Petrovich bears a number of other resemblances to Socrates in the area of method. During one of Porfiry's desultory remarks, as he is talking about the formal nature of the conventional investigation, he breaks off, musing: "Yes, . . . I am talking about forms again" (p. 350)—not formalities. This brief reference may be interpreted as an allusion to Socrates' much celebrated doctrine of Forms:[22] that is, knowledge of the whole truth and reality, and hence of the world of essential Forms, in contrast with the world of appearances. The Forms are ideals or patterns which exist apart from individual things in the visible world. The essence of the doctrine is the conviction that the differences between good and evil, right and wrong, true and false, are absolute, not 'relative' to the customs or tastes or desires of individual men or social groups. Dostoyevsky, of course, was a firm believer in absolute goodness, or absolute morality as he so forcefully expounded it in his last novel, *Brat'ya Karamazovy* (*The Brothers Karamazov*).

The hallmark of the Socratic dialogue is that at the conclusion of the argument both Socrates and his interlocutor are puzzled; in technical terms, they are in a state of *aporia,* a Greek word meaning "to be at a loss what course to pursue; having no way out". Dostoyevsky's Porfiry resembles Socrates in his ability to baffle and refute his opponent. In fact, his dialectical method, in which he probes the logical consequences of Raskolnikov's theory of crime, is very much akin to the Socratic disputation. It is not surprising therefore that Razumikhin describes Porfiry Petrovich's debate with his subject as "an old and well-tried method." (p. 255) Here, too, we may then conclude that Porfiry's role in *Crime and Punishment* is reminiscent of that of Socrates in Plato's dialogues.

Turning from Porfiry's method to his personality, we see an additional remarkable resemblance to Socrates. During his first meeting with Raskolnikov, Porfiry Petrovich recalls that only the night before they "had arrived at discussing the eternal verities, and soared into the clouds." (p. 264) The picture of a group of carousing revellers discussing the lofty subjects—Chaos, Broad-bosomed Earth, Love, and Harmony—constitutes the plot of the *Symposium,* including even the fact that Socrates in the *Symposium,* like Porfiry in *Crime and Punishment,* is the only one amongst the tipsy revellers who is not drunk. Furthermore, the reference "soared into the clouds" recalls the first scene of Aristophanes' satirical play *The Clouds,* in which Socrates slowly descends from the clouds in a basket after Strepsiades pleads with him to come down and teach him what he "needed to know".[23]

Like Porfiry, Socrates is supposed to have been awkward and strange in the eyes of other people. He was sceptical and critical of their assertions and inquiries, and claimed that he was wiser than all men because he fully realised that he knew very little. Wandering along the streets of Athens, he often succeeded in proving to those who considered themselves wise that their beliefs and opinions were ridiculously incongruous. These attitudes reappear in Razumikhin's portrayal of Porfiry, namely, that he is awkward, incredulous, sceptical and cynical; however, he knows what questions to ask, how to ask them, and how to respond to Raskolnikov's subterfuges and stratagems. Porfiry is also wise and experienced, also almost an artist in his own right, who step by step exposes Raskolnikov's psychological complexities and theoretical errors. In the following description (pp. 258-9) we can see a keen observer of people, a brilliant psychologist and dialectician, and a dangerous adversary, as he appears to Raskolnikov:

> He was a man of about thirty-five, shorter than average, corpulent and even paunchy, clean-shaven, with no mustache or sideburns, with closely cropped hair on a large round head which bulged out rather peculiarly at the back. He had a chubby, round, and somewhat snub-nosed face of a sickly dark yellow colour but rather hearty and even ironical. It would have been even benevolent but for the expression of his eyes, which had a sort of watery glint in them and were covered with almost white blinking eyelashes, which seemed to be winking at you. The expression of those eyes was strangely out of keeping with the rest of his figure, which even had something of an old woman about it and endowed it with something much more serious than one would have expected at first glance.

It is well known that whenever Dostoyevsky gave descriptions of his heroes' physical appearances, he did so to delineate their special qualities or, as George A. Panchias puts it in his informative study *The Burden of Vision: Dostoevsky's Spiritual Art,* he gave "an index to the total personality"[24] of the protagonist. The description of Porfiry Petrovich's appearance is indeed significant, for it is as incongruous as that of Socrates. They both possess great intellect, but their bodies appear so comical that people may become bewildered. Porfiry himself says that "God created me with such a figure that the only ideas I arouse in other people are comical ones; I am a clown." (p. 353) In the *Symposium,* Alcibiades says to Socrates: "you yourself will not deny that your face is that of a satyr,"[25] that is, of a man with the legs of a goat, pointed ears, and short horns, who comprised the choruses in the most scurrilous types of Greek comedy. "Aye, and there is a resemblance in other points too," Alcibiades continues. "For example, you are a bully, as I can prove by witnesses, if you won't confess."[26] In the banter which introduces the *Theaetetus,* we learn that Socrates had a snub-nose, like Porfiry. Theodorus states: "The remarkable Athenian youth whom I commend to you . . . is very much like you;

for he has a snub-nose and projecting eyes, although these features are less marked in him than you."[27] However, it is Socrates' and Porfiry's eyes that are their most striking, expressive and contradictory feature. Even though at first sight both characters may appear amusing and even harmless, their eyes reveal that they must be taken most seriously. Yet, at the same time, these eyes in some ways support Socrates' and Porfiry's generally funny physical appearance. In *The Clouds,* the chorus states that Socrates with his "swivel-eyes" walked barefoot down the streets of Athens.[28] Porfiry, too, suffers from a nervous tic around his eyes, as if screwing them up and winking at his interlocutor (p. 260). Other similarities between Socrates and Porfiry Petrovich, when added together, seem to form a coherent pattern.

When we consider these congruities together with the thematic correspondence and with Socrates' and Porfiry's methods of exploring the minds of their interlocutors, it should not appear too presumptuous to conclude that Dostoyevsky may have availed himself of the personality, doctrines and procedure of Socrates as the primary sources for his sagacious detective in **Crime and Punishment.** The Russian novelist introduced to us, in a most dramatic form, a new Socrates in our contemporary bleak surroundings.

Although it is, strictly speaking, outside the scope of this article, one might even go further and propose a parallel between Socrates and Dostoyevsky himself. With their steady concentration upon what is universally and basically human, Socrates and Dostoyevsky reveal an intellectual and spiritual complexity which is the essential characteristic of modern self-awareness. Probing into the mind of men, they acquaint the reader with a deeper psychological understanding of humanity, and focus his attention on those ethical and social involutions and perplexities which have not been solved even in twentieth-century society.

Notes

1. S. Yanovsky, *Russky vestnik* (Moscow), 1885, April, p. 806.

2. *The Unpublished Dostoevsky—Diaries and Notebooks (1860-81),* 3 Vols. General Editor Carl R. Proffer, with an Introduction by Robert L. Belknap, Ann Arbor, 1973. Vol. I, Notebook IV (1864-1865), translated by Ellendea Proffer, p. 113.

3. Loc. cit.

4. Ibid., p. 115.

5. Ibid., p. 123.

6. *SEEJ* [*Slavic and East European Journal*], Vol. 16, No. 1 (Spring 1972), p. 47.

7. Loc. cit.

8. Cf. Charles Passage, *Dostoevsky the Adapter: A Study of Dostoevsky's Use of the Tales of Hoffmann,* Chapel Hill, 1954, p. 145.

9. Donald Fanger, *Dostoevsky and Romantic Realism,* Chicago, 1967, p. 190.

10. F. M. Dostoevsky, *Crime and Punishment,* newly translated by Michael Scammell, New York, 1963, p. 478. Subsequent references in the text are to this edition. When it seemed advisable, changes were made in this translation.

11. See, for example, *The Republic of Plato,* translated, with Introduction and Notes, by Francis Macdonald Cornford, Oxford, 1941, Chapter III (1.336B-347E).

12. Plato, *Gorgias,* translated, with an Introduction, by W. C. Helmbold, Indianapolis, 1952, p. 52.

13. Ibid., p. 51.

14. Porfiry Petrovich summarizes the essence of Raskolnikov's article 'On Crime' in the *Periodical Review* in the following fashion:

> . . . The whole point of the matter is that in this gentleman's article all men are somehow divided up into 'ordinary' and 'extraordinary'. Ordinary men have to live in obedience to the law and have no right to overstep it, because, you see, they are ordinary. But extraordinary men have the right to commit all sort of crimes and overstep the law in all sorts of ways, because, in fact, they are extraordinary. That's the way you have it, I believe, if I'm not mistaken?
>
> (p. 268)

15. *Gorgias,* op. cit.,

> SOCRATES:
>
> Then a man who is punished suffers justly in being brought to justice.
>
> POLUS:
>
> It seems so.
>
> SOCRATES:
>
> And what is just, we have admitted to be beautiful.
>
> (p. 42)

16. Ibid., p. 52.

17. Ibid., p. 47.

18. *The Republic,* op. cit., Chapter XXV (VII. 514A-521B).

19. *Gorgias,* op. cit., p. 104.

20. Loc. cit.

21. Plato, *The Works of Plato—Symposium,* selected and edited by Irwin Edman, New York, 1956, p. 387.

22. *The Republic,* op. cit., Chapter XIX (V. 474B-480).

23. Aristophanes, *The Clouds,* tr. by William Arrowsmith with sketches by Thomas McClure, Ann Arbor, 1970, p. 26.

24. Grand Rapids, 1977, p. 29.

25. *Symposium,* op. cit., p. 383.

26. Loc. cit.

27. *The Works of Plato—Theaetetus,* op. cit. p. 483.

28. Of course, we should keep in mind that *The Clouds* is a satirical, grotesque and hilarious play that employs exaggeration and incongruity in presenting Socrates as merely a cipher, who disregarded all distinctions between doctrine and belief. According to Aristophanes, Socrates expounded the ideas of Protagoras, Anaxagoras, Diagoras, Gorgias, Prodikos and Thrasymachos, all at the same time, making them his own.

Robert Mann (essay date September 1981)

SOURCE: Mann, Robert. "Elijah the Prophet in *Crime and Punishment.*" *Canadian Slavonic Papers* 33, no. 3 (September 1981): 261-72.

[*In the following essay, Mann compares the character of the police magistrate, through whom Raskolnikov achieves his symbolic "resurrection," with the Biblical prophet Elijah.*]

Raskol'nikov's spiritual transformation in the epilogue of *Crime and Punishment* has elicited a wide range of responses among critics. Some see it as the logical culmination of a Christian theme that is developed throughout the novel. Others, including the Soviet critic Leonid Grossman, ignore the Christian motifs altogether.[1] Yet others, such as Konstantin Mochul'skii, argue that Raskol'nikov's transformation hardly follows from the earlier characterization of the hero. According to Mochul'skii, the epilogue is a poorly contrived appendage to the novel, hastily concocted in order to please the reader and publisher.[2]

In reply to such criticisms George Gibian has written:

> The epilogue has been called unprepared for, weak, and disjointed. These strictures are natural if we pay attention exclusively to "rational" aspects of the book

and look for connections between the epilogue and the body of the novel only in the realms of outward plot and explicit statement. It is true that the regeneration of Raskolnikov is not presented as fully or as dramatically as the events leading to its inception; yet its beginning and its future course are indicated sufficiently by other means. The frequent undervaluation of the epilogue may be symptomatic of the lack of attention to Dostoevsky's communication through the symbolic pattern of the novel.[3]

Gibian argues that Raskol'nikov's spiritual resurrection is artistically motivated by biblical symbolism which he traces throughout the novel. A still deeper examination of the spiritual themes and symbols of the novel may be found in Georgii Meier's *Svet v nochi,* probably the most valuable contribution to the study of *Crime and Punishment* written in this century.[4]

But biblical and Christian imagery in *Crime and Punishment* goes further than any critics have supposed. This study is concerned chiefly with the symbolic function of Il'ia Petrovich Porokh (Elijah Petrovich 'Gunpowder'), the assistant police superintendent to whom Raskol'nikov eventually confesses. A number of allegorical episodes linking Il'ia Petrovich with Elijah the Prophet show that the Christian theme of suffering and redemption is truly the pivotal theme of the novel and that Raskol'nikov's eventual resurrection was foreseen by Dostoevskii even in the early stages of his work on the novel.

An inner, spiritual awareness of the necessity to accept suffering for his sins leads Raskol'nikov to confess his crime, even though he knows there is no legally incriminating evidence against him. In Dostoevskii's view, all men share the spirit of Christ, and Raskol'nikov's spiritual path is not only that of Christ, but of mankind in general. His crime can be compared with original sin and the fall of man in the Bible.[5] A clerk at the police station remarks that the murderer escaped capture because the building where the old pawnbroker lived is "a Noah's ark" (p. 83).[6] The clerk simply means that the building is large, with plenty of places where the murderer might hide. But there is also a suggestion of the ark that saved the human race after Adam's fall and the corruption of his descendants.

Other biblical symbols mark Raskol'nikov's path and show that he is following in Christ's footsteps towards suffering and resurrection. He visits Sonia at the Kapernaumovs', whose name is derived from Capernaum, one of a series of towns Christ visited before his crucifixion, healing the afflicted and raising Lazarus from the dead.[7] In the novel Kapernaumov and his wife are both lame and they have a speech impediment; Kapernaumova is half deaf, their eldest child stutters, and their other children are sickly; the derelict building in which they live, the dwelling of cripples and a prostitute, recalls the biblical Capernaum, the fate of which would be worse than that of Sodom (Matthew, XI, 23-24). It is, of course, at the Kapernaumovs' that Sonia reads to Raskol'nikov about the resurrection of Lazarus.

Following Christ, Raskol'nikov "takes on the cross" given him by Sonia when he goes to confess. He then bows at the crossroads ("perekrestok"—from *krest* "cross") and kisses the ground.[8] As he enters the police station to confess, he speaks of "drinking the cup," a clear parallel to the "bitter cup" of Christ. Like Mary Magdalene, the prostitute who followed Christ to his crucifixion, an early draft states that she follows him "to Golgotha."[9] When he is sick and in delirium in Siberia, Sonia waits by his side, much as Mary Magdalene waited at Christ's tomb. Finally, his spiritual resurrection occurs shortly after Easter, the holiday of Christ's resurrection.

Il'ia Petrovich, the assistant police superintendent, figures in three highly symbolic episodes: first, when Raskol'nikov is summoned to the police station for not repaying his debt to his landlady; second, when he dreams that Il'ia Petrovich is beating his landlady; and third, when he finally confesses. *Pórokh* ("Gunpowder") is a nickname given to Il'ia Petrovich by his comrades in the army because of his fiery temperament. The police superintendent Nikodim Fomich first mentions the nickname in a passage that juxtaposes the words "porók" ("vice," "crime") and "pórokh" ("gunpowder"): "Бедность не порок, дружище, ну да уж что! Известно, порох не мог обиды перенести" (p. 80). The similarity between "porók" and "pórokh" points to an underlying word-play between Il'ia Pórokh and Il'ia Prorók (Elijah the Prophet) who, according to Russian folk belief, is the lord of thunder and lightning.[10] He doubtless inherited this function from the pagan thunder god Perun in Russia's early Christian period. His control over rain and lightning in the Bible and his godlike ascent into the heavens on a fiery chariot made him the most likely replacement for the pagan lord of thunder. Until recently, the Russian peasantry always expected a thunderstorm on the feast day of Elijah the prophet (July 20, O.S.).[11]

In the first scene at the police station, there are five allusions to Porokh's lightning. He looks at Raskol'nikov with a "lightning gaze" ("molnienosnyi vzgliad," p. 76; an earlier draft has the unusual formulation "thunderous gaze" ["gromovoi vzgliad"]).[12] When the superintendent first enters the station and finds that Il'ia Petrovich has "let loose with all his thunderbolts" against the brothel keeper Luiza Ivanovna ("nabrosilsia vsemi perunami," p. 78), he exclaims: "Опять грохот, опять гром и молния, смерч, ураган!" (p. 79). The whirlwind and hurricane recall the whirlwind in which the biblical Elijah ascends to heaven. Further thunder and lightning imagery is applied to Il'ia Petrovich throughout the

scene: "It was as though thunder and lightning had struck in the office;" "she (Luiza) was all atremble beneath Porokh's thunder and lightning" (p. 78). Porokh speaks in an "unnaturally loud" voice ("kak-to neestestvenno gromko") and emits a rain-like "spray" ("bryzgi") as he talks (p. 77). He smokes a cigarette and is repeatedly associated with heat and fire: "vspylil" (p. 77); "goriachii poruchik" (p. 77); "pylaia" (p. 78); "zakipel" (p. 79); "Vspylil, vskipel, sgorel" (p. 80). Near the end of the first scene at the police station, the narrator refers to Raskol'nikov's indifference to death by burning:

> О, какое ему дело теперь до собственной под-
> лости, до всех этих амбиций, поручиков, немок,
> взысканий, контор и проч, и проч! Если б его
> причоворили даже сжечб в эту минуту, то и тогда
> он не шевельнулся бы . . . !
>
> (p. 81)

At this point he disregards even the fire of God's wrath as it is embodied in Il'ia Petrovich Porokh, a symbolic Elijah the Prophet.

A subtle ambiguity is present in Nikodim Fomich's praise of Porokh:

> . . . на-и-бла-га-ар-р-роднейший, я вам скажу,
> человек, но порох, порох! Вспылил, вскипел,
> сгорел - и нет! И все прошло! И в результате одно
> только золото сердца!
>
> (p. 80)

The phrase "v rezul'tate" suggests that the "gold of the heart" refers to the heart of the suspect as well as that of Il'ia Petrovich. Of course, Nikodim Fomich is unaware of this *double entendre*, which was planted by the author himself. Porokh's lightning purifies the hearts of his suspects like gold in a furnace, recalling the evocation of Elijah in Malachi 3:2-3:

> . . . and who shall stand when he appeareth? for he is like a refiner's fire and like fullers' soap: And he shall sit as a refiner and purifier of silver: and he shall purify the sons of Levi, and purge them as gold and silver, that they may offer unto the Lord an offering in righteousness.

The first episode at the police station is an allegorical portrayal of Raskol'nikov's spiritual state. It is his first opportunity to confess, but he remains barricaded in his fortress of pride and weathers the storm of abuse which the symbolic Elijah the Prophet rains down on him. Popular belief places Elijah the Prophet somewhere in the heavenly heights. Raskol'nikov, appropriately enough, must climb up a winding stairway to the fifth story to reach the office of Il'ia Porokh. When Porokh admonishes him by saying, "Извольте ма-а-лчать! Вы в присутсвии" (p. 77), a second, symbolic meaning can be understood by the reader: "You are in His presence."

The word "dukh" ("spirit") and its cognates are emphasized as Raskol'nikov ascends the stairs to the police station. The stuffiness of the entryway ("strashnaia dukhota," "dukhota chrezvychainaia," p. 75) is mentioned twice. Inside the station, Raskol'nikov catches his breath ("perevel dukh svobodnee," p. 75). His head is swimming from the stuffiness: "dukhota . . . Golova eshche bol'she kruzhitsia . . . i um tozhe . . ." (p. 75). The room reeks of Luiza Ivanovna's perfume: "poneslo dukhami," "tak neset dukhami" (p. 76). The repetition of "dukh" and its cognates points to the spiritual significance of the episode.[13]

As Georgii Meier has shown, the heavily perfumed Luiza Ivanovna is a symbol of Raskol'nikov's sinful, fallen spirit.[14] Her dress, which is compared to a balloon and occupies almost half the room, gives her an airy, buoyant, amorphous aspect. The narrator refers to her with the formula "pyshnaia dama," which means "flamboyantly dressed lady" in the given context, but is suggestive of airiness, or fluffiness. Luiza Ivanovna takes buoyant little leaps as she walks, and she "flies" out of the room. She is half German and her speech is a comical blend of German and Russian, while Raskol'nikov is evidently steeped in German letters and is called a "German hatter" by a drunk who makes fun of his hat early in the novel. (p. 7)[15]

The scandal that was caused in Luiza Ivanovna's "noble house" ("blagorodnyi dom") by her "ignoble guest" ("neblagorodnyi gost'") parodies Raskol'nikov's crime, which is the result of nihilistic ideas infecting his spirit. The intruder who ran riot at Luiza Ivanovna's is a hack writer ("sochinitel'"). Symbolically, he is linked with the intellectual, reasoning side of Raskol'nikov's nature and with the ideas that have gained possession of Raskol'nikov's spirit. The connection between the hack writer and the "former student" Raskol'nikov is brought out in the same scene by Il'ia Petrovich:

> Вот они каковы, сочинители, литераторы, студенты, глашатаи . . . тьфу!
>
> (p. 79)

> . . . вот-с, изволите видеть: господин сочинитедь, то бишь студент, бывший то есть, денег не платит, векселей надавал, квартиру не очищает, ьесдрерывные на них поступают жалобы, а изволили в претензию войти, что я папироску при нзх иакурил!
>
> (p. 80)

Luiza Ivanovna's "noble house" is evidently a brothel, but she stands before Elijah Porokh persistently asserting her innocence. She symbolizes Raskol'nikov's spirit as he stands before the eternal tribunal of the Lord, refusing to confess his guilt.

Luiza Ivanovna's remarks concerning the "nobility" of her house and the "ignobility" of her guest refer symbolically to Raskol'nikov himself. Il'ia Petrovich makes repeated allusions to Raskol'nikov's noble background (pp. 407-8). His words doubtless ring ironically in the ears of the murderer. Similarly, when Raskol'nikov bows down at the crossroads on his way to confess, onlookers remark:

> -Ларнишка еще молодой!- ввернул третий.
> -Из благородных!- заметил кто-то солидным голосом.
> -Ноне их не разберешь, кто лиадорогный, кто нет.
>
> (p. 405)

Raskol'nikov is summoned to the police station because of his debt to his landlady, Zarnitsyna. However, as Meier notes, the Russian word "khoziaika" means not only "landlady," but "mistress," and so suggests that Raskol'nikov has neglected not only a financial debt, but also his duty to his inner "mistress," or conscience.[16] At the beginning of the novel, the narrator paraphrases Raskol'nikov's thoughts, stating that he was not afraid of *any* landlady (or: of any mistress) (p. 5). Why should he fear any other landlady besides the one to whom he owes money? This seemingly unmotivated formulation hints at her symbolic significance. Moreover, she is an "assessorsha"—literally, an assessor's wife; but on the symbolic plane she is Raskol'nikov's "moral assessor." The landlady's name in the early drafts is Sof'ia, the name later attached to Marmeladov's daughter. But the landlady remains another symbol of this "divine wisdom."[17] Her surname, Zarnitsyna, is derived from "zarnitsa" ("sheet lightning"). After his first visit to the police station, Raskol'nikov dreams that Il'ia Petrovich is brutally beating Zarnitsyna on the stairway outside his room. When the groans and cries of the landlady have stopped, Raskol'nikov lies in terror for half an hour, unaware that he has only been dreaming (pp. 90-91). Only the symbolic roles of Il'ia Petrovich and Zarnitsyna give this nightmare a clear meaning. Raskol'nikov's conscience, symbolized by the landlady, is tormented by a symbolic Elijah the Prophet. The quiet realizations of Raskol'nikov's conscience flash like sheet lightning beneath the bolts of divine vengeance. When the servant woman Nastas'ia comes to Raskol'nikov's room, he asks her who was beating the landlady. She replies that no beating took place. According to her, this is only "the blood crying out" in Raskol'nikov (p. 92). Of course, Nastas'ia's words are true in a sense which she does not intend: it is the blood of Raskol'nikov's victims crying out; that is, his conscience.

Two weeks pass between the murder and Raskol'nikov's confession. Throughout this time, the weather in Petersburg is unbearably hot and muggy. The stifling air bears down on Raskol'nikov physically, while the weight of his crime bears down on his spirit. But finally, on the fourteenth day the weather changes. That evening, in his last interview with Raskol'nikov, Porfirii Petrovich remarks: "Прогуляться собираетесь? Вечерокто будет хорош, только грозы бы вот не было. А впрочем, и лучше, кабы освежило . . ." (p. 352), referring perhaps as much to Raskol'nikov's spiritual state as to the weather.

That night, a spectacular thunderstorm lashes the earth for hours. The rain comes down "like a waterfall," forked lightning strikes time after time, and the flashes of sheet lightning last up to five seconds (p. 384). Raskol'nikov spends the whole night outdoors in the storm, and it is at this time that he finally decides to confess:

> Костюм его был ужасен: всё грязное, пробывшее всю ночь под дождём, изорванное, истрепанное. Лицо его было почти обезображено от усталости, непогоды, физическоло утомиения и чуть не суточной борьбы с самим собою. Всю эту ноч провел он один, Бог знает где. Но, по крайней мере, он решился.
>
> (p. 395)

After his thorough drenching in the thunderstorm, Raskol'nikov visits his mother and Dunia, who speaks of "washing away" his crime (p. 399). Then he confesses that evening to Il'ia Porokh, the symbolic Elijah the Prophet, master of thunder and lightning. The thunderstorm is clearly the spiritual storm of Elijah the Prophet which purifies the heart. Dostoevskii had in mind not only the general association of Elijah and thunderstorms in popular Russian lore, but also the specific folk belief that Elijah will unleash a storm each year on his feast day, July 20. The action in *Crime and Punishment* gets under way "at the beginning of July" (p. 5). If we assume this means the first week of the month (July 1-7), then the day of the storm and of Raskol'nikov's confession is July 15-21 (the fifteenth day in the novel); i.e., on or near the feast day of Elijah. We can probably assume that the storm, in Dostoevskii's conception, begins on the eve of Elijah's Day and that Raskol'nikov confesses to Il'ia Porokh on July 20.[18]

Instead of this symbolic cleansing by water in the thunderstorm, Dostoevskii had earlier planned a purification by fire. The notebooks refer to a housefire in which Raskol'nikov is burned while helping to save the tenants. Afterwards, he returns home to his mother, all scorched and singed, much as he comes back dishevelled and weatherbeaten by the thunderstorm in the final version. Then, still covered with soot from the fire, he goes to confess to Il'ia Porokh, who says: "Why are you all charred? Oh yes, of course! Good Lord!"[19] The housefire was doubtless associated symbolically with Elijah the Prophet, as the fire imagery in the first episode at the police station suggests. The notebooks also

refer to a whirlwind ("vikhr'") and a vision of Christ that were to precede the fire.[20] Like the whirlwind mentioned by Nikodim Fomich in describing Il'ia Porokh, this whirlwind might have been associated with the whirlwind of Elijah the Prophet.

After the storm in the final version, Raskol'nikov visits his mother and sister and goes to Sonia, where he "takes on the cross." Then he kisses the ground at the crossroads and goes to "drink the cup," while Sonia follows. As in the first episode at the police station, the word "dukh" and its cognates suggest a spiritual significance in Raskol'nikov's final encounter with Porokh. Once again he stops to catch his breath ("perevesti dukh") before entering the police station (p. 406). When he enters, Il'ia Petrovich greets him, exclaiming: "А-а-а! Слыхом не слыхать, видом не видать, а русский дух . . . как это там в сказке . . . забыл! (p. 496). The formula he is trying to recall from Russian folktales is *russkim dukhom pakhnet,* which means something like: "I smell the blood of a Russian!" However, a literal translation is: "It smells of a Russian spirit." The word "dukh" appears three more times in the confession episode: in reference to Porokh ("On byl . . . v vozbuzhdennom sostoianii dukha," pp. 406-7); in Porokh's characterization of Raskol'nikov ("uchenye issledovaniia—vot gde parit vash dukh!" pp. 407-8); and once again in reference to the stifling air in the police station ("U nas zdes' takoi spertyi dukh," p. 409), an authorial allusion to Raskol'nikov's entrapped spirit.

Near the end of both episodes at the police station, Raskol'nikov is offered a glass of water. He faints after his first interview with Porokh and wakes up to "a yellow glass filled with yellow water" (p. 83). In the second police station episode, as Raskol'nikov confesses, Il'ia Petrovich offers him a glass of water and enjoins him to drink (pp. 409-10). Both these drinking motifs, and especially the "yellow water," recall the "bitter cup" of suffering which Raskol'nikov resolves to drink when he ascends the spiral staircase to face "Elijah the Prophet." In neither case does he actually drink the water, but in confessing he accepts the "cup" of suffering. Compare Matthew 27:33-34: "When they had reached a place called Golgotha, that is, the place of the skull, they gave him wine to drink mixed with gall, which he tasted but refused to drink." Note that the Russian word for "yellow" ("zheltyi") shares the same root with the word for "gall" ("zhelch'").

Svidrigailov also spends part of the night in the thunderstorm. But unlike Raskol'nikov, his entire life has been consumed by debauched passions; visions of his past debauchery torment him when he tries to sleep. Illuminated by Elijah's lightning, even his passions become unbearable to him and he finally commits suicide.

While Raskol'nikov's path to suffering and resurrection resembles that of Christ, Svidrigailov follows the path of Judas, who accepted thirty pieces of silver for betraying Christ. Svidrigailov sells his soul to Marfa Petrovna for thirty thousand pieces of silver. (She ransoms him from jail for thirty thousand silver rubles.) When Judas hanged himself, he left the money in the sanctuary, and the priests used it to buy a field for a graveyard (Matthew 27:5-10). Before committing suicide, Svidrigailov pays for Katerina Ivanovna's funeral and leaves his money for the Marmeladovs' orphans.[21]

Il'ia Petrovich's function as a spiritual symbol in the novel helps to explain why Raskol'nikov confesses to him instead of to Porfirii Petrovich. Porfirii is a purely secular figure, as his first name—derived from the Roman purple symbolizing state authority—suggests. Unlike Il'ia Petrovich, his spirituality, on either the symbolic or realistic plane of portrayal, is open to question.[22]

When Raskol'nikov first speaks to Sonia of his decision to confess to Il'ia Petrovich, the demon of pride continues to make its voice heard:

> . . . Знаешь, я не к Порфирию иду; надоел он мне. Я лучше к моему приятелю Пороху пойду, то-то удивлю, то-то эффекта в своем роде достигну . . .

> (p. 403)

Later, as he climbs the spiral staircase leading to the police station, he debates:

> А для чего? зачем? - подумал он вдруг, осмыслив свое движение. - Если уж надо выпить эту чашу, то не всё ли уж равно? Чем гаже, тем лучше. В воображении его мелькнула в это мгновение юигура Ильи Петровича Пороха. - Неужели в самом деле к нему? А нельзя ли к другому? Нельзя ли к никодиму Фомичу? Поворотить сейчас и пойти к самому надзирателю на квартиру? По крайней мере, обойдется домашним образом . . . Нет, нет! К Пороху, к Пороху! Пить, так пить всё разом . . .

> (p. 406)

One might try to explain Raskol'nikov's behaviour in purely psychological terms and argue that his decision to go to Porokh is prompted by a masochistic impulse. But the world of *Crime and Punishment* reaches beyond the realm of body and mind alone, encompassing God and the human spirit. The symbolic biblical motifs throughout the novel all point to a deeper, spiritual need to atone for one's sins through suffering.

The symbolism associated with Elijah in both the final version and the drafts clearly shows that the murderer's spiritual resurrection was envisioned by Dostoevskii long before the writing of the novel was nearing its end. Raskol'nikov's transformation is slow and gradual; even in the epilogue it has barely begun. Nevertheless, some will still claim, along with Mochul'skii, that such a turnabout seems unlikely in a character of Raskol'nikov's type. But who really knows? As one of the drafts states, in what was foreseen as the final line of the novel: "неисповедимы пути, которыми находит Бог человека".[23]

Notes

1. See Leonid Grossman, *Dostoevsky: A Biography,* transl. Mary Mackler (Indianapolis and New York, 1975), p. 369.

2. See Konstantin Mochulsky, *Dostoevsky: His Life and Work,* transl. Michael A. Minihan (Princeton, 1967), p. 312.

3. George Gibian, "Traditional Symbolism in *Crime and Punishment,*" in George Gibian (Ed.), *Dostoevsky, Crime and Punishment: The Coulson Translation; Background and Sources; Essays in Criticism* (New York, 1964), p. 588.

4. See Georgii Meier, *Svet v nochi (o "Prestuplenii i nakazanii"). Opyt medlennogo chteniia* (Frankfurt/Main, 1967). Meier died in 1966 before completing the final chapter. His book has not been given the consideration it deserves. This is due in part to Meier's somewhat verbose style, which tends to veil many original and convincing observations.

5. This is a leitmotif in Meier's study. Raskol'nikov's function as a representative of mankind in general is reflected in his first name (Rodion, or Rodia), which resembles *rod* ("kind," "clan"), as in *rod chelovecheskii* ("mankind"). The use of the phrase "v rode" in conjunction with "iz raskol'nikov" in Porfirii's characterization of Mikolka is possibly intended by the author as a hint at the connection between *Rodia* and *rod*: "а известно ли вам, что он из раскольников, да и не то чтоб из раскольников, а просто сектант; у него в роде бегуны бывали . . ." F. M. Dostoevskii, *Polnoe sobranie sochinenii v tridtsati tomakh,* 19 vols. (Leningrad, 1972-), (hereafter *PSS*), 6 (1973), p. 347.

6. All citations from *Crime and Punishment* refer to page number in *PSS,* vol. 6. English translations are based on David Magarshack's rendition (Fyodor Dostoyevsky, *Crime and Punishment* [Baltimore, 1963]).

7. Mary Magdalene came from Magdal, a town near Capernaum, as noted by the editors in *PSS,* 7 (1973), pp. 365-66.

8. The juxtaposition of "krestami" and "perekrestok" in the following passage highlights the symbolic connection between the crossroads and the cross: ". . . я за твоими крестами, Соня. Сама же ты меня на перекресток посылала . . ." (*PSS,* 6, p. 403).

9. *PSS*, 7, p. 192.

10. Georgii Meier notes the parallel between the name Il'ia and the biblical Elijah, but he misses the word-play between "prorok" and "porokh" (*Svet v nochi*, pp. 43-45). The prototype for Il'ia Petrovich Porokh in real life was a policeman who helped Dostoevskii when he was threatened with jail for nonpayment of debts in June 1865. (See *PSS*, 7, p. 370.) For the biblical portrayal of Elijah see 1st Kings 17-21; 2nd Kings 1-2; Malachi 4:5-6; Matthew 17:10-12; Mark 9:11-13; Luke 1:17; Revelation 11:1-13.

11. See A. N. Afanas'ev, *Poèticheskie vozzreniia slavian na prirodu. Opyt sravnitel'nogo izucheniia slavianskikh predanii i verovanii, v sviazi s mificheskimi skazaniiami drugikh rodstvennykh narodov*, 3 vols. (Petersburg, 1865-1869), 1, pp. 469-83.

12. *PSS*, 7, p. 17.

13. Compare the toying with "dukh" ("smell" and "spirit") in "Bobok" (1873). (See F. M. Dostoevskii, *Dnevnik pisatelia za 1873 god* [Berlin, 1922], pp. 269-89, esp. p. 272.) One could point to numerous word-plays in *Crime and Punishment*, many of them replete with meaning for the reader. For example, there is Il'ia Petrovich's mistaken reference to Svidrigailov as Nil Pavlych immediately after speaking of nihilists and using the Latin *nihil est* in his characterization of Raskol'nikov (*PSS*, 6, pp. 407-8). This word-play suggests that the author saw a degree of irony in Svidrigailov's quotation from Terence: ". . . i ia chelovek esm', et nihil humanum . . ." (*PSS*, 6, p. 215). Another curious example is the name of the building in which Raskol'nikov formerly lived. Razumikhin's phrasing results in a variation on "obukha dom" ("the house of the blunt end of the axehead"): ". . . Искал, искал я этот Харламов дом, - а ведь вышпо потом, что он вовсе и не Харпамов дом, а Буха, - как иногда в звуках-то сбиваешся! . . ." (*PSS*, 6, p. 96). See also James L. Rice, "Raskol'nikov and Tsar Gorox," *Slavic and East European Journal*, 25, no. 3 (Fall 1981), in press.

14. Pointing to the clear contrast between the "pyshnaia dama" and the "traurnaia dama," Meier also notes that the woman in mourning is a symbol of the positive, godly aspect of Raskol'nikov's spirit; that is, of his conscience. (*Svet v nochi*, pp. 153-56.)

15. Raskol'nikov's German attributes were inherited in part from Pushkin's Hermann. See A. Bem, "Gogol' i Pushkin v tvorchestve Dostoevskogo," *Slavia*, VII, 1928-1929, pp. 63-86; VIII, 1929-1930, pp. 82-100, 297-311. Concerning the symbolic connection between Raskol'nikov's hat and the ideas inside his head, compare the allusions to his hat in *PSS*, 6, p. 7; p. 101; and p. 407.

16. Meier links the landlady with Raskol'nikov's own soul, which he has given over to torments. Meier does not note the symbolism of the landlady's name. (*Svet v nochi*, p. 44.)

17. Zarnitsyna's first name and patronymic are not specified in the final version. In one of the notebooks they are given as "Iuliia Prokhorovna," strikingly similar in sound to "Il'ia Porokh." (See *PSS*, 7, p. 153.) Raskol'nikov had been deeply concerned for the landlady's invalid daughter and had even intended to marry her. In a sense, she was the "daughter" of his own conscience, symbolized by Zarnitsyna.

18. In the early stages of writing *Crime and Punishment* (September 1865) Dostoevskii stated in a letter to Katkov that Raskol'nikov passes "almost a month" before confessing. (See Mochulsky, *Dostoevsky*, pp. 272-73.) Dostoevskii may have learned the folklore of Elijah from first-hand, oral sources. However, his source might have been Afanas'ev's *Poeticheskie vozzreniia slavian na prirodu*. (See vol. 1, pp. 469-83, 628, 630, 640, 698, 737, and 762.) Volume 1 came off the press in 1865, while Dostoevskii's work on *Crime and Punishment* began in the second half of 1865 and continued throughout 1866.

19. *PSS*, 7, p. 149. See also pp. 134-35, 137, 139, and 143.

20. See *ibid.*, p. 148.

21. Curiously, Raskol'nikov fears Svidrigailov as a potential betrayer. Svidrigailov is the only person who knows the murderer's identity and is liable to report. Raskol'nikov and Sonia also enter Judas's path (Sonia sells herself the first time for thirty rubles; Raskol'nikov virtually sells his soul in a nihilistic scheme to obtain 3,000 rubles), but they turn from the path of Judas to that of Christ.

22. These two "Petroviches" might be intended as ideological opposites. Il'ia is a family man and a Christian who reads the travel notes of the missionary Livingstone (a modern-day saint's life, so to speak); Porfirii is a bachelor and his own true beliefs are hard to pinpoint (even Razumikhin has trouble defining him). Il'ia states openly that his concern for Raskol'nikov comes from devotion to his country and to God, not from personal friendship; Porfirii tries (and fails) to win Raskol'nikov's confidence by appearing as his close friend. Il'ia is direct, honest, and spontaneous (even if he is hotheaded), while Porfirii is a wily fox who re-

sorts to ruse and deception to attain his goal. Il'ia Porokh is a prophet on the symbolic plane, while Raskol'nikov exclaims to Porfirii: "What sort of prophet are *you*?" (6, p. 352.)

Meier and other critics see Porfirii as a positive, compassionate figure. At times he *seems* compassionate and clearly shows much psychological insight. Yet, he betrays a predatory pleasure in the torments of his "victim" and an evident lack of concern for Raskol'nikov's spiritual well-being. (Consider, for example, his account of the pleasure he experiences, like a spider, when his suspects surrender to him like moths flying to a flame; or his dainty little request that Raskol'nikov leave a note if he decides to commit suicide.) When he says, "All is relative," one cannot be sure what his true attitude towards this sort of thinking really is. Porfirii's thinking is oriented around "nature" and the empirical sciences, including the "natural" science of the mind: psychology. If Porfirii and Porokh are not intended as ideological antipodes, then one can say, at least, that Porfirii is a spokesman for the "law of nature and man," while Porokh is a representative of the law of God. (See Dostoevskii's allusions to "Bozhiia pravda" and "zemnoi zakon" in *PSS*, 7, pp. 310-11; 154-55.)

23. *Ibid.*, p. 203.

Richard Gill (essay date 1982)

SOURCE: Gill, Richard. "The Bridges of St. Petersburg: A Motif in *Crime and Punishment*." *Dostoevsky Studies* 3 (1982): 145-55.

[*In the following essay, Gill argues that images of bridges in* Crime and Punishment *serve as symbols of Dostoevsky's central themes.*]

Read casually, the opening sentence of Dostoevsky's ***Crime and Punishment*** appears to be no more than a rather matter-of-fact statement, conventionally providing expository details of setting and character: "On an exceptionally hot evening early in July a young man came out of the garret in which he lodged in S. Place and walked slowly, as though in hesitation, towards K. bridge."[1] Nevertheless, as the Russian critic Vadim K. Kozhinov has observed, this initial sentence, though almost documentary in character, also has a symbolic function; and when reconsidered in the light of what follows later in the narrative, it represents indeed "the embryo of the whole huge novel," succinctly introducing images and motifs that are "linked organically" with Dostoevsky's total design and meaning.[2] The reference to the "exeptionally hot evening," Kozhinov goes

on to specify, is more than a weather report: it establishes not only the suffocating atmosphere of St. Petersburg in midsummer but also the infernal ambience of the crime itself.[3] The garret room, later described as a cupboard and a coffin, reappears throughout the novel as an emblem of Raskolnikov's withdrawal and isolation. Even the brief account of his slow and hesitant walk, Kozhinov notes, reveals the same irresolution that Raskolnikov will display before and after the crime.[4] Curiously, however, Kozhinov's meticulous explication of this pregnant sentence completely overlooks its final detail—namely, the bridge itself.[5]

If, as the Russian critic convincingly maintains, the opening sentence is meant to serve as a kind of overture to the novel, the bridge, like the other particulars, may also be interpreted as more than a matter of documentation. In fact, its climactic position implies that the movement of Raskolnikov towards the bridge and thus to the pawnbroker's room, in a calculated "rehearsal" (p. 5) of the crime, initiates the whole complex action of the novel. As with rooms and weather, moreover, allusions to bridges recur throughout the novel, not incidentally but in connection with nodal points of the action and motivation. My purpose here therefore is to show more fully how this hitherto neglected motif of the bridge functions in Dostoevsky's dialectical orchestration.

To be sure, given the topography of St. Petersburg—with its rivers, canals, and islands—bridges would naturally be mentioned in almost any novel set there. Dostoevsky's approach to the city, however, shuns reportorial naturalism. As more than one study has shown, Dostoevsky—like Balzac, Baudelaire, Dickens, and Gogol—was among the first to recognize the symbolic possibilities of city life and imagery drawn from the city. In *Crime and Punishment,* particularly, St. Petersburg becomes a *paysage moralisé*. The actual city, "rendered with a striking concreteness," is, to use Donald Fanger's words, "also a city of the mind in the way that its atmosphere answers Raskolnikov's spiritual condition and almost symbolizes it."[6] The crowded streets and squares, the shabby houses and taverns, the noise and stench, all are imaginatively transformed into a rich store of metaphors for states of mind. From this standpoint, the hump-backed bridges crisscrossing Czar Peter's labyrinthine city are, as found in the novel, likewise to be viewed as metaphorical and highly suitable for marking the stages of the tortuous course of Raskolnikov's internal drama.

Indeed, considered phenomenologically in terms of Gaston Bachelard's "poetics of space," bridges are potently expressive. As Bachelard writes, "space that has been seized upon by the imagination cannot remain indifferent space subject to the measures and estimates of the surveyor. It has been lived in, not in its positivity, but with all the partiality of the imagination."[7] Thus, "all great simple images reveal a psychic state"; they "speak" to us.[8] Bachelard himself concentrates on houses, without any references to bridges; nonetheless, his methodology—what he calls "topoanalysis" or "the systematic psychological study of the sites of our intimate lives"[9]—may be applied to bridges. Bridges also "speak," and with remarkable nuance. They suggest both union and separation, distance and contact. Linking and joining what would otherwise remain separate, they also evoke the "transitional," the state of being in-between. Crossing a bridge graphically accentuates the passage from one stage to another, just as pausing on a bridge offers a vantage point for looking backward or forward, localizing the uneasiness of indecision or the finality of commitment. Such phenomenological implications of bridges are particularly relevant to Raskolnikov's peculiar psychology, his obsession with taking a "new step," (p. 4) his vacillation between one extreme state of mind and another. All this, Dostoevsky would instinctively recognize.

In selecting the bridge as a motif, Dostoevsky may also have recalled—and perhaps intended ironic allusion to—the role bridges played in two well-known contemporary Russian works, both of which advanced sociopolitical ideas antagonistic to his own. The earlier one, Alexander Herzen's *From the Other Shore,* a book Dostoevsky admired for its poetic force despite his differences with the author's politics,[10] opens with the image of a bridge as an historical metaphor for the struggles of the nineteenth century. The liberal-minded Herzen, diagnosing the abortive revolution of 1848, still held fast to his own hopes for the future, "the other shore"; and, evidently remembering the words of his socialist friend Proudhon, who envisioned a new world where the injustices of the present would appear *"comme un pont magique jeté sur un fleuve d'oubli,"*[11] he began his own book with a plea to his son not to remain "on this shore":

> We do not build, we destroy. . . . Modern man, that melancholy *Pontifex Maximus,* only builds a bridge—it will be for the unknown man of the future to pass over it.[12]

Dostoevsky, with aspirations towards a future antithetical to that of Herzen, might very well have relished exploiting the liberal's image in the portrayal of his own ideological dissenter, Raskolnikov. The other book, *What Is To Be Done?* by N. G. Chernyshevskij, a veritable summa for the Nihilists of the 1860's and thus a target for Dostoevsky in both *Notes from Underground* and *Crime and Punishment,* opens with a dramatic scene on a St. Petersburg bridge. In the early hours of the morning, a flash is seen on the bridge, and a shot is heard. A man is then presumed to have killed himself, but when the bridge guard rushes to the spot, there are no traces of any one to be found. The suicide is now disputed, particularly because of the grotesque circumstances. "Does one blow his brains out on a bridge?" people ask. "Why a bridge? It would be stupid to do it on a bridge."[13] In Chernyshevskij's novel, it turns out of course that there has been no suicide; Lopukhov, one of the main characters, has simply staged one to deceive his wife.[14] But this incident, as narrated, closely resembles the actual suicide of Svidrigajlov by Tuchkov Bridge, and may be a possible source for the absurd manner of its execution: "Svidrigajlov took out the revolver and cocked it. Achilles (the bridge guard) raised his eyebrows. 'I say, this is not the place for such jokes.'" (p. 495)

In any case, whether Dostoevsky was mindful of these Russian works or not, a specific bridge in St. Petersburg is often the stage for a decisive moment in *Crime and Punishment.* (Indeed, as James M. Curtis points out, to appreciate the significance of Raskolnikov's whereabouts in the novel, it is helpful to keep a map of the city in mind.)[15] In the opening, to repeat briefly, Raskolnikov's crossing Kokushkin Bridge, in the first sentence, takes him from his own neighborhood into that of the pawnbroker; in fact, her house is just on the other side of the canal the bridge spans (p. 4). His actual encounter with the suspicious pawnbroker aggravates his indecision and self-loathing; and the days following are given over to tortured introspection. Then comes a moment of spiritual insight when he dreams of the mare being beaten to death. Here the topographical details correspond to his ambivalent psychological state:

> . . . he forgot at once what he had just been thinking about and even where he was going. In this way he walked right across Vasilevskij Ostrov, came out on to the Lesser Neva, crossed the bridge and turned toward the islands. The greenness and freshness were at first restful to his weary eyes after the dust of the town and the huge houses that hemmed him in and weighed him down.
>
> (p. 54)

The bridge he has crossed is Tuchkov Bridge, the same one later associated with Svidrigajlov's suicide. In this instance, its implications are positive: Raskolnikov's passage across the bridge from the stifling mainland of the city to the rather idyllic retreat of Peterburgskij Island represents, subjectively, a transition from the calculating and inhumanly cold side of his divided self to another and superior one open to spontaneous and generous feeling. This is borne out by the imagery and incidents of the sequence. Dostoevsky's presentation of the natural imagery of the setting, as Gibian has shown, draws upon the traditional symbolism of myth: the "greenness" of the vegetation and the "freshness" of the atmosphere are manifestations of the ancient life-giving elements of earth and air.[16] The natural surroundings, in contrast to the urban, release Raskolnikov's humane feelings, and after he falls asleep in the grass, the dream of the mare brutally slain by its master, prefiguring the murder of the pawnbroker, fills him with moral horror. Upon awakening, he abandons his criminal plan as vile and loathesome. Significantly, this decision is made on Tuchkov Bridge, the same one that brought him to the island. Now, during the moment of transformation, the bridge focuses his attention on water and light, two symbolic elements in sharp contrast with the dryness and darkness of the city:

> He rose to his feet, looked round in wonder as though surprised at finding himself in this place and went towards the bridge . . . "Lord," he prayed, "show me my path—I renounce this accursed . . . dream of mine."
>
> Crossing the bridge, he gazed quietly and calmy at the Neva, at the glowing red sun setting in the glowing sky.

(p. 61)

This decision—this healing of the split between intellect and feeling—is of course only temporary; the crime is actually committed just a short while later. But the sources of possible regeneration have been introduced, and like the course of the crime's preparation, key phases of its aftermath involve bridges. Raskolnikov's sense of isolation and his hostility toward everyone following the crime become painfully intensified during another bridge scene. On Nikolaevskij Bridge (p. 113), Raskolnikov walks absentmindedly in the middle of the traffic, and a coachman lashes him with a whip for nearly falling under the horses' hooves. As Raskolnikov recovers himself by the railing, a woman crossing the bridge charitably hands him a coin of twenty copecks—"in Christ's name." (p. 114) Her gesture is a reminder of Christian love and salvation, but at this point Raskolnikov is in too negative a mood to respond with gratitude. Indeed, the setting only accentuates his despair, for it poignantly reveals to him that his crime has divided him from his earlier self and what was best in his own past:

> He closed his hand on the twenty copecks, walked for ten paces, and turned facing the Neva . . . The cupola of the cathedral, which is seen at its best from the bridge about twenty paces from the chapel, glittered in the sunlight . . . He stood still, and gazed long and intently into the distance; this spot was especially familiar to him. When he was attending the university, he had hundreds of times—generally on his way home—stood still on this spot, gazed at this truly magnificent spectacle and always marvelled at a vague and mysterious emotion it roused in him . . . Deep down, hidden far away out of sight all that seemed to him now—all his old past, his old thoughts, his old problems and theories, his old impressions and that picture and himself and all, all.

(p. 114)

The images Raskolnikov sees from the bridge are rich with traditional associations: the cathedral represents orthodox religion and redemption; the waters of the Neva, the bright sunlight, the majestic beauty of the panorama—all are positive and life-giving.[17] His lingering receptivity to such images will be the source of regeneration later on; at this juncture, however, Raskolnikov gives in to despair and misanthropy: "He opened his hand, stared at the coin, and with a sweep of his arm flung it into the water; then he turned and went home. It seemed to him, he had cut himself off from every one and everything at that moment." (pp. 114-115) In contrast to the bridge scene before the crime, this one is a spiral turning in what now seems Raskolnikov's irreversible downward course.

Despair now leads Raskolnikov to consider suicide, and another bridge is pointedly made the setting for his morbid self-searching. Quarrelling with Razumikhin, he takes off on one of his solitary rambles through the city:

> Raskolnikov walked straight to X——Bridge, stood in the middle, and leaning both elbows on the rail stared into the distance . . . Bending over the water, he gazed mechanically at the last pink flush of the sunset, at the row of houses, growing dark in the gathering twilight, at one distant attic window on the left bank, flashing as though on fire in the last rays of the setting sun, at the darkening water in the canal, and the water seemed to attract his attention.

(p. 167)

This X-Bridge is actually Voznesenskij Bridge, which takes Voznesenskij Prospect across the canal near the house where Sonja lives.[18] Raskolnikov, standing Hamlet-like in the middle of the bridge, now faces the choice between life and suicide. These alternatives are symbolized, respectively, by "the one distant attic window on the left bank, flashing as though on fire" and "the darkening water of the canal." As James M. Curtis has pointed out, since Sonja's room is described later on in the novel as "looking out on to the canal," (p. 309) it is evident that it is Sonja's window that Raskolnikov looks at from the bridge; and "the fact that the ray of sunlight from her window catches his eye means that he will ultimately go to her apartment, confess his crime, and take upon himself the suffering which . . . leads to regeneration."[19] At this moment on the bridge, however, "the darkening water"—in contrast to the way water elsewhere in the novel implies salvation—suggests death. Indeed, as he gazes from the bridge, a woman suddenly appears and leaps over the railing into the canal. The woman, who has obviously been drinking, is soon rescued, but her attempt to drown herself objectifies the possibility of suicide that Raskolnikov has been pondering as an alternative to giving himself up. But the ignobility of death by drowning repels him, and he decides to go to the police, though his departure from the bridge reveals apathy rather than determination:

> He felt disgusted. "No, that's loathsome . . . water . . . it's not good enough," he muttered to himself.

"Nothing will come of it," he added, "no use to wait. What about the police office?" . . . He turned his back to the railing and looked about him.

"Very well then!" he said resolutely; he moved from the bridge and walked in the direction of the police office. His heart felt hollow and empty.

(p. 168)

Almost symphonically, this despair is soon counterpointed with hope. Shortly after witnessing the woman's attempted suicide, Raskolnikov enters the street where Marmeladov has been accidentally run over by a coach. Taking the dying man home, Raskolnikov meets Sonja for the first time, along with her small sister, Polenka. As he leaves, the child's grateful and affectionate embrace prompts Raskolnikov to ask for her prayers. Despair now begins to give way to hope, and it is more than a coincidence that Raskolnikov finds himself back at the same place where he considered suicide:

The child went away enchanted with him. It was past ten when he came out into the street. In five minutes he was standing on the bridge at the spot where the woman had jumped in.

"Enough," he pronounced resolutely and triumphantly. "I've done with fancies, imaginary terrors and phantoms! Life is real! Haven't I lived just now? My life has not yet died with that old woman"!

(p. 186)

But his hopeful realization is simply the beginning of his transformation, not its conclusion, as he here rather complacently assumes. The pride and self-confidence expressed by his words are belied by his bodily movements, for Dostoevsky immediately adds that "he walked with flagging footsteps from the bridge." (p. 186) Actually, Raskolnikov does not yet perceive that the true source of this new hope is, not his own presumed strength of will, but Sonja, whom he has just met and who will show him how regeneration must be earned through humility.

Even after his confession to Sonja, Raskolnikov still hesitates about giving himself up to the police. Till the last part of the novel he continues to oscillate between the extremes of hope and despair, now personified, respectively, by Sonja and the cynical, corrupt Svidrigajlov.[20] Toward the close of the novel, a bridge once more serves as a setting for a moment of near-paralyzing indecision. Rejecting Svidrigajlov's invitation to go for a carriage ride, Raskolnikov departs from him in disgust: "'To think that I could for one instant have looked for help from that coarse brute, that depraved sensualist and blackguard,' he cried." (p. 471) What follows is another moment of melancholy soul-searching that brings to mind similar bridge scenes earlier in the novel:

When he was alone, he had not gone twenty paces before he sank, as usual, into deep thought. On the bridge he stood by the railing and began gazing at the water.

(p. 471)

The bridge and the water are clearly reminders that, for Raskolnikov, suicide still remains "a way out," a serious temptation.

In fact, as his notebooks reveal, Dostoevsky originally intended to have Raskolnikov kill himself in despair.[21] In the novel itself, it is Svidrigajlov, his double, who commits suicide, vicariously acting out Raskolnikov's negativity. Svidrigajlov's last movements mirror earlier ones of Raskolnikov, as the precise topographical details help to emphasize. After leaving the apartment of his child-fiancée, which is on Vasilevskij Island, Svidrigajlov follows the identical route that Raskolnikov took before the crime:

. . . just at midnight, Svidrigajlov crossed the Tuchkov Bridge towards Peterburgskij Island . . . For a minute he gazed with a peculiar interest, and even with a questioning look, at the black water of the Little Neva, but he soon found it very cold standing near the water, and he turned and walked along Bolshoj Prospect.[22]

Tuchkov Bridge is of course the same one Raskolnikov crossed before the crime, and Peterburgskij Island is the place where he fell asleep on the grass and dreamed of the mare being beaten. The parallels to be found here accentuate the contrasts. Unlike Raskolnikov in the earlier scene, Svidrigajlov is incapable of appreciating nature. The storm, finally bringing relief from the summer heat and also symbolizing spiritual waters, only annoys him:

He remembered how he disliked it when he passed Petrovskij Park just now. This reminded him of the bridge over the Little Neva and he felt cold again as he had when standing there. "I have never liked water," he thought, "even in a landscape."

(p. 489)

Shunning the elements, he takes a room in a shabby hotel, where he has nightmares. Unlike Raskolnikov's dream outdoors, which revealed compassion for the victimized horse, these nightmares—particularly one about a small girl with the face of a harlot—only expose the depths of Svidrigajlov's depravity. Now, deciding to commit suicide without delay, he goes, not to Petrovskij Park as he intended, but back towards Tuchkov Bridge and, to the consternation of the guard, shoots himself. Thus he takes his own life, the reader is prompted to recall, near the bridge where Raskolnikov at least momentarily renounced his criminal intentions.

In contrast, Raskolnikov chooses to live. Later the same day, rain-soaked by the storm Svidrigajlov found so disagreeable, he revisits Sonja and, in spite of his pride, is psychologically compelled to surrender to the police, Significantly, this decision to give himself up means crossing one more bridge. Sonja has told him that he must not only go to the authorities, but also bow down at the crossroads of the Hay Market and humbly kiss the earth, confessing his crime publicly to all. Even after he leaves her, Raskolnikov still harbors doubts about such repentance. Nevertheless, he is unconsciously forced to come to a decision: "But still he went. He felt suddenly once for all that he mustn't ask himself questions." (p. 508) And what he finally decides is concretely dramatized in another bridge scene:

> He walked along the canal bank, and he had not much further to go. But on reaching the bridge he stopped and turning out of his way along it went to the Hay Market.
>
> He looked eagerly to right and left, gazed intently at every object . . . "In another week, another month I shall be driven in a prison van over this bridge, how shall I look at the canal then? I should like to remember this."
>
> (p. 508)

What immediately follows is Raskolnikov's kissing the crossroads at the Hay Market and, then, his confession in the police station.

Brief as this scene may be, it is analogous in its consequences to Raskolnikov's heading toward the bridge in the first sentence of the novel. Indeed, if a map of St. Petersburg is consulted, it appears that walking along the canal away from Sonja's room would bring Raskolnikov to none other than Kokushkin Bridge, the one he crossed to go to the pawnbroker's. By crossing this same bridge twice, Raskolnikov turns, literally and metaphorically, from his crime to his punishment.[23] In his beginning is his end, just as in this end there will be a new beginning.

This bridge scene is the last one in the novel. As such, it has a structural as well as symbolic function. Applying Joseph Frank's concept of "spatial form"[24] to ***Crime and Punishment***, James M. Curtis has pointed out that, while each one of Dostoevsky's references to any given element has meaning within the particular context where it occurs, the juxtaposition of all the separate references in a single instant of time reveals their organizational function as a system of "linkages" and reminds the reader of how "one must understand each reference in terms of all the others."[25] This illuminating observation is certainly relevant to the motif of the bridge. With the terminal bridge bringing to the mind the one in the opening along with the others in between, consideration of all of them together enhances the sense of the novel's formal coherence and provides a final cumulative impression transfixing Raskolnikov's phenomenal trajectory.

Upon the surrender of Raskolnikov to the police, the novel proper ends, and the epilogue shifts the setting to Siberia. Nonetheless, as Leonid P. Grossman emphasizes, "Petersburg is an inalienable part of Raskolnikov's private drama. It is the canvas upon which his ruthless dialectics draws its patterns. The Czarist capital sucks him into its drinking houses, police stations, taverns and hotels."[26] And to these portentous settings may be added the evocative bridges of St. Petersburg.

Notes

1. *Crime and Punishment,* trans. Constance Garnett (New York: Modern Library, 1950) p. 3. Subsequent page references to this edition will be given parenthetically in the text.

2. "The First Sentence in *Crime and Punishment,* the Word 'Crime,' and Other Matters," trans. Robert Louis Jackson, in *Twentieth Century Interpretations of Crime and Punishment,* ed. Robert Louis Jackson (Englewood Cliffs, N. J.: Prentice-Hall, 1974), p. 17. Kozhinov is, to my knowledge, the only one to interpret the opening sentence of the novel in this way, but several of the motifs that he finds in the sentence have been discussed by others. The motifs of weather, water, and drought have been explored in George Gibian's seminal study "Traditional Symbolism in *Crime and Punishment,*" *PMLA,* 70 (Dec. 1955), 979-996, *passim.* The function of rooms in the novel has also been noted by Pearl C. Nieme, "The Art of *Crime and Punishment,*" *Modern Fiction Studies,* 9, 4 (Winter 1963-1964), pp. 310-312.

3. Kozhinov, p. 19.

4. Kozhinov, pp. 17-18.

5. Dostoevsky's own text designated the bridge with only the initial as "K-Bridge," though some translations other than Garnett's identify the bridge, which is actually Kokushkin Bridge. For a convenient map of St. Petersburg during Dostoevsky's time and topographical information relevant to the novel, see the Norton Critical Edition of *Crime and Punishment,* ed. George Gibian (New York: W. W. Norton, 1964), pp. 53-31.

6. *Dostoevsky and Romantic Realism* (Cambridge, Mass.: Harvard University Press, 1965), p. 194. Though giving little attention to bridges, all of Fanger's Chapter 5, "The Most Fantastic City," pp. 137-151, is of great interest. Two early Russian studies cited by Fanger, but rarely elsewhere, are particularly relevant: N. K. Anciferov, *Dusha Peterburga* (Brockhaus-Efron, 1922) is a general treatment of the image of St. Petersburg in Russian literature with many references to Dostoevsky; the same author's *Petersburg Dostoevskogo* (St. Petersburg, 1923) is a monograph on the topography of St. Petersburg in relation to the novels, including *Crime and Punishment.* The bridges appearing in the novel are clearly identified and

related to the movements of the characters (pp. 63-72), but the analysis of their literary function is limited. For a balanced evaluation of Anciferov's approach in the two books, see George V. Florovsky's review, *Slavonic and East European Review* (London), (1926-1927): 193-198. Later Russian critics who have considered the topic of the city include Leonid Grossman, *Dostoevsky,* trans. Mary Macklet (Indianapolis/New York: Bobbs-Merrill, 1975), pp. 368-369; and I. F. I. Evnin, whose observations are presented in Vladimir Seduro's *Dostoevsky's Image in Russia Today* (Belmont, Mass.: Nordland, 1975), pp. 74-83. Of the studies done outside Russia, one of special interest, particularly because of its illustrations, is Ettore Lo Gatto, *Il mito Pietroburgo: Storia, leggenda, poesia* (Milano: Feltrinelli, 1960), especially pp. 196-205. A current publication, Marshall Berman, *All That Is Solid Melts into Air: The Experience of Modernity* (New York: Simon and Schuster, 1982), contains an extensive section on St. Petersburg and Russian Literature, pp. 173-286, with further bibliography, pp. 360-368. None of these studies, however, discuss the bridge motif as such. For specific references to *Crime and Punishment* and St. Petersburg having a direct bearing on my own thesis, see James. M. Curtis, "Spatial Form as the Intrinsic Genre of Dostoevsky's Novels," *Modern Fiction Studies,* 18, 2 (Summer 1972), pp. 151-153.

7. *The Poetics of Space,* trans. Maria Jolas (New York: Orion Press, 1964). p. xxxii.

8. Bachelard, p. 72 and p. xxiv.

9. Bachelard, p. 8.

10. See *The Diary of a Writer,* trans. Boris Brasol (New York: George Braziller, 1954), p. 4.

11. As quoted by James H. Billington, *The Icon and the Axe: An Interpretive History of Russian Culture* (New York: Alfred A. Knopf, 1966), pp. 741-742. I am also indebted to Billington, p. 364, for his reference to this connection between Proudhon and Herzen.

12. *From the Other Shore* and *The Russian People and Socialism* (New York: George Braziller, 1956), p. 3.

13. *What Is To Be Done?,* trans. Benjamin R. Tucker and rev. Ludmilla B. Turkevich (New York: Vintage Books, 1961), p. 5.

14. Lopukhov eventually reappears, after his wife, Vera, has married a young doctor; nonetheless, following a magnanimous reunion of all participants, a reasonable *menage à trois* is established.

15. James M. Curtis, p. 152.

16. Gibian, "Traditional Symbolism in *Crime and Punishment,*" p. 985.

17. For detailed analysis of this imagery, though not the bridge itself, see Gibian, 983.

18. I am indebted to Curtis, p. 153, for this point.

19. Curtis, p. 153.

20. For a detailed analysis of this interrelationship, see Edward Wasiolek, "On the Structure of *Crime and Punishment,*" *PMLA,* 74 (March 1959), 134-135).

21. See *The Notebooks for* Crime and Punishment, ed. and trans. Edward Wasiolek (Chicago & London: University of Chicago Press, 1967), p. 243. Raskolnikov's suicidal tendencies are examined by Ernest J. Simmons, *Dostoevsky: The Making of a Novelist* (New York: Vintage Books, 1962), pp. 151-152.

22. *Crime and Punishment,* The Coulson Translation, ed. George Gibian, p. 483. With respect to the topographical details in this passage, the Coulson translation is more accurate than the Garnett, p. 487, which is quite misleading.

23. It has often been pointed out that the English word "crime" (with its legalistic connotations) is an imprecise translation of Dostoevsky's Russian word "*prestuplenie,*" which might better be rendered by "transgression." Moreover, it is not without relevance to the many crossings of bridges in the novel that this word "*prestuplenie*" literally means "going over, going across." See editor's note, 8, to Kozhinov, p. 21.

24. See Joseph Frank, "Spatial Form in Modern Literature," *The Widening Gyre* (New Brunswick, N. J.: Rutgers University Press, 1963), pp. 3-104.

25. Curtis, p. 141.

26. Grossman, p. 368.

Steven Cassedy (essay date 1982)

SOURCE: Cassedy, Steven. "The Formal Problem of the Epilogue in *Crime and Punishment*: The Logic of Tragic and Christian Structures." *Dostoevsky Studies* 3 (1982): 171-90.

[*In the following essay, Cassedy discusses the purpose of the epilogue in* Crime and Punishment.]

One issue which has continued to capture the attention of readers of ***Crime and Punishment*** is the problematic nature of the Epilogue. Every Dostoevsky critic worth his salt, it seems, in discussing the structure and organization of this novel, has felt called upon either to condemn the novel's final pages as superfluous, anticlimactic, unworthy of the rest of the work, or to rush to the defense of the Epilogue, offering various ingenious schemes which conclusively prove its inevitability and necessity.[1] In the rush to take sides and offer normative pronouncements on the concluding section of the novel, however, no one has fully accounted for the problem itself. What is the source of the ambivalence towards the Epilogue which has given rise to this controversy? This is the question I propose to answer. The analysis I offer here does not pretend to resolve the question for or against the Epilogue. The most it can do in this regard is to show that the whole debate is in a sense misdirected, that the structure of *Crime and Punishment,* for reasons which I will detail, implicitly offers no resolution. It is my contention that *Crime and Punishment* is formally two distinct but closely related things, namely a particular type of tragedy in the classical Greek mold and a Christian resurrection tale; that it successfully superimposes the two forms because they are, *within clearly determined limits,* identical; finally, that the conflict between the two forms occurs at precisely the point where they cease to be superimposable. Briefly, the tragic form logically concludes with the hero's suffering (*pathos*), and thus corresponds to Raskolnikov's arrest at the end of Part VI; while for the Christian form suffering is merely an antecedent to another stage, namely *resurrection,* and this requires the inclusion of the Epilogue.

Some years ago, in an article in *Harper's,* W. H. Auden pointed out the formal similarities between the murder mystery and Greek tragedy.[2] Basing his analysis on the categories established by Aristotle in the *Poetics,* Auden showed how the standard mystery plot bears analogies to tragic logic, comprising *hybris* (the murder), recognition (the discovery of the villain), reversal or *peripeteia* (the change in the villain's fortune corresponding to his discovery and arrest), and suffering or *pathos* (the villain's punishment).

In so far as *Crime and Punishment* follows the pattern of the mystery novel one can see how it also contains the elements of this rudimentary model. But even on the internal, formal level there is a good deal more to be said than this, and here the critical literature on the subject is disappointing. Although a number of eminent writers have discussed the notion of tragedy in Dostoevsky, very few have made any effort to define the term carefully or to treat the formal aspect of the question in any rigorous or systematic way. Vjacheslav Ivanov, whose name immediately comes to mind in this context, briefly touches on the similarity of the plot of *Crime and Punishment* to a tragic plot of Aeschylus, refering to the progress of events in both from an act of *hybris* against the chthonic deess, "Mother Earth," to "knowledge in suffering" (*pathei mathos*).[3] But Ivanov

is ultimately too concerned with Nietzsche and Christian mysticism to draw on his erudition in the classics and pursue this remark further. Bicilli, in a well-known essay, is also disappointing on this subject. He refers to the tragi-comic in Dostoevsky and mentions the dramatic qualities of his works, but never really ties either notion to the "inner form" of the novels, as one might expect from the title of his article.[4] Nor are the others who have written on tragedy and Dostoevsky any more illuminating on the question of form.[5]

Let us be specific about the meaning of "tragic form." Richmond Lattimore has shown how futile it is to try to establish a single, simple, and universal formal model for Greek tragedy by simply gathering empirical data from the existing thirty-two tragic dramas and looking for a set of constants. Any such effort is bound to be frustrated, as Lattimore demonstrates, for the good and sufficient reason that almost none of the categories traditionally associated with tragedy occurs in all or even most of the surviving examples.[6] The formal pattern to which I refer holds for a limited number of Greek plays, but they are the plays which Western tradition has selected and canonized as the standard models which most frequently provide the norms for critical investigations of the nature of tragedy: Sophocles' *Oedipus the King* and the three plays in Aeschylus' *Oresteia* are representative of this model, and I will restrict my examples to them in this discussion. The point, after all, is not the simple resemblance of the formal structure of *Crime and Punishment* to that of Greek tragedy in its most general sense (to the limited degree that it is possible to have a clear sense of the formal structure of Greek tragedy that takes the entire extant corpus of plays into account). What is important is, first, the resemblance of the formal structure of *Crime and Punishment* to a particular, easily recognizable *type* of formal structure found in the most familiar examples of Greek tragic drama, and second, the degree to which aspects of this formal structure are governed and motivated by intrinsic and extrinsic factors common to Dostoevsky's novel and the Greek dramas under consideration. It should also be pointed out that in referring to a formal structure in Greek drama I refer not necessarily to the dramatic events alone in any single play, but to the entire *mythos,* or plot, much of which often merely precedes and predetermines the specific action of the play (most of the crucial events in Oedipus' story, for example, having taken place well before the action of Sophocles' play begins).

These, then, are the elements which make up the form to which I refer. First, there is an *act* which is legally and ethically ambiguous in the tragedy's own terms (it is also ambiguous in historically contemporary legal terms, but I will return to this shortly). Thus, before the action of Aeschylus' *Agamemnon* opens, Agamemnon has slain his daughter, but has done so in order to enable the Greek warships to depart for Troy. Clytemnestra slays her husband Agamemnon in the same play (thus preparing the way for the action of the *Choephoroe*), but does so, at least ostensibly, to avenge the death of their daughter. In the *Choephoroe* Orestes will commit matricide by slaying Clytemnestra, but in so doing will be avenging the death of his father, Agamemnon. In *Oedipus the King* the hero kills his father, but without knowing the identity of his victim any more than he knows the true identity of the woman with whom he commits incest.

It is not only the *character* of the act which must be ambiguous. The *motivation* of the perpetrator, his independence of action must also be unclear. This often takes the form of a conflict between destiny and free will, as for Oedipus, who attempts to defy the oracle dooming him to incest and parricide, but whom, in the end, "all-seeing times has found out, against (his) will."[7] The tragic hero's madness or blindness (*atē*), an error in judgment (*hamartia*) leading him to commit his act are conditions which deprive him of the rational capacity to choose and which are as inexorable as a decree from the gods.

The final stage of the tragic hero's progress is his suffering (*pathos*), the "punishment" for his transgression, to put it in legalistic terms. This is preceded in many cases (Aristotle maintains that it is a necessary part of good tragic form) by an understanding, a recognition (*anagnorisis*) by the hero of his mistake (*hamartia*). Agamemnon, as he goes in to the slaughter, begins to have glimmerings of the event which awaits him. This causes him to hesitate before accepting his wife's request to tread, like a god or an Oriental monarch, on a rich, purple carpet, thus overstepping his bounds and inviting destruction. The crucial moment of Sophocles' *Oedipus* is the scene of recognition where the hero's previous mistake (*hamartia*) concerning his own identity is corrected and he realizes that the oracle has already been accomplished. It is following this understanding, or simultaneously with it, that the hero experiences the reversal in fortune (*peripeteia*) which brings on his suffering (*pathos*). The sequence of events, then, looks like this: 1) the ambiguous criminal *act* accomplished in the partial absence of free will; 2) *recognition/understanding* of error by the hero; 3) *reversal* in fortune; and 4) *suffering*.

It is hardly necessary to point out the ambiguous character of Raskolnikov's crime. One can easily see the same clash of ethical convictions in Raskolnikov's act as in Greek tragedy—at least as Raskolnikov himself sees his act. For, while Raskolnikov's act might be called murder in the absolute sense, it is also, depending on the specific ideology Raskolnikov is defending, either a humanitarian act (which will benefit thousands of innocent unfortunates) or a right and privilege (for

the extraordinary man). And, just as the Greek hero seems in part led by forces beyond his control to commit the ambiguous act that later brings him great suffering, so it is with Raskolnikov. One of the last experiences Raskolnikov has before committing his crime follows the chance encounter that assures the safe accomplishment of that crime. After Raskolnikov overhears that Lizaveta, the pawnbroker's sister, will not be home at the appointed time, he *loses his reason* and the crime becomes a preordained thing. "It was only a couple of steps to his apartment. He went in like a man condemned to death. He did not reason about anything, and was completely incapable of reasoning; but he suddenly felt with his entire being that he no longer had either freedom of reason or will (*ni svobody rassudka, ni voli*) and that suddenly everything had been definitely decided."[8] Similarly, six weeks earlier, after overhearing the fateful conversation in the tavern in which his own thoughts concerning the pawnbroker were echoed exactly, Raskolnikov had had the sense that this was evidence of *predestination* (*predopredelenie*—**PSS** [*Polnoe sobranie sochinenij v tridcati tomakh*], VI, 55). And the same suggestion that the act was committed somehow in a way that escaped Raskolnikov's control is present in those Utopian Socialist statements that attribute the crime to environmental factors ("'low ceilings and close rooms oppress the soul and mind!'"— **PSS,** VI, 320) and in all Raskolnikov's other retrospective justifications that place the cause of his action outside himself ("it was the devil who was dragging me along then," as he later explains to Sonja. **PSS,** VI, 322).

But what is more important than this is the way in which Dostoevsky (perhaps unwittingly) shows the close logical connection between his hero's loss of reason and will, his crime, and his subsequent punishment. This is essential to tragedy, as the French classicist, Jean-Pierre Vernant says: "The hero's blindness, his criminal act and the punishment are not separate realities. It is the same supernatural power—blindness, *atē*, madness, *hubris*—which takes on different aspects while remaining the same. It is like a cloud in which man is enveloped and which makes him blind, makes him criminal, and then punishes him."[9] Raskolnikov loses his reason only the day before he performs the murder. That the loss of reason and the crime itself are in this sense continuous, part of the same "cloud" of *atē*, to use Vernant's expression, becomes clear when we consider the murder scene. For what do the myriad ways in which Raskolnikov bungles his plans, loses control, forgets essential details prove if not (and this clearly served Dostoevsky's ideological plans all too well) that the manner in which the crime is committed has defied all of its perpetrator's attempts to bend circumstances to his free will, that the whole thing in the end is "blindness, *atē*, madness, *hubris*"? And finally, as if to point up the logical proximity of the hero's crime to his later suffering, Dostoevsky shows Raskolnikov thinking to himself the day after the crime (not *two pages* after the conclusion of the murder scene), "What, can it be that it's already starting, that this is already the beginning of my punishment (*kazn'*)?" (*PSS,* VI, 72)

Aristotle maintains that, in tragedy, the best form of recognition scene (*anagnōrisis*) is one that is coincident with the reversal (*peripeteia*) in the hero's fortune, as in *Oedipus.*[10] The easiest way to apply this analogy to **Crime and Punishment** is to follow Auden's analysis of the mystery novel and locate the recognition scene in Raskolnikov's confession to the police. Here, as in many tragedies, an identity is revealed, and the reversal in fortune the hero experiences (as he is arrested) is clear and absolute. But there is an earlier scene which presents richer possibilities for this analogy: it is the scene of recognition where Raskolnikov reveals his true identity to Sonja in Part V. The scene is significant in this light partly because it leads to a clear turning point in Raskolnikov's life, one which, in turn, as the author tells us, leads directly to the hero's final downfall, and is thus similar to the Aristotelian reversal (*peripeteia*). Part VI, which follows the confession scene (and the brief exchange with Svidrigajlov, who has overheard the confession) opens like this: "A strange time began for Raskolnikov: it was as though a mist had suddenly descended before him and enclosed him in a hopeless, oppressive solitude. Long after, as he thought back on this time, he decided that his consciousness had occasionally grown dim and that this had continued, with only a few intervals, right up to the final catastrophe." (*PSS,* VI, 335)

But the chief interest of this scene is the degree to which the tragic recognition moves the plot along specifically by focusing on the problem of knowledge, learning, and discovery. Anyone who has studied Sophocles' *Oedipus* will remember how the same is true of the central dramatic scene in that play, the recognition scene where Oedipus learns his true identity from the herdsman who had rescued him as a baby. The whole passage from the entrance of the messenger bearing news of Oedipus' step-father's death, to the revelation of Oedipus' parentage, is peppered with words expressing various notions of *knowing, learning,* and *discovering.*

Exactly the same thing happens in Dostoevsky's "recognition" scene. The entire dialogue turns on the process whereby the truth of Raskolnikov's identity becomes known not only to Sonja but to himself as well. The same vocabulary occurs here as in Oedipus, starting with Raskolnikov's leading question:

> "*Ugadala?*" (*PSS,* VI, 315) "Nu chto tebe v tom, esli b ja i *soznalsja* sejchas, chto durno sdelal?" (318) "I zachem, zachem ja ej skazal, zachem ja ej *otkryl!*"

(318) "Da ved' i sam *znaju, chto ne vosh'.*" (320) ". . . ja ved' i sam *znaju* chto menja chert tashchil. . . . Ja vse *znaju.*" (321); Ja eto vse teper' *znaju . . . Poimi* menja: mozhet byt', toju zhe dorogoj idja, ja uzhe nikogda bolee ne povtoril by ubijstva. Mne drugoe nado bylo *uznat',* drugoe tolkalo menja pod ruki: mne nado bylo *uznt'* togda, i poskorej *uznat',* vosh' li ja kak vse, ili chelovek?"

(322; my emphasis throughout)

"Have you *guessed?*" (*PSS,* VI, 315) "What would it matter to you if I were to *confess* (the Russian word contains the verb *to know*) right now?" (318) "Why, why did I tell her, why did I *reveal* it to her!" (318) "I too *know* that she's not a louse." (320) "I *know* that the devil was dragging me along. . . . I *know* all that." (321) "I *know* all that now. . . . *Understand* me: perhaps if I had it all to do over I should never commit the murder again. There was something else I had to *know,* something else was urging me on: I had to *know* back then and *know* at once whether I was a louse like everyone else or whether I was a man."

(322; my emphasis throughout)

If Raskolnikov has a revelation for Sonja (the verb *otkryt'* is twice applied to Raskolnikov's confession in this scene—see pp. 316, 318), she has one for him, too. The final truth which Raskolnikov can only begin to learn now, and to which the dialogue leads precipitously, is contained in Sonja's sudden exclamation, "What suffering!" ("Ekoe stradanie!"—*PSS,* VI, 322), and in her equally abrupt exhortation to Raskolnikov to accept his suffering (*stradanie prinjat'*) and achieve atonement thereby. But suffering (*stradanie*) is the same thing as the *pathos* which concludes tragedy, and we see in this scene, too, as we see in the passage cited a moment ago from the opening of Part VI, how irresistibly, how tragically the recognition and simultaneous reversal now move toward this final stage.

About this final stage it is not necessary to say much. That Raskolnikov experiences suffering is obvious and has been obvious from the beginning. That his suffering now approaches tragic dimensions as he becomes conscious of it as an activity which will further his knowledge of himself and his deed is worth mentioning, since it bears out what Vjacheslav Ivanov says concerning the presence of the Aeschylean "learning through suffering" (*pathei mathos*) in **Crime and Punishment.**[11]

As Jean-Pierre Vernant has pointed out so concisely and lucidly, tragedy is not just a literary form, it is a historical "moment" which, as it almost appears, *causes* tragedy, but is also reflected back in all its issues and conflicts *by* tragedy. This is important to consider for two reasons. First, it helps explain *why* Dostoevsky should have generated a literary form that closely resembles classical tragedy, when we know full well that this was never his intention. The resemblance between the "moment" of **Crime and Punishment** (in the terms in which

Dostoevsky saw it) and that of Greek tragedy is striking indeed, and once we have seen this, it will no longer seem odd that Dostoevsky's novel presents such striking *formal* analogies to tragedy. The second reason is that the historical moment elucidates the form of tragedy specifically by providing the context and terms for many of the conflicts I have mentioned.

Here is how Vernant describes the moment of Greek tragedy: It is a moment, he says, where there is "a distance established between the heroic past, between the religious thought proper to an earlier epoch and the juridical and political thought which is that of the city performing the tragedy." At the same time, Vernant goes on to say, "for tragic man to appear, human action must have emerged as such, but the human agent must not have acquired too autonomous a status, the psychological category of the will must not be developed, and the distinction between voluntary and involuntary crime must not be clear enough for human action to be independent of the gods."[12] In Vernant's view, as this passage and the rest of his essay show, the moment and the form of tragedy are characterized by a number of tensions or clashes, religious, philosophical, social, and legal. We may extend Vernant's remarks and say that tragedy is a transitional form, occurring at the turning point from a religious outlook to a philosophical or scientific one, from a view of man as determined to a view of man as exercising free will, from a clan-based society where the individual is not recognized as such to an urban society where he is: thus the recurrent ambiguity of motivation and responsibility in tragedy. It is also the turning point from a primitive legal system where guilt is a *family* matter and is decided in relatively simplistic terms by custom, and a modern, juridical system where guilt involves the *individual* (and the City) and is decided on the basis of rational deliberations and fixed principles: thus the ambiguity in the *character* of the tragic act which is absolutely guilty by primitive standards, but at least partly justifiable by modern standards (where extenuating circumstances are considered). About the legal aspect of the question I will have more to say shortly.

For Dostoevsky the question is not only whether the same facts apply, but also whether he saw them that way. It is clear that he did. For what is the source of Dostoevsky's twenty-year polemic with the radical left if not the conflict between the new scientific and philosophical ideas and an older religious way of life? And, outside of the broader conflict of atheism and religious faith, what were the specific terms of this conflict if not determinism (destiny, fate, call it what you will) and freedom of will, just as in the age of tragedy in Greece? The only difference is that, for mid-century Russia, the chronological order of the philosophical conflict is reversed: freedom goes with the older, religious outlook, determinism with the new, scientific outlook.

There is no need to document Dostoevsky's privately held beliefs on this subject. It is sufficient to recall his antagonism towards his radical contemporaries in the 1860's, towards writings like Chernyshevskij's *Anthropological Principle in Philosophy,* that great, muddled assault on human freedom, towards the scientism of the nihilists, in short, towards any view which used the findings of modern science to reduce man to a cog in the mechanism of nature and thus deprive him of his individual freedom of action. What matters is that Dostoevsky made the conflict a thematic focus of so much of his post-exile work, starting with **Notes from the House of the Dead,** whose most important revelation is perhaps that no degree of physical restraint or hardship can ever be sufficient to extinguish the exercise of man's free will, even if the only form this takes is some utterly senseless act of self-destruction.

It is there in **Crime and Punishment,** too, where Dostoevsky has embodied the two poles of his conflict in his two central characters, Raskolnikov, who espouses the modern, "rational," scientific world-view, and Sonja, who represents the prescientific, pre-rational faith of an earlier religious word-view. And the central aspect of this conflict is the question of freedom. When Raskolnikov is speaking the language of positivism and social Darwinism, he reflects the views of his radical contemporaries who had mechanized not only man, but his environment, both natural and social, as well. "'Let them devour each other alive—what do I care'," Raskolnikov reflects, reproaching himself for having come to the aid of a young girl who has been molested. "'This is how it ought to be, they say. A certain percentage, they say, must go each year . . . somewhere . . . to the devil . . . Percentage! How glorious these words of theirs are: so reassuring, so scientific'." (**PSS,** VI, 42-43) "'People, by a law of nature, are *generally* divided into two categories. . . . The first category, that is the material, generally speaking, consists of people who are by their nature conservative, sedate, live in obedience and like to be obedient. In may opinion, they are obliged to be obedient because such is prescribed for them (*eto ikh naznachenie*). . . . But one thing is clear, and that is that the order governing the way in which people are conceived, governing all these categories and subdivisions, must be determined in a highly reliable and exact fashion by some law of nature'." (**PSS,** VI, 200-202)

Even when Raskolnikov speaks of the extraordinary men who *dare* to seize power, those who are not subject to nature's laws and prescriptions, who exercise their will over the rest of humanity, he continues nonetheless to embody the tragic conflict between free will and forces beyond man's control. There is a telling passage early in the novel which, especially if considered in light of succeeding events, points up the terms of this conflict with great clarity and with considerable tragic irony. Raskolnikov is preparing to set out for the pawnbroker's residence and perform the murder. The author tells us that Raskolnikov feels as though he were being dragged along now mechanically and irresistibly. As he prepares to go he ponders the question why criminals are always so easily caught, and comes to the conclusion that, "'the chief reason lies not so much in the material impossibility of concealing the crime as in the criminal himself. The criminal,'" he continues, "'at the moment of the crime falls victim to a *failure of will and reason* . . .'" Having arrived at these conclusions, he decided that with him personally, so far as his own affair was concerned, there could be no such upsets from illness, and that *his reason and will would not forsake him . . .*" (*PSS,* VI, 58-59; emphasis added).

The irony of this passage is occasioned by the events which take place a few pages later. But the passage is important also because it points up another dimension of the tragic conflict of freedom and destiny as it takes shape in Dostoevsky. If the events of **Crime and Punishment** prove anything, they prove that Raskolnikov is wrong in the passage just cited, and that he does *not* possess the will or freedom of action he desires. But this is not to deny the possibility of freedom in general. To have done so would have given victory to the positivists and social scientists whose doctrines Dostoevsky found so offensive. What is denied is a *specific kind* of freedom of will, namely the kind where the will aims to suppress the freedom of others and establish itself in a position of dominance. What the will *is* free to do is shown by Sonja in her ecstatic exhortation to Raskolnikov to rise up and atone for his sins. To speak the language of Christian theology, the will is free to strive to exchange its sinful essence for a pure essence by repenting.[13] In fact, one of the most tragic characteristics of the conclusion of **Crime and Punishment** without the Epilogue is that the truth of Raskolnikov's incapacity to act freely in *his* sense finally catches up with him there. As he resolves to abandon his confession to the police (that is, to reject the only freedom available to him), he hears the news of Svidrigajlov's suicide. It is undoubtedly no coincidence that this should occur precisely here at this point, since it proves to Raskolnikov once and for all, by showing the ultimate failure of a man whose very existence was devoted to the imposition of his will on others, that such freedom is *not* possible. Here truly, as for Oedipus, time has found the tragic hero out, and, with this understanding, Raskolnikov goes to meet the suffering that awaits him.

The moment of tragedy in Greece is also legal moment, as I mentioned earlier, and it is here that some of the most noteworthy parallels occur between Dostoevsky and the Greeks. Born in an age where the effects of the great change had become noticeable from earlier legal practices based on a vague but rigid notion of justice as determined by custom, to the modern Athenian juridical system instituted by the reforms of Solon in the early

sixth century, B.C., Greek tragedy reflects in form and substance many of the ethical and moral problems raised by this transition. It does so, moreover, in specifically *legal* terms. The whole change may be seen as a response to a need created by a larger social change, namely, from a society of clans to an urban society. As Louis Gernet pointed out many years ago, this broad change had an enormous impact on legal concepts and also on the vocabulary used to express such concepts.[14] Gernet demonstrates in his lengthy study of the subject that the changes in thought and language were occasioned above all by the emergence of the individual as a relatively autonomous entity, capable of, and responsible for, actions undertaken on his own volition. In primitive society notions like crime, guilt, "penality," had been family concerns, and the individual was seen as part of a *group* which became responsible for his actions. But with the breakdown of this structure accompanying the rise of an infinitely more abstract organization, namely the city, the individual comes into his own as a legal entity.

The ambiguity of both the character and motivation of the tragic hero's criminal act becomes clear in this historical context. For such acts include a component of absolute and unconditional guilt as determined by primitive customary law, and a component of justification, something which only a juridical system would even deign to consider. Similarly, if the motivation of the tragic act is ambiguous, it is undoubtedly because the very notion of motivation is undergoing a change from something beyond the individual's control towards something arising within the individual. The tragic situation seems specifically designed to isolate and explore these historical conflicts.

The true subject of Gernet's account, however, is one which concerns us more closely. It is the semantic shift that accompanies the social changes I have mentioned. For, as Gernet demonstrates with scrupulous thoroughness, terms of law and ethics vary in their usage to reflect the changing conceptions of their age. In the urban age of tragedy we find, for instance, a word like *hamartia,* whose primitive meaning had been simply "error" (that is, an involuntary mistake due, say, to madness), adopting the notion of voluntary, individual intention.[15] The word *timē,* which in its primitive sense means "honor," as something emanating from and owed to the gods, with the rise of urban society undergoes a process of generalization and abstraction, leading to a new conception of honor as something which attaches to the *individual* and reflects his relation not to the gods, but to the City.[16]

But in words like these one sense never fully replaces the other, and in the age of tragedy the same word is often used in two different senses, one reflecting the primitive, the other the modern, juridical usage. It is precisely this polyvalence in legal and ethical terms that tragedy exploits. As a product of an age of legal transition, tragedy sets itself up as a forum for exploring the ethical and moral implications of this transition. This is why, as Vernant points out in his essay, Greek tragedy is always so full of legal vocabulary, and legal vocabulary, moreover, which is tested and explored in all the ramifications of its polyvalent possibilities. When Orestes cries, at almost the exact midpoint of the central play of the *Oresteia,* that "Justice will vie with justice, Ares with Ares,"[17] he is using the dual meaning of justice (specifically, customary, blood-feud justice and modern justice of the law courts) to express the legal and ethical conflict at whose center he finds himself. And this is one of the central subjects of tragedy. As Vernant puts it, "A Greek tragedy is a tribunal. The institution of these tragic contests, with all of the practical organization implied, is but one institution and part of an institutional whole. Tragedy represents, specifically, a part of the establishment of a system of popular justice, a system of tribunals in which the City as City, with regard to individuals as individuals, now regulates what was formerly the object of a sort of contest among the *gene* of the noble families, a change resulting in the quite different system of arbitration. Tragedy is contemporaneous with the City and with its legal system."[18]

The sociological pattern is the same in Dostoevsky as in the age of tragedy in Greece. Dostoevsky's heroes begin to confront their metaphysical and ethical essence as individuals only when they have broken with the family. All of Dostoevsky's greatest heroes, from the underground man to the Karamazovs, come from broken families, from families in crisis, or seem to have severed all ties with a family that is never even mentioned.

Dostoevsky's "legal moment" speaks for itself in other respects. Greek tragedy, I said, is the product of an age following the extensive legal reforms of Solon. It is not surprising, then, to find Dostoevsky writing *Crime and Punishment* in the immediate wake of the Judicial Reform Act of 1864, a piece of legislation designed, like the Solonian reforms in Greece, to put an end to centuries of vaguely defined customary law and institute instead a codified body of law and a juridical system with courts, lawyers, and juries. The effects of the Judicial Reform Act were as far-reaching in Russia as the Solonian reforms had been in Greece,[19] and it is easy to see why many of the changes associated with the Reform would have troubled Dostoevsky. One of the most important aspects of the new system was that it was to be pervasively informed by the spirit of Western European science. This requirement was featured in the "Basic Principles" of 1862, a document designed at the request of Alexander II to lay the foundations for the reform.[20] For Dostoevsky, the injection of scientific rationalism into the law could hardly have been an appealing no-

tion. Nor was he favorably impressed, once the Reform had been instituted, with the creation of a new group of legal professionals trained to analyze and argue questions of ethics and morality according to "scientific" principles. For Dostoevsky this could only appear as the unwelcome intrusion of rational method into a realm of human experience where reason was powerless and incompetent to operate, and the only possible consequence of this intrusion would be the kind of quasi-scientific casuistry exemplified by Raskolnikov's own rhetoric. The reasons for Dostoevsky's subsequent hostility to the new breed of legal advocate as well as the intensity of that hostility appear clearly in his tirade some years later against the attorney in the much publicized Kroneberg trial in 1876. For in Dostoevsky's view this was a clear case of a keen and devious professional cynically mustering all the intellectual powers of a true casuist in order to exonerate a defendant who was manifestly guilty of child abuse.[21] The same hostility may be seen later in Dostoevsky's portrayal of Dmitrij Karamazov's defense attorney (patterned after the lawyer in the Kroneberg case), who uses "reason" in an equally deceitful way.

The point is that the force of the Judicial Reform is to create a conflict analogous to the tragic ethical conflict central to *Crime and Punishment*: in Russia it is the conflict between an older, Christian ethic, and a newer, rational ethic—utilitarianism, social Darwinism, or post-Reform law—which examines crime and personal responsibility rationally and intellectually. Oedipus' act of patricide is absolutely forbidden under a primitive ethic, but partly justifiable if extenuating circumstances are considered (he was not aware that it was his father), as they are only under Solonian principles of law. Similarly, Raskolnikov's murder is absolutely forbidden under Sonja's Christian ethic, but partly or wholly justifiable for Raskolnikov's utilitarian ethic when the circumstance is considered that this murder serves a higher end. In addition, Dostoevsky's account of the trial in the early pages of the Epilogue shows how not only utilitarianism, but also post-Reform legal rationalism was capable of coming to the defense of a murderer, for here too "various extenuating circumstances" are taken into account (*PSS,* VI, 412), many of them proposed by psychologists and adherents of the "recent fashionable theory of temporary derangement." (*PSS,* VI, 411)

The real purpose for discussing legal history here, however, is that, as in Greek tragedy, legal notions provide a context and a terminology for larger ethical questions. We find Dostoevsky, like the Greek tragedian, resorting to an exploration of legal terms which, because of historical changes in political, ethical, and legal thinking, have become polyvalent. It is as though Dostoevsky too is putting his community on trial.

This semantic play with legal terms surfaces most clearly in two scenes where Raskolnikov's views are presented "dialogically," that is, together with a point of view that challenges them. The first is the scene where Raskolnikov defends his article on crime against the attacks of Porfirij Petrovich (himself a man of the law). The entire argument is not merely filled with legal terms: *pravo* (right), *prestuplenie* (crime, transgression), *zakon* (law), *prestupnik* (criminal), *zakonodatel'* (law-giver). It is also noteworthy because the meaning of these terms is continually shifted and challenged. Raskolnikov's interlocutors, for example, are astonished at his notion of a "right to commit a crime" ("pravo na prestuplenie"—*PSS,* VI, 199) because, in Raskolnikov's mind, there is a distinction between an "official right" ("oficial'noe pravo"—*PSS,* VI, 199) and the intrinsic right of an extraordinary man to transgress. Similarly, it is possible for Raskolnikov to apply the terms "law-giver" ("zakonodatel'"—*PSS,* VI, 199) and "criminal" ("prestupnik"—*PSS,* VI, 200) to the same person, since here he plays on a new meaning of "law" (one which sanctions bloodshed) and juxtaposes it with a traditional meaning of "crime" (one which presupposes a prohibition on bloodshed). The same is true of Raskolnikov's "law of nature" ("zakon prirody"), which is distinguished in its modern sense from the laws that extraordinary men transgress.

The second scene is far more important. It is the confession scene with Sonja, which I have already mentioned. In this culminating scene, where "Justice vies with Justice," as it does for Orestes in the *Choephoroe,* we see a confrontation not only of ethical systems, but of the corresponding semantic systems as well. Once again Raskolnikov presents his terms in their modified sense and Sonja reacts with horror in each instance. "That is their *law* (*zakon*) . . . Law, Sonja!" (*PSS,* VI, 321) "Whoever dares much for them is *right* (*prav*). Whoever spits upon others the most is their *law-giver* (*zakonodatel'*), and whoever dares the most of all is the most *right* (*prav*)." (*PSS,* VI, 321) "Sonja realized that this gloomy catechism had become his faith and *law* (*zakon*)." (*PSS,* VI, 321, my emphasis throughout) Sonja challenges Raskolnikov with the inarticulate exclamations customary to her: Raskolnikov asks, "Was I a trembling creature or did I have the *right* . . ." Sonja interrupts him: "To kill? Did you have the right to kill?" (*PSS,* VI, 322) Even "kill" (*ubivat'*) has a dual meaning, for Sonja, who places an unconditional prohibition on bloodshed, understands the sense of the English "murder," while Raskolnikov has eliminated any necessary implication of moral fault from the verb. Sonja's usage is based on simple, unconditional ethical categories, and is, as it were, univalent.

Only one point remains to be made in reference to tragedy. In the tragic form I have used as a model, the central conflict is between a primitive system of justice characterized by customary and unconditional criteria for establishing guilt, and a modern system allowing for reasoned debate in the determination of guilt. The conclusion to this form of tragedy, I have said, is suffering. The effect of this is to deny any semblance of triumph to the modern system, giving victory instead to the primitive system. In *Oedipus,* for example, and in the *Oresteia,* it is as though moral order can be maintained in critical situations of conflict only if the primitive, unconditional criteria are reasserted in the end (this might be called the tragic irony of these plays).[22] So it is with Raskolnikov at the end of Part VI, for here he finds himself finally succumbing to the sentence of the older ethic (in this case a Christian one) and "accepting suffering." Here the tragic logic of **Crime and Punishment** is complete. All the steps of the form have been played out: 1) the ambiguous criminal act, 2) recognition/understanding, 3) reversal in fortune, and 4) suffering. They have been played out, moreover, in the same legal and historical terms as in Greek tragedy, and victory has been given to the primitive pole of the ethical conflict. As far as tragedy is concerned, nothing further is needed.

It is easy to see where this model is incomplete, however, and the reasons for this are both formal and historical. For to say that suffering concludes the logical demands of tragedy is to overlook one important thing in **Crime and Punishment,** and that is that the "suffering" we are speaking of is not a general term, nor is it exclusively the enlightening suffering born of ethical conflict that we find in Greek tragedy. Suffering here must be understood in a Christian sense, moreover in a *specific* Christian sense which the novel's own terms alone can fully supply.

But first it should be mentioned that the mere fact of providing a Christian context—*any* Christian context—for the notion of suffering entails certain assumptions. For Christian suffering or passion (*stradanie* in Russian means both), in the terms of the Gospel narratives, is not a finality but a *prius* to a finality: rebirth. Christ's sufferings, the crucible of doubt in Gethsemane and the passion on the cross, point always forward—not just to knowledge, as for the Greek hero, but to resurrection. Suffering in the Christian sense is an intrinsically incomplete activity, since it is necessarily directed towards an end.

The importance of this idea for Russian Christianity is borne out by the emphasis on voluntary physical suffering as a means towards participating in the ordeals of Christ. George P. Fedotov points out, in his study of the Kenotic tradition of Orthodoxy (the tradition which stresses the human, physical side of Christ as the one aspect of His being which man is capable of experiencing) how the one factor of major importance in the lives of canonized saints—the factor which *led* to their being canonized—was this voluntary acceptance of physical suffering as a means for imitating Christ.[23] In fact, in many of the accounts Fedotov gives of the lives of early saints, it is possible to notice a narrative pattern which resembles Raskolnikov's story. To begin with, many of the early saints did not display exemplary moral and religious characters during their lives. What truly sanctified them in the eyes of the Russian faithful, according to Fedotov, was nothing more than the violent nature of their death and their voluntary submission to it. But there is more to it than this, for it becomes clear from the accounts concerning the earliest saints, Boris, Gleb, and others that combined with voluntary suffering is a recognition, a sudden joyful understanding of the significance of that suffering. And the significance of that suffering is precisely that it brings the subject closer to Christ. In addition, it is essential to point out that the traditional consequence of such acts of non-resistance was eternal life, that is, a rebirth in Christ following the earthly death of the man in question. In this sense the stories closely resemble the final stages of the Gospels, where Christ emerges from his struggle in the garden with an understanding of his position and with the voluntary acceptance of his imminent suffering ("if this cup may not pass away from me, except I drink it, thy will be done"—Matthew 26:42).

It is easy to see how the pattern fits Raskolnikov, for, as I pointed out earlier, Raskolnikov's Christian acceptance of suffering is dependent on the understanding which grows from Sonja's teachings and from Svidrigajlov's suicide. This similarity is crucial to the present argument. The intrinsic narrative logic in the lives of the early Russian saints provides a *calque* not only for Raskolnikov's story, but for certain specifically tragic elements of that story. The Christian narrative involves a moment of recognition, like the tragic *anagnorisis*, which is followed by suffering, just as it is in the tragic forms I have discussed. The difference is that, where tragedy is content to *conclude* with suffering, Christian narrative is logically incomplete unless it goes beyond suffering to conclude with *resurrection*.

Still, it is almost unnecessary to turn to the Gospel narratives and the lives of the Russian saints to make this point, since the logic I speak of is already implicit in the terms in which the problem is presented in *Crime and Punishment*. What is more, in *Crime and Punishment* this logic more completely parallels the tragic model, since it is predicated on a criminal act or sin. When Sonja issues her rapturous command to Raskolnikov in the confession scene the notion of suffering, necessarily preceded by sin, a sinful act, is associated with an *act* of (self-) revelation and *recognition* ("I have murdered!"—*PSS,* VI, 322), then causally connected to redemption through *suffering* ("Accept suffering and redeem yourself through it . . ."—*PSS,* VI, 323) and rebirth ("Then God will send you life again"—*PSS,* VI,

322). This, in any case, is the logic implicit in Sonja's speech, even if she does not say it all in this order. All the important steps of the tragic model are thus present—crime (or sin), recognition, reversal, suffering—but the Christian order requires an additional step: resurrection. As a result, it is an order which is logically completed in *Crime and Punishment* only at the end of the Epilogue (or right *after* the end). Here the process from knowledge and suffering to rebirth is unquestionable. In exile, where "sufferings and tears are, after all, also life," (*PSS,* VI, 417) Raskolnikov finally reaches the knowledge of which he had had only a glimmer in confessing to Sonja and surrendering to the police. It is here that he casts himself at Sonja's feet, that he *knows* that he has been reborn (*PSS,* VI, 421), *knows* "with what infinite love he will redeem all (Sonja's) sufferings." (*PSS,* VI, 422) And, while the process is not yet complete, while further knowledge and suffering are still required ("He did not even know that his new life would not be reached easily . . ."—*PSS,* VI, 422) before the hero is entirely renewed, the promised rebirth is the image we are left with at the conclusion of the novel. And the image is reinforced in Russian, where the growing repetition of the word "resurrection" (*voskresenie*) in the last few pages leaves little doubt concerning Raskolnikov's fate.

So far, I have argued that there is an internal logic in *Crime and Punishment* which requires the element of resurrection with which the Epilogue concludes, and that this logic is given by certain forms of Christian narrative. There is a final argument which concerns the parallel between tragic and Christian narrative. I have mentioned that, in the tragic form that serves as a model for *Crime and Punishment,* the outcome of the central clash between two systems of justice is a relative victory for the historically earlier one. It seems to be a logical demand of this formal structure in Greek tragedy that the primitive, blood-feud ethic, with all its unconditional categories, prevail in the end over the modern, juridical ethic which allows for rational deliberations and debate. Now if Dostoevsky's "tragedy" follows the same logic, the outcome must give victory to the primitive and unconditional ethic. But in Dostoevsky's world the primitive ethic is the *Christian* one, and, while its categories are unconditional (just as its legal vocabulary is always univalent), justice is never satisfied (as the Furies are in Greek tragedy) with violence and suffering alone. It is satisfied only by something that is ultimately peaceful, that transcends violence.

The situation in Dostoevsky as compared with Greek tragedy may be illustrated in the following chart, which confronts the primitive and modern systems in both eras according to four categories: 1) underlying worldview (religious or humanistic); 2) complexity of conception of guilt (guilt as unconditional, or guilt as possible including extenuating circumstances); 3) the basis on which guilt is decided (popular custom or rational principles); and 4) the manner in which justice is restored (violence, attenuated violence, passive suffering and renewal).

GREEK TRAGEDY

	PRIMITIVE	MODERN (POST-SOLONIAN ATHENS)
WORLD-VIEW	RELIGIOUS	HUMANISTIC
COMPLEXITY OF GUILT	UNCONDITIONAL	ATTENUATED
BASIS OF VERDICT	CUSTOM	RATIONAL PRINCIPLE
JUSTICE RESTORED	VIOLENCE	ATTENUATED VIOLENCE

DOSTOEVSKY

	PRIMITIVE (CHRISTIAN)	MODERN
WORLD-VIEW	RELIGIOUS	HUMANISTIC
COMPLEXITY OF GUILT	UNCONDITIONAL	ATTENUATED
BASIS OF VERDICT	CUSTOM	RATIONAL PRINCIPLE
JUSTICE RESTORED	PASSIVE SUFFERING AND RENEWAL	ATTENUATED VIOLENCE

It should be noted that the "modern" categories for Dostoevsky will apply to any of the systems present in the book: Raskolnikov's utilitarian ethic, his extraordinary man theory, and even the principles of post-Reform law. The point is that in the tragic form the primitive member of each opposition must be part of the final solution. Oedipus, for example, suffers the guilt of one who has committed incest and murdered his father, not the attenuated guilt of one who committed these acts out of ignorance. This is because the older religious view did not sanction these crimes under *any* circumstances. Oedipus' violent suffering in the end is commensurate with the gravity of his offense, viewed unconditionally. Raskolnikov's crime is viewed in an equally unconditional fashion by Sonja, who represents the primitive, religious pole of the conflict in Dostoevsky's Russia. Here, however, justice is restored not through violent suffering alone, but through the voluntary acceptance of suffering *as a means to* atonement and new life.

The final picture is this. Dostoevsky's "Christian" tragedy is fundamentally similar to one prominent formal type of Greek tragic drama. This similarity owes its existence to the limited parallels which exist between the logic of events in tragedy and a "Christian" logic. This Christian logic may be seen partially in certain representative forms of narrative (the Gospels, the lives of saints), but it is ultimately generated simply by a religious ideology concerning sin and justice. Both forms include among their logical stages a crime or sin, an act of recognition or understanding, and suffering. But the Christian logic understands suffering as a means to an end, not as a finality, and thus departs from the tragic form at this point, adding its own final stage, namely rebirth. Moreover, it is in the very nature of the tragic model that its central ethical problem involve a conflict between a primitive and a modern system of beliefs, and that the primitive system prevail in the end. In Dostoevsky's Christian tragedy that primitive system is Christian, and thus logically requires as a final solution suffering leading to rebirth. In short, the logical demands of the tragic model as such are satisfied *without* the Epilogue in *Crime and Punishment.* Raskolnikov's catastrophic reversal in fortune and the suffering necessarily entailed by his arrest at the end of Part VI, are all that is needed. At the same time, this tragedy contains a Christian component, and the logical demands of this element are met only by the resurrection promised in the Epilogue.

Notes

1. There are really two questions at issue in the Epilogue: first, whether it is necessary at all, and second, given that it is there, whether there is a genuine conversion in the end. Konstantin Mochulsky gives perhaps the strongest negative answer to the second question, terming Raskolnikov's promised regeneration a "pious lie." See Mochulsky, *Dostoevsky: His Life and Works,* trans. Michael Minihan (Princeton: Princeton University Press, 1967), p. 312. Philip Rahv agrees with Mochulsky, maintaining that Sonja's faith offers no solution to Raskolnikov, but, where Mochulsky still finds a place for the Epilogue in his formal analysis of the novel (see below), Rahv uses this argument to attack the Epilogue as implausible. See his "Dostoevsky in *Crime and Punishment,*" in the Norton Critical Edition of *Crime and Punishment,* ed. George Gibian (New York: Norton, 1975), pp. 244-258. Edward Wasiolek deems the Epilogue an artistic failure, but argues for its structural necessity by showing that it completes an ascending movement by Sonja and what she represents, corresponding to a downward movement by her antithesis, Svidrigajlov. See "On the Structure of *Crime and Punishment,*" *PMLA,* 74 (1959), 131-136. The less ambivalent supporters of the Epilogue are virtually unanimous in their belief in the sincerity of Raskolnikov's conversion. Their arguments tend to concentrate on the Christian elements in the Epilogue as completing trends and patterns established earlier in the novel. This group includes: Maurice Beebe, who argues that "the ending is artistically and psychologically inevitable because the basic motive of regeneration is the same as the underlying motive for the crime" ("The Three Motives of Raskolnikov: A Reinterpretation of *Crime and Punishment,*" in Gibian, op. cit., p. 589); George Gibian, who says that the

Epilogue is necessary in order to complete religious symbolism developed earlier in the novel ("Traditional Symbolism in *Crime and Punishment*," in Gibian, pp. 519-536); and Maurita Willett, who concurs with Wasiolek in saying that the Epilogue presents the logical outcome of the conflict between what Sonja represents and what Svidrigajlov represents ("The 'Ending' of *Crime and Punishment*," *Orbis Litterarum*, 25, 1979, 244-258).

2. W. H. Auden, "The Guilty Vicarage: Notes on the Detective Story, by an Addict," *Harper's*, May, 1948, pp. 406-412.

3. Vyacheslav Ivanov, *Freedom and the Tragic Life*, trans. Norman Cameron (London: Harvill Press, 1952), p. 77.

4. Petr M. Bicilli, "K voprosu o vnutrennej forme romana Dostoevskogo," Sofia Universitet, Istorikofilologičeski Fakultet, *Godišnik*, 42 (1945/1946), 1-71. Rep. in Donald Fanger, ed., *O Dostoevskom: Stat'i*, Brown University Slavic Reprint IV (Providence: Brown University Press, 1966). See pp. 27, 45-46.

5. The most extensive discussion of the formal analogies between *Crime and Punishment* and tragedy is that of Mochulsky, who demonstrates that the novel obeys the three unities and fits the five-act structure of Renaissance and European classical tragedy (although Mochulsky simply uses the term "classical tragedy" as if these characteristics all applied to the Greeks as well). What vitiates Mochulsky's argument, however, is his failure to show that the five-part structure is anything but a happy accident. Apart from his implicit assumption that Raskolnikov's duality is an essential quality of tragic hero, Mochulsky has almost nothing to say about the content of the novel which might explain why it should be like a tragedy. See Konstantin Mochulsky, op. cit., pp. 270-313. Murray Krieger speaks of the "tragic vision" in Dostoevsky, but he discusses primarily *The Idiot* and, besides, has broadened his definition of the tragic so much that it is no longer strictly linked to any formal determinations. See Murray Krieger, *The Tragic Vision: Variations on a Theme in Literary Interpretation* (New York: Holt, Rinehart & Winston, 1960). S. I. Gessen's article on "The Tragedy of Good in *The Brothers Karamazov*" is actually not about tragedy as such, since the author is using the word "tragedy" in his title in a loose sense. See Sergej Josifovich Gessen, "Tragedija dobra v *Brat'jakh Karamazovykh*," in Donald Fanger, op. cit., pp. 197-229. A more recent article by Nina Gourfinkel, entitled, "Les éléments d'une tragédie moderne dans les romans de Dostoïevski," in *Dostoïevski*, ed. Jacques Catteau (Paris: Edi-

tions de l'Herne, 1973), pp. 235-251, is not a discussion of tragic elements in Dostoevsky at all, but a description of various modern stage adaptations of Dostoevsky's novels. Finally, there is a book-length study devoted to the subject of Christian tragedy in Dostoevsky and Shakespeare by Roger Cox: *Between Earth and Heaven: Shakespeare, Dostoevsky, and the Meaning of Christian Tragedy* (New York: Holt, Rinehart & Winston, 1969). One drawback I find in Cox's book is that, in developing the notion of "Christian tragedy," he shows at the outset why Christian narratives may be considered tragic, but does not return sufficiently to the idea of the tragic when he studies the individual novels and plays. Instead, he tends simply to concentrate on the Christian elements in the texts themselves, assuming that the point has already been made that what is Christian is also therefore tragic. Cox points out some interesting analogies between the Gospel narratives and tragedy, but I cannot agree with his belief that a narrative concluding with as positive an element as rebirth and spiritual renewal can be wholly tragic. My analysis differs from Cox's most significantly in emphasizing the distinction between tragic and Christian structure (although I recognize the parallels up to a very important limit).

6. Richmond Lattimore, *Story Patterns in Greek Tragedy* (Ann Arbor: University of Michigan Press, 1964).

7. *Oedipus Tyrannos*, 1. 1213; my translation.

8. F. M. Dostoevskii, *Polnoe sobranie sochinenij v tridcati tomakh* (Leningrad: Akademiia Nauk SSSR, 1972-), VI, 52. Hereafter cited in the text as *PSS*. Translations are my own throughout.

9. Jean-Pierre Vernant, "Greek Tragedy: Problems of Interpretation," in *The Structuralist Controversy: The Languages of Criticism and the Sciences of Man*, ed. Richard Macksey and Eugenio Donato (Baltimore and London: The John Hopkins University Press, 1970), p. 286.

10. Aristotle, *Poetics*, 1452 a.

11. Ivanov, loc. cit.

12. Vernant, op. cit., p. 288.

13. Cox, op. cit., pp. 34 ff., mentions this Johannine conception of sin, and the escape from the determinism of original sin it entails, as closely resembling Dostoevsky's view.

14. Louis Gernet, *Recherches sur le développement de la pensée juridique et morale en Grèce* (Paris: Ernst Leroux, 1917).

15. See Gernet, pp. 305, ff.

16. See Gernet, pp. 279, ff.

17. *Choephoroe,* l. 461; my translation.

18. Vernant, p. 278.

19. An account of the Reform and its consequences is given by Samuel Kucherov, who had been a lawyer under the old regime, in *Courts, Lawyers and Trials under the Last Three Tsars* (New York: Frederick A. Praeger, 1953).

20. Grigorij A. Dzhanishiev, *Osnovy sudebnoj reformy* (Moscow: Karinskoi, 1891), p. 47, cites the passage in the Basic Principles and discusses its importance in that document. Mentioned in Kucherov, p. 23.

21. See *Dnevnik Pisatelja za 1876 g.,* February article "Po povodu dela Kroneberga," ("On the Kroneberg Affair") and following articles, *PSS, XXII,* p. 50-73.

22. The conclusion of the Eumenides, where Athena gives the deciding vote to Orestes and not to the Furies, is an apparent exception to this. But it should be noted that even here the final accommodation rests on the inclusion of the Furies and their violent ethic. Moreover, even if the final tally does not officially point to guilt for the accused, Orestes' fate remains one of suffering.

23. George P. Fedotov, *The Russian Religious Mind (I): Kievan Christianity: The 10th to the 13th Centuries* (Cambridge, Mass., 146-166; rpt. Belmont, Mass.: Nordland, 1975), Chapter IV, "Russian Kenoticism," pp. 94-131.

Derek Offord (essay date 1983)

SOURCE: Offord, Derek. "The Causes of Crime and the Meaning of Law: *Crime and Punishment* and Contemporary Radical Thought." In *Fyodor Dostoevsky's* Crime and Punishment, edited by Harold Bloom, pp. 81-101. New York: Chelsea House Publishers, 1988.

[*In the following essay, originally published in 1983, Offord examines Dostoevsky's depiction of contemporary social issues in* Crime and Punishment. *According to Offord, Dostoevsky's ideas concerning the impact of crime on society are still relevant in the present day.*]

It is one of the qualities of the greatest writers of imaginative literature that they succeed in capturing in their works both what is of lasting, universal significance and what is of most pressing concern in their own age and for their own nation. They deepen our knowledge both of man's experience in general and of his condition in a given society in particular. Thus Turgenev, in *Fathers and Children,* the novel generally acclaimed as his masterpiece, recorded in the most topical terms a conflict between generations and classes which has a relevance far beyond the Russia of the 1860s. Similar praise may be accorded to Dostoevsky. His works have a profound bearing on some of the philosophical doctrines and political systems of the twentieth-century world and on the psychological condition of the individual in modern urban societies. They also throw light on problems such as crime, so central in Dostoevsky's major fiction, which have come increasingly to disturb those societies. There is much in his works, for example, that is portentous for a world in which antisocial behaviour often constitutes a pastime for the reasonably well-to-do rather than a matter of economic necessity for the destitute, and in which, perhaps even more importantly, indiscriminate violence is often accepted as a legitimate means to a supposedly worthy end. And yet the insights into these problems with which Dostoevsky can furnish us are the product of his participation in a debate about issues of great local and contemporary importance at the time when his novels were written. It is the relationship of *Crime and Punishment* to this debate that this [essay] is intended primarily to discuss.

II

Dostoevsky, when he came to write *Crime and Punishment* in 1865, had already made an extensive contribution, both in publicism and in imaginative literature, to the vigorous intellectual life of those years following the Crimean War and the death of Nicholas I when a more liberal regime flowered briefly in Russia and when the old order began to undergo irreversible change. In particular the hostility towards the radical camp which found expression in Dostoevsky's writing in the early sixties was to become one of the prime creative influences in his major fiction.

The radical camp, of course, contained individuals with divergent opinions. Moreover, the Western thinkers from whom the Russian radicals derived their convictions were themselves numerous and of varied complexion, ranging from the English utilitarian Jeremy Bentham, the early Welsh socialist Robert Owen, French utopian socialists such as Fourier, Cabet and Considérant, and the positivist Comte, to German philosophers and thinkers such as Feuerbach and L. Büchner, the contemporary English historian Buckle, scientists such as Darwin and popularizers of scientific thought, such as G. H. Lewes. But it is probably not grossly inaccurate to suggest that what was of most interest in Western thought to the Russian radicals of the sixties, and what constituted for Dostoevsky a core against which his creative energies should be directed, might be reduced to a fairly limited number of propositions which were given wide currency in the journal *Contemporary* and in the voluminous, wordy and extremely influential writings of Chernyshevsky in particular.

These propositions may be summarized as follows: firstly, that "no dualism is to be seen in man," that is to say man does not possess a spiritual dimension which is qualitatively different from his physical being; secondly, that man is governed by self-interest; thirdly, that he is at the same time a rational creature; fourthly, that he may therefore be made to see where his best interest lies and to act accordingly; fifthly, that since man is amenable to rational persuasion and since his best interest lies in cooperation with his fellows, one might realistically hope to construct in theory and then in practice a perfectly ordered society; sixthly, that the good is that which is useful, and the useful, for the radical "men of the sixties," was in turn that which promoted the dissemination and acceptance of the preceding propositions; and finally, that a scientific method of enquiry, and only that method of enquiry (with the help of which all the preceding propositions were supposedly formulated), could be applied successfully and profitably to the examination of human conduct, society and government.

Dostoevsky disagrees profoundly with every one of these propositions. In his first major novel, *Crime and Punishment,* he makes explicit or oblique references, which are caustic in their context, to thinkers who defend them, and vigorously disputes the propositions themselves. He implies, for example, that it is resurrection of the spiritual side of Raskolnikov's being which offers him his only hope of salvation after he has taken other lives. Furthermore, it is love of others, as preached and practised by Sonya, rather than love of self, which makes possible such regeneration. Raskolnikov is not capable of consistently rational conduct. His behaviour is frequently self-destructive. And Razumikhin inveighs bitterly against the socialist utopia (part 3, chap. 5). But in particular Dostoevsky sets out to test in his novel the strength and acceptability of the last two propositions of the radicals, which concern the equation of the good with the useful and the omnicompetence of the scientific method of enquiry. And it is through his examination of the subjects of the causes of crime and the nature and status of law that Dostoevsky explores the implications of these two propositions and concentrates his argument against those who defend them.

III

There are no doubt several reasons for Dostoevsky's choice of the subjects of crime and the law as his ground on which to do battle with the radicals.

Firstly, legal questions very much preoccupied educated people in Russia in the early 1860s and the novelist of the time, with his interest in contemporary reality, was entitled to devote attention to them. Overhaul of the judicial system was one aspect of the great reforms planned and carried out in Russia in the late 1850s and early 1860s. An ukase of 1864 finally provided for the establishment of new courts on the Western model. Numerous foreign books on jurisprudence were translated, published and reviewed in this period and the journals devoted much attention to legal questions. Dostoevsky's own journal *Epoch,* for example, carried lengthy articles on legal procedure, punishments, criminal law and lawyers, as well as the memoirs of an investigator, in the course of 1864-65. In 1865 Dostoevsky himself was contemplating an article on the courts, some notes for which are preserved in one of his notebooks. Thus references to changes in the law and its administration, the proliferation of the legal profession, litigation, the increase in crime—there are allusions to forgery, seduction and poisoning, as well as description of Raskolnikov's murders, in *Crime and Punishment*—help on one level to provide a broad social backcloth for the novel's main action.

Secondly, on a deeper level, the mentality of the criminal was a subject that already absorbed Dostoevsky, the novelist of profound psychological insight. He had intimate knowledge of the criminal, gained in his years in prison among hardened convicts and recorded in *Notes from the House of the Dead.* In the journal *Time,* which he had edited from 1861 to 1863, there had appeared transcripts of famous trials of the century, and Dostoevsky himself had written a preface to the first transcript, dealing with the trial of the French professional criminal Lacenaire, a murderer who exhibits striking similarities to Raskolnikov (both Lacenaire and Raskolnikov are educated but impoverished young men driven obsessively to dominate; both are influenced by Napoleon, atheistic, antisocial and vengeful; and both publish speculative articles. Raskolnikov on crime and Lacenaire on the penal system). It may also be that the great fictional possibilities of the subject of crime and its detection were underlined for Dostoevsky by the novels of Dickens, in so many of which crime, including murder, is a central feature.

Thirdly, on the polemical level, the question of crime was one which also preoccupied the socialists with whom Dostoevsky was taking issue. Like their Western European mentors, the Russian radicals of the 1860s expressed deterministic views on the causes of crime which seemed to Dostoevsky as oversimplified as their views on the nature of man and his society. Robert Owen—whom Chernyshevsky's hero, Lopukhov, describes as a "holy old man" and whose portrait hangs in Lopukhov's room—had taught the Russian radicals that crime was a natural product of the irrational organization of the British society of his day. The "poor and uneducated profligate among the working classes," he wrote in his *New View of Society,* "are now trained to commit crimes"; but with man's natural progression from a "state of ignorance to intelligence," and the consequent implementation of "rational plans for the education and general formation" of a society's members, crime would be eradicated. "Withdraw these circumstances which tend to create crime in the human character," he wrote with the ingenuous benevolence of the early socialists, "and crime will not be created," for the "worst formed disposition, short of incurable insanity," would not long resist a "firm, determined, well-directed, persevering kindness." Similarly, Büchner, who in the late fifties and early sixties exercised an influence on the Russian radical intelligentsia out of all proportion to his importance in the history of European thought, argued in *Kraft und Stoff*—a work much admired, incidentally, by Bazarov—that the "chief causes of crime" were "deficiency of intellect, poverty and want of education." In the Russia of the 1860s, where it became customary to explain a man's behaviour deterministically, as a product of his environment, views such as these were commonplace. Chernyshevsky, for example, in his major profession of faith, the article on the "anthropological principle in philosophy" asserted:

> After the need to breathe . . . man's most pressing need is to eat and drink. Very often, very many people lack the wherewithal for the proper satisfaction of this need, and this lack is the source of the greatest number of all bad actions, of almost all situations and institutions which are constant causes of bad actions. If one were to remove this cause of evil alone, at least nine tenths of all that is bad would quickly disappear from human society: the number of crimes would decrease ten times.

Likewise Dobrolyubov stated, in the tortuous style characteristic of the radical publicism of the time, that "any crime is not a consequence of man's nature, but a consequence of the abnormal relationship to society in which he is placed."

Dostoevsky's antagonism to such views is a major source of tension in *Crime and Punishment.*

IV

Now it is one of the qualities of Dostoevsky as a novelist that he seems rarely to come down decisively in his works of art on the side of those views which it is clear from his publicistic works that he wished to promote. His vision as an artist is too complex to permit him to be one-sided or tendentious. It is arguable, for example, that he failed adequately to rebut the arguments of Ivan Karamazov against acceptance of God's world, although he himself evidently needed to disbelieve them. And by emphasizing the loathsomeness of the pawnbroker Alyona and the exploitative Luzhin he sets up persuasive arguments in *Crime and Punishment* in favour of the crime whose moral inadmissibility he undoubtedly hoped eventually to demonstrate.

Similarly he does not simply reject out of hand the radicals' thesis that poverty was a possible cause of crime (or at least a cause of the derangement which might induce it). On the contrary, he points out on the very first page of the novel that Raskolnikov was "crushed by poverty"; for the second day running, we read shortly afterwards, he had eaten virtually nothing, and clearly his debility and illness are related. The oppressive and stinking milieu, moreover, "jarred the young man's nerves which were already disturbed without that" (part 1, chap. 1). And when Raskolnikov does refresh himself after his first visit to Alyona's, his thoughts clear and all that has been passing through his mind suddenly seems nonsense, the result of physical disorder (part 1, chap. 1). Furthermore, the view that crime and social conditions are related is openly advanced in those chapters of the novel in which characters, with the murder of Alyona and Lizaveta in mind, debate the causes of crime. Luzhin, trying to restore his rapidly dwindling credit when he visits Raskolnikov in part 2, delivers himself of a disquisition on the growth of crime in Russia, a phenomenon which Zosimov attributes to the fact that there have been "many economic changes" (part 2, chap. 5). Later, during Raskolnikov's first visit to Porfiry, Razumikhin refers to a heated debate that had taken place the night before, in which someone had expressed the view of the "socialists" that "crime is a protest against the abnormality of the social order—and only that, and nothing more, and no other causes are admitted." According to this view "all crimes" would disappear once society was organized "normally" (part 3, chap. 5). It is a view which even Porfiry appears to endorse: "'environment' means a lot in crime," he affirms. And he seems prepared to carry it to the extreme, since when Razumikhin asks him whether "environment" could be said to explain the seduction of a ten-year-old girl by a forty-year-old man, he replies "with surprising gravity": "Well, in a strict sense it very probably is environment, even a crime committed against a little girl may very well be explained by 'environment'" (part 3, chap. 5). Lebezyatnikov argues with even more conviction in favour of such social determinism. He believes that everything depends on man's "surroundings" and "environment." "All on the environment," he says in his broken Russian, "and man himself is nothing" (part 5, chap. 1). In the society of the future, therefore, when all is rationally arranged in the interests of equality, there will not even be any fights.

However, we are not expected to accept the deterministic view of man's behaviour and of the incidence of crime uncritically. We are put on our guard against it by the fact that its advocates are, in Dostoevsky's terms, unreliable. Zosimov, for example, merely voices the commonplaces fashionable among the younger generation. As a doctor he is the novel's main practitioner of the exact sciences which that generation exalted. He is the target of the invective of Razumikhin—the physically and spiritually healthy foil to the sickly Raskolnikov—against the "dumb progressives" who understand nothing and show disrespect for man because they take too narrow a view of him (part 2, chap. 4). And in practice Zosimov's judgement is repeatedly at fault: for instance he mistakenly assumes the murderer to be an experienced criminal (part 2, chap. 5); he wrongly predicts that the arrival of Raskolnikov's mother and sister will have a beneficial effect on Raskolnikov (part 3, chap. 1); and he fails to see in what way Luzhin is a bad suitor for Dunya (part 3, chap. 2). As for Lebezyatnikov, he is discredited morally—he beats Katerina Marmeladova (part 1, chap. 2)—and intellectually—he is the main apostle of Western rationalism in the novel but has great difficulty in talking coherently in his native language (part 5, chap. 3). And Porfiry, although he is by no means an object of Dostoevsky's criticism, does have a notorious capacity to mislead others for his own ends (part 3, chap. 5). On the other hand Razumikhin, the most vehement opponent of the view that "crime is a protest against the abnormality of the social order," and "nothing more" (part 3, chap. 5), is the champion of values close to Dostoevsky's own. Indeed in a sense he is the "positive hero" of the novel, Dostoevsky's fictional response to the hero of Chernyshevsky's *What Is to Be Done?*, Rakhmetov, with whom Dostoevsky even confuses him at one point in a rough draft for one of the scenes of *Crime and Punishment.* Like Rakhmetov, Razumikhin is physically strong, resourceful, independent, strong-willed and solicitous for his friends. He too is capable of feats of great endurance: Rakhmetov lies on a bed of nails to strengthen his will; Razumikhin has gone through a whole winter without heating his room (part 1, chap. 4).

More importantly, besides casting doubt on the reliability of those who uphold the deterministic explanation of crime or appear to do so, Dostoevsky underlines the limitations of the explanation itself by demonstrating—as was habitual with him—that the problem could be approached from the opposite angle. The radicals' hatred of existing society and their overriding desire to bring about its material transformation lead them to attribute even individual acts of wrongdoing to unsatisfactory social conditions. Dostoevsky, on the other hand, being concerned above all with the spiritual condition of the individual, seeks to direct the attention of those who would examine the incidence of crime in a given society not so much to any aspects of the material environment as to those psychological factors which allow the individual to commit crime or fail to prevent him from doing so. Thus in *Crime and Punishment* he is perhaps less interested in motives for murder, such as the desire of the impoverished Raskolnikov to "get rich quick" (part 1, chap. 3), than in the modern attitudes which appear to make it irrational for him not to kill, given the weakening or absence of conscience. In particular he has in mind the utilitarian morality of the radicals who, in the course of their endeavours to redefine concepts and transform values associated with the

established order, described the good as that which was useful and the greatest good as that which was useful to the greatest number, and commended the moral doctrine which they designated "rational and egoism."

As critics have frequently pointed out, Dostoevsky emphasizes the prevalence of the utilitarian morality of the radicals and makes clear its bearing on the murder which Raskolnikov commits. In the letter to his prospective publisher Katkov, which he drafted in September 1865 when *Crime and Punishment* was taking shape in his mind, Dostoevsky associated his hero's crime with current theories: the action was to take place in that year and the hero, who was to be a "man of the new generation," had been carried away by certain badly thought out ideas which were "in the air." Moreover, in order to emphasize that conversations about the possibility of killing in the interests of public utility were commonplace among the young generation, Dostoevsky has Raskolnikov overhear a student advancing "*exactly the same ideas*" as those he himself is pondering (part 1, chap. 6). (It is significant too that these ideas are put forward by a student, for it was in the higher educational institutions that the radicals found their most enthusiastic support.) Again, Porfiry emphasizes that the murder of the pawnbroker is a "modern" crime and that the murderer killed "in accordance with theory" (part 6, chap. 2).

But how precisely does the ascendancy of the new morality account for the commission of crimes which the proponents of that morality would attribute to social deprivation? The morality of the radicals, Dostoevsky seems to argue, may produce such destructive results in three ways. Firstly, the adoption of utility as the criterion by which to judge the value of actions makes for a blurring of distinctions between acts which are absolutely right and acts which are absolutely wrong, that is, right or wrong, moral or immoral, in all circumstances. Judgement of the quality of an action becomes dependent on extrinsic factors such as the value of its probable consequences. Seen from this point of view, acts which have traditionally appeared to be immoral are no longer necessarily held to be so. Lebezyatnikov exhibits this relativistic attitude when he says that what in the present society is "stupid" may in the rationally ordered society of the future be "intelligent" (part 5, chap. 1). But more importantly Raskolnikov himself applies it to crime. The murder, when its advantages have been calculated and the sum of its disadvantages subtracted, seems a useful act and is therefore "'not a crime'" (part 1, chap. 6).

Secondly, by asserting the preeminence of the greatest number, utilitarianism tends to reduce individual human beings to mere ciphers who have value not so much in themselves as in relation to the larger groups to which they belong. It was not difficult to decide, Chernyshevsky wrote, on whose side "theoretical justice" lay: the interests of mankind in general stood higher than the advantage of an individual nation, the general interest of a whole nation stood higher than the advantage of a single class, and the interest of a numerous class stood higher than that of a numerically inconsiderable group. This "theoretical justice" had about it an inflexible quality which precluded appeal by the minorities or individuals who might be the victims of its implementation; it represented merely an "application of geometrical axioms" such as the "'whole is greater than part of it.'" Likewise for Dostoevsky's student in part 1 of *Crime and Punishment* "justice" consists in the promotion of the interests of the many at the expense of the pawnbroker and may be expressed simply and indisputably in the form of an equation: "What do you think, wouldn't one tiny little crime be cancelled out by thousands of good deeds? For one life—thousands of lives, saved from rotting and decay. One death and a hundred lives in exchange—why it's arithmetic, isn't it?" (part 1, chap. 6).

Thirdly, by their doctrine of "rational egoism"—in which the Russian utilitarianism of the 1860s chiefly found expression—the radicals tended to vindicate *egoistic* actions if the consequences of those actions could be claimed to have general utility. In this doctrine—which appears oddly incompatible with the socialist convictions it was supposed to bolster—the radicals contrived to accommodate both the proposition that man was governed by self-interest and belief in the feasibility of a utopia based on cooperation, by maintaining that man, when properly enlightened, would derive his selfish pleasure from performing acts of general utility. Raskolnikov clearly finds justification for his crime in the doctrine's identification of pursuit of personal profit, on the one hand, and promotion of general wellbeing, on the other (even though later, when he hears Luzhin parrot the doctrine, he is repelled by this potentiality in it [part 2, chap. 5]). For Raskolnikov seems to believe, as it was Dostoevsky's intention that he should, that the murder of the pawnbroker and the theft of her money would benefit both himself and others: it would alleviate his own poverty but would also liberate his exploited sister from Luzhin and rid society of a louse.

Thus the radicals, far from providing a correct explanation of the incidence of crime in society, are putting forward moral views which are themselves responsible for crime's growth. The establishment of their doctrines, whose apparently incontestable veracity seemed to Chernyshevsky to preclude any "unsteadiness in convictions," has in the view of Dostoevsky and those who were likeminded had the opposite effect: it has actually produced a discernible "unsteadiness in the moral order." And far from tending to hasten the advent of a utopia in which acts hitherto considered criminal cease

to be perpetrated, these doctrines encourage the development of an anarchic society in which such acts merely cease to be considered criminal and therefore may proliferate.

V

From the early stages of *Crime and Punishment* Dostoevsky puts forward implicit arguments against the acceptability and even against the practicability of the utilitarian rationalization of crime. In the first place Raskolnikov himself tends to criticize rationalistic thinking when those he loves are the victims of its application. He is infuriated, for example, at the prospect of statisticians treating his sister as merely a number in a table indicating the percentage of the population which turns to prostitution each year (part 1, chap. 4). In the second place, there are strong indications that human behaviour is not so exclusively rational as the utilitarians believe: Raskolnikov's crime is logically planned—he even measures the distance ("exactly 730" paces [part 1, chap. 1]) between his lodging and the pawnbroker's—and yet over its actual commission his reason has very little control. (Indeed he is forced to commit another murder, the need for which he had planned to obviate by ensuring that Lizaveta would not be at home.) Moreover, the deliberate artistic confusion of the first part of the novel, with its disjointed time sequence and sometimes fractured style, serves to point up the disorientation of the character to whom issues seem in theory to be so clearcut. But although these factors serve from the beginning to undermine the value of the morality Raskolnikov has adopted, in fact the search for a sound explanation of his crime leads deeper into error. For the theories which Dostoevsky has Raskolnikov express in part 3 of the novel, concerning the right of certain individuals to "cross over" normal moral boundaries and to commit acts generally deemed criminal, represent an examination of some of the further implications of the new outlook. Whereas the first apparent explanation of the murder raises the question of how an act should be judged and affirms that its utility should be calculated, the second explanation raises the question as to who should make that judgement and calculation.

Commentators have drawn attention to the relationship between, on the one hand, the ideas Raskolnikov expresses in part 3 of the novel, and, on the other, those advanced in a book by Napoleon III and in the works of certain Russian radicals who wrote for the journal *Russian Word* and were by 1865 conducting an acrimonious polemic with the epigones of Chernyshevsky on *Contemporary*. It has also been noted that the use of the word *raskol,* chosen by Dostoevsky to denote the schism in the radical intelligentsia in the title of an article published in 1864 in his journal *Epoch* (which on more than one occasion mentioned the disagreements among the radicals with evident satisfaction), would seem to anticipate the name, Raskolnikov, chosen by him for the hero of the novel he began to write in the following year. And, of course, Lebezyatnikov refers obliquely to this schism in the novel itself (part 5, chap. 1). But since a few very striking similarities between the views expressed in *Russian Word* and those of Raskolnikov have not been fully brought out, it is worth briefly glancing again at this polemic and at the writings of Pisarev in particular.

In many respects Pisarev's views coincide with Chernyshevsky's. Pisarev preaches a materialistic doctrine similar to Chernyshevsky's; he believes that man is governed by self-interest; he repeatedly upholds the view that it is profitable for the individual to behave in socially useful ways; and he writes an extended encomium to the new men who practise this doctrine and whom Chernyshevsky had portrayed in his novel *What Is to Be Done?* But Pisarev's rebellion is altogether more iconoclastic than Chernyshevsky's. Whereas Chernyshevsky, writing in 1855 as the old order was just beginning to weaken, had given the cautious title *Aesthetic Relations of Art to Reality* to the dissertation in which he called in question the old belief that the beautiful was superior to everyday reality, Pisarev, writing in 1865, when the attack on the old order was well advanced, undertook nothing less than a "destruction" (*razrusheniye*) of aesthetics. Old barriers were to be torn down unceremoniously. Literature, Pisarev wrote in 1861, for example, should strive to emancipate man "from the various constraints imposed on him by the timidity of his own thought, by caste prejudice, by the authority of tradition, by the striving towards a common ideal and by all the obsolete lumber that prevents a living man from breathing freely and developing in every direction." His readers were exhorted to try to "live a full life," without stifling what was *original* in them in order to accommodate the established order and the taste of the crowd. He urged the destruction, together with other old values, of that "artificial system of morality" which crushed people from the cradle. In short, Pisarev's doctrines are partially similar to those of Chernyshevsky; but, as Dostoevsky jotted in his notebooks, probably under the impression of the article from which I have quoted, "Pisarev has gone further." In *Crime and Punishment* Lebezyatnikov, claiming that he would argue even with Dobrolyubov were he to rise from his grave, makes the same point in similar terms. "We have gone further in our convictions," he says, identifying himself with Pisarev and his supporters. "We reject more" (part 5, chap. 1).

Now it very often happened that ideas being expressed in the Russian publicism of the age were embodied in the fiction and that the fiction in turn stimulated the publicism. In fact between the publicism and the fiction there existed an intimate relationship; they responded to one another and moved forward together dialectically. And the freedom from traditional restraints already being advocated by Pisarev in 1861 found its fictional representation in Bazarov, the literary prototype of the new man to whom Turgenev applied the title "nihilist." Pisarev was delighted to accept Bazarov as an example for the new generation to follow, although in the second of the two substantial tracts he devoted to examination of Turgenev's novel he preferred the name "realist." The mission of the new man, as Bazarov saw it, was not to build but to destroy what impeded new construction, "to clear space," and Pisarev gleefully proceeded to elaborate on the freedom the destroyer would enjoy. Armed with an extreme materialism that obliged him to acknowledge only what his five senses could apprehend, and governed only by personal whim and self-interest, Bazarov acted "everywhere and in everything" only as he wished or as seemed to him "profitable and convenient." "Neither over himself, nor outside himself, nor within himself does he acknowledge any regulator, any moral law, any principle." That such freedom might be a basis for anarchy Pisarev plainly foresaw, since he considered it necessary to answer the question as to why Bazarov does not turn to crime. But his answer was unconvincing. Only circumstances and personal taste, he wrote, make such men as Bazarov "honest" or "dishonest," "civic dignitaries" or "inveterate swindlers." Nothing but personal taste, he continued in terms strikingly pertinent to *Crime and Punishment,* "prevents them from killing and robbing" and nothing but personal taste "prompts people of this stamp to make discoveries in the field of science and public life." Pisarev did invoke rational egoism as a restraining factor: intelligent people realize that "it is very profitable to be honest and that any crime, starting with a simple lie and ending with homicide, is dangerous and, consequently, inconvenient." But the die was cast. Pisarev, as Masaryk has put it, had "vindicated for the nihilists the right to kill and to rob."

Those who are capable of exercising the new moral freedom possess great power, as Turgenev, Pisarev and Dostoevsky all realized. They enjoy an implicit superiority over those who remain bound by conventional restraints. In his essay on Bazarov, Pisarev underlined this division of humanity. On the one hand he saw the mass, whose members never use their brains independently. The mass "neither makes discoveries, nor commits crimes"; it lives quietly from day to day "according to the established norm." On the other hand he saw the intelligent individuals who cannot come to terms so easily with all that the mass accepts. These individuals fall into three categories. Firstly, there are those who, being uneducated, are unable properly to take themselves in hand when they withdraw from the herd. Secondly, there are those who are educated but incapable of carrying their rebellion beyond a theoretical stage. And thirdly, there are those who are capable of implementing in practice their theoretical rebellion. These "people of the third category" (*tret'yego razryada*) "acknowledge their dissimilarity to the mass and boldly mark themselves off from it by their acts, by their habits, by their whole way of life. . . . Here the individual attains his full self-liberation, his full individuality and independence." Chernyshevsky, at the end of his publicistic career, draws a somewhat similar distinction in *What Is to Be Done?* between "ordinary people" and those who are by implication extraordinary, although now the rational egoists Lopukhov and Kirsanov (who, as their names imply, have grown symbolically out of Turgenev's representatives of the young generation) are themselves only ordinary before the epitome of independence, the iron-willed "special man" Rakhmetov.

Now Raskolnikov's speculative article on crime which is discussed in part 3 of *Crime and Punishment* owes much to current views such as Pisarev's on the division of mankind into the enslaved and the liberated. Indeed Raskolnikov says that what he is describing "has been printed and read a thousand times" (part 3, chap. 5). Like Pisarev, as Dostoevsky saw him, Raskolnikov has not merely flirted with rational egoism but has "gone further." He aspires, like Bazarov, to membership of that category of people who are bound by no moral law and who may waive those moral considerations that have generally restrained men from committing antisocial acts and continue to prevent the masses from doing so. Thus Raskolnikov has granted himself licence to destroy human life. He has committed the murder and robbery which Pisarev's destroyers might contemplate and has pondered the scientific discoveries and contributions to society which they might make if "personal taste" disposed them to such actions. And he has murdered, it now appears, for no sound financial reason, but merely to confirm the freedom Pisarev had exalted. He is one of those who might be able to say a "*new word*," the original contribution which Pisarev urged his readers not to stifle. His terms of reference are those of Pisarev too, although he has carried out a further simplification: the first category (*pervyy razryad*) is the mass, conservative by nature, which lies obediently; the second category (*vtoroy razryad*) consists of the "extraordinary" men and women, the "people of the future," the "destroyers" (*razrushiteli*) (part 3, chap. 5). Finally, the elitism implicit in Pisarev's schema is reflected in Raskolnikov's pride, his arrogance towards "ordinary" mortals. It is a trait which Dostoevsky is concerned to underline at this particular point in the novel. Thus in the notes for part 3 he remarks that the "thought of immeasurable pride, arrogance, and contempt for society" are expressed in Raskolnikov's personality; and in the finished work Razumikhin tells Raskolnikov's mother and sister that his friend is "arrogant and proud" (part 3, chap. 2).

Raskolnikov, then, represents Dostoevsky's conception of the man moulded by the new outlook and once all inhibitions have been properly stripped away. The self-will of this man accounts for a number of other traits in Raskolnikov's character which are brought out in the novel together with the explanation of the murder of Alyona as an attempt to test Raskolnikov's right to destroy, namely: the violence which threatens to erupt again at the expense of Luzhin; Raskolnikov's inflexible insistence on having his own way, manifested in his determination, of which his mother now speaks, to marry his landlady's crippled daughter (part 3, chap. 2) and his demand that Dunya reject Luzhin (part 3, chap. 3); and his own rejection of all authority, parental and divine, implied by his coolness towards and alienation from his mother and by spurning of prayer once he feels secure (part 2, chap. 7). But most importantly, self-will finds expression in his attitude towards crime which now seems only a further logical consequence of the thorough rejection of all those "constraints," "prejudices" and "traditions" execrated by Pisarev.

VI

As Dostoevsky deepens the examination of the implications of current radical theory, so he broadens his consideration of crime, or more correctly, as the Russian word *prestupleniye* implies, of transgression. He now broaches important questions concerning the general rules by which the conduct of all individuals in a society is circumscribed, namely the laws. There thus begins in his work that profound debate on the nature and status of law which culminates in his last novel and crowning achievement, *The Brothers Karamazov.*

The word "law," of course, may have not only a juridical sense of a "body of enacted or customary rules recognized by a community as binding," but also, among many others, a moral sense of "precepts" or "binding injunctions" to be followed because they are dictated by conscience rather than by statute; and, thirdly, a scientific sense of "correct statement of invariable sequence between specified conditions and specified phenomenon." The variety of meanings inherent in the English word "law" is also available in its Russian equivalent *zakon,* although in Soviet lexicography the moral sense tends to be either blurred, merging with the morally neutral concept of a "generally accepted rule," or simply classified as obsolete.

Numerous Western jurists have discussed the relationship of law in its juridical sense (which may be known as "human," "positive" or "temporal" law) to law in some broader and more abstract sense. They have considered whether there exists a "natural law," that is a "system of right or justice held to be common to all mankind," and have asked themselves whether human law is an expression of such "natural law." Does human law then embody some principles of absolute, universal and permanent validity, can it be evaluated against certain immutable standards? Or does it merely reflect the values and needs of a particular society, and therefore have little or no relevance in other times and places? (The debate is analogous to that on the question as to whether moral values are absolute or relative.) Now Dostoevsky, as a Russian Orthodox writer passionately critical of most tendencies in Western thought, cannot be closely identified with any Western exponents or opponents of theories of natural law, but he is preoccupied with the sort of questions to which Western jurists have addressed themselves, and on one level *Crime and Punishment* represents his first major attempt to deal with them.

Law in its juridical sense—and it is with the "juridical question" that Raskolnikov's remarks to Porfiry in part 3 begin; indeed Raskolnikov has been a student of this law—has little status for Dostoevsky's antihero in his murderous frame of mind. It is clear that the concept lacks absolute authority for him, since he treats it in the same relativistic fashion as crime in part 1 and again in part 3. All the great "lawgivers" to whom he refers—the Spartan Lycurgus, the Athenian Solon, Mohammed and Napoleon (remembered in Russia not only as an invader but also as the promulgator of a new legal code on which Speransky largely based the code he was preparing for Alexander I)—were at the same time "criminals" by virtue of the fact that they destroyed orders sanctified by their forebears. Conversely, just as an act which might normally be deemed a crime was "not a crime" when seen from Raskolnikov's utilitarian point of view in part 1, so the infringement of a law by a Lycurgus might with a similar change of perspective be seen as the establishment of a law. Lawbreakers or "destroyers" might also be designated "lawgivers" and "institutors" (*ustanoviteli*) of mankind (part 3, chap. 5).

Historically speaking, the view that human law had some absolute validity, derived from the existence of an immutable moral law which it expressed, was weakened by the promotion of law in its third, scientific, sense. For thinkers like Comte, who accepted only those concepts which could be verified empirically, rejected as obsolete unproven hypotheses about the existence of God or the nature of man on which moral law rested. They were interested not so much in assumptions about how man ought to behave as in the description and classification of the ways in which he in fact did behave. Again Darwin, in demonstrating scientifically the adaptability of organisms in the struggle for survival, provided a biological precedent for thinkers who urged institutional and legal change in response to external pressures. In this respect, therefore, he too helped to undermine the view that legal orders rest on some permanently valid principle.

The Russian radical thinkers of the 1860s, much influenced by Comte, Darwin and other Western writers who adopted a supposedly scientific approach to the problems that interested them, also treated as absolute and binding only the empirically verifiable scientific law and rejected any intuited natural *laws*. They insisted that a rational man could acknowledge only the empirical method of enquiry which proceeded along the lines of Comte's "positive philosophy" and treated "all phenomena as subject to immutable natural law." Such laws as had already been discovered in the natural sciences they propagated with enthusiasm and every effort was made to reveal equally immutable laws in disciplines such as the study of man's behaviour and even his aesthetic concepts, which had not previously been considered amenable to scientific treatment. Thus Chernyshevsky assured his readers that "all the diversity" in human motivation and in human life in general sprang "from one and the same nature in accordance with one and the same law" and set out to investigate the "laws in accordance with which the heart and the will operate." Pisarev's thought is coloured by the same admiration of the natural sciences and the same faith in the universal applicability of the scientific method.

It is clear from the way in which Raskolnikov frequently expresses his thoughts in *Crime and Punishment* that he too, like many other members of his generation, is a devotee of the scientific method. Just as the student has done in part 1, he presents in part 3 a mathematical equation, in which the discoveries of Kepler and Newton are weighed against the lives of "one, ten, a hundred and so forth people who might prevent this discovery or might stand in the way as an obstacle" (part 3, chap. 5). He neatly divides humanity into "two categories" and repeats the terms "first category" and "second category" and expresses qualifications parenthetically as if in a mathematical formula. And towards the end of his monologue he uses an image already popular with Dostoevsky to evoke the scientific approach (part 2, chap. 4), alluding to the "retort" in which the processes he has described are taking place. He also says now that there must exist some "law of nature" which determines the "order of appearance of people, of all these categories and subdivisions." He is convinced that an exact law governs the divisions of men into the categories he has postulated: "there certainly is and must be a definite law." Nor does the fact that such a law has not yet been discovered shake Raskolnikov's conviction that "it exists and may subsequently become known" (part 3, chap. 5).

In appealing to scientific law Raskolnikov is in effect arguing not only that people who have a new word to say will inevitably break the established criminal law, but also that such people will inevitably appear. This scientific explanation of lawbreaking in turn diminishes the status of any moral law from which human law might have derived from authority. For the scientific inevitability of lawbreaking tends to reduce the culpability of the lawbreakers. A moral choice is valuable if there is freedom to make it. But if actions, in Büchner's words, are in the final analysis "dependent upon a fixed necessity" and if therefore "in every individual case free choice has only an extremely limited, if any, sphere of action," then criminals "are rather deserving of pity than of disgust." And the smaller the degree of control a man has over his actions, the smaller becomes the burden of guilt he must bear for them. The legal implications of this argument were clear to the positivist criminologists of the second half of the nineteenth century, who "instead of assuming a moral stance that focussed on measuring the criminal's 'guilt' and 'responsibility,' . . . attempted a morally neutral and social interpretation of crime and its treatment." If crime was the result of abnormalities in the human organism or of inherited or environmental factors outside the control of the criminal, punishment was an inappropriate response to it. Raskolnikov himself, in invoking scientific law to confirm his right to kill, is brushing aside moral law and thereby detracting from his guilt: he seems, as the horrified Razumikhin notices, to permit the shedding of blood in accordance with the dictates of one's conscience, and he does not expect the "extraordinary" man to suffer if he kills; indeed the greater the calculable utility of his act, the less significant will be the burden of moral responsibility he will bear (part 3, chap. 5).

The ascendancy of a scientific law, then, allows certain people to break the moral law as well as human law with impunity. Thus as law in one of its senses is promoted, so the status of law in another of its senses is diminished. The "men of the sixties," who had shown such industry in redefining concepts and values such as the "beautiful" and the "good," had also shifted the emphasis of the concept of law from the morally binding to the scientifically inevitable. Indeed in so far as the "extraordinary" men are granted free will, it had become morally binding, Dostoevsky implies, for them to promote what was scientifically indisputable. For the establishment of scientific laws seems in part 3 of *Crime and Punishment* to have become the most pressing moral obligation. Kepler and Newton, to whom Raskolnikov refers in support of his thesis that "extraordinary people" may "step over" certain "obstacles," are unaggressive scientists whose association in Raskolnikov's mind with Napoleon seems at first sight strange. In fact they constitute classic examples of the discoverers of physical laws of motion of the sort admired for their apparent incontestability by the men of the sixties. (Thus in *What Is to Be Done?* Newton is extolled by Rakhmetov as the "most brilliant and the most sane mind of all the minds known to us.") And to Raskolnikov the promotion of the discoveries of these scientists had evidently seemed so important that what

might normally have been designated a "crime" could have been in a sense quite legitimately committed in order to assist it. Raskolnikov seems to imply by his choice of examples, then, that the cause of the transgression of the law may be the need to establish a scientific law and even that such a transgression is obligatory. For although in one breath he denies that he insists, as he thinks Porfiry has insinuated, that "extraordinary people inevitably must and always were bound to commit all sorts of excesses," he does in the next admit that a Newton, encountering obstacles to the dissemination of his discoveries, "would have the right, and would even be obliged" to eliminate the individuals standing in his way (part 3, chap. 5).

VII

It is a repeatedly asserted or implied belief of Dostoevsky's in the early 1860s that his radical contemporaries were wrong to concede omnicompetence to law in its scientific sense. By devising and upholding such law they neither provided an entirely accurate description of man's nature and conduct nor did they lay down sound rules about how he ought to behave.

Just as the observation of a utilitarian ethic tended to reduce to impersonal mathematical terms problems of human conduct which were properly speaking unquantifiable, so the attempt to bring all man's characteristics and behaviour under the jurisdiction of scientific laws resulted in an oversimplification of a very complex reality. In attempting to embrace reality in its entirety in some logically incontestable schema, the radicals failed properly to take into account aspects of man's being other than his reason; for phenomena which were not rational, or the existence of which could not be empirically demonstrated, did not seem to lend themselves to precise analysis. The exponents of the supposedly scientific doctrines, Dostoevsky wrote in his notebook, were "theoreticians" who wished to "clip" man, to shear off him those parts of his being which did not accord with the soothing theories they had devised in the isolation of their studies or which might serve to obstruct the development of the utopias they envisaged. There are references to such simplification in *Crime and Punishment* too: Razumikhin, for example, accuses the socialists of failing to take human nature into account when designing their phalansteries. "All the mysteries of life" they try to accommodate "on two printer's sheets" (part 3, chap. 5). In particular the radicals seemed to Dostoevsky to ignore man's often irrational craving to assert his individuality, to preserve at least that illusion of free will so cherished by the Underground Man. They also failed to take into consideration conscience, the "moral sense of right and wrong" which might inhibit harsh treatment of one's fellows. Individual conscience, having no bearing on the general utility of an action, is not a faculty to which the student in part 1 of *Crime and Punishment* is prepared to devote serious attention. And Raskolnikov, treating it more as an attribute of the oppressed mass than as an innate human characteristic, expects to remain free of the remorse it might arouse.

In opposition to the supposedly irrefutable scientific laws exalted by the radicals, Dostoevsky puts forward certain laws of his own which seem to him more accurately to describe reality as he perceives it. There is a "law of truth and human nature," he writes in his letter to Katkov, which leads the criminal voluntarily to accept "torments." The suffering required by the criminal and described by Porfiry as a "great thing" (part 6, chap. 2) contrasts with the pleasure which utilitarianism postulates as the only end of man's existence. It is a law of nature for Porfiry, moreover, that a criminal like Raskolnikov, pursued by psychological methods, and left at large in the uncertainty dreaded by the rationalist, will eventually trap himself (part 4, chap. 5). And "facts"—the investigator's equivalent of scientific data, which it is not really proper for him to question (part 6, chap. 2)—Porfiry treats with scepticism, for they may lead him into error no less than the "abstract arguments of reason" which have so beguiled Raskolnikov (part 4, chap. 5).

Not only does Dostoevsky suggest the existence of psychological laws at variance with those accepted by the radicals (whose approach to psychology, as Dostoevsky perceives it, is reflected in *Crime and Punishment* in the statements of Zosimov on the subject (e.g., part 3, chap. 1). More importantly Dostoevsky also reinstates the moral law which scientific law tended to ignore or to suppress. The moral law emanated not from the reason—only a "twentieth part" of the Underground Man's capacity for living—but from the spiritual side of man's nature which, Chernyshevsky had categorically stated, did not exist. In opposition to Chernyshevsky's supposedly scientific law, which asserted that egoism was the basic impulse of all human actions, Dostoevsky's moral law postulated in man a need for "sacrifice," the submission of one's ego to others in selfless love. It is clearly this law which Dostoevsky believes will prevail in the final stage of human development, designated "Christianity" and envisaged by him in plans for an article drafted shortly before he embarked on the writing of *Crime and Punishment.* The Christian phase would supplant and stand in opposition to a phase designated "civilization," characterized by the extreme development of the individual consciousness and crowned by the advent of socialism. And it is Christ's commandment "Thou shalt love thy neighbour as thyself," observed in *Crime and Punishment* by Sonya, which ultimately prohibits acts based on the supposedly scientific precept approved by Luzhin, "Love, above all, thyself alone" (part 2, chap. 5).

For Dostoevsky the moral law, not any scientific law, is sovereign: there is "one law—the moral law," he wrote in a rough draft of one of the scenes of the novel. Beside this law human law pales into insignificance. Thus Porfiry, although he is the chief agent of the human law in *Crime and Punishment,* is manifestly "less concerned with apprehending Raskolnikov as a criminal," as Richard Peace has aptly put it, "than with saving him as a human being." In any case the "[juridical] punishment for a crime," Dostoevsky wrote in his letter to Katkov, "frightens a criminal much less than they [the lawgivers] think, in part because *he himself morally requires* it." But the unimportance of the human law beside the moral law does not entitle one to break it. For whereas the promotion of supposedly scientific laws tended to weaken existing legal codes by making crime a relative concept, the reinstatement of moral law strengthened them by making acts such as killing absolutely wrong. Raskolnikov therefore does not have the right to disregard human law on the grounds that its authority is threatened by inevitable political, social or intellectual change; on the contrary, he is bound to obey it because it expresses a higher Christian principle.

VIII

The points I have made stand in need of three qualifications. Firstly, Dostoevsky was not a singleminded publicist, like Chernyshevsky, but first and foremost an artist committed to faithful and full representation of reality as he perceived it; he did not therefore give definitive answers to the questions he posed. Secondly, some of the views implicit in *Crime and Punishment* were not fully developed by Dostoevsky for more than another decade, until he presented that profound debate which takes place in *The Brothers Karamazov* on the relationship between the "laws of Christ" and the laws of the state and on the need to punish the criminal by cutting off not a limb but a soul. And thirdly, to read the novel primarily as a contribution to the intellectual life of the period is to illuminate it only partially and to leave out of consideration its artistic riches and other qualities.

Nevertheless it is true to say that Dostoevsky, unlike Turgenev, did have passionate convictions which find expression in his novels. Moreover, Dostoevsky's objections to the new radical *Weltanschauung* had on the whole become clear by the time he came to write *Crime and Punishment* in 1865. Most importantly, it was probably mainly out of a desire to state or at least to clarify these objections that Dostoevsky now raised numerous important questions. Is man's behaviour determined by circumstances outside his control? Is he bound, if placed in certain conditions, to commit crime? Should criminals be considered blameless for their actions? Is it unjust that criminals should suffer punishment? Is the individual unimportant by comparison with the larger group to which he belongs? Do affirmative answers to these questions help to promote crime by destroying in the individual a sense of responsibility for his actions and love and respect for his fellows? And it is in no small measure from Dostoevsky's examination of these questions—to which radical contemporaries seemed to give such crude and dogmatic answers—that *Crime and Punishment* derives its lasting and universal significance.

Gary Cox (essay date 1990)

SOURCE: Cox, Gary. "Part 2." In Crime and Punishment: *A Mind to Murder,* pp. 48-58. Boston: Twayne Publishers, 1990.

[*In the following essay, Cox examines the nihilistic qualities in Dostoevsky's various characters.*]

RUSSIAN NIHILISM

One cannot go far in understanding *Crime and Punishment* without coming to grips with what is termed "Russian nihilism," the version of left-wing ideology that was popular among Russian youth of the intelligentsia during the 1860s. As I explained earlier, Russian nihilism should not be confused with the nihilism ("nothingism," from the latin *nihil,* "nothing") associated with the later existentialist movement, developed by thinkers such as Nietzsche who were indebted to Dostoevsky in significant ways. The Russian nihilists, whom Dostoevsky opposed, were actually utilitarians, stimulated by the work of Jeremy Bentham, John Stuart Mill, and other positivistic philosophers; they were optimistic liberals who believed that a rational utopian society could be constructed based on the principle of the greatest good for the greatest number. The term *nihilist* was applied pejoratively at first, by their opponents, but the radical youth accepted it as it seemed to characterize accurately their vigorous rejection of everything in the old system. These nihilists had great respect for science and believed that ethics must be based on positivistic, materialist, or scientific principles rather than on religious ones. Medicine was a popular field of study among them (although some had received their early training in preseminary grammar schools), and they liked to apply medical metaphors to society, seeing it as a diseased organism in need of a cure. They came not only from the ranks of priests' families but from various segments of Russian society (they were sometimes called *raznochintsy,* "people of various ranks"), reflecting the diversification and democratization of the intelligentsia that was an important sociological phenomenon of the period. They liked to talk about "the laws of [human] nature," overcoming "prejudices," and "[enlightened] self-interest" (or "advantage" or "benefit") as

a scientific principle upon which a utopian society could be constructed. The careful reader will have recognized in this list terms already encountered in the early parts of *Crime and Punishment.*

But the nihilism of this novel is not a straightforward presentation of the typical features of the movement. (For this we have Turgenev's *Fathers and Sons,* whose controversial hero, Bazarov, is by common consent the quintessential Russian nihilist of the 1860s.) The only typical nihilist we meet in *Crime and Punishment* is Lebeziatnikov, who does not appear until part 5 (although we hear of him as early as 1:2), and who is a ridiculous, if good-hearted, figure. Most of the nihilists in *Crime and Punishment* come at the movement from some oblique angle: they have been nihilists in the past but are dismayed by the movement's naïveté and thick-headedness (not far from Dostoevsky's own position in *Notes from Underground*), or they are mouthing its catch phrases for their own purposes. In fact, Dostoevsky's characters often embody a contradiction between ideology and social type, and this is nowhere more evident than in the nihilists of *Crime and Punishment.*

Is Raskolnikov's murder a nihilist one, and is the novel, then, a straightforward attack on the nihilist movement? Most of Raskolnikov's intellectual rationalization of the murder comes after the fact and stays away from explicit nihilism. It is not the surface features of nihilism that are being attacked here, but the positivistic basis of its system of ethics—that is, the fact that it permits no ethical absolutes except a commitment to scientific rationality and the ever-shifting good of society, with the possible corollary that ends may justify means. This attack on the basis rather than the specifics of Russian nihilism raises the novel out of its place and time and enhances its universality. But it can also produce some confusion.

In fact, the young nihilists of *Crime and Punishment* are all *ex*-nihilists. We assume that they are nihilists because every detail about them as social types suggests this. They are ex-students, eking out an existence in the capital by translating, tutoring, and writing pieces for the liberal press. One of them (Zosimov) has just completed medical school. A number of their names sound religious, suggesting a family background in the clergy and an education in a pre-seminary grammar school. In the social history of the Russian Left this was the background of Vissarion Belinsky, Nikolai Dobrolyubov (whose name means "lover of the good"), and Joseph Dzhugashvili (Stalin). In *Crime and Punishment* it is suggested by the names Zosimov (after Saint Zosima; Dostoevsky later used the name for his hero of faith in *The Brothers Karamazov*), Kheruvimov (Cherubim), Razumikhin (from *rázum,* "wisdom," "good sense"; in reality the name ties his ancestral background to the clergy; symbolically it suggests that he bears qualities of wisdom and good sense in the novel), and Raskolnikov himself (from *raskól,* "schism," "split"; in reality the name ties his family background to the "schismatic" Old Believer sect; symbolically it suggests a neurotically divided character or a split with reality).

The tension between nihilist social type and antinihilistic or ex-nihilist opinion is clearest with Razumikhin. The reader hears about him in part 1, chapter 4, and, if he or she is a Russian reader in 1866, is immediately reminded of Rakhmetov, the nihilist hero of Chernyshevsky's pronihilist novel *What Is to Be Done?* In the notebooks for **Crime and Punishment,** Razumikhin is occasionally even called Rakhmetov. It is particularly the references to Razumikhin's extraordinary physical stamina that remind us of Rakhmetov.

> [Razumikhin's] external appearance was striking—he was tall, thin, always poorly shaved, black-haired. Occasionally he would get into a brawl, and he was known for his great strength. One night, carousing with friends, he laid out with a single blow a certain officer of the law who was well over six feet tall. He could drink endlessly, or just as easily abstain. He could be an outrageous practical joker, but could refrain from that as well. Razumikhin was also remarkable in that bad fortune never upset him and it seemed that no unpleasant circumstances could keep him down. He could lodge on a roof if necessary, tolerate terrible hunger or extraordinary cold. He was awfully poor, but insisted on supporting himself, coming by money with whatever jobs he could find. He knew a multitude of sources of income. Once he went a whole winter without heating his apartment, and he insisted that he liked that even better, since one sleeps better when chilly. Currently he had been obliged to discontinue his university studies [a draft states explicitly that he had been expelled, with the clear implication that it was for radical activities], but not for long, and he was exerting all his efforts to arrange things so that he could continue as soon as possible.
>
> (1:4)

Compare this with Chernyshevsky's Rakhmetov:

> Rakhmetov was at this time twenty-two; he had been a student since the age of sixteen, but had left the university for almost three years. . . . Everyone who knew him, knew him by [the] nickname . . . "the rigorist." At 16½ it occurred to him that he should develop his physical resources, and he began to work on himself. He began a serious program of gymnastic exercises. . . . He began to work as a physical laborer at jobs requiring exceptional strength; he went through many jobs and changed them often, since from every new job, with every change, he would develop a different muscle group. He took up a boxer's diet: he nourished himself . . . exclusively with things that had a reputation for enhancing physical strength, primarily beef, practically raw. He continued to live in this manner from that time on. . . . [H]e took up the most severe manner of living. . . . He would not waste a ko-

pek on food other than red meat. . . . With his own money he would buy nothing of the sort: "I haven't the right to spend money on whims I can do without." . . . He dressed quite modestly, although he loved fine things. And in everything else he lived a Spartan life: for instance, . . . he slept on a felt pad, not even permitting himself to fold it double. . . . Gymnastics, physically demanding work, reading: these were Rakhmetov's occupations, always observing the same rule that he observed in his readings, never to waste time on what was not essential.[1]

But Razumikhin's every statement exposes him as a former nihilist. His account of his relations with the pamphlet publisher Kheruvimov shows that although he is willing to make his living translating and ghost writing for the liberal press, he is contemptuous of their facile posturing, naive phrase mongering and slavish adoration of everything Western European.

> Look, I've got no pupils right now, but hell with them, there's this bookseller Kheruvimov in the Rag Market, and he's just as good as giving lessons. I wouldn't trade him for tutoring jobs with five wealthy merchants. He puts out these editions of trashy booklets on the natural sciences—and do they ever sell! The titles alone are priceless. You've always said I was stupid. Well, by God, here's somebody even dumber than me! Now he's crawled into the movement, although he doesn't understand a thing about it. But I encourage him, of course. Here's two and a half sheets of German text— the stupidist charlatanism in my opinion. Briefly, it examines the question, "Is woman a human being or not?" And of course it concludes triumphantly that she is. Kheruvimov is planning to issue it in his "Woman Question Department," and I'm translating it. . . . We'll finish this and then start translating something about whales, and a bit of the second part of Rousseau's *Confessions,* some dreary gossip he's marked out—we'll translate it. Someone told him that Rousseau is a sort of Radishchev [a major literary figure in the Russian radical left during the late eighteenth century]. I don't contradict him of course. To the devil with him! So, do you want to translate the second part of "Is Woman a Human Being?"
>
> (2:2)

In defense of his relations with the bribe-taking police clerk Zametov, Razumikhin excoriates the knee-jerk leftist Zosimov for writing off certain useful people because of their supposedly retrograde habits: "Principles! You're so obsessed by your principles, just as though you were on springs—you can't even turn around of your own volition. In my opinion, he's a good man. . . . So what if he takes bribes! . . . He needs to be won over, not pushed away. You won't improve a man by pushing him away, all the more so if he's just a kid, like Zametov. . . . You thick-headed progressives! You don't understand anything" [2:4]. In 3:5 Razumikhin attacks the Left for its emphasis on extenuating environmental circumstances in the prosecution of crime, and its consequent devaluation of the individual's personal moral responsibility (this was to become an increasingly important hobbyhorse for Dostoevsky in his own writings on Russian domestic affairs in the 1870s). Some of Razumikhin's statements sound quite like something from the more conservative Slavophile camp: "For almost two hundred years we've lost the knack for attending to practical matters!" he remarks to Luzhin, countering Luzhin's comment about the practicality of the "movement." He could only mean, "since the reforms of Peter the Great (1689-1725)." But that would be an antinihilist, Slavophile position.

It is Luzhin, after all, who enunciates most clearly the doctrines put forward by the nihilists. But, once again, there is no match between ideology and social type, for Luzhin is the opposite of a young radical—he is a self-serving, greedy lickspittle, ready to today, to connive, to mouth fashionable ideas, to take advantage of those in straitened circumstances, and, we finally learn, to frame an innocent person, in order to make his way in the world. His advocacy of utilitarian ethics argues against them more effectively than would any polemic, and he puts the young friends in an absolute rage. The "nihilistic" principle that he outlines is that of "enlightened self-interest" as the law of human nature that governs behaviour in society.

> For example, if someone said to me in the past, "Love thy neighbor!" and I did so, what was the result? . . . What happened was that I would tear my kaftan in half and share it with my neighbor, and both of us would remain half naked, just as in the old Russian proverb: "Chase several hares at the same time and you won't catch any." But how science tells us: Love yourself first of all, for all that happens in the world is based on self-interest. If you love yourself alone, then you will manage all your affairs sensibly and your kaftan will remain whole. The truths of scientific economics add that, the greater number of well-organized private affairs in society, the more, so to speak, whole kaftans, the firmer will be its foundations, and the better organized will be all that pertains to the common good. So it happens that, acquiring things solely and exclusively for myself, it is as though I am, by doing so, acquiring for everyone, and leading to a state of affairs in which my neighbor will get something more than a torn kaftan, and indeed, not from private, individual acts of charity but as a result of the general prosperity.
>
> (2:5)

The nihilists argued that an understanding of this "scientific" principle, and of the equivalence of individual interests and the common good, would lay the groundwork for a rational utopia. (American students may be surprised and baffled to recognize an argument we have seen characterized as "trickle down," which is supposedly a conservative rather than a liberal policy. This will not confuse us if we remember that what Luzhin is spouting is a fundamental premise of free-market economics or "liberalism." We tend to identify liberalism as a social conscience toward the poor, but this has only sporadically been a part of liberalism as an economic theory. In this classic sense, liberalism encompasses most of the spectrum of American politics from the far right to the moderate left.) A contemporary reader could not have missed the fundamental strangeness of part 2: a social-climbing, middle-aged lawyer advocating nihilist theory and a group of unshaven, disheveled students opposing it.

The radical Left, in advocating utilitarian economic theory and ethics, assumes that the interests of society and the common good are the ultimate goals; it assumes that the individual will make society's interest his own. Luzhin has done the opposite: he has made his own interest the goal of all. And what makes this abundantly clear is his treatment of Dunya. He wishes to choose a bride who has been disgraced and impoverished, as her condition will enhance her feeling toward him as benefactor and rescuer, which will ultimately lay a foundation for good family relations. As Mrs. Raskolnikov relates, "[H]e decided to take as a bride a girl who was honest but had no dowry, and particularly wanted to take a girl who had experienced an impoverished situation, since, as he explained, a husband should never feel obliged to his wife, and it is much better if the wife considers her husband her benefactor" (1:3). Raskolnikov is a little less polite about this theory: "[I]s it true that you said to your bride . . . that what made you happiest of all was that . . . she was poor . . . since it is more advantageous to take a wife out of poverty, so that you can exercise power over her later, and reproach her with the fact that she has been the beneficiary of your charity?" (2:5). If we view the family as a society in miniature, we then can see Luzhin's perversion of nihilist ethics more clearly: he has treated his own interest, the enhancement of his own position in the family, as the goal, as the common good of the whole family.

Raskolnikov's rage against Luzhin stems first of all from the fact that Luzhin has insulted his sister. But his feelings are more complex than that. We have already noticed that Raskolnikov relishes the role of benefactor, but recoils from that of beneficiary. We have seen that Dunya has made him a beneficiary by marrying Luzhin to save the family (the reverse of Luzhin's treatment of family—the common good really does come first for Dunya), and that Raskolnikov's recoil against the beneficiary role pushed him closer to committing the murder. This unwillingness to accept charity is echoed in part 2 by one of the nonplot incidents that form the thematic structure—when Raskolnikov is given alms because he looks so ragged and has been accidentally hit by the stray lash of a coachman's whip (2:2). In Luzhin, Raskolnikov faces a man who, like himself, enjoys the role of benefactor and who, in fact, has made Raskolnikov's own sister, and indirectly Raskolnikov, the beneficiaries of his charitable ministrations, but who has done so with base, self-serving motives. Small wonder that Luzhin drives Raskolnikov into a frenzy; there are complex personal and ideological reasons for his negative reaction. The relationship between benefactor and beneficiary, between rescuer and rescued, is a fundamental paradigm in this novel.

There is yet another dimension to Raskolnikov's revulsion toward Luzhin, one that relates directly to the murder Raskolnikov has committed. At the conclusion of Luzhin's disquisition on utilitarian economic ethics, Raskolnikov says to him: "Carry to its conclusions what you were just preaching and it follows that people may cut each other's throats!" (2:5). It is not immediately clear why this idea follows from Luzhin's principles. The idea that legal or moral boundaries could be overstepped for the cause, or even that ends justify means, was not a nihilist tenet, as such. Some of the middle premises of this syllogism are hidden, and thus need to be made evident. What utilitarian ethics does that ultimately makes murder permissible is to remove all ethical absolutes except for the common good and to make ethics a mechanistic and scientific, rather than a religious, system. It is in this sense that liberal economic theory implies, for Dostoevsky, that ends justify means, and that crime is permissible for the common good. This will become clearer as we look at Raskolnikov's article on crime in part 3.

Psychologically, what is interesting about Raskolnikov's statement, "If you carry what you were preaching to its logical conclusion, it follows that one may cut people's throats," is that he has found a veiled similarity between himself and the hated Luzhin, in terms of the ideological rationale for the murder he has just committed. Raskolnikov has left nihilism behind, yet gone ahead with the murder, originally planned with a utilitarian-based motive. He has repressed the motive, but gone ahead with the act, because he needs the act for another reason, a truer motive—the existential. In attacking Luzhin, Raskolnikov is attacking himself. Or viewed conversely, Raskolnikov is shifting the blame for the murder he has committed to Luzhin and his theory, one he once shared. These opposite meanings of the accusation can coexist in the world of the novel because they can coexist in Raskolnikov's unconscious mind. This kind of tension between opposite meanings is characteristic of Dostoevsky's writing; it is one of the things that makes his novels vibrate with the intensity of contradiction.

TWO RECURRENT IMAGES

There is nothing unique to Dostoevsky about using the crossing of a bridge or a river as a symbol for the decision-making process. Language itself, never mind literature, is full of examples of the image: "Crossing

the Rubicon," "Crossing your bridges before you come to them," "Burning your bridges behind you." But St. Petersburg/Leningrad, built on a river delta, is full of bridges, so it is natural that a novel intimately bound up with the life of that city will rely on the "decision on a bridge" paradigm as a special part of the symbolic system. Raskolnikov is constantly swinging back and forth between the extremes of the aggression/submission (murder/no murder, no confession/confession) polarity, and very often the shift occurs while he is on a bridge. In 1:4-5 he takes a long walk, crosses several bridges, has the dream of the horse beating on Petróvsky Island, and returns home via the Túchkov Bridge (near Razumikhin's old apartment) where the following reversal takes place.

> [He] walked onto the Túchkov Bridge. He was pale, his eyes burned, exhaustion filled all his limbs, but he suddenly began to breathe a bit more easily. He felt that he had thrown from his shoulders a horrible burden, which had been oppressing him for a long time, and his spirit suddenly felt lighter and more peaceful. "My Lord!," he prayed, "show me my path, and I renounce that accursed . . . dream of mine."

> Walking across the bridge, he quietly and peacefully looked at the Neva River, at the bright red sunset. . . . It was as though a boil on his heart, which had been swelling for a whole month, had suddenly burst. Freedom, freedom! He was free now from these spells, from this sorcery, witchcraft, from his obsession.

> (1:5)

Walking on home through the Haymarket (a detour) he overhears Lizaveta informing him of the perfect opportunity to commit the crime, and the reversal "is reversed."

In 2:5 he goes out for another walk, resolved to make an end of it some way or other. First he finds Zametov in the tavern called The Crystal Palace and mystifies him completely with his cryptic half-confession, then bumps into Razumikhin on the way out of the tavern. His next stop is the Voznesénsky (Resurrection) Bridge. "[He] stopped at the railing in the middle, rested his elbows on it and began to look into the distance. . . . Leaning over the water, he looked mechanically at the last pink reflection of the sunset, on a row of houses, growing dark in the thickening dusk, at one distant window, on a mansard on the left embankment, gleaming, just as though in flames, from the last ray of the sun, which was striking it for a moment." A careful calculation, on the basis of the text of the novel and the map of the city, shows convincingly that this is Sonya's window.[2] His reverie is interrupted by the suicide attempt of an alcoholic floozy named Afrosinya. As he observes this scene, he pulls back from the idea of suicide: "No, it's disgusting . . . water . . . it's not worth it." He is still motivated by the urge to bring things to some kind of conclusion ("All the same, I'll end it, because I wish to") but he will remain alive ("I'll still have my square yard of space"). He will end it by confessing, and he briefly half-looks for the police office, then incriminates himself in front of the workmen at the "scene of the crime." Only his discovery of the dying Marmeladov finally distracts him from his drive to "end it" (that is, kill himself or confess). In any case, his experience on the bridge does pull him back from the suicide option.

If bridges can represent a decision about whether or not to commit suicide, water certainly comes to represent the suicide option, as this Afrosinya episode makes clear. Kulidzhanov's excellent film of the novel depicts one fantasy in which Raskolnikov throws himself from a bridge; although the fantasy never occurs in the novel in precisely that form, the idea is certainly an active one in the system of images that comprise Raskolnikov's mental life. Watch for both of these linkages (bridge/decision, water/suicide) as part 6 progresses.

Notes

1. N. G. Chernyshevsky, *What Is to Be Done?*, 3:29, "An Extraordinary Person."

2. James Curtis, "Spatial Form [as the Intrinsic Genre of Dostoevsky's Novels," *Modern Fiction Studies* 18, no. 2 (summer 1972):] 152-53.

Gary Cox (essay date 1990)

SOURCE: Cox, Gary. "Part 4." In Crime and Punishment: *A Mind to Murder,* pp. 81-97. Boston: Twayne Publishers, 1990.

[*In the following essay, Cox argues that Dostoevsky's scrupulous depiction of Raskolnikov's consciousness forms a second, "abstract" plot in* Crime and Punishment, *one that forms an aesthetic counterpoint to the central action of the novel.*]

THE ABSTRACT PLOT

By the middle of the novel the murder has almost become a subplot, submerged in Raskolnikov's mind, surfacing only when events, other characters, or extraneous incidents bring it into his consciousness, and ours. The surface events of the novel have taken over by this time, and the structure consists of alternating scenes from the novel's various secondary plots and from the seemingly random life of St. Petersburg's Haymarket slum. Raskolnikov remains at the center, but it is his relations with family and acquaintances that provide the alternating scenes, serving to hide, and at the same time to intensify, the submerged tension we feel over the issue of whether or not he will confess. These alternating incidents are juxtaposed against each other, not so much to further the plot or plots on a realistic plane, but to

guide the reader through a series of issues and images close to the novel's central ideological concerns. We may call this the abstract structure, as distinguished from the realistic or dramatic structure. The abstract or thematic structure is an outgrowth of the novel's immersion in the stream of Raskolnikov's consciousness. Belinsky said "Art is thinking in images," and although this is not exactly what he meant, his formulation gives a pretty good idea of what is going on in this novel. The work presents conceptual relationships in aesthetic form.

The term "abstract" also suggests nonrepresentational art, and that, too, gives a good clue to what Dostoevsky is up to. Beyond the level of realistic events portrayed, *Crime and Punishment* is a pattern of relationships between ideas and images, and taken as such it is as abstract as a Kandinsky painting. Any realistic work has this level of abstract form—blur the focus on a slide of a painting by Boticelli or El Greco, and you get a nonrepresentational pattern of color, space, and form relationships. In Dostoevsky, one never loses sight of the realistic structure of the novel, the series of real events, realistically portrayed, that bring the novel to its dramatic conclusion. Yet the heightened interest in stream of consciousness gives the abstract structure more importance. The abstract structure complements, and at times even competes with, the realistic structure. This is why, despite his firm grounding in traditional, straightforward realism, Dostoevsky may be considered a true forerunner of much modern, avant-garde writing in the twentieth century.

The alternation between abstract and realistic structure resolves some of the conundrums about the novel. All events in the realistic plot are also part of the abstract structure. But it does not always work so neatly the other way around. Events that may seem to be irrelevant filler in realistic terms (the attempted drowning in 2:6, the accusation by the shopkeeper in 3:6) or contrived coincidence (the many overheard conversations; details of who lives where) make perfect sense in the context of the novel's thematic structure. In this sense, abstract or thematic structure even takes precedence over realistic or dramatic structure. But in general the two are conjoined and complement each other.

The novel's dreams form a vital part of its abstract structure. Psychoanalytic critics have noted that Dostoevsky's technique of "fantastic realism" is quite dreamlike,[1] and the patterns of imagery found in the dreams echo those of the waking sections, since all form part of Raskolnikov's consciousness. There are four dreams in the novel proper (I discuss the epilogue's one dream later), and three of them describe a beating. In each case a woman or female animal is being beaten by a man: in 1:5 Mikolka is beating the mare; in 2:2 Ilya Petrovich ("Officer Gunpowder," the volatile officer from the police station) is beating Raskolnikov's landlady; in 3:6 Raskolnikov beats the pawnbroker once again in the dream reenactment. This reinforces the idea of aggression, particularly male aggression against females, that underlies the entire novel. Other instances of such aggression in the waking sections include the murder itself (1:7), Raskolnikov's thoughts after "the rehearsal" (1:1), Svidrigailov's alleged beating of his late wife (3:1), Lebeziatnikov's beating of Katerina Ivanovna (we hear about it in 2:2), and humorous references such as Razumikhin's joke on the way into Porfiry's room in 3:5 ("I'll brain you") and Porfiry's pointed reference in 4:5 ("'whack him on the head, just as though with an axe-butt, right on the head, to use your happy metaphor . . .'"). Note that the eyes of the victimized females are often highlighted: the boy Raskolnikov is particularly eager to protect the mare's eyes from Mikolka's lash, and the man Raskolnikov notes that suffering women have soft, gentle eyes (3:6). In 1:2 Marmeladov notes that he cannot bear to look into Katerina Ivanovna's suffering eyes. Thus the themes highlighted in the dreams, and in the abstract structure generally, are always echoed in the realistic plot.

The dream of the oasis (1:6) seems not to fit this pattern. It is a dream of rest and of freedom from the ugliness of immediate surroundings. It occurs almost immediately *before* the murder and presents a striking contrast with his aggression there. Water is central to this dream, and elsewhere water is a symbol of suicide (2:6, 6:6). Although other meanings have been suggested for this dream, it seems most plausible to see it as expressing a death wish. Later in the novel suicide is seen as the alternative to confession for Raskolnikov. Here he is dreaming of the repose that death would afford. Even this "out-of-place" dream echoes the patterns of imagery that form the abstract structure.

I defer further discussion of abstract structure and the idea of situation rhyme until the treatment of part 5, as some important pieces of the puzzle do not appear until that part. But the phenomenon of character doubling—that is, thematic contrasts and parallels in relationships between characters—may be discussed profitably at this point and may be considered as a subcategory of abstract structure.

CHARACTER DOUBLING

A good deal has been written about the phenomenon of character doubling in Dostoevsky's writings, but the subject is a complex one and not always fully understood. Some critics speak of the double as simply a divided character, whose personality suffers from a split (*raskól,* "schism").[2] But generally speaking a character's double is another character who profoundly affects his/her identity in some fundamental way, an alter ego

or other self. But the relationship between the primary character and the double may take several forms. The double may echo elements of the major character's personality or life situation—it is similarity that binds them together. Or, the double may possess qualities that are the opposite of those possessed by the primary character—such contrasting or complementary doubles sometimes seem to be two halves making up a single whole. Often in Dostoevsky these types are mixed, and we have two characters who are opposites in every way save one, but the one similarity concerns an issue vitally important to the primary character's identity at the moment when the action of the novel takes place. This creates between the two an extraordinary bond, which is all the stronger because it is often secret. In some of Dostoevsky's works the double is even a supernatural figure. The chief thing to note is that this subterranean bond, beneath the surface of public life (like Raskolnikov's crime), is of crucial importance to the identity of the primary character. In a sense doubling emerges from the character's own inner dialogue and may be seen as an aspect of polyphony.[3]

Character doubling was not a new phenomenon with Dostoevsky; it has its roots in the Gothic novel and the tradition of horror literature. In fact, as literature began to take an interest in abnormal psychology, identity crises, and the like, the language of ghost stories was often what it first used to express these concerns. Writers like Edgar Allan Poe and Robert Louis Stevenson, along with Dostoevsky, psychologized the theme of the double in the Gothic tradition, making the encounter with the other self a psychic rather than a supernatural event. (Stevenson, in particular, was deeply moved by his later reading of *Crime and Punishment,* and his short story, "Markham," [1887] shows its influence.)

The first clearcut treatment of the double theme appeared in the writing of the German romantic E. T. A. Hoffmann, a master of the Gothic short novel. His novella *The Double* presents the main character's encounter with an exact physical double as a horrific event that produces profound emotional disturbance and, finally, ruin for the main character. The encounter with the self in the outside world is so unsettling that it destroys the self; this fact is not explained in the novella but is simply taken for granted. This is a little difficult for moderns to understand. In an age of every conceivable type of therapy and identity analysis, we have become comfortable, even blasé, about challenges to our identity. Our response to meeting an extraordinary lookalike would most likely be to laugh, not to shriek, faint, or run away. Nineteenth-century man did not see it this way, and the double in nineteenth-century literature is very much a spook. Dostoevsky's presentation of the appearance of a look-alike in his own early novella *The Double* (1846) is a good illustration of this attitude. In the course of a whole chapter of nocturnal wanderings and scene setting, along the lines of "it was a dark and stormy night," the pathetic protagonist continually encounters a mysterious stranger, to whom he always reacts roughly as follows: "he trembled in every muscle, his knees, not strong enough to support him, gave way under him, and he collapsed with a groan." He finally comes face to face with his double in his own flat: "All he had feared and foreseen had now become cold reality. It took his breath away and made his head spin. . . . His hair stood on end and he collapsed into a chair, numb with horror. . . . Mr. Golyadkin's nocturnal acquaintance was none other than himself" (5). The encounter with the mystic double was serious business for nineteenth-century man.

Dostoevsky, Poe ("William Wilson," 1839), and Stevenson (*Dr. Jekyll and Mr. Hyde,* 1886) still treat the double as a spooky creature, but they also begin to treat it as a psychological phenomenon—the double is beginning its transition from ghost to psychotic symptom. Furthermore, both Poe and Stevenson treat the double as a secret, evil self that is contrasted with the good, public self. In addition, Stevenson, writing quite a bit later, introduces another feature typical of the development of the Gothic novel in the late nineteenth century: the mechanism that introduces the "spook" is a scientific one, and the Gothic novel begins to move toward what we recognize as science fiction. In fact the double comes to be "explained" so thoroughly, whether in psychic or scientific terms, that by the early twentieth century, when Joseph Conrad wrote his contribution to the genre, "The Secret Sharer," it has moved completely out of the Gothic tradition. Conrad's "sharer" is a completely explicable, albeit somewhat mysterious, figure, and he is benevolent, not hostile. The chief thing is that he profoundly affects the hero's understanding of his own identity; he becomes a helper on the road to self-knowledge. It was Dostoevsky more than any other writer who contributed to this sort of treatment of the doubling theme.

For all its horrific passages when introducing the look-alike, Dostoevsky's *The Double* begins comically. Gogol had given the subject comic treatment in his story "The Nose," where a part of the self (a comic, yet potentially symbolic part—the nose) becomes detached and starts to confront and challenge the self. Dostoevsky's novella begins similarly, as we see the comically insecure hero taking extraordinary measures to bolster his sense of self. But there is no comedy when the double appears. At first he is only an exact physical double, but in time he begins to double the hero in other ways, usurping his position at work, supplanting him in his relations with his servant, and succeeding in a love relationship to which the hero has only aspired. He does this because he seems to possess all the personal qualities the hero lacks. At first it is suggested that the differences in their personalities will provide a basis for friendly complementation, but the double then moves to replace the hero rather than to support him. So the doubling begins with physical sameness but moves in the direction of psychological difference; and both conditions are seen as equally unsettling. Throughout, a balance is maintained between humor and horror. The work ends with the hero's insanity, but we never know the degree to which the whole story is his mad fantasy. At times Gothic explanations seem to fit; elsewhere, symptoms of abnormal psychology seem to be operating. The uncertainty over this issue keeps the novel on the borderline between Gothic and psychological literature, and it is one of the things that holds our interest as readers.

The Double was a work of Dostoevsky's youth; *Crime and Punishment* belongs to his mature period. Doubling is present, but it has become a more complex and sophisticated tool. It has moved away from the Gothic, except for a few scenic trappings, and toward the psychological. None of Raskolnikov's doubles are ghosts; none could even be mistaken for one, although Svidrigailov sometimes looks and acts like one. Raskolnikov's doubles are acquaintances who reflect in some way or other the most disturbing elements of his private emotional life. The event of chief importance in Raskolnikov's life at the time of the novel, his crime, is completely submerged, completely banished from the world of his public life. All the characters who may be seen as Raskolnikov's doubles are people who somehow echo that private event in the public world: they have committed comparable crimes (Svidrigailov) or have otherwise stepped across moral boundaries (Sonya) or the boundaries of traditional ethics (Luzhin). On the lowest level of doubling they are simply people who *know* about the murder (Porfiry, Razumikhin, Sonya, Svidrigailov, and, yes, even Alyona Ivanovna and Lizaveta—they, after all, know about the murder in the most intimate way possible: as its victims). Knowing Raskolnikov's secret makes these characters reflections of his private identity and sets up the strongest sort of bond between them. *Crime and Punishment* may be seen as a circle of doubles, knowers of the secret, surrounding a central Raskolnikov.

Razumikhin doubles Raskolnikov in a fairly superficial, yet important, way. He is a contrasting double for the most part. His personality is the opposite of Raskolnikov's. He is gregarious, well-adjusted, non-alienated, and he likes to charm, even to woo, old ladies, not kill them with axes. Even his name suggests the fundamental contrast with Raskolnikov: *rázum* means "good or common sense," "wisdom," while *raskól* means "split." Razumikhin is the close friend who complements or completes the intimate opposite. (Such relationships become particularly important in Dostoevsky's next four novels: *The Idiot, The Eternal Husband, The Devils* [or *The Possessed*], and *A Raw Youth.*) With regard to knowledge of Raskolnikov's secret, Razumikhin ought to know it—Raskolnikov tells him about it often enough. Each time he seems to take it in, but then later on behaves as though he does not know. From the perspective of the composition of the novel, one can accuse Dostoevsky of revising his plan in midstream, a vice to which he was susceptible, as we will see in the following chapter. Perhaps Dostoevsky simply savored too much the electric tension between the two friends in the revelation scene, for he keeps repeating the scene and then going back on it:

> "Once and for all: don't ever ask me about anything. There's nothing for me to answer. Don't come to me. Maybe I'll come here. Leave me alone. But *don't* leave them. Do you understand me?"
>
> It was dark in the corridor. They stood by the lamp. For about a minute they looked at each other silently. Raskolnikov's intent and anguished stare seemed to penetrate into his soul, into his consciousness. Suddenly Razumikhin shuddered. Something strange seemed to pass between them. Some idea slipped from one to the other, a sort of hint, something horrible, ugly, and suddenly understood on both sides. Razumikhin went as pale as a corpse.
>
> "Do you understand now?" said Raskolnikov with a painfully twisted face. "Go back, go to them."
>
> (4:3)

Yet a scene very like this is repeated in 6:1, where it looks as though Razumikhin still has not gotten the message. From the perspective of psychological realism, one could argue that Razumikhin continually represses his knowledge of his friend's crime since he cannot acknowledge in his friend an act that would be so impossible for himself—he cannot accept his friend's ultimate otherness. But that is a supposition. In fact we never see into Razumikhin's mind with enough clarity to know about such things for certain. This is Raskolnikov's novel, after all.

At first glance Luzhin could not be more opposite from Raskolnikov, but in at least two ways he may be seen as a secret double. I have already noted that Raskolnikov's negative response to Luzhin's exposition of utilitarian economic and ethical theory is an attack on an aspect of his own development, namely, the relationship between positivistic ethics and crime. Another link ties them together: both enjoy the role of "benefactor" in a "rescue triangle," that is, both like to see themselves saving a young woman in distress (for example, Luzhin:Dunya::Raskolnikov:Sonya). And yet this very characteristic, the smug enjoyment of his own benevolence, is one of the things that infuriates Raskolnikov most about Luzhin. Once again, his revulsion against Luzhin is a revulsion against an aspect of himself. On the other hand, Luzhin is the only one of the "doubles" who does not know Raskolnikov's secret. In general the doubling bond between them is weak. Luzhin echoes Raskolnikov as a reflection in a puddle. Could that be the reason for his peculiar name (*luzha* = "puddle")?

Raskolnikov has female doubles as well. We have already noticed doubling between female characters in the dream reenactment of 3:6 (Sonya and Lizaveta, Mrs. Raskolnikov and Alyona Ivanovna). And we noticed that Raskolnikov began at that point to identify with his victims, Lizaveta and Alyona, creating another sort of doubling. But the most important female double is of course Sonya.

Sonya and Raskolnikov seem unlike in every conceivable way, yet she, too, has "stepped across" a moral boundary and destroyed a human life, her own, as Raskolnikov is later to note. (The Russian word for "crime," *prestuplénie*, literally means "stepping across," or "transgression.") For Raskolnikov, this one similarity becomes a central bond, dealing as it does with his secret attempt to validate his identity through crime. Thus the doubling between Raskolnikov and Sonya becomes a strong bond.

For Sonya, on the other hand, the similarity between their acts is quite incomprehensible. Sonya's crime was a practical necessity for her; it was the only way to save her family. She has never had any motivation but that, and the idea of a crime committed for an intellectual motivation is not only repugnant, but simply incomprehensible to her. The scene in which Raskolnikov tries to explain his motives, in the face of her increasing bewilderment, is almost comic. She does see her own behavior as sinful, and she believes God will punish her, yet she does not allow this knowledge to deter her from her quite conventional piety. A modern sociologist would say that she experiences cognitive dissonance, that is, she persists in beliefs and behaviors that are mutually contradictory but keeps them in such separate compartments that they can coexist with only moderate personality disturbance.

Another sufferer who is a double of Raskolnikov is Mikolka (Nikolai), the house painter who confesses to Raskolnikov's crime. Mikolka is a member of an Old Believer sect noted for its extreme asceticism. Later on (6:2) when Porfiry tells Raskolnikov about this, he uses the word *raskólnik* ("schismatic") to mean "Old Believer," and it sounds almost as though he is saying "He comes out of Raskolnikov." Here is powerful linguistic evidence that Mikolka has become a double of Raskolnikov. Mikolka has accepted his suffering because of his participation in universal guilt; Raskolnikov's guilt is much more tangible, and he too must accept his suffering.

As his crime brings him suffering, Raskolnikov enters into a doubling relationship with his victims, both the pawnbroker (in the dream reenactment he calls himself "a louse," a term he has used earlier for the pawnbroker) and particularly Lizaveta, his accidental victim. He notes the doubling between Sonya and Lizaveta, and goes on to suggest that he will take on their characteristics: "They're both religious maniacs (*yuródivye*); I shall become one myself—it's infectious" (4:4). His identification with Lizaveta, and hers with Sonya, is dramatically symbolized by the exchange of crosses later on.

STEPPING ACROSS

It is one of the novel's great ironies that Sonya is the exemplar of Raskolnikov's theory on crime: she is a special person who can step across moral boundaries for the public good and do so without losing her own moral dignity. It is Sonya, not Raskolnikov, who is like Napoleon. The reason she can do this while Raskolnikov cannot is that she does it reflexively, totally without premeditation or rationalization. She is not trying to demonstrate any utilitarian theory. While Sonya and her counterpart Napoleon stride across moral boundaries instinctively, without taking thought for themselves, since their eyes are fixed on the goal, their contrasting double, Raskolnikov, surrounds his act with thought. He murders not really "for the public good" but to prove that he is a special person who can do so. The motive is not public utility but private identity. For Sonya and Napoleon the end *does* seem to justify the means because for them the end occupies the entire field of vision at the moment of the crime. For Raskolnikov, as for Luzhin, the self remains the ultimate object of the act, and thus their behavior seems morally invalid to us.

This line of reasoning ties Raskolnikov to the earlier work *Notes from Underground,* where the narrator declares that self-consciousness is the disease of modern man and proclaims his envy for those men of direct action who proceed boldly without rationalization: "Those people, for example, who know how to avenge their wrongs and generally stand up for themselves—how do they do it? . . . That sort of gentleman rushes straight for his goal like a mad bull charging with his horns down. . . . [I] am positively bilious with envy of such a man. He's stupid, I won't argue about that, but perhaps a normal man ought to be stupid, how do you know?" (*Notes from Underground* 1:3). Raskolnikov may be seen as another illustration of the underground man's dichotomy. In fact, existentialism, which is an outgrowth of these texts, is directly involved here. Existentialism is difficult to define, since it is not so much an idea as a relationship between idea and action. Existentialist theory argues that existence or identity must be authenticated through action. But in the light of Raskolnikov's experiences, and the underground man's, we find that the authentication of existence through action may only take place if it is unconscious, if it is free of theoretical rationalization, if only the goal, and not the means, is in sight. This places the existentialist in

an embarrassing position. Existentialist philosophical theory can only be valid if it is not a philosophical theory, that is, if it ceases to exist. The twentieth century is an age of contradictions, and perhaps it is Dostoevsky, more than any other writer, who introduces and foreshadows this contradictory age.

Is it not ironic to place Sonya in a class with Napoleon? This novel is chock-a-block with ironies, and one of the greatest of them is that once we cross that moral boundary into the category of special moral beings, we find it populated not with swaggering aggressors, but with self-denying victims who have taken upon themselves the burden of suffering humanity. Raskolnikov has already sensed this situation in the conversation with Porfiry in 3:5, when he notes that anyone committing crime for the benefit of humanity thereby takes upon himself a burden of suffering. He states that any genius/criminal with a conscience will suffer after his criminal act. Razumikhin quibbles that if crime is truly permitted to such a person, there should be no such suffering. Raskolnikov responds, "Let him suffer, if he pities his victim. Suffering and pain are always required of one with an expansive consciousness and a depth of spiritual emotion." And remember that this idea parallels what Dostoevsky himself had said about Bazarov in *Winter Notes on Summer Impressions.*

Elsewhere in Dostoevsky's work this idea surfaces in the treatment of convicts as "sufferers" in *Notes from the House of the Dead* and *The Diary of a Writer.* Furthermore, the Grand Inquisitor in *The Brothers Karamazov* is just such a self-denying sufferer—his control of his flock, and his reexecution of Christ, necessitates his acceptance of a burden of personal guilt that brings him true suffering. Mikolka (Nikolai) the house painter does much the same thing when he confesses to Raskolnikov's crime in order to "accept his suffering" (4:6, 6:2).

The special person is not the aggressor but the victim. It is the victim who has mana or spiritual power in Dostoevsky's world. The model, of course, is Christ. The novel implies the question of whether or not the end justifies the means, and although it takes no formal position, perhaps we can say that for Christ, or for the truly Christ-like character such as Sonya, it does. We cannot condemn Sonya for her moral turpitude because she is so completely Christ-like. For her there is no crime; all things are lawful for her. Any end that she would espouse would justify any means she would be willing to use.

The device of contrasting doubling brings about an inversion of the aggressor/victim paradigm. The aggressor becomes the victim, and the victim steps across and becomes the special person to whom all is permitted. This can even be seen as an inversion of nihilist ethics, a spiritual version of it, if you will. The self-victimizing character truly sees his or her advantage in the well-being of others, and when such a character commits a criminal act for the good of others, we do not stand in judgment. The implicit conclusion is that even positivistic ethics is redeemed by Christ-like self-denial. This idea is never explicit; in fact, Dostoevsky might not approve of this particular formulation of the idea, but in a sense it lies at the heart of Dostoevsky's quasi-Christian ethical system.

SVIDRIGAILOV

It is with Svidrigailov that the idea of the double is most fully developed. Apparently he had a real prototype; the notebooks call him "Aristov," after a character in the prison memoirs. He is surrounded with details connected with the Gothic tradition, underlining the emergence of "doubling" from the literature of the supernatural. The fact that we have heard many terrible things about this major character before he actually appears adds much to the suspense surrounding him. He appears (not "enters") at the end of a nightmare, the dream reenactment of 3:6, and Raskolnikov first entertains the idea that his appearance is a continuation of that dream. Note that this is precisely the halfway point of the novel, adding to the character's "centrality." Furthermore his appearance straddles a boundary, not only between chapters, but between parts, meaning that readers must wait for the next monthly installment (in this case it was two months) to find out more. Making readers wait for the next move of a mysterious character is a classic device to heighten suspense. Certain physical details add even more spookiness to the scene: silence and a buzzing fly (Dostoevsky liked this device—he used it again to ghoulish effect in the grisly and beautiful final scene of *The Idiot*).

And yet just what is it that is so spooky about Svidrigailov? He is dapper, jaunty, and good looking, with a wry wit and a talent for repartee. His opinions are paradoxical, not to say downright bizarre, but quite intentionally so, and he expresses them with charming flair and aplomb. In fact, everything about this character is contradictory; perhaps he is the best example of tension between personality and ideology. As a personality, Svidrigailov represents carnality. He is forthright and honest about his sensuality, and seems quite untroubled by guilt (one psychoanalytic critic sees this as the basis of Raskolnikov's attraction to him).[4] Yet the ideas Svidrigailov puts forward have to do with otherworldly matters. He sees ghosts, in particular the spirits of those for whose deaths he is responsible, to wit, his late wife Marfa Petrovna and a certain valet named Philippe. Asking Raskolnikov if he believes in ghosts, he explains that his late wife Marfa Petrovna "deigns to make visits." Likewise, Philippe appeared shortly after his burial and filled Svidrigailov's pipe.

So Svidrigailov's ideas of the spirit world war against his personality, that of the sensualist. To be sure, Svidrigailov is no ideologue; it is hard to call his comments on these ghosts an ideology as such. It is simply that these spirits, his spirits, are part of his current world, even his sensuous world, one might say. "All three times [Marfa Petrovna appeared when I was completely] awake. She'll come in, talk for a minute or so, then she'll go out through the door—always through the door. Just as though I could hear [or perceive] her." He even connects his belief in the spirit world with his peculiar ideas on mental illness: "I agree that ghosts appear only to the sick; but after all, that only shows that ghosts can't appear in any other way—only to the sick. It doesn't mean that they themselves do not exist."

He ties these ideas to his thoughts on the afterlife, although he is fully aware that he is making it all up as he goes along. The following speech appears within quotation marks, even within his larger quotation, and he refers to it as "literature":

> "Ghosts are, so to speak, bits and fragments of other worlds, the beginnings of those worlds. To a healthy man, of course, there's no reason to see them, for a healthy man is a more earthbound fellow, and as it happens, he must live only in this world, for the sake of wholeness and order. But once you've gotten sick, as soon as the normal earthly order has been destroyed in your organism, then the possibility of another world begins to be in evidence, and the sicker you are, the more contact with the other world becomes possible, so that, when you die, you go right over into the other world."

(4:1)

Another way of saying this is that sick people are special individuals in a way, that they step across some kind of boundary that divides them from the mass of humanity. Even Svidrigailov's thoughts have the same paradigmatic structure as Raskolnikov's.

But what a paradoxical afterlife Svidrigailov's is, an afterlife of the senses, if you will, for the horrors of Svidrigailov's hell are produced by disgusting sensuous details: "Everybody always imagines eternity as an idea that is impossible to understand, something huge, huge! But why should it necessarily be huge? For a change, instead of all that, imagine that there will be just one little room there, a room just like a country steam bath, blackened with soot, with spiders in all the corners, and there's your whole eternity. You know, it sometimes appears to me in that light."

Svidrigailov represents the sensualist's alternative, but his ideas are the most "spiritual" of the novel, outside of Sonya's. (Another paradoxical double, for the otherworldly Sonya is also a sensualist of sorts, by profession anyway, if not by conviction.)

In what way, then, does Svidrigailov double Raskolnikov? Both are murderers in a sense, for Svidrigailov appears to be morally, if not legally, responsible for the deaths of two individuals, or at least we are led to believe this by several characters—with the narrator's complicity. And yet during their first conversation, Svidrigailov is unaware of Raskolnikov's murder. Even so, it is Svidrigailov who presses the issue of their secret similarity in a criminal conscience. He seems to have prescient, not to say supernatural, knowledge of it. "Well, didn't I say that there was some point in common between us? . . . It seems to me I did say it. Just a moment ago, after I came in and saw that you were lying there with your eyes closed, and you yourself were pretending—right then I said to myself 'This is the very one!'" And later he adds: "Well, didn't I tell the truth when I said that we were like two peas in a pod?" (literally, "one field of berries"). Raskolnikov is in a better position to appreciate their shared blood-guilt, but it is he who resists most strongly the idea that they are doubles. (Another psychoanalytic critic states that Svidrigailov is Raskolnikov's id (*ono*).[5]

Of course Svidrigailov does find out about the murder, and after this point the doubling between the two increases apace toward the end of the novel. Svidrigailov's discovery of this fact comes at the end of Raskolnikov's first interview with Sonya, in which he all but confesses to the murder. The scene is eerie, right down to its chiaroscuro lighting. (This is another favorite Gothic device of Dostoevsky's: a single light source, often a candle, as here, illuminates a scene that is primarily in shadow, creating a visual effect quite like the chiaroscuro in Rembrandt's paintings.) At the end of the chapter the narrative tone changes from the eerie whisper of the conventional Gothic to a tone that is matter of fact, even jaunty. In that tone, the narrator informs us that Svidrigailov has heard the whole thing. This is another trick of the Dostoevskian Gothic, which he uses to good effect in all of his greatest late novels. When Dostoevsky wants to send us reeling with surprise, in a Gothic or suspenseful mode, he will relate frightening developments in just such a nonemotional tone.

A word on narrative point of view is in order with regard to Svidrigailov. Our opinions about him are formed by other characters, particularly Mrs. Raskolnikov, and even Luzhin, and the narrator does not correct them. We think of Svidrigailov as the chief villain in the novel, or perhaps he shares this (dis)honor with Luzhin. Yet he is not guilty of any crime in the legal sense. He may not even be guilty of any crime in the moral sense. Mrs. Raskolnikov, who introduces him, implies that he poisoned Marfa Petrovna, beat her regularly before that time, and of course, besieged Dunya's honor. (This last crime places him in a hoary tradition of villains in literature: middle-aged men who try to seduce governesses—the names Lovelace, Mr. B., Lothario are catchwords for sexual villainy within the novel tradition.) Svidrigailov himself insists that he did not poison Marfa Petrovna; he equivocates on the issue of wife-beating, implying that she encouraged it; he points out that their marital arrangement (in which his affairs were tolerated) was aboveboard, if a trifle unconventional; and he declares, convincingly at times, that his passion for Dunya is genuine. The other death on his conscience is the suicide of his valet Philippe, and we have little more than Svidrigailov's own comments to inform us on this matter. (What would a personality like Svidrigailov do to a servant that would drive the latter to suicide? Whenever we see him with subordinates he treats them with kind solicitude, although he has a propensity to seduce them. Could Svidrigailov have seduced Philippe? Certainly that would fit in with the general idea of Svidrigailov's sexual perversity.)

One hates to be in the position of defending a character who is obviously intended as the novel's villain, but it is worth pointing out that this novel's villains are guilty of no more than mental cruelty and sexual kinkiness in Svidrigailov's case, and intellectual dishonesty, selfish pride, and slander in Luzhin's case. They are guilty of these crimes primarily in the eyes of the hero, who is a murderer, and his friends and relations. In order to keep one's compass true while reading this novel, one ought to remember that the readers' judgments are being manipulated.

Notes

1. [A. L.] Bem, *Psikhoanaliticheskie etyudy* [(Prague: Petropolis, 1938)], 45.

2. Ernest Simmons, *Dostoevsky: The Making of a Novelist* (New York: Random House, 1940), 161-62; R. P. Blackmur, "*Crime and Punishment*: Murder in Your Own Room," in *Eleven Essays in the European Novel* (New York: Harcourt, Brace & World, 1964), 119-40.

3. [Robert] Lord, *Dostoevsky*[: *Essays and Perspectives* (London: Chatto and Windus, 1970)], 218.

4. Richard Rosenthal, "Raskolnikov's Transgression [and the Confusion between Destructiveness and Creativity," in *Do I Dare Disturb the Universe,* ed. James Grotstein (Beverly Hills, Calif.: Caesura Press, 1981)], 222.

5. Bem, *Psikhoanaliticheskie etyudy,* 180-86.

Kristin Eikeland (essay date 2000)

SOURCE: Eikeland, Kristin. "Authorial Rhetoric in *Crime and Punishment*." In *Severnyi sbornik: Proceedings of the NorFA Network in Russian Literature 1995-2000,* edited by Peter Alberg Jensen and Ingunn Lunde, pp. 80-89. Stockholm: Almqvist & Wiksell International, 2000.

[*In the following essay, Eikeland examines the extent to which the character of Raskolnikov serves as an expression of Dostoevsky's views of society and the individual.*]

Crime and Punishment is usually regarded as the most unified and the most organized of all of Dostoevsky's novels. This unity is normally ascribed to the use of an omniscient (or rather partially omniscient) narrator as opposed to the personalized "narrator-chroniclers" in Dostoevsky's later novels. Also, the fact that the entire novel is centred around one main character, Rodion Raskolnikov, adds to the impression of unity and completeness: "It is the story of one idea, one man, one fate [. . .] he [Raskolnikov] is the dynamic centre, it is from him that the beams go forth and diverge, and their reflections return to him."[1] The much criticized "monologic" epilogue[2] is another factor that has caused *Crime and Punishment* to be regarded as more "closed" and "finalized" than the later novels.

There is no doubt about Dostoevsky's personal, didactic intentions in this novel. One of the questions he wanted to explore was: "What happens to a young man who rationally plans and then commits a murder?" The writer's self-professed aim was to represent the psychological process of a crime, and show how the criminal is finally forced to confess. However, it is not fear of judicial punishment that should drive the criminal to do so, but "God's truth" and "the law of truth and of human nature," as Dostoevsky says in a letter to his publisher Katkov in 1865.[3] It is the power of this truth that Dostoevsky sets forth to demonstrate in *Crime and Punishment.*

In a recent analysis of the novel Valentina Vetlovskaia claims that Raskolnikov's argumentation, and his theories which are based on a casuistic logic, are reduced to a logical absurdity through the author's, that is Dostoevsky's form of argumentation.[4] Regarding the writer's novels as more "philosophic-publisistic" than purely artistic in terms of genre, Vetlovskaia disclaims Bakhtin's theory of polyphony, and finds that Dostoevsky's chief argumentative technique in his fiction as well as in his non-fiction is *argumentum ex concessis,* that is reasoning according to the premises of one's opponent.[5]

In Vetlovskaia's analysis then, we are dealing with an *ex concessis* form of argumentation where the orator (Dostoevsky) leads the argumentation of his opponent (Raskolnikov) *ad absurdum,* thereby gaining the audience's support for his own case, which is thus only *indirectly* proven rhetorically. "The falseness of one reasoning leads to the truth of the other."[6] From this perspective Vetlovskaia analyses rhetoric in *Crime and Punishment* as well as in *The Brothers Karamazov.* In her view, any analysis of the positive Christian discourse, which establishes the "illogicality" of spiritual truth or *istina,* is in fact superfluous, simply because the logical refutation of the negating ideas is so obvious.

According to Vetlovskaia the author agrees with Raskolnikov in his social criticism and his wish to change society; as is convincingly demonstrated by Vet-

lovskaia, the whole novel is permeated with examples of the unfairness and immorality of a society that is built on the need and greed for money. However, as Vetlovskaia points out, the real polemic in the novel arises only when it comes to the *means* of rebuilding society. In this dispute Raskolnikov's way is that of violence, that of the author is the way of love and redemption. In Vetlovskaia's analysis, the juxtaposition of these two principles leads to the triumph of one argument—the author's—through the realization of the obvious falseness of the other.

In this way Raskolnikov is compromised as a result of the inaccuracies in his casuistic logic. For instance, he does not for one second take into consideration the possibility of Lizaveta's making an early return and thus interrupting his plan. By the same token, in spite of his insistence on his own rational behaviour, he is convinced from the outset of the role of fate in his plans; he is in fact growing more and more superstitious as the moment of the execution of his plan draws closer. Vetlovskaia states that the inconsistency between Raskolnikov's plan and its implementation is a result of a *choice* made long before the murder itself, at the moment when he chooses to commit the crime, and thus, sin:

> Ever since his choice was made, events had been developing according to the logic of the natural consequences of the error which had led him to "mistake the apparition of goodness for goodness itself," that is, according to the logic of sin, which is based on false theories and incorrect calculations. It had to be like this. However complex and many-sided the hero's theoretical constructions may be, in the end, they all lead to a simple conclusion—to the justification of sophism, according to which sin is not sin, crime is not crime.[7]

A problem with Vetlovskaia's approach, however convincing and useful it may be in many respects, is that it does not make any distinction between rhetoric *per se* and rhetoric within the artistic context, thus reducing the poetic potential of literary personae. The strong emotional appeal of Raskolnikov, the reader's identification with him and sympathy for him in spite of his horrible rationalizations, is part of the appellative function of rhetoric, which is ignored in Vetlovskaia's argument. While we are familiar with the author's personal remarks regarding his own intentions in the novel (to express "God's truth" and "the law of truth and of human nature"), examining how these intentions materialize within the artistic context requires an analysis not only of the direct polemic between the author and his characters on the same level, but also of the persuasive discourse on the fictional level, between the characters themselves, as *represented* rhetorical discourses.

I will attempt to demonstrate in the following how the truth, the *istina* concerning Raskolnikov's "logic of sin," as Vetlovskaia calls it, is rhetorically unveiled in the novel. However, it is not the purely logical imperfections which are decisive for revealing the "truth" of Raskolnikov's idea, but rather a carefully constructed rhetoric based on what I shall refer to as *enthymematic argumentation.*

The *enthymeme* and the *example* are for Aristotle the two fundamental logical tools of rhetoric. The enthymeme is traditionally understood as "a concisely formulated argument, which seeks to substantiate the truth, or the plausibility of a statement about a particular fact or case, by deduction from other statements that are commonly accepted or hard to dispute."[8] As the rhetorical counterpart to the syllogism, the enthymeme, or the "rhetorical syllogism," is an apparently logical structure where the premises may be only generally true, or where one of the premises may be omitted as presupposed. Enthymemes provide "the connection between the strictest logic of syllogistic operations and the less rigorous 'logic' of probabilistic operations, ones that can be handled by rhetorical questions, authoritative proverbs, inductive method and grammatical analysis."[9] Quintilian gives this example of an enthymeme: "Can money be a blessing, seeing that people tend to misuse it?" This is a an enthymeme where the thesis is expressed in the form of a rhetorical question. As a full syllogism it would sound like this: "Nothing can be a blessing which may be misused; money may be misused, thus, money is not a blessing."[10] According to Aristotle, the absolute truth lying at the root of a syllogistic argument is not always comprehensible to the human mind. Therefore, the rhetorician must turn to the enthymeme as a way of providing proof. Moreover, an argument dealing with human behaviour, choices, and actions cannot rely on the kind of logical exactness of syllogistic reasoning. Thus the orator consequently has to depend on the logic of the enthymeme.

Art, in our case the novel, is permeated with this form of reasoning. A writer depicting not real life, but a representation of reality, or a "possible world," must present his argumentation in a manner that makes it appear convincing according to its *intrinsic logic.* In his exposition of Aristotle's aesthetics, the late Aleksei Losev defines a fictional story as a series of *topoi,* or, more specifically, as premises that may not be relevant in a strictly logical or syllogistic sense.[11] Thus, the logic of a novel, or the unfolding of its plot, does not have to correspond to the logic of the outside world, or "reality." It is the author's task to demonstrate that given the circumstances of the story and their assumptions, the "conclusive argument" or "message," if I may venture to use such an old-fashioned term, appears convincing to the reader.

Losev draws on Sophocles' tragedy *Oedipus Rex* in order to illustrate this *topological logic,* which constitutes the *aesthetics* of the plot. Here, the unfolding of the plot, with all its strange incidents and coincidences, makes sense only if one accepts the underlying premise: the power of fate over people's lives. This power Sophocles cannot prove scientifically or syllogistically, but only demonstrate enthymematically as the intrinsic logic underlying the represented events of the work itself. In *Antigone* one structuring premise is the impossibility of compatibility between the law of the state and *Realpolitik,* on the one hand, and the law of the family and the gods, on the other. In *Crime and Punishment,* Dostoevsky posits a similar problem of incongruity in at least two variants: Sonia's "overstepping" of the law in the form of her sacrificing herself, and Raskolnikov's transgression in committing a murder are both, in varying degrees and with different motivation, governed and made "logical," or conceivable, by the underlying premise of a moral, individual law superseding the written, factual law.

In *Crime and Punishment,* the "reasonable proofs" of Raskolnikov's mistake are presented in the form of an enthymematic argumentation. The enthymeme is, says Aristotle in his *Rhetoric,* especially suited to evoke and inspire the audience by making them participate in supplying missing or underlying premises. In *Crime and Punishment* the reader becomes involved in the process of gradually discovering Raskolnikov's true motive.

The motive is decisive in forming the audience's opinion of Raskolnikov. A noble motive is liable to provide some justification for the action itself. Through Dostoevsky's use of a mixed point of view, of an omniscient narrator combined with the limited point of view of the various characters, the reader is left in the dark from the outset concerning the real motive for the murder. Observing the criminal act as though from inside Raskolnikov's head, and taking part in Raskolnikov's disturbing thought processes, the reader identifies and sympathizes with him. Hints of several motives, varying from the altruistic to the existentialist, are given in the first part of the novel: Raskolnikov wants to "utter a new word," and to "leave a mark in history."

The real motive for the murder, however, is explored in more detail only in the third part of the novel, after the two murders. It is here that the Napoleonic theme is explicitly mentioned for the first time. The question of motive is strongly connected to this theme on several levels. Here Dostoevsky launches his rejoinder in the debate concerning the lawful right of the historical "genius" or "strong individual" to overstep moral laws, as it was put forward in Napoleon III's *History of Caesar* published in Russia in 1865. The myth of Napoleon is introduced into the novel as the strongest argument or "proof" against Raskolnikov.

It is above all in Raskolnikov's conversations with the court investigator Porfirii Petrovich and with Sonia Marmeladova that this motive is gradually revealed. In these conversations the author confronts the hero-villain directly with his spiritual and ideological adversaries. The author's voice, or rather an *authorial rhetoric,* is therefore more transparent here than, for instance, in **The Brothers Karamazov,** where the complex, multi-layered narrative structure only indirectly challenges Ivan with *his* spiritual opponent, Father Zosima, whose argument is refracted through the discourse of Alesha Karamazov. In **Crime and Punishment** the character or characters representing the positive ideas of the novel are juxtaposed with the ideas of their antagonists on the same narrative level.

As a representative of the new type of lawyer following the judicial reforms of 1864, the enigmatic character of Porfirii Petrovich seems to possess qualities which go beyond those of the social and psychological insights of a shrewd new advocate of the law.[12] Raskolnikov's conversations with the police investigator are, according to Bakhtin, examples of "authentic and remarkable polyphonic dialogue."[13] Here, Raskolnikov is not only unmasked and compromised, he is also inspired to embark on the road towards redemption. In contrast to Sonia's timid response, which has its climax in her reading of the story of Lazarus, Porfirii launches his own sharp polemic against Raskolnikov's theories. The reader is often left puzzled, however, by the witty and sarcastic interrogator's sudden sincerity and what appears to be a genuine interest in Raskolnikov's spiritual life and well-being. Bakhtin finds that Porfirii is governed by a "special dialogic intuition that allows him to penetrate the unfinalized and unresolved soul of Raskolnikov."[14] This quality in Porfirii, to peer into the soul of his interlocutor, seems to come close to the intriguing combination of psychological and spiritual intuition in some of the pious characters of Dostoevsky's other novels, such as Father Zosima, Bishop Tikhon and Makar Dolgorukii, who, like Porfirii, act as Socratic "midwives" of confession, their task being to "draw out" the truth.[15]

Porfirii seems to take pleasure in arguing; he insists for two months that he is to become a monk, at another time he pretends that he is getting married. He is, as it appears, a man who enjoys playing with argumentation and with logic—but not logic, however, in the strictest sense of the word, or in the sophistic sense of proving anything logically, as Razumikhin ironically suggests, gibing at the detective's argumentative skills:

> —Ну, да хочешь я тебе сейчас *ы еы* , [. . .] что у тебя белые резницы единственно оттого только, что в Иване великом тридцать пять сажен высоты, и выведу ясно, точно, прогрессивно и даже либеральным оттенком?
>
> (VI 197)[16]

The argumentative technique of Porfirii's verbal ensnaring of Raskolnikov is not based on this type of "logic-chopping," but rather on topological deduction or *en-*

thymematic argumentation. From a classical rhetorical perspective—from that of an orator trying to persuade an audience—we may say that it is both Porfirii's and Dostoevsky's task to reveal the possible consequences of Raskolnikov's theory when put into practice. With Gary Cox, it is possible to regard Porfirii Petrovich as Dostoevsky's double, in the sense that it is the author's task to make the reader, through his identification with Raskolnikov, "accept universal guilt and to seek redemption, just as Porfirii wants Raskolnikov to accept individual guilt and to confess."[17]

The point of departure for Porfirii is the article "On Crime" written by Raskolnikov six months earlier. Porfirii anticipates Raskolnikov's thoughts and ideas by presenting his own version of Raskolnikov's essay, by developing and amplifying what seems to be only *suggested* in the article. Raskolnikov is thus provoked to elaborate his present thoughts on his article:

> [Я] развиваю в моей статье, что все . . . ну, например, хоть законодатели и установители человечества, начиная с древнейших, продолжая Ликургами, Солонами, Магометами, Наполеонами и так далее, все до единнобо льиип преступники, уже тем одним, что, давая новый закон, тем самым нарушали древний, свято чтимий обществом и от отцов перешедший, и, уж конечно, не останавливались и перед кровью, если только кровь (иногда совсем невинная и доблестно пролитая за древний закон) могла им помочь.
>
> (VI 199-200)[18]

This is where the Napoleonic motive appears explicitly for the first time in the novel. The detective wants to reveal the possible consequences of Raskolnikov's theory. Thus, Porfirii Petrovich immediately turns the question away from the theoretical to the practical level, in order to exemplify and specify Raskolnikov's idea. The non-apodictic or plausible aspect of the enthymeme is made explicit in a series of tentative "what if" premises. He adheres to the military language, thus continuing the theme of Napoleon, using the word *pokhod* ("campaign," "crusade"):

> Ну как иной какой-нибудь муж, али юноша, вообразит, что он Ликург али магомет . . .—будущий, разумеется,—да и давай устранять к тому все препятствия . . . Предстоит, дескать, далекип дохоп, а в поход деньги нужны . . . ну и начнет добывать себе для похода . . . знаете?
>
> (VI 203)[19]

The detective zooms in on his target with a number of rhetorical questions, which seem to come as a natural consequence of the "what-if" premises. In his characteristically ironic style Porfirii poses the possibility of Raskolnikov believing himself to be one of the "extraordinary":

Ведь, вот-с, когда вы вашу статейку-то сочин-
яли,—ведь уж быть того не может, хе-хе! Чтобы
вы сами себя не считаи, ну хоть на капельку,—
тоже человеком «необыкновенным» и говорящим
о ое сло о,—в вашем то есть смысле-с . . . Ведь
так-с? [. . .]—а коль так-с, то неужели вы бы
сами решились—ну там ввиду житейских каких-
нибудь неудач и стеснений или для споспешество-
вания как-нибудь всему человечеству—перешаг-
нуть через препятствие-то? . . . Ну, например,
убить и ограбить? . . .

(VI 204)[20]

The policeman Semenov finally draws the now obvious parallel between Napoleon and Raskolnikov in a mocking rhetorical question: уж не наполеон ли какой будущий и нашу алену Ивановну на прошлой неделе топором укокошил? ("Is it not very likely that it was some future Napoleon who bumped off our Alena Ivanovna with an axe last week?" VI 204).

The parallel between the murderer Raskolnikov and the emperor Napoleon establishes a likely explanation for Raskolnikov's actions. The detective's enthymematic reasoning provides plausible arguments for the existence of such a young man as Raskolnikov, a man who may identify with and imitate an historical and mythical figure such as Bonaparte. At the same time, in the author's scheme, the irony of the argumentation, which enhances the awkwardness of the image of Bonaparte "bumping off" (укокошить) an old pawnbroker with an axe, compels the reader to question and distrust Raskolnikov's idea.

It is not, however, until Raskolnikov's confession to Sonia that Dostoevsky points to the ultimate consequence of the murderer's *imitatio*. This is where the parallel Raskolnikov-Napoleon reaches its climax, and where the writer delivers his final opinion of the cult of genius.

[Я] хотел налодеоном слеьатгся, оттоио и убил . . . Ну, понятно теперь? ("I wanted to become a Napoleon, that is why I committed a murder, do you get it now?" VI 318), Raskolnikov asks Sonia. Compelled to continue Porfirii's thought experiments, Raskolnikov compares Napoleon's main military quests (Toulon, Paris, Egypt, Moscow) with his own "crusade." An unbearable question arises: would the young Bonaparte kill an old "louse" of a pawnbroker, if that was his only way to launch his career? Seen in this perspective, the murder of the old pawnbroker, in all its absurdity, becomes problematic to Raskolnikov. Here he is confronted with what he calls an "aesthetic" problem: would Napoleon have crawled under the bed of "an old ridiculous pawnbroker" in order to steal her hidden money? (VI 211). Raskolnikov concludes that if Napoleon had had to kill the old lady, he would have done it without hesitation, without moral scruples. Ну и

я . . . вышел из задумчивости . . . задушил . . . по примеру авторитета . . . ("Hence, I too came out of reflection . . . I killed . . . following the example of an authority . . ." VI 319), Raskolnikov admits in his meeting with Sonia.

From this deduction there emerges an image of Napoleon stripped of any historical context of glorious military achievements. All that remains is the grotesque image of a man who is capable of killing without remorse, without conscience. In "his dark catechism that had become his faith and law"[21] Raskolnikov wanted to *dare*, like the Napoleon in Dostoevsky's version who эабывает армию в египте, трапит полмилиона людей в московском походе ("*forgets* an army in Egypt and *loses* half a million people in the march towards Moscow" VI 211).

Raskolnikov's *hubris* consists in the fact that he has succumbed to the temptation to become an extraordinary man. The young man's committing of a murder, in order to prove to himself that he is "more than a louse," betrays his utter egoism.

In the novel as a whole, an equivalence between Bonaparte and pure evil is established and made probable. Sonia exclaims: От бога вы отошли, и вас бог поразил, дьяволу передал! . . . ("you have turned away from God! And God has punished you and handed you over to the Devil!"); Raskolnikov answers: Кстати, соня, это когда я в темноте-то лежал и мне всё представлялось, это ведь дьявол смущал меня? ("Then Sonia, do you mean to infer that when those ideas came upon me in my room, it was the Devil who was tempting me?"), only to immediately confirm the question himself: [Я] ведь и сам знаю, что меня черт тащил. ("I know that it was the Devil who tempted me." VI 321).

This is Dostoevsky's fictional transformation of the romantic view of Napoleon as a "new poetic demon [who] represented an individualist devil freed of his traditional attachments to the Bible."[22] It is an image antithetically opposed to Belinskii's affirmative version of the cult of genius presented in his critique of Pushkin's "weak" Boris Godunov figure.[23] The image of the lonely demon suffering for humanity, or that of the chosen despot-genius, both of them *also* rhetorical constructions, are transformed in **Crime and Punishment** into an image of Satanic pride and self-centredness, into evil incarnate. [С]тарушонку эту черт убил, а не я ("I did not kill the old lady, the Devil did, not I" VI 322), Raskolnikov finally admits.

In this novel Dostoevsky continues the series of Napoleonic protagonists found in Russian literature. Eugene Onegin, Herman ("The Queen of Spades"), Pechorin (*A Hero of Our Time*) are all literary prototypes of

Raskolnikov.[24] However, in *Crime and Punishment,* the writer forces the meaning of the Napoleonic image further than anyone before him writing in this tradition.

It is interesting to observe the difference between the juxtaposition Raskolnikov-Napoleon and similar pairs of "doubles" in Dostoevsky's later works, notably that of Ivan Karamazov-the Grand Inquisitor. In *The Brothers Karamazov* the antagonist, Ivan, enters into a dialogue with *his* self-created phantoms, the Grand Inquisitor and later the Devil. In *Crime and Punishment,* however, Napoleon is never given a voice of his own. In *Crime and Punishment* the image of Bonaparte is rendered in the author's parodic discourse throughout. This infamous image, however, is born out of and made clear to Raskolnikov in the dialogues with Porfirii Petrovich (and subsequently with Sonia). These dialogues allow Raskolnikov to visualize the hideousness of his own ideas as represented in the image of Napoleon, and to engage with it and thus with his own inner being. This immanent polemic in the rhetorical structure is completely lost in Vetlovskaia's analysis.

The enthymematic logic establishing the evil universe of the novel is centred around Dostoevsky's recontextualization of the Napoleonic myth, where Napoleon appears as a Satanic figure. The existence of a constant struggle between this evil universe and its positive, affirming counterpart emerges as the presupposed premise, or to use Losev's term, the "supralogical" (*sverkhlogichnyi*) logic that underlies the "illogicality" of the plot of *Crime and Punishment.*

From here we could go on to analyse the function of enthymematic rhetoric in the story of Raskolnikov's redemption.

Notes

1. Konstantin Mochulsky, 1967, *Dostoevsky: His Life and Work,* Princeton, N.J., p. 298.

2. Mikhail Bakhtin, 1984, *Problems of Dostoevsky's Poetics,* trans. C. Emerson, Minneapolis, p. 92.

3. F. M. Dostoevskii, 1972-1990, *Polnoe sobranie sochinenii v tridtsati tomakh,* Leningrad, vol. 28 (2), p. 137. Further references made to this edition will be identified by volume and page. Here and elsewhere, unless otherwise noted, English translations are my own.

4. V. V. Vetlovskaia, 1996, "Priemy ideologicheskoi polemiki v 'Prestuplenii i nakazanii' Dostoevskogo," *Dostoevskii: Materialy i issledovaniia* 12, St Petersburg, pp. 78-98.

5. "Reasoning that the conclusion of an argument is sound, on the basis of the truth of the premises of one's opponent. He may have exaggerated the soundness of his premise for his purpose: you use the exaggeration for yours." Richard A. Lanham, 1991, *A Handlist of Rhetorical Terms,* Berkeley & Los Angeles, Calif., p. 22.

6. Vetlovskaia, 1996, p. 91.

7. Vetlovskaia, 1996, pp. 97-98.

8. Manfred Kraus, 1994, "Enthymem," *Historisches Wörterbuch der Rhetorik,* ed. G. Ueding, Tübingen, vol. 2, cols. 1197-1222; col. 1197.

9. Frederick W. Norris, 1991, *Faith Gives Fullness to Reasoning: The Five Theological Orations of Gregory Nazianzen,* intro. & comm. F. W. Norris, trans. L. Wickham & F. Williams, Leiden, p. 23.

10. Tormod Eide, 1990, *Retorisk leksikon,* Oslo, pp. 102-103.

11. A. F. Losev, 1975, *Aristotel' i pozdniaia klassika,* (*Istoriia antichnoi estetiki* 4), Moscow, p. 719ff.

12. See VII 340-341. Dostoevsky repeatedly portrays this new type of lawyer, especially the defence attorney, or the "hired conscience," as he preferred to call him. A famous fictional example of Dostoevsky's sarcastic presentation of this type is the defence attorney Fetiukovich in Dmitrii Karamazov's trial. The prototype for Fetiukovich is supposedly the famous V. D. Spasovich, of whom Dostoevsky draws an unflattering portrait in his *Diary of a Writer* (XXII 50-73).

13. Bakhtin, 1984, p. 62.

14. Bakhtin, 1984, p. 61.

15. It goes beyond the scope of this article to further analyse Porfirii's role in Raskolnikov's confession. Let it suffice here to mention that there are opposing views on the genuine spiritual aspect of Porfirii. See for instance Harriet Murav, 1992, *Holy Foolishness: Dostoevsky's Novels and the Poetics of Cultural Critique,* Stanford, Calif., p. 70. Although Murav traces features of the "holy fool" in Porfirii's buffoonery, constant mocking and gesture-making, she concludes that: "the question remains as to whether Porfirii is interested in Raskolnikov's salvation or in merely discharging his duty as an agent of the law."

16. "Well, then, let me deduce for you: you have white eyelashes only because the tower of Ivan the Great is thirty-five *sazhen* high, and I will draw this deduction clearly, precisely, progressively and even with a liberal touch."

17. Gary Cox, 1990, *Crime and Punishment: A Mind to Murder,* Boston, Mass., p. 70.

18. "In my article I develop the idea, that one and all . . . take for instance the legislators and rulers of

men, commencing with the earliest down to the Lycurguses, Solons, Mahomets, Napoleons, and so forth, that one and all were criminals, for whilst giving new laws, they have naturally broken the older ones, which had been faithfully observed by society and transmitted by its progenitors. These men most certainly never hesitated to shed blood, if only blood (sometimes innocent and valiantly shed for the sake of the old law) could help them."

19. "If a man or a youth fancies himself a Lycurgus or a Mahomet of the future, of course his first step will be to remove all obstacles in his way . . . Then he will say that he proposes undertaking a crusade, and in order to do so, he shall require money for the crusade . . . well, and then he starts acquiring money . . . you know?"

20. "Whilst composing this article of yours, isn't it very probable, ha-ha, that you looked upon yourself, perhaps for a second only, as one of those "extraordinary" men you were talking about, one of those who shall speak "the *new word*." Am I right? [. . .] If this is so—would you not be induced yourself—either in view of material embarrassments, or of assisting humanity in its onward course—to step over the obstacles? For instance to kill and to rob?"

21. Sonia's observation (Соня поняла, что этот мрачный катихизис стал его верой и законом. vi 321).

22. Valentin Boss, 1991, *Milton and the Rise of Russian Satanism,* Toronto, p. xxiii.

23. V. G. Belinskii, 1995, "Boris Godunov," *Polnoe sobranie sochinenii,* Moscow, vol. 7, pp. 505-534.

24. See vii 342-343 for a more detailed discussion of Raskolnikov's Napoleonic prototypes.

Jacqueline A. Zubeck (essay date 2004)

SOURCE: Zubeck, Jacqueline A. "Bakhtin's Ethics and an Iconographic Standard in *Crime and Punishment.*" In *Bakhtin: Ethics and Mechanics,* edited by Valerie Z. Nollan, pp. 33-55. Evanston, Ill.: Northwestern University Press, 2004.

[*In the following essay, Zubeck discusses the significance of iconography in* Crime in Punishment *within the framework of Mikhail Bakhtin's reading of the novel.*]

> *Behold, I send you forth as sheep in the midst of wolves: be ye therefore wise as serpents and harmless as doves.*
>
> —Mt. 10:16 KJV

Raskolnikov lies on a filthy sofa facing the wall in a stifling Petersburg attic, internalizing the tenets of a utilitarian nihilism—as if these theories might be his very meat and drink. He would make real the principles of these ideologies and accommodate their precepts, swallowing whole the assumptions expressed therein. His character and perspective are such that his ideas are intensified and epitomized as an "abstract cognition", which "seeks to pass itself off as the whole world."[1] Raskolnikov seems keenly suited to illustrate Bakhtin's concerns about theory divorced from practice, or what he refers to as the problem of theoretism. We see Raskolnikov bound to a set of utilitarian principles, which are consistent within a narrow rationalist framework and characterized by an "objective theoretical validity of judgment" ("TPA" ["Toward a Philosophy of the Act"] 9). But his theoretical standards are removed from actuality and "severed" from his own "answerable consciousness" ("TPA" 29). Raskolnikov obligates himself to a formalistic system and enacts the thinking that is intrinsic to that perspective, imagining that he might do so according to "an essential and fundamental abstraction from the fact" of his "unique being" ("TPA" 9). As such, Raskolnikov illustrates Bakhtin's concerns about a "disembodied theoretical consciousness" ("TPA" 73) which tries to ignore his individual "unique place . . . the answerable . . . concrete center of the concrete manifoldness of the world" ("TPA" 57).

While Raskolnikov's perceptions tend to be blinkered and narrowly focused, the action of the novel as a whole is geared toward a manifestation of the implications of his thinking and renders his theoretical word into flesh. Bakhtin noted that Dostoevsky had an ability to see the "potentialities" of the idea and could "divin[e] how a given idea would develop and function under certain . . . conditions,"[2] a divination that emerges according to his "word made flesh" aesthetics. Thus ideas for Dostoevsky, as for Bakhtin, are never merely theoretical constructs; rather, they reflect the contours of human consciousness and spill out into events.

In this essay I consider Bakhtin's ethical perspective as it is enunciated in "Toward a Philosophy of the Act" and argue that this work is related thematically to "The Idea in Dostoevsky" (from *Problems of Dostoevsky's Art*), in which the critic discusses "the image of the idea," or what he describes as the embodiment of thought in visual characterizations. Finally, I link Bakhtin and Dostoevsky to what I call an "iconographic standard," a perspective which is connected thematically, technically, narratively, and visually to the icon. Because Dostoevsky seeks to make meaning apparent through a "visible" image related to the embodiment of an ideology, it seems reasonable to consider this image in relation to Russian iconography—the wellspring of Russian pictorial and narrative art and the representation of ethical values as well. An iconographic approach pertains to the christological religious sense of both Dostoevsky and Bakhtin, and has bearing on the ideas that both author and critic express in their creative work. Let us historically contextualize the two Bakhtin works in question. Between 1919 and 1921, Bakhtin had worked on a philosophical essay which was published (at long last, in 1986) under the title "K filosofii postupka" ("Toward a Philosophy of the Act").[3] After the completion of this work, Bakhtin turned his attention to Dostoevsky and spent much of his time between 1921 and 1929 working on the Dostoevsky book. "The Idea in Dostoevsky," a chapter from *Problemy tvorchestva Dostoevskogo* (*Problems of Dostoevsky's Art*), was first published in Leningrad in 1929, and expanded and republished in 1963. His notes for further revision emerged in 1971. Caryl Emerson's English translation of the book appeared in 1984 as *Problems of Dostoevsky's Poetics,* and Vadim Liapunov's English translation of the earlier "Act" appeared in 1993. Thus while the publication of these two works seems to locate them in disparate time frames (especially to an English-speaking audience), their composition occurred consecutively and can be linked, I will argue, conceptually.

The historical period in which the two works were written also seems significant. The 1920s heralded the beginning of the long Soviet night. During this time, Bakhtin experienced firsthand the evolution of Marxism-Leninism. He witnessed the consequences of a theory run rampant, and saw actual practice made negligible in the primacy of a paradigm. One could not, of course, directly address the dangerous issue of political theory and actual practice during this period. But "Three Fragments from the 1929 Edition," which did not appear in the 1963 version, speaks to the terrifying concerns that Bakhtin had during the composition of these works and may signify his anticipation of official censorship of both topic and approach. In the foreword to the book, Bakhtin noted that he "had to exclude all historical problems," although "this approach to the material" cannot be considered "methodologically correct or normal"—in relation to socialist realism and its deterministic historical perspective. He makes a point of linking "every literary work" to "social evaluations" and seems eager to justify his own work in regard to an author whose art had managed to "outliv[e]" his suspect "philosophical and sociopolitical ideology" (*PDP* [*Problems of Dostoevsky's Poetics*] 276). Reading between the lines (a characteristic practice of the time) suggests that Bakhtin had concerns about the primacy of theory in Soviet Russia and the barbaric practices used to instill a monologic ideology into human consciousness and behavior. He had to mask these life-threatening matters with rhetoric that would appease Soviet censors, however, and emphasized, for example, Dostoevsky's "revolutionary innovation" in fiction.

We might also consider the thematic link between the two works. Some of the concerns in the Dostoevsky book about the *incarnation* of an idea resonate with the central problem of "Toward a Philosophy of the Act." In the latter, Bakhtin discusses the ethical problems, which accrue to the individual who embraces a theory that is consistent within a logical framework, but which does not take into account human consciousness and the particularity of context. Bakhtin thought in terms of the *word made flesh,* and in a typical first-person formulation insisted that "[e]very thought of mine, along with its content, is an act or deed that I perform—my own individually answerable act or deed [*postupok*]" ("TPA" 3). This statement, found in the first pages of "Act," informs the work as a whole. Bakhtin's "ethics of incarnation," if we may call it that, serves as a way to confront the dichotomy between theory and practice—by considering theory *as* practice. Theory as practice implies a weighted, active, individual acknowledgment of one's ideas in a way that "concentrates, correlates, and resolves within a unitary and unique and . . . *final context* both the sense and the fact, the universal and the individual, the real and the ideal" ("TPA" 28).

"The Idea in Dostoevsky" relates to this notion of a unitary and unique embodiment of thought as action. The "image of the idea"[4] suggests a literary visualization of theory in relation to the materiality of the world. It connotes that the idea has a palpability about it, a specificity which is played out in the world at large. Bakhtin suggests that Dostoevsky makes an idea tangible by personifying it—by making it an intrinsic part of a personality. Dostoevsky's hero is "inseparably linked with the image of an idea" so that the idea reaches into "the deepest recesses of his personality" ("Idea" 87). Raskolnikov's character illustrates this idea-driven personality—a character *particularly suited* to a self-lacerating adherence to formal structure. He experiences ideology at the level of *strast'*—with a passion that is related to compulsion, crucifixion, and love. But it is in the physical presentation and external manifestation of an inner intellectual and moral phenomenon that "[w]e *see* the hero in the idea and through the idea, and we *see* the idea in him and through him" ("Idea" 87). This kind of visual evocation is implied when Dostoevsky writes (in regard to another work): "the *dominating idea* of the Life must be visible . . . although *the entire dominating idea will not be explained in words. . . .*"[5] The dominating idea is the psychological stuff of the character himself, and suggests a unified context, an integration between ideology and psychology. Thus Dostoevsky "tried to perceive and formulate each thought in such a way that a whole person was expressed and began to sound in it." The "idea" involved "an entire spiritual orientation" which "emerged not [as] a system," but as "a concrete event" ("Idea" 93).

The enactment or contextualization of an idea was especially important to Dostoevsky in relation to *Crime and Punishment,* in which the author's artistic goal was, among other things, to make manifest the implications of radical theory. Joseph Frank notes that Dostoevsky had a "close personal contact . . . with a wide and diversified range of Russian social-cultural opinion. Indeed, he could see all its nuances *embodied in the flesh* as he spoke to the youthful members of the younger generation who swarmed into the editorial offices of his journal."[6] In other words, Dostoevsky saw various contemporary theories in terms of the particular individuals who held those ideas. But the author considered many of these philosophies to be simplistic in tone and naïve in conception. He was disturbed by the "strange, 'unfinished'" quality of the day's rhetoric and mourned an impoverished perspective, which, tragically, had little effect on the *sincerity* of the believers (*The Stir of Liberation* 42). Dostoevsky noted, for example, that the tremendous influence of nihilism in Russia came "in the name of honor, truth, and genuine usefulness." He empathized with this impulse and saw in it, it would seem, his own youthful goals and aspirations. Twenty years later, he also comprehended the "calamitous results" of naïvely conceived perspectives, while feeling "sorrow and pity for all the innocents who are being misled by such doctrines."[7] In *Crime and Punishment,* he creates a protagonist, a "man of the idea" ("Idea" 85), who embraces completely the tenets of radical thought, and, in the long process of the novel, comes to understand the ruinous consequences of his abstract conceptions—according to the weight of his own participation.

It is noteworthy that Bakhtin also considers the human personality as "unfinalized and inexhaustible" so that, in a sense, the "inexhaustible" nature of human identity speaks of the complexity of the idea and its various and variable consequences in the world. Bakhtin writes: "The idea is by nature dialogic." It "begins to live . . . to take shape, to develop . . . only when it enters into genuine dialogic relationships with other ideas, with the ideas of *others*" ("Idea" 86, 88). In Dostoevsky's novels, the meaning of an ideology is enacted or realized in relation to other consciousnesses within unique contexts in which "the idea is posed in terms beyond affirmation and repudiation, [and] at the same time [is] not reduced to simple psychical experience" ("Idea" 80). In *Crime and Punishment,* the embodied event, implied in ideological form, makes itself felt in such a way that the protagonist comes to acknowledge his "own participation in unitary Being-as-event," a "fact [which] cannot be adequately expressed in theoretical terms, but can only be . . . participatively experienced" ("TPA" 40). In the novel, Dostoevsky takes an ideology related to "utility," gives it to a personality that devours the idea and makes it part of his very being, and places him in the midst of other consciousnesses within specific

events. It is among these characters, within the unique texture of *their* particular contexts, that the significance of the idea is disclosed. All the characters, acting within the various associations of the novel, actualize the psychological, theoretical, and interactive potential of an ideology, associations which fatten into particular occurrences. Thus it is in the various manifestations of an "inexhaustible" human nature—in relation to other inexhaustible natures—in which the "image of the fully valid idea" emerges ("Idea" 86). In this way, the idea becomes "a live event, a dialogic meeting between two or several consciousnesses." And within this interactive field, ideas yield up their "various facts, nuances, [and] possibilities" ("Idea" 88). Dostoevsky manifests this individualized, yet dialogic quality of the idea in his signature scenes in which a group of characters, who embody "integral life positions," participate in a particular scene, "under conditions of living contact with another and alien thought . . . thought[s] embodied in someone else's voice" ("Idea" 88).

Raskolnikov, of course, strives to avoid these dialogic interactions and to hold the idea close to his chest, as if its workings affect him and him alone. His narcissistic deliberations regarding his own Napoleonic distinction and the utilitarian evaluations in regard to the pawnbroker provide little room for the consideration of the actual implications of his ideas, to be made incarnate with terrible effect in the world. Raskolnikov represses consideration of the consequences of thought and the particular contexts in which his philosophy is to be enacted. Instead, he struggles to maintain allegiance to his own theoretical formulations—and necessarily discards disorderly human particularity. Striving to confine himself to the "chief point,"[8] Raskolnikov bridles an acknowledgment of the physical reality of the murder and takes a disembodied perspective, which renders physical particularity and prosaic detail inconsequential. He wraps his ideas, like the decoy pledge, "carefully and daintily in clean, white paper," but "never for a single instant all that time could [he] believe in the carrying out of his plans" (*CP* [*Crime and Punishment*] 62) Fulfillment of the act, "the actual—individual and historical—self-activity of the performed act" ("TPA" 26) fades away in the light of a singular demonstration of his "will and reasoning power" (*CP* 64). But this "will-as-deed produces the law to which it submits," and as such, "describes a circle," that which "shuts itself in" from other human consciousnesses according to a "theoretism" that Bakhtin describes as "fatal" ("TPA" 27). Raskolnikov's decision is morally catastrophic because it neglects "an actual acknowledgment of one's own participation in unitary Being-as-event," and throws Raskolnikov, instead, into "irresponsible self-surrender" to his own Napoleonic pronouncements and theoretical formulations ("TPA" 27, 49). Thus he proceeds according to an "abstraction" from the self, as Bakhtin suggests, that is, from a sense of his own inescapable presentness within particular human interactions. He "doggedly, slavishly [seeks] arguments in all directions" to rationalize the murder within his Napoleonic framework, "as though someone were forcing and drawing him to it" (*CP* 63).

Robert Louis Jackson and Gary Saul Morson both discuss Raskolnikov's moral abdication in ways that are relevant to Bakhtin's perspective. Jackson notes that "Raskolnikov will never decide to commit the crime. He will never consciously, actively, and with his whole moral being choose to kill—or, the reverse, choose not to kill. . . . And yet he will kill! He will lose his freedom . . . and be pulled into crime and murder—so it will seem to him—by some 'unnatural power.'"[9] Caught up in the nihilist romance of Napoleon and the abstract numbers of "utility," Raskolnikov adopts an ideology whose workings are such that they justify even murder. Yet this weighted, bloody act is not something that the protagonist actively considers. His musings are not considered part of a "necessary moment in the composition of the performed act" and are kept strangely remote from the actual commission of the deed. As Morson argues, Raskolnikov "does not settle details *in order to* remain in uncertainty, *in order to* stay in the territory between deciding to act and deciding not to act."[10] Raskolnikov dreams of nihilistic power and utilitarian virtue, but never actually settles on the means for achieving these ends. (This is, in part, why he is fascinated by coincidence: when he overhears the conversation between the young officer and his friend proposing the murder of the pawnbroker, he feels that his role is justified and inevitable.) Raskolnikov "at last arrives at a moment when not renouncing the action necessitates doing it, *though without a decision to do so*" (emphasis added). It is as if the murders occur entropically, eked out in the "shrinking space between resolution and renunciation," as Raskolnikov "continues to do the sheer minimum necessary to keep the dream alive." Nevertheless, the "minimum is enough to bring [Raskolnikov] to the murder scene, axe in hand" (*Narrative and Freedom* 226).

Raskolnikov has adopted an alibi and falls into an "irresponsible self-surrender to being" in his blind adherence to a theory "governed by its own immanent laws" ("TPA" 7, 49). But he suppresses an "attitude of consciousness" which considers the theoretical along with the practical aspects of its exploration, the repercussions implied in the theory itself ("TPA" 24). Raskolnikov tries to divorce theory from practice even as he puts into effect the bloodiest kind of act in relation to his ideas, as if the purity of the concept releases him from the corruption of the deed. But in this division, he also abdicates "the uniqueness of [his] participation in Being" ("TPA" 41), a participation which Bakhtin characterizes as "answerability."

"Answerability" refers to a link between "the sense and the fact," "the real and the ideal." It involves "a thoughtful response to particular events," and has the sense of a "performed act [which] constitutes a going out *once and for all* from within possibility as such into *what is once-occurrent*" ("TPA" 28-29). In other words, answerability involves a willingness to see one's ideas (theoretical "possibility") in terms of a particular ("once-occurrent") event. Bakhtin writes that "the evaluation of a thought as an individual act . . . takes into account and includes within itself . . . the theoretical validity of a thought *qua* judgment" which must be considered in terms of a "necessary moment in the composition of the performed act" ("TPA" 3-4). In other words, one's theories occur with an intellectual substance and pith relating to how one spends the minutes of one's life. To disregard this weight is to be both dangerously naïve and morally remiss; to acknowledge responsibility for one's ideas is to be discerning and morally answerable. Answerability also implies an adoption of what Bakhtin calls "my non-alibi in Being" ("TPA" 40), which he characterizes as an "attitude of consciousness" ("TPA" 24) that affirms and acknowledges "the uniqueness of my participation in Being" ("TPA" 41). Answerability implies an active position, not an "irresponsible self-surrender to being" ("TPA" 49) nor a blind adherence to a theory "governed by its own laws" ("TPA" 7). The "non-alibi in Being" suggests moral struggle in relation to the daily and ongoing social events and interactions—that specific time and space in which moral responsibility has its place, and where "I assume answerability for my own uniqueness" ("TPA" 42). I must sign my name, Bakhtin says, to the events of daily interaction. This signing is related to "authorship" as well. One authors one's deeds as one would author one's books, the signing implying an acknowledgment of one's answerable participation.

Raskolnikov offers an "alibi in Being" when, for example, he comes upon the drunken young girl stalked by a well-dressed dandy. He wants to intercede on her behalf, but he quickly belittles this impulse and abandons the girl. Let them "devour each other," he decides; after all, a certain "percentage" will always be sacrificed (*CP* 45). In this case, Raskolnikov retreats into the abstract formulas of utilitarianism, a theory whose "autonomy" seems to be "justified and inviolable" ("TPA" 7), or "scientific" and backed by numerical "evidence." Raskolnikov declines to participate morally and, in regard to this unrepeatable event, will not "assume answerability for [his] own uniqueness" ("TPA" 42). He will not, as Bakhtin says, sign his name to that specific incident or be answerable for his involvement in it. Instead, he retreats into formulas: "once you've said 'percentage,' there's nothing more to worry about." Percentages "are so scientific, so consolatory" (*CP* 45).

In this interaction, Raskolnikov considers the young girl as an abstract entity. But this abstraction serves to effect an absenting of himself as well. He tells the bewildered policeman not to interfere with the girl and her pursuer and "long[s] to forget himself altogether, to forget everything" (*CP* 45). He does not want to be connected to this particular interaction or even be conscious of it, and "removes himself" by referring to his well-defined theoretical formula, which, as Bakhtin notes, "makes me myself useless" ("TPA" 9). Raskolnikov illustrates the neglect and negation of what Bakhtin calls "my own unique place in Being," the "actual center from which my act or deed can issue" ("TPA" 43). Thus he retreats from a sense of answerability, offers up a utilitarian "alibi," and funnels the girl into an element of an equation, into "an essential and fundamental abstraction from the fact of [her] unique Being . . . 'as if [she] did not exist'" ("TPA" 9). According to the strict dictates of his theory, her individuality, as is his, is beside the point. Porfiry Petrovich, the police investigator who pursues Raskolnikov, specifically deals with formal configurations in relation to actual practice. He reminds Raskolnikov that "the general case . . . calculated and laid down in books, does not exist at all, for the reason [that] every case, every crime . . . as soon as it actually occurs, at once becomes a thoroughly special case" (*CP* 294). Raskolnikov's "thoroughly special case" emerges despite its genesis according to a generalized, "universally valid" law, a law which cannot, however, accommodate the potential of a "unique and concrete, never to be repeated actuality" ("TPA" 73). Raskolnikov, putting his stock into utilitarian guidelines, proceeds according to "the detached content of the cognitional act . . . governed by its own immanent laws" ("TPA" 7).

"Act" translator Vadim Liapunov suggests that the problem with "universally valid" laws, especially those which espouse no specifically ethical norms, is that they demand a sense of obligation to the abstract paradigm or perspective itself ("TPA" 84). This commitment illustrates what Bakhtin called a "law of conformity to the law" ("TPA" 27). But the sense of obligation to an abstract paradigm can become, in Liapunov's words, "an inexhaustible source of moral nihilism"—in which the destruction of traditional moral ideas or standards of behavior becomes the "moral" act ("TPA" 84).[11] In Raskolnikov's case, the faithfulness to a utilitarian paradigm exists almost as a challenge: to put into effect its precepts according to a strict letter-of-the-law conformity, even if it means the annihilation of all other moral standards. This perspective is analogous to that of Nikolai Pisarev, when he suggested that nihilists should "[s]trike right and left; what resists the blow is worth keeping, what flies to pieces is rubbish anyway" (quoted in *MY* [*Dostoevsky: The Miraculous Years*] 70).

(This idea is paraphrased by Raskolnikov in the confession scene in which he tries to explain to Sonia why he committed the murders [*CP* 286-87].)

At this point I want to consider the dynamic which links Raskolnikov's nihilism to his utilitarianism, two concepts which may seem antithetical at first. Nihilism, with its distrust and rejection of all traditional moral teachings or perspectives, places a great deal of emphasis on the "extraordinary man" who has an ability to speak a "new word," as Raskolnikov says, and who is not constrained by "prejudice" or preexisting norms. The protagonist explains to Porfiry Petrovich that "ordinary people are conservative in temperament and law abiding. They live under control and love to be controlled." But the extraordinary man sees morality as a matter of personal discretion. He requires no consideration of other persons or the prosaic matters which interfere with his agenda. Rare individuals, like "Lycurgus, Solon, Mahomet, Napoleon . . . were all without exception criminals," says Raskolnikov, and "transgressed the ancient [law]" (*CP* 226). But it is their transgression which makes them great and their "greatness" which makes transgression a "moral act." Raskolnikov, similarly, constructs himself as paradigm and precedent and proceeds as if all individuals or ideas are subordinated to the measure of his self-regarded genius.

The "extraordinary" man, by definition an individual with an exaggerated sense of self and considered the foundation and yardstick of morality, has an odd kind of moral authority. Raskolnikov argues that if he "is forced for the sake of his idea to step over a corpse or wade through blood, he can . . . find within himself, *in his conscience,* a sanction for wading through blood" (*CP* 227). It is Razumikhin who understands the implications of Raskolnikov's idea (perhaps with Dostoevsky's sense of a higher "reality").[12] He notes that conscience-sanctioned murder is "more terrible than the official, legal sanction" because crime is then validated as a *principle*.

In seeking to make real in himself the ideal of the extraordinary man, Raskolnikov works with a single-mindedness akin to madness. The intense focus necessary for the enactment of his goal is attractive to Raskolnikov and complements his own personal characteristics, drawn as he is to isolation and, like the nihilist hero Bazarov, immensely conceited. He has systematically cut his social ties and retires to a cramped and filthy attic room, one more expression of his antisocial outlook. Here he cooks himself into a fevered frenzy so that he might demonstrate his "greatness." Raskolnikov "had gotten completely away from everyone, like a tortoise in its shell" and "was in the condition that overtakes some monomaniacs entirely concentrated upon one thing" (*CP* 25). Moreover, he jealously guards the isolation that produces his concentrated dream, the blinkered perception which blinds him to actual contexts and the prosaic actuality of events in the world. Again, Porfiry Petrovich provides the appropriate analysis of Raskolnikov's condition: "You lead such a solitary life that you know nothing of matters that concern you directly" (*CP* 225).

Raskolnikov, of course, refers to the rhetoric of utilitarianism, but this is a philosophy stripped down to bare essentials and simplistic in nature. Its very lack of complexity allows for attention to be paid to what really counts for Raskolnikov—himself. Like Emmerich in Don DeLillo's *The Names,* he is "self-taught, self-willed," but his theoretical guidelines form "endless material for speculation and self-knowledge."[13] This narcissistic emphasis on self is justified and supported by a rhetoric which stresses the abstract nature of the other (as a percentage or an expendable entity paving the way for a "better" future). Particularity, signaled by the prosaic, the earthy, and the contingent, fades away in the glare of the central concept. Thus even as he gathers the materials to commit the murder and descends the steps to the kitchen to pick up the axe, "he was thinking of the chief point, and put off trifling details" (*CP* 63). The "trifling details" are, Bakhtin might say, precisely the issue. Where Bakhtin would "linger intently" over the "valued manifoldness of Being as human" ("TPA" 64), Raskolnikov plays the role of the "superior man" and collapses other individuals into material made over in the service of his "chief point."

Both concepts that concern Raskolnikov—the notion of the exceptional man and utilitarianism—imply the necessity of an adherence or commitment to the law or standard—"for the sake of the law," as Bakhtin says. These ethical concepts are categorical in their absence of attention to circumstance or context, while having reference only to their own circumscribed form. They imply a "principle of abstract ought or obligation" in reference to their own form and posit "the good" in terms of the principle itself, but this hypothesis has nothing to do with behavior or a consideration of what one "ought" to do in relation to another person. And as Liapunov notes, "the principle of abstract ought or obligation has demonstrated a frightening perversity to conceive the "ought as the . . . *absence* of any ought." In other words, abstract perspectives which refer only to themselves can all too easily degenerate into the destruction of traditional moral behavior as the "proof" that the idea governs everything. Thus these perspectives prove to be "an inexhaustible source of moral nihilism" ("TPA" 84). It is important to note, of course, that Raskolnikov's sense of superiority and concomitant loathing for other people is only a part of his complex character. Frank argues that Raskolnikov's nihilism also "run[s] counter to the instinctive promptings of his moral-emotive sensibility" (*MY* 107), a sensibility which

relates, I would argue, to his Orthodox Christian background. This perspective makes itself apparent, for example, after Marmeladov is killed and Raskolnikov gives all of his money to his widow to pay for the funeral. Shortly thereafter, little Polenka clasps him about the neck and hugs him warmly; a tender feeling envelops Raskolnikov and moves him toward an uncharacteristic humility. He asks the child to pray for "thy servant Rodion," and after this brief interlude he feels that he "ha[s] not yet died with that old woman! The Kingdom of Heaven to her." In effect, he says a brief prayer for the repose of her soul and for himself.

Raskolnikov's very name implies a split within the character: *raskol* means "dissidence" or "schism." This dichotomy appears throughout the novel, in the scene with the drunken girl previously mentioned, and in the dream of the beaten mare as well. In the latter, Raskolnikov as a child sees the small, well-loved cemetery church in the distance. He remembers it tenderly for its "frameless icons" and green cupola. But the child moves on in the dream, away from the church, and comes to watch helplessly as the little mare is brutally beaten to death by her drunken master. Here we witness the mindless and obsessive enactment of the implications of another kind of utilitarian perspective. (Is the mare useful?) The point here is that Raskolnikov and the drunken peasant in the dream each behave in an "almost wholly mechanica[l]" fashion, "as if a piece of his clothing had been caught in the cogs of a machine and he were dragged into it."[14] It is as if Raskolnikov and the peasant cast themselves into the abyss of their intoxication, ideological or otherwise, an inebriation so complete that we might say it "describes a circle, shuts itself in, and exclude[s] the actual." This suggests a nihilistic intoxication, each man drunk with the power to destroy. And yet each one acts without the "actualization of a *decision*," as Bakhtin says ("TPA" 26, 7).

The novel, however, provides a ballast against the "weightlessness" of Raskolnikov's ideas. As a utilitarian nihilist, Raskolnikov is conceptually unable or unwilling to accommodate the heavy reality of human flesh and human context. He cannot imagine the form his ideas will eventually take because individual "form" itself is denigrated by the very notion of utilitarian percentages or nihilistic destruction. Morson notes that "[a]t the murder scene, [Raskolnikov] is 'almost unconscious of his body'" (*Narrative and Freedom* 227). And yet, the novel makes manifest the "image" of the protagonist's "idea"—his word represented in the bloody corpses of his victims. This grotesque incarnation of Raskolnikov's ideology in the novel occurs, I will argue, in relation to the Eastern Christian cultural-religious tradition implied in the text, a tradition which stresses the Incarnation of Jesus Christ and the "Word made flesh." Raskolnikov's ideology emerges in relation to other characters. But we might say that it also occurs as a conscious reaction to Christian thought and posits its diametrical opposition to the principles implied in Eastern Christianity and expressed visually in the icon.

In order to discuss these ideals, let us first consider a brief history of iconography. Icons, consisting of images of Christ and his disciples, various saints, and particular religious events, appeared from the earliest days of the Christian religion. By the fourth century, theologians and Christian thinkers such as John Chrysostom, Basil the Great, Gregory the Theologian, and Gregory of Nyssa refer "to images as to a normal and generally accepted institution of the Church."[15] Despite Jewish proscriptions against images, worries of church leaders regarding idolatry, and a bitter iconoclastic period, iconography took "its natural place in Church practice" (*Icons* 27). The logic and justification of iconography is related, I want to stress, to the Eastern Orthodox emphasis on the Incarnation of Jesus Christ, who was considered to be "the express image of (the Father's) person" (John 1:18, Heb. 1:3). This was the Son who was anticipated by the prophets and who embodied the ideals and teachings of the Father—*His* word made flesh. This Incarnation was seen as the fulfillment of a long Hebrew prophetic tradition. Christian theologians and thinkers thus considered it legitimate to move "from the symbols of the Old Testament . . . to a representation of what they symbolized, to the uncovering of their direct meaning." This "direct meaning" relates to a figure who was "accessible to sensory perception, representation, and description" (*Icons* 28). The materiality of the incarnate Christ, represented in the material form of the icon, is the message—because a keen sense of Christ's embodiment "lies at the foundation" of Orthodox "pictorial art" (*Icons* 31). As Ouspensky affirms, "the image not only does not contradict the essence of Christianity, but, being its basic truth, is inalienably connected with it" (*Icons* 28).

In this paper I connect the icon to what might be called a prosaic ethic, which we can think about in terms of Orthodox values related to the Incarnation. Prosaic ethics are related to both humility (*God* made man) and the possibility of an ennobled human reality (God made *man*). The icon speaks of the dignity and value of the human form and the best possibilities inherent therein. Its underlying theme of incarnation implies not only the embodiment of an ideal, but the possibility that the viewer might also embody a similar ideal. Iconography, using a sophisticated artistic technique, that of inverse perspective, seems to invite the viewer into the plane of the icon. Inverse perspective does not create depth and distance as does realistic perspective, but implies the inclusion of the viewer within the scene itself. Let us consider, for example, Andrei Rublev's depiction of the Holy Trinity, in which the three angels sit at a table facing the viewer. One has the impression that one might join them there and sit in their midst. This is precisely the point. The perspective of the icon suggests an invitation into the icon because it creates visually a liminal realm in which the viewer is given a place—as if the incarnation of an ideal might be the province of the individual viewer—as well as the province of Christ.

The icon's appeal to the individual viewer is related to the emphasis on individual identity in Eastern Christian art. Often described as "static," the depictions on icons actually attest to the physical image of the person. For nearly two thousand years, for example, John the Baptist has been depicted with a certain cowlick curl in his hair, peculiar to a man who lived in the desert and ate locusts. But this small feature is important because it identifies *this* particular man and his unique appearance in the world. Iconographic form pays attention to personality and detail. As Ouspensky notes, "[t]he Church does not reject particularities connected with human nature or with time and place . . . but sanctifies their content" [*Icons* 30]. Moreover, the concern with particular identity and the physical characteristics of a man is one indication of the valorization of the material body that is part of the Eastern Christian tradition. Orthodoxy proffers no Manichean dichotomy between flesh and spirit and no concentration on "original sin" as a fundamental basis of human existence. A much different approach to physical reality is implied, for example, in Orthodox liturgical services, which appeal to the eye and the ear, the nose and the palate, and use color, choreography, and the weighted distinctions of fasting and feast to underscore the ineluctable intersection of body and soul.

A prosaic ethic contrasts markedly, of course, with the denigration of the quotidian implied in "extraordinary man" scenarios or in Raskolnikov's conception of human beings as dissolute by definition and "truly defective by nature" ("Philosophical Pro and Contra in Part One of *Crime and Punishment*" 192). When he meets Marmeladov and hears about Sonia, Raskolnikov growls "man grows used to everything, the scoundrel!" And yet this divided character also asks: "What if I am wrong? What if man is not really a scoundrel, man in general . . . then all the rest is prejudice, simply artificial terror and there are no barriers and it's all as it should be" (*CP* 24). If man is not a scoundrel . . . then there are no barriers. First, the condition which affects "man in general" relates to a universal condition, one marked, in the nihilist mind, by natural law and the perimeters imposed by a human "species." If one cannot escape the boundaries of a deterministic science, then in order to be exceptional ("not a scoundrel"), one must acknowledge strictly materialist conditions and at the same time, epitomize the possibilities of the species. To do so, one must accept the premise of a deterministic law and put into practice—without fear or trembling—the implications of that understanding, which includes the leveling of all moral foundations or meaningful standards. Ethical standards are merely conventional in the face of materialist foundations and serve only to demonstrate "prejudice" and "artificial terror," as Raskolnikov says. But the epitome of the species—the exceptional man—enacts a laying waste of standards and acts according to a nihilistically conceived environment, taking at face value the materialist concepts which level ethics, leaving the ground free for the utterance of the "new word," the thing that "men most fear."

Raskolnikov's point of view, we might say, occurs according to an "exclusive" perspective, one which considers the value of "extraordinary" characters and relegates the "ordinary" to the ranks of the negligible and inconsequential. Putting himself into the extraordinary category, Raskolnikov develops an "exclusive" perspective, framed in terms of his ego, which becomes the "I" (or "eye") that sees outward into an immense world. He is the "one-eyed motionless person who is clearly detached from what he sees. [Realistic perspective] makes a god of the spectator, who becomes the person *on whom the world converges,* the Unmoved Onlooker."[16] We can think about Hughes's description in relation to Raskolnikov's overwhelming emphasis on self, as if we might imagine him at the "vanishing point" in a diagram which traces the point of view of realistic drawing on which all objects converge.

An iconographic point of view, created through inverse perspective, creates not depth and distance, but a sense of inclusion within the plane of the image, as mentioned earlier in the discussion in regard to Rublev's *Holy Trinity.* Continuing in this vein, we can consider the "inclusiveness" of iconographic art as a contiguous threshold created by inverse perspective. Consider the icons depicting the Nativity of Christ. There the infant Christ is situated at the very center of the icon (implying his semantic dominance in the image). Yet He is clearly a being of the earth, lying within a cave that houses an ox and ass. The inclusion of these animals relates to the prophet Isaiah's words "the ox and the ass know their master's crib" and implies the presence of the Old Testament prophecy within the depicted scene, linking two historical periods. Peripheral figures surround the infant but retain their own identities, the particularities of their individual characters working to broaden the story of the child and providing a hermeneutic direction in which to regard the central figure. Thus we see Mary, the Mother of Christ, pictured closest to her son, the three kings offering their gifts of frankincense, gold, and myrrh, indicative of his priesthood, kingship, and death, and the angels rejoicing in the heavens. The interaction implied here suggests a unity or unified realm between earth and heaven, birth and death, old and new. Sometimes we see the child being bathed, which again stresses the earthly quality of the heavenly king. We might also consider the various individuals depicted in

relation to their own threshold condition, on the edge of two realities. Humble shepherds behold an angelic choir and the kings are guided by a star. Perhaps most interesting is the figure of Joseph, the "just man" who had been plagued by doubt from the time of the Annunciation, when he was tempted to "put away" his pregnant betrothed "quietly." Here he sits on the very edge of the frameless icon, replicating the viewer's own misgivings about the virgin birth and the incarnation of God. But here, too, his connection to the viewer from within the plane of the icon itself implies another kind of threshold interaction and speaks of the importance of the viewer and his inclusion in the plane of the iconographic space.

Let us compare inverse perspective to its conceptual opposite, realistic perspective. Realistic perspective holds the viewer at arm's length and makes "the presentation . . . a view, a spectacle, an object of our gaze."[17] Inverse perspective, on the other hand, "presupposes an internal position of the artist" who "may be conceived of as being located *in the depths of the picture*" itself. From this perspective, "the artist is not isolated from the world he represents, but places himself in the position of an observer involved in it."[18] This internally located observer/artist depicts "not the object itself," but "the space surrounding this object (the world in which it is located)." Uspensky goes on to describes the multiple outlooks that this perspective generates, what he calls a "multilateral visual embrace" or "summation" of various internal points of view. This visual embrace does not create a single, fixed point of view, but encourages the eye to move around the image, as if it took up the various vantage points of the persons depicted within. But this summation suggests that "the entire picture as a whole becomes a SIGN of the reality represented, and its individual fragments are correlated to their *denotata* not directly, but through the relation of both to the whole" (Uspensky 34, 38). In other words, the icon presupposes the semantic importance of all the elements in the image so that their detachment (the detailed view) does not work for the icon, in contrast to realistic painting, in which "a detail can be removed" and still retain its "relation to the real world." People or items in realistic works can be isolated within the picture and continue to be meaningful in that isolation, whereas in the icon, where all the figures are postured around a semantic center, details appear somewhat distorted when taken out of context. Here artistic technique complements philosophical position as the icon constructs a world in which each of the persons inhabiting the iconographic scene lives a gestalt greater than the self. Thus iconography emphasizes the "relative correlation" of the human elements and "not so much in the concrete representation itself" (Uspensky 34, 35). What is important here is the sense of inclusion, the meaningful participation, of all those depicted within the embodied ideal of the icon.

We may note here that the sense of the inclusive realm incorporated into the iconographic approach to art is intimately related to Orthodox Christian ritual. There is constant participatory activity in the body of the church. (This is why traditional churches have no fixed seating in the center of the church.) During the services, people move throughout the space of the temple. They greet one another, venerate the icons, and light candles. And in the very center of the church, they are baptized, married, and mourned. Charles Lock considers the physically participatory nature of Orthodox worship and, in so doing, discusses the difference between depth-creating realistic perspective and an inclusive iconographic point of view. He writes:

> Perspective dissociates the image from the material by which it is constituted. What is within the frame is untouchable—and the frame is introduced as a condition of perspective (as the proscenium arch becomes a condition of theatre, and the isolation of the object of inquiry a condition of Baconian scientific method): the frame is that through which the subject of modernity is constituted, by a radical separation from the object of modernity—the object of modern knowledge. The optical becomes supreme, and the senses are valued insofar as they operate over distances. The immaterialization of the image, its disembodiment, leads to a disembodiment of the subject, whose body is reduced to being a pedestal for the eyes, and the ears.
>
> ("Iconic Space and the Materiality of the Sign" 2)

Here Lock lays out the modern, panoptic object of inquiry implied in realistic perspective. The distance suggested by realism isolates the viewer and disembodies him—because only the eyes are working. One can only *see* in the distance. There is no sense of being enveloped by the inverse perspective of the icon or by the choreography of the liturgical service. Counterintuitively, realistic perspective brings about "[t]he immaterialization of the image, its disembodiment" because, in a sense, one has no immediate connection to the milieu. There seems to be no physical body involved and therefore "the disembodiment of the subject is implied." And, as he says, this disembodiment "marks the end of ritual." Lock defines "ritual" thus: "a field of representation which includes the subject as a human body and which excludes the spectatorship of the subject. . . . In considering ritual we should speak of participation and of embodiment—that is, the valorization of the body as both ground and figure of semiotic value" ("Iconic Space and the Materiality of the Sign" 2).

Lock's definition implies the dignity of the human form and its expressive participation in liturgical services, again placing semiotic value on every individual. In a sense, the reality of the incarnation is evoked by ritualistic (or social) interaction within the church, calling upon the specificity of the flesh, considered noble within this inclusive sphere and appealed to by music, color, choreography, and scent.

That the liminality of the icon and the inclusionary, participatory realm created by iconographic technique, as well as the semantic importance of all the "participants," may be considered in relation to Bakhtin's ethics. Bakhtin considers "my actual participation in time and space from my unique place in Being" as the standpoint or foundation from which one might behave answerably ("TPA" 59). He affirms our particular situatedness in the world, and notes that this positioning implies all kinds of contiguous relations and threshold interactions. We cannot cut ourselves off from this liminal condition with respect to other individuals, for they, too, must be incorporated or considered within the whole picture. Thus he considers ethics not as a system or a "systematic inventory of values" or a matter of pure concepts, but a responsibility which occurs vis-à-vis "the actual, concrete architectonic of value-governed experiencing of the world . . . with that actual, concrete center (both spatial and temporal) from which valuations, assertions, and deeds come forth" ("TPA" 61). He speaks of the individual consciousness embodied, weighted and inescapably centered in the world, and yet conceived to be on a threshold with other embodied consciousnesses. This liminality is what makes all the factors pertinent, both human and contextual, and which is "iconographic" in its inclusivity, attentive to the uniqueness of both the individual and the circumstance. It is a perspective which suggests "a unitary and unique . . . *context*" which pays attention to "the sense and the fact, the universal and the individual, the real and the ideal" ("TPA" 28, 29).

The sense of a physical literalness within a participatory realm corresponds also to the ethical sense of Dostoevsky and Bakhtin, in their search for a unity between theory and practice. Dostoevsky's famous preference to remain with Christ, even if He is a "mistake," is a predilection which Bakhtin interprets in terms of the author's skepticism about "truth in the theoretical sense of the word . . . truth as formula, truth as proposition" ("Idea" 98). Dostoevsky wanted his truth incarnate, weighted and attentive to the prosaic necessities of life in the world. And yet, he also thought it essential to consider Christ as "the ideal image," but incarnate and related to practical activity in the world. "How would Christ have acted?" seems to be Dostoevsky's approach to ethical evaluation and ethical action ("Idea" 98). This is a prosaic approach to ethics, sensitive to the nuance of individual context—but firmly planted before an ideal that has also been embodied in the flesh.

Dostoevsky's ethical approach suggests an active and ongoing evaluation of thought and action with regard to the ideal of Jesus Christ, whose incarnate humility and weighted sense of earth are important to Russian Orthodox sensibilities. The effeminate, hands-folded, eyes-raised images of Christ which abound in Western art are completely alien in spirit to iconographic depictions, which stress a "sympathetic," "reasonable," and "courageous" image which seems to look directly at the observer.[19] This face-to-face positioning represents Christ or specific saints as "a personality entering into relationships with other personalities."[20] Bakhtin describes the personality of Christ as "the unique one" who shows mercy, "assuming the burden of sin and expiation—and all others as relieved of this burden and redeemed." This "burden" is recapitulated in Bakhtin's struggle, in his feeling that a moral life is related to an ongoing engagement in the world which is attentive to detail and particularity. And this is reflected in practice. "What I must be for the other, God is for me."[21] This can be thought about, again, in terms of the liminal space of the icon and its incarnation ethic: answerability as a practical form, in relation to an ideal. Sonia, of course, provides a Christ-like iconic presence for Raskolnikov. *She* is for Raskolnikov what *Christ* is for her. When she learns the truth of the murders, she cries out "There is no one—no one in the whole world now so unhappy as you!" It is her very compassion which implies an "inclusion" and allows Raskolnikov to reveal himself in the first place. She is a threshold figure—earth bound, yet free of those bonds—who embodies the spirit of the law rather than its letter, and provides that benevolent presence which allows Raskolnikov to be included within an iconographic ideal himself.

Raskolnikov's nihilistic ideal, on the other hand, accrues only to himself and his own turbulent personality. His isolation and his obsessive look *within* partakes of no liminal interaction or conception. Instead, he erects an *idol to self* which provides him with an unbalanced version of reality, but one which illustrates the solipsism implied in what Bakhtin called "the illusory nature of solitude." Solitude (or perhaps solitariness) is a problem for Bakhtin because "consciousness," in his view, "is in essence multiple." We proceed ethically and intellectually in the world in relation to other consciousnesses. We know who we are by our interactions with others. A character like Raskolnikov, who is monologic and narcissistic, effects a "[s]eparation, disassociation, and enclosure within the self" which become "the main reasons for the loss of one's self." Bakhtin points out that what is most important is, "Not that which takes place within, but that which takes place on the *boundary* between one's own and someone else's consciousness, on the *threshold*."[22]

Let us turn now to the Lazarus scene in *Crime and Punishment,* which prefigures Raskolnikov's emotional and spiritual resurrection (and, I would argue, makes the epilogue intrinsic to the novel as a whole). Roger Anderson considers Sonia's room an iconographic space and an example of how iconography's "technical optics" work in the novel.[23] Sonia's abode "was a large but exceedingly low pitched room . . . on the right

hand wall was another door . . . it was a very irregular quadrangle and this gave it a grotesque appearance. A wall with three windows looking out on to the canal ran aslant so that one corner formed a very acute angle. . . . The other corner was disproportionately obtuse." It had "scarcely any furniture." This "form and grouping" is typical of iconographic "architecture," which is "often contrary to logic and in separate details is emphatically illogical." In icons, for example, "[d]oors and windows are often pierced in wrong places, their size does not correspond to the functions" (*Icons* 41). But this spatial perspective recapitulates the liminal world of the icon, which is difficult to visualize in realistic form and "den[ies] the reader access to the illusion of objectivity" ("The Optics of Narration" 97). Yet the depiction corresponds to the overall reality of the central figure of the icon. In this scene we see Sonia's image within an iconographic geography, which provides another version of a threshold realm. (Svidrigailov, eavesdropping in the next room, represents an opposing image. He, too, might have been included in the invitation to "come forth," but he is "walled up" according to an exaggerated and grotesque carnality—embodiment gone bad—and proceeds to commit suicide in the most desolate setting imaginable.)

The architectural details of Sonia's room also relate to the field in which Raskolnikov hides his booty. There we see a "passage leading between two blank walls to a courtyard. On the right hand, the blank unwhitewashed wall of a four storied house stretched far into the court, on the left, a wooden boarding ran parallel with it for twenty paces into the court, and then turned sharply to the left." Anderson suggests that Dostoevsky "emphasiz[es] improbable angles and flat, empty spaces, with none of the visual depth common to realistic painting" ("The Optics of Narration" 97). More important, the architectural details imply "that the action taking place . . . is outside the laws of human logic, outside the laws of earthly existence" (*Icon* 41). Thus while Raskolnikov thinks he has erased all traces of his crime in the perfect hiding place (realistically speaking), the iconographic quality of the scene emphasizes the protagonist's moral conflict, which occurs here in the shadow of the four storied house (a visual echo of the fourth floor where the murders took place and the fourth floor from which the investigation originates). Raskolnikov hides his "treasure" under a rock in a field used as a toilet, an indication of where his heart is as well.

In Sonia's room, that "rock" begins to be dislodged as Raskolnikov hears the story of the raising of Lazarus and about the removal of a large stone from the mouth of a grave so that a man might leave its confines and "come forth!" This account also implies a threshold interaction as Lazarus emerges from the grave, stressing the earthiness of the man himself. (Again, his carnality is very much to the point. Otherwise, what is a resurrection for?) In some icons depicting this scene, the on-lookers cover their mouths and noses, because Lazarus, as his housewifely sister Martha notes, *stinketh,* being *four* days in the tomb. This condition, it would seem, has some relation to Raskolnikov's condition in the novel. It seems that these two scenes complement each other, not only in their iconographic perspective, but in their thematic content as well.

Frank contends that "[b]uilt into the narrative of *Crime and Punishment* is . . . a view of how it should be read, a hermeneutic of its interpretation" (*MY* 103). That is, the supporting characters provide an interpretive function regarding the protagonist, whose interactions are "organized so as to guide the reader toward a proper grasp of the significance of Raskolnikov's crime" (*MY* 98). This hermeneutic principle is implied in the iconographic form as well. Consider once again the Nativity icon where the figures in the periphery of the narrative image illustrate various aspects of the central figure (while retaining their individual status and importance). Similarly, the characters who surround Raskolnikov provide nuance and tone to the personality of the man and his ideas, and bring them into sharper focus while themselves remaining remarkably distinct characters. As he comes into contact with them, Raskolnikov becomes aware—from different angles and perspective—of the significance of his crime. This hermeneutic arrangement thus provides Dostoevsky with a way to flesh out the "unfinished" ideas of the radical theorists, and to thicken theory into practice by noting how ideas work in the world in relation to specific people within particular events. The "hermeneutic" characters play an "integral part" in making the significance of Raskolnikov's radical theory apparent and are tied, as Frank says, to the novel's "antiradical theme" (*MY* 103).

Part of this antiradical theme revolves around the denigration of the prosaic particularity already discussed. In Bakhtin's terms, radical frameworks like nihilism or (a less radical) utilitarianism do not consider "all the factors" ("TPA" 27)—the specific actors and their particular contexts and the irreplaceable self in relation to other such selves. Bakhtin typically puts his ideas into first-person formulation in order to reiterate to the reader that "I" which suggests specificity. And it is in the evocation of that grounded, particular being ("me") that he suggests the groundedness and particularity of other individuals and *their* "unique and utterly unrepeatable roles" ("TPA" 45). It is this perspective which speaks of Bakhtin's prosaic standard, an ethic which is related, I would suggest, to his consideration of "prose wisdom" or "prose vision."[24] It is significant that Bakhtin's discussion of "prose wisdom" occurs in relation to a "stupidity" which occurs as a "failure to understand languages" that are "generally accepted" and "have the *appearance* of being *universal*" ("Discourse in the Novel" 404, emphasis mine). In other words, stupidity (a harsh word for Bakhtin) accrues from the failure to understand the moral catastrophe of universal theories which are divorced from practice. But the opposition between stupidity and prose wisdom in the novel "teaches the novelist how to perceive them physically as *objects,* to see their relativity, to externalize them, to feel out their boundaries, that is, it teaches him how to expose and structure images of social languages" ("Discourse in the Novel" 404). Again Bakhtin stresses the visual dimension of this expression, as abstract theory is thrown against quotidian life, the contrast producing an image of sorts. This juxtaposition occurs, for example, when Raskolnikov is called to the police station after the murders. He has to dress himself and discovers that the only socks he owns are soaked with his victims' blood. He puts a sock on, takes it off, and puts it on again. It is all he has to wear. He wants to take comfort in this grotesque situation by noting that "this is all conditional, all relative, all merely forms." But the repulsive reality of this blood-soaked item is an expression of the contingent nature of Raskolnikov's act and reflects an almost ludicrous attempt to divorce himself from that act, based on "theoretical" dominance.

The visual and visionary power of Dostoevsky's writing as well as the ethical conceptions of Bakhtin find concomitant elements in the iconographic form. The common thematic, visual, narrative, and perspectival elements alluded to here in a rudimentary form suggest a common emphasis on embodiment, answerability, and a prosaic standard. I also posit that the iconographic perspective challenges the formulaic reading of religious discourse as monologic or authoritarian and suggests instead an active and answerable position in relation to an ideal, one that is, nevertheless, "embodiable" in the flesh. I think that Dostoevsky's fiction and Bakhtin's philosophy reflect the Christianity that puts married priests in parishes and takes note of the flesh in its yearly rhythms of fasting and feast, a Christianity which includes the earthy peasant and an enactment of Byzantine splendor. Characters like Polenka or Sonia (or Father Zossima or Alyosha Karamazov) express this prosaic ethic. They are inextricably inculcated in a peopled, physically insistent world. They regard the image of Christ and seek to embody that ideal in their actual dealings with the various and specific characters who come their way. And they evince a genuine humility. In this way they embody the inclusive perspective of the icon. Perhaps this is what Dostoevsky had in mind when he wrote in the *Crime and Punishment* notebooks: "The Orthodox point of view; what Orthodoxy consists of."[25]

I have, of course, only touched on these various subjects and have tried to suggest the outlines of a further discussion. I think that the powerful resonance of Dostoevsky's fiction and the response to it which is implied in Bakhtin's ethics find their conceptual match in the immediacy and inclusionary realm of an artistically sophisticated iconographic art. The icon embodies the ethics of incarnation and provides an inclusive plane. It pertains to a melding between theory and practice, and reflects the tendency of both writers to see the individual implied in the thought, the word made flesh. Iconography, with its emphasis on individual identity, an ennobled physical reality, threshold realms, and an inclusive perspective, provides a fruitful venue from which one can address the concerns of these writers.

Notes

This essay is adapted from my doctoral dissertation, *Murder in the Name of Theory: Theoretical Paradigms and Ethical Problems in Works by Dostoevsky, Gide and DeLillo,* Rutgers University, 1998.

1. M. M. Bakhtin, *Toward a Philosophy of the Act,* ed. Vadim Liapunov and Michael Holquist, trans. Vadim Liapunov (Austin: University of Texas Press, 1993) 7-8. Further references are to "TPA."

2. Mikhail Bakhtin, "The Idea in Dostoevsky," *Problems of Dostoevsky's Poetics,* ed. and trans. Caryl Emerson. (Minneapolis: University of Minnesota Press, 1984). Further references are to "Idea."

3. M. M. Bakhtin, "K filosofii postupka," *Filosofiia i sotsiologiia nauki i tekhniki* (Moscow: Nauka, 1986) 80-160.

4. Dostoevsky's skills as a writer of a "visual" text have been remarked upon by a number of critics. Bakhtin argues that the philosophical issues which concern the author "take shape" and "develop" and "begi[n] to live an authentic 'painterly' life" ("Idea" 88, 90). Dostoevsky's colleague Nikolay Strakhov noted that the author "*felt thought* with unusual liveliness," which he would "state" in "various forms, sometimes giving [them] a very sharp, graphic expression. . . . Above all, he was an artist, he thought in images." Thus Joseph Frank describes the author's work in terms of its "intellectual *physiognomy*" (Joseph Frank, *The Stir of Liberation: 1860-1865* [Princeton, N.J.: Princeton University Press, 1986] 42). And Robert Louis Jackson suggests that Dostoevsky's "philosophical credo" is such that "moral truth" is "embodied in real visual forms" (Robert Louis Jackson, "Two Kinds of Beauty," *Dostoevsky's Quest for Form* [New Haven and London: Yale University Press, 1966] 42, 45).

5. Dostoevsky writes this in relation to his proposed work *The Life of a Great Sinner,* an idea which became incorporated into *The Devils.* (Quoted in "Idea" 98.)

6. Joseph Frank, *The Stir of Liberation: 1860-1865* (Princeton, N.J.: Princeton University Press, 1986) 51 (emphasis mine).

7. Joseph Frank, *Dostoevsky: The Miraculous Years 1865-1871* (Princeton, N.J.: Princeton University Press, 1995) 51. Further references are to "*MY.*"

8. Fyodor Dostoevsky, *Crime and Punishment* (1866), trans. Constance Garnett (New York: Bantam Books, 1981) 63. Further references are to "*CP.*" See also Natalia Reed, "The Philosophical Roots of Polyphony: A Dostoevskian Reading," *Critical Essays on Mikhail Bakhtin,* ed. Caryl Emerson (New York: G. K. Hall and Co., 1999) 117-52, esp. 124-32 on Dostoevsky, self-sacrifice, and self-scapegoating.

9. Robert Louis Jackson, "Philosophical Pro and Contra in Part One of *Crime and Punishment,*" *The Art of Dostoevsky: Deliriums and Nocturnes* (Princeton, N.J.: Princeton University Press, 1981) 202.

10. Gary Saul Morson, *Narrative and Freedom: The Shadows of Time* (New Haven and London: Yale University Press, 1994) 226. Further references are to "Morson."

11. My thanks to Gerald Pirog for pointing out this note and its relevance to my theme.

12. Dostoevsky insisted that his "idealism" was "more real than [the realists'] realism." His own work is "realism, only deeper." Joseph Frank comments that Dostoevsky sees his own "'realism' as becoming 'fantastic' because it delves beneath the quotidian surface into the moral-spiritual depths of the human personality, while at the same time striving to incarnate a more-than-pedestrian or commonplace moral ideal" (*MY* 308-9). The name "Razumikhin," moreover, contains the word "reason" [*razum*] in Russian. Frank comments that the name "indicates Dostoevsky's desire to link the employment of this faculty not only with the cold calculations of Utilitarianism but also with spontaneous human warmth and generosity" (*MY* 99).

13. Don DeLillo, *The Names* (1982) (New York: Random House, Vintage Book edition, 1989) 290.

14. Morson 226-27. Gary Saul Morson notes that Constance Garnett omits this important part of the text in her translation, which refers to the last minutes before he commits the murders, as "he continues to do the sheer minimum necessary to keep the dream alive," as Morson says. Raskolnikov's and the peasant's "mechanical" behavior is reminiscent of Bakhtin's words in "*Art and Answerability*": "A whole is called "mechanical" when its constituent elements are united only in space and time by some external connection and are not imbued with the internal unity of meaning. The parts of such a whole are contiguous and touch each other, but in themselves they remain alien to each

other" (1). I thank Valerie Nollan for pointing out this connection to me.

15. Leonid Ouspensky and Vladimir Lossky, *The Meaning of Icons,* trans. G. E. H. Palmer and E. Kadloubovsky (Boston: Boston Book and Art Shop, Inc., 1969) 31. Further references are to *"Icons."*

16. Robert Hughes, *The Shock of the New* (New York: Alfred A. Knopf, 1991) 17.

17. Charles Lock, "Iconic Space and the Materiality of the Sign," unpublished article, 1.

18. Boris Uspensky, *The Semiotics of the Russian Icon,* ed. Stephen Rudy, trans. P. A. Reed (Lisse: Peter DeRidder Press, 1976) 38. Further references are to "Uspensky.)

19. Dostoevsky to N. D. Fonvizina, 1854, *Selected Letters of Fyodor Dostoyevsky,* ed. Joseph Frank and David I. Goldstein, trans. Andrew MacAndrew (New Brunswick, New Jersey, Rutgers University Press) 68. I use here Dostoevsky's description of the Christ with Whom he would stay even if He were a "mistake."

20. M. M. Bakhtin, "Dostoevsky's Polyphonic Novel," *Problems of Dostoevsky's Poetics,* ed. and trans. Caryl Emerson (Minneapolis: University of Minnesota Press, 1984) 31-32.

21. M. M. Bakhtin, *Art and Answerability,* ed. Michael Holquist and Vadim Liapunov, trans. Vadim Liapunov (Austin: University of Texas Press, 1990) 56.

22. M. M. Bakhtin, "Toward the Reworking of the Dostoevsky Book," *Problems of Dostoevsky's Poetics,* ed. and trans. Caryl Emerson, Theory and History of Literature, Volume 8 (Minneapolis: University of Minnesota Press, 1984) 287.

23. Roger Anderson, "The Optics of Narration: Visual Composition in *Crime and Punishment,"* *Russian Narrative and Visual Art: Varieties of Seeing,* ed. Roger Anderson and Paul Debreczeny (Gainesville: University Press of Florida, 1994) 95. Anderson's fascinating article prompted the direction of this paper.

24. M. M. Bakhtin, "Discourse in the Novel," *The Dialogic Imagination,* ed. Michael Holquist, trans. Caryl Emerson and Michael Holquist (Austin: University of Texas Press, 1981) 404.

25. Fyodor Dostoevsky, *The Notebooks for Crime and Punishment,* ed. and trans. Edward Wasiolek (Chicago: The University of Chicago Press, 1967) 188.

FURTHER READING

Criticism

Anderson, Roger B. "Raskolnikov and the Myth Experience." *Slavic and East European Journal* 20, no. 1 (spring 1976): 1-17.

　　Examines themes of rebellion and individuality in *Crime and Punishment.*

Bethea, David M. "Structure versus Symmetry in *Crime and Punishment."* In *Fearful Symmetry: Doubles and Doubling in Literature and Film,* edited by Eugene J. Cook, pp. 41-64. Tallahassee: University Press of Florida, 1981.

　　Discusses the ways in which the first half of *Crime and Punishment* serves as a mirror of the second half.

Busch, R. L. "*Crime and Punishment.*" In *Humor in the Major Novels of F. M. Dostoevsky,* pp. 21-38. Columbus, Ohio: Slavica Publishers, 1987.

　　Examines aspects of irony in *Crime and Punishment.* Busch asserts that Dostoevsky achieves a subtle comic effect through his juxtapositions of contrasting images.

Davydov, Sergei. "Dostoevsky and Nabokov: The Morality of Structure in *Crime and Punishment* and *Despair.*" *Dostoevsky Studies* 3 (1982): 157-70.

　　Compares *Crime and Punishment* with Vladimir Nabokov's 1934 novel *Otchayaniye (Despair).*

Fanger, Donald. *Dostoevsky and Romantic Realism: A Study of Dostoevsky in Relation to Balzac, Dickens, and Gogol.* Cambridge: Harvard University Press, 1965, 307 p.

　　Compares Dostoevsky's attitudes toward myth and literary realism with those of other significant nineteenth-century novelists.

Frank, Joseph. *Dostoevsky: The Miraculous Years, 1865-1871.* Princeton: Princeton University Press, 1995, 523 p.

　　Includes a close reading of *Crime and Punishment,* as well as an evaluation of the novel's sources.

Gibian, George. "Traditional Symbolism in *Crime and Punishment.*" *PMLA* 70, no. 5 (December 1955): 979-96.

　　Analyzes *Crime and Punishment*'s powerful anti-rationalist stance.

Hackel, Sergei. "Raskolnikov through the Looking-Glass: Dostoevsky and Camus's *L'Etranger.*" *Contemporary Literature* 9, no. 2 (spring 1968): 189-209.

Examines the impact of Dostoevsky's *Crime and Punishment* on Albert Camus's existential 1942 novel.

Holquist, Michael. *Dostoevsky and the Novel*. Princeton: Princeton University Press, 1977, 202 p.

Includes an analysis of the link between biography and narrative structure in *Crime and Punishment*.

Horsman, Dorothea. "*Crime and Punishment*: A Study in Technique." *New Zealand Slavonic Journal* 6 (summer 1970): 34-52.

Explores issues of style and structure in *Crime and Punishment*.

Johnson, Leslie A. *The Experience of Time in* Crime and Punishment. Columbus, Ohio: Slavica Publishers, 1984, 146 p.

Examines Dostoevsky's subjective attitude toward the nature of time in *Crime and Punishment*.

Jones, John. "*Crime and Punishment*: Theory and Life." 1983. Reprinted in *Fyodor Dostoevsky's* Crime and Punishment, edited by Harold Bloom, pp. 103-33. New York: Chelsea House Publishers, 1988.

Analyzes *Crime and Punishment*'s central characters through a careful reading of Dostoevsky's notebooks from the period.

Kasatkina, Tat'iana. "Lazarus Resurrected: A Proposed Exegetical Reading of Dostoevsky's *Crime and Punishment*." *Russian Studies in Literature* 40, no. 4 (fall 2004): 6-37.

Explores the relationship between Raskolnikov and Lazarus of Bethany through an examination of *Crime and Punishment*'s central themes.

Kim, Jung A. "Number Symbolism in the Story of Sonya." *Canadian-American Slavic Studies* 37, no. 4 (2003): 377-94.

Analyzes the character of Sonya within the framework of Biblical numerology.

Kiremidjian, David. "*Crime and Punishment*: Matricide and the Woman Question." *American Imago* 33, no. 4 (winter 1976): 403-33.

Examines the possible psychological origins of Raskolnikov's crime.

Langen, Tim. "The Fields and Walls of the Imagination: A Topographical Sketch of Tolstoy and Dostoevsky." *Partial Answers* 1, no. 2 (June 2003): 45-60.

Contrasts attitudes toward the physical world in the fiction of Dostoevsky and Leo Tolstoy.

Leatherbarrow, W. J. "Raskolnikov and the Enigma of Personality." *Forum for Modern Language Studies* 9, no. 2 (April 1973): 153-65.

Analyzes the character of Porfirii Petrovich as a symbol of Raskolnikov's desire to be punished.

Leighton, Lauren G. "The Crime and Punishment of Monstrous Coincidence." *Mosaic* 12, no. 1 (fall 1978): 93-106.

Examines Dostoevsky's use of realism to depict fantastic events in *Crime and Punishment*.

Nuttall, A. D. "*Crime and Punishment*: Christianity and Existentialism." 1978. Reprinted in *Fyodor Dostoevsky's* Crime and Punishment, edited by Harold Bloom, pp. 47-63. New York: Chelsea House Publishers, 1988.

Examines the ethical issues that lie at the heart of *Crime and Punishment* and finds that Dostoevsky struggles throughout the novel to reconcile notions of individual freedom with the central tenets of Christianity.

Peace, Richard. *Dostoevsky: An Examination of the Major Novels*. Cambridge: Cambridge University Press, 1971, 347 p.

Includes a close analysis of *Crime and Punishment*.

Pevear, Richard. Foreword to *Crime and Punishment*, by Fyodor Dostoevsky, translated and annotated by Richard Pevear and Larissa Volokhonsky. 1992. Reprint, pp. vii-xvii. New York: Vintage Books, 1993.

Examines the various factors that helped shape *Crime and Punishment*, including circumstances in Dostoevsky's personal and professional life at the time of the book's composition, as well as the social unrest that dominated Russia during the 1860s.

Rosenshield, Gary. "First- versus Third-Person Narrative in *Crime and Punishment*." *Slavic and East European Journal* 17 (1973): 399-407.

Evaluates Dostoevsky's handling of point of view in *Crime and Punishment*.

Rowe, W. W. "Dostoevskian Patterned Antinomy and Its Function in *Crime and Punishment*." *Slavic and East European Journal* 16 (1972): 287-96.

Investigates the conflicting impulses and beliefs that motivate *Crime and Punishment*'s central characters.

Stelleman, Jenny. "Raskol'nikov and His Women." *Russian, Croatian and Serbian, Czech and Slovak, Polish Literature* 54, nos. 1-3 (1 July-1 October 2003): 279-96.

Explores Dostoevsky's depiction of female characters in *Crime and Punishment*.

Straus, Nina Pelikan. "'Why Did I Say "Women!"'? Raskolnikov Reimagined." *Diacritics* 23, no. 1 (spring 1993): 54-65.

Examines Dostoevsky's attitudes toward masculinity and femininity in *Crime and Punishment*.

Wasiolek, Edward. "On the Structure of *Crime and Punishment*." *PMLA* 74, no. 1 (March 1959): 131-36.

Discusses the ways in which the structure of *Crime and Punishment* helps shape the identities and behavior of its central characters.

Welch, Lois M. "Luzhin's Crime and the Advantages of Melodrama in Dostoevsky's *Crime and Punishment*." *Texas Studies in Literature and Language* 18, no. 1 (1976): 135-46.

Argues that Luzhin's criminal behavior exerts a powerful impact on the subsequent behavior of Raskolnikov.

Zdanys, Jonas. "Raskolnikov and Frankenstein: The Deadly Search for a Rational Paradise." *Cithara* 16, no. 1 (1976): 57-67.

Discusses the relationship between heroism, individuality, and morality in *Crime and Punishment* and Mary Shelley's *Frankenstein*.

Additional coverage of Dostoevsky's life and career is contained in the following sources published by Thomson Gale: *Authors and Artists for Young Adults,* **Vol. 40;** *DISCovering Authors;* *DISCovering Authors: British Edition;* *DISCovering Authors: Canadian Edition;* *DISCovering Authors Modules: Most-studied Authors* **and** *Novelists;* *DISCovering Authors 3.0;* *European Writers,* **Vol. 7;** *Exploring Novels;* *Literature Resource Center;* *Nineteenth-Century Literature Criticism,* **Vols. 2, 7, 21, 33, 43, 119;** *Novels for Students,* **Vols. 3, 8;** *Reference Guide to Short Fiction,* **Ed. 2;** *Reference Guide to World Literature,* **Eds. 2, 3;** *Short Story Criticism,* **Vols. 2, 33, 44;** *Short Stories for Students,* **Vol. 8;** *Twayne's World Authors;* **and** *World Literature Criticism.***

How to Use This Index

Calvino, Italo
1923-1985 .... CLC **5, 8, 11, 22, 33, 39,
73; SSC 3, 48**

list all author entries in the following Thomson Gale Literary Criticism series:

AAL = Asian American Literature
BG = The Beat Generation: A Gale Critical Companion
BLC = Black Literature Criticism
BLCS = Black Literature Criticism Supplement
CLC = Contemporary Literary Criticism
CLR = Children's Literature Review
CMLC = Classical and Medieval Literature Criticism
DC = Drama Criticism
FL = Feminism in Literature: A Gale Critical Companion
GL = Gothic Literature: A Gale Critical Companion
HLC = Hispanic Literature Criticism
HLCS = Hispanic Literature Criticism Supplement
HR = Harlem Renaissance: A Gale Critical Companion
LC = Literature Criticism from 1400 to 1800
NCLC = Nineteenth-Century Literature Criticism
NNAL = Native North American Literature
PC = Poetry Criticism
SSC = Short Story Criticism
TCLC = Twentieth-Century Literary Criticism
WLC = World Literature Criticism, 1500 to the Present
WLCS = World Literature Criticism Supplement

The cross-references

See also CA 85-88, 116; CANR 23, 61;
DAM NOV; DLB 196; EW 13; MTCW 1, 2;
RGSF 2; RGWL 2; SFW 4; SSFS 12

list all author entries in the following Thomson Gale biographical and literary sources:

AAYA = Authors & Artists for Young Adults
AFAW = African American Writers
AFW = African Writers
AITN = Authors in the News
AMW = American Writers
AMWR = American Writers Retrospective Supplement
AMWS = American Writers Supplement
ANW = American Nature Writers
AW = Ancient Writers
BEST = Bestsellers
BPFB = Beacham's Encyclopedia of Popular Fiction: Biography and Resources
BRW = British Writers
BRWS = British Writers Supplement
BW = Black Writers
BYA = Beacham's Guide to Literature for Young Adults
CA = Contemporary Authors
CAAS = Contemporary Authors Autobiography Series
CABS = Contemporary Authors Bibliographical Series
CAD = Contemporary American Dramatists
CANR = Contemporary Authors New Revision Series
CAP = Contemporary Authors Permanent Series
CBD = Contemporary British Dramatists
CCA = Contemporary Canadian Authors
CD = Contemporary Dramatists
CDALB = Concise Dictionary of American Literary Biography

CDALBS = *Concise Dictionary of American Literary Biography Supplement*
CDBLB = *Concise Dictionary of British Literary Biography*
CMW = *St. James Guide to Crime & Mystery Writers*
CN = *Contemporary Novelists*
CP = *Contemporary Poets*
CPW = *Contemporary Popular Writers*
CSW = *Contemporary Southern Writers*
CWD = *Contemporary Women Dramatists*
CWP = *Contemporary Women Poets*
CWRI = *St. James Guide to Children's Writers*
CWW = *Contemporary World Writers*
DA = *DISCovering Authors*
DA3 = *DISCovering Authors 3.0*
DAB = *DISCovering Authors: British Edition*
DAC = *DISCovering Authors: Canadian Edition*
DAM = *DISCovering Authors: Modules*
   DRAM: *Dramatists Module;* **MST:** *Most-studied Authors Module;*
   MULT: *Multicultural Authors Module;* **NOV:** *Novelists Module;*
   POET: *Poets Module;* **POP:** *Popular Fiction and Genre Authors Module*
DFS = *Drama for Students*
DLB = *Dictionary of Literary Biography*
DLBD = *Dictionary of Literary Biography Documentary Series*
DLBY = *Dictionary of Literary Biography Yearbook*
DNFS = *Literature of Developing Nations for Students*
EFS = *Epics for Students*
EXPN = *Exploring Novels*
EXPP = *Exploring Poetry*
EXPS = *Exploring Short Stories*
EW = *European Writers*
FANT = *St. James Guide to Fantasy Writers*
FW = *Feminist Writers*
GFL = *Guide to French Literature,* Beginnings to 1789, 1798 to the Present
GLL = *Gay and Lesbian Literature*
HGG = *St. James Guide to Horror, Ghost & Gothic Writers*
HW = *Hispanic Writers*
IDFW = *International Dictionary of Films and Filmmakers: Writers and Production Artists*
IDTP = *International Dictionary of Theatre: Playwrights*
LAIT = *Literature and Its Times*
LAW = *Latin American Writers*
JRDA = *Junior DISCovering Authors*
MAICYA = *Major Authors and Illustrators for Children and Young Adults*
MAICYAS = *Major Authors and Illustrators for Children and Young Adults Supplement*
MAWW = *Modern American Women Writers*
MJW = *Modern Japanese Writers*
MTCW = *Major 20th-Century Writers*
NCFS = *Nonfiction Classics for Students*
NFS = *Novels for Students*
PAB = *Poets: American and British*
PFS = *Poetry for Students*
RGAL = *Reference Guide to American Literature*
RGEL = *Reference Guide to English Literature*
RGSF = *Reference Guide to Short Fiction*
RGWL = *Reference Guide to World Literature*
RHW = *Twentieth-Century Romance and Historical Writers*
SAAS = *Something about the Author Autobiography Series*
SATA = *Something about the Author*
SFW = *St. James Guide to Science Fiction Writers*
SSFS = *Short Stories for Students*
TCWW = *Twentieth-Century Western Writers*
WLIT = *World Literature and Its Times*
WP = *World Poets*
YABC = *Yesterday's Authors of Books for Children*
YAW = *St. James Guide to Young Adult Writers*

Literary Criticism Series
Cumulative Author Index

Alexie, Sherman (Joseph, Jr.)
1966- .... **CLC 96, 154; NNAL; PC 53**
See also AAYA 28; BYA 15; CA 138;
CANR 65, 95, 133; CN 7; DA3; DAM
MULT; DLB 175, 206, 278; LATS 1:2;
MTCW 2; MTFW 2005; NFS 17; SSFS
18

al-Farabi 870(?)-950 .... **CMLC 58**
See also DLB 115

Alfau, Felipe 1902-1999 .... **CLC 66**
See also CA 137

Alfieri, Vittorio 1749-1803 .... **NCLC 101**
See also EW 4; RGWL 2, 3; WLIT 7

Alfonso X 1221-1284 .... **CMLC 78**

Alfred, Jean Gaston
See Ponge, Francis

Alger, Horatio, Jr. 1832-1899 .... **NCLC 8, 83**
See also CLR 87; DLB 42; LAIT 2; RGAL
4; SATA 16; TUS

Al-Ghazali, Muhammad ibn Muhammad
1058-1111 .... **CMLC 50**
See also DLB 115

Algren, Nelson 1909-1981 ..... **CLC 4, 10, 33;
SSC 33**
See also AMWS 9; BPFB 1; CA 13-16R;
103; CANR 20, 61; CDALB 1941-1968;
CN 1, 2; DLB 9; DLBY 1981, 1982,
2000; EWL 3; MAL 5; MTCW 1, 2;
MTFW 2005; RGAL 4; RGSF 2

**al-Hariri, al-Qasim ibn 'Ali Abu
Muhammad al-Basri**
1054-1122 .... **CMLC 63**
See also RGWL 3

Ali, Ahmed 1908-1998 .... **CLC 69**
See also CA 25-28R; CANR 15, 34; CN 1,
2, 3, 4, 5; EWL 3

Ali, Tariq 1943- .... **CLC 173**
See also CA 25-28R; CANR 10, 99

Alighieri, Dante
See Dante
See also WLIT 7

al-Kindi, Abu Yusuf Ya'qub ibn Ishaq c.
801-c. 873 .... **CMLC 80**

Allan, John B.
See Westlake, Donald E(dwin)

Allan, Sidney
See Hartmann, Sadakichi

Allan, Sydney
See Hartmann, Sadakichi

Allard, Janet .... **CLC 59**

Allen, Edward 1948- .... **CLC 59**

Allen, Fred 1894-1956 .... **TCLC 87**

Allen, Paula Gunn 1939- .... **CLC 84, 202;
NNAL**
See also AMWS 4; CA 112; 143; CANR
63, 130; CWP; DA3; DAM MULT; DLB
175; FW; MTCW 2; MTFW 2005; RGAL
4; TCWW 2

Allen, Roland
See Ayckbourn, Alan

Allen, Sarah A.
See Hopkins, Pauline Elizabeth

Allen, Sidney H.
See Hartmann, Sadakichi

Allen, Woody 1935- .... **CLC 16, 52, 195**
See also AAYA 10, 51; AMWS 15; CA 33-
36R; CANR 27, 38, 63, 128; DAM POP;
DLB 44; MTCW 1; SSFS 21

Allende, Isabel 1942- ... **CLC 39, 57, 97, 170;
HLC 1; SSC 65; WLCS**
See also AAYA 18; CA 125; 130; CANR
51, 74, 129; CDWLB 3; CLR 99; CWW
2; DA3; DAM MULT, NOV; DLB 145;
DNFS 1; EWL 3; FL 1:5; FW; HW 1, 2;
INT CA-130; LAIT 5; LAWS 1; LMFS 2;
MTCW 1, 2; MTFW 2005; NCFS 1; NFS
6, 18; RGSF 2; RGWL 3; SATA 163;
SSFS 11, 16; WLIT 1

Alleyn, Ellen
See Rossetti, Christina

Alleyne, Carla D. .... **CLC 65**

Allingham, Margery (Louise)
1904-1966 .... **CLC 19**
See also CA 5-8R; 25-28R; CANR 4, 58;
CMW 4; DLB 77; MSW; MTCW 1, 2

Allingham, William 1824-1889 ...... **NCLC 25**
See also DLB 35; RGEL 2

Allison, Dorothy E. 1949- .... **CLC 78, 153**
See also AAYA 53; CA 140; CANR 66, 107;
CN 7; CSW; DA3; FW; MTCW 2; MTFW
2005; NFS 11; RGAL 4

Alloula, Malek .... **CLC 65**

Allston, Washington 1779-1843 .... **NCLC 2**
See also DLB 1, 235

Almedingen, E. M. .... **CLC 12**
See Almedingen, Martha Edith von
See also SATA 3

Almedingen, Martha Edith von 1898-1971
See Almedingen, E. M.
See also CA 1-4R; CANR 1

Almodovar, Pedro 1949(?)- .... **CLC 114;
HLCS 1**
See also CA 133; CANR 72; HW 2

Almqvist, Carl Jonas Love
1793-1866 .... **NCLC 42**
See also RGWL 3

**al-Mutanabbi, Ahmad ibn al-Husayn Abu
al-Tayyib al-Jufi al-Kindi**
915-965 .... **CMLC 66**
See Mutanabbi, Al-
See also RGWL 3

Alonso, Damaso 1898-1990 .... **CLC 14**
See also CA 110; 131; 130; CANR 72; DLB
108; EWL 3; HW 1, 2

Alov
See Gogol, Nikolai (Vasilyevich)

al'Sadaawi, Nawal
See El Saadawi, Nawal
See also FW

al-Shaykh, Hanan 1945- .... **CLC 218**
See also CA 135; CANR 111; WLIT 6

Al Siddik
See Rolfe, Frederick (William Serafino Aus-
tin Lewis Mary)
See also GLL 1; RGEL 2

Alta 1942- .... **CLC 19**
See also CA 57-60

Alter, Robert B(ernard) 1935- .... **CLC 34**
See also CA 49-52; CANR 1, 47, 100

Alther, Lisa 1944- .... **CLC 7, 41**
See also BPFB 1; CA 65-68; CAAS 30;
CANR 12, 30, 51; CN 4, 5, 6, 7; CSW;
GLL 2; MTCW 1

Althusser, L.
See Althusser, Louis

Althusser, Louis 1918-1990 .... **CLC 106**
See also CA 131; 132; CANR 102; DLB
242

Altman, Robert 1925- .... **CLC 16, 116**
See also CA 73-76; CANR 43

Alurista .... **HLCS 1; PC 34**
See Urista (Heredia), Alberto (Baltazar)
See also CA 45-48R; DLB 82; LLW

Alvarez, A(lfred) 1929- .... **CLC 5, 13**
See also CA 1-4R; CANR 3, 33, 63, 101,
134; CN 3, 4, 5, 6; CP 1, 2, 3, 4, 5, 6, 7;
DLB 14, 40; MTCW 2005

Alvarez, Alejandro Rodriguez 1903-1965
See Casona, Alejandro
See also CA 131; 93-96; HW 1

Alvarez, Julia 1950- .... **CLC 93; HLCS 1**
See also AAYA 25; AMWS 7; CA 147;
CANR 69, 101, 133; DA3; DLB 282;
LATS 1:2; LLW; MTCW 2; MTFW 2005;
NFS 5, 9; SATA 129; WLIT 1

Alvaro, Corrado 1896-1956 .... **TCLC 60**
See also CA 163; DLB 264; EWL 3

Amado, Jorge 1912-2001 ... **CLC 13, 40, 106;
HLC 1**
See also CA 77-80; 201; CANR 35, 74, 135;
CWW 2; DAM MULT, NOV; DLB 113,
307; EWL 3; HW 2; LAW; LAWS 1;
MTCW 1, 2; MTFW 2005; RGWL 2, 3;
TWA; WLIT 1

Ambler, Eric 1909-1998 .... **CLC 4, 6, 9**
See also BRWS 4; CA 9-12R; 171; CANR
7, 38, 74; CMW 4; CN 1, 2, 3, 4, 5, 6;
DLB 77; MSW; MTCW 1, 2; TEA

Ambrose, Stephen E(dward)
1936-2002 .... **CLC 145**
See also AAYA 44; CA 1-4R; 209; CANR
3, 43, 57, 83, 105; MTFW 2005; NCFS 2;
SATA 40, 138

Amichai, Yehuda 1924-2000 .. **CLC 9, 22, 57,
116; PC 38**
See also CA 85-88; 189; CANR 46, 60, 99,
132; CWW 2; EWL 3; MTCW 1, 2;
MTFW 2005; WLIT 6

Amichai, Yehudah
See Amichai, Yehuda

Amiel, Henri Frederic 1821-1881 .... **NCLC 4**
See also DLB 217

Amis, Kingsley (William)
1922-1995 ...... **CLC 1, 2, 3, 5, 8, 13, 40,
44, 129**
See also AITN 2; BPFB 1; BRWS 2; CA
9-12R; 150; CANR 8, 28, 54; CDBLB
1945-1960; CN 1, 2, 3, 4, 5, 6; CP 1, 2,
3, 4; DA; DA3; DAB; DAC; DAM MST,
NOV; DLB 15, 27, 100, 139; DLBY 1996;
EWL 3; HGG; INT CANR-8; MTCW 1,
2; MTFW 2005; RGEL 2; RGSF 2; SFW
4

Amis, Martin (Louis) 1949- .... **CLC 4, 9, 38,
62, 101, 213**
See also BEST 90:3; BRWS 4; CA 65-68;
CANR 8, 27, 54, 73, 95, 132; CN 5, 6, 7;
DA3; DLB 14, 194; EWL 3; INT CANR-
27; MTCW 2; MTFW 2005

Ammianus Marcellinus c. 330-c.
395 .... **CMLC 60**
See also AW 2; DLB 211

Ammons, A(rchie) R(andolph)
1926-2001 ...... **CLC 2, 3, 5, 8, 9, 25, 57,
108; PC 16**
See also AITN 1; AMWS 7; CA 9-12R;
193; CANR 6, 36, 51, 73, 107; CP 1, 2,
3, 4, 5, 6, 7; CSW; DAM POET; DLB 5,
165; EWL 3; MAL 5; MTCW 1, 2; PFS
19; RGAL 4; TCLE 1:1

Amo, Tauraatua i
See Adams, Henry (Brooks)

Amory, Thomas 1691(?)-1788 .... **LC 48**
See also DLB 39

Anand, Mulk Raj 1905-2004 ...... **CLC 23, 93**
See also CA 65-68; 231; CANR 32, 64; CN
1, 2, 3, 4, 5, 6, 7; DAM NOV; EWL 3;
MTCW 1, 2; MTFW 2005; RGSF 2

Anatol
See Schnitzler, Arthur

Anaximander c. 611B.C.-c.
546B.C. .... **CMLC 22**

Anaya, Rudolfo A(lfonso) 1937- ...... **CLC 23,
148; HLC 1**
See also AAYA 20; BYA 13; CA 45-48;
CAAS 4; CANR 1, 32, 51, 124; CN 4, 5,
6, 7; DAM MULT, NOV; DLB 82, 206,
278; HW 1; LAIT 4; LLW; MAL 5;
MTCW 1, 2; MTFW 2005; NFS 12;
RGAL 4; RGSF 2; TCWW 2; WLIT 1

Andersen, Hans Christian
1805-1875 .... **NCLC 7, 79; SSC 6, 56;
WLC**
See also AAYA 57; CLR 6; DA; DA3;
DAB; DAC; DAM MST, POP; EW 6;
MAICYA 1, 2; RGSF 2; RGWL 2, 3;
SATA 100; TWA; WCH; YABC 1

Anderson, C. Farley
See Mencken, H(enry) L(ouis); Nathan, George Jean

Anderson, Jessica (Margaret) Queale 1916- .... **CLC 37**
See also CA 9-12R; CANR 4, 62; CN 4, 5, 6, 7

Anderson, Jon (Victor) 1940- .... **CLC 9**
See also CA 25-28R; CANR 20; CP 1, 3, 4; DAM POET

Anderson, Lindsay (Gordon) 1923-1994 .... **CLC 20**
See also CA 125; 128; 146; CANR 77

Anderson, Maxwell 1888-1959 .... **TCLC 2, 144**
See also CA 105; 152; DAM DRAM; DFS 16, 20; DLB 7, 228; MAL 5; MTCW 2; MTFW 2005; RGAL 4

Anderson, Poul (William) 1926-2001 .... **CLC 15**
See also AAYA 5, 34; BPFB 1; BYA 6, 8, 9; CA 1-4R, 181; 199; CAAE 181; CAAS 2; CANR 2, 15, 34, 64, 110; CLR 58; DLB 8; FANT; INT CANR-15; MTCW 1, 2; MTFW 2005; SATA 90; SATA-Brief 39; SATA-Essay 106; SCFW 1, 2; SFW 4; SUFW 1, 2

Anderson, Robert (Woodruff) 1917- .... **CLC 23**
See also AITN 1; CA 21-24R; CANR 32; CD 6; DAM DRAM; DLB 7; LAIT 5

Anderson, Roberta Joan
See Mitchell, Joni

Anderson, Sherwood 1876-1941 .. **SSC 1, 46; TCLC 1, 10, 24, 123; WLC**
See also AAYA 30; AMW; AMWC 2; BPFB 1; CA 104; 121; CANR 61; CDALB 1917-1929; DA; DA3; DAB; DAC; DAM MST, NOV; DLB 4, 9, 86; DLBD 1; EWL 3; EXPS; GLL 2; MAL 5; MTCW 1, 2; MTFW 2005; NFS 4; RGAL 4; RGSF 2; SSFS 4, 10, 11; TUS

Andier, Pierre
See Desnos, Robert

Andouard
See Giraudoux, Jean(-Hippolyte)

Andrade, Carlos Drummond de ..... **CLC 18**
See Drummond de Andrade, Carlos
See also EWL 3; RGWL 2, 3

Andrade, Mario de .... **TCLC 43**
See de Andrade, Mario
See also DLB 307; EWL 3; LAW; RGWL 2, 3; WLIT 1

Andreae, Johann V(alentin) 1586-1654 .... **LC 32**
See also DLB 164

Andreas Capellanus fl. c. 1185- .... **CMLC 45**
See also DLB 208

Andreas-Salome, Lou 1861-1937 ... **TCLC 56**
See also CA 178; DLB 66

Andreev, Leonid
See Andreyev, Leonid (Nikolaevich)
See also DLB 295; EWL 3

Andress, Lesley
See Sanders, Lawrence

Andrewes, Lancelot 1555-1626 .... **LC 5**
See also DLB 151, 172

Andrews, Cicily Fairfield
See West, Rebecca

Andrews, Elton V.
See Pohl, Frederik

Andreyev, Leonid (Nikolaevich) 1871-1919 .... **TCLC 3**
See Andreev, Leonid
See also CA 104; 185

Andric, Ivo 1892-1975 .... **CLC 8; SSC 36; TCLC 135**
See also CA 81-84; 57-60; CANR 43, 60; CDWLB 4; DLB 147; EW 11; EWL 3; MTCW 1; RGSF 2; RGWL 2, 3

Androvar
See Prado (Calvo), Pedro

Angela of Foligno 1248(?)-1309 .... **CMLC 76**

Angelique, Pierre
See Bataille, Georges

Angell, Roger 1920- .... **CLC 26**
See also CA 57-60; CANR 13, 44, 70, 144; DLB 171, 185

Angelou, Maya 1928- ... **BLC 1; CLC 12, 35, 64, 77, 155; PC 32; WLCS**
See also AAYA 7, 20; AMWS 4; BPFB 1; BW 2, 3; BYA 2; CA 65-68; CANR 19, 42, 65, 111, 133; CDALBS; CLR 53; CP 4, 5, 6, 7; CPW; CSW; CWP; DA; DA3; DAB; DAC; DAM MST, MULT, POET, POP; DLB 38; EWL 3; EXPN; EXPP; FL 1:5; LAIT 4; MAICYA 2; MAICYAS 1; MAL 5; MAWW; MTCW 1, 2; MTFW 2005; NCFS 2; NFS 2; PFS 2, 3; RGAL 4; SATA 49, 136; TCLE 1:1; WYA; YAW

Angouleme, Marguerite d'
See de Navarre, Marguerite

Anna Comnena 1083-1153 .... **CMLC 25**

Annensky, Innokentii Fedorovich
See Annensky, Innokenty (Fyodorovich)
See also DLB 295

Annensky, Innokenty (Fyodorovich) 1856-1909 .... **TCLC 14**
See also CA 110; 155; EWL 3

Annunzio, Gabriele d'
See D'Annunzio, Gabriele

Anodos
See Coleridge, Mary E(lizabeth)

Anon, Charles Robert
See Pessoa, Fernando (Antonio Nogueira)

Anouilh, Jean (Marie Lucien Pierre) 1910-1987 . **CLC 1, 3, 8, 13, 40, 50; DC 8, 21**
See also AAYA 67; CA 17-20R; 123; CANR 32; DAM DRAM; DFS 9, 10, 19; DLB 321; EW 13; EWL 3; GFL 1789 to the Present; MTCW 1, 2; MTFW 2005; RGWL 2, 3; TWA

Anselm of Canterbury 1033(?)-1109 .... **CMLC 67**
See also DLB 115

Anthony, Florence
See Ai

Anthony, John
See Ciardi, John (Anthony)

Anthony, Peter
See Shaffer, Anthony (Joshua); Shaffer, Peter (Levin)

Anthony, Piers 1934- .... **CLC 35**
See also AAYA 11, 48; BYA 7; CA 200; CAAE 200; CANR 28, 56, 73, 102, 133; CPW; DAM POP; DLB 8; FANT; MAICYA 2; MAICYAS 1; MTCW 1, 2; MTFW 2005; SAAS 22; SATA 84, 129; SATA-Essay 129; SFW 4; SUFW 1, 2; YAW

Anthony, Susan B(rownell) 1820-1906 .... **TCLC 84**
See also CA 211; FW

Antiphon c. 480B.C.-c. 411B.C. .... **CMLC 55**

Antoine, Marc
See Proust, (Valentin-Louis-George-Eugene) Marcel

Antoninus, Brother
See Everson, William (Oliver)
See also CP 1

Antonioni, Michelangelo 1912- .... **CLC 20, 144**
See also CA 73-76; CANR 45, 77

Antschel, Paul 1920-1970
See Celan, Paul
See also CA 85-88; CANR 33, 61; MTCW 1; PFS 21

Anwar, Chairil 1922-1949 .... **TCLC 22**
See Chairil Anwar
See also CA 121; 219; RGWL 3

Anzaldua, Gloria (Evanjelina) 1942-2004 .... **CLC 200; HLCS 1**
See also CA 175; 227; CSW; CWP; DLB 122; FW; LLW; RGAL 4; SATA-Obit 154

Apess, William 1798-1839(?) .... **NCLC 73; NNAL**
See also DAM MULT; DLB 175, 243

Apollinaire, Guillaume 1880-1918 .... **PC 7; TCLC 3, 8, 51**
See Kostrowitzki, Wilhelm Apollinaris de
See also CA 152; DAM POET; DLB 258, 321; EW 9; EWL 3; GFL 1789 to the Present; MTCW 2; RGWL 2, 3; TWA; WP

Apollonius of Rhodes
See Apollonius Rhodius
See also AW 1; RGWL 2, 3

Apollonius Rhodius c. 300B.C.-c. 220B.C. .... **CMLC 28**
See Apollonius of Rhodes
See also DLB 176

Appelfeld, Aharon 1932- ... **CLC 23, 47; SSC 42**
See also CA 112; 133; CANR 86; CWW 2; DLB 299; EWL 3; RGSF 2; WLIT 6

Apple, Max (Isaac) 1941- .... **CLC 9, 33; SSC 50**
See also CA 81-84; CANR 19, 54; DLB 130

Appleman, Philip (Dean) 1926- .... **CLC 51**
See also CA 13-16R; CAAS 18; CANR 6, 29, 56

Appleton, Lawrence
See Lovecraft, H(oward) P(hillips)

Apteryx
See Eliot, T(homas) S(tearns)

Apuleius, (Lucius Madaurensis) 125(?)-175(?) .... **CMLC 1**
See also AW 2; CDWLB 1; DLB 211; RGWL 2, 3; SUFW

Aquin, Hubert 1929-1977 .... **CLC 15**
See also CA 105; DLB 53; EWL 3

Aquinas, Thomas 1224(?)-1274 ..... **CMLC 33**
See also DLB 115; EW 1; TWA

Aragon, Louis 1897-1982 .... **CLC 3, 22; TCLC 123**
See also CA 69-72; 108; CANR 28, 71; DAM NOV, POET; DLB 72, 258; EW 11; EWL 3; GFL 1789 to the Present; GLL 2; LMFS 2; MTCW 1, 2; RGWL 2, 3

Arany, Janos 1817-1882 .... **NCLC 34**

Aranyos, Kakay 1847-1910
See Mikszath, Kalman

Aratus of Soli c. 315B.C.-c. 240B.C. .... **CMLC 64**
See also DLB 176

Arbuthnot, John 1667-1735 .... **LC 1**
See also DLB 101

Archer, Herbert Winslow
See Mencken, H(enry) L(ouis)

Archer, Jeffrey (Howard) 1940- .... **CLC 28**
See also AAYA 16; BEST 89:3; BPFB 1; CA 77-80; CANR 22, 52, 95, 136; CPW; DA3; DAM POP; INT CANR-22; MTFW 2005

Archer, Jules 1915- .... **CLC 12**
See also CA 9-12R; CANR 6, 69; SAAS 5; SATA 4, 85

Archer, Lee
See Ellison, Harlan (Jay)

Archilochus c. 7th cent. B.C.- .... **CMLC 44**
See also DLB 176

Arden, John 1930- .... **CLC 6, 13, 15**
  See also BRWS 2; CA 13-16R; CAAS 4;
  CANR 31, 65, 67, 124; CBD; CD 5, 6;
  DAM DRAM; DFS 9; DLB 13, 245;
  EWL 3; MTCW 1

Arenas, Reinaldo 1943-1990 .. **CLC 41; HLC
  1**
  See also CA 124; 128; 133; CANR 73, 106;
  DAM MULT; DLB 145; EWL 3; GLL 2;
  HW 1; LAW; LAWS 1; MTCW 2; MTFW
  2005; RGSF 2; RGWL 3; WLIT 1

Arendt, Hannah 1906-1975 .... **CLC 66, 98**
  See also CA 17-20R; 61-64; CANR 26, 60;
  DLB 242; MTCW 1, 2

Aretino, Pietro 1492-1556 .... **LC 12**
  See also RGWL 2, 3

Arghezi, Tudor .... **CLC 80**
  See Theodorescu, Ion N.
  See also CA 167; CDWLB 4; DLB 220;
  EWL 3

Arguedas, Jose Maria 1911-1969 .... **CLC 10,
  18; HLCS 1; TCLC 147**
  See also CA 89-92; CANR 73; DLB 113;
  EWL 3; HW 1; LAW; RGWL 2, 3; WLIT
  1

Argueta, Manlio 1936- .... **CLC 31**
  See also CA 131; CANR 73; CWW 2; DLB
  145; EWL 3; HW 1; RGWL 3

Arias, Ron(ald Francis) 1941- .... **HLC 1**
  See also CA 131; CANR 81, 136; DAM
  MULT; DLB 82; HW 1, 2; MTCW 2;
  MTFW 2005

Ariosto, Lodovico
  See Ariosto, Ludovico
  See also WLIT 7

Ariosto, Ludovico 1474-1533 ... **LC 6, 87; PC
  42**
  See Ariosto, Lodovico
  See also EW 2; RGWL 2, 3

Aristides
  See Epstein, Joseph

Aristophanes 450B.C.-385B.C. .... **CMLC 4,
  51; DC 2; WLCS**
  See also AW 1; CDWLB 1; DA; DA3;
  DAB; DAC; DAM DRAM, MST; DFS
  10; DLB 176; LMFS 1; RGWL 2, 3; TWA

Aristotle 384B.C.-322B.C. .... **CMLC 31;
  WLCS**
  See also AW 1; CDWLB 1; DA; DA3;
  DAB; DAC; DAM MST; DLB 176;
  RGWL 2, 3; TWA

Arlt, Roberto (Godofredo Christophersen)
  1900-1942 .... **HLC 1; TCLC 29**
  See also CA 123; 131; CANR 67; DAM
  MULT; DLB 305; EWL 3; HW 1, 2;
  IDTP; LAW

Armah, Ayi Kwei 1939- . **BLC 1; CLC 5, 33,
  136**
  See also AFW; BRWS 10; BW 1; CA 61-
  64; CANR 21, 64; CDWLB 3; CN 1, 2,
  3, 4, 5, 6, 7; DAM MULT, POET; DLB
  117; EWL 3; MTCW 1; WLIT 2

Armatrading, Joan 1950- .... **CLC 17**
  See also CA 114; 186

Armitage, Frank
  See Carpenter, John (Howard)

Armstrong, Jeannette (C.) 1948- .... **NNAL**
  See also CA 149; CCA 1; CN 6, 7; DAC;
  SATA 102

Arnette, Robert
  See Silverberg, Robert

**Arnim, Achim von (Ludwig Joachim von
  Arnim)** 1781-1831 .. **NCLC 5, 159; SSC
  29**
  See also DLB 90

Arnim, Bettina von 1785-1859 ...... **NCLC 38,
  123**
  See also DLB 90; RGWL 2, 3

Arnold, Matthew 1822-1888 ..... **NCLC 6, 29,
  89, 126; PC 5; WLC**
  See also BRW 5; CDBLB 1832-1890; DA;
  DAB; DAC; DAM MST, POET; DLB 32,
  57; EXPP; PAB; PFS 2; TEA; WP

Arnold, Thomas 1795-1842 .... **NCLC 18**
  See also DLB 55

Arnow, Harriette (Louisa) Simpson
  1908-1986 .... **CLC 2, 7, 18**
  See also BPFB 1; CA 9-12R; 118; CANR
  14; CN 2, 3, 4; DLB 6; FW; MTCW 1, 2;
  RHW; SATA 42; SATA-Obit 47

Arouet, Francois-Marie
  See Voltaire

Arp, Hans
  See Arp, Jean

Arp, Jean 1887-1966 .... **CLC 5; TCLC 115**
  See also CA 81-84; 25-28R; CANR 42, 77;
  EW 10

Arrabal
  See Arrabal, Fernando

Arrabal (Teran), Fernando
  See Arrabal, Fernando
  See also CWW 2

Arrabal, Fernando 1932- ... **CLC 2, 9, 18, 58**
  See Arrabal (Teran), Fernando
  See also CA 9-12R; CANR 15; DLB 321;
  EWL 3; LMFS 2

Arreola, Juan Jose 1918-2001 .... **CLC 147;
  HLC 1; SSC 38**
  See also CA 113; 131; 200; CANR 81;
  CWW 2; DAM MULT; DLB 113; DNFS
  2; EWL 3; HW 1, 2; LAW; RGSF 2

Arrian c. 89(?)-c. 155(?) .... **CMLC 43**
  See also DLB 176

Arrick, Fran .... **CLC 30**
  See Gaberman, Judie Angell
  See also BYA 6

Arrley, Richmond
  See Delany, Samuel R(ay), Jr.

Artaud, Antonin (Marie Joseph)
  1896-1948 .... **DC 14; TCLC 3, 36**
  See also CA 104; 149; DA3; DAM DRAM;
  DFS 22; DLB 258, 321; EW 11; EWL 3;
  GFL 1789 to the Present; MTCW 2;
  MTFW 2005; RGWL 2, 3

Arthur, Ruth M(abel) 1905-1979 ..... **CLC 12**
  See also CA 9-12R; 85-88; CANR 4; CWRI
  5; SATA 7, 26

Artsybashev, Mikhail (Petrovich)
  1878-1927 .... **TCLC 31**
  See also CA 170; DLB 295

Arundel, Honor (Morfydd)
  1919-1973 .... **CLC 17**
  See also CA 21-22; 41-44R; CAP 2; CLR
  35; CWRI 5; SATA 4; SATA-Obit 24

Arzner, Dorothy 1900-1979 .... **CLC 98**

Asch, Sholem 1880-1957 .... **TCLC 3**
  See also CA 105; EWL 3; GLL 2

Ascham, Roger 1516(?)-1568 .... **LC 101**
  See also DLB 236

Ash, Shalom
  See Asch, Sholem

Ashbery, John (Lawrence) 1927- .. **CLC 2, 3,
  4, 6, 9, 13, 15, 25, 41, 77, 125; PC 26**
  See Berry, Jonas
  See also AMWS 3; CA 5-8R; CANR 9, 37,
  66, 102, 132; CP 1, 2, 3, 4, 5, 6, 7; DA3;
  DAM POET; DLB 5, 165; DLBY 1981;
  EWL 3; INT CANR-9; MAL 5; MTCW
  1, 2; MTFW 2005; PAB; PFS 11; RGAL
  4; TCLE 1:1; WP

Ashdown, Clifford
  See Freeman, R(ichard) Austin

Ashe, Gordon
  See Creasey, John

Ashton-Warner, Sylvia (Constance)
  1908-1984 .... **CLC 19**
  See also CA 69-72; 112; CANR 29; CN 1,
  2, 3; MTCW 1, 2

Asimov, Isaac 1920-1992 ..... **CLC 1, 3, 9, 19,
  26, 76, 92**
  See also AAYA 13; BEST 90:2; BPFB 1;
  BYA 4, 6, 7, 9; CA 1-4R; 137; CANR 2,
  19, 36, 60, 125; CLR 12, 79; CMW 4;
  CN 1, 2, 3, 4, 5; CPW; DA3; DAM POP;
  DLB 8; DLBY 1992; INT CANR-19;
  JRDA; LAIT 5; LMFS 2; MAICYA 1, 2;
  MAL 5; MTCW 1, 2; MTFW 2005;
  RGAL 4; SATA 1, 26, 74; SCFW 1, 2;
  SFW 4; SSFS 17; TUS; YAW

Askew, Anne 1521(?)-1546 .... **LC 81**
  See also DLB 136

Assis, Joaquim Maria Machado de
  See Machado de Assis, Joaquim Maria

Astell, Mary 1666-1731 .... **LC 68**
  See also DLB 252; FW

Astley, Thea (Beatrice May)
  1925-2004 .... **CLC 41**
  See also CA 65-68; 229; CANR 11, 43, 78;
  CN 1, 2, 3, 4, 5, 6, 7; DLB 289; EWL 3

Astley, William 1855-1911
  See Warung, Price

Aston, James
  See White, T(erence) H(anbury)

Asturias, Miguel Angel 1899-1974 .... **CLC 3,
  8, 13; HLC 1**
  See also CA 25-28; 49-52; CANR 32; CAP
  2; CDWLB 3; DA3; DAM MULT, NOV;
  DLB 113, 290; EWL 3; HW 1; LAW;
  LMFS 2; MTCW 1, 2; RGWL 2, 3; WLIT
  1

Atares, Carlos Saura
  See Saura (Atares), Carlos

Athanasius c. 295-c. 373 .... **CMLC 48**

Atheling, William
  See Pound, Ezra (Weston Loomis)

Atheling, William, Jr.
  See Blish, James (Benjamin)

Atherton, Gertrude (Franklin Horn)
  1857-1948 .... **TCLC 2**
  See also CA 104; 155; DLB 9, 78, 186;
  HGG; RGAL 4; SUFW 1; TCWW 1, 2

Atherton, Lucius
  See Masters, Edgar Lee

Atkins, Jack
  See Harris, Mark

Atkinson, Kate 1951- .... **CLC 99**
  See also CA 166; CANR 101; DLB 267

Attaway, William (Alexander)
  1911-1986 .... **BLC 1; CLC 92**
  See also BW 2, 3; CA 143; CANR 82;
  DAM MULT; DLB 76; MAL 5

Atticus
  See Fleming, Ian (Lancaster); Wilson,
  (Thomas) Woodrow

Atwood, Margaret (Eleanor) 1939- ... **CLC 2,
  3, 4, 8, 13, 15, 25, 44, 84, 135; PC 8;
  SSC 2, 46; WLC**
  See also AAYA 12, 47; AMWS 13; BEST
  89:2; BPFB 1; CA 49-52; CANR 3, 24,
  33, 59, 95, 133; CN 2, 3, 4, 5, 6, 7; CP 1,
  2, 3, 4, 5, 6, 7; CPW; CWP; DA; DA3;
  DAB; DAC; DAM MST, NOV, POET;
  DLB 53, 251; EWL 3; EXPN; FL 1:5;
  FW; GL 2; INT CANR-24; LAIT 5;
  MTCW 1, 2; MTFW 2005; NFS 4, 12,
  13, 14, 19; PFS 7; RGSF 2; SATA 50;
  SSFS 3, 13; TCLE 1:1; TWA; WWE 1;
  YAW

Aubigny, Pierre d'
  See Mencken, H(enry) L(ouis)

Aubin, Penelope 1685-1731(?) .... **LC 9**
  See also DLB 39

Barth, John (Simmons) 1930- ... CLC 1, 2, 3, 5, 7, 9, 10, 14, 27, 51, 89, 214; SSC 10, 89

See also AITN 1, 2; AMW; BPFB 1; CA 1-4R; CABS 1; CANR 5, 23, 49, 64, 113; CN 1, 2, 3, 4, 5, 6, 7; DAM NOV; DLB 2, 227; EWL 3; FANT; MAL 5; MTCW 1; RGAL 4; RGSF 2; RHW; SSFS 6; TUS

Barthelme, Donald 1931-1989 ... CLC 1, 2, 3, 5, 6, 8, 13, 23, 46, 59, 115; SSC 2, 55

See also AMWS 4; BPFB 1; CA 21-24R; 129; CANR 20, 58; CN 1, 2, 3, 4; DA3; DAM NOV; DLB 2, 234; DLBY 1980, 1989; EWL 3; FANT; LMFS 2; MAL 5; MTCW 1, 2; MTFW 2005; RGAL 4; RGSF 2; SATA 7; SATA-Obit 62; SSFS 17

Barthelme, Frederick 1943- ...... CLC 36, 117

See also AMWS 11; CA 114; 122; CANR 77; CN 4, 5, 6, 7; CSW; DLB 244; DLBY 1985; EWL 3; INT CA-122

Barthes, Roland (Gerard) 1915-1980 .... CLC 24, 83; TCLC 135

See also CA 130; 97-100; CANR 66; DLB 296; EW 13; EWL 3; GFL 1789 to the Present; MTCW 1, 2; TWA

Bartram, William 1739-1823 .... NCLC 145

See also ANW; DLB 37

Barzun, Jacques (Martin) 1907- ..... CLC 51, 145

See also CA 61-64; CANR 22, 95

Bashevis, Isaac

See Singer, Isaac Bashevis

Bashkirtseff, Marie 1859-1884 .... NCLC 27

Basho, Matsuo

See Matsuo Basho

See also RGWL 2, 3; WP

Basil of Caesaria c. 330-379 .... CMLC 35

Basket, Raney

See Edgerton, Clyde (Carlyle)

Bass, Kingsley B., Jr.

See Bullins, Ed

Bass, Rick 1958- .... CLC 79, 143; SSC 60

See also ANW; CA 126; CANR 53, 93, 145; CSW; DLB 212, 275

Bassani, Giorgio 1916-2000 .... CLC 9

See also CA 65-68; 190; CANR 33; CWW 2; DLB 128, 177, 299; EWL 3; MTCW 1; RGWL 2, 3

Bastian, Ann .... CLC 70

Bastos, Augusto (Antonio) Roa

See Roa Bastos, Augusto (Jose Antonio)

Bataille, Georges 1897-1962 .... CLC 29; TCLC 155

See also CA 101; 89-92; EWL 3

Bates, H(erbert) E(rnest) 1905-1974 .... CLC 46; SSC 10

See also CA 93-96; 45-48; CANR 34; CN 1; DA3; DAB; DAM POP; DLB 162, 191; EWL 3; EXPS; MTCW 1, 2; RGSF 2; SSFS 7

Bauchart

See Camus, Albert

Baudelaire, Charles 1821-1867 . NCLC 6, 29, 55, 155; PC 1; SSC 18; WLC

See also DA; DA3; DAB; DAC; DAM MST, POET; DLB 217; EW 7; GFL 1789 to the Present; LMFS 2; PFS 21; RGWL 2, 3; TWA

Baudouin, Marcel

See Peguy, Charles (Pierre)

Baudouin, Pierre

See Peguy, Charles (Pierre)

Baudrillard, Jean 1929- .... CLC 60

See also DLB 296

Baum, L(yman) Frank 1856-1919 .. TCLC 7, 132

See also AAYA 46; BYA 16; CA 108; 133; CLR 15; CWRI 5; DLB 22; FANT; JRDA; MAICYA 1, 2; MTCW 1, 2; NFS 13; RGAL 4; SATA 18, 100; WCH

Baum, Louis F.

See Baum, L(yman) Frank

Baumbach, Jonathan 1933- .... CLC 6, 23

See also CA 13-16R; CAAS 5; CANR 12, 66, 140; CN 3, 4, 5, 6, 7; DLBY 1980; INT CANR-12; MTCW 1

Bausch, Richard (Carl) 1945- .... CLC 51

See also AMWS 7; CA 101; CAAS 14; CANR 43, 61, 87; CN 7; CSW; DLB 130; MAL 5

Baxter, Charles (Morley) 1947- . CLC 45, 78

See also CA 57-60; CANR 40, 64, 104, 133; CPW; DAM POP; DLB 130; MAL 5; MTCW 2; MTFW 2005; TCLE 1:1

Baxter, George Owen

See Faust, Frederick (Schiller)

Baxter, James K(eir) 1926-1972 .... CLC 14

See also CA 77-80; CP 1; EWL 3

Baxter, John

See Hunt, E(verette) Howard, (Jr.)

Bayer, Sylvia

See Glassco, John

Baynton, Barbara 1857-1929 .... TCLC 57

See also DLB 230; RGSF 2

Beagle, Peter S(oyer) 1939- .... CLC 7, 104

See also AAYA 47; BPFB 1; BYA 9, 10, 16; CA 9-12R; CANR 4, 51, 73, 110; DA3; DLBY 1980; FANT; INT CANR-4; MTCW 2; MTFW 2005; SATA 60, 130; SUFW 1, 2; YAW

Bean, Normal

See Burroughs, Edgar Rice

Beard, Charles A(ustin) 1874-1948 .... TCLC 15

See also CA 115; 189; DLB 17; SATA 18

Beardsley, Aubrey 1872-1898 .... NCLC 6

Beattie, Ann 1947- ..... CLC 8, 13, 18, 40, 63, 146; SSC 11

See also AMWS 5; BEST 90:2; BPFB 1; CA 81-84; CANR 53, 73, 128; CN 4, 5, 6, 7; CPW; DA3; DAM NOV, POP; DLB 218, 278; DLBY 1982; EWL 3; MAL 5; MTCW 1, 2; MTFW 2005; RGAL 4; RGSF 2; SSFS 9; TUS

Beattie, James 1735-1803 .... NCLC 25

See also DLB 109

Beauchamp, Kathleen Mansfield 1888-1923

See Mansfield, Katherine

See also CA 104; 134; DA; DA3; DAC; DAM MST; MTCW 2; TEA

Beaumarchais, Pierre-Augustin Caron de 1732-1799 .... DC 4; LC 61

See also DAM DRAM; DFS 14, 16; DLB 313; EW 4; GFL Beginnings to 1789; RGWL 2, 3

Beaumont, Francis 1584(?)-1616 .. DC 6; LC 33

See also BRW 2; CDBLB Before 1660; DLB 58; TEA

Beauvoir, Simone (Lucie Ernestine Marie Bertrand) de 1908-1986 .... CLC 1, 2, 4, 8, 14, 31, 44, 50, 71, 124; SSC 35; WLC

See also BPFB 1; CA 9-12R; 118; CANR 28, 61; DA; DA3; DAB; DAC; DAM MST, NOV; DLB 72; DLBY 1986; EW 12; EWL 3; FL 1:5; FW; GFL 1789 to the Present; LMFS 2; MTCW 1, 2; MTFW 2005; RGSF 2; RGWL 2, 3; TWA

Becker, Carl (Lotus) 1873-1945 ..... TCLC 63

See also CA 157; DLB 17

Becker, Jurek 1937-1997 .... CLC 7, 19

See also CA 85-88; 157; CANR 60, 117; CWW 2; DLB 75, 299; EWL 3

Becker, Walter 1950- .... CLC 26

Beckett, Samuel (Barclay) 1906-1989 .. CLC 1, 2, 3, 4, 6, 9, 10, 11, 14, 18, 29, 57, 59, 83; DC 22; SSC 16, 74; TCLC 145; WLC

See also BRWC 2; BRWR 1; BRWS 1; CA 5-8R; 130; CANR 33, 61; CBD; CDBLB 1945-1960; CN 1, 2, 3, 4; CP 1, 2, 3, 4; DA; DA3; DAB; DAC; DAM DRAM, MST, NOV; DFS 2, 7, 18; DLB 13, 15, 233, 319, 321; DLBY 1990; EWL 3; GFL 1789 to the Present; LATS 1:2; LMFS 1; MTCW 1, 2; MTFW 2005; RGSF 2; RGWL 2, 3; SSFS 15; TEA; WLIT 4

Beckford, William 1760-1844 .... NCLC 16

See also BRW 3; DLB 39, 213; GL 2; HGG; LMFS 1; SUFW

Beckham, Barry (Earl) 1944- .... BLC 1

See also BW 1; CA 29-32R; CANR 26, 62; CN 1, 2, 3, 4, 5, 6; DAM MULT; DLB 33

Beckman, Gunnel 1910- .... CLC 26

See also CA 33-36R; CANR 15, 114; CLR 25; MAICYA 1, 2; SAAS 9; SATA 6

Becque, Henri 1837-1899 .... DC 21; NCLC 3

See also DLB 192; GFL 1789 to the Present

Becquer, Gustavo Adolfo 1836-1870 .... HLCS 1; NCLC 106

See also DAM MULT

Beddoes, Thomas Lovell 1803-1849 .. DC 15; NCLC 3, 154

See also BRWS 11; DLB 96

Bede c. 673-735 .... CMLC 20

See also DLB 146; TEA

Bedford, Denton R. 1907-(?) .... NNAL

Bedford, Donald F.

See Fearing, Kenneth (Flexner)

Beecher, Catharine Esther 1800-1878 .... NCLC 30

See also DLB 1, 243

Beecher, John 1904-1980 .... CLC 6

See also AITN 1; CA 5-8R; 105; CANR 8; CP 1, 2, 3

Beer, Johann 1655-1700 .... LC 5

See also DLB 168

Beer, Patricia 1924- .... CLC 58

See also CA 61-64; 183; CANR 13, 46; CP 1, 2, 3, 4; CWP; DLB 40; FW

Beerbohm, Max

See Beerbohm, (Henry) Max(imilian)

Beerbohm, (Henry) Max(imilian) 1872-1956 .... TCLC 1, 24

See also BRWS 2; CA 104; 154; CANR 79; DLB 34, 100; FANT; MTCW 2

Beer-Hofmann, Richard 1866-1945 .... TCLC 60

See also CA 160; DLB 81

Beg, Shemus

See Stephens, James

Begiebing, Robert J(ohn) 1946- .... CLC 70

See also CA 122; CANR 40, 88

Begley, Louis 1933- .... CLC 197

See also CA 140; CANR 98; DLB 299; TCLE 1:1

Behan, Brendan (Francis) 1923-1964 .... CLC 1, 8, 11, 15, 79

See also BRWS 2; CA 73-76; CANR 33, 121; CBD; CDBLB 1945-1960; DAM DRAM; DFS 7; DLB 13, 233; EWL 3; MTCW 1, 2

Behn, Aphra 1640(?)-1689 .. DC 4; LC 1, 30, 42; PC 13; WLC

See also BRWS 3; DA; DA3; DAB; DAC; DAM DRAM, MST, NOV, POET; DFS 16; DLB 39, 80, 131; FW; TEA; WLIT 3

Bishop, John Peale 1892-1944 ..... **TCLC 103**
See also CA 107; 155; DLB 4, 9, 45; MAL 5; RGAL 4

Bissett, Bill 1939- .... **CLC 18; PC 14**
See also CA 69-72; CAAS 19; CANR 15; CCA 1; CP 1, 2, 3, 4, 5, 6, 7; DLB 53; MTCW 1

Bissoondath, Neil (Devindra)
1955- .... **CLC 120**
See also CA 136; CANR 123; CN 6, 7; DAC

Bitov, Andrei (Georgievich) 1937- ... **CLC 57**
See also CA 142; DLB 302

Biyidi, Alexandre 1932-
See Beti, Mongo
See also BW 1, 3; CA 114; 124; CANR 81; DA3; MTCW 1, 2

Bjarme, Brynjolf
See Ibsen, Henrik (Johan)

Bjoernson, Bjoernstjerne (Martinius)
1832-1910 .... **TCLC 7, 37**
See also CA 104

Black, Robert
See Holdstock, Robert P.

Blackburn, Paul 1926-1971 .... **CLC 9, 43**
See also BG 1:2; CA 81-84; 33-36R; CANR 34; CP 1; DLB 16; DLBY 1981

Black Elk 1863-1950 .... **NNAL; TCLC 33**
See also CA 144; DAM MULT; MTCW 2; MTFW 2005; WP

Black Hawk 1767-1838 .... **NNAL**

Black Hobart
See Sanders, (James) Ed(ward)

Blacklin, Malcolm
See Chambers, Aidan

Blackmore, R(ichard) D(oddridge)
1825-1900 .... **TCLC 27**
See also CA 120; DLB 18; RGEL 2

Blackmur, R(ichard) P(almer)
1904-1965 .... **CLC 2, 24**
See also AMWS 2; CA 11-12; 25-28R; CANR 71; CAP 1; DLB 63; EWL 3; MAL 5

Black Tarantula
See Acker, Kathy

Blackwood, Algernon (Henry)
1869-1951 .... **TCLC 5**
See also CA 105; 150; DLB 153, 156, 178; HGG; SUFW 1

Blackwood, Caroline (Maureen)
1931-1996 .... **CLC 6, 9, 100**
See also BRWS 9; CA 85-88; 151; CANR 32, 61, 65; CN 3, 4, 5, 6; DLB 14, 207; HGG; MTCW 1

Blade, Alexander
See Hamilton, Edmond; Silverberg, Robert

Blaga, Lucian 1895-1961 .... **CLC 75**
See also CA 157; DLB 220; EWL 3

Blair, Eric (Arthur) 1903-1950 .... **TCLC 123**
See Orwell, George
See also CA 104; 132; DA; DA3; DAB; DAC; DAM MST, NOV; MTCW 1, 2; MTFW 2005; SATA 29

Blair, Hugh 1718-1800 .... **NCLC 75**

Blais, Marie-Claire 1939- .... **CLC 2, 4, 6, 13, 22**
See also CA 21-24R; CAAS 4; CANR 38, 75, 93; CWW 2; DAC; DAM MST; DLB 53; EWL 3; FW; MTCW 1, 2; MTFW 2005; TWA

Blaise, Clark 1940- .... **CLC 29**
See also AITN 2; CA 53-56, 231; CAAE 231; CAAS 3; CANR 5, 66, 106; CN 4, 5, 6, 7; DLB 53; RGSF 2

Blake, Fairley
See De Voto, Bernard (Augustine)

Blake, Nicholas
See Day Lewis, C(ecil)
See also DLB 77; MSW

Blake, Sterling
See Benford, Gregory (Albert)

Blake, William 1757-1827 . **NCLC 13, 37, 57, 127; PC 12, 63; WLC**
See also AAYA 47; BRW 3; BRWR 1; CD-BLB 1789-1832; CLR 52; DA; DA3; DAB; DAC; DAM MST, POET; DLB 93, 163; EXPP; LATS 1:1; LMFS 1; MAI-CYA 1, 2; PAB; PFS 2, 12; SATA 30; TEA; WCH; WLIT 3; WP

Blanchot, Maurice 1907-2003 .... **CLC 135**
See also CA 117; 144; 213; CANR 138; DLB 72, 296; EWL 3

Blasco Ibanez, Vicente 1867-1928 . **TCLC 12**
See Ibanez, Vicente Blasco
See also BPFB 1; CA 110; 131; CANR 81; DA3; DAM NOV; EW 8; EWL 3; HW 1, 2; MTCW 1

Blatty, William Peter 1928- .... **CLC 2**
See also CA 5-8R; CANR 9, 124; DAM POP; HGG

Bleeck, Oliver
See Thomas, Ross (Elmore)

Blessing, Lee (Knowlton) 1949- .... **CLC 54**
See also CA 236; CAD; CD 5, 6

Blight, Rose
See Greer, Germaine

Blish, James (Benjamin) 1921-1975 . **CLC 14**
See also BPFB 1; CA 1-4R; 57-60; CANR 3; CN 2; DLB 8; MTCW 1; SATA 66; SCFW 1, 2; SFW 4

Bliss, Frederick
See Card, Orson Scott

Bliss, Reginald
See Wells, H(erbert) G(eorge)

Blixen, Karen (Christentze Dinesen)
1885-1962
See Dinesen, Isak
See also CA 25-28; CANR 22, 50; CAP 2; DA3; DLB 214; LMFS 1; MTCW 1, 2; SATA 44; SSFS 20

Bloch, Robert (Albert) 1917-1994 .... **CLC 33**
See also AAYA 29; CA 5-8R; 179; 146; CAAE 179; CAAS 20; CANR 5, 78; DA3; DLB 44; HGG; INT CANR-5; MTCW 2; SATA 12; SATA-Obit 82; SFW 4; SUFW 1, 2

Blok, Alexander (Alexandrovich)
1880-1921 .... **PC 21; TCLC 5**
See also CA 104; 183; DLB 295; EW 9; EWL 3; LMFS 2; RGWL 2, 3

Blom, Jan
See Breytenbach, Breyten

Bloom, Harold 1930- .... **CLC 24, 103**
See also CA 13-16R; CANR 39, 75, 92, 133; DLB 67; EWL 3; MTCW 2; MTFW 2005; RGAL 4

Bloomfield, Aurelius
See Bourne, Randolph S(illiman)

Bloomfield, Robert 1766-1823 ..... **NCLC 145**
See also DLB 93

Blount, Roy (Alton), Jr. 1941- .... **CLC 38**
See also CA 53-56; CANR 10, 28, 61, 125; CSW; INT CANR-28; MTCW 1, 2; MTFW 2005

Blowsnake, Sam 1875-(?) .... **NNAL**

Bloy, Leon 1846-1917 .... **TCLC 22**
See also CA 121; 183; DLB 123; GFL 1789 to the Present

Blue Cloud, Peter (Aroniawenrate)
1933- .... **NNAL**
See also CA 117; CANR 40; DAM MULT

Bluggage, Oranthy
See Alcott, Louisa May

Blume, Judy (Sussman) 1938- .... **CLC 12, 30**
See also AAYA 3, 26; BYA 1, 8, 12; CA 29-32R; CANR 13, 37, 66, 124; CLR 2, 15, 69; CPW; DA3; DAM NOV, POP; DLB 52; JRDA; MAICYA 1, 2; MAICYAS 1; MTCW 1, 2; MTFW 2005; SATA 2, 31, 79, 142; WYA; YAW

Blunden, Edmund (Charles)
1896-1974 .... **CLC 2, 56; PC 66**
See also BRW 6; BRWS 11; CA 17-18; 45-48; CANR 54; CAP 2; DLB 20, 100, 155; MTCW 1; PAB

Bly, Robert (Elwood) 1926- .... **CLC 1, 2, 5, 10, 15, 38, 128; PC 39**
See also AMWS 4; CA 5-8R; CANR 41, 73, 125; CP 1, 2, 3, 4, 5, 6, 7; DA3; DAM POET; DLB 5; EWL 3; MAL 5; MTCW 1, 2; MTFW 2005; PFS 6, 17; RGAL 4

Boas, Franz 1858-1942 .... **TCLC 56**
See also CA 115; 181

Bobette
See Simenon, Georges (Jacques Christian)

Boccaccio, Giovanni 1313-1375 ... **CMLC 13, 57; SSC 10, 87**
See also EW 2; RGSF 2; RGWL 2, 3; TWA; WLIT 7

Bochco, Steven 1943- .... **CLC 35**
See also AAYA 11; CA 124; 138

Bode, Sigmund
See O'Doherty, Brian

Bodel, Jean 1167(?)-1210 .... **CMLC 28**

Bodenheim, Maxwell 1892-1954 .... **TCLC 44**
See also CA 110; 187; DLB 9, 45; MAL 5; RGAL 4

Bodenheimer, Maxwell
See Bodenheim, Maxwell

Bodker, Cecil 1927-
See Bodker, Cecil

Bodker, Cecil 1927- .... **CLC 21**
See also CA 73-76; CANR 13, 44, 111; CLR 23; MAICYA 1, 2; SATA 14, 133

Boell, Heinrich (Theodor)
1917-1985 ..... **CLC 2, 3, 6, 9, 11, 15, 27, 32, 72; SSC 23; WLC**
See Boll, Heinrich (Theodor)
See also CA 21-24R; 116; CANR 24; DA; DA3; DAB; DAC; DAM MST, NOV; DLB 69; DLBY 1985; MTCW 1, 2; MTFW 2005; SSFS 20; TWA

Boerne, Alfred
See Doeblin, Alfred

Boethius c. 480-c. 524 .... **CMLC 15**
See also DLB 115; RGWL 2, 3

Boff, Leonardo (Genezio Darci)
1938- .... **CLC 70; HLC 1**
See also CA 150; DAM MULT; HW 2

Bogan, Louise 1897-1970 .... **CLC 4, 39, 46, 93; PC 12**
See also AMWS 3; CA 73-76; 25-28R; CANR 33, 82; CP 1; DAM POET; DLB 45, 169; EWL 3; MAL 5; MAWW; MTCW 1, 2; PFS 21; RGAL 4

Bogarde, Dirk
See Van Den Bogarde, Derek Jules Gaspard Ulric Niven
See also DLB 14

Bogosian, Eric 1953- .... **CLC 45, 141**
See also CA 138; CAD; CANR 102; CD 5, 6

Bograd, Larry 1953- .... **CLC 35**
See also CA 93-96; CANR 57; SAAS 21; SATA 33, 89; WYA

Boiardo, Matteo Maria 1441-1494 .... **LC 6**

Boileau-Despreaux, Nicolas 1636-1711 . **LC 3**
See also DLB 268; EW 3; GFL Beginnings to 1789; RGWL 2, 3

Boissard, Maurice
See Leautaud, Paul

Bojer, Johan 1872-1959 .... **TCLC 64**
See also CA 189; EWL 3

Bok, Edward W(illiam)
1863-1930 .... **TCLC 101**
See also CA 217; DLB 91; DLBD 16

Boker, George Henry 1823-1890 . **NCLC 125**
See also RGAL 4

Boland, Eavan (Aisling) 1944- .. **CLC 40, 67, 113; PC 58**
See also BRWS 5; CA 143, 207; CAAE 207; CANR 61; CP 1, 7; CWP; DAM POET; DLB 40; FW; MTCW 2; MTFW 2005; PFS 12, 22

Boll, Heinrich (Theodor)
See Boell, Heinrich (Theodor)
See also BPFB 1; CDWLB 2; EW 13; EWL 3; RGSF 2; RGWL 2, 3

Bolt, Lee
See Faust, Frederick (Schiller)

Bolt, Robert (Oxton) 1924-1995 ...... **CLC 14; TCLC 175**
See also CA 17-20R; 147; CANR 35, 67; CBD; DAM DRAM; DFS 2; DLB 13, 233; EWL 3; LAIT 1; MTCW 1

Bombal, Maria Luisa 1910-1980 .... **HLCS 1; SSC 37**
See also CA 127; CANR 72; EWL 3; HW 1; LAW; RGSF 2

Bombet, Louis-Alexandre-Cesar
See Stendhal

Bomkauf
See Kaufman, Bob (Garnell)

Bonaventura .... **NCLC 35**
See also DLB 90

Bonaventure 1217(?)-1274 .... **CMLC 79**
See also DLB 115; LMFS 1

Bond, Edward 1934- .... **CLC 4, 6, 13, 23**
See also AAYA 50; BRWS 1; CA 25-28R; CANR 38, 67, 106; CBD; CD 5, 6; DAM DRAM; DFS 3, 8; DLB 13, 310; EWL 3; MTCW 1

Bonham, Frank 1914-1989 .... **CLC 12**
See also AAYA 1; BYA 1, 3; CA 9-12R; CANR 4, 36; JRDA; MAICYA 1, 2; SAAS 3; SATA 1, 49; SATA-Obit 62; TCWW 1, 2; YAW

Bonnefoy, Yves 1923- . **CLC 9, 15, 58; PC 58**
See also CA 85-88; CANR 33, 75, 97, 136; CWW 2; DAM MST, POET; DLB 258; EWL 3; GFL 1789 to the Present; MTCW 1, 2; MTFW 2005

Bonner, Marita .... **HR 1:2**
See Occomy, Marita (Odette) Bonner

Bonnin, Gertrude 1876-1938 .... **NNAL**
See Zitkala-Sa
See also CA 150; DAM MULT

Bontemps, Arna(ud Wendell)
1902-1973 .. **BLC 1; CLC 1, 18; HR 1:2**
See also BW 1; CA 1-4R; 41-44R; CANR 4, 35; CLR 6; CP 1; CWRI 5; DA3; DAM MULT, NOV, POET; DLB 48, 51; JRDA; MAICYA 1, 2; MAL 5; MTCW 1, 2; SATA 2, 44; SATA-Obit 24; WCH; WP

Boot, William
See Stoppard, Tom

Booth, Martin 1944-2004 .... **CLC 13**
See also CA 93-96; 188; 223; CAAE 188; CAAS 2; CANR 92; CP 1, 2, 3, 4

Booth, Philip 1925- .... **CLC 23**
See also CA 5-8R; CANR 5, 88; CP 1, 2, 3, 4, 5, 6, 7; DLBY 1982

Booth, Wayne C(layson) 1921-2005 . **CLC 24**
See also CA 1-4R; CAAS 5; CANR 3, 43, 117; DLB 67

Borchert, Wolfgang 1921-1947 .... **TCLC 5**
See also CA 104; 188; DLB 69, 124; EWL 3

Borel, Petrus 1809-1859 .... **NCLC 41**
See also DLB 119; GFL 1789 to the Present

Borges, Jorge Luis 1899-1986 ... **CLC 1, 2, 3, 4, 6, 8, 9, 10, 13, 19, 44, 48, 83; HLC 1; PC 22, 32; SSC 4, 41; TCLC 109; WLC**
See also AAYA 26; BPFB 1; CA 21-24R; CANR 19, 33, 75, 105, 133; CDWLB 3; DA; DA3; DAB; DAC; DAM MST,

MULT; DLB 113, 283; DLBY 1986; DNFS 1, 2; EWL 3; HW 1, 2; LAW; LMFS 2; MSW; MTCW 1, 2; MTFW 2005; RGSF 2; RGWL 2, 3; SFW 4; SSFS 17; TWA; WLIT 1

Borowski, Tadeusz 1922-1951 .... **SSC 48; TCLC 9**
See also CA 106; 154; CDWLB 4; DLB 215; EWL 3; RGSF 2; RGWL 3; SSFS 13

Borrow, George (Henry)
1803-1881 .... **NCLC 9**
See also DLB 21, 55, 166

Bosch (Gavino), Juan 1909-2001 ..... **HLCS 1**
See also CA 151; 204; DAM MST, MULT; DLB 145; HW 1, 2

Bosman, Herman Charles
1905-1951 .... **TCLC 49**
See Malan, Herman
See also CA 160; DLB 225; RGSF 2

Bosschere, Jean de 1878(?)-1953 ... **TCLC 19**
See also CA 115; 186

Boswell, James 1740-1795 ... **LC 4, 50; WLC**
See also BRW 3; CDBLB 1660-1789; DA; DAB; DAC; DAM MST; DLB 104, 142; TEA; WLIT 3

Bottomley, Gordon 1874-1948 ..... **TCLC 107**
See also CA 120; 192; DLB 10

Bottoms, David 1949- .... **CLC 53**
See also CA 105; CANR 22; CSW; DLB 120; DLBY 1983

Boucicault, Dion 1820-1890 .... **NCLC 41**

Boucolon, Maryse
See Conde, Maryse

Bourdieu, Pierre 1930-2002 .... **CLC 198**
See also CA 130; 204

Bourget, Paul (Charles Joseph)
1852-1935 .... **TCLC 12**
See also CA 107; 196; DLB 123; GFL 1789 to the Present

Bourjaily, Vance (Nye) 1922- .... **CLC 8, 62**
See also CA 1-4R; CAAS 1; CANR 2, 72; CN 1, 2, 3, 4, 5, 6, 7; DLB 2, 143; MAL 5

Bourne, Randolph S(illiman)
1886-1918 .... **TCLC 16**
See also AMW; CA 117; 155; DLB 63; MAL 5

Bova, Ben(jamin William) 1932- ...... **CLC 45**
See also AAYA 16; CA 5-8R; CAAS 18; CANR 11, 56, 94, 111; CLR 3, 96; DLBY 1981; INT CANR-11; MAICYA 1, 2; MTCW 1; SATA 6, 68, 133; SFW 4

Bowen, Elizabeth (Dorothea Cole)
1899-1973 . **CLC 1, 3, 6, 11, 15, 22, 118; SSC 3, 28, 66; TCLC 148**
See also BRWS 2; CA 17-18; 41-44R; CANR 35, 105; CAP 2; CDBLB 1945-1960; CN 1; DA3; DAM NOV; DLB 15, 162; EWL 3; EXPS; FW; HGG; MTCW 1, 2; MTFW 2005; NFS 13; RGSF 2; SSFS 5; SUFW 1; TEA; WLIT 4

Bowering, George 1935- .... **CLC 15, 47**
See also CA 21-24R; CAAS 16; CANR 10; CN 7; CP 1, 2, 3, 4, 5, 6, 7; DLB 53

Bowering, Marilyn R(uthe) 1949- .... **CLC 32**
See also CA 101; CANR 49; CP 4, 5, 6, 7; CWP

Bowers, Edgar 1924-2000 .... **CLC 9**
See also CA 5-8R; 188; CANR 24; CP 1, 2, 3, 4, 5, 6, 7; CSW; DLB 5

Bowers, Mrs. J. Milton 1842-1914
See Bierce, Ambrose (Gwinett)

Bowie, David .... **CLC 17**
See Jones, David Robert

Bowles, Jane (Sydney) 1917-1973 ..... **CLC 3, 68**
See Bowles, Jane Auer
See also CA 19-20; 41-44R; CAP 2; CN 1; MAL 5

Bowles, Jane Auer
See Bowles, Jane (Sydney)
See also EWL 3

Bowles, Paul (Frederick) 1910-1999 . **CLC 1, 2, 19, 53; SSC 3**
See also AMWS 4; CA 1-4R; 186; CAAS 1; CANR 1, 19, 50, 75; CN 1, 2, 3, 4, 5, 6; DA3; DLB 5, 6, 218; EWL 3; MAL 5; MTCW 1, 2; MTFW 2005; RGAL 4; SSFS 17

Bowles, William Lisle 1762-1850 . **NCLC 103**
See also DLB 93

Box, Edgar
See Vidal, (Eugene Luther) Gore
See also GLL 1

Boyd, James 1888-1944 .... **TCLC 115**
See also CA 186; DLB 9; DLBD 16; RGAL 4; RHW

Boyd, Nancy
See Millay, Edna St. Vincent
See also GLL 1

Boyd, Thomas (Alexander)
1898-1935 .... **TCLC 111**
See also CA 111; 183; DLB 9; DLBD 16; 316

Boyd, William (Andrew Murray)
1952- .... **CLC 28, 53, 70**
See also CA 114; 120; CANR 51, 71, 131; CN 4, 5, 6, 7; DLB 231

Boyesen, Hjalmar Hjorth
1848-1895 .... **NCLC 135**
See also DLB 12, 71; DLBD 13; RGAL 4

Boyle, Kay 1902-1992 .... **CLC 1, 5, 19, 58, 121; SSC 5**
See also CA 13-16R; 140; CAAS 1; CANR 29, 61, 110; CN 1, 2, 3, 4, 5; CP 1, 2, 3, 4; DLB 4, 9, 48, 86; DLBY 1993; EWL 3; MAL 5; MTCW 1, 2; MTFW 2005; RGAL 4; RGSF 2; SSFS 10, 13, 14

Boyle, Mark
See Kienzle, William X(avier)

Boyle, Patrick 1905-1982 .... **CLC 19**
See also CA 127

Boyle, T. C.
See Boyle, T(homas) Coraghessan
See also AMWS 8

Boyle, T(homas) Coraghessan
1948- .... **CLC 36, 55, 90; SSC 16**
See Boyle, T. C.
See also AAYA 47; BEST 90:4; BPFB 1; CA 120; CANR 44, 76, 89, 132; CN 6, 7; CPW; DA3; DAM POP; DLB 218, 278; DLBY 1986; EWL 3; MAL 5; MTCW 2; MTFW 2005; SSFS 13, 19

Boz
See Dickens, Charles (John Huffam)

Brackenridge, Hugh Henry
1748-1816 .... **NCLC 7**
See also DLB 11, 37; RGAL 4

Bradbury, Edward P.
See Moorcock, Michael (John)
See also MTCW 2

Bradbury, Malcolm (Stanley)
1932-2000 .... **CLC 32, 61**
See also CA 1-4R; CANR 1, 33, 91, 98, 137; CN 1, 2, 3, 4, 5, 6, 7; CP 1; DA3; DAM NOV; DLB 14, 207; EWL 3; MTCW 1, 2; MTFW 2005

Bradbury, Ray (Douglas) 1920- .... **CLC 1, 3, 10, 15, 42, 98; SSC 29, 53; WLC**
See also AAYA 15; AITN 1, 2; AMWS 4; BPFB 1; BYA 4, 5, 11; CA 1-4R; CANR 2, 30, 75, 125; CDALB 1968-1988; CN 1, 2, 3, 4, 5, 6, 7; CPW; DA; DA3; DAB; DAC; DAM MST, NOV, POP; DLB 2, 8;

EXPN; EXPS; HGG; LAIT 3, 5; LATS
1:2; LMFS 2; MAL 5; MTCW 1, 2;
MTFW 2005; NFS 1, 22; RGAL 4; RGSF
2; SATA 11, 64, 123; SCFW 1, 2; SFW 4;
SSFS 1, 20; SUFW 1, 2; TUS; YAW

Braddon, Mary Elizabeth
1837-1915 .... **TCLC 111**
See also BRWS 8; CA 108; 179; CMW 4;
DLB 18, 70, 156; HGG

Bradfield, Scott (Michael) 1955- .... **SSC 65**
See also CA 147; CANR 90; HGG; SUFW
2

Bradford, Gamaliel 1863-1932 .... **TCLC 36**
See also CA 160; DLB 17

Bradford, William 1590-1657 .... **LC 64**
See also DLB 24, 30; RGAL 4

Bradley, David (Henry), Jr. 1950- .... **BLC 1;**
CLC 23, 118
See also BW 1, 3; CA 104; CANR 26, 81;
CN 4, 5, 6, 7; DAM MULT; DLB 33

Bradley, John Ed(mund, Jr.) 1958- . **CLC 55**
See also CA 139; CANR 99; CN 6, 7; CSW

Bradley, Marion Zimmer
1930-1999 .... **CLC 30**
See Chapman, Lee; Dexter, John; Gardner,
Miriam; Ives, Morgan; Rivers, Elfrida
See also AAYA 40; BPFB 1; CA 57-60; 185;
CAAS 10; CANR 7, 31, 51, 75, 107;
CPW; DA3; DAM POP; DLB 8; FANT;
FW; MTCW 1, 2; MTFW 2005; SATA 90,
139; SATA-Obit 116; SFW 4; SUFW 2;
YAW

Bradshaw, John 1933- .... **CLC 70**
See also CA 138; CANR 61

Bradstreet, Anne 1612(?)-1672 ...... **LC 4, 30;**
PC 10
See also AMWS 1; CDALB 1640-1865;
DA; DA3; DAC; DAM MST, POET; DLB
24; EXPP; FW; PFS 6; RGAL 4; TUS;
WP

Brady, Joan 1939- .... **CLC 86**
See also CA 141

Bragg, Melvyn 1939- .... **CLC 10**
See also BEST 89:3; CA 57-60; CANR 10,
48, 89; CN 1, 2, 3, 4, 5, 6, 7; DLB 14,
271; RHW

Brahe, Tycho 1546-1601 .... **LC 45**
See also DLB 300

Braine, John (Gerard) 1922-1986 . **CLC 1, 3,**
41
See also CA 1-4R; 120; CANR 1, 33; CD-
BLB 1945-1960; CN 1, 2, 3, 4; DLB 15;
DLBY 1986; EWL 3; MTCW 1

Braithwaite, William Stanley (Beaumont)
1878-1962 .... **BLC 1; HR 1:2; PC 52**
See also BW 1; CA 125; DAM MULT; DLB
50, 54; MAL 5

Bramah, Ernest 1868-1942 .... **TCLC 72**
See also CA 156; CMW 4; DLB 70; FANT

Brammer, Billy Lee
See Brammer, William

Brammer, William 1929-1978 .... **CLC 31**
See also CA 235; 77-80

Brancati, Vitaliano 1907-1954 .... **TCLC 12**
See also CA 109; DLB 264; EWL 3

Brancato, Robin F(idler) 1936- .... **CLC 35**
See also AAYA 9, 68; BYA 6; CA 69-72;
CANR 11, 45; CLR 32; JRDA; MAICYA
2; MAICYAS 1; SAAS 9; SATA 97;
WYA; YAW

Brand, Dionne 1953- .... **CLC 192**
See also BW 2; CA 143; CANR 143; CWP

Brand, Max
See Faust, Frederick (Schiller)
See also BPFB 1; TCWW 1, 2

Brand, Millen 1906-1980 .... **CLC 7**
See also CA 21-24R; 97-100; CANR 72

Branden, Barbara .... **CLC 44**
See also CA 148

Brandes, Georg (Morris Cohen)
1842-1927 .... **TCLC 10**
See also CA 105; 189; DLB 300

Brandys, Kazimierz 1916-2000 .... **CLC 62**
See also CA 239; EWL 3

Branley, Franklyn M(ansfield)
1915-2002 .... **CLC 21**
See also CA 33-36R; 207; CANR 14, 39;
CLR 13; MAICYA 1, 2; SAAS 16; SATA
4, 68, 136

Brant, Beth (E.) 1941- .... **NNAL**
See also CA 144; FW

Brant, Sebastian 1457-1521 .... **LC 112**
See also DLB 179; RGWL 2, 3

Brathwaite, Edward Kamau
1930- .... **BLCS; CLC 11; PC 56**
See also BW 2, 3; CA 25-28R; CANR 11,
26, 47, 107; CDWLB 3; CP 1, 2, 3, 4, 5,
6, 7; DAM POET; DLB 125; EWL 3

Brathwaite, Kamau
See Brathwaite, Edward Kamau

Brautigan, Richard (Gary)
1935-1984 .... **CLC 1, 3, 5, 9, 12, 34, 42;**
TCLC 133
See also BPFB 1; CA 53-56; 113; CANR
34; CN 1, 2, 3; CP 1, 2, 3, 4; DA3; DAM
NOV; DLB 2, 5, 206; DLBY 1980, 1984;
FANT; MAL 5; MTCW 1; RGAL 4;
SATA 56

Brave Bird, Mary .... **NNAL**
See Crow Dog, Mary (Ellen)

Braverman, Kate 1950- .... **CLC 67**
See also CA 89-92; CANR 141

Brecht, (Eugen) Bertolt (Friedrich)
1898-1956 ..... **DC 3; TCLC 1, 6, 13, 35,**
169; WLC
See also CA 104; 133; CANR 62; CDWLB
2; DA; DA3; DAB; DAC; DAM DRAM,
MST; DFS 4, 5, 9; DLB 56, 124; EW 11;
EWL 3; IDTP; MTCW 1, 2; MTFW 2005;
RGWL 2, 3; TWA

Brecht, Eugen Berthold Friedrich
See Brecht, (Eugen) Bertolt (Friedrich)

Bremer, Fredrika 1801-1865 .... **NCLC 11**
See also DLB 254

Brennan, Christopher John
1870-1932 .... **TCLC 17**
See also CA 117; 188; DLB 230; EWL 3

Brennan, Maeve 1917-1993 ... **CLC 5; TCLC**
124
See also CA 81-84; CANR 72, 100

Brenner, Jozef 1887-1919
See Csath, Geza
See also CA 240

Brent, Linda
See Jacobs, Harriet A(nn)

Brentano, Clemens (Maria)
1778-1842 .... **NCLC 1**
See also DLB 90; RGWL 2, 3

Brent of Bin Bin
See Franklin, (Stella Maria Sarah) Miles
(Lampe)

Brenton, Howard 1942- .... **CLC 31**
See also CA 69-72; CANR 33, 67; CBD;
CD 5, 6; DLB 13; MTCW 1

Breslin, James 1930-
See Breslin, Jimmy
See also CA 73-76; CANR 31, 75, 139;
DAM NOV; MTCW 1, 2; MTFW 2005

Breslin, Jimmy .... **CLC 4, 43**
See Breslin, James
See also AITN 1; DLB 185; MTCW 2

Bresson, Robert 1901(?)-1999 .... **CLC 16**
See also CA 110; 187; CANR 49

Breton, Andre 1896-1966 .. **CLC 2, 9, 15, 54;**
PC 15
See also CA 19-20; 25-28R; CANR 40, 60;
CAP 2; DLB 65, 258; EW 11; EWL 3;
GFL 1789 to the Present; LMFS 2;
MTCW 1, 2; MTFW 2005; RGWL 2, 3;
TWA; WP

Breytenbach, Breyten 1939(?)- .. **CLC 23, 37,**
126
See also CA 113; 129; CANR 61, 122;
CWW 2; DAM POET; DLB 225; EWL 3

Bridgers, Sue Ellen 1942- .... **CLC 26**
See also AAYA 8, 49; BYA 7, 8; CA 65-68;
CANR 11, 36; CLR 18; DLB 52; JRDA;
MAICYA 1, 2; SAAS 1; SATA 22, 90;
SATA-Essay 109; WYA; YAW

Bridges, Robert (Seymour)
1844-1930 .... **PC 28; TCLC 1**
See also BRW 6; CA 104; 152; CDBLB
1890-1914; DAM POET; DLB 19, 98

Bridie, James .... **TCLC 3**
See Mavor, Osborne Henry
See also DLB 10; EWL 3

Brin, David 1950- .... **CLC 34**
See also AAYA 21; CA 102; CANR 24, 70,
125, 127; INT CANR-24; SATA 65;
SCFW 2; SFW 4

Brink, Andre (Philippus) 1935- . **CLC 18, 36,**
106
See also AFW; BRWS 6; CA 104; CANR
39, 62, 109, 133; CN 4, 5, 6, 7; DLB 225;
EWL 3; INT CA-103; LATS 1:2; MTCW
1, 2; MTFW 2005; WLIT 2

Brinsmead, H. F(ay)
See Brinsmead, H(esba) F(ay)

Brinsmead, H. F.
See Brinsmead, H(esba) F(ay)

Brinsmead, H(esba) F(ay) 1922- ...... **CLC 21**
See also CA 21-24R; CANR 10; CLR 47;
CWRI 5; MAICYA 1, 2; SAAS 5; SATA
18, 78

Brittain, Vera (Mary) 1893(?)-1970 . **CLC 23**
See also BRWS 10; CA 13-16; 25-28R;
CANR 58; CAP 1; DLB 191; FW; MTCW
1, 2

Broch, Hermann 1886-1951 .... **TCLC 20**
See also CA 117; 211; CDWLB 2; DLB 85,
124; EW 10; EWL 3; RGWL 2, 3

Brock, Rose
See Hansen, Joseph
See also GLL 1

Brod, Max 1884-1968 .... **TCLC 115**
See also CA 5-8R; 25-28R; CANR 7; DLB
81; EWL 3

Brodkey, Harold (Roy) 1930-1996 .. **CLC 56;**
TCLC 123
See also CA 111; 151; CANR 71; CN 4, 5,
6; DLB 130

Brodsky, Iosif Alexandrovich 1940-1996
See Brodsky, Joseph
See also AITN 1; CA 41-44R; 151; CANR
37, 106; DA3; DAM POET; MTCW 1, 2;
MTFW 2005; RGWL 2, 3

Brodsky, Joseph . **CLC 4, 6, 13, 36, 100; PC**
9
See Brodsky, Iosif Alexandrovich
See also AMWS 8; CWW 2; DLB 285;
EWL 3; MTCW 1

Brodsky, Michael (Mark) 1948- .... **CLC 19**
See also CA 102; CANR 18, 41, 58; DLB
244

Brodzki, Bella ed. .... **CLC 65**

Brome, Richard 1590(?)-1652 .... **LC 61**
See also BRWS 10; DLB 58

Bromell, Henry 1947- .... **CLC 5**
See also CA 53-56; CANR 9, 115, 116

Canfield, Dorothea F.
See Fisher, Dorothy (Frances) Canfield
Canfield, Dorothea Frances
See Fisher, Dorothy (Frances) Canfield
Canfield, Dorothy
See Fisher, Dorothy (Frances) Canfield
Canin, Ethan 1960- .... **CLC 55; SSC 70**
See also CA 131; 135; MAL 5
Cankar, Ivan 1876-1918 .... **TCLC 105**
See also CDWLB 4; DLB 147; EWL 3
Cannon, Curt
See Hunter, Evan
Cao, Lan 1961- .... **CLC 109**
See also CA 165
Cape, Judith
See Page, P(atricia) K(athleen)
See also CCA 1
Capek, Karel 1890-1938 .... **DC 1; SSC 36;
TCLC 6, 37; WLC**
See also CA 104; 140; CDWLB 4; DA;
DA3; DAB; DAC; DAM DRAM, MST,
NOV; DFS 7, 11; DLB 215; EW 10; EWL
3; MTCW 1, 2; MTFW 2005; RGSF 2;
RGWL 2, 3; SCFW 1, 2; SFW 4
Capote, Truman 1924-1984 . **CLC 1, 3, 8, 13,
19, 34, 38, 58; SSC 2, 47; TCLC 164;
WLC**
See also AAYA 61; AMWS 3; BPFB 1; CA
5-8R; 113; CANR 18, 62; CDALB 1941-
1968; CN 1, 2, 3; CPW; DA; DA3; DAB;
DAC; DAM MST, NOV, POP; DLB 2,
185, 227; DLBY 1980, 1984; EWL 3;
EXPS; GLL 1; LAIT 3; MAL 5; MTCW
1, 2; MTFW 2005; NCFS 2; RGAL 4;
RGSF 2; SATA 91; SSFS 2; TUS
Capra, Frank 1897-1991 .... **CLC 16**
See also CA 61-64; 135
Caputo, Philip 1941- .... **CLC 32**
See also AAYA 60; CA 73-76; CANR 40,
135; YAW
Caragiale, Ion Luca 1852-1912 ...... **TCLC 76**
See also CA 157
Card, Orson Scott 1951- .... **CLC 44, 47, 50**
See also AAYA 11, 42; BPFB 1; BYA 5, 8;
CA 102; CANR 27, 47, 73, 102, 106, 133;
CPW; DA3; DAM POP; FANT; INT
CANR-27; MTCW 1, 2; MTFW 2005;
NFS 5; SATA 83, 127; SCFW 2; SFW 4;
SUFW 2; YAW
Cardenal, Ernesto 1925- .... **CLC 31, 161;
HLC 1; PC 22**
See also CA 49-52; CANR 2, 32, 66, 138;
CWW 2; DAM MULT, POET; DLB 290;
EWL 3; HW 1, 2; LAWS 1; MTCW 1, 2;
MTFW 2005; RGWL 2, 3
Cardinal, Marie 1929-2001 .... **CLC 189**
See also CA 177; CWW 2; DLB 83; FW
Cardozo, Benjamin N(athan)
1870-1938 .... **TCLC 65**
See also CA 117; 164
Carducci, Giosue (Alessandro Giuseppe)
1835-1907 .... **PC 46; TCLC 32**
See also CA 163; EW 7; RGWL 2, 3
Carew, Thomas 1595(?)-1640 . **LC 13; PC 29**
See also BRW 2; DLB 126; PAB; RGEL 2
Carey, Ernestine Gilbreth 1908- ...... **CLC 17**
See also CA 5-8R; CANR 71; SATA 2
Carey, Peter 1943- .... **CLC 40, 55, 96, 183**
See also CA 123; 127; CANR 53, 76, 117;
CN 4, 5, 6, 7; DLB 289; EWL 3; INT CA-
127; MTCW 1, 2; MTFW 2005; RGSF 2;
SATA 94
Carleton, William 1794-1869 .... **NCLC 3**
See also DLB 159; RGEL 2; RGSF 2
Carlisle, Henry (Coffin) 1926- .... **CLC 33**
See also CA 13-16R; CANR 15, 85
Carlsen, Chris
See Holdstock, Robert P.

Carlson, Ron(ald F.) 1947- .... **CLC 54**
See also CA 105, 189; CAAE 189; CANR
27; DLB 244
Carlyle, Thomas 1795-1881 ..... **NCLC 22, 70**
See also BRW 4; CDBLB 1789-1832; DA;
DAB; DAC; DAM MST; DLB 55, 144,
254; RGEL 2; TEA
Carman, (William) Bliss 1861-1929 ... **PC 34;
TCLC 7**
See also CA 104; 152; DAC; DLB 92;
RGEL 2
Carnegie, Dale 1888-1955 .... **TCLC 53**
See also CA 218
Carossa, Hans 1878-1956 .... **TCLC 48**
See also CA 170; DLB 66; EWL 3
Carpenter, Don(ald Richard)
1931-1995 .... **CLC 41**
See also CA 45-48; 149; CANR 1, 71
Carpenter, Edward 1844-1929 .... **TCLC 88**
See also CA 163; GLL 1
Carpenter, John (Howard) 1948- ... **CLC 161**
See also AAYA 2; CA 134; SATA 58
Carpenter, Johnny
See Carpenter, John (Howard)
Carpentier (y Valmont), Alejo
1904-1980 . **CLC 8, 11, 38, 110; HLC 1;
SSC 35**
See also CA 65-68; 97-100; CANR 11, 70;
CDWLB 3; DAM MULT; DLB 113; EWL
3; HW 1, 2; LAW; LMFS 2; RGSF 2;
RGWL 2, 3; WLIT 1
Carr, Caleb 1955- .... **CLC 86**
See also CA 147; CANR 73, 134; DA3
Carr, Emily 1871-1945 .... **TCLC 32**
See also CA 159; DLB 68; FW; GLL 2
Carr, John Dickson 1906-1977 .... **CLC 3**
See Fairbairn, Roger
See also CA 49-52; 69-72; CANR 3, 33,
60; CMW 4; DLB 306; MSW; MTCW 1,
2
Carr, Philippa
See Hibbert, Eleanor Alice Burford
Carr, Virginia Spencer 1929- .... **CLC 34**
See also CA 61-64; DLB 111
Carrere, Emmanuel 1957- .... **CLC 89**
See also CA 200
Carrier, Roch 1937- .... **CLC 13, 78**
See also CA 130; CANR 61; CCA 1; DAC;
DAM MST; DLB 53; SATA 105
Carroll, James Dennis
See Carroll, Jim
Carroll, James P. 1943(?)- .... **CLC 38**
See also CA 81-84; CANR 73, 139; MTCW
2; MTFW 2005
Carroll, Jim 1951- .... **CLC 35, 143**
See also AAYA 17; CA 45-48; CANR 42,
115; NCFS 5
Carroll, Lewis ..... **NCLC 2, 53, 139; PC 18;
WLC**
See Dodgson, Charles L(utwidge)
See also AAYA 39; BRW 5; BYA 5, 13; CD-
BLB 1832-1890; CLR 2, 18; DLB 18,
163, 178; DLBY 1998; EXPN; EXPP;
FANT; JRDA; LAIT 1; NFS 7; PFS 11;
RGEL 2; SUFW 1; TEA; WCH
Carroll, Paul Vincent 1900-1968 ...... **CLC 10**
See also CA 9-12R; 25-28R; DLB 10; EWL
3; RGEL 2
Carruth, Hayden 1921- ..... **CLC 4, 7, 10, 18,
84; PC 10**
See also CA 9-12R; CANR 4, 38, 59, 110;
CP 1, 2, 3, 4, 5, 6, 7; DLB 5, 165; INT
CANR-4; MTCW 1, 2; MTFW 2005;
SATA 47
Carson, Anne 1950- .... **CLC 185; PC 64**
See also AMWS 12; CA 203; DLB 193;
PFS 18; TCLE 1:1
Carson, Ciaran 1948- .... **CLC 201**
See also CA 112; 153; CANR 113; CP 7

Carson, Rachel
See Carson, Rachel Louise
See also AAYA 49; DLB 275
Carson, Rachel Louise 1907-1964 .... **CLC 71**
See Carson, Rachel
See also AMWS 9; ANW; CA 77-80; CANR
35; DA3; DAM POP; FW; LAIT 4; MAL
5; MTCW 1, 2; MTFW 2005; NCFS 1;
SATA 23
Carter, Angela (Olive) 1940-1992 ...... **CLC 5,
41, 76; SSC 13, 85; TCLC 139**
See also BRWS 3; CA 53-56; 136; CANR
12, 36, 61, 106; CN 3, 4, 5; DA3; DLB
14, 207, 261, 319; EXPS; FANT; FW; GL
2; MTCW 1, 2; MTFW 2005; RGSF 2;
SATA 66; SATA-Obit 70; SFW 4; SSFS
4, 12; SUFW 2; WLIT 4
Carter, Nick
See Smith, Martin Cruz
Carver, Raymond 1938-1988 ..... **CLC 22, 36,
53, 55, 126; PC 54; SSC 8, 51**
See also AAYA 44; AMWS 3; BPFB 1; CA
33-36R; 126; CANR 17, 34, 61, 103; CN
4; CPW; DA3; DAM NOV; DLB 130;
DLBY 1984, 1988; EWL 3; MAL 5;
MTCW 1, 2; MTFW 2005; PFS 17;
RGAL 4; RGSF 2; SSFS 3, 6, 12, 13;
TCLE 1:1; TCWW 2; TUS
Cary, Elizabeth, Lady Falkland
1585-1639 .... **LC 30**
Cary, (Arthur) Joyce (Lunel)
1888-1957 .... **TCLC 1, 29**
See also BRW 7; CA 104; 164; CDBLB
1914-1945; DLB 15, 100; EWL 3; MTCW
2; RGEL 2; TEA
Casal, Julian del 1863-1893 .... **NCLC 131**
See also DLB 283; LAW
Casanova, Giacomo
See Casanova de Seingalt, Giovanni Jacopo
See also WLIT 7
Casanova de Seingalt, Giovanni Jacopo
1725-1798 .... **LC 13**
See Casanova, Giacomo
Casares, Adolfo Bioy
See Bioy Casares, Adolfo
See also RGSF 2
Casas, Bartolome de las 1474-1566
See Las Casas, Bartolome de
See also WLIT 1
Casely-Hayford, J(oseph) E(phraim)
1866-1903 .... **BLC 1; TCLC 24**
See also BW 2; CA 123; 152; DAM MULT
Casey, John (Dudley) 1939- .... **CLC 59**
See also BEST 90:2; CA 69-72; CANR 23,
100
Casey, Michael 1947- .... **CLC 2**
See also CA 65-68; CANR 109; CP 2, 3;
DLB 5
Casey, Patrick
See Thurman, Wallace (Henry)
Casey, Warren (Peter) 1935-1988 .... **CLC 12**
See also CA 101; 127; INT CA-101
Casona, Alejandro .... **CLC 49**
See Alvarez, Alejandro Rodriguez
See also EWL 3
Cassavetes, John 1929-1989 .... **CLC 20**
See also CA 85-88; 127; CANR 82
Cassian, Nina 1924- .... **PC 17**
See also CWP; CWW 2
Cassill, R(onald) V(erlin)
1919-2002 .... **CLC 4, 23**
See also CA 9-12R; 208; CAAS 1; CANR
7, 45; CN 1, 2, 3, 4, 5, 6, 7; DLB 6, 218;
DLBY 2002
Cassiodorus, Flavius Magnus c. 490(?)-c.
583(?) .... **CMLC 43**
Cassirer, Ernst 1874-1945 .... **TCLC 61**
See also CA 157

Cassity, (Allen) Turner 1929- .... **CLC 6, 42**
See also CA 17-20R, 223; CAAE 223;
CAAS 8; CANR 11; CSW; DLB 105

Castaneda, Carlos (Cesar Aranha)
1931(?)-1998 .... **CLC 12, 119**
See also CA 25-28R; CANR 32, 66, 105;
DNFS 1; HW 1; MTCW 1

Castedo, Elena 1937- .... **CLC 65**
See also CA 132

Castedo-Ellerman, Elena
See Castedo, Elena

Castellanos, Rosario 1925-1974 .... **CLC 66;**
HLC 1; SSC 39, 68
See also CA 131; 53-56; CANR 58; CD-
WLB 3; DAM MULT; DLB 113, 290;
EWL 3; FW; HW 1; LAW; MTCW 2;
MTFW 2005; RGSF 2; RGWL 2, 3

Castelvetro, Lodovico 1505-1571 .... **LC 12**

Castiglione, Baldassare 1478-1529 ...... **LC 12**
See Castiglione, Baldesar
See also LMFS 1; RGWL 2, 3

Castiglione, Baldesar
See Castiglione, Baldassare
See also EW 2; WLIT 7

Castillo, Ana (Hernandez Del)
1953- .... **CLC 151**
See also AAYA 42; CA 131; CANR 51, 86,
128; CWP; DLB 122, 227; DNFS 2; FW;
HW 1; LLW; PFS 21

Castle, Robert
See Hamilton, Edmond

Castro (Ruz), Fidel 1926(?)- .... **HLC 1**
See also CA 110; 129; CANR 81; DAM
MULT; HW 2

Castro, Guillen de 1569-1631 .... **LC 19**

Castro, Rosalia de 1837-1885 ... **NCLC 3, 78;**
PC 41
See also DAM MULT

Cather, Willa (Sibert) 1873-1947 . **SSC 2, 50;**
TCLC 1, 11, 31, 99, 132, 152; WLC
See also AAYA 24; AMW; AMWC 1;
AMWR 1; BPFB 1; CA 104; 128; CDALB
1865-1917; CLR 98; DA; DA3; DAB;
DAC; DAM MST, NOV; DLB 9, 54, 78,
256; DLBD 1; EWL 3; EXPN; EXPS; FL
1:5; LAIT 3; LATS 1:1; MAL 5; MAWW;
MTCW 1, 2; MTFW 2005; NFS 2, 19;
RGAL 4; RGSF 2; RHW; SATA 30; SSFS
2, 7, 16; TCWW 1, 2; TUS

Catherine II
See Catherine the Great
See also DLB 150

Catherine the Great 1729-1796 .... **LC 69**
See Catherine II

Cato, Marcus Porcius
234B.C.-149B.C. .... **CMLC 21**
See Cato the Elder

Cato, Marcus Porcius, the Elder
See Cato, Marcus Porcius

Cato the Elder
See Cato, Marcus Porcius
See also DLB 211

Catton, (Charles) Bruce 1899-1978 . **CLC 35**
See also AITN 1; CA 5-8R; 81-84; CANR
7, 74; DLB 17; MTCW 2; MTFW 2005;
SATA 2; SATA-Obit 24

Catullus c. 84B.C.-54B.C. .... **CMLC 18**
See also AW 2; CDWLB 1; DLB 211;
RGWL 2, 3

Cauldwell, Frank
See King, Francis (Henry)

Caunitz, William J. 1933-1996 .... **CLC 34**
See also BEST 89:3; CA 125; 130; 152;
CANR 73; INT CA-130

Causley, Charles (Stanley)
1917-2003 .... **CLC 7**
See also CA 9-12R; 223; CANR 5, 35, 94;
CLR 30; CP 1, 2, 3, 4; CWRI 5; DLB 27;
MTCW 1; SATA 3, 66; SATA-Obit 149

Caute, (John) David 1936- .... **CLC 29**
See also CA 1-4R; CAAS 4; CANR 1, 33,
64, 120; CBD; CD 5, 6; CN 1, 2, 3, 4, 5,
6, 7; DAM NOV; DLB 14, 231

Cavafy, C(onstantine) P(eter) .... **PC 36;**
TCLC 2, 7
See Kavafis, Konstantinos Petrou
See also CA 148; DA3; DAM POET; EW
8; EWL 3; MTCW 2; PFS 19; RGWL 2,
3; WP

Cavalcanti, Guido c. 1250-c.
1300 .... **CMLC 54**
See also RGWL 2, 3; WLIT 7

Cavallo, Evelyn
See Spark, Muriel (Sarah)

Cavanna, Betty .... **CLC 12**
See Harrison, Elizabeth (Allen) Cavanna
See also JRDA; MAICYA 1; SAAS 4;
SATA 1, 30

Cavendish, Margaret Lucas
1623-1673 .... **LC 30**
See also DLB 131, 252, 281; RGEL 2

Caxton, William 1421(?)-1491(?) .... **LC 17**
See also DLB 170

Cayer, D. M.
See Duffy, Maureen (Patricia)

Cayrol, Jean 1911-2005 .... **CLC 11**
See also CA 89-92; 236; DLB 83; EWL 3

Cela (y Trulock), Camilo Jose
See Cela, Camilo Jose
See also CWW 2

Cela, Camilo Jose 1916-2002 .... **CLC 4, 13,**
59, 122; HLC 1; SSC 71
See Cela (y Trulock), Camilo Jose
See also BEST 90:2; CA 21-24R; 206;
CAAS 10; CANR 21, 32, 76, 139; DAM
MULT; DLB 322; DLBY 1989; EW 13;
EWL 3; HW 1; MTCW 1, 2; MTFW
2005; RGSF 2; RGWL 2, 3

Celan, Paul .... **CLC 10, 19, 53, 82; PC 10**
See Antschel, Paul
See also CDWLB 2; DLB 69; EWL 3;
RGWL 2, 3

Celine, Louis-Ferdinand .. **CLC 1, 3, 4, 7, 9,**
15, 47, 124
See Destouches, Louis-Ferdinand
See also DLB 72; EW 11; EWL 3; GFL
1789 to the Present; RGWL 2, 3

Cellini, Benvenuto 1500-1571 .... **LC 7**
See also WLIT 7

Cendrars, Blaise .... **CLC 18, 106**
See Sauser-Hall, Frederic
See also DLB 258; EWL 3; GFL 1789 to
the Present; RGWL 2, 3; WP

Centlivre, Susanna 1669(?)-1723 .... **DC 25;**
LC 65
See also DLB 84; RGEL 2

Cernuda (y Bidon), Luis
1902-1963 .... **CLC 54; PC 62**
See also CA 131; 89-92; DAM POET; DLB
134; EWL 3; GLL 1; HW 1; RGWL 2, 3

Cervantes, Lorna Dee 1954- ..... **HLCS 1; PC**
35
See also CA 131; CANR 80; CWP; DLB
82; EXPP; HW 1; LLW

Cervantes (Saavedra), Miguel de
1547-1616 .... **HLCS; LC 6, 23, 93; SSC**
12; WLC
See also AAYA 56; BYA 1, 14; DA; DAB;
DAC; DAM MST, NOV; EW 2; LAIT 1;
LATS 1:1; LMFS 1; NFS 8; RGSF 2;
RGWL 2, 3; TWA

Cesaire, Aime (Fernand) 1913- .... **BLC 1;**
CLC 19, 32, 112; DC 22; PC 25
See also BW 2, 3; CA 65-68; CANR 24,
43, 81; CWW 2; DA3; DAM MULT,
POET; DLB 321; EWL 3; GFL 1789 to
the Present; MTCW 1, 2; MTFW 2005;
WP

Chabon, Michael 1963- ... **CLC 55, 149; SSC**
59
See also AAYA 45; AMWS 11; CA 139;
CANR 57, 96, 127, 138; DLB 278; MAL
5; MTFW 2005; SATA 145

Chabrol, Claude 1930- .... **CLC 16**
See also CA 110

Chairil Anwar
See Anwar, Chairil
See also EWL 3

Challans, Mary 1905-1983
See Renault, Mary
See also CA 81-84; 111; CANR 74; DA3;
MTCW 2; MTFW 2005; SATA 23; SATA-
Obit 36; TEA

Challis, George
See Faust, Frederick (Schiller)

Chambers, Aidan 1934- .... **CLC 35**
See also AAYA 27; CA 25-28R; CANR 12,
31, 58, 116; JRDA; MAICYA 1, 2; SAAS
12; SATA 1, 69, 108; WYA; YAW

Chambers, James 1948-
See Cliff, Jimmy
See also CA 124

Chambers, Jessie
See Lawrence, D(avid) H(erbert Richards)
See also GLL 1

Chambers, Robert W(illiam)
1865-1933 .... **TCLC 41**
See also CA 165; DLB 202; HGG; SATA
107; SUFW 1

Chambers, (David) Whittaker
1901-1961 .... **TCLC 129**
See also CA 89-92; DLB 303

Chamisso, Adelbert von
1781-1838 .... **NCLC 82**
See also DLB 90; RGWL 2, 3; SUFW 1

Chance, James T.
See Carpenter, John (Howard)

Chance, John T.
See Carpenter, John (Howard)

Chandler, Raymond (Thornton)
1888-1959 .... **SSC 23; TCLC 1, 7**
See also AAYA 25; AMWC 2; AMWS 4;
BPFB 1; CA 104; 129; CANR 60, 107;
CDALB 1929-1941; CMW 4; DA3; DLB
226, 253; DLBD 6; EWL 3; MAL 5;
MSW; MTCW 1, 2; MTFW 2005; NFS
17; RGAL 4; TUS

Chang, Diana 1934- .... **AAL**
See also CA 228; CWP; DLB 312; EXPP

Chang, Eileen 1921-1995 .... **AAL; SSC 28**
See Chang Ai-Ling; Zhang Ailing
See also CA 166

Chang, Jung 1952- .... **CLC 71**
See also CA 142

Chang Ai-Ling
See Chang, Eileen
See also EWL 3

Channing, William Ellery
1780-1842 .... **NCLC 17**
See also DLB 1, 59, 235; RGAL 4

Chao, Patricia 1955- .... **CLC 119**
See also CA 163

Chaplin, Charles Spencer
1889-1977 .... **CLC 16**
See Chaplin, Charlie
See also CA 81-84; 73-76

Chaplin, Charlie
See Chaplin, Charles Spencer
See also AAYA 61; DLB 44

Chapman, George 1559(?)-1634 . **DC 19; LC**
22, 116
See also BRW 1; DAM DRAM; DLB 62,
121; LMFS 1; RGEL 2

Chapman, Graham 1941-1989 .... **CLC 21**
See Monty Python
See also CA 116; 129; CANR 35, 95

Chapman, John Jay 1862-1933 .... **TCLC 7**
   See also AMWS 14; CA 104; 191

Chapman, Lee
   See Bradley, Marion Zimmer
   See also GLL 1

Chapman, Walker
   See Silverberg, Robert

Chappell, Fred (Davis) 1936- .... **CLC 40, 78, 162**
   See also CA 5-8R, 198; CAAE 198; CAAS 4; CANR 8, 33, 67, 110; CN 6; CP 7; CSW; DLB 6, 105; HGG

Char, Rene(-Emile) 1907-1988 .... **CLC 9, 11, 14, 55; PC 56**
   See also CA 13-16R; 124; CANR 32; DAM POET; DLB 258; EWL 3; GFL 1789 to the Present; MTCW 1, 2; RGWL 2, 3

Charby, Jay
   See Ellison, Harlan (Jay)

Chardin, Pierre Teilhard de
   See Teilhard de Chardin, (Marie Joseph) Pierre

Chariton fl. 1st cent. (?)- .... **CMLC 49**

Charlemagne 742-814 .... **CMLC 37**

Charles I 1600-1649 .... **LC 13**

Charriere, Isabelle de 1740-1805 .. **NCLC 66**
   See also DLB 313

Chartier, Alain c. 1392-1430 .... **LC 94**
   See also DLB 208

Chartier, Emile-Auguste
   See Alain

Charyn, Jerome 1937- .... **CLC 5, 8, 18**
   See also CA 5-8R; CAAS 1; CANR 7, 61, 101; CMW 4; CN 1, 2, 3, 4, 5, 6, 7; DLBY 1983; MTCW 1

Chase, Adam
   See Marlowe, Stephen

Chase, Mary (Coyle) 1907-1981 .... **DC 1**
   See also CA 77-80; 105; CAD; CWD; DFS 11; DLB 228; SATA 17; SATA-Obit 29

Chase, Mary Ellen 1887-1973 .... **CLC 2; TCLC 124**
   See also CA 13-16; 41-44R; CAP 1; SATA 10

Chase, Nicholas
   See Hyde, Anthony
   See also CCA 1

Chateaubriand, Francois Rene de 1768-1848 .... **NCLC 3, 134**
   See also DLB 119; EW 5; GFL 1789 to the Present; RGWL 2, 3; TWA

Chatelet, Gabrielle-Emilie Du
   See du Chatelet, Emilie
   See also DLB 313

Chatterje, Sarat Chandra 1876-1936(?)
   See Chatterji, Saratchandra
   See also CA 109

Chatterji, Bankim Chandra 1838-1894 .... **NCLC 19**

Chatterji, Saratchandra .... **TCLC 13**
   See Chatterje, Sarat Chandra
   See also CA 186; EWL 3

Chatterton, Thomas 1752-1770 .... **LC 3, 54**
   See also DAM POET; DLB 109; RGEL 2

Chatwin, (Charles) Bruce 1940-1989 .... **CLC 28, 57, 59**
   See also AAYA 4; BEST 90:1; BRWS 4; CA 85-88; 127; CPW; DAM POP; DLB 194, 204; EWL 3; MTFW 2005

Chaucer, Daniel
   See Ford, Ford Madox
   See also RHW

Chaucer, Geoffrey 1340(?)-1400 .. **LC 17, 56; PC 19, 58; WLCS**
   See also BRW 1; BRWC 1; BRWR 2; CD-BLB Before 1660; DA; DA3; DAB; DAC; DAM MST, POET; DLB 146; LAIT 1; PAB; PFS 14; RGEL 2; TEA; WLIT 3; WP

Chavez, Denise (Elia) 1948- .... **HLC 1**
   See also CA 131; CANR 56, 81, 137; DAM MULT; DLB 122; FW; HW 1, 2; LLW; MAL 5; MTCW 2; MTFW 2005

Chaviaras, Strates 1935-
   See Haviaras, Stratis
   See also CA 105

Chayefsky, Paddy .... **CLC 23**
   See Chayefsky, Sidney
   See also CAD; DLB 7, 44; DLBY 1981; RGAL 4

Chayefsky, Sidney 1923-1981
   See Chayefsky, Paddy
   See also CA 9-12R; 104; CANR 18; DAM DRAM

Chedid, Andree 1920- .... **CLC 47**
   See also CA 145; CANR 95; EWL 3

Cheever, John 1912-1982 ..... **CLC 3, 7, 8, 11, 15, 25, 64; SSC 1, 38, 57; WLC**
   See also AAYA 65; AMWS 1; BPFB 1; CA 5-8R; 106; CABS 1; CANR 5, 27, 76; CDALB 1941-1968; CN 1, 2, 3; CPW; DA; DA3; DAB; DAC; DAM MST, NOV, POP; DLB 2, 102, 227; DLBY 1980, 1982; EWL 3; EXPS; INT CANR-5; MAL 5; MTCW 1, 2; MTFW 2005; RGAL 4; RGSF 2; SSFS 2, 14; TUS

Cheever, Susan 1943- .... **CLC 18, 48**
   See also CA 103; CANR 27, 51, 92; DLBY 1982; INT CANR-27

Chekhonte, Antosha
   See Chekhov, Anton (Pavlovich)

Chekhov, Anton (Pavlovich) 1860-1904 .... **DC 9; SSC 2, 28, 41, 51, 85; TCLC 3, 10, 31, 55, 96, 163; WLC**
   See also AAYA 68; BYA 14; CA 104; 124; DA; DA3; DAB; DAC; DAM DRAM, MST; DFS 1, 5, 10, 12; DLB 277; EW 7; EWL 3; EXPS; LAIT 3; LATS 1:1; RGSF 2; RGWL 2, 3; SATA 90; SSFS 5, 13, 14; TWA

Cheney, Lynne V. 1941- .... **CLC 70**
   See also CA 89-92; CANR 58, 117; SATA 152

Chernyshevsky, Nikolai Gavrilovich
   See Chernyshevsky, Nikolay Gavrilovich
   See also DLB 238

Chernyshevsky, Nikolay Gavrilovich 1828-1889 .... **NCLC 1**
   See Chernyshevsky, Nikolai Gavrilovich

Cherry, Carolyn Janice 1942-
   See Cherryh, C. J.
   See also CA 65-68; CANR 10

Cherryh, C. J. .... **CLC 35**
   See Cherry, Carolyn Janice
   See also AAYA 24; BPFB 1; DLBY 1980; FANT; SATA 93; SCFW 2; SFW 4; YAW

Chesnutt, Charles W(addell) 1858-1932 .... **BLC 1; SSC 7, 54; TCLC 5, 39**
   See also AFAW 1, 2; AMWS 14; BW 1, 3; CA 106; 125; CANR 76; DAM MULT; DLB 12, 50, 78; EWL 3; MAL 5; MTCW 1, 2; MTFW 2005; RGAL 4; RGSF 2; SSFS 11

Chester, Alfred 1929(?)-1971 .... **CLC 49**
   See also CA 196; 33-36R; DLB 130; MAL 5

Chesterton, G(ilbert) K(eith) 1874-1936 . **PC 28; SSC 1, 46; TCLC 1, 6, 64**
   See also AAYA 57; BRW 6; CA 104; 132; CANR 73, 131; CDBLB 1914-1945; CMW 4; DAM NOV, POET; DLB 10, 19, 34, 70, 98, 149, 178; EWL 3; FANT; MSW; MTCW 1, 2; MTFW 2005; RGEL 2; RGSF 2; SATA 27; SUFW 1

Chettle, Henry 1560-1607(?) .... **LC 112**
   See also DLB 136; RGEL 2

Chiang, Pin-chin 1904-1986
   See Ding Ling
   See also CA 118

Chief Joseph 1840-1904 .... **NNAL**
   See also CA 152; DA3; DAM MULT

Chief Seattle 1786(?)-1866 .... **NNAL**
   See also DA3; DAM MULT

Ch'ien, Chung-shu 1910-1998 .... **CLC 22**
   See Qian Zhongshu
   See also CA 130; CANR 73; MTCW 1, 2

Chikamatsu Monzaemon 1653-1724 ... **LC 66**
   See also RGWL 2, 3

Child, L. Maria
   See Child, Lydia Maria

Child, Lydia Maria 1802-1880 .. **NCLC 6, 73**
   See also DLB 1, 74, 243; RGAL 4; SATA 67

Child, Mrs.
   See Child, Lydia Maria

Child, Philip 1898-1978 .... **CLC 19, 68**
   See also CA 13-14; CAP 1; CP 1; DLB 68; RHW; SATA 47

Childers, (Robert) Erskine 1870-1922 .... **TCLC 65**
   See also CA 113; 153; DLB 70

Childress, Alice 1920-1994 . **BLC 1; CLC 12, 15, 86, 96; DC 4; TCLC 116**
   See also AAYA 8; BW 2; BYA 2; CA 45-48; 146; CAD; CANR 3, 27, 50, 74; CLR 14; CWD; DA3; DAM DRAM, MULT, NOV; DFS 2, 8, 14; DLB 7, 38, 249; JRDA; LAIT 5; MAICYA 1, 2; MAICYAS 1; MAL 5; MTCW 1, 2; MTFW 2005; RGAL 4; SATA 7, 48, 81; TUS; WYA; YAW

Chin, Frank (Chew, Jr.) 1940- .... **AAL; CLC 135; DC 7**
   See also CA 33-36R; CAD; CANR 71; CD 5, 6; DAM MULT; DLB 206, 312; LAIT 5; RGAL 4

Chin, Marilyn (Mei Ling) 1955- .... **PC 40**
   See also CA 129; CANR 70, 113; CWP; DLB 312

Chislett, (Margaret) Anne 1943- ...... **CLC 34**
   See also CA 151

Chitty, Thomas Willes 1926- .... **CLC 11**
   See Hinde, Thomas
   See also CA 5-8R; CN 7

Chivers, Thomas Holley 1809-1858 .... **NCLC 49**
   See also DLB 3, 248; RGAL 4

Choi, Susan 1969- .... **CLC 119**
   See also CA 223

Chomette, Rene Lucien 1898-1981
   See Clair, Rene
   See also CA 103

Chomsky, (Avram) Noam 1928- ..... **CLC 132**
   See also CA 17-20R; CANR 28, 62, 110, 132; DA3; DLB 246; MTCW 1, 2; MTFW 2005

Chona, Maria 1845(?)-1936 .... **NNAL**
   See also CA 144

Chopin, Kate .... **SSC 8, 68; TCLC 127; WLCS**
   See Chopin, Katherine
   See also AAYA 33; AMWR 2; AMWS 1; BYA 11, 15; CDALB 1865-1917; DA; DAB; DLB 12, 78; EXPN; EXPS; FL 1:3; FW; LAIT 3; MAL 5; MAWW; NFS 3; RGAL 4; RGSF 2; SSFS 2, 13, 17; TUS

Chopin, Katherine 1851-1904
   See Chopin, Kate
   See also CA 104; 122; DA3; DAC; DAM MST, NOV

Chretien de Troyes c. 12th cent. - . **CMLC 10**
   See also DLB 208; EW 1; RGWL 2, 3; TWA

Christie
   See Ichikawa, Kon

DA3; DAM MULT, POET; DLB 5, 41;
EXPP; MAICYA 1, 2; MTCW 1, 2;
MTFW 2005; PFS 1, 14; SATA 20, 69,
128; WP

Clinton, Dirk
See Silverberg, Robert

Clough, Arthur Hugh 1819-1861 .. **NCLC 27, 163**
See also BRW 5; DLB 32; RGEL 2

Clutha, Janet Paterson Frame 1924-2004
See Frame, Janet
See also CA 1-4R; 224; CANR 2, 36, 76, 135; MTCW 1, 2; SATA 119

Clyne, Terence
See Blatty, William Peter

Cobalt, Martin
See Mayne, William (James Carter)

Cobb, Irvin S(hrewsbury)
1876-1944 .... **TCLC 77**
See also CA 175; DLB 11, 25, 86

Cobbett, William 1763-1835 .... **NCLC 49**
See also DLB 43, 107, 158; RGEL 2

Coburn, D(onald) L(ee) 1938- .... **CLC 10**
See also CA 89-92

Cocteau, Jean (Maurice Eugene Clement)
1889-1963 ...... **CLC 1, 8, 15, 16, 43; DC 17; TCLC 119; WLC**
See also CA 25-28; CANR 40; CAP 2; DA; DA3; DAB; DAC; DAM DRAM, MST, NOV; DLB 65, 258, 321; EW 10; EWL 3; GFL 1789 to the Present; MTCW 1, 2; RGWL 2, 3; TWA

Codrescu, Andrei 1946- .... **CLC 46, 121**
See also CA 33-36R; CAAS 19; CANR 13, 34, 53, 76, 125; CN 7; DA3; DAM POET; MAL 5; MTCW 2; MTFW 2005

Coe, Max
See Bourne, Randolph S(illiman)

Coe, Tucker
See Westlake, Donald E(dwin)

Coen, Ethan 1958- .... **CLC 108**
See also AAYA 54; CA 126; CANR 85

Coen, Joel 1955- .... **CLC 108**
See also AAYA 54; CA 126; CANR 119

The Coen Brothers
See Coen, Ethan; Coen, Joel

Coetzee, J(ohn) M(axwell) 1940- ..... **CLC 23, 33, 66, 117, 161, 162**
See also AAYA 37; AFW; BRWS 6; CA 77-80; CANR 41, 54, 74, 114, 133; CN 4, 5, 6, 7; DA3; DAM NOV; DLB 225; EWL 3; LMFS 2; MTCW 1, 2; MTFW 2005; NFS 21; WLIT 2; WWE 1

Coffey, Brian
See Koontz, Dean R.

Coffin, Robert P(eter) Tristram
1892-1955 .... **TCLC 95**
See also CA 123; 169; DLB 45

Cohan, George M(ichael)
1878-1942 .... **TCLC 60**
See also CA 157; DLB 249; RGAL 4

Cohen, Arthur A(llen) 1928-1986 ...... **CLC 7, 31**
See also CA 1-4R; 120; CANR 1, 17, 42; DLB 28

Cohen, Leonard (Norman) 1934- ...... **CLC 3, 38**
See also CA 21-24R; CANR 14, 69; CN 1, 2, 3, 4, 5, 6; CP 1, 2, 3, 4, 5, 6, 7; DAC; DAM MST; DLB 53; EWL 3; MTCW 1

Cohen, Matt(hew) 1942-1999 .... **CLC 19**
See also CA 61-64; 187; CAAS 18; CANR 40; CN 1, 2, 3, 4, 5, 6; DAC; DLB 53

Cohen-Solal, Annie 1948- .... **CLC 50**
See also CA 239

Colegate, Isabel 1931- .... **CLC 36**
See also CA 17-20R; CANR 8, 22, 74; CN 4, 5, 6, 7; DLB 14, 231; INT CANR-22; MTCW 1

Coleman, Emmett
See Reed, Ishmael (Scott)

Coleridge, Hartley 1796-1849 .... **NCLC 90**
See also DLB 96

Coleridge, M. E.
See Coleridge, Mary E(lizabeth)

Coleridge, Mary E(lizabeth)
1861-1907 .... **TCLC 73**
See also CA 116; 166; DLB 19, 98

Coleridge, Samuel Taylor
1772-1834 ...... **NCLC 9, 54, 99, 111; PC 11, 39, 67; WLC**
See also AAYA 66; BRW 4; BRWR 2; BYA 4; CDBLB 1789-1832; DA; DA3; DAB; DAC; DAM MST, POET; DLB 93, 107; EXPP; LATS 1:1; LMFS 1; PAB; PFS 4, 5; RGEL 2; TEA; WLIT 3; WP

Coleridge, Sara 1802-1852 .... **NCLC 31**
See also DLB 199

Coles, Don 1928- .... **CLC 46**
See also CA 115; CANR 38; CP 7

Coles, Robert (Martin) 1929- .... **CLC 108**
See also CA 45-48; CANR 3, 32, 66, 70, 135; INT CANR-32; SATA 23

Colette, (Sidonie-Gabrielle)
1873-1954 .... **SSC 10; TCLC 1, 5, 16**
See Willy, Colette
See also CA 104; 131; DA3; DAM NOV; DLB 65; EW 9; EWL 3; GFL 1789 to the Present; MTCW 1, 2; MTFW 2005; RGWL 2, 3; TWA

Collett, (Jacobine) Camilla (Wergeland)
1813-1895 .... **NCLC 22**

Collier, Christopher 1930- .... **CLC 30**
See also AAYA 13; BYA 2; CA 33-36R; CANR 13, 33, 102; JRDA; MAICYA 1, 2; SATA 16, 70; WYA; YAW 1

Collier, James Lincoln 1928- .... **CLC 30**
See also AAYA 13; BYA 2; CA 9-12R; CANR 4, 33, 60, 102; CLR 3; DAM POP; JRDA; MAICYA 1, 2; SAAS 21; SATA 8, 70; WYA; YAW 1

Collier, Jeremy 1650-1726 .... **LC 6**

Collier, John 1901-1980 . **SSC 19; TCLC 127**
See also CA 65-68; 97-100; CANR 10; CN 1, 2; DLB 77, 255; FANT; SUFW 1

Collier, Mary 1690-1762 .... **LC 86**
See also DLB 95

Collingwood, R(obin) G(eorge)
1889(?)-1943 .... **TCLC 67**
See also CA 117; 155; DLB 262

Collins, Billy 1941- .... **PC 68**
See also AAYA 64; CA 151; CANR 92; MTFW 2005; PFS 18

Collins, Hunt
See Hunter, Evan

Collins, Linda 1931- .... **CLC 44**
See also CA 125

Collins, Tom
See Furphy, Joseph
See also RGEL 2

Collins, (William) Wilkie
1824-1889 .... **NCLC 1, 18, 93**
See also BRWS 6; CDBLB 1832-1890; CMW 4; DLB 18, 70, 159; GL 2; MSW; RGEL 2; RGSF 2; SUFW 1; WLIT 4

Collins, William 1721-1759 .... **LC 4, 40**
See also BRW 3; DAM POET; DLB 109; RGEL 2

Collodi, Carlo .... **NCLC 54**
See Lorenzini, Carlo
See also CLR 5; WCH; WLIT 7

Colman, George
See Glassco, John

Colman, George, the Elder
1732-1794 .... **LC 98**
See also RGEL 2

Colonna, Vittoria 1492-1547 .... **LC 71**
See also RGWL 2, 3

Colt, Winchester Remington
See Hubbard, L(afayette) Ron(ald)

Colter, Cyrus J. 1910-2002 .... **CLC 58**
See also BW 1; CA 65-68; 205; CANR 10, 66; CN 2, 3, 4, 5, 6; DLB 33

Colton, James
See Hansen, Joseph
See also GLL 1

Colum, Padraic 1881-1972 .... **CLC 28**
See also BYA 4; CA 73-76; 33-36R; CANR 35; CLR 36; CP 1; CWRI 5; DLB 19; MAICYA 1, 2; MTCW 1; RGEL 2; SATA 15; WCH

Colvin, James
See Moorcock, Michael (John)

Colwin, Laurie (E.) 1944-1992 .... **CLC 5, 13, 23, 84**
See also CA 89-92; 139; CANR 20, 46; DLB 218; DLBY 1980; MTCW 1

Comfort, Alex(ander) 1920-2000 .... **CLC 7**
See also CA 1-4R; 190; CANR 1, 45; CN 1, 2, 3, 4; CP 1, 2, 3, 4, 5, 6, 7; DAM POP; MTCW 2

Comfort, Montgomery
See Campbell, (John) Ramsey

Compton-Burnett, I(vy)
1892(?)-1969 .... **CLC 1, 3, 10, 15, 34**
See also BRW 7; CA 1-4R; 25-28R; CANR 4; DAM NOV; DLB 36; EWL 3; MTCW 1, 2; RGEL 2

Comstock, Anthony 1844-1915 ...... **TCLC 13**
See also CA 110; 169

Comte, Auguste 1798-1857 .... **NCLC 54**

Conan Doyle, Arthur
See Doyle, Sir Arthur Conan
See also BPFB 1; BYA 4, 5, 11

Conde (Abellan), Carmen
1901-1996 .... **HLCS 1**
See also CA 177; CWW 2; DLB 108; EWL 3; HW 2

Conde, Maryse 1937- ..... **BLCS; CLC 52, 92**
See also BW 2, 3; CA 110, 190; CAAE 190; CANR 30, 53, 76; CWW 2; DAM MULT; EWL 3; MTCW 2; MTFW 2005

Condillac, Etienne Bonnot de
1714-1780 .... **LC 26**
See also DLB 313

Condon, Richard (Thomas)
1915-1996 .... **CLC 4, 6, 8, 10, 45, 100**
See also BEST 90:3; BPFB 1; CA 1-4R; 151; CAAS 1; CANR 2, 23; CMW 4; CN 1, 2, 3, 4, 5, 6; DAM NOV; INT CANR-23; MAL 5; MTCW 1, 2

Condorcet .... **LC 104**
See Condorcet, marquis de Marie-Jean-Antoine-Nicolas Caritat
See also GFL Beginnings to 1789

Condorcet, marquis de Marie-Jean-Antoine-Nicolas Caritat
1743-1794
See Condorcet
See also DLB 313

Confucius 551B.C.-479B.C. .... **CMLC 19, 65; WLCS**
See also DA; DA3; DAB; DAC; DAM MST

Congreve, William 1670-1729 ... **DC 2; LC 5, 21; WLC**
See also BRW 2; CDBLB 1660-1789; DA; DAB; DAC; DAM DRAM, MST, POET; DFS 15; DLB 39, 84; RGEL 2; WLIT 3

Conley, Robert J(ackson) 1940- .... **NNAL**
See also CA 41-44R; CANR 15, 34, 45, 96; DAM MULT; TCWW 2

Connell, Evan S(helby), Jr. 1924- . **CLC 4, 6, 45**
See also AAYA 7; AMWS 14; CA 1-4R; CAAS 2; CANR 2, 39, 76, 97, 140; CN 1, 2, 3, 4, 5, 6; DAM NOV; DLB 2; DLBY 1981; MAL 5; MTCW 1, 2; MTFW 2005

Connelly, Marc(us Cook) 1890-1980 . **CLC 7**
See also CA 85-88; 102; CAD; CANR 30;
DFS 12; DLB 7; DLBY 1980; MAL 5;
RGAL 4; SATA-Obit 25

Connor, Ralph .... **TCLC 31**
See Gordon, Charles William
See also DLB 92; TCWW 1, 2

Conrad, Joseph 1857-1924 ..... **SSC 9, 67, 69,
71; TCLC 1, 6, 13, 25, 43, 57; WLC**
See also AAYA 26; BPFB 1; BRW 6;
BRWC 1; BRWR 2; BYA 2; CA 104; 131;
CANR 60; CDBLB 1890-1914; DA; DA3;
DAB; DAC; DAM MST, NOV; DLB 10,
34, 98, 156; EWL 3; EXPN; EXPS; LAIT
2; LATS 1:1; LMFS 1; MTCW 1, 2;
MTFW 2005; NFS 2, 16; RGEL 2; RGSF
2; SATA 27; SSFS 1, 12; TEA; WLIT 4

Conrad, Robert Arnold
See Hart, Moss

Conroy, (Donald) Pat(rick) 1945- ... **CLC 30,
74**
See also AAYA 8, 52; AITN 1; BPFB 1;
CA 85-88; CANR 24, 53, 129; CN 7;
CPW; CSW; DA3; DAM NOV, POP;
DLB 6; LAIT 5; MAL 5; MTCW 1, 2;
MTFW 2005

Constant (de Rebecque), (Henri) Benjamin
1767-1830 .... **NCLC 6**
See also DLB 119; EW 4; GFL 1789 to the
Present

Conway, Jill K(er) 1934- .... **CLC 152**
See also CA 130; CANR 94

Conybeare, Charles Augustus
See Eliot, T(homas) S(tearns)

Cook, Michael 1933-1994 .... **CLC 58**
See also CA 93-96; CANR 68; DLB 53

Cook, Robin 1940- .... **CLC 14**
See also AAYA 32; BEST 90:2; BPFB 1;
CA 108; 111; CANR 41, 90, 109; CPW;
DA3; DAM POP; HGG; INT CA-111

Cook, Roy
See Silverberg, Robert

Cooke, Elizabeth 1948- .... **CLC 55**
See also CA 129

Cooke, John Esten 1830-1886 .... **NCLC 5**
See also DLB 3, 248; RGAL 4

Cooke, John Estes
See Baum, L(yman) Frank

Cooke, M. E.
See Creasey, John

Cooke, Margaret
See Creasey, John

Cooke, Rose Terry 1827-1892 ...... **NCLC 110**
See also DLB 12, 74

Cook-Lynn, Elizabeth 1930- .... **CLC 93;
NNAL**
See also CA 133; DAM MULT; DLB 175

Cooney, Ray .... **CLC 62**
See also CBD

Cooper, Anthony Ashley 1671-1713 .. **LC 107**
See also DLB 101

Cooper, Dennis 1953- .... **CLC 203**
See also CA 133; CANR 72, 86; GLL 1;
HGG

Cooper, Douglas 1960- .... **CLC 86**

Cooper, Henry St. John
See Creasey, John

Cooper, J(oan) California (?)- .... **CLC 56**
See also AAYA 12; BW 1; CA 125; CANR
55; DAM MULT; DLB 212

Cooper, James Fenimore
1789-1851 .... **NCLC 1, 27, 54**
See also AAYA 22; AMW; BPFB 1;
CDALB 1640-1865; DA3; DLB 3, 183,
250, 254; LAIT 1; NFS 9; RGAL 4; SATA
19; TUS; WCH

Cooper, Susan Fenimore
1813-1894 .... **NCLC 129**
See also ANW; DLB 239, 254

Coover, Robert (Lowell) 1932- ...... **CLC 3, 7,
15, 32, 46, 87, 161; SSC 15**
See also AMWS 5; BPFB 1; CA 45-48;
CANR 3, 37, 58, 115; CN 1, 2, 3, 4, 5, 6,
7; DAM NOV; DLB 2, 227; DLBY 1981;
EWL 3; MAL 5; MTCW 1, 2; MTFW
2005; RGAL 4; RGSF 2

Copeland, Stewart (Armstrong)
1952- .... **CLC 26**

Copernicus, Nicolaus 1473-1543 .... **LC 45**

Coppard, A(lfred) E(dgar)
1878-1957 .... **SSC 21; TCLC 5**
See also BRWS 8; CA 114; 167; DLB 162;
EWL 3; HGG; RGEL 2; RGSF 2; SUFW
1; YABC 1

Coppee, Francois 1842-1908 .... **TCLC 25**
See also CA 170; DLB 217

Coppola, Francis Ford 1939- ... **CLC 16, 126**
See also AAYA 39; CA 77-80; CANR 40,
78; DLB 44

Copway, George 1818-1869 .... **NNAL**
See also DAM MULT; DLB 175, 183

Corbiere, Tristan 1845-1875 .... **NCLC 43**
See also DLB 217; GFL 1789 to the Present

Corcoran, Barbara (Asenath)
1911- .... **CLC 17**
See also AAYA 14; CA 21-24R, 191; CAAE
191; CAAS 2; CANR 11, 28, 48; CLR
50; DLB 52; JRDA; MAICYA 2; MAIC-
YAS 1; RHW; SAAS 20; SATA 3, 77;
SATA-Essay 125

Cordelier, Maurice
See Giraudoux, Jean(-Hippolyte)

Corelli, Marie .... **TCLC 51**
See Mackay, Mary
See also DLB 34, 156; RGEL 2; SUFW 1

Corinna c. 225B.C.-c. 305B.C. ...... **CMLC 72**

Corman, Cid .... **CLC 9**
See Corman, Sidney
See also CAAS 2; CP 1, 2, 3, 4, 5, 6, 7;
DLB 5, 193

Corman, Sidney 1924-2004
See Corman, Cid
See also CA 85-88; 225; CANR 44; DAM
POET

Cormier, Robert (Edmund)
1925-2000 .... **CLC 12, 30**
See also AAYA 3, 19; BYA 1, 2, 6, 8, 9;
CA 1-4R; CANR 5, 23, 76, 93; CDALB
1968-1988; CLR 12, 55; DA; DAB; DAC;
DAM MST, NOV; DLB 52; EXPN; INT
CANR-23; JRDA; LAIT 5; MAICYA 1,
2; MTCW 1, 2; MTFW 2005; NFS 2, 18;
SATA 10, 45, 83; SATA-Obit 122; WYA;
YAW

Corn, Alfred (DeWitt III) 1943- .... **CLC 33**
See also CA 179; CAAE 179; CAAS 25;
CANR 44; CP 3, 4, 5, 6, 7; CSW; DLB
120, 282; DLBY 1980

Corneille, Pierre 1606-1684 ... **DC 21; LC 28**
See also DAB; DAM MST; DFS 21; DLB
268; EW 3; GFL Beginnings to 1789;
RGWL 2, 3; TWA

Cornwell, David (John Moore)
1931- .... **CLC 9, 15**
See le Carre, John
See also CA 5-8R; CANR 13, 33, 59, 107,
132; DA3; DAM POP; MTCW 1, 2;
MTFW 2005

Cornwell, Patricia (Daniels) 1956- . **CLC 155**
See also AAYA 16, 56; BPFB 1; CA 134;
CANR 53, 131; CMW 4; CPW; CSW;
DAM POP; DLB 306; MSW; MTCW 2;
MTFW 2005

Corso, (Nunzio) Gregory 1930-2001 . **CLC 1,
11; PC 33**
See also AMWS 12; BG 1:2; CA 5-8R; 193;
CANR 41, 76, 132; CP 1, 2, 3, 4, 5, 6, 7;
DA3; DLB 5, 16, 237; LMFS 2; MAL 5;
MTCW 1, 2; MTFW 2005; WP

Cortazar, Julio 1914-1984 ... **CLC 2, 3, 5, 10,
13, 15, 33, 34, 92; HLC 1; SSC 7, 76**
See also BPFB 1; CA 21-24R; CANR 12,
32, 81; CDWLB 3; DA3; DAM MULT,
NOV; DLB 113; EWL 3; EXPS; HW 1,
2; LAW; MTCW 1, 2; MTFW 2005;
RGSF 2; RGWL 2, 3; SSFS 3, 20; TWA;
WLIT 1

Cortes, Hernan 1485-1547 .... **LC 31**

Corvinus, Jakob
See Raabe, Wilhelm (Karl)

Corwin, Cecil
See Kornbluth, C(yril) M.

Cosic, Dobrica 1921- .... **CLC 14**
See also CA 122; 138; CDWLB 4; CWW
2; DLB 181; EWL 3

Costain, Thomas B(ertram)
1885-1965 .... **CLC 30**
See also BYA 3; CA 5-8R; 25-28R; DLB 9;
RHW

Costantini, Humberto 1924(?)-1987 . **CLC 49**
See also CA 131; 122; EWL 3; HW 1

Costello, Elvis 1954- .... **CLC 21**
See also CA 204

Costenoble, Philostene
See Ghelderode, Michel de

Cotes, Cecil V.
See Duncan, Sara Jeannette

Cotter, Joseph Seamon Sr.
1861-1949 .... **BLC 1; TCLC 28**
See also BW 1; CA 124; DAM MULT; DLB
50

Couch, Arthur Thomas Quiller
See Quiller-Couch, Sir Arthur (Thomas)

Coulton, James
See Hansen, Joseph

Couperus, Louis (Marie Anne)
1863-1923 .... **TCLC 15**
See also CA 115; EWL 3; RGWL 2, 3

Coupland, Douglas 1961- .... **CLC 85, 133**
See also AAYA 34; CA 142; CANR 57, 90,
130; CCA 1; CN 7; CPW; DAC; DAM
POP

Court, Wesli
See Turco, Lewis (Putnam)

Courtenay, Bryce 1933- .... **CLC 59**
See also CA 138; CPW

Courtney, Robert
See Ellison, Harlan (Jay)

Cousteau, Jacques-Yves 1910-1997 .. **CLC 30**
See also CA 65-68; 159; CANR 15, 67;
MTCW 1; SATA 38, 98

Coventry, Francis 1725-1754 .... **LC 46**

Coverdale, Miles c. 1487-1569 .... **LC 77**
See also DLB 167

Cowan, Peter (Walkinshaw)
1914-2002 .... **SSC 28**
See also CA 21-24R; CANR 9, 25, 50, 83;
CN 1, 2, 3, 4, 5, 6, 7; DLB 260; RGSF 2

Coward, Noel (Peirce) 1899-1973 . **CLC 1, 9,
29, 51**
See also AITN 1; BRWS 2; CA 17-18; 41-
44R; CANR 35, 132; CAP 2; CBD; CD-
BLB 1914-1945; DA3; DAM DRAM;
DFS 3, 6; DLB 10, 245; EWL 3; IDFW
3, 4; MTCW 1, 2; MTFW 2005; RGEL 2;
TEA

Cowley, Abraham 1618-1667 .... **LC 43**
See also BRW 2; DLB 131, 151; PAB;
RGEL 2

Cowley, Malcolm 1898-1989 .... **CLC 39**
See also AMWS 2; CA 5-8R; 128; CANR
3, 55; CP 1, 2, 3, 4; DLB 4, 48; DLBY
1981, 1989; EWL 3; MAL 5; MTCW 1,
2; MTFW 2005

Cowper, William 1731-1800 ..... **NCLC 8, 94;
PC 40**
See also BRW 3; DA3; DAM POET; DLB
104, 109; RGEL 2

Cox, William Trevor 1928-
See Trevor, William
See also CA 9-12R; CANR 4, 37, 55, 76, 102, 139; DAM NOV; INT CANR-37; MTCW 1, 2; MTFW 2005; TEA

Coyne, P. J.
See Masters, Hilary

Cozzens, James Gould 1903-1978 . **CLC 1, 4, 11, 92**
See also AMW; BPFB 1; CA 9-12R; 81-84; CANR 19; CDALB 1941-1968; CN 1, 2; DLB 9, 294; DLBD 2; DLBY 1984, 1997; EWL 5; MAL 5; MTCW 1, 2; MTFW 2005; RGAL 4

Crabbe, George 1754-1832 .... **NCLC 26, 121**
See also BRW 3; DLB 93; RGEL 2

Crace, Jim 1946- .... **CLC 157; SSC 61**
See also CA 128; 135; CANR 55, 70, 123; CN 5, 6, 7; DLB 231; INT CA-135

Craddock, Charles Egbert
See Murfree, Mary Noailles

Craig, A. A.
See Anderson, Poul (William)

Craik, Mrs.
See Craik, Dinah Maria (Mulock)
See also RGEL 2

Craik, Dinah Maria (Mulock)
1826-1887 .... **NCLC 38**
See Craik, Mrs.; Mulock, Dinah Maria
See also DLB 35, 163; MAICYA 1, 2; SATA 34

Cram, Ralph Adams 1863-1942 ..... **TCLC 45**
See also CA 160

Cranch, Christopher Pearse
1813-1892 .... **NCLC 115**
See also DLB 1, 42, 243

Crane, (Harold) Hart 1899-1932 .... **PC 3; TCLC 2, 5, 80; WLC**
See also AMW; AMWR 2; CA 104; 127; CDALB 1917-1929; DA; DA3; DAB; DAC; DAM MST, POET; DLB 4, 48; EWL 3; MAL 5; MTCW 1, 2; MTFW 2005; RGAL 4; TUS

Crane, R(onald) S(almon)
1886-1967 .... **CLC 27**
See also CA 85-88; DLB 63

Crane, Stephen (Townley)
1871-1900 ...... **SSC 7, 56, 70; TCLC 11, 17, 32; WLC**
See also AAYA 21; AMW; AMWC 1; BPFB 1; BYA 3; CA 109; 140; CANR 84; CDALB 1865-1917; DA; DA3; DAB; DAC; DAM MST, NOV, POET; DLB 12, 54, 78; EXPN; EXPS; LAIT 2; LMFS 2; MAL 5; NFS 4, 20; PFS 9; RGAL 4; RGSF 2; SSFS 4; TUS; WYA; YABC 2

Cranmer, Thomas 1489-1556 .... **LC 95**
See also DLB 132, 213

Cranshaw, Stanley
See Fisher, Dorothy (Frances) Canfield

Crase, Douglas 1944- .... **CLC 58**
See also CA 106

Crashaw, Richard 1612(?)-1649 .... **LC 24**
See also BRW 2; DLB 126; PAB; RGEL 2

Cratinus c. 519B.C.-c. 422B.C. ..... **CMLC 54**
See also LMFS 1

Craven, Margaret 1901-1980 .... **CLC 17**
See also BYA 2; CA 103; CCA 1; DAC; LAIT 5

Crawford, F(rancis) Marion
1854-1909 .... **TCLC 10**
See also CA 107; 168; DLB 71; HGG; RGAL 4; SUFW 1

Crawford, Isabella Valancy
1850-1887 .... **NCLC 12, 127**
See also DLB 92; RGEL 2

Crayon, Geoffrey
See Irving, Washington

Creasey, John 1908-1973 .... **CLC 11**
See Marric, J. J.
See also CA 5-8R; 41-44R; CANR 8, 59; CMW 4; DLB 77; MTCW 1

Crebillon, Claude Prosper Jolyot de (fils)
1707-1777 .... **LC 1, 28**
See also DLB 313; GFL Beginnings to 1789

Credo
See Creasey, John

Credo, Alvaro J. de
See Prado (Calvo), Pedro

Creeley, Robert (White) 1926-2005 .. **CLC 1, 2, 4, 8, 11, 15, 36, 78**
See also AMWS 4; CA 1-4R; 237; CAAS 10; CANR 23, 43, 89, 137; CP 1, 2, 3, 4, 5, 6, 7; DA3; DAM POET; DLB 5, 16, 169; DLBD 17; EWL 3; MAL 5; MTCW 1, 2; MTFW 2005; PFS 21; RGAL 4; WP

Crenne, Helisenne de 1510-1560 .... **LC 113**

Crevecoeur, Hector St. John de
See Crevecoeur, Michel Guillaume Jean de
See also ANW

Crevecoeur, Michel Guillaume Jean de
1735-1813 .... **NCLC 105**
See Crevecoeur, Hector St. John de
See also AMWS 1; DLB 37

Crevel, Rene 1900-1935 .... **TCLC 112**
See also GLL 2

Crews, Harry (Eugene) 1935- ..... **CLC 6, 23, 49**
See also AITN 1; AMWS 11; BPFB 1; CA 25-28R; CANR 20, 57; CN 3, 4, 5, 6, 7; CSW; DA3; DLB 6, 143, 185; MTCW 1, 2; MTFW 2005; RGAL 4

Crichton, (John) Michael 1942- .... **CLC 2, 6, 54, 90**
See also AAYA 10, 49; AITN 2; BPFB 1; CA 25-28R; CANR 13, 40, 54, 76, 127; CMW 4; CN 2, 3, 6, 7; CPW; DA3; DAM NOV, POP; DLB 292; DLBY 1981; INT CANR-13; JRDA; MTCW 1, 2; MTFW 2005; SATA 9, 88; SFW 4; YAW

Crispin, Edmund .... **CLC 22**
See Montgomery, (Robert) Bruce
See also DLB 87; MSW

Cristofer, Michael 1945- .... **CLC 28**
See also CA 110; 152; CAD; CD 5, 6; DAM DRAM; DFS 15; DLB 7

Criton
See Alain

Croce, Benedetto 1866-1952 .... **TCLC 37**
See also CA 120; 155; EW 8; EWL 3; WLIT 7

Crockett, David 1786-1836 .... **NCLC 8**
See also DLB 3, 11, 183, 248

Crockett, Davy
See Crockett, David

Crofts, Freeman Wills 1879-1957 .. **TCLC 55**
See also CA 115; 195; CMW 4; DLB 77; MSW

Croker, John Wilson 1780-1857 .... **NCLC 10**
See also DLB 110

Crommelynck, Fernand 1885-1970 .. **CLC 75**
See also CA 189; 89-92; EWL 3

Cromwell, Oliver 1599-1658 .... **LC 43**

Cronenberg, David 1943- .... **CLC 143**
See also CA 138; CCA 1

Cronin, A(rchibald) J(oseph)
1896-1981 .... **CLC 32**
See also BPFB 1; CA 1-4R; 102; CANR 5; CN 2; DLB 191; SATA 47; SATA-Obit 25

Cross, Amanda
See Heilbrun, Carolyn G(old)
See also BPFB 1; CMW; CPW; DLB 306; MSW

Crothers, Rachel 1878-1958 .... **TCLC 19**
See also CA 113; 194; CAD; CWD; DLB 7, 266; RGAL 4

Croves, Hal
See Traven, B.

Crow Dog, Mary (Ellen) (?)- .... **CLC 93**
See Brave Bird, Mary
See also CA 154

Crowfield, Christopher
See Stowe, Harriet (Elizabeth) Beecher

Crowley, Aleister .... **TCLC 7**
See Crowley, Edward Alexander
See also GLL 1

Crowley, Edward Alexander 1875-1947
See Crowley, Aleister
See also CA 104; HGG

Crowley, John 1942- .... **CLC 57**
See also AAYA 57; BPFB 1; CA 61-64; CANR 43, 98, 138; DLBY 1982; FANT; MTFW 2005; SATA 65, 140; SFW 4; SUFW 2

Crowne, John 1641-1712 .... **LC 104**
See also DLB 80; RGEL 2

Crud
See Crumb, R(obert)

Crumarums
See Crumb, R(obert)

Crumb, R(obert) 1943- .... **CLC 17**
See also CA 106; CANR 107

Crumbum
See Crumb, R(obert)

Crumski
See Crumb, R(obert)

Crum the Bum
See Crumb, R(obert)

Crunk
See Crumb, R(obert)

Crustt
See Crumb, R(obert)

Crutchfield, Les
See Trumbo, Dalton

Cruz, Victor Hernandez 1949- ... **HLC 1; PC 37**
See also BW 2; CA 65-68; CAAS 17; CANR 14, 32, 74, 132; CP 1, 2, 3, 4, 5, 6, 7; DAM MULT, POET; DLB 41; DNFS 1; EXPP; HW 1, 2; LLW; MTCW 2; MTFW 2005; PFS 16; WP

Cryer, Gretchen (Kiger) 1935- .... **CLC 21**
See also CA 114; 123

Csath, Geza .... **TCLC 13**
See Brenner, Jozef
See also CA 111

Cudlip, David R(ockwell) 1933- .... **CLC 34**
See also CA 177

Cullen, Countee 1903-1946 . **BLC 1; HR 1:2; PC 20; TCLC 4, 37; WLCS**
See also AFAW 2; AMWS 4; BW 1; CA 108; 124; CDALB 1917-1929; DA; DA3; DAC; DAM MST, MULT, POET; DLB 4, 48, 51; EWL 3; EXPP; LMFS 2; MAL 5; MTCW 1, 2; MTFW 2005; PFS 3; RGAL 4; SATA 18; WP

Culleton, Beatrice 1949- .... **NNAL**
See also CA 120; CANR 83; DAC

Cum, R.
See Crumb, R(obert)

Cumberland, Richard
1732-1811 .... **NCLC 167**
See also DLB 89; RGEL 2

Cummings, Bruce F(rederick) 1889-1919
See Barbellion, W. N. P.
See also CA 123

Cummings, E(dward) E(stlin)
1894-1962 .. **CLC 1, 3, 8, 12, 15, 68; PC 5; TCLC 137; WLC**
See also AAYA 41; AMW; CA 73-76; CANR 31; CDALB 1929-1941; DA; DA3; DAB; DAC; DAM MST, POET; DLB 4, 48; EWL 3; EXPP; MAL 5; MTCW 1, 2; MTFW 2005; PAB; PFS 1, 3, 12, 13, 19; RGAL 4; TUS; WP

Davies, William Henry 1871-1940 ... **TCLC 5**
See also BRWS 11; CA 104; 179; DLB 19,
174; EWL 3; RGEL 2

Da Vinci, Leonardo 1452-1519 ..... **LC 12, 57,
60**
See also AAYA 40

Davis, Angela (Yvonne) 1944- .... **CLC 77**
See also BW 2, 3; CA 57-60; CANR 10,
81; CSW; DA3; DAM MULT; FW

Davis, B. Lynch
See Bioy Casares, Adolfo; Borges, Jorge
Luis

Davis, Frank Marshall 1905-1987 ...... **BLC 1**
See also BW 2, 3; CA 125; 123; CANR 42,
80; DAM MULT; DLB 51

Davis, Gordon
See Hunt, E(verette) Howard, (Jr.)

Davis, H(arold) L(enoir) 1896-1960 . **CLC 49**
See also ANW; CA 178; 89-92; DLB 9,
206; SATA 114; TCWW 1, 2

Davis, Natalie Zemon 1928- .... **CLC 204**
See also CA 53-56; CANR 58, 100

Davis, Rebecca (Blaine) Harding
1831-1910 .... **SSC 38; TCLC 6**
See also CA 104; 179; DLB 74, 239; FW;
NFS 14; RGAL 4; TUS

Davis, Richard Harding
1864-1916 .... **TCLC 24**
See also CA 114; 179; DLB 12, 23, 78, 79,
189; DLBD 13; RGAL 4

Davison, Frank Dalby 1893-1970 ..... **CLC 15**
See also CA 217; 116; DLB 260

Davison, Lawrence H.
See Lawrence, D(avid) H(erbert Richards)

Davison, Peter (Hubert) 1928-2004 . **CLC 28**
See also CA 9-12R; 234; CAAS 4; CANR
3, 43, 84; CP 1, 2, 3, 4, 5, 6, 7; DLB 5

Davys, Mary 1674-1732 .... **LC 1, 46**
See also DLB 39

Dawson, (Guy) Fielding (Lewis)
1930-2002 .... **CLC 6**
See also CA 85-88; 202; CANR 108; DLB
130; DLBY 2002

Dawson, Peter
See Faust, Frederick (Schiller)
See also TCWW 1, 2

Day, Clarence (Shepard, Jr.)
1874-1935 .... **TCLC 25**
See also CA 108; 199; DLB 11

Day, John 1574(?)-1640(?) .... **LC 70**
See also DLB 62, 170; RGEL 2

Day, Thomas 1748-1789 .... **LC 1**
See also DLB 39; YABC 1

Day Lewis, C(ecil) 1904-1972 . **CLC 1, 6, 10;
PC 11**
See Blake, Nicholas; Lewis, C. Day
See also BRWS 3; CA 13-16; 33-36R;
CANR 34; CAP 1; CP 1; CWRI 5; DAM
POET; DLB 15, 20; EWL 3; MTCW 1, 2;
RGEL 2

Dazai Osamu .... **SSC 41; TCLC 11**
See Tsushima, Shuji
See also CA 164; DLB 182; EWL 3; MJW;
RGSF 2; RGWL 2, 3; TWA

de Andrade, Carlos Drummond
See Drummond de Andrade, Carlos

de Andrade, Mario 1892(?)-1945
See Andrade, Mario de
See also CA 178; HW 2

Deane, Norman
See Creasey, John

Deane, Seamus (Francis) 1940- ...... **CLC 122**
See also CA 118; CANR 42

**de Beauvoir, Simone (Lucie Ernestine Marie
Bertrand)**
See Beauvoir, Simone (Lucie Ernestine
Marie Bertrand) de

de Beer, P.
See Bosman, Herman Charles

De Botton, Alain 1969- .... **CLC 203**
See also CA 159; CANR 96

de Brissac, Malcolm
See Dickinson, Peter (Malcolm de Brissac)

de Campos, Alvaro
See Pessoa, Fernando (Antonio Nogueira)

de Chardin, Pierre Teilhard
See Teilhard de Chardin, (Marie Joseph)
Pierre

de Crenne, Helisenne c. 1510-c.
1560 .... **LC 113**

Dee, John 1527-1608 .... **LC 20**
See also DLB 136, 213

Deer, Sandra 1940- .... **CLC 45**
See also CA 186

De Ferrari, Gabriella 1941- .... **CLC 65**
See also CA 146

de Filippo, Eduardo 1900-1984 ... **TCLC 127**
See also CA 132; 114; EWL 3; MTCW 1;
RGWL 2, 3

Defoe, Daniel 1660(?)-1731 .... **LC 1, 42, 108;
WLC**
See also AAYA 27; BRW 3; BRWR 1; BYA
4; CDBLB 1660-1789; CLR 61; DA;
DA3; DAB; DAC; DAM MST, NOV;
DLB 39, 95, 101; JRDA; LAIT 1; LMFS
1; MAICYA 1, 2; NFS 9, 13; RGEL 2;
SATA 22; TEA; WCH; WLIT 3

de Gourmont, Remy(-Marie-Charles)
See Gourmont, Remy(-Marie-Charles) de

de Gournay, Marie le Jars
1566-1645 .... **LC 98**
See also FW

de Hartog, Jan 1914-2002 .... **CLC 19**
See also CA 1-4R; 210; CANR 1; DFS 12

de Hostos, E. M.
See Hostos (y Bonilla), Eugenio Maria de

de Hostos, Eugenio M.
See Hostos (y Bonilla), Eugenio Maria de

Deighton, Len .... **CLC 4, 7, 22, 46**
See Deighton, Leonard Cyril
See also AAYA 6; BEST 89:2; BPFB 1; CD-
BLB 1960 to Present; CMW 4; CN 1, 2,
3, 4, 5, 6, 7; CPW; DLB 87

Deighton, Leonard Cyril 1929-
See Deighton, Len
See also AAYA 57; CA 9-12R; CANR 19,
33, 68; DA3; DAM NOV, POP; MTCW
1, 2; MTFW 2005

Dekker, Thomas 1572(?)-1632 ..... **DC 12; LC
22**
See also CDBLB Before 1660; DAM
DRAM; DLB 62, 172; LMFS 1; RGEL 2

de Laclos, Pierre Ambroise Franois
See Laclos, Pierre-Ambroise Francois

Delacroix, (Ferdinand-Victor-)Eugene
1798-1863 .... **NCLC 133**
See also EW 5

Delafield, E. M. .... **TCLC 61**
See Dashwood, Edmee Elizabeth Monica
de la Pasture
See also DLB 34; RHW

de la Mare, Walter (John)
1873-1956 . **SSC 14; TCLC 4, 53; WLC**
See also CA 163; CDBLB 1914-1945; CLR
23; CWRI 5; DA3; DAB; DAC; DAM
MST, POET; DLB 19, 153, 162, 255, 284;
EWL 3; EXPP; HGG; MAICYA 1, 2;
MTCW 2; MTFW 2005; RGEL 2; RGSF
2; SATA 16; SUFW 1; TEA; WCH

de Lamartine, Alphonse (Marie Louis Prat)
See Lamartine, Alphonse (Marie Louis Prat)
de

Delaney, Franey
See O'Hara, John (Henry)

Delaney, Shelagh 1939- .... **CLC 29**
See also CA 17-20R; CANR 30, 67; CBD;
CD 5, 6; CDBLB 1960 to Present; CWD;
DAM DRAM; DFS 7; DLB 13; MTCW 1

Delany, Martin Robison
1812-1885 .... **NCLC 93**
See also DLB 50; RGAL 4

Delany, Mary (Granville Pendarves)
1700-1788 .... **LC 12**

Delany, Samuel R(ay), Jr. 1942- .... **BLC 1;
CLC 8, 14, 38, 141**
See also AAYA 24; AFAW 2; BPFB 1; BW
2, 3; CA 81-84; CANR 27, 43, 116; CN
2, 3, 4, 5, 6, 7; DAM MULT; DLB 8, 33;
FANT; MAL 5; MTCW 1, 2; RGAL 4;
SATA 92; SCFW 1, 2; SFW 4; SUFW 2

De la Ramee, Marie Louise (Ouida)
1839-1908
See Ouida
See also CA 204; SATA 20

de la Roche, Mazo 1879-1961 .... **CLC 14**
See also CA 85-88; CANR 30; DLB 68;
RGEL 2; RHW; SATA 64

De La Salle, Innocent
See Hartmann, Sadakichi

de Laureamont, Comte
See Lautreamont

Delbanco, Nicholas (Franklin)
1942- .... **CLC 6, 13, 167**
See also CA 17-20R, 189; CAAE 189;
CAAS 2; CANR 29, 55, 116; CN 7; DLB
6, 234

del Castillo, Michel 1933- .... **CLC 38**
See also CA 109; CANR 77

Deledda, Grazia (Cosima)
1875(?)-1936 .... **TCLC 23**
See also CA 123; 205; DLB 264; EWL 3;
RGWL 2, 3; WLIT 7

Deleuze, Gilles 1925-1995 .... **TCLC 116**
See also DLB 296

Delgado, Abelardo (Lalo) B(arrientos)
1930-2004 .... **HLC 1**
See also CA 131; 230; CAAS 15; CANR
90; DAM MST, MULT; DLB 82; HW 1,
2

Delibes, Miguel .... **CLC 8, 18**
See Delibes Setien, Miguel
See also DLB 322; EWL 3

Delibes Setien, Miguel 1920-
See Delibes, Miguel
See also CA 45-48; CANR 1, 32; CWW 2;
HW 1; MTCW 1

DeLillo, Don 1936- ..... **CLC 8, 10, 13, 27, 39,
54, 76, 143, 210, 213**
See also AMWC 2; AMWS 6; BEST 89:1;
BPFB 1; CA 81-84; CANR 21, 76, 92,
133; CN 3, 4, 5, 6, 7; CPW; DA3; DAM
NOV, POP; DLB 6, 173; EWL 3; MAL 5;
MTCW 1, 2; MTFW 2005; RGAL 4; TUS

de Lisser, H. G.
See De Lisser, H(erbert) G(eorge)
See also DLB 117

De Lisser, H(erbert) G(eorge)
1878-1944 .... **TCLC 12**
See de Lisser, H. G.
See also BW 2; CA 109; 152

Deloire, Pierre
See Peguy, Charles (Pierre)

Deloney, Thomas 1543(?)-1600 .... **LC 41**
See also DLB 167; RGEL 2

Deloria, Ella (Cara) 1889-1971(?) ..... **NNAL**
See also CA 152; DAM MULT; DLB 175

Deloria, Vine (Victor), Jr.
1933-2005 .... **CLC 21, 122; NNAL**
See also CA 53-56; CANR 5, 20, 48, 98;
DAM MULT; DLB 175; MTCW 1; SATA
21

del Valle-Inclan, Ramon (Maria)
See Valle-Inclan, Ramon (Maria) del
See also DLB 322

Del Vecchio, John M(ichael) 1947- .. **CLC 29**
See also CA 110; DLBD 9

Douglas, Leonard
See Bradbury, Ray (Douglas)
Douglas, Michael
See Crichton, (John) Michael
Douglas, (George) Norman
1868-1952 .... **TCLC 68**
See also BRW 6; CA 119; 157; DLB 34, 195; RGEL 2
Douglas, William
See Brown, George Douglas
Douglass, Frederick 1817(?)-1895 ..... **BLC 1; NCLC 7, 55, 141; WLC**
See also AAYA 48; AFAW 1, 2; AMWC 1; AMWS 3; CDALB 1640-1865; DA; DA3; DAC; DAM MST, MULT; DLB 1, 43, 50, 79, 243; FW; LAIT 2; NCFS 2; RGAL 4; SATA 29
Dourado, (Waldomiro Freitas) Autran
1926- .... **CLC 23, 60**
See also CA 25-28R; 179; CANR 34, 81; DLB 145, 307; HW 2
Dourado, Waldomiro Freitas Autran
See Dourado, (Waldomiro Freitas) Autran
Dove, Rita (Frances) 1952- . **BLCS; CLC 50, 81; PC 6**
See also AAYA 46; AMWS 4; BW 2; CA 109; CAAS 19; CANR 27, 42, 68, 76, 97, 132; CDALBS; CP 7; CSW; CWP; DA3; DAM MULT, POET; DLB 120; EWL 3; EXPP; MAL 5; MTCW 2; MTFW 2005; PFS 1, 15; RGAL 4
Doveglion
See Villa, Jose Garcia
Dowell, Coleman 1925-1985 .... **CLC 60**
See also CA 25-28R; 117; CANR 10; DLB 130; GLL 2
Dowson, Ernest (Christopher)
1867-1900 .... **TCLC 4**
See also CA 105; 150; DLB 19, 135; RGEL 2
Doyle, A. Conan
See Doyle, Sir Arthur Conan
Doyle, Sir Arthur Conan
1859-1930 . **SSC 12, 83; TCLC 7; WLC**
See Conan Doyle, Arthur
See also AAYA 14; BRWS 2; CA 104; 122; CANR 131; CDBLB 1890-1914; CMW 4; DA; DA3; DAB; DAC; DAM MST, NOV; DLB 18, 70, 156, 178; EXPS; HGG; LAIT 2; MSW; MTCW 1, 2; MTFW 2005; RGEL 2; RGSF; RHW; SATA 24; SCFW 1, 2; SFW 4; SSFS 2; TEA; WCH; WLIT 4; WYA; YAW
Doyle, Conan
See Doyle, Sir Arthur Conan
Doyle, John
See Graves, Robert (von Ranke)
Doyle, Roddy 1958- .... **CLC 81, 178**
See also AAYA 14; BRWS 5; CA 143; CANR 73, 128; CN 6, 7; DA3; DLB 194; MTCW 2; MTFW 2005
Doyle, Sir A. Conan
See Doyle, Sir Arthur Conan
Dr. A
See Asimov, Isaac; Silverstein, Alvin; Silverstein, Virginia B(arbara Opshelor)
Drabble, Margaret 1939- ...... **CLC 2, 3, 5, 8, 10, 22, 53, 129**
See also BRWS 4; CA 13-16R; CANR 18, 35, 63, 112, 131; CDBLB 1960 to Present; CN 1, 2, 3, 4, 5, 6, 7; CPW; DA3; DAB; DAC; DAM MST, NOV, POP; DLB 14, 155, 231; EWL 3; FW; MTCW 1, 2; MTFW 2005; RGEL 2; SATA 48; TEA
Drakulic, Slavenka 1949- .... **CLC 173**
See also CA 144; CANR 92
Drakulic-Ilic, Slavenka
See Drakulic, Slavenka

Drapier, M. B.
See Swift, Jonathan
Drayham, James
See Mencken, H(enry) L(ouis)
Drayton, Michael 1563-1631 .... **LC 8**
See also DAM POET; DLB 121; RGEL 2
Dreadstone, Carl
See Campbell, (John) Ramsey
Dreiser, Theodore (Herman Albert)
1871-1945 .... **SSC 30; TCLC 10, 18, 35, 83; WLC**
See also AMW; AMWC 2; AMWR 2; BYA 15, 16; CA 106; 132; CDALB 1865-1917; DA; DA3; DAC; DAM MST, NOV; DLB 9, 12, 102, 137; DLBD 1; EWL 3; LAIT 2; LMFS 2; MAL 5; MTCW 1, 2; MTFW 2005; NFS 8, 17; RGAL 4; TUS
Drexler, Rosalyn 1926- .... **CLC 2, 6**
See also CA 81-84; CAD; CANR 68, 124; CD 5, 6; CWD; MAL 5
Dreyer, Carl Theodor 1889-1968 ...... **CLC 16**
See also CA 116
Drieu la Rochelle, Pierre(-Eugene)
1893-1945 .... **TCLC 21**
See also CA 117; DLB 72; EWL 3; GFL 1789 to the Present
Drinkwater, John 1882-1937 .... **TCLC 57**
See also CA 109; 149; DLB 10, 19, 149; RGEL 2
Drop Shot
See Cable, George Washington
Droste-Hulshoff, Annette Freiin von
1797-1848 .... **NCLC 3, 133**
See also CDWLB 2; DLB 133; RGSF 2; RGWL 2, 3
Drummond, Walter
See Silverberg, Robert
Drummond, William Henry
1854-1907 .... **TCLC 25**
See also CA 160; DLB 92
Drummond de Andrade, Carlos
1902-1987 .... **CLC 18; TCLC 139**
See Andrade, Carlos Drummond de
See also CA 132; 123; DLB 307; LAW
Drummond of Hawthornden, William
1585-1649 .... **LC 83**
See also DLB 121, 213; RGEL 2
Drury, Allen (Stuart) 1918-1998 .... **CLC 37**
See also CA 57-60; 170; CANR 18, 52; CN 1, 2, 3, 4, 5, 6; INT CANR-18
Druse, Eleanor
See King, Stephen
Dryden, John 1631-1700 ..... **DC 3; LC 3, 21, 115; PC 25; WLC**
See also BRW 2; CDBLB 1660-1789; DA; DAB; DAC; DAM DRAM, MST, POET; DLB 80, 101, 131; EXPP; IDTP; LMFS 1; RGEL 2; TEA; WLIT 3
du Bellay, Joachim 1524-1560 .... **LC 92**
See also GFL Beginnings to 1789; RGWL 2, 3
Duberman, Martin (Bauml) 1930- ..... **CLC 8**
See also CA 1-4R; CAD; CANR 2, 63, 137; CD 5, 6
Dubie, Norman (Evans) 1945- .... **CLC 36**
See also CA 69-72; CANR 12, 115; CP 3, 4, 5, 6, 7; DLB 120; PFS 12
Du Bois, W(illiam) E(dward) B(urghardt)
1868-1963 ..... **BLC 1; CLC 1, 2, 13, 64, 96; HR 1:2; TCLC 169; WLC**
See also AAYA 40; AFAW 1, 2; AMWC 1; AMWS 2; BW 1, 3; CA 85-88; CANR 34, 82, 132; CDALB 1865-1917; DA; DA3; DAC; DAM MST, MULT, NOV; DLB 47, 50, 91, 246, 284; EWL 3; EXPP; LAIT 2; LMFS 2; MAL 5; MTCW 1, 2; MTFW 2005; NCFS 1; PFS 13; RGAL 4; SATA 42

Dubus, Andre 1936-1999 ..... **CLC 13, 36, 97; SSC 15**
See also AMWS 7; CA 21-24R; 177; CANR 17; CN 5, 6; CSW; DLB 130; INT CANR-17; RGAL 4; SSFS 10; TCLE 1:1
Duca Minimo
See D'Annunzio, Gabriele
Ducharme, Rejean 1941- .... **CLC 74**
See also CA 165; DLB 60
du Chatelet, Emilie 1706-1749 .... **LC 96**
See Chatelet, Gabrielle-Emilie Du
Duchen, Claire .... **CLC 65**
Duclos, Charles Pinot- 1704-1772 .... **LC 1**
See also GFL Beginnings to 1789
Dudek, Louis 1918-2001 .... **CLC 11, 19**
See also CA 45-48; 215; CAAS 14; CANR 1; CP 1, 2, 3, 4, 5, 6, 7; DLB 88
Duerrenmatt, Friedrich 1921-1990 ... **CLC 1, 4, 8, 11, 15, 43, 102**
See Durrenmatt, Friedrich
See also CA 17-20R; CANR 33; CMW 4; DAM DRAM; DLB 69, 124; MTCW 1, 2
Duffy, Bruce 1953(?)- .... **CLC 50**
See also CA 172
Duffy, Maureen (Patricia) 1933- ...... **CLC 37**
See also CA 25-28R; CANR 33, 68; CBD; CN 1, 2, 3, 4, 5, 6, 7; CP 7; CWD; CWP; DFS 15; DLB 14, 310; FW; MTCW 1
Du Fu
See Tu Fu
See also RGWL 2, 3
Dugan, Alan 1923-2003 .... **CLC 2, 6**
See also CA 81-84; 220; CANR 119; CP 1, 2, 3, 4, 5, 6, 7; DLB 5; MAL 5; PFS 10
du Gard, Roger Martin
See Martin du Gard, Roger
Duhamel, Georges 1884-1966 .... **CLC 8**
See also CA 81-84; 25-28R; CANR 35; DLB 65; EWL 3; GFL 1789 to the Present; MTCW 1
Dujardin, Edouard (Emile Louis)
1861-1949 .... **TCLC 13**
See also CA 109; DLB 123
Duke, Raoul
See Thompson, Hunter S(tockton)
Dulles, John Foster 1888-1959 .... **TCLC 72**
See also CA 115; 149
Dumas, Alexandre (pere)
1802-1870 .... **NCLC 11, 71; WLC**
See also AAYA 22; BYA 3; DA; DA3; DAB; DAC; DAM MST, NOV; DLB 119, 192; EW 6; GFL 1789 to the Present; LAIT 1, 2; NFS 14, 19; RGWL 2, 3; SATA 18; TWA; WCH
Dumas, Alexandre (fils) 1824-1895 ...... **DC 1; NCLC 9**
See also DLB 192; GFL 1789 to the Present; RGWL 2, 3
Dumas, Claudine
See Malzberg, Barry N(athaniel)
Dumas, Henry L. 1934-1968 .... **CLC 6, 62**
See also BW 1; CA 85-88; DLB 41; RGAL 4
du Maurier, Daphne 1907-1989 .. **CLC 6, 11, 59; SSC 18**
See also AAYA 37; BPFB 1; BRWS 3; CA 5-8R; 128; CANR 6, 55; CMW 4; CN 1, 2, 3, 4; CPW; DA3; DAB; DAC; DAM MST, POP; DLB 191; GL 2; HGG; LAIT 3; MSW; MTCW 1, 2; NFS 12; RGEL 2; RGSF 2; RHW; SATA 27; SATA-Obit 60; SSFS 14, 16; TEA
Du Maurier, George 1834-1896 ..... **NCLC 86**
See also DLB 153, 178; RGEL 2
Dunbar, Paul Laurence 1872-1906 ... **BLC 1; PC 5; SSC 8; TCLC 2, 12; WLC**
See also AFAW 1, 2; AMWS 2; BW 1, 3; CA 104; 124; CANR 79; CDALB 1865-1917; DA; DA3; DAC; DAM MST, MULT, POET; DLB 50, 54, 78; EXPP; MAL 5; RGAL 4; SATA 34

Empedocles 5th cent. B.C.- .... **CMLC 50**
See also DLB 176

Empson, William 1906-1984 ... **CLC 3, 8, 19, 33, 34**
See also BRWS 2; CA 17-20R; 112; CANR 31, 61; CP 1, 2, 3; DLB 20; EWL 3; MTCW 1, 2; RGEL 2

Enchi, Fumiko (Ueda) 1905-1986 ..... **CLC 31**
See Enchi Fumiko
See also CA 129; 121; FW; MJW

Enchi Fumiko
See Enchi, Fumiko (Ueda)
See also DLB 182; EWL 3

Ende, Michael (Andreas Helmuth)
1929-1995 .... **CLC 31**
See also BYA 5; CA 118; 124; 149; CANR 36, 110; CLR 14; DLB 75; MAICYA 1, 2; MAICYAS 1; SATA 61, 130; SATA-Brief 42; SATA-Obit 86

Endo, Shusaku 1923-1996 ..... **CLC 7, 14, 19, 54, 99; SSC 48; TCLC 152**
See Endo Shusaku
See also CA 29-32R; 153; CANR 21, 54, 131; DA3; DAM NOV; MTCW 1, 2; MTFW 2005; RGSF 2; RGWL 2, 3

Endo Shusaku
See Endo, Shusaku
See also CWW 2; DLB 182; EWL 3

Engel, Marian 1933-1985 .... **CLC 36; TCLC 137**
See also CA 25-28R; CANR 12; CN 2, 3; DLB 53; FW; INT CANR-12

Engelhardt, Frederick
See Hubbard, L(afayette) Ron(ald)

Engels, Friedrich 1820-1895 .. **NCLC 85, 114**
See also DLB 129; LATS 1:1

Enright, D(ennis) J(oseph)
1920-2002 .... **CLC 4, 8, 31**
See also CA 1-4R; 211; CANR 1, 42, 83; CN 1, 2; CP 1, 2, 3, 4, 5, 6, 7; DLB 27; EWL 3; SATA 25; SATA-Obit 140

Ensler, Eve 1953- .... **CLC 212**
See also CA 172; CANR 126

Enzensberger, Hans Magnus
1929- .... **CLC 43; PC 28**
See also CA 116; 119; CANR 103; CWW 2; EWL 3

Ephron, Nora 1941- .... **CLC 17, 31**
See also AAYA 35; AITN 2; CA 65-68; CANR 12, 39, 83; DFS 22

Epicurus 341B.C.-270B.C. .... **CMLC 21**
See also DLB 176

Epsilon
See Betjeman, John

Epstein, Daniel Mark 1948- .... **CLC 7**
See also CA 49-52; CANR 2, 53, 90

Epstein, Jacob 1956- .... **CLC 19**
See also CA 114

Epstein, Jean 1897-1953 .... **TCLC 92**

Epstein, Joseph 1937- .... **CLC 39, 204**
See also AMWS 14; CA 112; 119; CANR 50, 65, 117

Epstein, Leslie 1938- .... **CLC 27**
See also AMWS 12; CA 73-76; 215; CAAE 215; CAAS 12; CANR 23, 69; DLB 299

Equiano, Olaudah 1745(?)-1797 . **BLC 2; LC 16**
See also AFAW 1, 2; CDWLB 3; DAM MULT; DLB 37, 50; WLIT 2

Erasmus, Desiderius 1469(?)-1536 ..... **LC 16, 93**
See also DLB 136; EW 2; LMFS 1; RGWL 2, 3; TWA

Erdman, Paul E(mil) 1932- .... **CLC 25**
See also AITN 1; CA 61-64; CANR 13, 43, 84

Erdrich, (Karen) Louise 1954- .. **CLC 39, 54, 120, 176; NNAL; PC 52**
See also AAYA 10, 47; AMWS 4; BEST 89:1; BPFB 1; CA 114; CANR 41, 62, 118, 138; CDALBS; CN 5, 6, 7; CP 7; CPW; CWP; DA3; DAM MULT, NOV, POP; DLB 152, 175, 206; EWL 3; EXPP; FL 1:5; LAIT 5; LATS 1:2; MAL 5; MTCW 1, 2; MTFW 2005; NFS 5; PFS 14; RGAL 4; SATA 94, 141; SSFS 14; TCWW 2

Erenburg, Ilya (Grigoryevich)
See Ehrenburg, Ilya (Grigoryevich)

Erickson, Stephen Michael 1950-
See Erickson, Steve
See also CA 129; SFW 4

Erickson, Steve .... **CLC 64**
See Erickson, Stephen Michael
See also CANR 60, 68, 136; MTFW 2005; SUFW 2

Erickson, Walter
See Fast, Howard (Melvin)

Ericson, Walter
See Fast, Howard (Melvin)

Eriksson, Buntel
See Bergman, (Ernst) Ingmar

Eriugena, John Scottus c.
810-877 .... **CMLC 65**
See also DLB 115

Ernaux, Annie 1940- .... **CLC 88, 184**
See also CA 147; CANR 93; MTFW 2005; NCFS 3, 5

Erskine, John 1879-1951 .... **TCLC 84**
See also CA 112; 159; DLB 9, 102; FANT

Eschenbach, Wolfram von
See Wolfram von Eschenbach
See also RGWL 3

Eseki, Bruno
See Mphahlele, Ezekiel

Esenin, Sergei (Alexandrovich)
1895-1925 .... **TCLC 4**
See Yesenin, Sergey
See also CA 104; RGWL 2, 3

Eshleman, Clayton 1935- .... **CLC 7**
See also CA 33-36R; 212; CAAE 212; CAAS 6; CANR 93; CP 1, 2, 3, 4, 5, 6, 7; DLB 5

Espriella, Don Manuel Alvarez
See Southey, Robert

Espriu, Salvador 1913-1985 .... **CLC 9**
See also CA 154; 115; DLB 134; EWL 3

Espronceda, Jose de 1808-1842 ...... **NCLC 39**

Esquivel, Laura 1951(?)- ... **CLC 141; HLCS 1**
See also AAYA 29; CA 143; CANR 68, 113; DA3; DNFS 2; LAIT 3; LMFS 2; MTCW 2; MTFW 2005; NFS 5; WLIT 1

Esse, James
See Stephens, James

Esterbrook, Tom
See Hubbard, L(afayette) Ron(ald)

Estleman, Loren D. 1952- .... **CLC 48**
See also AAYA 27; CA 85-88; CANR 27, 74, 139; CMW 4; CPW; DA3; DAM NOV, POP; DLB 226; INT CANR-27; MTCW 1, 2; MTFW 2005; TCWW 1, 2

Etherege, Sir George 1636-1692 . **DC 23; LC 78**
See also BRW 2; DAM DRAM; DLB 80; PAB; RGEL 2

Euclid 306B.C.-283B.C. .... **CMLC 25**

Eugenides, Jeffrey 1960(?)- .... **CLC 81, 212**
See also AAYA 51; CA 144; CANR 120; MTFW 2005

Euripides c. 484B.C.-406B.C. .... **CMLC 23, 51; DC 4; WLCS**
See also AW 1; CDWLB 1; DA; DA3; DAB; DAC; DAM DRAM, MST; DFS 1, 4, 6; DLB 176; LAIT 1; LMFS 1; RGWL 2, 3

Evan, Evin
See Faust, Frederick (Schiller)

Evans, Caradoc 1878-1945 ... **SSC 43; TCLC 85**
See also DLB 162

Evans, Evan
See Faust, Frederick (Schiller)

Evans, Marian
See Eliot, George

Evans, Mary Ann
See Eliot, George
See also NFS 20

Evarts, Esther
See Benson, Sally

Everett, Percival
See Everett, Percival L.
See also CSW

Everett, Percival L. 1956- .... **CLC 57**
See Everett, Percival
See also BW 2; CA 129; CANR 94, 134; CN 7; MTFW 2005

Everson, R(onald) G(ilmour)
1903-1992 .... **CLC 27**
See also CA 17-20R; CP 1, 2, 3, 4; DLB 88

Everson, William (Oliver)
1912-1994 .... **CLC 1, 5, 14**
See Antoninus, Brother
See also BG 1:2; CA 9-12R; 145; CANR 20; CP 2, 3, 4; DLB 5, 16, 212; MTCW 1

Evtushenko, Evgenii Aleksandrovich
See Yevtushenko, Yevgeny (Alexandrovich)
See also CWW 2; RGWL 2, 3

Ewart, Gavin (Buchanan)
1916-1995 .... **CLC 13, 46**
See also BRWS 7; CA 89-92; 150; CANR 17, 46; CP 1, 2, 3, 4; DLB 40; MTCW 1

Ewers, Hanns Heinz 1871-1943 ..... **TCLC 12**
See also CA 109; 149

Ewing, Frederick R.
See Sturgeon, Theodore (Hamilton)

Exley, Frederick (Earl) 1929-1992 .... **CLC 6, 11**
See also AITN 2; BPFB 1; CA 81-84; 138; CANR 117; DLB 143; DLBY 1981

Eynhardt, Guillermo
See Quiroga, Horacio (Sylvestre)

Ezekiel, Nissim (Moses) 1924-2004 .. **CLC 61**
See also CA 61-64; 223; CP 1, 2, 3, 4, 5, 6, 7; EWL 3

Ezekiel, Tish O'Dowd 1943- .... **CLC 34**
See also CA 129

Fadeev, Aleksandr Aleksandrovich
See Bulgya, Alexander Alexandrovich
See also DLB 272

Fadeev, Alexandr Alexandrovich
See Bulgya, Alexander Alexandrovich
See also EWL 3

Fadeyev, A.
See Bulgya, Alexander Alexandrovich

Fadeyev, Alexander .... **TCLC 53**
See Bulgya, Alexander Alexandrovich

Fagen, Donald 1948- .... **CLC 26**

Fainzilberg, Ilya Arnoldovich 1897-1937
See Ilf, Ilya
See also CA 120; 165

Fair, Ronald L. 1932- .... **CLC 18**
See also BW 1; CA 69-72; CANR 25; DLB 33

Fairbairn, Roger
See Carr, John Dickson

Fairbairns, Zoe (Ann) 1948- .... **CLC 32**
See also CA 103; CANR 21, 85; CN 4, 5, 6, 7

French, Albert 1943- .... **CLC 86**
See also BW 3; CA 167

French, Antonia
See Kureishi, Hanif

French, Marilyn 1929- .. **CLC 10, 18, 60, 177**
See also BPFB 1; CA 69-72; CANR 3, 31, 134; CN 5, 6, 7; CPW; DAM DRAM, NOV, POP; FL 1:5; FW; INT CANR-31; MTCW 1, 2; MTFW 2005

French, Paul
See Asimov, Isaac

Freneau, Philip Morin 1752-1832 .. **NCLC 1, 111**
See also AMWS 2; DLB 37, 43; RGAL 4

Freud, Sigmund 1856-1939 .... **TCLC 52**
See also CA 115; 133; CANR 69; DLB 296; EW 8; EWL 3; LATS 1:1; MTCW 1, 2; MTFW 2005; NCFS 3; TWA

Freytag, Gustav 1816-1895 .... **NCLC 109**
See also DLB 129

Friedan, Betty (Naomi) 1921- .... **CLC 74**
See also CA 65-68; CANR 18, 45, 74; DLB 246; FW; MTCW 1, 2; MTFW 2005; NCFS 5

Friedlander, Saul 1932- .... **CLC 90**
See also CA 117; 130; CANR 72

Friedman, B(ernard) H(arper)
1926- .... **CLC 7**
See also CA 1-4R; CANR 3, 48

Friedman, Bruce Jay 1930- ...... **CLC 3, 5, 56**
See also CA 9-12R; CAD; CANR 25, 52, 101; CD 5, 6; CN 1, 2, 3, 4, 5, 6, 7; DLB 2, 28, 244; INT CANR-25; MAL 5; SSFS 18

Friel, Brian 1929- .... **CLC 5, 42, 59, 115; DC 8; SSC 76**
See also BRWS 5; CA 21-24R; CANR 33, 69, 131; CBD; CD 5, 6; DFS 11; DLB 13, 319; EWL 3; MTCW 1; RGEL 2; TEA

Friis-Baastad, Babbis Ellinor
1921-1970 .... **CLC 12**
See also CA 17-20R; 134; SATA 7

Frisch, Max (Rudolf) 1911-1991 ... **CLC 3, 9, 14, 18, 32, 44; TCLC 121**
See also CA 85-88; 134; CANR 32, 74; CD-WLB 2; DAM DRAM, NOV; DLB 69, 124; EW 13; EWL 3; MTCW 1, 2; MTFW 2005; RGWL 2, 3

Fromentin, Eugene (Samuel Auguste)
1820-1876 .... **NCLC 10, 125**
See also DLB 123; GFL 1789 to the Present

Frost, Frederick
See Faust, Frederick (Schiller)

Frost, Robert (Lee) 1874-1963 .. **CLC 1, 3, 4, 9, 10, 13, 15, 26, 34, 44; PC 1, 39; WLC**
See also AAYA 21; AMW; AMWR 1; CA 89-92; CANR 33; CDALB 1917-1929; CLR 67; DA; DA3; DAB; DAC; DAM MST, POET; DLB 54, 284; DLBD 7; EWL 3; EXPP; MAL 5; MTCW 1, 2; MTFW 2005; PAB; PFS 1, 2, 3, 4, 5, 6, 7, 10, 13; RGAL 4; SATA 14; TUS; WP; WYA

Froude, James Anthony
1818-1894 .... **NCLC 43**
See also DLB 18, 57, 144

Froy, Herald
See Waterhouse, Keith (Spencer)

Fry, Christopher 1907-2005 ... **CLC 2, 10, 14**
See also BRWS 3; CA 17-20R; 240; CAAS 23; CANR 9, 30, 74, 132; CBD; CD 5, 6; CP 1, 2, 3, 4, 5, 6, 7; DAM DRAM; DLB 13; EWL 3; MTCW 1, 2; MTFW 2005; RGEL 2; SATA 66; TEA

Frye, (Herman) Northrop
1912-1991 .... **CLC 24, 70; TCLC 165**
See also CA 5-8R; 133; CANR 8, 37; DLB 67, 68, 246; EWL 3; MTCW 1, 2; RGAL 4; TWA

Fuchs, Daniel 1909-1993 .... **CLC 8, 22**
See also CA 81-84; 142; CAAS 5; CANR 40; CN 1, 2, 3, 4, 5; DLB 9, 26, 28; DLBY 1993; MAL 5

Fuchs, Daniel 1934- .... **CLC 34**
See also CA 37-40R; CANR 14, 48

Fuentes, Carlos 1928- .. **CLC 3, 8, 10, 13, 22, 41, 60, 113; HLC 1; SSC 24; WLC**
See also AAYA 4, 45; AITN 2; BPFB 1; CA 69-72; CANR 10, 32, 68, 104, 138; CDWLB 3; CWW 2; DA; DA3; DAB; DAC; DAM MST, MULT, NOV; DLB 113; DNFS 2; EWL 3; HW 1, 2; LAIT 3; LATS 1:2; LAW; LAWS 1; LMFS 2; MTCW 1, 2; MTFW 2005; NFS 8; RGSF 2; RGWL 2, 3; TWA; WLIT 1

Fuentes, Gregorio Lopez y
See Lopez y Fuentes, Gregorio

Fuertes, Gloria 1918-1998 .... **PC 27**
See also CA 178, 180; DLB 108; HW 2; SATA 115

Fugard, (Harold) Athol 1932- . **CLC 5, 9, 14, 25, 40, 80, 211; DC 3**
See also AAYA 17; AFW; CA 85-88; CANR 32, 54, 118; CD 5, 6; DAM DRAM; DFS 3, 6, 10; DLB 225; DNFS 1, 2; EWL 3; LATS 1:2; MTCW 1; MTFW 2005; RGEL 2; WLIT 2

Fugard, Sheila 1932- .... **CLC 48**
See also CA 125

Fujiwara no Teika 1162-1241 .... **CMLC 73**
See also DLB 203

Fukuyama, Francis 1952- .... **CLC 131**
See also CA 140; CANR 72, 125

Fuller, Charles (H.), (Jr.) 1939- .... **BLC 2; CLC 25; DC 1**
See also BW 2; CA 108; 112; CAD; CANR 87; CD 5, 6; DAM DRAM, MULT; DFS 8; DLB 38, 266; EWL 3; INT CA-112; MAL 5; MTCW 1

Fuller, Henry Blake 1857-1929 .... **TCLC 103**
See also CA 108; 177; DLB 12; RGAL 4

Fuller, John (Leopold) 1937- .... **CLC 62**
See also CA 21-24R; CANR 9, 44; CP 1, 2, 3, 4, 5, 6, 7; DLB 40

Fuller, Margaret
See Ossoli, Sarah Margaret (Fuller)
See also AMWS 2; DLB 183, 223, 239; FL 1:3

Fuller, Roy (Broadbent) 1912-1991 ... **CLC 4, 28**
See also BRWS 7; CA 5-8R; 135; CAAS 10; CANR 53, 83; CN 1, 2, 3, 4, 5; CP 1, 2, 3, 4; CWRI 5; DLB 15, 20; EWL 3; RGEL 2; SATA 87

Fuller, Sarah Margaret
See Ossoli, Sarah Margaret (Fuller)

Fuller, Sarah Margaret
See Ossoli, Sarah Margaret (Fuller)
See also DLB 1, 59, 73

Fuller, Thomas 1608-1661 .... **LC 111**
See also DLB 151

Fulton, Alice 1952- .... **CLC 52**
See also CA 116; CANR 57, 88; CP 7; CWP; DLB 193

Furphy, Joseph 1843-1912 .... **TCLC 25**
See Collins, Tom
See also CA 163; DLB 230; EWL 3; RGEL 2

Fuson, Robert H(enderson) 1927- .... **CLC 70**
See also CA 89-92; CANR 103

Fussell, Paul 1924- .... **CLC 74**
See also BEST 90:1; CA 17-20R; CANR 8, 21, 35, 69, 135; INT CANR-21; MTCW 1, 2; MTFW 2005

Futabatei, Shimei 1864-1909 .... **TCLC 44**
See Futabatei Shimei
See also CA 162; MJW

Futabatei Shimei
See Futabatei, Shimei
See also DLB 180; EWL 3

Futrelle, Jacques 1875-1912 .... **TCLC 19**
See also CA 113; 155; CMW 4

Gaboriau, Emile 1835-1873 .... **NCLC 14**
See also CMW 4; MSW

Gadda, Carlo Emilio 1893-1973 ...... **CLC 11; TCLC 144**
See also CA 89-92; DLB 177; EWL 3; WLIT 7

Gaddis, William 1922-1998 ... **CLC 1, 3, 6, 8, 10, 19, 43, 86**
See also AMWS 4; BPFB 1; CA 17-20R; 172; CANR 21, 48; CN 1, 2, 3, 4, 5, 6; DLB 2, 278; EWL 3; MAL 5; MTCW 1, 2; MTFW 2005; RGAL 4

Gaelique, Moruen le
See Jacob, (Cyprien-)Max

Gage, Walter
See Inge, William (Motter)

Gaiman, Neil (Richard) 1960- .... **CLC 195**
See also AAYA 19, 42; CA 133; CANR 81, 129; DLB 261; HGG; MTFW 2005; SATA 85, 146; SFW 4; SUFW 2

Gaines, Ernest J(ames) 1933- .. **BLC 2; CLC 3, 11, 18, 86, 181; SSC 68**
See also AAYA 18; AFAW 1, 2; AITN 1; BPFB 2; BW 2, 3; BYA 6; CA 9-12R; CANR 6, 24, 42, 75, 126; CDALB 1968-1988; CLR 62; CN 1, 2, 3, 4, 5, 6, 7; CSW; DA3; DAM MULT; DLB 2, 33, 152; DLBY 1980; EWL 3; EXPN; LAIT 5; LATS 1:2; MAL 5; MTCW 1, 2; MTFW 2005; NFS 5, 7, 16; RGAL 4; RGSF 2; RHW; SATA 86; SSFS 5; YAW

Gaitskill, Mary (Lawrence) 1954- .... **CLC 69**
See also CA 128; CANR 61; DLB 244; TCLE 1:1

Gaius Suetonius Tranquillus
See Suetonius

Galdos, Benito Perez
See Perez Galdos, Benito
See also EW 7

Gale, Zona 1874-1938 .... **TCLC 7**
See also CA 105; 153; CANR 84; DAM DRAM; DFS 17; DLB 9, 78, 228; RGAL 4

Galeano, Eduardo (Hughes) 1940- . **CLC 72; HLCS 1**
See also CA 29-32R; CANR 13, 32, 100; HW 1

Galiano, Juan Valera y Alcala
See Valera y Alcala-Galiano, Juan

Galilei, Galileo 1564-1642 .... **LC 45**

Gallagher, Tess 1943- .... **CLC 18, 63; PC 9**
See also CA 106; CP 3, 4, 5, 6, 7; CWP; DAM POET; DLB 120, 212, 244; PFS 16

Gallant, Mavis 1922- ..... **CLC 7, 18, 38, 172; SSC 5, 78**
See also CA 69-72; CANR 29, 69, 117; CCA 1; CN 1, 2, 3, 4, 5, 6, 7; DAC; DAM MST; DLB 53; EWL 3; MTCW 1, 2; MTFW 2005; RGEL 2; RGSF 2

Gallant, Roy A(rthur) 1924- .... **CLC 17**
See also CA 5-8R; CANR 4, 29, 54, 117; CLR 30; MAICYA 1, 2; SATA 4, 68, 110

Gallico, Paul (William) 1897-1976 ..... **CLC 2**
See also AITN 1; CA 5-8R; 69-72; CANR 23; CN 1, 2; DLB 9, 171; FANT; MAI-CYA 1, 2; SATA 13

Gallo, Max Louis 1932- .... **CLC 95**
See also CA 85-88

Gallois, Lucien
See Desnos, Robert

Gallup, Ralph
See Whitemore, Hugh (John)

Galsworthy, John 1867-1933 .... **SSC 22; TCLC 1, 45; WLC**
See also BRW 6; CA 104; 141; CANR 75; CDBLB 1890-1914; DA; DA3; DAB; DAC; DAM DRAM, MST, NOV; DLB 10, 34, 98, 162; DLBD 16; EWL 3; MTCW 2; RGEL 2; SSFS 3; TEA

Galt, John 1779-1839 .... **NCLC 1, 110**
See also DLB 99, 116, 159; RGEL 2; RGSF 2

Galvin, James 1951- .... **CLC 38**
See also CA 108; CANR 26

Gamboa, Federico 1864-1939 .... **TCLC 36**
See also CA 167; HW 2; LAW

Gandhi, M. K.
See Gandhi, Mohandas Karamchand

Gandhi, Mahatma
See Gandhi, Mohandas Karamchand

Gandhi, Mohandas Karamchand
1869-1948 .... **TCLC 59**
See also CA 121; 132; DA3; DAM MULT; MTCW 1, 2

Gann, Ernest Kellogg 1910-1991 ..... **CLC 23**
See also AITN 1; BPFB 2; CA 1-4R; 136; CANR 1, 83; RHW

Gao Xingjian 1940- .... **CLC 167**
See Xingjian, Gao
See also MTFW 2005

Garber, Eric 1943(?)-
See Holleran, Andrew
See also CANR 89

Garcia, Cristina 1958- .... **CLC 76**
See also AMWS 11; CA 141; CANR 73, 130; CN 7; DLB 292; DNFS 1; EWL 3; HW 2; LLW; MTFW 2005

Garcia Lorca, Federico 1898-1936 ...... **DC 2; HLC 2; PC 3; TCLC 1, 7, 49; WLC**
See Lorca, Federico Garcia
See also AAYA 46; CA 104; 131; CANR 81; DA; DA3; DAB; DAC; DAM DRAM, MST, MULT, POET; DFS 4, 10; DLB 108; EWL 3; HW 1, 2; LATS 1:2; MTCW 1, 2; MTFW 2005; TWA

Garcia Marquez, Gabriel (Jose)
1928- .... **CLC 2, 3, 8, 10, 15, 27, 47, 55, 68, 170; HLC 1; SSC 8, 83; WLC**
See also AAYA 3, 33; BEST 89:1, 90:4; BPFB 2; BYA 12, 16; CA 33-36R; CANR 10, 28, 50, 75, 82, 128; CDWLB 3; CPW; CWW 2; DA; DA3; DAB; DAC; DAM MST, MULT, NOV, POP; DLB 113; DNFS 1, 2; EWL 3; EXPN; EXPS; HW 1, 2; LAIT 2; LATS 1:2; LAW; LAWS 1; LMFS 2; MTCW 1, 2; MTFW 2005; NCFS 3; NFS 1, 5, 10; RGSF 2; RGWL 2, 3; SSFS 1, 6, 16, 21; TWA; WLIT 1

Garcilaso de la Vega, El Inca
1539-1616 .... **HLCS 1**
See also DLB 318; LAW

Gard, Janice
See Latham, Jean Lee

Gard, Roger Martin du
See Martin du Gard, Roger

Gardam, Jane (Mary) 1928- .... **CLC 43**
See also CA 49-52; CANR 2, 18, 33, 54, 106; CLR 12; DLB 14, 161, 231; MAICYA 1, 2; MTCW 1; SAAS 9; SATA 39, 76, 130; SATA-Brief 28; YAW

Gardner, Herb(ert George)
1934-2003 .... **CLC 44**
See also CA 149; 220; CAD; CANR 119; CD 5, 6; DFS 18, 20

Gardner, John (Champlin), Jr.
1933-1982 ...... **CLC 2, 3, 5, 7, 8, 10, 18, 28, 34; SSC 7**
See also AAYA 45; AITN 1; AMWS 6; BPFB 2; CA 65-68; 107; CANR 33, 73; CDALBS; CN 2, 3; CPW; DA3; DAM NOV, POP; DLB 2; DLBY 1982; EWL 3;

FANT; LATS 1:2; MAL 5; MTCW 1, 2; MTFW 2005; NFS 3; RGAL 4; RGSF 2; SATA 40; SATA-Obit 31; SSFS 8

Gardner, John (Edmund) 1926- .... **CLC 30**
See also CA 103; CANR 15, 69, 127; CMW 4; CPW; DAM POP; MTCW 1

Gardner, Miriam
See Bradley, Marion Zimmer
See also GLL 1

Gardner, Noel
See Kuttner, Henry

Gardons, S. S.
See Snodgrass, W(illiam) D(e Witt)

Garfield, Leon 1921-1996 .... **CLC 12**
See also AAYA 8; BYA 1, 3; CA 17-20R; 152; CANR 38, 41, 78; CLR 21; DLB 161; JRDA; MAICYA 1, 2; MAICYAS 1; SATA 1, 32, 76; SATA-Obit 90; TEA; WYA; YAW

Garland, (Hannibal) Hamlin
1860-1940 .... **SSC 18; TCLC 3**
See also CA 104; DLB 12, 71, 78, 186; MAL 5; RGAL 4; RGSF 2; TCWW 1, 2

Garneau, (Hector de) Saint-Denys
1912-1943 .... **TCLC 13**
See also CA 111; DLB 88

Garner, Alan 1934- .... **CLC 17**
See also AAYA 18; BYA 3, 5; CA 73-76; 178; CAAE 178; CANR 15, 64, 134; CLR 20; CPW; DAB; DAM POP; DLB 161, 261; FANT; MAICYA 1, 2; MTCW 1, 2; MTFW 2005; SATA 18, 69; SATA-Essay 108; SUFW 1, 2; YAW

Garner, Hugh 1913-1979 .... **CLC 13**
See Warwick, Jarvis
See also CA 69-72; CANR 31; CCA 1; CN 1, 2; DLB 68

Garnett, David 1892-1981 .... **CLC 3**
See also CA 5-8R; 103; CANR 17, 79; CN 1, 2; DLB 34; FANT; MTCW 2; RGEL 2; SFW 4; SUFW 1

Garnier, Robert c. 1545-1590 .... **LC 119**
See also GFL Beginnings to 1789

Garos, Stephanie
See Katz, Steve

Garrett, George (Palmer, Jr.) 1929- . **CLC 3, 11, 51; SSC 30**
See also AMWS 7; BPFB 2; CA 1-4R; 202; CAAE 202; CAAS 5; CANR 1, 42, 67, 109; CN 1, 2, 3, 4, 5, 6, 7; CP 1, 2, 3, 4, 5, 6, 7; CSW; DLB 2, 5, 130, 152; DLBY 1983

Garrick, David 1717-1779 .... **LC 15**
See also DAM DRAM; DLB 84, 213; RGEL 2

Garrigue, Jean 1914-1972 .... **CLC 2, 8**
See also CA 5-8R; 37-40R; CANR 20; CP 1; MAL 5

Garrison, Frederick
See Sinclair, Upton (Beall)

Garrison, William Lloyd
1805-1879 .... **NCLC 149**
See also CDALB 1640-1865; DLB 1, 43, 235

Garro, Elena 1920(?)-1998 .. **HLCS 1; TCLC 153**
See also CA 131; 169; CWW 2; DLB 145; EWL 3; HW 1; LAWS 1; WLIT 1

Garth, Will
See Hamilton, Edmond; Kuttner, Henry

Garvey, Marcus (Moziah, Jr.)
1887-1940 ... **BLC 2; HR 1:2; TCLC 41**
See also BW 1; CA 120; 124; CANR 79; DAM MULT

Gary, Romain .... **CLC 25**
See Kacew, Romain
See also DLB 83, 299

Gascar, Pierre .... **CLC 11**
See Fournier, Pierre
See also EWL 3

Gascoigne, George 1539-1577 .... **LC 108**
See also DLB 136; RGEL 2

Gascoyne, David (Emery)
1916-2001 .... **CLC 45**
See also CA 65-68; 200; CANR 10, 28, 54; CP 1, 2, 3, 4, 5, 6, 7; DLB 20; MTCW 1; RGEL 2

Gaskell, Elizabeth Cleghorn
1810-1865 .... **NCLC 5, 70, 97, 137; SSC 25**
See also BRW 5; CDBLB 1832-1890; DAB; DAM MST; DLB 21, 144, 159; RGEL 2; RGSF 2; TEA

Gass, William H(oward) 1924- . **CLC 1, 2, 8, 11, 15, 39, 132; SSC 12**
See also AMWS 6; CA 17-20R; CANR 30, 71, 100; CN 1, 2, 3, 4, 5, 6, 7; DLB 2, 227; EWL 3; MAL 5; MTCW 1, 2; MTFW 2005; RGAL 4

Gassendi, Pierre 1592-1655 .... **LC 54**
See also GFL Beginnings to 1789

Gasset, Jose Ortega y
See Ortega y Gasset, Jose

Gates, Henry Louis, Jr. 1950- ... **BLCS; CLC 65**
See also BW 2, 3; CA 109; CANR 25, 53, 75, 125; CSW; DA3; DAM MULT; DLB 67; EWL 3; MAL 5; MTCW 2; MTFW 2005; RGAL 4

Gautier, Theophile 1811-1872 .. **NCLC 1, 59; PC 18; SSC 20**
See also DAM POET; DLB 119; EW 6; GFL 1789 to the Present; RGWL 2, 3; SUFW; TWA

Gay, John 1685-1732 .... **LC 49**
See also BRW 3; DAM DRAM; DLB 84, 95; RGEL 2; WLIT 3

Gay, Oliver
See Gogarty, Oliver St. John

Gay, Peter (Jack) 1923- .... **CLC 158**
See also CA 13-16R; CANR 18, 41, 77; INT CANR-18

Gaye, Marvin (Pentz, Jr.)
1939-1984 .... **CLC 26**
See also CA 195; 112

Gebler, Carlo (Ernest) 1954- .... **CLC 39**
See also CA 119; 133; CANR 96; DLB 271

Gee, Maggie (Mary) 1948- .... **CLC 57**
See also CA 130; CANR 125; CN 4, 5, 6, 7; DLB 207; MTFW 2005

Gee, Maurice (Gough) 1931- .... **CLC 29**
See also AAYA 42; CA 97-100; CANR 67, 123; CLR 56; CN 2, 3, 4, 5, 6, 7; CWRI 5; EWL 3; MAICYA 2; RGSF 2; SATA 46, 101

Geiogamah, Hanay 1945- .... **NNAL**
See also CA 153; DAM MULT; DLB 175

Gelbart, Larry
See Gelbart, Larry (Simon)
See also CAD; CD 5, 6

Gelbart, Larry (Simon) 1928- .... **CLC 21, 61**
See Gelbart, Larry
See also CA 73-76; CANR 45, 94

Gelber, Jack 1932-2003 ...... **CLC 1, 6, 14, 79**
See also CA 1-4R; 216; CAD; CANR 2; DLB 7, 228; MAL 5

Gellhorn, Martha (Ellis)
1908-1998 .... **CLC 14, 60**
See also CA 77-80; 164; CANR 44; CN 1, 2, 3, 4, 5, 6 7; DLBY 1982, 1998

Genet, Jean 1910-1986 .. **CLC 1, 2, 5, 10, 14, 44, 46; DC 25; TCLC 128**
See also CA 13-16R; CANR 18; DA3; DAM DRAM; DFS 10; DLB 72, 321; DLBY 1986; EW 13; EWL 3; GFL 1789 to the Present; GLL 1; LMFS 2; MTCW 1, 2; MTFW 2005; RGWL 2, 3; TWA

Green, Paul (Eliot) 1894-1981 .... **CLC 25**
See also AITN 1; CA 5-8R; 103; CAD;
CANR 3; DAM DRAM; DLB 7, 9, 249;
DLBY 1981; MAL 5; RGAL 4

Greenaway, Peter 1942- .... **CLC 159**
See also CA 127

Greenberg, Ivan 1908-1973
See Rahv, Philip
See also CA 85-88

Greenberg, Joanne (Goldenberg)
1932- .... **CLC 7, 30**
See also AAYA 12, 67; CA 5-8R; CANR
14, 32, 69; CN 6, 7; SATA 25; YAW

Greenberg, Richard 1959(?)- .... **CLC 57**
See also CA 138; CAD; CD 5, 6

Greenblatt, Stephen J(ay) 1943- ...... **CLC 70**
See also CA 49-52; CANR 115

Greene, Bette 1934- .... **CLC 30**
See also AAYA 7; BYA 3; CA 53-56; CANR
4, 146; CLR 2; CWRI 5; JRDA; LAIT 4;
MAICYA 1, 2; NFS 10; SAAS 16; SATA
8, 102, 161; WYA; YAW

Greene, Gael .... **CLC 8**
See also CA 13-16R; CANR 10

Greene, Graham (Henry)
1904-1991 .... **CLC 1, 3, 6, 9, 14, 18, 27,
37, 70, 72, 125; SSC 29; WLC**
See also AAYA 61; AITN 2; BPFB 2;
BRWR 2; BRWS 1; BYA 3; CA 13-16R;
133; CANR 35, 61, 131; CBD; CDBLB
1945-1960; CMW 4; CN 1, 2, 3, 4; DA;
DA3; DAB; DAC; DAM MST, NOV;
DLB 13, 15, 77, 100, 162, 201, 204;
DLBY 1991; EWL 3; MSW; MTCW 1, 2;
MTFW 2005; NFS 16; RGEL 2; SATA
20; SSFS 14; TEA; WLIT 4

Greene, Robert 1558-1592 .... **LC 41**
See also BRWS 8; DLB 62, 167; IDTP;
RGEL 2; TEA

Greer, Germaine 1939- .... **CLC 131**
See also AITN 1; CA 81-84; CANR 33, 70,
115, 133; FW; MTCW 1, 2; MTFW 2005

Greer, Richard
See Silverberg, Robert

Gregor, Arthur 1923- .... **CLC 9**
See also CA 25-28R; CAAS 10; CANR 11;
CP 1, 2, 3, 4, 5, 6, 7; SATA 36

Gregor, Lee
See Pohl, Frederik

Gregory, Lady Isabella Augusta (Persse)
1852-1932 .... **TCLC 1, 176**
See also BRW 6; CA 104; 184; DLB 10;
IDTP; RGEL 2

Gregory, J. Dennis
See Williams, John A(lfred)

Grekova, I. .... **CLC 59**
See Ventsel, Elena Sergeevna
See also CWW 2

Grendon, Stephen
See Derleth, August (William)

Grenville, Kate 1950- .... **CLC 61**
See also CA 118; CANR 53, 93; CN 7

Grenville, Pelham
See Wodehouse, P(elham) G(renville)

Greve, Felix Paul (Berthold Friedrich)
1879-1948
See Grove, Frederick Philip
See also CA 104; 141, 175; CANR 79;
DAC; DAM MST

Greville, Fulke 1554-1628 .... **LC 79**
See also BRWS 11; DLB 62, 172; RGEL 2

Grey, Lady Jane 1537-1554 .... **LC 93**
See also DLB 132

Grey, Zane 1872-1939 .... **TCLC 6**
See also BPFB 2; CA 104; 132; DA3; DAM
POP; DLB 9, 212; MTCW 1, 2; MTFW
2005; RGAL 4; TCWW 1, 2; TUS

Griboedov, Aleksandr Sergeevich
1795(?)-1829 .... **NCLC 129**
See also DLB 205; RGWL 2, 3

Grieg, (Johan) Nordahl (Brun)
1902-1943 .... **TCLC 10**
See also CA 107; 189; EWL 3

Grieve, C(hristopher) M(urray)
1892-1978 .... **CLC 11, 19**
See MacDiarmid, Hugh; Pteleon
See also CA 5-8R; 85-88; CANR 33, 107;
DAM POET; MTCW 1; RGEL 2

Griffin, Gerald 1803-1840 .... **NCLC 7**
See also DLB 159; RGEL 2

Griffin, John Howard 1920-1980 ..... **CLC 68**
See also AITN 1; CA 1-4R; 101; CANR 2

Griffin, Peter 1942- .... **CLC 39**
See also CA 136

Griffith, D(avid Lewelyn) W(ark)
1875(?)-1948 .... **TCLC 68**
See also CA 119; 150; CANR 80

Griffith, Lawrence
See Griffith, D(avid Lewelyn) W(ark)

Griffiths, Trevor 1935- .... **CLC 13, 52**
See also CA 97-100; CANR 45; CBD; CD
5, 6; DLB 13, 245

Griggs, Sutton (Elbert)
1872-1930 .... **TCLC 77**
See also CA 123; 186; DLB 50

Grigson, Geoffrey (Edward Harvey)
1905-1985 .... **CLC 7, 39**
See also CA 25-28R; 118; CANR 20, 33;
CP 1, 2, 3, 4; DLB 27; MTCW 1, 2

Grile, Dod
See Bierce, Ambrose (Gwinett)

Grillparzer, Franz 1791-1872 .... **DC 14;
NCLC 1, 102; SSC 37**
See also CDWLB 2; DLB 133; EW 5;
RGWL 2, 3; TWA

Grimble, Reverend Charles James
See Eliot, T(homas) S(tearns)

Grimke, Angelina (Emily) Weld
1880-1958 .... **HR 1:2**
See Weld, Angelina (Emily) Grimke
See also BW 1; CA 124; DAM POET; DLB
50, 54

Grimke, Charlotte L(ottie) Forten
1837(?)-1914
See Forten, Charlotte L.
See also BW 1; CA 117; 124; DAM MULT,
POET

Grimm, Jacob Ludwig Karl
1785-1863 .... **NCLC 3, 77; SSC 36, 88**
See also DLB 90; MAICYA 1, 2; RGSF 2;
RGWL 2, 3; SATA 22; WCH

Grimm, Wilhelm Karl 1786-1859 .. **NCLC 3,
77; SSC 36, 88**
See also CDWLB 2; DLB 90; MAICYA 1,
2; RGSF 2; RGWL 2, 3; SATA 22; WCH

**Grimmelshausen, Hans Jakob Christoffel
von**
See Grimmelshausen, Johann Jakob Christoffel von
See also RGWL 2, 3

**Grimmelshausen, Johann Jakob Christoffel
von** 1621-1676 .... **LC 6**
See Grimmelshausen, Hans Jakob Christof-
fel von
See also CDWLB 2; DLB 168

Grindel, Eugene 1895-1952
See Eluard, Paul
See also CA 104; 193; LMFS 2

Grisham, John 1955- .... **CLC 84**
See also AAYA 14, 47; BPFB 2; CA 138;
CANR 47, 69, 114, 133; CMW 4; CN 6,
7; CPW; CSW; DA3; DAM POP; MSW;
MTCW 2; MTFW 2005

Grosseteste, Robert 1175(?)-1253 . **CMLC 62**
See also DLB 115

Grossman, David 1954- .... **CLC 67**
See also CA 138; CANR 114; CWW 2;
DLB 299; EWL 3; WLIT 6

Grossman, Vasilii Semenovich
See Grossman, Vasily (Semenovich)
See also DLB 272

Grossman, Vasily (Semenovich)
1905-1964 .... **CLC 41**
See Grossman, Vasilii Semenovich
See also CA 124; 130; MTCW 1

Grove, Frederick Philip .... **TCLC 4**
See Greve, Felix Paul (Berthold Friedrich)
See also DLB 92; RGEL 2; TCWW 1, 2

Grubb
See Crumb, R(obert)

Grumbach, Doris (Isaac) 1918- . **CLC 13, 22,
64**
See also CA 5-8R; CAAS 2; CANR 9, 42,
70, 127; CN 6, 7; INT CANR-9; MTCW
2; MTFW 2005

Grundtvig, Nikolai Frederik Severin
1783-1872 .... **NCLC 1, 158**
See also DLB 300

Grunge
See Crumb, R(obert)

Grunwald, Lisa 1959- .... **CLC 44**
See also CA 120

Gryphius, Andreas 1616-1664 .... **LC 89**
See also CDWLB 2; DLB 164; RGWL 2, 3

Guare, John 1938- .... **CLC 8, 14, 29, 67; DC
20**
See also CA 73-76; CAD; CANR 21, 69,
118; CD 5, 6; DAM DRAM; DFS 8, 13;
DLB 7, 249; EWL 3; MAL 5; MTCW 1,
2; RGAL 4

Guarini, Battista 1537-1612 .... **LC 102**

Gubar, Susan (David) 1944- .... **CLC 145**
See also CA 108; CANR 45, 70, 139; FW;
MTCW 1; RGAL 4

Gudjonsson, Halldor Kiljan 1902-1998
See Halldor Laxness
See also CA 103; 164

Guenter, Erich
See Eich, Gunter

Guest, Barbara 1920- .... **CLC 34; PC 55**
See also BG 1:2; CA 25-28R; CANR 11,
44, 84; CP 1, 2, 3, 4, 5, 6, 7; CWP; DLB
5, 193

Guest, Edgar A(lbert) 1881-1959 ... **TCLC 95**
See also CA 112; 168

Guest, Judith (Ann) 1936- .... **CLC 8, 30**
See also AAYA 7, 66; CA 77-80; CANR
15, 75, 138; DA3; DAM NOV, POP;
EXPN; INT CANR-15; LAIT 5; MTCW
1, 2; MTFW 2005; NFS 1

Guevara, Che .... **CLC 87; HLC 1**
See Guevara (Serna), Ernesto

Guevara (Serna), Ernesto
1928-1967 .... **CLC 87; HLC 1**
See Guevara, Che
See also CA 127; 111; CANR 56; DAM
MULT; HW 1

Guicciardini, Francesco 1483-1540 ..... **LC 49**

Guild, Nicholas M. 1944- .... **CLC 33**
See also CA 93-96

Guillemin, Jacques
See Sartre, Jean-Paul

Guillen, Jorge 1893-1984 . **CLC 11; HLCS 1;
PC 35**
See also CA 89-92; 112; DAM MULT,
POET; DLB 108; EWL 3; HW 1; RGWL
2, 3

Guillen, Nicolas (Cristobal)
1902-1989 .... **BLC 2; CLC 48, 79; HLC
1; PC 23**
See also BW 2; CA 116; 125; 129; CANR
84; DAM MST, MULT, POET; DLB 283;
EWL 3; HW 1; LAW; RGWL 2, 3; WP

Guillen y Alvarez, Jorge
See Guillen, Jorge

Guillevic, (Eugene) 1907-1997 .... **CLC 33**
See also CA 93-96; CWW 2

Guillois
See Desnos, Robert

Guillois, Valentin
See Desnos, Robert

Guimaraes Rosa, Joao 1908-1967 .... **HLCS 2**
See Rosa, Joao Guimaraes
See also CA 175; LAW; RGSF 2; RGWL 2, 3

Guiney, Louise Imogen
1861-1920 .... **TCLC 41**
See also CA 160; DLB 54; RGAL 4

Guinizelli, Guido c. 1230-1276 ...... **CMLC 49**
See Guinizzelli, Guido

Guinizzelli, Guido
See Guinizelli, Guido
See also WLIT 7

Guiraldes, Ricardo (Guillermo)
1886-1927 .... **TCLC 39**
See also CA 131; EWL 3; HW 1; LAW;
MTCW 1

Gumilev, Nikolai (Stepanovich)
1886-1921 .... **TCLC 60**
See Gumilyov, Nikolay Stepanovich
See also CA 165; DLB 295

Gumilyov, Nikolay Stepanovich
See Gumilev, Nikolai (Stepanovich)
See also EWL 3

Gump, P. Q.
See Card, Orson Scott

Gunesekera, Romesh 1954- .... **CLC 91**
See also BRWS 10; CA 159; CANR 140;
CN 6, 7; DLB 267

Gunn, Bill .... **CLC 5**
See Gunn, William Harrison
See also DLB 38

Gunn, Thom(son William)
1929-2004 . **CLC 3, 6, 18, 32, 81; PC 26**
See also BRWS 4; CA 17-20R; 227; CANR
9, 33, 116; CDBLB 1960 to Present; CP
1, 2, 3, 4, 5, 6, 7; DAM POET; DLB 27;
INT CANR-33; MTCW 1; PFS 9; RGEL
2

Gunn, William Harrison 1934(?)-1989
See Gunn, Bill
See also AITN 1; BW 1, 3; CA 13-16R;
128; CANR 12, 25, 76

Gunn Allen, Paula
See Allen, Paula Gunn

Gunnars, Kristjana 1948- .... **CLC 69**
See also CA 113; CCA 1; CP 7; CWP; DLB
60

Gunter, Erich
See Eich, Gunter

Gurdjieff, G(eorgei) I(vanovich)
1877(?)-1949 .... **TCLC 71**
See also CA 157

Gurganus, Allan 1947- .... **CLC 70**
See also BEST 90:1; CA 135; CANR 114;
CN 6, 7; CPW; CSW; DAM POP; GLL 1

Gurney, A. R.
See Gurney, A(lbert) R(amsdell), Jr.
See also DLB 266

Gurney, A(lbert) R(amsdell), Jr.
1930- .... **CLC 32, 50, 54**
See Gurney, A. R.
See also AMWS 5; CA 77-80; CAD; CANR
32, 64, 121; CD 5, 6; DAM DRAM; EWL
3

Gurney, Ivor (Bertie) 1890-1937 ... **TCLC 33**
See also BRW 6; CA 167; DLBY 2002;
PAB; RGEL 2

Gurney, Peter
See Gurney, A(lbert) R(amsdell), Jr.

Guro, Elena (Genrikhovna)
1877-1913 .... **TCLC 56**
See also DLB 295

Gustafson, James M(oody) 1925- ... **CLC 100**
See also CA 25-28R; CANR 37

Gustafson, Ralph (Barker)
1909-1995 .... **CLC 36**
See also CA 21-24R; CANR 8, 45, 84; CP
1, 2, 3, 4; DLB 88; RGEL 2

Gut, Gom
See Simenon, Georges (Jacques Christian)

Guterson, David 1956- .... **CLC 91**
See also CA 132; CANR 73, 126; CN 7;
DLB 292; MTCW 2; MTFW 2005; NFS
13

Guthrie, A(lfred) B(ertram), Jr.
1901-1991 .... **CLC 23**
See also CA 57-60; 134; CANR 24; CN 1,
2, 3; DLB 6, 212; MAL 5; SATA 62;
SATA-Obit 67; TCWW 1, 2

Guthrie, Isobel
See Grieve, C(hristopher) M(urray)

Guthrie, Woodrow Wilson 1912-1967
See Guthrie, Woody
See also CA 113; 93-96

Guthrie, Woody .... **CLC 35**
See Guthrie, Woodrow Wilson
See also DLB 303; LAIT 3

Gutierrez Najera, Manuel
1859-1895 .... **HLCS 2; NCLC 133**
See also DLB 290; LAW

Guy, Rosa (Cuthbert) 1925- .... **CLC 26**
See also AAYA 4, 37; BW 2; CA 17-20R;
CANR 14, 34, 83; CLR 13; DLB 33;
DNFS 1; JRDA; MAICYA 1, 2; SATA 14,
62, 122; YAW

Gwendolyn
See Bennett, (Enoch) Arnold

H. D. .... **CLC 3, 8, 14, 31, 34, 73; PC 5**
See Doolittle, Hilda
See also FL 1:5

H. de V.
See Buchan, John

Haavikko, Paavo Juhani 1931- .. **CLC 18, 34**
See also CA 106; CWW 2; EWL 3

Habbema, Koos
See Heijermans, Herman

Habermas, Juergen 1929- .... **CLC 104**
See also CA 109; CANR 85; DLB 242

Habermas, Jurgen
See Habermas, Juergen

Hacker, Marilyn 1942- ...... **CLC 5, 9, 23, 72, 91; PC 47**
See also CA 77-80; CANR 68, 129; CP 3,
4, 5, 6, 7; CWP; DAM POET; DLB 120,
282; FW; GLL 2; MAL 5; PFS 19

Hadewijch of Antwerp fl. 1250- ... **CMLC 61**
See also RGWL 3

Hadrian 76-138 .... **CMLC 52**

Haeckel, Ernst Heinrich (Philipp August)
1834-1919 .... **TCLC 83**
See also CA 157

Hafiz c. 1326-1389(?) .... **CMLC 34**
See also RGWL 2, 3; WLIT 6

Hagedorn, Jessica T(arahata)
1949- .... **CLC 185**
See also CA 139; CANR 69; CWP; DLB
312; RGAL 4

Haggard, H(enry) Rider
1856-1925 .... **TCLC 11**
See also BRWS 3; BYA 4, 5; CA 108; 148;
CANR 112; DLB 70, 156, 174, 178;
FANT; LMFS 1; MTCW 2; RGEL 2;
RHW; SATA 16; SCFW 1, 2; SFW 4;
SUFW 1; WLIT 4

Hagiosy, L.
See Larbaud, Valery (Nicolas)

Hagiwara, Sakutaro 1886-1942 .... **PC 18;
TCLC 60**
See Hagiwara Sakutaro
See also CA 154; RGWL 3

Hagiwara Sakutaro
See Hagiwara, Sakutaro
See also EWL 3

Haig, Fenil
See Ford, Ford Madox

Haig-Brown, Roderick (Langmere)
1908-1976 .... **CLC 21**
See also CA 5-8R; 69-72; CANR 4, 38, 83;
CLR 31; CWRI 5; DLB 88; MAICYA 1,
2; SATA 12; TCWW 2

Haight, Rip
See Carpenter, John (Howard)

Hailey, Arthur 1920-2004 .... **CLC 5**
See also AITN 2; BEST 90:3; BPFB 2; CA
1-4R; 233; CANR 2, 36, 75; CCA 1; CN
1, 2, 3, 4, 5, 6, 7; CPW; DAM NOV, POP;
DLB 88; DLBY 1982; MTCW 1, 2;
MTFW 2005

Hailey, Elizabeth Forsythe 1938- ..... **CLC 40**
See also CA 93-96, 188; CAAE 188; CAAS
1; CANR 15, 48; INT CANR-15

Haines, John (Meade) 1924- .... **CLC 58**
See also AMWS 12; CA 17-20R; CANR
13, 34; CP 1, 2, 3, 4; CSW; DLB 5, 212;
TCLE 1:1

Hakluyt, Richard 1552-1616 .... **LC 31**
See also DLB 136; RGEL 2

Haldeman, Joe (William) 1943- .... **CLC 61**
See Graham, Robert
See also AAYA 38; CA 53-56, 179; CAAE
179; CAAS 25; CANR 6, 70, 72, 130;
DLB 8; INT CANR-6; SCFW 2; SFW 4

Hale, Janet Campbell 1947- .... **NNAL**
See also CA 49-52; CANR 45, 75; DAM
MULT; DLB 175; MTCW 2; MTFW 2005

Hale, Sarah Josepha (Buell)
1788-1879 .... **NCLC 75**
See also DLB 1, 42, 73, 243

Halevy, Elie 1870-1937 .... **TCLC 104**

Haley, Alex(ander Murray Palmer)
1921-1992 .... **BLC 2; CLC 8, 12, 76;
TCLC 147**
See also AAYA 26; BPFB 2; BW 2, 3; CA
77-80; 136; CANR 61; CDALBS; CPW;
CSW; DA; DA3; DAB; DAC; DAM MST,
MULT, POP; DLB 38; LAIT 5; MTCW
1, 2; NFS 9

Haliburton, Thomas Chandler
1796-1865 .... **NCLC 15, 149**
See also DLB 11, 99; RGEL 2; RGSF 2

Hall, Donald (Andrew, Jr.) 1928- ...... **CLC 1,
13, 37, 59, 151; PC 70**
See also AAYA 63; CA 5-8R; CAAS 7;
CANR 2, 44, 64, 106, 133; CP 1, 2, 3, 4,
5, 6, 7; DAM POET; DLB 5; MAL 5;
MTCW 2; MTFW 2005; RGAL 4; SATA
23, 97

Hall, Frederic Sauser
See Sauser-Hall, Frederic

Hall, James
See Kuttner, Henry

Hall, James Norman 1887-1951 ..... **TCLC 23**
See also CA 123; 173; LAIT 1; RHW 1;
SATA 21

Hall, Joseph 1574-1656 .... **LC 91**
See also DLB 121, 151; RGEL 2

Hall, (Marguerite) Radclyffe
1880-1943 .... **TCLC 12**
See also BRWS 6; CA 110; 150; CANR 83;
DLB 191; MTCW 2; MTFW 2005; RGEL
2; RHW

Hall, Rodney 1935- .... **CLC 51**
See also CA 109; CANR 69; CN 6, 7; CP
1, 2, 3, 4, 5, 6, 7; DLB 289

Harrison, James (Thomas) 1937- ...... **CLC 6, 14, 33, 66, 143; SSC 19**
See Harrison, Jim
See also CA 13-16R; CANR 8, 51, 79, 142; DLBY 1982; INT CANR-8
Harrison, Jim
See Harrison, James (Thomas)
See also AMWS 8; CN 5, 6; CP 1, 2, 3, 4, 5, 6, 7; RGAL 4; TCWW 2; TUS
Harrison, Kathryn 1961- .... **CLC 70, 151**
See also CA 144; CANR 68, 122
Harrison, Tony 1937- .... **CLC 43, 129**
See also BRWS 5; CA 65-68; CANR 44, 98; CBD; CD 5, 6; CP 2, 3, 4, 5, 6, 7; DLB 40, 245; MTCW 1; RGEL 2
Harriss, Will(ard Irvin) 1922- .... **CLC 34**
See also CA 111
Hart, Ellis
See Ellison, Harlan (Jay)
Hart, Josephine 1942(?)- .... **CLC 70**
See also CA 138; CANR 70; CPW; DAM POP
Hart, Moss 1904-1961 .... **CLC 66**
See also CA 109; 89-92; CANR 84; DAM DRAM; DFS 1; DLB 7, 266; RGAL 4
Harte, (Francis) Bret(t) 1836(?)-1902 ... **SSC 8, 59; TCLC 1, 25; WLC**
See also AMWS 2; CA 104; 140; CANR 80; CDALB 1865-1917; DA; DA3; DAC; DAM MST; DLB 12, 64, 74, 79, 186; EXPS; LAIT 2; RGAL 4; RGSF 2; SATA 26; SSFS 3; TUS
Hartley, L(eslie) P(oles) 1895-1972 ... **CLC 2, 22**
See also BRWS 7; CA 45-48; 37-40R; CANR 33; CN 1; DLB 15, 139; EWL 3; HGG; MTCW 1, 2; MTFW 2005; RGEL 2; RGSF 2; SUFW 1
Hartman, Geoffrey H. 1929- .... **CLC 27**
See also CA 117; 125; CANR 79; DLB 67
Hartmann, Sadakichi 1869-1944 ... **TCLC 73**
See also CA 157; DLB 54
Hartmann von Aue c. 1170-c. 1210 .... **CMLC 15**
See also CDWLB 2; DLB 138; RGWL 2, 3
Hartog, Jan de
See de Hartog, Jan
Haruf, Kent 1943- .... **CLC 34**
See also AAYA 44; CA 149; CANR 91, 131
Harvey, Caroline
See Trollope, Joanna
Harvey, Gabriel 1550(?)-1631 .... **LC 88**
See also DLB 167, 213, 281
Harwood, Ronald 1934- .... **CLC 32**
See also CA 1-4R; CANR 4, 55; CBD; CD 5, 6; DAM DRAM, MST; DLB 13
Hasegawa Tatsunosuke
See Futabatei, Shimei
Hasek, Jaroslav (Matej Frantisek) 1883-1923 .... **SSC 69; TCLC 4**
See also CA 104; 129; CDWLB 4; DLB 215; EW 9; EWL 3; MTCW 1, 2; RGSF 2; RGWL 2, 3
Hass, Robert 1941- ... **CLC 18, 39, 99; PC 16**
See also AMWS 6; CA 111; CANR 30, 50, 71; CP 3, 4, 5, 6, 7; DLB 105, 206; EWL 3; MAL 5; MTFW 2005; RGAL 4; SATA 94; TCLE 1:1
Hastings, Hudson
See Kuttner, Henry
Hastings, Selina .... **CLC 44**
Hathorne, John 1641-1717 .... **LC 38**
Hatteras, Amelia
See Mencken, H(enry) L(ouis)
Hatteras, Owen .... **TCLC 18**
See Mencken, H(enry) L(ouis); Nathan, George Jean

Hauptmann, Gerhart (Johann Robert) 1862-1946 .... **SSC 37; TCLC 4**
See also CA 104; 153; CDWLB 2; DAM DRAM; DLB 66, 118; EW 8; EWL 3; RGSF 2; RGWL 2, 3; TWA
Havel, Vaclav 1936- ..... **CLC 25, 58, 65, 123; DC 6**
See also CA 104; CANR 36, 63, 124; CD-WLB 4; CWW 2; DA3; DAM DRAM; DFS 10; DLB 232; EWL 3; LMFS 2; MTCW 1, 2; MTFW 2005; RGWL 3
Haviaras, Stratis .... **CLC 33**
See Chaviaras, Strates
Hawes, Stephen 1475(?)-1529(?) .... **LC 17**
See also DLB 132; RGEL 2
Hawkes, John (Clendennin Burne, Jr.) 1925-1998 .. **CLC 1, 2, 3, 4, 7, 9, 14, 15, 27, 49**
See also BPFB 2; CA 1-4R; 167; CANR 2, 47, 64; CN 1, 2, 3, 4, 5, 6; DLB 2, 7, 227; DLBY 1980, 1998; EWL 3; MAL 5; MTCW 1, 2; MTFW 2005; RGAL 4
Hawking, S. W.
See Hawking, Stephen W(illiam)
Hawking, Stephen W(illiam) 1942- . **CLC 63, 105**
See also AAYA 13; BEST 89:1; CA 126; 129; CANR 48, 115; CPW; DA3; MTCW 2; MTFW 2005
Hawkins, Anthony Hope
See Hope, Anthony
Hawthorne, Julian 1846-1934 .... **TCLC 25**
See also CA 165; HGG
Hawthorne, Nathaniel 1804-1864 ... **NCLC 2, 10, 17, 23, 39, 79, 95, 158; SSC 3, 29, 39, 89; WLC**
See also AAYA 18; AMW; AMWC 1; AMWR 1; BPFB 2; BYA 3; CDALB 1640-1865; CLR 103; DA; DA3; DAB; DAC; DAM MST, NOV; DLB 1, 74, 183, 223, 269; EXPN; EXPS; GL 2; HGG; LAIT 1; NFS 1, 20; RGAL 4; RGSF 2; SSFS 1, 7, 11, 15; SUFW 1; TUS; WCH; YABC 2
Hawthorne, Sophia Peabody 1809-1871 .... **NCLC 150**
See also DLB 183, 239
Haxton, Josephine Ayres 1921-
See Douglas, Ellen
See also CA 115; CANR 41, 83
Hayaseca y Eizaguirre, Jorge
See Echegaray (y Eizaguirre), Jose (Maria Waldo)
Hayashi, Fumiko 1904-1951 .... **TCLC 27**
See Hayashi Fumiko
See also CA 161
Hayashi Fumiko
See Hayashi, Fumiko
See also DLB 180; EWL 3
Haycraft, Anna (Margaret) 1932-2005
See Ellis, Alice Thomas
See also CA 122; 237; CANR 90, 141; MTCW 2; MTFW 2005
Hayden, Robert E(arl) 1913-1980 ..... **BLC 2; CLC 5, 9, 14, 37; PC 6**
See also AFAW 1, 2; AMWS 2; BW 1, 3; CA 69-72; 97-100; CABS 2; CANR 24, 75, 82; CDALB 1941-1968; CP 1, 2, 3; DA; DAC; DAM MST, MULT, POET; DLB 5, 76; EWL 3; EXPP; MAL 5; MTCW 1, 2; PFS 1; RGAL 4; SATA 19; SATA-Obit 26; WP
Haydon, Benjamin Robert 1786-1846 .... **NCLC 146**
See also DLB 110
Hayek, F(riedrich) A(ugust von) 1899-1992 .... **TCLC 109**
See also CA 93-96; 137; CANR 20; MTCW 1, 2

Hayford, J(oseph) E(phraim) Casely
See Casely-Hayford, J(oseph) E(phraim)
Hayman, Ronald 1932- .... **CLC 44**
See also CA 25-28R; CANR 18, 50, 88; CD 5, 6; DLB 155
Hayne, Paul Hamilton 1830-1886 . **NCLC 94**
See also DLB 3, 64, 79, 248; RGAL 4
Hays, Mary 1760-1843 .... **NCLC 114**
See also DLB 142, 158; RGEL 2
Haywood, Eliza (Fowler) 1693(?)-1756 .... **LC 1, 44**
See also DLB 39; RGEL 2
Hazlitt, William 1778-1830 ...... **NCLC 29, 82**
See also BRW 4; DLB 110, 158; RGEL 2; TEA
Hazzard, Shirley 1931- .... **CLC 18, 218**
See also CA 9-12R; CANR 4, 70, 127; CN 1, 2, 3, 4, 5, 6, 7; DLB 289; DLBY 1982; MTCW 1
Head, Bessie 1937-1986 ...... **BLC 2; CLC 25, 67; SSC 52**
See also AFW; BW 2, 3; CA 29-32R; 119; CANR 25, 82; CDWLB 3; CN 1, 2, 3, 4; DA3; DAM MULT; DLB 117, 225; EWL 3; EXPS; FL 1:6; FW; MTCW 1, 2; MTFW 2005; RGSF 2; SSFS 5, 13; WLIT 2; WWE 1
Headon, (Nicky) Topper 1956(?)- ..... **CLC 30**
Heaney, Seamus (Justin) 1939- ..... **CLC 5, 7, 14, 25, 37, 74, 91, 171; PC 18; WLCS**
See also AAYA 61; BRWR 1; BRWS 2; CA 85-88; CANR 25, 48, 75, 91, 128; CD-BLB 1960 to Present; CP 1, 2, 3, 4, 5, 6, 7; DA3; DAB; DAM POET; DLB 40; DLBY 1995; EWL 3; EXPP; MTCW 1, 2; MTFW 2005; PAB; PFS 2, 5, 8, 17; RGEL 2; TEA; WLIT 4
Hearn, (Patricio) Lafcadio (Tessima Carlos) 1850-1904 .... **TCLC 9**
See also CA 105; 166; DLB 12, 78, 189; HGG; MAL 5; RGAL 4
Hearne, Samuel 1745-1792 .... **LC 95**
See also DLB 99
Hearne, Vicki 1946-2001 .... **CLC 56**
See also CA 139; 201
Hearon, Shelby 1931- .... **CLC 63**
See also AITN 2; AMWS 8; CA 25-28R; CANR 18, 48, 103, 146; CSW
Heat-Moon, William Least .... **CLC 29**
See Trogdon, William (Lewis)
See also AAYA 9
Hebbel, Friedrich 1813-1863 . **DC 21; NCLC 43**
See also CDWLB 2; DAM DRAM; DLB 129; EW 6; RGWL 2, 3
Hebert, Anne 1916-2000 .... **CLC 4, 13, 29**
See also CA 85-88; 187; CANR 69, 126; CCA 1; CWP; CWW 2; DA3; DAC; DAM MST, POET; DLB 68; EWL 3; GFL 1789 to the Present; MTCW 1, 2; MTFW 2005; PFS 20
Hecht, Anthony (Evan) 1923-2004 .... **CLC 8, 13, 19; PC 70**
See also AMWS 10; CA 9-12R; 232; CANR 6, 108; CP 1, 2, 3, 4, 5, 6, 7; DAM POET; DLB 5, 169; EWL 3; PFS 6; WP
Hecht, Ben 1894-1964 ..... **CLC 8; TCLC 101**
See also CA 85-88; DFS 9; DLB 7, 9, 25, 26, 28, 86; FANT; IDFW 3, 4; RGAL 4
Hedayat, Sadeq 1903-1951 .... **TCLC 21**
See also CA 120; EWL 3; RGSF 2
Hegel, Georg Wilhelm Friedrich 1770-1831 .... **NCLC 46, 151**
See also DLB 90; TWA
Heidegger, Martin 1889-1976 .... **CLC 24**
See also CA 81-84; 65-68; CANR 34; DLB 296; MTCW 1, 2; MTFW 2005

Heyerdahl, Thor 1914-2002 .... **CLC 26**
See also CA 5-8R; 207; CANR 5, 22, 66, 73; LAIT 4; MTCW 1, 2; MTFW 2005; SATA 2, 52

Heym, Georg (Theodor Franz Arthur)
1887-1912 .... **TCLC 9**
See also CA 106; 181

Heym, Stefan 1913-2001 .... **CLC 41**
See also CA 9-12R; 203; CANR 4; CWW 2; DLB 69; EWL 3

Heyse, Paul (Johann Ludwig von)
1830-1914 .... **TCLC 8**
See also CA 104; 209; DLB 129

Heyward, (Edwin) DuBose
1885-1940 .... **HR 1:2; TCLC 59**
See also CA 108; 157; DLB 7, 9, 45, 249; MAL 5; SATA 21

Heywood, John 1497(?)-1580(?) .... **LC 65**
See also DLB 136; RGEL 2

Heywood, Thomas 1573(?)-1641 .... **LC 111**
See also DAM DRAM; DLB 62; LMFS 1; RGEL 2; TEA

Hibbert, Eleanor Alice Burford
1906-1993 .... **CLC 7**
See Holt, Victoria
See also BEST 90:4; CA 17-20R; 140; CANR 9, 28, 59; CMW 4; CPW; DAM POP; MTCW 2; MTFW 2005; RHW; SATA 2; SATA-Obit 74

Hichens, Robert (Smythe)
1864-1950 .... **TCLC 64**
See also CA 162; DLB 153; HGG; RHW; SUFW

Higgins, Aidan 1927- .... **SSC 68**
See also CA 9-12R; CANR 70, 115; CN 1, 2, 3, 4, 5, 6, 7; DLB 14

Higgins, George V(incent)
1939-1999 .... **CLC 4, 7, 10, 18**
See also BPFB 2; CA 77-80; 186; CAAS 5; CANR 17, 51, 89, 96; CMW 4; CN 2, 3, 4, 5, 6; DLB 2; DLBY 1981, 1998; INT CANR-17; MSW; MTCW 1

Higginson, Thomas Wentworth
1823-1911 .... **TCLC 36**
See also CA 162; DLB 1, 64, 243

Higgonet, Margaret ed. .... **CLC 65**

Highet, Helen
See MacInnes, Helen (Clark)

Highsmith, (Mary) Patricia
1921-1995 .... **CLC 2, 4, 14, 42, 102**
See Morgan, Claire
See also AAYA 48; BRWS 5; CA 1-4R; 147; CANR 1, 20, 48, 62, 108; CMW 4; CN 1, 2, 3, 4, 5; CPW; DA3; DAM NOV, POP; DLB 306; MSW; MTCW 1, 2; MTFW 2005

Highwater, Jamake (Mamake)
1942(?)-2001 .... **CLC 12**
See also AAYA 7; BPFB 2; BYA 4; CA 65-68; 199; CAAS 7; CANR 10, 34, 84; CLR 17; CWRI 5; DLB 52; DLBY 1985; JRDA; MAICYA 1, 2; SATA 32, 69; SATA-Brief 30

Highway, Tomson 1951- ...... **CLC 92; NNAL**
See also CA 151; CANR 75; CCA 1; CD 5, 6; CN 7; DAC; DAM MULT; DFS 2; MTCW 2

Hijuelos, Oscar 1951- .... **CLC 65; HLC 1**
See also AAYA 25; AMWS 8; BEST 90:1; CA 123; CANR 50, 75, 125; CPW; DA3; DAM MULT, POP; DLB 145; HW 1, 2; LLW; MAL 5; MTCW 2; MTFW 2005; NFS 17; RGAL 4; WLIT 1

Hikmet, Nazim 1902-1963 .... **CLC 40**
See Nizami of Ganja
See also CA 141; 93-96; EWL 3; WLIT 6

Hildegard von Bingen 1098-1179 . **CMLC 20**
See also DLB 148

Hildesheimer, Wolfgang 1916-1991 .. **CLC 49**
See also CA 101; 135; DLB 69, 124; EWL 3

Hill, Geoffrey (William) 1932- ...... **CLC 5, 8, 18, 45**
See also BRWS 5; CA 81-84; CANR 21, 89; CDBLB 1960 to Present; CP 1, 2, 3, 4, 5, 6, 7; DAM POET; DLB 40; EWL 3; MTCW 1; RGEL 2

Hill, George Roy 1921-2002 .... **CLC 26**
See also CA 110; 122; 213

Hill, John
See Koontz, Dean R.

Hill, Susan (Elizabeth) 1942- ...... **CLC 4, 113**
See also CA 33-36R; CANR 29, 69, 129; CN 2, 3, 4, 5, 6, 7; DAB; DAM MST, NOV; DLB 14, 139; HGG; MTCW 1; RHW

Hillard, Asa G. III .... **CLC 70**

Hillerman, Tony 1925- .... **CLC 62, 170**
See also AAYA 40; BEST 89:1; BPFB 2; CA 29-32R; CANR 21, 42, 65, 97, 134; CMW 4; CPW; DA3; DAM POP; DLB 206, 306; MAL 5; MSW; MTCW 2; MTFW 2005; RGAL 4; SATA 6; TCWW 2; YAW

Hillesum, Etty 1914-1943 .... **TCLC 49**
See also CA 137

Hilliard, Noel (Harvey) 1929-1996 ... **CLC 15**
See also CA 9-12R; CANR 7, 69; CN 1, 2, 3, 4, 5, 6

Hillis, Rick 1956- .... **CLC 66**
See also CA 134

Hilton, James 1900-1954 .... **TCLC 21**
See also CA 108; 169; DLB 34, 77; FANT; SATA 34

Hilton, Walter (?)-1396 .... **CMLC 58**
See also DLB 146; RGEL 2

Himes, Chester (Bomar) 1909-1984 .. **BLC 2; CLC 2, 4, 7, 18, 58, 108; TCLC 139**
See also AFAW 2; BPFB 2; BW 2; CA 25-28R; 114; CANR 22, 89; CMW 4; CN 1, 2, 3; DAM MULT; DLB 2, 76, 143, 226; EWL 3; MAL 5; MSW; MTCW 1, 2; MTFW 2005; RGAL 4

Himmelfarb, Gertrude 1922- .... **CLC 202**
See also CA 49-52; CANR 28, 66, 102

Hinde, Thomas .... **CLC 6, 11**
See Chitty, Thomas Willes
See also CN 1, 2, 3, 4, 5, 6; EWL 3

Hine, (William) Daryl 1936- .... **CLC 15**
See also CA 1-4R; CAAS 15; CANR 1, 20; CP 1, 2, 3, 4, 5, 6, 7; DLB 60

Hinkson, Katharine Tynan
See Tynan, Katharine

Hinojosa(-Smith), Rolando (R.)
1929- .... **HLC 1**
See Hinojosa-Smith, Rolando
See also CA 131; CAAS 16; CANR 62; DAM MULT; DLB 82; HW 1, 2; LLW; MTCW 2; MTFW 2005; RGAL 4

Hinton, S(usan) E(loise) 1950- ... **CLC 30, 111**
See also AAYA 2, 33; BPFB 2; BYA 2, 3; CA 81-84; CANR 32, 62, 92, 133; CDALBS; CLR 3, 23; CPW; DA; DA3; DAB; DAC; DAM MST, NOV; JRDA; LAIT 5; MAICYA 1, 2; MTCW 1, 2; MTFW 2005 !**; NFS 5, 9, 15, 16; SATA 19, 58, 115, 160; WYA; YAW

Hippius, Zinaida (Nikolaevna) .... **TCLC 9**
See Gippius, Zinaida (Nikolaevna)
See also DLB 295; EWL 3

Hiraoka, Kimitake 1925-1970
See Mishima, Yukio
See also CA 97-100; 29-32R; DA3; DAM DRAM; GLL 1; MTCW 1, 2

Hirsch, E(ric) D(onald), Jr. 1928- .... **CLC 79**
See also CA 25-28R; CANR 27, 51; DLB 67; INT CANR-27; MTCW 1

Hirsch, Edward 1950- .... **CLC 31, 50**
See also CA 104; CANR 20, 42, 102; CP 7; DLB 120; PFS 22

Hitchcock, Alfred (Joseph)
1899-1980 .... **CLC 16**
See also AAYA 22; CA 159; 97-100; SATA 27; SATA-Obit 24

Hitchens, Christopher (Eric)
1949- .... **CLC 157**
See also CA 152; CANR 89

Hitler, Adolf 1889-1945 .... **TCLC 53**
See also CA 117; 147

Hoagland, Edward (Morley) 1932- .. **CLC 28**
See also ANW; CA 1-4R; CANR 2, 31, 57, 107; CN 1, 2, 3, 4, 5, 6, 7; DLB 6; SATA 51; TCWW 2

Hoban, Russell (Conwell) 1925- ... **CLC 7, 25**
See also BPFB 2; CA 5-8R; CANR 23, 37, 66, 114, 138; CLR 3, 69; CN 4, 5, 6, 7; CWRI 5; DAM NOV; DLB 52; FANT; MAICYA 1, 2; MTCW 1, 2; MTFW 2005; SATA 1, 40, 78, 136; SFW 4; SUFW 2; TCLE 1:1

Hobbes, Thomas 1588-1679 .... **LC 36**
See also DLB 151, 252, 281; RGEL 2

Hobbs, Perry
See Blackmur, R(ichard) P(almer)

Hobson, Laura Z(ametkin)
1900-1986 .... **CLC 7, 25**
See also BPFB 2; CA 17-20R; 118; CANR 55; CN 1, 2, 3, 4; DLB 28; SATA 52

Hoccleve, Thomas c. 1368-c. 1437 ...... **LC 75**
See also DLB 146; RGEL 2

Hoch, Edward D(entinger) 1930-
See Queen, Ellery
See also CA 29-32R; CANR 11, 27, 51, 97; CMW 4; DLB 306; SFW 4

Hochhuth, Rolf 1931- .... **CLC 4, 11, 18**
See also CA 5-8R; CANR 33, 75, 136; CWW 2; DAM DRAM; DLB 124; EWL 3; MTCW 1, 2; MTFW 2005

Hochman, Sandra 1936- .... **CLC 3, 8**
See also CA 5-8R; CP 1, 2, 3, 4; DLB 5

Hochwaelder, Fritz 1911-1986 .... **CLC 36**
See Hochwalder, Fritz
See also CA 29-32R; 120; CANR 42; DAM DRAM; MTCW 1; RGWL 3

Hochwalder, Fritz
See Hochwaelder, Fritz
See also EWL 3; RGWL 2

Hocking, Mary (Eunice) 1921- .... **CLC 13**
See also CA 101; CANR 18, 40

Hodgins, Jack 1938- .... **CLC 23**
See also CA 93-96; CN 4, 5, 6, 7; DLB 60

Hodgson, William Hope
1877(?)-1918 .... **TCLC 13**
See also CA 111; 164; CMW 4; DLB 70, 153, 156, 178; HGG; MTCW 2; SFW 4; SUFW 1

Hoeg, Peter 1957- .... **CLC 95, 156**
See also CA 151; CANR 75; CMW 4; DA3; DLB 214; EWL 3; MTCW 2; MTFW 2005; NFS 17; RGWL 3; SSFS 18

Hoffman, Alice 1952- .... **CLC 51**
See also AAYA 37; AMWS 10; CA 77-80; CANR 34, 66, 100, 138; CN 4, 5, 6, 7; CPW; DAM NOV; DLB 292; MAL 5; MTCW 1, 2; MTFW 2005; TCLE 1:1

Hoffman, Daniel (Gerard) 1923- . **CLC 6, 13, 23**
See also CA 1-4R; CANR 4, 142; CP 1, 2, 3, 4, 5, 6, 7; DLB 5; TCLE 1:1

Hoffman, Eva 1945- .... **CLC 182**
See also CA 132; CANR 146

Hoffman, Stanley 1944- .... **CLC 5**
See also CA 77-80

Hoffman, William 1925- .... **CLC 141**
See also CA 21-24R; CANR 9, 103; CSW; DLB 234; TCLE 1:1

MULT, NOV; DFS 6; DLB 51, 86; EWL 3; EXPN; EXPS; FL 1:6; FW; LAIT 3; LATS 1:1; LMFS 2; MAL 5; MAWW; MTCW 1, 2; MTFW 2005; NFS 3; RGAL 4; RGSF 2; SSFS 1, 6, 11, 19, 21; TUS; YAW

Husserl, E. G.
See Husserl, Edmund (Gustav Albrecht)

Husserl, Edmund (Gustav Albrecht)
1859-1938 .... **TCLC 100**
See also CA 116; 133; DLB 296

Huston, John (Marcellus)
1906-1987 .... **CLC 20**
See also CA 73-76; 123; CANR 34; DLB 26

Hustvedt, Siri 1955- .... **CLC 76**
See also CA 137

Hutten, Ulrich von 1488-1523 .... **LC 16**
See also DLB 179

Huxley, Aldous (Leonard)
1894-1963 .... **CLC 1, 3, 4, 5, 8, 11, 18, 35, 79; SSC 39; WLC**
See also AAYA 11; BPFB 2; BRW 7; CA 85-88; CANR 44, 99; CDBLB 1914-1945; DA; DA3; DAB; DAC; DAM MST, NOV; DLB 36, 100, 162, 195, 255; EWL 3; EXPN; LAIT 5; LMFS 2; MTCW 1, 2; MTFW 2005; NFS 6; RGEL 2; SATA 63; SCFW 1, 2; SFW 4; TEA; YAW

Huxley, T(homas) H(enry)
1825-1895 .... **NCLC 67**
See also DLB 57; TEA

Huygens, Constantijn 1596-1687 .... **LC 114**
See also RGWL 2, 3

Huysmans, Joris-Karl 1848-1907 ... **TCLC 7, 69**
See also CA 104; 165; DLB 123; EW 7; GFL 1789 to the Present; LMFS 2; RGWL 2, 3

Hwang, David Henry 1957- .... **CLC 55, 196; DC 4, 23**
See also CA 127; 132; CAD; CANR 76, 124; CD 5, 6; DA3; DAM DRAM; DFS 11, 18; DLB 212, 228, 312; INT CA-132; MAL 5; MTCW 2; MTFW 2005; RGAL 4

Hyde, Anthony 1946- .... **CLC 42**
See Chase, Nicholas
See also CA 136; CCA 1

Hyde, Margaret O(ldroyd) 1917- ..... **CLC 21**
See also CA 1-4R; CANR 1, 36, 137; CLR 23; JRDA; MAICYA 1, 2; SAAS 8; SATA 1, 42, 76, 139

Hynes, James 1956(?)- .... **CLC 65**
See also CA 164; CANR 105

Hypatia c. 370-415 .... **CMLC 35**

Ian, Janis 1951- .... **CLC 21**
See also CA 105; 187

Ibanez, Vicente Blasco
See Blasco Ibanez, Vicente
See also DLB 322

Ibarbourou, Juana de
1895(?)-1979 .... **HLCS 2**
See also DLB 290; HW 1; LAW

Ibarguengoitia, Jorge 1928-1983 ..... **CLC 37; TCLC 148**
See also CA 124; 113; EWL 3; HW 1

Ibn Battuta, Abu Abdalla
1304-1368(?) .... **CMLC 57**
See also WLIT 2

Ibn Hazm 994-1064 .... **CMLC 64**

Ibsen, Henrik (Johan) 1828-1906 .... **DC 2; TCLC 2, 8, 16, 37, 52; WLC**
See also AAYA 46; CA 104; 141; DA; DA3; DAB; DAC; DAM DRAM, MST; DFS 1, 6, 8, 10, 11, 15, 16; EW 7; LAIT 2; LATS 1:1; MTFW 2005; RGWL 2, 3

Ibuse, Masuji 1898-1993 .... **CLC 22**
See Ibuse Masuji
See also CA 127; 141; MJW; RGWL 3

Ibuse Masuji
See Ibuse, Masuji
See also CWW 2; DLB 180; EWL 3

Ichikawa, Kon 1915- .... **CLC 20**
See also CA 121

Ichiyo, Higuchi 1872-1896 .... **NCLC 49**
See also MJW

Idle, Eric 1943- .... **CLC 21**
See Monty Python
See also CA 116; CANR 35, 91

Idris, Yusuf 1927-1991 .... **SSC 74**
See also AFW; EWL 3; RGSF 2, 3; RGWL 3; WLIT 2

Ignatow, David 1914-1997 .... **CLC 4, 7, 14, 40; PC 34**
See also CA 9-12R; 162; CAAS 3; CANR 31, 57, 96; CP 1, 2, 3, 4, 5, 6; DLB 5; EWL 3; MAL 5

Ignotus
See Strachey, (Giles) Lytton

Ihimaera, Witi (Tame) 1944- .... **CLC 46**
See also CA 77-80; CANR 130; CN 2, 3, 4, 5, 6, 7; RGSF 2; SATA 148

Ilf, Ilya .... **TCLC 21**
See Fainzilberg, Ilya Arnoldovich
See also EWL 3

Illyes, Gyula 1902-1983 .... **PC 16**
See also CA 114; 109; CDWLB 4; DLB 215; EWL 3; RGWL 2, 3

Imalayen, Fatima-Zohra
See Djebar, Assia

Immermann, Karl (Lebrecht)
1796-1840 .... **NCLC 4, 49**
See also DLB 133

Ince, Thomas H. 1882-1924 .... **TCLC 89**
See also IDFW 3, 4

Inchbald, Elizabeth 1753-1821 ...... **NCLC 62**
See also DLB 39, 89; RGEL 2

Inclan, Ramon (Maria) del Valle
See Valle-Inclan, Ramon (Maria) del

Infante, G(uillermo) Cabrera
See Cabrera Infante, G(uillermo)

Ingalls, Rachel (Holmes) 1940- .... **CLC 42**
See also CA 123; 127

Ingamells, Reginald Charles
See Ingamells, Rex

Ingamells, Rex 1913-1955 .... **TCLC 35**
See also CA 167; DLB 260

Inge, William (Motter) 1913-1973 ..... **CLC 1, 8, 19**
See also CA 9-12R; CAD; CDALB 1941-1968; DA3; DAM DRAM; DFS 1, 3, 5, 8; DLB 7, 249; EWL 3; MAL 5; MTCW 1, 2; MTFW 2005; RGAL 4; TUS

Ingelow, Jean 1820-1897 .... **NCLC 39, 107**
See also DLB 35, 163; FANT; SATA 33

Ingram, Willis J.
See Harris, Mark

Innaurato, Albert (F.) 1948(?)- ... **CLC 21, 60**
See also CA 115; 122; CAD; CANR 78; CD 5, 6; INT CA-122

Innes, Michael
See Stewart, J(ohn) I(nnes) M(ackintosh)
See also DLB 276; MSW

Innis, Harold Adams 1894-1952 .... **TCLC 77**
See also CA 181; DLB 88

Insluis, Alanus de
See Alain de Lille

Iola
See Wells-Barnett, Ida B(ell)

Ionesco, Eugene 1912-1994 ... **CLC 1, 4, 6, 9, 11, 15, 41, 86; DC 12; WLC**
See also CA 9-12R; 144; CANR 55, 132; CWW 2; DA; DA3; DAB; DAC; DAM DRAM, MST; DFS 4, 9; DLB 321; EW

13; EWL 3; GFL 1789 to the Present; LMFS 2; MTCW 1, 2; MTFW 2005; RGWL 2, 3; SATA 7; SATA-Obit 79; TWA

Iqbal, Muhammad 1877-1938 .... **TCLC 28**
See also CA 215; EWL 3

Ireland, Patrick
See O'Doherty, Brian

Irenaeus St. 130- .... **CMLC 42**

Irigaray, Luce 1930- .... **CLC 164**
See also CA 154; CANR 121; FW

Iron, Ralph
See Schreiner, Olive (Emilie Albertina)

Irving, John (Winslow) 1942- ... **CLC 13, 23, 38, 112, 175**
See also AAYA 8, 62; AMWS 6; BEST 89:3; BPFB 2; CA 25-28R; CANR 28, 73, 112, 133; CN 3, 4, 5, 6, 7; CPW; DA3; DAM NOV, POP; DLB 6, 278; DLBY 1982; EWL 3; MAL 5; MTCW 1, 2; MTFW 2005; NFS 12, 14; RGAL 4; TUS

Irving, Washington 1783-1859 . **NCLC 2, 19, 95; SSC 2, 37; WLC**
See also AAYA 56; AMW; CDALB 1640-1865; CLR 97; DA; DA3; DAB; DAC; DAM MST; DLB 3, 11, 30, 59, 73, 74, 183, 186, 250, 254; EXPS; GL 2; LAIT 1; RGAL 4; RGSF 2; SSFS 1, 8, 16; SUFW 1; TUS; WCH; YABC 2

Irwin, P. K.
See Page, P(atricia) K(athleen)

Isaacs, Jorge Ricardo 1837-1895 ... **NCLC 70**
See also LAW

Isaacs, Susan 1943- .... **CLC 32**
See also BEST 89:1; BPFB 2; CA 89-92; CANR 20, 41, 65, 112, 134; CPW; DA3; DAM POP; INT CANR-20; MTCW 1, 2; MTFW 2005

Isherwood, Christopher (William Bradshaw)
1904-1986 .... **CLC 1, 9, 11, 14, 44; SSC 56**
See also AMWS 14; BRW 7; CA 13-16R; 117; CANR 35, 97, 133; CN 1, 2, 3; DA3; DAM DRAM, NOV; DLB 15, 195; DLBY 1986; EWL 3; IDTP; MTCW 1, 2; MTFW 2005; RGAL 4; RGEL 2; TUS; WLIT 4

Ishiguro, Kazuo 1954- . **CLC 27, 56, 59, 110, 219**
See also AAYA 58; BEST 90:2; BPFB 2; BRWS 4; CA 120; CANR 49, 95, 133; CN 5, 6, 7; DA3; DAM NOV; DLB 194; EWL 3; MTCW 1, 2; MTFW 2005; NFS 13; WLIT 4; WWE 1

Ishikawa, Hakuhin
See Ishikawa, Takuboku

Ishikawa, Takuboku 1886(?)-1912 ..... **PC 10; TCLC 15**
See Ishikawa Takuboku
See also CA 113; 153; DAM POET

Iskander, Fazil (Abdulovich) 1929- .. **CLC 47**
See Iskander, Fazil' Abdulevich
See also CA 102; EWL 3

Iskander, Fazil' Abdulevich
See Iskander, Fazil (Abdulovich)
See also DLB 302

Isler, Alan (David) 1934- .... **CLC 91**
See also CA 156; CANR 105

Ivan IV 1530-1584 .... **LC 17**

Ivanov, Vyacheslav Ivanovich
1866-1949 .... **TCLC 33**
See also CA 122; EWL 3

Ivask, Ivar Vidrik 1927-1992 .... **CLC 14**
See also CA 37-40R; 139; CANR 24

Ives, Morgan
See Bradley, Marion Zimmer
See also GLL 1

Izumi Shikibu c. 973-c. 1034 .... **CMLC 33**

J. R. S.
See Gogarty, Oliver St. John

Jabran, Kahlil
See Gibran, Kahlil
Jabran, Khalil
See Gibran, Kahlil
Jackson, Daniel
See Wingrove, David (John)
Jackson, Helen Hunt 1830-1885 .... **NCLC 90**
See also DLB 42, 47, 186, 189; RGAL 4
Jackson, Jesse 1908-1983 .... **CLC 12**
See also BW 1; CA 25-28R; 109; CANR
27; CLR 28; CWRI 5; MAICYA 1, 2;
SATA 2, 29; SATA-Obit 48
Jackson, Laura (Riding) 1901-1991 .... **PC 44**
See Riding, Laura
See also CA 65-68; 135; CANR 28, 89;
DLB 48
Jackson, Sam
See Trumbo, Dalton
Jackson, Sara
See Wingrove, David (John)
Jackson, Shirley 1919-1965 . **CLC 11, 60, 87;**
SSC 9, 39; WLC
See also AAYA 9; AMWS 9; BPFB 2; CA
1-4R; 25-28R; CANR 4, 52; CDALB
1941-1968; DA; DA3; DAC; DAM MST;
DLB 6, 234; EXPS; HGG; LAIT 4; MAL
5; MTCW 2; MTFW 2005; RGAL 4;
RGSF 2; SATA 2; SSFS 1; SUFW 1, 2
Jacob, (Cyprien-)Max 1876-1944 .... **TCLC 6**
See also CA 104; 193; DLB 258; EWL 3;
GFL 1789 to the Present; GLL 2; RGWL
2, 3
Jacobs, Harriet A(nn)
1813(?)-1897 .... **NCLC 67, 162**
See also AFAW 1, 2; DLB 239; FL 1:3; FW;
LAIT 2; RGAL 4
Jacobs, Jim 1942- .... **CLC 12**
See also CA 97-100; INT CA-97-100
Jacobs, W(illiam) W(ymark)
1863-1943 .... **SSC 73; TCLC 22**
See also CA 121; 167; DLB 135; EXPS;
HGG; RGEL 2; RGSF 2; SSFS 2; SUFW
1
Jacobsen, Jens Peter 1847-1885 .... **NCLC 34**
Jacobsen, Josephine (Winder)
1908-2003 .... **CLC 48, 102; PC 62**
See also CA 33-36R; 218; CAAS 18; CANR
23, 48; CCA 1; CP 2, 3, 4, 5, 6, 7; DLB
244; PFS 23; TCLE 1:1
Jacobson, Dan 1929- .... **CLC 4, 14**
See also AFW; CA 1-4R; CANR 2, 25, 66;
CN 1, 2, 3, 4, 5, 6, 7; DLB 14, 207, 225,
319; EWL 3; MTCW 1; RGSF 2
Jacqueline
See Carpentier (y Valmont), Alejo
Jacques de Vitry c. 1160-1240 ...... **CMLC 63**
See also DLB 208
Jagger, Michael Philip
See Jagger, Mick
Jagger, Mick 1943- .... **CLC 17**
See also CA 239
Jahiz, al- c. 780-c. 869 .... **CMLC 25**
See also DLB 311
Jakes, John (William) 1932- .... **CLC 29**
See also AAYA 32; BEST 89:4; BPFB 2;
CA 57-60, 214; CAAE 214; CANR 10,
43, 66, 111, 142; CPW; CSW; DA3; DAM
NOV, POP; DLB 278; DLBY 1983;
FANT; INT CANR-10; MTCW 1, 2;
MTFW 2005; RHW; SATA 62; SFW 4;
TCWW 1, 2
James I 1394-1437 .... **LC 20**
See also RGEL 2
James, Andrew
See Kirkup, James
James, C(yril) L(ionel) R(obert)
1901-1989 .... **BLCS; CLC 33**
See also BW 2; CA 117; 125; 128; CANR
62; CN 1, 2, 3, 4; DLB 125; MTCW 1

James, Daniel (Lewis) 1911-1988
See Santiago, Danny
See also CA 174; 125
James, Dynely
See Mayne, William (James Carter)
James, Henry Sr. 1811-1882 .... **NCLC 53**
James, Henry 1843-1916 .... **SSC 8, 32, 47;**
TCLC 2, 11, 24, 40, 47, 64, 171; WLC
See also AMW; AMWC 1; AMWR 1; BPFB
2; BRW 6; CA 104; 132; CDALB 1865-
1917; DA; DA3; DAB; DAC; DAM MST,
NOV; DLB 12, 71, 74, 189; DLBD 13;
EWL 3; EXPS; GL 2; HGG; LAIT 2;
MAL 5; MTCW 1, 2; MTFW 2005; NFS
12, 16, 19; RGAL 4; RGEL 2; RGSF 2;
SSFS 9; SUFW 1; TUS
James, M. R.
See James, Montague (Rhodes)
See also DLB 156, 201
James, Montague (Rhodes)
1862-1936 .... **SSC 16; TCLC 6**
See James, M. R.
See also CA 104; 203; HGG; RGEL 2;
RGSF 2; SUFW 1
James, P. D. .... **CLC 18, 46, 122**
See White, Phyllis Dorothy James
See also BEST 90:2; BPFB 2; BRWS 4;
CDBLB 1960 to Present; CN 4, 5, 6; DLB
87, 276; DLBD 17; MSW
James, Philip
See Moorcock, Michael (John)
James, Samuel
See Stephens, James
James, Seumas
See Stephens, James
James, Stephen
See Stephens, James
James, William 1842-1910 .... **TCLC 15, 32**
See also AMW; CA 109; 193; DLB 270,
284; MAL 5; NCFS 5; RGAL 4
Jameson, Anna 1794-1860 .... **NCLC 43**
See also DLB 99, 166
Jameson, Fredric (R.) 1934- .... **CLC 142**
See also CA 196; DLB 67; LMFS 2
James VI of Scotland 1566-1625 .... **LC 109**
See also DLB 151, 172
Jami, Nur al-Din 'Abd al-Rahman
1414-1492 .... **LC 9**
Jammes, Francis 1868-1938 .... **TCLC 75**
See also CA 198; EWL 3; GFL 1789 to the
Present
Jandl, Ernst 1925-2000 .... **CLC 34**
See also CA 200; EWL 3
Janowitz, Tama 1957- .... **CLC 43, 145**
See also CA 106; CANR 52, 89, 129; CN
5, 6, 7; CPW; DAM POP; DLB 292;
MTFW 2005
Japrisot, Sebastien 1931- .... **CLC 90**
See Rossi, Jean-Baptiste
See also CMW 4; NFS 18
Jarrell, Randall 1914-1965 .... **CLC 1, 2, 6, 9,**
13, 49; PC 41
See also AMW; BYA 5; CA 5-8R; 25-28R;
CABS 2; CANR 6, 34; CDALB 1941-
1968; CLR 6; CWRI 5; DAM POET;
DLB 48, 52; EWL 3; EXPP; MAICYA 1,
2; MAL 5; MTCW 1, 2; PAB; PFS 2;
RGAL 4; SATA 7
Jarry, Alfred 1873-1907 .... **SSC 20; TCLC 2,**
14, 147
See also CA 104; 153; DA3; DAM DRAM;
DFS 8; DLB 192, 258; EW 9; EWL 3;
GFL 1789 to the Present; RGWL 2, 3;
TWA
Jarvis, E. K.
See Ellison, Harlan (Jay)
Jawien, Andrzej
See John Paul II, Pope

Jaynes, Roderick
See Coen, Ethan
Jeake, Samuel, Jr.
See Aiken, Conrad (Potter)
Jean Paul 1763-1825 .... **NCLC 7**
Jefferies, (John) Richard
1848-1887 .... **NCLC 47**
See also DLB 98, 141; RGEL 2; SATA 16;
SFW 4
Jeffers, (John) Robinson 1887-1962 .. **CLC 2,**
3, 11, 15, 54; PC 17; WLC
See also AMWS 2; CA 85-88; CANR 35;
CDALB 1917-1929; DA; DAC; DAM
MST, POET; DLB 45, 212; EWL 3; MAL
5; MTCW 1, 2; MTFW 2005; PAB; PFS
3, 4; RGAL 4
Jefferson, Janet
See Mencken, H(enry) L(ouis)
Jefferson, Thomas 1743-1826 . **NCLC 11, 103**
See also AAYA 54; ANW; CDALB 1640-
1865; DA3; DLB 31, 183; LAIT 1; RGAL
4
Jeffrey, Francis 1773-1850 .... **NCLC 33**
See Francis, Lord Jeffrey
Jelakowitch, Ivan
See Heijermans, Herman
Jelinek, Elfriede 1946- .... **CLC 169**
See also AAYA 68; CA 154; DLB 85; FW
Jellicoe, (Patricia) Ann 1927- .... **CLC 27**
See also CA 85-88; CBD; CD 5, 6; CWD;
CWRI 5; DLB 13, 233; FW
Jelloun, Tahar ben 1944- .... **CLC 180**
See Ben Jelloun, Tahar
See also CA 162; CANR 100
Jemyma
See Holley, Marietta
Jen, Gish .... **AAL; CLC 70, 198**
See Jen, Lillian
See also AMWC 2; CN 7; DLB 312
Jen, Lillian 1955-
See Jen, Gish
See also CA 135; CANR 89, 130
Jenkins, (John) Robin 1912- .... **CLC 52**
See also CA 1-4R; CANR 1, 135; CN 1, 2,
3, 4, 5, 6, 7; DLB 14, 271
Jennings, Elizabeth (Joan)
1926-2001 .... **CLC 5, 14, 131**
See also BRWS 5; CA 61-64; 200; CAAS
5; CANR 8, 39, 66, 127; CP 1, 2, 3, 4, 5,
6, 7; CWP; DLB 27; EWL 3; MTCW 1;
SATA 66
Jennings, Waylon 1937-2002 .... **CLC 21**
Jensen, Johannes V(ilhelm)
1873-1950 .... **TCLC 41**
See also CA 170; DLB 214; EWL 3; RGWL
3
Jensen, Laura (Linnea) 1948- .... **CLC 37**
See also CA 103
Jerome, Saint 345-420 .... **CMLC 30**
See also RGWL 3
Jerome, Jerome K(lapka)
1859-1927 .... **TCLC 23**
See also CA 119; 177; DLB 10, 34, 135;
RGEL 2
Jerrold, Douglas William
1803-1857 .... **NCLC 2**
See also DLB 158, 159; RGEL 2
Jewett, (Theodora) Sarah Orne
1849-1909 .... **SSC 6, 44; TCLC 1, 22**
See also AMW; AMWC 2; AMWR 2; CA
108; 127; CANR 71; DLB 12, 74, 221;
EXPS; FL 1:3; FW; MAL 5; MAWW;
NFS 15; RGAL 4; RGSF 2; SATA 15;
SSFS 4
Jewsbury, Geraldine (Endsor)
1812-1880 .... **NCLC 22**
See also DLB 21

Khayyam, Omar 1048-1131 ... **CMLC 11; PC 8**
See Omar Khayyam
See also DA3; DAM POET; WLIT 6

Kherdian, David 1931- .... **CLC 6, 9**
See also AAYA 42; CA 21-24R, 192; CAAE 192; CAAS 2; CANR 39, 78; CLR 24; JRDA; LAIT 3; MAICYA 1, 2; SATA 16, 74; SATA-Essay 125

Khlebnikov, Velimir .... **TCLC 20**
See Khlebnikov, Viktor Vladimirovich
See also DLB 295; EW 10; EWL 3; RGWL 2, 3

Khlebnikov, Viktor Vladimirovich 1885-1922
See Khlebnikov, Velimir
See also CA 117; 217

Khodasevich, Vladislav (Felitsianovich) 1886-1939 .... **TCLC 15**
See also CA 115; DLB 317; EWL 3

Kielland, Alexander Lange 1849-1906 .... **TCLC 5**
See also CA 104

Kiely, Benedict 1919- ... **CLC 23, 43; SSC 58**
See also CA 1-4R; CANR 2, 84; CN 1, 2, 3, 4, 5, 6, 7; DLB 15, 319; TCLE 1:1

Kienzle, William X(avier) 1928-2001 .... **CLC 25**
See also CA 93-96; 203; CAAS 1; CANR 9, 31, 59, 111; CMW 4; DA3; DAM POP; INT CANR-31; MSW; MTCW 1, 2; MTFW 2005

Kierkegaard, Soren 1813-1855 ..... **NCLC 34, 78, 125**
See also DLB 300; EW 6; LMFS 2; RGWL 3; TWA

Kieslowski, Krzysztof 1941-1996 .... **CLC 120**
See also CA 147; 151

Killens, John Oliver 1916-1987 .... **CLC 10**
See also BW 2; CA 77-80; 123; CAAS 2; CANR 26; CN 1, 2, 3, 4; DLB 33; EWL 3

Killigrew, Anne 1660-1685 .... **LC 4, 73**
See also DLB 131

Killigrew, Thomas 1612-1683 .... **LC 57**
See also DLB 58; RGEL 2

Kim
See Simenon, Georges (Jacques Christian)

Kincaid, Jamaica 1949- ...... **BLC 2; CLC 43, 68, 137; SSC 72**
See also AAYA 13, 56; AFAW 2; AMWS 7; BRWS 7; BW 2, 3; CA 125; CANR 47, 59, 95, 133; CDALBS; CDWLB 3; CLR 63; CN 4, 5, 6, 7; DA3; DAM MULT, NOV; DLB 157, 227; DNFS 1; EWL 3; EXPS; FW; LATS 1:2; LMFS 2; MAL 5; MTCW 2; MTFW 2005; NCFS 1; NFS 3; SSFS 5, 7; TUS; WWE 1; YAW

King, Francis (Henry) 1923- .... **CLC 8, 53, 145**
See also CA 1-4R; CANR 1, 33, 86; CN 1, 2, 3, 4, 5, 6, 7; DAM NOV; DLB 15, 139; MTCW 1

King, Kennedy
See Brown, George Douglas

King, Martin Luther, Jr. 1929-1968 . **BLC 2; CLC 83; WLCS**
See also BW 2, 3; CA 25-28; CANR 27, 44; CAP 2; DA; DA3; DAB; DAC; DAM MST, MULT; LAIT 5; LATS 1:2; MTCW 1, 2; MTFW 2005; SATA 14

King, Stephen 1947- .... **CLC 12, 26, 37, 61, 113; SSC 17, 55**
See also AAYA 1, 17; AMWS 5; BEST 90:1; BPFB 2; CA 61-64; CANR 1, 30, 52, 76, 119, 134; CN 7; CPW; DA3; DAM NOV, POP; DLB 143; DLBY 1980; HGG; JRDA; LAIT 5; MTCW 1, 2; MTFW 2005; RGAL 4; SATA 9, 55, 161; SUFW 1, 2; WYAS 1; YAW

King, Stephen Edwin
See King, Stephen
King, Steve
See King, Stephen
King, Thomas 1943- .... **CLC 89, 171; NNAL**
See also CA 144; CANR 95; CCA 1; CN 6, 7; DAC; DAM MULT; DLB 175; SATA 96

Kingman, Lee .... **CLC 17**
See Natti, (Mary) Lee
See also CWRI 5; SAAS 3; SATA 1, 67

Kingsley, Charles 1819-1875 .... **NCLC 35**
See also CLR 77; DLB 21, 32, 163, 178, 190; FANT; MAICYA 2; MAICYAS 1; RGEL 2; WCH; YABC 2

Kingsley, Henry 1830-1876 .... **NCLC 107**
See also DLB 21, 230; RGEL 2

Kingsley, Sidney 1906-1995 .... **CLC 44**
See also CA 85-88; 147; CAD; DFS 14, 19; DLB 7; MAL 5; RGAL 4

Kingsolver, Barbara 1955- .... **CLC 55, 81, 130, 216**
See also AAYA 15; AMWS 7; CA 129; 134; CANR 60, 96, 133; CDALBS; CN 7; CPW; CSW; DA3; DAM POP; DLB 206; INT CA-134; LAIT 5; MTCW 2; MTFW 2005; NFS 5, 10, 12; RGAL 4; TCLE 1:1

Kingston, Maxine (Ting Ting) Hong 1940- .... **AAL; CLC 12, 19, 58, 121; WLCS**
See also AAYA 8, 55; AMWS 5; BPFB 2; CA 69-72; CANR 13, 38, 74, 87, 128; CDALBS; CN 6, 7; DA3; DAM MULT, NOV; DLB 173, 212, 312; DLBY 1980; EWL 3; FL 1:6; FW; INT CANR-13; LAIT 5; MAL 5; MAWW; MTCW 1, 2; MTFW 2005; NFS 6; RGAL 4; SATA 53; SSFS 3; TCWW 2

Kinnell, Galway 1927- ..... **CLC 1, 2, 3, 5, 13, 29, 129; PC 26**
See also AMWS 3; CA 9-12R; CANR 10, 34, 66, 116, 138; CP 1, 2, 3, 4, 5, 6, 7; DLB 5; DLBY 1987; EWL 3; INT CANR-34; MAL 5; MTCW 1, 2; MTFW 2005; PAB; PFS 9; RGAL 4; TCLE 1:1; WP

Kinsella, Thomas 1928- .... **CLC 4, 19, 138; PC 69**
See also BRWS 5; CA 17-20R; CANR 15, 122; CP 1, 2, 3, 4, 5, 6, 7; DLB 27; EWL 3; MTCW 1, 2; MTFW 2005; RGEL 2; TEA

Kinsella, W(illiam) P(atrick) 1935- . **CLC 27, 43, 166**
See also AAYA 7, 60; BPFB 2; CA 97-100; 222; CAAE 222; CAAS 7; CANR 21, 35, 66, 75, 129; CN 4, 5, 6, 7; CPW; DAC; DAM NOV, POP; FANT; INT CANR-21; LAIT 5; MTCW 1, 2; MTFW 2005; NFS 15; RGSF 2

Kinsey, Alfred C(harles) 1894-1956 .... **TCLC 91**
See also CA 115; 170; MTCW 2

Kipling, (Joseph) Rudyard 1865-1936 . **PC 3; SSC 54, 125; TCLC 8, 17, 167; WLC**
See also AAYA 32; BRW 6; BRWC 1, 2; BYA 4; CA 105; 120; CANR 33; CDBLB 1890-1914; CLR 39, 65; CWRI 5; DA; DA3; DAB; DAC; DAM MST, POET; DLB 19, 34, 141, 156; EWL 3; EXPS; FANT; LAIT 3; LMFS 1; MAICYA 1, 2; MTCW 1, 2; MTFW 2005; NFS 21; PFS 22; RGEL 2; RGSF 2; SATA 100; SFW 4; SSFS 8, 21; SUFW 1; TEA; WCH; WLIT 4; YABC 2

Kircher, Athanasius 1602-1680 .... **LC 121**
See also DLB 164

Kirk, Russell (Amos) 1918-1994 .. **TCLC 119**
See also AITN 1; CA 1-4R; 145; CAAS 9; CANR 1, 20, 60; HGG; INT CANR-20; MTCW 1, 2

Kirkham, Dinah
See Card, Orson Scott
Kirkland, Caroline M. 1801-1864 . **NCLC 85**
See also DLB 3, 73, 74, 250, 254; DLBD 13

Kirkup, James 1918- .... **CLC 1**
See also CA 1-4R; CAAS 4; CANR 2; CP 1, 2, 3, 4, 5, 6, 7; DLB 27; SATA 12

Kirkwood, James 1930(?)-1989 .... **CLC 9**
See also AITN 2; CA 1-4R; 128; CANR 6, 40; GLL 2

Kirsch, Sarah 1935- .... **CLC 176**
See also CA 178; CWW 2; DLB 75; EWL 3

Kirshner, Sidney
See Kingsley, Sidney
Kis, Danilo 1935-1989 .... **CLC 57**
See also CA 109; 118; 129; CANR 61; CDWLB 4; DLB 181; EWL 3; MTCW 1; RGSF 2; RGWL 2, 3

Kissinger, Henry A(lfred) 1923- ..... **CLC 137**
See also CA 1-4R; CANR 2, 33, 66, 109; MTCW 1

Kivi, Aleksis 1834-1872 .... **NCLC 30**

Kizer, Carolyn (Ashley) 1925- ... **CLC 15, 39, 80; PC 66**
See also CA 65-68; CAAS 5; CANR 24, 70, 134; CP 1, 2, 3, 4, 5, 6, 7; CWP; DAM POET; DLB 5, 169; EWL 3; MAL 5; MTCW 2; MTFW 2005; PFS 18; TCLE 1:1

Klabund 1890-1928 .... **TCLC 44**
See also CA 162; DLB 66

Klappert, Peter 1942- .... **CLC 57**
See also CA 33-36R; CSW; DLB 5

Klein, A(braham) M(oses) 1909-1972 .... **CLC 19**
See also CA 101; 37-40R; CP 1; DAB; DAC; DAM MST; DLB 68; EWL 3; RGEL 2

Klein, Joe
See Klein, Joseph
Klein, Joseph 1946- .... **CLC 154**
See also CA 85-88; CANR 55

Klein, Norma 1938-1989 .... **CLC 30**
See also AAYA 2, 35; BPFB 2; BYA 6, 7, 8; CA 41-44R; 128; CANR 15, 37; CLR 2, 19; INT CANR-15; JRDA; MAICYA 1, 2; SAAS 1; SATA 7, 57; WYA; YAW

Klein, T(heodore) E(ibon) D(onald) 1947- .... **CLC 34**
See also CA 119; CANR 44, 75; HGG

Kleist, Heinrich von 1777-1811 ...... **NCLC 2, 37; SSC 22**
See also CDWLB 2; DAM DRAM; DLB 90; EW 5; RGSF 2; RGWL 2, 3

Klima, Ivan 1931- .... **CLC 56, 172**
See also CA 25-28R; CANR 17, 50, 91; CDWLB 4; CWW 2; DAM NOV; DLB 232; EWL 3; RGWL 3

Klimentev, Andrei Platonovich
See Klimentov, Andrei Platonovich
Klimentov, Andrei Platonovich 1899-1951 .... **SSC 42; TCLC 14**
See Platonov, Andrei Platonovich; Platonov, Andrey Platonovich
See also CA 108; 232

Klinger, Friedrich Maximilian von 1752-1831 .... **NCLC 1**
See also DLB 94

Klingsor the Magician
See Hartmann, Sadakichi
Klopstock, Friedrich Gottlieb 1724-1803 .... **NCLC 11**
See also DLB 97; EW 4; RGWL 2, 3

Kluge, Alexander 1932- .... **SSC 61**
See also CA 81-84; DLB 75

Knapp, Caroline 1959-2002 .... **CLC 99**
See also CA 154; 207

Knebel, Fletcher 1911-1993 .... **CLC 14**
See also AITN 1; CA 1-4R; 140; CAAS 3;
CANR 1, 36; CN 1, 2, 3, 4, 5; SATA 36;
SATA-Obit 75

Knickerbocker, Diedrich
See Irving, Washington

Knight, Etheridge 1931-1991 ... **BLC 2; CLC 40; PC 14**
See also BW 1, 3; CA 21-24R; 133; CANR
23, 82; CP 1, 2, 3, 4; DAM POET; DLB
41; MTCW 2; MTFW 2005; RGAL 4;
TCLE 1:1

Knight, Sarah Kemble 1666-1727 .... **LC 7**
See also DLB 24, 200

Knister, Raymond 1899-1932 .... **TCLC 56**
See also CA 186; DLB 68; RGEL 2

Knowles, John 1926-2001 ... **CLC 1, 4, 10, 26**
See also AAYA 10; AMWS 12; BPFB 2;
BYA 3; CA 17-20R; 203; CANR 40, 74,
76, 132; CDALB 1968-1988; CLR 98; CN
1, 2, 3, 4, 5, 6, 7; DA; DAC; DAM MST,
NOV; DLB 6; EXPN; MTCW 1, 2;
MTFW 2005; NFS 2; RGAL 4; SATA 8,
89; SATA-Obit 134; YAW

Knox, Calvin M.
See Silverberg, Robert

Knox, John c. 1505-1572 .... **LC 37**
See also DLB 132

Knye, Cassandra
See Disch, Thomas M(ichael)

Koch, C(hristopher) J(ohn) 1932- .... **CLC 42**
See also CA 127; CANR 84; CN 3, 4, 5, 6,
7; DLB 289

Koch, Christopher
See Koch, C(hristopher) J(ohn)

Koch, Kenneth (Jay) 1925-2002 .... **CLC 5, 8, 44**
See also AMWS 15; CA 1-4R; 207; CAD;
CANR 6, 36, 57, 97, 131; CD 5, 6; CP 1,
2, 3, 4, 5, 6, 7; DAM POET; DLB 5; INT
CANR-36; MAL 5; MTCW 2; MTFW
2005; PFS 20; SATA 65; WP

Kochanowski, Jan 1530-1584 .... **LC 10**
See also RGWL 2, 3

Kock, Charles Paul de 1794-1871 . **NCLC 16**

Koda Rohan
See Koda Shigeyuki

Koda Rohan
See Koda Shigeyuki
See also DLB 180

Koda Shigeyuki 1867-1947 .... **TCLC 22**
See Koda Rohan
See also CA 121; 183

Koestler, Arthur 1905-1983 ... **CLC 1, 3, 6, 8, 15, 33**
See also BRWS 1; CA 1-4R; 109; CANR 1,
33; CDBLB 1945-1960; CN 1, 2, 3;
DLBY 1983; EWL 3; MTCW 1, 2; MTFW
2005; NFS 19; RGEL 2

Kogawa, Joy Nozomi 1935- ...... **CLC 78, 129**
See also AAYA 47; CA 101; CANR 19, 62,
126; CN 6, 7; CP 1; CWP; DAC; DAM
MST, MULT; FW; MTCW 2; MTFW
2005; NFS 3; SATA 99

Kohout, Pavel 1928- .... **CLC 13**
See also CA 45-48; CANR 3

Koizumi, Yakumo
See Hearn, (Patricio) Lafcadio (Tessima
Carlos)

Kolmar, Gertrud 1894-1943 .... **TCLC 40**
See also CA 167; EWL 3

Komunyakaa, Yusef 1947- .. **BLCS; CLC 86, 94, 207; PC 51**
See also AFAW 2; AMWS 13; CA 147;
CANR 83; CP 7; CSW; DLB 120; EWL
3; PFS 5, 20; RGAL 4

Konrad, George
See Konrad, Gyorgy

Konrad, Gyorgy 1933- .... **CLC 4, 10, 73**
See also CA 85-88; CANR 97; CDWLB 4;
CWW 2; DLB 232; EWL 3

Konwicki, Tadeusz 1926- .... **CLC 8, 28, 54, 117**
See also CA 101; CAAS 9; CANR 39, 59;
CWW 2; DLB 232; EWL 3; IDFW 3;
MTCW 1

Koontz, Dean R. 1945- .... **CLC 78, 206**
See also AAYA 9, 31; BEST 89:3, 90:2; CA
108; CANR 19, 36, 52, 95, 138; CMW 4;
CPW; DA3; DAM NOV, POP; DLB 292;
HGG; MTCW 1; MTFW 2005; SATA 92,
165; SFW 4; SUFW 2; YAW

Koontz, Dean Ray
See Koontz, Dean R.

Koontz, Dean Ray
See Koontz, Dean R.

Kopernik, Mikolaj
See Copernicus, Nicolaus

Kopit, Arthur (Lee) 1937- ...... **CLC 1, 18, 33**
See also AITN 1; CA 81-84; CABS 3;
CAD; CD 5, 6; DAM DRAM; DFS 7, 14;
DLB 7; MAL 5; MTCW 1; RGAL 4

Kopitar, Jernej (Bartholomaus)
1780-1844 .... **NCLC 117**

Kops, Bernard 1926- .... **CLC 4**
See also CA 5-8R; CANR 84; CBD; CN 1,
2, 3, 4, 5, 6, 7; CP 1, 2, 3, 4, 5, 6, 7; DLB
13

Kornbluth, C(yril) M. 1923-1958 .... **TCLC 8**
See also CA 105; 160; DLB 8; SCFW 1, 2;
SFW 4

Korolenko, V. G.
See Korolenko, Vladimir Galaktionovich

Korolenko, Vladimir
See Korolenko, Vladimir Galaktionovich

Korolenko, Vladimir G.
See Korolenko, Vladimir Galaktionovich

Korolenko, Vladimir Galaktionovich
1853-1921 .... **TCLC 22**
See also CA 121; DLB 277

Korzybski, Alfred (Habdank Skarbek)
1879-1950 .... **TCLC 61**
See also CA 123; 160

Kosinski, Jerzy (Nikodem)
1933-1991 .... **CLC 1, 2, 3, 6, 10, 15, 53, 70**
See also AMWS 7; BPFB 2; CA 17-20R;
134; CANR 9, 46; CN 1, 2, 3, 4; DA3;
DAM NOV; DLB 2, 299; DLBY 1982;
EWL 3; HGG; MAL 5; MTCW 1, 2;
MTFW 2005; NFS 12; RGAL 4; TUS

Kostelanetz, Richard (Cory) 1940- .. **CLC 28**
See also CA 13-16R; CAAS 8; CANR 38,
77; CN 4, 5, 6; CP 2, 3, 4, 5, 6, 7

Kostrowitzki, Wilhelm Apollinaris de
1880-1918
See Apollinaire, Guillaume
See also CA 104

Kotlowitz, Robert 1924- .... **CLC 4**
See also CA 33-36R; CANR 36

Kotzebue, August (Friedrich Ferdinand) von
1761-1819 .... **NCLC 25**
See also DLB 94

Kotzwinkle, William 1938- ..... **CLC 5, 14, 35**
See also BPFB 2; CA 45-48; CANR 3, 44,
84, 129; CLR 6; CN 7; DLB 173; FANT;
MAICYA 1, 2; SATA 24, 70, 146; SFW
4; SUFW 2; YAW

Kowna, Stancy
See Szymborska, Wislawa

Kozol, Jonathan 1936- .... **CLC 17**
See also AAYA 46; CA 61-64; CANR 16,
45, 96; MTFW 2005

Kozoll, Michael 1940(?)- .... **CLC 35**

Kramer, Kathryn 19(?)- .... **CLC 34**

Kramer, Larry 1935- .... **CLC 42; DC 8**
See also CA 124; 126; CANR 60, 132;
DAM POP; DLB 249; GLL 1

Krasicki, Ignacy 1735-1801 .... **NCLC 8**

Krasinski, Zygmunt 1812-1859 .... **NCLC 4**
See also RGWL 2, 3

Kraus, Karl 1874-1936 .... **TCLC 5**
See also CA 104; 216; DLB 118; EWL 3

Kreve (Mickevicius), Vincas
1882-1954 .... **TCLC 27**
See also CA 170; DLB 220; EWL 3

Kristeva, Julia 1941- .... **CLC 77, 140**
See also CA 154; CANR 99; DLB 242;
EWL 3; FW; LMFS 2

Kristofferson, Kris 1936- .... **CLC 26**
See also CA 104

Krizanc, John 1956- .... **CLC 57**
See also CA 187

Krleza, Miroslav 1893-1981 .... **CLC 8, 114**
See also CA 97-100; 105; CANR 50; CD-
WLB 4; DLB 147; EW 11; RGWL 2, 3

Kroetsch, Robert (Paul) 1927- .... **CLC 5, 23, 57, 132**
See also CA 17-20R; CANR 8, 38; CCA 1;
CN 2, 3, 4, 5, 6, 7; CP 7; DAC; DAM
POET; DLB 53; MTCW 1

Kroetz, Franz
See Kroetz, Franz Xaver

Kroetz, Franz Xaver 1946- .... **CLC 41**
See also CA 130; CANR 142; CWW 2;
EWL 3

Kroker, Arthur (W.) 1945- .... **CLC 77**
See also CA 161

Kroniuk, Lisa
See Berton, Pierre (Francis de Marigny)

Kropotkin, Peter (Aleksieevich)
1842-1921 .... **TCLC 36**
See Kropotkin, Petr Alekseevich
See also CA 119; 219

Kropotkin, Petr Alekseevich
See Kropotkin, Peter (Aleksieevich)
See also DLB 277

Krotkov, Yuri 1917-1981 .... **CLC 19**
See also CA 102

Krumb
See Crumb, R(obert)

Krumgold, Joseph (Quincy)
1908-1980 .... **CLC 12**
See also BYA 1, 2; CA 9-12R; 101; CANR
7; MAICYA 1, 2; SATA 1, 48; SATA-Obit
23; YAW

Krumwitz
See Crumb, R(obert)

Krutch, Joseph Wood 1893-1970 ..... **CLC 24**
See also ANW; CA 1-4R; 25-28R; CANR
4; DLB 63, 206, 275

Krutzch, Gus
See Eliot, T(homas) S(tearns)

Krylov, Ivan Andreevich
1768(?)-1844 .... **NCLC 1**
See also DLB 150

Kubin, Alfred (Leopold Isidor)
1877-1959 .... **TCLC 23**
See also CA 112; 149; CANR 104; DLB 81

Kubrick, Stanley 1928-1999 .... **CLC 16; TCLC 112**
See also AAYA 30; CA 81-84; 177; CANR
33; DLB 26

Kumin, Maxine (Winokur) 1925- ..... **CLC 5, 13, 28, 164; PC 15**
See also AITN 2; AMWS 4; ANW; CA
1-4R; CAAS 8; CANR 1, 21, 69, 115,
140; CP 2, 3, 4, 5, 6, 7; CWP; DA3; DAM
POET; DLB 5; EWL 3; EXPP; MTCW 1,
2; MTFW 2005; PAB; PFS 18; SATA 12

Kundera, Milan 1929- . **CLC 4, 9, 19, 32, 68, 115, 135; SSC 24**
See also AAYA 2, 62; BPFB 2; CA 85-88; CANR 19, 52, 74, 144; CDWLB 4; CWW 2; DA3; DAM NOV; DLB 232; EW 13; EWL 3; MTCW 1, 2; MTFW 2005; NFS 18; RGSF 2; RGWL 3; SSFS 10

Kunene, Mazisi (Raymond) 1930- ... **CLC 85**
See also BW 1, 3; CA 125; CANR 81; CP 1, 7; DLB 117

Kung, Hans .... **CLC 130**
See Kung, Hans

Kung, Hans 1928-
See Kung, Hans
See also CA 53-56; CANR 66, 134; MTCW 1, 2; MTFW 2005

Kunikida Doppo 1869(?)-1908
See Doppo, Kunikida
See also DLB 180; EWL 3

Kunitz, Stanley (Jasspon) 1905- .. **CLC 6, 11, 14, 148; PC 19**
See also AMWS 3; CA 41-44R; CANR 26, 57, 98; CP 1, 2, 3, 4, 5, 6, 7; DA3; DLB 48; INT CANR-26; MAL 5; MTCW 1, 2; MTFW 2005; PFS 11; RGAL 4

Kunze, Reiner 1933- .... **CLC 10**
See also CA 93-96; CWW 2; DLB 75; EWL 3

Kuprin, Aleksander Ivanovich 1870-1938 .... **TCLC 5**
See Kuprin, Aleksandr Ivanovich; Kuprin, Alexandr Ivanovich
See also CA 104; 182

Kuprin, Aleksandr Ivanovich
See Kuprin, Aleksander Ivanovich
See also DLB 295

Kuprin, Alexandr Ivanovich
See Kuprin, Aleksander Ivanovich
See also EWL 3

Kureishi, Hanif 1954- .. **CLC 64, 135; DC 26**
See also BRWS 11; CA 139; CANR 113; CBD; CD 5, 6; CN 6, 7; DLB 194, 245; GLL 2; IDFW 4; WLIT 4; WWE 1

Kurosawa, Akira 1910-1998 ..... **CLC 16, 119**
See also AAYA 11, 64; CA 101; 170; CANR 46; DAM MULT

Kushner, Tony 1956- .... **CLC 81, 203; DC 10**
See also AAYA 61; AMWS 9; CA 144; CAD; CANR 74, 130; CD 5, 6; DA3; DAM DRAM; DFS 5; DLB 228; EWL 3; GLL 1; LAIT 5; MAL 5; MTCW 2; MTFW 2005; RGAL 4; SATA 160

Kuttner, Henry 1915-1958 .... **TCLC 10**
See also CA 107; 157; DLB 8; FANT; SCFW 1, 2; SFW 4

Kutty, Madhavi
See Das, Kamala

Kuzma, Greg 1944- .... **CLC 7**
See also CA 33-36R; CANR 70

Kuzmin, Mikhail (Alekseevich) 1872(?)-1936 .... **TCLC 40**
See also CA 170; DLB 295; EWL 3

Kyd, Thomas 1558-1594 .... **DC 3; LC 22**
See also BRW 1; DAM DRAM; DFS 21; DLB 62; IDTP; LMFS 1; RGEL 2; TEA; WLIT 3

Kyprianos, Iossif
See Samarakis, Antonis

L. S.
See Stephen, Sir Leslie

Laȝamon
See Layamon
See also DLB 146

Labe, Louise 1521-1566 .... **LC 120**

Labrunie, Gerard
See Nerval, Gerard de

La Bruyere, Jean de 1645-1696 .... **LC 17**
See also DLB 268; EW 3; GFL Beginnings to 1789

Lacan, Jacques (Marie Emile) 1901-1981 .... **CLC 75**
See also CA 121; 104; DLB 296; EWL 3; TWA

Laclos, Pierre-Ambroise Francois 1741-1803 .... **NCLC 4, 87**
See also DLB 313; EW 4; GFL Beginnings to 1789; RGWL 2, 3

Lacolere, Francois
See Aragon, Louis

La Colere, Francois
See Aragon, Louis

La Deshabilleuse
See Simenon, Georges (Jacques Christian)

Lady Gregory
See Gregory, Lady Isabella Augusta (Persse)

Lady of Quality, A
See Bagnold, Enid

La Fayette, Marie-(Madelaine Pioche de la Vergne) 1634-1693 .... **LC 2**
See Lafayette, Marie-Madeleine
See also GFL Beginnings to 1789; RGWL 2, 3

Lafayette, Marie-Madeleine
See La Fayette, Marie-(Madelaine Pioche de la Vergne)
See also DLB 268

Lafayette, Rene
See Hubbard, L(afayette) Ron(ald)

La Flesche, Francis 1857(?)-1932 ...... **NNAL**
See also CA 144; CANR 83; DLB 175

La Fontaine, Jean de 1621-1695 .... **LC 50**
See also DLB 268; EW 3; GFL Beginnings to 1789; MAICYA 1, 2; RGWL 2, 3; SATA 18

Laforet, Carmen 1921-2004 .... **CLC 219**
See also CWW 2; DLB 322; EWL 3

Laforgue, Jules 1860-1887 . **NCLC 5, 53; PC 14; SSC 20**
See also DLB 217; EW 7; GFL 1789 to the Present; RGWL 2, 3

Lagerkvist, Paer (Fabian) 1891-1974 ..... **CLC 7, 10, 13, 54; TCLC 144**
See Lagerkvist, Par
See also CA 85-88; 49-52; DA3; DAM DRAM, NOV; MTCW 1, 2; MTFW 2005; TWA

Lagerkvist, Par .... **SSC 12**
See Lagerkvist, Paer (Fabian)
See also DLB 259; EW 10; EWL 3; RGSF 2; RGWL 2, 3

Lagerloef, Selma (Ottiliana Lovisa) .... **TCLC 4, 36**
See Lagerlof, Selma (Ottiliana Lovisa)
See also CA 108; MTCW 2

Lagerlof, Selma (Ottiliana Lovisa) 1858-1940
See Lagerloef, Selma (Ottiliana Lovisa)
See also CA 188; CLR 7; DLB 259; RGWL 2, 3; SATA 15; SSFS 18

La Guma, (Justin) Alex(ander) 1925-1985 . **BLCS; CLC 19; TCLC 140**
See also AFW; BW 1, 3; CA 49-52; 118; CANR 25, 81; CDWLB 3; CN 1, 2, 3; CP 1; DAM NOV; DLB 117, 225; EWL 3; MTCW 1, 2; MTFW 2005; WLIT 2; WWE 1

Laidlaw, A. K.
See Grieve, C(hristopher) M(urray)

Lainez, Manuel Mujica
See Mujica Lainez, Manuel
See also HW 1

Laing, R(onald) D(avid) 1927-1989 . **CLC 95**
See also CA 107; 129; CANR 34; MTCW 1

Laishley, Alex
See Booth, Martin

Lamartine, Alphonse (Marie Louis Prat) de 1790-1869 .... **NCLC 11; PC 16**
See also DAM POET; DLB 217; GFL 1789 to the Present; RGWL 2, 3

Lamb, Charles 1775-1834 ..... **NCLC 10, 113; WLC**
See also BRW 4; CDBLB 1789-1832; DA; DAB; DAC; DAM MST; DLB 93, 107, 163; RGEL 2; SATA 17; TEA

Lamb, Lady Caroline 1785-1828 ... **NCLC 38**
See also DLB 116

Lamb, Mary Ann 1764-1847 .... **NCLC 125**
See also DLB 163; SATA 17

Lame Deer 1903(?)-1976 .... **NNAL**
See also CA 69-72

Lamming, George (William) 1927- ... **BLC 2; CLC 2, 4, 66, 144**
See also BW 2, 3; CA 85-88; CANR 26, 76; CDWLB 3; CN 1, 2, 3, 4, 5, 6, 7; CP 1; DAM MULT; DLB 125; EWL 3; MTCW 1, 2; MTFW 2005; NFS 15; RGEL 2

L'Amour, Louis (Dearborn) 1908-1988 .... **CLC 25, 55**
See also AAYA 16; AITN 2; BEST 89:2; BPFB 2; CA 1-4R; 125; CANR 3, 25, 40; CPW; DA3; DAM NOV, POP; DLB 206; DLBY 1980; MTCW 1, 2; MTFW 2005; RGAL 4; TCWW 1, 2

Lampedusa, Giuseppe (Tomasi) di .... **TCLC 13**
See Tomasi di Lampedusa, Giuseppe
See also CA 164; EW 11; MTCW 2; MTFW 2005; RGWL 2, 3

Lampman, Archibald 1861-1899 ... **NCLC 25**
See also DLB 92; RGEL 2; TWA

Lancaster, Bruce 1896-1963 .... **CLC 36**
See also CA 9-10; CANR 70; CAP 1; SATA 9

Lanchester, John 1962- .... **CLC 99**
See also CA 194; DLB 267

Landau, Mark Alexandrovich
See Aldanov, Mark (Alexandrovich)

Landau-Aldanov, Mark Alexandrovich
See Aldanov, Mark (Alexandrovich)

Landis, Jerry
See Simon, Paul (Frederick)

Landis, John 1950- .... **CLC 26**
See also CA 112; 122; CANR 128

Landolfi, Tommaso 1908-1979 .... **CLC 11, 49**
See also CA 127; 117; DLB 177; EWL 3

Landon, Letitia Elizabeth 1802-1838 .... **NCLC 15**
See also DLB 96

Landor, Walter Savage 1775-1864 .... **NCLC 14**
See also BRW 4; DLB 93, 107; RGEL 2

Landwirth, Heinz 1927-
See Lind, Jakov
See also CA 9-12R; CANR 7

Lane, Patrick 1939- .... **CLC 25**
See also CA 97-100; CANR 54; CP 3, 4, 5, 6, 7; DAM POET; DLB 53; INT CA-97-100

Lang, Andrew 1844-1912 .... **TCLC 16**
See also CA 114; 137; CANR 85; CLR 101; DLB 98, 141, 184; FANT; MAICYA 1, 2; RGEL 2; SATA 16; WCH

Lang, Fritz 1890-1976 .... **CLC 20, 103**
See also AAYA 65; CA 77-80; 69-72; CANR 30

Lange, John
See Crichton, (John) Michael

Langer, Elinor 1939- .... **CLC 34**
See also CA 121

Langland, William 1332(?)-1400(?) .... **LC 19, 120**
See also BRW 1; DA; DAB; DAC; DAM MST, POET; DLB 146; RGEL 2; TEA; WLIT 3

Langstaff, Launcelot
See Irving, Washington

Lanier, Sidney 1842-1881 . **NCLC 6, 118; PC 50**
See also AMWS 1; DAM POET; DLB 64; DLBD 13; EXPP; MAICYA 1; PFS 14; RGAL 4; SATA 18

Lanyer, Aemilia 1569-1645 .... **LC 10, 30, 83; PC 60**
See also DLB 121

Lao Tzu c. 6th cent. B.C.-3rd cent. B.C. .... **CMLC 7**

Lao-Tzu
See Lao Tzu

Lapine, James (Elliot) 1949- .... **CLC 39**
See also CA 123; 130; CANR 54, 128; INT CA-130

Larbaud, Valery (Nicolas) 1881-1957 .... **TCLC 9**
See also CA 106; 152; EWL 3; GFL 1789 to the Present

Lardner, Ring
See Lardner, Ring(gold) W(ilmer)
See also BPFB 2; CDALB 1917-1929; DLB 11, 25, 86, 171; DLBD 16; RGAL 4; RGSF 2

Lardner, Ring W., Jr.
See Lardner, Ring(gold) W(ilmer)

Lardner, Ring(gold) W(ilmer) 1885-1933 .... **SSC 32; TCLC 2, 14**
See Lardner, Ring
See also AMW; CA 104; 131; MAL 5; MTCW 1, 2; MTFW 2005; TUS

Laredo, Betty
See Codrescu, Andrei

Larkin, Maia
See Wojciechowska, Maia (Teresa)

Larkin, Philip (Arthur) 1922-1985 ... **CLC 3, 5, 8, 9, 13, 18, 33, 39, 64; PC 21**
See also BRWS 1; CA 5-8R; 117; CANR 24, 62; CDBLB 1960 to Present; CP 1, 2, 3, 4; DA3; DAB; DAM MST, POET; DLB 27; EWL 3; MTCW 1, 2; MTFW 2005; PFS 3, 4, 12; RGEL 2

La Roche, Sophie von 1730-1807 .... **NCLC 121**
See also DLB 94

La Rochefoucauld, Francois 1613-1680 .... **LC 108**

Larra (y Sanchez de Castro), Mariano Jose de 1809-1837 .... **NCLC 17, 130**

Larsen, Eric 1941- .... **CLC 55**
See also CA 132

Larsen, Nella 1893(?)-1963 .... **BLC 2; CLC 37; HR 1:3**
See also AFAW 1, 2; BW 1; CA 125; CANR 83; DAM MULT; DLB 51; FW; LATS 1:1; LMFS 2

Larson, Charles R(aymond) 1938- ... **CLC 31**
See also CA 53-56; CANR 4, 121

Larson, Jonathan 1960-1996 .... **CLC 99**
See also AAYA 28; CA 156; MTFW 2005

La Sale, Antoine de c. 1386-1460(?) . **LC 104**
See also DLB 208

Las Casas, Bartolome de 1474-1566 .... **HLCS; LC 31**
See Casas, Bartolome de las
See also DLB 318; LAW

Lasch, Christopher 1932-1994 .... **CLC 102**
See also CA 73-76; 144; CANR 25, 118; DLB 246; MTCW 1, 2; MTFW 2005

Lasker-Schueler, Else 1869-1945 ... **TCLC 57**
See Lasker-Schuler, Else
See also CA 183; DLB 66, 124

Lasker-Schuler, Else
See Lasker-Schueler, Else
See also EWL 3

Laski, Harold J(oseph) 1893-1950 . **TCLC 79**
See also CA 188

Latham, Jean Lee 1902-1995 .... **CLC 12**
See also AITN 1; BYA 1; CA 5-8R; CANR 7, 84; CLR 50; MAICYA 1, 2; SATA 2, 68; YAW

Latham, Mavis
See Clark, Mavis Thorpe

Lathen, Emma .... **CLC 2**
See Hennissart, Martha; Latsis, Mary J(ane)
See also BPFB 2; CMW 4; DLB 306

Lathrop, Francis
See Leiber, Fritz (Reuter, Jr.)

Latsis, Mary J(ane) 1927-1997
See Lathen, Emma
See also CA 85-88; 162; CMW 4

Lattany, Kristin
See Lattany, Kristin (Elaine Eggleston) Hunter

Lattany, Kristin (Elaine Eggleston) Hunter 1931- .... **CLC 35**
See Hunter, Kristin
See also AITN 1; BW 1; BYA 3; CA 13-16R; CANR 13, 108; CLR 3; CN 7; DLB 33; INT CANR-13; MAICYA 1, 2; SAAS 10; SATA 12, 132; YAW

Lattimore, Richmond (Alexander) 1906-1984 .... **CLC 3**
See also CA 1-4R; 112; CANR 1; CP 1, 2, 3; MAL 5

Laughlin, James 1914-1997 .... **CLC 49**
See also CA 21-24R; 162; CAAS 22; CANR 9, 47; CP 1, 2, 3, 4; DLB 48; DLBY 1996, 1997

Laurence, (Jean) Margaret (Wemyss) 1926-1987 . **CLC 3, 6, 13, 50, 62; SSC 7**
See also BYA 13; CA 5-8R; 121; CANR 33; CN 1, 2, 3, 4; DAC; DAM MST; DLB 53; EWL 3; FW; MTCW 1, 2; MTFW 2005; NFS 11; RGEL 2; RGSF 2; SATA-Obit 50; TCWW 2

Laurent, Antoine 1952- .... **CLC 50**

Lauscher, Hermann
See Hesse, Hermann

Lautreamont 1846-1870 .. **NCLC 12; SSC 14**
See Lautreamont, Isidore Lucien Ducasse
See also GFL 1789 to the Present; RGWL 2, 3

Lautreamont, Isidore Lucien Ducasse
See Lautreamont
See also DLB 217

Lavater, Johann Kaspar 1741-1801 .... **NCLC 142**
See also DLB 97

Laverty, Donald
See Blish, James (Benjamin)

Lavin, Mary 1912-1996 . **CLC 4, 18, 99; SSC 4, 67**
See also CA 9-12R; 151; CANR 33; CN 1, 2, 3, 4, 5, 6; DLB 15, 319; FW; MTCW 1; RGEL 2; RGSF 2

Lavond, Paul Dennis
See Kornbluth, C(yril) M.; Pohl, Frederik

Lawes, Henry 1596-1662 .... **LC 113**
See also DLB 126

Lawler, Ray
See Lawler, Raymond Evenor
See also DLB 289

Lawler, Raymond Evenor 1922- .... **CLC 58**
See Lawler, Ray
See also CA 103; CD 5, 6; RGEL 2

Lawrence, D(avid) H(erbert Richards) 1885-1930 .... **PC 54; SSC 4, 19, 73; TCLC 2, 9, 16, 33, 48, 61, 93; WLC**
See Chambers, Jessie
See also BPFB 2; BRW 7; BRWR 2; CA 104; 121; CANR 131; CDBLB 1914-1945; DA; DA3; DAB; DAC; DAM MST, NOV, POET; DLB 10, 19, 36, 98, 162, 195; EWL 3; EXPP; EXPS; LAIT 2, 3; MTCW 1, 2; MTFW 2005; NFS 18; PFS 6; RGEL 2; RGSF 2; SSFS 2, 6; TEA; WLIT 4; WP

Lawrence, T(homas) E(dward) 1888-1935 .... **TCLC 18**
See Dale, Colin
See also BRWS 2; CA 115; 167; DLB 195

Lawrence of Arabia
See Lawrence, T(homas) E(dward)

Lawson, Henry (Archibald Hertzberg) 1867-1922 .... **SSC 18; TCLC 27**
See also CA 120; 181; DLB 230; RGEL 2; RGSF 2

Lawton, Dennis
See Faust, Frederick (Schiller)

Layamon fl. c. 1200- .... **CMLC 10**
See Lazamon
See also DLB 146; RGEL 2

Laye, Camara 1928-1980 ..... **BLC 2; CLC 4, 38**
See Camara Laye
See also AFW; BW 1; CA 85-88; 97-100; CANR 25; DAM MULT; MTCW 1, 2; WLIT 2

Layton, Irving 1912-2006 ..... **CLC 2, 15, 164**
See also CA 1-4R; CANR 2, 33, 43, 66, 129; CP 1, 2, 3, 4, 5, 6, 7; DAC; DAM MST, POET; DLB 88; EWL 3; MTCW 1, 2; PFS 12; RGEL 2

Layton, Irving Peter
See Layton, Irving

Lazarus, Emma 1849-1887 ...... **NCLC 8, 109**

Lazarus, Felix
See Cable, George Washington

Lazarus, Henry
See Slavitt, David R(ytman)

Lea, Joan
See Neufeld, John (Arthur)

Leacock, Stephen (Butler) 1869-1944 .... **SSC 39; TCLC 2**
See also CA 104; 141; CANR 80; DAC; DAM MST; DLB 92; EWL 3; MTCW 2; MTFW 2005; RGEL 2; RGSF 2

Lead, Jane Ward 1623-1704 .... **LC 72**
See also DLB 131

Leapor, Mary 1722-1746 .... **LC 80**
See also DLB 109

Lear, Edward 1812-1888 ..... **NCLC 3; PC 65**
See also AAYA 48; BRW 5; CLR 1, 75; DLB 32, 163, 166; MAICYA 1, 2; RGEL 2; SATA 18, 100; WCH; WP

Lear, Norman (Milton) 1922- .... **CLC 12**
See also CA 73-76

Leautaud, Paul 1872-1956 .... **TCLC 83**
See also CA 203; DLB 65; GFL 1789 to the Present

Leavis, F(rank) R(aymond) 1895-1978 .... **CLC 24**
See also BRW 7; CA 21-24R; 77-80; CANR 44; DLB 242; EWL 3; MTCW 1, 2; RGEL 2

Leavitt, David 1961- .... **CLC 34**
See also CA 116; 122; CANR 50, 62, 101, 134; CPW; DA3; DAM POP; DLB 130; GLL 1; INT CA-122; MAL 5; MTCW 2; MTFW 2005

Leblanc, Maurice (Marie Emile) 1864-1941 .... **TCLC 49**
See also CA 110; CMW 4

Lebowitz, Fran(ces Ann) 1951(?)- ... **CLC 11, 36**
See also CA 81-84; CANR 14, 60, 70; INT CANR-14; MTCW 1

Lebrecht, Peter
See Tieck, (Johann) Ludwig

le Carre, John .... **CLC 3, 5, 9, 15, 28**
See Cornwell, David (John Moore)
See also AAYA 42; BEST 89:4; BPFB 2; BRWS 2; CDBLB 1960 to Present; CMW 4; CN 1, 2, 3, 4, 5, 6, 7; CPW; DLB 87; EWL 3; MSW; MTCW 2; RGEL 2; TEA

Le Clezio, J(ean) M(arie) G(ustave)
1940- .... **CLC 31, 155**
See also CA 116; 128; CWW 2; DLB 83; EWL 3; GFL 1789 to the Present; RGSF 2

Leconte de Lisle, Charles-Marie-Rene
1818-1894 .... **NCLC 29**
See also DLB 217; EW 6; GFL 1789 to the Present

Le Coq, Monsieur
See Simenon, Georges (Jacques Christian)

Leduc, Violette 1907-1972 .... **CLC 22**
See also CA 13-14; 33-36R; CANR 69; CAP 1; EWL 3; GFL 1789 to the Present; GLL 1

Ledwidge, Francis 1887(?)-1917 .... **TCLC 23**
See also CA 123; 203; DLB 20

Lee, Andrea 1953- .... **BLC 2; CLC 36**
See also BW 1, 3; CA 125; CANR 82; DAM MULT

Lee, Andrew
See Auchincloss, Louis (Stanton)

Lee, Chang-rae 1965- .... **CLC 91**
See also CA 148; CANR 89; CN 7; DLB 312; LATS 1:2

Lee, Don L. .... **CLC 2**
See Madhubuti, Haki R.
See also CP 2, 3, 4

Lee, George W(ashington)
1894-1976 .... **BLC 2; CLC 52**
See also BW 1; CA 125; CANR 83; DAM MULT; DLB 51

Lee, (Nelle) Harper 1926- . **CLC 12, 60, 194; WLC**
See also AAYA 13; AMWS 8; BPFB 2; BYA 3; CA 13-16R; CANR 51, 128; CDALB 1941-1968; CSW; DA; DA3; DAB; DAC; DAM MST, NOV; DLB 6; EXPN; LAIT 3; MAL 5; MTCW 1, 2; MTFW 2005; NFS 2; SATA 11; WYA; YAW

Lee, Helen Elaine 1959(?)- .... **CLC 86**
See also CA 148

Lee, John .... **CLC 70**

Lee, Julian
See Latham, Jean Lee

Lee, Larry
See Lee, Lawrence

Lee, Laurie 1914-1997 .... **CLC 90**
See also CA 77-80; 158; CANR 33, 73; CP 1, 2, 3, 4; CPW; DAB; DAM POP; DLB 27; MTCW 1; RGEL 2

Lee, Lawrence 1941-1990 .... **CLC 34**
See also CA 131; CANR 43

Lee, Li-Young 1957- .... **CLC 164; PC 24**
See also AMWS 15; CA 153; CANR 118; CP 7; DLB 165, 312; LMFS 2; PFS 11, 15, 17

Lee, Manfred B(ennington)
1905-1971 .... **CLC 11**
See Queen, Ellery
See also CA 1-4R; 29-32R; CANR 2; CMW 4; DLB 137

Lee, Nathaniel 1645(?)-1692 .... **LC 103**
See also DLB 80; RGEL 2

Lee, Shelton Jackson 1957(?)- .. **BLCS; CLC 105**
See Lee, Spike
See also BW 2, 3; CA 125; CANR 42; DAM MULT

Lee, Spike
See Lee, Shelton Jackson
See also AAYA 4, 29

Lee, Stan 1922- .... **CLC 17**
See also AAYA 5, 49; CA 108; 111; CANR 129; INT CA-111; MTFW 2005

Lee, Tanith 1947- .... **CLC 46**
See also AAYA 15; CA 37-40R; CANR 53, 102, 145; DLB 261; FANT; SATA 8, 88, 134; SFW 4; SUFW 1, 2; YAW

Lee, Vernon .... **SSC 33; TCLC 5**
See Paget, Violet
See also DLB 57, 153, 156, 174, 178; GLL 1; SUFW 1

Lee, William
See Burroughs, William S(eward)
See also GLL 1

Lee, Willy
See Burroughs, William S(eward)
See also GLL 1

Lee-Hamilton, Eugene (Jacob)
1845-1907 .... **TCLC 22**
See also CA 117; 234

Leet, Judith 1935- .... **CLC 11**
See also CA 187

Le Fanu, Joseph Sheridan
1814-1873 .... **NCLC 9, 58; SSC 14, 84**
See also CMW 4; DA3; DAM POP; DLB 21, 70, 159, 178; GL 3; HGG; RGEL 2; RGSF 2; SUFW 1

Leffland, Ella 1931- .... **CLC 19**
See also CA 29-32R; CANR 35, 78, 82; DLBY 1984; INT CANR-35; SATA 65

Leger, Alexis
See Leger, (Marie-Rene Auguste) Alexis Saint-Leger

Leger, (Marie-Rene Auguste) Alexis Saint-Leger 1887-1975 .. **CLC 4, 11, 46; PC 23**
See Perse, Saint-John; Saint-John Perse
See also CA 13-16R; 61-64; CANR 43; DAM POET; MTCW 1

Leger, Saintleger
See Leger, (Marie-Rene Auguste) Alexis Saint-Leger

Le Guin, Ursula K(roeber) 1929- ..... **CLC 8, 13, 22, 45, 71, 136; SSC 12, 69**
See also AAYA 9, 27; AITN 1; BPFB 2; BYA 5, 8, 11, 14; CA 21-24R; CANR 9, 32, 52, 74, 132; CDALB 1968-1988; CLR 3, 28, 91; CN 2, 3, 4, 5, 6, 7; CPW; DA3; DAB; DAC; DAM MST, POP; DLB 8, 52, 256, 275; EXPS; FANT; FW; INT CANR-32; JRDA; LAIT 5; MAICYA 1, 2; MAL 5; MTCW 1, 2; MTFW 2005; NFS 6, 9; SATA 4, 52, 99, 149; SCFW 1, 2; SFW 4; SSFS 2; SUFW 1, 2; WYA; YAW

Lehmann, Rosamond (Nina)
1901-1990 .... **CLC 5**
See also CA 77-80; 131; CANR 8, 73; CN 1, 2, 3, 4; DLB 15; MTCW 2; RGEL 2; RHW

Leiber, Fritz (Reuter, Jr.)
1910-1992 .... **CLC 25**
See also AAYA 65; BPFB 2; CA 45-48; 139; CANR 2, 40, 86; CN 2, 3, 4, 5; DLB 8; FANT; HGG; MTCW 1, 2; MTFW 2005; SATA 45; SATA-Obit 73; SCFW 1, 2; SFW 4; SUFW 1, 2

Leibniz, Gottfried Wilhelm von
1646-1716 .... **LC 35**
See also DLB 168

Leimbach, Martha 1963-
See Leimbach, Marti
See also CA 130

Leimbach, Marti .... **CLC 65**
See Leimbach, Martha

Leino, Eino .... **TCLC 24**
See Lonnbohm, Armas Eino Leopold
See also EWL 3

Leiris, Michel (Julien) 1901-1990 ..... **CLC 61**
See also CA 119; 128; 132; EWL 3; GFL 1789 to the Present

Leithauser, Brad 1953- .... **CLC 27**
See also CA 107; CANR 27, 81; CP 7; DLB 120, 282

le Jars de Gournay, Marie
See de Gournay, Marie le Jars

Lelchuk, Alan 1938- .... **CLC 5**
See also CA 45-48; CAAS 20; CANR 1, 70; CN 3, 4, 5, 6, 7

Lem, Stanislaw 1921- ...... **CLC 8, 15, 40, 149**
See also CA 105; CAAS 1; CANR 32; CWW 2; MTCW 1; SCFW 1, 2; SFW 4

Lemann, Nancy (Elise) 1956- .... **CLC 39**
See also CA 118; 136; CANR 121

Lemonnier, (Antoine Louis) Camille
1844-1913 .... **TCLC 22**
See also CA 121

Lenau, Nikolaus 1802-1850 .... **NCLC 16**

L'Engle, Madeleine (Camp Franklin)
1918- .... **CLC 12**
See also AAYA 28; AITN 2; BPFB 2; BYA 2, 4, 5, 7; CA 1-4R; CANR 3, 21, 39, 66, 107; CLR 1, 14, 57; CPW; CWRI 5; DA3; DAM POP; DLB 52; JRDA; MAICYA 1, 2; MTCW 1, 2; MTFW 2005; SAAS 15; SATA 1, 27, 75, 128; SFW 4; WYA; YAW

Lengyel, Jozsef 1896-1975 .... **CLC 7**
See also CA 85-88; 57-60; CANR 71; RGSF 2

Lenin 1870-1924
See Lenin, V. I.
See also CA 121; 168

Lenin, V. I. .... **TCLC 67**
See Lenin

Lennon, John (Ono) 1940-1980 .. **CLC 12, 35**
See also CA 102; SATA 114

Lennox, Charlotte Ramsay
1729(?)-1804 .... **NCLC 23, 134**
See also DLB 39; RGEL 2

Lentricchia, Frank, (Jr.) 1940- .... **CLC 34**
See also CA 25-28R; CANR 19, 106; DLB 246

Lenz, Gunter .... **CLC 65**

Lenz, Jakob Michael Reinhold
1751-1792 .... **LC 100**
See also DLB 94; RGWL 2, 3

Lenz, Siegfried 1926- .... **CLC 27; SSC 33**
See also CA 89-92; CANR 80; CWW 2; DLB 75; EWL 3; RGSF 2; RGWL 2, 3

Leon, David
See Jacob, (Cyprien-)Max

Leonard, Elmore (John, Jr.) 1925- . **CLC 28, 34, 71, 120**
See also AAYA 22, 59; AITN 1; BEST 89:1, 90:4; BPFB 2; CA 81-84; CANR 12, 28, 53, 76, 96, 133; CMW 4; CN 5, 6, 7; CPW; DA3; DAM POP; DLB 173, 226; INT CANR-28; MSW; MTCW 1, 2; MTFW 2005; RGAL 4; SATA 163; TCWW 1, 2

Leonard, Hugh .... **CLC 19**
See Byrne, John Keyes
See also CBD; CD 5, 6; DFS 13; DLB 13

Leonov, Leonid (Maximovich)
1899-1994 .... **CLC 92**
See Leonov, Leonid Maksimovich
See also CA 129; CANR 76; DAM NOV; EWL 3; MTCW 1, 2; MTFW 2005

MacDiarmid, Hugh .... **CLC 2, 4, 11, 19, 63; PC 9**
See Grieve, C(hristopher) M(urray)
See also CDBLB 1945-1960; CP 1, 2; DLB 20; EWL 3; RGEL 2

MacDonald, Anson
See Heinlein, Robert A(nson)

Macdonald, Cynthia 1928- .... **CLC 13, 19**
See also CA 49-52; CANR 4, 44, 146; DLB 105

MacDonald, George 1824-1905 .... **TCLC 9, 113**
See also AAYA 57; BYA 5; CA 106; 137; CANR 80; CLR 67; DLB 18, 163, 178; FANT; MAICYA 1, 2; RGEL 2; SATA 33, 100; SFW 4; SUFW; WCH

Macdonald, John
See Millar, Kenneth

MacDonald, John D(ann)
1916-1986 .... **CLC 3, 27, 44**
See also BPFB 2; CA 1-4R; 121; CANR 1, 19, 60; CMW 4; CPW; DAM NOV, POP; DLB 8, 306; DLBY 1986; MSW; MTCW 1, 2; MTFW 2005; SFW 4

Macdonald, John Ross
See Millar, Kenneth

Macdonald, Ross ..... **CLC 1, 2, 3, 14, 34, 41**
See Millar, Kenneth
See also AMWS 4; BPFB 2; CN 1, 2, 3; DLBD 6; MSW; RGAL 4

MacDougal, John
See Blish, James (Benjamin)

MacDougal, John
See Blish, James (Benjamin)

MacDowell, John
See Parks, Tim(othy Harold)

MacEwen, Gwendolyn (Margaret)
1941-1987 .... **CLC 13, 55**
See also CA 9-12R; 124; CANR 7, 22; CP 1, 2, 3, 4; DLB 53, 251; SATA 50; SATA-Obit 55

Macha, Karel Hynek 1810-1846 .... **NCLC 46**

Machado (y Ruiz), Antonio
1875-1939 .... **TCLC 3**
See also CA 104; 174; DLB 108; EW 9; EWL 3; HW 2; PFS 23; RGWL 2, 3

Machado de Assis, Joaquim Maria
1839-1908 .... **BLC 2; HLCS 2; SSC 24; TCLC 10**
See also CA 107; 153; CANR 91; DLB 307; LAW; RGSF 2; RGWL 2, 3; TWA; WLIT 1

Machaut, Guillaume de c.
1300-1377 .... **CMLC 64**
See also DLB 208

Machen, Arthur .... **SSC 20; TCLC 4**
See Jones, Arthur Llewellyn
See also CA 179; DLB 156, 178; RGEL 2; SUFW 1

Machiavelli, Niccolo 1469-1527 ... **DC 16; LC 8, 36; WLCS**
See also AAYA 58; DA; DAB; DAC; DAM MST; EW 2; LAIT 1; LMFS 1; NFS 9; RGWL 2, 3; TWA; WLIT 7

MacInnes, Colin 1914-1976 .... **CLC 4, 23**
See also CA 69-72; 65-68; CANR 21; CN 1, 2; DLB 14; MTCW 1, 2; RGEL 2; RHW

MacInnes, Helen (Clark)
1907-1985 .... **CLC 27, 39**
See also BPFB 2; CA 1-4R; 117; CANR 1, 28, 58; CMW 4; CN 1, 2; CPW; DAM POP; DLB 87; MSW; MTCW 1, 2; MTFW 2005; SATA 22; SATA-Obit 44

Mackay, Mary 1855-1924
See Corelli, Marie
See also CA 118; 177; FANT; RHW

Mackay, Shena 1944- .... **CLC 195**
See also CA 104; CANR 88, 139; DLB 231, 319; MTFW 2005

Mackenzie, Compton (Edward Montague)
1883-1972 .... **CLC 18; TCLC 116**
See also CA 21-22; 37-40R; CAP 2; CN 1; DLB 34, 100; RGEL 2

Mackenzie, Henry 1745-1831 .... **NCLC 41**
See also DLB 39; RGEL 2

Mackey, Nathaniel (Ernest) 1947- .... **PC 49**
See also CA 153; CANR 114; CP 7; DLB 169

MacKinnon, Catharine A. 1946- .... **CLC 181**
See also CA 128; 132; CANR 73, 140; FW; MTCW 2; MTFW 2005

Mackintosh, Elizabeth 1896(?)-1952
See Tey, Josephine
See also CA 110; CMW 4

MacLaren, James
See Grieve, C(hristopher) M(urray)

MacLaverty, Bernard 1942- .... **CLC 31**
See also CA 116; 118; CANR 43, 88; CN 5, 6, 7; DLB 267; INT CA-118; RGSF 2

MacLean, Alistair (Stuart)
1922(?)-1987 .... **CLC 3, 13, 50, 63**
See also CA 57-60; 121; CANR 28, 61; CMW 4; CP 2, 3, 4, 5, 6, 7; CPW; DAM POP; DLB 276; MTCW 1; SATA 23; SATA-Obit 50; TCWW 2

Maclean, Norman (Fitzroy)
1902-1990 .... **CLC 78; SSC 13**
See also AMWS 14; CA 102; 132; CANR 49; CPW; DAM POP; DLB 206; TCWW 2

MacLeish, Archibald 1892-1982 ... **CLC 3, 8, 14, 68; PC 47**
See also AMW; CA 9-12R; 106; CAD; CANR 33, 63; CDALBS; CP 1, 2; DAM POET; DFS 15; DLB 4, 7, 45; DLBY 1982; EWL 3; EXPP; MAL 5; MTCW 1, 2; MTFW 2005; PAB; PFS 5; RGAL 4; TUS

MacLennan, (John) Hugh
1907-1990 .... **CLC 2, 14, 92**
See also CA 5-8R; 142; CANR 33; CN 1, 2, 3, 4; DAC; DAM MST; DLB 68; EWL 3; MTCW 1, 2; MTFW 2005; RGEL 2; TWA

MacLeod, Alistair 1936- .... **CLC 56, 165**
See also CA 123; CCA 1; DAC; DAM MST; DLB 60; MTCW 2; MTFW 2005; RGSF 2; TCLE 1:2

Macleod, Fiona
See Sharp, William
See also RGEL 2; SUFW

MacNeice, (Frederick) Louis
1907-1963 .... **CLC 1, 4, 10, 53; PC 61**
See also BRW 7; CA 85-88; CANR 61; DAB; DAM POET; DLB 10, 20; EWL 3; MTCW 1, 2; MTFW 2005; RGEL 2

MacNeill, Dand
See Fraser, George MacDonald

Macpherson, James 1736-1796 .... **LC 29**
See Ossian
See also BRWS 8; DLB 109; RGEL 2

Macpherson, (Jean) Jay 1931- .... **CLC 14**
See also CA 5-8R; CANR 90; CP 1, 2, 3, 4, 5, 6, 7; CWP; DLB 53

Macrobius fl. 430- .... **CMLC 48**

MacShane, Frank 1927-1999 .... **CLC 39**
See also CA 9-12R; 186; CANR 3, 33; DLB 111

Macumber, Mari
See Sandoz, Mari(e Susette)

Madach, Imre 1823-1864 .... **NCLC 19**

Madden, (Jerry) David 1933- .... **CLC 5, 15**
See also CA 1-4R; CAAS 3; CANR 4, 45; CN 3, 4, 5, 6, 7; CSW; DLB 6; MTCW 1

Maddern, Al(an)
See Ellison, Harlan (Jay)

Madhubuti, Haki R. 1942- ... **BLC 2; CLC 6, 73; PC 5**
See Lee, Don L.
See also BW 2, 3; CA 73-76; CANR 24, 51, 73, 139; CP 5, 6, 7; CSW; DAM MULT, POET; DLB 5, 41; DLBD 8; EWL 3; MAL 5; MTCW 2; MTFW 2005; RGAL 4

Madison, James 1751-1836 .... **NCLC 126**
See also DLB 37

Maepenn, Hugh
See Kuttner, Henry

Maepenn, K. H.
See Kuttner, Henry

Maeterlinck, Maurice 1862-1949 ..... **TCLC 3**
See also CA 104; 136; CANR 80; DAM DRAM; DLB 192; EW 8; EWL 3; GFL 1789 to the Present; LMFS 2; RGWL 2, 3; SATA 66; TWA

Maginn, William 1794-1842 .... **NCLC 8**
See also DLB 110, 159

Mahapatra, Jayanta 1928- .... **CLC 33**
See also CA 73-76; CAAS 9; CANR 15, 33, 66, 87; CP 4, 5, 6, 7; DAM MULT

Mahfouz, Naguib (Abdel Aziz Al-Sabilgi)
1911(?)- .... **CLC 153; SSC 66**
See Mahfuz, Najib (Abdel Aziz al-Sabilgi)
See also AAYA 49; BEST 89:2; CA 128; CANR 55, 101; DA3; DAM NOV; MTCW 1, 2; MTFW 2005; RGWL 2, 3; SSFS 9

Mahfuz, Najib (Abdel Aziz al-Sabilgi)
.... **CLC 52, 55**
See Mahfouz, Naguib (Abdel Aziz Al-Sabilgi)
See also AFW; CWW 2; DLBY 1988; EWL 3; RGSF 2; WLIT 6

Mahon, Derek 1941- .... **CLC 27; PC 60**
See also BRWS 6; CA 113; 128; CANR 88; CP 1, 2, 3, 4, 5, 6, 7; DLB 40; EWL 3

Maiakovskii, Vladimir
See Mayakovski, Vladimir (Vladimirovich)
See also IDTP; RGWL 2, 3

Mailer, Norman (Kingsley) 1923- . **CLC 1, 2, 3, 4, 5, 8, 11, 14, 28, 39, 74, 111**
See also AAYA 31; AITN 2; AMW; AMWC 2; AMWR 2; BPFB 2; CA 9-12R; CABS 1; CANR 28, 74, 77, 130; CDALB 1968-1988; CN 1, 2, 3, 4, 5, 6, 7; CPW; DA; DA3; DAB; DAC; DAM MST, NOV, POP; DLB 2, 16, 28, 185, 278; DLBD 3; DLBY 1980, 1983; EWL 3; MAL 5; MTCW 1, 2; MTFW 2005; NFS 10; RGAL 4; TUS

Maillet, Antonine 1929- .... **CLC 54, 118**
See also CA 115; 120; CANR 46, 74, 77, 134; CCA 1; CWW 2; DAC; DLB 60; INT CA-120; MTCW 2; MTFW 2005

Maimonides, Moses 1135-1204 ..... **CMLC 76**
See also DLB 115

Mais, Roger 1905-1955 .... **TCLC 8**
See also BW 1, 3; CA 105; 124; CANR 82; CDWLB 3; DLB 125; EWL 3; MTCW 1; RGEL 2

Maistre, Joseph 1753-1821 .... **NCLC 37**
See also GFL 1789 to the Present

Maitland, Frederic William
1850-1906 .... **TCLC 65**

Maitland, Sara (Louise) 1950- .... **CLC 49**
See also BRWS 11; CA 69-72; CANR 13, 59; DLB 271; FW

Major, Clarence 1936- ... **BLC 2; CLC 3, 19, 48**
See also AFAW 2; BW 2, 3; CA 21-24R; CAAS 6; CANR 13, 25, 53, 82; CN 3, 4, 5, 6, 7; CP 2, 3, 4, 5, 6, 7; CSW; DAM MULT; DLB 33; EWL 3; MAL 5; MSW

Major, Kevin (Gerald) 1949- .... **CLC 26**
See also AAYA 16; CA 97-100; CANR 21,
38, 112; CLR 11; DAC; DLB 60; INT
CANR-21; JRDA; MAICYA 1, 2; MAIC-
YAS 1; SATA 32, 82, 134; WYA; YAW
Maki, James
See Ozu, Yasujiro
Makine, Andrei 1957- .... **CLC 198**
See also CA 176; CANR 103; MTFW 2005
Malabaila, Damiano
See Levi, Primo
Malamud, Bernard 1914-1986 .. **CLC 1, 2, 3,
5, 8, 9, 11, 18, 27, 44, 78, 85; SSC 15;
TCLC 129; WLC**
See also AAYA 16; AMWS 1; BPFB 2;
BYA 15; CA 5-8R; 118; CABS 1; CANR
28, 62, 114; CDALB 1941-1968; CN 1, 2,
3, 4; CPW; DA; DA3; DAB; DAC; DAM
MST, NOV, POP; DLB 2, 28, 152; DLBY
1980, 1986; EWL 3; EXPS; LAIT 4;
LATS 1:1; MAL 5; MTCW 1, 2; MTFW
2005; NFS 4, 9; RGAL 4; RGSF 2; SSFS
8, 13, 16; TUS
Malan, Herman
See Bosman, Herman Charles; Bosman,
Herman Charles
Malaparte, Curzio 1898-1957 .... **TCLC 52**
See also DLB 264
Malcolm, Dan
See Silverberg, Robert
Malcolm, Janet 1934- .... **CLC 201**
See also CA 123; CANR 89; NCFS 1
Malcolm X .... **BLC 2; CLC 82, 117; WLCS**
See Little, Malcolm
See also LAIT 5; NCFS 3
Malherbe, Francois de 1555-1628 .... **LC 5**
See also GFL Beginnings to 1789
Mallarme, Stephane 1842-1898 ...... **NCLC 4,
41; PC 4**
See also DAM POET; DLB 217; EW 7;
GFL 1789 to the Present; LMFS 2; RGWL
2, 3; TWA
Mallet-Joris, Francoise 1930- .... **CLC 11**
See also CA 65-68; CANR 17; CWW 2;
DLB 83; EWL 3; GFL 1789 to the Present
Malley, Ern
See McAuley, James Phillip
Mallon, Thomas 1951- .... **CLC 172**
See also CA 110; CANR 29, 57, 92
Mallowan, Agatha Christie
See Christie, Agatha (Mary Clarissa)
Maloff, Saul 1922- .... **CLC 5**
See also CA 33-36R
Malone, Louis
See MacNeice, (Frederick) Louis
Malone, Michael (Christopher)
1942- .... **CLC 43**
See also CA 77-80; CANR 14, 32, 57, 114
Malory, Sir Thomas 1410(?)-1471(?) . **LC 11,
88; WLCS**
See also BRW 1; BRWR 2; CDBLB Before
1660; DA; DAB; DAC; DAM MST; DLB
146; EFS 2; RGEL 2; SATA 59; SATA-
Brief 33; TEA; WLIT 3
Malouf, (George Joseph) David
1934- .... **CLC 28, 86**
See also CA 124; CANR 50, 76; CN 3, 4,
5, 6, 7; CP 1, 3, 4, 5, 6, 7; DLB 289; EWL
3; MTCW 2; MTFW 2005
Malraux, (Georges-)Andre
1901-1976 ...... **CLC 1, 4, 9, 13, 15, 57**
See also BPFB 2; CA 21-22; 69-72; CANR
34, 58; CAP 2; DA3; DAM NOV; DLB
72; EW 12; EWL 3; GFL 1789 to the
Present; MTCW 1, 2; MTFW 2005;
RGWL 2, 3; TWA
Malthus, Thomas Robert
1766-1834 .... **NCLC 145**
See also DLB 107, 158; RGEL 2

Malzberg, Barry N(athaniel) 1939- ... **CLC 7**
See also CA 61-64; CAAS 4; CANR 16;
CMW 4; DLB 8; SFW 4
Mamet, David (Alan) 1947- .. **CLC 9, 15, 34,
46, 91, 166; DC 4, 24**
See also AAYA 3, 60; AMWS 14; CA 81-
84; CABS 3; CAD; CANR 15, 41, 67, 72,
129; CD 5, 6; DA3; DAM DRAM; DFS
2, 3, 6, 12, 15; DLB 7; EWL 3; IDFW 4;
MAL 5; MTCW 1, 2; MTFW 2005;
RGAL 4
Mamoulian, Rouben (Zachary)
1897-1987 .... **CLC 16**
See also CA 25-28R; 124; CANR 85
Mandelshtam, Osip
See Mandelstam, Osip (Emilievich)
See also EW 10; EWL 3; RGWL 2, 3
Mandelstam, Osip (Emilievich)
1891(?)-1943(?) .... **PC 14; TCLC 2, 6**
See Mandelshtam, Osip
See also CA 104; 150; MTCW 2; TWA
Mander, (Mary) Jane 1877-1949 ... **TCLC 31**
See also CA 162; RGEL 2
Mandeville, Bernard 1670-1733 .... **LC 82**
See also DLB 101
Mandeville, Sir John fl. 1350- ...... **CMLC 19**
See also DLB 146
Mandiargues, Andre Pieyre de .... **CLC 41**
See Pieyre de Mandiargues, Andre
See also DLB 83
Mandrake, Ethel Belle
See Thurman, Wallace (Henry)
Mangan, James Clarence
1803-1849 .... **NCLC 27**
See also RGEL 2
Maniere, J.-E.
See Giraudoux, Jean(-Hippolyte)
Mankiewicz, Herman (Jacob)
1897-1953 .... **TCLC 85**
See also CA 120; 169; DLB 26; IDFW 3, 4
Manley, (Mary) Delariviere
1672(?)-1724 .... **LC 1, 42**
See also DLB 39, 80; RGEL 2
Mann, Abel
See Creasey, John
Mann, Emily 1952- .... **DC 7**
See also CA 130; CAD; CANR 55; CD 5,
6; CWD; DLB 266
Mann, (Luiz) Heinrich 1871-1950 ... **TCLC 9**
See also CA 106; 164, 181; DLB 66, 118;
EW 8; EWL 3; RGWL 2, 3
Mann, (Paul) Thomas 1875-1955 . **SSC 5, 80,
82; TCLC 2, 8, 14, 21, 35, 44, 60, 168;
WLC**
See also BPFB 2; CA 104; 128; CANR 133;
CDWLB 2; DA; DA3; DAB; DAC; DAM
MST, NOV; DLB 66; EW 9; EWL 3; GLL
1; LATS 1:1; LMFS 1; MTCW 1, 2;
MTFW 2005; NFS 17; RGSF 2; RGWL
2, 3; SSFS 4, 9; TWA
Mannheim, Karl 1893-1947 .... **TCLC 65**
See also CA 204
Manning, David
See Faust, Frederick (Schiller)
Manning, Frederic 1882-1935 .... **TCLC 25**
See also CA 124; 216; DLB 260
Manning, Olivia 1915-1980 .... **CLC 5, 19**
See also CA 5-8R; 101; CANR 29; CN 1,
2; EWL 3; FW; MTCW 1; RGEL 2
Mano, D. Keith 1942- .... **CLC 2, 10**
See also CA 25-28R; CAAS 6; CANR 26,
57; DLB 6
Mansfield, Katherine .... **SSC 9, 23, 38, 81;
TCLC 2, 8, 39, 164; WLC**
See Beauchamp, Kathleen Mansfield
See also BPFB 2; BRW 7; DAB; DLB 162;
EWL 3; EXPS; FW; GLL 1; RGEL 2;
RGSF 2; SSFS 2, 8, 10, 11; WWE 1

Manso, Peter 1940- .... **CLC 39**
See also CA 29-32R; CANR 44
Mantecon, Juan Jimenez
See Jimenez (Mantecon), Juan Ramon
Mantel, Hilary (Mary) 1952- .... **CLC 144**
See also CA 125; CANR 54, 101; CN 5, 6,
7; DLB 271; RHW
Manton, Peter
See Creasey, John
Man Without a Spleen, A
See Chekhov, Anton (Pavlovich)
Manzano, Juan Francisco
1797(?)-1854 .... **NCLC 155**
Manzoni, Alessandro 1785-1873 ... **NCLC 29,
98**
See also EW 5; RGWL 2, 3; TWA; WLIT 7
Map, Walter 1140-1209 .... **CMLC 32**
Mapu, Abraham (ben Jekutiel)
1808-1867 .... **NCLC 18**
Mara, Sally
See Queneau, Raymond
Maracle, Lee 1950- .... **NNAL**
See also CA 149
Marat, Jean Paul 1743-1793 .... **LC 10**
Marcel, Gabriel Honore 1889-1973 . **CLC 15**
See also CA 102; 45-48; EWL 3; MTCW 1,
2
March, William .... **TCLC 96**
See Campbell, William Edward March
See also CA 216; DLB 9, 86, 316; MAL 5
Marchbanks, Samuel
See Davies, (William) Robertson
See also CCA 1
Marchi, Giacomo
See Bassani, Giorgio
Marcus Aurelius
See Aurelius, Marcus
See also AW 2
Marguerite
See de Navarre, Marguerite
Marguerite d'Angouleme
See de Navarre, Marguerite
See also GFL Beginnings to 1789
Marguerite de Navarre
See de Navarre, Marguerite
See also RGWL 2, 3
Margulies, Donald 1954- .... **CLC 76**
See also AAYA 57; CA 200; CD 6; DFS 13;
DLB 228
Marie de France c. 12th cent. - ..... **CMLC 8;
PC 22**
See also DLB 208; FW; RGWL 2, 3
Marie de l'Incarnation 1599-1672 ...... **LC 10**
Marier, Captain Victor
See Griffith, D(avid Lewelyn) W(ark)
Mariner, Scott
See Pohl, Frederik
Marinetti, Filippo Tommaso
1876-1944 .... **TCLC 10**
See also CA 107; DLB 114, 264; EW 9;
EWL 3; WLIT 7
Marivaux, Pierre Carlet de Chamblain de
1688-1763 .... **DC 7; LC 4, 123**
See also DLB 314; GFL Beginnings to
1789; RGWL 2, 3; TWA
Markandaya, Kamala .... **CLC 8, 38**
See Taylor, Kamala (Purnaiya)
See also BYA 13; CN 1, 2, 3, 4, 5, 6, 7;
EWL 3
Markfield, Wallace (Arthur)
1926-2002 .... **CLC 8**
See also CA 69-72; 208; CAAS 3; CN 1, 2,
3, 4, 5, 6, 7; DLB 2, 28; DLBY 2002
Markham, Edwin 1852-1940 .... **TCLC 47**
See also CA 160; DLB 54, 186; MAL 5;
RGAL 4
Markham, Robert
See Amis, Kingsley (William)

Markoosie .... **NNAL**
See Patsauq, Markoosie
See also CLR 23; DAM MULT

Marks, J.
See Highwater, Jamake (Mamake)

Marks, J
See Highwater, Jamake (Mamake)

Marks-Highwater, J
See Highwater, Jamake (Mamake)

Marks-Highwater, J.
See Highwater, Jamake (Mamake)

Markson, David M(errill) 1927- .... **CLC 67**
See also CA 49-52; CANR 1, 91; CN 5, 6

Marlatt, Daphne (Buckle) 1942- .... **CLC 168**
See also CA 25-28R; CANR 17, 39; CN 6, 7; CP 4, 5, 6, 7; CWP; DLB 60; FW

Marley, Bob .... **CLC 17**
See Marley, Robert Nesta

Marley, Robert Nesta 1945-1981
See Marley, Bob
See also CA 107; 103

Marlowe, Christopher 1564-1593 . **DC 1; LC 22, 47, 117; PC 57; WLC**
See also BRW 1; BRWR 1; CDBLB Before 1660; DA; DA3; DAB; DAC; DAM DRAM, MST; DFS 1, 5, 13, 21; DLB 62; EXPP; LMFS 1; PFS 22; RGEL 2; TEA; WLIT 3

Marlowe, Stephen 1928- .... **CLC 70**
See Queen, Ellery
See also CA 13-16R; CANR 6, 55; CMW 4; SFW 4

Marmion, Shakerley 1603-1639 .... **LC 89**
See also DLB 58; RGEL 2

Marmontel, Jean-Francois 1723-1799 .. **LC 2**
See also DLB 314

Maron, Monika 1941- .... **CLC 165**
See also CA 201

Marquand, John P(hillips)
1893-1960 .... **CLC 2, 10**
See also AMW; BPFB 2; CA 85-88; CANR 73; CMW 4; DLB 9, 102; EWL 3; MAL 5; MTCW 2; RGAL 4

Marques, Rene 1919-1979 .. **CLC 96; HLC 2**
See also CA 97-100; 85-88; CANR 78; DAM MULT; DLB 305; EWL 3; HW 1, 2; LAW; RGSF 2

Marquez, Gabriel (Jose) Garcia
See Garcia Marquez, Gabriel (Jose)

Marquis, Don(ald Robert Perry)
1878-1937 .... **TCLC 7**
See also CA 104; 166; DLB 11, 25; MAL 5; RGAL 4

Marquis de Sade
See Sade, Donatien Alphonse Francois

Marric, J. J.
See Creasey, John
See also MSW

Marryat, Frederick 1792-1848 .... **NCLC 3**
See also DLB 21, 163; RGEL 2; WCH

Marsden, James
See Creasey, John

Marsh, Edward 1872-1953 .... **TCLC 99**

Marsh, (Edith) Ngaio 1895-1982 .. **CLC 7, 53**
See also CA 9-12R; CANR 6, 58; CMW 4; CN 1, 2, 3; CPW; DAM POP; DLB 77; MSW; MTCW 1, 2; RGEL 2; TEA

Marshall, Allen
See Westlake, Donald E(dwin)

Marshall, Garry 1934- .... **CLC 17**
See also AAYA 3; CA 111; SATA 60

Marshall, Paule 1929- .. **BLC 3; CLC 27, 72; SSC 3**
See also AFAW 1, 2; AMWS 11; BPFB 2; BW 2, 3; CA 77-80; CANR 25, 73, 129; CN 1, 2, 3, 4, 5, 6, 7; DA3; DAM MULT; DLB 33, 157, 227; EWL 3; LATS 1:2; MAL 5; MTCW 1, 2; MTFW 2005; RGAL 4; SSFS 15

Marshallik
See Zangwill, Israel

Marsten, Richard
See Hunter, Evan

Marston, John 1576-1634 .... **LC 33**
See also BRW 2; DAM DRAM; DLB 58, 172; RGEL 2

Martel, Yann 1963- .... **CLC 192**
See also CA 146; CANR 114; MTFW 2005

Martens, Adolphe-Adhemar
See Ghelderode, Michel de

Martha, Henry
See Harris, Mark

Marti, Jose
See Marti (y Perez), Jose (Julian)
See also DLB 290

Marti (y Perez), Jose (Julian)
1853-1895 .... **HLC 2; NCLC 63**
See Marti, Jose
See also DAM MULT; HW 2; LAW; RGWL 2, 3; WLIT 1

Martial c. 40-c. 104 .... **CMLC 35; PC 10**
See also AW 2; CDWLB 1; DLB 211; RGWL 2, 3

Martin, Ken
See Hubbard, L(afayette) Ron(ald)

Martin, Richard
See Creasey, John

Martin, Steve 1945- .... **CLC 30, 217**
See also AAYA 53; CA 97-100; CANR 30, 100, 140; DFS 19; MTCW 1; MTFW 2005

Martin, Valerie 1948- .... **CLC 89**
See also BEST 90:2; CA 85-88; CANR 49, 89

Martin, Violet Florence 1862-1915 .. **SSC 56; TCLC 51**

Martin, Webber
See Silverberg, Robert

Martindale, Patrick Victor
See White, Patrick (Victor Martindale)

Martin du Gard, Roger
1881-1958 .... **TCLC 24**
See also CA 118; CANR 94; DLB 65; EWL 3; GFL 1789 to the Present; RGWL 2, 3

Martineau, Harriet 1802-1876 ...... **NCLC 26, 137**
See also DLB 21, 55, 159, 163, 166, 190; FW; RGEL 2; YABC 2

Martines, Julia
See O'Faolain, Julia

Martinez, Enrique Gonzalez
See Gonzalez Martinez, Enrique

Martinez, Jacinto Benavente y
See Benavente (y Martinez), Jacinto

Martinez de la Rosa, Francisco de Paula
1787-1862 .... **NCLC 102**
See also TWA

Martinez Ruiz, Jose 1873-1967
See Azorin; Ruiz, Jose Martinez
See also CA 93-96; HW 1

Martinez Sierra, Gregorio
1881-1947 .... **TCLC 6**
See also CA 115; EWL 3

Martinez Sierra, Maria (de la O'LeJarraga)
1874-1974 .... **TCLC 6**
See also CA 115; EWL 3

Martinsen, Martin
See Follett, Ken(neth Martin)

Martinson, Harry (Edmund)
1904-1978 .... **CLC 14**
See also CA 77-80; CANR 34, 130; DLB 259; EWL 3

Martyn, Edward 1859-1923 .... **TCLC 131**
See also CA 179; DLB 10; RGEL 2

Marut, Ret
See Traven, B.

Marut, Robert
See Traven, B.

Marvell, Andrew 1621-1678 .... **LC 4, 43; PC 10; WLC**
See also BRW 2; BRWR 2; CDBLB 1660-1789; DA; DAB; DAC; DAM MST, POET; DLB 131; EXPP; PFS 5; RGEL 2; TEA; WP

Marx, Karl (Heinrich)
1818-1883 .... **NCLC 17, 114**
See also DLB 129; LATS 1:1; TWA

Masaoka, Shiki -1902 .... **TCLC 18**
See Masaoka, Tsunenori
See also RGWL 3

Masaoka, Tsunenori 1867-1902
See Masaoka, Shiki
See also CA 117; 191; TWA

Masefield, John (Edward)
1878-1967 .... **CLC 11, 47**
See also CA 19-20; 25-28R; CANR 33; CAP 2; CDBLB 1890-1914; DAM POET; DLB 10, 19, 153, 160; EWL 3; EXPP; FANT; MTCW 1, 2; PFS 5; RGEL 2; SATA 19

Maso, Carole (?)- .... **CLC 44**
See also CA 170; CN 7; GLL 2; RGAL 4

Mason, Bobbie Ann 1940- ... **CLC 28, 43, 82, 154; SSC 4**
See also AAYA 5, 42; AMWS 8; BPFB 2; CA 53-56; CANR 11, 31, 58, 83, 125; CDALBS; CN 5, 6, 7; CSW; DA3; DLB 173; DLBY 1987; EWL 3; EXPS; INT CANR-31; MAL 5; MTCW 1, 2; MTFW 2005; NFS 4; RGAL 4; RGSF 2; SSFS 3, 8, 20; TCLE 1:2; YAW

Mason, Ernst
See Pohl, Frederik

Mason, Hunni B.
See Sternheim, (William Adolf) Carl

Mason, Lee W.
See Malzberg, Barry N(athaniel)

Mason, Nick 1945- .... **CLC 35**

Mason, Tally
See Derleth, August (William)

Mass, Anna .... **CLC 59**

Mass, William
See Gibson, William

Massinger, Philip 1583-1640 .... **LC 70**
See also BRWS 11; DLB 58; RGEL 2

Master Lao
See Lao Tzu

Masters, Edgar Lee 1868-1950 ...... **PC 1, 36; TCLC 2, 25; WLCS**
See also AMWS 1; CA 104; 133; CDALB 1865-1917; DA; DAC; DAM MST, POET; DLB 54; EWL 3; EXPP; MAL 5; MTCW 1, 2; MTFW 2005; RGAL 4; TUS; WP

Masters, Hilary 1928- .... **CLC 48**
See also CA 25-28R, 217; CAAE 217; CANR 13, 47, 97; CN 6, 7; DLB 244

Mastrosimone, William 1947- .... **CLC 36**
See also CA 186; CAD; CD 5, 6

Mathe, Albert
See Camus, Albert

Mather, Cotton 1663-1728 .... **LC 38**
See also AMWS 2; CDALB 1640-1865; DLB 24, 30, 140; RGAL 4; TUS

Mather, Increase 1639-1723 .... **LC 38**
See also DLB 24

Matheson, Richard (Burton) 1926- .. **CLC 37**
See also AAYA 31; CA 97-100; CANR 88, 99; DLB 8, 44; HGG; INT CA-97-100; SCFW 1, 2; SFW 4; SUFW 2

Mathews, Harry (Burchell) 1930- ..... **CLC 6, 52**
See also CA 21-24R; CAAS 6; CANR 18, 40, 98; CN 5, 6, 7

McFadden, David 1940- .... **CLC 48**
See also CA 104; CP 1, 2, 3, 4, 5, 6, 7; DLB
60; INT CA-104

McFarland, Dennis 1950- .... **CLC 65**
See also CA 165; CANR 110

McGahern, John 1934- ... **CLC 5, 9, 48, 156;
SSC 17**
See also CA 17-20R; CANR 29, 68, 113;
CN 1, 2, 3, 4, 5, 6, 7; DLB 14, 231, 319;
MTCW 1

McGinley, Patrick (Anthony) 1937- . **CLC 41**
See also CA 120; 127; CANR 56; INT CA-
127

McGinley, Phyllis 1905-1978 .... **CLC 14**
See also CA 9-12R; 77-80; CANR 19; CP
1, 2; CWRI 5; DLB 11, 48; MAL 5; PFS
9, 13; SATA 2, 44; SATA-Obit 24

McGinniss, Joe 1942- .... **CLC 32**
See also AITN 2; BEST 89:2; CA 25-28R;
CANR 26, 70; CPW; DLB 185; INT
CANR-26

McGivern, Maureen Daly
See Daly, Maureen

McGrath, Patrick 1950- .... **CLC 55**
See also CA 136; CANR 65; CN 5, 6, 7;
DLB 231; HGG; SUFW 2

McGrath, Thomas (Matthew)
1916-1990 .... **CLC 28, 59**
See also AMWS 10; CA 9-12R; 132; CANR
6, 33, 95; CP 1, 2, 3, 4; DAM POET;
MAL 5; MTCW 1; SATA 41; SATA-Obit
66

McGuane, Thomas (Francis III)
1939- .... **CLC 3, 7, 18, 45, 127**
See also AITN 2; BPFB 2; CA 49-52;
CANR 5, 24, 49, 94; CN 2, 3, 4, 5, 6, 7;
DLB 2, 212; DLBY 1980; EWL 3; INT
CANR-24; MAL 5; MTCW 1; MTFW
2005; TCWW 1, 2

McGuckian, Medbh 1950- .... **CLC 48, 174;
PC 27**
See also BRWS 5; CA 143; CP 4, 5, 6, 7;
CWP; DAM POET; DLB 40

McHale, Tom 1942(?)-1982 .... **CLC 3, 5**
See also AITN 1; CA 77-80; 106; CN 1, 2,
3

McHugh, Heather 1948- .... **PC 61**
See also CA 69-72; CANR 11, 28, 55, 92;
CP 4, 5, 6, 7; CWP

McIlvanney, William 1936- .... **CLC 42**
See also CA 25-28R; CANR 61; CMW 4;
DLB 14, 207

McIlwraith, Maureen Mollie Hunter
See Hunter, Mollie
See also SATA 2

McInerney, Jay 1955- .... **CLC 34, 112**
See also AAYA 18; BPFB 2; CA 116; 123;
CANR 45, 68, 116; CN 5, 6, 7; CPW;
DA3; DAM POP; DLB 292; INT CA-123;
MAL 5; MTCW 2; MTFW 2005

McIntyre, Vonda N(eel) 1948- .... **CLC 18**
See also CA 81-84; CANR 17, 34, 69;
MTCW 1; SFW 4; YAW

McKay, Claude .... **BLC 3; HR 1:3; PC 2;
TCLC 7, 41; WLC**
See McKay, Festus Claudius
See also AFAW 1, 2; AMWS 10; DAB;
DLB 4, 45, 51, 117; EWL 3; EXPP; GLL
2; LAIT 3; LMFS 2; MAL 5; PAB; PFS
4; RGAL 4; WP

McKay, Festus Claudius 1889-1948
See McKay, Claude
See also BW 1, 3; CA 104; 124; CANR 73;
DA; DAC; DAM MST, MULT, NOV,
POET; MTCW 1, 2; MTFW 2005; TUS

McKuen, Rod 1933- .... **CLC 1, 3**
See also AITN 1; CA 41-44R; CANR 40;
CP 1

McLoughlin, R. B.
See Mencken, H(enry) L(ouis)

McLuhan, (Herbert) Marshall
1911-1980 .... **CLC 37, 83**
See also CA 9-12R; 102; CANR 12, 34, 61;
DLB 88; INT CANR-12; MTCW 1, 2;
MTFW 2005

McManus, Declan Patrick Aloysius
See Costello, Elvis

McMillan, Terry (L.) 1951- . **BLCS; CLC 50,
61, 112**
See also AAYA 21; AMWS 13; BPFB 2;
BW 2, 3; CA 140; CANR 60, 104, 131;
CN 7; CPW; DA3; DAM MULT, NOV,
POP; MAL 5; MTCW 2; MTFW 2005;
RGAL 4; YAW

McMurtry, Larry 1936- .... **CLC 2, 3, 7, 11,
27, 44, 127**
See also AAYA 15; AITN 2; AMWS 5;
BEST 89:2; BPFB 2; CA 5-8R; CANR
19, 43, 64, 103; CDALB 1968-1988; CN
2, 3, 4, 5, 6, 7; CPW; CSW; DA3; DAM
NOV, POP; DLB 2, 143, 256; DLBY
1980, 1987; EWL 3; MAL 5; MTCW 1,
2; MTFW 2005; RGAL 4; TCWW 1, 2

McNally, T. M. 1961- .... **CLC 82**

McNally, Terrence 1939- ... **CLC 4, 7, 41, 91;
DC 27**
See also AAYA 62; AMWS 13; CA 45-48;
CAD; CANR 2, 56, 116; CD 5, 6; DA3;
DAM DRAM; DFS 16, 19; DLB 7, 249;
EWL 3; GLL 1; MTCW 2; MTFW 2005

McNamer, Deirdre 1950- .... **CLC 70**

McNeal, Tom .... **CLC 119**

McNeile, Herman Cyril 1888-1937
See Sapper
See also CA 184; CMW 4; DLB 77

McNickle, (William) D'Arcy
1904-1977 .... **CLC 89; NNAL**
See also CA 9-12R; 85-88; CANR 5, 45;
DAM MULT; DLB 175, 212; RGAL 4;
SATA-Obit 22; TCWW 1, 2

McPhee, John (Angus) 1931- .... **CLC 36**
See also AAYA 61; AMWS 3; ANW; BEST
90:1; CA 65-68; CANR 20, 46, 64, 69,
121; CPW; DLB 185, 275; MTCW 1, 2;
MTFW 2005; TUS

McPherson, James Alan 1943- . **BLCS; CLC
19, 77**
See also BW 1, 3; CA 25-28R; CAAS 17;
CANR 24, 74, 140; CN 3, 4, 5, 6; CSW;
DLB 38, 244; EWL 3; MTCW 1, 2;
MTFW 2005; RGAL 4; RGSF 2

McPherson, William (Alexander)
1933- .... **CLC 34**
See also CA 69-72; CANR 28; INT
CANR-28

McTaggart, J. McT. Ellis
See McTaggart, John McTaggart Ellis

McTaggart, John McTaggart Ellis
1866-1925 .... **TCLC 105**
See also CA 120; DLB 262

Mead, George Herbert 1863-1931 . **TCLC 89**
See also CA 212; DLB 270

Mead, Margaret 1901-1978 .... **CLC 37**
See also AITN 1; CA 1-4R; 81-84; CANR
4; DA3; FW; MTCW 1, 2; SATA-Obit 20

Meaker, Marijane (Agnes) 1927-
See Kerr, M. E.
See also CA 107; CANR 37, 63, 145; INT
CA-107; JRDA; MAICYA 1, 2; MAIC-
YAS 1; MTCW 1; SATA 20, 61, 99, 160;
SATA-Essay 111; YAW

Medoff, Mark (Howard) 1940- .... **CLC 6, 23**
See also AITN 1; CA 53-56; CAD; CANR
5; CD 5, 6; DAM DRAM; DFS 4; DLB
7; INT CANR-5

Medvedev, P. N.
See Bakhtin, Mikhail Mikhailovich

Meged, Aharon
See Megged, Aharon

Meged, Aron
See Megged, Aharon

Megged, Aharon 1920- .... **CLC 9**
See also CA 49-52; CAAS 13; CANR 1,
140; EWL 3

Mehta, Deepa 1950- .... **CLC 208**

Mehta, Gita 1943- .... **CLC 179**
See also CA 225; CN 7; DNFS 2

Mehta, Ved (Parkash) 1934- .... **CLC 37**
See also CA 1-4R, 212; CAAE 212; CANR
2, 23, 69; MTCW 1; MTFW 2005

Melanchthon, Philipp 1497-1560 .... **LC 90**
See also DLB 179

Melanter
See Blackmore, R(ichard) D(oddridge)

Meleager c. 140B.C.-c. 70B.C. ...... **CMLC 53**

Melies, Georges 1861-1938 .... **TCLC 81**

Melikow, Loris
See Hofmannsthal, Hugo von

Melmoth, Sebastian
See Wilde, Oscar (Fingal O'Flahertie Wills)

Melo Neto, Joao Cabral de
See Cabral de Melo Neto, Joao
See also CWW 2; EWL 3

Meltzer, Milton 1915- .... **CLC 26**
See also AAYA 8, 45; BYA 2, 6; CA 13-
16R; CANR 38, 92, 107; CLR 13; DLB
61; JRDA; MAICYA 1, 2; SAAS 1; SATA
1, 50, 80, 128; SATA-Essay 124; WYA;
YAW

Melville, Herman 1819-1891 ..... **NCLC 3, 12,
29, 45, 49, 91, 93, 123, 157; SSC 1, 17,
46; WLC**
See also AAYA 25; AMW; AMWR 1;
CDALB 1640-1865; DA; DA3; DAB;
DAC; DAM MST, NOV; DLB 3, 74, 250,
254; EXPN; EXPS; GL 3; LAIT 1, 2; NFS
7, 9; RGAL 4; RGSF 2; SATA 59; SSFS
3; TUS

Members, Mark
See Powell, Anthony (Dymoke)

Membreno, Alejandro .... **CLC 59**

Menand, Louis 1952- .... **CLC 208**
See also CA 200

Menander c. 342B.C.-c. 293B.C. .... **CMLC 9,
51; DC 3**
See also AW 1; CDWLB 1; DAM DRAM;
DLB 176; LMFS 1; RGWL 2, 3

Menchu, Rigoberta 1959- .. **CLC 160; HLCS
2**
See also CA 175; CANR 135; DNFS 1;
WLIT 1

Mencken, H(enry) L(ouis)
1880-1956 .... **TCLC 13**
See also AMW; CA 105; 125; CDALB
1917-1929; DLB 11, 29, 63, 137, 222;
EWL 3; MAL 5; MTCW 1, 2; MTFW
2005; NCFS 4; RGAL 4; TUS

Mendelsohn, Jane 1965- .... **CLC 99**
See also CA 154; CANR 94

Mendoza, Inigo Lopez de
See Santillana, Inigo Lopez de Mendoza,
Marques de

Menton, Francisco de
See Chin, Frank (Chew, Jr.)

Mercer, David 1928-1980 .... **CLC 5**
See also CA 9-12R; 102; CANR 23; CBD;
DAM DRAM; DLB 13, 310; MTCW 1;
RGEL 2

Merchant, Paul
See Ellison, Harlan (Jay)

Meredith, George 1828-1909 .. **PC 60; TCLC
17, 43**
See also CA 117; 153; CANR 80; CDBLB
1832-1890; DAM POET; DLB 18, 35, 57,
159; RGEL 2; TEA

Meredith, William (Morris) 1919- .... **CLC 4, 13, 22, 55; PC 28**
See also CA 9-12R; CAAS 14; CANR 6, 40, 129; CP 1, 2, 3, 4, 5, 6, 7; DAM POET; DLB 5; MAL 5

Merezhkovsky, Dmitrii Sergeevich
See Merezhkovsky, Dmitry Sergeyevich
See also DLB 295

Merezhkovsky, Dmitry Sergeevich
See Merezhkovsky, Dmitry Sergeyevich
See also EWL 3

Merezhkovsky, Dmitry Sergeyevich 1865-1941 .... **TCLC 29**
See Merezhkovsky, Dmitrii Sergeevich; Merezhkovsky, Dmitry Sergeevich
See also CA 169

Merimee, Prosper 1803-1870 ... **NCLC 6, 65; SSC 7, 77**
See also DLB 119, 192; EW 6; EXPS; GFL 1789 to the Present; RGSF 2; RGWL 2, 3; SSFS 8; SUFW

Merkin, Daphne 1954- .... **CLC 44**
See also CA 123

Merleau-Ponty, Maurice 1908-1961 .... **TCLC 156**
See also CA 114; 89-92; DLB 296; GFL 1789 to the Present

Merlin, Arthur
See Blish, James (Benjamin)

Mernissi, Fatima 1940- .... **CLC 171**
See also CA 152; FW

Merrill, James (Ingram) 1926-1995 .. **CLC 2, 3, 6, 8, 13, 18, 34, 91; PC 28; TCLC 173**
See also AMWS 3; CA 13-16R; 147; CANR 10, 49, 63, 108; CP 1, 2, 3, 4; DA3; DAM POET; DLB 5, 165; DLBY 1985; EWL 3; INT CANR-10; MAL 5; MTCW 1, 2; MTFW 2005; PAB; PFS 23; RGAL 4

Merriman, Alex
See Silverberg, Robert

Merriman, Brian 1747-1805 .... **NCLC 70**

Merritt, E. B.
See Waddington, Miriam

Merton, Thomas (James) 1915-1968 . **CLC 1, 3, 11, 34, 83; PC 10**
See also AAYA 61; AMWS 8; CA 5-8R; 25-28R; CANR 22, 53, 111, 131; DA3; DLB 48; DLBY 1981; MAL 5; MTCW 1, 2; MTFW 2005

Merwin, W(illiam) S(tanley) 1927- ... **CLC 1, 2, 3, 5, 8, 13, 18, 45, 88; PC 45**
See also AMWS 3; CA 13-16R; CANR 15, 51, 112, 140; CP 1, 2, 3, 4, 5, 6, 7; DA3; DAM POET; DLB 5, 169; EWL 3; INT CANR-15; MAL 5; MTCW 1, 2; MTFW 2005; PAB; PFS 5, 15; RGAL 4

Metastasio, Pietro 1698-1782 .... **LC 115**
See also RGWL 2, 3

Metcalf, John 1938- .... **CLC 37; SSC 43**
See also CA 113; CN 4, 5, 6, 7; DLB 60; RGSF 2; TWA

Metcalf, Suzanne
See Baum, L(yman) Frank

Mew, Charlotte (Mary) 1870-1928 .. **TCLC 8**
See also CA 105; 189; DLB 19, 135; RGEL 2

Mewshaw, Michael 1943- .... **CLC 9**
See also CA 53-56; CANR 7, 47; DLBY 1980

Meyer, Conrad Ferdinand 1825-1898 .... **NCLC 81; SSC 30**
See also DLB 129; EW; RGWL 2, 3

Meyer, Gustav 1868-1932
See Meyrink, Gustav
See also CA 117; 190

Meyer, June
See Jordan, June (Meyer)

Meyer, Lynn
See Slavitt, David R(ytman)

Meyers, Jeffrey 1939- .... **CLC 39**
See also CA 73-76, 186; CAAE 186; CANR 54, 102; DLB 111

Meynell, Alice (Christina Gertrude Thompson) 1847-1922 .... **TCLC 6**
See also CA 104; 177; DLB 19, 98; RGEL 2

Meyrink, Gustav .... **TCLC 21**
See Meyer, Gustav
See also DLB 81; EWL 3

Michaels, Leonard 1933-2003 ..... **CLC 6, 25; SSC 16**
See also CA 61-64; 216; CANR 21, 62, 119; CN 3, 45, 6, 7; DLB 130; MTCW 1; TCLE 1:2

Michaux, Henri 1899-1984 .... **CLC 8, 19**
See also CA 85-88; 114; DLB 258; EWL 3; GFL 1789 to the Present; RGWL 2, 3

Micheaux, Oscar (Devereaux) 1884-1951 .... **TCLC 76**
See also BW 3; CA 174; DLB 50; TCWW 2

Michelangelo 1475-1564 .... **LC 12**
See also AAYA 43

Michelet, Jules 1798-1874 .... **NCLC 31**
See also EW 5; GFL 1789 to the Present

Michels, Robert 1876-1936 .... **TCLC 88**
See also CA 212

Michener, James A(lbert) 1907(?)-1997 .. **CLC 1, 5, 11, 29, 60, 109**
See also AAYA 27; AITN 1; BEST 90:1; BPFB 2; CA 5-8R; 161; CANR 21, 45, 68; CN 1, 2, 3, 4, 5, 6; CPW; DA3; DAM NOV, POP; DLB 6; MAL 5; MTCW 1, 2; MTFW 2005; RHW; TCWW 1, 2

Mickiewicz, Adam 1798-1855 . **NCLC 3, 101; PC 38**
See also EW 5; RGWL 2, 3

Middleton, (John) Christopher 1926- .... **CLC 13**
See also CA 13-16R; CANR 29, 54, 117; CP 1, 2, 3, 4, 5, 6, 7; DLB 40

Middleton, Richard (Barham) 1882-1911 .... **TCLC 56**
See also CA 187; DLB 156; HGG

Middleton, Stanley 1919- .... **CLC 7, 38**
See also CA 25-28R; CAAS 23; CANR 21, 46, 81; CN 1, 2, 3, 4, 5, 6, 7; DLB 14

Middleton, Thomas 1580-1627 ...... **DC 5; LC 33, 123**
See also BRW 2; DAM DRAM, MST; DFS 18, 22; DLB 58; RGEL 2

Migueis, Jose Rodrigues 1901-1980 . **CLC 10**
See also DLB 287

Mikszath, Kalman 1847-1910 .... **TCLC 31**
See also CA 170

Miles, Jack .... **CLC 100**
See also CA 200

Miles, John Russiano
See Miles, Jack

Miles, Josephine (Louise) 1911-1985 .... **CLC 1, 2, 14, 34, 39**
See also CA 1-4R; 116; CANR 2, 55; CP 1, 2, 3, 4; DAM POET; DLB 48; MAL 5; TCLE 1:2

Militant
See Sandburg, Carl (August)

Mill, Harriet (Hardy) Taylor 1807-1858 .... **NCLC 102**
See also FW

Mill, John Stuart 1806-1873 .... **NCLC 11, 58**
See also CDBLB 1832-1890; DLB 55, 190, 262; FW 1; RGEL 2; TEA

Millar, Kenneth 1915-1983 .... **CLC 14**
See Macdonald, Ross
See also CA 9-12R; 110; CANR 16, 63, 107; CMW 4; CPW; DA3; DAM POP; DLB 2, 226; DLBD 6; DLBY 1983; MTCW 1, 2; MTFW 2005

Millay, E. Vincent
See Millay, Edna St. Vincent

Millay, Edna St. Vincent 1892-1950 ..... **PC 6, 61; TCLC 4, 49, 169; WLCS**
See Boyd, Nancy
See also AMW; CA 104; 130; CDALB 1917-1929; DA; DA3; DAB; DAC; DAM MST, POET; DLB 45, 249; EWL 3; EXPP; FL 1:6; MAL 5; MAWW; MTCW 1, 2; MTFW 2005; PAB; PFS 3, 17; RGAL 4; TUS; WP

Miller, Arthur 1915-2005 ..... **CLC 1, 2, 6, 10, 15, 26, 47, 78, 179; DC 1; WLC**
See also AAYA 15; AITN 1; AMW; AMWC 1; CA 1-4R; 236; CABS 3; CAD; CANR 2, 30, 54, 76, 132; CD 5, 6; CDALB 1941-1968; DA; DA3; DAB; DAC; DAM DRAM, MST; DFS 1, 3, 8; DLB 7, 266; EWL 3; LAIT 1, 4; LATS 1:2; MAL 5; MTCW 1, 2; MTFW 2005; RGAL 4; TUS; WYAS 1

Miller, Henry (Valentine) 1891-1980 .... **CLC 1, 2, 4, 9, 14, 43, 84; WLC**
See also AMW; BPFB 2; CA 9-12R; 97-100; CANR 33, 64; CDALB 1929-1941; CN 1, 2; DA; DA3; DAB; DAC; DAM MST, NOV; DLB 4, 9; DLBY 1980; EWL 3; MAL 5; MTCW 1, 2; MTFW 2005; RGAL 4; TUS

Miller, Hugh 1802-1856 .... **NCLC 143**
See also DLB 190

Miller, Jason 1939(?)-2001 .... **CLC 2**
See also AITN 1; CA 73-76; 197; CAD; CANR 130; DFS 12; DLB 7

Miller, Sue 1943- .... **CLC 44**
See also AMWS 12; BEST 90:3; CA 139; CANR 59, 91, 128; DA3; DAM POP; DLB 143

Miller, Walter M(ichael, Jr.) 1923-1996 .... **CLC 4, 30**
See also BPFB 2; CA 85-88; CANR 108; DLB 8; SCFW 1, 2; SFW 4

Millett, Kate 1934- .... **CLC 67**
See also AITN 1; CA 73-76; CANR 32, 53, 76, 110; DA3; DLB 246; FW; GLL 1; MTCW 1, 2; MTFW 2005

Millhauser, Steven (Lewis) 1943- .... **CLC 21, 54, 109; SSC 57**
See also CA 110; 111; CANR 63, 114, 133; CN 6, 7; DA3; DLB 2; FANT; INT CA-111; MAL 5; MTCW 2; MTFW 2005

Millin, Sarah Gertrude 1889-1968 ... **CLC 49**
See also CA 102; 93-96; DLB 225; EWL 3

Milne, A(lan) A(lexander) 1882-1956 .... **TCLC 6, 88**
See also BRWS 5; CA 104; 133; CLR 1, 26; CMW 4; CWRI 5; DA3; DAB; DAC; DAM MST; DLB 10, 77, 100, 160; FANT; MAICYA 1, 2; MTCW 1, 2; MTFW 2005; RGEL 2; SATA 100; WCH; YABC 1

Milner, Ron(ald) 1938-2004 ..... **BLC 3; CLC 56**
See also AITN 1; BW 1; CA 73-76; 230; CAD; CANR 24, 81; CD 5, 6; DAM MULT; DLB 38; MAL 5; MTCW 1

Milnes, Richard Monckton 1809-1885 .... **NCLC 61**
See also DLB 32, 184

Milosz, Czeslaw 1911-2004 .... **CLC 5, 11, 22, 31, 56, 82; PC 8; WLCS**
See also AAYA 62; CA 81-84; 230; CANR 23, 51, 91, 126; CDWLB 4; CWW 2;

DA3; DAM MST, POET; DLB 215; EW 13; EWL 3; MTCW 1, 2; MTFW 2005; PFS 16; RGWL 2, 3

Milton, John 1608-1674 ..... **LC 9, 43, 92; PC 19, 29; WLC**
See also AAYA 65; BRW 2; BRWR 2; CD-BLB 1660-1789; DA; DA3; DAB; DAC; DAM MST, POET; DLB 131, 151, 281; EFS 1; EXPP; LAIT 1; PAB; PFS 3, 17; RGEL 2; TEA; WLIT 3; WP

Min, Anchee 1957- .... **CLC 86**
See also CA 146; CANR 94, 137; MTFW 2005

Minehaha, Cornelius
See Wedekind, (Benjamin) Frank(lin)

Miner, Valerie 1947- .... **CLC 40**
See also CA 97-100; CANR 59; FW; GLL 2

Minimo, Duca
See D'Annunzio, Gabriele

Minot, Susan (Anderson) 1956- ...... **CLC 44, 159**
See also AMWS 6; CA 134; CANR 118; CN 6, 7

Minus, Ed 1938- .... **CLC 39**
See also CA 185

Mirabai 1498(?)-1550(?) .... **PC 48**

Miranda, Javier
See Bioy Casares, Adolfo
See also CWW 2

Mirbeau, Octave 1848-1917 .... **TCLC 55**
See also CA 216; DLB 123, 192; GFL 1789 to the Present

Mirikitani, Janice 1942- .... **AAL**
See also CA 211; DLB 312; RGAL 4

Mirk, John (?)-c. 1414 .... **LC 105**
See also DLB 146

Miro (Ferrer), Gabriel (Francisco Victor) 1879-1930 .... **TCLC 5**
See also CA 104; 185; DLB 322; EWL 3

Misharin, Alexandr .... **CLC 59**

Mishima, Yukio ... **CLC 2, 4, 6, 9, 27; DC 1; SSC 4; TCLC 161**
See Hiraoka, Kimitake
See also AAYA 50; BPFB 2; GLL 1; MJW; RGSF 2; RGWL 2, 3; SSFS 5, 12

Mistral, Frederic 1830-1914 .... **TCLC 51**
See also CA 122; 213; GFL 1789 to the Present

Mistral, Gabriela
See Godoy Alcayaga, Lucila
See also DLB 283; DNFS 1; EWL 3; LAW; RGWL 2, 3; WP

Mistry, Rohinton 1952- ... **CLC 71, 196; SSC 73**
See also BRWS 10; CA 141; CANR 86, 114; CCA 1; CN 6, 7; DAC; SSFS 6

Mitchell, Clyde
See Ellison, Harlan (Jay)

Mitchell, Emerson Blackhorse Barney 1945- .... **NNAL**
See also CA 45-48

Mitchell, James Leslie 1901-1935
See Gibbon, Lewis Grassic
See also CA 104; 188; DLB 15

Mitchell, Joni 1943- .... **CLC 12**
See also CA 112; CCA 1

Mitchell, Joseph (Quincy) 1908-1996 .... **CLC 98**
See also CA 77-80; 152; CANR 69; CN 1, 2, 3, 4, 5, 6; CSW; DLB 185; DLBY 1996

Mitchell, Margaret (Munnerlyn) 1900-1949 .... **TCLC 11, 170**
See also AAYA 23; BPFB 2; BYA 1; CA 109; 125; CANR 55, 94; CDALBS; DA3; DAM NOV, POP; DLB 9; LAIT 2; MAL 5; MTCW 1, 2; MTFW 2005; NFS 9; RGAL 4; RHW; TUS; WYAS 1; YAW

Mitchell, Peggy
See Mitchell, Margaret (Munnerlyn)

Mitchell, S(ilas) Weir 1829-1914 .... **TCLC 36**
See also CA 165; DLB 202; RGAL 4

Mitchell, W(illiam) O(rmond) 1914-1998 .... **CLC 25**
See also CA 77-80; 165; CANR 15, 43; CN 1, 2, 3, 4, 5, 6; DAC; DAM MST; DLB 88; TCLE 1:2

Mitchell, William (Lendrum) 1879-1936 .... **TCLC 81**
See also CA 213

Mitford, Mary Russell 1787-1855 ... **NCLC 4**
See also DLB 110, 116; RGEL 2

Mitford, Nancy 1904-1973 .... **CLC 44**
See also BRWS 10; CA 9-12R; CN 1; DLB 191; RGEL 2

Miyamoto, (Chujo) Yuriko 1899-1951 .... **TCLC 37**
See Miyamoto Yuriko
See also CA 170, 174

Miyamoto Yuriko
See Miyamoto, (Chujo) Yuriko
See also DLB 180

Miyazawa, Kenji 1896-1933 .... **TCLC 76**
See Miyazawa Kenji
See also CA 157; RGWL 3

Miyazawa Kenji
See Miyazawa, Kenji
See also EWL 3

Mizoguchi, Kenji 1898-1956 .... **TCLC 72**
See also CA 167

Mo, Timothy (Peter) 1950- .... **CLC 46, 134**
See also CA 117; CANR 128; CN 5, 6, 7; DLB 194; MTCW 1; WLIT 4; WWE 1

Modarressi, Taghi (M.) 1931-1997 ... **CLC 44**
See also CA 121; 134; INT CA-134

Modiano, Patrick (Jean) 1945- .... **CLC 18, 218**
See also CA 85-88; CANR 17, 40, 115; CWW 2; DLB 83, 299; EWL 3

Mofolo, Thomas (Mokopu) 1875(?)-1948 .... **BLC 3; TCLC 22**
See also AFW; CA 121; 153; CANR 83; DAM MULT; DLB 225; EWL 3; MTCW 2; MTFW 2005; WLIT 2

Mohr, Nicholasa 1938- .... **CLC 12; HLC 2**
See also AAYA 8, 46; CA 49-52; CANR 1, 32, 64; CLR 22; DAM MULT; DLB 145; HW 1, 2; JRDA; LAIT 5; LLW; MAICYA 2; MAICYAS 1; RGAL 4; SAAS 8; SATA 8, 97; SATA-Essay 113; WYA; YAW

Moi, Toril 1953- .... **CLC 172**
See also CA 154; CANR 102; FW

Mojtabai, A(nn) G(race) 1938- ..... **CLC 5, 9, 15, 29**
See also CA 85-88; CANR 88

Moliere 1622-1673 ..... **DC 13; LC 10, 28, 64; WLC**
See also DA; DA3; DAB; DAC; DAM DRAM, MST; DFS 13, 18, 20; DLB 268; EW 3; GFL Beginnings to 1789; LATS 1:1; RGWL 2, 3; TWA

Molin, Charles
See Mayne, William (James Carter)

Molnar, Ferenc 1878-1952 .... **TCLC 20**
See also CA 109; 153; CANR 83; CDWLB 4; DAM DRAM; DLB 215; EWL 3; RGWL 2, 3

Momaday, N(avarre) Scott 1934- ...... **CLC 2, 19, 85, 95, 160; NNAL; PC 25; WLCS**
See also AAYA 11, 64; AMWS 4; ANW; BPFB 2; BYA 12; CA 25-28R; CANR 14, 34, 68, 134; CDALBS; CN 2, 3, 4, 5, 6, 7; CPW; DA; DA3; DAB; DAC; DAM MST, MULT, NOV, POP; DLB 143, 175, 256; EWL 3; EXPP; INT CANR-14;

LAIT 4; LATS 1:2; MAL 5; MTCW 1, 2; MTFW 2005; NFS 10; PFS 2, 11; RGAL 4; SATA 48; SATA-Brief 30; TCWW 1, 2; WP; YAW

Monette, Paul 1945-1995 .... **CLC 82**
See also AMWS 10; CA 139; 147; CN 6; GLL 1

Monroe, Harriet 1860-1936 .... **TCLC 12**
See also CA 109; 204; DLB 54, 91

Monroe, Lyle
See Heinlein, Robert A(nson)

Montagu, Elizabeth 1720-1800 .... **NCLC 7, 117**
See also FW

Montagu, Mary (Pierrepont) Wortley 1689-1762 .... **LC 9, 57; PC 16**
See also DLB 95, 101; FL 1:1; RGEL 2

Montagu, W. H.
See Coleridge, Samuel Taylor

Montague, John (Patrick) 1929- ..... **CLC 13, 46**
See also CA 9-12R; CANR 9, 69, 121; CP 1, 2, 3, 4, 5, 6, 7; DLB 40; EWL 3; MTCW 1; PFS 12; RGEL 2; TCLE 1:2

Montaigne, Michel (Eyquem) de 1533-1592 .... **LC 8, 105; WLC**
See also DA; DAB; DAC; DAM MST; EW 2; GFL Beginnings to 1789; LMFS 1; RGWL 2, 3; TWA

Montale, Eugenio 1896-1981 ... **CLC 7, 9, 18; PC 13**
See also CA 17-20R; 104; CANR 30; DLB 114; EW 11; EWL 3; MTCW 1; PFS 22; RGWL 2, 3; TWA; WLIT 7

Montesquieu, Charles-Louis de Secondat 1689-1755 .... **LC 7, 69**
See also DLB 314; EW 3; GFL Beginnings to 1789; TWA

Montessori, Maria 1870-1952 ...... **TCLC 103**
See also CA 115; 147

Montgomery, (Robert) Bruce 1921(?)-1978
See Crispin, Edmund
See also CA 179; 104; CMW 4

Montgomery, L(ucy) M(aud) 1874-1942 .... **TCLC 51, 140**
See also AAYA 12; BYA 1; CA 108; 137; CLR 8, 91; DA3; DAC; DAM MST; DLB 92; DLBD 14; JRDA; MAICYA 1, 2; MTCW 2; MTFW 2005; RGEL 2; SATA 100; TWA; WCH; WYA; YABC 1

Montgomery, Marion H., Jr. 1925- .... **CLC 7**
See also AITN 1; CA 1-4R; CANR 3, 48; CSW; DLB 6

Montgomery, Max
See Davenport, Guy (Mattison, Jr.)

Montherlant, Henry (Milon) de 1896-1972 .... **CLC 8, 19**
See also CA 85-88; 37-40R; DAM DRAM; DLB 72, 321; EW 11; EWL 3; GFL 1789 to the Present; MTCW 1

Monty Python
See Chapman, Graham; Cleese, John (Marwood); Gilliam, Terry (Vance); Idle, Eric; Jones, Terence Graham Parry; Palin, Michael (Edward)
See also AAYA 7

Moodie, Susanna (Strickland) 1803-1885 .... **NCLC 14, 113**
See also DLB 99

Moody, Hiram (F. III) 1961-
See Moody, Rick
See also CA 138; CANR 64, 112; MTFW 2005

Moody, Minerva
See Alcott, Louisa May

Moody, Rick .... **CLC 147**
See Moody, Hiram (F. III)

Mott, Michael (Charles Alston)
1930- .... CLC 15, 34
See also CA 5-8R; CAAS 7; CANR 7, 29

Mountain Wolf Woman 1884-1960 . CLC 92;
NNAL
See also CA 144; CANR 90

Moure, Erin 1955- .... CLC 88
See also CA 113; CP 7; CWP; DLB 60

Mourning Dove 1885(?)-1936 .... NNAL
See also CA 144; CANR 90; DAM MULT;
DLB 175, 221

Mowat, Farley (McGill) 1921- .... CLC 26
See also AAYA 1, 50; BYA 2; CA 1-4R;
CANR 4, 24, 42, 68, 108; CLR 20; CPW;
DAC; DAM MST; DLB 68; INT CANR-
24; JRDA; MAICYA 1, 2; MTCW 1, 2;
MTFW 2005; SATA 3, 55; YAW

Mowatt, Anna Cora 1819-1870 ..... NCLC 74
See also RGAL 4

Moyers, Bill 1934- .... CLC 74
See also AITN 2; CA 61-64; CANR 31, 52

Mphahlele, Es'kia
See Mphahlele, Ezekiel
See also AFW; CDWLB 3; CN 4, 5, 6; DLB
125, 225; RGSF 2; SSFS 11

Mphahlele, Ezekiel 1919- ... BLC 3; CLC 25,
133
See Mphahlele, Es'kia
See also BW 2, 3; CA 81-84; CANR 26,
76; CN 1, 2, 3; DA3; DAM MULT; EWL
3; MTCW 2; MTFW 2005; SATA 119

Mqhayi, S(amuel) E(dward) K(rune Loliwe)
1875-1945 .... BLC 3; TCLC 25
See also CA 153; CANR 87; DAM MULT

Mrozek, Slawomir 1930- .... CLC 3, 13
See also CA 13-16R; CAAS 10; CANR 29;
CDWLB 4; CWW 2; DLB 232; EWL 3;
MTCW 1

Mrs. Belloc-Lowndes
See Lowndes, Marie Adelaide (Belloc)

Mrs. Fairstar
See Horne, Richard Henry Hengist

M'Taggart, John M'Taggart Ellis
See McTaggart, John McTaggart Ellis

Mtwa, Percy (?)- .... CLC 47
See also CD 6

Mueller, Lisel 1924- .... CLC 13, 51; PC 33
See also CA 93-96; CP 7; DLB 105; PFS 9,
13

Muggeridge, Malcolm (Thomas)
1903-1990 .... TCLC 120
See also AITN 1; CA 101; CANR 33, 63;
MTCW 1, 2

Muhammad 570-632 .... WLCS
See also DA; DAB; DAC; DAM MST;
DLB 311

Muir, Edwin 1887-1959 . PC 49; TCLC 2, 87
See Moore, Edward
See also BRWS 6; CA 104; 193; DLB 20,
100, 191; EWL 3; RGEL 2

Muir, John 1838-1914 .... TCLC 28
See also AMWS 9; ANW; CA 165; DLB
186, 275

Mujica Lainez, Manuel 1910-1984 ... CLC 31
See Lainez, Manuel Mujica
See also CA 81-84; 112; CANR 32; EWL
3; HW 1

Mukherjee, Bharati 1940- ..... AAL; CLC 53,
115; SSC 38
See also AAYA 46; BEST 89:2; CA 107,
232; CAAE 232; CANR 45, 72, 128; CN
5, 6, 7; DAM NOV; DLB 60, 218; DNFS
1, 2; EWL 3; FW; MAL 5; MTCW 1, 2;
MTFW 2005; RGAL 4; RGSF 2; SSFS 7;
TUS; WWE 1

Muldoon, Paul 1951- .... CLC 32, 72, 166
See also BRWS 4; CA 113; 129; CANR 52,
91; CP 2, 3, 4, 5, 6, 7; DAM POET; DLB
40; INT CA-129; PFS 7, 22; TCLE 1:2

Mulisch, Harry (Kurt Victor)
1927- .... CLC 42
See also CA 9-12R; CANR 6, 26, 56, 110;
CWW 2; DLB 299; EWL 3

Mull, Martin 1943- .... CLC 17
See also CA 105

Muller, Wilhelm .... NCLC 73

Mulock, Dinah Maria
See Craik, Dinah Maria (Mulock)
See also RGEL 2

Multatuli 1820-1887 .... NCLC 165
See also RGWL 2, 3

Munday, Anthony 1560-1633 .... LC 87
See also DLB 62, 172; RGEL 2

Munford, Robert 1737(?)-1783 .... LC 5
See also DLB 31

Mungo, Raymond 1946- .... CLC 72
See also CA 49-52; CANR 2

Munro, Alice (Anne) 1931- .... CLC 6, 10, 19,
50, 95; SSC 3; WLCS
See also AITN 2; BPFB 2; CA 33-36R;
CANR 33, 53, 75, 114; CCA 1; CN 1, 2,
3, 4, 5, 6, 7; DA3; DAC; DAM MST,
NOV; DLB 53; EWL 3; MTCW 1, 2;
MTFW 2005; RGEL 2; RGSF 2; SATA
29; SSFS 5, 13, 19; TCLE 1:2; WWE 1

Munro, H(ector) H(ugh) 1870-1916 .... WLC
See Saki
See also AAYA 56; CA 104; 130; CANR
104; CDBLB 1890-1914; DA; DA3;
DAB; DAC; DAM MST, NOV; DLB 34,
162; EXPS; MTCW 1, 2; MTFW 2005;
RGEL 2; SSFS 15

Murakami, Haruki 1949- .... CLC 150
See Murakami Haruki
See also CA 165; CANR 102, 146; MJW;
RGWL 3; SFW 4

Murakami Haruki
See Murakami, Haruki
See also CWW 2; DLB 182; EWL 3

Murasaki, Lady
See Murasaki Shikibu

Murasaki Shikibu 978(?)-1026(?) .. CMLC 1,
79
See also EFS 2; LATS 1:1; RGWL 2, 3

Murdoch, (Jean) Iris 1919-1999 ... CLC 1, 2,
3, 4, 6, 8, 11, 15, 22, 31, 51; TCLC 171
See also BRWS 1; CA 13-16R; 179; CANR
8, 43, 68, 103, 142; CBD; CDBLB 1960
to Present; CN 1, 2, 3, 4, 5, 6; CWD;
DA3; DAB; DAC; DAM MST, NOV;
DLB 14, 194, 233; EWL 3; INT CANR-8;
MTCW 1, 2; MTFW 2005; NFS 18;
RGEL 2; TCLE 1:2; TEA; WLIT 4

Murfree, Mary Noailles 1850-1922 .. SSC 22;
TCLC 135
See also CA 122; 176; DLB 12, 74; RGAL
4

Murnau, Friedrich Wilhelm
See Plumpe, Friedrich Wilhelm

Murphy, Richard 1927- .... CLC 41
See also BRWS 5; CA 29-32R; CP 1, 2, 3,
4, 5, 6, 7; DLB 40; EWL 3

Murphy, Sylvia 1937- .... CLC 34
See also CA 121

Murphy, Thomas (Bernard) 1935- ... CLC 51
See Murphy, Tom
See also CA 101

Murphy, Tom
See Murphy, Thomas (Bernard)
See also DLB 310

Murray, Albert L. 1916- .... CLC 73
See also BW 2; CA 49-52; CANR 26, 52,
78; CN 7; CSW; DLB 38; MTFW 2005

Murray, James Augustus Henry
1837-1915 .... TCLC 117

Murray, Judith Sargent
1751-1820 .... NCLC 63
See also DLB 37, 200

Murray, Les(lie Allan) 1938- .... CLC 40
See also BRWS 7; CA 21-24R; CANR 11,
27, 56, 103; CP 1, 2, 3, 4, 5, 6, 7; DAM
POET; DLB 289; DLBY 2001; EWL 3;
RGEL 2

Murry, J. Middleton
See Murry, John Middleton

Murry, John Middleton
1889-1957 .... TCLC 16
See also CA 118; 217; DLB 149

Musgrave, Susan 1951- .... CLC 13, 54
See also CA 69-72; CANR 45, 84; CCA 1;
CP 2, 3, 4, 5, 6, 7; CWP

Musil, Robert (Edler von)
1880-1942 .... SSC 18; TCLC 12, 68
See also CA 109; CANR 55, 84; CDWLB
2; DLB 81, 124; EW 9; EWL 3; MTCW
2; RGSF 2; RGWL 2, 3

Muske, Carol .... CLC 90
See Muske-Dukes, Carol (Anne)

Muske-Dukes, Carol (Anne) 1945-
See Muske, Carol
See also CA 65-68, 203; CAAE 203; CANR
32, 70; CWP

Musset, (Louis Charles) Alfred de
1810-1857 .... DC 27; NCLC 7, 150
See also DLB 192, 217; EW 6; GFL 1789
to the Present; RGWL 2, 3; TWA

Mussolini, Benito (Amilcare Andrea)
1883-1945 .... TCLC 96
See also CA 116

Mutanabbi, Al-
See al-Mutanabbi, Ahmad ibn al-Husayn
Abu al-Tayyib al-Jufi al-Kindi
See also WLIT 6

My Brother's Brother
See Chekhov, Anton (Pavlovich)

Myers, L(eopold) H(amilton)
1881-1944 .... TCLC 59
See also CA 157; DLB 15; EWL 3; RGEL
2

Myers, Walter Dean 1937- .. BLC 3; CLC 35
See also AAYA 4, 23; BW 2; BYA 6, 8, 11;
CA 33-36R; CANR 20, 42, 67, 108; CLR
4, 16, 35; DAM MULT, NOV; DLB 33;
INT CANR-20; JRDA; LAIT 5; MAICYA
1, 2; MAICYAS 1; MTCW 2; MTFW
2005; SAAS 2; SATA 41, 71, 109, 157;
SATA-Brief 27; WYA; YAW

Myers, Walter M.
See Myers, Walter Dean

Myles, Symon
See Follett, Ken(neth Martin)

Nabokov, Vladimir (Vladimirovich)
1899-1977 .... CLC 1, 2, 3, 6, 8, 11, 15,
23, 44, 46, 64; SSC 11, 86; TCLC 108;
WLC
See also AAYA 45; AMW; AMWC 1;
AMWR 1; BPFB 2; CA 5-8R; 69-72;
CANR 20, 102; CDALB 1941-1968; CN
1, 2; CP 2; DA; DA3; DAB; DAC; DAM
MST, NOV; DLB 2, 244, 278, 317; DLBD
3; DLBY 1980, 1991; EWL 3; EXPS;
LATS 1:2; MAL 5; MTCW 1, 2; MTFW
2005; NCFS 4; NFS 9; RGAL 4; RGSF
2; SSFS 6, 15; TUS

Naevius c. 265B.C.-201B.C. .... CMLC 37
See also DLB 211

Nagai, Kafu .... TCLC 51
See Nagai, Sokichi
See also DLB 180

Nagai, Sokichi 1879-1959
See Nagai, Kafu
See also CA 117

Nagy, Laszlo 1925-1978 .... CLC 7
See also CA 129; 112

Naidu, Sarojini 1879-1949 .... TCLC 80
See also EWL 3; RGEL 2

Naipaul, Shiva(dhar Srinivasa)
1945-1985 .... **CLC 32, 39; TCLC 153**
See also CA 110; 112; 116; CANR 33; CN
2, 3; DA3; DAM NOV; DLB 157; DLBY
1985; EWL 3; MTCW 1, 2; MTFW 2005

Naipaul, V(idiadhar) S(urajprasad)
1932- .... **CLC 4, 7, 9, 13, 18, 37, 105,
199; SSC 38**
See also BPFB 2; BRWS 1; CA 1-4R;
CANR 1, 33, 51, 91, 126; CDBLB 1960
to Present; CDWLB 3; CN 1, 2, 3, 4, 5,
6, 7; DA3; DAB; DAC; DAM MST,
NOV; DLB 125, 204, 207; DLBY 1985,
2001; EWL 3; LATS 1:2; MTCW 1, 2;
MTFW 2005; RGEL 2; RGSF 2; TWA;
WLIT 4; WWE 1

Nakos, Lilika 1903(?)-1989 .... **CLC 29**

Napoleon
See Yamamoto, Hisaye

Narayan, R(asipuram) K(rishnaswami)
1906-2001 .... **CLC 7, 28, 47, 121, 211;
SSC 25**
See also BPFB 2; CA 81-84; 196; CANR
33, 61, 112; CN 1, 2, 3, 4, 5, 6, 7; DA3;
DAM NOV; DNFS 1; EWL 3; MTCW 1,
2; MTFW 2005; RGEL 2; RGSF 2; SATA
62; SSFS 5; WWE 1

Nash, (Frediric) Ogden 1902-1971 . **CLC 23;
PC 21; TCLC 109**
See also CA 13-14; 29-32R; CANR 34, 61;
CAP 1; CP 1; DAM POET; DLB 11;
MAICYA 1, 2; MAL 5; MTCW 1, 2;
RGAL 4; SATA 2, 46; WP

Nashe, Thomas 1567-1601(?) .... **LC 41, 89**
See also DLB 167; RGEL 2

Nathan, Daniel
See Dannay, Frederic

Nathan, George Jean 1882-1958 .... **TCLC 18**
See also Hatteras, Owen
See also CA 114; 169; DLB 137; MAL 5

Natsume, Kinnosuke
See Natsume, Soseki

Natsume, Soseki 1867-1916 .... **TCLC 2, 10**
See also Natsume Soseki; Soseki
See also CA 104; 195; RGWL 2, 3; TWA

Natsume Soseki
See Natsume, Soseki
See also DLB 180; EWL 3

Natti, (Mary) Lee 1919-
See Kingman, Lee
See also CA 5-8R; CANR 2

Navarre, Marguerite de
See de Navarre, Marguerite

Naylor, Gloria 1950- ..... **BLC 3; CLC 28, 52,
156; WLCS**
See also AAYA 6, 39; AFAW 1, 2; AMWS
8; BW 2, 3; CA 107; CANR 27, 51, 74,
130; CN 4, 5, 6, 7; CPW; DA; DA3;
DAC; DAM MST, MULT, NOV, POP;
DLB 173; EWL 3; FW; MAL 5; MTCW
1, 2; MTFW 2005; NFS 4, 7; RGAL 4;
TCLE 1:2; TUS

Neal, John 1793-1876 .... **NCLC 161**
See also DLB 1, 59, 243; FW; RGAL 4

Neff, Debra .... **CLC 59**

Neihardt, John Gneisenau
1881-1973 .... **CLC 32**
See also CA 13-14; CANR 65; CAP 1; DLB
9, 54, 256; LAIT 2; TCWW 1, 2

Nekrasov, Nikolai Alekseevich
1821-1878 .... **NCLC 11**
See also DLB 277

Nelligan, Emile 1879-1941 .... **TCLC 14**
See also CA 114; 204; DLB 92; EWL 3

Nelson, Willie 1933- .... **CLC 17**
See also CA 107; CANR 114

Nemerov, Howard (Stanley)
1920-1991 .... **CLC 2, 6, 9, 36; PC 24;
TCLC 124**
See also AMW; CA 1-4R; 134; CABS 2;
CANR 1, 27, 53; CN 1, 2, 3; CP 1, 2, 3,
4; DAM POET; DLB 5, 6; DLBY 1983;
EWL 3; INT CANR-27; MAL 5; MTCW
1, 2; MTFW 2005; PFS 10, 14; RGAL 4

Neruda, Pablo 1904-1973 .. **CLC 1, 2, 5, 7, 9,
28, 62; HLC 2; PC 4, 64; WLC**
See also CA 19-20; 45-48; CANR 131; CAP
2; DA; DA3; DAB; DAC; DAM MST,
MULT, POET; DLB 283; DNFS 2; EWL
3; HW 1; LAW; MTCW 1, 2; MTFW
2005; PFS 11; RGWL 2, 3; TWA; WLIT
1; WP

Nerval, Gerard de 1808-1855 ... **NCLC 1, 67;
PC 13; SSC 18**
See also DLB 217; EW 6; GFL 1789 to the
Present; RGSF 2; RGWL 2, 3

Nervo, (Jose) Amado (Ruiz de)
1870-1919 .... **HLCS 2; TCLC 11**
See also CA 109; 131; DLB 290; EWL 3;
HW 1; LAW

Nesbit, Malcolm
See Chester, Alfred

Nessi, Pio Baroja y
See Baroja (y Nessi), Pio

Nestroy, Johann 1801-1862 .... **NCLC 42**
See also DLB 133; RGWL 2, 3

Netterville, Luke
See O'Grady, Standish (James)

Neufeld, John (Arthur) 1938- .... **CLC 17**
See also AAYA 11; CA 25-28R; CANR 11,
37, 56; CLR 52; MAICYA 1, 2; SAAS 3;
SATA 6, 81, 131; SATA-Essay 131; YAW

Neumann, Alfred 1895-1952 .... **TCLC 100**
See also CA 183; DLB 56

Neumann, Ferenc
See Molnar, Ferenc

Neville, Emily Cheney 1919- .... **CLC 12**
See also BYA 2; CA 5-8R; CANR 3, 37,
85; JRDA; MAICYA 1, 2; SAAS 2; SATA
1; YAW

Newbound, Bernard Slade 1930-
See Slade, Bernard
See also CA 81-84; CANR 49; CD 5; DAM
DRAM

Newby, P(ercy) H(oward)
1918-1997 .... **CLC 2, 13**
See also CA 5-8R; 161; CANR 32, 67; CN
1, 2, 3, 4, 5, 6; DAM NOV; DLB 15;
MTCW 1; RGEL 2

Newcastle
See Cavendish, Margaret Lucas

Newlove, Donald 1928- .... **CLC 6**
See also CA 29-32R; CANR 25

Newlove, John (Herbert) 1938- .... **CLC 14**
See also CA 21-24R; CANR 9, 25; CP 1, 2,
3, 4, 5, 6, 7

Newman, Charles (Hamilton) 1938- . **CLC 2,
8**
See also CA 21-24R; CANR 84; CN 3, 4,
5, 6

Newman, Edwin (Harold) 1919- ...... **CLC 14**
See also AITN 1; CA 69-72; CANR 5

Newman, John Henry 1801-1890 . **NCLC 38,
99**
See also BRWS 7; DLB 18, 32, 55; RGEL
2

Newton, (Sir) Isaac 1642-1727 ...... **LC 35, 53**
See also DLB 252

Newton, Suzanne 1936- .... **CLC 35**
See also BYA 7; CA 41-44R; CANR 14;
JRDA; SATA 5, 77

New York Dept. of Ed. .... **CLC 70**

Nexo, Martin Andersen
1869-1954 .... **TCLC 43**
See also CA 202; DLB 214; EWL 3

Nezval, Vitezslav 1900-1958 .... **TCLC 44**
See also CA 123; CDWLB 4; DLB 215;
EWL 3

Ng, Fae Myenne 1957(?)- .... **CLC 81**
See also BYA 11; CA 146

Ngema, Mbongeni 1955- .... **CLC 57**
See also BW 2; CA 143; CANR 84; CD 5,
6

Ngugi, James T(hiong'o) . **CLC 3, 7, 13, 182**
See Ngugi wa Thiong'o
See also CN 1, 2

Ngugi wa Thiong'o
See Ngugi wa Thiong'o
See also CD 3, 4, 5, 6, 7; DLB 125; EWL 3

Ngugi wa Thiong'o 1938- ... **BLC 3; CLC 36,
182**
See Ngugi, James T(hiong'o); Ngugi wa
Thiong'o
See also AFW; BRWS 8; BW 2; CA 81-84;
CANR 27, 58; CDWLB 3; DAM MULT,
NOV; DNFS 2; MTCW 1, 2; MTFW
2005; RGEL 2; WWE 1

Niatum, Duane 1938- .... **NNAL**
See also CA 41-44R; CANR 21, 45, 83;
DLB 175

Nichol, B(arrie) P(hillip) 1944-1988 . **CLC 18**
See also CA 53-56; CP 1, 2, 3, 4; DLB 53;
SATA 66

Nicholas of Cusa 1401-1464 .... **LC 80**
See also DLB 115

Nichols, John (Treadwell) 1940- .... **CLC 38**
See also AMWS 13; CA 9-12R, 190; CAAE
190; CAAS 2; CANR 6, 70, 121; DLBY
1982; LATS 1:2; MTFW 2005; TCWW 1,
2

Nichols, Leigh
See Koontz, Dean R.

Nichols, Peter (Richard) 1927- .... **CLC 5, 36,
65**
See also CA 104; CANR 33, 86; CBD; CD
5, 6; DLB 13, 245; MTCW 1

Nicholson, Linda ed. .... **CLC 65**

Ni Chuilleanain, Eilean 1942- .... **PC 34**
See also CA 126; CANR 53, 83; CP 7;
CWP; DLB 40

Nicolas, F. R. E.
See Freeling, Nicolas

Niedecker, Lorine 1903-1970 ..... **CLC 10, 42;
PC 42**
See also CA 25-28; CAP 2; DAM POET;
DLB 48

Nietzsche, Friedrich (Wilhelm)
1844-1900 .... **TCLC 10, 18, 55**
See also CA 107; 121; CDWLB 2; DLB
129; EW 7; RGWL 2, 3; TWA

Nievo, Ippolito 1831-1861 .... **NCLC 22**

Nightingale, Anne Redmon 1943-
See Redmon, Anne
See also CA 103

Nightingale, Florence 1820-1910 ... **TCLC 85**
See also CA 188; DLB 166

Nijo Yoshimoto 1320-1388 .... **CMLC 49**
See also DLB 203

Nik. T. O.
See Annensky, Innokenty (Fyodorovich)

Nin, Anais 1903-1977 ..... **CLC 1, 4, 8, 11, 14,
60, 127; SSC 10**
See also AITN 2; AMWS 10; BPFB 2; CA
13-16R; 69-72; CANR 22, 53; CN 1, 2;
DAM NOV, POP; DLB 2, 4, 152; EWL
3; GLL 2; MAL 5; MAWW; MTCW 1, 2;
MTFW 2005; RGAL 4; RGSF 2

Nisbet, Robert A(lexander)
1913-1996 .... **TCLC 117**
See also CA 25-28R; 153; CANR 17; INT
CANR-17

Nishida, Kitaro 1870-1945 .... **TCLC 83**

Nishiwaki, Junzaburo 1894-1982 .... **PC 15**
See Junzaburo, Nishiwaki
See also CA 194; 107; MJW; RGWL 3

Nissenson, Hugh 1933- .... **CLC 4, 9**
See also CA 17-20R; CANR 27, 108; CN
5, 6; DLB 28

Nister, Der
See Der Nister
See also EWL 3

Niven, Larry .... **CLC 8**
See Niven, Laurence Van Cott
See also AAYA 27; BPFB 2; BYA 10; DLB
8; SCFW 1, 2

Niven, Laurence Van Cott 1938-
See Niven, Larry
See also CA 21-24R, 207; CAAE 207;
CAAS 12; CANR 14, 44, 66, 113; CPW;
DAM POP; MTCW 1, 2; SATA 95; SFW
4

Nixon, Agnes Eckhardt 1927- .... **CLC 21**
See also CA 110

Nizan, Paul 1905-1940 .... **TCLC 40**
See also CA 161; DLB 72; EWL 3; GFL
1789 to the Present

Nkosi, Lewis 1936- .... **BLC 3; CLC 45**
See also BW 1, 3; CA 65-68; CANR 27,
81; CBD; CD 5, 6; DAM MULT; DLB
157, 225; WWE 1

Nodier, (Jean) Charles (Emmanuel)
1780-1844 .... **NCLC 19**
See also DLB 119; GFL 1789 to the Present

Noguchi, Yone 1875-1947 .... **TCLC 80**

Nolan, Christopher 1965- .... **CLC 58**
See also CA 111; CANR 88

Noon, Jeff 1957- .... **CLC 91**
See also CA 148; CANR 83; DLB 267;
SFW 4

Norden, Charles
See Durrell, Lawrence (George)

Nordhoff, Charles Bernard
1887-1947 .... **TCLC 23**
See also CA 108; 211; DLB 9; LAIT 1;
RHW 1; SATA 23

Norfolk, Lawrence 1963- .... **CLC 76**
See also CA 144; CANR 85; CN 6, 7; DLB
267

Norman, Marsha (Williams) 1947- . **CLC 28,
186; DC 8**
See also CA 105; CABS 3; CAD; CANR
41, 131; CD 5, 6; CSW; CWD; DAM
DRAM; DFS 2; DLB 266; DLBY 1984;
FW; MAL 5

Normyx
See Douglas, (George) Norman

Norris, (Benjamin) Frank(lin, Jr.)
1870-1902 .... **SSC 28; TCLC 24, 155**
See also AMW; AMWC 2; BPFB
2; CA 110; 160; CDALB 1865-1917; DLB
12, 71, 186; LMFS 2; NFS 12; RGAL 4;
TCWW 1, 2; TUS

Norris, Leslie 1921- .... **CLC 14**
See also CA 11-12; CANR 14, 117; CAP 1;
CP 1, 2, 3, 4, 5, 6, 7; DLB 27, 256

North, Andrew
See Norton, Andre

North, Anthony
See Koontz, Dean R.

North, Captain George
See Stevenson, Robert Louis (Balfour)

North, Captain George
See Stevenson, Robert Louis (Balfour)

North, Milou
See Erdrich, (Karen) Louise

Northrup, B. A.
See Hubbard, L(afayette) Ron(ald)

North Staffs
See Hulme, T(homas) E(rnest)

Northup, Solomon 1808-1863 ...... **NCLC 105**

Norton, Alice Mary
See Norton, Andre
See also MAICYA 1; SATA 1, 43

Norton, Andre 1912-2005 .... **CLC 12**
See Norton, Alice Mary
See also AAYA 14; BPFB 2; BYA 4, 10,
12; CA 1-4R; 237; CANR 68; CLR 50;
DLB 8, 52; JRDA; MAICYA 2; MTCW
1; SATA 91; SUFW 1, 2; YAW

Norton, Caroline 1808-1877 .... **NCLC 47**
See also DLB 21, 159, 199

Norway, Nevil Shute 1899-1960
See Shute, Nevil
See also CA 102; 93-96; CANR 85; MTCW
2

Norwid, Cyprian Kamil
1821-1883 .... **NCLC 17**
See also RGWL 3

Nosille, Nabrah
See Ellison, Harlan (Jay)

Nossack, Hans Erich 1901-1978 .... **CLC 6**
See also CA 93-96; 85-88; DLB 69; EWL 3

Nostradamus 1503-1566 .... **LC 27**

Nosu, Chuji
See Ozu, Yasujiro

Notenburg, Eleanora (Genrikhovna) von
See Guro, Elena (Genrikhovna)

Nova, Craig 1945- .... **CLC 7, 31**
See also CA 45-48; CANR 2, 53, 127

Novak, Joseph
See Kosinski, Jerzy (Nikodem)

Novalis 1772-1801 .... **NCLC 13**
See also CDWLB 2; DLB 90; EW 5; RGWL
2, 3

Novick, Peter 1934- .... **CLC 164**
See also CA 188

Novis, Emile
See Weil, Simone (Adolphine)

Nowlan, Alden (Albert) 1933-1983 ... **CLC 15**
See also CA 9-12R; CANR 5; CP 1, 2, 3;
DAC; DAM MST; DLB 53; PFS 12

Noyes, Alfred 1880-1958 ...... **PC 27; TCLC 7**
See also CA 104; 188; DLB 20; EXPP;
FANT; PFS 4; RGEL 2

Nugent, Richard Bruce
1906(?)-1987 .... **HR 1:3**
See also BW 1; CA 125; DLB 51; GLL 2

Nunn, Kem .... **CLC 34**
See also CA 159

Nussbaum, Martha Craven 1947- .. **CLC 203**
See also CA 134; CANR 102

Nwapa, Flora (Nwanzuruaha)
1931-1993 .... **BLCS; CLC 133**
See also BW 2; CA 143; CANR 83; CD-
WLB 3; CWRI 5; DLB 125; EWL 3;
WLIT 2

Nye, Robert 1939- .... **CLC 13, 42**
See also BRWS 10; CA 33-36R; CANR 29,
67, 107; CN 1, 2, 3, 4, 5, 6, 7; CP 1, 2, 3,
4, 5, 6, 7; CWRI 5; DAM NOV; DLB 14,
271; FANT; HGG; MTCW 1; RHW;
SATA 6

Nyro, Laura 1947-1997 .... **CLC 17**
See also CA 194

Oates, Joyce Carol 1938- .. **CLC 1, 2, 3, 6, 9,
11, 15, 19, 33, 52, 108, 134; SSC 6, 70;
WLC**
See also AAYA 15, 52; AITN 1; AMWS 2;
BEST 89:2; BPFB 2; BYA 11; CA 5-8R;
CANR 25, 45, 74, 113, 129; CDALB
1968-1988; CN 1, 2, 3, 4, 5, 6, 7; CP 7;
CPW; CWP; DA; DA3; DAB; DAC;
DAM MST, NOV, POP; DLB 2, 5, 130;
DLBY 1981; EWL 3; EXPS; FL 1:6; FW;
GL 3; HGG; INT CANR-25; LAIT 4;
MAL 5; MAWW; MTCW 1, 2; MTFW
2005; NFS 8; RGAL 4; RGSF 2; SATA
159; SSFS 1, 8, 17; SUFW 2; TUS

O'Brian, E. G.
See Clarke, Arthur C(harles)

O'Brian, Patrick 1914-2000 .... **CLC 152**
See also AAYA 55; CA 144; 187; CANR
74; CPW; MTCW 2; MTFW 2005; RHW

O'Brien, Darcy 1939-1998 .... **CLC 11**
See also CA 21-24R; 167; CANR 8, 59

O'Brien, Edna 1932- ..... **CLC 3, 5, 8, 13, 36,
65, 116; SSC 10, 77**
See also BRWS 5; CA 1-4R; CANR 6, 41,
65, 102; CDBLB 1960 to Present; CN 1,
2, 3, 4, 5, 6, 7; DA3; DAM NOV; DLB
14, 231, 319; EWL 3; FW; MTCW 1, 2;
MTFW 2005; RGSF 2; WLIT 4

O'Brien, Fitz-James 1828-1862 ..... **NCLC 21**
See also DLB 74; RGAL 4; SUFW

O'Brien, Flann .... **CLC 1, 4, 5, 7, 10, 47**
See O Nuallain, Brian
See also BRWS 2; DLB 231; EWL 3;
RGEL 2

O'Brien, Richard 1942- .... **CLC 17**
See also CA 124

O'Brien, (William) Tim(othy) 1946- . **CLC 7,
19, 40, 103, 211; SSC 74**
See also AAYA 16; AMWS 5; CA 85-88;
CANR 40, 58, 133; CDALBS; CN 5, 6,
7; CPW; DA3; DAM POP; DLB 152;
DLBD 9; DLBY 1980; LATS 1:2; MAL
5; MTCW 2; MTFW 2005; RGAL 4;
SSFS 5, 15; TCLE 1:2

Obstfelder, Sigbjoern 1866-1900 .... **TCLC 23**
See also CA 123

O'Casey, Sean 1880-1964 .... **CLC 1, 5, 9, 11,
15, 88; DC 12; WLCS**
See also BRW 7; CA 89-92; CANR 62;
CBD; CDBLB 1914-1945; DA3; DAB;
DAC; DAM DRAM, MST; DFS 19; DLB
10; EWL 3; MTCW 1, 2; MTFW 2005;
RGEL 2; TEA; WLIT 4

O'Cathasaigh, Sean
See O'Casey, Sean

Occom, Samson 1723-1792 .... **LC 60; NNAL**
See also DLB 175

Ochs, Phil(ip David) 1940-1976 .... **CLC 17**
See also CA 185; 65-68

O'Connor, Edwin (Greene)
1918-1968 .... **CLC 14**
See also CA 93-96; 25-28R; MAL 5

O'Connor, (Mary) Flannery
1925-1964 .... **CLC 1, 2, 3, 6, 10, 13, 15,
21, 66, 104; SSC 1, 23, 61, 82; TCLC
132; WLC**
See also AAYA 7; AMW; AMWR 2; BPFB
3; BYA 16; CA 1-4R; CANR 3, 41;
CDALB 1941-1968; DA; DA3; DAB;
DAC; DAM MST, NOV; DLB 2, 152;
DLBD 12; DLBY 1980; EWL 3; EXPS;
LAIT 5; MAL 5; MAWW; MTCW 1, 2;
MTFW 2005; NFS 3, 21; RGAL 4; RGSF
2; SSFS 2, 7, 10, 19; TUS

O'Connor, Frank .... **CLC 23; SSC 5**
See O'Donovan, Michael Francis
See also DLB 162; EWL 3; RGSF 2; SSFS
5

O'Dell, Scott 1898-1989 .... **CLC 30**
See also AAYA 3, 44; BPFB 3; BYA 1, 2,
3, 5; CA 61-64; 129; CANR 12, 30, 112;
CLR 1, 16; DLB 52; JRDA; MAICYA 1,
2; SATA 12, 60, 134; WYA; YAW

Odets, Clifford 1906-1963 ..... **CLC 2, 28, 98;
DC 6**
See also AMWS 2; CA 85-88; CAD; CANR
62; DAM DRAM; DFS 3, 17, 20; DLB 7,
26; EWL 3; MAL 5; MTCW 1, 2; MTFW
2005; RGAL 4; TUS

O'Doherty, Brian 1928- .... **CLC 76**
See also CA 105; CANR 108

O'Donnell, K. M.
See Malzberg, Barry N(athaniel)

O'Donnell, Lawrence
See Kuttner, Henry

O'Donovan, Michael Francis
1903-1966 .... **CLC 14**
See O'Connor, Frank
See also CA 93-96; CANR 84

Oe, Kenzaburo 1935- .. **CLC 10, 36, 86, 187; SSC 20**
See Oe Kenzaburo
See also CA 97-100; CANR 36, 50, 74, 126; DA3; DAM NOV; DLB 182; DLBY 1994; LATS 1:2; MJW; MTCW 1, 2; MTFW 2005; RGSF 2; RGWL 2, 3

Oe Kenzaburo
See Oe, Kenzaburo
See also CWW 2; EWL 3

O'Faolain, Julia 1932- .... **CLC 6, 19, 47, 108**
See also CA 81-84; CAAS 2; CANR 12, 61; CN 2, 3, 4, 5, 6, 7; DLB 14, 231, 319; FW; MTCW 1; RHW

O'Faolain, Sean 1900-1991 ...... **CLC 1, 7, 14, 32, 70; SSC 13; TCLC 143**
See also CA 61-64; 134; CANR 12, 66; CN 1, 2, 3, 4; DLB 15, 162; MTCW 1, 2; MTFW 2005; RGEL 2; RGSF 2

O'Flaherty, Liam 1896-1984 .... **CLC 5, 34; SSC 6**
See also CA 101; 113; CANR 35; CN 1, 2, 3; DLB 36, 162; DLBY 1984; MTCW 1, 2; MTFW 2005; RGEL 2; RGSF 2; SSFS 5, 20

Ogai
See Mori Ogai
See also MJW

Ogilvy, Gavin
See Barrie, J(ames) M(atthew)

O'Grady, Standish (James)
1846-1928 .... **TCLC 5**
See also CA 104; 157

O'Grady, Timothy 1951- .... **CLC 59**
See also CA 138

O'Hara, Frank 1926-1966 .... **CLC 2, 5, 13, 78; PC 45**
See also CA 9-12R; 25-28R; CANR 33; DA3; DAM POET; DLB 5, 16, 193; EWL 3; MAL 5; MTCW 1, 2; MTFW 2005; PFS 8, 12; RGAL 4; WP

O'Hara, John (Henry) 1905-1970 . **CLC 1, 2, 3, 6, 11, 42; SSC 15**
See also AMW; BPFB 3; CA 5-8R; 25-28R; CANR 31, 60; CDALB 1929-1941; DAM NOV; DLB 9, 86; DLBD 2; EWL 3; MAL 5; MTCW 1, 2; MTFW 2005; NFS 11; RGAL 4; RGSF 2

O Hehir, Diana 1922- .... **CLC 41**
See also CA 93-96

Ohiyesa
See Eastman, Charles A(lexander)

Okada, John 1923-1971 .... **AAL**
See also BYA 14; CA 212; DLB 312

Okigbo, Christopher (Ifenayichukwu)
1932-1967 .. **BLC 3; CLC 25, 84; PC 7; TCLC 171**
See also AFW; BW 1, 3; CA 77-80; CANR 74; CDWLB 3; DAM MULT, POET; DLB 125; EWL 3; MTCW 1, 2; MTFW 2005; RGEL 2

Okri, Ben 1959- .... **CLC 87**
See also AFW; BRWS 5; BW 2, 3; CA 130; 138; CANR 65, 128; CN 5, 6, 7; DLB 157, 231, 319; EWL 3; INT CA-138; MTCW 2; MTFW 2005; RGSF 2; SSFS 20; WLIT 2; WWE 1

Olds, Sharon 1942- .. **CLC 32, 39, 85; PC 22**
See also AMWS 10; CA 101; CANR 18, 41, 66, 98, 135; CP 7; CPW; DAM POET; DLB 120; MAL 5; MTCW 2; MTFW 2005; PFS 17

Oldstyle, Jonathan
See Irving, Washington

Olesha, Iurii
See Olesha, Yuri (Karlovich)
See also RGWL 2

Olesha, Iurii Karlovich
See Olesha, Yuri (Karlovich)
See also DLB 272

Olesha, Yuri (Karlovich) 1899-1960 . **CLC 8; SSC 69; TCLC 136**
See Olesha, Iurii; Olesha, Iurii Karlovich; Olesha, Yury Karlovich
See also CA 85-88; EW 11; RGWL 3

Olesha, Yury Karlovich
See Olesha, Yuri (Karlovich)
See also EWL 3

Oliphant, Mrs.
See Oliphant, Margaret (Oliphant Wilson)
See also SUFW

Oliphant, Laurence 1829(?)-1888 .. **NCLC 47**
See also DLB 18, 166

Oliphant, Margaret (Oliphant Wilson)
1828-1897 .... **NCLC 11, 61; SSC 25**
See Oliphant, Mrs.
See also BRWS 10; DLB 18, 159, 190; HGG; RGEL 2; RGSF 2

Oliver, Mary 1935- .... **CLC 19, 34, 98**
See also AMWS 7; CA 21-24R; CANR 9, 43, 84, 92, 138; CP 4, 5, 6, 7; CWP; DLB 5, 193; EWL 3; MTFW 2005; PFS 15

Olivier, Laurence (Kerr) 1907-1989 . **CLC 20**
See also CA 111; 150; 129

Olsen, Tillie 1912- ... **CLC 4, 13, 114; SSC 11**
See also AAYA 51; AMWS 13; BYA 11; CA 1-4R; CANR 1, 43, 74, 132; CDALBS; CN 2, 3, 4, 5, 6, 7; DA; DA3; DAB; DAC; DAM MST; DLB 28, 206; DLBY 1980; EWL 3; EXPS; FW; MAL 5; MTCW 1, 2; MTFW 2005; RGAL 4; RGSF 2; SSFS 1; TCLE 1:2; TCWW 2; TUS

Olson, Charles (John) 1910-1970 .. **CLC 1, 2, 5, 6, 9, 11, 29; PC 19**
See also AMWS 2; CA 13-16; 25-28R; CABS 2; CANR 35, 61; CAP 1; CP 1; DAM POET; DLB 5, 16, 193; EWL 3; MAL 5; MTCW 1, 2; RGAL 4; WP

Olson, Toby 1937- .... **CLC 28**
See also CA 65-68; CANR 9, 31, 84; CP 3, 4, 5, 6, 7

Olyesha, Yuri
See Olesha, Yuri (Karlovich)

Olympiodorus of Thebes c. 375-c. 430 .... **CMLC 59**

Omar Khayyam
See Khayyam, Omar
See also RGWL 2, 3

Ondaatje, (Philip) Michael 1943- .... **CLC 14, 29, 51, 76, 180; PC 28**
See also AAYA 66; CA 77-80; CANR 42, 74, 109, 133; CN 5, 6, 7; CP 1, 2, 3, 4, 5, 6, 7; DA3; DAB; DAC; DAM MST; DLB 60; EWL 3; LATS 1:2; LMFS 2; MTCW 2; MTFW 2005; PFS 8, 19; TCLE 1:2; TWA; WWE 1

Oneal, Elizabeth 1934-
See Oneal, Zibby
See also CA 106; CANR 28, 84; MAICYA 1, 2; SATA 30, 82; YAW

Oneal, Zibby .... **CLC 30**
See Oneal, Elizabeth
See also AAYA 5, 41; BYA 13; CLR 13; JRDA; WYA

O'Neill, Eugene (Gladstone)
1888-1953 ... **DC 20; TCLC 1, 6, 27, 49; WLC**
See also AAYA 54; AITN 1; AMW; AMWC 1; CA 110; 132; CAD; CANR 131; CDALB 1929-1941; DA; DA3; DAB;

DAC; DAM DRAM, MST; DFS 2, 4, 5, 6, 9, 11, 12, 16, 20; DLB 7; EWL 3; LAIT 3; LMFS 2; MAL 5; MTCW 1, 2; MTFW 2005; RGAL 4; TUS

Onetti, Juan Carlos 1909-1994 ... **CLC 7, 10; HLCS 2; SSC 23; TCLC 131**
See also CA 85-88; 145; CANR 32, 63; CD-WLB 3; CWW 2; DAM MULT, NOV; DLB 113; EWL 3; HW 1, 2; LAW; MTCW 1, 2; MTFW 2005; RGSF 2

O Nuallain, Brian 1911-1966
See O'Brien, Flann
See also CA 21-22; 25-28R; CAP 2; DLB 231; FANT; TEA

Ophuls, Max 1902-1957 .... **TCLC 79**
See also CA 113

Opie, Amelia 1769-1853 .... **NCLC 65**
See also DLB 116, 159; RGEL 2

Oppen, George 1908-1984 ..... **CLC 7, 13, 34; PC 35; TCLC 107**
See also CA 13-16R; 113; CANR 8, 82; CP 1, 2, 3; DLB 5, 165

Oppenheim, E(dward) Phillips
1866-1946 .... **TCLC 45**
See also CA 111; 202; CMW 4; DLB 70

Opuls, Max
See Ophuls, Max

Orage, A(lfred) R(ichard)
1873-1934 .... **TCLC 157**
See also CA 122

Origen c. 185-c. 254 .... **CMLC 19**

Orlovitz, Gil 1918-1973 .... **CLC 22**
See also CA 77-80; 45-48; CN 1; CP 1, 2; DLB 2, 5

O'Rourke, P(atrick) J(ake) 1947- .. **CLC 209**
See also CA 77-80; CANR 13, 41, 67, 111; CPW; DAM POP; DLB 185

Orris
See Ingelow, Jean

Ortega y Gasset, Jose 1883-1955 ...... **HLC 2; TCLC 9**
See also CA 106; 130; DAM MULT; EW 9; EWL 3; HW 1, 2; MTCW 1, 2; MTFW 2005

Ortese, Anna Maria 1914-1998 .... **CLC 89**
See also DLB 177; EWL 3

Ortiz, Simon J(oseph) 1941- ... **CLC 45, 208; NNAL; PC 17**
See also AMWS 4; CA 134; CANR 69, 118; CP 3, 4, 5, 6, 7; DAM MULT, POET; DLB 120, 175, 256; EXPP; MAL 5; PFS 4, 16; RGAL 4; TCWW 2

Orton, Joe ...... **CLC 4, 13, 43; DC 3; TCLC 157**
See Orton, John Kingsley
See also BRWS 5; CBD; CDBLB 1960 to Present; DFS 3, 6; DLB 13, 310; GLL 1; RGEL 2; TEA; WLIT 4

Orton, John Kingsley 1933-1967
See Orton, Joe
See also CA 85-88; CANR 35, 66; DAM DRAM; MTCW 1, 2; MTFW 2005

Orwell, George ...... **SSC 68; TCLC 2, 6, 15, 31, 51, 128, 129; WLC**
See Blair, Eric (Arthur)
See also BPFB 3; BRW 7; BYA 5; CDBLB 1945-1960; CLR 68; DAB; DLB 15, 98, 195, 255; EWL 3; EXPN; LAIT 4, 5; LATS 1:1; NFS 3, 7; RGEL 2; SCFW 1, 2; SFW 4; SSFS 4; TEA; WLIT 4; YAW

Osborne, David
See Silverberg, Robert

Osborne, George
See Silverberg, Robert

Osborne, John (James) 1929-1994 .... **CLC 1, 2, 5, 11, 45; TCLC 153; WLC**
See also BRWS 1; CA 13-16R; 147; CANR 21, 56; CBD; CDBLB 1945-1960; DA; DAB; DAC; DAM DRAM, MST; DFS 4, 19; DLB 13; EWL 3; MTCW 1, 2; MTFW 2005; RGEL 2

Osborne, Lawrence 1958- .... **CLC 50**
See also CA 189

Osbourne, Lloyd 1868-1947 .... **TCLC 93**

Osgood, Frances Sargent
1811-1850 .... **NCLC 141**
See also DLB 250

Oshima, Nagisa 1932- .... **CLC 20**
See also CA 116; 121; CANR 78

Oskison, John Milton
1874-1947 .... **NNAL; TCLC 35**
See also CA 144; CANR 84; DAM MULT;
DLB 175

Ossian c. 3rd cent. - .... **CMLC 28**
See Macpherson, James

Ossoli, Sarah Margaret (Fuller)
1810-1850 .... **NCLC 5, 50**
See Fuller, Margaret; Fuller, Sarah Margaret
See also CDALB 1640-1865; FW; LMFS 1;
SATA 25

Ostriker, Alicia (Suskin) 1937- .... **CLC 132**
See also CA 25-28R; CAAS 24; CANR 10,
30, 62, 99; CWP; DLB 120; EXPP; PFS
19

Ostrovsky, Aleksandr Nikolaevich
See Ostrovsky, Alexander
See also DLB 277

Ostrovsky, Alexander 1823-1886 .. **NCLC 30,
57**
See Ostrovsky, Aleksandr Nikolaevich

Otero, Blas de 1916-1979 .... **CLC 11**
See also CA 89-92; DLB 134; EWL 3

O'Trigger, Sir Lucius
See Horne, Richard Henry Hengist

Otto, Rudolf 1869-1937 .... **TCLC 85**

Otto, Whitney 1955- .... **CLC 70**
See also CA 140; CANR 120

Otway, Thomas 1652-1685 ... **DC 24; LC 106**
See also DAM DRAM; DLB 80; RGEL 2

Ouida .... **TCLC 43**
See De la Ramee, Marie Louise (Ouida)
See also DLB 18, 156; RGEL 2

Ouologuem, Yambo 1940- .... **CLC 146**
See also CA 111; 176

Ousmane, Sembene 1923- ... **BLC 3; CLC 66**
See Sembene, Ousmane
See also BW 1, 3; CA 117; 125; CANR 81;
CWW 2; MTCW 1

Ovid 43B.C.-17 .... **CMLC 7; PC 2**
See also AW 2; CDWLB 1; DA3; DAM
POET; DLB 211; PFS 22; RGWL 2, 3;
WP

Owen, Hugh
See Faust, Frederick (Schiller)

Owen, Wilfred (Edward Salter)
1893-1918 ... **PC 19; TCLC 5, 27; WLC**
See also BRW 6; CA 104; 141; CDBLB
1914-1945; DA; DAB; DAC; DAM MST,
POET; DLB 20; EWL 3; EXPP; MTCW
2; MTFW 2005; PFS 10; RGEL 2; WLIT
4

Owens, Louis (Dean) 1948-2002 .... **NNAL**
See also CA 137, 179; 207; CAAE 179;
CAAS 24; CANR 71

Owens, Rochelle 1936- .... **CLC 8**
See also CA 17-20R; CAAS 2; CAD;
CANR 39; CD 5, 6; CP 1, 2, 3, 4, 5, 6, 7;
CWD; CWP

Oz, Amos 1939- ...... **CLC 5, 8, 11, 27, 33, 54;
SSC 66**
See also CA 53-56; CANR 27, 47, 65, 113,
138; CWW 2; DAM NOV; EWL 3;
MTCW 1, 2; MTFW 2005; RGSF 2;
RGWL 3; WLIT 6

Ozick, Cynthia 1928- .... **CLC 3, 7, 28, 62,
155; SSC 15, 60**
See also AMWS 5; BEST 90:1; CA 17-20R;
CANR 23, 58, 116; CN 3, 4, 5, 6, 7;
CPW; DA3; DAM NOV, POP; DLB 28,

152, 299; DLBY 1982; EWL 3; EXPS;
INT CANR-23; MAL 5; MTCW 1, 2;
MTFW 2005; RGAL 4; RGSF 2; SSFS 3,
12

Ozu, Yasujiro 1903-1963 .... **CLC 16**
See also CA 112

Pabst, G. W. 1885-1967 .... **TCLC 127**

Pacheco, C.
See Pessoa, Fernando (Antonio Nogueira)

Pacheco, Jose Emilio 1939- .... **HLC 2**
See also CA 111; 131; CANR 65; CWW 2;
DAM MULT; DLB 290; EWL 3; HW 1,
2; RGSF 2

Pa Chin .... **CLC 18**
See Li Fei-kan
See also EWL 3

Pack, Robert 1929- .... **CLC 13**
See also CA 1-4R; CANR 3, 44, 82; CP 1,
2, 3, 4, 5, 6, 7; DLB 5; SATA 118

Padgett, Lewis
See Kuttner, Henry

Padilla (Lorenzo), Heberto
1932-2000 .... **CLC 38**
See also AITN 1; CA 123; 131; 189; CWW
2; EWL 3; HW 1

Page, James Patrick 1944-
See Page, Jimmy
See also CA 204

Page, Jimmy 1944- .... **CLC 12**
See Page, James Patrick

Page, Louise 1955- .... **CLC 40**
See also CA 140; CANR 76; CBD; CD 5,
6; CWD; DLB 233

Page, P(atricia) K(athleen) 1916- ...... **CLC 7,
18; PC 12**
See Cape, Judith
See also CA 53-56; CANR 4, 22, 65; CP 1,
2, 3, 4, 5, 6, 7; DAC; DAM MST; DLB
68; MTCW 1; RGEL 2

Page, Stanton
See Fuller, Henry Blake

Page, Stanton
See Fuller, Henry Blake

Page, Thomas Nelson 1853-1922 .... **SSC 23**
See also CA 118; 177; DLB 12, 78; DLBD
13; RGAL 4

Pagels, Elaine Hiesey 1943- .... **CLC 104**
See also CA 45-48; CANR 2, 24, 51; FW;
NCFS 4

Paget, Violet 1856-1935
See Lee, Vernon
See also CA 104; 166; GLL 1; HGG

Paget-Lowe, Henry
See Lovecraft, H(oward) P(hillips)

Paglia, Camille (Anna) 1947- .... **CLC 68**
See also CA 140; CANR 72, 139; CPW;
FW; GLL 2; MTCW 2; MTFW 2005

Paige, Richard
See Koontz, Dean R.

Paine, Thomas 1737-1809 .... **NCLC 62**
See also AMWS 1; CDALB 1640-1865;
DLB 31, 43, 73, 158; LAIT 1; RGAL 4;
RGEL 2; TUS

Pakenham, Antonia
See Fraser, Antonia (Pakenham)

Palamas, Costis
See Palamas, Kostes

Palamas, Kostes 1859-1943 .... **TCLC 5**
See Palamas, Kostis
See also CA 105; 190; RGWL 2, 3

Palamas, Kostis
See Palamas, Kostes
See also EWL 3

Palazzeschi, Aldo 1885-1974 .... **CLC 11**
See also CA 89-92; 53-56; DLB 114, 264;
EWL 3

Pales Matos, Luis 1898-1959 .... **HLCS 2**
See Pales Matos, Luis
See also DLB 290; HW 1; LAW

Paley, Grace 1922- .. **CLC 4, 6, 37, 140; SSC
8**
See also AMWS 6; CA 25-28R; CANR 13,
46, 74, 118; CN 2, 3, 4, 5, 6, 7; CPW;
DA3; DAM POP; DLB 28, 218; EWL 3;
EXPS; FW; INT CANR-13; MAL 5;
MAWW; MTCW 1, 2; MTFW 2005;
RGAL 4; RGSF 2; SSFS 3, 20

Palin, Michael (Edward) 1943- .... **CLC 21**
See Monty Python
See also CA 107; CANR 35, 109; SATA 67

Palliser, Charles 1947- .... **CLC 65**
See also CA 136; CANR 76; CN 5, 6, 7

Palma, Ricardo 1833-1919 .... **TCLC 29**
See also CA 168; LAW

Pamuk, Orhan 1952- .... **CLC 185**
See also CA 142; CANR 75, 127; CWW 2;
WLIT 6

Pancake, Breece Dexter 1952-1979
See Pancake, Breece D'J
See also CA 123; 109

Pancake, Breece D'J .... **CLC 29; SSC 61**
See Pancake, Breece Dexter
See also DLB 130

Panchenko, Nikolai .... **CLC 59**

Pankhurst, Emmeline (Goulden)
1858-1928 .... **TCLC 100**
See also CA 116; FW

Panko, Rudy
See Gogol, Nikolai (Vasilyevich)

Papadiamantis, Alexandros
1851-1911 .... **TCLC 29**
See also CA 168; EWL 3

Papadiamantopoulos, Johannes 1856-1910
See Moreas, Jean
See also CA 117

Papini, Giovanni 1881-1956 .... **TCLC 22**
See also CA 121; 180; DLB 264

Paracelsus 1493-1541 .... **LC 14**
See also DLB 179

Parasol, Peter
See Stevens, Wallace

Pardo Bazan, Emilia 1851-1921 .... **SSC 30**
See also EWL 3; FW; RGSF 2; RGWL 2, 3

Pareto, Vilfredo 1848-1923 .... **TCLC 69**
See also CA 175

Paretsky, Sara 1947- .... **CLC 135**
See also AAYA 30; BEST 90:3; CA 125;
129; CANR 59, 95; CMW 4; CPW; DA3;
DAM POP; DLB 306; INT CA-129;
MSW; RGAL 4

Parfenie, Maria
See Codrescu, Andrei

Parini, Jay (Lee) 1948- .... **CLC 54, 133**
See also CA 97-100, 229; CAAE 229;
CAAS 16; CANR 32, 87

Park, Jordan
See Kornbluth, C(yril) M.; Pohl, Frederik

Park, Robert E(zra) 1864-1944 ..... **TCLC 73**
See also CA 122; 165

Parker, Bert
See Ellison, Harlan (Jay)

Parker, Dorothy (Rothschild)
1893-1967 . **CLC 15, 68; PC 28; SSC 2;
TCLC 143**
See also AMWS 9; CA 19-20; 25-28R; CAP
2; DA3; DAM POET; DLB 11, 45, 86;
EXPP; FW; MAL 5; MAWW; MTCW 1,
2; MTFW 2005; PFS 18; RGAL 4; RGSF
2; TUS

Parker, Robert B(rown) 1932- .... **CLC 27**
See also AAYA 28; BEST 89:4; BPFB 3;
CA 49-52; CANR 1, 26, 52, 89, 128;
CMW 4; CPW; DAM NOV, POP; DLB
306; INT CANR-26; MSW; MTCW 1;
MTFW 2005

Parkin, Frank 1940- .... **CLC 43**
See also CA 147

PEPECE
See Prado (Calvo), Pedro

Pepys, Samuel 1633-1703 ... **LC 11, 58; WLC**
See also BRW 2; CDBLB 1660-1789; DA;
DA3; DAB; DAC; DAM MST; DLB 101,
213; NCFS 4; RGEL 2; TEA; WLIT 3

Percy, Thomas 1729-1811 .... **NCLC 95**
See also DLB 104

Percy, Walker 1916-1990 .... **CLC 2, 3, 6, 8,
14, 18, 47, 65**
See also AMWS 3; BPFB 3; CA 1-4R; 131;
CANR 1, 23, 64; CN 1, 2, 3, 4; CPW;
CSW; DA3; DAM NOV, POP; DLB 2;
DLBY 1980, 1990; EWL 3; MAL 5;
MTCW 1, 2; MTFW 2005; RGAL 4; TUS

Percy, William Alexander
1885-1942 .... **TCLC 84**
See also CA 163; MTCW 2

Perec, Georges 1936-1982 .... **CLC 56, 116**
See also CA 141; DLB 83, 299; EWL 3;
GFL 1789 to the Present; RGWL 3

**Pereda (y Sanchez de Porrua), Jose Maria
de** 1833-1906 .... **TCLC 16**
See also CA 117

Pereda y Porrua, Jose Maria de
See Pereda (y Sanchez de Porrua), Jose
Maria de

Peregoy, George Weems
See Mencken, H(enry) L(ouis)

Perelman, S(idney) J(oseph)
1904-1979 .. **CLC 3, 5, 9, 15, 23, 44, 49;
SSC 32**
See also AITN 1, 2; BPFB 3; CA 73-76;
89-92; CANR 18; DAM DRAM; DLB 11,
44; MTCW 1, 2; MTFW 2005; RGAL 4

Peret, Benjamin 1899-1959 .... **PC 33; TCLC
20**
See also CA 117; 186; GFL 1789 to the
Present

Peretz, Isaac Leib
See Peretz, Isaac Loeb
See also CA 201

Peretz, Isaac Loeb 1851(?)-1915 ...... **SSC 26;
TCLC 16**
See Peretz, Isaac Leib
See also CA 109

Peretz, Yitzkhok Leibush
See Peretz, Isaac Loeb

Perez Galdos, Benito 1843-1920 ..... **HLCS 2;
TCLC 27**
See Galdos, Benito Perez
See also CA 125; 153; EWL 3; HW 1;
RGWL 2, 3

Peri Rossi, Cristina 1941- .. **CLC 156; HLCS
2**
See also CA 131; CANR 59, 81; CWW 2;
DLB 145, 290; EWL 3; HW 1, 2

Perlata
See Peret, Benjamin

Perloff, Marjorie G(abrielle)
1931- .... **CLC 137**
See also CA 57-60; CANR 7, 22, 49, 104

Perrault, Charles 1628-1703 .... **LC 2, 56**
See also BYA 4; CLR 79; DLB 268; GFL
Beginnings to 1789; MAICYA 1, 2;
RGWL 2, 3; SATA 25; WCH

Perry, Anne 1938- .... **CLC 126**
See also CA 101; CANR 22, 50, 84; CMW
4; CN 6, 7; CPW; DLB 276

Perry, Brighton
See Sherwood, Robert E(mmet)

Perse, St.-John
See Leger, (Marie-Rene Auguste) Alexis
Saint-Leger

Perse, Saint-John
See Leger, (Marie-Rene Auguste) Alexis
Saint-Leger
See also DLB 258; RGWL 3

Persius 34-62 .... **CMLC 74**
See also AW 2; DLB 211; RGWL 2, 3

Perutz, Leo(pold) 1882-1957 .... **TCLC 60**
See also CA 147; DLB 81

Peseenz, Tulio F.
See Lopez y Fuentes, Gregorio

Pesetsky, Bette 1932- .... **CLC 28**
See also CA 133; DLB 130

Peshkov, Alexei Maximovich 1868-1936
See Gorky, Maxim
See also CA 105; 141; CANR 83; DA;
DAC; DAM DRAM, MST, NOV; MTCW
2; MTFW 2005

Pessoa, Fernando (Antonio Nogueira)
1888-1935 ..... **HLC 2; PC 20; TCLC 27**
See also CA 125; 183; DAM MULT; DLB
287; EW 10; EWL 3; RGWL 2, 3; WP

Peterkin, Julia Mood 1880-1961 ...... **CLC 31**
See also CA 102; DLB 9

Peters, Joan K(aren) 1945- .... **CLC 39**
See also CA 158; CANR 109

Peters, Robert L(ouis) 1924- .... **CLC 7**
See also CA 13-16R; CAAS 8; CP 1, 7;
DLB 105

Petofi, Sandor 1823-1849 .... **NCLC 21**
See also RGWL 2, 3

Petrakis, Harry Mark 1923- .... **CLC 3**
See also CA 9-12R; CANR 4, 30, 85; CN
1, 2, 3, 4, 5, 6, 7

Petrarch 1304-1374 .... **CMLC 20; PC 8**
See also DA3; DAM POET; EW 2; LMFS
1; RGWL 2, 3; WLIT 7

Petronius c. 20-66 .... **CMLC 34**
See also AW 2; CDWLB 1; DLB 211;
RGWL 2, 3

Petrov, Evgeny .... **TCLC 21**
See Kataev, Evgeny Petrovich

Petry, Ann (Lane) 1908-1997 .. **CLC 1, 7, 18;
TCLC 112**
See also AFAW 1, 2; BPFB 3; BW 1, 3;
BYA 2; CA 5-8R; 157; CAAS 6; CANR
4, 46; CLR 12; CN 1, 2, 3, 4, 5, 6; DLB
76; EWL 3; JRDA; LAIT 1; MAICYA 1,
2; MAICYAS 1; MTCW 1; RGAL 4;
SATA 5; SATA-Obit 94; TUS

Petursson, Halligrimur 1614-1674 .... **LC 8**

Peychinovich
See Vazov, Ivan (Minchov)

Phaedrus c. 15B.C.-c. 50 .... **CMLC 25**
See also DLB 211

Phelps (Ward), Elizabeth Stuart
See Phelps, Elizabeth Stuart
See also FW

Phelps, Elizabeth Stuart
1844-1911 .... **TCLC 113**
See Phelps (Ward), Elizabeth Stuart
See also DLB 74

Philips, Katherine 1632-1664 . **LC 30; PC 40**
See also DLB 131; RGEL 2

Philipson, Morris H. 1926- .... **CLC 53**
See also CA 1-4R; CANR 4

Phillips, Caryl 1958- .... **BLCS; CLC 96**
See also BRWS 5; BW 2; CA 141; CANR
63, 104, 140; CBD; CD 5, 6; CN 5, 6, 7;
DA3; DAM MULT; DLB 157; EWL 3;
MTCW 2; MTFW 2005; WLIT 4; WWE
1

Phillips, David Graham
1867-1911 .... **TCLC 44**
See also CA 108; 176; DLB 9, 12, 303;
RGAL 4

Phillips, Jack
See Sandburg, Carl (August)

Phillips, Jayne Anne 1952- .... **CLC 15, 33,
139; SSC 16**
See also AAYA 57; BPFB 3; CA 101;
CANR 24, 50, 96; CN 4, 5, 6, 7; CSW;
DLBY 1980; INT CANR-24; MTCW 1,
2; MTFW 2005; RGAL 4; RGSF 2; SSFS
4

Phillips, Richard
See Dick, Philip K(indred)

Phillips, Robert (Schaeffer) 1938- .... **CLC 28**
See also CA 17-20R; CAAS 13; CANR 8;
DLB 105

Phillips, Ward
See Lovecraft, H(oward) P(hillips)

Philostratus, Flavius c. 179-c.
244 .... **CMLC 62**

Piccolo, Lucio 1901-1969 .... **CLC 13**
See also CA 97-100; DLB 114; EWL 3

Pickthall, Marjorie L(owry) C(hristie)
1883-1922 .... **TCLC 21**
See also CA 107; DLB 92

Pico della Mirandola, Giovanni
1463-1494 .... **LC 15**
See also LMFS 1

Piercy, Marge 1936- .... **CLC 3, 6, 14, 18, 27,
62, 128; PC 29**
See also BPFB 3; CA 21-24R; 187; CAAE
187; CAAS 1; CANR 13, 43, 66, 111; CN
3, 4, 5, 6, 7; CP 1, 2, 3, 4, 5, 6, 7; CWP;
DLB 120, 227; EXPP; FW; MAL 5;
MTCW 1, 2; MTFW 2005; PFS 9, 22;
SFW 4

Piers, Robert
See Anthony, Piers

Pieyre de Mandiargues, Andre 1909-1991
See Mandiargues, Andre Pieyre de
See also CA 103; 136; CANR 22, 82; EWL
3; GFL 1789 to the Present

Pilnyak, Boris 1894-1938 . **SSC 48; TCLC 23**
See Vogau, Boris Andreyevich
See also EWL 3

Pinchback, Eugene
See Toomer, Jean

Pincherle, Alberto 1907-1990 ...... **CLC 11, 18**
See Moravia, Alberto
See also CA 25-28R; 132; CANR 33, 63,
142; DAM NOV; MTCW 1; MTFW 2005

Pinckney, Darryl 1953- .... **CLC 76**
See also BW 2, 3; CA 143; CANR 79

Pindar 518(?)B.C.-438(?)B.C. .... **CMLC 12;
PC 19**
See also AW 1; CDWLB 1; DLB 176;
RGWL 2

Pineda, Cecile 1942- .... **CLC 39**
See also CA 118; DLB 209

Pinero, Arthur Wing 1855-1934 .... **TCLC 32**
See also CA 110; 153; DAM DRAM; DLB
10; RGEL 2

Pinero, Miguel (Antonio Gomez)
1946-1988 .... **CLC 4, 55**
See also CA 61-64; 125; CAD; CANR 29,
90; DLB 266; HW 1; LLW

Pinget, Robert 1919-1997 .... **CLC 7, 13, 37**
See also CA 85-88; 160; CWW 2; DLB 83;
EWL 3; GFL 1789 to the Present

Pink Floyd
See Barrett, (Roger) Syd; Gilmour, David;
Mason, Nick; Waters, Roger; Wright, Rick

Pinkney, Edward 1802-1828 .... **NCLC 31**
See also DLB 248

Pinkwater, D. Manus
See Pinkwater, Daniel Manus

Pinkwater, Daniel
See Pinkwater, Daniel Manus

Pinkwater, Daniel M.
See Pinkwater, Daniel Manus

Pinkwater, Daniel Manus 1941- .... **CLC 35**
See also AAYA 1, 46; BYA 9; CA 29-32R;
CANR 12, 38, 89, 143; CLR 4; CSW;
FANT; JRDA; MAICYA 1, 2; SAAS 3;
SATA 8, 46, 76, 114, 158; SFW 4; YAW

Pinkwater, Manus
See Pinkwater, Daniel Manus

Pinsky, Robert 1940- .... **CLC 9, 19, 38, 94,
    121, 216; PC 27**
    See also AMWS 6; CA 29-32R; CAAS 4;
    CANR 58, 97, 138; CP 3, 4, 5, 6, 7; DA3;
    DAM POET; DLBY 1982, 1998; MAL 5;
    MTCW 2; MTFW 2005; PFS 18; RGAL
    4; TCLE 1:2
Pinta, Harold
    See Pinter, Harold
Pinter, Harold 1930- .. **CLC 1, 3, 6, 9, 11, 15,
    27, 58, 73, 199; DC 15; WLC**
    See also BRWR 1; BRWS 1; CA 5-8R;
    CANR 33, 65, 112, 145; CBD; CD 5, 6;
    CDBLB 1960 to Present; CP 1; DA; DA3;
    DAB; DAC; DAM DRAM, MST; DFS 3,
    5, 7, 14; DLB 13, 310; EWL 3; IDFW 3,
    4; LMFS 2; MTCW 1, 2; MTFW 2005;
    RGEL 2; TEA
Piozzi, Hester Lynch (Thrale)
    1741-1821 .... **NCLC 57**
    See also DLB 104, 142
Pirandello, Luigi 1867-1936 .. **DC 5; SSC 22;
    TCLC 4, 29, 172; WLC**
    See also CA 104; 153; CANR 103; DA;
    DA3; DAB; DAC; DAM DRAM, MST;
    DFS 4, 9; DLB 264; EW 8; EWL 3;
    MTCW 2; MTFW 2005; RGSF 2; RGWL
    2, 3; WLIT 7
Pirsig, Robert M(aynard) 1928- ... **CLC 4, 6,
    73**
    See also CA 53-56; CANR 42, 74; CPW 1;
    DA3; DAM POP; MTCW 1, 2; MTFW
    2005; SATA 39
Pisarev, Dmitrii Ivanovich
    See Pisarev, Dmitry Ivanovich
    See also DLB 277
Pisarev, Dmitry Ivanovich
    1840-1868 .... **NCLC 25**
    See Pisarev, Dmitrii Ivanovich
Pix, Mary (Griffith) 1666-1709 .... **LC 8**
    See also DLB 80
Pixerecourt, (Rene Charles) Guilbert de
    1773-1844 .... **NCLC 39**
    See also DLB 192; GFL 1789 to the Present
Plaatje, Sol(omon) T(shekisho)
    1878-1932 .... **BLCS; TCLC 73**
    See also BW 2, 3; CA 141; CANR 79; DLB
    125, 225
Plaidy, Jean
    See Hibbert, Eleanor Alice Burford
Planche, James Robinson
    1796-1880 .... **NCLC 42**
    See also RGEL 2
Plant, Robert 1948- .... **CLC 12**
Plante, David (Robert) 1940- . **CLC 7, 23, 38**
    See also CA 37-40R; CANR 12, 36, 58, 82;
    CN 2, 3, 4, 5, 6, 7; DAM NOV; DLBY
    1983; INT CANR-12; MTCW 1
Plath, Sylvia 1932-1963 ..... **CLC 1, 2, 3, 5, 9,
    11, 14, 17, 50, 51, 62, 111; PC 1, 37;
    WLC**
    See also AAYA 13; AMWR 2; AMWS 1;
    BPFB 3; CA 19-20; CANR 34, 101; CAP
    2; CDALB 1941-1968; DA; DA3; DAB;
    DAC; DAM MST, POET; DLB 5, 6, 152;
    EWL 3; EXPN; EXPP; FL 1:6; FW; LAIT
    4; MAL 5; MAWW; MTCW 1, 2; MTFW
    2005; NFS 1; PAB; PFS 1, 15; RGAL 4;
    SATA 96; TUS; WP; YAW
Plato c. 428B.C.-347B.C. .... **CMLC 8, 75;
    WLCS**
    See also AW 1; CDWLB 1; DA; DA3;
    DAB; DAC; DAM MST; DLB 176; LAIT
    1; LATS 1:1; RGWL 2, 3
Platonov, Andrei
    See Klimentov, Andrei Platonovich
Platonov, Andrei Platonovich
    See Klimentov, Andrei Platonovich
    See also DLB 272

Platonov, Andrey Platonovich
    See Klimentov, Andrei Platonovich
    See also EWL 3
Platt, Kin 1911- .... **CLC 26**
    See also AAYA 11; CA 17-20R; CANR 11;
    JRDA; SAAS 17; SATA 21, 86; WYA
Plautus c. 254B.C.-c. 184B.C. ...... **CMLC 24;
    DC 6**
    See also AW 1; CDWLB 1; DLB 211;
    RGWL 2, 3
Plick et Plock
    See Simenon, Georges (Jacques Christian)
Plieksans, Janis
    See Rainis, Janis
Plimpton, George (Ames)
    1927-2003 .... **CLC 36**
    See also AITN 1; CA 21-24R; 224; CANR
    32, 70, 103, 133; DLB 185, 241; MTCW
    1, 2; MTFW 2005; SATA 10; SATA-Obit
    150
Pliny the Elder c. 23-79 .... **CMLC 23**
    See also DLB 211
Pliny the Younger c. 61-c. 112 ...... **CMLC 62**
    See also AW 2; DLB 211
Plomer, William Charles Franklin
    1903-1973 .... **CLC 4, 8**
    See also AFW; BRWS 11; CA 21-22; CANR
    34; CAP 2; CN 1; CP 1, 2; DLB 20, 162,
    191, 225; EWL 3; MTCW 1; RGEL 2;
    RGSF 2; SATA 24
Plotinus 204-270 .... **CMLC 46**
    See also CDWLB 1; DLB 176
Plowman, Piers
    See Kavanagh, Patrick (Joseph)
Plum, J.
    See Wodehouse, P(elham) G(renville)
Plumly, Stanley (Ross) 1939- .... **CLC 33**
    See also CA 108; 110; CANR 97; CP 3, 4,
    5, 6, 7; DLB 5, 193; INT CA-110
Plumpe, Friedrich Wilhelm
    1888-1931 .... **TCLC 53**
    See also CA 112
Plutarch c. 46-c. 120 .... **CMLC 60**
    See also AW 2; CDWLB 1; DLB 176;
    RGWL 2, 3; TWA
Po Chu-i 772-846 .... **CMLC 24**
Podhoretz, Norman 1930- .... **CLC 189**
    See also AMWS 8; CA 9-12R; CANR 7,
    78, 135
Poe, Edgar Allan 1809-1849 ..... **NCLC 1, 16,
    55, 78, 94, 97, 117; PC 1, 54; SSC 1,
    22, 34, 35, 54, 88; WLC**
    See also AAYA 14; AMW; AMWC 1;
    AMWR 2; BPFB 3; BYA 5, 11; CDALB
    1640-1865; CMW 4; DA; DA3; DAB;
    DAC; DAM MST, POET; DLB 3, 59, 73,
    74, 248, 254; EXPP; EXPS; GL 3; HGG;
    LAIT 2; LATS 1:1; LMFS 1; MSW; PAB;
    PFS 1, 3, 9; RGAL 4; RGSF 2; SATA 23;
    SCFW 1, 2; SFW 4; SSFS 2, 4, 7, 8, 16;
    SUFW; TUS; WP; WYA
Poet of Titchfield Street, The
    See Pound, Ezra (Weston Loomis)
Pohl, Frederik 1919- .... **CLC 18; SSC 25**
    See also AAYA 24; CA 61-64, 188; CAAE
    188; CAAS 1; CANR 11, 37, 81, 140; CN
    1, 2, 3, 4, 5, 6; DLB 8; INT CANR-11;
    MTCW 1, 2; MTFW 2005; SATA 24;
    SCFW 1, 2; SFW 4
Poirier, Louis 1910-
    See Gracq, Julien
    See also CA 122; 126; CANR 141
Poitier, Sidney 1927- .... **CLC 26**
    See also AAYA 60; BW 1; CA 117; CANR
    94
Pokagon, Simon 1830-1899 .... **NNAL**
    See also DAM MULT
Polanski, Roman 1933- .... **CLC 16, 178**
    See also CA 77-80

Poliakoff, Stephen 1952- .... **CLC 38**
    See also CA 106; CANR 116; CBD; CD 5,
    6; DLB 13
Police, The
    See Copeland, Stewart (Armstrong); Sum-
    mers, Andrew James
Polidori, John William 1795-1821 . **NCLC 51**
    See also DLB 116; HGG
Poliziano, Angelo 1454-1494 .... **LC 120**
    See also WLIT 7
Pollitt, Katha 1949- .... **CLC 28, 122**
    See also CA 120; 122; CANR 66, 108;
    MTCW 1, 2; MTFW 2005
Pollock, (Mary) Sharon 1936- .... **CLC 50**
    See also CA 141; CANR 132; CD 5; CWD;
    DAC; DAM DRAM, MST; DFS 3; DLB
    60; FW
Pollock, Sharon 1936- .... **DC 20**
    See also CD 6
Polo, Marco 1254-1324 .... **CMLC 15**
    See also WLIT 7
Polonsky, Abraham (Lincoln)
    1910-1999 .... **CLC 92**
    See also CA 104; 187; DLB 26; INT CA-
    104
Polybius c. 200B.C.-c. 118B.C. ...... **CMLC 17**
    See also AW 1; DLB 176; RGWL 2, 3
Pomerance, Bernard 1940- .... **CLC 13**
    See also CA 101; CAD; CANR 49, 134;
    CD 5, 6; DAM DRAM; DFS 9; LAIT 2
Ponge, Francis 1899-1988 .... **CLC 6, 18**
    See also CA 85-88; 126; CANR 40, 86;
    DAM POET; DLBY 2002; EWL 3; GFL
    1789 to the Present; RGWL 2, 3
Poniatowska, Elena 1933- . **CLC 140; HLC 2**
    See also CA 101; CANR 32, 66, 107; CD-
    WLB 3; CWW 2; DAM MULT; DLB 113;
    EWL 3; HW 1, 2; LAWS 1; WLIT 1
Pontoppidan, Henrik 1857-1943 .... **TCLC 29**
    See also CA 170; DLB 300
Ponty, Maurice Merleau
    See Merleau-Ponty, Maurice
Poole, Josephine .... **CLC 17**
    See Helyar, Jane Penelope Josephine
    See also SAAS 2; SATA 5
Popa, Vasko 1922-1991 . **CLC 19; TCLC 167**
    See also CA 112; 148; CDWLB 4; DLB
    181; EWL 3; RGWL 2, 3
Pope, Alexander 1688-1744 ...... **LC 3, 58, 60,
    64; PC 26; WLC**
    See also BRW 3; BRWC 1; BRWR 1; CD-
    BLB 1660-1789; DA; DA3; DAB; DAC;
    DAM MST, POET; DLB 95, 101, 213;
    EXPP; PAB; PFS 12; RGEL 2; WLIT 3;
    WP
Popov, Evgenii Anatol'evich
    See Popov, Yevgeny
    See also DLB 285
Popov, Yevgeny .... **CLC 59**
    See Popov, Evgenii Anatol'evich
Poquelin, Jean-Baptiste
    See Moliere
Porete, Marguerite (?)-1310 .... **CMLC 73**
    See also DLB 208
Porphyry c. 233-c. 305 .... **CMLC 71**
Porter, Connie (Rose) 1959(?)- .... **CLC 70**
    See also AAYA 65; BW 2, 3; CA 142;
    CANR 90, 109; SATA 81, 129
Porter, Gene(va Grace) Stratton .. **TCLC 21**
    See Stratton-Porter, Gene(va Grace)
    See also BPFB 3; CA 112; CWRI 5; RHW
Porter, Katherine Anne 1890-1980 ... **CLC 1,
    3, 7, 10, 13, 15, 27, 101; SSC 4, 31, 43**
    See also AAYA 42; AITN 2; AMW; BPFB
    3; CA 1-4R; 101; CANR 1, 65; CDALBS;
    CN 1, 2; DA; DA3; DAB; DAC; DAM
    MST, NOV; DLB 4, 9, 102; DLBD 12;
    DLBY 1980; EWL 3; EXPS; LAIT 3;

MAL 5; MAWW; MTCW 1, 2; MTFW 2005; NFS 14; RGAL 4; RGSF 2; SATA 39; SATA-Obit 23; SSFS 1, 8, 11, 16; TCWW 2; TUS

Porter, Peter (Neville Frederick)
1929- .... **CLC 5, 13, 33**
See also CA 85-88; CP 1, 2, 3, 4, 5, 6, 7; DLB 40, 289; WWE 1

Porter, William Sydney 1862-1910
See Henry, O.
See also CA 104; 131; CDALB 1865-1917; DA; DA3; DAB; DAC; DAM MST; DLB 12, 78, 79; MAL 5; MTCW 1, 2; MTFW 2005; TUS; YABC 2

Portillo (y Pacheco), Jose Lopez
See Lopez Portillo (y Pacheco), Jose

Portillo Trambley, Estela 1927-1998 .. **HLC 2**
See Trambley, Estela Portillo
See also CANR 32; DAM MULT; DLB 209; HW 1

Posey, Alexander (Lawrence)
1873-1908 .... **NNAL**
See also CA 144; CANR 80; DAM MULT; DLB 175

Posse, Abel .... **CLC 70**

Post, Melville Davisson
1869-1930 .... **TCLC 39**
See also CA 110; 202; CMW 4

Potok, Chaim 1929-2002 ... **CLC 2, 7, 14, 26, 112**
See also AAYA 15, 50; AITN 1, 2; BPFB 3; BYA 1; CA 17-20R; 208; CANR 19, 35, 64, 98; CLR 92; CN 4, 5, 6; DA3; DAM NOV; DLB 28, 152; EXPN; INT CANR-19; LAIT 4; MTCW 1, 2; MTFW 2005; NFS 4; SATA 33, 106; SATA-Obit 134; TUS; YAW

Potok, Herbert Harold -2002
See Potok, Chaim

Potok, Herman Harold
See Potok, Chaim

Potter, Dennis (Christopher George)
1935-1994 .... **CLC 58, 86, 123**
See also BRWS 10; CA 107; 145; CANR 33, 61; CBD; DLB 233; MTCW 1

Pound, Ezra (Weston Loomis)
1885-1972 .. **CLC 1, 2, 3, 4, 5, 7, 10, 13, 18, 34, 48, 50, 112; PC 4; WLC**
See also AAYA 47; AMW; AMWR 1; CA 5-8R; 37-40R; CANR 40; CDALB 1917-1929; CP 1; DA; DA3; DAB; DAC; DAM MST, POET; DLB 4, 45, 63; DLBD 15; EFS 2; EWL 3; EXPP; LMFS 2; MAL 5; MTCW 1, 2; MTFW 2005; PAB; PFS 2, 8, 16; RGAL 4; TUS; WP

Povod, Reinaldo 1959-1994 .... **CLC 44**
See also CA 136; 146; CANR 83

Powell, Adam Clayton, Jr.
1908-1972 .... **BLC 3; CLC 89**
See also BW 1, 3; CA 102; 33-36R; CANR 86; DAM MULT

Powell, Anthony (Dymoke)
1905-2000 .... **CLC 1, 3, 7, 9, 10, 31**
See also BRW 7; CA 1-4R; 189; CANR 1, 32, 62, 107; CDBLB 1945-1960; CN 1, 2, 3, 4, 5, 6; DLB 15; EWL 3; MTCW 1, 2; MTFW 2005; RGEL 2; TEA

Powell, Dawn 1896(?)-1965 .... **CLC 66**
See also CA 5-8R; CANR 121; DLBY 1997

Powell, Padgett 1952- .... **CLC 34**
See also CA 126; CANR 63, 101; CSW; DLB 234; DLBY 01

Powell, (Oval) Talmage 1920-2000
See Queen, Ellery
See also CA 5-8R; CANR 2, 80

Power, Susan 1961- .... **CLC 91**
See also BYA 14; CA 160; CANR 135; NFS 11

Powers, J(ames) F(arl) 1917-1999 ..... **CLC 1, 4, 8, 57; SSC 4**
See also CA 1-4R; 181; CANR 2, 61; CN 1, 2, 3, 4, 5, 6; DLB 130; MTCW 1; RGAL 4; RGSF 2

Powers, John J(ames) 1945-
See Powers, John R.
See also CA 69-72

Powers, John R. .... **CLC 66**
See Powers, John J(ames)

Powers, Richard (S.) 1957- .... **CLC 93**
See also AMWS 9; BPFB 3; CA 148; CANR 80; CN 6, 7; MTFW 2005; TCLE 1:2

Pownall, David 1938- .... **CLC 10**
See also CA 89-92, 180; CAAS 18; CANR 49, 101; CBD; CD 5, 6; CN 4, 5, 6, 7; DLB 14

Powys, John Cowper 1872-1963 ... **CLC 7, 9, 15, 46, 125**
See also CA 85-88; CANR 106; DLB 15, 255; EWL 3; FANT; MTCW 1, 2; MTFW 2005; RGEL 2; SUFW

Powys, T(heodore) F(rancis)
1875-1953 .... **TCLC 9**
See also BRWS 8; CA 106; 189; DLB 36, 162; EWL 3; FANT; RGEL 2; SUFW

Pozzo, Modesta
See Fonte, Moderata

Prado (Calvo), Pedro 1886-1952 ... **TCLC 75**
See also CA 131; DLB 283; HW 1; LAW

Prager, Emily 1952- .... **CLC 56**
See also CA 204

Pratchett, Terry 1948- .... **CLC 197**
See also AAYA 19, 54; BPFB 3; CA 143; CANR 87, 126; CLR 64; CN 6, 7; CPW; CWRI 5; FANT; MTFW 2005; SATA 82, 139; SFW 4; SUFW 2

Pratolini, Vasco 1913-1991 .... **TCLC 124**
See also CA 211; DLB 177; EWL 3; RGWL 2, 3

Pratt, E(dwin) J(ohn) 1883(?)-1964 . **CLC 19**
See also CA 141; 93-96; CANR 77; DAC; DAM POET; DLB 92; EWL 3; RGEL 2; TWA

Premchand .... **TCLC 21**
See Srivastava, Dhanpat Rai
See also EWL 3

Prescott, William Hickling
1796-1859 .... **NCLC 163**
See also DLB 1, 30, 59, 235

Preseren, France 1800-1849 .... **NCLC 127**
See also CDWLB 4; DLB 147

Preussler, Otfried 1923- .... **CLC 17**
See also CA 77-80; SATA 24

Prevert, Jacques (Henri Marie)
1900-1977 .... **CLC 15**
See also CA 77-80; 69-72; CANR 29, 61; DLB 258; EWL 3; GFL 1789 to the Present; IDFW 3, 4; MTCW 1; RGWL 2, 3; SATA-Obit 30

Prevost, (Antoine Francois)
1697-1763 .... **LC 1**
See also DLB 314; EW 4; GFL Beginnings to 1789; RGWL 2, 3

Price, (Edward) Reynolds 1933- ... **CLC 3, 6, 13, 43, 50, 63, 212; SSC 22**
See also AMWS 6; CA 1-4R; CANR 1, 37, 57, 87, 128; CN 1, 2, 3, 4, 5, 6, 7; CSW; DAM NOV; DLB 2, 218, 278; EWL 3; INT CANR-37; MAL 5; MTFW 2005; NFS 18

Price, Richard 1949- .... **CLC 6, 12**
See also CA 49-52; CANR 3; CN 7; DLBY 1981

Prichard, Katharine Susannah
1883-1969 .... **CLC 46**
See also CA 11-12; CANR 33; CAP 1; DLB 260; MTCW 1; RGEL 2; RGSF 2; SATA 66

Priestley, J(ohn) B(oynton)
1894-1984 .... **CLC 2, 5, 9, 34**
See also BRW 7; CA 9-12R; 113; CANR 33; CDBLB 1914-1945; CN 1, 2, 3; DA3; DAM DRAM, NOV; DLB 10, 34, 77, 100, 139; DLBY 1984; EWL 3; MTCW 1, 2; MTFW 2005; RGEL 2; SFW 4

Prince 1958- .... **CLC 35**
See also CA 213

Prince, F(rank) T(empleton)
1912-2003 .... **CLC 22**
See also CA 101; 219; CANR 43, 79; CP 1, 2, 3, 4, 5, 6, 7; DLB 20

Prince Kropotkin
See Kropotkin, Peter (Aleksieevich)

Prior, Matthew 1664-1721 .... **LC 4**
See also DLB 95; RGEL 2

Prishvin, Mikhail 1873-1954 .... **TCLC 75**
See Prishvin, Mikhail Mikhailovich

Prishvin, Mikhail Mikhailovich
See Prishvin, Mikhail
See also DLB 272; EWL 3

Pritchard, William H(arrison)
1932- .... **CLC 34**
See also CA 65-68; CANR 23, 95; DLB 111

Pritchett, V(ictor) S(awdon)
1900-1997 ... **CLC 5, 13, 15, 41; SSC 14**
See also BPFB 3; BRWS 3; CA 61-64; 157; CANR 31, 63; CN 1, 2, 3, 4, 5, 6; DA3; DAM NOV; DLB 15, 139; EWL 3; MTCW 1, 2; MTFW 2005; RGEL 2; RGSF 2; TEA

Private 19022
See Manning, Frederic

Probst, Mark 1925- .... **CLC 59**
See also CA 130

Procaccino, Michael
See Cristofer, Michael

Proclus c. 412-485 .... **CMLC 81**

Prokosch, Frederic 1908-1989 ...... **CLC 4, 48**
See also CA 73-76; 128; CANR 82; CN 1, 2, 3, 4; CP 1, 2, 3, 4; DLB 48; MTCW 2

Propertius, Sextus c. 50B.C.-c. 16B.C. .... **CMLC 32**
See also AW 2; CDWLB 1; DLB 211; RGWL 2, 3

Prophet, The
See Dreiser, Theodore (Herman Albert)

Prose, Francine 1947- .... **CLC 45**
See also CA 109; 112; CANR 46, 95, 132; DLB 234; MTFW 2005; SATA 101, 149

Proudhon
See Cunha, Euclides (Rodrigues Pimenta) da

Proulx, Annie
See Proulx, E. Annie

Proulx, E. Annie 1935- .... **CLC 81, 158**
See also AMWS 7; BPFB 3; CA 145; CANR 65, 110; CN 6, 7; CPW 1; DA3; DAM POP; MAL 5; MTCW 2; MTFW 2005; SSFS 18

Proulx, Edna Annie
See Proulx, E. Annie

Proust, (Valentin-Louis-George-Eugene) Marcel 1871-1922 ..... **SSC 75; TCLC 7, 13, 33; WLC**
See also AAYA 58; BPFB 3; CA 104; 120; CANR 110; DA; DA3; DAB; DAC; DAM MST, NOV; DLB 65; EW 8; EWL 3; GFL 1789 to the Present; MTCW 1, 2; MTFW 2005; RGWL 2, 3; TWA

Prowler, Harley
See Masters, Edgar Lee

Ralegh, Sir Walter
  See Raleigh, Sir Walter
  See also BRW 1; RGEL 2; WP
Raleigh, Richard
  See Lovecraft, H(oward) P(hillips)
Raleigh, Sir Walter 1554(?)-1618 .... **LC 31, 39; PC 31**
  See Ralegh, Sir Walter
  See also CDBLB Before 1660; DLB 172; EXPP; PFS 14; TEA
Rallentando, H. P.
  See Sayers, Dorothy L(eigh)
Ramal, Walter
  See de la Mare, Walter (John)
Ramana Maharshi 1879-1950 .... **TCLC 84**
Ramoacn y Cajal, Santiago 1852-1934 .... **TCLC 93**
Ramon, Juan
  See Jimenez (Mantecon), Juan Ramon
Ramos, Graciliano 1892-1953 .... **TCLC 32**
  See also CA 167; DLB 307; EWL 3; HW 2; LAW; WLIT 1
Rampersad, Arnold 1941- .... **CLC 44**
  See also BW 2, 3; CA 127; 133; CANR 81; DLB 111; INT CA-133
Rampling, Anne
  See Rice, Anne
  See also GLL 2
Ramsay, Allan 1686(?)-1758 .... **LC 29**
  See also DLB 95; RGEL 2
Ramsay, Jay
  See Campbell, (John) Ramsey
Ramuz, Charles-Ferdinand 1878-1947 .... **TCLC 33**
  See also CA 165; EWL 3
Rand, Ayn 1905-1982 ...... **CLC 3, 30, 44, 79; WLC**
  See also AAYA 10; AMWS 4; BPFB 3; BYA 12; CA 13-16R; 105; CANR 27, 73; CDALBS; CN 1, 2, 3; CPW; DA; DA3; DAC; DAM MST, NOV, POP; DLB 227, 279; MTCW 1, 2; MTFW 2005; NFS 10, 16; RGAL 4; SFW 4; TUS; YAW
Randall, Dudley (Felker) 1914-2000 . **BLC 3; CLC 1, 135**
  See also BW 1, 3; CA 25-28R; 189; CANR 23, 82; CP 1, 2, 3, 4; DAM MULT; DLB 41; PFS 5
Randall, Robert
  See Silverberg, Robert
Ranger, Ken
  See Creasey, John
Rank, Otto 1884-1939 .... **TCLC 115**
Ransom, John Crowe 1888-1974 .. **CLC 2, 4, 5, 11, 24; PC 61**
  See also AMW; CA 5-8R; 49-52; CANR 6, 34; CDALBS; CP 1, 2; DA3; DAM POET; DLB 45, 63; EWL 3; EXPP; MAL 5; MTCW 1, 2; MTFW 2005; RGAL 4; TUS
Rao, Raja 1909- .... **CLC 25, 56**
  See also CA 73-76; CANR 51; CN 1, 2, 3, 4, 5, 6; DAM NOV; EWL 3; MTCW 1, 2; MTFW 2005; RGEL 2; RGSF 2
Raphael, Frederic (Michael) 1931- ... **CLC 2, 14**
  See also CA 1-4R; CANR 1, 86; CN 1, 2, 3, 4, 5, 6, 7; DLB 14, 319; TCLE 1:2
Ratcliffe, James P.
  See Mencken, H(enry) L(ouis)
Rathbone, Julian 1935- .... **CLC 41**
  See also CA 101; CANR 34, 73
Rattigan, Terence (Mervyn) 1911-1977 .... **CLC 7; DC 18**
  See also BRWS 7; CA 85-88; 73-76; CBD; CDBLB 1945-1960; DAM DRAM; DFS 8; DLB 13; IDFW 3, 4; MTCW 1, 2; MTFW 2005; RGEL 2
Ratushinskaya, Irina 1954- .... **CLC 54**
  See also CA 129; CANR 68; CWW 2

Raven, Simon (Arthur Noel) 1927-2001 .... **CLC 14**
  See also CA 81-84; 197; CANR 86; CN 1, 2, 3, 4, 5, 6; DLB 271
Ravenna, Michael
  See Welty, Eudora (Alice)
Rawley, Callman 1903-2004
  See Rakosi, Carl
  See also CA 21-24R; 228; CANR 12, 32, 91
Rawlings, Marjorie Kinnan 1896-1953 .... **TCLC 4**
  See also AAYA 20; AMWS 10; ANW; BPFB 3; BYA 3; CA 104; 137; CANR 74; CLR 63; DLB 9, 22, 102; DLBD 17; JRDA; MAICYA 1, 2; MAL 5; MTCW 2; MTFW 2005; RGAL 4; SATA 100; WCH; YABC 1; YAW
Ray, Satyajit 1921-1992 .... **CLC 16, 76**
  See also CA 114; 137; DAM MULT
Read, Herbert Edward 1893-1968 ..... **CLC 4**
  See also BRW 6; CA 85-88; 25-28R; DLB 20, 149; EWL 3; PAB; RGEL 2
Read, Piers Paul 1941- .... **CLC 4, 10, 25**
  See also CA 21-24R; CANR 38, 86; CN 2, 3, 4, 5, 6, 7; DLB 14; SATA 21
Reade, Charles 1814-1884 .... **NCLC 2, 74**
  See also DLB 21; RGEL 2
Reade, Hamish
  See Gray, Simon (James Holliday)
Reading, Peter 1946- .... **CLC 47**
  See also BRWS 8; CA 103; CANR 46, 96; CP 7; DLB 40
Reaney, James 1926- .... **CLC 13**
  See also CA 41-44R; CAAS 15; CANR 42; CD 5, 6; CP 1, 2, 3, 4, 5, 6, 7; DAC; DAM MST; DLB 68; RGEL 2; SATA 43
Rebreanu, Liviu 1885-1944 .... **TCLC 28**
  See also CA 165; DLB 220; EWL 3
Rechy, John (Francisco) 1934- ...... **CLC 1, 7, 14, 18, 107; HLC 2**
  See also CA 5-8R, 195; CAAE 195; CAAS 4; CANR 6, 32, 64; CN 1, 2, 3, 4, 5, 6, 7; DAM MULT; DLB 122, 278; DLBY 1982; HW 1, 2; INT CANR-6; LLW; MAL 5; RGAL 4
Redcam, Tom 1870-1933 .... **TCLC 25**
Reddin, Keith 1956- .... **CLC 67**
  See also CAD; CD 6
Redgrove, Peter (William) 1932-2003 .... **CLC 6, 41**
  See also BRWS 6; CA 1-4R; 217; CANR 3, 39, 77; CP 1, 2, 3, 4, 5, 6, 7; DLB 40; TCLE 1:2
Redmon, Anne .... **CLC 22**
  See Nightingale, Anne Redmon
  See also DLBY 1986
Reed, Eliot
  See Ambler, Eric
Reed, Ishmael (Scott) 1938- . **BLC 3; CLC 2, 3, 5, 6, 13, 32, 60, 174; PC 68**
  See also AFAW 1, 2; AMWS 10; BPFB 3; BW 2, 3; CA 21-24R; CANR 25, 48, 74, 128; CN 1, 2, 3, 4, 5, 6, 7; CP 1, 2, 3, 4, 5, 6, 7; CSW; DA3; DAM MULT; DLB 2, 5, 33, 169, 227; DLBD 8; EWL 3; LMFS 2; MAL 5; MSW; MTCW 1, 2; MTFW 2005; PFS 6; RGAL 4; TCWW 2
Reed, John (Silas) 1887-1920 .... **TCLC 9**
  See also CA 106; 195; MAL 5; TUS
Reed, Lou .... **CLC 21**
  See Firbank, Louis
Reese, Lizette Woodworth 1856-1935 . **PC 29**
  See also CA 180; DLB 54
Reeve, Clara 1729-1807 .... **NCLC 19**
  See also DLB 39; RGEL 2
Reich, Wilhelm 1897-1957 .... **TCLC 57**
  See also CA 199

Reid, Christopher (John) 1949- .... **CLC 33**
  See also CA 140; CANR 89; CP 4, 5, 6, 7; DLB 40; EWL 3
Reid, Desmond
  See Moorcock, Michael (John)
Reid Banks, Lynne 1929-
  See Banks, Lynne Reid
  See also AAYA 49; CA 1-4R; CANR 6, 22, 38, 87; CLR 24; CN 1, 2, 3, 7; JRDA; MAICYA 1, 2; SATA 22, 75, 111, 165; YAW
Reilly, William K.
  See Creasey, John
Reiner, Max
  See Caldwell, (Janet Miriam) Taylor (Holland)
Reis, Ricardo
  See Pessoa, Fernando (Antonio Nogueira)
Reizenstein, Elmer Leopold
  See Rice, Elmer (Leopold)
  See also EWL 3
Remarque, Erich Maria 1898-1970 . **CLC 21**
  See also AAYA 27; BPFB 3; CA 77-80; 29-32R; CDWLB 2; DA; DA3; DAB; DAC; DAM MST, NOV; DLB 56; EWL 3; EXPN; LAIT 3; MTCW 1, 2; MTFW 2005; NFS 4; RGWL 2, 3
Remington, Frederic S(ackrider) 1861-1909 .... **TCLC 89**
  See also CA 108; 169; DLB 12, 186, 188; SATA 41; TCWW 2
Remizov, A.
  See Remizov, Aleksei (Mikhailovich)
Remizov, A. M.
  See Remizov, Aleksei (Mikhailovich)
Remizov, Aleksei (Mikhailovich) 1877-1957 .... **TCLC 27**
  See Remizov, Alexey Mikhaylovich
  See also CA 125; 133; DLB 295
Remizov, Alexey Mikhailovich
  See Remizov, Aleksei (Mikhailovich)
  See also EWL 3
Renan, Joseph Ernest 1823-1892 . **NCLC 26, 145**
  See also GFL 1789 to the Present
Renard, Jules(-Pierre) 1864-1910 .. **TCLC 17**
  See also CA 117; 202; GFL 1789 to the Present
Renault, Mary .... **CLC 3, 11, 17**
  See Challans, Mary
  See also BPFB 3; BYA 2; CN 1, 2, 3; DLBY 1983; EWL 3; GLL 1; LAIT 1; RGEL 2; RHW
Rendell, Ruth (Barbara) 1930- .. **CLC 28, 48**
  See Vine, Barbara
  See also BPFB 3; BRWS 9; CA 109; CANR 32, 52, 74, 127; CN 5, 6, 7; CPW; DAM POP; DLB 87, 276; INT CANR-32; MSW; MTCW 1, 2; MTFW 2005
Renoir, Jean 1894-1979 .... **CLC 20**
  See also CA 129; 85-88
Resnais, Alain 1922- .... **CLC 16**
Revard, Carter (Curtis) 1931- .... **NNAL**
  See also CA 144; CANR 81; PFS 5
Reverdy, Pierre 1889-1960 .... **CLC 53**
  See also CA 97-100; 89-92; DLB 258; EWL 3; GFL 1789 to the Present
Rexroth, Kenneth 1905-1982 .... **CLC 1, 2, 6, 11, 22, 49, 112; PC 20**
  See also BG 1:3; CA 5-8R; 107; CANR 14, 34, 63; CDALB 1941-1968; CP 1, 2, 3; DAM POET; DLB 16, 48, 165, 212; DLBY 1982; EWL 3; INT CANR-14; MAL 5; MTCW 1, 2; MTFW 2005; RGAL 4
Reyes, Alfonso 1889-1959 .... **HLCS 2; TCLC 33**
  See also CA 131; EWL 3; HW 1; LAW

Robbins, Tom .... CLC 9, 32, 64
   See Robbins, Thomas Eugene
   See also AAYA 32; AMWS 10; BEST 90:3;
   BPFB 3; CN 3, 4, 5, 6, 7; DLBY 1980
Robbins, Trina 1938- .... CLC 21
   See also AAYA 61; CA 128
Roberts, Charles G(eorge) D(ouglas)
   1860-1943 .... TCLC 8
   See also CA 105; 188; CLR 33; CWRI 5;
   DLB 92; RGEL 2; RGSF 2; SATA 88;
   SATA-Brief 29
Roberts, Elizabeth Madox
   1886-1941 .... TCLC 68
   See also CA 111; 166; CLR 100; CWRI 5;
   DLB 9, 54, 102; RGAL 4; RHW; SATA
   33; SATA-Brief 27; TCWW 2; WCH
Roberts, Kate 1891-1985 .... CLC 15
   See also CA 107; 116; DLB 319
Roberts, Keith (John Kingston)
   1935-2000 .... CLC 14
   See also BRWS 10; CA 25-28R; CANR 46;
   DLB 261; SFW 4
Roberts, Kenneth (Lewis)
   1885-1957 .... TCLC 23
   See also CA 109; 199; DLB 9; MAL 5;
   RGAL 4; RHW
Roberts, Michele (Brigitte) 1949- .... CLC 48,
   178
   See also CA 115; CANR 58, 120; CN 6, 7;
   DLB 231; FW
Robertson, Ellis
   See Ellison, Harlan (Jay); Silverberg, Robert
Robertson, Thomas William
   1829-1871 .... NCLC 35
   See Robertson, Tom
   See also DAM DRAM
Robertson, Tom
   See Robertson, Thomas William
   See also RGEL 2
Robeson, Kenneth
   See Dent, Lester
Robinson, Edwin Arlington
   1869-1935 .... PC 1, 35; TCLC 5, 101
   See also AMW; CA 104; 133; CDALB
   1865-1917; DA; DAC; DAM MST,
   POET; DLB 54; EWL 3; EXPP; MAL 5;
   MTCW 1, 2; MTFW 2005; PAB; PFS 4;
   RGAL 4; WP
Robinson, Henry Crabb
   1775-1867 .... NCLC 15
   See also DLB 107
Robinson, Jill 1936- .... CLC 10
   See also CA 102; CANR 120; INT CA-102
Robinson, Kim Stanley 1952- .... CLC 34
   See also AAYA 26; CA 126; CANR 113,
   139; CN 6, 7; MTFW 2005; SATA 109;
   SCFW 2; SFW 4
Robinson, Lloyd
   See Silverberg, Robert
Robinson, Marilynne 1944- ...... CLC 25, 180
   See also CA 116; CANR 80, 140; CN 4, 5,
   6, 7; DLB 206; MTFW 2005
Robinson, Mary 1758-1800 .... NCLC 142
   See also DLB 158; FW
Robinson, Smokey .... CLC 21
   See Robinson, William, Jr.
Robinson, William, Jr. 1940-
   See Robinson, Smokey
   See also CA 116
Robison, Mary 1949- .... CLC 42, 98
   See also CA 113; 116; CANR 87; CN 4, 5,
   6, 7; DLB 130; INT CA-116; RGSF 2
Roches, Catherine des 1542-1587 ...... LC 117
Rochester
   See Wilmot, John
   See also RGEL 2
Rod, Edouard 1857-1910 .... TCLC 52

Roddenberry, Eugene Wesley 1921-1991
   See Roddenberry, Gene
   See also CA 110; 135; CANR 37; SATA 45;
   SATA-Obit 69
Roddenberry, Gene .... CLC 17
   See Roddenberry, Eugene Wesley
   See also AAYA 5; SATA-Obit 69
Rodgers, Mary 1931- .... CLC 12
   See also BYA 5; CA 49-52; CANR 8, 55,
   90; CLR 20; CWRI 5; INT CANR-8;
   JRDA; MAICYA 1, 2; SATA 8, 130
Rodgers, W(illiam) R(obert)
   1909-1969 .... CLC 7
   See also CA 85-88; DLB 20; RGEL 2
Rodman, Eric
   See Silverberg, Robert
Rodman, Howard 1920(?)-1985 .... CLC 65
   See also CA 118
Rodman, Maia
   See Wojciechowska, Maia (Teresa)
Rodo, Jose Enrique 1871(?)-1917 .... HLCS 2
   See also CA 178; EWL 3; HW 2; LAW
Rodolph, Utto
   See Ouologuem, Yambo
Rodriguez, Claudio 1934-1999 .... CLC 10
   See also CA 188; DLB 134
Rodriguez, Richard 1944- .... CLC 155; HLC
   2
   See also AMWS 14; CA 110; CANR 66,
   116; DAM MULT; DLB 82, 256; HW 1,
   2; LAIT 5; LLW; MTFW 2005; NCFS 3;
   WLIT 1
Roelvaag, O(le) E(dvart) 1876-1931
   See Rolvaag, O(le) E(dvart)
   See also CA 117; 171
Roethke, Theodore (Huebner)
   1908-1963 .... CLC 1, 3, 8, 11, 19, 46,
   101; PC 15
   See also AMW; CA 81-84; CABS 2;
   CDALB 1941-1968; DA3; DAM POET;
   DLB 5, 206; EWL 3; EXPP; MAL 5;
   MTCW 1, 2; PAB; PFS 3; RGAL 4; WP
Rogers, Carl R(ansom)
   1902-1987 .... TCLC 125
   See also CA 1-4R; 121; CANR 1, 18;
   MTCW 1
Rogers, Samuel 1763-1855 .... NCLC 69
   See also DLB 93; RGEL 2
Rogers, Thomas Hunton 1927- .... CLC 57
   See also CA 89-92; INT CA-89-92
Rogers, Will(iam Penn Adair)
   1879-1935 .... NNAL; TCLC 8, 71
   See also CA 105; 144; DA3; DAM MULT;
   DLB 11; MTCW 2
Rogin, Gilbert 1929- .... CLC 18
   See also CA 65-68; CANR 15
Rohan, Koda
   See Koda Shigeyuki
Rohlfs, Anna Katharine Green
   See Green, Anna Katharine
Rohmer, Eric .... CLC 16
   See Scherer, Jean-Marie Maurice
Rohmer, Sax .... TCLC 28
   See Ward, Arthur Henry Sarsfield
   See also DLB 70; MSW; SUFW
Roiphe, Anne (Richardson) 1935- .. CLC 3, 9
   See also CA 89-92; CANR 45, 73, 138;
   DLBY 1980; INT CA-89-92
Rojas, Fernando de 1475-1541 ... HLCS 1, 2;
   LC 23
   See also DLB 286; RGWL 2, 3
Rojas, Gonzalo 1917- .... HLCS 2
   See also CA 178; HW 2; LAWS 1
Roland (de la Platiere), Marie-Jeanne
   1754-1793 .... LC 98
   See also DLB 314

Rolfe, Frederick (William Serafino Austin
   Lewis Mary) 1860-1913 .... TCLC 12
   See Al Siddik
   See also CA 107; 210; DLB 34, 156; RGEL
   2
Rolland, Romain 1866-1944 .... TCLC 23
   See also CA 118; 197; DLB 65, 284; EWL
   3; GFL 1789 to the Present; RGWL 2, 3
Rolle, Richard c. 1300-c. 1349 ...... CMLC 21
   See also DLB 146; LMFS 1; RGEL 2
Rolvaag, O(le) E(dvart) .... TCLC 17
   See Roelvaag, O(le) E(dvart)
   See also DLB 9, 212; MAL 5; NFS 5;
   RGAL 4
Romain Arnaud, Saint
   See Aragon, Louis
Romains, Jules 1885-1972 .... CLC 7
   See also CA 85-88; CANR 34; DLB 65,
   321; EWL 3; GFL 1789 to the Present;
   MTCW 1
Romero, Jose Ruben 1890-1952 .... TCLC 14
   See also CA 114; 131; EWL 3; HW 1; LAW
Ronsard, Pierre de 1524-1585 . LC 6, 54; PC
   11
   See also EW 2; GFL Beginnings to 1789;
   RGWL 2, 3; TWA
Rooke, Leon 1934- .... CLC 25, 34
   See also CA 25-28R; CANR 23, 53; CCA
   1; CPW; DAM POP
Roosevelt, Franklin Delano
   1882-1945 .... TCLC 93
   See also CA 116; 173; LAIT 3
Roosevelt, Theodore 1858-1919 .... TCLC 69
   See also CA 115; 170; DLB 47, 186, 275
Roper, William 1498-1578 .... LC 10
Roquelaure, A. N.
   See Rice, Anne
Rosa, Joao Guimaraes 1908-1967 ... CLC 23;
   HLCS 1
   See Guimaraes Rosa, Joao
   See also CA 89-92; DLB 113, 307; EWL 3;
   WLIT 1
Rose, Wendy 1948- . CLC 85; NNAL; PC 13
   See also CA 53-56; CANR 5, 51; CWP;
   DAM MULT; DLB 175; PFS 13; RGAL
   4; SATA 12
Rosen, R. D.
   See Rosen, Richard (Dean)
Rosen, Richard (Dean) 1949- .... CLC 39
   See also CA 77-80; CANR 62, 120; CMW
   4; INT CANR-30
Rosenberg, Isaac 1890-1918 .... TCLC 12
   See also BRW 6; CA 107; 188; DLB 20,
   216; EWL 3; PAB; RGEL 2
Rosenblatt, Joe .... CLC 15
   See Rosenblatt, Joseph
   See also CP 3, 4, 5, 6, 7
Rosenblatt, Joseph 1933-
   See Rosenblatt, Joe
   See also CA 89-92; CP 1, 2; INT CA-89-92
Rosenfeld, Samuel
   See Tzara, Tristan
Rosenstock, Sami
   See Tzara, Tristan
Rosenstock, Samuel
   See Tzara, Tristan
Rosenthal, M(acha) L(ouis)
   1917-1996 .... CLC 28
   See also CA 1-4R; 152; CAAS 6; CANR 4,
   51; CP 1, 2, 3, 4; DLB 5; SATA 59
Ross, Barnaby
   See Dannay, Frederic
Ross, Bernard L.
   See Follett, Ken(neth Martin)
Ross, J. H.
   See Lawrence, T(homas) E(dward)
Ross, John Hume
   See Lawrence, T(homas) E(dward)

Ryder, Jonathan
See Ludlum, Robert

Ryga, George 1932-1987 .... **CLC 14**
See also CA 101; 124; CANR 43, 90; CCA
1; DAC; DAM MST; DLB 60

S. H.
See Hartmann, Sadakichi

S. S.
See Sassoon, Siegfried (Lorraine)

Sa'adawi, al- Nawal
See El Saadawi, Nawal
See also AFW; EWL 3

Saadawi, Nawal El
See El Saadawi, Nawal
See also WLIT 2

Saba, Umberto 1883-1957 .... **TCLC 33**
See also CA 144; CANR 79; DLB 114;
EWL 3; RGWL 2, 3

Sabatini, Rafael 1875-1950 .... **TCLC 47**
See also BPFB 3; CA 162; RHW

Sabato, Ernesto (R.) 1911- .... **CLC 10, 23;
HLC 2**
See also CA 97-100; CANR 32, 65; CD-
WLB 2; CWW 2; DAM MULT; DLB 145;
EWL 3; HW 1, 2; LAW; MTCW 1, 2;
MTFW 2005

Sa-Carneiro, Mario de 1890-1916 . **TCLC 83**
See also DLB 287; EWL 3

Sacastru, Martin
See Bioy Casares, Adolfo
See also CWW 2

Sacher-Masoch, Leopold von
1836(?)-1895 .... **NCLC 31**

Sachs, Hans 1494-1576 .... **LC 95**
See also CDWLB 2; DLB 179; RGWL 2, 3

Sachs, Marilyn 1927- .... **CLC 35**
See also AAYA 2; BYA 6; CA 17-20R;
CANR 13, 47; CLR 2; JRDA; MAICYA
1, 2; SAAS 2; SATA 3, 68, 164; SATA-
Essay 110; WYA; YAW

Sachs, Marilyn Stickle
See Sachs, Marilyn

Sachs, Nelly 1891-1970 .... **CLC 14, 98**
See also CA 17-18; 25-28R; CANR 87;
CAP 2; EWL 3; MTCW 2; MTFW 2005;
PFS 20; RGWL 2, 3

Sackler, Howard (Oliver)
1929-1982 .... **CLC 14**
See also CA 61-64; 108; CAD; CANR 30;
DFS 15; DLB 7

Sacks, Oliver (Wolf) 1933- .... **CLC 67, 202**
See also CA 53-56; CANR 28, 50, 76;
CPW; DA3; INT CANR-28; MTCW 1, 2;
MTFW 2005

Sackville, Thomas 1536-1608 .... **LC 98**
See also DAM DRAM; DLB 62, 132;
RGEL 2

Sadakichi
See Hartmann, Sadakichi

Sa'dawi, Nawal al-
See El Saadawi, Nawal
See also CWW 2

Sade, Donatien Alphonse Francois
1740-1814 .... **NCLC 3, 47**
See also DLB 314; EW 4; GFL Beginnings
to 1789; RGWL 2, 3

Sade, Marquis de
See Sade, Donatien Alphonse Francois

Sadoff, Ira 1945- .... **CLC 9**
See also CA 53-56; CANR 5, 21, 109; DLB
120

Saetone
See Camus, Albert

Safire, William 1929- .... **CLC 10**
See also CA 17-20R; CANR 31, 54, 91

Sagan, Carl (Edward) 1934-1996 .... **CLC 30,
112**
See also AAYA 2, 62; CA 25-28R; 155;
CANR 11, 36, 74; CPW; DA3; MTCW 1,
2; MTFW 2005; SATA 58; SATA-Obit 94

Sagan, Francoise .... **CLC 3, 6, 9, 17, 36**
See Quoirez, Francoise
See also CWW 2; DLB 83; EWL 3; GFL
1789 to the Present; MTCW 2

Sahgal, Nayantara (Pandit) 1927- .... **CLC 41**
See also CA 9-12R; CANR 11, 88; CN 1,
2, 3, 4, 5, 6, 7

Said, Edward W. 1935-2003 .... **CLC 123**
See also CA 21-24R; 220; CANR 45, 74,
107, 131; DLB 67; MTCW 2; MTFW
2005

Saint, H(arry) F. 1941- .... **CLC 50**
See also CA 127

St. Aubin de Teran, Lisa 1953-
See Teran, Lisa St. Aubin de
See also CA 118; 126; CN 6, 7; INT CA-
126

Saint Birgitta of Sweden c.
1303-1373 .... **CMLC 24**

Saint Gregory of Nazianzus
329-389 .... **CMLC 82**

Sainte-Beuve, Charles Augustin
1804-1869 .... **NCLC 5**
See also DLB 217; EW 6; GFL 1789 to the
Present

**Saint-Exupery, Antoine (Jean Baptiste
Marie Roger) de** 1900-1944 .... **TCLC 2,
56, 169; WLC**
See also AAYA 63; BPFB 3; BYA 3; CA
108; 132; CLR 10; DA3; DAM NOV;
DLB 72; EW 12; EWL 3; GFL 1789 to
the Present; LAIT 3; MAICYA 1, 2;
MTCW 1, 2; MTFW 2005; RGWL 2, 3;
SATA 20; TWA

St. John, David
See Hunt, E(verette) Howard, (Jr.)

St. John, J. Hector
See Crevecoeur, Michel Guillaume Jean de

Saint-John Perse
See Leger, (Marie-Rene Auguste) Alexis
Saint-Leger
See also EW 10; EWL 3; GFL 1789 to the
Present; RGWL 2

Saintsbury, George (Edward Bateman)
1845-1933 .... **TCLC 31**
See also CA 160; DLB 57, 149

Sait Faik .... **TCLC 23**
See Abasiyanik, Sait Faik

Saki .... **SSC 12; TCLC 3**
See Munro, H(ector) H(ugh)
See also BRWS 6; BYA 11; LAIT 2; RGEL
2; SSFS 1; SUFW

Sala, George Augustus 1828-1895 . **NCLC 46**

Saladin 1138-1193 .... **CMLC 38**

Salama, Hannu 1936- .... **CLC 18**
See also EWL 3

Salamanca, J(ack) R(ichard) 1922- .. **CLC 4,
15**
See also CA 25-28R; 193; CAAE 193

Salas, Floyd Francis 1931- .... **HLC 2**
See also CA 119; CAAS 27; CANR 44, 75,
93; DAM MULT; DLB 82; HW 1, 2;
MTCW 2; MTFW 2005

Sale, J. Kirkpatrick
See Sale, Kirkpatrick

Sale, Kirkpatrick 1937- .... **CLC 68**
See also CA 13-16R; CANR 10

Salinas, Luis Omar 1937- ... **CLC 90; HLC 2**
See also AMWS 13; CA 131; CANR 81;
DAM MULT; DLB 82; HW 1, 2

Salinas (y Serrano), Pedro
1891(?)-1951 .... **TCLC 17**
See also CA 117; DLB 134; EWL 3

Salinger, J(erome) D(avid) 1919- .. **CLC 1, 3,
8, 12, 55, 56, 138; SSC 2, 28, 65; WLC**
See also AAYA 2, 36; AMW; AMWC 1;
BPFB 3; CA 5-8R; CANR 39, 129;
CDALB 1941-1968; CLR 18; CN 1, 2, 3,
4, 5, 6, 7; CPW 1; DA; DA3; DAB; DAC;
DAM MST, NOV, POP; DLB 2, 102, 173;
EWL 3; EXPN; LAIT 4; MAICYA 1, 2;
MAL 5; MTCW 1, 2; MTFW 2005; NFS
1; RGAL 4; RGSF 2; SATA 67; SSFS 17;
TUS; WYA; YAW

Salisbury, John
See Caute, (John) David

Sallust c. 86B.C.-35B.C. .... **CMLC 68**
See also AW 2; CDWLB 1; DLB 211;
RGWL 2, 3

Salter, James 1925- .. **CLC 7, 52, 59; SSC 58**
See also AMWS 9; CA 73-76; CANR 107;
DLB 130

Saltus, Edgar (Everton) 1855-1921 . **TCLC 8**
See also CA 105; DLB 202; RGAL 4

Saltykov, Mikhail Evgrafovich
1826-1889 .... **NCLC 16**
See also DLB 238:

Saltykov-Shchedrin, N.
See Saltykov, Mikhail Evgrafovich

Samarakis, Andonis
See Samarakis, Antonis
See also EWL 3

Samarakis, Antonis 1919-2003 .... **CLC 5**
See Samarakis, Andonis
See also CA 25-28R; 224; CAAS 16; CANR
36

Sanchez, Florencio 1875-1910 .... **TCLC 37**
See also CA 153; DLB 305; EWL 3; HW 1;
LAW

Sanchez, Luis Rafael 1936- .... **CLC 23**
See also CA 128; DLB 305; EWL 3; HW 1;
WLIT 1

Sanchez, Sonia 1934- .... **BLC 3; CLC 5, 116,
215; PC 9**
See also BW 2, 3; CA 33-36R; CANR 24,
49, 74, 115; CLR 18; CP 2, 3, 4, 5, 6, 7;
CSW; CWP; DA3; DAM MULT; DLB 41;
DLBD 8; EWL 3; MAICYA 1, 2; MAL 5;
MTCW 1, 2; MTFW 2005; SATA 22, 136;
WP

Sancho, Ignatius 1729-1780 .... **LC 84**

Sand, George 1804-1876 ..... **NCLC 2, 42, 57;
WLC**
See also DA; DA3; DAB; DAC; DAM
MST, NOV; DLB 119, 192; EW 6; FL 1:3;
FW; GFL 1789 to the Present; RGWL 2,
3; TWA

Sandburg, Carl (August) 1878-1967 . **CLC 1,
4, 10, 15, 35; PC 2, 41; WLC**
See also AAYA 24; AMW; BYA 1, 3; CA
5-8R; 25-28R; CANR 35; CDALB 1865-
1917; CLR 67; DA; DA3; DAB; DAC;
DAM MST, POET; DLB 17, 54, 284;
EWL 3; EXPP; LAIT 2; MAICYA 1, 2;
MAL 5; MTCW 1, 2; MTFW 2005; PAB;
PFS 3, 6, 12; RGAL 4; SATA 8; TUS;
WCH; WP; WYA

Sandburg, Charles
See Sandburg, Carl (August)

Sandburg, Charles A.
See Sandburg, Carl (August)

Sanders, (James) Ed(ward) 1939- .... **CLC 53**
See Sanders, Edward
See also BG 1:3; CA 13-16R; CAAS 21;
CANR 13, 44, 78; CP 1, 2, 3, 4, 5, 6, 7;
DAM POET; DLB 16, 244

Sanders, Edward
See Sanders, (James) Ed(ward)
See also DLB 244

Sanders, Lawrence 1920-1998 .... **CLC 41**
See also BEST 89:4; BPFB 3; CA 81-84;
165; CANR 33, 62; CMW 4; CPW; DA3;
DAM POP; MTCW 1

Shepherd, Michael
See Ludlum, Robert

Sherburne, Zoa (Lillian Morin)
1912-1995 .... **CLC 30**
See also AAYA 13; CA 1-4R; 176; CANR 3, 37; MAICYA 1, 2; SAAS 18; SATA 3; YAW

Sheridan, Frances 1724-1766 .... **LC 7**
See also DLB 39, 84

Sheridan, Richard Brinsley
1751-1816 .... **DC 1; NCLC 5, 91; WLC**
See also BRW 3; CDBLB 1660-1789; DA; DAB; DAC; DAM DRAM, MST; DFS 15; DLB 89; WLIT 3

Sherman, Jonathan Marc 1968- .... **CLC 55**
See also CA 230

Sherman, Martin 1941(?)- .... **CLC 19**
See also CA 116; 123; CAD; CANR 86; CD 5, 6; DFS 20; DLB 228; GLL 1; IDTP

Sherwin, Judith Johnson
See Johnson, Judith (Emlyn)
See also CANR 85; CP 2, 3, 4; CWP

Sherwood, Frances 1940- .... **CLC 81**
See also CA 146, 220; CAAE 220

Sherwood, Robert E(mmet)
1896-1955 .... **TCLC 3**
See also CA 104; 153; CANR 86; DAM DRAM; DFS 11, 15, 17; DLB 7, 26, 249; IDFW 3, 4; MAL 5; RGAL 4

Shestov, Lev 1866-1938 .... **TCLC 56**

Shevchenko, Taras 1814-1861 .... **NCLC 54**

Shiel, M(atthew) P(hipps)
1865-1947 .... **TCLC 8**
See Holmes, Gordon
See also CA 106; 160; DLB 153; HGG; MTCW 2; MTFW 2005; SCFW 1, 2; SFW 4; SUFW

Shields, Carol (Ann) 1935-2003 ...... **CLC 91, 113, 193**
See also AMWS 7; CA 81-84; 218; CANR 51, 74, 98, 133; CCA 1; CN 6, 7; CPW; DA3; DAC; MTCW 2; MTFW 2005

Shields, David (Jonathan) 1956- .... **CLC 97**
See also CA 124; CANR 48, 99, 112

Shiga, Naoya 1883-1971 .... **CLC 33; SSC 23; TCLC 172**
See Shiga Naoya
See also CA 101; 33-36R; MJW; RGWL 3

Shiga Naoya
See Shiga, Naoya
See also DLB 180; EWL 3; RGWL 3

Shilts, Randy 1951-1994 .... **CLC 85**
See also AAYA 19; CA 115; 127; 144; CANR 45; DA3; GLL 1; INT CA-127; MTCW 2; MTFW 2005

Shimazaki, Haruki 1872-1943
See Shimazaki Toson
See also CA 105; 134; CANR 84; RGWL 3

Shimazaki Toson .... **TCLC 5**
See Shimazaki, Haruki
See also DLB 180; EWL 3

Shirley, James 1596-1666 .... **DC 25; LC 96**
See also DLB 58; RGEL 2

Sholokhov, Mikhail (Aleksandrovich)
1905-1984 .... **CLC 7, 15**
See also CA 101; 112; DLB 272; EWL 3; MTCW 1, 2; MTFW 2005; RGWL 2, 3; SATA-Obit 36

Shone, Patric
See Hanley, James

Showalter, Elaine 1941- .... **CLC 169**
See also CA 57-60; CANR 58, 106; DLB 67; FW; GLL 2

Shreve, Susan
See Shreve, Susan Richards

Shreve, Susan Richards 1939- .... **CLC 23**
See also CA 49-52; CAAS 5; CANR 5, 38, 69, 100; MAICYA 1, 2; SATA 46, 95, 152; SATA-Brief 41

Shue, Larry 1946-1985 .... **CLC 52**
See also CA 145; 117; DAM DRAM; DFS 7

Shu-Jen, Chou 1881-1936
See Lu Hsun
See also CA 104

Shulman, Alix Kates 1932- .... **CLC 2, 10**
See also CA 29-32R; CANR 43; FW; SATA 7

Shuster, Joe 1914-1992 .... **CLC 21**
See also AAYA 50

Shute, Nevil .... **CLC 30**
See Norway, Nevil Shute
See also BPFB 3; DLB 255; NFS 9; RHW; SFW 4

Shuttle, Penelope (Diane) 1947- .... **CLC 7**
See also CA 93-96; CANR 39, 84, 92, 108; CP 3, 4, 5, 6, 7; CWP; DLB 14, 40

Shvarts, Elena 1948- .... **PC 50**
See also CA 147

Sidhwa, Bapsi
See Sidhwa, Bapsy (N.)
See also CN 6, 7

Sidhwa, Bapsy (N.) 1938- .... **CLC 168**
See Sidhwa, Bapsi
See also CA 108; CANR 25, 57; FW

Sidney, Mary 1561-1621 .... **LC 19, 39**
See Sidney Herbert, Mary

Sidney, Sir Philip 1554-1586 . **LC 19, 39; PC 32**
See also BRW 1; BRWR 2; CDBLB Before 1660; DA; DA3; DAB; DAC; DAM MST, POET; DLB 167; EXPP; PAB; RGEL 2; TEA; WP

Sidney Herbert, Mary
See Sidney, Mary
See also DLB 167

Siegel, Jerome 1914-1996 .... **CLC 21**
See Siegel, Jerry
See also CA 116; 169; 151

Siegel, Jerry
See Siegel, Jerome
See also AAYA 50

Sienkiewicz, Henryk (Adam Alexander Pius)
1846-1916 .... **TCLC 3**
See also CA 104; 134; CANR 84; EWL 3; RGSF 2; RGWL 2, 3

Sierra, Gregorio Martinez
See Martinez Sierra, Gregorio

Sierra, Maria (de la O'LeJarraga) Martinez
See Martinez Sierra, Maria (de la O'LeJarraga)

Sigal, Clancy 1926- .... **CLC 7**
See also CA 1-4R; CANR 85; CN 1, 2, 3, 4, 5, 6, 7

Siger of Brabant 1240(?)-1284(?) . **CMLC 69**
See also DLB 115

Sigourney, Lydia H.
See Sigourney, Lydia Howard (Huntley)
See also DLB 73, 183

Sigourney, Lydia Howard (Huntley)
1791-1865 .... **NCLC 21, 87**
See Sigourney, Lydia H.; Sigourney, Lydia Huntley
See also DLB 1

Sigourney, Lydia Huntley
See Sigourney, Lydia Howard (Huntley)
See also DLB 42, 239, 243

Siguenza y Gongora, Carlos de
1645-1700 .... **HLCS 2; LC 8**
See also LAW

Sigurjonsson, Johann
See Sigurjonsson, Johann

Sigurjonsson, Johann 1880-1919 ... **TCLC 27**
See also CA 170; DLB 293; EWL 3

Sikelianos, Angelos 1884-1951 .... **PC 29; TCLC 39**
See also EWL 3; RGWL 2, 3

Silkin, Jon 1930-1997 .... **CLC 2, 6, 43**
See also CA 5-8R; CAAS 5; CANR 89; CP 1, 2, 3, 4, 5, 6; DLB 27

Silko, Leslie (Marmon) 1948- .... **CLC 23, 74, 114, 211; NNAL; SSC 37, 66; WLCS**
See also AAYA 14; AMWS 4; ANW; BYA 12; CA 115; 122; CANR 45, 65, 118; CN 4, 5, 6, 7; CP 4, 5, 6, 7; CPW 1; CWP; DA; DA3; DAC; DAM MST, MULT, POP; DLB 143, 175, 256, 275; EWL 3; EXPP; EXPS; LAIT 4; MAL 5; MTCW 2; MTFW 2005; NFS 4; PFS 9, 16; RGAL 4; RGSF 2; SSFS 4, 8, 10, 11; TCWW 1, 2

Sillanpaa, Frans Eemil 1888-1964 ... **CLC 19**
See also CA 129; 93-96; EWL 3; MTCW 1

Sillitoe, Alan 1928- .. **CLC 1, 3, 6, 10, 19, 57, 148**
See also AITN 1; BRWS 5; CA 9-12R; 191; CAAE 191; CAAS 2; CANR 8, 26, 55, 139; CDBLB 1960 to Present; CN 1, 2, 3, 4, 5, 6; CP 1, 2, 3, 4; DLB 14, 139; EWL 3; MTCW 1, 2; MTFW 2005; RGEL 2; RGSF 2; SATA 61

Silone, Ignazio 1900-1978 .... **CLC 4**
See also CA 25-28; 81-84; CANR 34; CAP 2; DLB 264; EW 12; EWL 3; MTCW 1; RGSF 2; RGWL 2, 3

Silone, Ignazione
See Silone, Ignazio

Silver, Joan Micklin 1935- .... **CLC 20**
See also CA 114; 121; INT CA-121

Silver, Nicholas
See Faust, Frederick (Schiller)

Silverberg, Robert 1935- .... **CLC 7, 140**
See also AAYA 24; BPFB 3; BYA 7, 9; CA 1-4R, 186; CAAE 186; CAAS 3; CANR 1, 20, 36, 85, 140; CLR 59; CN 6, 7; CPW; DAM POP; DLB 8; INT CANR-20; MAICYA 1, 2; MTCW 1, 2; MTFW 2005; SATA 13, 91; SATA-Essay 104; SCFW 1, 2; SFW 4; SUFW 2

Silverstein, Alvin 1933- .... **CLC 17**
See also CA 49-52; CANR 2; CLR 25; JRDA; MAICYA 1, 2; SATA 8, 69, 124

Silverstein, Shel(don Allan)
1932-1999 .... **PC 49**
See also AAYA 40; BW 3; CA 107; 179; CANR 47, 74, 81; CLR 5, 96; CWRI 5; JRDA; MAICYA 1, 2; MTCW 2; MTFW 2005; SATA 33, 92; SATA-Brief 27; SATA-Obit 116

Silverstein, Virginia B(arbara Opshelor)
1937- .... **CLC 17**
See also CA 49-52; CANR 2; CLR 25; JRDA; MAICYA 1, 2; SATA 8, 69, 124

Sim, Georges
See Simenon, Georges (Jacques Christian)

Simak, Clifford D(onald) 1904-1988 . **CLC 1, 55**
See also CA 1-4R; 125; CANR 1, 35; DLB 8; MTCW 1; SATA-Obit 56; SCFW 1, 2; SFW 4

Simenon, Georges (Jacques Christian)
1903-1989 .... **CLC 1, 2, 3, 8, 18, 47**
See also BPFB 3; CA 85-88; 129; CANR 35; CMW 4; DA3; DAM POP; DLB 72; DLBY 1989; EW 12; EWL 3; GFL 1789 to the Present; MSW; MTCW 1, 2; MTFW 2005; RGWL 2, 3

Simic, Charles 1938- .... **CLC 6, 9, 22, 49, 68, 130; PC 69**
See also AMWS 8; CA 29-32R; CAAS 4; CANR 12, 33, 52, 61, 96, 140; CP 2, 3, 4, 5, 6, 7; DA3; DAM POET; DLB 105; MAL 5; MTCW 2; MTFW 2005; PFS 7; RGAL 4; WP

Simmel, Georg 1858-1918 .... **TCLC 64**
See also CA 157; DLB 296

Simmons, Charles (Paul) 1924- .... **CLC 57**
See also CA 89-92; INT CA-89-92

Simmons, Dan 1948- .... **CLC 44**
See also AAYA 16, 54; CA 138; CANR 53, 81, 126; CPW; DAM POP; HGG; SUFW 2

Simmons, James (Stewart Alexander)
1933- .... **CLC 43**
See also CA 105; CAAS 21; CP 1, 2, 3, 4, 5, 6, 7; DLB 40

Simms, William Gilmore
1806-1870 .... **NCLC 3**
See also DLB 3, 30, 59, 73, 248, 254; RGAL 4

Simon, Carly 1945- .... **CLC 26**
See also CA 105

Simon, Claude 1913-2005 ... **CLC 4, 9, 15, 39**
See also CA 89-92; 241; CANR 33, 117; CWW 2; DAM NOV; DLB 83; EW 13; EWL 3; GFL 1789 to the Present; MTCW 1

Simon, Claude Eugene Henri
See Simon, Claude

Simon, Claude Henri Eugene
See Simon, Claude

Simon, Myles
See Follett, Ken(neth Martin)

Simon, (Marvin) Neil 1927- ... **CLC 6, 11, 31, 39, 70; DC 14**
See also AAYA 32; AITN 1; AMWS 4; CA 21-24R; CAD; CANR 26, 54, 87, 126; CD 5, 6; DA3; DAM DRAM; DFS 2, 6, 12, 18; DLB 7, 266; LAIT 4; MAL 5; MTCW 1, 2; MTFW 2005; RGAL 4; TUS

Simon, Paul (Frederick) 1941(?)- ..... **CLC 17**
See also CA 116; 153

Simonon, Paul 1956(?)- .... **CLC 30**

Simonson, Rick ed. .... **CLC 70**

Simpson, Harriette
See Arnow, Harriette (Louisa) Simpson

Simpson, Louis (Aston Marantz)
1923- .... **CLC 4, 7, 9, 32, 149**
See also AMWS 9; CA 1-4R; CAAS 4; CANR 1, 61, 140; CP 1, 2, 3, 4, 5, 6, 7; DAM POET; DLB 5; MAL 5; MTCW 1, 2; MTFW 2005; PFS 7, 11, 14; RGAL 4

Simpson, Mona (Elizabeth) 1957- ... **CLC 44, 146**
See also CA 122; 135; CANR 68, 103; CN 6, 7; EWL 3

Simpson, N(orman) F(rederick)
1919- .... **CLC 29**
See also CA 13-16R; CBD; DLB 13; RGEL 2

Sinclair, Andrew (Annandale) 1935- . **CLC 2, 14**
See also CA 9-12R; CAAS 5; CANR 14, 38, 91; CN 1, 2, 3, 4, 5, 6, 7; DLB 14; FANT; MTCW 1

Sinclair, Emil
See Hesse, Hermann

Sinclair, Iain 1943- .... **CLC 76**
See also CA 132; CANR 81; CP 7; HGG

Sinclair, Iain MacGregor
See Sinclair, Iain

Sinclair, Irene
See Griffith, D(avid Lewelyn) W(ark)

Sinclair, Mary Amelia St. Clair 1865(?)-1946
See Sinclair, May
See also CA 104; HGG; RHW

Sinclair, May .... **TCLC 3, 11**
See Sinclair, Mary Amelia St. Clair
See also CA 166; DLB 36, 135; EWL 3; RGEL 2; SUFW

Sinclair, Roy
See Griffith, D(avid Lewelyn) W(ark)

Sinclair, Upton (Beall) 1878-1968 ..... **CLC 1, 11, 15, 63; TCLC 160; WLC**
See also AAYA 63; AMWS 5; BPFB 3; BYA 2; CA 5-8R; 25-28R; CANR 7; CDALB 1929-1941; DA; DA3; DAB; DAC; DAM MST, NOV; DLB 9; EWL 3; INT CANR-7; LAIT 3; MAL 5; MTCW 1, 2; MTFW 2005; NFS 6; RGAL 4; SATA 9; TUS; YAW

Singe, (Edmund) J(ohn) M(illington)
1871-1909 .... **WLC**

Singer, Isaac
See Singer, Isaac Bashevis

Singer, Isaac Bashevis 1904-1991 .. **CLC 1, 3, 6, 9, 11, 15, 23, 38, 69, 111; SSC 3, 53, 80; WLC**
See also AAYA 32; AITN 1, 2; AMW; AMWR 2; BPFB 3; BYA 1, 4; CA 1-4R; 134; CANR 1, 39, 106; CDALB 1941-1968; CLR 1; CN 1, 2, 3, 4; CWRI 5; DA; DA3; DAB; DAC; DAM MST, NOV; DLB 6, 28, 52, 278; DLBY 1991; EWL 3; EXPS; HGG; JRDA; LAIT 3; MAI-CYA 1, 2; MAL 5; MTCW 1, 2; MTFW 2005; RGAL 4; RGSF 2; SATA 3, 27; SATA-Obit 68; SSFS 2, 12, 16; TUS; TWA

Singer, Israel Joshua 1893-1944 .... **TCLC 33**
See also CA 169; EWL 3

Singh, Khushwant 1915- .... **CLC 11**
See also CA 9-12R; CAAS 9; CANR 6, 84; CN 1, 2, 3, 4, 5, 6, 7; EWL 3; RGEL 2

Singleton, Ann
See Benedict, Ruth (Fulton)

Singleton, John 1968(?)- .... **CLC 156**
See also AAYA 50; BW 2, 3; CA 138; CANR 67, 82; DAM MULT

Siniavskii, Andrei
See Sinyavsky, Andrei (Donatevich)
See also CWW 2

Sinjohn, John
See Galsworthy, John

Sinyavsky, Andrei (Donatevich)
1925-1997 .... **CLC 8**
See Siniavskii, Andrei; Sinyavsky, Andrey Donatovich; Tertz, Abram
See also CA 85-88; 159

Sinyavsky, Andrey Donatovich
See Sinyavsky, Andrei (Donatevich)
See also EWL 3

Sirin, V.
See Nabokov, Vladimir (Vladimirovich)

Sissman, L(ouis) E(dward)
1928-1976 .... **CLC 9, 18**
See also CA 21-24R; 65-68; CANR 13; CP 2; DLB 5

Sisson, C(harles) H(ubert)
1914-2003 .... **CLC 8**
See also BRWS 11; CA 1-4R; 220; CAAS 3; CANR 3, 48, 84; CP 1, 2, 3, 4, 5, 6, 7; DLB 27

Sitting Bull 1831(?)-1890 .... **NNAL**
See also DA3; DAM MULT

Sitwell, Dame Edith 1887-1964 ..... **CLC 2, 9, 67; PC 3**
See also BRW 7; CA 9-12R; CANR 35; CDBLB 1945-1960; DAM POET; DLB 20; EWL 3; MTCW 1, 2; MTFW 2005; RGEL 2; TEA

Siwaarmill, H. P.
See Sharp, William

Sjoewall, Maj 1935- .... **CLC 7**
See Sjowall, Maj
See also CA 65-68; CANR 73

Sjowall, Maj
See Sjoewall, Maj
See also BPFB 3; CMW 4; MSW

Skelton, John 1460(?)-1529 ..... **LC 71; PC 25**
See also BRW 1; DLB 136; RGEL 2

Skelton, Robin 1925-1997 .... **CLC 13**
See Zuk, Georges
See also AITN 2; CA 5-8R; 160; CAAS 5; CANR 28, 89; CCA 1; CP 1, 2, 3, 4; DLB 27, 53

Skolimowski, Jerzy 1938- .... **CLC 20**
See also CA 128

Skram, Amalie (Bertha)
1847-1905 .... **TCLC 25**
See also CA 165

Skvorecky, Josef (Vaclav) 1924- ...... **CLC 15, 39, 69, 152**
See also CA 61-64; CAAS 1; CANR 10, 34, 63, 108; CDWLB 4; CWW 2; DA3; DAC; DAM NOV; DLB 232; EWL 3; MTCW 1, 2; MTFW 2005

Slade, Bernard 1930- .... **CLC 11, 46**
See Newbound, Bernard Slade
See also CAAS 9; CCA 1; CD 6; DLB 53

Slaughter, Carolyn 1946- .... **CLC 56**
See also CA 85-88; CANR 85; CN 5, 6, 7

Slaughter, Frank G(ill) 1908-2001 ... **CLC 29**
See also AITN 2; CA 5-8R; 197; CANR 5, 85; INT CANR-5; RHW

Slavitt, David R(ytman) 1935- ..... **CLC 5, 14**
See also CA 21-24R; CAAS 3; CANR 41, 83; CN 1, 2; CP 1, 2, 3, 4, 5, 6, 7; DLB 5, 6

Slesinger, Tess 1905-1945 .... **TCLC 10**
See also CA 107; 199; DLB 102

Slessor, Kenneth 1901-1971 .... **CLC 14**
See also CA 102; 89-92; DLB 260; RGEL 2

Slowacki, Juliusz 1809-1849 .... **NCLC 15**
See also RGWL 3

Smart, Christopher 1722-1771 . **LC 3; PC 13**
See also DAM POET; DLB 109; RGEL 2

Smart, Elizabeth 1913-1986 .... **CLC 54**
See also CA 81-84; 118; CN 4; DLB 88

Smiley, Jane (Graves) 1949- ...... **CLC 53, 76, 144**
See also AAYA 66; AMWS 6; BPFB 3; CA 104; CANR 30, 50, 74, 96; CN 6, 7; CPW 1; DA3; DAM POP; DLB 227, 234; EWL 3; INT CANR-30; MAL 5; MTFW 2005; SSFS 19

Smith, A(rthur) J(ames) M(arshall)
1902-1980 .... **CLC 15**
See also CA 1-4R; 102; CANR 4; CP 1, 2, 3; DAC; DLB 88; RGEL 2

Smith, Adam 1723(?)-1790 .... **LC 36**
See also DLB 104, 252; RGEL 2

Smith, Alexander 1829-1867 .... **NCLC 59**
See also DLB 32, 55

Smith, Anna Deavere 1950- .... **CLC 86**
See also CA 133; CANR 103; CD 5, 6; DFS 2, 22

Smith, Betty (Wehner) 1904-1972 .... **CLC 19**
See also BPFB 3; BYA 3; CA 5-8R; 33-36R; DLBY 1982; LAIT 3; RGAL 4; SATA 6

Smith, Charlotte (Turner)
1749-1806 .... **NCLC 23, 115**
See also DLB 39, 109; RGEL 2; TEA

Smith, Clark Ashton 1893-1961 .... **CLC 43**
See also CA 143; CANR 81; FANT; HGG; MTCW 2; SCFW 1, 2; SFW 4; SUFW

Smith, Dave .... **CLC 22, 42**
See Smith, David (Jeddie)
See also CAAS 7; CP 3, 4, 5, 6, 7; DLB 5

Smith, David (Jeddie) 1942-
See Smith, Dave
See also CA 49-52; CANR 1, 59, 120; CSW; DAM POET

Smith, Florence Margaret 1902-1971
See Smith, Stevie
See also CA 17-18; 29-32R; CANR 35; CAP 2; DAM POET; MTCW 1, 2; TEA

Smith, Iain Crichton 1928-1998 .... **CLC 64**
See also BRWS 9; CA 21-24R; 171; CN 1,
2, 3, 4, 5, 6; CP 1, 2, 3, 4; DLB 40, 139,
319; RGSF 2

Smith, John 1580(?)-1631 .... **LC 9**
See also DLB 24, 30; TUS

Smith, Johnston
See Crane, Stephen (Townley)

Smith, Joseph, Jr. 1805-1844 .... **NCLC 53**

Smith, Lee 1944- .... **CLC 25, 73**
See also CA 114; 119; CANR 46, 118; CN
7; CSW; DLB 143; DLBY 1983; EWL 3;
INT CA-119; RGAL 4

Smith, Martin
See Smith, Martin Cruz

Smith, Martin Cruz 1942- .. **CLC 25; NNAL**
See also BEST 89:4; BPFB 3; CA 85-88;
CANR 6, 23, 43, 65, 119; CMW 4; CPW;
DAM MULT, POP; HGG; INT CANR-
23; MTCW 2; MTFW 2005; RGAL 4

Smith, Patti 1946- .... **CLC 12**
See also CA 93-96; CANR 63

Smith, Pauline (Urmson)
1882-1959 .... **TCLC 25**
See also DLB 225; EWL 3

Smith, Rosamond
See Oates, Joyce Carol

Smith, Sheila Kaye
See Kaye-Smith, Sheila

Smith, Stevie .... **CLC 3, 8, 25, 44; PC 12**
See Smith, Florence Margaret
See also BRWS 2; CP 1; DLB 20; EWL 3;
PAB; PFS 3; RGEL 2

Smith, Wilbur (Addison) 1933- .... **CLC 33**
See also CA 13-16R; CANR 7, 46, 66, 134;
CPW; MTCW 1, 2; MTFW 2005

Smith, William Jay 1918- .... **CLC 6**
See also AMWS 13; CA 5-8R; CANR 44,
106; CP 1, 2, 3, 4, 5, 6, 7; CSW; CWRI
5; DLB 5; MAICYA 1, 2; SAAS 22;
SATA 2, 68, 154; SATA-Essay 154; TCLE
1:2

Smith, Woodrow Wilson
See Kuttner, Henry

Smith, Zadie 1976- .... **CLC 158**
See also AAYA 50; CA 193; MTFW 2005

Smolenskin, Peretz 1842-1885 .... **NCLC 30**

Smollett, Tobias (George) 1721-1771 ... **LC 2,
46**
See also BRW 3; CDBLB 1660-1789; DLB
39, 104; RGEL 2; TEA

Snodgrass, W(illiam) D(e Witt)
1926- .... **CLC 2, 6, 10, 18, 68**
See also AMWS 6; CA 1-4R; CANR 6, 36,
65, 85; CP 1, 2, 3, 4, 5, 6, 7; DAM POET;
DLB 5; MAL 5; MTCW 1, 2; MTFW
2005; RGAL 4; TCLE 1:2

Snorri Sturluson 1179-1241 .... **CMLC 56**
See also RGWL 2, 3

Snow, C(harles) P(ercy) 1905-1980 ... **CLC 1,
4, 6, 9, 13, 19**
See also BRW 7; CA 5-8R; 101; CANR 28;
CDBLB 1945-1960; CN 1, 2; DAM NOV;
DLB 15, 77; DLBD 17; EWL 3; MTCW
1, 2; MTFW 2005; RGEL 2; TEA

Snow, Frances Compton
See Adams, Henry (Brooks)

Snyder, Gary (Sherman) 1930- . **CLC 1, 2, 5,
9, 32, 120; PC 21**
See also AMWS 8; ANW; BG 1:3; CA 17-
20R; CANR 30, 60, 125; CP 1, 2, 3, 4, 5,
6, 7; DA3; DAM POET; DLB 5, 16, 165,
212, 237, 275; EWL 3; MAL 5; MTCW
2; MTFW 2005; PFS 9, 19; RGAL 4; WP

Snyder, Zilpha Keatley 1927- .... **CLC 17**
See also AAYA 15; BYA 1; CA 9-12R;
CANR 38; CLR 31; JRDA; MAICYA 1,
2; SAAS 2; SATA 1, 28, 75, 110, 163;
SATA-Essay 112, 163; YAW

Soares, Bernardo
See Pessoa, Fernando (Antonio Nogueira)

Sobh, A.
See Shamlu, Ahmad

Sobh, Alef
See Shamlu, Ahmad

Sobol, Joshua 1939- .... **CLC 60**
See Sobol, Yehoshua
See also CA 200

Sobol, Yehoshua 1939-
See Sobol, Joshua
See also CWW 2

Socrates 470B.C.-399B.C. .... **CMLC 27**

Soderberg, Hjalmar 1869-1941 ...... **TCLC 39**
See also DLB 259; EWL 3; RGSF 2

Soderbergh, Steven 1963- .... **CLC 154**
See also AAYA 43

Sodergran, Edith (Irene) 1892-1923
See Soedergran, Edith (Irene)
See also CA 202; DLB 259; EW 11; EWL
3; RGWL 2, 3

Soedergran, Edith (Irene)
1892-1923 .... **TCLC 31**
See Sodergran, Edith (Irene)

Softly, Edgar
See Lovecraft, H(oward) P(hillips)

Softly, Edward
See Lovecraft, H(oward) P(hillips)

Sokolov, Alexander V(sevolodovich) 1943-
See Sokolov, Sasha
See also CA 73-76

Sokolov, Raymond 1941- .... **CLC 7**
See also CA 85-88

Sokolov, Sasha .... **CLC 59**
See Sokolov, Alexander V(sevolodovich)
See also CWW 2; DLB 285; EWL 3; RGWL
2, 3

Solo, Jay
See Ellison, Harlan (Jay)

Sologub, Fyodor .... **TCLC 9**
See Teternikov, Fyodor Kuzmich
See also EWL 3

Solomons, Ikey Esquir
See Thackeray, William Makepeace

Solomos, Dionysios 1798-1857 .... **NCLC 15**

Solwoska, Mara
See French, Marilyn

Solzhenitsyn, Aleksandr I(sayevich)
1918- .. **CLC 1, 2, 4, 7, 9, 10, 18, 26, 34,
78, 134; SSC 32; WLC**
See Solzhenitsyn, Aleksandr Isaevich
See also AAYA 49; AITN 1; BPFB 3; CA
69-72; CANR 40, 65, 116; DA; DA3;
DAB; DAC; DAM MST, NOV; DLB 302;
EW 13; EXPS; LAIT 4; MTCW 1, 2;
MTFW 2005; NFS 6; RGSF 2; RGWL 2,
3; SSFS 9; TWA

Solzhenitsyn, Aleksandr Isaevich
See Solzhenitsyn, Aleksandr I(sayevich)
See also CWW 2; EWL 3

Somers, Jane
See Lessing, Doris (May)

Somerville, Edith Oenone
1858-1949 .... **SSC 56; TCLC 51**
See also CA 196; DLB 135; RGEL 2; RGSF
2

Somerville & Ross
See Martin, Violet Florence; Somerville,
Edith Oenone

Sommer, Scott 1951- .... **CLC 25**
See also CA 106

Sommers, Christina Hoff 1950- ...... **CLC 197**
See also CA 153; CANR 95

Sondheim, Stephen (Joshua) 1930- . **CLC 30,
39, 147; DC 22**
See also AAYA 11, 66; CA 103; CANR 47,
67, 125; DAM DRAM; LAIT 4

Sone, Monica 1919- .... **AAL**
See also DLB 312

Song, Cathy 1955- .... **AAL; PC 21**
See also CA 154; CANR 118; CWP; DLB
169, 312; EXPP; FW; PFS 5

Sontag, Susan 1933-2004 ... **CLC 1, 2, 10, 13,
31, 105, 195**
See also AMWS 3; CA 17-20R; 234; CANR
25, 51, 74, 97; CN 1, 2, 3, 4, 5, 6, 7;
CPW; DA3; DAM POP; DLB 2, 67; EWL
3; MAL 5; MAWW; MTCW 1, 2; MTFW
2005; RGAL 4; RHW; SSFS 10

Sophocles 496(?)B.C.-406(?)B.C. .... **CMLC 2,
47, 51; DC 1; WLCS**
See also AW 1; CDWLB 1; DA; DA3;
DAB; DAC; DAM DRAM, MST; DFS 1,
4, 8; DLB 176; LAIT 1; LATS 1:1; LMFS
1; RGWL 2, 3; TWA

Sordello 1189-1269 .... **CMLC 15**

Sorel, Georges 1847-1922 .... **TCLC 91**
See also CA 118; 188

Sorel, Julia
See Drexler, Rosalyn

Sorokin, Vladimir .... **CLC 59**
See Sorokin, Vladimir Georgievich

Sorokin, Vladimir Georgievich
See Sorokin, Vladimir
See also DLB 285

Sorrentino, Gilbert 1929- .. **CLC 3, 7, 14, 22,
40**
See also CA 77-80; CANR 14, 33, 115; CN
3, 4, 5, 6, 7; CP 1, 2, 3, 4, 5, 6, 7; DLB 5,
173; DLBY 1980; INT CANR-14

Soseki
See Natsume, Soseki
See also MJW

Soto, Gary 1952- ... **CLC 32, 80; HLC 2; PC
28**
See also AAYA 10, 37; BYA 11; CA 119;
125; CANR 50, 74, 107; CLR 38; CP 4,
5, 6, 7; DAM MULT; DLB 82; EWL 3;
EXPP; HW 1, 2; INT CA-125; JRDA;
LLW; MAICYA 2; MAICYAS 1; MAL 5;
MTCW 2; MTFW 2005; PFS 7; RGAL 4;
SATA 80, 120; WYA; YAW

Soupault, Philippe 1897-1990 .... **CLC 68**
See also CA 116; 147; 131; EWL 3; GFL
1789 to the Present; LMFS 2

Souster, (Holmes) Raymond 1921- .... **CLC 5,
14**
See also CA 13-16R; CAAS 14; CANR 13,
29, 53; CP 1, 2, 3, 4, 5, 6, 7; DA3; DAC;
DAM POET; DLB 88; RGEL 2; SATA 63

Southern, Terry 1924(?)-1995 .... **CLC 7**
See also AMWS 11; BPFB 3; CA 1-4R;
150; CANR 1, 55, 107; CN 1, 2, 3, 4, 5,
6; DLB 2; IDFW 3, 4

Southerne, Thomas 1660-1746 .... **LC 99**
See also DLB 80; RGEL 2

Southey, Robert 1774-1843 .... **NCLC 8, 97**
See also BRW 4; DLB 93, 107, 142; RGEL
2; SATA 54

Southwell, Robert 1561(?)-1595 .... **LC 108**
See also DLB 167; RGEL 2; TEA

Southworth, Emma Dorothy Eliza Nevitte
1819-1899 .... **NCLC 26**
See also DLB 239

Souza, Ernest
See Scott, Evelyn

Soyinka, Wole 1934- .. **BLC 3; CLC 3, 5, 14,
36, 44, 179; DC 2; WLC**
See also AFW; BW 2, 3; CA 13-16R;
CANR 27, 39, 82, 136; CD 5, 6; CDWLB
3; CN 6, 7; CP 1, 2, 3, 4, 5, 6 ,7; DA;
DA3; DAB; DAC; DAM DRAM, MST,
MULT; DFS 10; DLB 125; EWL 3;
MTCW 1, 2; MTFW 2005; RGEL 2;
TWA; WLIT 2; WWE 1

Spackman, W(illiam) M(ode)
1905-1990 .... **CLC 46**
See also CA 81-84; 132

Stringer, David
See Roberts, Keith (John Kingston)

Stroheim, Erich von 1885-1957 ..... **TCLC 71**

Strugatskii, Arkadii (Natanovich)
1925-1991 .... **CLC 27**
See Strugatsky, Arkadii Natanovich
See also CA 106; 135; SFW 4

Strugatskii, Boris (Natanovich)
1933- .... **CLC 27**
See Strugatsky, Boris (Natanovich)
See also CA 106; SFW 4

Strugatsky, Arkadii Natanovich
See Strugatskii, Arkadii Natanovich
See also DLB 302

Strugatsky, Boris (Natanovich)
See Strugatskii, Boris (Natanovich)
See also DLB 302

Strummer, Joe 1952-2002 .... **CLC 30**

Strunk, William, Jr. 1869-1946 ...... **TCLC 92**
See also CA 118; 164; NCFS 5

Stryk, Lucien 1924- .... **PC 27**
See also CA 13-16R; CANR 10, 28, 55, 110; CP 1, 2, 3, 4, 5, 6, 7

Stuart, Don A.
See Campbell, John W(ood, Jr.)

Stuart, Ian
See MacLean, Alistair (Stuart)

Stuart, Jesse (Hilton) 1906-1984 ... **CLC 1, 8, 11, 14, 34; SSC 31**
See also CA 5-8R; 112; CANR 31; CN 1, 2, 3; DLB 9, 48, 102; DLBY 1984; SATA 2; SATA-Obit 36

Stubblefield, Sally
See Trumbo, Dalton

Sturgeon, Theodore (Hamilton)
1918-1985 .... **CLC 22, 39**
See Queen, Ellery
See also AAYA 51; BPFB 3; BYA 9, 10; CA 81-84; 116; CANR 32, 103; DLB 8; DLBY 1985; HGG; MTCW 1, 2; MTFW 2005; SCFW; SFW 4; SUFW

Sturges, Preston 1898-1959 .... **TCLC 48**
See also CA 114; 149; DLB 26

Styron, William 1925- .... **CLC 1, 3, 5, 11, 15, 60; SSC 25**
See also AMW; AMWC 2; BEST 90:4; BPFB 3; CA 5-8R; CANR 6, 33, 74, 126; CDALB 1968-1988; CN 1, 2, 3, 4, 5, 6, 7; CPW; CSW; DA3; DAM NOV, POP; DLB 2, 143, 299; DLBY 1980; EWL 3; INT CANR-6; LAIT 2; MAL 5; MTCW 1, 2; MTFW 2005; NCFS 1; NFS 22; RGAL 4; RHW; TUS

Su, Chien 1884-1918
See Su Man-shu
See also CA 123

Suarez Lynch, B.
See Bioy Casares, Adolfo; Borges, Jorge Luis

Suassuna, Ariano Vilar 1927- .... **HLCS 1**
See also CA 178; DLB 307; HW 2; LAW

Suckert, Kurt Erich
See Malaparte, Curzio

Suckling, Sir John 1609-1642 . **LC 75; PC 30**
See also BRW 2; DAM POET; DLB 58, 126; EXPP; PAB; RGEL 2

Suckow, Ruth 1892-1960 .... **SSC 18**
See also CA 193; 113; DLB 9, 102; RGAL 4; TCWW 2

Sudermann, Hermann 1857-1928 .. **TCLC 15**
See also CA 107; 201; DLB 118

Sue, Eugene 1804-1857 .... **NCLC 1**
See also DLB 119

Sueskind, Patrick 1949- .... **CLC 44, 182**
See Suskind, Patrick

Suetonius c. 70-c. 130 .... **CMLC 60**
See also AW 2; DLB 211; RGWL 2, 3

Sukenick, Ronald 1932-2004 ..... **CLC 3, 4, 6, 48**
See also CA 25-28R, 209; 229; CAAE 209; CAAS 8; CANR 32, 89; CN 3, 4, 5, 6, 7; DLB 173; DLBY 1981

Suknaski, Andrew 1942- .... **CLC 19**
See also CA 101; CP 3, 4, 5, 6, 7; DLB 53

Sullivan, Vernon
See Vian, Boris

Sully Prudhomme, Rene-Francois-Armand
1839-1907 .... **TCLC 31**
See also GFL 1789 to the Present

Su Man-shu .... **TCLC 24**
See Su, Chien
See also EWL 3

Sumarokov, Aleksandr Petrovich
1717-1777 .... **LC 104**
See also DLB 150

Summerforest, Ivy B.
See Kirkup, James

Summers, Andrew James 1942- .... **CLC 26**

Summers, Andy
See Summers, Andrew James

Summers, Hollis (Spurgeon, Jr.)
1916- .... **CLC 10**
See also CA 5-8R; CANR 3; CN 1, 2, 3; CP 1, 2, 3, 4; DLB 6; TCLE 1:2

Summers, (Alphonsus Joseph-Mary Augustus) Montague
1880-1948 .... **TCLC 16**
See also CA 118; 163

Sumner, Gordon Matthew .... **CLC 26**
See Police, The; Sting

Sun Tzu c. 400B.C.-c. 320B.C. ...... **CMLC 56**

Surrey, Henry Howard 1517-1574 ... **LC 121; PC 59**
See also BRW 1; RGEL 2

Surtees, Robert Smith 1805-1864 .. **NCLC 14**
See also DLB 21; RGEL 2

Susann, Jacqueline 1921-1974 .... **CLC 3**
See also AITN 1; BPFB 3; CA 65-68; 53-56; MTCW 1, 2

Su Shi
See Su Shih
See also RGWL 2, 3

Su Shih 1036-1101 .... **CMLC 15**
See Su Shi

Suskind, Patrick .... **CLC 182**
See Sueskind, Patrick
See also BPFB 3; CA 145; CWW 2

Sutcliff, Rosemary 1920-1992 .... **CLC 26**
See also AAYA 10; BYA 1, 4; CA 5-8R; 139; CANR 37; CLR 1, 37; CPW; DAB; DAC; DAM MST, POP; JRDA; LATS 1:1; MAICYA 1, 2; MAICYAS 1; RHW; SATA 6, 44, 78; SATA-Obit 73; WYA; YAW

Sutro, Alfred 1863-1933 .... **TCLC 6**
See also CA 105; 185; DLB 10; RGEL 2

Sutton, Henry
See Slavitt, David R(ytman)

Suzuki, D. T.
See Suzuki, Daisetz Teitaro

Suzuki, Daisetz T.
See Suzuki, Daisetz Teitaro

Suzuki, Daisetz Teitaro
1870-1966 .... **TCLC 109**
See also CA 121; 111; MTCW 1, 2; MTFW 2005

Suzuki, Teitaro
See Suzuki, Daisetz Teitaro

Svevo, Italo .... **SSC 25; TCLC 2, 35**
See Schmitz, Aron Hector
See also DLB 264; EW 8; EWL 3; RGWL 2, 3; WLIT 7

Swados, Elizabeth (A.) 1951- .... **CLC 12**
See also CA 97-100; CANR 49; INT CA-97-100

Swados, Harvey 1920-1972 .... **CLC 5**
See also CA 5-8R; 37-40R; CANR 6; CN 1; DLB 2; MAL 5

Swan, Gladys 1934- .... **CLC 69**
See also CA 101; CANR 17, 39; TCLE 1:2

Swanson, Logan
See Matheson, Richard (Burton)

Swarthout, Glendon (Fred)
1918-1992 .... **CLC 35**
See also AAYA 55; CA 1-4R; 139; CANR 1, 47; CN 1, 2, 3, 4, 5; LAIT 5; SATA 26; TCWW 1, 2; YAW

Swedenborg, Emanuel 1688-1772 ..... **LC 105**

Sweet, Sarah C.
See Jewett, (Theodora) Sarah Orne

Swenson, May 1919-1989 ..... **CLC 4, 14, 61, 106; PC 14**
See also AMWS 4; CA 5-8R; 130; CANR 36, 61, 131; CP 1, 2, 3, 4; DA; DAB; DAC; DAM MST, POET; DLB 5; EXPP; GLL 2; MAL 5; MTCW 1, 2; MTFW 2005; PFS 16; SATA 15; WP

Swift, Augustus
See Lovecraft, H(oward) P(hillips)

Swift, Graham (Colin) 1949- ...... **CLC 41, 88**
See also BRWC 2; BRWS 5; CA 117; 122; CANR 46, 71, 128; CN 4, 5, 6, 7; DLB 194; MTCW 2; MTFW 2005; NFS 18; RGSF 2

Swift, Jonathan 1667-1745 ..... **LC 1, 42, 101; PC 9; WLC**
See also AAYA 41; BRW 3; BRWC 1; BRWR 1; BYA 5, 14; CDBLB 1660-1789; CLR 53; DA; DA3; DAB; DAC; DAM MST, NOV, POET; DLB 39, 95, 101; EXPN; LAIT 1; NFS 6; RGEL 2; SATA 19; TEA; WCH; WLIT 3

Swinburne, Algernon Charles
1837-1909 ... **PC 24; TCLC 8, 36; WLC**
See also BRW 5; CA 105; 140; CDBLB 1832-1890; DA; DA3; DAB; DAC; DAM MST, POET; DLB 35, 57; PAB; RGEL 2; TEA

Swinfen, Ann .... **CLC 34**
See also CA 202

Swinnerton, Frank (Arthur)
1884-1982 .... **CLC 31**
See also CA 202; 108; CN 1, 2, 3; DLB 34

Swinnerton, Frank Arthur
1884-1982 .... **CLC 31**
See also CA 108; DLB 34

Swithen, John
See King, Stephen

Sylvia
See Ashton-Warner, Sylvia (Constance)

Symmes, Robert Edward
See Duncan, Robert (Edward)

Symonds, John Addington
1840-1893 .... **NCLC 34**
See also DLB 57, 144

Symons, Arthur 1865-1945 .... **TCLC 11**
See also CA 107; 189; DLB 19, 57, 149; RGEL 2

Symons, Julian (Gustave)
1912-1994 .... **CLC 2, 14, 32**
See also CA 49-52; 147; CAAS 3; CANR 3, 33, 59; CMW 4; CN 1, 2, 3, 4, 5; CP 1, 3, 4; DLB 87, 155; DLBY 1992; MSW; MTCW 1

Synge, (Edmund) J(ohn) M(illington)
1871-1909 .... **DC 2; TCLC 6, 37**
See also BRW 6; BRWR 1; CA 104; 141; CDBLB 1890-1914; DAM DRAM; DFS 18; DLB 10, 19; EWL 3; RGEL 2; TEA; WLIT 4

Syruc, J.
See Milosz, Czeslaw

1945; CLR 56; CN 1; CPW 1; CWRI 5;
DA; DA3; DAB; DAC; DAM MST, NOV,
POP; DLB 15, 160, 255; EFS 2; EWL 3;
FANT; JRDA; LAIT 1; LATS 1:2; LMFS
2; MAICYA 1, 2; MTCW 1, 2; MTFW
2005; NFS 8; RGEL 2; SATA 2, 32, 100;
SATA-Obit 24; SFW 4; SUFW; TEA;
WCH; WYA; YAW

Toller, Ernst 1893-1939 .... **TCLC 10**
See also CA 107; 186; DLB 124; EWL 3;
RGWL 2, 3

Tolson, M. B.
See Tolson, Melvin B(eaunorus)

Tolson, Melvin B(eaunorus)
1898(?)-1966 .... **BLC 3; CLC 36, 105**
See also AFAW 1, 2; BW 1, 3; CA 124; 89-
92; CANR 80; DAM MULT, POET; DLB
48, 76; MAL 5; RGAL 4

Tolstoi, Aleksei Nikolaevich
See Tolstoy, Alexey Nikolaevich

Tolstoi, Lev
See Tolstoy, Leo (Nikolaevich)
See also RGSF 2; RGWL 2, 3

Tolstoy, Aleksei Nikolaevich
See Tolstoy, Alexey Nikolaevich
See also DLB 272

Tolstoy, Alexey Nikolaevich
1882-1945 .... **TCLC 18**
See Tolstoy, Aleksei Nikolaevich
See also CA 107; 158; EWL 3; SFW 4

Tolstoy, Leo (Nikolaevich)
1828-1910 . **SSC 9, 30, 45, 54; TCLC 4,
11, 17, 28, 44, 79, 173; WLC**
See Tolstoi, Lev
See also AAYA 56; CA 104; 123; DA; DA3;
DAB; DAC; DAM MST, NOV; DLB 238;
EFS 2; EW 7; EXPS; IDTP; LAIT 2;
LATS 1:1; LMFS 1; NFS 10; SATA 26;
SSFS 5; TWA

Tolstoy, Count Leo
See Tolstoy, Leo (Nikolaevich)

Tomalin, Claire 1933- .... **CLC 166**
See also CA 89-92; CANR 52, 88; DLB
155

Tomasi di Lampedusa, Giuseppe 1896-1957
See Lampedusa, Giuseppe (Tomasi) di
See also CA 111; DLB 177; EWL 3; WLIT
7

Tomlin, Lily .... **CLC 17**
See Tomlin, Mary Jean

Tomlin, Mary Jean 1939(?)-
See Tomlin, Lily
See also CA 117

Tomline, F. Latour
See Gilbert, W(illiam) S(chwenck)

Tomlinson, (Alfred) Charles 1927- .... **CLC 2,
4, 6, 13, 45; PC 17**
See also CA 5-8R; CANR 33; CP 1, 2, 3, 4,
5, 6, 7; DAM POET; DLB 40; TCLE 1:2

Tomlinson, H(enry) M(ajor)
1873-1958 .... **TCLC 71**
See also CA 118; 161; DLB 36, 100, 195

Tonna, Charlotte Elizabeth
1790-1846 .... **NCLC 135**
See also DLB 163

Tonson, Jacob fl. 1655(?)-1736 .... **LC 86**
See also DLB 170

Toole, John Kennedy 1937-1969 ..... **CLC 19,
64**
See also BPFB 3; CA 104; DLBY 1981;
MTCW 2; MTFW 2005

Toomer, Eugene
See Toomer, Jean

Toomer, Eugene Pinchback
See Toomer, Jean

Toomer, Jean 1894-1967 .. **BLC 3; CLC 1, 4,
13, 22; HR 1:3; PC 7; SSC 1, 45;
TCLC 172; WLCS**
See also AFAW 1, 2; AMWS 3, 9; BW 1;
CA 85-88; CDALB 1917-1929; DA3;
DAM MULT; DLB 45, 51; EWL 3; EXPP;
EXPS; LMFS 2; MAL 5; MTCW 1, 2;
MTFW 2005; NFS 11; RGAL 4; RGSF 2;
SSFS 5

Toomer, Nathan Jean
See Toomer, Jean

Toomer, Nathan Pinchback
See Toomer, Jean

Torley, Luke
See Blish, James (Benjamin)

Tornimparte, Alessandra
See Ginzburg, Natalia

Torre, Raoul della
See Mencken, H(enry) L(ouis)

Torrence, Ridgely 1874-1950 .... **TCLC 97**
See also DLB 54, 249; MAL 5

Torrey, E(dwin) Fuller 1937- .... **CLC 34**
See also CA 119; CANR 71

Torsvan, Ben Traven
See Traven, B.

Torsvan, Benno Traven
See Traven, B.

Torsvan, Berick Traven
See Traven, B.

Torsvan, Berwick Traven
See Traven, B.

Torsvan, Bruno Traven
See Traven, B.

Torsvan, Traven
See Traven, B.

Tourneur, Cyril 1575(?)-1626 .... **LC 66**
See also BRW 2; DAM DRAM; DLB 58;
RGEL 2

Tournier, Michel (Edouard) 1924- .... **CLC 6,
23, 36, 95; SSC 88**
See also CA 49-52; CANR 3, 36, 74; CWW
2; DLB 83; EWL 3; GFL 1789 to the
Present; MTCW 1, 2; SATA 23

Tournimparte, Alessandra
See Ginzburg, Natalia

Towers, Ivar
See Kornbluth, C(yril) M.

Towne, Robert (Burton) 1936(?)- ..... **CLC 87**
See also CA 108; DLB 44; IDFW 3, 4

Townsend, Sue .... **CLC 61**
See Townsend, Susan Lilian
See also AAYA 28; CA 119; 127; CANR
65, 107; CBD; CD 5, 6; CPW; CWD;
DAB; DAC; DAM MST; DLB 271; INT
CA-127; SATA 55, 93; SATA-Brief 48;
YAW

Townsend, Susan Lilian 1946-
See Townsend, Sue

Townshend, Pete
See Townshend, Peter (Dennis Blandford)

Townshend, Peter (Dennis Blandford)
1945- .... **CLC 17, 42**
See also CA 107

Tozzi, Federigo 1883-1920 .... **TCLC 31**
See also CA 160; CANR 110; DLB 264;
EWL 3; WLIT 7

Tracy, Don(ald Fiske) 1905-1970(?)
See Queen, Ellery
See also CA 1-4R; 176; CANR 2

Trafford, F. G.
See Riddell, Charlotte

Traherne, Thomas 1637(?)-1674 .. **LC 99; PC
70**
See also BRW 2; BRWS 11; DLB 131;
PAB; RGEL 2

Traill, Catharine Parr 1802-1899 .. **NCLC 31**
See also DLB 99

Trakl, Georg 1887-1914 .... **PC 20; TCLC 5**
See also CA 104; 165; EW 10; EWL 3;
LMFS 2; MTCW 2; RGWL 2, 3

Trambley, Estela Portillo .... **TCLC 163**
See Portillo Trambley, Estela
See also CA 77-80; RGAL 4

Tranquilli, Secondino
See Silone, Ignazio

Transtroemer, Tomas Gosta
See Transtromer, Tomas (Goesta)

Transtromer, Tomas (Gosta)
See Transtromer, Tomas (Goesta)
See also CWW 2

Transtromer, Tomas (Goesta)
1931- .... **CLC 52, 65**
See Transtromer, Tomas (Gosta)
See also CA 117; 129; CAAS 17; CANR
115; DAM POET; DLB 257; EWL 3; PFS
21

Transtromer, Tomas Gosta
See Transtromer, Tomas (Goesta)

Traven, B. 1882(?)-1969 .... **CLC 8, 11**
See also CA 19-20; 25-28R; CAP 2; DLB
9, 56; EWL 3; MTCW 1; RGAL 4

Trediakovsky, Vasilii Kirillovich
1703-1769 .... **LC 68**
See also DLB 150

Treitel, Jonathan 1959- .... **CLC 70**
See also CA 210; DLB 267

Trelawny, Edward John
1792-1881 .... **NCLC 85**
See also DLB 110, 116, 144

Tremain, Rose 1943- .... **CLC 42**
See also CA 97-100; CANR 44, 95; CN 4,
5, 6, 7; DLB 14, 271; RGSF 2; RHW

Tremblay, Michel 1942- .... **CLC 29, 102**
See also CA 116; 128; CCA 1; CWW 2;
DAC; DAM MST; DLB 60; EWL 3; GLL
1; MTCW 1, 2; MTFW 2005

Trevanian .... **CLC 29**
See Whitaker, Rod(ney)

Trevor, Glen
See Hilton, James

Trevor, William .. **CLC 7, 9, 14, 25, 71, 116;
SSC 21, 58**
See Cox, William Trevor
See also BRWS 4; CBD; CD 5, 6; CN 1, 2,
3, 4, 5, 6, 7; DLB 14, 139; EWL 3; LATS
1:2; RGEL 2; RGSF 2; SSFS 10; TCLE
1:2

Trifonov, Iurii (Valentinovich)
See Trifonov, Yuri (Valentinovich)
See also DLB 302; RGWL 2, 3

Trifonov, Yuri (Valentinovich)
1925-1981 .... **CLC 45**
See Trifonov, Iurii (Valentinovich); Trifonov, Yury Valentinovich
See also CA 126; 103; MTCW 1

Trifonov, Yury Valentinovich
See Trifonov, Yuri (Valentinovich)
See also EWL 3

Trilling, Diana (Rubin) 1905-1996 . **CLC 129**
See also CA 5-8R; 154; CANR 10, 46; INT
CANR-10; MTCW 1, 2

Trilling, Lionel 1905-1975 ..... **CLC 9, 11, 24;
SSC 75**
See also AMWS 3; CA 9-12R; 61-64;
CANR 10, 105; CN 1, 2; DLB 28, 63;
EWL 3; INT CANR-10; MAL 5; MTCW
1, 2; RGAL 4; TUS

Trimball, W. H.
See Mencken, H(enry) L(ouis)

Tristan
See Gomez de la Serna, Ramon

Tristram
See Housman, A(lfred) E(dward)

Usk, Thomas (?)-1388 .... **CMLC 76**
  See also DLB 146
Ustinov, Peter (Alexander)
  1921-2004 .... **CLC 1**
  See also AITN 1; CA 13-16R; 225; CANR
  25, 51; CBD; CD 5, 6; DLB 13; MTCW
  2
U Tam'si, Gerald Felix Tchicaya
  See Tchicaya, Gerald Felix
U Tam'si, Tchicaya
  See Tchicaya, Gerald Felix
Vachss, Andrew (Henry) 1942- .... **CLC 106**
  See also CA 118, 214; CAAE 214; CANR
  44, 95; CMW 4
Vachss, Andrew H.
  See Vachss, Andrew (Henry)
Vaculik, Ludvik 1926- .... **CLC 7**
  See also CA 53-56; CANR 72; CWW 2;
  DLB 232; EWL 3
Vaihinger, Hans 1852-1933 .... **TCLC 71**
  See also CA 116; 166
Valdez, Luis (Miguel) 1940- ..... **CLC 84; DC**
  10; HLC 2
  See also CA 101; CAD; CANR 32, 81; CD
  5, 6; DAM MULT; DFS 5; DLB 122;
  EWL 3; HW 1; LAIT 4; LLW
Valenzuela, Luisa 1938- .... **CLC 31, 104;**
  HLCS 2; SSC 14, 82
  See also CA 101; CANR 32, 65, 123; CD-
  WLB 3; CWW 2; DAM MULT; DLB 113;
  EWL 3; FW; HW 1, 2; LAW; RGSF 2;
  RGWL 3
Valera y Alcala-Galiano, Juan
  1824-1905 .... **TCLC 10**
  See also CA 106
Valerius Maximus fl. 20- .... **CMLC 64**
  See also DLB 211
Valery, (Ambroise) Paul (Toussaint Jules)
  1871-1945 .... **PC 9; TCLC 4, 15**
  See also CA 104; 122; DA3; DAM POET;
  DLB 258; EW 8; EWL 3; GFL 1789 to
  the Present; MTCW 1, 2; MTFW 2005;
  RGWL 2, 3; TWA
Valle-Inclan, Ramon (Maria) del
  1866-1936 .... **HLC 2; TCLC 5**
  See del Valle-Inclan, Ramon (Maria)
  See also CA 106; 153; CANR 80; DAM
  MULT; DLB 134; EW 8; EWL 3; HW 2;
  RGSF 2; RGWL 2, 3
Vallejo, Antonio Buero
  See Buero Vallejo, Antonio
Vallejo, Cesar (Abraham)
  1892-1938 .... **HLC 2; TCLC 3, 56**
  See also CA 105; 153; DAM MULT; DLB
  290; EWL 3; HW 1; LAW; RGWL 2, 3
Valles, Jules 1832-1885 .... **NCLC 71**
  See also DLB 123; GFL 1789 to the Present
Vallette, Marguerite Eymery
  1860-1953 .... **TCLC 67**
  See Rachilde
  See also CA 182; DLB 123, 192
Valle Y Pena, Ramon del
  See Valle-Inclan, Ramon (Maria) del
Van Ash, Cay 1918-1994 .... **CLC 34**
  See also CA 220
Vanbrugh, Sir John 1664-1726 .... **LC 21**
  See also BRW 2; DAM DRAM; DLB 80;
  IDTP; RGEL 2
Van Campen, Karl
  See Campbell, John W(ood, Jr.)
Vance, Gerald
  See Silverberg, Robert
Vance, Jack .... **CLC 35**
  See Vance, John Holbrook
  See also DLB 8; FANT; SCFW 1, 2; SFW
  4; SUFW 1, 2

Vance, John Holbrook 1916-
  See Queen, Ellery; Vance, Jack
  See also CA 29-32R; CANR 17, 65; CMW
  4; MTCW 1
Van Den Bogarde, Derek Jules Gaspard
  Ulric Niven 1921-1999 .... **CLC 14**
  See Bogarde, Dirk
  See also CA 77-80; 179
Vandenburgh, Jane .... **CLC 59**
  See also CA 168
Vanderhaeghe, Guy 1951- .... **CLC 41**
  See also BPFB 3; CA 113; CANR 72, 145;
  CN 7
van der Post, Laurens (Jan)
  1906-1996 .... **CLC 5**
  See also AFW; CA 5-8R; 155; CANR 35;
  CN 1, 2, 3, 4, 5, 6; DLB 204; RGEL 2
van de Wetering, Janwillem 1931- ... **CLC 47**
  See also CA 49-52; CANR 4, 62, 90; CMW
  4
Van Dine, S. S. .... **TCLC 23**
  See Wright, Willard Huntington
  See also DLB 306; MSW
Van Doren, Carl (Clinton)
  1885-1950 .... **TCLC 18**
  See also CA 111; 168
Van Doren, Mark 1894-1972 .... **CLC 6, 10**
  See also CA 1-4R; 37-40R; CANR 3; CN
  1; CP 1; DLB 45, 284; MAL 5; MTCW
  1, 2; RGAL 4
Van Druten, John (William)
  1901-1957 .... **TCLC 2**
  See also CA 104; 161; DLB 10; MAL 5;
  RGAL 4
Van Duyn, Mona (Jane) 1921-2004 .. **CLC 3,**
  7, 63, 116
  See also CA 9-12R; 234; CANR 7, 38, 60,
  116; CP 1, 2, 3, 4, 5, 6, 7; CWP; DAM
  POET; DLB 5; MAL 5; MTFW 2005;
  PFS 20
Van Dyne, Edith
  See Baum, L(yman) Frank
van Itallie, Jean-Claude 1936- .... **CLC 3**
  See also CA 45-48; CAAS 2; CAD; CANR
  1, 48; CD 5, 6; DLB 7
Van Loot, Cornelius Obenchain
  See Roberts, Kenneth (Lewis)
van Ostaijen, Paul 1896-1928 .... **TCLC 33**
  See also CA 163
Van Peebles, Melvin 1932- .... **CLC 2, 20**
  See also BW 2, 3; CA 85-88; CANR 27,
  67, 82; DAM MULT
van Schendel, Arthur(-Francois-Emile)
  1874-1946 .... **TCLC 56**
  See also EWL 3
Vansittart, Peter 1920- .... **CLC 42**
  See also CA 1-4R; CANR 3, 49, 90; CN 4,
  5, 6, 7; RHW
Van Vechten, Carl 1880-1964 ... **CLC 33; HR**
  1:3
  See also AMWS 2; CA 183; 89-92; DLB 4,
  9, 51; RGAL 4
van Vogt, A(lfred) E(lton) 1912-2000 . **CLC 1**
  See also BPFB 3; BYA 13, 14; CA 21-24R;
  190; CANR 28; DLB 8, 251; SATA 14;
  SATA-Obit 124; SCFW 1, 2; SFW 4
Vara, Madeleine
  See Jackson, Laura (Riding)
Varda, Agnes 1928- .... **CLC 16**
  See also CA 116; 122
Vargas Llosa, (Jorge) Mario (Pedro)
  1936- .... **CLC 3, 6, 9, 10, 15, 31, 42, 85,**
  181; HLC 2
  See Llosa, (Jorge) Mario (Pedro) Vargas
  See also BPFB 3; CA 73-76; CANR 18, 32,
  42, 67, 116, 140; CDWLB 3; CWW 2;
  DA; DA3; DAB; DAC; DAM MST,
  MULT, NOV; DLB 145; DNFS 2; EWL

3; HW 1, 2; LAIT 5; LATS 1:2; LAW;
  LAWS 1; MTCW 1, 2; MTFW 2005;
  RGWL 2; SSFS 14; TWA; WLIT 1
Varnhagen von Ense, Rahel
  1771-1833 .... **NCLC 130**
  See also DLB 90
Vasari, Giorgio 1511-1574 .... **LC 114**
Vasiliu, George
  See Bacovia, George
Vasiliu, Gheorghe
  See Bacovia, George
  See also CA 123; 189
Vassa, Gustavus
  See Equiano, Olaudah
Vassilikos, Vassilis 1933- .... **CLC 4, 8**
  See also CA 81-84; CANR 75; EWL 3
Vaughan, Henry 1621-1695 .... **LC 27**
  See also BRW 2; DLB 131; PAB; RGEL 2
Vaughn, Stephanie .... **CLC 62**
Vazov, Ivan (Minchov) 1850-1921 . **TCLC 25**
  See also CA 121; 167; CDWLB 4; DLB
  147
Veblen, Thorstein B(unde)
  1857-1929 .... **TCLC 31**
  See also AMWS 1; CA 115; 165; DLB 246;
  MAL 5
Vega, Lope de 1562-1635 ... **HLCS 2; LC 23,**
  119
  See also EW 2; RGWL 2, 3
Vendler, Helen (Hennessy) 1933- ... **CLC 138**
  See also CA 41-44R; CANR 25, 72, 136;
  MTCW 1, 2; MTFW 2005
Venison, Alfred
  See Pound, Ezra (Weston Loomis)
Ventsel, Elena Sergeevna 1907-2002
  See Grekova, I.
  See also CA 154
Verdi, Marie de
  See Mencken, H(enry) L(ouis)
Verdu, Matilde
  See Cela, Camilo Jose
Verga, Giovanni (Carmelo)
  1840-1922 .... **SSC 21, 87; TCLC 3**
  See also CA 104; 123; CANR 101; EW 7;
  EWL 3; RGSF 2; RGWL 2, 3; WLIT 7
Vergil 70B.C.-19B.C. ... **CMLC 9, 40; PC 12;**
  WLCS
  See Virgil
  See also AW 2; DA; DA3; DAB; DAC;
  DAM MST, POET; EFS 1; LMFS 1
Vergil, Polydore c. 1470-1555 .... **LC 108**
  See also DLB 132
Verhaeren, Emile (Adolphe Gustave)
  1855-1916 .... **TCLC 12**
  See also CA 109; EWL 3; GFL 1789 to the
  Present
Verlaine, Paul (Marie) 1844-1896 .. **NCLC 2,**
  51; PC 2, 32
  See also DAM POET; DLB 217; EW 7;
  GFL 1789 to the Present; LMFS 2; RGWL
  2, 3; TWA
Verne, Jules (Gabriel) 1828-1905 ... **TCLC 6,**
  52
  See also AAYA 16; BYA 4; CA 110; 131;
  CLR 88; DA3; DLB 123; GFL 1789 to
  the Present; JRDA; LAIT 2; LMFS 2;
  MAICYA 1, 2; MTFW 2005; RGWL 2, 3;
  SATA 21; SCFW 1, 2; SFW 4; TWA;
  WCH
Verus, Marcus Annius
  See Aurelius, Marcus
Very, Jones 1813-1880 .... **NCLC 9**
  See also DLB 1, 243; RGAL 4
Vesaas, Tarjei 1897-1970 .... **CLC 48**
  See also CA 190; 29-32R; DLB 297; EW
  11; EWL 3; RGWL 3
Vialis, Gaston
  See Simenon, Georges (Jacques Christian)

Wain, John (Barrington) 1925-1994 . **CLC 2, 11, 15, 46**
> See also CA 5-8R; 145; CAAS 4; CANR 23, 54; CDBLB 1960 to Present; CN 1, 2, 3, 4, 5; CP 1, 2, 3, 4; DLB 15, 27, 139, 155; EWL 3; MTCW 1, 2; MTFW 2005

Wajda, Andrzej 1926- .... **CLC 16, 219**
> See also CA 102

Wakefield, Dan 1932- .... **CLC 7**
> See also CA 21-24R, 211; CAAE 211; CAAS 7; CN 4, 5, 6, 7

Wakefield, Herbert Russell
> 1888-1965 .... **TCLC 120**
> See also CA 5-8R; CANR 77; HGG; SUFW

Wakoski, Diane 1937- ...... **CLC 2, 4, 7, 9, 11, 40; PC 15**
> See also CA 13-16R, 216; CAAE 216; CAAS 1; CANR 9, 60, 106; CP 1, 2, 3, 4, 5, 6, 7; CWP; DAM POET; DLB 5; INT CANR-9; MAL 5; MTCW 2; MTFW 2005

Wakoski-Sherbell, Diane
> See Wakoski, Diane

Walcott, Derek (Alton) 1930- ... **BLC 3; CLC 2, 4, 9, 14, 25, 42, 67, 76, 160; DC 7; PC 46**
> See also BW 2; CA 89-92; CANR 26, 47, 75, 80, 130; CBD; CD 5, 6; CDWLB 3; CP 1, 2, 3, 4, 5, 6, 7; DA3; DAB; DAC; DAM MST, MULT, POET; DLB 117; DLBY 1981; DNFS 1; EFS 1; EWL 3; LMFS 2; MTCW 1, 2; MTFW 2005; PFS 6; RGEL 2; TWA; WWE 1

Waldman, Anne (Lesley) 1945- .... **CLC 7**
> See also BG 1:3; CA 37-40R; CAAS 17; CANR 34, 69, 116; CP 1, 2, 3, 4, 5, 6, 7; CWP; DLB 16

Waldo, E. Hunter
> See Sturgeon, Theodore (Hamilton)

Waldo, Edward Hamilton
> See Sturgeon, Theodore (Hamilton)

Walker, Alice (Malsenior) 1944- .... **BLC 3; CLC 5, 6, 9, 19, 27, 46, 58, 103, 167; PC 30; SSC 5; WLCS**
> See also AAYA 3, 33; AFAW 1, 2; AMWS 3; BEST 89:4; BPFB 3; BW 2, 3; CA 37-40R; CANR 9, 27, 49, 66, 82, 131; CDALB 1968-1988; CN 4, 5, 6, 7; CPW; CSW; DA; DA3; DAB; DAC; DAM MST, MULT, NOV, POET, POP; DLB 6, 33, 143; EWL 3; EXPN; EXPS; FL 1:6; FW; INT CANR-27; LAIT 3; MAL 5; MAWW; MTCW 1, 2; MTFW 2005; NFS 5; RGAL 4; RGSF 2; SATA 31; SSFS 2, 11; TUS; YAW

Walker, David Harry 1911-1992 ...... **CLC 14**
> See also CA 1-4R; 137; CANR 1; CN 1, 2; CWRI 5; SATA 8; SATA-Obit 71

Walker, Edward Joseph 1934-2004
> See Walker, Ted
> See also CA 21-24R; 226; CANR 12, 28, 53

Walker, George F(rederick) 1947- .. **CLC 44, 61**
> See also CA 103; CANR 21, 43, 59; CD 5, 6; DAB; DAC; DAM MST; DLB 60

Walker, Joseph A. 1935-2003 .... **CLC 19**
> See also BW 1, 3; CA 89-92; CAD; CANR 26, 143; CD 5, 6; DAM DRAM, MST; DFS 12; DLB 38

Walker, Margaret (Abigail)
> 1915-1998 .... **BLC; CLC 1, 6; PC 20; TCLC 129**
> See also AFAW 1, 2; BW 2, 3; CA 73-76; 172; CANR 26, 54, 76, 136; CN 1, 2, 3, 4, 5, 6; CP 1, 2, 3, 4; CSW; DAM MULT; DLB 76, 152; EXPP; FW; MAL 5; MTCW 1, 2; MTFW 2005; RGAL 4; RHW

Walker, Ted .... **CLC 13**
> See Walker, Edward Joseph
> See also CP 1, 2, 3, 4, 5, 6, 7; DLB 40

Wallace, David Foster 1962- ... **CLC 50, 114; SSC 68**
> See also AAYA 50; AMWS 10; CA 132; CANR 59, 133; CN 7; DA3; MTCW 2; MTFW 2005

Wallace, Dexter
> See Masters, Edgar Lee

Wallace, (Richard Horatio) Edgar
> 1875-1932 .... **TCLC 57**
> See also CA 115; 218; CMW 4; DLB 70; MSW; RGEL 2

Wallace, Irving 1916-1990 .... **CLC 7, 13**
> See also AITN 1; BPFB 3; CA 1-4R; 132; CAAS 1; CANR 1, 27; CPW; DAM NOV, POP; INT CANR-27; MTCW 1, 2

Wallant, Edward Lewis 1926-1962 ... **CLC 5, 10**
> See also CA 1-4R; CANR 22; DLB 2, 28, 143, 299; EWL 3; MAL 5; MTCW 1, 2; RGAL 4

Wallas, Graham 1858-1932 .... **TCLC 91**

Waller, Edmund 1606-1687 .... **LC 86**
> See also BRW 2; DAM POET; DLB 126; PAB; RGEL 2

Walley, Byron
> See Card, Orson Scott

Walpole, Horace 1717-1797 .... **LC 2, 49**
> See also BRW 3; DLB 39, 104, 213; GL 3; HGG; LMFS 1; RGEL 2; SUFW 1; TEA

Walpole, Hugh (Seymour)
> 1884-1941 .... **TCLC 5**
> See also CA 104; 165; DLB 34; HGG; MTCW 2; RGEL 2; RHW

Walrond, Eric (Derwent) 1898-1966 . **HR 1:3**
> See also BW 1; CA 125; DLB 51

Walser, Martin 1927- .... **CLC 27, 183**
> See also CA 57-60; CANR 8, 46, 145; CWW 2; DLB 75, 124; EWL 3

Walser, Robert 1878-1956 ..... **SSC 20; TCLC 18**
> See also CA 118; 165; CANR 100; DLB 66; EWL 3

Walsh, Gillian Paton
> See Paton Walsh, Gillian

Walsh, Jill Paton .... **CLC 35**
> See Paton Walsh, Gillian
> See also CLR 2, 65; WYA

Walter, Villiam Christian
> See Andersen, Hans Christian

Walters, Anna L(ee) 1946- .... **NNAL**
> See also CA 73-76

Walther von der Vogelweide c.
> 1170-1228 .... **CMLC 56**

Walton, Izaak 1593-1683 .... **LC 72**
> See also BRW 2; CDBLB Before 1660; DLB 151, 213; RGEL 2

Wambaugh, Joseph (Aloysius), Jr.
> 1937- .... **CLC 3, 18**
> See also AITN 1; BEST 89:3; BPFB 3; CA 33-36R; CANR 42, 65, 115; CMW 4; CPW 1; DA3; DAM NOV, POP; DLB 6; DLBY 1983; MSW; MTCW 1, 2

Wang Wei 699(?)-761(?) .... **PC 18**
> See also TWA

Warburton, William 1698-1779 .... **LC 97**
> See also DLB 104

Ward, Arthur Henry Sarsfield 1883-1959
> See Rohmer, Sax
> See also CA 108; 173; CMW 4; HGG

Ward, Douglas Turner 1930- .... **CLC 19**
> See also BW 1; CA 81-84; CAD; CANR 27; CD 5, 6; DLB 7, 38

Ward, E. D.
> See Lucas, E(dward) V(errall)

Ward, Mrs. Humphry 1851-1920
> See Ward, Mary Augusta
> See also RGEL 2

Ward, Mary Augusta 1851-1920 ... **TCLC 55**
> See Ward, Mrs. Humphry
> See also DLB 18

Ward, Nathaniel 1578(?)-1652 .... **LC 114**
> See also DLB 24

Ward, Peter
> See Faust, Frederick (Schiller)

Warhol, Andy 1928(?)-1987 .... **CLC 20**
> See also AAYA 12; BEST 89:4; CA 89-92; 121; CANR 34

Warner, Francis (Robert le Plastrier)
> 1937- .... **CLC 14**
> See also CA 53-56; CANR 11; CP 1, 2, 3, 4

Warner, Marina 1946- .... **CLC 59**
> See also CA 65-68; CANR 21, 55, 118; CN 5, 6, 7; DLB 194; MTFW 2005

Warner, Rex (Ernest) 1905-1986 ...... **CLC 45**
> See also CA 89-92; 119; CN 1, 2, 3, 4; CP 1, 2, 3, 4; DLB 15; RGEL 2; RHW

Warner, Susan (Bogert)
> 1819-1885 .... **NCLC 31, 146**
> See also DLB 3, 42, 239, 250, 254

Warner, Sylvia (Constance) Ashton
> See Ashton-Warner, Sylvia (Constance)

Warner, Sylvia Townsend
> 1893-1978 .. **CLC 7, 19; SSC 23; TCLC 131**
> See also BRWS 7; CA 61-64; 77-80; CANR 16, 60, 104; CN 1, 2; DLB 34, 139; EWL 3; FANT; FW; MTCW 1, 2; RGEL 2; RGSF 2; RHW

Warren, Mercy Otis 1728-1814 ..... **NCLC 13**
> See also DLB 31, 200; RGAL 4; TUS

Warren, Robert Penn 1905-1989 .. **CLC 1, 4, 6, 8, 10, 13, 18, 39, 53, 59; PC 37; SSC 4, 58; WLC**
> See also AITN 1; AMW; AMWC 2; BPFB 3; BYA 1; CA 13-16R; 129; CANR 10, 47; CDALB 1968-1988; CN 1, 2, 3, 4; CP 1, 2, 3, 4; DA; DA3; DAB; DAC; DAM MST, NOV, POET; DLB 2, 48, 152, 320; DLBY 1980, 1989; EWL 3; INT CANR-10; MAL 5; MTCW 1, 2; MTFW 2005; NFS 13; RGAL 4; RGSF 2; RHW; SATA 46; SATA-Obit 63; SSFS 8; TUS

Warrigal, Jack
> See Furphy, Joseph

Warshofsky, Isaac
> See Singer, Isaac Bashevis

Warton, Joseph 1722-1800 .... **NCLC 118**
> See also DLB 104, 109; RGEL 2

Warton, Thomas 1728-1790 .... **LC 15, 82**
> See also DAM POET; DLB 104, 109; RGEL 2

Waruk, Kona
> See Harris, (Theodore) Wilson

Warung, Price .... **TCLC 45**
> See Astley, William
> See also DLB 230; RGEL 2

Warwick, Jarvis
> See Garner, Hugh
> See also CCA 1

Washington, Alex
> See Harris, Mark

Washington, Booker T(aliaferro)
> 1856-1915 .... **BLC 3; TCLC 10**
> See also BW 1; CA 114; 125; DA3; DAM MULT; LAIT 2; RGAL 4; SATA 28

Washington, George 1732-1799 .... **LC 25**
> See also DLB 31

Wassermann, (Karl) Jakob
> 1873-1934 .... **TCLC 6**
> See also CA 104; 163; DLB 66; EWL 3

Wessel, Johan Herman 1742-1785 .... **LC 7**
See also DLB 300

West, Anthony (Panther)
1914-1987 .... **CLC 50**
See also CA 45-48; 124; CANR 3, 19; CN 1, 2, 3, 4; DLB 15

West, C. P.
See Wodehouse, P(elham) G(renville)

West, Cornel (Ronald) 1953- .... **BLCS; CLC 134**
See also CA 144; CANR 91; DLB 246

West, Delno C(loyde), Jr. 1936- .... **CLC 70**
See also CA 57-60

West, Dorothy 1907-1998 ...... **HR 1:3; TCLC 108**
See also BW 2; CA 143; 169; DLB 76

West, (Mary) Jessamyn 1902-1984 ... **CLC 7, 17**
See also CA 9-12R; 112; CANR 27; CN 1, 2, 3; DLB 6; DLBY 1984; MTCW 1, 2; RGAL 4; RHW; SATA-Obit 37; TCWW 2; TUS; YAW

West, Morris L(anglo) 1916-1999 ..... **CLC 6, 33**
See also BPFB 3; CA 5-8R; 187; CANR 24, 49, 64; CN 1, 2, 3, 4, 5, 6; CPW; DLB 289; MTCW 1, 2; MTFW 2005

West, Nathanael 1903-1940 .. **SSC 16; TCLC 1, 14, 44**
See also AMW; AMWR 2; BPFB 3; CA 104; 125; CDALB 1929-1941; DA3; DLB 4, 9, 28; EWL 3; MAL 5; MTCW 1, 2; MTFW 2005; NFS 16; RGAL 4; TUS

West, Owen
See Koontz, Dean R.

West, Paul 1930- .... **CLC 7, 14, 96**
See also CA 13-16R; CAAS 7; CANR 22, 53, 76, 89, 136; CN 1, 2, 3, 4, 5, 6, 7; DLB 14; INT CANR-22; MTCW 2; MTFW 2005

West, Rebecca 1892-1983 ... **CLC 7, 9, 31, 50**
See also BPFB 3; BRWS 3; CA 5-8R; 109; CANR 19; CN 1, 2, 3; DLB 36; DLBY 1983; EWL 3; FW; MTCW 1, 2; MTFW 2005; NCFS 4; RGEL 2; TEA

Westall, Robert (Atkinson)
1929-1993 .... **CLC 17**
See also AAYA 12; BYA 2, 6, 7, 8, 9, 15; CA 69-72; 141; CANR 18, 68; CLR 13; FANT; JRDA; MAICYA 1, 2; MAICYAS 1; SAAS 2; SATA 23, 69; SATA-Obit 75; WYA; YAW

Westermarck, Edward 1862-1939 . **TCLC 87**

Westlake, Donald E(dwin) 1933- . **CLC 7, 33**
See also BPFB 3; CA 17-20R; CAAS 13; CANR 16, 44, 65, 94, 137; CMW 4; CPW; DAM POP; INT CANR-16; MSW; MTCW 2; MTFW 2005

Westmacott, Mary
See Christie, Agatha (Mary Clarissa)

Weston, Allen
See Norton, Andre

Wetcheek, J. L.
See Feuchtwanger, Lion

Wetering, Janwillem van de
See van de Wetering, Janwillem

Wetherald, Agnes Ethelwyn
1857-1940 .... **TCLC 81**
See also CA 202; DLB 99

Wetherell, Elizabeth
See Warner, Susan (Bogert)

Whale, James 1889-1957 .... **TCLC 63**

Whalen, Philip (Glenn) 1923-2002 .... **CLC 6, 29**
See also BG 1:3; CA 9-12R; 209; CANR 5, 39; CP 1, 2, 3, 4, 5, 6, 7; DLB 16; WP

Wharton, Edith (Newbold Jones)
1862-1937 ... **SSC 6, 84; TCLC 3, 9, 27, 53, 129, 149; WLC**
See also AAYA 25; AMW; AMWC 2; AMWR 1; BPFB 3; CA 104; 132; CDALB 1865-1917; DA; DA3; DAB; DAC; DAM MST, NOV; DLB 4, 9, 12, 78, 189; DLBD 13; EWL 3; EXPS; FL 1:6; GL 3; HGG; LAIT 2, 3; LATS 1:1; MAL 5; MAWW; MTCW 1, 2; MTFW 2005; NFS 5, 11, 15, 20; RGAL 4; RGSF 2; RHW; SSFS 6, 7; SUFW; TUS

Wharton, James
See Mencken, H(enry) L(ouis)

Wharton, William (a pseudonym)
1925- .... **CLC 18, 37**
See also CA 93-96; CN 4, 5, 6, 7; DLBY 1980; INT CA-93-96

Wheatley (Peters), Phillis
1753(?)-1784 .. **BLC 3; LC 3, 50; PC 3; WLC**
See also AFAW 1, 2; CDALB 1640-1865; DA; DA3; DAC; DAM MST, MULT, POET; DLB 31, 50; EXPP; FL 1:1; PFS 13; RGAL 4

Wheelock, John Hall 1886-1978 .... **CLC 14**
See also CA 13-16R; 77-80; CANR 14; CP 1, 2; DLB 45; MAL 5

Whim-Wham
See Curnow, (Thomas) Allen (Monro)

White, Babington
See Braddon, Mary Elizabeth

White, E(lwyn) B(rooks)
1899-1985 .... **CLC 10, 34, 39**
See also AAYA 62; AITN 2; AMWS 1; CA 13-16R; 116; CANR 16, 37; CDALBS; CLR 1, 21; CPW; DA3; DAM POP; DLB 11, 22; EWL 3; FANT; MAICYA 1, 2; MAL 5; MTCW 1, 2; MTFW 2005; NCFS 5; RGAL 4; SATA 2, 29, 100; SATA-Obit 44; TUS

White, Edmund (Valentine III)
1940- .... **CLC 27, 110**
See also AAYA 7; CA 45-48; CANR 3, 19, 36, 62, 107, 133; CN 5, 6, 7; DA3; DAM POP; DLB 227; MTCW 1, 2; MTFW 2005

White, Hayden V. 1928- .... **CLC 148**
See also CA 128; CANR 135; DLB 246

White, Patrick (Victor Martindale)
1912-1990 ...... **CLC 3, 4, 5, 7, 9, 18, 65, 69; SSC 39, TCLC 176**
See also BRWS 1; CA 81-84; 132; CANR 43; CN 1, 2, 3, 4; DLB 260; EWL 3; MTCW 1; RGEL 2; RGSF 2; RHW; TWA; WWE 1

White, Phyllis Dorothy James 1920-
See James, P. D.
See also CA 21-24R; CANR 17, 43, 65, 112; CMW 4; CN 7; CPW; DA3; DAM POP; MTCW 1, 2; MTFW 2005; TEA

White, T(erence) H(anbury)
1906-1964 .... **CLC 30**
See also AAYA 22; BPFB 3; BYA 4, 5; CA 73-76; CANR 37; DLB 160; FANT; JRDA; LAIT 1; MAICYA 1, 2; RGEL 2; SATA 12; SUFW 1; YAW

White, Terence de Vere 1912-1994 ... **CLC 49**
See also CA 49-52; 145; CANR 3

White, Walter
See White, Walter F(rancis)

White, Walter F(rancis) 1893-1955 ... **BLC 3; HR 1:3; TCLC 15**
See also BW 1; CA 115; 124; DAM MULT; DLB 51

White, William Hale 1831-1913
See Rutherford, Mark
See also CA 121; 189

Whitehead, Alfred North
1861-1947 .... **TCLC 97**
See also CA 117; 165; DLB 100, 262

Whitehead, E(dward) A(nthony)
1933- .... **CLC 5**
See Whitehead, Ted
See also CA 65-68; CANR 58, 118; CBD; CD 5; DLB 310

Whitehead, Ted
See Whitehead, E(dward) A(nthony)
See also CD 6

Whiteman, Roberta J. Hill 1947- ...... **NNAL**
See also CA 146

Whitemore, Hugh (John) 1936- .... **CLC 37**
See also CA 132; CANR 77; CBD; CD 5, 6; INT CA-132

Whitman, Sarah Helen (Power)
1803-1878 .... **NCLC 19**
See also DLB 1, 243

Whitman, Walt(er) 1819-1892 .. **NCLC 4, 31, 81; PC 3; WLC**
See also AAYA 42; AMW; AMWR 1; CDALB 1640-1865; DA; DA3; DAB; DAC; DAM MST, POET; DLB 3, 64, 224, 250; EXPP; LAIT 2; LMFS 1; PAB; PFS 2, 3, 13, 22; RGAL 4; SATA 20; TUS; WP; WYAS 1

Whitney, Phyllis A(yame) 1903- .... **CLC 42**
See also AAYA 36; AITN 2; BEST 90:3; CA 1-4R; CANR 3, 25, 38, 60; CLR 59; CMW 4; CPW; DA3; DAM POP; JRDA; MAICYA 1, 2; MTCW 2; RHW; SATA 1, 30; YAW

Whittemore, (Edward) Reed, Jr.
1919- .... **CLC 4**
See also CA 9-12R; 219; CAAE 219; CAAS 8; CANR 4, 119; CP 1, 2, 3, 4, 5, 6, 7; DLB 5; MAL 5

Whittier, John Greenleaf
1807-1892 .... **NCLC 8, 59**
See also AMWS 1; DLB 1, 243; RGAL 4

Whittlebot, Hernia
See Coward, Noel (Peirce)

Wicker, Thomas Grey 1926-
See Wicker, Tom
See also CA 65-68; CANR 21, 46, 141

Wicker, Tom .... **CLC 7**
See Wicker, Thomas Grey

Wideman, John Edgar 1941- ... **BLC 3; CLC 5, 34, 36, 67, 122; SSC 62**
See also AFAW 1, 2; AMWS 10; BPFB 4; BW 2, 3; CA 85-88; CANR 14, 42, 67, 109, 140; CN 4, 5, 6, 7; DAM MULT; DLB 33, 143; MAL 5; MTCW 2; MTFW 2005; RGAL 4; RGSF 2; SSFS 6, 12; TCLE 1:2

Wiebe, Rudy (Henry) 1934- .. **CLC 6, 11, 14, 138**
See also CA 37-40R; CANR 42, 67, 123; CN 1, 2, 3, 4, 5, 6, 7; DAC; DAM MST; DLB 60; RHW; SATA 156

Wieland, Christoph Martin
1733-1813 .... **NCLC 17**
See also DLB 97; EW 4; LMFS 1; RGWL 2, 3

Wiene, Robert 1881-1938 .... **TCLC 56**

Wieners, John 1934- .... **CLC 7**
See also BG 1:3; CA 13-16R; CP 1, 2, 3, 4, 5, 6, 7; DLB 16; WP

Wiesel, Elie(zer) 1928- .... **CLC 3, 5, 11, 37, 165; WLCS**
See also AAYA 7, 54; AITN 1; CA 5-8R; CAAS 4; CANR 8, 40, 65, 125; CDALBS; CWW 2; DA; DA3; DAB; DAC; DAM MST, NOV; DLB 83, 299; DLBY 1987; EWL 3; INT CANR-8; LAIT 4; MTCW 1, 2; MTFW 2005; NCFS 4; NFS 4; RGWL 3; SATA 56; YAW

Literary Criticism Series
Cumulative Topic Index

This index lists all topic entries in Thompson Gale's *Children's Literature Review* (CLR), *Classical and Medieval Literature Criticism* (CMLC), *Contemporary Literary Criticism* (CLC), *Drama Criticism* (DC), *Literature Criticism from 1400 to 1800* (LC), *Nineteenth-Century Literature Criticism* (NCLC), *Short Story Criticism* (SSC), and *Twentieth-Century Literary Criticism* (TCLC). The index also lists topic entries in the Gale Critical Companion Collection, which includes the following publications: *The Beat Generation* (BG), and *Harlem Renaissance* (HR).

Topic Index

Topic Index

Topic Index

NCLC Cumulative Nationality Index

Nationality Index

NCLC-167 Title Index

ISBN 0-7876-8651-4